THE BERG
COMPANION
TO FASHION

THE BERG COMPANION TO FASHION

Edited by Valerie Steele

Oxford • New York

This edition first
published in 2010 by

Berg

Editorial offices:
First Floor, Angel Court, 81 St Clements Street, Oxford OX4 1AW, UK
175 Fifth Avenue, New York, NY 10010, USA

© Berg 2010

Edited (including preface) by Valerie Steele

All rights reserved.

Entries are from *Encyclopedia of Clothing and Fashion*. © 2005
Gale, Cengage Learning. Entries that have been updated for this
edition are indicated by an asterisk "*."

No part of this publication may be reproduced in any form or by
any means without the written permission of Gale (for all entries)
or Berg (for the preface and all updated entries).

Berg is the imprint of Oxford International Publishers Ltd.

Library of Congress Cataloging-in-Publication Data
A catalogue record for this book is available from the Library of Congress.

British Library Cataloguing-in-Publication Data
A catalogue record for this book is available from the British Library.

ISBN 978 1 84788 592 0 (Cloth)
978 1 84788 563 0 (Paper)

Typeset by Apex CoVantage, LLC, Madison, WI, USA

Printed in the UK by the MPG Books Group

www.bergpublishers.com

Contents

E

F

U

V

W

Preface

Some Middle Eastern women wear *burqas* so voluminous that not a single square inch of skin is exposed to the gaze of others. In the highlands of New Guinea, some men go completely naked except for a penis sheath made from a long, narrow gourd, and a circlet of brightly colored feathers in their hair. Between these extremes, every culture in the world has its own customs and rules of dress. There are few (if any) societies in the world in which people wear no clothing at all, and none in which people do not fashion their appearance in one way or another, whether through hairdressing, cosmetics, tattooing, jewelry, or some other form of adornment. "Fashion" is the key word here; used as a verb, it means "to make" or "to create." Throughout the world, people employ clothing and adornment to fashion an identity. Clothing is obviously worn for practical reasons as well, such as keeping warm, and social considerations, such as conforming to any given society's rules of modesty and propriety. However, functional considerations fall far short of being able to explain what clothing means to the people who wear it and to others who see it.

Dress and adornment are thus a universal feature of human behavior (along with such things as language and tool-making) and, as such, have long been a subject of extraordinary interest. For many years, however, the study of dress and adornment (generally under the rubric of "Costume History") was essentially descriptive and antiquarian. The production, in the nineteenth century, of lavishly illustrated books on historical costume or folk costumes revealed a lively interest in the phenomenon of dress, but asked a limited range of questions about it. The formation in the twentieth century of museum-based costume collections showed a laudable spirit of historic preservation, but the exhibition of such collections seldom went beyond a somewhat romanticized impulse to illustrate the past. The new field of Fashion Studies, which takes as its subject fashion in the most inclusive sense of "the cultural construction of the embodied identity," emerged in the 1980s, in part from a realization that dress and adornment offered possibilities of interpretation and understanding that went far beyond the purview of traditional costume studies.

Fashion Studies, sometimes known as the "new fashion history," is above all an interdisciplinary field that welcomes insight and analysis from multiple perspectives, embracing anthropology, art history, cultural and intellectual history, economics, gender and queer studies, material culture, and other fields, some of them also newly emerging. *Fashion Theory: The Journal of Dress, Body and Culture* (founded in 1997) has played an important role in legitimating the field of Fashion Studies, and in bringing the methods and insights of Fashion Studies to the attention of a steadily widening academic audience. The rapid development and intellectual liveliness of this new approach to fashion has contributed to a growing popular interest in fashion as a field of enquiry. Every year brings a new crop of books on fashion, some scholarly, others aimed at a general audience, and, increasingly, many written from a perspective that takes fashion seriously as a social, cultural, and artistic phenomenon.

The field of Fashion Studies has also given rise to serious reference works. The two most important of these are *The Encyclopedia of Clothing and Fashion* (Scribner's, 2005), which I edited several years ago, and the massive ten-volume *Berg Encyclopedia of World Dress and Fashion* (Berg, 2010) under the editorship of Joanne B.

Eicher. The first of these ranges widely across time and cultures, but focuses primarily on the modern fashion system, going beyond traditional dictionaries of fashion designers to include themes such as Dandyism and Subcultures. *The Berg Encyclopedia of World Dress and Fashion* focuses on in-depth explorations of regional and ethnic dress and adornment around the world. These two works thus complement each other, and both are available not only in print but on-line as part of the *Berg Fashion Library* (www.bergfashionlibrary.com).

The Berg Companion to Fashion draws primarily on *The Encyclopedia of Clothing and Fashion*, featuring selected and updated entries from that work in a convenient, reasonably priced single-volume format. It contains insightful and informative profiles of fashion designers from Adrian to Yohji Yamamoto; articles on components of the fashion system (Fashion Magazines, Supermodels); entries on particular items of dress (High Heels, Jeans); essays on fashion personalities (Diana Vreeland, the Duke and Duchess of Windsor); and much more. I am delighted to present this work to the growing audience of people who understand that clothes do not grow in our closets, and that how we choose to dress and present ourselves to the world every day—how we fashion ourselves—is a vital part of what makes us who we are.

Valerie Steele

ACADEMIC DRESS

Academic dress is the formal attire worn by students and officials at a commencement or graduation ceremony. The most common styles emulate the everyday clothing worn by scholars at the first universities in the eleventh and twelfth centuries. Typically, this included a flowing gown, a hood or cape, and some sort of head wear; the contemporary form of this ensemble depends on the rules dictated by the institution with which the student or official is associated.

Origin and History

The ancient universities were established in Italy and France in the late eleventh and early twelfth centuries, with the University of Oxford following in circa 1115 and Cambridge in circa 1209. It was these two English schools that set the tradition for academic dress by establishing strict decrees for their students and officials; the subsequent influence of the British Empire spread this tradition to many parts of the world.

Historically, schools of higher learning were referred to as *stadium generale* or *universitas*; titles conferred by the Pope of the day, with the latter being the higher honor. This early association with religion can still be seen in the similarities between academic dress and church robes. However, the early schools were not religious orders as a rule, but rather scholastic guilds made up of students and teachers organized around a cathedral or monastery. Not necessarily priests, the scholars wore clothes that were a sober reflection of lay fashions. In this respect, it was the degree that signified the scholar's full membership in the learned corporation, not the robe.

In medieval times the term "bachelor" was used to describe the assistant of a small landowner; the apprentice as opposed to the master who was already skilled, hence the academic use of the term "master" as well. Both of these titles were in widespread use in the universities during the thirteenth century. As such, there was a structure within these institutions related specifically to the degree of knowledge obtained by the scholar. This hierarchy, along with the medieval style of clothing, became the basis of academic dress.

The Cap and Gown

Medieval dress consisted of a flowing gown or *cappa clausa*, with a cape or cloak draped over the top. This often had a cowl-like appendage that could be pulled over the head, much like a hooded cape or *capitium*. By the second half of the fifteenth century, the fashion had progressed toward an open gown, said to be an expression of the new acceptance of academic learning and the arts. From 1490 onward this gown became standard academic dress, with the hooded cape becoming more ornamental than practical. Most commonly, bachelors and masters scholars wore black gowns made of "princes stuff" or "crape," with the senior man's garment having wider sleeves to allow for movement while teaching. The dress hood took the form of a drooping cape, lined with silk or fur to denote the scholar's faculty or social status. For example, in 1432 Oxford forbade the use of miniver for anyone except Masters of the Arts and those of great wealth or noble birth. Variations in sleeve style and lining continued to mirror fashionable dress, and by the sixteenth century academics followed professionals and the clergy in the wearing of caps.

It is difficult to pinpoint the origins of the academic cap, but it is thought to have evolved as a variation on the ecclesiastic *pileus* cap and the medieval head scarf. Most contemporary graduates wear the trencher form of the *pileus quadratus*—or the Oxford mortarboard. This consists of a small skullcap, shaped to fit the head, and a flat, square top, adorned with a silk tassel. This form of headwear became popular with the clergy after the Restoration, when it was thought that emphasizing "squareness" denoted greater dedication. However, the modern academic form was not popularized until the eighteenth century, when wood or card was used to stiffen the square. Some philosophical doctors or secular doctors may wear a variation of the Tudor Bonnet, a softer, fuller hat, or if of Scottish origin, the John Knox cap.

Contemporary Academic Dress

Most contemporary graduates wear a variation of the Oxford or Cambridge bachelor of arts gown. The Cambridge gown is knee-length, "princes stuff" and has pointed, open sleeves: the seam on the forearm is unsewn to the cuff, allowing a generous hole for the arm to pass through. The hood is partly lined with white fur or silk that is colored to denote the degree of the wearer. The sleeveless Oxford "commoners" gown sits a little below the knee and is expected to be worn with lay clothes that conform to a strict code. The lining of the hood is again appropriate to status. Hugh Smith's *Academic Dress and Insignia of the World* (1970) provides a thorough reference for those interested in all dress variations.

In the United States most universities accept the Inter-Collegiate Code (1895) of academic dress, a variation on the Cambridge style, but with an extensive system of color coding that denotes both the degree and the university. In many other countries students do not wear any academic dress: in Germany, it is seen as a sign of respect for the teachings of Martin Luther; in the former Soviet Union, students receive medallions; in Finland, doctors don swords for their commencement. And in many more countries, adaptations have been made to the English model, with Native Americans adding traditional jewelry and head wear, New Zealand Maoris wearing feathered capes, and Australian Aborigines adopting red, yellow, and black capes. Certainly, the fact that academic dress pays homage to establishment and tradition makes it the perfect dress for subversion.

Dress in American High Schools

The use of the cap and gown in American high schools originated in 1911 as a means of providing an economical and egalitarian code of dress. American educators joined with the academic dress companies to design an official ensemble for the high school graduate. It was gray, with long, pointed sleeves and the Oxford mortarboard cap. One of those who pushed for such dress in schools was the principal of Englewood High, Chicago,

James Armstrong. He believed that the adoption of academic dress would ease the burden on parents to provide fashionable and expensive graduation outfits. By the early 2000s, traditional gray had been replaced by the official colors of the particular school, with religious or private girls' schools opting for white, grammar schools for maroon. Across America the cap and gown has been adopted by many institutions, with even nursery schools conferring honors on their infant graduates. This practice has not been widely emulated beyond the United States; however, some schools in Australia and Asia have adopted the practice.

As a means of historical record, academic dress encapsulates medieval fashion, preserving its character and form for what is an important modern occasion, both to the graduates and to those who have carried them through their time as a scholar. Hence, this form of dress is both steeped in tradition and very distinct from everyday clothes—such contrast clearly conveys significant achievement.

See also Uniforms, School.

Bibliography

Goff, Philip. *University of London Academic Dress.* London: University of London, 1999.

Smith, Hugh. *Academic Dress and Insignia of the World.* 3 vols. Cape Town, South Africa: Balkema, 1970.

Walters, Helen. *The Story of Caps and Gowns.* Chicago and New York: E. R. Moore Publishing Company, 1939.

Internet Resources

Cox, Noel. "Academic Dress in New Zealand." Auckland: Private Monograph. Available from <http://www.geocities.com/noelcox/Introduction.htm>.

Joanne McCallum

ACTIVEWEAR

The clothing known as activewear in the early 2000s traces its origins back to the high-performance sportswear designed for mountaineering, sailing, and hiking that became popular among urban youth during the 1970s. By the 1980s, such utilitarian styles swept through college campuses in North America, and, subsequently, sneakers were worn with suits, back-packs replaced briefcases, anoraks were paired with deck shoes, and sweatshirts were combined with khaki trousers or jeans. As the style began to characterize the sporty chic of city dwellers and coed campus life, activewear became a staple of the modern wardrobe.

While activewear is often regarded as a contemporary style, the combination of street clothes, travel accessories, and sportswear is nothing new. In the 1930s and 1940s, the American designers Bonnie Cashin, Claire McCardell, and Vera Maxwell updated garments produced for travel, leisure, and sport with vestiges of high fashion. The designers made functionality a statement of style by producing easy-fit, loosely constructed clothing in fabrics such as wool, denim, and calico. One of Cashin's signature garments was an overcoat with an integral purse, while Maxwell designed a jacket with builtin bags rather than pockets. Such garments were conceived as urban tools that expanded into wearable luggage, widening the appeal of apparel that could maximize the performance of clothing as well as the body's ability to transport necessities with ease.

For several decades, activewear was characterized by bulky, loose-fitting garments. As the body-conscious styles of the 1990s took hold, activewear gradually became more tailored and form-fitting, yet continued to suit the active leisure interests of urban dwellers. Dress codes became more fluid as Rollerbladers, inner-city cyclists, and speed-walking pedestrians dressed in smart basics that moved easily and provided protection from adverse weather. Mobility and versatility became key considerations for professionals, who started commuting to work in sneakers and multifunctional outer garments. Many were made with detachable hoods that transformed overcoats into raincoats as they were buttoned or zipped into place, or designed with removable collars and detachable sleeves that could be adapted to weather changes.

The hoods, zip-front seams, windproof jackets, pouch pockets, Velcro, and magnetic fastenings of activewear have become part of the everyday fashion vocabulary, along with drawstrings fitted at the neck, sleeve, and waist to make zippers and buttons redundant. Maharishi popularized these tailoring details on the catwalk as the 1990s drew to a close, updating them with elements of occupational uniforms to create a signature militaristic style. The rise of activewear's popularity throughout the 1990s indicated that the traditional compartmentalized wardrobe no longer sustained shifting social and cultural needs. As the style formed an essential part of the modern wardrobe, it encouraged

the movement of materials and technologies across disciplines, moving high-tech fabrics into the collections of forward-thinking fashion designers. Activewear's multifunctional, dynamic features seemed to herald the dawn of twenty-first century fashion in garments that fused fashion with high-performance sportswear.

Labels such as CP Company, Mandarina Duck, Issey Miyake, Vexed Generation, and Final Home were among the first to use advanced textile technology to create an edgy, urban aesthetic in designs as durable as they were chic. CP Company led the pack with designs that transcended fashion altogether; their overcoats transformed into one-person tents or inflated into air mattresses, and their parkas puffed up into armchairs. The garments are transformed by the wearers themselves, introducing a notion of technical skill required beyond the point of purchase. Likewise, the "Jackpack," designed by Mandarina Duck in Italy, integrated a backpack's straps, fastenings, and compartments within the fabric of the jacket's back panel. By taking the jacket off, turning it inside out, and folding the sleeves, lapels, and fabric panels into an internal pouch, the structure of the garment was completely transformed. The pouch contains other zippered compartments for stowing away shopping or other items of clothing. Issey Miyake, for his "Transformer" series, also designed cotton jackets that concealed a nylon raincoat within.

The British fashion duo Vexed Generation countered the problems of modern life with clothing crafted from bullet-proof and slash-proof materials. Their designs combined high-performance fabrics with cutting-edge street style in garments incorporating many of the functions associated with protective clothing. Temperature-regulating materials manufactured for sportswear were incorporated into their winter coats, ending the need for bulky layering. By lining jackets and overcoats with phase-change materials such as Outlast, Vexed Generation created outer garments that could function as personal thermostats. Tiny paraffin capsules in the phase-change fabrics expand when body temperature climbs, absorbing the heat. Once body temperature drops below 98.6° F (37° C), they contract, releasing the heat they have stored. By maintaining a mean temperature within changing climatic environments, Vexed Generation created a comfort zone for the wearer.

The Japanese designer Kosuke Tsumura's signature garment, the Final Home jacket, expands the mobility of activewear into an expression of architecture as he claims that clothing constitutes the ultimate shelter. The multi-functional, transparent jacket is a nylon sheath equipped with forty-four zippered pockets that can be lined with warm materials for extra insulation, or cushion the wearer when sitting or reclining. Tsumura sees the jacket as a protective shell that enables the wearer to withstand harsh weather conditions. Along with personal items and accessories, Tsumura suggests that some of the pockets be filled with survival rations and practical supplies, eliminating the need for backpacks, shopping bags, luggage, and even tool kits.

As fashion consumers continue looking to activewear to reconcile the demands of the modern lifestyle, the boundaries between street clothes, office attire, and sportswear are blurring even further. High-performance designs and technologically advanced textiles are common to all three, as comfort, flexibility, and protection become central to all parts of the modern wardrobe. As the garments are updated with innovations that transcend conventional clothing, activewear is proving to be one of the fastest moving areas of fashion in the early 2000s. New tailoring techniques radically streamline the designs each season, and future styles of activewear portend such sophistication that the gym is probably the last place one can expect to see them.

See also Outerwear; Sportswear.

Bibliography

Barnard, Malcolm. *Fashion as Communication*. London: Routledge, 1996.

Bolton, Andrew. *The Supermodern Wardrobe*. London: V & A Publications, 2001.

Jones, Terry, and Avril Mair. *Fashion Now*. Cologne, Germany: Taschen, 2003.

McDowell, Colin. *The Fashion Book*. London: Phaidon Press, Ltd., 2000.

Quinn, Bradley. *Techno Fashion*. Oxford: Berg, 2002.

Bradley Quinn

ACTORS AND ACTRESSES, IMPACT ON FASHION

Professional actors and actresses have long fascinated their audiences, but until the twentieth century, they were often associated with licentious sexual behavior, making them problematic role models. Perhaps the first true stage professionals, in the modern sense, were the men and women who made up the repertory companies of the Italian commedia dell'arte in the sixteenth and seventeenth centuries. The stock characters they impersonated, such as Harlequin, Columbine, and Pierrot, left their mark on fashion. Shirts for women in the twentieth century have sported an extravagantly ruffled collar like that of Pierrot, while the diamond-patterned fabric of Harlequin's costume is now part of the fashion lexicon.

In England, theaters were established in London during the Elizabethan Age, but the first thing the Puritans did upon taking control of the city of London in 1620 was to close them. After the Royalist defeat in the English Civil War, Charles II, the future king of England, had to flee to Paris. He remained in exile there for a decade at the court of Louis XIV, where he saw actresses, whose costumes reflected current trends in fashion, on stage both at court and in the fashionable playhouses. When he returned to London in 1660, theater flourished; his most famous mistress was the actress Nell Gwyn. It was during his reign that the "first

A tailor makes adjustments to a gown for actress Betty Grable. Hollywood stars of the 1930s and 1940s had a great impact on style, setting many fashion trends both onscreen and off. © JERRY COOKE/CORBIS. REPRODUCED BY PERMISSION.

night" of a new play became both a social event and a dress parade, as it has remained ever since.

In the eighteenth century, the English actress Mrs. Sheridan (1754–1792), wife of the playwright Richard Brinsley Sheridan, was painted by Sir Joshua Reynolds and Thomas Gainsborough. Other actresses sat for fashionable portraitists, and their dress and hairstyles were widely copied. Caroline Abington, who married into the aristocracy, was perhaps the first fashion consultant; she was driven around London to advise her wealthy, titled friends on sartorial matters, particularly if a ball or marriage was imminent.

Many French actresses also had an influence on fashion. Sarah Bernhardt (1844–1923), in particular, was famed for her stylish clothes. She toured the world and was the first actress to be dressed for the screens of the new cinema by a couturier. In 1913, when her play *Elizabeth I* was filmed, she asked Paul Poiret to create her wardrobe, setting a trend that other couturiers would follow, from Coco Chanel and Hubert de Givenchy to the more recent long-term collaboration on- and off-screen between Yves St. Laurent and Catherine Deneuve.

The actor, writer, and director Noel Coward (1899–1973) made a polka-dotted silk Sulka dressing-gown part of every well-dressed man's wardrobe. His favored actress, Gertrude Lawrence, wore a backless dress on stage in *Private Lives* in 1930 and the style instantly became fashionable. Jean Harlow set trends in hair and makeup—the "silver screen" succeeded where the stage had always failed: it made the wearing of makeup not only respectable but a fashionable necessity.

In the early twenty-first century, the stage has less impact than film in fashion terms. The fashionable theatrical couples of the 1930s and 1940s—the Oliviers and the Lunts, for example—were eclipsed by the cinematic duos of the second half of the twentieth century and beginning of the twenty-first century. However, the stage door still has its appeal: its glittering first nights, its gala evenings, and its award ceremonies—all of which, like the Academy Awards, demand "occasion dressing," and act as yet another showcase for designers and stylists canny enough to offer up their services.

See also Animal Prints; Film and Fashion; Theatrical Costume; Theatrical Makeup.

Bibliography

Bruzzi, Stella. *Undressing Cinema: Clothing and Identity in the Movies*. London: Routledge, 1997.

Hartnoll, Phyllis. *The Theatre: A Concise History*. Rev. ed. London: Thames and Hudson, Inc., 1985.

Laver, James. *Costume in the Theatre*. New York: Hill and Wang, 1965.

Pointon, Marcia. *Hanging the Head: Portraiture and Social Formation in Eighteenth-Century England*. New Haven, Conn.: Yale University Press, 1993.

Ribeiro, Aileen. *The Art of Dress: Fashion in England and France, 1750 to 1820*. New Haven, Conn.: Yale University Press, 1995.

Pamela Church Gibson

ADRIAN

Adrian, the great American film and fashion designer, was born Adrian Adolph Greenberg in Connecticut in 1903. Stage-struck at an early age, he had worked in summer stock and sold costume sketches to the producers of a Broadway show by the time he was eighteen. In 1921 he entered the New York School of Fine and Applied Arts (now the Parsons School of Design) to study stage design. He transferred to the Paris branch of the school in 1922.

Adrian returned to New York after three months to design costumes for Irving Berlin's *Music Box Revue*. He had designed costumes for his first movie and a number of Broadway shows by 1924, when he accepted a job designing costumes for Rudolph Valentino. Relocating to Los Angeles with Valentino, Adrian created costumes for three more of his films. He freelanced on *Her Sister from Paris*, starring Constance Talmadge, in 1925 and on Howard Hawks's *Fig Leaves* for Fox in 1926, a film that featured a two-color Technicolor fashion show sequence. Adrian signed a contract with Cecil B. DeMille the same year, moved with DeMille to Metro-Goldwyn-Mayer (MGM) in 1928, and subsequently signed with MGM. He stayed there until 1941, when he terminated his contract and left the movie business. In 1939 Adrian married Janet Gaynor, winner of the first Academy Award for best actress, and they had one son.

As MGM's chief designer, Adrian designed costumes for all the major stars in every important movie. Greta Garbo, Norma Shearer, Joan Crawford, Jean Harlow, Jeanette MacDonald, and Katharine Hepburn all wore his designs. Adrian was so important to the stars that Joan Crawford once said he should have been given cobilling on her movies. Film costumes had to make the stars look their best, be suitable for the character, and conform to the technical dictates of lighting, film stock, and sound recording. Period costumes had to be reasonably authentic but also accessible to the audience's eye. Modern wardrobes had to be of their time but independent of any specific fashion, for several reasons. First, the time lag between the production of a movie and its release meant that using current styles on a star would make her look out of fashion when the film was released months later. More important, each star's screen persona was carefully developed by the studio, and her roles never varied widely from it. For example, Norma Shearer represented the conservative-young-woman type; Garbo was always the unpredictable, mysterious exotic; and Joan Crawford typified sophisticated young America.

Film styles had influenced fashion since the silent movie era, but their impact was intensified by the advent of sound. With the "talkies," films became more realistic, and film costuming became less focused on theatrical effects. The European fashion world watched to see what Adrian put on Garbo, Shearer, and Crawford. Designs that Adrian introduced on individual stars frequently returned to America as "the latest from Paris."

The studios allowed manufacturers to market garments based on a star's film wardrobe, and thousands of dresses, blouses, and coats named for *Letty Lynton* (Joan Crawford, 1932) or *Queen Christina* (Greta Garbo, 1933) were sold. A number of Garbo's hats—the cloche from *A Woman of Affairs*, the plumed cap from *Romance*, and the pillbox and turban from *Painted Veil*—created new trends.

In 1930 the Modern Merchandising Bureau was established to organize the manufacture of styles introduced in a film before the picture's release, in order to have copies available in stores as soon as audiences saw the movie. Macy's in New York was the first store to open a Cinema Fashions shop, and crowds would gather on the sidewalk to see the new styles in the display windows. During the Great Depression, Hollywood further capitalized on film fashions by licensing patterns for home sewing based on them. The success of Condé Nast's *Hollywood Pattern Book* led to its becoming a whole new magazine, *Glamour of Hollywood*, in 1939; the title was subsequently shortened to *Glamour*. Movies exerted an enormous influence on world fashion, and Adrian was the leading Hollywood designer of his era.

After retiring from films, Adrian opened a couture and ready-to-wear business in Beverly Hills, which manufactured his designs and sold them to specialty stores throughout the United States. He showed his first collection in February 1942. Having designed suit variations for years in his movies on stars from Garbo to Hedy Lamarr—but most famously on Joan Crawford—he now produced the classic, square-shouldered, 1940s suit for which he is best known. Antecedents of this "V" silhouette throughout the 1930s had included such devices as the pagoda shoulder and the horizontal extension of the sleeve cap through pleating. To avoid both the faddish effect of the pagoda shoulder and the boxiness of the widened sleeve cap, Adrian squared the shoulder with pads of his own design, narrowing and neatening the silhouette to give it a classic line. As well as suits, he included a wide variety of day dresses, cocktail and evening wear, and coats in his collections.

In 1947 Adrian refused to follow the example of Paris when the New Look was introduced by Christian Dior. He found sloping shoulders, a cinched waist, padded hips, and long, full skirts unattractive on the average woman as well as cumbersome and impractical. Although he never significantly varied the "V" cut of his suits, he reduced the shoulder pads in his suits—never removing them altogether—and lengthened and slimmed the skirt. For evening wear, as opposed to daytime, Adrian had no quarrel with the New Look and encouraged women to go "all out." His wartime evening silhouette—a neoclassic column of rayon crepe with the same slim, squared shoulders as his suits—mutated into a softer silk sheath. Adrian's evening collections expanded to include everything from voluminous ball gowns to variations on the sari to dinner dresses draped with bustle variations.

Throughout the collections of Adrian's fashion career, certain themes reappeared. He frequently designed prints of animals, such as the famous "Roan Stallion" evening gown or *The Egg and I* at-home dress with its furious barnyard chickens. After Adrian's trip to Africa in 1949, animal and reptile prints appeared in a ball gown of tiger-skin taffeta and a hooded evening suit made from heavy silk that looked like an iridescent python skin. His "Americana" theme included a quilted silk hostess gown appliquéd with cotton gingham motifs and a long gingham evening coat with a matching skirt and sequined bodice. He referenced modern art movements such as futurism with inset streamers that emerged from the gown's surface to drape and flutter and cubism in the extraordinary "Modern Museum" series of rayon crepe gowns executed in pieced, multicolor, biomorphic shapes. In 1952 Adrian suffered a heart attack that forced him to close his business. He died in 1959.

Adrian's career was unique among designers in that he conquered both the film and fashion worlds. He worked entirely in California, far off the beaten track for couture or ready-to-wear. In film he worked as a couturier, designing costumes to highlight a star's individuality and conceal her figure flaws. These singular creations in turn engendered worldwide fashion trends. After leaving films his greatest achievement lay in his mastery of the ready-to-wear market. As a film designer Adrian gave fashion inspiration and hours of entertainment to millions of people all over the world. As a fashion designer he set a standard both for originality of design and quality of workmanship.

See also Actors and Actresses, Impact on Fashion; Costume Designer; Film and Fashion; Hollywood Style; Ready-to-Wear.

Bibliography

Gutner, Howard. *Gowns by Adrian.* New York: Harry N. Abrams, 2001.

Lee, Sarah Tomerlin, ed. *American Fashion: The Life and Lines of Adrian, Mainbocher, McCardell, Norell, and Trigère.* New York: Quadrangle/New York Times Book Company, 1975.

Jane Trapnell

AESTHETIC DRESS

In 1851, London celebrated the Great Exhibition, showcasing the latest innovations in manufacture and design. Its warm reception by the public and the media confirmed, in many people's eyes, the triumph of increased industrialization and mass production. However, some, who found this way of life increasingly abhorrent, sought an alternative lifestyle by looking to the past.

Three years earlier, in 1848, the young artists William Holman Hunt, John Everett Millais, and Dante Gabriel Rosetti established the Pre-Raphaelite Brotherhood, taking inspiration from the art of the late medieval and early renaissance periods, which they felt produced a purer and more naturalistic style. As such, dress played an important role in the depiction of the subjects, but with no extant examples, references came

from tomb effigies, illustrated manuscripts, and the artist's own inventions. The type of dress that emerged was worn by female members of the artists' circle.

Early styles of aesthetic dress took the form of flowing fabric with soft pleating falling from the neckline. The folds then gently gathered in at the natural, uncorseted waistline and fell into a small train at the back. The sleeves were a defining feature; unlike those of fashionable dress, they were set at the natural shoulder line and often decorated with puffs of fabric at the sleeve head, or gathered down the length of the arm. This enabled freedom of movement, as did the abandonment of the corset, which was felt to offer a more natural figure along the lines of the Venus de Milo, although critics noted "had Venus herself been compelled by a cold climate to drape herself, we have little doubt she would have worn stays, to give her clothes the shape they lacked" (Douglas, pp. 123–124). As such, the style found favor with dress reformers who spoke out against the damaging effects of tightly laced corseting. The two movements became closely allied and by 1890 the Healthy and Artistic Dress Union was established, publishing their ideas in their journal *Aglaia*.

Color was an all important element of the style, with soft browns, reds, blues, and—a popular choice and most recognizable of them all—a sage green, which was often referred to as "greenery yallery." Aesthetic dress was relatively unadorned, the only decoration appearing in the form of smocking or floral and organically inspired embroidery, with the sunflower and the lily being popular motifs. Accessories were kept to a minimum, with amber beads seen as the most appropriate choice, along with eastern or oriental-inspired pieces. The aesthetic woman herself was epitomized by the red-haired, pale-skinned beauties with their defined jawlines and sorrowful eyes as seen in Rosetti's *La Ghirlandata* (1877). A photograph of Jane Morris, the wife of the designer William Morris, taken in 1865, depicts her as the perfect embodiment of this ideal. Her untamed hair is loosely tied back, her dress draping in heavy folds.

By the 1870s, the style had really come to the attention of the public. In 1877, Mrs. Eliza Haweis published her book *The Art of Beauty* in which she outlined the drawbacks of contemporary fashion and commended the lines of historical dress. She was approached in 1878 by the ladies magazine *The Queen* to write some articles on the subject of Pre-Raphaelite dress. *The Queen* reported: "A great change has come over the style of English dressing within the last, say, five years. . . . The world of artists first started the idea of their wives and daughters dressing in harmony with ... [their] surroundings, and thence the grandes dames of fashion were influenced" (pp. 139–140).

As fashion conscripted artistic dress, historic periods were plundered with a myriad of styles indiscriminately thrown together under the term "aesthetic"; Greek tunics, medieval sleeves, and Elizabethan ruffs became popular adornments for fashionable dress. The Watteau-back dress, a partly fashionable style, was characterized by a large pleat of fabric falling loosely from the shoulders and caught up above the hem; it was inspired by eighteenth-century sacque dresses, depicted in the works of Watteau. These styles were a feature of the tea gown, a loose informal garment that could be worn at home or while receiving guests for afternoon tea.

The year 1877 also saw the opening of the Grosvenor Gallery and the first of the satirist George Du Maurier's series of cartoons, published in *Punch*, and based around a family known as the Cimabue Browns. The images portrayed the wearers of aesthetic dress as lank and languid men and women—the men in velvet jackets and long hair, the ladies with frizzed hair in long drooping garments—who always seemed to be contemplating the emotional impact of art on life.

The International Exhibition held in London in 1862 had stimulated the growing interest in oriental and exotic foreign goods. Arthur Lasenby Liberty, a young employee of Farmer and Roger's Shawl Emporium in Regent Street, persuaded his employers to open an oriental department. Owing to its huge success, Liberty left to set up his own department store in 1875. His imported fabrics and unusual artifacts were extremely popular with many artists, such as George Frederick Watts, James Whistler, and Frederick Leighton, who frequented the shop. Liberty soon began to produce his own fabrics suitable to the English climate yet with the qualities and colors of imported Eastern examples. In 1884, he opened a dressmaking department, overseen by E. W. Godwin, an architect and honorable secretary of the Costume Society. Godwin had designed many of the costumes for his partner, the famous actress Ellen Terry, whose choice of aesthetic dress was well known.

In 1881, the aesthetic craze was at its height with the production of Gilbert and Sullivan's *Patience* and the start of Oscar Wilde's lecture tours in America. His lectures included the importance of Liberty to the aesthetic movement and, as Alison Adburgham notes, this could "be said to have sown the first seeds that germinated into the long love affair between the Americans and Liberty's of London" (pp. 32–33).

May Morning, **Jane Morris, taken by J. Robert Parsons.** The heavily draped, unadorned dress, minimal accessories, and sorrowful expression are all typical of aesthetic fashion. © Stapleton Collection/Corbis. Reproduced by permission.

The aesthetic movement had a popular following in America, the most noted proponent being Annie Jenness Miller who published *Dress: The Jenness Miller Magazine*. The society painter W. P. Frith captured the aesthetic scene in his painting *Private View* (1881), which depicted many of the leading proponents of the movement, such as Wilde and Ellen Terry. In his memoirs of 1887, Frith recalled,

> Seven years ago certain ladies delighted to display themselves at public gatherings in what are called aesthetic dresses; in some cases the costumes were pretty enough, in others they seemed to rival each other in ugliness of form and oddity of color (p. 256).

This telling quote also illustrates how aesthetic dress was now somewhat passé. Many of its elements had entered the mainstream, with the popularity of the tea gown and the ready availability of "artistic dress" in most department stores. A guide to London of 1889 recommends Hamilton's of Regent Street for "those triumphs of needlework: smocked frocks and smocked tea gowns. But it is by no means only in so-called artistic dress that they excel" (Pascoe, p. 351). By the turn of the century, aesthetic dress was no longer seen as radical or revolutionary. While its themes may have lingered in the work of early twentieth-century designers, such as Mariano Fortuny, whose pleated fabrics seem directly inspired by the dress worn in Rosetti's painting *A Vision of Fiametta* (1878), or the draped velvets of Maria Monaci Gallenga, the sumptuous sophisticated style of art nouveau had captured the artistic imagination, and the soft muted colors and trailing drapery of aesthetic dress were considered démodé.

See also Art and Fashion; Fortuny, Mariano; Wilde, Oscar.

Bibliography

Adburgham, Alison. *Shops and Shopping.* London: George Allen and Unwin Ltd., 1964.

——. *Liberty: A Biography of a Shop.* London: George Allen and Unwin Ltd., 1975.

Costume: The Journal of the Costume Society 1 (1967), 2 (1968), 13 (1979), 21 (1987).

Douglas, Mrs. J. *The Gentlewoman's Book of Dress.* London: Henry and Company, 1895.

Frith, W. P. *My Autobiography and Reminiscences.* Vol. 2. London: Richard Bentley and Son, 1887.

Haweis, Eliza. *The Art of Beauty and The Art of Dress.* New York and London: Garland, 1978.

MacDonald, Margaret F., et al. *Whistler, Women and Fashion.* New Haven, Conn.: Yale University Press, 2003.

Newton, Stella Mary. *Health, Art and Reason: Dress Reformers of the 19th Century.* London: John Murray, 1974.

Pascoe, Charles Eyre. *London of Today: An Illustrated Handbook for the Season.* London: Hamilton Adams and Company, 1889.

Punch. 14 September 1878, 9 April 1881, 30 April 1881.

The Queen. 24 August 1878.

Squire, Geo. *Dress, Art and Society.* London: Macmillan, 1974.

Thieme, Otto Charles, E. A. Coleman, M. Oberly, and P. Cunningham. *With Grace and Favour: Victorian and Edwardian Fashion in America.* Cincinnati, Ohio: Cincinnati Art Museum, 1993.

Oriole Cullen

AFRICAN AMERICAN DRESS

African American dress intertwines with the history of Africans, who arrived in the Virginia colony in 1619. Within that century, southern codes forced the children of any enslaved woman to remain enslaved for life. West Africans continued to come unwillingly until the 1830s. President Abraham Lincoln proclaimed the emancipation of all enslaved peoples in 1863; but after the Civil War, African Americans lived on the margins of American society with poor jobs, substandard living and educational conditions, disenfranchisement, and public segregation. Nearly one hundred years later, in 1954, a Supreme Court decision began the desegregation process and in the 1960s, Federal legislation gave equal rights to African Americans.

Under enslavement, white owners demanded a certain form of dress for those in bondage: better dress for house servants and managers; poorer attire for field hands, children, and those too old to continue working. In spite of these constrictions, the nineteenth-century autobiographies and narratives, collected in the 1930s from formerly enslaved people, relate that African Americans put a great deal of thought into their dress. The narrators emphasized what clothing they had and did not have and described the clothing styles they desired and how they obtained them. "Correct" dress was especially important when "stepping out" for social occasions with community members, a habit that continues in the early 2000s. Narrators offered vivid depictions of dressing well for church, dances, and marriage.

Evidence shows that some retained West African forms of bodily adornment, particularly in the form of jewelry. From the African Burial Ground (1712–1795) in New York City, the remains of an adult female and an infant wore waistbeads as do West African women. Archaeological evidence from known slave sites sometimes includes cowries, seashells of economic importance before currencies became available in Africa and apparently worn as jewelry by the enslaved. The beads most often found at these sites consist of blue glass beads, worn as amulets in much of Africa and the Middle East. Former slaves provided testimony of wearing jewelry for both adornment and protection. Several Sea Islands narrators, for instance, describe single gold, loop earrings worn to protect the eyesight, retention of an African belief.

More outstanding as an African holdover than specific items of jewelry or clothing has been the interest in hairstyle and headwear by African American men and women. Documentation for West Africans' concern for well-groomed hair and ornamented heads is long-standing and survives among African Americans. Black men continue to sport ever-changing styles of facial hair and hairdos; the "conk" (straightened hair that is flattened down or slightly waved) of the 1930s remains a primary example. And, into the early twenty-first century, African American men consistently wear some type of headgear.

African American women also show a marked interest in their hairstyles and headwear. The slave narratives explain various ways of styling hair even under the most adverse conditions. Photographs of prominent women after the Civil War show them wearing the elegant, long, straight hairstyles in general fashion at the time. In 1906, this processing of the natural hair texture into straight hair spread across the country when Madame C. J. Walker began to market her highly profitable hair formula for managing African American women's hair. Black women also choose to wear hats, especially prevalent for church attendance.

With one exception, portraits from the eighteenth and nineteenth centuries, and nineteenth-century photographs, of African Americans show them wearing dress appropriate in general society. The exception is the African American woman's headwrap, the oldest extant specific dress item of any immigrant group

Headwraps. Beginning in the 1960s, African American women began wearing traditional headwraps as an acknowledgment of their West African ancestral roots. This fashion trend, among others, became popular with white Americans as well. © BJ Formento/ Corbis. Reproduced by permission.

worn in the early 2000s. But over time, its meaning changed.

In the antebellum South, several states legally enforced the code that ordered black women to wear a cloth head covering in public and not the hats and feathers worn by white women. These codes thus marked certain females as a subservient class. During enslavement, women working in onerous conditions wore the head wrap to keep the hair cleaner and to absorb perspiration. Use of the head wrap at home continued after the Civil War, but for public wear it was discarded. Beginning with the civil rights movement of the 1960s and 1970s, the head wrap took on other meanings. Young African American women again tied elaborate head wraps around their heads and publicly wore them in acknowledgment of their enslaved ancestors and as a reference to Africa and the way West African women adorn their heads.

During the civil rights movement, along with the head wrap, other young black revolutionaries adopted what they perceived to be West African attire, such as caftans and male head caps. Men and women grew their hair into enormous styles called "Afros," allowing for the natural texture to be emphasized in direct reaction against conks and Walker's straightening products that attempted to simulate European hair. Since the 1960s, some black men have continued to look back to Africa by wearing Rasta locks while black women have their hair intricately braided into elaborate African styles, often adding hairpieces.

African Americans generally have dressed in the prevailing fashions along with other Americans. Portraits of early black clergymen offer examples. Slave narrative frontispieces, however, illustrate the author in either slave clothing or formally dressed as a freed person, the choice obviously expressed what the author wanted to portray about his or her place in society. After the invention of photography, the images of eminent leaders such as Frederick Douglass and Booker T. Washington always show them dressed in formal, gentleman's clothing. Between 1895 and 1925, black intellectuals, literati, and artists strove to present themselves as quite different from the racist stereotypical cartoon illustrations of "Mammys" and "Sambos" drawn by whites. Many illustrations show these "New Negroes" groomed and adorned in conservative, mainstream dress.

Although African Americans adopted the prevailing cultural dress of each period, their style often sets them apart. For instance, travelers' accounts about the South prior to emancipation describe African Americans' dress as more flamboyant and colorful than that of whites. Contemporary African Americans similarly prefer to be well dressed for most occasions and have not adopted the white population's sartorial trends to casual and even sloppy dress.

In general, American fashions came from Europe until about 1950. But at the same time, black styles began to influence white American dress, particularly men's; for example, the zoot suit of the 1940s, highlighted by the popular singers Billy Eckstein and Frank Sinatra. In the 1960s, expensive, stylized brands of tennis shoes, first worn by professional African American athletes, notably basketball players, were adopted by the larger, adolescent community. In the 1990s, white, suburban youth began wearing the hip-hop clothing first worn by young, urban, black males. And in the early twenty-first century, white males wear the doo rag, for decades the African American male's inner-city hair tamer.

Since the mid-1950s, African Americans have become part of the greater American cultural scene. And, in a very real sense, this larger society in the early 2000s adopts African American culture in many aspects of life, not the least in styles of dress.

See also Afro Hairstyle; Afrocentric Fashion; Ethnic Dress; Zoot Suit.

Bibliography

Cunningham, Michael, and Craig Marberry. *Crowns: Portraits of Black Women in Church Hats*. New York: Algonquin Books of Chapel Hill, 2001.

Foster, Helen Bradley. *"New Raiments of Self"*: *African American Clothing in the Antebellum South*. Oxford: Berg, 1997.

———. "African American Jewelry Before the Civil War." In *Beads and Bead Makers: Gender, Material Culture and Meaning*. Edited by Lidia D. Sciama and Joanne B. Eicher 177–192. Oxford: Berg, 1998.

Gates, Henry Louis, Jr. "The Trope of the New Negro and the Reconstruction of the Image of the Black." *Representations* 24 (Fall 1988): 129–155.

Genovese, Eugene. "Clothes Make the Man and the Woman." In *Roll, Jordan, Roll: The World the Slaves Made*, 550–561. New York: Pantheon Books, 1974.

Rawick, George P., ed. *The American Slave: A Composite Autobiography*. Westport, Conn.: Greenwood, 1972, 1977, 1979.

Starke, Barbara M., Lillian O. Holloman, and Barbara K. Nordquist, eds. *African American Dress and Adornment: A Cultural Perspective*. Dubuque, Iowa: Kendall/Hunt, 1990.

White, Shane, and Graham White. *Stylin': African American Expressive Culture*. Ithaca, N.Y.: Cornell University Press, 1998.

Helen Bradley Foster

AFRO HAIRSTYLE

At the end of the 1950s, a small number of young black female dancers and jazz singers broke with prevailing black community norms and wore unstraightened hair. The hairstyle they wore had no name and when noticed by the black press, was commonly referred to as wearing hair "close-cropped." These dancers and musicians were sympathetic to or involved with the civil rights movement and felt that unstraightened hair expressed their feelings of racial pride. Around 1960, similarly motivated female student civil rights activists at Howard University and other historically black colleges stopped straightening their hair, had it cut short, and generally suffered ridicule from fellow students. Over time the close-cropped style developed into a large round shape, worn by both sexes, and achieved by lifting longer unstraightened hair outward with a wide-toothed comb known as an Afro pick. At the peak of its popularity in the late 1960s and early 1970s the Afro epitomized the black is beautiful movement. In those years the style represented a celebration of black beauty and a repudiation of Eurocentric beauty standards. It also created a sense of commonality among its wearers who saw the style as the mark of a person who was willing to take a defiant stand against racial injustice. As the Afro increased in popularity its association with black political movements weakened and so its capacity to communicate the political commitments of its wearers declined.

Pre-Existing Norms

In the 1950s black women were expected to straighten their hair. An unstraightened black female hairstyle constituted a radical rejection of black community norms. Black women straightened their hair by coating it with protective pomade and combing it with a heated metal comb. This technique transformed the tight curls of African American hair into completely straight hair with a pomaded sheen. Straightened hair remained straight until it had contact with water. Black women made every effort to lengthen the time between touch-ups. They protected their hair from rain, did not go swimming, and washed their hair only immediately before straightening it again. If a woman could not straighten her hair, she covered it with a scarf.

The technology of hair straightening served prevailing gender norms that defined long wavy hair as beautifully feminine. While hair straightening could not lengthen hair and may have contributed to breakage, it transformed tightly curled hair into straight hair that could be set into waves. Tightly curled hair was disparaged as "nappy" or "bad hair," while straight hair was praised as "good hair." The Eurocentric underpinnings of these black community judgments have led many to characterize the practice of hair straightening as a black attempt to imitate whites. Cultural critics have countered by arguing that hair straightening represented much more than an imitation of whites. Black women modeled themselves after other black women who straightened their hair to present themselves as urban, modern, and well groomed.

In the post–World War II period, when the vast majority of black women straightened their hair, most black men wore short unstraightened hair. The male straightened hairstyle that was known as the conk was highly visible because it was the style favored by many black entertainers. The conk, however, was a rebellious style associated with entertainers and with men in criminal subcultures. Conventional black men and men with middle-class aspirations kept their hair short and did not straighten it.

Origins

In the late 1950s and early 1960s, awareness of newly independent African nations and the victories and setbacks of the civil rights movement encouraged feelings of hope and anger, as well as exploration of identity among young African Americans. The Afro originated in that political and emotional climate. The style fit with a broader generational rejection of artifice but more importantly, it expressed defiance of racist beauty norms, rejection of middle-class conventions, and pride in black beauty. The unstraightened hair of the Afro was simultaneously a way to celebrate the cultural and physical distinctiveness of the race and to reject practices associated with emulation of whites.

Dancers, jazz and folk musicians, and university students may have enjoyed greater freedom to defy conventional styles than ordinary working women and were the first to wear unstraightened styles. In the late 1950s a few black modern dancers who tired of continually touching-up straightened hair that perspiration had returned to kinkiness, decided to wear short unstraightened hair. Ruth Beckford, who performed with Katherine Dunham, recalled the confused reactions she received when she wore a short unstraightened haircut. Strangers offered her cures to help her hair grow and a young student asked the shapely Miss Beckford if she was a man.

Around 1960, in politically active circles on the campuses of historically black colleges and in civil rights movement organizations, a few young black women adopted natural hairstyles. As early as 1961 the jazz musicians Abbey Lincoln, Melba Liston, Miriam Makeba, Nina Simone and folk singer Odetta were performing wearing short unstraightened hair. Though these women are primarily known as performing artists, political commitments were integral to their work. They sang lyrics calling for racial justice and performed at civil rights movement rallies and fund-raisers. In 1962 and 1963 Abbey Lincoln toured with Grandassa, a group of models and entertainers whose fashion shows promoted the link between black pride and what had begun to be called variously the "au naturel," "au naturelle," or "natural" look. When the mainstream black press took note of unstraightened hair, reporters generally insinuated that wearers of "au naturelle" styles had sacrificed their sex appeal for their politics. They could not yet see unstraightened hair as beautiful.

Activist Angela Davis, without and with an Afro. By the late 1960s, the Afro was less frequently associated with black political movements, but the notoriety of Davis caused many to refer to the Afro as the "Angela Davis look." © BETTMANN/CORBIS. REPRODUCED BY PERMISSION.

Early Reactions

Though they received support for the style among fellow activists, the first women who wore unstraightened styles experienced shocked stares, ridicule, and insults for wearing styles that were perceived as appalling rejections of community standards. Many of these women had conflicts with their elders who thought of hair straightening as essential good grooming. Ironically, a few black female students who were isolated at predominantly white colleges experienced acceptance from white radicals who were unfamiliar with black community norms. More mainstream whites, however, saw the style as shockingly unconventional and some employers banned Afros from the workplace. As more women abandoned hair straightening, the natural became a recognizable style and a frequent topic of debate in the black press. Increasing numbers of women stopped straightening their hair as the practice became emblematic of racial shame. At a 1966 rally, the black leader Stokely Carmichael fused style, politics, and self-love when he told the crowd: "We have to stop being ashamed of being black. A broad nose, a thick lip, and nappy hair is us and we are going to call that beautiful whether they like it or not. We are not going to fry our hair anymore" (Bracey, Meier, and Rudwick 1970, p. 472). The phrase "black is beautiful" was everywhere and it summed up a new aesthetic ranking that valued the beauty of dark brown skin and the tight curls of unstraightened hair.

Increasing numbers of activists adopted the hairstyle and the media disseminated their images. By 1966 the Afro was firmly associated with political activism. Women who wore unstraightened hair could feel that their hair identified them with the emerging black power movement. Televised images of Black Panther Party members wearing black leather jackets, black berets, sunglasses, and Afros projected the embodiment of black radicalism. Some men and many women began to grow larger Afros. Eventually only hair that was cut in a large round shape was called an Afro, while other unstraightened haircuts were called naturals.

Popularization

As larger numbers of black men and women wore the Afro, workplace and intergenerational conflicts lessened. In 1968 Kent cigarettes and Pepsi-cola developed print advertisements featuring women with large Afros. Decorative Afro picks with black power fist-shaped handles or African motifs were popular fashion items. While continuing to market older products for straightening hair, manufacturers of black hair-care products formulated new products for Afro care. The electric "blow-out comb" combined a blow-dryer and an Afro pick for styling large Afros. Wig manufacturers introduced Afro wigs. Though the Afro's origins were in the United States, Johnson Products, longtime manufacturer of hair-straightening products, promoted its new line of Afro Sheen products with the Swahili words for "beautiful people" in radio and print advertisements that stated "Wantu Wazuri use Afro Sheen." In 1968 a large Afro was a crucial element of the style of Clarence Williams III, star of the popular television series, *The Mod Squad*. In 1969 British *Vogue* published Patrick Lichfield's photograph of Marsha Hunt, who posed nude except for arm and ankle bands and her grand round Afro. This widely celebrated image fit with an emerging fashion industry pattern of featuring black models associated with signifiers of the primitive, wildness, or exotica.

One wearer of a large Afro was the activist and scholar Angela Davis who wore the style in keeping with the practices of other politically active black women. When, in 1970, she was placed on the FBI's most wanted list, her image circulated internationally. During her time as a fugitive and prisoner she became a heroine for many black women as a wide campaign worked for her release. The large Afro became indelibly associated with Angela Davis and increasingly described as the "Angela Davis look." Ironically the popularization of her image contributed to the transformation of the Afro from a practice that expressed the political commitments of dedicated activists to a style that could be worn by the merely fashion-conscious.

The style that became the Afro originated with black women. Since most black men wore short unstraightened hair in the late 1950s, short unstraightened hair could only represent something noteworthy for black women. When, in the mid-1960s, the style evolved into a large round shape, it became a style for men as well as women. Since black men customarily wore unstraightened hair, an Afro was only an Afro when it was large. During the late 1960s and early 1970s, when men and women wore Afros, commercial advertising and politically inclined artwork generally reasserted gender distinctions that had been challenged by the first women who dared to wear short unstraightened hair. Countless images of the era showed the head and shoulders of a black man wearing a large Afro behind a black woman with a larger Afro. Typically, the woman's shoulders were bare and she wore large earrings.

Declining Popularity and Enduring Significance

In the late 1960s the black radical H. Rap Brown complained that underneath their natural hairstyles too many blacks had "processed minds." By the end of the decade many blacks would agree with his observation that the style said little about a wearer's political views. As fashion incorporated the formerly shocking style, it detached the Afro from its political origins. The hair-care industry worked to position the Afro as one option among many and to reassert hair straightening as the essential first step of black women's hair care. In 1970 a style known as the Curly Afro, which required straightening and then curling hair, became popular for black women. In 1972 Ron O'Neal revived pre-1960s subcultural images of black masculinity when he wore long wavy hair as the star of the film *Superfly*. Large Afros continued to be popular through the 1970s but their use in the era's blaxploitation films introduced new associations with Hollywood's parodic representations of black subcultures.

While the large round Afro is so strongly associated with the 1970s that it is most frequently revived in comical retro contexts, the Afro nonetheless had enduring consequences. It permanently expanded prevailing images of beauty. In 2003 the black singer Erykah Badu stepped onstage at Harlem's Apollo Theater wearing a large Afro wig. After a few songs she removed the wig to reveal her short unstraightened hair. Reporters described her hair using the language employed by those who had first attempted to describe the styles worn by singer Nina Simone, Abbey Lincoln, and Odetta at the beginning of the 1960s. They called it "close-cropped." Prior to the popularity of the Afro black women hid unstraightened hair under scarves. Through the Afro the public grew accustomed to seeing the texture of unstraightened hair as beautiful and the way was opened for a proliferation of unstraightened African American styles.

See also African American Dress; Afrocentric Fashion; Barbers; Hair Accessories; Hairdressers; Hairstyles.

Bibliography

Bracey, John H., Jr., August Meier, and Elliott Rudwick, eds. *Black Nationalism in America*. New York: Bobbs-Merrill Company, 1970.

Craig, Maxine Leeds. *Ain't I a Beauty Queen: Black Women, Beauty, and the Politics of Race*, New York: Oxford University Press, 2002. Includes a detailed history of the emergence of the Afro.

Davis, Angela Y. "Afro Images: Politics, Fashion, and Nostalgia." *Critical Inquiry* 21 (Autumn 1994): 37–45. Davis reflects on the use of photographs of her Afro in fashion images devoid of political content.

Kelley, Robin D. G. "Nap Time: Historicizing the Afro." *Fashion Theory* 1, no. 4 (1997): 339–351. Kelley traces the black bohemian origins of the Afro and its transformation from a feminine to masculine style.

Mercer, Kobena. "Black Hair/Style Politics." In *Out There: Marginalization and Contemporary Cultures*, edited by Russell Ferguson, Martha Gever, Trinh T. Minh-ha, and Cornel West, 247–264. Cambridge, Mass.: MIT Press, 1990. Mercer places the Afro in the context of earlier black hair care practices and challenges the widely held view that hair-straightening represented black self-hatred.

Maxine Leeds Craig

AFROCENTRIC FASHION

An Afrocentric perspective references African history and applies it to all creative, social, and political activity.

Negritude and Afrocentricity

Afrocentricity was founded in the 1940s when Aimé Césaire and Léopold Sédar Senghor, president of Senegal and poet, used the term "negritude" to describe the effects of Western colonization upon black people without any reference to their culture, language, or place. The most significant example of colonization was the Atlantic slave trade that started in the fourteenth century and lasted for 400 years. However, the effects of colonization have arguably caused Africa to become economically underdeveloped and culturally bereft. For the descendants of slaves living in Western countries Atlantic slavery had resulted in them experiencing disadvantage and intolerance, which was based upon their physical dissimilarity from the indigenous population. These points are at the kernel of Aimé Césaire and Léopold Sédar Senghor's idea that negritude is defined by the physical state of the black person, which is blackness.

Afrocentrism gained gravitas when Cheikh Anta Diop (1974) argued that ancient Africans and modern Africans share similar physical appearances and other genetic similarities, as well as cultural patterns and language structures. Diop and others have used this insight to sponsor the idea of ancient Egypt (Kemet) as a black civilization and a reference point for modern Africans.

Frantz Fanon (1967) used the term "negritude" to illustrate the existence of black psychological pathologies that hindered black individuals from attaining liberation within Western modernism and the way all black people are affected by colonialism. An example of black psychological pathology in self-expression is found in the way fashion provides a visual backdrop to the engagement between mask and identity, image and identification. The purpose of fashion in the African setting is precise; it enables black individuals to attain status positions that are outside of their usual habitus. In doing so blacks use some of the visual tools of their oppression and liberation when creating their fashioned self image. Fanon provides a sketch of a black Caribbean man who arrives in the West after leaving his homeland. He leaves behind a way of life symbolized by the bandanna and the straw hat. Once in the West the man shifts into a position, which is manifest by his unease of existing in the West and perhaps from wearing Western clothes. Fanon's rather harsh indictment offers blacks in the West only two possibilities, either to stand with the white world or to reject it. This concept of negritude contributed to the conceptual basis of Afrocentrism.

Expression of Self

The way that black people use apparel in personal representations of *self* may differ and be dependent upon location and perspective. Afrocentric fashion is analogous to Western fashion. Both appropriate much from oppositional fashion expressions; consequently both expressions are fragmented and perennially incomplete. Avid Afrocentrists reject the idea that Afrocentricism might be influenced or contain traces of Western culture, though it is perceptible that Afrocentric fashion is less absolute than other expressive forms, such as music and art.

In Africa and in the African diaspora, disparate elements may be united by their adoption of Afrocentric apparel. Visualizations of Afrocentric clothing are made with reference to Kemet and are therefore mental constructions that are mimetic because they draw upon the idea of an ancient African self and its accompanied gestures, which are of course an aberration, occasioned by the pathology that Fanon alluded to. Around the time of the 1960s American civil rights movement, Afrocentricism became important and sometimes central to the fashion expressions of black people living in America, the Caribbean, and Britain.

Ordinarily, Afrocentric clothing does not feature fine linen dresses, kilts, collars, or the wearing of kohl on one's eyes; yet Afrocentric dressing does feature selected apparel motifs and long-established textiles, production, and cutting methods from the rest of Africa. Afrocentric fashion references the apparel traditions of multicultural Africa, including the traditions of both the colonizers and the colonized. The story of batik (which is Indonesian in origin) is an example of the former.

For Afrocentrists, Afrocentric dress is the norm; consequently Western dress is "ethnic" and therefore "exotic." For that reason, Afrocentric dress has become a virtuoso expression of African diaspora culture. Political and cultural activities like black cultural nationalism have adopted Afrocentric fashion for its visual symbolism. African and black identity and black nationalism are expressed by the wearing of African and African-inspired dress such as the dashiki, Abacos (Mao-styled suit), Kanga, caftan, wraps, and Buba. All of these items are cultural products of the black diaspora and are worn exclusively or integrated into Western dress.

These fashions connote a dissonance. The combination of Afrocentric and Western styles in a single garment or outfit is a direct confrontation of Western fashion, especially if the clothing does not simultaneously promote an Afrocentric leitmotiv or theme. Within its configuration, Afrocentric dress co-opts a number of textiles. Ghanaian kente cloth, batik, mud cloth, indigo cloth, and, to a lesser extent, bark cloth are used. Interestingly, dashikis, Abacos, Kangas, caftans, wraps, and Saki robes are all made in kente, batik, and mud cloth, but are also made in plain cottons, polyesters, and glittery novelty fabrics and tiger, leopard, and zebra prints.

Less popular are apparel items that do not assimilate well in everyday life; these are grand items such the West African Buba, which can be a voluminous floor-length robe that is often embroidered at the neckline and worn both by men and women. Various types of accessories such as skullcaps, kofis, turbans, and Egyptian- and Ghanaian-inspired jewelry are worn with other Afrocentric items or separately with Western

Trio modeling Afrocentric clothing. The women wear *bubas*, a type of floor-length West African garment, and the man wears a loose-fitting *dashiki* shirt and wooden jewelry. © BETTMANN/CORBIS. REPRODUCED BY PERMISSION.

items. Afrocentric fabrics that are made into ties, purses, graduation cowls, and pocket-handkerchiefs have special significance within the middle-class African diaspora.

Who Has Worn Afrocentric Fashion?

The most significant expression of Afrocentricity outside of Africa existed in America during the 1960s and 1970s. The Black Panthers and other black nationalist and civil rights groups used clothing as a synthesis of protest and self-affirmation. Prototype items consisted of men's berets, knitted tams, black leather jackets, black turtleneck sweaters, Converse sneakers, and Afrocentric items including dashikis, various versions of Afro hairstyles, and to a lesser extent Nehru jackets, caftans, and djellabas for men. Women adopted tight black turtleneck sweaters, leather trousers, dark shades, Yoruba-style head wraps, batik wrap skirts, and African inspired jewelry. For both men and women, the latter items were Afrocentric; the former were incorporated

into Afrocentricity because the constituency wore them and popularized them, and they became idiomatic of black protest.

In 1962, Kwame Brathwaite and the African Jazz-Art Society and Studios in Harlem presented a fashion and cultural show that featured the Grandassa Models. The show became an annual event. The purpose was to explore the idea that "black is beautiful." It did so by using dark-skinned models with kinky hair wearing clothes that used African fabrics cut in shapes derivative of African dress. The impetus for the popularity of Afrocentric fashion in America arose from this event. The Grandassa Models explored the possibilities of kente, mud cloth, batik, tie-dye, and indigo cloths, and numerous possibilities of wrapping cloth, as opposed to cut-and-sewn apparel. Subsequently, such entertainers as Nina Simone, Aretha Franklin, the Voices of East Harlem, and Stevie Wonder on occasion wore part or full Afrocentric dress. In America, the Caribbean, and Britain, Afrocentric fashion was most popular during the 1960s and 1970s. Turbans, dashikis, large hooped earrings, and cowrie shell jewelry became the most popular Afrocentric fashion items.

Similar to the Black Panthers, Jamaican Rastafarians wear "essentialized" fashion items. However, spiritual, aesthetic, and cultural values of Rastafarianism are implied through various apparel items. The material culture of Rastafarianism is directly linked to cultural resistance, signified by military combat pants, battle jackets, and berets. These items were introduced in the 1970s and provided Rastafarians with a sense of identity that is further supported and symbolized by dreadlocks, the red, green, and gold Ethiopian flag, and the image of the Lion of Judah, which represents strength and dread.

Jamaican Dancehall, a music-led subculture that started with picnics and tea dances in the 1950s, features a wide repertoire of fashion themes. One widely used theme is African. African dress is omnipresent in Dance-hall fashion; items such as the baggy "Click Suits," worn by men in the mid-1990s, were based on the African Buba top and Sokoto pants. Women's fashions—including baggy layered clothing made in vibrant and sometimes gaudy colors; transparent, plastic, or stretchable fabrics; and decorations, such as beading, fringing, or rickrack—were shaped into discordant Western silhouettes. Dancehall fashions of the 1990s symbolized sexuality, self-determination; and freedom. Wearers rejected apparel that was comfortable and practical in favor of clothing that celebrated hedonism.

Wearers of Afrocentric dress distinguish themselves and celebrate "Africanness" within the context of the West. Adoption of Afrocentric clothing is a way of casting aside the deep psychological rift of topographical past and modern present that the psychiatrist Frantz Fanon writes of in *Black Skin, White Masks* (1967). Afrocentric dress is also present in black music cultures of the Caribbean, United States, and the United Kingdom. In the early 2000s B-boys and girls, Flyboys and girls, Dancehall Kings and Queens, Daisy Agers, Rastafarians, neo-Panthers, Funki Dreds, and Junglist all include Afro-centicity in their fashion choices. Afrocentric fashion features combinations of commonplace apparel items that represent dissonance with selected preeminent pieces from Africa's primordial past and its present.

See also African American Dress; Batik; Boubou; Dashiki; Kente.

Bibliography

Diop, Cheikh Anta. *The African Origin of Civilization: Myth or Reality*. New York: Lawrence Hill and Company, 1974.

Fanon, Frantz. *Black Skin, White Masks*. New York: Grove Press, 1967.

Vaillant, Janet G. *Black, French, and African: A Life of Leopold Sedar Senghor*. Cambridge, Mass.: Harvard University Press, 1990.

Van Dyk Lewis

ALAÏA, AZZEDINE

Azzedine Alaïa was born in southern Tunisia in about 1940 to a farming family descended from Spanish Arabic stock. He was brought up by his maternal grandparents in Tunis and, at the age of fifteen, enrolled at l'École des beaux-arts de Tunis to study sculpture. However, his interest in form soon diverted him toward fashion. Alaïa's career started with a part-time job finishing hems (assisted at first by his sister, who also studied fashion). He became a dressmaker's assistant, helping to copy couture gowns by such Parisian couturiers as Christian Dior, Pierre Balmain, and Cristóbal Balenciaga for wealthy Tunisian clients; these luxurious and refined creations set a standard for excellence that Alaïa has emulated ever since.

In 1957 Alaïa moved to Paris. His first job, for Christian Dior, lasted only five days; the Algerian war had just begun and Alaïa, being Arabic, was probably not welcome. He then worked on two collections at Guy Laroche, learning the essentials of dress construction. Introduced to the cream of Parisian society by a Paris-based compatriot (Simone Zehrfuss, wife of the architect Bernard Zehrfuss), Alaïa began to attract private commissions. Between 1960 and 1965 he lived as a housekeeper and dressmaker for the comtesse Nicole de Blégiers and then established a small salon on the Left Bank, where he built up a devoted private clientele. He remained there until 1984, fashioning elegant clothing for, among others, the French actress Arlette-Leonie Bathiat, the legendary cinema star Greta Garbo, and the socialite Cécile de Rothschild, a cousin of the famous French banking family. Alaïa also worked on commissions for other designers; for example, he created the prototype for Yves Saint Laurent's Mondrian-inspired shift dress.

Ready-to-Wear Collections

By the 1970s, in response to the changing climate in fashion, Alaïa's focus shifted from custom-made gowns to ready-to-wear for an emerging clientele of young, discerning customers. Toward the end of the decade he designed for Thierry Mugler and produced a group of leather garments for Charles Jourdan. Rejected for being too provocative, they have been kept ever since in Alaïa's extensive archive. In 1981 he launched his first collection; already favored by the French fashion press, he soon found international success. In 1982 he showed his prêt-à-porter, or ready-to-wear, line at Bergdorf Goodman in New York, and in 1983 he opened a boutique in Beverly Hills. The French Ministry of Culture honored him with the Designer of the Year award in 1985. He has dressed many famous women, such as the model Stephanie Seymour, the entertainer and model Grace Jones, and the 1950s Dior model Bettina. Moreover, Alaïa was the first to feature the supermodel Naomi Campbell on the catwalk.

In the early 1990s Alaïa relocated his Paris showroom to a large, nineteenth-century, glass-roofed, iron-frame building on the rue de Moussy. There he lives and works, accompanied by various dogs, and his staff, regardless of status, eat lunch together every day. Partly designed by Julian Schnabel and adorned with his artwork, the building's calm, pared-down interior, glass-roofed gallery, and intense workshops resemble a shrine to fashion. Alaïa has always been a nonconformist; since 1993 he has eschewed producing a new collection every season, preferring to show his creations at his atelier when they are ready, which is often months later than announced.

King of Cling

Alaïa's technique was formed through traditional couture practice, but his style is essentially modern. He is best known for his svelte, clinging garments that fit like a second skin. Although he is revered in the early 2000s, the 1980s were in many ways Alaïa's time; his use of stretch Lycra, silk jersey knits, and glove leather and suede suited the sports- and body-conscious decade. The singer Tina Turner said of his work, "He gives you the very best line you can get out of your body. . . . Take any garment he has made. You can't drop the hem, you can't let it out or take it in. It's a piece of sculpture" (Howell, p. 256).

Alaïa has described himself as a *bâtisseur*, or builder, and his tailoring is exceptional. He cuts the pattern and assembles the prototype for every single dress that he creates, sculpting and draping the fabric on a live model. As he explains, "I have to try my things on a living body because the clothes I make must respect the body" (Mendes, p. 113). Although his clothes appear simple, many contain numerous discrete components, all constructed with raised, corsetry stitching and curved seaming to achieve a perfect sculptural form. Georgina Howell wrote in *Vogue* in March 1990:

> He worked out dress in terms of touch. He abolished all underclothes and made one garment do the work. The technique is dazzling, for just as a woman's body is a network of surface tensions, hard here, soft there, so Azzedine Alaïa's clothes are a force field of give and resistance. (p. 258)

Utilizing fabric technology first designed for sportswear to skim the body in stretch fabric that made women's bodies look as smooth as possible, Alaïa produced a stunning variety of fashions. They included jersey sheath dresses with flesh-exposing zippers, dresses made of stretch Lycra bands, taut jackets and short skirts, stretch chenille and lace body suits, leggings, skinny jumper dresses with cutouts, and dresses with spiraling zippers. To this oeuvre he added bustiers and cinched, perforated leather belts; cowl-neck gowns; *broderie anglaise* or gold-mesh minidresses; and stiffened tulle wedding gowns. His palette favored muted colors, in particular, black, uncluttered and unadorned with jewelry.

Alaïa's Influence

Whether applied to his haute couture, tailoring, or ready-to-wear lines, Alaïa's work is typified by precision and control; these characteristics apply even to his designs for mail-order companies, such as Les 3 Suisses and La redoute. He survived the 1990s without glossy advertising campaigns and without compromise, and in 2001 Helmut Lang paid tribute to Alaïa's work in his spring and summer 2001 collection.

Alaïa is a perfectionist and has been known to sew women into their outfits in order to get the most perfect fit. Often accompanied by his friend, confidante, and muse, the model and actress Farida Khelfa, he is of small stature and invariably dresses in a black Chinese silk jacket and trousers and black cotton slippers, declaring that he would look far too macho in a suit. Alaïa's work has been shown in retrospectives at the Bordeaux Museum of Contemporary Art (1984–1985) and the Groninger Museum in the Netherlands (1998), and in the exhibition *Radical Fashion* at the Victoria and Albert Museum in London (2001). In 2000 Prada acquired a stake in Alaïa; the agreement contains the promise of creating a foundation in Paris for the Alaïa archive, which includes not only his own creations but also designs by many twentieth-century couturiers, such as Madeleine Vionnet and Cristóbal Balenciaga. Alaïa said, "When I see beautiful clothes I want to keep them, preserve them. . . . clothes, like architecture and art, reflect an era" (Wilcox, p. 56).

See also Fashion Designer; Fashion Models; Jersey; Super-models.

Bibliography

Alaïa, Azzedine, ed. *Alaïa*. Göttingen, Germany: Steidl, 1999.

Baudot, François. *Alaïa*. London: Thames and Hudson, Inc., 1996.

Howell, Georgina. "The Titan of Tight." *Vogue*, March 1990, pp. 456–459.

Mendes, Valerie. *Black in Fashion*. London: V & A Publications, 1999.

Wilcox, Claire, ed. *Radical Fashion*. London: V & A Publications, 2001.

Claire Wilcox

ALBINI, WALTER

Walter Albini (1941–1983) was born Gualtiero Angleo Albini in Busto Arsizio, Lombardy, in northern Italy. In 1957 he interrupted his study of the classics, which his family had encouraged him to pursue, and enrolled in the Istituto d'Arte, Disegno e Moda in Turin, the only male student admitted to the all-girls school. A gifted student, Albini studied drawing and specialized in ink and tempera, at which he excelled. He took a degree in fashion design in 1960.

Fashion design remained an abiding interest for Albini. Even as an adolescent he worked as an artist for newspapers and magazines, to whom he sent sketches of the fashion shows held in Rome and Paris, a city for which he felt an intense and profound affinity. Paris was a fundamental step in his creative and emotional development, as evidenced by the many references to the French designers Paul Poiret and Coco Chanel in his work. In Paris, where he remained from 1961 to 1965, Albini met Chanel—a designer he admired throughout his life and to whom he dedicated his 1975 haute couture show in Rome. He was inspired by the importance Chanel gave to freeing the woman's body, to mixing and coordinating different pieces, and to accessorizing. While still in Paris he became friends with Mariucci Mandelli, who started the Krizia line and with whom he had a lifelong friendship. After Albini's return to Italy, he worked for three years (1965–1968) designing sweaters for Krizia. The designer, Karl Lagerfeld was also working for Krizia in this period. Mandelli once said of Albini, "I was never disappointed with Walter. He never gave in to vulgarity, pettiness, or mediocrity; he was a character straight out of (F. Scott) Fitzgerald, maybe the last. He gave us a lesson in style" (Bocca, p. 138).

Albini worked as a consultant for several companies and designed for Billy Ballo, Cadette, Trell, and Montedoro. He selected fabrics and designs for Etro and created several collections for Basile. In 1967 *Vogue Italia* published a six-page spread of his work for the Krizia collection, and by 1968 he was already well known to other designers. The next year he presented his own Mister Fox line, a name that had been suggested by his friend the journalist Anna Piaggi. The collection comprised sixteen elegant suits, eight of which (all black) were called "the widows" and the other eight (all flesh-colored), "the wives." The garments were made in collaboration with the industrialist, Luciano Papini.

Albini was the first to initiate a series of innovative reforms in Italian fashion that responded to a changing market. These innovations included freeing the designer from the anonymity of the world of production and treating him as a creator, as in the world of haute couture, and recognizing the need for the fashion industry to provide styles and images and not only clothing, so that it could reach new market segments in a rapidly changing world. Albini worked closely with fabric manufacturers and enhanced the presence of the designer in industrial production.

He also helped create specialized companies in different sections of industry, so that they could collaborate to produce a collection with a recognizable brand name. These companies included well-known names like Basile for coats, skirts, and jackets; Escargots for jersey; Callaghan for knitwear, Mister Fox for evening dress; Diamant's for shirts. An agreement with FTM (Ferrante, Tositti, Monti) gave rise to a new label—"Walter Albini for," followed by the name of the manufacturer. At the Circolo del Giardino in Milan (28 April 1971), a prêt-àporter collection was presented for the first time. The collection, made of dresses, shirts, coats, trousers, evening dress, hats, shoes, and jewelry was designed by just one designer in coordination with producers from different industries, each of them specialized in its own field of production. The collection was then sold as a whole to shops, which sold them as they were conceived. It was the system of prêt-à-porter as we currently know it. The 7 June 1971 issue of *Women's Wear Daily*, entitled "Putting It Together," reported on this epochal change in fashion.

In 1971 Albini was the first designer to abandon the Sala Bianca at Palazzo Pitti in Florence—together with Caumont, Trell, Ken Scott, Missoni, Krizia—which was still associated with the older fashion tradition, in favor of Milan. That year, 1971, is considered the official birth of prêt-à-porter. Bianca was a place strictly connected to the name of Giovanni Battista Giorgini and to the official birth of Italian fashion with the collective catwalk shows of January 1952. Sala Bianca continued its activities until 1982, when Milan, already the center of the emerging new design prêt-à-porter, took over.

The 1973 Venice catwalk show took place among the tables of the celebrated Caffè Florian, which had been closed for the day. It was a magical moment for Albini. "It had been a long time since so much tweed, velvet, silk, and lamé, worn by these elegant women, had grazed the exquisitely decorated woodwork of the Caffè Florian in Piazza san Marco" (Vercelloni 1984, p. 90).

There are a number of constants in Walter Albini's designs and inspiration: the deco style, Poiret interpretation of liberty, Bauhaus, futurism, constructivism, the art of the 1910s to 1930s when a new feminine representation emerged especially with the work of Chanel. Albini's constants in design are jackets with half belts, flat collars, wide pants, the famous shirt jacket that was to become a classic of Italian men's clothing, sandals, two-tone shoes, Bermuda shorts, sports jackets, knit caps worn low on the forehead, and the first waterproof boots. He invented the image of the woman in pants, jacket, and shirt and reintroduced the use of print designs, both abstract and figurative. His favorite themes were the zodiac, the ballerina, the Scottish terrier, and the Madonna.

Albini is considered the inventor of the "total look," derived from his single-minded emphasis on accessories and details that became almost more important than the garment itself. It was Albini who first developed the idea of using music in place of an announcer during fashion shows. He also conceived the idea of grouping advertising pages in fashion magazines. But Albini was even more tied to the past, to the historical roots that inspired him, to the perfect elegance that is never achieved without a fanatical attention to the search for perfection in the intelligent and ironic use of older styles.

When Albini's agreement with FTM terminated in 1973, he founded Albini Srl with Papini. The new company produced and distributed the WA label, with MISTERFOX as their commercial line of clothing. In this endeavor, too, Albini was ahead of his time. His love of fashion went hand in hand with his interest in research and traveling to Asia—India, in particular, and also Tunisia, where he found inspiration for his creations. He bought apartments in his favorite cities, one on the Grand Canal in Venice, another on Piazza Borromeo in Milan, and a third in Sidi-fu-Said in Tunisia. Each of them, in its own way, expressed the aesthetics of the surrounding environment.

In 1975 Albini presented his first fall collection for men—another area in which he was a precursor of later designers. But the fashion world was not quite ready for Albini's innovations. When Albini was at the height of his success, there was not sufficient financial support in a still immature clothing and textile market. Toward the end of his career, his manufacturers could not live up to their commitments; Paolo Rinaldi, his companion and press agent, remained his only supporter. Albini died in Milan at the age of forty-two.

Walter Albini cannot easily be categorized, because of the richness and variety of his designs, their intimacy and complexity, and the fact that the designs were ahead of their time. "A creative genius in the pure state," wrote Isa Vercelloni, Albini "is always somewhere else, at least one step ahead of what is predictable, and a thousand miles ahead of what we anticipate" (1984, p. 235). A key figure of Italian artistic culture, Albini still evokes deep admiration. His memory lingers on in the images taken by the many photographers who worked with him: Aldo Ballo, Maria Vittoria Corradi Backhaus, Giampaolo Barbieri, and Alfa Castaldi.

See also Chanel, Gabrielle (Coco); Fashion Designer; Fashion Shows; Italian Fashion; Ready-to-Wear.

Bibliography

Bianchino, Gloria, and Arturo Quintavalle. *Moda: Dalla fiaba al design. Italia 1951–1989.* Novara, Italy: Istituto geografico De Agostini, 1989.

Bocca, N. "La coerenza dello stile." In *Walter Albini: Lo stile nella moda.* Edited by Paolo Rinaldi. Modena, Italy: Zanfi Editori, 1988.

Gastel, Minnie. *50 anni di moda italiana.* Milan: Vallardi, 1995.

Morini, E., and N. Bocca. *La moda italiana.* Volume 2: *Dall'antimoda allo stilismo.* Milan: Electa, 1987.

Vercelloni, Isa Tutino. "Walter Albini 1968." In *Il genio antipatico: Creatività e tecnologia della moda italiana 1951/1983.* Edited by Pia Soli. Milan: Mondadori, 1984.

——. "Albini Walter." In *Dizionario della moda.* Edited by Guido Vergani. Milan: Baldini and Castoldi, 1999.

Simona Segre Reinach

A-LINE DRESS

The term "A-line" is used to describe a dress, skirt, or coat with a triangular silhouette, narrow and fitted at the top and widening out from the bust or waist in a straight line to the hem. More specifically, it is understood to mean a structured garment, which stands away from the body to form the sides of the *A.* The fronts of A-line garments are often cut in one piece, with darts for fitting, and the skirts often have no waistband.

The term first entered the vocabulary of fashion via the couturier Christian Dior's collection for Spring 1955, which he named the "A-Line." In the 1950s, the international fashion press looked to Paris, and Dior in particular, to set the direction fashion would take each season. Dior obliged by organizing each new collection around a specific idea, and giving each a name that described or evoked that idea. In 1954 and 1955, he designed three closely related collections, based on the shapes of the letters *H*, *A*, and *Y*, which marked a move away from the strongly emphasized, nipped-in waist that had been the dominant silhouette since his 1947 "Corolle Line" (or "New Look") collection. The most influential of these was the "A-Line" collection, characterized by narrow shoulders and a smooth, trumpetlike flare toward the hem; the elongated waistline, either high under the bust or dropped toward the hips, formed the crossbar of the *A*. The signature look of this collection (the "most wanted silhouette in Paris," according to *Vogue*, 1 March 1995, p. 95) was a fingertip-length flared jacket worn over a dress with a very full, pleated skirt; while it was clearly an A-shape, this silhouette was quite different from what was later meant by "A-line."

Though the example set by the A-Line collection was not immediately followed, and Christian Dior explored other ideas in subsequent collections, the idea of the A-shape was a success, and the term quickly entered common usage. The A-line was one of a series of controversial mid- to late-1950s looks that de-emphasized the waist and brought an easier, more casual look to fashion; chemise and sack dresses, loose tunics, and boxy suits were shown by Dior, but also by other couturiers, most notably Balenciaga and Chanel. The most dramatic of these, in which the A-line idea was given its ultimate expression, was the Spring 1958 "Trapeze Line" introduced by Dior's successor, Yves Saint Laurent, in his first collection for the house of Dior. The Trapeze silhouette, in which dresses flared out dramatically from a fitted shoulder line, was considered extreme by many, but it did establish the A-line dress, with its highly structured, clean lines, as a suitable look for modern times. A more subdued version of the A-line shape was introduced in the early 1960s, and A-line dresses and skirts remained a popular style choice through the mid-1970s.

By the early 1980s, however, A-line garments, and flared shapes in general, had almost completely disappeared. The new loose silhouette was an update of the sack shape, with dresses and tunics falling loosely from an exaggerated shoulder line. Some 1960s styles received a retro revival later in the decade, but as long as the shoulders remained padded and the tops loose-fitting, straight skirts were required to balance the look. A-line skirts and dresses were not revived until the late 1990s, when the retro trend embraced the styles of the 1970s, and closely fitted garments with narrow shoulders and fitted sleeves came back into fashion. By this time, following almost twenty years of straight skirts and dresses, the term had been out of use for so long that its earlier, more specific meanings had been forgotten. It is used loosely to describe any dress wider at the hips than at the bust or waist, and a variety of flared skirt styles. With the revival of true A-line shapes in the early 2000s, however, there are signs that the terms originally used to describe them are beginning to return as well.

See also Chemise Dress; Dior, Christian; Saint Laurent, Yves.

Bibliography

Keenan, Brigid. *Dior in Vogue*. London: Octopus Books, 1981. Excellent chronological and thematic guide to the Dior collections and their influence.

Musheno, Elizabeth J., ed. *The Vogue Sewing Book*. Rev. ed. New York: Vogue Patterns, 1975. Contains helpful typology, with illustrations, of 1960s–1970s garments and style terms.

Susan Ward

AMIES, HARDY

The British couturier Hardy Amies is best known as Queen Elizabeth II's longest-serving dressmaker. Supported by a highly skilled team in the workrooms at Savile Row, Amies dressed the queen and a small clientele of aristocratic and wealthy women for half a century. His men's wear and international licensee business had a lower profile but were crucial to the financial viability of the company. The licensee business benefited from Amies's position as dressmaker to the queen and from his staff's expertise, but its success ensured the survival of the couture house.

Early Life

Edwin Hardy Amies was born in London on 17 July 1909. Although he had some knowledge of dressmaking through his mother's work as a saleswoman for Miss Gray, Ltd., a London court dressmaker, it was not his chosen career. He wanted to be a journalist and on the advice of the editor of the *Daily Express* went to work in Europe to learn French and German. Back in Britain in 1931 he joined W. and T. Avery, selling industrial weighing machines and hoping to be posted to Germany, but dressmaking was clearly his destiny. A chance letter describing a dress worn by Miss Gray led to the offer of a job as designer at Lachasse, a sportswear shop owned by Miss Gray's husband, Fred Shingleton. In late 1933, Amies was invited by Mr. and Mrs. Shingleton (Miss Gray) to join their party at a dance given in aid of the Middlesex Hospital. At Christmas 1933, Amies wrote a letter to Mlle. Louise Probet-Piolat (Aunt Louie), a friend of his mother, describing the dress worn by Mrs. Shingleton at the dance. Aunt Louie in turn wrote to Mrs. Shingleton, reporting "how vivid she found my description." Mrs Shingleton threw the letter across the table to her husband and said, "You ought to get that boy into the business in Digby Morton's place" (Amies 1954, pp. 52–53). Undeterred by his complete ignorance of practical dressmaking, Amies boldly grabbed the opportunity.

Lachasse and the War

Lachasse was set up in 1928 as an offshoot of Fred Shingleton's company Gray and Paulette, Ltd. The firm specialized in custom-made daywear designed for members of the British upper classes, who divided their time between London and the country. When Amies joined in 1934 he replaced the Irish designer Digby Morton, whom he credited with transforming the classic country tweed suit "into an intricately cut and carefully designed garment that was so fashionable that it could be worn with confidence at the Ritz" (Amies 1954, p. 54). Following Morton, Amies concentrated on producing stylish, feminine, tailored clothes. The year 1937 was a turning point. The April edition of British *Vogue* featured a Lachasse suit, and Amies made his first sales to U.S. buyers, in London for King George VI's coronation. *Vogue* praised Amies's facility with pattern and color but noted the comparatively static silhouette of his suits, which now incorporated the slightly low waist that became characteristic of

his cut. This slowly evolving line was, in fact, exactly what Amies's customers wanted. They were looking for clothes that were in tune with fashion but that would blend with their existing wardrobe, that were smart but not ostentatious, and that were well cut, immaculately fitted, and hard wearing. Amies catered to this particularly English approach to dressing throughout his career. His customers at Lachasse included the society hostess Mrs. Ernest Guinness and the actress Virginia Cherrill.

By 1939 sales at Lachasse had doubled but Amies's appeals to design in his own name were rebuffed. Restless and frustrated, he saw World War II as an escape. He joined the Intelligence Corps, transferring in 1941 to the Belgian section of the Special Operations Executive, where he rose to the rank of lieutenant colonel. Amies designed throughout the war, contributing to government-backed export collections and, after resigning from Lachasse, selling through the London house of Worth. He was a founding member of the Incorporated Society of London Fashion Designers and served as the society's chairman from 1959 to 1960.

Savile Row

After demobilization, Amies set up his own house in November 1945 at 14 Savile Row, in the heart of London's tailoring district. Staff from Lachasse, Worth, and Miss Gray joined him, bringing their clients and skills and enabling Amies to establish a reputation for all-around excellence. Although nearly forty, he was considered young in couture terms. Amies played on this, promoting himself and his house as vigorous, youthful, and progressive. In 1950 he was among the first London couturiers to set up a boutique line aimed at export buyers, selected provincial retail buyers, and the general public. Within two years the new business was half the size of the couture business.

In 1950 Amies received his first order from the future Queen Elizabeth II. In 1955 he successfully applied for the coveted royal warrant, which he held until his death. Norman Hartnell was still the queen's premier dressmaker but Amies's position at the top of his profession was secure. Designing for the queen gave him international standing, attracted prestigious clients, and guaranteed his own personal acceptability in the highest echelons of society. He later designed for Princess Michael of Kent and Diana, Princess of Wales.

> "I understand and admire the Englishwoman's attitude to dress . . . just as our great country houses always look lived in and not [like] museums, so do our ladies refuse to look like fashion plates." (Amies 1954, p. 239)

Men's Wear

Amies entered the men's wear market in 1959, when he designed a range of silk ties for Michelson's. During the 1950s the preference of young adult men for more informal, body-conscious clothes and the popularity of American and Italian styles persuaded British manufacturers to reformulate their image and product. Hepworths, a middle-market multiple tailoring group, approached Amies. His first collection for Hepworths in 1961 was designed "to make the customer feel younger and richer than they were, and more attractive" (Amies 1984, p. 68). His designs were never cutting edge but formulated to attract a broad customer base. By 1964 the annual sales of his men's wear was about £15 million, compared with £0.75 million for women's wear. His collaboration with Hepworths led to a string of licensee agreements selling men's wear and some women's wear across the globe from the United States and Canada to Australia, New Zealand, Japan, Taiwan, and Korea. As Amies dedicated more time to the licensee business, the women's wear design was taken over by his codirector, Ken Fleetwood (d. 1996). Amies sold Hardy Amies, Ltd., to Debenhams in 1973 to develop a ready-to-wear business but bought the company back in 1980.

Hardy Amies was appointed a Commander of the Victorian Order (CVO) in 1977 and honored with a knighthood in 1989. He was elected a Royal Designer for Industry in 1964. He received the *Harper's Bazaar* Award in 1962, the *Sunday Times* Special Award in 1965, and the British Fashion Council Hall of Fame award in 1989. He sold Hardy Amies, Ltd., to the Luxury Brands Group in 2001. Amies died on 5 March 2003.

See also Diana, Princess of Wales; Haute Couture; Savile Row; Travel Clothing; Tweed.

Bibliography

Amies, Hardy. *Just So Far*. London: Collins, 1954. Detailed account of the first ten years of the house of Hardy Amies, and considers London fashion in relation to Paris.

——. *Still Here: An Autobiography*. London: Weidenfeld and Nicolson, 1984. Covers Amies's involvement in menswear and the development of his licensee business and his work for Queen Elizabeth II.

——. *The Englishman's Suit: A Personal View of Its History, Its Place in the World Today, Its Future, and the Accessories Which Support It*. London: Quartet, 1994. Describes the evolution of the suit and Amies's taste in menswear.

Cohn, Nik. *Today There Are No Gentlemen: The Changes in Englishmen's Clothes since the War*. London: Weidenfeld and Nicolson, 1971.

Ehrman, Edwina. "The Spirit of English Style: Hardy Amies, Royal Dressmaker and International Businessman." In *The Englishness of English Dress*. Edited by Christopher Breward, Becky Conekin, and Caroline Cox. Oxford: Berg, 2002. Considers how Englishness informed Amies's style and how he used his association with Englishness as a marketing tool.

Edwina Ehrman

APRONS

"Apron" means an over-garment covering the front of the body (from the French *naperon*, a small tablecloth). For centuries, people worldwide have worn them as protective garments, as ceremonial indicators of marital and parental status, rank and group affiliation, and as decorations.

Cretan fertility goddesses and Assyrian priests wore sacred aprons. Egyptian rulers broadcast their status by wearing jewel-encrusted aprons. In Europe during the Middle Ages, women placed extra swaths of cloth in their laps to protect their skirts during rowdy communal meals, and tradesmen and artisans began wearing aprons to protect their clothing and their flesh. In fact, tradesmen in general were called "apron men," as aprons were so common that several trades boasted distinguishing styles. Gardeners, spinners, weavers, and garbagemen wore blue aprons; butlers wore green; butchers wore blue stripes; cobblers wore "black flag" aprons for protection from the black wax they used; and English barbers were known as "checkered apron men." Stonemasons wore white aprons as protection against the dust of their trade, and even in the twenty-first century, aprons survive as part of Masonic ceremonial attire. In contemporary South Africa, young women wear beaded aprons to celebrate their coming of age.

By 1500, decorative aprons had become fashion accessories for European women with lifestyles permitting such luxury and display. Their popularity waxed and waned over the centuries. By the time colonists settled in North America, aprons were firmly established in European women's wardrobes.

United States Aprons

Aprons were worn by some Native American women and men, for both practical and ceremonial reasons. Through the centuries, colonial immigrants and their descendants have worn functional aprons for work, while decorative aprons have fallen in and out of fashion.

Looking back just one century, from 1900 through the 1920s, well-heeled women wore ornate, heavily embroidered aprons. In the 1930s and 1940s, women working outside the home wore whatever protective garments their jobs required, including coveralls, smocks, or aprons. At home, they worked in full-length aprons with hefty pockets.

In the United States in the early 2000s, many people consider aprons 1950s kitsch, but aprons deserve more serious and thorough consideration than that. Many aprons are fine examples of textile craft; and most importantly, aprons are icons—symbols within popular culture. They conjure twin images: the mythology of motherhood and family in the cozy, homemade good old days; and the reality of the endless hard work those times required. Through a blend of individual and collective memory and fantasy, aprons have come to represent an idealized, apple-pie, June Cleaver–esque mom. Cartoonists adorn a stick figure with an apron to communicate that she's a mom and probably a housewife. Though this character is a manufactured stereotype, she has held great sway as a role model—often wearing an apron.

The heyday of this archetypal housewife—and U.S. women's aprons—was the post war era of the 1940s and 1950s. Rosie the Riveter lost her well-paying job, and the media and government—thus the job market—encouraged her to be a housewife and mom. Sewing machines and cloth became available, and aprons—both commercial and homemade—became ubiquitous as the uniform of the professional housewife. Many 1950s aprons addressed housework and were decorated with sewing, cleaning, cooking, and "mom" themes.

This apron-wearing housewife served as family hostess and wore decorative serving aprons for holidays.

She wore a more utilitarian model while in the kitchen getting things ready, but right before she entered the dining room, she donned her holiday froth. Commercial aprons were certainly available, but many holiday aprons were homemade. Not only were they made by the housewife herself, but they were also the stuff of church and neighborhood bazaars, often made of netting and festooned with ribbons, sequins, and felt. The at-the-ready hostess had at least one all-season party apron. In fact, if possible, she had several to match her outfits. They were flashy and flirtatious and often sheer. Aprons were common hostess gifts, as well.

The postwar archetypal housewife was practical and creative. She made aprons out of remnants, extra kitchen curtains, dish towels, handkerchiefs, and flour sacks. When she made her aprons, she considered design as well as function. Many handmade aprons from the 1950s have one-of-a-kind designs and details.

The apron-wearing mom collected souvenir aprons—from maps of every state to "Indian aprons" that bore slight if any resemblance to authentic ethnic garb. At home, when she had "had enough," she donned her letting-off-steam apron that said, "The hell with housework," or the one that pictured a frazzled washerwoman and the caption, "Life can be beautiful." And in the 1950s, when "the man of the house" was back from the war, he was supposed to spend weekends at home, so "men's" aprons printed with barbecue and bartender themes became available.

By the early 1960s, the era of glorified housework was passing and with it the heyday of aprons. But aprons *are* still worn. At-home kitchen aprons have evolved into the unisex butcher/barbecue style. And aprons are filling a new at-work role as "the instant uniform." An apron tied over any assortment of clothes produces a consistent look for a fast food chain or discount store. Generic aprons are shipped in from Central Supply and stamped with corporate logos, and gone is the variety, the visual delight, and the individual expression that aprons once provided.

Aprons can reveal a lot about women's lives. Examining a store-bought apron found at an estate sale or antique shop may yield information about the time from which the garment came and the woman who bought and wore it; and besides meriting study as a handcrafted one-of-a-kind item, a homemade apron may also contain clues about the life and times of the woman who made and wore it.

See also Protective Clothing.

Bibliography

Barber, Elizabeth Wayland. *Women's Work. The First 20,000 Years, Women, Cloth, and Society in Early Times.* New York: W. W. Norton and Company, 1994.

Cheney, Joyce. *Aprons: Icons of the American Home.* Philadelphia: Running Press, 2000.

——. *Aprons: A Celebration.* Philadelphia: Running Press, 2001.

Florence, Judy. *Aprons of the Mid-Twentieth Century, To Serve and Protect.* Atglen, Pa.: Schiffer Books, 2002.

McKissack, Patricia. *Ma Dear's Aprons.* New York: Alfred A. Knopf, 1997.

Joyce Cheney

ARMANI, GIORGIO

Giorgio Armani, one of the most authoritative names in Italian ready-to-wear design, was born in Piacenza, Italy, in 1934. He became interested in fashion in 1957, when he left the school of medicine at the University of Piacenza to become a buyer for the La Rinascete chain in Milan. In 1964 Armani met Nino Cerruti, owner of Hitman, the Italian men's clothing producer. After a brief period to see how Armani worked with materials, Cerruti asked him to restructure completely the company's approach to clothing. Armani worked with Cerruti for six years, developing a simplified form of menswear that could be reproduced in series.

In the late 1960s Armani met Sergio Galeotti, which was the beginning of a relationship that lasted for years. In 1973 Galeotti persuaded him to open a design office in Milan, at 37 corso Venezia. This led to a period of extensive collaboration, during which Armani worked as a freelance designer for a number of fashion houses, including Allegri, Bagutta, Hilton, Sicons, Gibò, Montedoro, and Tendresse. The international press was quick to acknowledge Armani's importance following the runway shows at the Sala Bianca in the Pitti Palace in Florence. The experience provided Armani with an opportunity to develop his own style in new ways. He was now ready to devote his energy to his own label, and in 1975 he founded Giorgio Armani Spa in Milan with his friend Galeotti. In October of that same year he presented his first collection of men's ready-to-wear for spring and summer 1976 under his own name. He also produced a women's line for the same season.

International Recognition

The secret of Armani's great success seems to derive from his having introduced, at the right moment, a new approach to clothing design that reflected the changes

Giorgio Armani with pieces from his collection. After freelancing for a number of fashion houses, Armani founded his own label in 1976, quickly capitalizing on a reputation for producing high-quality, distinctive clothing at affordable prices. AP/WIDE WORLD PHOTOS. REPRODUCED BY PERMISSION.

in post-1968 society, which was composed essentially of a middle class that could no longer afford to wear couture clothing but at the same time wanted to construct a distinctive image for itself. With this in mind, Armani established an innovative relationship with industry, characterized by the 1978 agreement with Gruppo finanzario Tessile (GFT), which made it possible to produce luxury ready-to-wear in a manufacturing environment under the attentive supervision of the company's designer. In 1979, after founding the Giorgio Armani Corporation, Armani began producing for the United States and introduced the Mani line for men and women. The label became one of the leading names in international fashion with the introduction of several new product lines, including G. A. Le Collezioni, and Giorgio Armani Underwear and Swimwear, and Giorgio Armani Accessories.

In the early 1980s the company signed an important agreement with L'Oréal to create perfumes and introduced the Armani Junior, Armani Jeans, and Emporio Armani lines, followed in 1982 by the introduction of Emporio Underwear, Swimwear, and Accessories. A new store was opened in Milan for the Emporio line, followed by the first Giorgio Armani boutique. Armani's concern for the end user culminated in the development of a more youthful product with the same level of stylistic quality as his high-end line, but at a more accessible price.

Because of the democratic nature of the Emporio line, Armani felt that he had to make use of new and unconventional advertising methods. These included television spots and enormous street ads, together with a house magazine that was sent out by mail to consumers, faithful Armani eaglet wearers. Armani also felt that a relationship with the cinema was essential, both for promotional reasons and for the stimulus to creativity. He designed the costumes for *American Gigolo*, directed by Paul Schrader (1980), the success of which led to a long-term collaboration with the world of film. Armani designed costumes for more than one hundred films, one of the most important of which was *The Untouchables*, directed by Brian De Palma and released in 1987.

In 1983 the designer modified his agreement with GFT. They began to produce both the Mani line for the United States and his high-end ready-to-wear line, rechristened Borgonuovo 21, after the address of the company's headquarters. During the late 1980s, despite Galeotti's death (1985), Armani continued to expand commercial horizons and licensing agreements. He opened Armani Japan and introduced a line of

eyeglasses (1988), socks (1987), a gift collection (1989), and a new "basic" men's and women's line for America known as A/X Armani Exchange (1991). After the frenetic expansion of the 1990s (sportswear, eyeglasses, cosmetics, home, and new accessories collections), the year 2000, the twenty-fifth anniversary of the brand, saw a flurry of investment activity, including stock sales and the acquisition of new manufacturing capacity intended to increase Armani's control over the quality and distribution of his products.

Style and Innovation

There is a common thread running through Armani's stylistic development that is closely associated with the change in contemporary society. It led to the creation of clothing and accessories that aimed at a clean, simple style, beyond fashion, designed to enhance the personality of the person who wore it. When, in 1976, the designer presented the first unstructured jackets for men, unlined and unironed, the product of years of experience in production design, they were intended to lower labor costs and simplify tailoring. But in introducing them Armani opened a third way in men's clothing, an alternative to the traditional approach of English tailoring and the expectations associated with Italian made-to-measure clothing, realizing an innovative synthesis between formal wear and loose, flexible sportswear. With the invention of the blazer worn as a pullover, Armani offered men a new identity that rejected rigid professional divisions and allowed them to present themselves as young, attractive, and vaguely feminine. Referred to as the "first postmodern designer," by several Italian newspapers, for his radically unstructured garments, Armani had simply softened men's wear and made women's wear more concise and modern, transforming changing social roles into an "Armani look," making the casual look authoritative.

Official recognition of his fame came in 1982 when he appeared on the cover of *Time* magazine, only the second fashion designer, after Christian Dior, to do so. Armani had freed women from their stiff suits, providing them with soft jackets without collars and with comfortable pants. Although initially somewhat severe, as if intended to assist women in their climb to professional credibility, these outfits greatly enhanced a type of femininity that, because it was not ostentatious, was ultimately more real. Armani sought to establish an image of a woman who was strong but not harsh (a mix of the film stars Greta Garbo and Marlene

Dietrich in modern dress) and who could be practical and indispensable as well as glamorous. Over time the jacket has continued to remain the centerpiece of the Armani wardrobe, changing year by year through the use of new materials, new proportions, and new colors. For Armani the "greige" (somewhere between gray and beige) of 1997 remained the most typical element in a palette often centered on shades of white and black, soft earth tones, dusty blues, and occasional unexpected bursts of color.

The search for fabrics has always been one of the distinctive elements of Armani's collections for men and women, becoming a key design element in 1986, together with embroidery and the return to evening wear that he brought about. Here the look was precious and exclusive but always in a minimalist key, demystified through the use of low-heeled shoes or sneakers. An attentive analyst of past cultures and Eastern influences, Armani's clothing has never been a collage of banal ideas. Throughout his career he has always succeeded in providing new images of how men and women dress and in translating elegant, decorative patterns into a unique but accessible style.

See also Film and Fashion; Italian Fashion; Jacket; Ready-to-Wear; Sports Jacket.

Bibliography

Bianchino, Gloria, and Arturo Carlo Quintavalle. *Moda: Dalla fiaba al design italia 1951–1989*. Novara, Italy: De Agostini, 1989.

Bucci, Ampelio. *Moda a Milano: Stile e impresa nella città che cambia*. Milan: Abitare Segesta, 2002.

Celant, Germano, and Harold Koda, eds. *Giorgio Armani*. New York: Guggenheim Museum Publications, 2000.

Sollazzo, Lucia. "Armani, Giorgio." In *Dizionario della moda*. Edited by Guido Vergani. Milan: Baldini and Castoldi, 1999.

White, Nicola. *Giorgio Armani*. London: Carlton, 2000.

Aurora Fiorentini

ARMOR

Accommodating and enclosing the human form, body armor has a direct connection with costume. Over the centuries, and in cultures worldwide, armor has been made from virtually all natural and many man-made media. During the Middle Ages and the Renaissance, armor was an effective defense and became one of the most elaborate and complex bodily adornments. It both identified and concealed its wearer and made a definitive statement about personal fashion.

The Earliest Armor

Humans' earliest supplemental protection was probably skins and hides. However, the earliest purpose-built defense, found in Europe and western Asia, was a type of belly plate made originally of organic material and later in bronze or metal-reinforced fabric. The Sumerians employed metal helmets and a metal-reinforced cloak. In about 2000 B.C.E. textile coverings appeared with applied, overlapping metal scales, which continued in occasional use until the eighteenth century.

A rather similar defense was lamellar armor. This probably first appeared in eighth century B.C.E. Assyria, composed of interconnected plaques or hoops, all worn over an undergarment. The Roman legionary's metal lorica *segmentata* is an example, as is the lacquered leather armor of Japanese samurai. The remarkable terra-cotta tomb figures of emperor Qin Shih Huang (221–210 B.C.E.) demonstrate China's use of lamellar armor for various troops identified by rank via color-coding and tassels. Mycenaean warriors during the Trojan War, and Greek hoplite infantry who fought the Persians wore body armor of layered linen. The Greeks and the inhabitants of the Italian peninsula also made use of bronze cuirasses (torso armor) embossed with musculature. All types were worn over an undergarment resembling period male ensembles.

Mail also appeared in classical times. Probably a Celtic innovation of the fifth or sixth century B.C.E., this network of riveted metal rings spread throughout Europe and into the East, and was widely used by the Romans and their allies. Mail's use steadily increased in Europe, particularly after the collapse of the Roman military system in the fifth century C.E., and among those who experienced its use by invading Hunnish cavalry.

The Middle Ages

Leather and textile armor were used throughout the Middle Ages, and not surprisingly, their form and style conformed to prevailing civilian fashion. The most common metal armor in Europe until the thirteenth century was mail, the name derived from the French *maille*, or "mesh." Mail shirts, worn over a heavily padded undergarment, or *aketon*, eventually covered the thighs, and developed long sleeves with mittens. Mail hoods (*coifs*), leggings, a conical helmet or a barrel-shaped helm that covered all but the eyes, completed the defense. As extra protection against powerful weapons, a long, wooden shield was carried. Such warriors were expensive to maintain, and of great wealth—deriving this from lands given to them in return for military service. These armored men thus became the horse-mounted knights of popular imagination, and in many European languages, the words "knight" and "horseman" are identical. Each warrior was identified by a system of symbolism called heraldry. A knight's "coat of arms" appeared on his shield and, from the twelfth century, on a gownlike surcoat over his mail. The surcoat's length followed civilian fashion; some could actually trip up a warrior in combat.

However, better defenses were needed. By the early thirteenth century pieces of plate armor reappeared on a scale not seen since Classical Rome and became increasingly common on the torso and legs by mid to late century. Plate appeared in various forms—horn, bone, molded leather—but most often in iron. It offered rigidity and better resistance to weapons. It was shaped to the individual, thick where needed or thin to reduce weight, and its smooth, curving surfaces deflected weapons. It increasingly covered the body, although there seems to have been reluctance by some knights to be encased in rigid metal. Thus, there was a "transition" throughout the fourteenth century to mix mail and plate armor for the knight and his horse. This interim defense remained the primary form of protection in the armies of Islamic cultures and the Indian subcontinent until well into the nineteenth century.

Armor makers were divided into plate, mail, and textile (cloth armorers) specialists and tightly regulated. The transitional knight was a graceless, stout figure in

Those who wore armor recognized its importance and appreciated the expertise required in its manufacture. During a test-fitting of a new armor "his Majesty [Charles V] said that they [his armor parts] were more precious to him than a city . . . and they were so excellent that . . . if he [the armorer] had taken the measurement a thousand times they could not fit better" (Hayward, p. 11).

During the seventeenth century, a militia officer was struck by an arrow in the chest. His only defense was a hard piece of cheese inside his shirt. Almost unbelievably, the arrow hit the cheese. Informed of his subordinate's luck, his captain replied that this "may verify the old saying, A little Armour would serve if a Man knew where to place it" (Mason, p. 22).

layered textiles and iron, much of it cloth-covered. The plate edges had ribs to protect the armpits, elbows, and other vulnerable spots, with mail worn on the undergarment at these points.

By the beginning of the fifteenth century, the transition was complete. An individual wanting the latest in armor could have full plate—often without the textile covering, and with surfaces polished gleaming bright—virtually head to toe. The status of knights saw their clothing needs increasingly influencing male fashion, and vice versa. The change to all plate gradually produced a wasp-waisted appearance. This slim, hard-body look increasingly mirrored elegant male attire at the end of the century, and each complemented the other. For example, tubular arm defenses required slim sleeves on the undergarment, while shoulders broadened to accommodate extra padding for the load of a cuirass. Some armor elements were fastened to the aketon with laces called points. These also appeared on male apparel, to attach sleeves and hose. The aketon assimilated the new forms and was worn alone as knightly clothing. The surcoat became the short, form-fitting *jupon* (overgarment).

The Renaissance and Armor's Decline

The fifteenth through seventeenth centuries saw both armor's acme and nadir. Plate armor remained paramount, changing with the demands of war, sport, and ceremony, and the continuing influence of civilian fashion. Centers in Italy (the term "milliner" originally meant a Milanese armor vendor) and Germany grew wealthy from the production and sale of armor. Master armorers throughout Europe crafted spectacular suits through the tailorlike handwork of specialists, including locksmiths (for hinges and fasteners), artists (Holbein and Dürer provided themes for armor decoration), and cloth armorers (the cloth tabs of internal linings were called *pickadils*, inspiring the name of the London district where makers were centered). The slim, angular, and rippled form of fifteenth-century German "Gothic" armor is regarded as the peak moment, in which pure form blended perfectly with function. However, in the early part of the sixteenth century, this gave way in some areas to the rounded, "Maximilian" style whose fluted cuirass imitated a globose doublet cinched by a waistbelt. The average weight was about forty to sixty well-distributed, balanced pounds in which a trained individual could do the same as in everyday clothing, especially mounting a horse unaided. Aketons became arming doublets and hose, an affair of durable material, padded with grasses, wool waste, or cotton especially at the load-bearing shoulders and hips, with points and garters to secure components. Some clothing, such as the kiltlike "base" skirt, gave texture and color to plain metal. Fashions again changed with the times, as once-pointed foot defenses (that imitated the *poulaine* shoe) became broadly rounded, then narrower and more contemporary. Breastplates followed doublet changes, also placing acid-etched decorative bands to imitate embroidery, and by the end of the century developing the grotesquely dipped "peascod" shape. Mail continued as a secondary defense, or primary for the less wealthy. Textiles and plate combined in the vest-like brigandine used by all classes, differing only in the quality of materials and finish. The jack was similar, but generally of cruder stuff, and both defenses mimicked the doublet lines. A wide range of helmets was worn, from visored types that enclosed the head, to hatlike open forms. Foot soldiers favored the latter, and wore pieces of munitions-grade armor, sometimes little more than helmet and breastplate, or as much as a half armor to the hips.

Armor was also made for jousts and tournaments. Formerly training for war, these equestrian events became pure sport during the fifteenth century and required highly protective equipment that could reach 100 pounds. These suits have fueled the erroneous stereotype of the heavy, awkward knight, unable to mount without aid, and helpless if unhorsed.

From about the 1530s into the second half of the century, "Roman" and "antique" style armor became popular for festivals and spectacles. Other types of ceremonial armors flourished, even for children, as armorers experimented in fantastic creations, using a range of precious or fragile media to embellish the products of wealthy clients. Some were so extravagant as to be moving examples of decorative art or metal costume and were built by goldsmiths rather than armorers. Most armor was embellished to some degree. The entire decorative arts vocabulary was employed, including plating, enameling, encrusting with gems, but most often acid-etching.

The armorer's craft culminated in the garniture, a set of various components together with a basic armor and creating a versatile ensemble for war, sport, and ceremony. While each element had a designated function, it had to harmonize structurally and artistically with dozens of others. Such sets were extremely expensive and available only to very wealthy individuals.

Armor was also used by bodyguards, representing the patron's importance, good taste, and artistic refinement. Guard armor was sometimes limited to helmets, but embellished body armor was worn by those like the Vatican's papal guard.

Throughout much of the sixteenth century developments in firearms and changing battlefield tactics had an impact on armor's use. Powerful handguns required bulletproof armor that could weigh some eighty pounds, but retained its fashion relevance of its form. The lines of certain armor elements, such as the form of breastplates, tended to follow those of male civilian fashion. Complete head-to-toe armor became rare, with protection concentrated on the head and torso. By the seventeenth century, half or three-quarter armor (to the knees) became typical for horsemen, who now carried firearms themselves. Some troops wore "buff" leather coats, or padded textiles, and by the end of the century it was rare to see armor in war.

The Enlightenment to the Present

Although most troops ceased wearing armor by the eighteenth century, military engineers (sappers) wore bullet-proof helmets during sieges, and some horsemen wore breastplates and helmets against sword cuts and firearms. The knight's neck defense, or gorget, became a symbol of officer's rank, and many armors became theatrical props. The Napoleonic wars briefly revived the use of some cavalry armor, but by the middle of the nineteenth century, its military use was again largely ceremonial. There were some exceptions, such as the breastplates privately acquired by both sides in the American Civil War (1861–1865), and Australian outlaw Ned Kelly's crude 100-pound body armor worn during a shootout. World Wars I and II revived interest in protective armor on a large scale. Allied and Axis physicians and scientists worked with curators to develop helmets and body defenses for ground troops and "flak jackets" for aircrew, but they used media and technologies little different from those of centuries earlier.

Armor developments late in World War II and the Korean Conflict benefited from new plastic polymers. Soldiers' needs in Vietnam led to better armor, but it remained rather heavy and hot. The invention of Kevlar in the 1980s provided a material five times stronger than steel. Produced in fabriclike sheets, then laminated and encased in textiles, this has produced a new range of highly protective and light armor and helmets for the military, sport, law enforcement, and individuals. However, even more remarkable systems are under development in commercial and governmental laboratories, striving to produce another breakthrough technology, one just as dramatic as the suit of knightly plate armor that continues to fascinate us.

See also Military Style; Protective Clothing; Techno-Textiles; Uniforms, Military.

Bibliography

Blair, Claude. *European Armour.* New York: Crane, Russak, and Company, 1972; also published in 1958 by B. T. Batsford, Ltd., London. Remains the standard work.

Blair, Claude, and Leonid Tarassuk, eds. *The Complete Encyclopedia of Arms and Weapons.* New York: Simon and Schuster, 1982. Best one-volume source of information on a range of arms and armor terms.

Dean, Bashford. *Helmets and Body Armor in Modern Warfare.* Reprint of the 1920 edition, including the World War II Supplement. Tuckahoe, N.Y.: Carl J. Pugliese, 1977. Fascinating study of the development and use of personal armor in both World Wars.

Edge, David, and John Paddock. *Arms and Armour of the Medieval Knight.* Greenwich Conn.: Crescent Books, 1988. Well-illustrated and accessible to a general audience.

Ffoulkes, Charles. *The Armourer and His Craft.* Several printings available, the most recent by Dover Publications. Somewhat dated, but remains an important work on the topic.

Hayward, J. F. "Filippo Orsoni, Designer, and Caremolo Modrone, Armourer, of Mantua." *Waffen und Kostümkunde*, 3rd ser., 24, no.1 (1982): 11.

Mason, John. *A Brief History of the Pequot War.* Boston, 1736.

Pfaffenbichler, Matthias. *The Armourers.* Toronto: University of Toronto Press, 1992. Well-illustrated and excellent resource.

Pyhrr, Stuart W., and José-A. Godoy. *Heroic Armor of the Italian Renaissance.* New York: Metropolitan Museum of Art, 1998. Beautifully illustrated, premier study of Italian Renaissance parade armor.

Robinson, H. Russell. *The Armour of Imperial Rome.* New York: Charles Scribner's Sons, 1975. Excellent, and accessible to the general reader.

Snodgrass, A. M. *Arms and Armour of the Greeks.* Ithaca N.Y.: Cornell University Press, 1967. Scholarly and thorough.

Walter Karcheski Jr.

ART AND FASHION

When one considers "fashion," as distinct from "clothing," "costume," or "dress," it is as a socially shared concept of what is to be worn at a particular point in time rather than an esoteric, ritualistic, or utilitarian cover or decoration of the body. The concept of fashion's point of origin in the mid-nineteenth century is contemporary with a fundamental change in the market for works of art. This was not accidental, since the institution of fashion, as clothing that adheres to particular modes of production, representation, and consumption, was connected to the emergence of similar structures in the creation and dissemination of works of art. Fashion came into being with the advent of the couture industry in Paris in the second half of the nineteenth century, when a bourgeois audience began to demand constant change as an intellectual, aesthetic, and, above all, economic stimulus for modern times. This is not to say that the notion of fashion did not exist previously. The timing qualifies the term as denoting clothing that is produced according to a certain seasonal rhythm, in quantities large enough to have an effect on sartorial appearances within a society, that can be exported as a "style," and that is consumed according to a prescribed agenda. Correspondingly, art as an autonomous production of subjective expression not bound directly to ecclesiastical or monarchist decrees emerged through the foundation of a bourgeois culture after the European revolutions between 1830 and 1848, when artistic education, independent structures of display, and expanded commercial possibilities allowed for a new creation and distribution of art. Thus, there exists a shared point of origin due to socioeconomic foundations in western Europe. Although fashion was produced elsewhere, too, it was this "Western" concept that eventually determined its global idiom and reception.

History I

The year 1868 saw "La Chambre syndicale de la confection de la couture pour dames et fillettes" establish the guidelines for the production and promotion of high fashion and the popularization of complex new fabrics through weavers such as Joseph Marie Jacquard and through the development of the sewing machine by men such as Thimonnier Barthélemy. It was also the time when the art market expanded significantly due to technical advances in the reproduction of artworks, the establishment of museums such as le Louvre (which became property of the French state in 1848), and the opening of commercial galleries by the Durand-Ruels and Bernheim-Jeune (late 1850s, early 1860s) in the French capital. Therefore, art and fashion together began to leave the confines of private spaces and made the consumption of commodities public. Paintings were no longer exclusive to collections in haute bourgeois drawing rooms, and clothing was no longer individually commissioned from the comfort of one's own home. To view art and to buy gowns one had to venture out into the public, into a commercial setting. Contrary to the social and political impetus of the bourgeois toward increased privacy, the consumption of fashion in particular ran as part of a wide social current—being *à la mode* became a highly publicized statement in art as well as in clothing.

History II

Art and fashion differ significantly in their respective attitudes to history. Art looks at its own historical tradition and, importantly, at the communication of history (historiography), as points of friction and contrast. History for artists consists of mythical or ideological narratives that can be illustrated, debated, and reassessed in the context of artistic tradition. Styles or motifs are quoted, as in the historicism of academic painting, for example, but this process is consciously reflected upon. The costumes in European history paintings of the nineteenth century are often remodeled and redrawn to fit contemporary ideals of the past. Thus, for example, a subject wearing Roman toga is depicted with a contemporary hairstyle and contemporary makeup, and the face and body of the painterly subject follows modern perceptions rather than adhering to any archaeological evidence. The beholder of such artworks understands that historical authenticity is impossible but expects the painter or sculptor to communicate both the spirit of the past and its present interpretation. For fashion, too, authenticity is regarded as impossible; moreover, it is undesirable for the material impact of the design. Fashion's imperative, that is, its absolute contemporariness, has to be observed always. A costume for the stage might endeavor to evoke historical accuracy, but a piece of clothing created within the fashion industry has to transcend historical copy and be an absolute part of the present. In contrast to art, fashion is not expected to conform to ideals of reflection or visual truthfulness and integrity. Fashion is afforded a liberal view of history as a stylistic, pictorial sourcebook. The design of a dress or accessory can be a willful quotation that uses only one particular aspect of the history (such as the cut of a sleeve or waistline, or the setting for a jewel) while operating overall in a deliberately ahistorical manner. In fashion the evocation of a historical period has to be immediate yet not necessarily correct in its aspects; visual impact and easy reading of the design take preference over historical accuracy in material or shape. History is filtered in fashion through the present; it is constantly updated and thus rewritten.

Inspiration

These diverging attitudes to history within art and fashion are not simply due to material reasoning, although the dress in fashion, as opposed to costume design, has to exist in the contemporary market and can thus not be seen as only retrospective or pedantic in its historical detail. The purported seriousness of art in its relation to history and its Platonic equation of truth with beauty renders art the established basis from which fluctuating fashions can draw inspiration. Fashion uses art, analogous to history, as a visual model for its contemporary interpretation. The elevated position that is given to the fine arts in occidental culture is employed by fashion to raise the cultural capital of its creations. When fashion design displays an overt reference to a painterly style or motif, or quotes a particular artwork, the standing and value that the artist or work has accrued in the course of history is also transferred to the fashion design. This transferral occurs in a number of ways: (1) the artist becomes fashion (not costume) designer. One example is Giacomo Balla's menswear of 1914, which cites his own paintings; (2) the designer employs artists for the decoration of the garment, as when Salvador Dalí worked for Elsa Schiaparelli in 1937; (3) fashion renders a contemporary style in painting a decorative motif on the dress, as in Yves Saint Laurent's

Pop Art collection of 1966; (4) the presentation of the collection becomes an art-historical *tableaux vivant*, such as Vivienne Westwood's catwalk of 1994, which cited the works of Franz-Xaver Winterhalter and other artists of the Second Empire; (5) the rendition of fashion in a magazine or other promotional media inserts the design into an art environment, as in Karl Lagerfeld's photos of 1997 that deliberately copy Bauhaus motifs. Conversely, fashion—in dress, accessories, makeup, and so forth—provides the source of inspiration for artists, especially in portraiture. The depiction of women in couture clothing on the canvases of Henri Matisse or Pablo Picasso, for example, show how the extravagant shapes or colors of the designer's creation guide the pictorial representation by the painter. Here, the new perception of the body that fashion can instigate through vibrant textiles, constricting or revealing fabrics, elongation of members through extravagant sleeves or extensions or forms through bustles and padded hips, for example, inspires the artist to take a new look at corporeal representation.

Production I

Art and sartorial fashion have always shared terms to describe their procedure. Both the pictorial work of art as well as the couture dress are traditionally sketched out, and both are then transferred from a paper template to canvas (the *toile*). And while the painting exists as the final outcome of the artist's vision, the toile in couture subsequently needs a further transposition into fabrics in order to appear finished. These procedural similarities do not exclusively define the character of modern painting or contemporary couture, but they go some way to explain why fashion designers have traditionally felt a strong kinship with painters and sculptors in regard to the making of their garments. In the nineteenth century haute couturiers saw themselves as artists in the development of their designs and their frames of reference (shown, for example, in the titles of dresses that allude to pieces of music, histories, allegories, motifs, or styles in painting), but also in subjective perception of the body, which in turn prompted the challenge to sexual mores. By the early 2000s this challenge had become less important than the recourse to and structural engagement with the traditional kinship of couturier and artist, evidenced when the Maison Martin Margiela proposed the paper template or toile to be worn as dress proper.

Avants-gardes

The parallels in the development of art and fashion in the avants-gardes of the nineteenth and twentieth centuries thus became visible through shared patterns and methods and styles of production, but also in adopting moral reflection, oppositional expressions, and attitudes toward commodification. At first the comparatively small group of couturiers and couturières of the second half of the 1800s, styled themselves along the established lines of artistic bohemians. From Charles Frederick Worth and Émile Pingat in the 1870s to John Redfern in the 1880s, they occupied studios and received clients in salons—thus echoing the environment for working and exhibiting in the fine arts (for example, the Parisian Salon as seasonal event). The furnishing of these rooms with collections of portrait paintings and assorted wall hangings indicate the cross-references and quotations that underscore the relationship between art and fashion.

While fashion used from the outset painterly tradition as a culturally established frame of reference and stylistic sourcebook, art looked to fashion for decorative solution in three dimensions and for structural inspiration in regard to repeatedly coined styles and the constant propagating of "originality" as a commodity. With the subjectivism and professed decadence of the fin de siècle, the profusion of decoration was shared between artworks and clothes; expressive hyperbole was de rigueur for both fields, as seen in fashion by Jacques Doucet or the Callot Sisters.

The turn of the century saw an emancipation of the body and simultaneously that of fashion's female clientele. More couturières established economic independence within the fashion industry (for instance, Jeanne Lanvin or Jeanne Paquin), and this was reflected in the cultural climate on the whole. An emerging performativity in art (for example, opera and ballet became much more dynamic), and the sense of physical experimentation that pervaded performances by, for example, the Ballets Russes, combined with the abolition of the corset through the commercial adaptation of non-Western costume, freed the body for new movements outside socially prescribed spaces. This led to a rapid succession of art movements that proclaimed the breaking up of corporeality (cubism), its progression in space (futurism), or the construction of a communal body politic (constructivism, Bauhaus)—efforts that were structurally inspired by and became visually reflected in contemporary couture. Fashion presented the body as a fluid concept that could be determined through a sartorial shell, not as mere social agency but as an aesthetic concept. Madeleine Vionnet, for instance, demonstrated how dress shapes the proportion of the body, and Gabrielle Chanel showed how to liberate its posture.

With political mass movements in the years between the wars the uniformity of dress became significant. Politically committed artists used the unifying potential of clothes to demonstrate equality, and nonobjective painting provided, literally, a pattern book for the abstraction in cut and decoration, which dispensed with societal signifiers. Postwar artistic reflections of consumer society and the culture industry caused an ambivalent intimacy between art and fashion, as the former looked at the latter for the expression of codified consumption that was to be critically assessed, while the latter viewed painterly solutions, for example in Pop Art, as affirmation of its structural significance. The art market in the 1950s, 1960s, and 1970s coined in quick succession a series of artistic styles that resembled seasonal proclamation in couture.

With the creative expansion of ready-to-wear, the need for stylistic inspirations multiplied, and the past and recent history of art was increasingly required to serve as source material. Now, the concept of using the fashion industry not for its structural and procedural differences but employing its tropes directly for the production and representation of art has become widespread. Contemporary art cites fashion not just as an aesthetic model, but also as a field of reference in which the challenges and perils of modern life are glamorously played out. The engagement with fashion in contemporary art is also curatorial, that is, in displaying—often experimental—clothing in museums and galleries, pairing dress and art in exhibitions about material objects or notions of beauty, or using the fashion industry to fund art projects. The curatorial awareness of fashion leads in some cases to the institutional support of collections; for example, the first catwalks of the Dutch duo Viktor and Rolf were made possible only through the support and acquisition policies of the Centraal Museum in Utrecht and the Groninger Museum in Groningen. This implies the positioning of fashion in contemporary culture as one of many interchangeable manifestations, rather than as a structurally distinct medium within a cultural hierarchy. The use of fashion's material basis (textiles, fabrics) and, significantly, its mode of representation through particular photographs, catwalk performances, and so forth, is used in contemporary art to play along with the late modernist staging of the culture industry.

Production II

The production of couture adopted the idea of the independent, subjective artist and developed this stance despite the growing commercial pressure and industrialization of the industry's progress toward ready-to-wear. In the fashion industry there exists a pronounced dialectic that is expressed in the need for stylistic, some would say artistic, innovation that cannot be catered for by the manufacturing process that had given rise to couture as the basis for the fashion market established in the early twenty-first century. Designers perceive themselves as removed from the production process in auxiliary industries like weaving in a way that is similar to the painter who professes to be removed from the maker of the canvas or paper. Thus, from the birth of haute couture onward, fashion has had to accommodate the problem of relying on a design process that contradicts its procedural basis. This is the reason for the oscillating parameters of art and fashion and for the curious hovering of the latter around the former. The dialectic of fashion found in an individualized creation that exists within mass manufacture (which establishes its social coinage in the first place) was recognized willingly by the art market itself. The dialectic does not necessarily show itself in creation, although there has been, at least since Marcel Duchamp and Andy Warhol, a profusion of objects that covet a "designed" look and that are alienated from the artists through their handing over of the actual production to others (such as craftsmen, designers, studio assistants), but it is evidenced in representation, promotion, and consumption, in which fashion's principle is increasingly approximated by art in its advertising, gallery openings, growth of multiples, or museum shops, and in the fact that more and more foundations for contemporary art, as well as for music, architecture, and so forth, are now run by fashion companies, who thus embrace the cultural credibility that rests on the consumption of "high" art.

Within the realm of fashion it is at times difficult to separate neatly the production process from reception and consumption because the interrelation of the three segments constitutes its methodological core. Fashion is largely conceived through trend prediction and marketing analyses that attempt to anticipate as correctly as possible its manner and level of consumption. Correspondingly, fashion coverage, even outside identifiable promotional vehicles, reflects directly the interests of the designer or manufacturer. This, of course, appears as very different from artistic creation that might be influenced by demands from gallerists or commissions—increasingly so in late modernism—but still asserts subjectivism to guarantee itself creative autonomy and institutional independence.

Consumption I

The parallel consumption of art (in exhibitions) and fashion (in catwalk shows or shops) comes at the tail end of the change in modernity that moved from acquiring material goods for their functional purpose, through conspicuous consumption, in which objects are bought for their societal significance, to consuming the products as a spectacle, as entertainment within a saturated market. At the beginning art was consumed for "educational" purposes, to instruct the senses in what was understood to be morally just. It celebrated the dominant spirituality of the culture and favorably documented the established political system. Throughout the Enlightenment (as well as comparable tendencies outside occidental culture) the consumption of art began to operate along lines of individualized perception, and the communication of ideal beauty was understood to be based on temporal and spatial aspects and no longer as an unchangeable cogent. With the rise of a middle class that was socially mobile and less culturally dependent on one structure alone, art turned to the reflection and subsequent critique of its consumers. It no longer presented an unobtainable ideal of sentimental or spiritual perfection but introduced the vernacular, the popular, and the visceral into its discourse. The personal worldview of a particular consumer base took over from the universal understanding that had been propagated for the whole of a culture before. Western modernism challenged such particularity by looking again at quasi-scientific inquiries that should establish general principles for the aesthetic and social meaning of art. Yet such "empirical" principles were subject to change with every art movement that was usurping the one before and wiping the sociocultural slate clean for new individualized rules to be inscribed onto it. In the early 2000s, with the tropes of later modernism determining our understanding of art, its consumption has shifted from edification to entertainment.

Consumption II

In contrast, the consumption of fashion originates in the pragmatic triumvirate of protection, modesty, and decoration. Clothes were first acquired for their utilitarian value, providing warmth, pious cover of the body, and adornment. The latter quickly became the ubiquitous signifier of consumption in which social status was shown through the splendor and profusion of fabrics and accessories. However, sartorial aspirations were still constricted by sumptuary laws and customs. No matter how much money the consumer might spend, certain colors or materials remained the proviso of nobility or clergy. In the eighteenth and nineteenth centuries consumption became increasingly conspicuous; that is, fashion was consumed as the most obvious sign of material wealth. More than carriages or town houses, sumptuous garments acted as an immediate signpost of the social position that its wearer desired. Because fashion is a more direct but less expensive manifestation of wealth, compared with architecture or art collections, conspicuous consumption of clothes could be used by the nouveaux riches to present a façade of financial and social success that did not necessarily exist. Unlike art, the consumption of fashion is not based primarily on knowledge or education but functions through visual awareness, a type of sensuality and perception of the corporeal self. Obviously, couture, like fine art, was acquired originally by the most affluent parts of society, but fashion was still comparatively affordable for the aspiring middle classes, even if its constant change meant seasonal outlay rather than a one-off investment in a painting or sculpture.

Art can be consumed through beholding the object in a (more or less) public space without having to purchase it. The subsequent mental consumption, that is, its appreciation, possible interpretation, analysis or debate, occurs within the subjective personal domain. (This is apart from the art "professional"—artist, gallerist, critic, curator, for instance—who has to publicly communicate the result of such consumption.) In a reverse fashion, clothing is consumed by slipping on the dress or jacket and moving from personal confines, such as a changing room or bedroom, into a public space that is the shop, workplace, or social gathering. Modern media allows individuals to increasingly consume art in the privacy of their own homes. Concerts recorded on CD, films on DVD, and virtual museums on the Internet remove the necessity to withdraw from public space into one's own imagination. However, the principle of moving from the public to the private in art, and conversely from the private to the public in fashion, still separates the two fields. To consume clothes conspicuously and to consume art self-effacingly show a divide between materialist objective and subjective contemplation. Here, fashion's ontology marks it out as a public commodity, despite its very proximity to the individual, while the work of art ambiguously remains a more distant ideal (socially as well as physically) that is integrated into a wider cultural discourse and cannot readily be appropriated for personal consumption.

Consumption III

Consumption in the culture industry habitually operated between the poles of ephemeral following of fashion and the establishment of permanent structures in art. The distinction between understanding an object as "consumable," accepting its limited life span as characteristic, and the understanding object as a document or illustration of such consumption, separates fashion from art. When an object has become accepted *as fashion* it immediately ceases to exist. As sociologist Georg Simmel postulated at the beginning of the last century, fashion dies at the very moment it comes into being, in the instance when the cut of a dress or the shape of a coat is accepted into the cultural mainstream. In order to guarantee its survival in commodity culture, fashion has to constantly reinvent itself and proclaim a new style that supplants the previous one. Modern art, in contrast, is seen to come into being only when its progressive shapes are canonized. Even in its most fugitive performance it always claims its right to lasting values—whereas clothes cannot mean to be permanent; otherwise parts of the textile and fashion industries would have to cease production. The dialectic (not binary pairing) of ephemerality and permanence shape the respective reception of modern art and modern fashion. Art has to remain mobile to reflect and interpret the ever-increasing speed of changes in modernity, yet it must appear permanent, lest it would be regarded as insubstantial. Fashion intends to be lasting—the greatest achievement of a designer is to create a "classic"—in order to be accepted as a substantial cultural fact, yet simultaneously needs to be ephemeral for immanent material as well as conceptual reasons.

See also Caricature and Fashion; Music and Fashion.

Bibliography

Anna, Susanne, and Markus Heinzelmann, eds. *Untragbar*. Ostfildern-Ruit, Germany: HatjeCantz, 2001.

Art/Fashion. New York: Guggenheim Soho, 1997.

Brandstätter, Christian. *Klimt and die Mode*. Vienna: Brandstätter, 1998.

Celant, Germanom, et al., eds. *Looking at Fashion*. Florence, Italy: Cantz/Skira, 1996.

De Givry, Valérie. *Art et mode*. Paris: Editions du Regard, 1998.

Evans, Caroline. *Fashion at the Edge*. New Haven, Conn.: Yale University Press, 2003.

Fausch, Deborah, et al., eds. *Architecture: In Fashion*. Princeton, N.J.: Princeton University Press, 1994.

Felshin, Nina, ed. *Empty Dress*. New York: Independent Curators Incorporated, 1993.

——. "Clothing as Subject." *Art Journal* 1 (1995).

Guillaume, Valérie, ed. *Europe 1910–1939*. Paris: Les Musées de la Ville de Paris, 1996.

Hollander, Anne. *Seeing through Clothes*. New York: Penguin Group, 1980.

Martin, Richard. *Fashion and Surrealism*. New York: Rizzoli, 1989.

——. *Cubism and Fashion*. New York: Abrams/Metropolitan Museum, 1998.

Mode et art 1960–1990. Brussels: Palais des Beaux-Arts, 1995.

Müller, Florence. *L'Art et la mode*. Paris: Assouline, 1999.

Ribeiro, Eileen. *Ingres in Fashion*. New Haven, Conn.: Yale University Press: 1999.

——. *The Gallery of Fashion*. Princeton, N.J.: Princeton University Press, 2000.

Simon, Marie. *Fashion in Art: The Second Empire and Impressionism*. London: Zwemmer, 2003.

Smulders, Caroline. *Sous le manteau*. Paris: Galerie Thaddeus Ropac, 1997.

Smulders, Caroline, and Catherine Millet, eds. *Art et Mode*. *Art Press* 18 (1997).

Steele, Valerie. *Paris Fashion*. New York: Oxford University Press, 1988.

Steele, Valerie, and John S. Mayor. *China Chic*. New Haven, Conn.: Yale University Press, 1999.

Stern, Radu. *Against Fashion*. Cambridge, Mass., and London: MIT Press, 2003.

Troy, Nancy. *Couture Culture*. Cambridge, Mass., and London: MIT Press, 2003.

Wollen, Peter, ed. *Addressing the Century*. London: South Bank, 1998.

Ulrich Lehmann

ART NOUVEAU AND ART DECO

Art nouveau design penetrated into all types of modern, luxury European decorative arts in the period from 1895 to 1905. Its undulating vegetal curves and graceful floral swirls were also a design gift to the Parisian couturiers and until about 1908 or 1909 art nouveau style was energetically appropriated for seasonal, high-fashion use.

Evening garments were the most lavishly attuned to art nouveau. Couturiers swathed their evening wear with a profusion of silk brocade, appliqué, embroidery, and lace. From neckline to hem, the designers played art nouveau swirls around the voluptuousness of the fashionable figure, which itself was curvaceously shaped by "S"-bend corsets. Even tailored woolen walking costumes were trimmed with swirlings of appliqué. By 1907–1909, the style's popularity had waned, replaced by a more upright figure styled with a geometric simplicity drawn from the Vienna Werkstatte, a fashion drawing from *Les Modes* of August 1909 by Gaby, *Toilettes pour Le Casino*.

Historical Content

This appropriation of art nouveau styling coincided with the moment in the history of couture when a united business structure was firmly established by the Chambre Syndicale de la Couture Parisienne. Unrivaled elsewhere in the Western world, Paris couturiers dressed the women of international royal courts and high society including in Japan and tsarist Russia, the wives of the wealthiest international plutocrats, and the great actresses of the Paris stage. Commercial clients already included the grandest department stores at an international level.

The art nouveau "look" was at the cutting edge of modern style. Only the most fashionable wore it in its fullest manifestation, while others preferred moderated versions. These styles were spread internationally through fashion journals, such as *Les Modes* and down through middle-class oriented magazines such as *The Ladies Field* and *La Mode illustrée*. *Les Modes* of July 1902 featured, for example, an art nouveau ball dress by Maggy Rouff with full-length swirls in silver and diamante, on a straw-colored silk ground trimmed with alençon lace.

Designers

From 1895 all the top twenty or so Paris salons were developing art nouveau fashions, from the House of Worth (whose designer was by then Jean-Philippe Worth) through the salons of Doucet, Maggy Rouff, Jeanne Paquin, and Laferriere to cite just a few. They launched season after season of art nouveau–styled garments on to the international fashion market. Examples survive in the great fashion collections of museums in Paris and the United States.

High Art and Popular Versions

Within middle-class levels of ready-to-wear manufacture (for department stores and top levels of wholesale manufacturers), the style was watered down but clearly visible, as in a tailored woolen walking costume featured in *La Mode illustrée, journal de la famille* in January 1901 for example. The swirl did not, however, penetrate the cheapest levels of mass manufacture of tailored clothing for women. At the level of John Noble's *Half Guinea Costume*, as seen in the *Lady's Companion* of 19 September 1896, there was no trimming or decoration at all. Described as "dainty and durable," consumers were concerned with little other than a vaguely stylish silhouette and issues of durability.

Art Deco Fashion

Following the demise of art nouveau as fashion inspiration, the appropriation of art deco design by Paris couturiers informed the next fashion look. This had two phases. The first ran from about 1910 to 1924 and was built around neoclassical/oriental/peasant styling. The second ran from 1924 to about 1930—a more minimalist style, with modernist design touches

Paul Poiret led the first art deco fashion phase. His life was absorbed by orientalism, even as the Ballets Russes arrived in Paris, in 1909. He launched his slim, simple, high-waisted line in 1908, with its less-structured cut and delicately layered exotic style. Poiret was a collector of fauve paintings, which inspired his use of purples, pinks, blues, greens, and golds. Poiret's passion for orientalism, chinoiserie, European peasant, and North African design introduced a fresh bold simplicity to the cut and decoration. His 1911 *One Thousand and One Night Ball* set off a lasting vogue for the exotic, with use of light silks, gold tassels, turbans, tunic dresses, and bold use embroidery. Poiret unwillingly shared his limelight with other couturiers such as Jeanne Lanvin, Lucile, and the Callot Soeurs, who all created versions of the slender, high waisted and often sumptuous exotic look.

Art Deco—Phase Two

From about 1924 Paris fashion crystalized into the hipless garçonne look, reflected in the new sportive couture client, with her flat chest, bobbed hair, and less socially restricted lifestyle. The new generation of key designers included Jean Patou and Chanel, who both borrowed elements from Sonia Delaunay's far more extreme Orphic cubist designs. Madeleine Vionnet developed her skillful bias cut while Lelong produced the first ready-to-wear to come from a couture salon These short-skirted, simple, art-deco garments were nevertheless always made from the finest wool or the most sophisticated gilded, flowered Lyon silks and embellished with complex beading or tucking to identify their couture provenance. Patou ended the look when he lowered the hemline in 1929.

Fashion Illustration

A group of young struggling fauve artists produced a generation of fashion illustration of lasting quality and celebrity. Under the original inspiration of Paul Poiret, and his pochoir printed *Les Choses de Paul Poiret of 1909 and 1911* this period launched the careers of Barbier, Lepape, Iribe, Dufy, Erté, Marty, Benito, and Bonfils.

Couture and popular versions. The short skirt and dropped waistline were copied at all levels of the fashion trade, this time right down to the cheapest ready-to-wear, as seen in Sears and Roebuck and English ready-to-wear wholesalers' catalogs. Fashion knowledge and consumption opportunities were spread to a mass audience through the movies, through new cheap fashion journals, through home dressmaking, and through the wide availability of artificial silk or rayon (albeit still an unreliable fashion fabric). All of this accelerated the demand for mass, machine-made ready-to-wear and thus "up and coming" working-class girls on both sides of the Atlantic embraced moderated forms of art deco fashion even though their financial means were limited.

Retro Versions

While historical styling is never repeated in the same way, both art nouveau and art deco styles have been subject to fashion revivals. As the maxi hemline became accepted from the late 1960s, in Britain new psychedelic styles were linked to a subversive nostalgia for the imperial Edwardian period, for art nouveau, and for the work of Aubrey Beardsley. This is evident in the original art nouveau brand logo selected by Barbara Hulanicki for her fashion company Biba, founded in 1964. This is also clear in the art nouveau romanticism of her fashionable evening silhouette and use of feather boas, though she fused this with early 1930s style in her use of slinky satins and the bias cut. John Galliano presented several Edwardian-styled fashions in 1996–1997.

Art Deco

Art deco design is far more deeply etched on the public mind as epitomizing a mythical ideal of free, youthful gaiety, glamour, and sexuality. This image has been strengthened by a stream of popular movies set in the 1920s, including *Singin' in the Rain* (1952), *Some Like It Hot* (1959), and *Thoroughly Modern Millie* (1967), brought to the stage in New York in 2002 and in London in 2003. A filmed version of F. Scott Fitzgerald's *The Great Gatsby* in 1974, while the *Chicago* of 2002 and the Art Deco exhibition at the Victoria and Albert Museum of the same year, further escalated public fascination. The mid-1960s revival was led by Yves Saint Laurent with his African art deco collection in 1967, which perfectly suited that period's young, androgynous style. At the turn of the second millennium, Galliano reworked the flapper style in 1994, while Diane von Furstenberg showed flapper dresses with dropped waists and beaded fringing in New York on 17 September 2003.

See also Appliqué; Doucet, Jacques; Galliano, John; Orientalism; Poiret, Paul; Saint Laurent, Yves.

Bibliography

Benton, Charlotte, Tim Benton, and Gislaine Wood. *Art Deco, 1910–1939.* London: Victoria and Albert Museum, 2002.

Charles-Roux, Edmonde. *Chanel and Her World.* New York: Vendome Press, 1981.

Coleman, E. A. *The Opulent Era, the Work of Worth, Doucet and Pingat.* London and New York: Thames and Hudson, Inc., Brooklyn Museum, 1989.

Greenhalgh Paul, ed. *Art Nouveau: 1890–1914.* London: Victoria and Albert Museum, 2000.

Musée de la Mode et du Costume. *Paul Poiret et Nicole Groult: maîtres de la mode art deco.* Paris: Paris Musées, 1986.

Troy, Nancy J. *Modernism and the Decorative Arts in France: Art Nouveau to Le Corbusier.* New Haven, Conn.: Yale University Press, 1991.

———. *Couture Culture, A Study in Modern Art and Fashion.* Cambridge, Mass.: Massachusetts Institute of Technology, 2002.

White, Palmer. *Poiret.* London: Studio Vista, 1974.

Lou Taylor

AVEDON, RICHARD*

Richard Avedon (1923–2004) was one of the most important and prolific photographers of the second half of the twentieth century, and in the eyes of many photography and fashion specialists, he was the most important fashion photographer of all time. In a career spanning sixty years he showed himself capable of almost constant stylistic reinvention, yet in retrospect his oeuvre also demonstrated a remarkable coherence and strength that far surpassed the narrow confines of fashion photography. He was acknowledged by his peers for his superb work as early as 1950, when he won the Highest Achievement Medal of the Art Directors Club in New York. Only eight years later he was named by *Popular Photography* magazine as one of the ten most important photographers in the world. By the end of the twentieth century, having garnered handfuls of honorary degrees, lifetime achievement awards, and other prestigious prizes, Avedon was identified by the *Photo District News* as "the most influential photographer of the past twenty years." These successes were due in no small measure to his acute sensitivity to the social and artistic revolutions in American culture. As the historian Nancy Hall-Duncan observed in 1979, "This sense of timing and flexibility—representing the desires of our society and reflecting its mood with uncanny sympathy—was Avedon's forte from the start of his career." This talent also helps to explain why he was never displaced by a younger pretender, as happened to so many of his rivals. John Durniak once reported in *Time* magazine that an admiring colleague considered Avedon "the white mechanical rabbit that all other photographers tried to catch" but never could. Even allowing for the hyperbolic language of the fashion industry itself, which anointed him the king of fashion photography, Avedon could claim a towering record of achievement.

Richard Avedon was born in New York City, the son of Russian Jewish immigrants who owned a department store in Manhattan. His school years revealed a marked literary aptitude: he was coeditor with James Baldwin of the De Witt Clinton High School literary magazine, and he was named poet laureate of the New York City high schools in 1941. A brief period of study in philosophy at Columbia University was followed by two years in the U.S. Merchant Marine (1942–1944), after which Avedon undertook intensive visual studies with Alexey Brodovitch at the Design Laboratory of the New School for Social Research. New York had everything the ambitious young man wanted: "theater, movies, music, dance." Part of Avedon's visual education had come from his love of photography. As a teenager he had decorated his room with the work of the masters; as a mature professional, he benefited from the lessons of his predecessors. This keen awareness of the accomplishments of previous artists in the field, and a philosophical bent that allowed him to consider the medium of photography in abstract as well as practical terms, encouraged him to explore the full gamut of the medium's possibilities. For example, switching to a large-format camera after he had started his career in fashion photography with the more flexible Rolleiflex made him realize that throwing the background of a shot out of focus reduced the sum of detail and created "an ambiguous narrative relationship between the knowable (what's sharp), and the unknowable (what's blurred)" (Thurman and Avedon).

Avedon's arrival on the scene coincided with the final years of the dominance of haute couture. In 1945 Carmel Snow invited him to join *Harper's Bazaar* as staff photographer, where his mentor Brodovitch was already working as art director. Avedon thus stepped into the shoes (but not the footsteps) of the great neoclassicist image-maker George Hoyningen-Huene, who was convinced high fashion was dead. Hoyningen-Huene greeted his young rival disdainfully with the phrase, "Too bad . . . Too late!" It was this atmosphere of ennui that Snow wished to dispel in and with her magazine. The visionary editor wanted to reinvigorate the Parisian luxury business by opening the vast American market to it, and she needed an interpreter of French taste who was less aloof than Hoyningen-Huene—someone who could temper the classicism of French couture with American zest.

It was not surprising that Avedon always acknowledged the Hungarian photojournalist-turned-fashion photographer Martin Munkacsi, rather than the patrician Hoyningen-Huene, as a key influence on his style. Munkacsi was a pioneer of the out-of-doors realistic fashion photograph, a major stimulus to Avedon's own approach, although the fact that Avedon skillfully combined the exuberance of outdoor photography with the static tradition of the studio showed that he had absorbed lessons from the Baron Adolf de Meyer, Edward Steichen, and George Hoyningen-Huene as well.

For the next four decades Avedon's name was synonymous with the best of fashion photography. Between 1947 and 1984 he photographed the Paris collections for either *Harper's Bazaar* or *Vogue*, and he worked exclusively for the latter from 1966 to 1990. Avedon preferred to work repeatedly with the same models, establishing a rapport that, in his words, was "built from sitting to sitting and from season to season." Whether the sitter was Suzy Parker wearing Gres, Dovima wearing Dior—"Dovima Among the Elephants" (1955) is arguably Avedon's most famous photograph—or Jean Shrimpton and Veruschka dressed in psychedelic whimsies, the models wore the clothes as if they were born to them. Avedon's earliest photographs showed women dancing, partying, skipping about from one lively *boîte* to another on the arm of debonair escorts, the images always striking a careful balance between factual information about the dresses and impressions of how the women looked—and more important, it was implied, felt—wearing them. Despite the seemingly spontaneous character of the images, however, the photographer carefully researched his outdoor and indoor settings before he undertook the sittings.

Avedon's intense early commitment inevitably took its toll. After twenty years in fashion photography, he decided that there was "too much narcissism and disenchantment" in the work. The outdoor images gave way to a harsher minimalist aesthetic that was even described as "cruel," the fabrication of which was possible only in the studio. "I've worked out a series of no's," Avedon wrote in 1994, ". . . no to exquisite light, no to apparent compositions, no to the seduction of poses or narrative. And all these no's force me to the yes. I have a white background. I have the person I am interested in and the thing that happens between us." If he continued to work in the arena of fashion, it was to support his family and his "art"—namely, portrait photography.

Avedon's sitters essentially comprised a gallery of the rich, the famous, and the powerful. All were treated equally, in such a way that fellow photographer Henri Cartier-Bresson could call them "inhabitants of an Avedon world." Avedon's twentieth-century gallery has been acknowledged as one of the greatest projects of its kind—in historian and curator Maria Hambourg's words, "a gallery of modern souls as intense and vivid as any ever achieved." Yet somehow, the portraits in the aggregate comprised Avedon's self-portrait, or as Thomas Hess wrote, Avedon seemed always to be "trying to climb into his image." After 1990, his portraits of the past and the present were regular features of the *New Yorker* magazine. Avedon's work was also exhibited in such prestigious institutions as the Metropolitan Museum of Art, the Smithsonian Institution, the Museum of Modern Art in New York, the Minneapolis Institute of Fine Arts, the Seibu Museum in Tokyo, the Museum "La Caixa" in Barcelona, and the University Art Museum in Berkeley, California.

See also Celebrities; Fashion Museums and Collections; Fashion Photography; Hoyningen-Huene, George; Vogue.

Bibliography

Avedon, Richard. "The Family." Special bicentennial issue of *Rolling Stone*, 21 October 1976.
——. *Photographs 1947–1977*. New York: Farrar, Straus and Giroux, 1978.
——. *In the American West 1979–1984*. New York: Harry N. Abrams, Inc., 1985.
——. *Evidence 1944–1994*. New York: Random House, 1994.
——. *Portraits*. New York: Metropolitan Museum of Art and Harry N. Abrams, Inc., 2002.
Avedon, Richard, and Truman Capote. *Observations*. New York: Simon and Schuster, 1959.
Avedon, Richard, and Arbus Doon. *The Sixties*. New York: Random House, 1999.
Baldwin, James, and Richard Avedon. *Nothing Personal*. New York: Dell Publishing Company, 1964.
Thurman, Judith, and Richard Avedon. *Richard Avedon: Made in France*. San Francisco: Fraenkel Gallery, 2001.

William Ewing

B

BALENCIAGA, CRISTÓBAL

Born in 1895 in Guetaria (Getaria), a small fishing village on the tempestuous northern coast of Spain, Cristóbal Balenciaga Eisaguirre (1895–1972) was to become, in his own lifetime, the most famous Spanish fashion designer of his generation. He died in the mellower climate of Jávea, on the eastern coast of Spain, twelve years after receiving the Légion d'honneur for services to the French fashion industry and only four years after closing down his prestigious business in Paris. The contrast between Balenciaga's places of birth and death offers a touching analogy to his journey from rags to riches or, at the very least, from a relatively obscure, fairly modest, and extremely hardworking provincial background to the sunny prominence of an established position in international fashion. While he gained considerable material comfort, he did not lose his work ethic. He owned a flat in central Paris, an estate near Orléans (France), and a substantial house in Igueldo, near Guetaria. He was able to fill his homes with collections of decorative and fine arts and, from time to time, with friends from different walks of life.

Balenciaga evidently achieved this major change in circumstance, initially, through the patronage of a member of the Spanish aristocracy, the marquesa de Casa Torres, who recognized his talent at sewing—a skill learned from his seamstress mother— and apprenticed him to a tailor in fashionable San Sebastián (Donostia). From this training, he went on to become chief designer in a local dressmaking establishment, before opening his own house in Madrid. Armed with financial backing from a fellow Basque, he subsequently successfully established, directed, and designed for the Parisian couture house that bore his name. At the same time, he maintained three high-class dressmaking establishments in Spain, in San Sebastián, Barcelona, and Madrid. They functioned under the label Eisa, an abbreviated form of his mother's patronymic.

Balenciaga's formative experiences in Spain were fundamental to both his design practice and his ultimate move to Paris. His tailoring apprenticeship gave him a mastery of cut and construction and an obsession with perfection of fit. He was one of the few couturiers who was capable of "cutting material, assembling a creation and sewing it by hand," as even his archrival Coco Chanel acknowledged (Miller, p. 14). His fascination with certain simple forms (the manipulation of circles, semicircles, and tunics) may well have derived from familiarity with the cut of the ecclesiastical vestments and clerical dress so common in Spain. His use of certain colors (black, shades of gray, earth colors, brilliant reds, fuchsia, and purple), certain forms of decoration (heavy embroidery and braid), and certain fabrics (lace used voluptuously in flounces and heavy woolens or new synthetics "sculpted" into extraordinary shapes) owed much to the aesthetic of Spanish regional dress and to the drapery and costume depicted in Spanish painting and sculpture from 1500 to 1900. His early working experience in San Sebastián alerted him to the dominance of Paris in international women's fashion, as one of his responsibilities was to travel to the center of couture to the seasonal collections, to make drawings of models that might subsequently be translated into garments for Spanish clients. In this second, transitional, stage of his career, he was copyist or translator rather than originator of designs.

Historical Context

While the reasons for Balenciaga's departure from Spain in 1935 at the age of forty, and his subsequent establishment in Paris, are not clear, it is probable that the commercial and political situation in Europe contributed to his move. In the 1930s Paris was the fashion mecca not only for ambitious designers but also for the cosmopolitan women they dressed. The French government fostered couture and its ancillary trades because they were important national export industries.

Subsidies encouraged the use of French textiles, and textile manufacturers supplied short runs of rare fabrics for couture collections. The trade organization Chambre Syndicale de la couture parisienne guided the regulation of conditions of employment, training for prospective couturiers, and the efficient coordination of the twice-yearly showings of all couturiers' collections. This arrangement made the trade desirable, as private clients and commercial buyers from department stores and wholesale companies from other parts of Europe, the United States, and Japan could plan their visits in advance and make the most of their time in Paris. Before World War II, no other country boasted such a highly organized and prestigious fashion system, a fact of which Balenciaga must have been aware as early as about 1920.

That Balenciaga chose to "defect" some fifteen years later was probably linked to the increasingly difficult political situation in Spain, a state of affairs that did not bode well for those who made their living from fashion. In 1931 the Spanish monarchy fell, and a period of un-

certainty preceded the Spanish Civil War (1936–1939). Balenciaga lost his main clientele of the 1920s, the Spanish royal family and the aristocracy who summered in San Sebastián and wintered in Madrid. Consequently, he closed down his branch in the north of Spain just after it opened. The advent of war did not improve his prospects, so his move to Paris (via London) was timely. By 1939, when he reopened his houses in Spain, he had made a reputation in Paris, gaining an international clientele that far outstripped the captive following he had had in Spain.

During World War II, he moved back and forth between the two countries, keeping a connection with his familial and cultural roots and control of his modest fashion empire. At the end of the war he continued this practice. Even when he spent long periods in Paris, he did not lose contact with Spaniards, as both his business and home were in the district frequented by Spanish émigrés, many of his business associates or employees were Spanish, and his friends included his fellow countrymen the artists Pablo Picasso, Joan Miró, and Pablo Palazuelo.

The Businesses

Haute couture businesses are secretive about their internal workings, if not their ambitions, and often it is the design records rather than the accounts that survive. In the absence of financial or administrative archives for the house of Balenciaga, it is possible to reconstruct its organization and strategy only through its public registration, its rich design archive, and limited oral and written testimony from the salon, some of the more illustrious members of its clientele, and a few of the designer's colleagues or pupils. Tradition and continuity were particular characteristics of the house, in terms of its internal structure and workforce, its design output and quality of production, and its maintenance of a faithful and prestigious customer base. Gimmickry was avoided at all costs—even in the postwar period of consumerism, when many of Balenciaga's competitors engaged freely in a variety of new sales tactics, including the development of ranges of ready-to-wear clothing, accessories, and numerous fragrances and the use of advertising.

As was relatively common in Parisian couture, Balenciaga was a limited company, in the form of a partnership between Balenciaga himself, his hat designer and friend Vladzio Zawrorowski (d. 1946), and Nicolas Bizcarrondo, the Basque businessman who provided

Woman modeling Balenciaga coat and dress. This ensemble smartly conveys several Balenciaga trademarks, such as elegance and grandeur, monochromatic colors, and a perfect fit. HENRY CLARKE/VOGUE © 1995 CONDÉ NAST PUBLICATIONS, INC. REPRODUCED BY PERMISSION.

the initial capital. Balenciaga's previous success in Spain and the existence of three houses there (albeit that they were in limbo in 1937) might well account for Bizcarrondo's faith in Balenciaga and his willingness to support him. Established in 1937 on an initial investment of Fr 100,000, the value of Balenciaga's couture house rose to Fr 2 million in 1946 and to Fr 30 million in 1960. Injections of funding coincided with expansion in its activities. The investment reflected the size—large by couture standards but small relative to industrial enterprises before or after World War II.

The structure of the design house followed to the letter a traditional couture model, conforming without difficulty to the new haute couture regulations implemented in 1947. Throughout Balenciaga's reign, the seat of business was at 10 avenue Georges V—a suitable location in the golden triangle of Parisian luxury production. This six-story building served all functions—aesthetic, craft, commercial, and administrative. Discretion was the key to both the exterior and interior, with little overt reference to the house's sales function. On the outside, classical pillars flanked the shop windows, which never contained any hint of clothes for sale but rather pretended to a certain artistry.

On the ground floor the entrance was through the boutique (shop), which stocked accessories, such as gloves, foulards, and the perfumes Le Dix (1947), La Fuite des Heures (1948), and Quadrille (1955). This floor had the appearance of the hallway of a grand house, with a black-and-white tiled floor, rich carpets, and dark wooden and gilded furniture and fittings. On the first floor, reached by an elevator lined in red Cordoban leather and studded with brass pins, were the salon and fitting rooms, decorated in 1937 in the fashionable Parisian taste of the day, with upholstered settees, curvaceous free-standing ashtrays, and mirrored doors. Presided over by Madame Renée, this floor was home to the *vendeuses* (saleswomen), who greeted their own specially designated clients, consulted with them about their vestmental needs and social calendar, introduced them to the models that might suit them (specially paraded by a house mannequin), and then watched over their three fittings once they had placed their orders. Above the salons were the workshops where the clothes were cut and constructed; only occasionally were certain garments farmed out for special treatment, for example, to the embroidery firms of Bataille, Lesage, or Rébé for embellishment. Higher still in the building were the offices occupied by the administration.

Expansion and continuity. Workshop space expanded beyond the four workshops set up in 1937 (two for dresses, one for suits, and one for dresses and suits). During the war (1941) Balenciaga added two millinery ateliers; then, after the war (1947–1948), another two workshops for dresses and one for suits; and, finally, in 1955, another for dresses, bringing the total to ten. Just before the opening of the final workshop, Balenciaga's employees numbered 318. In the scheme of things, Balenciaga valued his cutters more highly than his workshop heads, paying the former 20–30 percent more than the latter between 1953 and 1954. Given the reputation of the house for high-quality tailoring, this prioritization is not surprising, nor is the fact that skilled employees in positions of trust remained with the firm over a prolonged period. In the case of the known workshop heads, the majority stayed for twenty to thirty years. Moreover, "new" senior staff members seem to have arrived from the Spanish houses, possibly because Balenciaga could rely on their standards and experience.

Client Base

Continuity was also an aspect of the client base, satisfying Balenciaga's firm belief that women should find and remain with the dressmaker who best served their needs and understood their personal styles. Many private and professional clients patronized the house for thirty years. At his height, Balenciaga showed his collections to two hundred wholesale buyers and made to measure about 2,325 garments per annum for private clients. Some of the latter bought as many as fifty to eighty items per year. They made their choices from the four hundred models he created, a number in line with the output of other top couturiers of the time.

Major department stores bought Balenciaga models with particular customers in mind and then reproduced as closely as possible the couture experience in their salons, offering fashion shows, personal advice on customers' social and practical needs, and high standards of fitting and making. At different times these firms included Lydia Moss, Fortnum and Mason, and Harrods in London; Hattie Carnegie, Henri Bendel, Bloomingdale's, Saks Fifth Avenue, and Bergdorf Goodman in New York; I. Magnin in Los Angeles and San Francisco; and Holt Renfrew in Toronto. In contrast, wholesalers bought with batch production in mind, spreading Balenciaga styles through their adaptation of toiles from the house. The wholesalers who attended

Balenciaga's shows included many members of the London Model House Group, the elite of ready-to-wear. For them, every model had about eight to ten derivatives, each of which was reproduced four hundred to five hundred times. Some Balenciaga models, however, were considered too complex for reproduction, whether in department stores or factories, and too outré for the tastes of more conservative clients.

Balenciaga's loyal band of private clients belonged to the wealthiest titled and untitled families across the globe and embraced both professional women and socialites. Some customers combined buying from him with purchases from other made-to-measure or ready-made sources or found his garments in special secondhand outlets. His true devotees developed a close relationship, even friendship, with "The Master," who provided for their every need: some daughters followed their mothers into the house, among them the future Queen Fabiola of Belgium, daughter of his patron, the marquesa de Casa Torres; Sonsoles, daughter of his most consistent client, the marquesa de Llanzol; and General Francisco Franco's wife and granddaughter, whose wedding dress was the last designed by Balenciaga. Others grew into Balenciaga through familiarity with his house in Paris, for example, Mona Bismarck, widow of Harrison Williams, one of the wealthiest men in America, who consistently acquired her wardrobe from him every season for twenty years, even the shorts she wore for yachting or gardening. Perhaps, like Barbara "Bobo" Rockefeller, she believed that a Balenciaga dress gave its wearer a sense of security. A cheaper way of buying made-to-measure Balenciaga fashions was open to those who knew his Spanish operations, where labor costs were lower and local fabrics sometimes were substituted for those used in Paris (and a favorable exchange rate prevailed for most foreign visitors). The film star Ava Gardner, a regular visitor to Spain in the 1950s, patronized Eisa, for example, as well as the Parisian house.

Balenciaga's final— and perhaps most intriguing— client was Air France. In 1966 the world's biggest airline asked him to design air stewardesses' summer and winter uniforms to a brief that probably appealed to him: "elegance, freedom of movement, adaptability to sudden changes of climate, and maintenance of a smart appearance even after a long journey" (Miller pp. 57–59). His experience of dealing with the soigné jet set and his fashion philosophy of practicality prepared him well for this request.

Fashion Philosophy and Signature Designs

Balenciaga was reticent in talking about himself and his craft, so the nature of his business, the identity of his clients, and actual surviving garments and designs are necessary to supplement his occasional observations about his fashion philosophy. Evolution rather than revolution, elegance and decorum rather than novelty and flash-in-the-pan fashion, practicality, wearability, and "breathability" were guiding principles in his design and, no doubt, suited a discerning, largely mature clientele. At his apogee in the 1950s and 1960s Balenciaga created designs that bear witness to his keen attention to the effects achieved by combining different colors and textures. Often the intrinsic qualities of fabrics, whether traditional woolens and silks or innovative synthetics, led the design process, as Balenciaga pondered their potential in tailored, draped, or sculpted forms. He was prepared to forgo the French government subsidy, granted to couturiers whose collections comprised 90 percent French-made textiles, in order to acquire the best-quality and most groundbreaking textiles from whichever part of Europe they came.

Balenciaga gradually honed his design in daywear, building out from the base of apparently traditional tailored suits with neat, fitted bodies and sleeves that sat perfectly at the shoulder into experimentation that led to the minimalist "no-seam coat" (1961), crafted from a single piece of fabric by the artful use of darts and tucks. This garment hung loose on the body and embodied the culmination of a range of loose or semifitted lines in various garments that probably constituted Balenciaga's most important contribution to fashion. These designs emerged gradually during the 1950s, flattering different female figures (mature and youthful) and allowing the wearer to move easily. The tunic (1955), chemise or sack (1957), and Empire styles (1958) drew attention away from the natural waist through the creation of a tubular line or the emphasis that a bloused back laid on the hip line or that a high waist laid on the bust. Suit jackets were judiciously cut, and their matching skirts were often gathered slightly into the waistband at the front to accommodate middle-age spread. Three-quarter- and seven-eighth-length sleeves and necklines set away from the neck sought to flatter the wrists and the neck, both graceful at any age. They also proved practical for busy lifestyles. In the 1960s a range of different lengths and fits of jackets and coats featured in Balenciaga's collections, from the very fitted to the loose.

Similar paring down is evident in Balenciaga's cocktail and evening wear; so, too, is a taste for the grandeur and elaboration appropriate to the purpose. For these gowns he drew on historical and non-European sources and sought his own version of modernism. Initially, for all their apparent ease, these dresses were often built on a corset base with boning, an understructure that was not obvious under the complex confections of drapery, puffs, and flounces popular in the 1950s. By the 1960s, however, shapes simplified and did not cling to or mold the body. The contrast between the slim black sheaths of the late 1940s and early 1950s and the outstanding models of gazar, zibeline, faille, and matelassé of the 1960s is absolute. The former took their drama from the swathes of contrasting satin in jewel colors that were attached at waist or neckline and could be draped to the wearer's fancy. The latter relied for their éclat on the sculptural simplicity of their lines and the substance of the fabric rather than on artificial flowers, feathers, or polychrome embroidery. While three-dimensional decoration was not obsolete, the shapes to which it adhered became tunic-like. The frills, ballooning skirts, and sack backs had given way to a more austere, almost monastic aesthetic.

Importance and Legacy

The fashion cognoscenti, from couturiers to journalists, still accord Balenciaga the laurel of the "designers' designer." They use his name to evoke certain standards in fashion—evolution in style, ease of dress, and meticulous attention to detail (visible or otherwise). Balenciaga's former apprentices (André Courrèges and Emanuel Ungaro), colleagues (Hubert de Givenchy), and aficionados (Oscar de la Renta and Paco Rabanne) have inherited and propagated certain elements of his philosophy and style. In the last quarter of the twentieth century approximately eight major exhibitions worldwide perpetuated his fame, many facilitated by the archivist of the house of Balenciaga, owned by Bogart perfumes from 1987 to 2001 and since then by the Gucci Group (91 percent) and the in-house designer, Nicolas Ghesquière (9 percent). Ghesquière's widely acknowledged talent and vitality revived the fortunes of Balenciaga in the late 1990s, and by the early 2000s the designer himself had begun to explore the riches of the archives and appreciate more fully the shadow in which he labored. He was quick to draw parallels between his own work and that of the "The Master," although couture represents a tiny element of his output.

In Spain, Balenciaga's reputation contributed to initiatives to encourage the Spanish fashion industry: in 1987 the Spanish Ministry of Industry and Energy named the first (and only) national prize for fashion design after him and in 2000 injected $3.2 million into the charitable foundation set up in Guetaria in his name. The overall objective of this trust is "to foster, spread and emphasize the transcendence, importance, and prominence that Don Cristóbal Balenciaga has had in the world of fashion," (www.fundacionbalenciaga.com) an objective that is meant to be achieved through the construction and development of a museum in Guetaria, the establishment of an international center for design training, the foundation of a research and documentation center, the publication of a fashion periodical, and the development of touring exhibitions about Balenciaga, fashion design, and haute couture.

With such sustained efforts at maintaining Balenciaga's reputation and values, his impact on fashion is bound to survive, disseminated through a range of techniques from which the reserved and publicity-shy Balenciaga himself might well have recoiled. The ramifications of his dedication to fashion for that once small fishing town of Guetaria are likely to be impressive.

See also Chanel, Gabrielle (Coco); Courrèges, André; Ecclesiastical Dress; Haute Couture; Paris Fashion; Spanish Dress.

Bibliography

Ballard, Bettina. *In My Fashion*. New York: D. McKay Company, 1960. A contemporary fashion editor's autobiography, which incorporates substantial portraits of many Parisian couturiers, including Balenciaga, whom the author knew well.

Beaton, Cecil. *The Glass of Fashion*. Garden City, N.Y.: Doubleday, 1954. The fashion world seen through the eyes of the society fashion photographer Cecil Beaton, a friend of Balenciaga's.

Bertin, Célia. *Paris à la Mode: A Voyage of Discovery*. Translated by Marjorie Deans. London: V. Gollancz, 1956. A contemporary view of haute couture and its main protagonists.

De Marly, Diana. *The History of Haute Couture, 1850–1950*. New York: Holmes and Meier, 1980. Classic overview of the development of French haute couture.

Jouve, Marie-Andrée. *Balenciaga*. Text by Jacqueline Demornex. New York: Rizzoli International, 1989. The first major account of Balenciaga from the archivist of the house, with superb illustrations.

——. *Balenciaga*. New York: Universal/Vendome, 1997. A brief and useful introduction to Balenciaga, largely through images but also containing new data on clients.

Latour, Anny. *Kings of Fashion*. Translated by Mervyn Savill. New York: Coward-McCann, 1958. A contemporary fashion journalist's investigation of haute couture and its main protagonists.

Menkes, Suzy. "Temple to a Monk of Fashion: Museum to Open in Basque Designer's Birthplace." *International Herald Tribune*, 23 May 2000. An overview of the Fundación Balenciaga in Guetaria.

Miller, Lesley Ellis. *Cristóbal Balenciaga*. New York: Holmes and Meier, 1993. A historically contextualized account of the man and his background, clothes, clients, business, and legacy.

Palmer, Alexandra. *Couture and Commerce: The Transatlantic Fashion Trade in the 1950s*. Vancouver, Canada: University of British Columbia Press, 2001. A multidisciplinary approach to haute couture that unpacks many of its myths by delving into the dissemination of haute couture through transatlantic (especially Torontonian) outlets, the uses and meanings of couture clothing to clients (achieved through oral history), and the examination of objects in the Royal Ontario Museum's textile collection. Useful references to the reception of Balenciaga's designs.

Spindler, Amy M. "Keys to the Kingdom: A Fashion Fairy Tale Wherein Nicolas Ghesquière Finally Inherits the Throne." *New Yorker*, 14 April 2002, pp. 53–58. Ghesquière encounters the Balenciaga archives at last.

Exhibition Catalogs

Cristóbal Balenciaga. Tokyo: Fondation de la Mode, 1987.

de Petri Stephen, and Melissa Leventon, eds. *New Look to Now: French Haute Couture 1947–1987*. New York: Rizzoli International, 1989. A case study of haute couture and its San Francisco customers, with an excellent essay explaining how department stores adapted garments for their clients.

Ginsburg, Madeleine, comp. *Fashion: An Anthology by Cecil Beaton*. London: Victoria and Albert Museum, 1971. A short section of catalog entries on the Balenciaga clothes lent to the exhibition.

Healy, Robyn. *Balenciaga: Masterpieces of Fashion Design*. Melbourne, Australia: National Gallery of Victoria, 1992. An overview of Balenciaga and his oeuvre and its importance.

Jouve, Marie-Andrée. *Homage à Balenciaga*. Lyons, France: Musée Historique des Tissus, 1985. Emphasis on Balenciaga's relationship to the textile industry.

——. *Mona Bismarck, Cristobal Balenciaga, Cecil Beaton*. Paris: Mona Bismarck Foundation, 1994. An intriguing glimpse into the relationship of a major client, her couturier, and their mutual friend. Well-documented record of designs chosen and worn by Bismarck.

El mundo de Balenciaga. Madrid: Palacio de Bellas Artes, 1974.

Vreeland, Diana, curator. *The World of Balenciaga*. New York: Metropolitan Museum of Art, 1973.

Internet Resources

Cristóbal Balenciaga Fundazioa-Fundación. Available from <http://www.fundacionbalenciaga.com>. General information on the aims and objectives of the trust and the temporary displays of clothes.

Lesley Ellis Miller

BALL DRESS

Ball dress is simply defined as a gown worn to a ball or formal dance. Beyond this fundamental description, there are remarkably intricate conventions related to appropriateness of ball dress. The most extravagant within the category of evening dress, a ball gown functions to dazzle the viewer and augment a woman's femininity. Ball gowns typically incorporate a low décolletage, a constricted bodice, bared arms, and long bouffant skirts. Ball gowns are visually distinguishable from other evening gowns by their lavishly designed surfaces—with layers of swags and puffs and such trim details as artificial flowers, ribbons, rosettes, and lace.

Additionally, ball gowns permit a woman to inhabit more space, as the especially billowing and expansive skirts extend the dimensions of her body. Fabric surfaces vary from reflective to matte, textured to smooth, and soft to rigid. Through the decades, undergarments have played a vital role in reshaping the natural structure of the body into the desired silhouette, from the corsets and petticoats of the nineteenth century to the control-top panty hose and padded bras of the twenty-first century.

Historical Significance

Balls have existed for centuries among royalty and the social elite, dating back to the Middle Ages. During the mid-1800s, the ball re-emerged as a desirable manner of entertainment among the upper and middle classes. Through the 1800s, the ball served as a means to bring together people of similar social backgrounds, often for purposes of introducing young women and men of marriageable age. Coming-out balls, debutante balls, or cotillion balls became standard events by the mid-1800s, and have continued in some form or another into the twenty-first century, with the high school prom added as a more middle-class and democratized version of a coming-out ball.

As popularity of the ball increased, ball gowns materialized and developed as a category of evening dress.

Designer Madame Lucille fitting ball gown. Lavish works of fashion art, ball gowns are designed to emphasize femininity by drawing attention to the wearer's décolletage, bare arms, and small waist. © HULTON-DEUTSCH COLLECTION/CORBIS. REPRODUCED BY PERMISSION.

Fashions during the first half of the nineteenth century included expansive skirts and tiny waistlines, and these characteristics were incorporated into the ball dress. Bouffant skirts functioned beautifully in the ballroom, as women skimmed across the floor as if they were floating on air. At all social levels and through the decades competition for the most opulent gown has remained a central ingredient of the event, as the finest ball gown may possibly result in the attentions of the most eligible suitor.

Contemporary Use

As the most splendid among evening dresses, ball gowns represent the romantic dreams of young women. *Cinderella* and *Beauty and the Beast* are recognizable fairy tales that instill in children the magnificence and fantasy of the ball, complete with appropriate full-skirted gown and a handsome prince. These ideas are reinforced and incorporated into our cultural consciousness. The profile of the traditional ball gown is evident in gowns for such modern-day events as weddings (bride and bride's attendants), high school proms, and the most elegant of evening occasions. Not surprisingly, designers of contemporary ball gowns continue to emphasize feminine curves while at the same time drawing from the nostalgic styles of expansive and lavishly decorated skirts, thereby establishing the wearer as a work of art.

See also Evening Dress.

Bibliography

Boucher, François. *20,000 Years of Fashion: The History of Costume and Personal Adornment.* New York: Harry N. Abrams, 1987.

Laver, James. *Costume and Fashion: A Concise History.* London: Thames and Hudson, 1982.

Milbank, Caroline Rennolds. *New York Fashion: The Evolution of American Style.* New York: Harry N. Abrams, 1989.

Payne, Blanche, Geitel Winakor, and Jane Farrell-Beck. *The History of Costume.* 2nd ed. New York: HarperCollins, 1992.

Russell, Douglas A. *Costume History and Style.* New Jersey: Prentice-Hall, 1983.

Steele, Valerie. *Women of Fashion: Twentieth-Century Designers.* New York: Rizzoli International, 1991.

——. *Fifty Years of Fashion.* New Haven, Conn., and London: Yale University Press, 2000.

——. *The Corset*. New Haven, Conn., and London: Yale University Press, 2001.

Watson, Linda. *Vogue: Twentieth Century Fashion*. London: Carlton Books Ltd., 1999.

Jane E. Hegland

BALLET COSTUME

Ballet costumes constitute an essential part of stage design and can be considered as a visual record of a performance. They are often the only survival of a production, representing a living imaginary picture of the scene.

Renaissance and Baroque

The origins of ballet lie in the court spectacles of the Renaissance in France and Italy, and evidence of costumes specifically for ballet can be dated to the early fifteenth century. Illustrations from this period show the importance of masks and clothing for spectacles. Splendor at court was strongly reflected in luxuriously designed ballet costumes. Cotton and silk were mixed with flax woven into semitransparent gauze.

From the beginning of the sixteenth century, public theaters were being built in Venice (1637), Rome (1652), Paris (1660), Hamburg (1678), and other important cities. Ballet spectacles were combined in these venues with processional festivities and masquerades, as stage costumes became highly decorated and made from expensive materials. The basic costume for a male dancer was a tight-fitting, often brocaded cuirass, a short draped skirt and feather-decorated helmets. Female dancers wore opulently embroidered silk tunics in several layers with fringes. Important components of the ballet dress were tightly laced, high-heeled and wedged boots for both dancers, which constituted characteristic footwear for this period.

From 1550, classical Roman dress had a strong influence on costume design: silk skirts were voluminous; positioning of necklines and waistlines and the design of hairstyles were based on the components of everyday dress, although on the stage key details were often exaggerated. Male dancers' dresses were influenced by Roman armor. Typical colors of ballet costumes ranged from dark copper to maroon and purple. A more detailed description of the theatrical dress in the Renaissance and Baroque periods may be found in Lincoln Kirstein's *Four Centuries of Ballet* (1984, p. 34).

Seventeenth Century

From the seventeenth century onward, silks, satins, and fabrics embroidered with real gold and precious stones increased the level of spectacular decoration associated with ballet costumes. Court dress remained the standard costume for female performers while male dancers' costumes had developed into a kind of uniform embellished with symbolic decoration to denote character or occupation; for example, scissors represented a tailor.

The first Russian ballet performance was staged in 1675, and the Russians adopted European ballet designs. Although costumes for male performers permitted complete freedom of movement, heavy garments and supporting structures for female dancers did not allow graceful gestures. However, male dancers *en travesti*, often wore knee-long skirts. The luxuriously decorated costumes of this period reflected the glory of the court; details of dresses and silhouettes were exaggerated to be visible and identifiable to spectators viewing from a distance.

Eighteenth Century

From the early eighteenth century, European ballet was centered in the Paris Opéra. Stage costumes were still very similar in outline to the ones in ordinary use at Court, but more elaborate. Around 1720, the *panier*, a hooped petticoat, appeared, raising skirts a few inches off the ground. During the reign of Louis XVI, court dress, ballet costumes, and fashionable architectural design incorporated decorative rococo prints and ornamental garlands. Flowers, flounces, ribbons, and lace emphasized this opulent feminine style, as soft pastel tones in citron, peach, pink, azure, and pistachio dominated the color range of stage costumes. Female dancers in male roles became popular, and, after the French Revolution in 1789 in particular, male costumes reflected the more conservative and sober Neoclassical style, which dominated the design of everyday fashionable dress. However, massive wigs and headdresses still restricted the mobility of dancers. In the eighteenth and nineteenth centuries, Russian ballet and European ballet developed similarly and were often considered an integral part of the opera.

Nineteenth Century

From the early nineteenth century, the ideals of Romanticism were reflected in female stage costumes through the introduction of close-fitting bodices, floral crowns, corsages, and pearls on fabrics, as well as necklace and bracelets; Neoclassical style still dominated the design of male costumes. Moreover, the role of the ballerina as star dancer became more important and was emphasized with tight-fitting corsets, bejeweled bodices, and opulent headdresses. In 1832, Marie Taglioni's gauze-layered white tutu in *La Sylphide* set a new trend in ballet costumes, in which silhouettes became tighter, revealing the legs and the permanently toe-shoed feet. From this point on, the silhouette of ballet costumes became more tight fitting. The choreography required that ballerinas to wear pointe shoes all the time. The Russian ballet continued to develop in the nineteenth century and such writers and composers as Tolstoy, Dostoevsky, and Tchaikovsky changed the meaning of ballet through the composition of narrative productions. Choreographers of classical ballet, such as Marius Petipa, created fairy-tale ballets, including *The Sleeping Beauty* (1890), *Swan Lake* (1895), and *Raymonde* (1898), making fantasy costumes very popular.

Twentieth Century

At the turn of the twentieth century, ballet costumes reformed again under the more liberal influence of the Russian choreographer Michel Fokine. Ballerina skirts changed gradually to become knee-length tutus designed to show off the point work and multiple turns, which formed the focus of dance practice. The dancer Isadora Duncan freed ballerinas from corsets and introduced a revolutionary natural silhouette. The Russian impresario and producer Serge Diaghilev marked this era with his creative innovations, and professional costumers like Alexandre Benois and Léon Bakst demonstrated, in performances such as *Schéhérezade* (1910), that the influence of Orientalism had spread from fashion to the stage and vice versa. Indeed, fashion designers like Jean Poiret had already used the tunic shape taken up by dancers in the prewar era, and, in the 1920s, costume designers updated classical Russian story ballets with exotic tunics and veils wrapped around the body. Ballet dancers were dressed in loose tunics, harem pants, and turbans, rather than in the established tutu and feather headdress. Instead of discreet pastel colors vibrant shades, such as yellow, orange, or red, often in

---

THE MASK IN BALLET SPECTACLES

Mary Clarke's and Clement Crisp's Design for Ballet (London 1978, p. 34) serves to illustrate a vivid description of the importance of masks in ballet performances to stylize characters: "For demons, this was properly hideous; for nymphs it would be sweetly naïve, rivers wore venerable bearded masks, while dwarfs and juveniles might be encumbered with massive heads. Masks were also sometimes placed upon knees, elbows, and the chest to indicate something more of the character." Half-masks were still worn until the 1770s and were from then on replaced by facial makeup.

---

wild patterns, gave an unprecedented visual impression of exciting exoticism to the spectator.

Modernism and Postmodernism

Modernism liberalized the rules of ballet costumes, and, after Diaghilev's death in 1929, costume design was no longer impeded by restrictions imposed by traditionalists. Nowadays ballet dancers perform in various costumes, which can still include traditional Diaghilev designs. In postmodern productions like Matthew Bourne's *Swan Lake*, the costume designer Lez Brotherston turned the traditional gracile female cygnets into topless, feather-legged male swans. However, fashion designers of the 1990s have picked up the theme of ballerina shoes. The house of Chanel designed elegant, heelless slippers tied up with ribbons and brought the ballerina shoe from the stage to the street.

See also Dance and Fashion; Dance Costume; Theatrical Costume.

Bibliography

André, Paul. *The Great History of Russian Ballet*. Bournemouth, U.K.: Parkstone Publishers, 1998.

Chazin-Bennahum, Judith. *A Longing for Perfection: Neoclassic Fashion and Ballet*. Oxford: *Fashion Theory* 6, no. 4 (2002): 369–386.

Clarke, Mary, and Clement Crisp. *Design for Ballet*. London: Cassell and Collier, Macmillan Publishers, Ltd., 1978.

Kirstein, Lincoln. *Four Centuries of Ballet*. New York: Dover Publications, Inc., 1984.

Morrison, Kirsty. *From Russia with Love*. Canberra: National Gallery of Australia, 1998.

Reade, Brian. *Ballet Designs and Illustrations 1581–1940*. London: Her Majesty's Stationery Office, 1967.

Schouvaloff, Alexander. *The Art of Ballet Russes*. New Haven, Conn., and London: Yale University Press, 1997.

Williams, Peter. *Masterpieces of Ballet Design*. Oxford: Phaidon Press, Ltd, 1981.

Wulf, Helena. *Ballet Across Borders*. Oxford and New York: Berg Publishers, 1998.

Thomas Hecht

BALMAIN, PIERRE*

Pierre Balmain (1914–1982) was born in the Savoie region of France in 1914. He studied architecture for a year in Paris before taking a position as a sketch artist with the fashion house of Robert Piguet in 1934. He worked at the House of Molyneux as an assistant designer from 1934 to 1938, and as a designer with Lucien Lelong in Paris in 1939 and from 1941 to 1945. During this time he worked alongside another young designer at Lelong, Christian Dior. In 1945 Balmain founded the Maison Balmain as a couture house with a lucrative sideline in fragrances. He expanded into the American market in 1953, showing his collections under the brand name Jolie Madame. The Balmain perfume business was sold to Revlon in 1960, but Pierre Balmain continued as the proprietor and chief designer of the Maison Balmain until his death in 1982.

The fashion historian Farid Chenoune described Pierre Balmain as one of "the supreme practitioners of the New Look generation," along with Christian Dior and Jacques Fath. During the 1950s and 1960s, Balmain's clients included some of the world's most elegant and best-dressed women, such as Katharine Hepburn, Vivien Leigh, Marlene Dietrich, and Queen Sirikit of Thailand.

Balmain's work was characterized by an emphasis on impeccable construction and simple elegance. He is credited with popularizing the stole as an accessory. He once said, "Keep to the basic principles of fashion and you will always be in harmony with the latest trends without falling prey to them."

The Maison Balmain continued in business after Pierre Balmain's death, with several designers and under shifting ownership throughout the 1980s. A ready-to-wear line was added in 1982. The company reacquired its perfume business from Revlon but unwisely entered into extensive licensing agreements that put the Balmain name on a wide range of products, diluting the company's image. In 1993 Oscar de la Renta took on the position of chief designer for the Maison Balmain—the first American to become head designer for a Paris couture house. De la Renta's first collection for the company, which appeared on the runway in February 1994, was a critical and commercial success. Critics generally agree that de la Renta, who spent nearly a decade at Balmain, succeeded not only in reviving the company's fortunes, but also in restoring the house's old reputation for elegance. Oscar de la Renta presented his final collection for Balmain in July 2002. He was succeeded by Laurent Mercier, who was artistic director from 2002 to 2003, and Christophe Lebourg, who was appointed in 2003. Christophe Decarnin joined Maison Balmain as Chief Designer in 2005.

See also De la Renta, Oscar; Dior, Christian; Fath, Jacques; New Look; Paris Fashion; Perfume.

Bibliography

Benbow-Pfalzgraf, Taryn, ed. *Contemporary Fashion*. 2nd ed. Farmington Hills, Mich.: St. James Press, 2002.

Buxbaum, Gerda, ed. *Icons of Fashion: The 20th Century*. Munich, London, and New York: Prestel Verlag, 1999.

Milbank, Caroline Rennolds. *Couture: The Great Designers*. New York: Stewart, Tabori and Chang, 1985.

Pierre Balmain: 40 années de création. Paris: Musée de la Mode et du Costume, 1985.

John S. Major

BARBIE

Since the Mattel corporation introduced Barbie in 1959, the doll's relation to fashion, sex, femininity, and cultural values has been a subject of spin control, change, and controversy.

Early official accounts of Barbie's beginnings emphasized the desire of Ruth Handler, Mattel's cofounder, to produce a three-dimensional version of the paper fashion dolls her daughter, Barbara, loved. But Barbie's body actually originated elsewhere: with a German character named Lilli, who appeared in cartoon and doll form primarily as a sexpot plaything for adult men.

Mattel bought all the rights and patents required to remove Lilli from that context of meaning and turned her into Barbie, the "shapely teenage Fashion Model!" announced in early catalogs.

Changes followed soon after the doll's launch, as Mattel worked to gear Barbie's persona to sales and supplementary products. In a 1961 television ad, Barbie, although still described as a fashion model, had acquired a school life, a boyfriend, and outfits for activities ranging from school lunches to frat parties: "Think of the fun you'll have taking Barbie and Ken on dates, dressing each one just right." The ad's invitation to "see where the romance will lead" illustrated Barbie's dreamy future by showing her in a wedding dress, a costume that would recur in many subsequent versions. Other outfits to come included the latest in formal wear, casual attire, sports gear, and lingerie. Many fashions were modeled after the work of contemporary designers. Sometimes Mattel enlisted designers directly, especially for the high-end offerings later created to cash in on the ever-increasing traffic in Barbie collectibles. Like designer Bob Mackie's 1991 "Limited Edition Platinum Barbie," these sometimes sold for up to several hundred dollars each.

Careers and Colors

Over the years, too, Barbie saw expanding options in one type of costume that would generate praise, humor, doubt, and derision: the career outfit. In the early 1960s, Barbie's career identities were primarily traditionally female, like nurse; largely unattainable, like astronaut; or both, like ballerina. Barbie had less work, ironically, during the burgeoning of popular feminism in the 1970s.

Her career life took off in the mid-1980s, however, with the Day-to-Night Barbie line. Its first incarnation presented Barbie as an executive, whose pink suit could be transformed into evening wear. She came with the slogan "We Girls Can Do Anything," a catchphrase relevant also to the range of careers that Barbie adopted into the 1990s, which included doctor, veterinarian, UNICEF ambassador, rock star, rap musician, teacher, chef, Marine Corps sergeant, and professional basketball player for the WNBA.

Besides addressing concerns about whether a girl with few apparent interests other than fashion, fun, and spending a vast amount of cash on clothes, cars (like the Barbie Ferrari), and real estate (like the famed Barbie Dream House) provided a good role model, career

Barbies on display. Since her introduction in 1959, Barbie has been marketed with many different looks to entice children to buy multiple dolls. This strategy appears to have paid off, as the average number of Barbies owned per child grew to ten in the 1990s. © BETTMANN/CORBIS. REPRODUCED BY PERMISSION.

Barbies suited an important change in Mattel's marketing strategy. Initially, Mattel wanted consumers to supplement their first Barbie with outfits, accessories, and other characters such as Ken and Midge, Barbie's close yet distinctly unglamorous friend. In fact, the promotion for the 1967 Twist 'N Turn Barbie even offered a trade-in deal. Later, promotions became geared to the purchase of multiple Barbies. In 1992, for example, a Barbie owner interested in the rapper outfit had to buy Rappin' Rockin' Barbie, or four of them to get each of the different boom boxes. Another trend sponsored by Mattel that catered simultaneously to sales and social consciousness was the increase in Barbies of color and Barbies representing countries outside the United States. Changing statistics about how many Barbies the "average child" owns suggest Mattel's success at shifting multiple acquisitions to Barbie herself, with the number climbing from seven to ten over the course of the 1990s.

Controversies

With Barbie's popularity has come increasing controversy, both about Barbie's (unrecyclable) plastic body and about the flesh to which it does, or does not, refer. To a number of critics, Barbie represents shallow feminism, focused primarily on individual success and fulfillment, and Barbie's world looks like diversity lite, peopled by innumerable white, blond Barbies, unquestionably front and center, and a much smaller number of Barbies who look like white Barbies with skin and hair dye jobs. Detractors have advanced other arguments as well: that Mattel's restriction of Barbie's dating life to boys adds yet another set of cultural narratives guiding young people to see heterosexuality as the desired, perhaps required, norm; that Barbie's impossible-to-attain proportions contribute to cultural ideals of beauty that invite self-loathing and unhealthy eating practices; and that Barbie promotes an undue focus on looks in general. Why give a girl Soccer Barbie (1999) instead of a soccer ball?

Yet as other commentators have noted, Barbie has generated a lot of play far from Mattel's official sponsorship. Mattel's WNBA Barbie may not emerge from the box with the characteristic butch flair displayed by many of her charming human counterparts, but in the hands and minds of many consumers, Barbie has been butched out, turned out, fixed up with diverse sex mates, and, of course, undressed; for a doll whose wardrobe forms the centerpiece of her reputation, she spends quite a lot of time naked. Then again, for some critics, this is Mattel's fault, too. People who like to imagine children as innocent of sexual desires have accused the company of turning their children's minds to sex with its bigbreasted adult doll. Others, conversely, have mourned what Mattel couldn't do: inspire femininity in their daughters or distaste in insufficiently truck-minded sons.

Object of Attention

From all these diverse uses and assessments of Barbie, one certainty emerges. Barbie remains an object of attention, fascination, and, of course, purchase. Whatever her influence has been—and surely it has varied among individuals and over time—she has successfully convinced many of her importance as a symbol of femininity, as a catalyst for fantasy, and as a marker and agent of cultural values.

See also Fashion and Identity; Fashion Dolls.

Bibliography

BillyBoy. *Barbie: Her Life and Times*. New York: Crown Publishers, 1987. Excellent source of fashion study and illustrations.

Du Cille, Ann. *Skin Trade*. Cambridge, Mass.: Harvard University Press, 1996. Critical issues including race.

Lord, M. G. *Forever Barbie: The Unauthorized Biography of a Real Doll*. New York: Morrow and Company, 1994. History.

Rand, Erica. *Barbie's Queer Accessories*. Durham, N.C., and London: Duke University Press, 1995. History, consumers, subversions.

Erica Rand

BARBIER, GEORGES*

The French illustrator, painter, and theatrical designer Georges Barbier (1882–1932) was born in the seaport city of Nantes. The city's seventeenth-and eighteenth-century architecture, as well as its art museum collections, with works by Antoine Watteau and Jean-Auguste-Dominique Ingres, influenced Barbier's aesthetic sensibilities. As a young man he moved to Paris where, between 1908 and 1910, he studied at l'École des beaux-arts in the atelier of the academic history painter, Jean-Paul Laurens. Although Barbier's artistic style differed significantly from that of his teacher, his appreciation of the past as a source of inspiration was undoubtedly reinforced by Laurens's subjects.

In the galleries of the Louvre, Barbier discovered the art of classical antiquity. His enduring admiration for Greek and Etruscan vases, Tanagra figurines, and small Egyptian sculptures is evident in his depiction of the human body and resonates overall in the clarity and restraint of his graphic work. His refined color sense and use of strong colors, influenced by costumes of the Ballets Russes, which was founded in Paris in 1909, also characterize his work.

Barbier first exhibited at the Salon des humoristes in 1911, where his drawings were immediately acclaimed; subsequently, he was a regular contributor to the Salon des artistes décorateurs. Barbier was a prolific and skillful artist whose sophisticated style was in great demand. Over the course of his brief career, he contributed to most of the leading French fashion journals and almanacs; illustrated numerous publications of classic and contemporary French prose and poetry issued in limited, deluxe editions; and designed costumes for stage productions, including ballet, film, and revues, such as the Folies Bergère and the Casino de Paris. In addition, Barbier wrote essays on fashion that appeared in *La Gazette du bon ton* and other journals, and as a member of the Société des artistes décorateurs, he produced designs for jewelry, glass, and wallpaper. One of the most well-known and highly regarded artists working in the second and third decades of the twentieth century, Barbier died in Paris at the peak of his profession in 1932.

Barbier and Art Deco

In Michael Arlen's best-selling 1924 novel, *The Green Hat*, the heroine Iris March is compared to a figure in a Barbier fashion illustration: "She stood carelessly like the women in Georges Barbier's almanacs, *Falbalas et Fanfreluches*, who know how to stand carelessly. Her hands were thrust into the pockets of a light brown leather jacket—pour le sport" (Steele, p. 247). The casual elegance ascribed to Arlen's character, a quintessential element of the 1920s fashion ideal, epitomizes Barbier's figures. With their strong yet lithe forms and dark-lidded, slightly exotic eyes, Barbier's women embody the notions of female beauty and grace of the time.

Beginning with the innovative and influential *Le Journal des dames et des modes* (1912–1914), launched by Lucien Vogel, Barbier's talents were sought after by the publishers and editors of avant-garde fashion magazines. Following the lead of the couturier Paul Poiret, whose collaboration with the artists Paul Iribe and Georges Lepape in 1908 and 1911, respectively, set the standard for a new, modernist presentation of fashion, these publications showcased the emerging art deco aesthetic. Rather than realistic, fussily detailed renderings of dress, Barbier and his fellow illustrators (Lepape, Iribe, Bernard Boutet de Monvel, Pierre Brissaud, and Charles Martin, among others) created bold, stylized images that conveyed mood and atmosphere. The laborious technique of *pochoir* printing used for these illustrations (a hand-stenciled process whereby layers of color are built up in gouache paint) enhanced their visual impact.

In addition to *Le Journal des dames*, Barbier contributed widely to other luxury fashion periodicals including *La Gazette du bon ton* (1912–1925), *Les Feuillets d'art* (1919–1922), and *Art goût beauté* (1920–1933), as well as *Vogue*, *Femina*, and *La Vie parisienne*. Barbier was also commissioned to illustrate more specialized fashion publications: couturiers' albums and almanacs, such as *Modes et manières d'aujourd'hui* (1912–1923), *La Guirlande des mois* (1917–1920), *Le Bonheur du jour* (1920–1924), and *Falbalas et fanfreluches* (1922–1926). Modeled after the early nineteenth-century publication *Le Bon genre* that chronicles the modes and lifestyle of the First Empire and the Bourbon restoration, Barbier's refined and often witty drawings for particular almanacs not only depict Parisian haute couture but also record the social scene and fashionable activities in charming vignettes.

Set Designs and Costumes

Although it is primarily through Barbier's fashion illustrations that one is familiar with his work, in his lifetime his book illustrations and theatrical costume designs contributed significantly to his artistic reputation and success. Both authors with whom he collaborated and critics agreed that Barbier was able to distill the essence of a literary text and give it visual form. His interpretations of historic dress and interiors for the stage (including *Casanova* and *La Dernière nuit de Don Juan* by Edmond Rostand, *Marion Delorme* by Victor Hugo, and *Lysistrata* by Maurice Donnay) were admired for their imaginative evocation of a particular time and place, rather than representing merely a scrupulous imitation or pastiche. Barbier's love of the exotic resulted in spectacular beribboned, furred, feathered, and jeweled fantasy costumes for revue performers at popular Paris nightclubs.

Legacy

In the preface to *Personnages de comédie* (1922), illustrated by Barbier, Albert Flament refers to him as "One of the most precious and significant artists of our era. . . . When our times are lost . . . in the dust . . . some of his water-colours and drawings will be all that is necessary to resurrect the taste and the spirit of the years in which we have lived" (Ginsburg, p. 3). Barbier was undoubtedly one of the preeminent fashion illustrators of the early twentieth century. Among the group of artists including Lepape, Iribe, and Monvel, dubbed "The Knights of the Bracelet" by *Vogue* in 1922 (a reference to their "dandyism . . . and love of luxury" [Barbier, p. 6]), Barbier was in the forefront of the alliance between art and fashion. His superb draftsmanship, color sense, and ability to infuse freshness into historic influences combine to produce distinctive images that define the modernity of the art deco style.

See also Art Nouveau and Art Deco; Fashion Illustrators; Fashion Magazines.

Bibliography

Barbier, Georges. *Art Deco Costumes.* New York: Crescent Books, 1988.

Mackrell, Alice. *An Illustrated History of Fashion: 500 Years of Fashion Illustration.* New York: Costume and Fashion Press, 1997.

Martorelli, Barbara. *Georges Barbier: The Birth of Art Deco.* Venezia: Marsilio, 2009.

Steele, Valerie. *Paris Fashion: A Cultural History.* New York: Oxford University Press, 1988.

Vaudoyer, Jean-Louis, and Henri de Régnier. *George Barbier: Étude Critique.* Paris: Henry Babou, 1929.

Weill, Alain. *Parisian Fashion: La Gazette du bon ton, 1912–1925.* Paris: Bibliothèque de l'Image, 2000.

Michele Majer

BARTHES, ROLAND

Better than anyone else, the author of *Roland Barthes par Roland Barthes* (1974) as well as of *Le Degré zéro de l'écriture* (1953) pointed out the illusory nature of the work of biography. Here, we will therefore merely recall a few fragments of a life whose intellectual twists and turns accompanied and helped to transform all facets of French, if not European, thought in the second half of the twentieth century. His publications easily demonstrate his role as developer—in the photographic sense of the term—of the founding questions of so-called postmodern thought. They reveal even more the qualities of a refined and elliptical writer haunted by *The Pleasure of the Text* (1973). Well known for works, alternately journalistic and scholarly, on the political use of myths, literary creation, mass culture, photography, semiological methods, and romantic desire, Barthes also wrote many diverse works on fashion. Often referred to but very little read for themselves, these works still call for a radically novel approach to the phenomena of fashion.

Fragments of Life

Following Jean-Baptiste Farges and Andy Stafford, one can try to distinguish three moments—but they are also three directions, closely connected but not successive—in the activities and the life of Barthes: the polemical journalist immediately after the war, the triumphant yet marginal university professor of the postwar boom, and the elusive "novelist" celebrated by the entire intelligentsia of the left in the 1970s.

More than the details of these moments, it is important to note the intellectual influences that guided Barthes. He himself, in the "Phases" section of his pseudo-autobiography, *Roland Barthes par Roland Barthes*, played with establishing a correspondence of these stages (he counted two more) with an "intertext" of those who inspired him: Gide gave him the wish to write ("the desire for a work"); the trio Sartre-Marx-Brecht drove him to deconstruct our social mythologies (*Mythologies* was published in 1957); Saussure guided him in his work in semiology; the dialogue with Sollers, Kristeva, Derrida, and Lacan led him to take intertextuality as a subject; as for Nietzsche, his influence corresponded to the pleasure of writing during and about his last years, when he produced books dedicated to the enigma of pleasure: *L'Empire des signes* (1970), *S/Z* (1970), *Sade, Fourier, Loyola* (1971), and *Fragments d'un discours amoureux* (1977). *La Chambre claire* (1980), written shortly after the death of his mother, offers a restrained emotional reading of the illusions of the resurrection of reality through photography and concludes with an alternative: accept the spectacle of the false, or "confront untreatable reality."

This represents a program of investigation, both political and aesthetic, that all the works and the very life of Barthes seem to have put into practice, even including the part of his work devoted to speaking about clothes and fashion, "stable ephemera."

Genealogy of an Interest

It has been little noticed how early Barthes developed a curiosity about clothing (at least the clothing of others), about its communicative functions, and about the problems of approach and reconstruction to which those functions give rise. His contribution was that of a student of sociology, considering a massive and poorly understood phenomenon that had been seldom studied in France. This contribution could be decoded on many levels, but it was also that of an aesthete, enamored with the feel of fabrics and the flaring of a white dress on the beach at Bayonne in the 1930s. This is the image—a blurry photograph of his mother—that opens (and closes on "a moment of pleasure") the introduction to *Roland Barthes par Roland Barthes*. Here, it is difficult to avoid noticing the trace of a nostalgic identification with the mother and a personal dandyism maintained with and by discreet and elegant companions. D. A.

Miller (1992) may be right to regret that this geneal-ogy, in part based on an unequivocal homosexuality ("L'adjectif," "La déesse H.," "Actif/Passif," and other vignettes in *Roland Barthes*), was never made explicit or "brought out."

However, attention to the body, to its costumes, and to the functions and imagery of those costumes, obsesses—literally—all aspects of the work of Barthes, and this is true beginning with his earliest theater criticism ("Les maladies du costume de théâtre" of 1955, reprinted in *Essais critiques* [1964]), and his various analyses of Brecht's staging of *Mother Courage* from 1957 to 1960. As late as 1980, some fashion details of the photographs illustrating his last book, *La Chambre claire*, become the focus of his reflective emotion and serve as a *punctum*.

In parallel, as early as 1957, he published in *Annales* the seminal article "Histoire et sociologie du vêtement," followed in 1960 by "Pour une sociologie du vêtement," and in 1959, *Critique*, under the title "Langage et vête-ment," he published his review of books by J. C. Flügel, F. Kiener, H. H. Hansen, and N. Truman, writers then unknown to French specialists in the field. Other ar-ticles, such as "Le bleu est à la mode cette année" (*Revue française de sociologie*, 1960), "Des joyaux aux bijoux" (*Jardin des Arts*, 1961), and "Le dandysme et la mode" (*United States Lines Paris Review*, July 1962) exhibit the development of a semiological approach to cloth-ing and the concern for a multifaceted way of writing able to adapt with virtuosity to diverse audiences. For example, he published in the women's magazine *Marie-Claire* (1967) "Le match Chanel-Courrèges," an article similar to one of the last of the *Mythologies*. Finally, although after that date, the language connected to fashion was no longer directly questioned, the last lines of *Roland Barthes* are still concerned with the weight of appearances: "Writing the body. Neither the skin, nor the muscles, nor the bones, nor the nerves, but the rest, a clumsy, stringy, fluffy, frayed thing, the cloak of a clown."

For a Systemic Approach to Fashion

Le Système de la mode (1967) is an austere and baroque book that came out of a planned thesis, in which a lin-guistic theory ("the dress code") develops, flourishes, and self-destructs. The book's luxurious jargon and absence of iconography has repelled many and led to various misunderstandings. Its author—famous and praised for other more "literary" publications—plays the role of the proponent of a hard and fast scientism,

which he nevertheless declares in the preface is already outdated. He counters and even contradicts this by em-bellishing the text with precious formulations ("Le bleu est à la mode"), and with a second part (one fourth of the book) unexpected in a work with a methodological purpose: an essay on the rhetoric of fashion journalists along with caustic sociological commentary. "Fashion makes something out of nothing," and that "something" is first of all words, as Stéphane Mallarmé had shown. Hence, it is only the vocabulary and syntax of the cap-tions for fashion pictures presented in the magazines of the 1960s that form the basis for the analyses—legiti-mately linguistic—offered by *Le Système*.

One should never forget that this was a practical ex-ercise: the ingenious and inventive application of a new technique of reading (semiology) to a limited object but one requiring the creation of novel concepts. Those limits, explicitly set out by Barthes in his book and in contemporaneous interviews, were not understood by many readers who criticize the book for not speak-ing directly of the non-verbal communication carried out through clothing. Barthes is interested neither in clothing as artifact (clothing as made) nor in its figu-rative representations (iconic clothing), although those diverse subjects were part of the research program—too broad but more cautious on questions of linguistic analogy—proposed by the 1957 article. His aim is thus to find out "what happens when a real or imaginary ob-ject is converted into language" and thus becomes litera-ture capable of being appropriated.

This lack of understanding—often unrecognized—and various ambiguities of expression making a faith-ful translation difficult, explain in part the delay of the book's publication in English (1985), and a limited re-ception (in quantity and quality), which needs, however, to be analyzed country by country and generation by generation. The book nevertheless remains an essential reference, at least in France, for sociologists and histo-rians of clothing, but even, or perhaps especially, there, *Le Système* has not acquired a following, except among a few French ethnologists, like Yves Delaporte, Jeanne Martinet, and Marie-Thérèse Duflos-Priot, who do not restrict themselves to studying "spoken," that is, written clothing. It is a fashionable reference in a bibliography, but it has not really been assimilated, even though it has inspired several descriptive systems of clothing used by museums and it has provided a number of convenient metaphors for experts in fashion.

As Barthes wished, the book has to be read first of all as a historical monument, a dated polemic, focused on methodological questions. But it is also a book in which one may take pleasure in digressing, while acquiring expertise and understanding about the state of fashion rhetoric in the 1960s, the state of innovative practices linked to structuralism, and also the state of French backwardness in research on clothing and the still novel efforts to introduce into the field the indispensable theory required for any study of a cultural phenomenon. The phraseology of the fashion magazine signifies a "fashionable" representation of reality, the ideology of which is unveiled by breaking it down into subsets and elements and by the concomitant variations (combined or opposed) of signifier and signified: "A cardigan is sporty or formal depending on whether the collar is open or closed."

Barthes was a pioneer by rejecting the elitist linearity and the facile psychologism of "histories of costume," by engaging in contemporary, not nostalgic, analysis of consumerist ideologies, and by carrying out high-risk interdisciplinary work taking into account individual choices and collective tendencies, the *longue durée* and differential rhythms of transformation of forms and customs, as well as the ephemeral character of the analyses of those who produced them: all knowledge is by definition "Heraclitean." Even more, *Le Système de la mode* should be seen as an invitation to dissect (or possibly de-construct) the discourse on other discourses that we fabricate with respect to all our objects of investigation. It should be done without illusions, but always with seriousness and irony.

See also Fashion, Historical Studies of; Fashion, Theories of.

Bibliography

Barthes, Roland. *Œuvres complètes*. 3 vols. Paris: Seuil, 1993–1995.
——. *The Fashion System*. New York: Hill & Wang, 1983.
Boultwood, Anne, and Robert Jerrard. "Ambivalence, and Its Relation to Fashion and the Body." *Fashion Theory* 4, no. 3 (2000): 301–322.
Delaporte, Y. "Le signe vestimentaire." *L'Homme* 20, no. 3 (1980): 109–142.
Delaporte, Y., ed. "Vêtement et Sociétés 2." *L'Ethnographie* 130, nos. 92, 93, 94 (1984). Special issue.
Fages, Jean Baptiste. *Comprendre Roland Barthes*. Toulouse, France: Privat, 1979.
Harvey, John. *Men in Black*. Chicago: University of Chicago Press, 1995.
Hollander, Anne. *Seeing Through Clothes*. Berkeley: University of California Press, 1993.
Martinet, J. "Du sémiologique au sein des fonctions vestimentaires," *L'Ethnographie* 130, nos. 92, 93, 94 (1984): pp. 141–251.
Miller, D. A. *Bringing Out Roland Barthes*. Berkeley: University of California Press, 1992.
Stafford, Andy. *Roland Barthes, Phenomenon and Myth: An Intellectual Biography*. Edinburgh: Edinburgh University Press, 1998.
Wilson, Elizabeth. *Adorned in Dreams: Fashion and Modernity*. London: Virago, 1985. Rutgers University Press issued a revised edition in 2003.

Nicole Pellegrin

BAUDELAIRE, CHARLES

Charles-Pierre Baudelaire (1821–1867) was perhaps the greatest French poet of the nineteenth century. He is most famous for a volume of poetry, *Les fleurs du mal* (Flowers of evil), published in 1857, which was prosecuted for blasphemy as well as obscenity. Baudelaire was also an important art critic and translator. He appears in an encyclopedia of fashion because he proved to be an influential theorist of fashion and dandyism.

In his youth, Baudelaire devoted considerable time and money to his appearance. At a time when the masculine wardrobe was becoming ever more sober, he adopted an austere form of dandyism that was neither foppish nor bohemian. Whereas many of his contemporaries deplored the trend toward dark, severe clothing for men, he embraced and even exaggerated the style by wearing all-black clothing. But dandyism involved more than clothing for Baudelaire; he would certainly not have agreed with Thomas Carlyle's definition of the dandy as "a clothes-wearing man." Although Baudelaire's poetry does not touch on dandyism per se, he explored the topic both in his intimate journals, under such headings as "The eternal superiority of the Dandy. What is the Dandy?", and in two of his most famous essays, "On the Heroism of Modern Life," a section of his *Salon of 1846*, and *The Painter of Modern Life* (1863).

The modernity of dandyism is central to Baudelaire's analysis. Dandyism, he wrote, "is a modern thing, resulting from causes entirely new." It appears "when democracy is not yet all-powerful, and aristocracy is just beginning to fall." Like many artists during the nineteenth century, Baudelaire was ambivalent about the rise of democracy and capitalism. He described contemporary middle-class masculine attire as "a uniform livery of affliction [that] bears witness to equality." It was, he suggested, "a symbol of perpetual mourning." On the other hand, Baudelaire insisted that one should be of one's own time. "But all the same, has not this much-abused garb its own beauty?" The modern man's frock coat had both a "political beauty, which is an expression of universal equality," and also a "poetic beauty."

In place of the equality which modern men's uniform attire seemed to proclaim, Baudelaire suggested that dandyism announced a new type of intellectual elitism. "In the disorder of these times, certain men . . . may conceive the idea of establishing a new kind of aristocracy . . . based . . . on the divine gifts which work and money are unable to bestow. Dandyism is the last spark of heroism amid decadence." Baudelaire's modern dandy eschewed not only the foppish paraphernalia of prerevolutionary aristocratic dress, but also denied the bourgeois capitalist dominance of wealth. The Baudelairean dandy was not just a wealthy man who wore fashionable and expensive dark suits.

"Dandyism does not . . . consist, as many thoughtless people seem to believe, in an immoderate taste for . . . material elegance," declared Baudelaire. "For the perfect dandy these things are no more than symbols of his aristocratic superiority of mind. Furthermore, to his eyes, which are in love with distinction above all things, the perfection of his toilet will consist in absolute simplicity." Part of Baudelaire's minimalist aesthetic involved the elimination of color in favor of black, a noncolor that remains strongly associated with both authority and rebellion, as witnessed by the following lines from Quentin Tarantino's film *Reservoir Dogs*:

> MR. PINK: Why can't we pick out our own color?
> JOE: I tried that once. It don't work. You get four guys fighting over who's gonna be Mr. Black.

If modern men's clothing— and still more so the clothing of the dandy—was characterized by simplicity, the same could not be said of nineteenth-century women's fashion, which was highly complicated and decorative. It was only in the twentieth century that such women as Coco Chanel created a radically simplified style of female fashion epitomized by the little black dress. Indeed, it could be said that Chanel was one of the first female dandies. Yet Baudelaire's attitudes toward women are problematic for modern feminists. "Woman is the opposite of the dandy," declared Baudelaire, because she is "natural." Only to the extent that she creates an artificial persona through dress and cosmetics is she admirable, and, even then, Baudelaire describes her as "a kind of idol, stupid perhaps, but dazzling."

Putting aside his ambivalence towards women, Baudelaire analyzed fashion in ways that illuminate both modern life and modern art. In particular, his essay *The Painter of Modern Life* was one of the first and most penetrating analyses of the relationship between *la mode* (fashion) and *la modernité* (modernity). For Baudelaire, fashion was the key to modernity, and one simply could not paint modern individuals if one did not understand their dress. Baudelaire argued that it was simply "laziness" that led so many artists to "dress all their subjects in the garments of the past." "The draperies of Rubens or Veronese will in no way teach you how to depict . . . fabric of modern manufacture," he wrote. "Furthermore, the cut of skirt and bodice is by no means similar. . . . Finally, the gesture and bearing of the woman of today gives her dress a life and a special character which are not those of the woman of the past."

According to Baudelaire, there were two aspects to beauty—the eternal and the ephemeral. The fact that fashion was so transitory, constantly changing into something new, made it the hallmark of modernity. The modern artist, whether painter or poet, had to be able "to distill the eternal from the transitory." As Baudelaire wrote, "What poet would dare, in depicting the pleasure caused by the appearance of a great beauty, separate the woman from her dress?"

As a theorist of fashion, Baudelaire moved far beyond such other dandies and writers of his era as George ("Beau") Brummell, Jules Barbey d'Aurevilly, and Théophile Gautier. He inspired such modernist poets as Stéphane Mallarmé and such philosophers as Georg Simmel and Walter Benjamin. Indeed, it is virtually impossible to imagine the modern study of fashion without taking account of Baudelaire's contribution.

See also Benjamin, Walter; Brummell, George (Beau); Dandyism; Fashion, Theories of; Little Black Dress; Mallarmé, Stéphane; Simmel, Georg; Wilde, Oscar.

Bibliography

Baudelaire, Charles. *The Painter of Modern Life and Other Essays.* Edited and translated by Jonathan Mayne. London: Phaidon Press Ltd., 1964.

Lehmann, Ulrich. *Tigersprung: Fashion in Modernity.* Cambridge, Mass.: MIT Press, 2000.

Moers, Ellen. *The Dandy: Brummell to Beerbohm.* London: Secker and Warburg, 1960.

Steele, Valerie. *Paris Fashion: A Cultural History.* 2nd ed. New Haven, Conn.: Berg, 1999.

Valerie Steele

BAUDRILLARD, JEAN

The French intellectual Jean Baudrillard (b. 1929) is widely acclaimed as one of the master visionary thinkers of postmodernism and post-structuralism. He was trained as a sociologist, and his early critique was influenced by a certain style of radicalism that appeared in France after 1968, which included critical challenge to the disciplines, methods, theories, styles, and discourses of the academic intellectual establishment. After the late 1960s Baudrillard's social theory witnessed major paradigm shifts. The theory of consumption that he began to articulate in the 1970s fore-saw the development of consumer society, with its dual focus first on the visual culture (material objects) and, later, on the virtual (electronic and cyberspace) culture.

Baudrillard's fashion-relevant theorizing dates from his earlier writing: it forms part of his broader analysis of objects in consumer society. This scheme postulated a transition from "dress," in which sartorial meaning (of differentiation and distinction) resided in natural signs, through "fashion," in which meaning resided in oppositional (structuralist) signs, to "post-fashion," in which signs are freed from the link to referents and to meaning (poststructuralist). Baudrillard's early work is divided into three phases: (*a*) the reworking of Marxist social theory, as evident in *The System of Objects* (1968), *The Consumer Society* (1970), and *For a Critique of the Political Economy of the Sign* (1972) and with an emphasis on the "sign"; (*b*) a critique of Marxism, as seen in *The Mirror of Production* (1975) and *Symbolic Exchange and Death* (1976), where Baudrillard substitutes symbolic exchange for utilitarian exchange as an explanation of

consumerism; (*c*) a break with Marxism, as manifest in *Seduction* (1979), *Simulations* (1983), *Fatal Strategies* (1983), and *The Transparency of Evil: Essays on Extreme Phenomena* (1993), which substitutes the carnival-esque principle (celebration, pleasure, excess, and waste) for the utility principle.

Signification

Initially, Baudrillard argued that when products move from the realm of function (reflecting use value and exchange value) to the realm of signification (reflecting sign value), they become carriers of social meaning. Specifically, they become "objects." Baudrillard's notion of sign value is based on an analogy between a system of objects (commodity) and a system of sign (language). He applied Ferdinand de Saussure's structural linguistics to the study of fashion, media, ideologies, and images. If consumption is a communication system (messages and images), commodities are no longer defined by their use but by what they signify—not individually but as "set" in a total configuration. The meaning of signs, according to de Saus-sure, is made up of two elements: *signifiers* (sound images), which index the *signifieds* (referent). Saussurian structural linguistics is based on two principles: a metaphysics of depth and a metaphysics of surface. The metaphysics of depth assumes that meaning links a signifier with an underlying signified. The metaphysics of surface implies that signs do not have inherent meaning but rather gain their meaning through their relation to other signs.

Using a linguistic (semiotic) analogy to analyze commodities, Baudrillard developed a genealogy of sign structures consisting of three orders. The first order, founded on *imitation*, presupposes a dualism where appearances mask reality. In the second order, founded on *production*, appearances create an illusion of reality. In the third order, founded on *simulation*, appearances invent reality. No longer concerned with the real, images are reproduced from a model, and it is this lack of a reference point that threatens the distinction between true and false. There are parallels between Baudrillard's historical theory of sign structures and historical theorizing of European sartorial signification. The order of imitation corresponds to the premodern stage, the order of production corresponds to the modern stage, and the order of simulation corresponds to the postmodern stage.

Premodern stage. Throughout European fashion history the scarcity of resources symbolized rank in dress. Costly materials were owned and displayed by the privileged classes. Technological and social developments from the fourteenth century onward challenged the rigid hierarchy of feudal society. This challenge triggered the legislation of sumptuary laws that attempted to regulate clothing practices along status lines by defining precisely the type and quality of fabrics allowed to each class. Since styles were not sanctioned by law, toward the end of the fourteenth century clothes began to take on new forms. This tendency set in motion a process of differentiation (along the lines of Georg Simmel's "trickle-down theory" of fashion), whereby the aristocracy could distinguish itself by the speed with which it adopted new styles.

Modern stage. The technological developments that characterized industrial capitalism (among them, the invention of the sewing machine and wash-proof dyes), popularized fashion by reducing the price of materials. Mass production of clothes increased homogeneity of style and decreased their indexical function. The industrial revolution created the city and the mass society, improved mobility, and multiplied social roles. A new order was created in which work (achieved status) rather than lineage (ascribed status) determined social positioning. Uniforms were introduced to the workplace to denote rank, as dress no longer reflected rank order (but instead defined time of day, activities, occasions, or gender). As a result, a subtle expert system of status differentiation through appearance between the aristocracy and "new money" evolved. This system coded the minutiae of appearance and attributed symbolic meanings that reflected a person's character or social standing. It also anchored certain sartorial practices to moral values (for example, the notion of noblesse oblige).

Postmodern stage. Postmodernism denotes a radical break with the dominant culture and aesthetics. In architecture it represented plurality of forms, fragmentation of styles, and diffuse boundaries. It has substituted disunity, subjectivity, and ambiguity for the modernist unity, absolutism, and certainty. In the sciences it stands for a "crisis in representation." This challenge to the "correspondence theory of truth" resulted in totalizing theories of universal claims giving way to a plurality of "narrative truths" that reflect, instead, the conventions of discourse (for example, rules of grammar that construct gender, metaphors and expressions encode cultural assumptions and worldview, notions of what makes a "good" story). The postmodern cultural

shift has left its mark on the fashion world through its rejection of tradition, relaxation of norms, emphasis on individual diversity, and variability of styles.

Baudrillard characterized postmodern fashion by a shift from the modern *order of production* (functionality and utility) to the aristocratic *order of seduction*. Seduction derives pleasure from excess (sumptuary useless consumption of surplus, such as is displayed by celebrities). Baudrillard posits seduction as a system that marks the end of the structuralist principle of opposition as a basis for meaning. His notion of seduction is that of a libido that is enigmatic and enchanted. It is not a passion for desire but a passion for games and ritual. Seduction takes place on the level of appearance, surface, and signs and negates the seriousness of reality, meaning, morality, and truth.

Analysis. Analysis of the three stages of sartorial representation in terms of Baudrillard's signification relations produces Figure 1. In the order of *imitation* that characterized the premodern stage, clothes refer unequivocally to status. They signify the natural order of things without ambiguity. The order of *production* characterized the modern stage, where mass-produced clothes ceased to be indexical of status. It became important to establish whether people were what they claimed to be or rather were just pretending. In the orders of imitation and production, the signifier indexes an underlying meaning, either inherent or constructed. In contrast, the order of *simulation* refers to the principle of the postmodern dress that is indifferent to any traditional social order and is completely self-referential, that is, fashion for its own sake. For Baudrillard, the effacing of real history as a referent leaves us nothing but empty signs and marks the end of signification itself. In sum, as simulation substitutes for production, it replaces the linear order with a cyclical order and frees the signifier from its link to the signified. Thus, fashion as a form of pleasure takes the place of fashion as a form of communication.

See also Benjamin, Walter; Brummell, George (Beau); Fashion, Theories of; Mallarmé, Stéphane; Simmel, Georg; Wilde, Oscar.

Bibliography

Baudrillard, Jean. *The Mirror of Production.* Translated by Mark Poster. St. Louis, Mo.: Telos Press, 1975.
——. *For a Critique of the Political Economy of the Sign.* Translated by Charles Levin. St. Louis, Mo.: Telos Press, 1981.

——. *Simulations.* Translated by Paul Foss, Paul Patton, and Philip Beitchman. New York: Semiotext (e), 1983.

——. *Fatal Strategies.* Translated by Philip Beitchman and W. G. J. Niesluchowski. New York: Semiotext (e), 1990.

——. *Seduction.* Translated by Brian Singer. New York: St. Martin's Press, 1990.

——. *Symbolic Exchange and Death.* Translated by Iain Hamilton Grant. Thousand Oaks, Calif.: Sage Publications, 1993.

——. *The Transparency of Evil: Essays on Extreme Phenomena.* Translated by James Benedict. London and New York: Verso, 1993.

——. *The System of Objects.* Translated by James Benedict. New York: Verso, 1996.

——. *The Consumer Society: Myths and Structures.* Thousand Oaks, Calif.: Sage Publications, 1998.

Works about Jean Baudrillard

Gane, Mike, ed. *Jean Baudrillard.* 4 vols. Sage Masters of Modern Social Thought. Thousand Oaks, Calif.: Sage Publications, 2000.

Kellner, Douglas. "Baudrillard, Semiurgy and Death." *Theory, Culture, and Society* 4, no. 1 (1987): 125–146.

——. *Jean Baudrillard: From Marxism to Postmodernism and Beyond.* Stanford, Calif.: Stanford University Press, 1989.

Kellner, Douglas, ed. *Baudrillard: A Critical Reader.* Oxford and Cambridge, Mass.: Blackwell, 1989.

Poster, Mark, ed. *Jean Baudrillard: Selected Writings.* Stanford, Calif.: Stanford University Press, 1988.

Efrat Tseëlon

BEARDS AND MUSTACHES

Because facial hair is strongly associated with masculinity, beards and mustaches carry powerful and complex cultural meanings. Growing a beard or mustache, or being clean-shaven, can communicate information about religion, sexual identity, and orientation, and other important aspects of cultural heritage.

In many cultures, the wearing (or not) of facial hair has been a marker of membership in a tribe, ethnic group, or culture, implying acceptance of the group's cultural values and a rejection of the values of other groups. This distinction sometimes admitted a certain ambiguity; in ancient Greece, a neatly trimmed beard was a mark of a philosopher, but the Greeks also distinguished themselves from the *barbaroi* ("barbarians," literally "hairy ones") to their north and east. In early imperial China some powerful men (magistrates and military officers, for example) wore beards, but in general hairiness was associated with the "uncivilized" pastoral peoples of the northern frontier; by later imperial times, most Chinese men were clean-shaven. As Frank Dikotter puts it, "the hairy man was located beyond the limits of the cultivated field, in the wilderness, the mountains, and the forests: the border of human society, he hovered on the edge of bestiality. Body hair indicated physical regression, generated by the absence of cooked food, decent clothing and proper behaviour" (p. 52).

Conversely, in ancient Egypt beards were associated with high rank, and they were braided and cultivated to curl upward at the ends. False beards were worn by rulers, both male and female, and fashioned of gold. In the ancient Mesopotamian, Assyrian, Sumerian, and Hittite empires, curled and elaborately decorated beards were indicators of high social status while slaves were clean-shaven. In his book *Hair: The First Five Thousand Years*, Richard Corson analyzes the complexities of facial hair across history and points out that in the ancient world, "during shaven periods, beards were allowed to grow as a sign of mourning." Also, in a period of shaven faces such as early in the first century, "slaves were required to wear beards as a sign of their subjugation" but when free men wore beards in the second and third centuries slaves had to distinguish themselves free by shaving (p. 71). Long mustaches were the norm amongst Goths, Saxons, and Gauls and were worn "hanging down upon their breasts like wings" (p. 91) and by the Middle Ages again were a mark of noble birth.

Facial hair has been an issue for many religions. Pope Gregory VII issued a papal edict banning bearded clergymen in 1073. In Hasidic Jewish culture beards are worn as an emblem of obedience to religious law. Muslim men who shave their facial hair are, in some places, subject to intense criticism from more religiously conservative Muslims for whom growing a beard is an indication of clean-liness, obedience to God, and male gender. In some Muslim countries (such as Afghanistan under the Taliban), the wearing of untrimmed beards has been obligatory for men.

In Western culture in recent centuries, however, the wearing or shaving of facial hair has tended to become more a matter of fashion than of cultural identity. For most of history, the shaving of facial hair and the shaping of beards and mustaches has depended on the skills of barbers and personal servants who knew how to whet a razor and to use hot water and emollients to soften a beard. Jean-Jacques Perret created the first safety razor in 1770. It consisted of a blade with a wooden guard, which was sold together with a book of instruction in its use entitled *La Pogotomie* (The Art of Self-Shaving). In 1855 the Gillette razor was invented, the T-shape taking over from the cutthroat razor. Self-shaving became increasingly popular as the century progressed, especially after Gillette's further modification of his original design in 1895 with the introduction of the disposable razor blade.

The nineteenth and twentieth centuries have seen a myriad of different styles of beards and mustaches as facial hair took over as a focal point of male personal fashion, together with complementary hairstyles. Men might choose to wear their whiskers as muttonchops (so-called because of their shape), Piccadilly weepers (very long side-whiskers), Burnsides (that eventually evolved into sideburns), or the short and pointed Vandyke beard (alluding to a style popular in Renaissance Holland). Full mustaches that grew down over the top lip were dubbed soup strainers.

Many products, such as tonics, waxes, and pomades, were developed to help groom and style facial hair, and small industries grew up to manufacture and distribute them. Stylish mustaches and beards could be a point of personal pride. Charles Dickens wrote of his own facial ornamentation, "the moustaches are glorious, glorious. I have cut them shorter and trimmed them a little at the ends to improve their shape" (Corson 1965, p. 405).

In much of western Europe and America, facial hair was considered dashing and masculine because of its long associations with the military. By the mid-nineteenth century, doctors warned men that the clean-shaven look could be deleterious to their health; for example, it was said that bronchial problems could result if a mustache and beard were not worn to filter the air to the lungs. Thus to be clean-shaven was almost an act of rebellion, taken at the end of the century by bohemians and artists such as Aubrey Beardsley and the playwright Oscar Wilde. By the 1920s, however, the clean-shaven look had taken hold in mainstream fashion. Facial hair then became a mark of rebellion or artistic self-definition. Salvador Dali confirmed his artist status with an elaborate waxed mustache by the late 1920s. Mustaches continued to be worn by military men, and this is reflected in the names of styles such as Guardsman, Major, and Captain.

The beard had become rare by the mid-twentieth century, and was thus taken up by young bohemians in the 1950s as a gesture of nonconformity. Beards continued as a countercultural statement in the late 1960s with the hippie movement, when many young men saw facial hair as a sign of "naturalness," or a gesture of admiration for revolutionaries such as Che Guevara and the Cuban leader Fidel Castro. Hells Angels and bikers added a leather-clad hypermasculinity to the beard. Bearded hypermasculinity also was embraced within some subsets of gay culture. By the 1970s the clone look emanating from the streets of San Francisco included tight jeans, short hair, and mustaches. This look was adopted in mainstream fashion as seen on the actor Tom Selleck in *Magnum P.I.*, a popular television program.

By the mid-1980s, in place of full beards or mustaches designer stubble became de rigueur for actors and male models, as seen on the face of the pop star George Michael and the actor Bruce Willis, an effect achieved by going unshaven for a day or two. The 1990s witnessed a renaissance of beards and stubble as a result of the grunge movement emanating from Seattle and the New Age Traveler alliance in Europe. Both groups, one associated with rock music and the other with environmental protest, advocated a return to "authenticity" and eschewed regular shaving. Stubble and short beards appeared on the singer Kurt Cobain, front man for the band Nirvana. Swampy, a well-known British environmental protester, sported a head of dreadlocks and a matching "natural" beard in protest against environmental destruction.

The most popular contemporary permutations of facial hair are the goatee or love bud (in which a small patch of beard is allowed to grow below the lower lip). The full beard with side-whiskers, now found mainly on the faces of men who were young in the 1950s and 1960s, has been generally rejected by men of later generations, most of whom are clean-shaven.

See also Fashion and Identity; Hairstyles.

Bibliography

Corson, Richard. *Hair: The First Five Thousand Years*. London: Peter Owen, 1965.

Dikotter, Frank. "Hairy Barbarian, Furry Primates, and Wild Men: Medical Science and Cultural Representations of Hair in China." In *Hair: Its Power and Meaning in Asian Cultures*. Edited by Alf Hiltebeitel and Barbara D. Miller. Albany: State University of New York Press, 1998.

Peterkin, Allan. *One Thousand Beards: A Cultural History of Facial Hair.* Vancouver, Canada: Arsenal Pulp Press, 2001.

Caroline Cox

BEATON, CECIL

Cecil Beaton (1904–1980) was one of the most original and prolific creative talents of the twentieth century. Born in London and educated at Harrow and Cambridge University, he worked not only as a fashion photographer but also as a writer, artist, and actor and in his primary field of interest as a stage and costume designer for ballet, opera, and theater. Beaton was a self-taught photographer: he was given a simple Kodak 3A camera for his twelfth birthday and soon was eagerly photographing his young sisters, Nancy and Barbara ("Baba"), in "period" costumes and sets he made from fish-scale tissues and pseudo-Florentine brocades, tinsel nets, and imitation leopard skins. His nanny developed his negatives in the bathtub. In 1927, at the age of twenty-three, he went to work for *Vogue* as a cartoonist, but he soon began freelancing as a photographer for Condé Nast Publications and *Harper's Bazaar*, taking fashion shots and portraits of royalty and personalities in the arts and literature.

Influences on Beaton

The most important influence on Beaton's fashion photography was his interest in stage design and theatrical production, in which he was extremely accomplished. He did costume design for the film *Gigi* and set and costume design for the play and the film *My Fair Lady*, receiving Oscars for both. He also designed for the Metropolitan Opera, the Comédie Française, the Royal Ballet (London), and the American Ballet Theatre. "Completely stage struck" at an early age, he wrote in his *Photobiography* that he felt "a keen perverse enjoyment in scrutinizing photographs of stage scenery. The more blatantly these showed the tricks and artifices of the stage, which would never be obvious to a theatre audience, the greater my pleasure" (p. 16). This interest explains some of Beaton's most unusual fashion photographs, which include hanging wires and large sheets of pasted paper as backdrops for high-fashion outfits.

Beaton also had an extensive knowledge of Victorian and Edwardian photography and drew for inspiration on the costume depiction of such nineteenth-century portrait photographers as Camille Silvy and the collaborators D. O. Hill and Robert Adamson. He was also inspired by the soft-focus technique of the photographer E. O. Hoppé, the opalescent lighting of Baron Adolf de Meyer, and conventions of English portraiture and Renaissance painting. Beaton combined these influences with his innate taste for Victorian surface ornamentation and opulent effects, or what the critic Hilton Kramer has termed "extravagant and overripe artifice" (p. 28).

Beaton first traveled to Hollywood in 1931, and the world of tinsel as well as the influence of surrealism he encountered there were well suited to his insatiable taste for the theatrical and exotic. "My first impressions of a film studio were so strange and fantastic that I felt I could never drain their photographic possibilities," he wrote. "The vast sound stages, with the festoons of ropes, chains, and the haphazard impedimenta, were as lofty and aweinspiring as cathedrals; the element of paradox and surprise was never-ending, and the juxtaposition of objects and people gave me my first glimpse of Surrealism" (*Photobiography*, p. 61).

Beaton began introducing strong shadows into his work, a motif he may well have borrowed from Hollywood productions. The use of such shadows was popular in movies and advertising photography of the 1930s, so much so that articles such as one entitled "Shadows in Commercial Photography" were devoted to it (Hall-Duncan, p. 61). A famous pair of pendant photographs taken by Beaton in 1935 each shows an elegant model attended by three debonair phantoms created by backlighting three tuxedoed male models against a white muslin screen (Hall-Duncan, pp. 114–115).

Beaton's Work at *Vogue*

Returning to New York for his *Vogue* assignments in 1934, Beaton took his always fussy sets to a new level of fantastic overindulgence. He combed the antique shops of Madison and Third Avenues for carved arabesques, gesticulating cupids, silver studio work, and ceilings in imitation of the Italian rococo painter Giovanni Battista Tiepolo. "His baroque is worse than his bite," was a comment heard around the Condé Nast studios.

At the same time, under the influence of surrealism, which advocated the surprising juxtaposition of objects as a way to release the subconscious, he began incorporating bizarre combinations that created some of the most unusual fashion photographs of the century. The commonest object became grist for Beaton's creative mill: expensive gowns were posed against backgrounds of eggbeaters and cutlet frills, wire bedsprings, and kitchen utensils. Models appeared wearing hats composed of eggshells or carrying baskets of tree twigs. Beaton was even accused of using toilet paper, though his background was actually made of what is called "cartridge" paper.

The most extreme example was one that would have profound implications for fashion photography decades later, particularly in the work of Guy Bourdin and Deborah Turbeville. In 1937 Beaton discovered an office building under construction on the Champs-Elysées in Paris that revealed a "fantastic décor" (*Photobiography*, p. 73) of cement sacks, mortar, bricks, and half-finished walls. The resulting prints, in which Beaton showed mannequins nonchalantly reading newspapers or idling elegantly in this debris, were published with much hesitation on the part of the magazine's editors. Yet even much later, as Beaton noted, "fashion photographers are still searching for corners of desolation and decay, for peeling walls, scabrous bill-boardings and rubble to serve as a background for the latest and most expensive dresses" (*Photobiography*, p. 73).

By the middle of the 1930s Beaton was starting to be disturbed by *Vogue's* restrictions on his creativity. He was called into the *Vogue* offices for posing models in "unladylike" poses with their feet planted well apart. Then it was found that Beaton had incorporated anti-Semitic words into the border of a pen-and-ink sketch done for the February 1938 issue of *Vogue*. The offending line read, "Mr. R. Andrew's ball at the El Morocco brought out all the dirty kikes in town." The result, after 150,000 copies of *Vogue* were on newsstands, was catastrophic. Condé Nast recalled and reprinted 130,000 copies of the questionable issue and quickly issued a legal disclaimer. Walter Winchell wrote a snide review, as did many other columnists. As a result, Beaton "resigned." In time, the incident blew over and Beaton was reinstated at *Vogue*, where he continued to do fashion photography for several more decades. During World War II he was the official photographer to the British Ministry of Information, photographing the fronts in Africa and in the Near and Far East.

Beaton's Importance

Beaton had a long and extremely productive career in fashion photography, costume, and set design and writing and illustrating many books with his own witty drawings, based on the detailed diaries he kept all his life. Yet his work is of uneven quality. "When Cecil Beaton is good," the photography critic Gene Thornton said, "he is very, very good, but when he's bad, he's horrid. . . . It takes a kind of genius to be that bad" (p. 33). Indeed, the excesses of Beaton's style can be cloying, naive, and even trite, but few have questioned the inventive range of work or the important influence it would have on subsequent fashion photographers, particularly in the 1970s.

See also Fashion Photography; Film and Fashion; Theatrical Costume; Vogue.

Bibliography

Beaton, Cecil. *Photobiography*. London: Odhams Press, 1951.

Danziger, James. *Beaton*. New York: Viking Press, 1980.

Garner, Philippe, and David Alan Mellor. *Cecil Beaton: Photographs 1920–1970*. New York: Stuart, Tabori, and Chang, 1995.

Hall-Duncan, Nancy. *The History of Fashion Photography*. New York: Alpine Book Company, 1979.

Kramer, Hilton. "The Dubious Art of Fashion Photography." *New York Times*, 28 December 1975.

Ross, Josephine. *Beaton in Vogue*. New York: Clarkson N. Potter, 1986.

Thornton, Gene. "It's Hard to Miss with a Show of the '30s." *New York Times*, 18 April 1976.

Nancy Hall-Duncan

BEENE, GEOFFREY

Geoffrey Beene was born Samuel Albert Bozeman Jr. in Haynesville, Louisiana, on 30 August 1927, into a family of doctors. He dutifully enrolled in the premed program at Tulane University in New Orleans in 1943. Three years later he dropped out of Tulane and enrolled in the University of Southern California, Los Angeles, to pursue his lifelong interest in fashion design. However, he never attended classes as he decided to accept a job working in the display department of the I. Magnin department store, and then moved to New York to study at the Traphagen School of Fashion. By 1948 Beene had moved to Paris, where he attended the École de la Syndicale d'Haute Couture, the traditional training ground for European fashion designers. He then served a two-year apprenticeship with a tailor from the couture house of Molyneux. Beene returned to New York in 1951 and worked for a series of Seventh Avenue fashion houses before being hired by Teal Traina in 1954. He remained at Teal Traina until 1963, when he decided it was time to strike out on his own, opening Geoffrey Beene, Inc., offering high-quality ready-to-wear women's clothing. Beene's business partner was Leo Orlandi, who had been the production manager for Teal Traina.

An American Aesthetic

Beene started his career during the era when Parisian designers still dominated the fashion world and Americans were expected to look to them for inspiration. However, though Beene was trained in the traditional manner, educated in New York and Paris, he broke out of the mold after his training and apprenticeship working for other designers. His creativity and skill were soon rewarded with a Coty award in 1964, after just one year in business, thus beginning one of the most award-winning careers in American fashion. His first collection made the cover of *Vogue*, and he has been regarded as a dean of American design ever since. His high-profile clients have included several First Ladies, and he designed the wedding dress of President Lyndon B. Johnson's daughter, Lynda Bird Johnson, in 1967.

Beene's distinctive creative vision manifested itself fully in 1966 when he designed ballgowns using gray flannel and wool jersey. He went on to design a series of dresses inspired by athletic jerseys, most notably a sequined full-length football-jersey gown in 1968. Generally, his clothes did display a respect for traditional dress-making, which manifested itself in details such as delicate collars and cuffs, and minutely tucked blouses, applied to a paired-down silhouette.

By the mid-1970s Beene had a number of licensing agreements for products as diverse as eyeglasses and bed sheets. The Beene Bag line of women's wear, introduced in 1971, used the same silhouettes as his couture line, but he employed inexpensive fabrics such as mattress ticking and muslin. Everyday fabrics continued to make their way into his higher-priced line as they had since the late 1960s, as he used sweatshirt fabric and denim for evening dresses in his 1970 collection.

Beene considers the years 1972–1973 as a turning point in his career. It was then that he set aside

traditional Parisian tailoring methods and began to explore softer silhouettes. He commented on these years in the catalog to a 1988 retrospective of his work at the National Academy of Design:

> At that time there was so much construction in my clothes they could stand alone. I believed inner structure and weight were synonymous with form and shape. My sketches were dictating the design, not the fabric. When I became aware that my clothes lacked modernity, I began to experiment more with fabric, working with textile mills abroad, commissioning new weights, textures and fiber mixes. (Beene 1988, p. 4)

By 1975 Beene had been awarded a fifth Coty and had launched Grey Flannel, one of the first and perennially most successful designer men's fragrances. He was able to buy out his partner and obtain complete control over his business by the early 1980s.

Influence Abroad

In 1976 Beene became the first American designer to show in Milan, Italy, set up manufacturing facilities there, and successfully compete in the European fashion market. This success led to his sixth Coty in 1977, which was awarded for giving impetus to American fashion abroad. It is the Coty award that he treasured most, as the challenge of success in Europe was significant to his development as an artist—he proved to himself that his designs and his unique American vision had validity in the international arena. The European success also brought the added benefit of prestige and significantly increased sales of the couture line in the United States. But by this point in his career, Geoffrey Beene Couture, Beene Bag, and two fragrances accounted for only one-third of Beene's sales; the remainder was from licensing royalties for Beene-designed men's clothes, sheets, furs, jewelry, and eyeglasses.

While Beene has always been regarded as a master of form silhouette, it has been his use of color and fabric mixtures that garner the most comment. In a 1977 article for *The New Yorker*, Kennedy Fraser stated: "The distinctive quality of Geoffrey Beene's work which at the same time reflects an immediate sensuous response to the color and texture of beautiful fabrics must be characterized as a variety of intellectualism" (Fraser, p. 181). His ability to push experiments with color and texture was remarked upon again by the *Cleveland Plain Dealer* in 1987: "In the hands of a less adept designer, a collection that encompasses everything from bedspread chenille and gold spattered faille or silver leather to monk's cloth would be a nightmare" (Cullerton, p. 181). Beene consistently revealed hidden characteristics of the fabrics that he chooses.

In 1982 Geoffrey Beene received his eighth Coty award—the most awarded to any one designer as of the early 2000s— and professional recognition continued through the 1980s as he was named Designer of the Year in 1986 by the Council of Fashion Designers of America.

The vocabulary of sportswear appeared consistently in Beene's work as he strove for a balance between comfort and style. During the 1980s, when jumpsuits began to appear frequently in his women's collection, he stated that "the jumpsuit is the ballgown of the next century." Neither hard-edged nor futuristic, Beene's jumpsuits emphasize the comfort and versatility of this form of garment. The same is true for his use of men's wear influences in women's wear—bow ties, vests, and suiting fabrics are used with whimsy.

Later Career

In 1988 a retrospective at the National Academy of Design opened to coincide with the anniversary of Beene's twenty-five years in business. During this time, an article appeared in the *Village Voice* by Amy Fine Collins, who took on the role of Beene's muse through the 1990s.

Geoffrey Beene selecting shoes. Geoffrey Beene, a fashion designer whose career has spanned more than four decades, introduced an innovative mix of color and new fabrics to haute couture. His creations earned him eight prestigious Coty Awards. © DAVID LEES/CORBIS. REPRODUCED BY PERMISSION.

In analyzing Beene's work as an artist, she focused on his seemingly contradictory combinations of materials and influences, praising his courage to "regularly descend into the depths of taste in order to reemerge with his vision replenished" (Fine Collins, p. 34). In 1988 the Council of Fashion Designers of America gave Beene a newly created award, the Special Award for Fashion as Art.

Beene continued his innovations with fabric, treating humble textiles regally and using luxurious materials with throwaway ease. For example, a 1989 sheared mink coat for the furrier Goldin-Feldman in a bathrobe-like silhouette was created in fur dyed hot pink, edged with electric blue ribbon in a giant rickrack pattern, and lined with an abstract print in coordinating colors.

The year 1989 saw the opening of Geoffrey Beene on the Plaza, Beene's flagship retail shop on Fifth Avenue. He envisioned the shop as a design laboratory where he could "put in something new and in a few days have enough feedback to know if it's a success or if it has to go back to the drawing board" (Morris, p. B11).

Beene had shown a special interest in lace, for its combination of sheerness and strength along with its ability to stretch. In the late 1980s he began utilizing strategically placed sheer and cutout panels, especially in his evening clothes, culminating in the matte-wool-jerseyand-sequins lace-insertion gowns of 1991, which exemplify the exacting cut and technical intricacy of his work. His spiraling designs, which consider the body in the round rather than using flat pieces and treating the front and back as separate entities, reveal his admiration for and study of the work of the French couturier Madeleine Vionnet.

In 1994 Beene was honored again with an exhibition at the Fashion Institute of Technology to celebrate thirty years in business and was awarded the first-ever Award of Excellence by the Costume Council of the Los Angeles County Museum of Art. In 1997 and 1998 exhibitions of his work were featured at the Toledo Museum of Art, the Philadelphia Museum of Art, and the Rhode Island School of Design Museum.

Beene's clothes have consistently been praised for their individuality and wearability. In a 1994 interview with Grace Mirabella he explained his philosophy of design:

> The biggest change in fashion and the world has probably come in the past and present decade— the collapse of rules and their rigidity. This had to happen. There were too many illogical rules.

I have never wished to impose or dictate with design. Its meaning for me is to affect people's lives with a certain joy, and not to impose questions of right and wrong. (Mirabella, p. 7)

Beene's lifetime achievement awards include the Smithsonian's Cooper-Hewitt National Design Museum's American Original award, presented in 2002. In 2003 he became the first recipient of the Gold Medal of Honor for Lifetime Achievement in Fashion from the National Arts Club. He received a career excellence award from the Rhode Island School of Design, which awarded him an honorary doctorate in 1992.

Beene weathered a famous seventeen-year feud with *Women's Wear Daily*, during which the publication refused to mention his name. By early 2002, Geoffrey Beene pulled his couture line out of retail stores; he continued to produce clothing for a select group of private clients.

See also Fashion Designer; Paris Fashion; Vionnet, Madeleine; Women's Wear Daily.

Bibliography

Anderson, Susan Heller. "Geoffrey Beene Takes On Europe." *New York Times*, 20 November 1977.

Beene, Geoffrey. *Geoffrey Beene: The First Twenty-five Years: An Exhibition of the National Academy of Design, New York City, September 20 till October 9, 1988. Geoffrey Beene, Inc. Essay by Marylou Luther*. New York: National Academy of Design, 1988.

———. *Geoffrey Beene Unbound*. New York: Museum at the Fashion Institute of Technology, 1994. Interview by Grace Mirabella.

Cocks, Jay. "Geoffrey Beene's Amazing Grace." *Time*, 10 October 1988.

Cullerton, Brenda. *Geoffrey Beene*. New York: Harry N. Abrams, 1995.

Dennis, Harry. "Geoffrey Beene," *TWA Ambassador*, September 1989.

Fine Collins, Amy. "The Wearable Rightness of Beene." *Village Voice*, 10 January 1989.

Fraser, Kennedy. *The Fashionable Mind: Reflections on Fashion, 1970–1981*. New York: Alfred A. Knopf, 1981.

Martin, Richard. *American Ingenuity: Sportswear, 1930s–1970s*. New York: Metropolitan Museum of Art, 1998.

Milbank, Caroline Rennolds. *Couture, The Great Designers*. New York: Stewart, Tabori, and Chang, 1985.

Morris, Bernadine. "In New Retail Shop, Beene Envisions a Laboratory of Fashion." *New York Times*, 19 December 1989.

Schiro, Anne-Marie. "Geoffrey Beene Shows the Way." *New York Times*, 2 November 1996.

Melinda Watt

BELGIAN FASHION*

In October 2003, the American newspaper *Women's Wear Daily* asked, "Is Belgian Avant-Garde Out of Fashion?" Twenty years after Belgian fashion design, with Antwerp as its epicenter, had won its place on the world scene, it was time to ask how things now stood with the avant-garde character of the Belgians. The Belgian designers, who had instigated a small revolution in the early 1980s with their unexpected images and conceptual approaches, were by 2003 counted by critics among the classic designers in their field. During the intervening two decades, the perception of Belgian fashion evolved from avant-garde, edgy, and against-the-grain toward a generally accepted classic style. "Antwerp" and "Belgian" became prefixes laden with high symbolic— and in some cases financial—capital and had successfully earned themselves a secure place alongside "French," "Italian," "Japanese," and "American."

Writing about Belgian fashion in terms of nationality is, however, not without its problems. Where the first-generation designers were still quite literally "Belgian," younger generations have taken on an increasingly international character; consequently the word does not refer to nationality in the strict sense, but rather to a certain identity that manifests itself at different levels—varying from visual imagery and graphic design to training and corporate culture— and which is perceived as characteristically "Belgian."

Early History

Prior to the 1980s, there was in fact no Belgian fashion. One precursor of the 1980s generation, however, was Ann Salens, an Antwerp designer who for a short time in the 1960s generated international furor and is an important point of reference for Belgian designers. Her extravagant, brilliantly colored dresses and wigs in artificial silk, her flamboyant lifestyle, risqué fashion shows, and happenings at unusual locations earned her the title of "Belgian Fashion's Bird of Paradise."

During the first half of the twentieth century, fashion in Belgium had primarily reflected what was taking place on the Paris runways. Parisian chic also dominated the Belgian image of fashion. Until 1950, creativity was restricted to the realm of interpretation, which frequently amounted to all but literal copying of the creations from the great French houses, which were in fact geared to this form of commercial reproduction. Smaller and less resounding names outside France could select from among various formulas with associated price tags, beginning with attending the presentation of the collection—where it was strictly forbidden to take notes—up to the purchase of the patterns and original fabrics. If desired, the purchased design could be further sold under the new name. Even after the 1950s, however, it remained commercially uninteresting to advertise Belgian origins. In the early 1980s, established Belgian brands, such as Olivier Strelli, Cortina, and Scapa of Scotland, were choosing more exotic names that sooner disguised rather than emphasized their Belgian roots.

The Golden 1980s

At the beginning of the 1980s, the Belgian government launched a plan to give new incentives to the stagnating textiles industry. On 1 January 1981, the Instituut voor Textiel en Confectie van België (ITCB, Institute for Belgian Textiles and Fashion) was established to provide constructive guidance for the various economic, commercial, and creative initiatives of the government's *textiles plan*. On the one hand, the Belgian textiles and apparel industry could call on government support in order to modernize and introduce new technology. On the other hand, a wide-ranging commercial campaign was begun, under the motto, "Fashion: It's Belgian." Its purpose was to provide Belgian fashion with a new and convincing image. At the same time, there was growing awareness that such a campaign had to be supported by a creative substructure, in which young talent was given every possible opportunity. In 1982, this led to the establishment of the annual Golden Spindle competition, the first of which was won by Ann Demeulemeester. Other laureates of that first edition were Martin Margiela, Dries Van Noten, Walter Van Beirendonck, Marina Yee, Dirk Van Saene, and Dirk Bikkembergs. Along with the requisite attention from the press and an article in the *Fashion: It's Belgian* magazine, the laureates

were given the opportunity to collaborate with manufacturers to produce their collections, resulting in the first important reciprocal overtures between Belgian manufacturers and the new avant-garde designers.

During the late 1970s and early 1980s, Paris reached an apex with spectacular shows by Jean-Paul Gaultier and Thierry Mugler, among others, and with creations by Comme des Garçons and Yohji Yamamoto, which were lauded as works of art. Italy also brought innovation, with Gianni Versace and Romeo Gigli. In both ladies' and men's apparel, Italy established itself as a trendsetter, and Italian men's collections presented a new, nonchalant man, designed by Romeo Gigli or Dolce & Gabbana. This passion for pushing fashion to its peak and the exuberance of these collections in turn stimulated academy graduates and young designers in Antwerp.

There was a growing sense that Belgians could also produce fashion, and do so without the show elements so dependent on extravagant budgets. *Les gens du Nord*, or "the folks from the North," presented an avant-garde reversal to fashion, or *l'Anvers de la mode*—as the journalist Elisabeth Paillée aptly wrote in a wordplay on the French name for Antwerp. This was the backside, the recycled, throwaway fashion, an underground phenomenon, the underdog: not so extroverted as English fashion, not so sexy as Italian fashion, not so cerebral as Japanese fashion.

As the only member of this group to do so, Martin Margiela went to Paris to apprentice with Gaultier (1984–1987) and eventually established his own Maison Martin Margiela in 1988. Maison Margiela developed an impressive oeuvre comprising differing lines, with recurring focus on such themes as tailoring, haute couture, recycling, and deconstruction. Margiela's story is a tale about the system that underlies fashion, a journey to discover alternatives that remain economically alive and which, in the fashion world, give new substance to the supposedly unassailable notion of innovation.

The remaining six designers decided to pool their resources and in 1987, left together for London's *British Designer Show*, where they were quickly noticed by the press, who referred to them as the "The Antwerp Six"—purportedly because the difficult Flemish names were such tongue-twisters. Success was not long to follow. After London, they stormed Paris. By the late 1980s and early 1990s, most had their own fashion lines and retail outlets, as well as a permanent place on the Parisian fashion week calendar, with growing numbers of international selling points as a result.

Presenting these designers as a group, as the "Antwerp Six" or the "Belgians," indeed overlooks their individual styles and identities. Where content, form, and image are concerned, it can in fact be difficult to find something they share in common. Dries Van Noten is known for the ethnic or historic tone of his designs, with an almost naïve and at the same time touching exoticism. His flower motifs and the strong silhouette structure of his fashion shows are a trademark. In Ann Demeulemeester, there is a super-cooled romanticism, with a color palette reduced to the bare essentials: black and white. For her, the study of form is crucial, resulting in a union of such contrasts as masculine toughness and feminine elegance. Walter Van Beirendonck holds to an extreme eccentricity, with sources of inspiration ranging from science fiction to performance, comic books, and politics. From 1992 through 1999, he designed his W&LT line, followed by the introduction of his "Aestheticterrorists." Dirk Van Saene seems to harbor a love-hate relationship with couture. His image of women is fickle, even cynical, yet his apparel designs demonstrate great love and attention to craftsmanship. Finally, Dirk Bikkembergs initially created a sensation with heavy men's shoes with laces pulled through the heel. This subsequently evolved into an image that is sporty and sexy, perhaps most akin to Italian fashion.

What Is Belgian?

If Belgian fashion cannot be understood in terms of a single style and if nationality itself is not the determining factor, what do these different designers have in common that makes their work recognizably Belgian? It is not the intention here to formulate a definition as such, but rather to indicate a number of aspects that contribute to the specific identity of the Belgian designers. One important factor is undoubtedly their training at the Royal Academy in Antwerp, with "individuality" and "creativity" being the principle concepts. Personal growth and creative development of the student are fundamental at school, without this one loses sight of the link between professional life. The personal approach also extends to the various peripheral activities that come along with the presentation of a collection, ranging from exceptional attention to the graphic design for the invitations and catalogs and particular focus on the location and design of the fashion show to a warm welcome in the showroom. One need only think of the now historic presentations of Martin Margiela's collections in an abandoned Metro station or Salvation Army depots, Dries Van Noten's

delight-to-behold, beautiful shows, or the art performance tone of the presentations by Bernhard Willhelm and Jurgi Persoons for illustrations of this approach.

Nonetheless, the collection and the love and passion for clothing always take first place. With the Belgians, there is no superstar allure, or coquetry, but a healthy mix of humility, sobriety, and daring, and this translates first and foremost in the apparel itself. There is no blinding haute couture for the Belgians, but there is attention to professional craftsmanship, the study of form and concept; no out-of-control profits in the wake of the luxury houses, but a self-sufficiently structured enterprise in which as many factors as possible are kept under the designers' own control; no top models whose star status relegates the clothes to subservient status, but real girls with character.

The Next Generation

The generation following the "Belgian Six" found themselves faced with a very difficult challenge: how to create a profile and where to position oneself in the presence of such a strong avant-garde. Several responded by choosing not to present collections of their own. Perhaps the first to prove that there really was life after the Six was Raf Simons, who set his aims high with collections that indeed generated long-term changes in men's fashion. With images based on youth culture, the influence his work has had on the fashion field must not be underestimated.

In 1997, Véronique Branquinho presented a new woman: dreamy, young, mysterious, fascinating, and pure. Branquinho appeared on the scene as a young business-woman with talent, and has been a pleasure to watch as her collections have grown together with their maker. Her collections are unpretentious and refined. Her label, James, refers to class—class without the glamour. In 2009 Véronique Branquinho's James label went out of business.

The A. F. Vandevorst designer team of An Vandevorst and Filip Arickx drew considerable press attention with the presentation of their second collection, in which girls slumbered and awoke in hospital beds. When the girls woke, their clothes still had the same pleats they had had when they lay down. It was an endearing and human image.

Bernhard Willhelm did not hesitate to begin by infusing his collection with humor. It was intended to provoke thought and balanced at the edge of cynicism, using new shapes and colors, and not be categorized in any single style. After only a few seasons, Willhelm was designing for the Italian house, Capucci, in addition to producing his own line.

Among the youngest designers, Haider Ackermann, of Colombian-French origins, has attracted particular attention. In 2002, he showed his first women's collection on the Paris catwalk. In 2003, he designed a collection for the Italian leather designers, Ruffo Research. His experiments with leather were astonishing, combining superb knowledge of material and form, along with the necessary dose of elegance and craftsmanship.

Brussels, too, is making itself heard. The super-talent Olivier Theyskens, who was designing for Rochas, prematurely broke off his training at the La Cambre School for Fashion in Brussels and almost immediately became a center of attention when the pop icon Madonna appeared in one of his creations. Theyskens achieved wonders in linking Parisian elegance to a certain Belgian conceptuality and sobriety. His designs are exquisitely beautiful, approaching perfection, yet at the same time possessing a dark underside, a gothic edge. After working for Rochas, which was closed down by owner Procter & Gamble in 2006, Theyskens worked for Nina Ricci, which he left in 2009.

The Fashion Nation

With the achievements of the 1980s generation in mind, Antwerp became increasingly conscious of the fact that a number of structures had to be brought into play if the unique position that the city enjoyed in the fashion world were to be maintained. The starting bell rang in 2001, during Antwerp's "Year of Fashion," with the hosting of a broad-ranged series of artistic events curated by Walter Van Beirendonck. At the same time, the "Fashion Nation" opened its doors in the heart of Antwerp. By way of three different organizations, the Fashion Nation unites three influences on fashion: education, culture, and economics. The fashion department of the Royal Academy is located on the top floor and also symbolically stands for "top floor" and creative input. The next story down is home to the MoMu Museum of Fashion and the Flanders Fashion Institute (FFI). The MoMu unites heritage and tradition with an innovative approach, while the FFI has the task of bridging a link with the financial world, by way of a production fund for starting designers and countless other activities to help Belgian designers achieve the aura they need at both national and international levels.

See also Italian Fashion; Japanese Fashion; London Fashion; Margiela, Martin; Paris Fashion.

Bibliography

Coppens, Marguerite, ed. *Les Années 80: L'Essor d'une mode Belge* [The 1980s: The Rise of a Belgian Fashion]. Brussels, Belgium: Musées Royaux d'Art et Histoire, 1995.

Debo, Kaat, ed. *The Fashion Museum Backstage*. Ghent, Belgium, and Amsterdam: Ludion, 2002.

Derycke, Luc, and Sandra Van De Veire, eds. *Belgian Fashion Design*. Ghent, Belgium, and Amsterdam: Ludion, 1999.

Esch, Gerdi, and Agnes Goyvaerts. *Mode in de Lage Landen: België* [Fashion in the Low Countries: Belgium]. Antwerp, Belgium: Hadewijch, 1989.

Weekend Knack 20 Years Fashion It's Belgian. Issue 37. Roeselaere: Roularta Media Group, 2003. Jubilee issue with an excellent overview of who's who in Belgian fashion.

Windels, Veerle. *Jonge Belgische Mode* [Young Belgian Fashion]. Ghent, Belgium, and Amsterdam: Ludion, 2001.

Kaat Debo and Linda Loppa

BENJAMIN, WALTER

The German writer and cultural critic Walter Benjamin (1892–1940) was born in Berlin, one of three children of assimilated Jewish parents. In 1912 he began his studies in philosophy, German literature, and art history at the University of Freiburg and then moved back to Berlin, where he encountered the teachings of the philosopher Georg Simmel. In 1914 he continued his studies at the universities in Munich and Bern, Switzerland. Benjamin married Dora Kellner in 1917; they had one son, Stefan, in 1918, before the marriage ended in divorce in 1930. Benjamin's doctoral dissertation on German Romanticism was accepted by the University of Bern in 1919. In 1923 he met his closest intellectual friends, the philosopher Theodor Wiesengrund Adorno and the cultural historian Siegfried Kracauer. His attempts to submit another professional dissertation to the University of Frankfurt, on the origin of German tragic drama, were not successful. The work was published in 1928 under the title *Ursprung des deutschen Trauerspiels* (*The Origin of the German Tragic Drama*).

Benjamin eked out a precarious existence as writer, translator, and journalist. In 1925–1927 he journeyed to Moscow, to visit Asja Lascis, whom he had fallen in love with. In 1933, in the wake of the rise of Hitler and Nazism, he left Germany for Paris, where he stayed except for brief visits to the German dramatist Bertolt Brecht in Denmark. Before his exile to France, Benjamin had begun to formulate *Das Passagenwerk* (*The Arcades Project*), his work on Paris in the nineteenth century; he would devote the remainder of his life to this incomplete magnum opus.

In 1936 he wrote the famous essay "Das Kunstwerk im Zeitalter seiner technischen Reproduzierbarkeit" ("The Work of Art in the Age of Mechanical Reproduction"). The text is the first to postulate the loss of the work's aura, that is the demise of its multi-tiered authenticity in view of the cultural implications of art's reproducibility in modern media. The German occupation of Paris in 1939 drove Benjamin from the French capital, but his manuscripts remained hidden in the vaults of the Bibliothèque Nationale until after the war. Border police halted his attempt to escape to Spain across the Pyrenees in September of 1940. Mentally and physically exhausted, Benjamin committed suicide in Port Bou, Spain. He carried with him a black bag with what is rumored to have been a final version of *The Arcades Project*. It was never recovered.

Benjamin on Fashion

Benjamin's significance for the interpretation of fashion resides in his unfinished chef-d'œuvre, *Das Passagenwerk*. A vast array of fragments, excerpts, aphorisms, quotations, metaphysical musings, and sociopolitical observations constitute the material for this book on Paris in the nineteenth century, the "pre-history of modernity," as Adorno called it. Fashion, both as an economic force and a visual signifier, is one of the most important features of *The Arcades Project*. Benjamin collected some hundred entries that deal with couture, dress codes and the art, literature, philosophy, and sociology of clothing (including a wealth of quotations from Simmel). His works on French literature; translations of Charles Baudelaire and Marcel Proust, with whom he shared sensibilities in regard to fashion; and essays on visual art in France were preparatory to the project, and his collections *Thesen über den Begriff der Geschichte* (1942; *Theses on the Philosophy of History*) and *Zentralpark* (1955; *Central Park*) are methodological spin-offs. A number of abstracts that he produced over the course of a decade explain and modify his conceptual approach.

Common to all these writings is the centrality of fashion as a historical fact—not simply as a historicized element of the past but more as a force that through its constant self-reference and quotation breaks the historical continuum and activates, at times even revolutionizes, past occurrences for the present. It is Benjamin's principal achievement to use dialectical materialism—that is, the materialist philosophy that regards the process of development in thought, nature, and history as coined by the necessary contradiction of ideas (albeit rather unorthodoxically) in this context as a structuring device against historicism, which uses styles, ornamentation, and motifs from the past often in eclectic and not reflective combination, and also against the notion of history marked by linear progress toward constantly higher levels of technical proficiency and material satisfaction. The potency of Georg Friedrich Wilhelm Hegel's and Karl Marx's concept of history as turning from quantitative progression to qualitative change is used by Benjamin to create an analogy in fashion's willful quotations from its own source book, where a particular style or stylistic element is taken from costume history and brought into present fashion to create reference and friction simultaneously, along with new commodities. This method is seen as particular to fashion, not just as the result of the seasonal structure of haute couture but because fashion operates differently from the historicism inherent in other decorative or applied arts. Thus, for example, quotations in Empire furniture are different from citations of Greek dress in the Directoire fashion. Through the stylistic quote, the console or chair merely offers a consolidation of historical substance, while the high-waisted dress presents the direct impression of the democratic ideal on the body politic.

In his *Theses on the Philosophy of History* Benjamin finds a poetic definition of fashion in history, a definition that moves from metaphysical to material questions and perceives fashion as a structural device. Through the sartorial quotation, fashion fuses the thesis of the eternal or "classical" ideal with its antithesis, which is the openly contemporary. The apparent opposition between the eternal and the ephemeral is rendered obsolete by the leap that needs the past for any continuation of the present. Correspondingly, the transhistorical describes the position of fashion as detached both from the eternal, that is, an aesthetic ideal, and the continuous progression of history. Benjamin conjures up the image of the "*Tiger-sprung*" to explain how fashion is able to leap from the contemporary to the ancient and back again without coming to rest exclusively in one temporal or aesthetic configuration. This generates a novel view of historical development. Coupled with the dialectical image, the tiger's leap under the open skies of history marks a convergence that is revolutionary in its essence.

The text that contains the *Tigersprung* thesis indicates what *The Arcades Project* could have constituted in terms of a radical rethinking of fashion in modern culture, if Benjamin had finished it. Its excerpts demonstrate the leap from a sociological, art historical, or material observation of clothes to an understanding of fashion's unique character as a historical constituent, a structuring device, potentially even a revolutionary force. Benjamin tempts us in his unfinished work with glimpses of a new abstract perception of fashion viewed independently of its material basis (textile industry, haute couture, distribution, representation, and so forth), but retaining its materialism, that is, its sociopolitical significance. It is seen as part of intellectual culture, to be debated and interpreted simultaneously as sensuous and poetic, that is, as an expression of contemporary beauty, and on an abstract and metaphysical level, as an independent structure of modern existence and cognition.

See also Fashion, Historical Studies of; Fashion, Theories of; Historicism and Historical Revival; Simmel, Georg.

Bibliography

Works by Walter Benjamin

"Theses on the Philosophy of History." *Illuminations*. London: Cape, 1970: 263.
The Correspondence of Walter Benjamin 1910–1940. Edited by Gershom Scholem and Theodor W. Adorno. Translated by Manfred R. Jacobson and Evelyn M. Jacobson. Chicago: University of Chicago Press, 1994.
The Arcades Project. Translated by Howard Eiland and Kevin McLaughlin. Cambridge, Mass.: Belknap Press, 1999.
Selected Writings of Walter Benjamin. 4 vols. Cambridge, Mass.: Belknap Press, 1996–2003.

Works about Walter Benjamin

Bolz, Norbert W., and Richard Faber, eds. *Antike und Moderne: Zu Walter Benjamins "Passagen."* Würzburg, Germany: Königshausen and Neumann, 1986.
Buck-Morss, Susan. *The Dialectics of Seeing: Walter Benjamin and the Arcades Project*. Cambridge, Mass.: MIT Press, 1989.
Bulthaupt, Peter, ed. *Materialien zu Benjamins Thesen "Über den Begriff der Geschichte": Text, Varianten, Briefstel-*
len, Inter-pretationen. Frankfurt, Germany: Suhrkamp, 1975.
Frisby, David. *Fragments of Modernity: Theories of Modernity in the Work of Simmel, Kracauer, and Benjamin*. Cambridge, U.K.: Polity, 1985.
Lehmann, Ulrich. *Tigersprung: Fashion in Modernity*. Cambridge, Mass.: MIT Press, 2000.
Smith, Gary, ed. *On Walter Benjamin: Critical Essays and Recollections*. Cambridge, Mass.: MIT Press, 1988.
———. *Benjamin: Philosophy, Aesthetics, History*. Chicago: University of Chicago Press, 1990.
Steinberg, Michael P. *Walter Benjamin and the Demands of History*. Ithaca, N.Y.: Cornell University Press, 1996.
Vinken, Barbara. "Eternity—A Frill on the Dress." *Fashion Theory* 1, no. 1 (1997): 59–67.
Wismann, Heinz, ed. *Walter Benjamin et Paris: Colloque international 27–29 Jun 1983*. Paris: Le Cerf, 1986.
Wolin, Richard. *Walter Benjamin: An Aesthetic of Redemption*. Berkeley: University of California Press, 1994.

Ulrich Lehmann

BERET

A beret is a round, flat, visorless cap worn by both sexes over centuries. Berets are made from circular pieces of knitted, woven, or felted cloth, occasionally velvet, and drawn underneath by a string, thread band, or leather thong so as to fit around the head. They may be decorated with objects, such as ribbons, plumes, pins, tassels, jewelry, precious stones, fabrics, and cords.

Options for wearing the beret include set back on the head (halo style), flat on the head (pancake style), pulled down covering the ears (winter version), dipping diagonally to one side (fashion style), or pulling over the eyes for sleeping (oversized practical type).

Archaeological and art historical evidence indicates that variations of the beret have been worn by Bronze Age inhabitants of northern Europe, Ancient Cretans, Etruscans, English aristocrats such as Henry VIII, along with baroque and modern artists (Rembrandt to Picasso).

Basque Beret

The modern "Basque" beret originated with shepherds living on both sides of the Pyrenees in southern France and northern Spain. Little is known of Basque peoples' origins, and in the Spanish Provincias Vascongadas, different color berets were worn: red in Guipúzcoa, white in Ávala, blue in Vizcaya. Eventually, the Basques all adopted blue, while red berets were taken over as part of the provincial folk costume in neighboring Navarre. The wearing of black berets spread to villages throughout Spain, and by the 1920s they were associated with working classes in France.

Production

Basque beret production dates back to the seventeenth century in the non-Basque area of Oloron-Sainte-Marie, a small town in southern France, where sheep grazed on nearby mountainsides. Locals, like many other peoples, discovered that when wetted and rubbed together, small bits of wool became felted. While still moist, the felt could be hand manipulated by pulling it over the knee, thereby creating a rounded shape appropriate for covering the head.

Originally made by hand for male villagers, beret making became industrialized in the nineteenth century, with the first factory, Beatex-Laulhere, claiming production records dating back to 1810. Other factories followed and, by 1928, over twenty were producing millions of berets for international markets, stimulated by World War I military and civilian migrations. French sheep wool was originally used; later merino was imported from Australia and South Africa. By the mid-twentieth century, softer berets made of angora (molted rabbit fur) mixed with thermofibers attracted female wearers.

Basque berets are usually made during winter months and involve ten steps: knitting, sewing, felting, blocking, drying, checking, brushing, shaving, "confection" or finishing, and delivery. In 1996, a beret museum opened in the village of Nay, sponsored by the manufacturer Blancq-Olibet, which provides public educational tours on Basque beret manufacture.

Beret Usage

Over time, berets have been worn for political, military, religious, and aesthetic reasons. Symbolic meanings developed that were associated with color. The black beret became so popular with French urban workers that beret-wearing resistance movement fighters (Maquis) during World War II were able to blend into crowds without raising suspicion among German occupation forces. The dark beret became the trademark of Che Guevara, leader in the 1959 Cuban Revolution, and many of his later followers. A Che beret is preserved at the Museum of the Revolution in Havana.

Because of its flexibility, the beret was ideal for low-ranking military uniforms. Originally worn by nineteenth-century French seamen, it was adopted during World War I for alpine troops. British Field Marshal Montgomery popularized the beret during World War II as a badge of honor for elite military units. Since the Korean Conflict, berets have identified Special Forces as the "Green Berets," paratroopers trained to drop behind enemy lines (maroon beret) and the U.S. Army Rangers (whose beret was changed from black to tan). During the 1960s Vietnam War, "The Ballad of the Green Berets" brought to public attention the exploits and heritage of these courageous units, symbolized through their caps and shoulder badges.

A controversy broke out in 2000 C.E. when black berets became standard issue to all incoming U.S. Army recruits in an effort to attract and boost morale for an all-volunteer army. Some traditionalists felt the beret as an elite symbol had become compromised. Additionally, to meet the several million beret orders, manufacturers overseas were contracted, which required waiving a U.S. law requiring all clothing and textiles purchased by the military to be produced in the United States.

Over the past half century, United Nations troops have been identified by their baby-blue berets, and peace-keeping forces by orange ones. The beret is worn by modern armies worldwide, including Russia, Iraq, Pakistan, Venezuela, Democratic Republic of the Congo, and South Africa.

In an effort to combat urban crime during the 1990s, volunteer units known as Guardian Angels or "Red Berets" began patrolling city streets in the United States and Europe, later in urban centers in Africa, South America, and Japan. Their bright red berets serve as warnings to petty criminals and reassurance to community residents.

Jamaican Rastafari, and later followers in Central America and the United States, motivated by Black Religious Nationalism, follow biblical prescription by wearing long-uncut, uncombed, and matted hair (dreadlocks) covered by a knitted or crocheted black beret with red, gold, and green circles. Rastafari consider the beret and dreadlocks as an individual's crown, symbols of power representing the Biblical Covenant of God with His Chosen People, Black Israelites (Genesis 9:13).

As a Western fashion statement, the beret has been worn as "classic" sportswear by adults of both sexes and children since the 1920s and is especially popular during wartime and the winter olympics. As part of the U.S. Girl Scouts' required uniform, the beret was adopted in 1936 and only replaced in 1994 by the universally popular visor baseball cap.

Variations of the beret include the Scotch Bonnet, a flat, woven or knitted woolen cap with ribbon cockade and feathers that serve to identify the wearer's clan and rank. Worn at an angle and usually dark blue, called "Bluebonnet" for Scotland's national color, it has been a symbol of Scottish patriotism. The entire Highlander costume including the Bluebonnet was outlawed for many years by the British government. After construction of Balmoral Castle at Aberdeenshire, Scotland, in 1855, the Bonnet came to be called the "Balmoral" because of recognition given the Highlanders by Queen Victoria and Prince Albert.

Other Scottish types include the tam-o'-shanter, made of brushed wool with a large pompom in the center and named after a Robert Burns poem, and the striped woolen Kilmarnock Cap, also with pompom, named for a town in Strathclyde.

See also Afrocentric Fashion; Felt; Hats, Men's; Hats, Women's; Military Style.

Bibliography

Denford, Carole. "Le Vrai Basque." *The Hat Magazine* (April/May/June 2001): 34–37.
Wilcox, R. Turner. *The Mode in Hats and Headdress.* New York and London: Charles Scribner's Sons, 1945.

Beverly Chico

BERTIN, ROSE

Rose Bertin was born Marie-Jeanne Bertin (1747–1813) in Abbeville, a textile town in the Picardy region of France. Her family was not wealthy, and so she was apprenticed to a *marchande de modes* (fashion merchant) at a young age. By 1772 she had worked her way up to the exclusive rue Saint-Honoré in Paris, where she opened her own shop under the name of the *Grand Mogol*. She quickly won the patronage of several influential courtiers, including the duchess of Chartres, Louise Marie Adélaïde de Bourbon, who introduced Bertin to the newly crowned queen, Marie Antoinette, in the summer of 1774.

The queen of France quickly became Bertin's most famous customer. Sources of the day (including Bertin's surviving business records) document more than 1,500 clients; undoubtedly, there were many more of whom no credible record survives. In addition to Marie Antoinette, Bertin dressed the queens of Spain, Sweden, and Portugal; Grand-Duchess Maria-Fëdorovna of Russia; and many European aristocrats. The latter group included Marie Jeanne Bécu, the comtesse Du Barry; the duchess of Devonshire; Georgina Cavendish and the cross-dressing Charles Geneviève Louis D'Eon de Beaumont, Chevalier d'Eon. Bertin also dressed celebrities like the Vestris family of dancers and the actress Mademoiselle de Sainval of the Comédie-Française, who were fashion plates both onstage and off. Indeed, Bertin was the first "fashion designer" to become a celebrity in her own right.

In the twenty-first century, it is taken for granted that fashion designers can achieve international fame. But the ancien régime offered few avenues for social mobility, particularly for unmarried women of humble birth. Bertin overcame these obstacles with equal measures of talent and ambition, manipulating the young queen and the emerging fashion press to make her name and her creations known throughout the world.

Minister of Fashion

Marie Antoinette is remembered as a woman preoccupied with fashion. In fact, before she met Bertin, she was not considered particularly well dressed. Bertin was not Marie Antoinette's only *marchande de modes*; the task of clothing the queen was far too demanding for just one person, and Bertin had hundreds of other clients to accommodate. But no other *marchande de modes* enjoyed such easy access to the queen or to the royal purse. Thus, Rose Bertin and Marie Antoinette were inextricably linked in the public imagination.

When the *marchandes de modes* of Paris were incorporated in 1776, Bertin was elected as the guild's first mistress. In this post, she earned the right to dress the life-sized fashion doll that toured the mercantile centers of Europe and beyond, advertising French fashions. In 1777 Bertin had a staff of forty employees, not including dozens of subcontractors and suppliers. By 1778 Bertin had grown so powerful at court that the press dubbed her France's *ministre des modes*, or "minister of fashion." The unofficial title underlined Bertin's position as a trusted royal adviser as well as a representative of France to other nations.

Bertin's partnership with the queen ensured her success, but it would also prove to be her undoing. As Marie Antoinette's popularity waxed and waned, so did that of her favorite minister. Courtiers were outraged by Bertin's privileged place in the royal circle, unprecedented for a commoner. Furthermore, her success at court gave her an ego of princely proportions. Soon Bertin was as famous for her arrogance and astronomical prices as she was for her fashions and celebrity clients. Previously, labor had represented only a fraction of the cost of a garment. By demanding star status and a star's salary, Bertin helped elevate fashion from a trade to an art.

French Revolution

The outbreak of the French Revolution forced hundreds of fashion workers out of business or out of the country. Some left voluntarily, following their aristocratic clients; others feared that they would be persecuted if they remained in France. With her ties to queen and court, Bertin had every reason to fear for her life as well as her livelihood. While the aristocracy saw Bertin as an upstart and an interloper, to the revolutionaries she was no better than an aristocrat herself. Royalists and Republicans alike blamed Bertin for encouraging Marie Antoinette's excesses, which she continued to do right up until the queen's imprisonment.

Bertin fled Paris in 1792 and spent the next three years in such émigré havens as Brussels, Frankfurt, and London, where she continued to dress fashionable foreigners and French exiles. Unlike her royal muse, Bertin managed to survive the French Revolution unscathed. Although she was twice put on the government's émigré list, she managed to prove that she had left France on legitimate business both times. The émigré list was the official record of people who had emigrated, thus forfeiting their property and, in some cases, their lives. Effectively, Bertin was declared a fugitive.

By the time Bertin returned to Paris, she was out of danger but also out of fashion. Bertin could still count a few English, Russian, and Spanish aristocrats among her clients, but hardly any Frenchwomen. Indeed, many of her French clients had perished on the scaffold, leaving their bills unpaid. The Revolution cut Bertin's career short at the height of her power, and she never recovered financially or emotionally. She died at her country retreat in Épinay-sur-Seine just a few months too soon to see restoration of the monarchy in 1814. Even after her death Bertin remained a potent and provocative symbol of the elegance and excess of the ancien régime.

See also Court Dress; Fashion Designer.

Bibliography

Chrisman, Kimberly. "Rose Bertin in London?" *Costume* 32 (1999): 45–51.

Langlade, Émile. *La marchande de modes de Marie-Antoinette: Rose Bertin*. Paris: Albin Michel, 1911. Entertaining but unreliable biography.

——. *Rose Bertin: The Creator of Fashion at the Court of Marie-Antoinette*. Translated by Dr. Angelo S. Rappoport. New York: Charles Scribner's Sons, 1913. An English-language biography adapted from the French version.

Nouvion, Pierre de, and Émile Liez. *Un Ministre des modes sous Louis XVI: Mademoiselle Bertin, marchande de modes de la reine, 1747–1813*. Paris: Henri Leclerc, 1911. Contains detailed information about Bertin's family history.

Sapori, Michelle. *Rose Bertin: Ministre des modes de Marie-Antoinette*. Paris: Regard/Institut Français de la Mode, 2004. Illustrated monograph incorporating recent research on Bertin's career, competitors, and clients.

Kimberly Chrisman-Campbell

BEST-DRESSED LISTS

Since their inception in the first half of the twentieth century, best-dressed lists have become a popular barometer of international style. By publishing best-dressed lists in the mainstream media, fashion editors and style arbiters have established a steady market for information about the wardrobes, grooming, and comportment of smartly dressed men and women.

Perhaps the most eminent best-dressed list was the "International Best-Dressed Poll," the brainchild of Eleanor Lambert (1903–2003), a New York City publicist considered the doyenne of fashion publicity. Lambert first penned the list in 1940 as a press release for the New York Dress Institute, a trade organization she helped establish to stimulate dress sales during

World War II. Lambert claimed that her list was patterned after an anonymous poll of the world's ten best-dressed women issued by the Paris couture starting in the 1920s.

Lambert's annual list became a widely heralded tally of the world's most beautifully dressed people, derided as frivolous, yet eagerly anticipated. She coordinated the poll by canvassing a coterie of fashion insiders to nominate the contenders, and then revealed the winners in a press release to the media. Lambert elevated repeat winners to her own fashion Hall of Fame. Finally, at nearly 100 years old, she stopped coordinating her celebrated list in 2002.

Another important best-dressed list has been the domain of Richard Blackwell. In 1958, Blackwell established a line of evening gowns under the label "Mr. Blackwell," which attracted high-profile buyers like Nancy Reagan and Zsa Zsa Gabor. In 1960, *American Weekly* magazine, a national Sunday newspaper supplement, hired him to compile a list of Hollywood's best-and worst-dressed stars. Mr. Blackwell's list became notorious for his willingness to criticize icons like Brigitte Bardot and Queen Elizabeth II. The lists established Blackwell as a popular arbiter of taste, and he continues to issue his controversial fashion pronouncements as of the early 2000s.

Given the visibility of Lambert's and Blackwell's lists, fashion editors were inspired to publish best-dressed lists of their own. Among the publications that have published, or continue to publish, best-dressed lists are *Vogue*, *Harper's Bazaar*, *Vanity Fair*, and *Prima*.

People magazine publishes an annual special issue featuring best-and worst-dressed celebrities, while the annual Academy Awards show has spawned its own best-dressed subcategory. Other best-dressed lists have been printed by non-fashion publications like *Fortune* magazine and the *New York Post*.

Best-dressed lists allow readers to imagine that a winning profile is open to all, when in fact the top spots invariably go to wealthy people in the public eye: film stars and fashion industry or society figures. But the lists continue to fascinate as they impart lessons in style, self-presentation, and the ineffable quality of individual chic.

See also Fashion.

Bibliography

Blackwell, Richard. *Mr. Blackwell's Worst: 30 Years of Fashion Fiascos*. New York: Pharos Books, 1991.

Haugland, H. Kristina, and Dilys E. Blum. *Best Dressed: Fashion from the Birth of Couture to Today*. Philadelphia: Philadelphia Museum of Art, 1997.

Nemy, Enid. "Eleanor Lambert, Empress of Fashion, Dies at 100." *The New York Times*, 8 October 2003.

Wilson, Eric. "Eleanor Lambert Celebrates an American Fashion Century." *WWD* 186, no. 26 (6 August 2003).

Kathleen Paton

PERENNIALLY BEST-DRESSED

Marella and Gianni Agnelli
Fred Astaire
Marisa Berenson
Tina Chow
Cary Grant
C. Z. Guest
Gloria Guinness
Audrey Hepburn
Slim Keith
Jackie Kennedy
Babe Paley
Millicent Rogers
John Hay "Jock" Whitney
The Duke and Duchess of Windsor

BIBA

Biba has become a potent legend quite out of proportion with its relatively brief life in the mid-twentieth century. It was a shop and a label—but it was more than either or both of these: it came to stand for the "swinging chick," the ideal, running, jumping and never-standing-still girl, the image that dominated fashion from the mid-1960s until about 1974. That one word, "Biba" calls up from memory the long-legged, zany, crop-haired Twiggy morphing into the druggy, Pre-Raphaelite hippie of 1970: from the futuristic to the retro in four short years.

Biba was the creation of Barbara Hulanicki and her husband, Stephen Fitz-Simon. It began as a mail-order firm, selling gamine gingham shifts with matching head scarf in the wake of Brigitte Bardot. In 1964 the couple followed the just emerging trend for the fashion boutique as opposed to the department store where most women bought their clothes in the 1950s. (Small dress shops, known in Britain as "madam shops," still existed, but were by this time considered very old-fashioned, and small dressmakers were also dying out.) Biba's first outlet opened in the smart Kensington district of London. The young couple rented what had been a chemist's shop, retained in the window the big period bottles of ruby-and topaz-colored liquids that traditionally decorated such shops at that time (suggestive of magical potions), and created a dark blue interior with William Morris curtains, more like an Aladdin's cave than an ordinary shop. This was a totally different shopping experience from the department store or the "madam shop." There were no assistants pressuring you to buy by peering into the claustrophobic changing room and commenting on the clothes; instead there was a communal changing room free for all, more reminiscent of the school locker room than of adult life—but in an exciting way. The message was always that these fashions were for the young and carefree.

Biba really began to make an impact just as the mood of the 1960s began to change. From 1966 on, a creeping sense of economic discontent and social unrest in Britain was beginning to supersede the optimism of the first half of the decade. One of the ways in which this was expressed stylistically was in the mutation from future to past. By 1967 the Courrèges look—flat white boots and a square-cut tunic, reminiscent of cinematic fashions of the future—was being displaced by much dreamier clothes. The two other most influential British fashion designers of the period, Mary Quant and Ozzie Clark, began to use such "old-fashioned" textiles as crêpe and satin in art deco colors of eau de nil, cream, rust, and even maroon. Biba was at the epicenter of this trend from the beginning. The shops had a distinctly period feel, with bentwood furniture, vases of ostrich feathers, Tiffany-style lamps, Victorian china pedestal jardinières, and even—in Biba's third shop—the Victorian gothic paneling from a recently relocated boys' school.

The clothes were subtly period, too. Minidresses looked like something out of Mabel Lucie Atwell, childishly high-waisted, with sleeves tight at the shoulder but ballooning out toward the cuff. Trousers flapped out at the hem, like men's "Oxford bags" of the 1920s; slithery satin evening dresses looked like gowns Jean Harlow might have worn in a 1930s' Hollywood melodrama. Then there were T-shirts, exaggeratedly long of hem

and sleeve, and knee-high suede boots all in matching offbeat colors of dirty pink, brick dust, sage green, aubergine, and chocolate; and a makeup range that made the wearer look like the silent film star Theda Bara, with black lips and glistening eyes.

Biba was a way of life as much as a dress shop, and its greatest moment became its ultimate tragedy. From the original shop, it moved—still in Kensington—first to a grocer's shop, retaining all the period wooden shelving, then to a yet larger shop that had been a school outfitters, and finally to what had been Derry and Toms department store, a fabulous art deco building, complete with roof garden and all the original fittings, carpets, and staircases. On these five floors, Biba aimed to sell not just clothes but a whole lifestyle. As well as the dresses, there were to be aubergine refrigerators, Biba dinner services, art deco carpets, a food department complete with coffee, tea, flour, and sugar in Biba packaging, and—on the ground floor—all manner of trinkets, purses, scarves, accessories and, of course, the makeup range.

It was a magnificent vision. Unfortunately the hordes of young women who came to hang out among the satin bolsters on the tiger-print sofas of the ground floor, with its dark walls and druggy ambience, did not necessarily come to buy but simply to be Biba. By this time, Barbara Hulanicki and her husband had lost financial control of the enterprise to the multichain fashion company Dorothy Perkins, and the returns were not high enough to satisfy its board of directors. In 1975 Biba folded— and not only that; in an act of the utmost philistinism, the magnificent original Derry and Toms interiors were destroyed to make way for a utilitarian Marks & Spencer and British Home Stores.

Barbara Hulanicki and her husband moved to the United States, and Hulanicki made a second successful career designing interiors for the art deco mansions of Miami, Florida. In 1993, the Laing Art Gallery in Newcastle decided to hold a Biba exhibition. Many Biba aficionados previously donated the outfits they had treasured for thirty years. There were examples of the coffee— and even baked bean—tins, the cosmetics, and the soft furnishings, and the interiors of the shops were re-created. But what was extraordinary about the exhibition was the visitors' book. Visitors were invited to comment in any way they wished. Unlike other visitors' books, its pages were filled with loving reminiscences of how a Biba outfit had defined a major experience, a period, an identity, and although Biba the shop spanned only a decade, the memory gave promise of living on forever.

See also Boutique; Clark, Ossie; Quant, Mary; Twiggy.

Bibliography

Fogg, Marnie. *Boutique: A '60s Cultural Icon.* London: Phaidon Press Ltd., 2003.
Hulanicki, Barbara. *From A to Biba.* London: Hutchinson, 1983.

Elizabeth Wilson

BICYCLE CLOTHING

The bicycle was invented in Europe, but American ingenuity increased its usability and widespread use. Kirkpatrick Macmillan of Scotland is credited with inventing the first mechanical bicycle, while Pierre Michaux and son Ernest of Paris were the first to manufacture bicycles on a large scale in the mid-1860s. The aptly named "boneshaker" or velocipede was quickly followed by the high-wheeler and then the safety bicycle. In July 1865 Pierre Lallement brought the bicycle to America resulting in a wave of bicycle-related patents. The bicycle craze flourished through the end of the century. Clothing specifically designed for wear while bicycling has changed dramatically over the years.

Early bicycle riding was a man's activity due to the fact that in order to ride the velocipede, essentially two wheels connected by a frame and suspended seat, the rider had to wear bifurcated apparel to straddle the mechanism. With the introduction of the pneumatic tire in 1888, the popularity of the bicycle for transportation and leisure increased dramatically. In the same year the drop-frame bike was introduced in America. This new model made bicycle riding in a skirt much easier and more women participated in the activity. By the 1890s, clothing developed specifically for bicycling was being designed and produced. Racing clubs for men were formed and appropriate attire was required. Typical clothing included the "wheelman" or sleeveless vest with insignia worn over a shirt, long shorts (to the knee), and shoes without socks. In 1874 Charles Bennet, an avid bicyclist, decided to tackle "the delicate

problem that men faced as they were jounced on their penny farthings" (Norcliffe, p. 128). He designed the "bike web," a knit and elastic garment to provide support and cushioning. Because the garment was worn by bicycle "jockeys" it was called the "jockey strap," soon shortened to "jock strap." Headgear and footwear were also designed specifically for bicyclists. Headgear varied from a small flat crown hat with visor brim to a pith helmet that might provide protection in a crash. Shoes were designed to prevent slipping on the bike pedals. One shoe model incorporated leather pleats on the sole that served this function.

Mid-Victorian society did not approve of women riding bicycles, but the activity became more accepted after 1881 when Queen Victoria ordered tricycles for her daughters. Besides the immodesty and physicality of women straddling a bicycle, the independence allowed the individual woman was unprecedented. By the late 1800s, women were becoming enthusiastic bicyclists. Soon many adventurous women started wearing shorter skirts to avoid catching them in the pedals. Barbara Schreier (1989, p. 112) declared "bicycling helped to smooth the way for future clothing changes and dramatically advanced the position of women in sports." Knickerbockers made bicycle riding even easier for women, but the style was ridiculed as being unfeminine and unattractive. More shocking was the association of bifurcated garments and immorality. P. Russell suggests, "the forked body astride a modern machine could be represented as an essentially sexual image" (p. 66).

By the 1920s, new trends in sportswear introduced new forms and fabrics that permeated all sports activities. The new casual lifestyle eliminated the need for specific bicycle wear. Practical, comfortable sportswear was now fashionable and accepted. From the 1920s to the 1960s bicyclists wore all varieties of readily available sportswear with the exception of professional bike racers who wore close-fitting knit tops and pants to facilitate speed.

Bicycle clothing in the early 2000s combines elements of function, fashion, and advertising. Function centers on the most aerodynamic ensemble while providing comfort for the rider. Fashion is evident in color choices while professional and leisure riders sport clothing with company names and logos. The avid bicyclist wears form-fitting shorts and jerseys with appropriate accessories. Bicycle shorts rely on properties of nylon and spandex fibers to provide the closest fit possible. A major functional feature of bicycle shorts is the pad sewn into the crotch of the shorts, providing cushioning between body and bike seat. Chamois leather was originally used for the pad, but synthetic chamois or gel inserts are used in the twenty-first century. The bicycle shirt or jersey is also body-conforming for the all-important aerodynamic form. Shirts are typically brightly colored making the rider highly visible. The well-known yellow jersey worn by the leader in the Tour de France bicycle race was introduced in 1919. The Tour de France uses other signifier color jerseys including the green "points" jersey for the race's most consistent sprinter or points winner, the red polkadot jersey for the most consistent climber, and the reintroduced white jersey distinguishes the best young rider.

Bicycle helmets, when properly worn, prevent head injuries and are becoming more accepted as the "look" for riders. Indeed, bicycle helmets are required wear for child bicyclists in some states. Helmets vary in cost and design, but most are aerodynamic in shape. Cycling shoes are designed with a rigid sole to efficiently transfer energy from the downward push of the leg to the ball of the foot and so to the pedal. Shoes worn by professional racers can be almost impossible to walk in as the sole of the shoe is contoured to mesh with the pedal of the bicycle. Gloves and eyewear often provide the finishing touch to the cyclist's look. Gloves facilitate grip on the handlebars and may prevent injury in a fall. Eyewear provides protection from sun, wind, and insects.

Since the introduction of the bicycle to the general public, bicycle clothing has influenced everyday fashion. Bifurcated garments for bicycle wear in the late 1800s assisted in liberating women from cumbersome full-length skirts. The body-conforming look provided by modern materials, especially nylon and spandex knits, is evident in bicycle wear and fashion forms worn in the twenty-first century.

See also Activewear; Elastomers; Nylon.

Bibliography

Norcliffe, Glen. *The Ride to Modernity: The Bicycle in Canada, 1869–1900*. Toronto: University of Toronto Press, 2001.

Russell, P. "Recycling Femininity: Old Ladies and New Women." *Australian Cultural History* 13 (1994): 31.

Schreier, Barbara. "Sporting Wear." In *Men and Women: Dressing the Part*. Edited by Claudia Kidwell and Valerie Steele, 93–123. Washington D.C.: Smithsonian Institution Press, 1989.

Simpson, Claire. "Respectable Identities: New Zealand Nineteenth Century—'New Women'—on Bicycles." *The International Journal of the History of Sport* 18, no. 2 (2001): 54–77.

Karen L. LaBat

BIKINI

The bikini, a two-piece bathing suit of diminutive proportions, first appeared on the fashion scene in the summer of 1946. Its impact was compared to that of the atomic bomb tests conducted that same summer by the United States at Bikini Atoll in the Pacific Islands, which was arguably the source of its name. Both the French couturier Jacques Heim and the Swiss engineer Louis Reard are credited with launching the skimpy two-piece, which they dubbed the *atome* and bikini, respectively. The French model Michele Bernardini wore the first bikini at a fashion show in Paris. Her suit consisted of little more than two triangles of fabric for the bra, with strings that tied around the neck and back, and two triangles of fabric for the bottom, connected by strings at the hips.

The legendary fashion editor Diana Vreeland dubbed the bikini the "swoonsuit," and declared that it was the most important thing since the A-bomb, revealing "everything about a girl except her mother's maiden name." Vreeland worked at the time for *Harper's Bazaar*, which was the first magazine to showcase the bikini in America. The May 1947 issue featured a Toni Frissell photograph of a model wearing a rayon green-and-white-polka-dot bikini by the American sportswear designer Carolyn Schnurer.

Vreeland's comments about the bikini speak to the controversy that erupted when it first appeared. Unlike its two-piece counterparts, first seen on beaches in the late 1920s and 1930s, which exposed only a small section of midriff, the bikini bared a number of erogenous zones—the back, upper thigh, and for the first time, the navel—all at once. It was almost immediately banned, for religious reasons, in such countries as Spain, Portugal, and Italy and was shunned by American women as lacking in decency. Many public parks and beaches prohibited bikinis, and wearing them in private clubs and resorts was looked upon with disfavor.

The bikini remained a taboo novelty throughout the 1950s. Made even of such unusual fabrics as mink, grass, and porcupine quills, bikinis were worn mostly by screen sirens and pin-up girls like Brigitte Bardot, Jayne Mansfield, and Diana Dors, along with sophisticates on the beaches of resorts along the Riviera. They were also showcased in bathing suit beauty contests in vacation spots like Florida and California. One-piece and more modest two-piece suits, resembling the highly structured undergarments of the period, held favor with the majority of women until the end of the decade, when bikini sales started to rise.

An increased number of private pools in suburban backyards and a growing awareness of health and fitness were cited as possible causes for increased acceptance of bikini-wearing, at least within the privacy of one's own home. *Harper's Bazaar* touted the bikini as putting one close to the elements. American retailers, however, who reportedly sold more sleepwear resembling bikinis than actual bikini swimsuits, were ambivalent about the extent to which they should promote the sale of bikinis.

It was not until the 1960s that the bikini gained more widespread acceptance. Youth culture, celebrity endorsements, and innovations in textile technology such as the manufacture of spandex, helped establish the bikini, and its variations, as a mainstay in swimwear fashion. In 1960, the singer Brian Hyland immortalized the bikini with his hit song, "Itsy Bitsy Teenie Weenie Yellow Polka Dot Bikini." A crop of beach movies with bikini-clad teenagers, including the former Mouseketeer Annette Funicello, appeared. Ursula Andress wore one of the most famous bikinis, with a hip holster, in the 1962 James Bond film *Dr. No*—a variation of which was worn by Halle Berry in the 2002 Bond movie *Die Another Day*. *Sports Illustrated* published its first swimsuit issue in 1964, with Babette March wearing a bikini on the cover; appearing on the cover of *Sports Illustrated's* much-anticipated, annual swimsuit issue is now a coveted rite of passage for fashion models. The prevailing form of the early 1960s bikini was a structured bra top and low-slung, hip-hugging briefs, often embellished with ruffles and fringe.

Relaxing sexual mores and shifting views on modesty brought about more daring variations of the bikini in the late 1960s and early 1970s. In 1964, the American fashion designer Rudi Gernreich, whose progressive, androgynous clothing pushed fashion's boundaries, debuted his "monokini" or topless bathing suit. The black wool knit suit consisted of briefs with suspenders that extended between bared breasts and around the neck,

reminiscent of a bathing suit illustrated in 1940 by the Italian designer Umberto Brunescelli. Gernreich sold 3,000 of the monokinis by the end of the season. He again shocked the public when he unveiled his unisex thong bathing suits in 1974, and the "pubikini" in the mid 1980s. The thong bikini, which revealed the buttocks, has since become the unofficial uniform of professional bodybuilders, boxing ring girls who announce the rounds, and female dancers in music videos.

In 1974, the string bikini, or "tanga," consisting of little more than tiny triangles of cloth held together with ties at the hip and around the neck and back, emerged from Rio de Janeiro. Topless bathing, which had been accepted for some time in exotic beach locales such as Rio and Saint Tropez, started to gain popularity on public beaches in the 1970s, particularly in the United States.

By the late 1970s, the bikini, which had been pushed to extremely minimal proportions, had lost some of its shock value and allure, and in response the one-piece suit came into favor again. However, new one-piece styles were strongly influenced by the bikini phenomenon. A year after Gernreich's monokini was unveiled, "scandal suits" by Cole of California, also known as net bikinis, were popular, at once playfully revealing and concealing the body with solid patches of fabric connected with patches of net. The thong was also a clear antecedent of figure revealing one-pieces of the late 1970s and 1980s, which were cut high on the thigh, low at the neck and down the back, and open at the sides.

The trend toward less-structured, more figure-revealing suits such as the bikini corresponded with the sports and fitness craze that emerged in the 1970s and 1980s. Sport bikinis with racer-back tops and high-cut briefs appeared in the 1980s and were popular into the 1990s, worn, for example, as the official uniform for women's volleyball teams in the 1996 Olympics. In the twenty-first century, the bikini has regained popularity through new incarnations, many of which are, paradoxically, made with more fabric.

The "tankini," a two-piece that can provide as much coverage as a one-piece, has appeared, along with the "boy short" bottoms and surfer styles reminiscent of 1960s bikinis. High-end fashion houses such as Chanel, which debuted its minimal "eye-patch" bikini in 1995, contributed to the surfer craze with logo-emblazoned bikinis and surfboards in their Spring/Summer 2002 collection.

Despite the initial controversy, the bikini has become a perennial in swimwear fashion, particularly among the young. Youth-oriented culture, sexual emancipation, innovation in textile technology, an emphasis on sports and fitness, and the overarching societal shift to a more relaxed style of dress have all contributed to the bikini's success.

See also Swimwear; Teenage Fashions; Vreeland, Diana.

Bibliography

Esten, John. *Diana Vreeland Bazaar Years.* New York: Universe Books, 2001.

Lencek, Lena, and Gideon Bosker. *Making Waves: Swimsuits and the Undressing of America.* San Francisco: Chronicle Books, 1988.

Martin, Richard, and Harold Koda. *Splash!: A History of Swimwear.* New York: Rizzoli International, 1990.

Poli, Doretta Davanzo. *Beachwear and Bathing-Costume.* Modena, Italy: Zanfi Editori, 1995.

Probert, Christina. *Swimwear in Vogue Since 1910.* New York: Abbeville Press, 1981.

Tiffany Webber-Hanchett

BLAHNIK, MANOLO

Manolo Blahnik (b. 1942) was a designer and manufacturer of what were called "the sexiest shoes in the world"—beautiful, expensive, and highly coveted by many of the world's most fashionable women. Heir to a tradition of luxury shoemaking epitomized by André Perugia, Salvatore Ferragamo, and Roger Vivier, Blahnik produced shoes—"Manolos," to the cognoscenti—that became icons of the fashion culture at the turn of the twenty-first century. In the words of retailer Jeffrey Kalinsky, "There's never been a shoe designer whose reign as No. 1 shoe designer has lasted so long. His hold on the throne has no sign of doing anything but growing" (Larson, p. 6).

Manolo Blahnik was born on 27 November 1942 in the small village of Santa Cruz de la Palma in the Canary Islands, where his family—his Spanish mother, Manuela, his Czechoslovakian father, Enan, and his younger sister, Evangelina—had a banana plantation. Manuela, a voracious consumer of fashion magazines, bought clothes on shopping trips to Paris and Madrid

CEO of Neiman Marcus Direct, Karen Katz. Katz sits near a display of Manolo Blahnik shoes that are now available for purchase online. Manolo Blahnik's shoes are universally recognized. © AP/WORLD WIDE PHOTOS. REPRODUCED BY PERMISSION.

and had the island's dressmaker copy styles from fashion magazines. She designed her own shoes with the help of the local cobbler.

Manolo Blahnik moved to Geneva at the age of fifteen to live with his father's cousin. Here he had his first experiences of the theater, opera, and fine restaurants. He studied law for a short period but soon switched to literature and art history. Blahnik left Geneva for Paris in 1965 to study art and theater design. He worked at the trendy Left Bank shop GO, where he met the actress Anouk Aimée and the jewelry designer Paloma Picasso.

With Picasso's encouragement, Blahnik soon moved to London. While working at Feathers, a trendy boutique, he continued to cultivate his connections to the worlds of fashion and culture and was known for his unique style. But Blahnik was still searching for a specific vocation; the search then took him to New York City.

Blahnik arrived in New York City in 1969. Hired by the store Zapata, he began designing men's saddle shoes. In 1972 Blahnik was introduced to Ossie Clark, then one of London's most fashionable designers, who asked him to design the shoes for his women's collection. While the shoes were not commercially successful, the press noticed their originality of design. Blahnik had no formal training as a shoe maker and initally his designs were structually weak. He consulted with a London shoe manufacture in order to correct his lack of technical skills. Also during this time Blahnik met Diana Vreeland, who declared, "Young man, do things, do accessories. Do shoes" (McDowell, p. 84). This endorsement was seconded by China Machado, the fashion editor of *Harper's Bazaar*. *Women's Wear Daily* proclaimed Blahnik "one of the most exotic spirits in London" in 1973, and *Footwear News* described the Manolo Blahnik shoe on its front page as "the most talked about shoe in London." Blahnik purchased Zapata from its owner in 1973. In 1978 he introduced a line exclusive to Bloomingdale's, a well-known American retailer. Blahnik opened a second free-standing store a year later on New York's Madison Avenue.

Blahnik's creations received considerable publicity in the early 1980s, but his business was not running smoothly. Searching for alternatives, he was introduced by Dawn Mello, the vice president of Bergdorf Goodman, to an advertising copywriter named George Malkemus. Malkemus and his partner, Anthony Yurgaitis, went into business with Blahnik in 1982. They closed the Madison Avenue shop, opened a store on West Fifty-Fourth Street, and limited the distribution of Blahnik's shoes to such prestigious retailers as Barneys, Bergdorf Goodman, and Neiman Marcus. By 1984 the newspaper *USA Today* projected earnings of a million dollars for the New York shop alone. Manolo Blahnik shoes began to appear on the runways of designers from Yves Saint Laurent, Bill Blass, and Geoffrey Beene to Perry Ellis, Calvin Klein, Isaac Mizrahi, and John Galliano.

Manolo Blahnik's shoes became more popular than ever in the early twenty-first century. They appealed to an increasingly broad audience, in part because of their star billing on the television show *Sex and the City*. With production of "Manolos" limited to 10,000 to 15,000 pairs per month by four factories outside of Milan, the demand for these shoes exceeded the supply.

EXCELLENCE IN DESIGN

Manolo Blahnik won three awards from the Council of Fashion Designers of America in the 1980s and 1990s. The first special award was given in 1987; the second, for outstanding excellence in accessory design, in 1990. The third award came with the following tribute in 1997: "Blahnik has done for footwear what Worth did for the couture, making slippers into objects of desire, collectibles for women for whom Barbies are too girlish and Ferraris not girlish enough. . . . an incredible piston in the engine of fashion, there is almost no designer he has not collaborated with, no designer who has not turned to him to transform a collection into a concert."

The December 2003 issue of *Footwear News* quoted Alice Rawsthorn, the director of London's Design Museum, which had been the site of a recent Blahnik retrospective: "Technically, aesthetically and conceptually, he is one of the most accomplished designers of our time in any field, and is undeniably the world's most influential footwear designer" (Anniss, p. 16).

See also Clark, Ossie; Ferragamo, Salvatore; London Fashion; Shoes, Women's; Vreeland, Diana.

Bibliography

Anniss, Elisa. "Prince Charming." *Footwear News*, 8 December 2003.

Larson, Kirsten. "Blahnik Holds Reins Tight on His Manolos." *Footwear News*, 10 November 2003.

McDowell, Colin. *Manolo Blahnik*. New York: HarperCollins, 2000.

Reed, Julia. "Walk This Way." *Vogue*, November 2003.

Liz Gessner

BLASS, BILL*

William Ralph (Bill) Blass (1922–2002) was born in Fort Wayne, Indiana, in 1922. At the age of nineteen he left the Midwest and moved to New York City, where he studied briefly at Parsons School of Design. He worked as a sketch artist for a sportswear firm in 1940–1941, but his budding career was interrupted for military service in a counterintelligence unit in World War II. After the war Blass began working as a fashion designer, mainly for the firm of Maurice Rentner, Ltd. In 1970 he purchased the Rentner firm, renamed it Bill Blass Ltd., and saw the company take off as one of the most successful American fashion houses of the late twentieth century.

Blass created a glamorous but restrained look that won him a faithful following among women of style, including Nancy Reagan, Barbara Bush, Candice Bergen, and Barbara Walters. His day outfits drew heavily on tailoring and fabrics usually associated with menswear, including pinstriped gabardines, worsteds, and houndstooth checks. His eveningwear referenced Hollywood glamour. One of his most famous evening gowns consisted of a cashmere sweater top and a bouffant satin skirt.

Blass showed great business acumen in making Bill Blass Ltd. one of the leaders of the licensing boom that took off in the fashion industry in the 1980s. In rapid succession the firm concluded lucrative licensing deals for eyeglasses, executive gifts, fragrances, and a wide range of other fashion-related products. Blass retired from his business after suffering a stroke in 1998, and the company was sold to its backers in 1999. Blass died in 2002. Since then Bill Bass Ltd. has experienced a rapid turnover of designers, with the founder's first successor, Lars Nilsson, being replaced as the firm's chief designer by Michael Vollbracht in 2003, and Michael Bastian having since taken over from Vollbracht.

See also Celebrities; Fashion Marketing and Merchandising; First Ladies' Gowns; Perfume; Twentieth-Century Fashion.

Bibliography

Blass, Bill. *Bare Blass*. New York: HarperCollins, 2002.

Daria, Irene. *The Fashion Cycle: A Behind-the-Scenes Look at a Year with Bill Blass, Liz Claiborne, Donna Karan, Arnold Scaasi, and Adrienne Vittadini*. New York: Simon and Schuster, 1990.

O'Hagen, Helen, Kathleen Rowald, and Michael Vollbracht. *Bill Blass: An American Designer*. New York: Harry N. Abrams, 2002.

Wilson, Eric. "Bill Blass Receives a Retrospective." *Women's Wear Daily*, 16 May 2000.

John S. Major

BLAZER

Possibly a development of the nautical reefer jacket, a blazer is a loose-fitting and lightweight flannel sports jacket. Coming in both double-or single-breasted styles, although most are double-breasted, a blazer is generally tailored in either plain navy or black, has brass buttons, two side vents, is thigh length and in many cases has a breast-pocket badge. A well-constructed blazer can make even a pair of jeans appear smart. The blazer is generally considered to be a vital component of the "preppy" or "British look."

History

The familiar navy blazer traces its origins back to the captain of the frigate HMS *Blazer*, who had short double-breasted jackets cut in navy blue serge for his scruffy-looking crew when Queen Victoria visited his ship in 1837. The crew's "blazers" with their shining brass Royal Navy buttons impressed the Queen and soon became part of their dress uniform.

It is believed that the heavier double-breasted reefer jacket was the inspiration for the captain's original blazer design. What is less clear is how and why the naval blazer came to be worn by civilians. One likely explantion, and probably why so many owners of yachts and other sailing vessels wear blazers, is that many people who had no obvious association with the sea or indeed the navy could still have blazer jackets made originally for maritime experiences. With traditional outfitters such as Gieves and Hawkes, on London's Savile Row, cutting blazers for Royal Naval officers it is likely that many civilians would get their own tailors to copy a version for them. If buttons with emblems were not used then simple flat brass buttons were, although it would then become difficult to distinguish the blazer from the other sports jackets.

Divorced from any military background, the single-breasted blazer was the favored style of club jacket worn by rowing clubs in the nineteenth century. These would be made up in college, school, or club colors to be worn at special outdoor sporting events, such as the Henley Royal Regatta. Crests and other insignia were often embroidered in heavy gold thread on the left breast pocket, and the buttons were similar to those used by the navy. Men who were not in a sporting club might still wear a blazer but, as with the naval-inspired version, more likely using enamel buttons instead of brass.

Worn by many Europeans for both work and leisure and popularized by Brooks Brothers for the American market in the early twentieth century (and later in bright colors, such as bottle green or yellow, for golf attire), the authentic British blazer (and its imitations) have held a minor but consistent place in the male wardrobe for decades. The blazer's most recent revival was as essential executive dress in the 1980s, often worn with open shirt and cravat. Its popularity is limited somewhat by its reputation as being too formal for the young, and too stuffy for the "casual dress" office.

See also Jacket; Sports Jacket.

Bibliography

Amies, Hardy. *A, B, C of Men's Fashion*. London: Cahill and Company Ltd., 1964.

Byrde, Penelope. *The Male Image:—Men's Fashion in England 1300–1970*. London: B. T. Batsford Ltd., 1979.

Chenoune, Farid. *A History of Men's Fashion*. Paris: Flammarion, 1993.

De Marley, Diana. *Fashion for Men: An Illustrated History*. London: B. T. Batsford Ltd., 1985.

Keers, Paul. *A Gentleman's Wardrobe*. London: Weidenfeld and Nicolson, 1987.

Roetzel, Bernhard. *Gentleman: A Timeless Fashion*. Cologne, Germany: Konemann, 1999.

Schoeffler, O. E., and William Gale. *Esquire's Encyclopedia of 20th Century Fashions*. New York: McGraw-Hill, 1973.

Wilkins, Christobel. *The Story of Occupational Costume*. Poole: Blandford Press, 1982.

Tom Greatrex

BLOOMER COSTUME

In the spring of 1851, three leading women's rights activists, Elizabeth Cady Stanton (1815–1902), Cady's cousin, Elizabeth Smith Miller (1822–1911), and Amelia Jenks Bloomer (1818–1894), editor of the *Lily, a Ladies' Journal Devoted to Temperance and Literature*, wore similar outfits on the streets of Seneca Falls, New York—ensembles consisting of knee-length dresses over full trousers. In nineteenth-century America, trousers were an exclusively male garment and women wearing trousers in public caused a sensation. The national press quickly linked this dress reform style to Amelia Bloomer, who had been writing articles about it. Soon both the costume and its wearers were popularly identified as "Bloomers."

Amelia Bloomer's strong association with the freedom dress, as it was known by women's rights advocates, began with an article in the *Lily* in February 1851. Bloomer wrote more pieces about the outfit over the next several months, particularly emphasizing its advantages as a healthful, convenient alternative to the many petticoats, long skirts, and tight corsets of current fashionable dress. In response to readers' inquiries, Bloomer described the costume in detail in the *Lily's* May issue, and when it sold out, repeated the description the following month, stating:

Our skirts have been robbed of about a foot of their former length, and a pair of loose trousers of the same material as the dress, substituted. These latter extend from the waist to the ankle, and may be gathered into a band . . . We make our *dress* the same as usual, except that we wear no bodice, or a very slight one, the waist is loose and easy, and without whalebones . . . Our skirt is full, and falls a little below the knee.

But however closely she was connected with the Bloomer costume by the press and the public, Amelia Bloomer did not invent the style. Bloomer's full trousers gathered in at the ankle were called "Turkish trousers" and patterned after those worn by women in the Middle East. Since the eighteenth century, European and American women had also worn such trousers for fancy dress. French fashion plates of the 1810s show similar full trousers, called pantalets or pantaloons, peeking out under calf-length fashionable dresses. Although this style was far too daring for American women, by the 1820s children of both sexes were wearing short dresses over narrow, straight-legged trousers, also called pantalets. Boys exchanged pantalets for regular trousers when they grew too old for dresses (typically at five or six), while girls wore them throughout childhood. In their late teens, girls graduated to long dresses and continued to wear pantalets as underwear beneath their skirts.

Amelia Bloomer credited Elizabeth Smith Miller with introducing the freedom dress. There are differing accounts of how Miller came to design her outfit, but it is likely that Miller was aware of similar attire worn by women in utopian communities or sanatoriums. Beginning in 1827 with Community of Equality in New Harmony, Indiana, women in several American religious and utopian groups wore straight-legged trousers like children's pantalets under knee-length loose-fitting dresses. Variously styled similar outfits were also promoted for women performing calisthenic exercises and patients at water cure sanatoriums. These early instances of women wearing short dresses over trousers did cause occasional comment in the press, but because the garments were worn in closed societies or in women-only situations, they did not challenge the basic social order, unlike the public displays of the Bloomer costume in the 1850s.

The initial press coverage of Bloomer wearers during the summer of 1851 was not completely negative but before long the reality of women publicly wearing trousers brought out underlying fears of gender role reversals. In a society based on male dominance and female submission, men saw the Bloomer costume as a threat to the status quo and male leaders from newspaper editors to ministers decried the fashion. Satirical cartoons depicted Bloomer-clad women as crude louts indulging in the worst male vices or bossy wives holding sway over their husbands.

Although women's rights activists generally favored dress reform, they came to view the Bloomer costume as a counterproductive force. When activists lectured wearing the Bloomer costume, audiences focused on the controversial trousers instead of radical change in women's education, employment, and suffrage. Consequently, by the mid-1850s, most women's rights advocates had stopped wearing the Bloomer costume in public. Amelia Bloomer herself continued to wear it until 1858, when she cited a move to a new community

> Yesterday afternoon, Main street was thrown into intense commotion by the sudden appearance . . . of a pretty young woman, rigged out in the Bloomer costume—her dress being composed of a pink silk cap, pink skirt reaching to the knees and large white silk trousers, fitting compactly around the ankle, and pink coloured gaiters. . . . Old and young, grave and gay, descended into the street to catch a glimpse of the Bloomer as she passed leisurely and gracefully down the street, smiling at the sensation which her appearance had created. The boys shouted, the men laughed and the ladies smiled at the singular spectacle. . . . Few inquired the name of the Bloomer, because all who visited the Theatre during the last season, recognized in her a third or fourth rate actress, whose real or assumed name appeared in the bills as "Miss O'Neil." During the Season, however, we learn she severed her connexion with Mr. Potter's corps of Super numeraries and entered a less respectable establishment in this city.
>
> *Richmond Dispatch*, Tuesday, 8 July 1851, p. 2, c. 6.

The Bloomer Quick Step. The "Bloomer" described in the *Daily Richmond Times* account wore an outfit similar to the one seen on the girl illustrating the "Bloomer Quick Step." A publisher of dance scores apparently mistook the Bloomer costume as a fashion fad and released a series of illustrated "Bloomer" dances late in 1851. LIBRARY OF CONGRESS. REPRODUCED BY PERMISSION.

and the newly introduced cage crinoline, which eliminated the need for heavy petticoats, as the reasons she abandoned the freedom dress and returned to long skirts.

The Bloomer costume and a similar outfit called the American costume, which featured mannish, straight-legged trousers, were viable alternatives to constrictive fashionable dress during the second half of the nineteenth century. Although the number of women who wore such attire in public was very small, there are accounts of women wearing it in private when doing housework, farming, or traveling, especially in the west. In 1858 *Godey's Lady's Book* promoted a Bloomer-style costume for calisthenics and similar clothing was worn as bathing costume. Physical training educators used the Bloomer costume as a prototype in developing garments for increasingly active women's sports programs. The full trousers themselves became known as bloomers and, by the 1880s, were an essential element of the gymnasium or gym suit; short bloomers continued to be worn as part of gym suits into the 1970s. Bloomers reappeared in public during the bicycling craze of the 1890s, now worn as part of a suit with a jacket instead of a short dress. Women wearing bicycling bloomers in the 1890s were less controversial than when Amelia Bloomer and her friends donned their famous outfits in the 1850s, but not until the mid-twentieth century did women routinely wear trousers in public without criticism.

See also Dress Reform; Gender, Dress, and Fashion; Trousers.

Bibliography

Bloomer, Amelia. *The Lily, a Ladies' Journal Devoted to Temperance and Literature.* The February, March, April, May, and June 1851 issues of *The Lily* have articles by Amelia Bloomer related to female dress reform.

Cunningham, Patricia A. *Reforming Women's Fashion, 1850–1920: Politics, Health, and Art.* Kent, Ohio, and London: Kent State University Press, 2003. Comprehensive social history of women's dress reform with an excellent overview of the role of the Bloomer costume.

Fischer, Gayle V. *Pantaloons and Power: A Nineteenth-Century Dress Reform in the United States.* Kent, Ohio, and London: Kent State University Press, 2001. Detailed analysis of the cultural role of trousers in nineteenth-century American society.

Sims, Sally. "The Bicycle, the Bloomer and Dress Reform in the 1890s." In *Dress and Popular Culture.* Edited by Patricia A. Cunningham and Susan Vosco Lab, 125–145. Bowling Green, Ohio: Bowling Green State University Popular Press, 1991. Article about women wearing bloomers during the bicycle craze of the 1890s.

Colleen R. Callahan

BLOUSE

Although the term "blouse" now refers to a woman's separate bodice of a different material than the skirt, the word derives from the French name for a workman's loose smock and was first used in English for men's and boy's shirts. The feminine blouse has its antecedents in the undergarment known as a smock, shift, or chemise, which served the same purposes as the male shirt: worn next to the skin, it absorbed bodily soil and protected outer garments.

In the early 1860s full-sleeved loose bodices came into vogue, called Garibaldi shirts since they were modeled on the famous red shirt of the Italian nationalist and freedom fighter. *Peterson's Magazine* in May 1862 (p. 421) thought these blouses, often made in red or black wool or white or striped cotton, were warm, comfortable, inexpensive, and practical, extending the life of a silk skirt which outlived its matching bodice. Puffed "in bag fashion" at the waist, Garibaldi shirts sometimes created an ungainly silhouette with a hooped skirt, but a boned waistband called a Swiss belt could be worn to gracefully ease the transition between top and bottom. The idea of fashionable separates for women had emerged. In January 1862 *Godey's Lady's Magazine* (p. 21) predicted that the advent of the feminine shirt was "destined to produce a change amounting to a revolution in ladies' costume."

By the 1890s, these bodices, now called shirtwaists or waists, had indeed dramatically increased the average woman's clothing options. Shirtwaists could be severely tailored with masculine-style detachable starched collars and cuffs, or very feminine in lightweight fabrics trimmed with lace, insertion, and other lavish decoration. Shirt-waists were suitable with tailored suits, with a skirt for housework and sportswear, and with bloomers for cycling or as gym costumes, while dressier versions were worn for afternoon receptions, the theater, and evening wear. In 1895, Montgomery Ward's spring and summer catalog (p. 37) told customers, "Your old dress skirt worn with a neat laundered waist provides you with a cool, comfortable and up-to-date costume that will quite astonish you." They commended the shirtwaist as "by far the most becoming and sensible article of woman's attire to receive fashion's universal approval."

Although they could be made at home and commercial patterns were widely available, shirtwaists, with their loose fit, were the first women's garment to be successfully mass-produced. Ready-made waists could be purchased at incredibly low prices—as little as twenty-five cents from Sears, Roebuck and Company in 1897. The burgeoning apparel industry utilized economies of scale and power machinery, but cheap garments were also the result of sweatshop production by unskilled and often exploited labor. Workers could toil seventy hours a week for as little as thirty cents a day, frequently in egregious conditions.

One of the many sweatshops in Manhattan churning out these popular garments was the Triangle Shirtwaist Company, which occupied the top three floors of a ten-story building and ensured maximum production by locking the exit doors. When fire broke out on 25 March 1911, many of the 500 workers, mainly Jewish immigrants aged thirteen to twenty-three, were trapped; 146 women died in less than fifteen minutes.

While this tragedy helped crystallize calls for reform, led by organizations such as the International Ladies Garment Workers Union founded in 1900, mass production continued to create victims as well as affordable clothing.

Many sweatshop workers no doubt wore shirtwaists, for these practical, inexpensive, and unobtrusive garments were a boon to women in factories, offices, and those who would later be dubbed "pink collar" workers. Yet at the turn of the century, the well-to-do, imperiously handsome women immortalized by illustrator Charles Dana Gibson were often depicted wearing immaculate starched shirtwaists during vigorous walks or rounds of golf. The "Gibson girl" soon became such an American icon that she gave her name to styles of waists and the preferred high stand collars. As fashion evolved, shirtwaists gradually became more relaxed; by the 1910s the "middy blouse," modeled on the loose sailor-collared shirts of seamen, was especially popular with girls and for general sport and utility wear.

The shirtwaist, now also called a blouse, proved remarkably accommodating in style and price. By 1915 Gimbel's catalog (p. 44) could state, "The shirtwaist has become an American institution. The women of other lands occasionally wear a shirtwaist—the American woman occasionally wears something else." Mass-produced or custom-made, serviceable or dainty, the versatile blouse played an essential role in the democratization of fashion. *Suiting Everyone* (Kidwell and Christman, p. 145) states, "For the first time in America, women dressed with a uniformity of look which blurred economic and social distinctions."

While not as universally worn, the feminine blouse adapted itself to almost every occasion through the mid-twentieth century. The haute couture ensembles of elegant matrons often featured blouses to match suit jacket linings, while college girls coordinated Peter-Pan collared permanent-press blouses with casual skirts or slacks. As more women joined the labor force—nearly a third of the American labor force was female by 1960—the blouse continued to be the workhorse of clerical workers, teachers, and those in service industries. In 1977 John T. Molloy in *The Woman's Dress for Success Book* (pp. 54, 55) famously advocated a "uniform" for the executive woman consisting of a skirted suit and blouse—but warned that removing the jacket would make her look like a secretary. He argued that since the blouse made a

measurable difference in the psychological impact of the suit, it should not be selected for emotional or aesthetic reasons, but for its message. Molloy claimed his research showed a white blouse gave high authority and status, and his recommended styles included man-tailored shirts with one button open and the "acceptable nonfrilly style" with a built-in bow tie at the neck—the so-called floppy bow that soon became a "dress for success" cliché.

While blouses were important in reflecting the wearer's personal style, this message was sometimes over-simplified. Toby Fischer-Mirkin's 1995 book *Dress Code* (p. 94), for example, definitively states that an unbuttoned shirt collar indicates an open-minded, flexible woman, a loose collar reflects a casual woman who may be slack in her work, while an angular or oddly shaped collar proclaims a highly creative and unconventional individual.

In the late twentieth and early twenty-first century, the blouse—like the earlier Garibaldi shirt and shirtwaist—has been overshadowed by trendier permutations of feminine tops, from T-shirts and turtlenecks to sweaters and man-tailored shirts. Introduced less than one hundred and fifty years ago, the concept of women's separates has become a democratic sartorial style.

See also Shirtwaist; T-Shirt.

Bibliography

1897 Sears Roebuck Catalogue. Reprint edited by Fred L. Israel. New York: Chelsea House Publisher, 1968.

Fischer-Mirkin, Toby. *Dress Code.* New York: Clarkson Potter, 1995.

Gimbel's Illustrated 1915 Fashion Catalog. Reprint, New York: Dover Publications, Inc., 1994.

Kidwell, Claudia B., and Margaret C. Christman. *Suiting Everyone: The Democratization of Clothing in America.* Washington, D.C.: Smithsonian Institution Press, 1974.

Molloy, John T. *The Woman's Dress for Success Book.* New York: Warner Books, 1977.

Montgomery Ward & Company's Spring and Summer 1895 Catalogue. Reprint, New York: Dover Publications, Inc., 1969.

Schreier, Barbara A. *Becoming American Women: Clothing and the Jewish Immigrant Experience, 1880–1920.* Chicago: Chicago Historical Society, 1994.

H. Kristina Haugland

BODY PIERCING

Body piercing is the practice of inserting jewelry (usually metal, though wood, glass, bone, or ivory, and certain plastics are used as well) completely through a hole in the body. Piercing is often combined with other forms of body art, such as tattooing or branding, and many studios offer more than one of these services. While virtually any part of the body can be, and has been, pierced and bejeweled (for evidence, see the well-known Web site http://www.bmezine.com) widely pierced sites include ear, eyebrow, nose, lip, tongue, nipple, navel, and genitals.

Much of what popularly passes for the history of body piercing is in fact fictitious. In the 1970s, the Los Angeles resident Doug Malloy, an eccentric and wealthy proponent of piercing, set forth with charismatic authority a set of historical references connecting contemporary Western body piercing to numerous ancient practices. He declared, for example, that ancient Egyptian royalty pierced their navels (consequently valuing deep navels), Roman soldiers hung their capes from rings through their nipples, the *hafada* (a piercing through the skin of the scrotum) was a puberty rite brought back from the Middle East by French legionnaires, and that the *guiche* (a male piercing of the perineum) was a Tahitian puberty rite performed by respected transvestite priests. No anthropological accounts bear out these claims.

What facts can be sorted from the fiction nonetheless attest to the remarkable antiquity of piercing. The oldest fully preserved human being found, the 5,300-year-old "ice-man" of the Alps, shows evidence of ear-lobe piercing. Like many with a serious interest in piercing in the twenty-first century, the ice-man has stretched his lobes, in his case to a diameter of about seven millimeters. Artifacts as well as bodies offer evidence of ancient single and multiple ear piercings from as early as the ninth century B.C.E.

While Malloy's claims are largely imaginative, there are geographically diverse cultures in which piercing has been continually practiced for quite some time. Ear and nose piercing seem to be, and seem to have been, the most popular; indeed, there are far too many examples to list here, and the following instances should be taken as representative rather than anything close to exhaustive. Many Native American peoples practiced ear or nose—generally septum—piercing (the latter most famously among the Nez Percé of the American

Northwest). Multiple ear piercing was practiced by both men and women in the ancient Middle East, and a mummy believed to be that of Queen Nefertiti of Egypt, sports two piercings in each ear. The Maoris of New Zealand, though better known for their intricate and elegant tattoo designs, have also long practiced ear piercing, which along with nose piercing is widespread among native peoples of both New Zealand and Australia. Ear piercing for girls forms part of traditional rites in Thai and Polynesian cultures. Ear piercing among the Alaskan Tlingits could be an indication of social status, as could nose piercing.

Stretched ear piercings—in which the hole is gradually enlarged by the use of weights or by the insertion of successively larger pieces of jewelry—appear in diverse cultures as well. In Africa, the Masai and Fulani are known for ear-cartilage piercings, which may be stretched (a much slower and more difficult process than stretching earlobe piercings). Images and artifacts from native Central American cultures show stretched lobes with jewelry much like that used by contemporary enthusiasts. East Asian images and sculptures, some many centuries old, show long stretched lobes as well; these are emblematic especially of Buddhist saints. The Dayaks of Borneo traditionally pierce and dramatically stretch the earlobe; other piercings—including the *ampallang*, a horizontal piercing through the penis—have also been attributed to them.

Nostril piercing may have originated in the Middle East, and has been practiced in India for thousands of years, particularly among women. It may be through their interest in Eastern cultures that the hippies of North America took to nostril piercing around the 1970s.

While not as prevalent as the piercing of the ears or nose, lip piercing is also geographically widespread. Women in many regions of East Africa have traditionally worn lip piercings with plugs, while Dogon women may pierce their lips with rings. The men among some native Alaskan peoples also pierced the lower lip, either doubly or singly.

Other piercings are much less attested to in older or more traditional contexts. There is some indication of Central American tongue piercing, for example among the Mayas, but this may have been temporary, intended to draw blood for ceremonial purposes rather than for the lasting insertion of jewelry. More reliable is the evidence of the Indian Kama Sutra (written by the sixth century C.E.) where penis piercings resembling the contemporary *apadravya*—a vertical piercing through the penis—are described as enhancing the pleasure of both the penis-bearer and his partner.

There may also have been temporary upsurges of interest prior to contemporary versions—some sources, for example, report a fad for nipple piercings among women in the late nineteenth century in both London and Paris. (See both Kern and Harwood.) Here, as in its contemporary form, piercing is removed from its more traditional social functions, such as marking one as a member of a community or as being of a particular status, and more specifically erotic as well as decorative functions are noted.

Recent History and Subcultures

"Body piercing" is generally distinguished from (unstretched) earlobe piercing, and is more recent in popularity. In its late-twentieth-century version, the interest in such piercing can be traced largely to a handful of figures, particularly Doug Malloy along with Jim Ward and Fakir Musafar (Roland Loomis) in the United States and Mr. Sebastian (Alan Oversby) in the United Kingdom.

With Malloy serving as patron and in some respects teacher, Ward began making specialized piercing jewelry in the early 1970s (Ward is credited with the design of the ubiquitous captive-bead ring, also called the ball-closure ring). He and Musafar opened the Gauntlet, a piercing shop that seemed a natural outgrowth of the jewelry business, in Los Angeles in 1975. Gauntlet shops in other major cities opened in succeeding years. Later he began the journal *PFIQ* (*Piercing Fans International Quarterly*), an important source of both information and community for those interested in body piercing. Mr. Sebastian, likewise taught at first by Malloy, was more secretive with his techniques, but was widely known as a piercer. For both, the initial clientele was largely gay men from the sadomasochistic (s/m) community.

In the 1980s, Elayne Binnie (known as Elayne Angel in the early 2000s) joined the staff of the Gauntlet, attracting many more women clients. Angel, who was the first person to obtain the "Master Piercer" certificate from the Gauntlet, is also widely credited with popularizing the tongue piercing (having five herself). Along with the navel, the tongue is one of the most popular piercings in the early twenty-first century.

Musafar, who later fell out with his former partner, is responsible for the term "modern primitive," with which a number of highly pierced people have identified.

Musafar emphasizes commonalities between contemporary and older, particularly tribal, traditions; he also emphasizes the psychological and spiritual elements of all sorts of body modifications, including piercing. Many serious piercers in the early 2000s are trained in his seminars. Modern primitives may ritualize the processes and meaning of their body art and often draw on traditional cultures for design in both piercing jewelry and other arts, such as tattooing.

From its start among gay leathermen, piercing grew in popularity to include a number of communities. Among the most influential in the spread of piercing's popularity was punk. The punks in both the United States and the United Kingdom were fond of non-ear piercings, particularly on the face (lip, nostril, and cheek piercings attained popularity early in this group). The punk emphasis is on rebellion and unconventionality; the modern primitive emphasis on cross-cultural connection and spirituality is quite absent here, replaced by punk's interesting combination of outrage and playfulness.

Music and cultural styles that emerged out of punk often have a place for piercing as well. The straightedge movement, generally dated to the early 1980s, though it attained more popularity later on, provides today a large subset of the heavily pierced. Along with tattoos (often of straightedge symbols such as XXX or sXe) piercings show both the punk influence on straightedge music and the subculture's deep interest in the body (most who identify as straightedge are vegetarian or vegan and abstain from the use of alcohol and other recreational drugs). Straightedge thinking may emphasize the slightly mind-altering sensation of the piercing experience, incorporating elements of the modern primitive emphasis on ecstasies (overcoming the limits of time and selfhood in experience) alongside punk unconventionality. The Goth scene emergent in the early 1980s and again in the 1990s has a religious sensibility very different from modern primitive spirituality, tending toward highly stylized and cultivated artifice in its use of religious, particularly Catholic and Wiccan, imagery. As these associations suggest, Goth style tends toward intense theatricality, and visually striking piercings are widespread; the "dark" emphasis of much Goth culture also meets up with an acceptance of s/m imagery and the pain that may be inherent in body piercing.

The rave scene emergent in the 1990s also includes an interest in visually compelling piercings, particularly facial and navel piercings. Often glow-in-the-dark or battery-powered flashing jewelry is used, giving the piercings a hypnotic effect in dimly lit spaces and playing off the more rapid pulse of the very high beats-per-minute music generally favored.

Not all highly pierced groups or scenes are connected to particular species of music, of course. S/m communities remain strongholds of piercing. Here both the physicality of the piercing experience (and the enhanced sensation often provided by healed piercings) and the symbolism of the jewelry are significant—with the significance ranging from pain-tolerance to community affiliation to ownership. Piercing is also popular, though not so much as tattooing, in biker culture. Here large-gauge (thickness) piercings are often favored, complimenting the traditional bold lines of biker tattooing. Finally, many people also simply understand themselves as members of a body-modification or body-art community, with a respect for body modification and an interest in its being practiced well—as well as in having their own bodies modified.

The Move to the Mainstream

Most piercers, however, will emphasize that the people who get pierced do not often fit into any of these groups, and may indeed be, for example, corporate or grandparental types whose under-the-clothes piercings almost certainly go unsuspected. The more fashionable piercings—particularly tongue, navel, nostril, and eyebrow—tend to attract a younger and more specifically (or overtly) fashion-oriented clientele. A significant influence on the entry of body piercing into mainstream fashion has been popular music, as formerly "edgy" or marginal looks were assimilated into pop and made widely visible in music videos. The most famous instance here is undoubtedly the inspirationally pierced navel of the singer Britney Spears, which has taken thousands if not millions of young women into piercing shops they might not otherwise have frequented.

In general, "mainstream" body piercing involves relatively small-gauge jewelry, often (particularly for navel piercings) with ornamental, even jeweled, beads. Gold, while expensive, may be used as well as more commonly used nonreactive metals including stainless steel and titanium. Perhaps in response, those who identify as more marginal or as members of the body-art community tend to prize piercings that are unusual in location or style, such as surface piercings (piercings that go under the skin rather than through a protruding part of the body—the eyebrow is a surface piercing, but less common versions include the nape or front of the neck, the back along the spine, and the wrists), multiple piercings in a single location (even the navel offers top, bottom, left, and right options), or very large-gauge piercings.

As body piercing has grown in popularity, it has come to be increasingly regulated, though it is still much less so than tattooing. In most of the United States, and in parts of Canada and Australia, local legislation sets hygienic standards via departments of health, and limits the piercing permitted to minors, either banning it outright or requiring parental permission. Interestingly, earlobe piercing is almost invariably excluded from this legislation, a reflection of its well-established and unthreatening presence. The Association of Professional Piercers, a voluntary organization, promotes self-regulation regarding cleanliness standards and piercing practices, and many piercers are members.

Legislation in the United Kingdom is somewhat ambiguous, although piercing seems in general to be legal so long as its purpose is solely cosmetic. In 1991, Mr. Sebastian was found guilty of "gross bodily harm" to thirteen of his clients (they had not complained, but their names were located in his records), on the principle that one cannot assent to assault or mutilation. Cosmetic piercing is regulated in London, and ear piercing elsewhere in the United Kingdom, but it is not quite clear how or whether laws on injury, surgery, or female circumcision might apply (see Tameside Metropolitan Borough Council).

Despite occasional suggestions that the proper legislation regarding body piercing is to ban it outright, the phenomenon seems unlikely to disappear altogether. Undoubtedly its popularity will wane, perhaps to wax again at some point, but the longevity of the practice among human beings suggests that it has an enduring, as well as cross-cultural, appeal.

See also Plastic and Cosmetic Surgery; Punk; Scarification; Tattoos.

Bibliography

Camphausen, Rufus C. *Return of the Tribal*. Rochester, Vt.: Inner Traditions Ltd., 1997.

Harwood, Bernhardt. *The Golden Age of Erotica*. New York: Paperback Library, 1968.

Kern, Stephen. *Anatomy and Destiny*. Indianapolis, Ind.: Bobbs-Merrill Company, 1974.

Larratt, Shannon. *ModCon: The Secret World of Extreme Body Modification*. Toronto: BME Books, 2002.

Vale, V., and Andrea Juno. *Modern Primitives*. San Francisco: V/Search, 1989.

Internet Resource

Tameside Metropolitan Borough Council. 2000. "Guidelines for the Practice of Body Piercing." Available from <http:// www.tameside.gov.uk/licensing/bodypiercingguidelines. html>.

Karmen MacKendrick

BOHEMIAN DRESS

"Bohemian" was the label attached to artists, writers, students, and intellectuals in early nineteenth-century France after the turbulent years of the Revolution. The reason for the name was that these artists were likened to wandering gypsies, and it was believed (incorrectly) that gypsies came from Bohemia in central Europe. With rapid economic and social change, the

Greenwich Village café. The Gaslight coffee house in New York's Greenwich Village in the late 1950s, and others like it, provided the setting for the Bohemian movement throughout the years. Artists, writers and students used their dress to illustrate both their poverty and their originality. © BETTMANN/CORBIS. REPRODUCED BY PERMISSION.

artist's status became financially insecure as the market replaced the old system of patronage. At the same time the Romantic Movement introduced the seductive notion of the "Artist as Genius." An artist was no longer someone with a particular talent, but became a special kind of person. In earlier times dress had signified social status, a trade, membership of a princely retinue, or a profession. Now for the first time, dress became part of the performance of an individual personality, as the young bohemians used costume to signify their poverty and originality.

There was no single chronological line of development in bohemian dress; rather, there were several different strategies. In the 1830s the styles of dress favored by French bohemians had echoes of the Romantics' love of the medieval and of orientalism. Influenced by the fevered poetry of Byron, they favored rich materials and colors, wide-brimmed hats, and long flowing curls.

A second style, described by the novelist Henri Murger (1822–1861), whose bohemian tales are best-known today as the basis for Giacomo Puccini's opera, *La Bohème*, was simply the uniform of abject poverty, threadbare coats and trousers, leaking shoes, and general dishevelment. A third influential style was the restrained black and white of the male dandy. Dandyism originated in Regency England and, although distinct from bohemian dress, was influential in that dandies, such as George Bryan "Beau" Brummell (1778–1840), developed a cult of the self. They went to such lengths that their appearances became almost works of art in their own right, blurring the dividing line between life and art. This was significant for the bohemian way of life, since for many bohemians this line was blurred in any case, and style, surroundings, and dress became as stylized and carefully wrought as any more conventional artwork.

Then there were those who were influenced by the nineteenth-century movements for dress reform. Dress reformers advocated an end to the distortions and restrictions of fashion, especially women's fashions, and searched for a permanently beautiful form of clothing that would put an end to the fashion cycle. The English Pre-Raphaelites were the best known such group. One of their members, William Morris (1834–1896), who built a successful business on the design and sale of alternative textiles, wallpapers, and embroidery, designed robes for his wife, Jane, that were far removed from the crinolines and corsets of the mid-Victorian period. These innovators were part of the Arts and Crafts movement that spread throughout Europe during the second half of the nineteenth century and by the 1890s had reached Germany, where the styles were combined with art nouveau motifs. The painter Vasily Kandinsky (1866–1944), for example, designed dresses for his lover, the artist Gabriele Munter (1877–1962), which had the natural Pre-Raphaelite line, with full sleeves and loose waists for ease of movement.

Kandinsky and Munter belonged to the artistic and bohemian culture that flourished in and around Munich during this time, where bohemianism was taken to extremes seldom seen before or since. Some of these eccentrics and revolutionaries expressed themselves by adopting what amounted to fancy dress, in imitation of ancient Greece and Rome, or sometimes borrowing from peasant culture.

Bohemian dress, like the whole bohemian counterculture, underwent many vicissitudes during the course of the twentieth century. Between World War I and II, bohemianism became for many young people little more than a phase during which they would dress in a picturesquely rebellious manner, live in artists' studios, and go to bohemian parties—a way of life not so different from that of students in the twenty-first century. The link between genuine creativity and a style of life became attenuated. The idea of "lifestyle" was developing, even if the word did not come into use until after World War II. Yet the idea of bohemia as a privileged and special place—or even just an idea—remained as a kind of umbrella concept beneath which society's dissidents, geniuses, misfits, and eccentrics still gathered to encourage and support one another. For example, lesbians in the 1930s often regarded themselves as bohemians rather than as belonging to a distinct "lesbian subculture."

After 1945 this changed. Bohemia had always effectively been a land of youth, but it was only with the development of the mass media and popular music that the existence and costuming of the generational divide became explicit. Jazz, swing, and rock and roll came with their own uniforms of rebellion. Then came beatniks with, for young women, white lips, black kohl-ringed eyes, peasant skirts, black stockings, and "arty" jewelry—but now for the first time such styles were quickly broadcast via the mass media to a much wider circle of bohemian wanna-bes. The 1957 Audrey Hepburn film, *Funny Face*, for example, satirized Greenwich Village style—at the beginning of the film the star is shown working in a bookshop, dressed in a tweed jumper, black turtleneck sweater, horn-rimmed-glasses, and flat ballerina shoes.

Artists and writers that were displaced as minority groups took center stage in the creation of countercultural dress. Alongside the huge influence of black American style, beginning with the zoot suit of the 1940s, the emergent lesbian and gay culture began to make an impact. Although the most familiar form of alternative dress in the 1960s and 1970s was the hippie style, which boasted bricolage, secondhand clothes, and ethnic items to create a statement about an alternative lifestyle opposed to the consumer society.

Yet at the dawn of the third millennium, it hardly seems as if rebellion can any longer be expressed in the wearing of outrageous garments. Bohemian dress was always a provocation, but in Western, or westernized urban settings, at least, there hardly exists a style of dress that can shock anymore. Grunge, and the styles of Nirvana in the early 1990s, was the last form of dress that aimed to express dissent of the traditional kind. But, like every style, it was no sooner seen on stage than it appeared in every mass-market fashion store in the Western world.

Some have suggested that rebellion of the old bohemian sort is no longer possible, since there no longer exists a single mainstream or dominant form of society against which to rebel. Instead we have what one French sociologist terms "neo-tribes,"—groups with fluid membership of young people who are no longer confrontational, but have an allegiance to certain styles of music, dress, and clubbing. There are exceptions: Goth style and the accoutrements of the anti-globalization movement single out participants fairly definitively. Yet what was once the casual originality of bohemian dress has become the height of celebrity fashion and of high-street style. It therefore follows that in the twenty-first century, when everyone is bohemian, no one can any longer be.

See also Brummell, George (Beau); Subcultures.

Bibliography

Beard, Rick, and Leslie Cohen Berlowitz, eds. *Greenwich Village: Culture and Counter Culture.* Camden, N.J.: Rutgers University Press, 1993.

David, Hugh. *The Fitzrovians: A Portrait of Bohemian Society, 1900–1955.* London: Michael Joseph, 1988.

Siegel, Jerrold. *Bohemian Paris: Culture, Politics and the Boundaries of Bourgeois Life, 1830-1890.* New York: Viking Press, 1986.

Wilson, Elizabeth. *Bohemians: The Glamorous Outcasts.* Camden, N.J.: Rutgers University Press, 2001.

Elizabeth Wilson

BOOTS

The modern definition of the term "boots" is a loose one; footwear covering the entire foot and lower leg. This is believed to have developed from one of the earliest forms of footwear—a two-piece unit covering the foot and lower leg. This wrapping of the leg formed the building block on which all modern forms of the boot have derived.

Throughout history the essential form of the boot has been adapted to fit the needs of the wearer and the culture. Materials vary as does form—but the essential purpose of the boot remains the same throughout most cultures; to provide protection from the elements. Boots are usually made of leather, but have been made of many other materials, including silk, cotton, wool, felt, and furs. A perfect example of this is the *kamiks* of the Inuits. The Inuits pride themselves on their efficient use of their resources and their traditional boots, called *kamiks*, are no exception. Crafted of caribou hide or sealskin (their two main food sources), these boots are warm and waterproof thanks to an ingenious raised band of stitching with sinews that ensures a waterproof join at the sole and upper.

The oldest known depiction of boots is in a cave painting from Spain, which has been dated between 12,000 and 15,000 B.C.E. This painting seems to depict man in boots of skin and a woman in boots of fur. Persian funerary jars have been found which date from around 3000 B.C.E. and are made in the shape of boots. Boots were also found in the tomb of Khnumhotep (2140–1785 B.C.E.) in Egypt. The Scythians of about 1000 B.C.E. were reported by the Greeks to have worn simple boots of untanned leather with the fur turned in against the leg. These simple baglike boots were then lashed to the leg by a thong of leather. This basic form can be found in the traditional dress of many Asiatic and Artic cultures as well.

In the ancient world, boots represented ruling power and military might. Emperors and kings wore ornate and colorful examples; this was a significant distinction when the majority of the population went barefoot. Leather was expensive, and roman emperors were cited as wearing colorful jeweled and embroidered examples—even with gold soles. Boots were also already associated with the military—the *campagnus* was worn by the highest-ranking officers and some senators in ancient Rome, the height of the boot denoting rank. Other styles, such as the high, white leather *phaecasim*, were worn as ceremonial garb.

During the Middle Ages, the styles shoes and boots established by the ancient world continued. Courtiers of the Carolingian period were depicted wearing high boots laced halfway up the leg. Under Charlemagne the term *brodequin* is first used for these laced boots and roman terms rejected. The *huese*, a high, soft leather shoe and forerunner to the boot appeared toward the ninth century. During the twelfth through fourteenth centuries, a short, soft boot called the *estivaux* was popular. Toward the middle of the fourteenth century, people often wore soled hose, which precluded the need for shoes and boots.

In the fifteenth century, men wore long boots that reached the thighs and were usually of brown leather. This style was prevalent among all of the classes. Despite this widespread popularity, this was emphatically not an appropriate style for women; in fact this was one of the chief criminal charges against Joan of Arc in 1431. It was more common for women of the fourteenth century to wear laced ankle boots, which were often lined in fur.

By the sixteenth century, high boots of soft perfumed leather were worn to meet upper stocks and would soon develop into the wide, floppy cavalier styles of the first half of the seventeenth century. Soft boots folded down— and slouchy boots worn with boot hose elaborately trimmed with lace flaring out into wide funnel shapes to fold down over the boots—characterized these fashions. Boot hose was worn both for its decorative qualities and to protect the costly silk stockings. These high boots featured a leather strap on the instep (the *surpied*), and a strap under the foot, which anchored the spur in place (the *soulette*). They had funnel tops, which covered the knee for riding and could be turned down for town wear. Under Louis XIII a shorter, lighter model of boot emerged, the *ladrine* (Boucher, p. 266). In the early years of the eighteenth century, under the influence of the French court, boots disappeared except for those worn by laborers, soldiers, and devotees of active sports, such as hunting and riding.

The seventeenth century had seen the emergence of the first military uniforms, and the boot had played an essential role in this standardization. The high-legged cavalier boot of the previous century was transformed by a highly polished and rigid leg—the prototypical military jackboot. The high top and rigid finish was supremely practical and successful at protecting legs while on horseback. This style was seen as early as 1688 and continued to be worn into the 1760s. Other popular styles were essentially military in origin. One notable example was the Hessian or Souvaroff, which was brought to England by German soldiers circa 1776. This style featured a trademark center front dip and was trimmed with tassels and braid.

For the more gentlemanly pursuit of sport riding, the high cavalier boot of the seventeenth century developed into a softer and closer fitting "jockey" style boot with the top folded down under the knee for mobility which showed the brown leather or cotton lining. This style originated in 1727 and became increasingly fashionable into the 1770s. The popularity of the English style riding boot was a part of the greater Anglomania of the eighteenth century and foreshadows the "Great Masculine Renunciation" that would follow in the wake of the French Revolution and the early years of the nineteenth century.

The vogue for democratic, English style dress had made the boot more popular than ever. Beau Brummel epitomized the radical simplicity of the dandy. His typical morning dress was reported as "Hessians and pantaloons or top boots and buckskins" (Swann, p. 35). Despite this endorsement, the shape and design of the boot inevitably shifted with fashion. The Wellington supplanted the Hessian since the tassels and braid of the Hessian were difficult to wear with the newly fashionable trousers. The Wellington boot was essentially a Hessian that had had its curved top cut straight across with a simple binding. This style was reputedly developed by the Duke of Wellington in 1817 and dominated menswear in the first quarter of the nineteenth century. The success of the Wellington was so pronounced that it was said in 1830, "the Hessian is a boot only worn with tight pantaloons. The top boot is almost entirely a sporting fashion ... although they are worn by gentlemen in hunting, they are in general use among the lower orders, such as jockeys, grooms, and butlers. The Wellington ... the only boot in general wear" (*The Whole Art of Dress* as quoted in Swann, p. 43).

The Blucher was another important style of the early nineteenth century named for a popular war hero. The Blucher was a practical, front-laced ankle boot worn by laborers in the eighteenth century, which had popularly been known as the "high-low." After 1817 this style was known as the Blucher and was worn for casual and sport wear. This basic laced-front style would prove to be popular in modified forms to this day, and has served as the basis of the modern high-top sneaker, hiking boot, and combat boot.

The popularity of boots began to influence women's fashions during the early years of the nineteenth century. Women had been wearing masculine-style boots for riding and driving during the eighteenth century, and by the 1790s their styles had become distinctly feminine with tight lacing, high heels, and pointed toes. By 1815 fashion periodicals begin to suggest boots for walking and daywear; boots were widespread by 1830. The most common style was the Adelaide, a flat, heelless ankle boot with side lacing. This style would remain in use for more than fifty years.

During the Victorian period boots of all kinds reached the peak of their popularity. The trend was for greater comfort and practicality in footwear for both men and women and was aided by technological advances like the sewing machine and vulcanized rubber. In 1837 the British inventor J. Sparkes Hall presented Queen Victoria with the first pair of boots with an elasticized side boot gusset. This easy to wear slip on style would be popular throughout the rest of the century with both men and women. By mid-century the two most popular styles were the elastic side—also known as the congress, side-spring, Chelsea, or garibaldi— and the front-lacing boot. The two most popular styles for front lace were the Derby and the Balmoral. The latter boot was designed for Prince Albert and was similar in style to the modern wrestling or boxing shoe. By the late Victorian period, balmorals or "bals" were most popular and frequently featured contrasting cloth tops and pearl button closures.

Although the Wellington had been almost entirely abandoned in England in favor of the short ankle boot by the 1860s, the style survived in United States and contributed to the development of the cowboy boot. The cowboy boot is believed to have originated in Kansas, and is considered to be a combination of the Wellington and the high heeled boots of the Mexican *vaqueros*. In the United States the Hessian continued to be worn as well and can be seen in photographs of the outlaw "Billy the Kid" from the 1870s.

For women in the mid-century, the majority of footwear was in boot form. The elastic side was a popular choice for daywear, but by the 1860s was replaced by front lace balmorals in satin or colored leather for dressy occasions. Tightly laced boots gave the impression of modesty but also accentuated the curves of the ankle and calf. Increasingly boot styles emphasized this aspect. By 1870 the principal styles worn were side springs, balmorals, and high-button boots. A new development was the barrette boot, which can be viewed as an extension of the shoe since so much of the stocking could be seen through the delicate straps.

In the early years of the twentieth century, boots were still prevalent but soon abandoned by fashionable dress in the 1920s. In this period boots returned to their functional role, and traditional forms remained in use for specific military and sport activities. The exception to this was the vogue among women for knee-high leather Russian boots which featured relatively high heels and a side zipper for a close fit. In the second half of the twentieth century, boots reemerged as an important element in the counterculture fashions favored by the young. Early rebels adopted the sturdy Engineer or Motorcycle boot as a visible sign of their rebellion inspired by films such as *The Wild One* and *Rebel Without a Cause*. In the late 1950s a trend developed for elastic side boots copied from the nineteenth-century originals, but with the addition of a high heel and a pointed toe which were worn with the new slim-fitting tapered trouser. These were the Chelsea boots and would later become known as "Beatle boots."

Women saw an explosion of fashion boots after 1960. While the flat-heeled, white kid leather boots launched by Parisian couturier André Courrèges was the ubiquitous boot of the decade, many styles of boot were popular. Go-Go boots could be ankle, knee, or thigh high and with or without heels, they all served as the perfect accompaniment to the miniskirt. By the end of the decade, retro styles became popular, and the front lacing granny boot became an essential part of the hippie style.

Styles were increasingly unisex in the 1970s, with both genders wearing suede chukka boots, cowboy boots, and high zip-up platform boots. The Dr. Martens boot, originally designed as an orthopedic shoe in the 1940s, was adopted by the punk counter-culture in the 1970s, but by the 1990s had been assimilated into popular fashion. Masculine-styled boots worn by women have been considered extremely provocative, especially when paired with more conventional symbols of femininity.

While traditional forms of boots continue to be worn throughout the world for specific functions, they have also played an important role in fashion throughout history.

See also Inuit and Arctic Footwear; Sandals; Shoes.

Bibliography

Cunnington, C. Willett. *English Women's Clothing in the Nineteenth Century*. New York: Dover Publications, Inc., 1990.

McDowell, Colin. *Shoes: Fashion and Fantasy*. New York: Thames and Hudson, 1989.

Pratt, Lucy, and Linda Woolley. *Shoes*. London: V & A Publications, 1999.

Swann, Julie. *Shoes*. London: Butler and Tanner Ltd., 1982.

Wilcox, R. Turner. *The Mode in Footwear*. New York: Charles Scribner's Sons, 1948.

Clare Sauro

BOURDIN, GUY

Guy Bourdin (1928–1991) has an extraordinary cult following within the field of fashion photography, expanded by the 2003 retrospective of his work at London's Victoria and Albert Museum. Critical, autocratic, dictatorial, and quirky, he had a personal life that was chaotic and probably sadistic, pushed his models to the point of tears and passing out, and even under-mined his reputation during his lifetime and his legacy upon his death. Yet despite—or possibly because of—the morbidity and violence of his personal and professional life, Bourdin has had a profound influence on photo-graphic and artistic currents of the late twentieth century.

Bourdin's Background

Guy Bourdin was born in Paris. His mother abandoned him when he was still an infant, and he was alternately raised by his grandparents in Normandy and Paris and placed in a boarding school. Bourdin was the only child to the age of fifteen, when his brother, Michael, was born, and he spent much time in the solitary pursuits of reading and drawing.

At age twenty Bourdin joined the French air force for his mandatory two years of military service, working as an aerial photographer in Dakar, Senegal. After he completed his service, he wanted to buy a small wedding photography business in Magny-en-Vexin, near the family home in Normandy. Refused a loan by his father, Bourdin worked at Bon Marché, the Paris department store, selling lenses and at a variety of odd jobs, including cleaning floors, acting as a messenger at the U.S. Embassy, and washing dishes at the Brasserie Lipp. During this period, he continued to draw, photograph, and produce paintings inspired by Balthus, Francis Bacon, and Stanley Spencer.

In the late 1940s Edward Weston's photograph of a pepper showed Bourdin that photography could be art. He was also inspired by the monumental landscapes of Ansel Adams and developed a friendship with the dada painter and photographer Man Ray, who wrote the gallery announcement for Bourdin's 1952 exhibition at Galerie 29 on the rue de Seine in Paris. It was undoubtedly through Man Ray that Bourdin became acquainted with surrealism, which was to infuse his photography throughout his life.

Bourdin's Editorial and Advertising Photography

In 1954 Bourdin took his work to French *Vogue*, where he was given a fashion assignment on hats. It included a shot, which has become one of Bourdin's early classics, showing a model walking by a butcher shop, three skinned and bloodied calves' heads swinging just above her impeccably turned head. Bourdin continued his exclusive editorial work for French *Vogue* from 1955 through 1987. Bourdin's advertising work for Charles Jourdan shoes from 1967 to 1981 was extremely important. He also did advertising work for the designer Grès and in 1976 photographed the controversial Bloomingdale's "Sighs and Whispers" lingerie brochure, which has become a collector's item.

The Charles Jourdan shoe campaign was groundbreaking in its approach, originality, and daring. In Bourdin's hands, the shoe was presented as a fetishistic object, both as an object of desire and the focal point of scenarios of violence. Bourdin's infamous 1975 photograph depicting the scene of a bloody automobile fatality, the body marked in chalk on the pavement next to the featured shoes, was a benchmark in the history of attraction by shock. The power and perversity of this image were legendary: that an image of death and tragedy (though fictitious) would be used to sell shoes was unthinkable, yet unforgettable. The image itself possessed the same power of attraction that causes a crowd to gather at the scene of a gory accident. In other shots Bourdin juxtaposed gigantic shoes and tiny shoes, which had been made especially for this purpose by the Jourdan company. In this way, Bourdin played on the type of size discrepancies often used in surrealist works, such as the paintings of René Magritte.

Background of Bourdin's Style

Bourdin clearly transformed his personal obsessions into a body of work that was stunningly daring and visually unforgettable. "What Guy did," his stylist Serge Lutens has said, "was conduct his own psychoanalysis in *Vogue* " (Hayden-Guest, p. 143). Abandoned as an infant by an unloving woman, he obsessively depicted women tied up, in compromising situations, or dead. He was said to favor models with pale red hair, because they reminded him of his mother, and he was renowned for making bizarre, macabre, and sometimes cruel demands on them. Stories abound about models being made to balance on a rock during an electrical storm, being subjected to props that cut into their flesh, and passing out after being suspended to appear as if they were flying.

One model, Louise Despointes, was said to have been kept waiting in a freezing studio, then wrapped in plastic and lowered into a bathtub of extremely cold water on which black enamel paint had been floated. She emerged from the tub "enameled" in black paint, uncomfortable and unable to work for days. Bourdin even reputedly placed models in life-threatening positions and delighted in the idea of their deaths. In another famous story, Bourdin initially smeared the faces of Despointes and another model with a thin layer of glue as a way to stick dozens of pearls to their faces. When he decided to cover their entire bodies with pearls, they passed out because they were not getting enough oxygen to their skin and could not breathe, and the editor stopped the shoot, thinking the models would die. Bourdin was reputed to have said, "Oh, it would be beautiful—to have them dead in bed!" (Hayden-Guest, p. 136).

Eroticism and Violence in Bourdin's Photography

Eroticism—and the link between sex and violence—is a major component of Bourdin's photography. The foundation had been laid by the imagery of the preceding decade, particularly the sexual emancipation of Richard Avedon's work of the 1960s. Yet the brilliant and sensitive use of nudity and sexual innuendo that Avedon and Bob Richardson had introduced into fashion depiction in those years—confronting lesbianism and the ménage à trois, for instance—was tame by 1970s' standards. The time was ripe for Bourdin's stylized violence and the darker realities of voyeurism, death, and rape.

Bourdin's photographic violence is thematically akin to the bloody climax of the film *Bonnie and Clyde*, the dental torture in *Marathon Man*, or the orgiastic violence of *The Wild Bunch*. This brand of violent depiction plays with the audience's attraction to the escalating brutality and demands that the viewer consider violence glamorous. The new brand of violent fashion photography and film supplies the viewer with a fantasy fulfillment unavailable in everyday life. As Stephen Farber explains in his *New Yorker* article "The Bloody Movies: Why Film Violence Sells":

> One of the functions of popular art has always been to give people some notion of experiences denied them in reality—a taste of romance, glamour, adventure, danger. But perhaps as everyday life becomes more smoothly homogenized, people need splashier, more grotesque vicarious thrills. Today, . . . [we only experience violence] at professional hockey and football games, at high-powered rock concerts, or at the movies. (p. 44)

Or, one might add, in fashion photography.

Guy Bourdin's violence against women—both actual and photographic—played on their vulnerability, which is a leitmotif in his work. Shadows are an effective device often used for creating an air of mystery, implied physical threat, and even frenzy. Bourdin used such shadows as early as 1966 to suggest the presence of Batman—normally a hero figure and protector—chasing a confused, worried woman through the streets. The thrown shadows, used repeatedly in Bourdin's oeuvre, represent the woman's living nightmare of vulnerability, of being threatened by indistinguishable forms and unseen presences.

Influence of Bourdin's Personal Life on His Work

Bourdin even materialized the reality of violence toward women into his personal life: his first wife is thought to have committed suicide, his second hanged herself, one girlfriend lived after slashing her wrists, and another died after falling out of a tree. As Tim Blanks suggested

in his *New York Times Magazine* article, "Both masochism and sadism were bedfellows." Bourdin also seemed bent on undermining himself and his own reputation. He was infamous for not allowing his work to be used in books and exhibitions and for refusing to grant interviews. In 1985 he rejected the $9,000 Grand prix national de la photographie, given by the French Ministry of Culture.

In his article "The Return of Guy Bourdin," Anthony Hayden-Guest explained how Bourdin, when he died of cancer at age sixty-two, left his estate in disarray, compounding a horrendous tax situation and further paralyzing his legacy (p. 137). He had deeded his pictures to Martine Victoire, his common-law wife of seven years, in a signed and witnessed (but not notarized) contract; Samuel Bourdin, the photographer's estranged only child, contested the action. The legal decision gave Victoire possession of the archives but allowed Samuel to exercise his discretion in their use. Without his consent, Victoire could not publish, sell, or exhibit the photographs she owned. Subsequently, the reproduction rights were contested in court.

Bourdin's Influence

The vast influence Bourdin had on subsequent art and photography is only now becoming clear. Like it or not, Bourdin broke taboos and reflected the escalating violence in society, blazing the path for contemporary artists like Paul McCarthy and Matthew Barney in combining the disgusting with the exalted. He pioneered the narrative approach to photography that has become one of its dominant strains, from the work of Gregory Crewdson to that of David Leventhal. Bourdin created pictures filled with what seemed to be clues in a mystery, hinting at meanings rather than articulating them. We are often unsure of what is going on; we know only that we are dealing with a specific moment in which something has happened or is about to happen. Bourdin scatters clues in his pictures, such as water spurting from a pool with a shoe by its edge, a girl "talking" to a shark, or two girls dressed only in lingerie watching as items fall from a purse, frozen in midair.

Bourdin was also one of only a handful of photographers who had almost complete creative freedom within the field of editorial and advertising fashion photography. In both realms Bourdin was a technical virtuoso. His brilliance in producing a wide range of ideas with a continually fresh vision was equaled by his mastery of technique and execution. His background as a painter influenced his approach, particularly the way he built his compositions. Each shape and color was painstakingly and thoughtfully composed to contribute to the whole.

Bourdin's concern for the final effect of his work, including the exact placement on the printed page, is evidence of his commitment to fashion photography. With respect to the photograph itself as a compositional element, he created some of the most unusual and visually exciting layouts ever published in fashion periodicals. Particularly effective was his frequent grouping of photographs in multiples or sequences, repeating sections of the picture or making unexpected juxtapositions to heighten interest.

See also Art and Fashion; Avedon, Richard; Fashion Advertising; Fashion Magazines; Fashion Photography; Vogue.

Bibliography

Blanks, Tim. "Beauty and the Beast." *New York Times Magazine*, 23 February 2003.

DeLano, Sharon. "Dead Girls." *New Yorker*, 3 September 2001, 58.

Farber, Stephen. "The Bloody Movies, Why Film Violence Sells." *New Yorker*, 29 November 1976, 39–45.

Hall-Duncan, Nancy. *The History of Fashion Photography*. New York: Alpine Book Company, 1979.

Hayden-Guest, Anthony. "The Return of Guy Bourdin." *New Yorker*, 7 November 1994, 136–146.

Nancy Hall-Duncan

BOUTIQUE

Synonymous with the youth movement and counterculture fashions of the "Swinging Sixties," the boutique radically changed ways of making, marketing, displaying, and buying clothing. Names and places such as Mary Quant, Biba, Paraphernalia, the King's Road, and Carnaby Street evoke the spirit of freedom, individuality, and rebellion that characterized the social upheaval of that decade, and defined a style of dressing. As a retailing concept, the boutique is associated with a distinct identity that reflects the taste of the designer or owner; small-scale production with rapid turnover

of merchandise; fashion novelty and experimentation; innovative displays and interiors; and an informality among owner, salespeople, and clientele. Although the boutique phenomenon of the 1960s played itself out by the mid-1970s, boutiques remain a vital part of the commercial world of fashion—whether as an individual enterprise or incorporated into a larger setting, such as a department store.

Origins

Small retailing establishments were not new to the post-World War II period. In the first half of the twentieth century, Paris, London, and New York all had specialty shops. Usually owned by a single designer or proprietor, these operated between the highly exclusive couture houses and the large department stores, and catered to a well-to-do clientele with an emphasis on personal attention to the customer.

As early as the 1920s, Parisian designers began to open small shops within the premises of their *maisons de couture* where they sold a variety of (often less expensive) merchandise including accessories. In 1925 Jean Patou, for example, opened *Le Coin des Sports* (The Sports Corner), a series of rooms on the ground floor of his couture house that offered specialized sports clothing. From its opening in 1935, Elsa Schiaparelli's boutique featured unorthodox and whimsical window arrangements that anticipated the eye-catching, frankly outré displays and interior decor of 1960s boutiques. By the 1950s, boutiques were well-established venues for selling designer clothes and accessories.

New Consumers, New Producers

The coming of age of the baby boomers in the late 1950s and early 1960s created a new consumer market that significantly affected the boutique explosion. The economic hardships of the war years had ended and a period of prosperity began in both Europe and America. Young men and women not only had money to spend but also sought to distinguish—and distance—themselves sartorially from their parents. Dissatisfied with what they saw as outmoded, irrelevant, and conformist styles promoted by the Parisian haute couture, emerging young designers, particularly in Britain, began to create clothing that reflected a new aesthetic and attitude toward dressing. Equally significant was their determination to produce clothing that was affordable to their peers. Rather than work within the restrictions

A novel window display in the "Lady Jane" boutique on London's Carnaby Street, 1966. Boutiques in the 1960s changed the way merchandise was displayed and sold. The shops reflected an informality between the owner and clientele and included novelty fashions, smaller retail volumes, and innovative displays and interiors. © HULTON-DEUTCH COLLECTION/CORBIS. REPRODUCED BY PERMISSION.

imposed by a couture house or a large manufacturing company, these designers often began by sewing garments in their homes and opening boutiques in out-of-the-way locations.

Dubbed the "Swinging City" by *Time* magazine in 1966, London was the undisputed capital of the youth movement in the early and mid-1960s, and young British designers were in the vanguard of the boutique scene. Of this group, Mary Quant was the highly influential pioneer. Her boutique, Bazaar, which she opened on King's Road in 1955 in partnership with her publicist husband, Alexander Plunkett-Green, and business manager Archie McNair, was the first of its kind. Bazaar offered clothing and accessories aimed at a youthful audience ready for fashion that emphasized informality, irreverence, and playfulness.

Quant's Bazaar set the standard for the many boutiques that opened in London and New York in the following decade, including Barbara Hulanicki's Biba; Alice Pollock's Quorum, which featured clothes by the celebrated husband-and-wife team of Ozzie Clark and Celia Birtwell; the entrepreneur John Stephen's numerous emporia on Carnaby Street; and Paraphernalia, where Betsey Johnson's exhibitionist designs were modeled by Warhol "superstar" Edie Sedgwick.

Boutique Shopping

Inventive window displays and interior decor not only formed a particular boutique's image and identity, they also added a sense of fun and discovery to the shopping experience. Unconventional windows were designed to engage—even shock—passersby. At Bazaar, Quant created whimsical vignettes using attenuated, stylized mannequins in awkward poses, props, large-scale photographs, and banners. Historicism was the hallmark at Biba that would become famous for its art nouveau and art deco inspired interiors (and fashions). Paraphernalia was characterized by a space-age minimalism in which white and silver predominated. In these varied settings, clothes and accessories might be hung on walls or old-fashioned coat stands (as at Biba), or tucked away in dimly lit corners. The unexpected juxtaposition of different types of merchandise also encouraged the boutique shopper to linger and explore.

Although Biba's clientele was primarily working-class while Quorum was patronized by the Rolling Stones lead singer Mick Jagger, Marianne Faithfull, and other pop stars, boutique shopping in the 1960s was a shared social experience among young men and women. Strolling down King's Road or Carnaby Street and frequenting the "in" shops were part of the hip lifestyle. Boutiques were first and foremost places to see and purchase the most up-to-the-minute styles, but they were also "happening" places where one went to meet friends and listen to the latest rock music. Their generally small, often dark interiors and casual atmosphere fostered an intimate ambience. Some boutiques (such as Paraphernalia) stayed open late at night; music and live models dancing on platforms further blurred the distinction between store and party scene.

Boutiques and Fashion in the Early 2000s

By the late 1960s and early 1970s, the success and popularity of boutiques resulted in their being co-opted by mainstream fashion and big business. In New York, large department stores such as Bloomingdale's opened designer boutiques aimed at attracting a share of the enormous youth market. Geraldine Stutz, president of Henri Bendel, transformed the staid specialty shop into a highly visible showcase for the work of young British, American, and French designers, each with their own boutique space. By the time it closed in 1976, Biba had moved twice from its original, small location in Abingdon Road to occupy the former premises of Derry and Toms, a 1930s multi-storied department store in Kensington High Street.

In the "Swinging Sixties," fashion was a defining aspect of the counterculture movement, and boutiques were the matrix in the creation and dissemination of those fashions. The boutique scene introduced a new set of expectations regarding fashion and shopping that is still a factor in the early twenty-first century. Boutiques expanded the concept of fashion as catering to more individualized—and adventurous—tastes. Along with the multiplicity of styles available was the possibility for creative self-expression through clothing, while the shopping experience became part of fashionable behavior. Boutiques continue to offer alternative fashions to elitist haute couture and mass-produced, mass-distributed ready-to-wear.

See also Biba; Quant, Mary.

Bibliography

Bernard, Barbara. *Fashions in the 60s.* London: Academy Editions, 1978.

Fogg, Marnie. *Boutique: A '60s Cultural Phenomenon.* London: Mitchell Beazley, 2003.

Fraser, Kennedy. *The Fashionable Mind: Reflections on Fashion 1970–1982.* Boston: David R. Godine, Publisher, 1985.

Lobenthal, Joel. *Radical Rags: Fashions of the Sixties.* New York: Abbeville Press, 1990.

Mendes, Valerie, and Amy de la Haye. *20th Century Fashion.* London: Thames and Hudson, Inc., 1999.

Steele, Valerie. *Fifty Years of Fashion: New Look to Now.* New Haven, Conn.: Yale University Press, 1997.

Michele Majer

BRANDS AND LABELS

Brands developed as a means of commercial distinction within the marketplace in the mid-to late-nineteenth century. The process of branding begins with the attachment of a name to a business, product, or a family of products, and involves the creation of an image for that business which sets it apart from its competitors. Brand image is usually disseminated through advertising, but the value of a brand generally resides in its reputation and the level of loyalty or desirability it can generate amongst consumers. In the fashion industry, a desirable brand name allows companies to bridge the gap between expensive, high-fashion garments and affordable mass-market goods such as perfumes, accessories, and ready-to-wear diffusion lines.

The emergence of brands is closely linked to the establishment of copyright, patent, and trademark legislation in the nineteenth century, as this allowed companies to legally protect their names, and seek redress from their imitators. Many other factors affected the emergence of modern brands, such as the growth of new distribution and retail networks; the increased dominance of fixedpricing, the concomitant growth of the advertising and packaging trades, and the shift from local to national (and international) markets for consumer goods.

The fashion industry can seek legal protection for designs through patents legislation, which protects the unauthorized use of original designs for manufacture. It also benefits from complex trademark legislation, which protects the words, names, symbols, sounds, or colors that are used to distinguish goods and services. Effectively, this covers the use of a company's logo and brand identity from both counterfeit and "look-alike" goods, where the visual identity of brand is suggested rather than exactly copied.

One celebrated early example of branded clothing is Levi Strauss and Co., who incorporated many trademarked features into their garments (such as rivets and stitching) and gave proof of authenticity in the form of a patent and trademark "certificate" with each garment (later to be sewn on as a label). Authenticity is a central promise of branded goods, and the fashion industry has used it to generate high cultural value in a world of rapid turnover, fluctuating consumer loyalties, and the seemingly incessant demand for novelty. Fashion branding has become synonymous with a late-capitalist consumerist culture where it is the experience rather than the product that drives demand.

Many fashion houses developed as brands through the practice of franchising and licensed copying. In the period 1880–1914, couture businesses such as Worth and Paquin sold through an international network of department stores. In their attempts to cut down on illegal copying, they also sold reproduction rights to private dressmaking salons. The copying of models was a fundamental part of the nineteenth century fashion trade, and designer "names" such as Worth would produce models specifically for copy by retailers in both Europe and America, in order to gain some financial benefit from this practice. By the 1860s it was necessary for Worth to incorporate a house label into products, carrying the Worth name and address either stamped or woven into garments (labels were in turn copied by counterfeit producers).

This two-tier system of couture models and more accessible ready-to-wear lines bearing the same label was exploited by successive generations of designers, including Paul Poiret and Coco Chanel, who used it to build their international reputations. The "signature label" became a defining characteristic of twentieth-century fashion, allowing fashion houses and named designers to attach their names to goods including fashion, perfume, cosmetics, and even household products in order to give these goods distinction. In this way, fashion branding moved beyond the "naming" of a product into the creation of desirable lifestyle scenarios, which could supposedly be replicated by consumers purchasing even the smallest named item. During the 1930s, most of the major couture labels including Elsa Schiaparelli, Coco Chanel, and Jean Patou successfully marketed their signature perfumes well beyond the market for couture.

Franchising became a more widespread activity in the postwar period. Designers such as Dior used the success of franchise agreements in the 1940s to underpin the more risky business of couture. In the 1970s and 1980s designers such as Paco Rabanne, Pierre Cardin, Calvin Klein, and Ralph Lauren capitalized on the value of their brands by franchising their names to the producers of housewares, accessories, and beauty lines. Some labels quickly became debased by the lack of quality control, and crossed the fine line from exclusivity to down-market ubiquity. Now that the practice is more commonplace, it is also more heavily controlled by the presence of major global conglomerates such as LVMH and the Gucci Group. Many brands, such as Donna Karan, have successfully created a family of brands or diffusion lines, each of which has a specific character and target market (Donna Karan and the various DKNY lines including Kids, City, Sport, and Pure).

Aside from the diversification of fashion houses, brand culture has also been driven by the expansion of the sports and leisure sectors into fashion. Despite its claim to be motivated only by the needs of athletes, the global sportswear brand Nike has become synonymous with street fashion since its diversification in the mid-1980s. Nike's phenomenal expansion was also due to its direct appeal to a sense of personal achievement through its "Just Do It" slogan and highly emotive advertising. It also fueled overt brand loyalty on the part of its wearers. The popularity of branded goods amongst closely defined "style tribes" has resulted in a profusion of goods where the logo is prominently displayed.

By the twenty-first century, investment in brand building has reached unprecedented levels, with many familiar brand names reinventing themselves by the hire of celebrity designers and radical company overhauls. Fashion and luxury brands have been most affected, as brands known for a particular product category (such as leather goods) launch couture and ready-to-wear collections. With a combination of business acumen and designer credentials, brand "auteurs" such as Tom Ford have transformed the fortunes of a company such as Gucci in a few short years. Many individual designers now work in several capacities at once: creating their own couture and ready-to-wear collections, producing a collection for another fashion house (John Galliano and Alexander McQueen have both held this post at Givenchy) and perhaps acting as consultant to a department store's own label (Betty Jackson for Marks & Spencer, Jasper Conran for Debenhams in the United Kingdom). These designers may risk their individual reputations on the success of named collections, but the companies behind them are now multinational conglomerates, each with a huge portfolio of brands.

See also Logos.

Bibliography

Clifton, Rita, and John Simmons, eds. *Brands and Branding.* Princeton, N.J.: Bloomberg Press, 2004.

Mendes, Valerie, and Amy de la Haye. *20th Century Fashion.* London: Thames and Hudson, 1999.

Pavitt, Jane, ed. *Brand New.* London: V & A Publications, 2000.

Troy, Nancy J. *Couture Culture: A Study in Modern Art and Fashion.* Cambridge, Mass.: MIT Press, 2003.

White, Nicola, and Ian Griffiths, eds. *The Fashion Business: Theory, Practice, Image.* Oxford: Berg, 2000.

Jane M. Pavitt

BRASSIERE

A brassiere is a garment worn next to the skin with two shaped cups or pockets to hold female breast tissue; it is supported by a chest bandeau and generally two over-the-shoulder straps. It may have elastic, wire, padding, lace trim, and a variety of other parts. Strapless versions are also used on occasions where the shoulders are exposed. Specialized brassieres are made for holding breast prostheses of those with surgical removal of one or both breasts, in addition to the particular needs of maternity and nursing mothers. Brassiere styles are often dependent on the fashionable silhouette of the time: breast-flattening bands of the early 1920s, softly curved bias-cut styles of the 1930s, structured and circular stitched "torpedo" shapes of the 1940s and 1950s, unstructured and naturally shaped bras of the 1960s and 1970s, until the introduction of the Lycra-based knitted fabric sports bras of the 1980s. Any of those could be found in lingerie wardrobes, along with the ultimate in uplift and underwire by Wonderbra, Victoria's Secret, Warnaco, and others. It is not anatomically or physiologically necessary to support the breasts, but is strictly a fashionable or socially demanded item.

Breast coverings, in the form of tight bandeaus, have been worn throughout history and by many different ethnic groups of women, but the particularly designed and shoulder-supported garment we know today was a product of the nineteenth-century Dress Reform. United States patent #40,907 issued to Luman L. Chapman in 1863 may be the first recorded design in America, but is almost certainly not the first such garment produced for women wishing to substitute a more comfortable garment for their fashionable tight-laced corsets.

A Norman French word for a child's undershirt, the term "brassiere" was adopted in America about 1904 when it appeared in New York advertising copy of the DeBevoise Company to describe their latest bust supporter, thus giving it French cachet. Prior to that time, the garments specifically designed for breast covering and support were designated variously as bust, bosom, or breast supporters or corsets. Occasionally they were patented as braces, waists, foundation garments, halters, or simply covers. The term "brassiere" became widespread in English-speaking nations within a few years, but the French have maintained their designation of *soutien-gorge* (literally "bosom supporter"). In the 1930s, when slang shortened words like pajamas

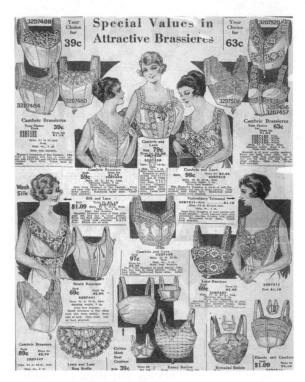

Brassiere advertisement. This advertisement shows the soft, curved bias-cut styles popular in the 1930s. The French word *brassiere*, adopted in the United States about 1904 when it appeared in an advertisement in New York, gave the garment a French quality. They were previously known as "bust, bosom, or breast supporters/corsets." © BETTMANN/CORBIS. REPRODUCED BY PERMISSION.

to "pj's," brassieres became "bras." Custom-made in the nineteenth century, the brassiere made its entrance into mass production in the early twentieth century in the United States, England, western Europe, and other countries influenced by Western lifestyles.

The brassiere had early prototypes in undergarments worn by late eighteenth-century Western European women with the lightweight columnar fashions that emphasized the breasts and deemphasized the natural waist. Those unstructured pouchlike garments, fitted by draw-strings, and commonly held by shoulder straps, may have inspired the dressmakers and reformers who attempted to produce garments later in the nineteenth century. One function that corsets provided was to help disperse from the waist, the weight of the crinolines, petticoats, and skirts, which may have been as much as thirty-five pounds. A garment with shoulder straps could transfer this weight to the shoulders by hitching lower garments to hooks and tapes. Dress Reformers, including about half of the doctors in a survey of the mid-nineteenth-century medical literature, encouraged women to wear garments that would not impede their digestion, lung capacity, or reproductive system; the new designs maintained the fashionable shape without harming the physique.

Several dozen American entrepreneurs patented breast-supporting garments in the decades up to World War I; about half were women. Olivia Flynt, Marie Tucek, Caroline Newell, and Gabrielle Poix Yerkes were early patentees and producers, with dozens following in the twentieth century. In the undergarment industry, enterprising women found opportunities in design, production, and management not readily available to them in other clothing manufacture. Dr. Jeanne Walters patented rubber brassiere designs with weight-loss claims; and Herma Dozier, R.N., patented three maternity and nursing bras for her company Fancee Free. The latter employed adjustable flaps to allow nipple access without removing the supporting garment. By the end of World War II, the vast majority of fashion-conscious women in America and Europe were wearing brassieres. Western fashions introduced the brassiere to Asia, Africa, and Latin America.

There have been many attributions about the invention of the brassiere. One oft-repeated story concerns Mary Phelps Jacob (a.k.a. Caresse Crosby), a self-described New York socialite who patented a bias-cut brassiere in 1914; it was neither first nor successful. Frenchwoman Herminie (Hermoinie) Cadolle set up a lingerie business in Argentina just as rubber fabric became available and parlayed her elastic insert brassieres (not unlike L. L. Chapman's 1863 design) into a fortune and eventually moved back to Paris, where her business survives in the early 2000s. Claims to her invention of the shoulder strap are misplaced. The Warner Corset Company of Bridgeport, Connecticut, also professed invention, but can only declare innovation and patents for several excellent designs, mostly after 1890. The Gossard Company dominated the English market for many years, with many unique adaptations in brassieres. In fact, there were hundreds of innovators. Not all patented designs, but many found success in the marketplace as women demanded more comfort in their clothing and fashion moved away from the rigid silhouettes of the nineteenth century. In a changing society, women entered universities and work places in great numbers, they took part in sports like hiking, tennis and bicycling, and they drove cars, activities that demanded greater freedom of movement and lung capacity than allowed by restrictive corsets.

As the idea of the brassiere became popular, patterns for the home seamstress were available, but the intricacy of stitching required skills practiced by specialists. Dozens of small entrepreneurial firms entered the market to supply the growing demands for brassieres. Production could be mastered and as assembly lines using readily available components were set up in small quarters, the industry flourished. Designs were patented by the hundreds, along with specialized machinery for cutting, sewing, making fasteners, and even packaging as sales of brassieres increased. Special industries produced the rust-proof wires, hooks, fasteners, and straps in addition to the fabrics, elastics, lace trims, stitching machines, and molding units. Brassiere construction involves up to forty components per garment, using specialized machines for cutting and sewing. In early designs, chromium wire fasteners were the norm; these have been largely replaced by plastic components, which like straps are produced by specialized firms. Improvements in rubber and synthetic elastics have resulted in their almost universal use in brassieres. Fabric selection for brassieres has evolved from the firm coutil and twill weaves used in the nineteenth century to the fine cottons, embroidered polyester blends, delicate silks, fiberfill, and soft knits of the twenty-first century. The brassiere business gave opportunity to women in ownership, administration, design, and manufacturing not readily available in other fields. There were some self-regulatory aspects within the industry, particularly regarding nomenclature. What differentiated a bandeau from a brassiere was more than two inches of length below the breasts. Until war shortages created problems with supplies, there were few government regulations for work standards or for wages.

By the 1910s, retailers featured specialist "fitters" in departments devoted to corsets and brassieres, which did not have universal cup sizing until the early 1930s. Brassieres, like other items of clothing, were sewn in small production companies, often by sweated labor. Despite demands of complicated designs, sewers were expected to produce items of uniform style and size. The term "cup" was not used until 1916, and letter designation for cup size was first used about 1933 by S. H. Camp and Company to imply progression in volume of breast tissue to be replaced with their prostheses. The under-breast circumference or band dimension is one part of early twenty-first-century brassiere size, with the cup volume designated in letters AA thru I available in retail outlets. Introduction of the minimally shaped "training bra" in the 1950s opened the fashion door for countless adolescents.

Fabrics that could be sewn with flat-felled or bias-tape covered seams were used to ensure comfort to the wearer. In pre-1900 brassieres, linen, cotton broadcloth, and twill weaves were favored. "Whirlpool," or concentric, stitching shaped the bra structure of some designs after 1940. As man-made fibers were introduced, these were quickly adopted by the industry because of their properties of easy care. Since a brassiere must be laundered frequently, this was of great importance. Zippers were used in some designs, as well as Velcro, but these fasteners caused discomfort or caught on clothing and complicated laundering.

Small, medium, and large companies were making brassieres in America during the 1930s and 1940s. Some fell prey to shortages of material during World War II, others to changes in business practices in the drive for export markets. There were union problems, and in later decades challenges switching to computer-aided design. The need to supply and advertise to a nationwide market stretched some firms to the breaking point. Offshore production was initiated to save labor costs following the war, eroding influence of garment workers' unions. Introduction of self-service in lingerie departments was another cost-cutting measure, but did not stem the loss of declining brands. Individual brand-name manufacturers have been taken over by conglomerates, which resulted in fewer available designs and less attention paid to quality, in part due to manufacturing processes being moved offshore. Brassiere manufacturing companies like Kabo of Chicago and Kops of New York were in business from the 1890s until the mid-1960s. Many like G. M. Poix, Treo, Model, Dorothy Bickum, Van Raalte, and Lovable lasted fifty or more years, often run by successive family generations. Maiden Form (until 1948, when it changed to Maidenform) began production in 1922 as a direct competitor to the New York–based Boyshform Company, who made bandeau flatteners for the slim styles of the times. After being a leader in the industry and developing through their advertising campaigns one of the best recognized brand names in history, Maidenform continues eighty years later with a smaller market share. Familiar names like Olga, Bali, Exquisite Form, and Play-tex played important roles in the brassiere industry but are now owned by conglomerates.

Eroticism is associated with breasts and brassieres, and brassieres do play a role in the fetish and transvestite dressing by males; however, the garment was designed with the female shape in mind. One prominent promoter of eroticism with a twist of humor was Frederick's of Hollywood, who has been almost eclipsed in the early 2000s by the very market-savvy Victoria's Secret Company. The latter has parlayed lingerie into an art form, taking eroticism from the boudoir to the front parlor in an upward thrust of lace. Décolletage, whether natural or enhanced by padding, is emphasized with the underwired push-up brassiere and by silicone gel in the cups. The metallic wire in many brassieres has been replaced by flexible plastic, perhaps in an attempt to increase comfort and durability. Brassiere designs have been adapted over the decades to fashions of backless dresses, open to the waist in center front, or completely strapless. The Bleumette brassiere and other brands featured gummed cup-shaped supports to the breasts directly when both bandeaus and straps were eschewed.

In 1969, a planned demonstration by a group of feminists who protested the proceedings at the Miss America pageant in Atlantic City, to call attention to their cause resulted in the myth of bra-burning; however, no fire was ever lit, and participants claimed that the bra, high heels, cosmetics, and girdles thrown into the "freedom trash can" were to be a non-pyrotechnic display. The assembled press reported the incident in ambiguous terms, leading many to believe the fire had consumed the offending brassieres. A few more aggressive feminists urged the disposal of all bras; however the majority of American women clung to their familiar fashions, if not their personal comfort.

The elasticized knitted fabric bras introduced in the 1970s and 1980s are now widely worn by athletes and nonathletes alike as comfortable substitutes for the underwired wonders of this age. As female athletes doff their jerseys to reveal brand-name sports bras, few eyebrows are lifted. In the later decades of the twentieth century, the structured brassiere continued its popularity with the majority of women in the middle of the age spectrum, but the youngest and oldest have often either resisted or refused to wear them. Whether for reasons of comfort or personal choice, many women in the twenty-first century are choosing not to wear brassieres.

See also Fasteners; Lingerie; Underwear.

Bibliography

Banner, Lois W. *American Beauty: A Social History Through Two Centuries of the American Ideal, and the Image of*

Beautiful Women. Chicago: University of Chicago Press, 1983.

Boucher, Françoise, and Yvonne Deslandres. *20,000 Years of Fashion: The History of Costume and Personal Adornment.* New York: Harry N. Abrams, 1987.

Cunnington, Cecil Willette. *The Perfect Lady.* London: Max Parrish and Company, 1948.

——. *Feminine Attitudes in the Nineteenth Century.* London: Heinemann, 1955.

Cunnington, Cecil Willette, and Phillis Cunnington. *The History of Underclothes.* New York: Dover Publications, Inc., 1992.

Ecob, Helen Gilbert. *The Well-Dressed Woman.* New York: Fowler, 1982.

Ewing, Elizabeth. *Underwear: A History.* New York: Theater Arts Books, 1972.

——. *Dress and Undress: A History of Women's Underwear.* New York: Drama Book Specialists, 1978.

Farrell-Beck, Jane, and Colleen R. Grace. *Uplift: The Bra in America.* Philadelphia: University of Pennsylvania Press, 2002.

Flower, B. O. "The Next Step Forward; or Thoughts on the Movement for Rational Dress." *The Arena* 6 (1892): 635–644.

Flynt, Olivia. *Manual of Underdressing for Women and Children.* Boston: C. M. S. Twitchell, 1882.

Gersheim, Alison. *Victorian and Edwardian Fashions.* New York: Dover Publications, Inc., 1981.

Lane-Claypon, Janet E. *Hygiene of Women and Children.* London: Henry Frowde and Hodder and Stoughton, 1921.

Newton, S. M. Health. *Art and Reason: Dress Reformers of the Nineteenth Century.* London: John Murray, 1974.

Payne, Blanche, Geitel Winakor, and Jane Farrell-Beck. *The History of Costume: From Ancient Mesopotamia through the Twentieth Century.* 2nd ed. New York: HarperCollins, 1992.

Steele, Valerie Fahnestock. *Fashion and Eroticism: Ideals of Feminine Beauty from the Victorian Era to the Jazz Age.* New York: Oxford University Press, 1985.

——. *The Corset: A Cultural History.* New Haven, Conn.: Yale University Press, 2001.

Treves, Frederick. *Dress of the Period and Its Relations to Health.* London: Hillman and Son, 1882.

Verbrugge, M. H. *Able-Bodied Women: Personal and Social Change in Nineteenth Century Boston.* Oxford: Oxford University Press, 1988.

Vicinus, M., ed. *Suffer and Be Still: Women in the Victorian Age.* Bloomington: University of Indiana Press, 1973.

Woolson, Anna G., and C. Hastings, eds. *Five Essays on Women's Health: Dress Reform,* 1874. New York: Arno Press., Reprint, 1984.

Colleen Gau

BRUMMELL, GEORGE (BEAU)*

George Bryan Brummell (or Brummel), most famously known as "Beau" Brummell, was born in Britain in 1778 and died in 1840 in France. His dress and demeanor established many of the canons of dandyism. Although he was not an aristocrat by birth, he rose in the ranks of Regency society (1795–1820) and belonged to the circle of the Prince of Wales, known as the Prince Regent, who became King George IV. His father was a civil servant and secretary to Lord North, though his grandfather was probably a valet. Brummell was educated at Eton and left Oxford at the age of sixteen when he inherited a sum from his father estimated to have been 15,000 to 65,000 pounds. He became a cornet in the Tenth Hussars, the Prince's regiment, known as "the Elegant Extracts," and was a captain by the time of his retirement from the military in 1798. He then began his life as a stylish gentleman in his houses in Chesterfield and Chapel Streets in London and was a member of Brooks's and White's on St. James's Street, the most exclusive gentlemen's clubs of his day in an elite founded on the principle of exclusivity.

Brummell lived above his means, but his association with the Prince of Wales and his personal sense of style and cutting wit assured him a privileged place among the fashionable set. Many anecdotes mythologize his life, and though there is speculation as to his possible homosexuality, he was never linked specifically with a man or a woman, which the writer Jules Barbey d'Aurevilly took as a sign of his narcissism. In the second decade of the nineteenth century he fell out with the Prince Regent, and his creditors became more insistent. On 16 May 1816 he left Britain for Calais, France, because of his mounting debts and spent his last twenty-four years as an impoverished exile in Calais and then in Caen, Normandy, where he finished his life in a sanatorium.

Brummell's dress was austere and elegant. It was not flamboyant or extravagant but consisted of impeccably clean linen and finely tailored clothes. As Captain

William Jesse (who published his biography in 1886) noted and Robert Dighton's portrait of 1805 illustrates, "His morning dress was similar to that of every other gentleman—top boots and buckskins, with a blue coat and a light or buff coloured waistcoat. . . . His dress of an evening was a blue coat and white waistcoat, black pantaloons which buttoned tight to the ankle, striped silk stockings and opera hat." Although this description suggests that his attire was not extraordinary in the context of Regency society, Brummell's personal attention to detail, function, and cleanliness as well as the fine materials, rare craftsmanship, dignified bearing, and mastery of social etiquette required to maintain such a wardrobe set him apart. The casual equestrian origins of his dress challenged courtly protocol and heralded the pared-down simplicity of masculine attire in the later nineteenth and early twentieth centuries.

Even in his lifetime Brummell was becoming a figure of fiction. A wide range of anecdotes and sayings were attributed to him. Sir Edward Bulwer-Lytton satirized him in his 1828 novel *Pelham; or, The Adventures of a Gentleman*. Mr. Russelton, a thinly disguised Brummell figure, boasts that he employs three tradesmen to make his gloves: "one for the hand, a second for the fingers, and a third for the thumb!"

Brummell's reputation spread to France, where Honoré de Balzac fictionalized him in his *Traité de la vie élégante* (Treatise on the Elegant Life), first published as a serial in *La mode* in 1830. The most important French writing on Brummell is Jules Amédée Barbey d'Aurevilly's short tract of 1845 entitled *Du Dandysme et de Georges Brummell* (On Dandyism and George Brummell). It celebrates Brummell's dandyism as a spiritual achievement of the highest order and raises the dandy's status to that of the poet or artist. This text shifts the terrain of dandyism to a superior intellectual and philosophical ground. Later nineteenth-century texts highlighted the artistic nature of the dandy and his cultivation of both his environment and his dress as works of art. These literary interpretations preserved the heritage of Brummell through the nineteenth century and brought him, transformed, to twentieth-century audiences.

In the first half of the twentieth century, his life would be reenacted in new venues, in the theater and on the silver screen. The playwright Clyde Fitch was commissioned by the matinee idol Richard Mansfield to write a play based on Brummell's legend. *Beau Brummell* premiered on 17 May 1890 at the Madison Square Theatre in New York City, starring Richard Mansfield

and Beatrice Cameron. An illustrated version of the play was published in 1908 and remained popular into the second decade of the century.

Three Hollywood films loosely based on Fitch's play were made in the first half of the twentieth century. The first, just sixteen minutes long and directed by and starring James Young, was released in 1913. The second film, produced by Warner Brothers in 1924, was a star vehicle for John Barrymore. This lavish costume movie was released worldwide and was on the *New York Times* topten list of films in 1924. In 1954 MGM studios came out with an even more extravagant production. This version cast the swashbuckling hero Stewart Granger in the starring role, alongside Elizabeth Taylor and Peter Ustinov, who is wonderfully petulant as the Prince Regent. Although it was produced in America, it featured both British and American actors and drew on the talents of the celebrated British costume designer Elizabeth Haffenden, who worked in collaboration with Walter Plunkett on this film. Despite the British cast and costumes, this Americanized Brummell is presented as a social and sartorial reformer who leads Britain from outdated, luxurious aristocratic mores into the more democratic, industrial, and progressive era of the nineteenth century. This was the final cinematic version of the Brummell legend, which has found new currency in literary accounts, such as George Walden's essay and translation of Barbey d'Aurevilly's text, entitled *Who Is a Dandy?*

William Jesse referred to Brummel as "cool and impertinent." Brummell's self-mastery and calculated sense of cool, his rise to fame in Regency society, and his sartorial perfection are his hallmarks. His name has become synonymous with dandyism, and the plaque marking his house in Chesterfield Street reads simply and appropriately, "A Man of Fashion."

See also Art and Fashion; Dandyism; Fancy Dress; Fashion, Theories of.

Bibliography

Barbey d'Aurevilly, Jules. *Who Is a Dandy?* Translated by George Walden. London: Gibson Square Books, 2002.

Bulwer-Lytton, Edward. *Pelham; or, The Adventures of a Gentleman*. 3 vols. London: Colburn, 1828.

Fitch, Clyde. *Beau Brummel: A Play in Four Acts*. New York: John Lane, 1908.

Jesse, Captain William. *The Life of George Brummell, Esq., Commonly Called Beau Brummell*. London: John Nimmo, 1886.

Kelly, Ian. *Beau Brummell: The Ultimate Man of Style*. New York: Free Press, 2007.

Moers, Ellen. *The Dandy: Brummell to Beerbohm*. London: Secker and Warburg, 1960.

Alison Matthews David

BURBERRY*

Although overtly recognized by its trademark check of red, black, white, and camel, Burberry is principally renowned for its innovation in waterproof clothing, rather than for the design of the lining material that traditionally lies beneath the outer gabardine cloth. Yet such is the power of reinvention, that to many the reverse is true. Burberry as a company is a rare thing—a British brand of clothing and goods that has successfully held on to its traditions while being able to remold itself into a covetable luxury brand that competes in a worldwide market. Thomas Burberry's invention of waterproof gabardine cloth has ensured that the form of apparel his company sold became bound to his name, so that the definition of Burberry in the Oxford English Dictionary reads "a distinguished type of raincoat."

Burberry's chief executive officer from 1997 to 2005, Rosemary Bravo. Bravo transformed the financially ailing company in 1997. Her decision to use the company's trademark check on the outer fabric of their famous raincoats, instead of on the lining material, marked the turning point for the company's bottom line. © REUTERS NEWMEDIA INC./CORBIS. REPRODUCED BY PERMISSION.

Born in 1835, Thomas Burberry opened an outfitters shop in Basingstoke in 1856 at the relatively young age of twenty-one. As an ambitious country draper, Burberry was inspired by metropolitan ideas of fashionable dress, but drew upon local examples of work clothing to develop his ideas. His starting point was a loose-fitting linen smock that farmers and shepherds wore all year-round. Noticing that it kept the workers cool in summer yet warm in winter, he found on closer inspection that the close weave of the fabric helped to keep out the wet, while the looseness of the garment allowed for the circulation of air without inhibiting movement. By 1879 Burberry had refined his prototype fabric from his own mill to a cloth woven from long-staple Egyptian cotton. It created a fabric that was waterproof, breathable, rip-resistant and crease-proof. Burberry termed it gabardine cloth, reviving an old term for a loose coat or cloak. It soon came to the attention of motorists, travelers, and explorers who used the weatherproof overcoat, often referred to as a "slip-on," in all weather conditions. When supported on four sticks, many an intrepid Colonial knew its additional use as an impromptu bathtub.

With a London store opening on Haymarket in 1890 (it remains the company headquarters to this day), the company grew to include a wholesale division and shops in Paris and New York by the turn of the century. Ever ready to protect the interests of his business and its products, Burberry registered the logo in 1904 and the eponymous check in 1920 (it did not appear on the lining of the raincoat until 1924). Further, in 1932 the company pioneered the department-store concession devoted exclusively to the sale of Burberry's goods.

The British War Office in 1900 commissioned Burberry to design an overcoat to replace the heavily rubberized mackintoshes that were then standard issue. The lightweight cotton raincoat designed incorporated D-ring belt clasps, straps, and epaulettes for better function in combat and it soon gained popularity when endorsed by Lord Kitchener. As the most suitable protection from the appalling conditions of trench warfare, it is the origin of what we now refer to as the trench coat.

In 1970, Burberry opened a New York flagship store on east Fifty-Seventh Street. With the resurgence of the luxury goods market in the last decade of the twentieth century, the financially flailing company appointed Rosemary Bravo in 1997 from Saks, New York as Chief Executive whose responsibility was to revive the brand. According to a story in the *Daily Telegraph*, her American friends dismissed her new job as "selling raincoats in London," but within five years the value of the company rose from £200 million to £1.5 billion ($350 million to $2.67 billion). The linchpin of this transformation was the decision to use the check of the lining on the outer gabardine cloth of the raincoat in the first collection shown at London Fashion Week for A/W 1999/2000. When the model Kate Moss was caught by the paparazzi wearing the raincoat in the street rather than on the catwalk, demand for the item was unparalleled. In being worn in such a casual way, the raincoat signaled a metropolitan savvy that claimed as much an understanding of the visual heritage of British clothing, as an understanding of fashionable taste. Rosemary Bravo resigned as CEO in 2005.

Although credited to Roberto Menichetti, the first appointed fashion designer for the company, the fashionability of the item was influenced by the subversive ideas of American fashion designer Miguel Androver and British fashion designer Russell Sage, who had both flaunted the inside-out Burberry raincoat in their catwalk collections for A/W 2000/1. While Androver mined the cachet of the checked lining in terms of the selling of vintage goods and their reuse, Sage questioned the legal permissibility of appropriating registered goods, sardonically titling his collection "So Sue Me." Later in the same year, Burberry commissioned Mario Testino to photograph their campaigns, astutely hiring Kate Moss as the chief model.

The allure of the check reached unprecedented heights: young mothers dressed their babies in checked bibs, hooligans wore Burberry scarves in tribute to the Casuals who wore them on football terraces in the 1980s, and even Cherie Blair, prime minister Tony Blair's wife, once sported a handbag. Menichetti's response to this popular exposure was to make the high-end Prosorum range showcased in Milan even more directional, causing him to be replaced by Christopher Bailey in 2000, who brought a more commercial and digestible level of reinvention to the product range. To this end, the variation on a raincoat remains core to the company's design repertoire.

From the water-logged trenches of military warfare at the beginning of the twentieth century to the swimming-pool terraces of the twenty-first century, the insatiable demand for the Burberry bikini in 2001 indicates that the kind of water protection the company is now investing in may have diversified considerably, but it remains curiously consistent with Thomas Burberry's sense of reinvention.

See also London Fashion; Raincoat; Rainwear.

Bibliography

Barrow, Becky. "£10m Ride from Bronx to Burberry's." *Daily Telegraph*, 24 June 2002.

Ewing, Elizabeth. *History of Twentieth Century Fashion*. London: Batsford, 1974.

Sudjic, Deyan. *Cult Objects: The Complete Guide to Having It All*. London: Paladin, 1985.

Thornton, Phil. *Casuals: The Story of Terrace Fashion*. Lytham, U.K.: Milo Books, 2003.

Alistair O'Neill

BUSTLE

Exaggeration of the feminine posterior has been a periodic theme in Western fashion for several hundred years. The pulled-back overskirts of late-seventeenth and early-eighteenth-century mantuas (loose-fitting gowns) emphasized this area, and pads or "cork rumps" sometimes supported the swagged-up styles of the late 1770s and 1780s. Even early-nineteenth-century neoclassical dresses often featured a small back pad—a socalled artificial hump—to give the high-waisted line a graceful flow. As waists lowered and skirts widened, the pad was retained, and by the late 1820s it was called a bustle. Throughout the mid-nineteenth century full skirts were enhanced by a small bustle made of padding, whalebone, or even inflatable rubber. In the 1870s and 1880s, however, both the skirt support and the silhouette created by the bustle became the focus of fashion.

In an age when men and women were considered to have distinct social roles, the late nineteenth century assumed the natural forms of the two genders also diverged. One arbiter of etiquette and aesthetics, "Professor" Thomas E. Hill, explained that, in contrast to the broad-shouldered male, the female figure is characterized by narrow, sloped shoulders but width across "the lower portion of the form." He stated that to avoid looking "masculine and unnatural," women's dresses should be tight on top while dressmakers are "permitted to arrange tuck and bow and flounce without stint below the waist." These enhanced derrieres proportionately lessened women's small waists, produced by corseting. The idea that women are naturally steatopygous or fat-buttocked is no more aberrant than the late-twentieth-century idea that all women should have "buns of steel."

The bustle, also known as a tournure, pannier, or dress improver, could be made in a wide variety of materials and shapes. Some types were full length, such as sprung steel half hoopskirts called crinolettes and petticoats with adjustable inset steels. Many bustles, however, were made to pad only the rump area, secured to the wearer by a buckled waistband. These could be simple rectangular- or crescent-shaped pads filled with horsehair or other stuffing, but more intricate forms included down-filled devices and puffed or ruffled constructions of crinoline or stiff fabric such as tampico hemp. Woven wire mesh bustles were advertised as not only cooler than padding, but uncrushable, eliminating the need for furtive rearrangement after sitting. Other structures featured several metal springs arranged vertically, placed a large crescent-shaped spring horizontally below the waist, or had projecting steel half hoops that adjusted with lacing and claimed to cleverly fold up when the wearer sat down.

The material used to create bustles was seemingly endless: M. V. Hughes in her memoir *A London Child of the Seventies* (Oxford University Press, p. 84) recalls that an acquaintance used *The Times* newspaper to achieve her effective bustle, saying, "I find its paper so good, far more satisfactory than the *Daily News*." Petticoats, often with layers of ruffles down the back, helped smooth the line of the bustle pad and support bustled skirts.

By 1868, the fullness of women's skirts had moved to the back, and a bustle was needed to support fashionable puffed overskirts and large sashes. The high back interest continued in the early 1870s as the bustle gradually swelled in size. Although the back of the skirt remained the dominant feature, the silhouette slimmed down after about 1875, when the skirt and petticoats, drawn back low and close to the figure and usually flowing into a long train, were often unsupported by a bustle. In the early 1880s, the bustle returned in dramatic proportions, often forming a shelflike protuberance at right angles to the wearer's body. An examination of images of fashionable women in extreme bustle dresses would lead an impartial observer to conclude—as Bernard Rudofsky proposed in the 1940s—that skirts shaped in this peculiar way must contain a second pair of legs behind the women's normal ones.

The wardrobe of a woman of the time included a chemise, drawers, corset, corset cover, stockings, and several petticoats, as well as a bustle. The bustle's size was accentuated by all the features of fashionable dresses, including tight sleeves, tight-fitting bodices with back

Women wearing bustles. Bustles have been an element of Western fashion intermittently since the seventeenth century. Women's dresses were form-fitting on top and created with a tuck and flounce in the back, below the waist, to avoid appearing masculine. © BETTMAN/CORBIS. REPRODUCED BY PERMISSION.

tails, and elaborately constructed skirts with back poufs, swags, gathering, pleating, draperies, and asymmetrical effects. While a few called for reform of feminine dress for artistic and health reasons, most accepted women's convoluted clothing as in accord with High Victorian taste, with its love of the ornate, ostentatious, and overdone. A fashionable woman, dressed in a horsehair or spring bustle, layers of undergarments, and rich, heavy fabrics trimmed with fringe, did present an upholstered effect, similar to an overstuffed sofa of the time, both expensive, decorative objects. In 1899, Thorstein Veblen's *The Theory of the Leisure Class* introduced ideas, such as the conferring of status by "conspicuous consumption," reflecting the bustle period's excesses. Yet to most contemporaries, highly contrived feminine clothing was not seen as contradictory to the spirit of this "age of progress," but rather as a concomitant of civilization, showing commercial enterprise and mechanical ingenuity and firmly establishing the "civilized" division of the sexes. Throughout the period, although ridiculed, the bustle silhouette was widely accepted and worn by women from all classes, as well as by little girls with their short skirts. As *The Delineator* noted in February 1886 (p. 99), some women did not wear a bustle pad, "except when such an adjunct if necessitated by a ceremonious toilette," relying instead on a flounced petticoat to support the drapery of simpler dresses.

After about 1887 the bustle reduced in size and skirts began to slim. The skirts of the early 1890s featured some back fullness, but emphasis had shifted to flared skirt hems and enormous leg-of-mutton sleeves, and bustle supports were not as fashionable. With skirts fitting snugly to the hips and derriere in the late 1890s, however, some women relied on skirt supports to achieve a gracefully rounded hipline that set off a small waist. While not as extreme as examples from the mid-1880s, the woven wire or quilted hip pads worn beyond the turn of century show the tenacity of the full-hipped female ideal.

Despite some historians' view that bustle fashions were surely the most hideous ever conceived, this very feminine silhouette has continued to fascinate. In the late 1930s, Elsa Schiaparelli made playful homage to the bustle in some of her sleek evening dresses, while late-twentieth-century bustle interpretations by avant-garde designers, such as Yohji Yamamoto and Vivienne Westwood, have utilized the form with historically informed irony.

See also Mantua; Skirt Supports.

Bibliography

Blum, Stella. *Victorian Fashions and Costumes from Harper's Bazar 1867–1898*. New York: Dover Publications, Inc., 1974.

Cunnington, C. Willett. *English Women's Clothing in the Nineteenth Century*. London: Faber and Faber, 1937. Reprint, New York: Dover Publications, Inc., 1990.

Gernsheim, Alison. *Fashion and Reality: 1840–1914*. London: Faber and Faber, 1963. Reprint as *Victorian and Edwardian Fashion: A Photographic Survey*. New York: Dover Publications, Inc., 1981.

Hill, Thomas E. *Never Give a Lady a Restive Horse*. From *Manual of Social and Business Forms: Selections*. 1873. Also from *Album of Biography and Art*. 1881. Reprint, Berkeley, Calif.: Diablo Press, 1967.

Hughes, Mary Vivian. *A London Child of the Seventies*. London: Oxford University Press, 1934.

Rudofsky, Bernard. *The Unfashionable Human Body*. New York: Doubleday and Company, 1971.

Severa, Joan. *Dressed for the Photographer: Ordinary Americans and Fashion, 1840–1900*. Kent, Ohio: Kent State University Press, 1995.

Waugh, Norah. *Corsets and Crinolines*. New York: Theatre Arts Books, 1954.

H. Kristina Haugland

BUTTONS

Button-like objects of stone, glass, bone, ceramic, and gold have been found at archaeological sites dating as early as 2000 B.C.E., but evidence suggests that these objects were used as decoration on cloth or strung like beads. Nevertheless, they have the familiar holes through which to pass a thread, which gives them the appearance of the button currently known as a fastener.

Buttons can be divided into two types according to the way they are attached to a garment. Shank buttons have a pierced knob or shaft on the back through which passes the sewing thread. The majority of buttons are this type. The shank can be a separate piece that is attached to the button or part of the button material itself, as in a molded button. Pierced buttons have a hole from front to back of the button so that the thread used to attach the button is visible on the face.

Almost every material that has been used in the fine and decorative arts has been used historically in the production of buttons. Buttons exist in a variety of materials: metals (precious or otherwise), gemstones, ivory, horn, wood, bone, mother-of-pearl, glass, porcelain, paper, and silk. In the late nineteenth and twentieth centuries, celluloid and other artificial materials have been used to imitate natural materials.

Early History

The precursor to the button fastener was the fibula, a brooch or pin used to hold two pieces of clothing on the shoulder or chest. The button began to replace the fibula at least by the early Middle Ages, if not sooner.

Buttons functioned as primary fastenings for men's dress earlier than for women's. This may be due to the fact that the women's, from the late Middle Ages into the twentieth century, was required to be tight and smoothly fitted. Lacings and hooks are better suited to providing the strong hold and smooth appearance necessary for tight-fitting garments.

One of the earliest extant pieces of clothing to show the use of buttons as fastenings is the pourpoint of Charles of Blois (c. 1319–1364). This new outer garment was fitted in the body and sleeves, with buttons used to close the front and the sleeves from the elbow. At this point, however, men's lower garments (hose, and, later, breeches) were still fastened to their upper garments, or to an interior belt, by points (laces of ribbon or cord decorated with metal tips). These points with metal tips were often attached as purely decorative pieces to both male and female apparel.

There are records of buttons in documents relating to nobility during the late Middle Ages and the Renaissance. For example, Philip the Good, Duke of Burgundy (1396–1497) ordered Venetian glass buttons decorated with pearls, and Francis I of France (1494–1547) is said to have ordered a set of black enamel buttons mounted on gold from a Parisian goldsmith. These were obviously special buttons of the same quality as contemporary jewelry. Buttons of any material were generally round in shape and made of decorated metal or covered with needlework in silk or metal threads on a wooden core. The ball-shaped toggle button is probably the type of button that replaced the fibula as a fastening for cloaks, capes, and other outer garments. A sixteenth-century example exists in Nuremberg hallmarked silver, attached to a thin bar by a flexible chain link.

The Eighteenth Century

The eighteenth century is considered the Golden Age of buttons by collectors, as the variety of styles, as well as the physical size of buttons increase dramatically. Men's coats required buttons at the front opening, sleeves, pockets, and back vents. Waistcoats and breeches were also fastened with buttons. The size of the button grows and the shape generally flattens during the course of the century, ending in the flat disk as large as 1.38 inch (3.5 cm) in diameter. The value of decorations on a man's ensemble during this period, composed of metal thread embroidery and jeweled buttons, could account for as much as 80 percent of the cost of the suit of clothes. Thus, luxurious buttons became an increasingly essential part of the expression of status in upper-class men's dress. In Denis Diderot's *Encyclopédie* (c. 1746) the creativity of button-makers is exalted, though for moralists costly buttons became one sign of excess in fashion.

The newly fashionable paste jewels (imitation gemstones) appeared in the 1730s and were used to create some of the most highly prized buttons of the nineteenth century. Georges Frédéric Strass, a Parisian jeweler, perfected techniques of making these glass jewels.

As the button evolved from a ball to a flat disk, another notable change in decorative technique was the use of the button as a palette for painting. Representational images became immensely popular in the second

Women shop for buttons in London, 1953. Buttons have been a mainstay of fashion since 2000 B.C.E. and continue to hold their place as an object of function and style. Buttons are created in a variety of materials, including metals, plastics, gem stones, ivory, horn, wood, bone, mother-of-pearl, glass, porcelain, paper, and silk. © Hulton-Deutsch Collection/Corbis. Reproduced by permission.

half of the eighteenth century and are related to the miniature portraits that were worn as pendants or pins during the period. Portraits and subjects like rococo genre scenes, historical events, tourist views, and architectural monuments were produced. An extraordinary set of French portrait miniature buttons was made about 1790 and included portraits of personalities from the French Revolutionary period; each portrait was set in silver with paste-diamond border and the name of the sitter engraved on the back. Artists of note participated in the production of portrait buttons; Jean-Baptiste Isabey (1767–1855), a miniature painter and pupil of Jacques-Louis David, records that he painted decorative buttons at the beginning of his career.

By the second half of the eighteenth century, button making in Europe fell into two categories: French button production remained a craft tradition allied with other high-quality decorative arts, while the English button industry developed mass-production techniques. Probably the most influential of the new English technologies was the development of cut-steel buttons and accessories by the steel manufacturer Matthew Bolton (1728–1809) of Birmingham in the 1760s. Bolton's cut-steel or faceted steel buttons were one of the most prevalent styles of the last three decades of the eighteenth century. The polished and faceted surface was created to imitate that of faceted gems or glass and the effect was quite successful.

The ceramic manufacturer Josiah Wedgwood began producing buttons made of his popular jasperware in 1773 as part of a collaboration with Matthew Bolton, who created cut-steel settings for the ceramic buttons. Jasper-ware ceramics, with their neoclassical motifs derived from cameos, had become the trademark product of the Wedg-wood factory and the buttons were available in five colors and a variety of shapes. Another innovation in the ceramic industry, that of transfer printing, created a new type of ceramic button decorated with designs derived from copperplate engravings. At the end of the eighteenth century, buttons made from mother-of-pearl began to rival in popularity those of steel.

The eighteenth-century Enlightenment sensibility manifested itself in several unique types of buttons. Faithfully depicted insects and animals became the subject of button sets, as did buttons created from semiprecious materials such as agate, in which the natural patterns of the stones were the only decoration. The highlight of this natural history trend is probably the so-called Habitat buttons, which contain actual specimens of insects, plants, or pieces of minerals encased under glass domes.

Nineteenth and Twentieth Century

The standardization of military uniforms in eighteenth-century Europe led to the production of specialized buttons that continues to be a major portion of the button industry today. The number of buttons required for a soldier's coat could be as many as twenty to thirty. Each country, region, and specialization within the armed services required their own individual designs. Uniform buttons carried over into civilian life, as modern businesses, such as airlines, and local law enforcement agencies required special buttons for their uniforms.

Beginning in the early nineteenth century men's dress became much plainer and less ostentatious. Portraits by Jean-Auguste-Dominique Ingres (1780–1867) show men's fashion in the first half of the nineteenth century with plain gold metal or fabric buttons of the same color as the garment on which they are sewn.

Women's bodices and outerwear became the outlet for the display of decorative buttons by the mid-nineteenth century. Women's buttons followed trends in jewelry: colored enamel, porcelain, pearl, silver, and jewels were used. Jet and black glass, introduced during Queen Victoria's mourning for Prince Albert, remained popular to the end of the century.

The nineteenth-century button industry continued along the two lines that had been established in the eighteenth century; industrial progress continued concurrently with handcraft techniques, which generally followed the historical revival styles of nineteenth-century decorative arts.

In 1812, Aaron Benedict established a metal button-making factory in Waterbury, Connecticut, to supply metal buttons for the military. Until that time many metal buttons were still coming from England, but the War of 1812 brought trade between the United States and Britain to a halt. As of 2003, Benedict's company, which became known as Waterbury Buttons, had been in business for 191 years. It is the oldest and largest producer of stamped metal buttons in the United States. Statistics from 1996 show that they produced 100 million buttons—about one-half for fashion trade and the remainder for military and commercial clients. Metal remains the main type of mass-produced button because the material lends itself to mass-production techniques.

The French firm Albert Parent et Cie, founded in 1825, exemplifies the brilliance of French manufacturers who combined mass-production techniques with the hand-finished details to produce luxury buttons in the manner of the eighteenth century. The company left an archive of sample books showing over 80,000 examples of buttons in every available technique of the time.

While more buttons were mass-produced in the nineteenth century that did not mean that fewer materials were employed in the creation of buttons. Natural materials like horn and shells, which had been used for centuries, were rediscovered as mass-produced items. New materials such as celluloid, the first plastic, were used as early as the 1870s to imitate other materials.

Representational picture buttons, first introduced in the late eighteenth century, reached their peak between 1870 and 1914. The nineteenth-century scenes were generally mass-produced stamped metal designs depicting any motif imaginable, but contemporary marvels like the Eiffel Tower were especially popular.

The late nineteenth and early twentieth centuries saw more and more men and women wearing suits with linen or cotton shirts underneath, the new uniform for the emerging white-collar working class. Both suit jackets and shirts required buttons as fastenings and they created the need for large numbers of inexpensive buttons. Thus, the four-holed pierced button was introduced to both men's and women's fashions. However, fine jewelry quality buttons were still produced by some of the best-known retailers of the day such as Cartier, Liberty's of London, and Georg Jensen.

Buttons received competition in the form of the new zipper that was patented in 1903 but did not come into general use until the 1930s. The zipper was considered a novelty at first and played a prominent role as decoration in the designs of top designers.

Bakelite was invented in 1907 and by the 1930s had replaced almost all other synthetics for accessories. Durable and versatile, Bakelite was the medium for some of the most extravagant buttons of the twentieth century, but other plastics eventually replaced it. Three-dimensional accessories, such as fruit shapes, were created in the 1930s and 1940s when small accessories like buttons were especially popular. The designer Elsa Schiaparelli (1890–1973), who was allied with surrealist artists in the 1930s, is notable for her use of extraordinary custom-made buttons.

Plastics replaced most inexpensive glass and pearl buttons by the 1960s. That coupled with the fact that natural materials such as ivory and tortoiseshell are now banned in the United States and other countries has led to the dominance of plastic buttons made to imitate these materials. Mother-of-pearl is still used but in much smaller quantities than in the past. American-made pearl buttons can cost from twenty-five cents to three dollars apiece, as some of the work must still be done by hand and the best shells are imported from the Pacific Ocean coastlines.

The use of stretch fabrics and increasingly informal dressing have led to a decrease in the demand for button fasteners. They have become a symbol of nostalgia and anachronistic tradition, as evidenced by retro button-fly jeans introduced by denim manufacturers in the 1990s and the continued use of rows of tiny buttons on the back of bridal gowns.

Buttons have become extremely collectible. The National Button Society exists for collectors and publishes a quarterly bulletin and holds an annual meeting and show. There are similar societies in Britain and Australia and elsewhere in the world. Military buttons represent a specialty among collectors, as the challenge of identifying the insignias of segments of the armed services adds to the interest of these items.

See also Fasteners; Zipper.

Bibliography

Boucher, Francois. 20,000. *Years of Fashion: The History of Costume and Personal Adornment.* New York: Harry N. Abrams, 1987.

DeMasters, Karen. "New Jersey & Co. Out of the Dust Emerge Lustrous Buttons." *New York Times,* 4 April 1999.

Epstein, Diana, and Millicent Safro. *Buttons.* New York: Harry N. Abrams, 1991.

Houart, Victor. *Buttons: A Collector's Guide.* London: Souvenir Press Ltd., 1977.

Pearsall, Susan. "In Waterbury, Buttons Are Serious Business." *New York Times,* 3 August 1997.

Roche, Daniel. *The Culture of Clothing: Dress and Fashion in the Ancient Régime.* New York: Cambridge University Press, 1996.

Melinda Watt

C

CACHE-SEXE

The term "cache-sexe" refers to a covering for the female genitals. The term is derived from the French *cacher*, which means to hide, and *sexe*, which means genitals. Other terms used synonymously are modesty apron, marriage apron, modesty skirt, loincloth, string skirt, and girdle. The choice of term appears to be related to the country of origin or discipline of the observer. In this case, "cache-sexe" appears to be the term used in those areas of the African continent that were colonized by the French, such as the region from western Mali to southern Cameroon. Cache-sexe are used throughout much of West Africa and parts of East Asia, where the term modesty apron is more commonly used. In short, a wide variety of terms are employed to describe an article of dress that offers insight into the life ways of women in some small-scale societies.

Cache-sexe are constructed of a variety of materials including woven fabric, leather, beads, leaves, and metals. For example, cache-sexe created by the Kirdi (Fulani) women in northern Cameroon are skirts beaded with a fantastic range of colors. Cowry shells and brass beads ornament and give weight to the fringe. Cowry shells originate in the Maldive Islands, off the western coast of India, indicating Kirdi linkages to long distance trade. Cache-sexe are worn low on the hip and tied with a cord. Regardless of materials, the skirts measure approximately twelve to eighteen inches in length and twenty to twenty-two inches in width, excluding the cord.

The cache-sexe can be traced to the Paleolithic period, where stone carvings of fecund women, such as the Venus of Lespugue, depict panels of string fore and aft. String skirts dating from the fourteenth century B.C.E. have been uncovered in burial sites in Denmark. These skirts are wool, also ride low on the hip, fall to just above the knees, and wrap around the body twice. The cords of the skirt are thickly plied and knotted at the bottom, so that the skirt "must have had quite a swing to it" (Barber, p. 57). One of the oldest African examples of cache-sexe is described as a girdle from twelfth-century Mali. It can be described as a three-layer belt with very long fringes. The inner bark of the baobab tree is believed to be the source of the strands of fiber, which are plaited and twined into a solid chevron pattern. Its manufacture is closely related to the techniques used to produce snares, nets, and baskets. This specific article of dress is significant because it was once believed that dress was introduced to sub-Saharan Africa by the spread of Islam. However, this object predates the expansion of Islam and is made of local, not imported, materials.

Cache-sexe appear to be exclusive to females. When and how a woman wears a cache-sexe varies from society to society. In some, a girl begins to wear the skirt after menarche; in others menarche is recognized by a change from a small leather panel skirt to a fringed skirt that wraps all the way around the body. In visual sources of information, cache-sex are part of an ensemble that includes necklaces or supplements to the nose. In parts of New Guinea and Irian Jaya, women use knitted net bags that hang from a strap across the forehead. In twentieth-century images women can be seen wearing brassieres, T-shirts, and blouses.

Female informants report that protection from the environment is the main reason they wear cache-sexe. However, because of the open styling of the of the skirt, either as panels hanging in front and back or as fringes, it may be less effective as physical protection than as spiritual protection. For example, in Papua New Guinea, the Doni believe that ghosts can attack vulnerable areas like the anal opening. Articles of dress with ritual power, such as the cache-sexe, are used to protect, if not actually conceal, the lower body against evil.

Like the penis sheath, one function of the cache-sexe was thought to be modesty. A more likely interpretation of this act of dressing has more to do with fulfilling a group aesthetic about standards of public appearance. Not wearing a cache-sexe is a visible statement of a woman's inability or unwillingness to participate in social interaction, as when ill or in mourning.

Indeed, the main function of the cache sexe, like the penis sheath, appears to be one of drawing attention to the female secondary sex characteristics by intermittently concealing them. In her contemplation of Paleolithic string skirts, Barber states:

> To solve the mystery of why they were [worn], I think we must follow our eyes. Not only do the skirts hide nothing of importance, but also if anything, they attract the eye precisely to the specifically female sexual areas by framing them, presenting them, or playing peekaboo with them.... Our best guess, then is that string skirts indicated something about the childbearing ability or readiness of a woman, . . . that she was in some sense "available" as a bride. (p. 59)

Thus, the cache sexe, by any other name, is exclusively a female symbol. Like the penis sheath, it is more than a covering or a display. It is a unique form of material culture that draws one in to an understanding of the physical, social, and aesthetic life of women in some small-scale cultures.

See also Penis Sheath.

Bibliography

Barber, Elizabeth Wayland. *Women's Work: The First 20,000 Years.* New York: W. W. Norton and Company, 1994.

Heider, Karl G. "Attributes and Categories in the Study of Material Culture: New Guinea Dani Attire." *Man* 4, no. 3 (1969): 379–391.

Hersey, Irwin. "The Beaded Cache-Sexe of Northern Cameroon." *African Arts* 8, no. 2 (winter 1975): 64.

O'Neill, Thomas. "Irian Jaya: Indonesia's Wild Side." *National Geographic* 189, no. 2 (February 1996): 2–34.

Steinmetz, George. "Irian Jaya's People of the Trees." *National Geographic* 189, no. 2 (February 1996): 35–43.

Symonds, Patricia V. *Calling the Soul: Gender and the Cycle of Life in a Hmong Village.* Seattle: University of Washington Press, 2003.

Sandra Lee Evenson

CALLOT SISTERS

The Paris couture house Callot Sisters was founded in 1895 by four sisters, Marie Gerber, Marthe Bertrand, Régine Tennyson-Chantrelle, and Joséphine Crimont, at 24, rue Taitbout. The sisters came from an artistic family; their mother was a talented lace maker and embroiderer, and their father, Jean-Baptiste Callot, was an artist who came from a family of lace makers and engravers (including the esteemed seventeenth-century artist Jacques Callot) and taught at the École nationale supérieure des beaux-arts. Before opening the couture salon, the sisters owned a shop that sold antique laces, ribbons, and lingerie. Madame Gerber was generally acknowledged as the head designer and had worked as a *modéliste* (a designer who works under the house name but is not credited) with the firm Raudnitz et cie. By 1900 Callot Sisters was employing six hundred workers and had clientele in Europe and America. The house's inclusion in the 1900 Paris Exposition Universelle, where it displayed dresses alongside such venerable couture firms as Doucet, Paquin, Redfern, Rouff, and Worth, demonstrates the sisters' respected place within the industry.

A number of designers, including Madeleine Vionnet and Georgette Renal, began their careers at Callot Sisters before launching their own couture houses. According to Vionnet, who worked at the house from 1901 to 1907, Madame Gerber was a friend of the art collector and critic Edmond de Goncourt, with whom she shared an interest in the Orient and eighteenth-century rococo design. The decor of the sisters' salon reflected these two influences, and they received their clients in a Chinese-style room adorned with Coromandel lacquer, Song dynasty silks, and Louis XV furniture. The house's design repertoire encompassed daywear, tailored suits, and evening dresses, but it was best known for its ethereal, eighteenth-century-inspired dishabille and exotic evening dress influenced by the East.

The sisters' luxurious tea gowns, produced in the early part of the century, were made of silk, chiffon, and organdy and often incorporated costly antique laces into their designs. Their penchant for such delicate materials prompted Marcel Proust to write, in *Remembrance of Things Past*, that the sisters "go in rather too freely for lace" (p. 675). Their layered, filmy, pastel-toned garments were very fashionable;

such contemporaries as Jacques Doucet and Lucile also created such "confections," as they were often described.

In the 1910s and early 1920s the house's garments also drew upon the brilliant fauvist colors and Eastern-inspired design that were a vital part of the visual culture of the period. While this exotic mode is commonly associated with the designer Paul Poiret, the sisters also created clothing that incorporated embellishment and construction techniques derived from Asia and Africa. Some of these dresses (sometimes referred to as *robes phéniciennes*) integrated design elements from the two continents into one garment. For example, a kimono sleeve might be used with an Algerian burnoose form. Madeleine Vionnet recalls that the adoption of the kimono sleeve was Madame Gerber's innovation and that she was incorporating the cylindrical sleeve into art nouveau dresses in the early part of the century.

The year 1914 was significant for the design house, in that it marked both a move to 9–11, avenue Matignon and the sisters' involvement in Le syndicat de défense de la grande couture française. Through this organization, Callot Sisters, along with the designers Paul Poiret, Jacques Worth, Jeanne Paquin, Madeleine Cheruit, Paul Rodier, and Bianchini and Ferier, put in place controls to protect their original designs from copy houses that sold them to ready-to-wear manufacturers without their permission. This is the period when the Callot Sisters, and many other designers, began to date their labels. While fashion activity in Paris subsided somewhat during World War I, the house of Callot remained open, and the sisters continued to promote their clothing in America by exhibiting at the 1915 Pacific Panama International Exposition in San Francisco, California. By the 1920s the house also expanded its operations to include branches in Nice, Biarritz, Buenos Aires, and London, further extending the international recognition of their label.

Callot Sisters remained active throughout the 1920s and participated in the 1925 Exposition internationale des arts décoratifs et industriels modernes in Paris, along with Jeanne Lanvin, the house of Worth, and the jeweler Cartier in the Pavilion of Elegance. By 1926, however, the fashionability of the house was on the wane. The American designer Elizabeth Hawes, who was working as a copyist in Paris in 1926, writes of dressing herself at Callot for some time and "getting some beautiful bargains in stylish clothes which

> "There are very few firms at present, one or two only, Callot—although they go in rather too freely for lace—Doucet, Cheruit, Paquin sometimes. The others are all horrible. . . . . Then is there a vast difference between a Callot dress and one from any ordinary shop?" Albertine responds that there is a great difference because what one could buy for three hundred francs in an ordinary shop will cost two thousand at Callot soeurs (Proust, p. 675).

lasted me for years. I had an extra fondness for Callot because the American buyers found her out of date and unfashionable. She was. She just made simple clothes with wonderful embroidery. Embroidery wasn't chic" (Hawes p. 66). The sisters retained their interest in fashionable detail and luxurious materials even when the more graphic lines of the art deco silhouette were in ascendance.

In 1928 Madame Gerber's son Pierre took over the firm and moved it to 41, avenue Montaigne, where it remained until Madame Gerber retired in 1937. At that time the company was absorbed into the house of Calvet, although labels with the Callot Sisters name appeared until the closing of Calvet in 1948.

See also Art and Fashion; Haute Couture; Orientalism; Paris Fashion; Proust, Marcel; Vionnet, Madeleine.

Bibliography

Chantrell, Maria Lyding. *Les Moires-Mesdames Callot Soeurs*. Paris: Paris Presses du Palais-Royal, 1978.

Hawes, Elizabeth. *Fashion Is Spinach*. New York: Random House, 1938.

Kirke, Betty. *Madeleine Vionnet*. San Francisco: Chronicle Books, 1998.

Milbank, Caroline Rennolds. *Couture: The Great Designers*. New York: Stewart, Tabori and Chang, Inc., 1985.

Proust, Marcel. *Remembrance of Things Past*. Vol. 2: *Within a Budding Grove*. Translated by C. K. Scott Moncrieff and Frederick A. Blossom. New York: Random House, 1927–1932.

Steele, Valerie. *Paris Fashion: A Cultural History*. New York and Oxford: Oxford University Press, 1988.

Michelle Tolini Finamore

CAMOUFLAGE CLOTH

Camouflage cloth was developed during the twentieth century to make military personnel less visible to enemy forces. The word "camouflage" (from a French expression meaning "puffing smoke") refers to a process of evading visual detection through some combination of blend-in coloration, cryptic patterning, and blurring of the silhouette. Camouflage is widespread in the natural world, from the barklike coloration and patterning of many moths to the stripes of tigers and zebras. Used by predators and prey alike, camouflage is all about gaining a survival edge in situations of conflict.

Human beings have no natural camouflage features, but it is likely that some forms of camouflage have been used by humans for thousands of years. Prehistoric hunters would readily have learned to attach pieces of brush or clumps of grass to their clothing in order to approach prey undetected. In historic times, Indian hunters of the American Great Plains practiced a related technique, mimicry, by draping themselves in bison skins to approach herds of bison without alarming them.

The same techniques of camouflage that were employed by early hunters were applicable to small-scale tribal warfare and raiding. However, the development of large-scale military operations, which accompanied the rise of civilization and the invention of metal weapons, made camouflage less important. Warfare for many centuries consisted largely of combat between forces in plain view of each other; camouflage has no role in an army of massed swordsmen or spearmen. Well into the nineteenth century, many armies wore brightly colored uniforms (such as the British redcoats) to aid in maintaining formations and to boost morale.

Armies fighting colonial and frontier wars, however, found such uniforms a disadvantage when dealing with irregular forces who fought from hidden places and employed time-honored camouflage techniques used in hunting and raiding. The development of improved firearms capable of accurate long-distance fire at individual targets also made it important for troops to make themselves less conspicuous.

During the nineteenth century, British military forces in India encountered khaki (Urdu for "dustcolored") cloth, which they began to adopt for field use. Khaki uniforms were standard-issue for British troops in the South African Boer War in the 1890s, which featured widespread use of guerrilla tactics by the Boer forces.

Camouflage paint in various colors and cryptic patterns was used by German, French, and other forces during World War I to decrease the visibility of bunkers, tanks, and even ships, but camouflage was not widely used to protect troops during that war. In the 1920s, the French military conducted extensive research into camouflage, and other armed forces soon followed suit; camouflage cloth as such dates to the period between the two World Wars. During World War II, camouflage paint and netting were extensively used to disguise combat vehicles and forward bases, and troops on all sides used camouflage-cloth combat uniforms or tunics in some situations (including white outfits for winter, arctic, and mountain operations). A problem arose in that camouflage cloth made it difficult for troops to distinguish friend from foe under combat conditions. Partly for that reason, American soldiers in WWII largely abandoned camouflage gear except for their helmets, with netting covers into which twigs, grass, and leaves could be inserted.

American troops continued to avoid camouflage cloth in the Korean War, but camouflage gear became ubiquitous in military forces worldwide during the 1950s. Camouflage outfits were widely used by American troops during the Vietnam War, the Gulf War, and other operations. Patterns and color schemes have been continually refined to produce better results in different environments, including jungle, grasslands, and desert.

Camouflage cloth entered the civilian wardrobe in the late 1960s as part of the counterculture appropriation of military surplus clothing for street wear—an ironic response to the Vietnam War. The trend faded but then resumed in the street styles of the 1980s. In the 1990s, in the wake of the Gulf War, camouflage cloth (including some pseudo-military patterns and colors developed especially for the civilian market) again entered civilian wardrobes. It was occasionally used even for such non-military clothing styles as sports jackets for men and dresses and skirts for women. In the second half of the decade, camouflage cloth was incorporated into the collections of several prominent designers, including John Galliano, Anna Sui, and Rei Kawakubo.

In the twenty-first century, camouflage cloth is firmly entrenched in the military wardrobe and continues to appear in civilian clothing from time to time. Though its military connotations are never absent, in some respects camouflage has become just another type of patterned cloth, like animal prints or plaid, available for optional use.

See also Galliano, John; Protective Clothing; Uniforms, Military.

Bibliography

Newark, Tim, Quentin Newark, and J. F. Borsarello. *Brassey's Book of Camouflage*. London: Brassey's (U.K.) Ltd., 1996.

John S. Major

CARDIN, PIERRE

During the last half of the twentieth century, Pierre Cardin (1922–) became a prominent and widely admired designer as well as a highly successful businessman. Cardin is known for his acute intuition, which often made him a trendsetter and design leader. Cardin has expanded his design operations far beyond fashions for both men and women to encompass all aspects of modern living. The name Cardin has become synonymous with his brand as he has expanded his commercial operations through timely licensing. As of the early

Pierre Cardin displays his designs. Cardin's fashion empire is known the world over. He is one of the first designers to "brand" his products, which include accessories and handbags, home interiors, luxury cars, and luggage. © Reuters/Corbis. Reproduced by Permission.

2000s, Cardin's corporate empire held 900 licenses for production in 140 countries.

Early Training

Born in Italy of French parents on 2 July 1922, the designer was originally named Pietro Cardini. After several years in Venice, however, his family relocated to France. As a young man Cardin briefly studied architecture before joining the house of Paquin in 1945. His tenure there gave him the opportunity of working with Christian Bérard and Jean Cocteau on the 1946 film *La Belle et la bête*, for which he created the velvet costume for the Beast, played by Jean Marais. After a brief stint with Elsa Schiaparelli, Cardin worked under the auspices of Christian Dior from 1946 until he went out on his own in 1950. Cardin honed his superb tailoring skills heading up Dior's coat and suit workroom. Cardin's own business was first located on the rue Richepanse (renamed rue du Chevalier de Saint-George), but later moved to the famed rue du Faubourg Saint-Honoré, where the designer launched his first couture collection in 1953. In 1954 Cardin opened a boutique called Eve, followed by Adam for men in 1957.

From the beginning, Cardin showed himself to be an innovator and a rebel. He was quoted as saying, "For me, the fabric is nearly secondary. I believe first in shape, architecture, the geometry of a dress" (Lobenthal, p. 151). His experimentation with fabrics embraced geometric abstraction without losing sight of the human figure. Cardin's ability to sculpt fabric with an architectural sensibility became his signature. Making garments with impeccable craftsmanship, Cardin possessed the skills and vision to make his dreams a wearable reality. Even during the 1970s, when his dresses shifted from a sculpted look to a more draped silhouette, the fluidity of his work remained formal. Cardin was highly successful as a couturier, but he also sought to redefine the field of fashion design commercially. For his efforts in launching a ready-to-wear line alongside his couture collection, however, Cardin's membership in the prestigious Chambre Syndicale was revoked in 1959. Cardin was soon reinstated, but voluntarily resigned from the Chambre in 1966.

Cardin's Men's Wear

Cardin's early training as a tailor's apprentice shaped his approach to fashion design for men as he matured throughout the 1950s. Cardin deconstructed the traditional business suit. He subtracted collars, cuffs, and lapels, creating one of the most compelling images of the early 1960s. This look became instantly famous when Dougie Millings, the master tailor who made stage outfits for numerous British rock musicians, dressed the Beatles in his version of matching collarless suits.

Cardin's men's wear line was housed in a separate building on the Place Beauvau by 1962. He was inspired by his travels; after seeing the traditional high-collared jacket of India and Pakistan, he distilled its form into another popular innovation in men's fashions of the 1960s, the so-called Nehru jacket. Cardin further disrupted men's customary suiting by heralding the wearing of neck scarves in place of ties, and turtlenecks instead of button-down shirts. Yet he also was capable of designing men's clothing in the classic tradition, such as the costumes worn by the character John Steed in the British television series *The Avengers*.

Space Age and Unisex Styles

Advances in fabric production and technology during the 1960s coincided with a widespread fascination with space exploration. Cardin's Space Age or Cosmocorps collection of 1964 synthesized his streamlined, minimal dressing for both men and women. This body-skimming apparel resembling uniforms featured cutouts inspired by op art. Cardin was innovative in his use of vinyl and metal in combination with wool fabric. Not just unisex, Cardin's clothing often seemed asexual. Unlike such other fashion minimalists as Rudi Gernreich and André Courrèges, Cardin did not promote pants for women. He often used monotone-colored stockings or white patterned tights to compliment his minidresses. The "Long Longuette," which was dubbed the maxidress, was Cardin's 1970 response to the miniskirt. In 1971, Cardin obtained an exclusive agreement with a German firm to use its stretch fabric, declaring that "stretch fabrics would revolutionize fashion" (Weir, p. 5). Continuing his reputation as a trendsetter, he showed white cotton T-shirts paired with couture gowns on the runway in 1974 and introduced exaggerated shoulders in 1979.

Licensing and Global Marketing

Cardin learned much about the business side of fashion from his mentor Christian Dior. Dior had been very successful in trading on his name to license his designs

> "The job of fashion is not just to make pretty suits or dresses, it is to change the face of the world by cut and line. It is to make another aspect of men evident."
>
> Pierre Cardin (in Lobenthal, p. 153)

internationally. Cardin took this approach further when he sought and found a global acceptance of his designs in countries as diverse as the Soviet Union, India, and Japan. Cardin was an exponent of what is now called branding long before other fashion designers followed suit. He was the first designer to sell ready-to-wear clothing in the Soviet Union as early as 1971. While Cardin's men's wear lines were ultimately more successful than his women's fashions in the United States during the 1970s, he still owned more than two hundred American retail outlets. Cardin was embraced by the Japanese market with special enthusiasm. At the peak of his expansion in 1969, Cardin boasted of having 192 factories throughout the world.

Cardin's fashion empire spanned the globe with his trademark licensing as of the early 2000s. Products identified by the Cardin brand ranged from accessories and handbags to home interiors, luxury cars, and luggage, as well as to such personal items as Fashion Tress wigs, introduced in 1973. The ubiquitous brand name was recognized around the world. As Caroline Milbank stated, "It is difficult to name something that Pierre Cardin has yet to design or transform with his imprint" (Milbank, p. 338). In 1971, Cardin transformed the former Théâtre des Ambassadeurs into L'Espace Cardin to promote new talent in performance art and fashion design. Cardin capitalized again on his fame in 1981 by purchasing Maxim's, the famous Paris restaurant, and using its name to build a worldwide chain of restaurants in the mid-1980s.

Brand Identity and Logos

During the early 1960s, Cardin was a pioneer in designing clothing conspicuously adorned with his company's logo. This trend was picked up by many other designers from the 1970s onward. Cardin's logos, consisting of his initials or a circular bull's eye, were often three-dimensional vinyl appliqués or quilted directly into the garment. Cardin's unrestrained licensing, while symbolic of his success, may have resulted in untimely diluting his name brand image.

Many fashion writers criticized Cardin for overexposure, especially given the very rapid expansion of his product lines during the 1980s and 1990s. Nevertheless, Cardin's name was known throughout the world, and identified by the public with quality and high standards. Cardin stood out as one of the most complex designers of the twentieth century because he was one of a handful who understood that fashion is above all a business. His skills as an entrepreneur, and especially his creative licensing, made Pierre Cardin one of the richest people in the fashion world.

See also Brands and Labels; Dior, Christian; Fashion Marketing and Merchandising; Logos; Nehru Jacket; Paquin, Jeanne; Paris Fashion; Schiaparelli, Elsa; Space Age Styles; Unisex Clothing; Vinyl as Fashion Fabric.

Bibliography

Lobenthal, Joel. *Radical Rags: Fashions of the Sixties.* New York: Abbeville Press, 1990.

Lynam, Ruth, ed. *Couture: An Illustrated History of the Great Paris Designers and Their Creations.* Garden City, N.Y.: Doubleday, 1972.

Mendes, Valerie. *Pierre Cardin: Past, Present, Future.* London and Berlin: Dirk Nishen Publishing, 1990.

Milbank, Caroline Rennolds. *Couture: The Great Designers.* New York: Stewart, Tabori, and Chang, Inc., 1985.

Weir, June. "Cardin Today . . . A New Freedom." *Women's Wear Daily* (26 January 1971): 5.

Myra Walker

CARICATURE AND FASHION

From the Italian for "charge" or "loaded," the caricature print emerged in large numbers in the eighteenth century in industrializing western Europe. It was in the second half of the twentieth century that the caricature that concerned itself primarily with the subject of fashion and manners, rather than political or portrait themes, developed. The origins and conventions of the fashion caricature include over-lapping literary, theatrical, and popular religious and artistic traditions. Greco-Roman theorizations, performances, and artistic depictions of the cosmic world turned upside down,

and late medieval woodcuts, in which memento mori themes of the dance of death and the bonfire of the vanities established the tropes of the veneer of civilization and the futility of dress and cosmetics in arresting earthly time. The European carnival tradition, commedia dell'arte and puppetry, which highlight human foibles, and the figure of the hag who deploys fashion and makeup in an act of sartorial and spiritual delusion provided subjects for major artists working in the etching media such as Giambattista Tiepolo (1696–1770), Domenico Tiepolo (1727–1804), and Francisco de Goya (1746–1828). Not fashion caricatures as such, nor were these images widely available, but their themes recur in the eighteenth-century caricature print.

Caricature fashion prints also exist in a relationship to respectful engravings of the cries or occupations of the town, plates depicting national dress, and "costume plates" depicting courtier men and "women of quality" by seventeenth-century artists including Abraham Bosse and J. D. de Saint-Jean in France and the Bohemian Wenceslaus Hollar (1607–1677) working in England. The work of Jacques Callot (1592–1635) in France crosses the boundary between observation and satire. Etched images take on new meanings when pointed titles or moralizing verse are appended; the caricature generally makes use of a combination of word and image. Although censorship restricted production in France, prints were produced in neighboring Holland, and an early eighteenth-century fashion caricature entitled "The Powdered Poodle" survives in which the high-heeled shoes, forward posture, and long blond wig popularized by the court of Louis XIV is mocked in both image and appended verse (Paris, Bibliothèque Nationale).

Eighteenth-Century Caricature

Drawing on Renaissance physiognomic studies or "caprices" by Leonardo da Vinci, Giuseppe Arcimboldo, and Albrecht Dürer, and the baroque caricatures of Annibale and Agostoni Carracci (*Heads,* c. 1590) and Gianlorenzo Bernini, eighteenth-century Italy saw a rise in the production of recognizable portrait caricatures. They included carefully delineated costumes etched by Pier Leone Ghezzi (1674–1755) and Pietro Longhi (1702–1785), and painted in Rome by the English artists Sir Joshua Reynolds (1723–1792) and Thomas Patch (1725–1782). These works did not circulate widely in the public realm but were designed for the amusement of aristocratic circles participating in the Grand Tour who understood the dialectic of the ideal and the debased explored in this work. Furnishing their sitters with hideous physiognomies and ill-formed bodies loaded with fine clothing and airs, the works depict the dress and demeanor of the aristocrat abroad when the mask of civility has slipped under the influence of alcohol and other vice. The paintings of Patch and Reynolds drew upon the painted "modern moral subject" and subsequent etching cycles produced in England by William Hogarth (*The Harlot's Progress* 1731; *The Rake's Progress* 1733–1734; *Marriage à la Mode* 1743). Cinematic in its scenic narrative, Hogarth's finely produced work included satirical details of fashionable dress and deportment that were used to emphasize more general political, aesthetic, and moral questions.

As new and cheaper forms of reproduction and literate audiences for periodicals and prints arose in Enlightenment western Europe, there was a marked increase in the output of satirical printmaking from the 1760s in France, Germany, and the Dutch Republic, but notably England. England's freedom of the press and involvement of the public in political and cultural affairs through coffeehouse, print, and exhibition culture encouraged the production of thousands of caricatures. Fashion had two principal functions in these prints. In the first half of the century, the English political print included dress to indicate class, political party, geographic, ethnic, and national identity. In tandem with theatrical precedents, the shorthand device for a Frenchman was elaborate court dress and a simpering posture, for a Spaniard a ruff, and a Dutchman round breeches. Nationalist Tories and the English John Bull figure wore rustic frock coats and boots, in contrast to the rich court dress of Whigs which resembled that of continental court culture.

In the second half of the century, numerous English printmakers who were also printsellers switched their output from political caricatures to social ones in which fashion formed the principal and not the secondary subject. Matthew and Mary Darly, John Dawes, William Humphrey, William Holland, Samuel W. Fores, Carington and John Bowles, and John Raphael Smith exhibited their wares publicly in shop windows and printed single sheet caricatures that were sold in folio sets, reproducing the designs of others such as John Collett, Robert Dighton, Henry W. Bunbury, and Thomas Rowlandson. Themes include the speed of new fashionable items, textiles, patterns, and bodily silhouettes; the alleged spread of fashionability to the lower orders including the servant

class; the concomitant difficulty of reading the social sphere; themes of metropolitan urbanity versus rustic simplicity; the role of the appearance trades, such as wigmaking and hairdressing, in promoting fashion; and alleged relationships between national fashions and character. The disjunction between the applied finery of fashion and the lumpen, deluded, or immoral physical body beneath continued older Christian themes.

The caricature print from 1760 extends the more general cultural association of women with extremes of fashion to that of men, as they scrutinize extensively the airs and dress of the macaroni (c. 1760–1780) and later the buck and the dandy (c. 1800–1820). Prints included both fictive and recognizable metropolitan individuals as well as referring to stock theatrical types such as the fop, the German friseur (an aged and ugly male hairdresser whose physiognomy was interchangeable with the Jew), the dancing-master (French and effete), the rustic, and the Scotsman, a "Billingsgate Moll" (a market woman), and a "Lady of the Town" (prostitute). In the etched prints of Matthew Darly, the more lowborn the person depicted, the more crude the illustrative style, suggesting a cruder imitation or performance of fashionability. These differences perpetuate the belief that the orders are inherently either vulgar or superior depending on rank, as well as highlighting the joke contained in the overstepping of sartorial boundaries from class to class. Just as the development of caricature demands its opposite, idealized aesthetics, so the convoluted forms, surprising gestures, and novel departures of caricature perfectly reflected contemporary notions of the chicanery of fashion.

Caricature prints appeared in the expanding number of English periodicals, such as *The London Museum*, *The Oxford Magazine*, and *The Town and Country Magazine*. Sometimes hand-colored, many such prints were also sold or hired out in suites. Etching and engraving were the dominant techniques until the 1770s, when the mezzotint was developed and during the 1780s aquatint and stipple engraving appeared. The latter techniques permitted longer print-runs of more than one thousand and conveyed detailed messages about the texture of clothing and the tone of complexion. Carington Bowles's and John Raphael Smith's figures were also set in backgrounds such as paved streetscapes and neoclassical dressing-rooms and masquerade venues which comment on the spread of consumption, comfort, and new design novelties, including dress.

Caricature prints were relatively expensive, sought out by the aristocracy, the gentry, and collected even by the king. If generally too expensive for the artisan, prints were available for viewing in print shops, on the walls of taverns, coffeehouses, and clubs, or in the 1790s, visited in exhibitions. Satirical prints were generally kept in folios, and it is unclear how often they were glazed and hung. Pasted on walls they made "print-rooms" (Calke Abbey, Derbyshire) and ladies' fans were occasionally composed of them. English prints were imported by French dealers and sent as far as St. Petersburg. Ambassadorial missions reported on their contents to rulers such as Louis XVI.

Although the circuits of exchange between English, French, Dutch, and German fashion caricature have not been clarified by scholars (most work has been done on revolutionary political imagery), it is apparent that the subject and style of English and continental work is interrelated. Hogarth derived much of his compositional virtuosity from a study of the French rococo fashion drawing and print by Boitard, Cochin, Coypel, Watteau, and Gravelot. The Matthew and Mary Darlys' calligraphic linear style set upon evacuated white backgrounds was copied around Europe. A group of crude French engravings on the topic of fops, fashion absurdities, and touristic interactions in the street are virtually indistinguishable in subject matter from English work, and the Darlys were copied in Germany. The French also produced caricature engravings of superb technical perfection and elegance in the 1770s, in which the style and format mocks both high fashion's perfection and the engravings of manners seen in Rétif de la Bretonne's *Monument du costume* (1789).

Meanings of Caricature Fashion Prints

In Germany, Daniel Nikolaus Chodowiecki's engravings for almanacs possess an elegant and animated line that epitomizes the ambiguity of some fashion caricatures. His paired contrasting images on the themes of artifice (court dress) and naturalism (neoclassical dressing) does not necessarily castigate the former: perhaps his suggestion is that pastoral dress is just as much an affectation for leisured peoples. His illustrations for Johann Kaspar Lavater's highly influential study of character and physiognomy (1775–1778) with a considerable focus on dress, do function as explicit attacks on ancien régime manners and morals and argue that the new man must reject the set of the courtier.

Eighteenth-century prints were often reproduced in the nineteenth century without the context of their original verbal text banners. This led to different interpretations that were frequently sentimental and nostalgic. Approaches to the caricature reflect shifts in twentieth-century art-historical and social analysis. A reflection model used exhaustively by British Museum cataloger and historian M. Dorothy George analyzed caricature prints as representations of real events such as the launch and spread of a new fashion. This approach is reductive in that prints had multiple meanings to different audiences and may have helped create the dynamic of an event. Whereas the art historian Ernst Gombrich argued that the aim of the printmaker and dealer was to sell the product and not unsettle the purchaser overly, the Hogarth historian Ronald Paulson argued that within graphic satire a range of explanations are true and not mutually exclusive. Paulson argued that Hogarth's work was designed for more than one audience and one reading. Like the theater, which assumed different reading positions from its multiple publics, the power of the caricature print is to function on several levels simultaneously. Although Brewer notes that there is almost no surviving evidence of how the common people viewed popular imagery, such as the caricature prints, there are many contemporary descriptions of the street and the theater, which emphasize that the fashionable and wealthy were often mocked or even abused for their pretension. Fashion caricatures participated in this dialogue.

Some men and women "of family and estate" such as W. H. Bunbury, Lady Diana Beauclerc, and the Marquis Townshend produced sketches which were engraved and distributed by professionals. Many of them laugh at the pretensions of the lower orders that emulate the manners and dress previously reserved for their social betters. This is not the only meaning, however. As Maidment notes of the early-nineteenth-century "literary dustman" type, in form and technique such prints might simultaneously highlight the energy and ingenuity of laboring class subjects at the same time as mocking aspirational behavior. It partly explains the longevity of the caricature print in periodicals for all classes. Caricature fashion prints also provided information about the mood or set of a fashion such as the insouciance of the *Incroyable*, a fop of the Directoire period. As Anne Hollander noted of Renaissance art, forms such as engravings might teach people what it was to look fashionable. In the eighteenth century, high-art painting and caricature were both means through which fashion was read, experienced, and modulated.

Nineteenth-Century Caricature

Master illustrators in the nineteenth century continued the themes on fashion laid down in the 1760s, notably Thomas Rowlandson (1756–1827) who worked for publisher Ackermann, James Gillray (1757–1815), Robert Dighton (1752–1814) and son Richard; Isaac Cruikshank (1756–1811) and sons Robert (1789–1856) and George (1792–1878). In the Revolutionary and Napoleonic period, dress featured as part of the textual jokes in political caricature. Respectful fashion plates and caricatures issued from the same hand of experienced illustrators: Jean-Francois Bosio (1764–1827) and Philibert Louis Debu-court (1755–1832), who deployed an extremely elegant style and fine coloring as part of the joke. In Paris the famed series by Horace Vernet, *Le Supreme bon ton* from *Caricatures parisiennes* (c. 1800) used the figure types and linear illustrative style of the contemporary fashion periodical, but distorted the figures, poses, and situations to expose the ludicrous nature of contemporary manners. H. Vernet provided "serious" fashion plates for Pierre La Mésangère, who was both the publisher of *Le journal des dames et des modes* (c. 1810) as well as the famous caricature series *Incroyables et merveilleuses* (1810–1818), which continued the work of his father, Carle Vernet (1758–1836), from the 1790s. The paradox and collisions of exoticism and historicism of early-nineteenth-century dress is extremely well conveyed in these French images. The series *Le bon genre* (French periodical 1814–1816) set English and French fashions side by side, subject to some distortion, in order to have a ready-made caricature that also provides fashion information and comments on national identity. Louis-Léopold Boilly's exquisite painted genre scenes of fashionable life often verge on caricature with rather too much male and female buttock revealed through the chamois leather and muslin, and this interest was made explicit in his *Recueil de grimaces* (Paris, 1823–1828), caricature physiognomy lithographic studies.

Nineteenth-Century Journalism and the Caricature

In the nineteenth century, reading publics and leisure time increased and the costs of printing decreased, with a massive expansion of cheap periodicals and news-sheets including journals who now took the caricature as their very subject: in France *La caricature* (1830–1835) and its successor *Le charivari* (1832–1842) were run by Charles Philipon. Technical developments in lithographic, steel engraving, and wood-block reproductions meant that the caricature proliferated within these formats and ceased to be sold primarily within folio sets. When from 1835 political censorship was introduced in France, the caricature of Parisian manners became the screen through which other events might be filtered. Social, economic, and technological developments had major impacts upon fashion and there is no social topic in which the caricature did not participate. These included, but were not restricted to, male dandyism; the rise of the demimonde or courtesan class; sweatshops and the production of clothing; shopping and the department store; makeup and artifice; swells or dandies; middle-class hypocrisy and propriety; immodesty and the ball gown; women's participation in sport and education; feminism and the suffragette movement; dress reform; emancipation and embourgeoisement of slaves; issues of class and the "servant problem"; the aesethetic movement of the 1880s; and the general spread of consumer goods. Extremes and novelties of fashion, such as the women's crinoline and the bustle, the nature of fashionability and the *Parisienne*, and the interaction of the classes in the new public spaces of the metropoli of Paris, London, and New York, were delineated by highly accomplished artists working in lithography, notably Gustave Doré (1832–1883), J. J. Grandville (1803–1846), Joseph Traviès, Paul Gavarni (1804–1866), and Cham and J. L. Forain (1852–1931) Honoré Daumier (1808–1879) produced a massive output of 4,000 lithographs, many appearing in *Le charivari* and *Le Journal amusant*. His human comedy in which the same characters reappear relates to that of Balzac's literature. Nineteenth-century caricature employed novel compositional formats with overlapping vignettes and asymmetrical strip formats, as seen in the periodical *La Vie parisienne*. In England Max Beerbohm and George du Maurier provided the journal *Punch*, or the *The London Charivari* (from 1841) with a constant stream of caricatures that contributed to the tenacious idea that fashions for both men and women represented an absurdity. Its illustrator John Leech termed the word "cartoon" within *Punch* in 1843. The German middle-class public had numerous journals in which fashion caricatures recurred—*Punsch* (1847), *Leipziger Charivari* (1858), *Berliner Charivari* (1847), and *Kladderadatsch* (1848);

the generic term "Biedermeier" for the period referred to a middle-class everyman fictional figure. The journal *Simplizissimus* (from 1896) led to the milieu in which expressionists like Georg Grosz (1893–1959) produced stinging comments on the human condition, using dress to mark out issues of class, gender, and sexuality. In North America enormous amounts of fashion-related caricature were produced for journals after the 1820s such as *American Comic Almanach* (from 1841), *Punchinello, Harper's Weekly*, and *Vanity Fair*. At the turn of the century the work of Charles Dana Gibson blurred the distinction between satire and the exaggerated fashionability of the Gibson girl, a gentle caricature that might be emulated for the turn of a head or silhouette of a skirt. In that the cartoon strip, comic book, and Disney film rely on caricature for their conventions, North America generated several industries from this form.

Until the post-World War II period when photography eclipsed line and other drawing in the media, the fashion caricature continued to be prominent within twentieth-century periodicals for all classes. Many of the fashion images commissioned by French couturiers including Paul Poiret approach the mannerism of caricature. The work of Erté (Romain de Tirtoff) also blurs the division between the fashion plate and the caricature in order to express a mood. Caricature images constitute important documents of relatively submerged topics including lesbianism and mannish dressing for women in the 1920s and male dress within homosexual communities. The commodification of dress and the rise of the fashion parade as a theatrical spectacle are documented in caricatures by figures such as Sem (Georges Goursat). The ironies of modernist lifestyle were documented by the British caricaturist Osbert Lancaster (*Homes Sweet Homes*, London, 1939). Wartime Britain and America used the caricature as propaganda to castigate wasteful female consumers. The emergence of the New Look was mocked as absurd or extravagant and unsuitable to matronly women in the late 1940s. Illustrator-designers, such as Cecil Beaton, provided high-style magazines like *Vanity Fair* and *Vogue* with both drawn and composite photographic or collaged backdrop renditions of real society women (Elsa Maxwell, the Duchess of Windsor, Coco Chanel) which teetered upon caricature, as well as producing cutting versions for private consumption (Violet Trefusis).

Although caricatures continue to be included as cartoons in newspaper and periodicals, their power declined with the advent of television as an alternative form of entertainment in the 1950s. It could be argued, however, that the techniques of the caricature, related as they were to the theater and vaudeville stereotype, continued within popular culture forms of television and film. Many 1950s and 1960s situation comedies such as *Green Acres* and *I Love Lucy* feature absurd situations involving dress; the 1990s comedy series *Absolutely Fabulous*, written and acted by Dawn French and Jennifer Saunders, made the fashion industry and absurd fashions in dress and lifestyle its subject, as did the Robert Altman film *Pret-à-Porter*. Other popular situation comedies, such as *Designing Women* from the 1980s, *Seinfeld*, and the overdressed and shopping-addicted figure of Karen in the queer sitcom *Will and Grace*, deploy caricature-like exaggeration of dress, pose, and identity which is intertwined with both ancient tropes of theatrical farce and the caricature print of modern culture.

Much postmodern high-fashion illustration in the 1980s and 1990s used the form of the caricature to comment ironically on the place of fashion in contemporary life. The designers Moschino, Christian Lacroix (spring–summer 1994), and Karl Lagerfeld utilize a caricature-like irony in some of their illustration derived from Directoire imagery by the likes of Louis LeCoeur and Debucourt, as well as studying the genre for ideas; some fashion parades and styling by John Galliano and Vivienne Westwood resemble a caricature suite brought to life as a conscious strategy. Galliano's degree show (1984) and some subsequent collections (spring–summer 1986) were directly inspired by *Incroyables et merveilleuses*. Forms that are directly derived from the eighteenth-century caricature continue to be published in daily newspapers (the political cartoon in which prominent figures are characterized through their dress), journals such as *Country Life* (Annie Tempest's Tottering-by-Gently series) and *The New Yorker* (established 1925). Although amusing and trenchant, such caricatures now have an archaic air and may be replaced in the future by the three-dimensional and new temporal possibilities of digital technology. In that surrealism found fertile pickings in English Georgian and nineteenth-century French and German caricature, it could be said that surrealist-inspired contemporary digital fashion photography by Phil Poynter and Andrea Giacobbe continues the ludic project of the fashion caricature consumed in multidimensional ways.

See also Fashions; Historical Studies of.

Bibliography

D'Oench, Ellen G. "Copper into Gold." Prints by John Raphael Smith 1751–1812. New Haven, Conn., and London: Yale University Press, 1999.

Donald, Diana. The Age of Caricature: Satirical Prints in the Reign of George III. New Haven, Conn., and London: Yale University Press, 1996.

——. Followers of Fashion. Graphic Satires from the Georgian Period. London: Hayward Gallery Publishing, 2002.

Duffy, Michael. The Englishman and the Foreigner: The English Satirical Print 1600–1832. Cambridge, Mass.: Chadwyck-Healey, 1986.

George, Mary Dorothy. Hogarth to Cruikshank: Social Change in Graphical Satire. London: Allen Lane; Penguin, 1967.

Hallett, Mark. The Spectacle of Difference: Graphic Satire in the Age of Hogarth. New Haven, Conn., and London: Yale University Press, 1999.

Maidment, B. E. Reading Popular Prints, 1790–1870. Manchester. U.K., and New York: Manchester University Press, 1996.

Paston, George [pseudonym for Miss E. M. Symonds]. Social Caricature in the Eighteenth Century. London: Methuen and Company, 1905.

Paulson, Ronald. Hogarth: His Life, Art, and Times. 2 vols. New Haven, Conn., and London: Yale University Press, 1971.

Perrot, Philippe. Fashioning the Bourgeoisie: A History of Clothing in the Nineteenth Century. Translated by Richard Bienvenu. Princeton, N.J.: Princeton University Press, 1994.

Sanders, Mark, et al. The Impossible Image: Fashion Photography in the Digital Age. London: Phaidon Press Ltd., 2000.

Peter McNeil

CARNIVAL DRESS

In its broadest sense, "carnival" refers to a pageant, festival, or public celebration found all over the world. It originates in prehistoric times, varying in content, form, function, and significance from one culture to another. But in Europe and the Americas, "carnival" refers specifically to the period of feasting and revelry preceding Lent. The general consensus is that it began during the Middle Ages, evolving from the burlesque celebrations associated with Easter, Christmas, and other European festivities such as *Maypole*, *Quadrille Ball*, *Entrudo*, and *Hallowmas*. The word is said to derive from the Latin *carnem levare*, meaning abstention from meat or farewell to flesh, reflecting the self-denial such as fasting and penitence associated with Lent. Its synonyms are the French *carementrant* (approaching Lent), the German *fastnacht* (night of fasting) and the English Shrovetide (referring to the three days set aside for confession before Lent).

Another school of thought links the word "carnival" to the Latin *carrus navalis*, a horse-drawn wagon for transporting revelers, arguing that its Christian aspects grew out of the seasonal Dionysian or Bacchanalian fertility rites of Greco-Roman times. These rites are noted for their emphasis on revelry, masquerading, satirical displays, and periods of symbolic inversion of the social order that provided an outlet for celebrants to let off steam.

In any event, while most of the principles underlying carnival remain more or less intact, its form, content, context, and dress modes have changed drastically over the centuries. This is particularly the case in the Americas where carnival was introduced after the fifteenth century following European colonization. Since then, it has absorbed new elements from the aboriginal populations, Africans and other ethnic groups. The emphasis here is on the carnival dress of the black diaspora in the Caribbean, United States, and Brazil where carnival is known by other names such as *Rara* in Haiti, Mardi Gras in New Orleans, and *Carnaval* in Cuba and Brazil.

The African contribution to carnival in the Americas began when the European slave masters allowed their African captives to display their ancestral heritage in the visual and performing arts on special occasions for recreational and therapeutic purposes. These occasions include the Day of the Kings in Cuba, the *Jonkonnu*, 'Lection Day and Pinkster celebrations in the United States and the Caribbean as well as the *Batuque* (recreational drumming) in Brazil. The various attempts by enslaved blacks to revive African festival costumes in the Americas are well documented. Early eyewitness accounts describe slaves as donning horned masks and feathered headdresses, wearing shredded strips of cloth or painting their faces and bodies in assorted colors, just as they had done in their homeland. Some of these elements survive in the modern carnival, though in new forms and materials. Several sketches of carnival masquerades in nineteenth-century Jamaica by Isaac Belisario document African carryovers. One of them done during the Christmas celebrations in Kingston in 1836, depicts a mask with a palm leaf costume similar to that of the *Sangbeto* mask of the Yoruba and Fon of Nigeria and Republic of Benin respectively. A painting of the Day of the Kings celebration in Cuba executed in the 1870s by the Spanish-born artist Victor Patricio de Landaluze shows not only black figures playing African drums, but also dancers wearing raffia skirts and animal skins. Near the drummers is a masquerade with a conical headdress introduced to Cuba by Ekoi, Abakpa, and Ejagham slaves from the Nigerian–Cameroon border where the masquerade is associated with the *Ekpe* leader-ship society. Now called *Abakua*, this masquerade is still a feature of the twenty-first-century carnival in Cuba. Another African retention in the modern carnival among blacks in the Americas and Europe is the *Moco Jumbie*, a masquerade on stilts. Apart from the fact that this masquerade type abounds all over Africa, it appears in the prehistoric rock art of the Sahara desert as early as the Round Head period, created about eight thousand years ago.

At first, the public celebrations by free and enslaved blacks in the Americas during the slavery era occurred on the fringes of the white space. However, by the beginning of the twentieth century, emancipation had brought about various degrees of racial integration, allowing blacks, whites, Creoles, Amerindians, and new immigrants from Europe, Middle East, Asia, and the South Pacific to perform the carnival together. Each group has since contributed significantly to the repertoire of carnival dress, while at the same time borrowing elements from one another. For instance, even though the emphasis on feathers in some masquerades has African precedents, influences from Amerindian costumes are apparent as well, most especially in the black Indian Mardi Gras costumes of New Orleans.

In the early 2000s a typical carnival is a public procession of musicians, lavishly attired dancers and colorful masquerades. Some are transported on decorated floats. The areas to be covered by the parade are usually closed to traffic. The costumes often combine assorted materials—fabrics, plastic beads, feathers, sequins, colorful ribbons, glass mirrors, horns, and shells—all aimed at creating a dazzling spectacle. In some areas, the parade lasts one, two, or three days; and in others, a whole week. There is usually a grand finale at a public square or sports stadium where all participants perform in turn before thousands of spectators. In Trinidad,

Brazil, and other countries, a panel of judges selects and awards prizes to the most innovative groups and to the masquerades with the best costumes. As a result, carnival has turned into a tourist attraction—a big business, requiring elaborate preparations. In most cases, participants are expected to belong to established groups or specific clubs such as the Zulu of New Orleans, Hugga Bunch of St. Thomas (U.S. Virgin Islands), Ile Aye of Salvador (Brazil) and African Heritage of Notting Hill Gate (United Kingdom) whose members are expected to appear in identical costumes. Each group usually has a professional designer who is responsible not only for its costume themes, styles, colors, and forms, but also the group's dance movements. In Brazil, where African-derived festivals have been assimilated into the carnival, religious groups (*Candomble*) associated with the worship of Yoruba deities (*orixa*) may emphasize the sacred color of a particular deity in their carnival costumes. Thus, white honors *Obatala* (creation deity), blue, *Yemaja* (the Great Mother), red, *Xango* (thunder deity), and yellow, *Oxun* (fertility and beauty deity). Designers such as Fernando Pinto and Joaosinho Trinta of Brazil and Hilton Cox, Peter Minshall, Lionell Jagessar and Ken Morris—all of Trinidad—have become world-famous for their innovations. Some of Peter Minshall's costumes, for example, are monumental, modernistic puppetlike constructions whose articulated parts respond rhythmically to dance movements. Other costumes by him incorporate elements of traditional African art in an attempt to relate the black diaspora to its roots in Africa. This nationalism has led a number of black designers to seek inspiration from African costumes and headdresses, recalling the original contributions of African captives to carnival during the ancient *Jonkonnu*, Pinkster and Day of the Kings celebrations when they improvised with new materials.

In the recent past, grasses, leaves, raffia, flowers, beads, furs, animal skins, feathers, and cotton materials were used for the costumes. These materials are increasingly being replaced by synthetic substitutes, partly to reduce cost and partly to facilitate mass production. Some costumes or masquerades depict animals, birds, insects, sea creatures, or characters from myths and folklore. Others represent kings, Indians, celebrities, African or European culture heroes, historical figures, clowns, and other characters. Cross-dressing and masquerades with grotesque features are rampant. So too is seductive dancing. The loud music—calypso in the Caribbean and samba in Brazil—adds to the frenzy, allowing performers and spectators alike to release pent up emotion.

See also America, South: History of Dress; Cross-Dressing; Masquerade and Masked Balls.

Bibliography

Besson, Gerard A., ed. *The Trinidad Festival.* Port of Spain, Trinidad and Tobago: Paria, 1988.

Cowley, John. *Carnival, Canboulay and Calypso: Traditions in the Making.* Cambridge, U.K.: Cambridge University Press, 1996.

Golby, J. M., and A. W. Purdue. *The Making of the Modern Christmas.* Athens: University of Georgia Press, 1986.

Harris, Max. *Carnival and Other Christian Festivals: Folk Theology and Folk Performance.* Austin: University of Texas Press, 2003.

Hill, Errol. *Trinidad Festival: Mandate for a National Theatre.* Austin: University of Texas Press, 1972.

Huet, Michel, and Claude Savary. *The Dances of Africa.* New York: Harry N. Abrams, 1996.

Humphrey, Chris. *The Politics of Carnival.* Manchester, U.K.: Manchester University Press, 2001.

Lawal, Babatunde. *The Gèlèdé Spectacle: Art, Gender, and Social Harmony in an African Culture.* Seattle: Washington University Press, 1996.

Mason, Peter. *Bacchanal! The Carnival Culture of Trinidad.* Philadelphia: Temple University Press, 1998.

Minshall, Peter. *Callaloo an de Crab: A Story.* Trinidad and Tobago: Peter Minshall, 1984.

Nettleford, Rex M. *Dance Jamaica: Cultural Definition and Artistic Discovery.* New York: Grove Press, 1986.

Nicholls, Robert W. *Old-Time Masquerading in the U.S. Virgin Islands.* St. Thomas, U.S. Virgin Islands: Virgin Islands Humanities Council, 1998.

Nunely, John W., and Judith Bettelheim. *Caribbean Festival Arts: Each and Every Bit of Difference.* Seattle: University of Washington Press, 1988.

Orloff, Alexander. *Carnival: Myth and Cult.* Wörgl, Austria: Per-linger, 1981.

Poppi, Cesare. "Carnival." In *The Dictionary of Art.* Edited by Jane Turner. Vol. 5. London: Macmillan Publishers, 1996.

Teissl, Helmut. *Carnival in Rio.* New York: Abbeville Press Publishers, 2000.

Turner, Victor, ed. *Celebration: Studies in Festivity and Ritual.* Washington, D.C.: Smithsonian Institution Press, 1982.

Babatunde Lawal

CASHIN, BONNIE

One of America's foremost designers in the second half of the twentieth century, Bonnie Cashin (1908–2000) was a pioneer in the sportswear industry, specializing in modular wardrobes for the modern woman "on the go." Her lifelong interest in clothing design, however, encompassed a number of careers on both American coasts. Growing up in California, Cashin worked as an apprentice in a series of dressmaking shops owned and operated by her mother, Eunice. In her teens she worked as a fashion illustrator and dance costume designer. Between 1943 and 1949 she costumed more than sixty films at Twentieth Century–Fox. It was not until midcentury, when she was over forty years old, that she began designing the ready-to-wear for which she became best known.

Cashin favored timeless shapes from the history of clothing, such as ponchos, tunics, Noh coats, and kimonos, which allowed for ease of movement and manufacture. Approaching dress as a form of collage or kinetic art, she favored luxurious, organic materials that she could "sculpt" into shape, such as leather, suede, mohair, wool jersey, and cashmere, as well as nonfashion materials, including upholstery fabrics. Cashin's aim was to create "simple art forms for living in, to be re-arranged as mood and activity dictates" (Interview 1999).

Early Years

As a girl moving along the California coastline, Cashin developed a love for travel and a keen eye for the clothing of different cultures, which would underpin her later professional work. This interest in "why people looked the way they did" placed her in good stead to begin work in 1924, alongside Helen Rose, as a costume designer for the Los Angeles dance troupe Fanchon and Marco. In 1934 her producers took over performances at New York's Roxy Theater and asked Cashin to join them as costumer for the Roxyette dance line, the precursors and rivals to the Rockettes.

Fashion and Film

In 1937 the *Harper's Bazaar* editor Carmel Snow, an admirer of Cashin's costume designs, encouraged Bonnie to work in fashion and arranged for her to become the head designer for the prestigious coat and suit manufacturer Adler and Adler. Owing to the wartime focus on American fashion design, she became so well recognized that she was commissioned to design World War II civilian defense uniforms and was featured in a Coca-Cola advertisement. By 1942, however, Cashin felt boxed in by wartime restrictions. She returned to California to sign a six-year contract as a costume designer with Twentieth Century–Fox.

Cashin designed costumes for the female characters in more than sixty films. Her favorite projects, *Laura* (1944), *A Tree Grows in Brooklyn* (1945), and *Anna and the King of Siam* (1946), also became American cinematic classics. Designing for the lavish productions that typified Hollywood's golden age, she was expected to make innovative use of the day's finest materials to create historical, fantasy, and contemporary wardrobes. She used the resources at the Fox studios to experiment with designs for "real" clothing that she wore and made in custom versions for her leading ladies' offscreen wardrobes.

Return to Ready-to-Wear

Cashin returned to New York, and to Adler and Adler, in 1949. She received the unprecedented honor of earning both the Neiman Marcus Award and the Coty Fashion Critic's Award within the same year (1950). Displeased, however, with her manufacturer's control over her creativity, she decided to challenge the setup of the fashion industry. Working with multiple manufacturers, she designed a range of clothing at different price points, thereby specializing in complete wardrobes for "my kind of a girl for a certain kind of living."

In 1953 Cashin teamed with the leather importer and craftsman Philip Sills and initiated the use of leather for high fashion. She made her name through her unconventional choices in materials as well as her inexhaustible variations on her favorite theme of adapting the flat, graphic patterns of Asian and South American clothing to contemporary global living. Through her work for Sills and Company, she is credited with introducing "layering" into the fashion lexicon. In turn, she credited the Chinese tradition of dressing for, and interpreting the weather as, a "one-shirt day" or a "seven-shirt day." Her layered garments snugly nestled within one another and were easily converted to suit different temperatures and activities by donning or removing a layer. Cashin's objective was to create a flexible wardrobe for her own globe-trotting lifestyle, wherein seasonal changes were only a plane trip away. Frustrated by the categorization of sportswear designer, she declared that travel was her "favorite sport."

Coach and the Cashin Look

In 1962 Cashin became the first designer of Coach handbags and initiated the use of hardware on clothing and accessories, including the brass toggle that became Coach's hallmark. She revolutionized the handbag industry. Unlike contemporary rigid, hand-held bags, her vividly colored "Cashin-Carries" for Coach packed flat and had wide straps, attached coin purses, industrial zippers, and the famous sturdy brass toggles, the last inspired by the hardware used to secure the top on her convertible sports car.

Without licensing her name, Cashin designed cashmere separates, gloves, canvas totes, at-home gowns and robes, raincoats, umbrellas, and furs. She also ran the Knittery, a consortium of British mills that produced one-of-a-kind sweaters knit to shape, rather than cut and sewn. Among many other industry awards, she received the Coty award five times and entered their hall of fame in 1972; in 2001 was honored with a plaque on the Fashion Walk of Fame on Seventh Avenue in New York City.

Cashin worked until 1985, when she decided to focus on painting and philanthropy. Among several scholarships and educational programs, she established the James Michelin Lecture Series at the California Institute of Technology. Cashin died in New York on 3 February 2000 from complications during heart surgery. In 2003 the Bonnie Cashin Collection, consisting of her entire design archive and endowments for design-related lecture series and symposia, was donated to the Department of Special Collections within the Charles E. Young Research Library at the University of California, Los Angeles.

See also Costume Designer; Dance Costume; Film and Fashion; Ready-to-Wear; Sportswear.

Bibliography

Cashin, Bonnie. Interview by Stephanie Day Iverson. 12 September 1999.

Iverson, Stephanie Day. "'Early' Bonnie Cashin, before Bonnie Cashin Designs, Inc." *Studies in the Decorative Arts* 8, no. 1 (2001–2002): 108–124.

Steele, Valerie. *Women of Fashion: Twentieth-Century Designers*. New York: Rizzoli International, 1991.

Stephanie Day Iverson

CELEBRITIES

In November 2003, the Prince's Trust, an organization set up by Prince Charles to help disadvantaged young people, organized a charity event in the Albert Hall: "Fashion Rocks," a collaboration between the worlds of music and fashion. It was hosted by Elizabeth Hurley, the epitome of a new type of celebrity. She has been photographed constantly for nearly ten years, and used for countless magazine covers, including British *Vogue*. She has a multimillion-dollar contract with Estée Lauder, and her private life is constantly subject to close tabloid scrutiny. Everyone, it seems, knows who she is—she is often named in headlines as, simply, "Liz." If a job description is ever necessary, she is referred to as "model and actress." Yet apart from magazine covers where she is used because of her celebrity, and the Lauder campaign, she does no modeling. The films in which she has appeared—with the exception of *Austin Powers: The Spy Who Shagged Me* (1999) have done very badly at the box office. It would be more accurate to say that she is part of a new group of celebrities who have been instantly created by and perpetuated within the media. She is, quite simply, a construct—and, paradoxically, it is this that makes her a celebrity.

Her career in fact began in 1994, at the London premiere of *Four Weddings and a Funeral*. She accompanied her boyfriend, Hugh Grant, and borrowed a dress from the London offices of Versace. The black dress was short and revealing—held together by large, strategically placed safety pins. The following day she appeared on the front page of all tabloid and middle-market newspapers in Britain, while even the broadsheets saw fit to include the "story" on their inside pages. Since then, she has been continually photographed, and the dress has been retrospectively discussed as "That Dress." Indeed, when Grant was convicted of an indiscretion with a Hollywood prostitute, the English Sunday paper found the woman in question and photographed her wearing a red version of the Versace dress, which they put on their front page. Unsurprisingly, Versace has offered Hurley clothes for every subsequent photo opportunity, and she has repaid them by being photographed in all of them. One of the dresses was slit so high up the thigh that it revealed a pair of knickers in a leopard-print fabric to match the dress. Hurley is a perfect example of the new breed of fashion celebrity for, unlike fashion celebrities of the past, her taste is often deemed to be questionable. On this particular occasion, she was censured in the press for having worn this outfit, since it was to a "society wedding," and it was suggested that she had wished to divert attention away from the bride. This is in direct contrast to the former notion of a fashion celebrity who attained his or her status precisely because their taste in clothes was deemed to be excellent.

While there are still fashion celebrities who have been selected for their ability to look stylish—the model Kate Moss is a perfect example—the majority of today's celebrities are seen as legitimate targets for sartorial criticism. A weekly staple of journalism is now a roundup of the past week's fashion triumphs and disasters; if a celebrity wears a particularly unbecoming or unsuitable outfit, an appearance in the papers the very next morning is guaranteed.

A "celebrity," however, as opposed to an "icon," has always had a notoriety over and above the sum of their talent. But one of the many problems with today's culture of celebrity is a seeming disregard for the absence of any particular talent apart from the simple fact of being photogenic. Another is the disproportionate amount of media attention given over to celebrity stories. The past decade has seen an unprecedented growth in the cult of the celebrity—it is very different from the carefully controlled interest in "stars" that characterized the heyday of Hollywood.

Interestingly, it has meant huge shifts within the fashion industry, which seem to have gone at times unremarked. For instance, it was traditional within magazine journalism—from its infancy at the end of the last century until the late 1990s—for leading fashion journalists to have some effect on the success or failure of a particular collection, a particular look, and for the journalists themselves, if prestigious enough, to be able to assist the career of new designers. Some journalists are still sufficiently well known to be photographed as celebrities in their own right, known for their own particular style. Just as from the 1930s to the 1950s the characteristic "look" of Diana Vreeland was frequently discussed, so today Anna Piaggi of Italian *Vogue* is still photographed, as is Suzy Menkes of the *International Herald Tribune*. However, these are among a few exceptions—arguably the photographs from the collections are now of the celebrities in the front row—and it is their choice of designer or outfit which makes for success. Julien Macdonald owes his career as a designer to the fact that he was asked, early on, to design for Kylie Minogue. Donatella Versace has ensured the continued good fortunes of the house for which she designs not only through her shrewd use of different celebrities—she organized a wedding party for Jennifer Lopez, and always dresses singers for music award ceremonies—but through the fact that she has become a fashion celebrity in her own right. Her characteristic heavy makeup, long bleached-blonde hair, and year-round suntan are the constant focus of media comment.

Not only have journalists lost their power over designers, they have watched their employers make radical changes to cope with the new obsession with celebrity. The magazine *In Style*, launched in America in 1998 by the publishers of *People*, has been extremely successful and has created a new template for fashion journalism both in America and the United Kingdom. Celebrities, rather than models, are now used for many cover shots, while the fashion and beauty pages tell their readers how to emulate particular star "looks."

Journalism has gone through extraordinary changes over the last century. A hundred years ago, "celebrity photographs" were rare within magazine journalism, and tended to involve the aristocracy or royalty. There was still some use of sketches; the British magazine *Queen* was specifically set up to portray the weekly activities of Queen Victoria and her companions and to depict the lifestyle of the very uppermost echelons of British society, and these scenes could not be photographed. But the development of the cinema brought the royal family onto the screen in newsreels, and they became the subject of special short films on ceremonial occasions. Princess Alexandra—later Queen herself—was of great interest because of her elegance in dress—royalty and aristocracy continued to be of interest as the new media forms developed. In the period between the two World Wars, Pond's ran a famous advertising campaign which used "society ladies," invariably titled, to endorse their range of skin-care products. But tastes gradually changed—celebrity endorsement for cosmetics and beauty products was more likely, by 1939, to involve a Hollywood star.

As advertising has become more sophisticated, so it has cast its net more widely. Not only has it used celebrities from every sphere of activity—the first sportsman to appear in a fashion-related advertisement was Henry Cooper, the British boxing champion, who advertised the aftershave, Brut, in the 1970s—but it has also created its own minor, usually transient, celebrities through its campaigns. A perfect example within the fashion sphere was the Calvin Klein men's underwear campaign, which ran during 2002–2003 and used an obscure young surfer, Travis, rather than a well-known model or a famous figure. Research showed that although women responded very positively to his image, men found his long hair and soft features off-putting. He was replaced in the Autumn 2003 campaign by the Arsenal soccer star, Fredrik Ljung-berg, who has a more macho image—his hair is shaved, he wears a medallion, and the pictures all show clearly the large black panther tattooed on his lower abdomen.

Interestingly, despite the growing popularity of sports over the past century, fashion advertising was relatively slow to involve sportsmen and women. Things changed during the 1980s and 1990s—arguably Nike owes its global dominance to its use of the basketball star Michael Jordan, and more recently they have used international footballers such as Edgar Davits. The tennis stars Venus and Serena Williams have appeared on magazine covers and lent their names to sportswear, while the Russian Anna Kournikova was used for a Berlei bra campaign with the tag line "Only the balls should bounce."

The most notable development within the 1990s, however, has been the link forged between fashion and soccer. Eric Cantona appeared on the catwalk for John Paul Gaultier, while younger stars have modeled in men's fashion magazines. David Beckham's enormous popularity has meant that he has moved from fashion-related advertising—sunglasses, watches, children's clothes—and magazine shoots to becoming a global brand in himself. He and his wife, the former Posh Spice, went on a tour of America in 2003 when their agents advised them that it was necessary, given the fact that many Americans are unfamiliar with soccer stars. He and his wife are important because they are among the new "celebrity couples" whose activities the media can chronicle and whose image is of interest. Their American counterparts are perhaps Brad Pitt and Jennifer Aniston—she was voted "The Most Popular Person in America" in the *Forbes* poll of July 2003. However, apart from Aniston's early contract with L'Oreal, neither she nor Pitt has taken part in direct advertising. Nevertheless, they can "endorse" products simply by wearing them when snapped on the street—they have popularized Maharishi trousers and Birkenstock sandals.

Celebrities within the music industry have been courted, too, both in the 1960s and more recently. In the past singers were used in fashion spreads or asked to lend their name to a range of merchandise—now they are directly approached by leading fashion brands to join film stars in rendering "luxury brands" more democratic. Donna Karan used Bruce Willis, action-man hero, in the 1990s, while Madonna modeled Tom Ford's early designs for Gucci. She also appeared in a Versace campaign photographed by Herb Ritts—but recently she has lent her celebrity to the high street, in a Gap television commercial with Missy Elliott. The high-fashion brands have tried to widen their appeal through the use of singers such as Christina Aguilera, in the Versace campaign for Autumn 2003, and Jennifer Lopez, used by Louis Vuitton in the same season. At the same moment, Tommy Hilfiger announced that he wanted to create a new image for his sportswear and had recruited the musician David Bowie and his wife, the ex-model Iman, currently working for Bulgari. Hilfiger sportswear is currently popular among the young and has some "street credibility"—this latest celebrity appointment suggests an attempt to interest forty-somethings in his sportswear, based perhaps on the success of Juicy Couture tracksuits after Madonna and Jennifer Lopez were photographed wearing them. Rap stars have been courted assiduously in an attempt to gain the kind of appeal Hilfiger's range possesses; the singer P. Diddy has launched a collection of casual wear, Sean Jean—while in another attempt to give expensive brands a broader appeal, Missy Elliott has been used as the face of Garrards, the royal jewelers.

This new reliance on celebrities for high-fashion endorsement is not worrying in itself—what is problematic, both within the industry and, more importantly, in a wider sociological context, are the sociological and psychological implications of celebrity obsession. It is tempting and not too far-fetched to suggest that the current climate owes much to the life—and unfortunate death—of Diana, Princess of Wales. In the early 1980s, she was far from being a glamorous fashion icon—and it was this perceived "ordinariness" that made her so appealing to the press at first. She had a haircut and a taste for frilly blouses that set trends precisely because this Earl's daughter seemed to the public to be "one of them," however false

that assumption was. Her experiments with different hairstyles and her fashion education—she received guidance from the staff of British *Vogue*—were avidly followed. So too was the developing drama within her personal life. She featured in newspapers worldwide, and magazine editors found that her face on a cover guaranteed sales. Her battles with her weight—and her admission of her bulimia—were chronicled as carefully as the problems within her private life. When she died, the scenes in England were both extraordinary and unprecedented.

Arguably, the public had developed over two decades a need, even a craving, for celebrity worship—and the press has responded. The current pathological interest in body image, with its accounts of the different diets and fitness regimes followed by particular celebrities, seems to be spiraling out of control. And certainly in Britain, there is concern about the size of individual credit-card debt. A recent survey showed that the average woman now spends far more on shoes than in the past, and this is possibly linked to the fact that "Manolos" have become a household name through the television program "Sex and the City." They were worn not only on-screen by the heroine, Carrie Bradshaw, but by the actress Sarah Jessica Parker, who herself became a style icon. The new attempts to copy star images, decor, and lifestyle, the hours spent scouring celebrity websites, can only make for a stifling of individuality in dress, a feeling of discontent, and, more disturbingly, an unhappiness with faces or bodies that are not perfect.

See also Actors and Actresses, Impact on Fashion; Fashion Icons; Models; Supermodels.

Bibliography

Berger, Maurice, Brian Wallis, and Simon Watson, eds. *Constructing Masculinity*. London and New York: Routledge, 1995.

Bruzzi, Stella. "Football, Fashion and That Sarong." In *Fashion Cultures: Theories, Explorations, and Analysis*. Edited by Stella Bruzzi and Church Gibson. London: Routledge, 2000.

Dyer, Richard. *Stars*. London: BFI Publishing, 1986/1998.

Gritten, David. *Fame*. London: Allen Lane, 2002.

Hilfiger, Tommy. *Rock Style*. London: Barbican Centre, 2000.

Macdonald, Paul. *The Star System*. London: Wallflower Press, 2000.

Rojek, Chris. *Celebrity*. London: Reaktion Books, 2002.
Thesander, Marianne. *The Feminine Ideal*. London: Reaktion, 1997.

Pamela Church Gibson

CEREMONIAL AND FESTIVAL COSTUMES

Ceremonies, festivals, and other rituals provide a structure for an individual or a group to reaffirm social values and ties. They tend to be public events, seen as different from everyday, which spotlight an important personal or cultural happening. Ritual helps to give meaning to the world in part by linking the past to the present and the present to the future. Ritual works through the senses to structure our perception of reality and the world around us; it is often when a society's deepest values emerge in the form of activity, objects, and dress. Ceremonies often combine religious belief with social and political concerns. Although rituals tend to evolve very slowly, cultures do change over time, and possible disjunctures may develop between a ceremony and the attitudes of the society, resulting in the modification or even elimination of the ceremony. The costumes worn at these times are frequently special to the occasion and dramatically symbolic; they can reflect historical or cultural preferences that are no longer in vogue. Different stages or events characterize some celebrations, requiring many changes of costume or dress. Dress is an inclusive concept that involves modifying the body by the use of textiles, cosmetics, scars, coiffures, apparel, jewelry, and accessories held by or for a person. Although in general dress can range from temporary acts of covering and adorning to permanent acts of modification, such as scarification, ceremonial dress is usually of a temporary nature.

Unlike masquerading, dress is not meant to transform an individual into something else but to enhance the identity of the individual. In many cultures, costumes have been used in a wide range of festivals stressing community solidarity or declaring the right of a person or group to a particular status, office, or possession. Since the nineteenth century, the Zulu of South Africa have used clothing and jewelry made from imported beads to demarcate changes in status associated with different life-cycle stages. Children and married women usually wear less beadwork. Young girls attire themselves in square or rectangular beaded loincloth panels attached to a bead string; pregnant women dress in leather aprons decorated with beadwork; and married women wear a knee-length skirt made of pleated goat skin or ox hide, hoop-like circular necklaces, and a flared headdress in the shape of a crown covered with red ocher or red beads and a beaded band around its base. The color schemes of beaded necklaces convey social messages about stages of physical and social development. Small rectangles, zigzag or vertical bands, diamonds, triangles, and lozenges are the most widespread motifs.

Rites of Passage

A rite of passage is a common ceremony that involves a transition from one status or condition to another. For an individual, these include birth, puberty, marriage, and death. Scholars usually divide this type of ritual into three stages: separation, a transitional or liminal one, and rein-corporation; the latter two are most often associated with distinctive dress. For a community, annual rites of passage mark seasonal changes or cycles of renewal and regeneration. Individual and community rites of passage serve to enhance social solidarity, confirm membership in a group, and channel any anxiety resulting from the potential dangers of the transition. Societies throughout the world institutionalize the physical and social transformation that boys and girls undergo at the time of puberty by marking their passage from childhood to adulthood. There is, however, considerable variation in the timing of the ritual, length of ritual, and age of initiate.

As part of the puberty ceremony carried out among Sepik River peoples in New Guinea, newly initiated boys enter a men's meetinghouse, the political and religious center of the community; after passing across the threshold, the boys encounter sacred cult objects that play a role in their introduction to appropriate beliefs and behavior. The young men are also given body paint in the course of initiation. After residing in the cult house for months, the boys return to their village as adults when all male members of the house elaborately decorate their bodies as a statement of their own attractiveness, to display characteristics identified with being a successful male and to identify themselves as sacred beings from the world of the ancestors. The men—dressed in fiber skirts—paint their bodies with yellow, black, red, and white curvilinear patterns. Paint is believed to be sacred and clearly adds to the seriousness of the occasion. Red and white are especially favored because these colors are associated with brightness and are viewed as auspicious. A wicker headdress adorned with flowers and feathers as well as large shells worn on the chest and forehead enhance the brilliance of the costume. In addition, other accessories of shell, bone, boar-tusk, seeds, and feathers are worn. Feathers are noteworthy for symbolizing growth and power.

In the early 2000s, the most important Apache ceremony is the girl's four-day puberty rite—sometimes referred to as the Sunrise Dance—that was taught to the Apache by White Painted Woman, an important deity in the American Southwest. A similar ritual is held by the Navajo, but the Apache put greater stress on the benefit of the ritual to the community. The ceremony is organized by a shaman hired by the girl's family who also select godparents to assist the young girl during the ceremony and throughout her life. On the second night, male masqueraders called Gan, wearing plank headdresses made of slats of agave stalk, impersonate Mountain Spirits who bless the area and help protect the community from dangers and disease. During the Apache puberty ceremony, the young girl is dressed in either a buckskin skirt or a long cotton skirt and a buckskin smock or cape painted yellow, the color of sacred pollen said to symbolize fertility. These garments are decorated with symbols of the moon, sun, and stars. Both skirt and smock utilize fringes that could represent sunbeams. An abalone shell is worn on the fore-head along with shell necklaces, shell earrings, and feathers for the hair. Metal bells, buttons, and decorative metal cones cut from cans dangling from the dress have been used since the early nineteenth century. Buckskin moccasins and leggings might be added to the ensemble. The various items of dress must be put on in a prescribed sequence and draped in a particular way. The outfit of the girl, based on traditional female dress, is now specific to this ceremony; in the past, the Apache wore various items of dress made only from animal skins. The use of an older material or clothing style for ceremonies is not uncommon.

At the time of puberty in the West African country of Sierra Leone, Mende girls begin an initiation process into the female Sande association where they learn traditional songs and dances and are educated about their future roles as wives and mothers. During seclusion, the girls are covered with a white pigment of crushed shell and chalk and wear ornaments that define their status as novice and indicate that they are under the protection of the association. Formerly, this period lasted for several months, but in recent decades, the period has been reduced to a few weeks. After successfully completing all initiation obligations, the girls with similar hairstyles and dressed in fine clothing form a procession and parade back to town accompanied by masked dancers. Sande is the only documented African association in which women both own and perform masquerades. The masks—characterized by a shiny black surface, fleshy neck rolls, delicately carved features, a smooth, high forehead, and an elaborate coiffure—are seen as expressing a Mende feminine ideal. The coiffures of the mask are actually based on popular types of Mende hairstyles, especially those worn on special occasions by women of high status. The arrangement of the hair into a series of longitudinal ridges is a common coiffure and has been documented on women at the turn of the fifteenth century; it indicates the role of women as cultivators and bearers of culture.

Elaborately painted body decoration and scarification are customarily associated with initiation ceremonies in many parts of the world. Among the We of the Ivory Coast, the faces of young female initiates are painted when they leave the excision camp by initiated women, skilled in body painting. They paint the faces of the young girls with schematic designs in black, blue, red, and white. The girls' torsos are sprinkled with oil and rubbed with snail shell or porcelain to make their bodies shine; they will also wear a woven wrapper, necklaces, and bracelets. The purpose of such embellishment is to make the girls look attractive. After emerging from the camp, the initiated girls sit in state, displaying their newly acquired social status as marriageable women. Changes in role and status have been correlated with irreversible forms of body art to emphasize the accumulative and unalterable nature of the transition. Among the Ga'anda of Nigeria, girls are given facial and body scarification to mark different stages of their transition into adulthood. This procedure begins when a girl is five or six and at each stage consists of rows of slightly raised dots that form linear and geometric patterns. The scarification is displayed at each stage and when completed expresses the permanent nature of the transition as well as a visual identification with the group. At these times, the girls wear only a simple woven cloth apron allowing for maximum visibility of the body designs.

For centuries, the Kalabari people of southeastern Nigeria have worn an assortment of both foreign and indigenous items of dress. These they assemble into a distinctive ensemble that for women consists of an imported lace or eyelet blouse and a combination of wrappers embellished with bead, gold, or coral jewelry. The Kalabari do not produce textiles themselves, but purchase hand-woven textiles made in Nigeria and Ghana along with imported, factory-made textiles. This type of composite dress is especially apparent during *iria*, a series of ceremonies that mark several stages of a woman's life. When women reach both physical and social maturity, they are allowed to tie and layer a series of short cloth wrappers around their waist to increase the bulk of their midsection, symbolizing their role as society's procreators. Textiles signify a family's wealth and are stored in special cloth boxes that are passed down from one generation to the next. The Kalabari also make use of these textiles by decorating funerary chambers of socially prominent elders with rich displays of heirloom textiles. The degree of a chamber's elaboration is directly related to the deceased's success in life. A group of elderly women, skilled in selecting and arranging textiles, completely drape the ceiling and walls with cloth. The bed, where the corpse is laid in state, is the visual focus of the chamber. Personal accessories that belonged to the deceased, such as beads, fans, canes, and textiles are folded and layered on the bed to reveal a variety of patterns, textures, and colors. The display of the family's textile collection in the funerary chambers is believed to facilitate an elder's transition from the human community to the realm of the ancestors.

Many societies or cultures associate a particular color or type of costume with mourning appropriate for wearing at funerary or memorial ceremonies. The Frafra of northern Ghana have elaborate funerary rituals that emphasize dress. The ordinary male funerary costume consists of a smock, quiver, bow, flute, and headdress. This costume, which is based on the dress worn by both hunters and warriors, symbolizes the origins of Frafra society and its early history. The most common funerary headdress, worn by any male old enough to be a hunter or warrior, is a wicker cap with a hole in the top for inserting a stick or bundle of reeds covered with the hair from the neck of a sheep. The use of sheep hair reflects the importance of domesticated animals, especially for sacrifices. Such a helmet may be made by the owner or purchased in the market. On the other hand, the wicker helmet with horns can be worn only by a hunter. The female funerary costume is based on traditional female dress. In much of northeastern Ghana, women in the past wore woven grass waistbands with small forked leafy branches attached to the front and rear. This leaf form has been replaced almost entirely

by a tail made of dyed grass or leather strands. Women would receive such elaborate "tails" during courtship as signs of admiration and intent. The grass or leather "tails" are viewed as proper dress for special occasions. Today, a commercially printed cloth for the upper torso or head tie is often added. In addition, a woman may wear stone or ivory armlets to reflect pride in her family and household.

A wedding ritual not only unites two individuals, but provides a permanent linkage between families and kin groups. Ceremonies marking marriage put considerable emphasis on elaborate and often colorful dress. In Central Asia, special garments tailored from silk cloth were worn at marriage by high-status, wealthy women during the nineteenth century. Because Central Asians viewed silk attire as accumulated wealth, dresses and robes were seen as important components of a woman's dowry. For the marriage ceremony, women attired themselves in a series of dresses, worn in a layered manner so that the richly patterned sleeves of each dress were visibly displayed; an outer robe completed the bride's dress ensemble. This collarless robe, which was close-fitting in the torso with a flaring outward toward the hem, was worn open in the front to reveal the bride's brightly colored dresses; outer robes, considered the most sumptuous of all of the bride's garments, were held in such high esteem, that one or two of them were even draped over the owner's body during her funeral ceremony. The garments were fashioned from handloomed silk cloth, decorated with designs made using the ikat-dying technique in which the thread is tie-dyed prior to being woven. The designs were usually created through a process of tie-dying the lengthwise or warp threads before plain colored crosswise or weft threads were woven into them. In the finished textile, the edges where the warp threads had been bound together for dyeing, show a blurred, irregular outline.

The traditional dress for a Tunisian woman consists of a silk, cotton, or wool wrapper draped around the body and attached on the chest with one or two fibulae and gathered at the waist with a sash. The wrapper is covered by a loose-fitting tunic with seams on either side and, for some, sleeves made from another more exquisite material. This type of outfit is now used only for weddings with each region having its own specific patterns and colors. Women are allowed to express their own individual taste and preference. Tunisian wedding tunics are decorated with elaborate embroidery, sequins, and gold-covered wire thread. There is an increasing emphasis on such gold work, especially in the urban areas. Embroidered designs may represent popular symbols of luck such as a star, birds, fish, and crescents. Similar tunics are found in other parts of North Africa. The wedding costumes and jewelry, which have become increasingly expensive, may be borrowed from neighboring families or rented from a female specialist who helps plan wedding ceremonies. For jewelry, silver is preferred because it is believed to be pure and propitious. Women wear a variety of tunics with different types of decoration and design at distinct ceremonies during the wedding ritual. In Tunisia an important part of the wedding ceremony is for a bride to be displayed formally to the groom, her relatives, and the relatives of the groom. At these times she is dressed in several different tunics that she removes one by one until she is in the last one, the richest of all. For North Africans, marriages represent a significant change of status and require considerable expense and attention; they last for several days and most people of the village will turn out for the event.

Identity, Status, and Leadership

Costumes may also express cultural identity or member-ship in a group. For the Yoruba of Nigeria there are a number of secular occasions where dress plays a prominent role in affirming a person's Yoruba identity. Both family and community ceremonies, including funerals, childbirth, and child-naming occasions, weddings, chief-taincy celebrations, and house-opening feasts are important social events where members of different extended families come together and dress in their finest clothing. Men wear a gown ensemble consisting of tailored gowns, trousers, and hats made from strip-woven cloth while women wear a wrapper ensemble, blouse, and a head tie. The Yoruba have a custom called *aso-ebi*, where male and female members of families and social clubs appear together in dress made of the same type of cloth. *Aso-ebi* cloth may be special-ordered or purchased at the market and when worn, it visually reinforces the group's cohesion.

In the northwest coast of America, the confirmation of an inherited privilege or the authentication of a new rank or status occurs during a special type of public ceremony called a potlatch, which is especially well developed among the Kwakiutl, Haida, and Tlingit. A potlatch is often held over a period of days and accompanied by the display of objects and the giving of gifts to the guests. The acceptance of these gifts and the acknowledgment of their purpose are critical components of a potlatch. Although the ordinary dress of the northwest coast in the eighteenth century consisted of fairly plain cedar bark capes and blankets, when attending potlatch events, people dressed in their best clothing and seated themselves according to rank. Ceremonial garments in this area are colorful, elaborately decorated, and spectacular. A wealthy man might wear a Chilkat or button blanket, a waist robe or apron, a shirt, leggings, and a headdress, often made of woven spruce root or cedar bark. To the headdress, a carved frontlet, ermine strips, or basketry rings could be added. Trousers are currently worn under the garments. The costume of wealthy women is similar to that of men except for the substitution of a plain dress for the trousers or robe. Shredded cedar bark and mountain goat wool are used for weaving the Chilkat blanket, considered as a family heirloom. This garment is rectangular at the top and the sides and from the bottom edge in the shape of a shallow V, there extends a long warp fringe about one-quarter the length of the blanket. The surface design is clearly a transfer from another medium (painting) and has the effect of a low relief. In addition, the curvilinear forms, characteristic of northwest coast art, is successfully achieved. Black, blue, white, and yellow are the colors that establish the patterns. A newer ceremonial covering is the button blanket consisting of a dark blue blanket—usually Hudson's Bay blanket—decorated with red flannel border and appliqué outlined in small iridescent pearl buttons. Buttons are used as well for creating the details of an image. Dentalium shells—a symbol of wealth—could also ornament a button blanket. The images are normally crest animals, such as a raven, whale, beaver, or eagle, which connect to clan myths.

Ceremonial dress associated with identity and renewal can also reflect social and political points of view or be used for other functions such as protection. Although metal armor was worn by warriors and rulers in Europe as far back as ancient times, in the fourteenth century, overlapping plates of steel were developed to produce a more effective way for covering the entire body. Since plate armor was quite expensive to make, it was limited to warriors of noble birth and became an indicator of status. During the following two centuries, knights and kings who rode into battle on horseback both protected and defined themselves with full suits of plate combat armor while providing a festive element to the occasion. For tournaments or jousting events, knights needed to wear armor made of even heavier metal and often more elaborately decorated. Armor served to protect an individual as well as to enhance appearance. Therefore, decoration, based on a variety of metalworking techniques such as embossing, engraving, and etching, expressed the wealth and status of the wearer. The most commonly used technique in decorating armor was etching.

The Great Plains of North America consisted of many tribes sharing a dependence on the buffalo as a source of food and raw materials. The standard ceremonial regalia for a Plains' warrior included a painted buffalo robe, quill shirt, leggings, moccasins, and some kind of feathered headdress. Plains ritual, which encompassed songs and special dress including body and face painting, were performed for a war campaign, a major buffalo hunt, and a community ceremony such as the sun dance, which focused on renewal. All clothing was made by women who were responsible for tanning animal skins and tailoring the various garments. For the American Plains, the buffalo robe was a distinctive type of dress, which could be painted by men with figurative designs illustrating historical events—especially military exploits—hunting scenes or, in some cases, supernatural visions. Plains cultures attached great importance to these visions and animals were frequently involved, especially buffalo, elk, bears, eagles, and sparrow hawks. The designs, which can symbolize less visually obvious ideas, were usually arranged horizontally without any overall composition. The actual painting of a buffalo robe was the responsibility of the owner. Originally the colors, each applied with a separate brush, were made from mineral or vegetable material. Quillwork and beadwork embroidery were also employed to adorn a robe. For the people of the Plains, robes served as an expression of both individual and community exploits. A men's robe is similar in form and construction to a woman's dress except it is shorter and has full sleeves.

The symbolic power of traditional Plains clothing was acknowledged again in the late nineteenth century with the Ghost Dance movement, a revitalization movement based on a belief that the Great Spirit would clear away the wreckage of the white man, bring back the buffalo herds, and reunite the Native American people—both living and dead—in a regenerated Earth. The ceremony, which originated among the Paiutes but quickly spread north and east to other Plains groups, began either late in the afternoon or after sundown and involved a circular dance, from East to West, following the movement of the sun. Preliminary activities included painting and dressing the body that took about two hours. The painted designs were an inspiration from a trance vision and consisted of elaborate designs in red, yellow, green, or blue upon the face or a yellow line along the parting of the hair. Suns, crescents, stars, crosses, and birds (especially crows) were the designs usually associated with both painting and clothing. Stars were the most common motif and consisted of a variety of forms such as the traditional four-pointed star, the five-pointed star of the American flag, dashes of paint representing falling stars or the many stars in the heaven. It was by wearing Ghost Dance shirts and dresses that the Great Spirit would recognize his people. Both shirts and dresses were usually made of muslin or cotton but garments of elk, deer, or antelope skins were also produced. These garments were decorated with painted designs, cones, bone, quillwork, and feathers. An eagle feather was also worn on the head.

Social status in most societies is usually expressed through the display of ornaments on the body; yet for a number of cultures, the permanent modification of the skin can exhibit societal membership or high status through scar and tattoo designs. For the Maori of New Zealand, tattooing was characterized by a dense, overall, and interrelated series of motifs organized into spiral and curvilinear patterns. In general, a tattoo results from pricking or piercing the skin and then pigmenting the punctured spots with a coloring substance. Pigment made from soot mixed with spring water, light fish oil, or plant sap, was rubbed into the cut skin. The entire process usually took months or even years to complete. Facial tattooing identified a man as belonging to a particular group and indicated the magnitude of his mana or spiritual power. Although permanent, tattooing was seen as a necessary item of dress for ceremonial occasions: each design had a specific name, and every tattooed individual was marked differently. People of high status had the right to be tattooed while those of lesser status had to earn that right. Wealth, position in the community, and the level of a person's courage would determine the extent and nature of the tattoos. The facial tattooing of a chief were considered so distinctive and varied that the chief would draw them at the bottom of European documents as his signature.

Frequently, leaders of the community will dress in a distinctive fashion, especially during ceremonial occasions. An individual's political power, social position, and wealth can be made visible by dress expressing prominent status or indicating particular social roles such as warrior, judge, and police officer. We must not forget that ordinary people also wear special dress for important events, including weddings, funerals, high school proms, or even gallery openings. Usually it is the entire ensemble of clothing and accessories that project authority and status. But at times, a single item of dress may announce social position and political power. For example, among the Yoruba of Nigeria, a conical, beaded crown with fringe veil is the primary symbol of kingship and must be worn by the ruler on all ceremonial occasions. The veil obscures the face of the living king while a face motif on the crown reveals the dynastic ancestors. In this way, the crown represents the spiritual and political force of the dynasty. Crowns also reference royal power in European cultures.

Royal dress and regalia has characterized the Asante people of Ghana since the seventeenth century. The two most spectacular elements of Asante dress are kente cloth and elaborate gold jewelry. Kente is a brightly colored, hand-loomed, narrow band cloth woven by men on a four-heddle horizontal loom. The weavers use silk or rayon thread to create bright color in a predominantly cotton textile. The names and meanings of kente designs can allude to proverbs, historical events, or important characteristics of leadership. During their reigns, Asante kings were expected to invent new kente designs. Kente is a good example of how a dress form that is adopted by another culture can shift meaning. In the United States, kente has become identified with African American culture and has been used in multiple forms and ceremonial contexts. The Asante have used gold extensively to adorn and glorify rulers as well as to validate their positions. The Asante king and various categories of chiefs wear many items of gold, such as necklaces, anklets, large armlets, and rings. Magnificently attired rulers, encumbered with as many gold ornaments as they can wear or carry while participating in religious or state ceremonies can be identified with the proverb "Great men move slowly." Gold objects are produced by the lost wax process or repoussé technique.

In Polynesia the spiritual power of rulers and other high-ranking people was often expressed by wearing apparel made of feathers, which associated it with the gods. In Hawaii, one of the most centralized and status-conscious societies in Polynesia, feather cloaks, sashes, and helmets were important components of ceremonial dress, enhancing the authority and divine status of a ruler. Cloaks, worn on state occasions and during battle, provided spiritual, and to some extent physical, protection to the wearer. Capturing an enemy's feathered cloak was a particularly powerful symbol of defeat. The size of a cloak was directly related to the amount

of power a noble person possessed. Because so many feathers were required to produce a cloak, only individuals of great wealth could afford them. Feathers were in part collected as tribute paid by commoners to the chiefs each year. Although ordinary clothing was made by women, the cloaks were made by high-ranking men. Passing a cloak to a descendant involved a transfer of mana (power) from one generation to the next. Feathered cloaks were worn wrapped around the body so that the edges come together unifying the motifs that flank each edge. Many cloaks were decorated with four yellow, bladelike motifs set against a red background. With the imposition of American rule in the late nineteenth century, feathered cloaks were no longer used for warfare but continued to be indicative of chiefly rank. Also, red feathers, associated with the god of war, were used less and yellow became more common as yellow feathers were rarer and more valuable.

A complete clothing ensemble, consisting of cloak, robe, and turban, expresses religious identity as well as high social status for the Muslim Hausa-Fulani rulers of northern Nigeria and is worn for religious celebrations and major political events. On such occasions, the lavishly dressed ruler and officials of high rank appear in a public procession, mounted on richly adorned horses, to symbolically establish superiority over those they rule. Their dress not only sets the ruling aristocracy apart from the rest of the population, but also identifies the wearer with the larger Muslim world both within Africa and beyond. Robes, the most distinct part of the dress ensemble, are often worn layered, creating an imposing image of physical bulk and majesty. The visual focus of the robe, tailored from hand-woven or factory-made cloth, is a large pocket densely embroidered with geometric designs that are loosely inspired by Islamic calligraphy and believed to offer spiritual protection to the wearer. A turban is wrapped numerous times around the wearer's head and chin, creating an aesthetic effect that visually complements the bulky robe. The turban signifies that the man has completed the most important obligation of Islam—a pilgrimage to the sacred city of Mecca. Items in a ruler's dress ensemble are valued heir-looms that belong to the state; like the feathered cloaks of Hawaiian leaders, they can be passed on to descendants in the royal line or given as gifts to other rulers and officials to seal political alliances.

Symbolic dress is not limited to other times and cultures. The dress of modern political leaders and their families shapes the public image as well. A case in point is the wardrobe of Jacqueline Kennedy during the campaign and presidency of her husband, John F. Kennedy. Kennedy was criticized for her extravagant wardrobe and use of foreign designers—especially when compared to the plain style of the Republican candidate's wife, Pat Nixon. Soon after the election, Kennedy worked with the American designer Oleg Cassini to re-create her image. As First Lady, Kennedy established a unique style that was dignified and elegant but also photogenic and recognizable. For her husband's swearing-in ceremony in January 1961, Jacqueline Kennedy wore a Cassinidesigned beige wool crepe dress. She also wore a pillbox hat from Bergdorf Goodman's millinery salon, in what was to become her trademark style—on the back of her head rather than straight and high, as was the fashion. Jacqueline Kennedy's style became widely popular and helped define the image of the Kennedy presidency as innovative, dynamic, and glamorous.

Viewed globally, ceremonial dress involves many acts of body modification that reflect both indigenous development and outside influences. As cultural artifacts, the specific elements of apparel and body adornment have many aspects of meaning; they serve as vehicles for the expression of values, symbols of identity and social status, and statements of aesthetic preference. Each item of a costume has its own history and sociocultural significance and must be considered along with the total ensemble. By looking at ceremonial costumes in other cultures, it becomes possible to understand better the form and function of similar types of dress in one's own culture.

See also Carnival Dress; Kente; Masks; Masquerade and Masked Balls.

Bibliography

Adams, Monni. "Women's Art as a Gender Strategy among the Wé of Canton Boo." *African Arts* 26, no. 4 (1993): 32–43.

D'Alleva, Anne. *Art of the Pacific*. London: Calmann and King Ltd., 1998.

Eicher, Joanne B., and Tonye V. Erekosima. "Final Farewells: The Fine Art of Kalabari Funerals." In *Ways of the River: Arts and Environment of the Niger Delta*. Edited by Martha G. Anderson and Philip M. Peek, 307–329. Los Angeles: UCLA Fowler Museum of Cultural History, 2002.

Jonaitis, Aldona, ed. *Chiefly Feasts: The Enduring Kwakiutl Potlatch*. New York: American Museum of Natural History, 1991.

Mack, John, ed. *African Arts and Cultures*. London: British Museum Press, 2000.

Perani, Judith, and Fred T. Smith. *The Visual Arts of Africa: Gender Power and Life Cycle Rituals*. Upper Saddle River, N.J.: Prentice Hall, 1998.

Rose, Roger G., and Adrienne L. Kaeppler. *Hawai'i: The Royal Islands*. Honolulu, Hawaii: Bishop Museum Press, 1980.

Ross, Doran. *Wrapped in Pride: Ghanaian Kente and African American Identity*. Los Angeles: UCLA Fowler Museum of Cultural History, 1998.

Rubin, Arnold, ed. *Marks of Civilization*. Los Angeles: UCLA Fowler Museum of Cultural History, 1988.

Spring, Christopher, and Julie Hudson. *North African Textiles*. London: British Museum Press, 1995.

Turner, Victor, ed. *Celebration: Studies in Festivity and Ritual*. Washington, D.C.: Smithsonian Institution Press, 1982.

Fred T. Smith

CHALAYAN, HUSSEIN*

Hussein Chalayan's fascination with architecture, spatial dynamics, urban identity, and aerodynamics is expressed in garments based on concepts, technological systems, historical dress, and theories of the body. His clothes are minimal in look but maximal in thought.

Early Career

Chalayan was born in the Turkish community of Nicosia on the island of Cyprus in 1970. His parents separated when he was a child. At the age of eight, he joined his father, who had moved to the United Kingdom. Chalayan was sent to a private school in London when he was twelve, but returned to Cyprus to study for his A-level examinations. He went back to London and attended Central Saint Martin's College at the age of nineteen to study fashion. Chalayan rose to fashion fame soon after he received his B.A. degree from Central Saint Martin's in 1993. His graduating collection, titled The Tangent Flows, was the now infamous series of buried garments that were exhumed just before the show and presented with a text that explained the process.

The rituals of burial and resurrection gave the garments a dimension of reference to life, death, and urban decay in a process that transported the garments from the world of fashion to the kingdom of nature. Since then, Chalayan has collaborated with architects, artists, textile technologists and aerospace engineers; has won awards; and has been recognized as an artist in numerous museum presentations of his work.

The genius of Chalayan's work lies in his ability to explore visual and intellectual principles that chart the spectral orientations of urban societies through such tangibles as clothing, buildings, vehicles, and furniture and through such abstractions as beauty, philosophy and feeling. Chalayan's Aeroplane and Kite dresses (autumn–winter 1995) used the spatial relationship between the fabric and the body to reflect the relative meanings of speed and gravity. The dresses became dynamic interfaces between the human body and its surroundings; the Kite dress actually flew and was reunited with its wearer when it returned to earth.

In Chalayan's eyes, all garments are externalizations of the body in the same way that vehicles and buildings are proportioned to contain the human form. "Everything around us either relates to the body or to the environment," Chalayan explained. "I think of modular systems where clothes are like small parts of an interior, the interiors are part of architecture, which is then a part of an urban environment. I think of fluid space where they are all a part of each other, just in different scales and proportions" (Quinn, p. 120). These sentiments were amplified in the Echoform collection (autumn–winter 1999) in dresses that mimicked airplane interiors. Chalayan attached padded headrests to the shoulders of the garments, evoking thoughts on the role of clothing as a component of a larger spatial system.

Likewise, the Geotrophics collection (spring–summer 1999) made chairs into wearable extensions of the human form. The chair dresses represented the idea of a nomadic existence facilitated by living within completely transportable environments. Determined to express "how the meaning of a nation evolves through conflict or natural boundaries," Chalayan explored the body's role as a locus for the construction of identity, highlighting the ways in which its appropriation by national regimes would orient and indoctrinate it according to the space in which it "belongs."

The relationship between space and identity was further explored in the groundbreaking After Words (autumn–winter 2000) collection. Chalayan based the collection on the necessity of evacuating one's home during wartime and having to hide possessions when a raid was impending. The theme evoked

the 1974 Turkish military intervention that displaced both Turkish and Greek Cypriots from their homes and led indirectly to Chalayan's emigration to Britain several years later. The collection introduced the idea of urban camouflage through clothing, whereby fashion functions as a means of hiding objects in obvious places. After Words featured dresses-cum-chair covers that disguised their role as fashionable garments while simultaneously concealing the furniture beneath them. The collection included a table designed to be worn as a skirt, with chairs that were transformed into suitcases and carried away by the models.

For his before minus now collection (spring–summer 2000), Chalayan returned to the architectural theme expressed in Echoform and Geotrophics, designing a series of dresses in collaboration with an architectural firm. The dresses featured wire-frame architectural prints against static white backgrounds generated by a computer program designed to draw three-dimensional perspectives within an architectural landscape. The renderings' geo-metric dimensions suppress the depiction of real space and create a reality independent of the shapes and textures found in the organic world. Such absolute symmetry and concise angles create the illusion of a realm that is carefully ordered and controlled, yet the architectonic expressions correspond to physical registrations of surfaces and programmatic mappings.

The Remote Control Dress, which was commissioned in 2000 by Judith Clark Costume in London, was designed by means of the composite technology used by aircraft engineers, mirroring the systems that enable airplanes to fly by remote control. Crafted from a combination of fiberglass and resin, the dress was molded into two smooth and glossy pink-colored front and back panels fastened together by metal clips. The facade-like structure of the dress forms an exoskeleton around the body, arcing dramatically inward at the waist and out-ward in the hip region, echoing the silhouette produced by a corset. This structure gives the dress a well-defined hourglass shape that incorporates principles of corsetry into its design, emphasizing a conventionally feminine shape while creating a solid structure that simultaneously masks undesirable body proportions.

Chalayan's Importance

While Chalayan's work continues to question traditional readings of dress and to generate exciting interdisciplinary collaborations, he also opens new frontiers for other designers to explore. As many of his ground-breaking ideas begin to influence wider trends, Chalayan's work is gaining recognition in the mainstream fashion market while continuing to receive acclaim in fashion circles. Since Chalayan signed a licensing agreement with the Italian manufacturing company Gibo in 2002, his label has grown into a strong retail brand. The designer's appointment as creative director of fashion for the classically inclined British luxury retailer Asprey brought his conceptual oeuvre to a wider public, as did his collaboration with Adidas. But his own label still requires an audience with the confidence to carry off clothes heavy with the thought processes behind them.

See also Fashion Designer; Fashion and Identity; Fashion Shows; Haute Couture.

Bibliography

Frankel, Susannah. *Fashion Visionaries: Interviews with Fashion Designers*. London: V and A Publications, 2001.
Quinn, Bradley. *The Fashion of Architecture*. Oxford: Berg, 2003.

Bradley Quinn

CHANEL, GABRIELLE (COCO)

Gabrielle Chanel (1883–1971) was born out of wedlock in the French town of Saumur in the Loire Valley on 19 August 1883 to Albert Chanel, an itinerant salesman, and Jeanne Devolle. Her parents were finally married in July of 1884. Her mother died of asthma at the age of thirty-three. When Chanel was just twelve years old, she was sent along with her two sisters to an orphanage at Aubazine. During the holidays the girls stayed with their grandparents in Moulins. In 1900 Chanel moved there permanently and attended the local convent school with her aunt Adrienne, who was of a similar age. Having been taught to sew by the nuns, both girls found work as dressmakers, assisting Monsieur Henri Desboutin of the House of Grampayre.

Early Career

Chanel sang during evening concerts at a fashionable café called La Rotonde. It is believed that her rendition of the song "Qui qu'a vu Coco dans le Trocadéro" earned her the nickname "Coco." Chanel started to mix in fashionable circles when she went to live in 1908 with Étienne Balsan, who bred racehorses on his vast estate at La Croix-Saint-Ouen. Chanel's astute choice of clothing—her neat tailor-made suits and masculine riding dress—and modest demeanor served to mark her out from the other courtesans. Thus from an early age Chanel demonstrated great confidence in her own sense of style, a formula that proved irresistible to other women. Soon Balsan's friends asked her to make them copies of the boater hats that she trimmed and wore herself. Seizing upon this opportunity for financial independence, in 1908–1909 Chanel persuaded Balsan to let her use his Paris apartment at 160, boulevard Malesherbes to set up a millinery business. She employed a professional milliner and she engaged her sister Antoinette and two other assistants as the business grew.

While Chanel was in Paris, her friendship with the millionaire entrepreneur and polo player Arthur Capel, known as "Boy," developed into love. It was Boy who lent her the money to rent commercial premises on the rue Cambon—where the House of Chanel was still located in the early 2000s—in the heart of Paris's couture district. Chanel modes opened at 21, rue Cambon in 1910. From the outset, Chanel was the perfect model for her own designs, and she was photographed for the fall 1910 issue of the magazine *Le théâtre: Revue mensuelle illustrée*. By 1912 hats by Chanel appeared in the popular press, worn by such leading actresses of the day as Lucienne Roger and Gabrielle Dorziat. Chanel had achieved financial independence. The terms of her lease, however, prevented her from selling clothes, as there was a dressmaker already working in the building.

First Collections, 1913–1919

While on vacation in Deauville on the west coast of France in the summer of 1913, Boy Capel found a shop for Chanel to open on the fashionable rue Gontaut-Biron, and it was here that she presented her first fashion collections. With the outbreak of World War I in July 1914, many wealthy and fashionable Parisians decamped to Deauville and shopped at Chanel's boutique. It is believed that she sold only ready-to-wear clothing at this date. Chanel had cut her hair short during this period and many other women copied her bobbed hairstyle as well as bought her clothes. Chanel's time had come: radical in their understatement, her versatile and sporty designs were to prove perfect for the more active lives led by many wealthy women during wartime.

In 1916 Chanel purchased a stock of surplus jersey fabric from the manufacturer Rodier, which she made into unstructured three-quarter-length coats belted at the waist and embellished with luxurious fabrics or furs, worn with matching skirts. That fall Chanel presented her first complete couture collection. The March 1917 issue of *Les élégances parisiennes* illustrates a group of jersey suits by Chanel, some of which are delicately embroidered, while others are strictly plain and accessorized with a saddlery-style double belt. All are worn with open-neck blouses with deep sailor collars. A 1918 design consisted of a coat of tan jersey banded with brown rabbit fur, with a lining and blouse of white-dotted rose foulard: this matching of the coat lining to the dress or blouse was to become a Chanel trademark. Striking in their simplicity and modernity, Chanel's jersey fashions caused a sensation.

While Chanel's daywear was characterized by its stylish utility, her evening wear was unashamedly romantic. In 1919 she presented fragile gowns in black Chantilly lace with gold-spun net and jet tassels and other gowns in silver lace brocade. Capes of black velvet adorned with rows of ostrich fringe revealed a Spanish influence—the very height of fashion that winter. This was the year that Chanel would announce, "I woke up famous," but it was also the year that Boy Capel was killed in an automobile accident.

The 1920s

Fashions of the early 1920s. From 1920 to 1923 Chanel conducted a liaison with the grand duke Dmitri Pavlovitch, grandson of Russia's Tsar Alexander II, and her collections during these years were imbued with Russian influences. Particularly noteworthy were loose shift dresses, waistcoats, blouses, and evening coats made in dark and neutral colors with exquisite, brightly colored, folkloric Russian embroideries stitched by exiled aristocrats. In 1922 Chanel showed long, lean, belted blouses based on Russian peasant wear.

By 1923 she had further simplified the cut of her clothes and offered fewer brocaded fabrics, while her embroideries—red and beige were favorite colors that year—displayed more restrained and modernistic designs. Chanel led the international trend toward shorter hemlines. Her premises on the rue Cambon, which had already expanded in 1919, grew to include numbers 27, 29, and 31 during the early 1920s.

Perfumes. Chanel launched her first perfume, Chanel No. 5, in 1921. Reputedly named for the designer's lucky number, No. 5 was blended by Ernest Beaux, who used aldehydes (an organic compound which yields acids when oxidized and alcohols when reduced) to enhance the fragrance of such costly natural ingredients as jasmine, the perfume's base note. Chanel designed the modern pharmaceutical-style bottle and monochrome packaging herself. Chanel No. 5 was the first perfume to bear a designer's name. Building upon the success of No. 5, Chanel introduced Cuir de Russie (1924), Bois des Îles (1926), and Gardénia (1927) before the end of the decade.

La garçonne. Chanel's interpretation of masculine styles and sportswear—her blazers, waistcoats, and shirts with cufflinks, as well as her choice of fabrics—were greatly inspired by the garments worn by the duke of Westminster (an Englishman with whom she was involved between 1923 and 1930) and his aristocratic friends. Following a fishing holiday in Scotland, she introduced her customers to Fair Isle woolens and tweeds. The duke bought her a mill to secure exclusive fabrics for her new styles. Chanel was also inspired by humbler items of masculine apparel, including berets, reefer jackets, mechanics' dungarees, stonemasons' neckerchiefs, and sailor suits, which she rendered utterly luxurious for her wealthy clients. Chanel herself often wore loose sailor-style trousers, flouting the rules of sartorial etiquette that generally restricted women from wearing trousers to the beach or within the home as evening pajamas.

In 1927 *Vogue* recommended Chanel's jersey suit in soft tan wool, with collar, cuffs, blouse, and jacket lining in rose jersey, for the woman who wanted to look chic on board ship. The long-line jacket buttoned diagonally, while the skirt was box-pleated at the front. Throughout her career Chanel paid great attention to the cut of her sleeves, ensuring that they permitted the wearer to move with ease without distorting the lines of the garment. By the fall of 1929 her sports costumes were still slim but longer, with hemlines reaching below the calf.

The little black dress. Chanel had designed black dresses as early as 1913, when she made a black velvet dress with a white petal collar for Suzanne Orlandi. In April 1919 British *Vogue* reported that "Chanel takes into account the lack of motors and the general difficulty of living in Paris just now by her almost invariably black evening dresses" (p. 48). But it was not until American *Vogue* (1 October 1926) described a *garçonnestyle* black day dress as "The Chanel 'Ford'—the frock that all the world will wear" (p. 69) that the little black dress took the fashion world by storm. And although the use of black in fashion has a long history, Chanel has been credited as its originator ever since.

Theatrical costume. The stage was a prominent showcase for fashion designers during the nineteenth and early twentieth centuries. Chanel always moved in artistic circles, and she often supported the work of her friends both financially and by working collaboratively with them. In 1922 she designed Grecian-style costumes in coarse wool for Jean Cocteau's adaptation of Sophocles's *Antigone*; the designs were featured in French *Vogue* (1 February 1923). The following year she dressed the dancers of the Ballets russes in jersey bathing costumes and sports clothes similar to those seen in her fashion collections for the modern-realist production *Le train bleu* (1924). And in 1926 the actresses in Cocteau's *Orphée* were dressed head to toe in Chanel's latest fashions.

Jewelry. Chanel believed the role of jewelry was to decorate an ensemble rather than to flaunt wealth, and she challenged convention by wearing heaps of jewelry, often precious, during the day—even for sailing—while for evening she sometimes wore no jewelry at all. The loose, straight-cut shapes of Chanel's fashions and her use of many plain fabrics provided the perfect foil for the lavish costume jewelry that she introduced in the early 1920s. Lacking any desire to replicate precious jewels, Chanel's designs, initially made by Maison Gripoix, defied nature in their bold use of color and size. In 1924 she opened her own jewelry workshop, which was managed by the comte Étienne de Beaumont. Beaumont designed the long chains with colored stones and cross-shaped pendants that became a classic of her house. Chanel was fond of Byzantine crosses, and she was also inspired by the buttons, chains, and tassels of military costumes.

Her oversized fake pearls, worn in multiple strands, were an instant success. In 1926 Chanel created a vogue for mismatched earrings by wearing a black pearl in one ear and a white one in the other. In 1928 she introduced diamond paste jewelry and in 1929 offered "gypsy" necklaces—triple strands of red, green, and yellow beads, as well as colored beads combined with chunky wooden chains.

Fashions of the later 1920s. By the late 1920s Chanel's fashions were adorned with geometric designs. For day-wear she used stripes and checks as well as patterns inspired by Fair Isle knitwear; for evening many of her black lace fabrics were combined with metallic, embroidered, or beaded laces.

At the height of her fame and with the demand for Paris couture at its peak, Chanel employed between two and three thousand workers during the mid-to late 1920s. She was said, however, to be a hard taskmaster and to pay poor wages. In 1927 she opened her London house. British *Vogue* pointed out in early June 1927 that, while the conception and feel of Chanel's current collection was essentially French, the designer had adapted it for London social life. For the Royal Ascot racing meet she offered a long-sleeved black lace dress with trailing scarf detail and, for presentation at court, an understated white taffeta dress with a train that was cut in one piece with the skirt, complemented by a simple headdress based on the Prince of Wales feathers. In September 1929 *Vogue* wrote, "When Chanel, the sponsor of the straight, chemise dress and the boyish silhouette, uses little, rippling capes on her fur coats and a high waist-line and numerous ruffles on an evening gown, then you may be sure that the feminine mode is a fact and not a fancy" (p. 35).

In tune with her modernist fashion aesthetic, Chanel installed faceted glass mirrors in her Paris couture salon around 1928. These mirrors brought the advantage of allowing her to sit out of sight to watch her shows. In complete contrast to the salon, her private apartment on the third floor of 31, rue Cambon was lavish and ornate. It is now carefully preserved, decorated with Coromandel screens, Louis XIV furniture, Venetian mirrors, black-amoor sculptures, and smoked crystal and amethyst chandeliers. When designing clothes, Chanel would pare away the nonessentials for the sake of the wearer's comfort; when designing domestic interiors, on the other hand, she believed that clutter was a necessity—that it was essential to be surrounded by the objects one needed and loved.

The 1930s

Fashions of the early 1930s. Although Chanel's business may have suffered during the depression—she is said to have halved her prices in 1932—her workforce increased to around four thousand employees by 1935. Chanel's saleswomen as well as her seamstresses went on strike in June 1936 to protest their poor wages and working conditions. In April 1936 the French people voted in a left-wing coalition government headed by Leon Blum, which was followed by a number of strikes including the workers at Chanel. Chanel refused to implement the Matignon Agreement, which introduced wage increases of 7 to 15 percent, the right to collective bargaining and unionize, a 40-hour week and a 2-week paid annual holiday. Instead she fired 300 women who refused to leave the building and only later, in order to produce her next collection, agreed to introduce a workers cooperative on the understanding that she managed it (Madsen, p. 216).

From 1930 Chanel's hemlines became longer and were slightly flared; she emphasized her waists, and her jackets had soft, bloused bodices. Bows were to become a signature motif, used as decorative details on the shoulders and skirts of her garments. Cravat bows provided a feminine touch to her blouses, and crisp white frills were added around the collars and cuffs of her black suits and dresses. From 1934 Chanel used American elasticized fabrics made with a brand of yarn with a latex core called Lastex in her collections to create clothes with a crepe-like surface, and she frequently combined these with jersey.

During the 1930s she launched her cosmetics line and introduced a new perfume called Glamour. She further boosted her revenue by endorsing other manufacturers' products and designing for other companies. In 1931 she promoted Ferguson Brothers' cottons—her spring collection included cotton evening gowns—and she designed knitwear for Ellaness and raincoats for David Mosley and Sons. She also earned $2 million for her work in Hollywood that year.

Screen and stage. When hemlines dropped in 1929, Hollywood's movie studios were devastated, as thousands of reels of film were instantly rendered old-fashioned. Rather than continue to follow Parisian fashions slavishly, the studio magnate Samuel Goldwyn invited Chanel to design costumes directly for his leading female stars, including Greta Garbo, Gloria Swanson, and Marlene Dietrich. Chanel, however, produced designs for just three Metro-Goldwyn-Mayer productions: *Palmy Days* (1931), *Tonight or Never* (1931), and *The Greeks Had a Word for Them* (1932). Many actresses refused to have Chanel's style imposed on them, and her designs were either overlooked or criticized for being too understated for the screen.

In Paris, Chanel continued to design for progressive plays, providing costumes for Cocteau's *La machine infernale* (1934) as well as *Les chevaliers de la table ronde* and *Oedipe-Roi*, both of which appeared in 1937. In addition,

despite her dislike of left-wing politics, she created the costumes for Jean Renoir's radical film *La marseillaise* and for *La règle du jeu*, both produced in 1938.

Jewelry. In 1932 the International Guild of Diamond Merchants commissioned Chanel to design a collection of diamonds set in platinum called Bijoux de Diamants. Having designed fake jewels during affluent times, Chanel now declared that diamonds were an investment. Along with her current lover, Paul Iribe, she presented a line of jewelry based on the themes of knots, stars, and feathers. The collection was exhibited in her own home in the rue du Faubourg-Saint-Honoré in Paris.

During the 1930s, Fulco di Santostefano della Cerda, duc di Verdura, started to design jewelry for Chanel. He had been designing textiles for her since 1927. Most significantly, di Verdura pioneered the revival of baked enamel jewelry: his chunky, baked enamel bracelets inset with jeweled Maltese crosses were particularly successful. Christian Bérard also designed occasional pieces for her, and Maison Gripoix continued to make up many of her designs—notably those in romantic floral and rococo-revival styles. From the mid-to late 1930s Chanel's heavy triangular bibs of colored stones and coins and her silk cord necklaces with tassels of brilliantly colored stones showed influences from India and Southeast Asia.

Fashions of the later 1930s. Chanel's daywear continued to be characterized by its simplicity, but—perhaps surprisingly—she participated in the vogue for Victorian-revival styles, presenting cinch-waisted, full-skirted, and bustle-backed evening gowns worn with shoulder-length lace gloves and floral accessories. Decidedly more modern was the trouser suit worn by the fashion editor Diana Vreeland in 1937–1938 that consisted of a black bolero-style jacket and high-waisted trousers entirely covered with overlapping sequins. The metallic sheen of the sequins contrasted with a soft cream silk chiffon and lace blouse with ruffled neckline and fastened with pearl buttons. Chanel's dramatic combinations of black with white or scarlet remained popular. In the late 1930s her evening wear revealed influences from gypsy and peasant sources: skirts in multicolored taffetas, sometimes striped or checked, and worn with puff-sleeved, embroidered blouses.

The war years. Chanel closed her fashion house during World War II but continued to sell her perfumes. For the duration of the war she lived in Paris at the Hotel Ritz with her German lover, an officer in the German army named Hans-Gunther von Dincklage. When Paris was liberated in 1944, Chanel fled to Switzerland and did not return to the rue Cambon for almost a decade.

The 1950s

Fashions of the 1950s. Chanel started working again at the age of seventy in 1953, partly to boost her flagging perfume sales. Her fashion philosophy remained unchanged: she extolled function and comfort in dress and declared her aim of making women look pretty and young. On 5 February 1954 she presented her first postwar collection, a line of understated suits and dresses. The general press response, however, was that Chanel was too old and out of touch with the modern market, and only a few models sold. On the other hand, American *Vogue* (15 February 1954) thought "the great revolutionist" sufficiently important to justify a three-and-a-half-page article devoted to her career and fashion philosophy: "A dress isn't right if it is uncomfortable. . . . A dress must function; place the pockets accurately for use, never a button without a button-hole. A sleeve isn't right unless the arm moves easily. Elegance in clothes means freedom to move freely" (American *Vogue*, p. 84).

By modernizing the formulas that had brought her so much success earlier in her career, Chanel succeeded in reestablishing herself as a fashion designer of international stature. For spring–summer 1955 she presented a gray jersey suit consisting of a softly-fitted jacket complete with pockets and a full box-pleated skirt, worn with a bow-tied white blouse. Navy jersey suits had schoolgirl-style blazer jackets and were banded with white trim or worn with knitwear striped in navy and white. Buttons were often covered in fabrics that matched the suit, and sometimes meticulously trimmed with the contrasting fabric that was used to outline the pockets and form the attached shirt cuffs. Other buttons were molded in bold brass, sometimes featuring a lion's head—Chanel's birth sign was Leo—or made in more delicate gilt, perhaps with a cutwork floral motif.

In 1957 Chanel introduced braid trimmings to her cardigan-style jackets. For fall–winter 1957–1958 her suits had a wrap pleat that ran down the side of the skirt and concealed a trouser-style pocket. Unusually, she showed a hat with every model—these were upturned sailor-style hats made in soft fabrics that matched the

> "The maison Chanel might be called the 'Jersey House', for the creations of Mlle. Chanel have long been and long will be in jersey. Of late, a thin firm quality of cotton velvet has been used by Chanel for cloaks and certain frocks." (British *Vogue*, early October 1917, p. 30)

suits with which they were worn. As always, she paid great attention to the linings of her coats and suits: this season, camel hair was lined with red guanaco, gray tweed with white squirrel, and red velour with fluffy gray goatskin. Her coats were cut in the same style as her suit jackets, simply lengthened to the same level as the skirt hem.

Chanel's modern suits in nubby wools, tweeds, or jersey fabrics with their multiple functional pockets, teamed with gilt chains and fake pearl jewelry; her distinctive handbags; and her sling-back shoes with contrasting toe caps, became fashion staples for the affluent. And as before, her designs were widely copied for the mass market: the company sold toiles to the British chain store Wallis so that it could legitimately reproduce Chanel's designs.

For evening Chanel offered variations on her suits in such lavish materials as gold-trimmed brocade, and she remained faithful to her love of black-and-white laces for dresses. A cocktail dress from the spring–summer 1958 collection had a bodice of navy-and-white-striped silk with a large bow at the neckline and a full skirt of white organdy, banded at the hem with the same striped fabric.

For spring–summer 1959 she presented a black lace dress, dipping low at the back and molded to the hipline, which was threaded with black ribbon and flared into a full skirt; it was accessorized with a long chain with linked pearls and chunky, colored stones. That season the collection was modeled by the designer's friends—stylish young women who were accustomed to wearing her clothes.

Perfumes and accessories. In 1954 Chanel introduced a man's fragrance, Pour Monsieur. The same year Pierre and Paul Wertheimer, who already owned Parfums Chanel, bought her entire business, and it remained within the Wertheimer family as of the early 2000s.

In 1955 Chanel introduced quilted handbags with shoulder straps of leather plaited with gilt chains with flattened links, similar to those used to weight her jackets. The bags were offered in leather or jersey and were initially available in beige, navy, brown, and black, lined with red grosgrain or leather—Chanel chose a lighter color for the interior to help women find small items in their bags. Updated each season, Chanel's distinctive handbags were still top sellers in the early 2000s.

The 1960s

By 1960 fashions by Chanel were no longer at the forefront of style. She abhorred the miniskirt, believing that a woman's knees were always best concealed. But nonetheless she continued to clothe a faithful clientele in suits that were subtly reworked each season. One of her most high-profile and stylish clients from this period was Jacqueline Kennedy.

A suit that Chanel herself wore during the mid-1960s (model 37750) was purchased by London's Victoria and Albert Museum. It consists of a three-quarter-length jacket and a dress made of black worsted crepe that reaches just below the knee, accessorized with a black silk stockinette-brimmed hat. Pristine white collar and cuffs are integral to the jacket—some clients complained that these touches wore out long before the jacket itself. Neat, unadorned, monochrome, and entirely functional, the suit has echoes of a school uniform.

In 1962 Chanel was again invited to design for the cinema, this time to dress Romy Schneider in Luchino Visconti's film *Boccaccio '70* and Delphine Seyrig in Alain Resnais's film *Last Year at Marienbad*. In 1969 Chanel herself became the subject of a Broadway musical called *Coco*, written by Alan Jay Lerner. With Chanel's permission, the title role was played by Katharine Hepburn.

Chanel died on 10 January 1971 in the midst of preparing her spring–summer 1971 collection. Her personal clothing and jewelry was sold at auction in London in December 1978.

Postscript

Following Chanel's death, Gaston Berthelot was appointed to design classic garments in the Chanel tradition between 1971 and 1973. The perfume No. 19, named after Chanel's birthday, was launched in 1970. From 1974 Jean Cazaubon and Yvonne Dudel designed the couture line; in 1978 a ready-to-wear range was designed by Philippe Guibourgé; and in 1980 Ramon Esparza joined the couture team. But it was not until 1983, when Karl Lagerfeld was appointed chief designer, that the House of Chanel once again made fashion headlines: it

remains the ultimate in desirability for a clientele of all ages in the early 2000s.

Since his appointment, Lagerfeld has continued to reference the Chanel style, sometimes offering classic interpretations and at other times making witty and ironic statements. Ultimately, he has developed the label to make it relevant to the contemporary market. Like its founder, he draws on sportswear for inspiration: surfing and cycling outfits inspired his fall–winter 1990–1991 collection; training shoes bearing the distinctive interlocked CC logo were shown for fall–winter 1993–1994; nautical styles were shown for spring–summer 1994; and skiwear styles were featured in fall–winter 2003–2004. While Chanel looked to the utilitarian dress of the working man, Lager-feld derives his ideas from contemporary social subcultures. He has presented fetishistic PVC jeans, lace-up bustiers, dog collars, and plastic raincoats (fall–winter 1991–1992); biker-style leather jackets, trousers, and boots (fall–winter 1992–1993 and fall–winter 2002–2003); B-Boy-and Ragga-inspired styles (spring–summer 1994); and a more eclectic "rock chic" (fall–winter 2003–2004). The tweed suit continues to be a mainstay of the collections, satisfying classic tastes with cardigan styles and the more adventurous younger clients with tweed bra tops and micro-miniskirts. The classic cardigan-style suit has also been offered in terry cloth, while denim jackets are trimmed with Chanel's favorite camellia flowers (both for spring–summer 1991). Costume jewelry is used in abundance, and the little black dress is still inextricably associated with the name of Chanel.

To ensure the survival of the refined craft skills of the couture industry, the House of Chanel purchased five artisan workshops in 2002: the top embroiderer François Lesage, the expert shoemaker Raymond Massaro, the flamboyant milliner Maison Michel, the feather specialist André Lemarié, and the leading costume jeweler Desrues.

Chanel perfumes remain top sellers. Since the founder died, the company has launched Cristalle (1974), Coco (1984), No. 5 Eau de Parfum (1986), Allure (1996), Coco Mademoiselle (2001), and Chance (2002) for women and Antaeus pour Homme (1981), Egoïste (1990), Platinum Egoïste (1993), and Allure Homme (1999) for men.

See also Costume Jewelry; Handbags and Purses; Lagerfeld, Karl; Little Black Dress; Paris Fashion; Perfume; Vreeland, Diana.

Bibliography

Charles-Roux, Edmonde. *Chanel and Her World*. London: Weidenfeld and Nicolson, 1979. Extensively illustrated in black and white, a standard text covering Chanel's major design achievements as well as her private and social life.

———. *Chanel*. London: Collins Harvill, 1989.

de la Haye, Amy, and Shelley Tobin. *Chanel: The Couturière at Work*. London: V and A Publications, 1994. Detailed analysis of Chanel's designs and working practice. Extensively illustrated in color, including many museum garments in detail.

Madsen, Axel. *Coco Chanel: A Biography*. London: Bloomsbury, 1990. Comprehensive account of Chanel's life.

Morand, Paul. *L'allure de Chanel*. London: Herman, 1976. An insight into Chanel's life written by an author friend.

Mauriès, Patrick. *Jewellery by CHANEL*. London: Thames and Hudson, Inc., 1993.

Amy de la Haye

CHEMISE DRESS

The term "chemise dress" has traditionally been used to describe a dress cut straight at the sides and left unfitted at the waist, in the manner of the undergarment known as a chemise. This term has most often been used to describe outer garments during transitional periods in fashion (most notably during the 1780s and the 1950s), in order to distinguish new, unfitted styles from the prevailing, fitted silhouette.

In the eighteenth century, the primary female undergarment was the chemise, or shift, a knee-length, loose-fitting garment of white linen with a straight or slightly triangular silhouette. The term chemise was first used to describe an outer garment in the 1780s, when Queen Marie Antoinette of France popularized a kind of informal, loose-fitting gown of sheer white cotton, resembling a chemise in both cut and material, which became known as the *chemise à la reine*. After chemise dresses, cut straight and gathered to a high waist with a sash or drawstring, became the dominant fashion, around 1800, there was no longer a need to describe their silhouette, and the term "chemise" reverted almost exclusively to its former meaning.

Dresses were next described as chemises around 1910, when loosely belted, columnar dresses recalling early-nineteenth-century styles became popular. (The chemise was still worn as lingerie, but by the 1920s, it evolved into a hip-length, tubular, camisole-like garment with narrow straps.) Though the straight, unbelted dresses of the 1920s were more like chemises than any previous dress style, and have since been called chemise dresses by historians, the term was only occasionally used at the time. After fashion returned to a more fitted silhouette in the 1930s, the chemise dress reappeared around 1940, this time in the form of a dress cut to fall straight from the shoulders, or gathered into a yoke, but always meant to be worn belted at the waist.

The most important decade of the twentieth century for the chemise dress, however, was the 1950s. Early in that decade, the Parisian couturiers Christian Dior and Cristóbal Balenciaga, along with other designers in Europe and the United States, began experimenting with unfitted sheath and tunic dresses, and belted chemise dresses continued to be popular. The major change, however, came in 1957, when both Dior and Balenciaga presented straight, unbelted chemise dresses that bypassed the waist entirely. Called chemises or sacks, these dresses were considered a revolutionary change of direction in fashion, and became the subject of heated debate in the American press; many commentators, particularly men, considered such figure-concealing styles ugly and unnatural, while proponents praised their ease and clean-lined, modern look. (The term "sack" may have been a reference to the eighteenth-century sacque, or sack-back gown, which Balenciaga revived in the form of chemises with back fullness, but it was also an apt description of the bag-like chemise silhouette.)

Waistless styles, both straight and A-line, continued to be controversial over the next several years, but they were gradually incorporated into most wardrobes, and became a staple of 1960s fashion. The term "chemise," however, faded from use early in the 1960s, possibly because the press uproar of 1957 and 1958 had given it negative connotations (or because the lingerie chemise was a distant memory, having last been worn in the 1920s). Straight-cut dresses were now called shifts; more voluminous variants were the muumuu and tent dress. After another period of more fitted garments in the 1970s, unfitted dresses were again revived in the 1980s. Since then, however, women have had the option of choosing from a variety of silhouettes, and unfitted styles have simply been described as straight, or loose-fitting.

See also A-Line Dress; Dior, Christian.

Bibliography

Keenan, Brigid. *Dior in Vogue*. London: Octopus Books, 1981.

Miller, Lesley Ellis. *Cristóbal Balenciaga*. London: B. T. Batsford, Ltd., 1993.

"Topics of the Times." *New York Times* (28 May 1958). Good contemporary overview and summary of the chemise controversy.

Susan Ward

CHILDREN'S CLOTHING

All societies define childhood within certain parameters. From infancy to adolescence, there are societal expectations throughout the various stages of children's development concerning their capabilities and limitations, as well as how they should act and look. Clothing plays an integral role of the "look" of childhood in every era. An overview history of children's clothing provides insights into changes in child-rearing theory and practice, gender roles, the position of children in society, and similarities and differences between children's and adults' clothing.

Before the early-twentieth century, clothing worn by infants and young children shared a distinctive common feature—their clothing lacked sex distinction. The origins of this aspect of children's clothing stem from the sixteenth century, when European men and older boys began wearing doublets paired with breeches. Previously, both males and females of all ages (except for swaddled infants) had worn some type of gown, robe, or tunic. Once men began wearing bifurcated garments, however, male and female clothing became much more distinct. Breeches were reserved for men and older boys, while the members of society most subordinate to men—all females and the youngest boys—continued to wear skirted garments. To modern eyes, it may appear that when little boys of the past were attired in skirts or dresses, they were dressed "like girls," but to their contemporaries, boys and girls were simply dressed alike in clothing appropriate for small children.

New theories put forth in the late seventeenth and the eighteenth centuries about children and childhood greatly influenced children's clothing. The custom of swaddling—immobilizing newborn infants with linen

wrappings over their diapers and shirts—had been in place for centuries. A traditional belief underlying swaddling was that babies' limbs needed to be straightened and supported or they would grow bent and misshapen. In the eighteenth century, medical concerns that swaddling weakened rather than strengthened children's limbs merged with new ideas about the nature of children and how they should be raised to gradually reduce the use of swaddling. For example, in philosopher John Locke's influential 1693 publication, *Some Thoughts Concerning Education*, he advocated abandoning swaddling altogether in favor of loose, lightweight clothing that allowed children freedom of movement. Over the next century, various authors expanded on Locke's theories and by 1800, most English and American parents no longer swaddled their children.

When swaddling was still customary in the early years of the eighteenth century, babies were taken out of swaddling at between two and four months and put into "slips," long linen or cotton dresses with fitted bodices and full skirts that extended a foot or more beyond the children's feet; these long slip outfits were called "long clothes." Once children began crawling and later walking, they wore "short clothes"—ankle-length skirts, called petticoats, paired with fitted, back-opening bodices that were frequently boned or stiffened. Girls wore this style until thirteen or fourteen, when they put on the front-opening gowns of adult women. Little boys wore petticoat outfits until they reached at least age four through seven, when they were "breeched" or considered mature enough to wear miniature versions of adult male clothing—coats, vests, and the exclusively male breeches. The age of breeching varied, depending on parental choice and the boy's maturity, which was defined as how masculine he appeared and acted. Breeching was an important rite of passage for young boys because it symbolized they were leaving childhood behind and beginning to take on male roles and responsibilities.

As the practice of swaddling declined, babies wore the long slip dresses from birth to about five months old. For crawling infants and toddlers, "frocks," ankle-length versions of the slip dresses, replaced stiffened bodices and petticoats by the 1760s. The clothing worn by older children also became less constricting in the latter part of the eighteenth century. Until the 1770s, when little boys were breeched, they essentially went from the petticoats of childhood into the adult male clothing appropriate for their station in life. Although boys were still breeched by about six or seven during the 1770s, they now began to wear somewhat more relaxed versions of adult clothing—looser-cut coats and open-necked shirts with ruffled collars—until their early teen years. Also in the 1770s, instead of the more formal bodice and petticoat combinations, girls continued to wear frock-style dresses, usually accented with wide waist sashes, until they were old enough for adult clothing.

These modifications in children's clothing affected women's clothing—the fine muslin chemise dresses worn by fashionable women of the 1780s and 1790s look remarkably similar to the frocks young children had been wearing since mid-century. However, the development of women's chemise dresses is more complex than the garments simply being adult versions of children's frocks. Beginning in the 1770s, there was general movement away from stiff brocades to softer silk and cotton fabrics in women's clothing, a trend that converged with a strong interest in the dress of classical antiquity in the 1780s and 1790s. Children's sheer white cotton frocks, accented with waist sashes giving a high-waisted look, provided a convenient model for women in the development of neoclassical fashions. By 1800, women, girls, and toddler boys all wore similarly styled, high-waisted dresses made up in lightweight silks and cottons.

A new type of transitional attire, specifically designed for small boys between the ages of three and seven, began to be worn about 1780. These outfits, called "skeleton suits" because they fit close to the body, consisted of ankle-length trousers buttoned onto a short jacket worn over a shirt with a wide collar edged in ruffles. Trousers, which came from lower class and military clothing, identified skeleton suits as male clothing, but at the same time set them apart from the suits with knee-length breeches worn by older boys and men. In the early 1800s, even after trousers had supplanted breeches as the fashionable choice, the jumpsuit-like skeleton suits, so unlike men's suits in style, still continued as distinctive dress for young boys. Babies in slips and toddlers in frocks, little boys in skeleton suits, and older boys who wore frilled collar shirts until their early teens, signaled a new attitude that extended childhood for boys, dividing it into the three distinct stages of infancy, boyhood, and youth.

In the nineteenth century, infants' clothing continued trends in place at the end of the previous century. Newborn layettes consisted of the ubiquitous long dresses (long clothes) and numerous undershirts, day and night caps, napkins (diapers), petticoats, nightgowns, socks, plus one or two outerwear cloaks. These garments were made by mothers or commissioned from seamstresses, with ready-made layettes available by the late 1800s. While it is possible to date nineteenth-century baby dresses based on subtle variations in cut and the type and placement of trims, the basic dresses changed little over the century. Baby dresses were generally made in white cotton because it was easily washed and bleached and were styled with fitted bodices or yokes and long full skirts. Because many dresses were also ornately trimmed with embroidery and lace, today such garments are often mistaken as special occasion attire. Most of these dresses, however, were everyday outfits—the standard baby "uniforms" of the time. When infants became more active at between four and eight months, they went into calf-length white dresses (short clothes). By mid-century, colorful prints gained popularity for older toddlers' dresses.

The ritual of little boys leaving off dresses for male clothing continued to be called "breeching" in the nineteenth century, although now trousers, not breeches, were the symbolic male garments. The main factors determining breeching age were the time during the century when a boy was born, plus parental preference and the boy's maturity. At the beginning of the 1800s, little boys went into their skeleton suits at about age three, wearing these outfits until they were six or seven. Tunic suits with knee-length tunic dresses over long trousers began to replace skeleton suits in the late 1820s, staying in fashion until the early 1860s. During this period, boys were not considered officially breeched until they wore trousers without the tunic overdresses at about age six or seven. Once breeched, boys dressed in cropped, waist-length jackets until their early teens, when they donned cutaway frock coats with knee-length tails, signifying they had finally achieved full adult sartorial status.

From the 1860s to the 1880s, boys from four to seven wore skirted outfits that were usually simpler than girls' styles with more subdued colors and trim or "masculine" details such as a vest. Knickerbockers or knickers, knee-length pants for boys aged seven to fourteen, were introduced about 1860. Over the next thirty years, boys were breeched into the popular knickers outfits at younger and younger ages. The knickers worn by the youngest boys from three to six were paired with short jackets over lace-collared blouses, belted tunics, or sailor tops. These outfits contrasted sharply to the versions worn by their older brothers, whose knickers suits had tailored wool jackets, stiff-collared shirts, and four-in-hand ties. From the 1870s to the 1940s, the major difference between men's and schoolboys' clothing was that men wore long trousers and boys, short ones. By the end of the 1890s, when the breeching age had dropped from a mid century high of six or seven to between two and three, the point at which boys began wearing long trousers was frequently seen as a more significant event than breeching.

Unlike boys, as nineteenth-century girls grew older their clothing did not undergo a dramatic transformation. Females wore skirted outfits throughout their lives from infancy to old age; however, the garments' cut and style details did change with age. The most basic difference between girls' and women's dresses was that the children's dresses were shorter, gradually lengthening to floor length by the mid-teen years. When neoclassical styles were in fashion in the early years of the century, females of all ages and toddler boys wore similarly styled, high-waisted dresses with narrow columnar skirts. At this time, the shorter length of the children's dresses was the main factor distinguishing them from adult clothing.

From about 1830 and into the mid-1860s, when women wore fitted waist-length bodices and full skirts in various styles, most dresses worn by toddler boys and preadolescent girls were more similar to each other than to women's fashions. The characteristic "child's" dress of this period featured a wide off-the-shoulder neckline, short puffed or cap sleeves, an unfitted bodice that usually gathered into an inset waistband, and a full skirt that varied in length from slightly-below-knee length for toddlers to calf length for the oldest girls. Dresses of this design, made up in printed cottons or wool challis, were typical daywear for girls until they went into adult women's clothing in their mid-teens. Both girls and boys wore white cotton ankle-length trousers, called pantaloons or pantalets, under their dresses. In the 1820s, when pantalets were first introduced, girls wearing them provoked controversy because bifurcated garments of any style represented masculinity. Gradually pantalets became accepted for both girls and women as underwear, and as "private" female dress did not pose a threat to male power. For little boys, pantalets' status as feminine underwear meant that, even though pantalets were technically trousers, they were not viewed as comparable to the trousers boys put on when they were breeched.

Some mid-nineteenth-century children's dresses, especially best dresses for girls over ten, were reflective of women's styles with currently fashionable sleeve, bodice, and trim details. This trend accelerated in the late 1860s when bustle styles came into fashion. Children's dresses echoed women's clothing with additional back fullness, more elaborate trims, and a new cut that used princess seaming for shaping. At the height of the bustle's popularity in the 1870s and 1880s, dresses for girls between nine and fourteen had fitted bodices with skirts that draped over small bustles, differing only in length from women's garments. In the 1890s, simpler, tailored outfits with pleated skirts and sailor blouses or dresses with full skirts gathered onto yoked bodices signaled that clothing was becoming more practical for increasingly active schoolgirls.

New concepts of child rearing emphasizing children's developmental stages had a significant impact on young children's clothing beginning in the late-nineteenth century. Contemporary research supported crawling as an important step in children's growth, and one-piece rompers with full bloomer-like pants, called "creeping aprons," were devised in the 1890s as cover-ups for the short white dresses worn by crawling infants. Soon, active babies of both sexes were wearing rompers without the dresses underneath. Despite earlier controversy about females wearing pants, rompers were accepted without debate as playwear for toddler girls, becoming the first unisex pants outfits.

Baby books into the 1910s had space for mothers to note when their babies first wore "short clothes," but this time-honored transition from long white dresses to short ones was quickly becoming a thing of the past. By the 1920s, infants wore short, white dresses from birth to about six months with long dresses relegated to ceremonial wear as christening gowns. New babies continued to wear short dresses into the 1950s, although by this time, boys only did so for the first few weeks of their lives.

As rompers styles for both day and night wear replaced dresses, they became the twentieth century's "uniforms" for babies and young children. The first rompers were made up in solid colors and gingham checks, providing a lively contrast to traditional baby white. In the 1920s, whimsical floral and animal motifs began to appear on children's clothing. At first these designs were as unisex as the rompers they decorated, but gradually certain motifs were associated more with one sex or the other—for example, dogs and drums with boys and kittens and flowers with girls. Once such sex-typed motifs appeared on clothing, they designated even styles that were identical in cut as either a "boy's" or a "girl's" garment. Today, there is an abundance of children's clothing on the market decorated with animals, flowers, sports paraphernalia, cartoon characters, or other icons of popular culture—most of these motifs have masculine or feminine connotations in our society and so do the garments on which they appear.

Colors used for children's clothing also have gender symbolism—today, this is most universally represented by blue for infant boys and pink for girls. Yet it took many years for this color code to be come standardized. Pink and blue were associated with gender by the 1910s, and there were early efforts to codify the colors for one sex or the other, as illustrated by this 1916 statement from the trade publication *Infants' and Children's Wear Review*: "[T]he generally accepted rule is pink for the boy and blue for the girl." As late as 1939, a *Parents Magazine* article rationalized that because pink was a pale shade of red, the color of the war god Mars, it was appropriate for boys, while blue's association with Venus and the Madonna made it the color for girls. In practice, the colors were used interchangeably for both young boys' and girls' clothing until after World War II, when a combination of public opinion and manufacturer's clout ordained pink for girls and blue for boys—a dictum that still holds true today.

Even with this mandate, however, blue continues to be permissible for girls' clothing while pink is rejected for boys' attire. The fact that girls can wear both pink (feminine) and blue (masculine) colors, while boys wear only blue, illustrates an important trend begun in the late 1800s: over time, garments, trims, or colors once worn by both young boys and girls, but traditionally associated with female clothing, have become unacceptable for boys' clothing. As boys' attire grew less "feminine" during the twentieth century, shedding trimmings and ornamental details such as lace and ruffles, girls' clothing grew ever more "masculine." A paradoxical example of this progression occurred in the 1970s, when parents involved in "nonsexist" child-rearing pressed manufacturers for "gender-free" children's clothes. Ironically, the resulting pants outfits were only gender-free in the sense that they used styles, colors, and trims currently acceptable for boys, eliminating any "feminine" decorations such as pink fabrics or ruffled trim.

Over the course of the twentieth century, those formerly male-only garments—trousers—became increasingly accepted attire for girls and women. As toddler girls outgrew their rompers in the 1920s, new play clothes for three-to five-year-olds, designed with full bloomer pants underneath short dresses, were the first outfits to extend the age at which girls could wear pants. By the 1940s, girls of all ages wore pants outfits at home and for casual public events, but they were still expected—if not required—to wear dresses and skirts for school, church, parties, and even for shopping. About 1970, trousers' strong masculine connection had eroded to the point that school and office dress codes finally sanctioned trousers for girls and women. Today, girls can wear pants outfits in nearly every social situation. Many of these pant styles, such as blue jeans, are essentially unisex in design and cut, but many others are strongly sex-typed through decoration and color.

Adolescence has always been a time of challenge and separation for children and parents but, before the twentieth century, teenagers did not routinely express their independence through appearance. Instead, with the exception of a few eccentrics, adolescents accepted current fashion dictates and ultimately dressed like their parents. Since the early twentieth century, however, children have regularly conveyed teenage rebellion through dress and appearance, often with styles quite at odds with conventional dress. The jazz generation of the 1920s was the first to create a special youth culture, with each succeeding generation concocting its own unique crazes. But teenage vogues such as bobby sox in the 1940s or poodle skirts in the 1950s did not exert much influence on contemporary adult clothing and, as teens moved into adulthood, they left behind such fads. It was not until the 1960s, when the baby-boom generation entered adolescence that styles favored by teenagers, like miniskirts, colorful male shirts, or "hippie" jeans and T-shirts, usurped more conservative adult styles and became an important part of mainstream fashion. Since that time, youth culture has continued to have an important impact on fashion, with many styles blurring the lines between children's and adult clothing.

See also Shoes, Children's; Teenage Fashions.

Bibliography

Ashelford, Jane. *The Art of Dress: Clothes and Society, 1500–1914.* London: National Trust Enterprises Limited, 1996. General history of costume with a well-illustrated chapter on children's dress.

Buck, Anne. *Clothes and the Child: A Handbook of Children's Dress in England, 1500–1900.* New York: Holmes and Meier, 1996. Comprehensive look at English children's clothing, although the organization of the material is somewhat confusing.

Callahan, Colleen, and Jo B. Paoletti. *Is It a Girl or a Boy? Gender Identity and Children's Clothing.* Richmond, Va.: The

Valentine Museum, 1999. Booklet published in conjunction with an exhibition of the same name.

Calvert, Karin. *Children in the House: The Material Culture of Early Childhood, 1600–1900*. Boston: Northeastern University Press, 1992. Excellent overview of child-rearing theory and practice as they relate to the objects of childhood, including clothing, toys, and furniture.

Rose, Clare. *Children's Clothes Since 1750*. New York: Drama Book Publilshers, 1989. Overview of children's clothing to 1985 that is well illustrated with images of children and actual garments.

Colleen R. Callahan

CLARK, OSSIE

British designer Raymond (Ossie) Clark (1942–1996) was born on 9 June 1942 in Liverpool, England. He was known by his nickname Ossie, after Oswaldtwistle, the Lancashire village to which the family was evacuated during World War II. Clark started making clothes at the age of ten for his niece and nephew. Although he was not regarded as academically promising—he went to a secondary modern school where he learned building skills—he began to draw and developed a love of glamour and beauty, encouraged by his art teacher and mentor, who lent him copies of *Vogue* and *Harper's Bazaar*. For Clark, Diana Vreeland was always "top dog."

Early Career

Clark's copies of fashion pictures and ballet dancers showed skill. In 1958 he enrolled at the Regional College of Art in Manchester, where he was the only male student in the fashion course. The college emphasized technical training, so that Clark learned pattern cutting, construction, tailoring, and glove making—skills in which he excelled and which formed the basis of his distinctive style. In 1959 he saw a Pierre Cardin collection in Paris; he was struck by chiffon "peacock" dresses cut in what he described as a "spiral line," which influenced his later work. In 1960 Clark became friends with Celia Birtwell, who was studying textile design at Salford College, and with the artist Mo McDermott, through whom he met David Hockney in 1961. Clark began a postgraduate course in fashion design at the Royal College of Art in London in 1962, under the aegis of Professor Janey Ironside.

The Royal College of Art produced not only such leading artists as Peter Blake and David Hockney, but also fashion designers who became well known in their own right: Janice Wainwright, Marian Foale, Sally Tuffin, Leslie Poole, Bill Gibb, Zandra Rhodes, and Anthony Price. Textile designer Bernard Nevill taught the students the history of fashion, taking them to the Victoria and Albert Museum, where they observed the collections, particularly those of clothing from the 1920s and 1930s. The students were introduced to the *Gazette du bon ton*, and Neville had them produce illustrations in the styles of George Barbier, Georges Lepape, and other artists of the period. Clark became an admirer of Madeleine Vionnet and Charles James; both designers influenced him, as did Adrian, who had designed the costumes for the film version of *The Women* (1939). "Bernard Nevill . . . opened all the students' eyes to the fact that fashion wasn't about rejecting what your parents stood for. . . . the glamour of the thirties and the satin bias; we thought, why can't people on the street wear them?"

Clark graduated from the Royal College in 1965, the only student in his class to complete the course with distinction. He was photographed by David Bailey for *Vogue*, with the model Chrissie Shrimpton wearing his Robert Indiana op art–print dress. His degree collection was sold at the Woollands 21 boutique; he also began designing for Alice Pollock, part owner of the boutique Quorum in Kensington, close to Barbara Hulanicki's Biba and the Kings Road. Quorum quickly became part of "the most exciting city in the world," as described by writer John Crosby in a 1965 article that discussed youth, talent, and sexual freedom in "swinging London." The new post-Profumo society had a Labour government; unemployment was low, exports were high, and young working women were wearing Mary Quant's miniskirts. Clark and Pollock articulated the new freedom through their clothes. In 1966 Clark's Hoopla dress, a short shift cut to fit without darts and influenced by John Kloss, was featured in *Vogue*.

Success

In 1967 Clark's Rocker jackets and culottes defined the look of "Chelsea Girls" like Patti Harrison, Anita Pallenberg, Marianne Faithfull, Amanda Lear, and Jane Rainey, who was married to Michael Rainey, the proprietor of the Kings Road boutique Hung On You.

All were friends for whom Clark made clothes. At this time Alice Pollock suggested to Celia Birtwell that she should design fabrics for Quorum, especially for Clark's styles. Birtwell's floral patterns were influenced in color and design by the work of the Russian artist Leon Bakst as well as by flowers, naturalistic early imagery from manuscripts, and the textiles from collections at the Victoria and Albert Museum, consisting of printed silk chiffon, marrocain crepes, and velvets. Birtwell's fabrics were discharge-printed at Ivo Printers, and used to create such dresses as "Acapulco Gold" or "Ouidjita Banana." Clark cut chiffons and crepes on the straight and turned them to fit the body on the bias, to form the "spiral line" that he had seen at Cardin's show. He also experimented with alternatives to zippers, in particular ties or numerous covered buttons. His versatility in the period from 1967 to 1968 was best illustrated by his use of a range of materials as well as by the clothes themselves. Clark made use of snakeskin and leather as well as chiffon, satin, crepe, tweed, and furs. In 1967, the year in which the film *Bonnie and Clyde* was released and marked a return to nostalgia in fashion, Clark dropped his hemlines, shifting the focus to the wearer's bosom and shoulders, back, or waist to "find a new permutation and erogenous zones," he said. In 1968 *Vogue* featured his tailored redingote in a new "maxi" length. At the end of the same year he launched his "Nude Look," transparent chiffon dresses worn with little or no underwear. His couture pieces, made for such friends as Kari-Anne Jagger, had small hidden pockets, just big enough to hold a key and a five-pound note to pay the cab fare home. At the same time, a Clark menswear range was launched, which included ruffled shirts and printed chiffon scarves that were worn by the Rolling Stones, David Hockney, and Jimi Hendrix.

Both Quorum and the Ossie Clark name were sold to a middle-market company, Radley Gowns, in 1968. There were now three Clark lines: a couture line, Ossie Clark for Quorum, and Ossie Clark for Radley—which retailed at an accessible price not only at Quorum, which had relocated to the Kings Road, but also at other boutiques and department stores. In 1969 Clark and Birtwell were married when she became pregnant with their first child. Prudence Glyn, the fashion editor of *The Times*, chose a nude-look ruffled top and matching satin trousers made in Birtwell's trefoil print as the dress of the year for the Museum of Costume in Bath. "Ossie Clark is I believe in the world class for talent; in fact I think that we should build a completely modern idea of British high fashion around him," she wrote. Clark's contemporary Leslie Poole argued his importance at this point in his career: "He liberated women by constructing the low neckline with a bib front, tied at the back that could fit anybody. He borrowed lots of things like pointy sleeves and bias cut, but he effectively altered fashion through this new construction."

In 1970 Clark was invited to design a ready-to-wear collection by the French manufacturer Mendes, to be distributed in France and the United States. It was launched at the musée du Louvre on 22 April 1971 to high acclaim. Clark's collection featured top-quality chiffons, velvets, and silks, cut into frills and parachute pleats, 1940s-in-spired panels and plunging necklines, floating shapes and tightly tailored wools. He produced one collection, for reasons still unclear, but continued to show and work in London, dressing Mick Jagger in jumpsuits based on anatomical drawings by Leonardo da Vinci, and making trouser suits for Bianca Jagger. David Hockney's portrait *Mr and Mrs Clark and Percy* (1970–1971) commemorated one of the most famous couples in fashionable London—and their pet cat.

Last Years

Clark's early success did not last. In 1974 he separated from business partner Alice Pollock, and was divorced by Birtwell, who had grown tired of his affairs with men. In October 1974, Clark was the featured speaker at a fashion forum at the Institute of Contemporary Arts in London; he discussed marketing opportunities for the future on that occasion while admitting that he was living the lifestyle of a rock star. Unfortunately his work became disjointed by depression and alcohol abuse in the mid-1970s and appeared in magazines only intermittently. A relaunch in 1977 was not a success because Clark's clothes were not in touch with the London of Vivienne Westwood and punk style. Clark had little business sense, and declared bankruptcy in 1981. Shortly before his death however, he had started to make clothes again. Clark was stabbed to death in October 1996 by a former lover, Diego Cogolato. Designers working today influenced by Clark include Anna Sui, John Galliano, Christian Lacroix, Dries van Noten, Marc Jacobs and Clements Ribeiro.

See also Adrian; Biba; Cardin, Pierre; Celebrities; Galliano, John; Lacroix, Christian; London Fashion; Rhodes, Zandra; Vreeland, Diana.

Bibliography

Clark, Ossie. Recording of Ossie Clark at the Institute of Contemporary Arts, 16 October 1974, possession of this writer and with thanks to Ted Polhemus, host of the event.

———. Recording of Ossie Clark lecture at the Royal College of Art, 1996, courtesy of Dr. Susannah Handley and the RCA.

Green, Jonathon. *All Dressed Up: The Sixties and the Counter-culture.* London: Jonathan Cape, 1998.

Vogue (British) August 1965.

Watson, Linda. *Ossie Clark.* Warrington, U.K.: Warrington Museum and Art Gallery, 2000.

Watt, Judith. *Ossie Clark 1965–1974.* London: Victoria and Albert Museum, 2003.

Judith Watt

CLOTHING, COSTUME, AND DRESS

Clothing, costume, and dress indicate what people wear, along with related words like "apparel," "attire," "accessories," "garments," "garb," "outfits," and "ensembles." Many writers have tried to figure out why and when human beings began to decorate and cover their bodies; the reasons go beyond obvious considerations of temperature and climate, because some people dress skimpily in cold weather and others wear heavy garments in hot weather. Common reasons given are for protection, modesty, decoration, and display. One can only conjecture or speculate about origins, however, because no records exist detailing why early humans chose to dress their bodies.

Dress functions as a silent communication system that provides basic information about age, gender, marital status, occupation, religious affiliation, and ethnic background for everyday, special occasions and events, or participation in cinema, television, live theater, burlesque, circus, or dance productions. What people wear also can indicate personality characteristics and aesthetic preferences. People understand most clearly the significance and meaning of clothing, costume, and dress when the wearers and observers share the same cultural background. The words "clothing," "costume," and "dress" are sometimes used interchangeably to refer to what is being worn, but the words differ in several ways.

Clothing

"Clothing" as a noun refers generally to articles of dress that cover the body. "Clothing" as a verb refers to the act of putting on garments. Examples of clothing around the world include articles for the torso such as caftans, wrappers, sarongs, shirts, trousers, dresses, blouses, and skirts, as well as accessories for the head, hands, and feet such as turbans, hats, gloves, mittens, sandals, clogs, and shoes.

Costume

"Costume" as a noun describes garments of many types, particularly when worn as an ensemble. "Costume" as a verb often refers to designing an ensemble for an individual to wear. Frequently, "costume" refers to the clothing items, accessories, and makeup for actors, dancers, and people dressing up for special events such as Halloween, masquerade balls, Carnival, and Mardi Gras. A useful distinction between clothing and costume results when clothing refers to specific garments and costume refers to the ensemble that allows individuals to perform in dance, theater, or a masquerade, hiding or temporarily canceling an individual's everyday identity.

The words "costume" and "custom" are closely related, and the word "costume" can also refer to ensembles of clothing (folk costume) worn by members of an ethnic group for special occasions that serve as an affirmation of the group's traditions and solidarity.

Dress

As a noun, "dress" is used in several ways: to indicate a woman's one-piece garment, to indicate a category of garments such as "holiday dress" or "military dress," or as a general reference to an individual's overall appearance or various identities. As a verb, "dress" indicates the process of using various items to cover, adorn, and modify the body. The act of dress involves all five senses and encompasses more than wearing clothes. Getting dressed includes arranging hair, applying scent, lotion, and cosmetics, as well as putting on clothing of various textures and colors and jewelry, such as necklaces, earrings, and jangling bracelets. Dress ordinarily communicates aspects of a person's identity.

Distinctions among Clothing, Costume, and Dress

Items of clothing are components utilized in both costume and dress and designate specific garments and other apparel items such as footwear, headwear, and accessories. Costume is an ensemble created to allow an individual to present a performance identity for the theater, cinema, or masquerade, or to assert an identity as a member of an ethnic group on special occasions or for special events. Dress is the totality of body alterations and additions that help an individual establish credibility of identity in everyday life. In the United States, the term "costume history" ordinarily indicates the chronological study of dress, but in the United Kingdom, the term "dress history" is most frequently used.

Requirements for Costume and Dress

Costume. Designers for theater, cinema, and dance carefully plan the array of costumes to represent and highlight various roles to be played; principal characters are set apart and highlighted by costume from the rest of the cast or dance troupe. Some costumes designed for single-time use also involve countless hours of fastidious design and construction for adults in high-visibility and prestige Halloween or Mardi Gras events. For example, members of organized groups such as the various Krewes (masking and parading clubs) celebrating a New Orleans Mardi Gras or the San Antonio debutantes selected to be the duchess or princesses in their special ball engage in advance planning and execute intricate costume designs. In contrast, some Halloween costumes for adults or children may be quickly, even carelessly, made and worn for a short evening of venturing out for "trick or treat" candy or a casual masquerade party.

Costumes for the theater, dance, Halloween, and Mardi Gras have special requirements in fit, color, and effect. Garments must allow the performer's body to move easily and be well made. For example, costumes of professional actors and dancers often receive hard wear. Constant use or vigorous movement for dancers, circus clowns, and acrobats can put a strain on garments, thus requiring sturdy fabrics and specific construction considerations like seam reinforcement. When many viewers see costumes from afar, colors or other aspects of design may be exaggerated for effect. Some colors, therefore, may be more bold or brilliant than choices for everyday dress. Others may be drab. Such choices

depend on the interpretation of the costume designer in planning the garb for each performer's individual role and for the interaction among the performers.

Dress. In contrast to costume, dress establishes individual identity within a cultural context, emphasizing common social characteristics: age and gender, marital status, and occupation. Much information about identity is communicated through sensory cues provided by dress without the observer asking questions. Most individuals, especially in urban settings, have a variety of identities that are connected to dress, such as occupation, leisure-time activities (sports), and religious affiliation.

Costume, dress, and the body. Costumes and dress can reveal or conceal the body. Costumes or dress reveals the body by allowing bare skin to be displayed; for example, shoulders, arms, legs, and feet in the case of the classic ballerina tutu or a swimsuit. In such examples as an iceskater's bodysuit or dancer's leotard, the costume may cover but closely conform to and reveal the body shape. Sometimes aspects of a costume are exaggerated for ridicule and irony, as in the giant shoes seen on circus clowns or the padded bosoms of drag queens. In variations of Carnival and Mardi Gras costume, the body, including the head and face, is completely covered and the body is not easily discernible. Among the Kalabari people in the Niger delta of Nigeria one masquerade costume representing an elephant is made of massive palm fronds that eclipse the dancer's body. A small, carved sculpture of an elephant nestles among them, barely visible.

See also Fashion.

Bibliography

Eicher, Joanne B. "Classification of Dress and Costume for African Dance." In *The Spirit's Dance in Africa*. Edited by E. Dagan. Montreal. Galerie Amrad African Art Publication, 1997.

——, and Mary E. Roach-Higgins. "Describing Dress: A System of Classifying and Defining." In *Dress and Gender: Making and Meaning in Cultural Context.* Edited by Ruth Barnes and Joanne B. Eicher. Oxford and Washington, D.C: Berg Publishers, 1992–1993.

Laver, James. *Costume in the Theatre.* London: George G. Harrap and Company, Ltd., 1964.

Joanne B. Eicher

COCKTAIL DRESS

During the 1920s, newfound concepts of individuality and a repudiation of the Edwardian matronly ideal of respectable womanhood gave rise to the new phenomenon of the "Drinking Woman," who dared to enjoy cocktails in mixed company (Clark, p. 212). She emerged at private cocktail soirées and lounges, and the cocktail dress, as a short evening sheath with matching hat, shoes, and gloves was designated to accompany her. The cocktail affair generally took place between six and eight P.M., yet by manipulating one's accessories, the cocktail ensemble could be converted to appropriate dress for every event from three o'clock until late in the evening. Cocktail garb, by virtue of its flexibility and functionality, became the 1920s uniform for the progressive fashionable elite.

Birth of the Cocktail Ensemble

By the end of World War I, the French couture depended rather heavily on American clientele and to an even greater extent on American department stores that copied and promoted the French *créateurs* (Steele, p. 253). As cocktailing had originated in the United States, the French paid less attention to the strict designations of line, cut, and length that American periodicals promoted for their *heure de l'aperitif*. Instead, the couturières Chanel and Vionnet created garments for the late afternoon, or "after five," including beach pajamas—silk top and palazzo pant outfits worn with a mid-calf-length wrap jacket. Louise Boulanger produced *les robes du studio*, chic but rather informal sheaths that suited the hostess of private or intimate cocktail gatherings.

As the popularity of travel grew, both in American resort cities like Palm Beach, "the Millionaire's Playground," and abroad with the luxury of the Riviera, these French cocktail garments gained favor in wealthy American circles. But while America's elite were promoting the exclusive designs of the French couture, the majority of the United States relied on the advertisements of *Vanity Fair* and American *Vogue*, as well as their patronage of American department stores to dress for the cocktail hour. Created by Chanel in 1926, the little black dress was translated to ready-to-wear as a staple of late afternoon and cocktail hours; American women at every level of consumption knew the importance of a practical "Well-mannered Black" (*Vogue*, 1 May 1943, p. 75).

Mid-1920s skirt lengths were just below the knee for all hours and affairs. Though cocktail attire featured the longer sleeves, modest necklines, and sparse ornamentation of daytime clothing, it became distinguished by executions in evening silk failles or satins, rather than wool crepes or gabardines. Often the only difference between a day dress and a cocktail outfit was a fabric *noir* and a stylish cocktail hat. Hats in the 1920s varied little from the cloche shape, but cocktail and evening models were adorned with plumes, rhinestones, and beaded embroideries that indicated a more formal aesthetic. Short gloves were worn universally for cocktail attire during this period and could be found in many colors, though white and black were the most popular.

From Day to Evening

In the early 1930s, Hollywood sirens like Greta Garbo embodied a casual, sporty American chic that paired easily with the separates ensembles favored by the French. The more privatized cocktail party of the silver screen began to gain popularity, replacing the smoking rooms of Paris and the dance clubs of New York. The stock market crash of 1929 and the resulting economic depression dictated that it was no longer fashionable to display wealth by throwing ostentatious public affairs. Exclusive lounges emerged rapidly on the Paris scene; Bergère, the Blue Room, and Florence's were as popular for after-dinner cocktails as for the private affairs of the early evening. *Dames du Vogue* like Vicomtesse Marie-Laure de Noailles and Mrs. Reginald (Daisy) Fellowes, members of the elite international café society, became notorious for their exclusive soirées. Their patronage of Chanel, Patou, and Elsa Schiaparelli, all made famous by separates designs, helped popularize day-into-evening wear for upper-class Parisians and American socialites.

While Mademoiselle Cheruit had her *smoking*, a fitted jacket ensemble for early evening affairs, Schiaparelli was the most famous purveyor of the cocktail-appropriate dinner suit. Her suit consisted of a bolero or flared jacket that could be removed for the evening, revealing a sleeveless sheath dress. Unlike the previous decade, the 1930s dictated different skirt lengths for different hours: the silk, rayon, or wool crepe sheath of the dinner suit was steadfastly ankle or cocktail length.

In light of the economic hardships of the early 1930s, American designers like Muriel King designed "day-intoevening" clothes by championing a simple, streamlined silhouette and emphasizing the importance of accessories. Cartwheel hats, made of straw or silk and decorated with velvet ribbons or feathers, and slouchy fedoras of black felt were equally acceptable for the cocktail hour. Gloves were a bit longer than in the previous decade, but were still mandatory for late afternoon and evening. Costume jewelry, whether as a daytime pin or an evening parure, became the definitive cocktail accessory. Excessive jewelry was promoted as both daring and luxurious when clothing itself was regulated to be modest and unfettered.

During World War II, the hemline of the cocktail dress rose again to just below the knee, but the convenience and accessibility of the fashionable cocktail accessory sustained. Parisian milliners like Simone Naudet (Claude Saint-Cyr) produced elegant chapeaus with black silk net veils for the cocktail hour. In New York, Norman Norell attached rhinestone buttons to vodka gray or billiard green day suits to designate them cocktail ensembles. By the mid-1940s, cocktailing was made easy by the adaptability of cocktail clothing and the availability of the indispensable cocktail accessory.

A New Look for Cocktails

With his New Look collection of 1947, Christian Dior brought romanticism back to the catwalk. His cinched waists and full, mid-calf length frocks enforced a demure feminine aesthetic (Arnold, p. 102). The cocktail hour began to represent universal social identities for women: the matron, the wife, and the hostess. Cocktail parties rose to the height of sociability, and cocktail clothing was defined by strict rules of etiquette. While invitees were required to wear gloves, the hostess was forbidden the accessory. Guests were obligated to travel to an engagement in a cocktail hat (which had retained the veil made popular in the 1940s), but they were never to wear their hats indoors.

Parisian cocktail dresses were executed in black velvets and printed voiles alike, but they all retained the short-length of the original 1920s cocktail dress. American designers like Anne Fogarty and Ceil Chapman emulated the "New Look" line, but used less luxurious fabrics and trims. Dior, along with Jacques Fath and milliners Lilly Daché and John-Fredericks, quickly saw the advantages of promoting cocktail clothing in the American ready-to-wear market, designing specifically for their more inexpensive lines: Dior New York, Jacques Fath for Joseph Halpert, Dachettes, and John Fredericks Charmers.

Dior was the first to name the early evening frock a "cocktail" dress, and in doing so allowed periodicals, department stores, and rival Parisian and American designers to promote fashion with cocktail-specific terminology. *Vogue Paris* included articles entitled "*Pour le Coktail: L'Organdi,*" while advertisements in *Vogue* out of New York celebrated "cocktail cotton" textiles (*Vogue Paris*, April 1955, p. 77). Cocktail sets, martini-printed interiors fabrics, and cocktail advertisements all fostered an obsessively consumer-driven cocktail culture in America and, to some extent, abroad.

Though Pauline Trigère, Norman Norell, and countless Parisian couturiers continued to produce cocktail models well into the 1960s, the liberated lines of Gallitzine's palazzo pant ensembles and Emilio Pucci's jumpsuits easily replaced formal cocktail garb in privatized European and American social circuits. Often direct appropriations of midcentury designs, the cocktail dress and its partner accessories exist today on runways and in trendy boutiques as reminders of the etiquette and formality of 1950s cocktail fashions.

See also Chanel, Gabrielle (Coco); Dior, Christian; Little Black Dress.

Bibliography

Arnold, Rebecca. *Fashion, Desire, and Anxiety: Image and Morality in the Twentieth Century.* New Brunswick, N.J.: Rutgers University Press, 2001.

Clark, Norman H. *Deliver Us From Evil: An Interpretation of the American Prohibition.* New York: W. W. Norton and Company, 1976.

"Dior's Convertible Costumes." *Vogue* (1 September 1951): 183a.

Kirkham, Pat. *Women Designers in the USA 1900–2000.* New York: Yale University Press, 2000.

"Les Décolleté de sept heures." *Vogue Paris* (September 1948): 141.

"Les Pyjamas et les robes du studio." *Vogue Paris* (June 1930): 47.

Milbank, Caroline Rennolds. *New York Fashion: The Evolution of American Style.* New York: Harry N. Abrams, 1989.

Seeling, Charlotte. *Fashion: The Century of the Designer, 1900–1999.* Cologne, Germany: Konemann, 1999.

Steele, Valerie. *Paris Fashion: A Cultural History.* New York: Oxford University Press, 1988.

"The Well-Dressed Woman." *Vanity Fair* (June 1928): 87.

Elyssa Schram Da Cruz

CODPIECE

The codpiece was a distinguishing feature of men's dress from 1408 to about 1575 C.E. Originally a triangle of cloth used to join the individual legs of men's hose, the codpiece emerged as a nonverbal statement of political and economic power.

The codpiece began as a solution to changing fashion. Throughout the Renaissance, various forms of the doublet-and-hose combination characterized men's dress. A doublet was a fitted, often quilted jacket that varied in length from above the knee to the natural waist. Hose were individually tailored legs of woven fabric cut on the bias grain. Each leg was stitched up the back and laced to the doublet, similar to the system of garter belts and stockings used by women in the middle twentieth century. An early version of underpants made of linen or wool was worn underneath. As doublets shortened, hose were cut longer and wider to cover the underpants up to the waist. Across the genitals, a triangular gusset laced to the front of the hose between the legs. It satisfied decency requirements and calls of nature. By the sixteenth century, the codpiece was both shaped and padded. Squire and Baynes report that the term "cod" was both a Renaissance-era word for bag and a slang word for testicles. By the mid-1500s, the embellishment of the codpiece with jewels and embroidery exaggerated the genitals so that little was left to the imagination.

Once the codpiece achieved a pouch shape, it was used for a variety of purposes, including as a purse for small objects. When the fitted doublet/hose/codpiece combination is compared with the ankle-length, draped, and pleated robes of earlier periods, Renaissance men's dress appears slim and ready for action. However, the bias cut of woven hose, while more elastic than straight grain, does not allow for a full range of movement. The successful application of knitting to create fine, well-fitting hose contributed to the decline of the codpiece by the turn of the seventeenth century.

Clear examples of the codpiece can be seen in sixteenth-century court portraits by Clouet, Titian, and Holbein. During this period, men's dress extended the body into an overall horizontal silhouette. Codpiece, shoulders, and doublet were padded; luxury fabrics were slashed and their contrasting linings pulled out through the slits; and heavy gold chains were draped from shoulder to shoulder. Squire and Baynes describe the "aggressive solidity of appearance" and the "fantastic

air of brutality" (1975, p. 66). Squire describes the fashionable man as, "broad-shouldered and barrel-chested, while a proudly displayed virility between his legs projected forcefully through the skirts of his jerkin" (1974, p. 52). In fact, the sixteenth century was a period of aggressive kingdom building in which more and more power was consolidated into the hands of fewer, very strong individuals. The codpiece contributed, in part, to the visible, and not at all subtle, expression of the power and the spirit of those times.

See also Doublet; Penis Sheath.

Bibliography

Boucher, François. *20,000 Years of Fashion: The History of Costume and Personal Adornment.* New York: Harry N. Abrams, 1987.

Squire, Geoffrey. *Dress and Society: 1560–1970.* New York: Viking, 1974.

Squire, Geoffrey, and Pauline Baynes. *The Observer's Book of European Costume.* London: Frederick Warne and Company, Ltd., 1975.

Tortora, Phyllis, and Keith Eubank. *Survey of Historic Costume.* 3rd ed. New York: Fairchild Publications, 1998.

Sandra Lee Evenson

COLONIALISM AND IMPERIALISM

The term "empire" covers a range of ways of incorporating and managing different populations under the rule of a single dominant state or polity, as for example in the Roman Empire, the Carolingan Empire, and the British Empire. A more detailed categorization might distinguish between colonialism as the ruling by an external power over subject populations and imperialism as intervention in or dominating influence over another polity without actually governing it. The two processes differ largely in terms of the extent to which they transform the institutions and organization of life in the societies subject to their intrusion; the transformations of colonialism tend to be more direct than those of imperialism.

Many European nations, the United States, China, and Japan have at one time or another exerted colonial rule over subject populations as part of regionally shifting geopolitical strategies combined with economic motives for gain. Although they applied diverse approaches to governing local societies, most colonial powers considered the people they ruled to be alien and different. Entering into the affairs of other societies, differentiating between groups and individuals in racial, ethnic, and gender terms, colonial rule reorganized local life, affecting colonized people's access to land, property, and resources, authority structures and institutions, family life and marriage, among many others. These vast transformations of livelihoods had numerous cultural ramifications, including on dress.

Colonial powers have tended in recent centuries to be developed countries with strong agricultural and manufacturing economies and powerful urban centers. Their populations, and especially individuals directly involved in the colonial enterprise, have often regarded colonized indigenous peoples as "backward," both culturally and socioeconomically. Appearance was a strongly contested area in the relations between colonizers and colonized. Indigenous people in many colonized societies adorned their bodies with cosmetics, tattooing, or scarification, wore feathers and other forms of ornament, and habitually went naked or dressed in animal skins or other non-woven materials. When they did wear woven cloth, it was often in the form of clothing that was draped, wrapped, or folded rather than cut, stitched, and shaped to the contours of the body. Dress and textiles conveyed information about gender and rank in terms different from those familar to the colonizers. Such vastly different dress practices, especially nakedness, struck colonizers as evidence of the inferiority of subject populations. Because colonizers considered their own norms and lifestyles to be proof of their superior status, dress became an important boundary-marking mechanism.

Clothing Encounters

The cultural norms that guided the West's colonial encounters were shaped importantly by Christian notions of morality and translated into action across the colonial world by missionary societies from numerous denominations. The colonial conquest by Spain and Portugal of today's Latin America developed caste-like socioeconomic and political systems in which indigenous people and African slaves were forced to convert to Christianity and to wear Western styles of dress. Yet the rich weaving traditions of the Maya and Andean regions did not disappear but developed creative designs combining local

and Christian symbols. When the Dutch colonized Indonesia in the seventeenth century and introduced Christianity, Islam was already long established. Subsequent interactions encompassed three distinct cultural spheres: Dutch and European, Muslim, and non-Muslim indigenous. The Dutch initially reserved Western-style dress for Europeans and for Christian converts.

Clothing "the natives" was a central focus of the missionary project in the early encounters between the West and the non-West, for example in Africa. In Bechuanaland, a frontier region between colonial Botswana and South Africa, the struggle for souls entailed dressing African bodies in European clothes to cover their nakedness and managing those bodies through new hygiene regimes. Missionaries were pleased when indigenous peoples accepted their clothing proposals, seeing it as a sign of religious conversion in the new moral economy of mind and body. In the Pacific, the encounter between missionary and indigenous clothing preferences sometimes produced striking results, as in the cultural synthesis in Samoan Christians' bark cloth "ponchos" that not only expressed new ideas of modesty but also in fact made modesty possible by providing new ways to cover bodies. In a number of island societies, Pacific Islanders' innovations and transformations of clothing resulted in new styles and designs.

In Melanesia, missionaries saw the eager adoption of printed calico as an outward sign of conversion, or at least openness to conversion, while Melanesians interpreted these patterns with reference to ideas about empowered bodies. Native peoples in North America also found floral designs on European printed cloth to be very attractive, incorporating them in embroidery on garments and crafts objects in increasingly stylized and abstract forms. Throughout the colonial world, missionary-inspired dress, often with links to traditional dress, developed in many directions. European styles and fabrics were incorporated in many places, such as in the smocked *Sotho* dress and the *Herero* long dress that serve as visible markers for "traditional" dress in southern Africa. Following independence from colonial rule, many such dress practices have come close to being considered national dress and are associated with notions of proper womanhood.

Colonial Behavior

Western civilization set the standards of dress for colonizers in foreign outposts in a way that stereotyped the differences between colonizer and subject populations.

British soldiers in naval uniforms attack Malay villagers. Indigenous peoples were often considered inferior by colonizers, in part because of their different dress practices, causing dress to become a status-defining mechanism. JOHN S. MAJOR. REPRODUCED BY PERMISSION.

For example, Westerners often made a point of dressing in full European attire (woolen suits for men, corseted dresses for women) when touring up-country in the African bush or the jungles of Java; they wished their willingness to endure discomfort for the sake of dressing "properly" to be viewed as evidence of moral and cultural superiority. Although some Europeans in early encounter situations adopted local elements of dress, for example loose-stitched gowns of cotton and silk in India, colonial dress practice became increasingly rigid and formal. As time went by, colonial dress codes regarded cultural cross-dressing (a sign of "going native") to be an affront to the standards of the ruling group. Obsessions over dress extended to climate and disease. The British in India and Africa wore special underwear to guard themselves against sudden weather changes. They wore *sola topis*, flannel-lined solar helmets, to protect themselves against the dangerous rays of the sun. The fears associated with the physical environment provoked a form of a sometimes suicidal depression that contemporary medical doctors in east and southern Africa described as tropical neurasthenia.

Oppression and Resistance

In cases where colonial rulers regarded indigenous dress as a potential focus of resistance to the occupying

power, suppression of local dress might be rigidly enforced. For example, when Korea was a Japanese colony (1910–1945), all markers of Korean cultural identity, including the use of the spoken and written Korean language and the wearing of the national *hanbok* costume, were ruthlessly suppressed. In contrast, in the Japanese colony of Taiwan (ruled 1895–1945), there was no readily identifiable national dress, and so the Japanese authorities did not pay particular attention to what Taiwanese people wore.

Colonizers often could not fully control how subjected people dressed. Migrant labor, urban life, and education introduced new consumption practices and desires, among them factory-produced textiles and European-styled fashions. Local people sometimes wore the new garments as they saw fit. They were highly selective about which items of foreign dress they absorbed into their local dress repertoires. With new clothes also came new etiquettes that might be at variance with local ways, such as the practice in India and Indonesia of removing one's shoes when entering a building and covering one's head as signs of respect.

Indigenous persons of high rank, the new elite, and men were among the first to incorporate items of Western clothing into their wardrobes. Because the suit was a hallmark of colonial authority, jackets and trousers signified status, education, and colonial employment. In India, some men who adopted Western fabrics retained Indian dress styles while others had Indian garments tailored to take on a European look. New combination garments consisted of both Indian and European clothes—for example, shoes and trousers worn with coats in local styles and distinctive hats, a Western-style jacket on top of locally styled trousers or a sarong. In parts of Africa, highly decorated military uniforms were worn by kings and paramount chiefs on special occasions in combination with other styles of dress and accessories such as animal skins. The big robes, *boubous*, worn by Muslim men in West Africa, were not widely abandoned in favor of Western suits and are today worn with pride as evidence of a different dress aesthetic than the strong linear form of the Western suit.

Except for the elite, women in many parts of the colonial world were more resistant to adopt the new dress styles. Adopting European fabrics while retaining regional styles was popular among Indian women, who might add new accessories such as shoes, petticoats, and jackets to their Indian dress. Their saris might incorporate the latest trends in color and design from Europe. European suit jackets, often acquired in the used-clothing trade, are combined with indigenous garments in hybrid styles of men's clothing from Africa to Afghanistan. Across most of Africa, women eagerly appropriated factory-produced cloth, much of it manufactured in Europe incorporating "African" designs, into their everyday dress style of wrapper and headtie, tailored and highly constructed dresses, alongside a variety of Western-style garments.

Exoticizing Dress Practices

In early colonial encounters, the British in India and the Dutch in Indonesia mapped and organized the diversity of the peoples they ruled in terms of dress. In late nine- tenth- and early-twentieth-century Paris, Brussels, London, and Chicago, among other places, preoccupations with the racial attributes of dress were showcased at expositions displaying colonial subjects in "traditional" clothes. The contemporary desire to catalog the world by parading exotic people in "traditional" dress as ethno-graphic specimens helped to accentuate the difference between the familiar and exotic in highly stereotypical ways. Postcards, produced for example in Algeria and Indonesia, displaying women in erotic stances and exotic clothing, made women's dress central to the marking of cultural difference. With the West as voyeur, such postcards projected invidious images of the exotic onto women's dressed bodies.

Dress as Artifact and Cultural Revival

Not all segments of colonial society advocated the adoption of Western dress for their local subjects. Some, who were able to adopt an attitude of cultural pluralism, appreciated differences in dress without assuming the superiority of European styles, while others promoted the revival of local dress and adornment as a way of safeguarding threatened cultures and their aesthetics. In northeast Canada, French Ursuline nuns promoted pictorial and floral imagery among Native Americans in sewing and embroidery, stimulating a commodification of Indian curios. Over time, these depictions shifted from images of "noble savages" to colonial nostalgia scenes depicting the imminent disappearance of a way of life dependent on nature. Similar managed efforts in support of cultural survival were instituted in many places in Latin Americia, Africa, India, South and Southeast Asia, and the Pacific. Products of these cultural revival movements often did

not remain within the societies that produced them, but were acquired for private and public collections and museums of textile arts. Although they all have given rise to interpretations about authenticity, such artifacts were everywhere the products of complex interactions and influences that demonstrate continuous incorporation of new developments and inspirations into "tradition."

The retention or revival of some of these clothing and textile traditions sometimes served to express rejection of colonialism, such as in Gandhi's call on Indians to wear homespun cloth. Some dress and textile traditions are used to make claims for political representation in states where indigenous people are subordinated or threatenend, for example in the Amazon region of Brazil. Another development of the cultural revival of textiles and dress practices has turned the process into fashion, in which newly developed styles that are considered ethnically chic attract consumers in former colonies and the world beyond.

The Seductions of Imperialism

Imperialism, which in the modern usage of the term usually involves influence on another country or culture but not direct colonial control, can have a powerful effect on the clothing of the subject culture. The effect is usually voluntary (as opposed to the actual imposition of new forms of dress by missionaries and colonial administrators), but it can be seen as a form of cultural coercion in which voluntarism is compromised. The effects can take a wide range of forms.

In Japan during the Meiji Period (1868–1912), the government energetically promoted modernization as a way of strengthening the country, with a twofold goal: to prevent Japan's being taken over as a colony by any European power, and to prepare Japan to compete on equal terms with Europe as a colonial power itself. The effort to emulate the strength of the West included a promotion of beef-eating (formerly nearly unknown in Japan) and a wholesale adoption of Western-style clothing, at least by urban elites.

In China at the end of the nineteenth century, a deliberate effort was made to design a new-style military and school uniform that would be "modern" but not too "Western." The result was an early version of the Sun Yat-sen suit (later to be known in the West as the Mao Zedong suit), based on the Prussian military uniform but with a collar derived from that of the traditional Chinese long gown.

A third example, one so ubiquitous as to be part of the common wisdom about the modern world, has been the worldwide spread of sartorial markers of Western popular culture: the T-shirt, jeans, and running shoes. No one has forced any teenager in the Third World to wear these garments; almost no one (short of fanatical religious dictatorships such as the Taliban in Afghanistan) has succeeded in preventing them from doing so. Denounced by nationalists and cultural conservatives as "cultural imperialism," the trend nevertheless seems irreversible.

Transformative Encounters and Contesting Clothes

Colonies and empires exerted a limited form of rule over subject populations both in relation to the exercise of power and the will and ability to transform society. The clothing practices colonialism inspired in many parts of the world demonstrate an important lesson about the relation between colonialism and dress. Colonialism was always a transformative encounter in which subject people were active participants rather then passive respondents to sartorial impositions from the outside. When dress served as a boundary-making mechanism, it did so in ways that were contested. Because the meanings of the dressed body everywhere are ambiguous, the colonial encounter enabled local people to take pride in long-held aesthetics expressed in new dress media and forms. It enabled the creation of styles of "national dress" that as invented traditions have served as cultural assertions for shifting claims to political voice and representation between the late colonial period and the present. Last but not least, colonial dress practices from Latin America, to India, to Japan have become part of everyday wardrobes everywhere, opening a world of dress for which everyone is the richer.

See also Africa, North: History of Dress; Africa, Sub-Saharan: History of Dress; America, Central, and Mexico: History of Dress; America, North: History of Dress; Americas, South: History of Dress; Asia, East: History of Dress; Asia, South: History of Dress; Asia, Southeastern Islands and the Pacific: History of Dress; Asia, Southeastern Mainland: History of Dress.

Bibliography

Alloula, Malek. "The Colonial Harem." In *Theory and History of Literatures*. Manchester University Press, 1986.

Colchester, Cloe, ed. *Clothing the Pacific*. Oxford: Berg, 2003.

Nordholt, Henk Schulte, ed. *Outward Appearances: Dressing State and Society in Indonesia*. Leiden, Netherlands: KITLV Press, 1997.

Phillips, Ruth B. *Trading Identities: The Souvenir in Native North American Art from the Northeast, 1700–1900*. Hong Kong: University of Washington Press, 1998.

Steele, Valerie, and John Major, eds. *China Chic: East Meets West*. New Haven, Conn.: Yale University Press, 1999.

Tarlo, Emma. *Clothing Matters: Dress and Identity in India*. London: Hurst and Company, 1996.

Karen Tranberg Hansen

COLOR IN DRESS

Color attracts attention, creates an emotional connection, and leads the consumer to the product (Brannon, p. 117). Color is often a primary reason why a person is attracted to and buys a particular item of clothing. A new T-shirt in a different color can help transform the look of a product year after year. Color captures a viewer's interest because it is both easily recognizable and distinctive. We often describe clothing in terms of color, such as "a blue suit."

The study of color is complex and involves light, vision, and pigment as well as science, technology, and art. In addition, colored pigment behaves differently than colored light. Although there are many models of color classification, the Munsell color system with its numeric notation for each color is widely used and accepted to describe color pigments and the color properties that relate to dress.

Color Dimensions

All pigment color systems recognize that three dimensions describe color—hue (the name), intensity (brightness/dullness), and value (lightness/darkness). All three dimensions are present in every color and every color starts with hue. Value and intensity are adjectives that describe variations of any hue (light bright green, or deep dull red, for instance).

Hue. The name of the color as designated on the color wheel is its hue—the visual sensation of blue, for example. Each hue has an individual physical character:

primary pigment hues are red, yellow, and blue. No other colors combine to make them, but these colors combine to make all other hues. The secondary hues, orange, green, and violet are mixtures of the adjacent primary hues; orange is a mixture of red and yellow; violet is a mixture of red and blue. The hue spectrum runs from red to violet, and is usually depicted as a circle of hues with the primary hues separated by the secondary. Tertiary hues (sometimes called intermediate) result from mixing a primary and a secondary, that is, red-orange or blue-violet.

Groups or categories of colors that share common sensory effects are often called families. Related hues (sometimes called analogous) such as blue-violet, violet, and red-violet, are adjacent on the color wheel and constitute a color family. Contrasting colors are separated from each other on the color wheel. Contrasting color schemes include complementary and split-complementary. Hues opposite each other, such as yellow and purple-blue, are called complementary because they complete the spectrum; each contains primaries the other lacks. Complementary hues can produce an afterimage of each other. If you stare at one hue for several seconds, when you glance away to a neutral surface, you will see an image of its complement. In a split-complementary scheme the color on either side of the complement is selected, green, red-orange, and red-violet, for example.

Value. Each hue has a specific normal or home value; the home value of yellow is close to white or light gray, and violet is as dark as very dark gray. Values have an effect upon colors in combination. For example, the complements red and green have similar values, offering hue contrast but not value contrast. However, the complementary hues of yellow and violet at normal value offer both hue and value contrast.

Contrasting values can affect the perception of edge in adjacent surfaces. A light value surface placed next to a dark one offers a strong visual pull to the difference between the two surfaces. Applications can be found in the value contrast between a white shirt and black trousers, light skin and dark hair, or dark hair and skin and pastel suit.

Intensity. The relative purity or saturation of a color is its intensity, sometimes referred to as chroma. This dimension describes the strength of a color. Saturated colors are primary and secondary hues at their purest and strongest on the color wheel. Each hue has a range of saturation from full intensity to neutral gray.

Intensity provides hue with its vividness or neutrality. Intensity yields a variety of expressions. A saturated hue is intense and usually evokes a response of excitement or energy. Less saturated hues range from nearly bright to almost muted incorporating many moods. Hues in the lowest intensities are neutral colors and often are the foundation of a wardrobe. If used together at full strength, complementary colors can vibrate. The addition of a hue's complement lowers its saturation toward neutral gray and can increase its livability.

Intensity is influenced by surface texture. Even minor surface irregularities reflect minute areas of light that cast miniature shadows; this has the effect of dulling the intensity of a color. If a fabric with a distinct weave or surface were dipped into the same dye bath as a smooth material, it would appear duller in color because of the softening effect of the napped texture. Conversely, a smooth shiny surface will make a soft color appear stronger (Goldstein and Goldstein 1960, pp. 184–185).

Psychophysical Effects of Color

Psychophysical effects can be tied to hue characteristics. The temperature of a hue, the space from which it is viewed, and the color combinations used to create it can influence perception.

COLOR FOR THE INDIVIDUAL

Packaging of colors for individual selection has been used to market color (Jackson 1981; Pinckney and Swenson 1981). Color selection for clothing is based upon colors that are grouped according to some easily remembered system, such as nature's seasons. Winter and spring colors are described as clear, vivid, and bright, while summer and fall are less intense. Winter and summer colors are cool; spring and fall colors are warm. Personal color analysis systems range from offering small pre-packaged color palettes, to specifically selected colors for each individual.

The Color Key system categorizes color according to warm or cool overtones that contain all basic hues, values, and intensities (Brannon 2000). Color Key 1 consists of cool, clear colors and Color Key 2 includes warm, earth tone colors; each has a corresponding color fan of paint chips that can be used to coordinate paint for interiors and apparel colors. This color key system implies that people will look and feel better when surrounded by colors that reflect their personal coloring.

Warm and cool. Warm hues, light values, and strong intensities seem to advance while cool hues, dark values, and desaturated hues recede. Hues that advance also expand a shape. Warm colors and dark values are perceived as dense or solid and are often associated with muted earth tones such as brick or red-orange, ocher, or golden brown. Cool colors seem to reduce a shape. Cool hues and light values are associated with air, distant mountains, and water and may present an appearance of distance, depth, shadow, coolness, and lightness.

Warm hues, light values, and saturated colors such as bright orange or shocking pink can seem loud or noisy. Cool hues, dark values, and desaturated colors like deep taupe or dark violet are quiet by comparison.

Spatial position. Hues viewed singly can produce an afterimage and this affects colors on the body. When the viewer concentrates on a clothing surface and then glances at the face, the skin can appear to take on tinges of the complement to the hue of the clothing. Thus after looking intensely at a green sweater, a viewer who glances up at the face may find it tinged with the complement, red.

Whether a hue is directly surrounded by another hue or is separated in some way will influence its perceptual effect. When individual colors are separated by black or white, both their singleness of character and their inter-action are suppressed somewhat. Black causes adjacent hues to seem lighter and more brilliant; a surround of white often appears to darken them.

Visual mixing. Colors combined in very small patterns or woven together appear to mix visually. When two or more colors are interwoven onto one surface the result can be more vibrant than a surface of just one color. Complementary hues or black and white threads woven together will create a surface that appears gray or neutral when viewed from a distance. If the size of the black and white threads is increased, a salt-and-pepper effect is created.

Color and the Body

Color and dress enter a relationship with color and the body. As a composite of colors, human coloration can be analyzed in the same way as other pigments to predict the effects of color in dress. Similarity of any of the attributes of colors placed upon the body can form a powerful visual relationship with the body.

A person's appearance is a combination of the surfaces placed upon the body and the individual's personal body coloring. Included in appearance are the body colors of skin, hair, and eyes. What surrounds a particular color affects how it appears. The pre-existing colors of the body are influenced by other colors placed upon it, so the body colors affect the surfaces placed upon it and the reverse is also true. In addition, the clothed body can be greatly influenced by colors of the surrounding environment and by lighting effects.

By matching, naming, and locating personal body colors, an individual can begin to understand color relationships. Intensity is a difficult dimension of color to describe when applied to body colors because the skin surface requires noting small and subtle differences. "Highlights" in one's personal coloring may include areas of the hair, skin, or eyes that seem more intense than other areas. "Undertone" is used to describe underlying colors of skin and hair. Identifying both highlights and undertones for an individual helps in placing colors on the body that are related by similarity or contrast.

Color as a source of association. Color is associated with many natural objects of similar color and therefore can acquire similar meaning according to that association. Sunshine is yellow and warm: yellow is warm. Blue is cool and distant as the mountains and water. Red is exciting like fire and in many cultures red signals danger. Mood is associated with color, too; we have the "blues," or we are "green" with envy.

Colors may be associated symbolically with specific peoples or historic periods. In the 1960s in the United States, psychedelic colors were symbolic of the decade and included combinations of intense hues of pink, yellow, blue, green, and purple. Koreans favor celadon green, a pastel blue-green, because of its traditional association with pottery and ceramics, and white is used for mourning dress in Korea (Geum and DeLong).

Color preferences. Human response to colors can be measured and identified both collectively and individually, and psychologists have studied the formation of and reaction to color preferences. Eysenck (Brannon 2000) published research in 1941 that showed a consistent order of color preferences in adults: blue, red, green, purple, yellow, orange. According to Itten (1973) people have subjective individual preferences that include dimensions of hue, value, and intensity. The Lüscher Color Test (1969) links personality to color preferences. Subjects are asked to arrange color chips in order of preference and the results are analyzed to take into consideration both the meaning and impact of the colors as selected.

Color Marketing

Color is rated as the most important aesthetic criterion in consumer preference (Eckman, Damhorst, and Kadolph 1990). Because color is a complex phenomenon, marketers can present merchandise in coordinated colors in an effort to help the consumer select purchases. When a line of clothing is color coordinated, wardrobe planning may seem less difficult to the consumer. Designers and manufacturers may coordinate colors within a season, or from one fashion season to another so that colors of a suit from the past season will coordinate with a shirt the next season. Selections of cosmetics are a part of color coordination of the body in a clothing ensemble and may be linked to personal coloring or to one's wardrobe colors.

Fashion in colors. Color has had a fashionable aspect historically. Editors of contemporary fashion often cite a color for a season as a means of marketing clothing. History is often recognized by the colors or color combinations fashionable at the time. Examples include the raspberry pink and lime green of mid-twentieth century, or the pastels and filmy light tints at the end of the nineteenth century.

Forecasters take advantage of the importance attached to color by advancing a color palette for a given season. Color forecasting began in 1915 (Brannon 2000) and is based upon analysis of cultural demographics and color patterns. A cyclical pattern of color coordination occurs from High Chroma, Multicolored, Subdued, Earth Tones, Achromatic, Purple, and then back to High Chroma (Brannon 2000).

Target markets. Color is used for brand identification. Conceived broadly, this could include a designer's line of clothing or the introduction of a single color. Ralph Lauren tends to select middle value hues of low intensity for his depiction of "traditional" values. Elsa Schiaparelli introduced a single identifier, "shocking pink."

See also Aesthetic Dress; Appearance; Dyeing.

Bibliography

Arnheim, Rudolf. *Art and Visual Perception*. Berkeley and Los Angeles: University of California Press, 1974.

Brannon, Evelyn. *Fashion Forecasting*. New York: Fairchild Publications, 2000.

Davis, Marian. *Visual Design in Dress*. 2nd ed. Englewood Cliffs, N.J.: Prentice-Hall, Inc., 1987.

DeLong, Marilyn Revell. *The Way We Look*. 2nd ed. New York: Fairchild Publications, 1998.

Eckman, Molly, Mary Lynn Damhorst, and Sara Kadolph. "To-ward a Model of the In-store Purchase Decision Process: Consumer Use of Criteria for Evaluating Women's Apparel." *Clothing and Textiles Research Journal* 8, 2 (1990): 13–22.

Eiseman, Leatrice. *Alive With Color*. Washington, D.C.: Acropolis Books, Ltd., 1983.

Geum, Keysook, and Marilyn DeLong. "Korean Traditional Dress as an Expression of Heritage." *Dress* 19 (1992): 57–68.

Goldstein, Harriet, and Vetta Goldstein. *Art in Everyday Life*. 4th ed. New York: MacMillan, 1960.

Itten, Johannes. *The Art of Color*. New York: Van Nostrand Reinhold Company, 1973.

Jackson, Carole. *Color Me Beautiful*. New York: Ballantine Books, 1981.

Luke, Joy Turner. *The Munsell® Color System: A Language for Color*. New York: Fairchild Publications, 1996.

Lüscher, Max. *The Lüscher Color Test*. New York: Pocket Books, 1969.

Mathis, Carla Mason, and Helen VillaConnor. *The Triumph of Individual Style: A Guide to Dressing Your Body, Your Beauty, Your Self*. Cali, Colombia: Timeless Editions, 1993.

Meyers, Jack Fredrick. *The Language of Visual Art: Perception as a Basis for Design*. Chicago: Holt, Rinehart and Winston, Inc., 1989.

Munsell, A. *A Book of Color: Neighboring Hues Edition, Matte Finish Collection*. Newburgh, N.Y.: Kollmmorgen, 1973.

Pinckney, Gerrie. *Your New Image Through Color and Line*. Costa Mesa, Calif.: Crown Summit Books, 1981.

Pooser, Doris. *Always in Style with Color Me Beautiful*. Washington, D.C.: Acropolis Books, Ltd., 1985.

Marilyn Revell DeLong and
Barbara Perso Heinemann

COMME DES GARÇONS*

Rei Kawakubo was born in Tokyo in 1942, the daughter of a senior academic at Keio University. She studied fine art (both Japanese and Western) at Keio and, after graduating in 1964, joined the advertising department of the Japanese chemical company Asahi Kasei, which produced acrylic fabrics. From 1967 she worked as a freelance fashion stylist, but, critical of the selection of clothes available in Japan, she started designing them herself.

> I wanted to have some kind of job to earn money because at that time, having money meant being free. I never dreamt of being a fashion designer like other people. When I was young, it was just a way of earning a living by doing something I found I could do: making clothes and taking them around the shops to sell them. (Frankel, p. 8)

By 1969 she was producing clothing under the label Comme des Garçons, and in 1973 she formed a limited company. The moniker was typically enigmatic; named after the title of a French soldier's song meaning "Like the Boys," she designed clothes that eschewed conventional sexuality.

Distinctive Looks and Products

In 1975 Kawakubo showed her first collection in Tokyo, and in 1976, in a collaboration with the architect Takao Kawasaki, who has since designed most of Comme's typically calm and austere outlets, the first Comme des Garçons shop opened in the Minami-Aoyama district. The first shop did not even have mirrors, because Kawakubo wanted women to buy clothes because of how they felt rather than the way they looked. In 1978 Kawakubo introduced the Homme line; she followed it with Tricot and Robe de Chambre in 1981 and Noir in 1987. In 1981 Kawakubo launched her first women's collection in Paris at the same time as her compatriot Yohji Yamamoto, and soon afterward she joined the Chambre Syndicale du Pret-a-Porter.

Although the West was aware of other Japanese designers, such as Kenzo Takada and Issey Miyake, who had trained in Paris and New York, Kawakubo's vision was uncompromisingly severe and challenging. Her early shows made an indelible impression on the fashion world with their monochrome palette and distressed fabrics, with exposed seams and fraying edges influenced by Japanese work wear. Rather than echoing the contours of the body, she enclosed it in oversized swathes of fabric. The voluminous, layered, asymmetrical forms were accessorized with flat footwear, and the

cosmetics and hair styles seemed apocalyptic to many, but the influence of her clothes soon spread, particularly for those who were prepared to be challenged by clothing, "I think that pieces that are difficult to wear are very interesting, because if people make the effort and wear them, then they can feel a new form of energy and a certain strength. I want to give people that chance" (Petronio, pp. 154–155).

Early supporters included Joan Burstein, proprietress of Browns, who stocked Comme des Garçons beginning in 1981, and more recent enthusiasts from the art and media world include contemporary art gallery owner and collector Charles Saatchi, furniture designer Tom Dixon, chef Ruth Rogers, Lucy Ferrry (rock-star Brian Ferry's wife), the actress Miranda Richardson, the rock star Sting, and Sting's wife, Trudi Styler. Kawakubo has explored color, and her silhouettes tend to be more fitted, but her work continues to be typified by complex patternmaking and experimentation with natural and man-made textiles. For those uncomfortable with overt sexuality in fashion and intrigued by her cerebral approach to material and form, Kawakubo's work offers an alternative aesthetic language to mainstream Western fashion. Kawakubo's clothes are architectonic, concentrating on structure rather than surface. A black pullover with holes in it in the Victoria and Albert Museum's collection of 1982 is an essay on deconstruction of form and the contained chaos that it inhabits.

Consistent Image

Kawakubo's aesthetic vision extends beyond clothes to embrace every facet of her company, giving consistency to her image all around the world. The controlled presentation of her clothes within the architecture of her shops includes photography, graphics, and packaging. She explains, "Everything that I do or that is seen as the result of Comme des Garçon's work is the same. They are all different ways of expressing the same shared values, from a collection to a museum, a shop or even a perfume" (Petronio, pp. 154–155). (Rather than having a name, each fragrance is simply numbered, based on its chemical components, and then vacuum packed like coffee in a plastic sachet.) Kawakubo's innovative graphics have been evident from early on in her career in a series of photographic catalogs of the collections and numerous brochures, posters, greetings, and announcement cards.

In 1988 she launched the biannual magazine *Six*, which is characterized by having little text, for

Kawakubo prefers the images to speak for themselves. *Six* mixes images of clothes with portraits, photographic features, and shots of things that she finds beautiful, such as wildflowers growing beside a road or plastic sheeting flapping in the wind. This aesthetic was emulated in the photographic essay she designed for the exhibition catalog of the Victoria and Albert Museum's exhibition *Radical Fashion* (2001).

Creative Collaborations

Kawakubo's creativity has extended to many events and collaborations, from museum and gallery exhibitions to performances to collaborations with architects, photographers, graphic designers, and even a floral artist. She has worked with the artists Cindy Sherman and Jean-Pierre Raynaud, and in 1997 she designed the set and costumes for Merce Cunningham's work *Scenario*, performed at the Brooklyn Academy of Music and the Palais Garnier in Paris. Kawakubo said that fashion and modern dance are

> really the same. With a collection presentation, I think about the total concept, the environment, the lighting and the make-up as well as the clothes. And the pressure to create something new and beautiful is similarly the same. Of course, the added dimension is the dancers' movements which was the risk. When I saw the rehearsal for the first time, I was fascinated how the shapes changed and came alive with the movements of the dancers. (Johnson, p. 49)

The designs for *Scenario* derived from Kawakubo's spring 1997 collection, Body Becomes Dress, Dress Becomes Body, in which she used feather padding to produce bulges under the clothes, an effect that altered the natural silhouette of the body. Kawakubo said, "It is always stimulating to do new things. The goal of my work for 'Scenario' is the same as my goal for everything: to create something strong, and beautiful and new" (Johnson, pp. 48–53).

Distinctive Collections

Although Kawakubo's clothes are typified by an independence from mainstream fashion, the collections often obliquely reflect current styles. For example, she included strips of camouflage (which was fashionable

at the time) in her Optical Shock collection of 2001. Her autumn–winter 2002 collection parodied overtly provocative clothing with large, tulle, 1950s skirts and bras with squashed-in cups worn on top of jackets or even slung around the posterior, while the back seams of billowing trousers gaped open to reveal an arc of flesh. This was really modern erotica. She remarked,

> What I would love to transmit and tell people isn't so much in my working method or creative approach, but more in the values in which I believe. It wouldn't be interesting if everyone wore the same clothes or worked the same ways. I would want to convince people to be courageous and try things differently. (Petronio, pp. 154–155)

Kawakubo's spring–summer 2004 collection featured skirt after skirt shaped like inverted flowers, teamed with a simple gauze top over bared breasts, radical because of its insistence on presenting only one form. The effect was to make the viewer focus on the variations on form and cloth, which varied from beige cotton to bright, bold patterns, completed with tricorn fabric headgear. Kawakubo described the collection as abstract excellence. Suzy Menkes described it as "an expression of artistry, imagination and a certain sweet elegance. And it represented the power of Paris to accommodate ideology in the industry."

Overview of Company

In the early twenty-first century Comme des Garçons is an extremely successful company. Its various lines are designed to appeal to audiences in both the West and the East, all overseen by Kawakubo herself. In 1982 and 1983 she opened her first shops in Paris and New York, and in 1984 the Comme des Garçons Homme plus collection was introduced. In 1986 an American subsidiary company was launched, and in 1988 the shirt line, which was manufactured in France and provided affordable garments to a European audience, was introduced. In 1989 the Comme des Garçons flagship store opened in Aoyama, Tokyo. In 1992 along with her protégé Junya Watanabe she launched the Junya Watanabe Comme des Garçons collection, and in 2005 with Tao Kurihara she launched Tao Comme des Garçons.

Recognitions and Legacy

Kawakubo has received many honors in recognition of her achievements. They include the following: Night of the Stars award from the Fashion Group, New York (1986); the Mainichi Newspaper award (1988); the Business Woman of the Year award from Veuve Clicquot (1991); and Chevalier de l'Ordre des arts et des lettres, awarded by the French Ministry of Culture (1993). In 1997 she received an honorary doctorate from the Royal College of Art, London, and in 2000, the Excellence in Design Award from the Harvard University Graduate School of Design, Cambridge, Massachusetts. Her work has also been celebrated in many museum and gallery exhibitions, such as *Mode et photo*, an exhibition of Comme des Garçons photography at the Centre Georges Pompidou, Paris (1986), and *Three Voices: Franco Albini, Kris Ruhs, Rei Kawakubo*, Paris (1993). She has had a furniture exhibition at the Galleria Carla Sozzani, Milan, and the *Essence of Quality* exhibition of Comme des Garçons Noir with the Kyoto Costume Institute, Kyoto, Japan. In 1995 she participated in the *Mode and Art* exhibition in Brussels, Belgium. In 1996 she participated in the *Art and Fashion* exhibition at the Florence Biennale Internazionale dell' Arte Contemporanea in Italy. She featured in the *Three Women: Madeleine Vionnet, Claire McCardell and Rei Kawakubo* exhibition at the Fashion Institute of Technology, New York, and in *Radical Fashion* at the Victoria and Albert Museum in 2001.

Since Rei Kawakubo's first show in Paris, Comme des Garçons clothes have continued to be characterized by complex patternmaking and an unmistakable mix of the hand-crafted and technology. Her role in the history of twentieth- and twenty-first-century fashion is about the creative fusion of two cultures and two audiences. In her words, "If my ultimate goal was to achieve financial success, I would have done things differently, but I want to create something new. I want to suggest to people different aesthetics and values. I want to question their being" (Frankel, p. 158).

See also Art and Fashion; Dance and Fashion; Fashion Designer; Fashion Magazines.

Bibliography

Fashion Institute of Technology. *Three Women: Madeleine Vionnet, Claire McCardell, and Rei Kawakubo*. New York: Fashion Institute of Technology, 1987. An exhibition catalog.

Frankel, Susannah. *Visionaries: Interviews with Fashion Designers*. London: V&A Publications, 2001.

——. "Quiet Storm." *The Independent Magazine* (2002): 8.

Grand, France. *Comme des Garçons*. London: Thames and Hudson, Inc., 1998.

Johnson, Robert. "The Bulges. Merce Cunningham's 'Scenario.'" In *Ballett International/Tanz Aktuell* (December 1997): 48–51.

Koda, Harold et al. *ReFusing Fashion: Rei Kawakubo*. Detroit: Museum of Contemporary Art, 2008.

Mendes, Valerie. *Black in Fashion*. London: V&A Publications, 1999.

Menkes, Suzy. "Abstract Artistry from Kawakubo." International Herald Tribune, October 10, 2003.

Petronio, Ezra. *Self Service* 13 (Autumn/Winter 2000): 154.

Sudjic, Deyan. *Rei Kawakubo and Comme des Garçons*. New York: Rizzoli International.

Claire Wilcox

CORSET

The corset is a garment with a long and controversial history. A rigid bodice, usually incorporating vertical and diagonal boning, and laced together, the corset was designed to shape the female torso to the fashionable silhouette of the period. Corsets have been worn by women in the Western world from the sixteenth century through the early twentieth century, at which point girdles and brassieres replaced them. Men, especially dandies and military officers, have also sometimes worn corsets. The primary significance of the corset, however, is its role as an essential element of women's fashionable dress for a period of about 400 years.

Throughout its history, the corset was frequently criticized as an "instrument of torture" and a cause of ill health and even death. Feminist historians have often argued that corsetry functioned as a coercive apparatus through which patriarchal society controlled women and exploited their sexuality. Recently, some historians have questioned this interpretation, arguing that corsetry was not one monolithic, unchanging experience that all women endured, but rather a situated practice that meant different things to different people at different times. Some women did experience the corset as an assault on the body. But for others, the corset also had positive connotations of social status, self-discipline, respectability, beauty, youth, and erotic allure. This revisionist view, which aims for a balanced and non-ideological history of corsetry based on carefully considered evidence, must not be confused with the uncritical defenses of corsetry that have been published by corset "enthusiasts." As for the long-standing claim that corsets were a source of disease and death, historians continue to disagree about the medical consequences of corsetry.

The word "corset" derives from the French *corse*, which simply designated a bodice. Early corsets were known as *corps à la baleine* (or in English, whalebone bodies), because strips of whalebone, or, more accurately, whale baleen, were inserted into the fabric (usually linen or canvas) to stiffen the cloth bodice. As whalebone became more expensive in the nineteenth century, lengths of steel increasingly replaced it. Traditionally, down the center front of the corset was inserted a *busk*, which, in shape and size, was not unlike a ruler. Busks were variously made of wood, horn, and whalebone; they were often elaborately carved and given as lovers' gifts. By 1850 the traditional, inflexible one-piece busk had been replaced by a steel, front-opening style, which made it much easier for women to put on and take off their corsets. Prior to this, women had usually relied on assistance to lace and unlace their corsets.

Corsets were also known as "stays," a term probably derived from the French *estayer* (to support), since they were thought to support the body. Because women were looked upon as the "weaker sex," it was commonly believed that their bodies habitually needed additional support. For similar reasons, children were also often placed in stiffened bodices, which were supposed to make them grow up straight. However, by the eighteenth century, many doctors argued that children's bodies were more likely to be deformed by corsets that were too tight. They also increasingly warned that women were endangering their health (and that of their unborn children) by wearing corsets. Over the course of the nineteenth century, medical journals published numerous articles criticizing corsetry. Yet the vast majority of middle- and upper-class women continued to wear corsets, and increasing numbers of working-class women also adopted corsets.

In her book, *Health and Beauty; or, Corsets and Clothing Constructed in Accordance with the Physiological Laws of the Human Body* (London, 1854), the English corsetière Madame Roxey A. Caplin defended corsets—at least if they were well-made: "It never seems to have occurred to the Doctors that ladies must and will wear stays, in spite of all the medical men of Europe." Because women "desire to retain as long as possible the charm of beauty and the appearance of youth," they wear corsets, which conceal "defects" (such as a thick waist or belly) and give support "where it is needed" (for example, in the absence of brassieres, corsets support "the fullness of the breasts"). Caplin even claimed that a French doctor had told her, "Madame, your corset is more like a new layer of muscles than an artificial extraneous article of dress!" It would be many years, however, before the majority of women stopped relying on corsets and started developing their own muscles.

The history of the corset is replete with myths and exaggerations. For example, the notorious "iron corsets" of the Renaissance were not fashion items worn by the ladies at the court of Catherine de Médicis, as is often claimed. Rather, they were orthopedic braces meant to correct spinal deformities. (Some of these metal corsets are also modern forgeries.) Accounts of extreme tight lacing are also problematic. During the second half of the nineteenth century, several English periodicals, most famously *The Englishwoman's Domestic Magazine*, published numerous letters purporting to describe how the authors had achieved waists of fifteen inches or even less. Although fashion historians and journalists have frequently quoted excerpts from this "corset correspondence," they cannot be taken at face value. Both internal and external evidence indicate that many of these letters represent sexual fantasies rather than descriptions of authentic experiences. Certainly the scenarios described, which often focused on coercive practices at anonymous boarding schools, were not typical of the average Victorian girl or woman, although they may reflect the role-playing practices of fetishistic subcultures.

Thorstein Veblen, author of *The Theory of the Leisure Class* (1899), famously described the corset as "a mutilation undergone for the purpose of lowering the subject's vitality and rendering her permanently and obviously unfit for work." In reality, however, ladies of the leisure class were not the only ones to wear corsets. By the mid-nineteenth century, with the development of cheap, mass-produced corsets, many urban working-class women also wore corsets. Clearly, the corset did not render them unfit for work, but did it lower their vitality?

Certainly many eighteenth- and nineteenth-century doctors regarded the corset as a health hazard. They blamed the corset for causing dozens of diseases, including apoplexy, asthma, cancer, chlorosis (a type of anemia), curvature of the spine, deformities of the ribs, damage to internal organs such as the liver, digestive disorders, respiratory and circulatory diseases, and birth defects and miscarriages. Other doctors, however, approved of "moderate" corsetry, condemning only "tight lacing" (a notoriously imprecise term). In 1785, Dr. von Soemmering published comparative illustrations of corseted and uncorseted rib cages, which indicated that corsetry caused permanent deformity. Twentieth-century X-rays also show that a tightly laced corset compresses the ribs and moves the internal organs, although when the corset is removed, the body seems to revert to its normal appearance.

During the nineteenth century, relatively little was understood about the causes of various diseases, to say nothing of the treatments. One cannot, therefore, automatically accept the diagnoses of nineteenth-century doctors, many of which are patently absurd. This is not to say that corsets were totally harmless. Most authorities today agree that extremely tight corsets might risk various kinds of physical impairment or harm. There is no consensus among experts, however, on what risks were involved in ordinary corset wearing. Although contemporary scholars disagree about how dangerous corsets really were, corsets undoubtedly did contribute to some health problems. Spirometry (lung volume) testing conducted by Colleen Gau and her associates has demonstrated that corseted women suffered depleted lung volume, as well as changes in breathing (from normal diaphragmatic breathing to reliance on the accessory muscles of the chest wall). Lessened lung capacity would not necessarily contribute to respiratory disease, but it could certainly lower vitality and cause fainting. This would seem to lend credence to nineteenth-century accounts that associated corsetry with shallow breathing and fainting. In the 1880s, using an adaptation of the sphygmomanometer (blood pressure machine), the New York obstetrician Robert L. Dickinson measured corset pressure on several hundred women, recording pressures as high as eighty-two pounds per square inch. He believed that corset pressure caused digestive and breathing problems, as well as serious effects on the reproductive organs, such as prolapse of the uterus. It is sometimes alleged that some women underwent the dangerous surgical procedure of having their lower ribs removed in order to achieve a smaller corseted waist. There is, however, no evidence at all that any Victorian woman ever had her ribs removed; rib removal appears to be entirely mythical.

Some doctors and corsetieres tried (or claimed) to develop safer and more comfortable corsets. During the 1890s, for example, Dr. Inez Josephine Gaches-Sarraute designed the so-called straight-front corset, which she described as a "health" corset. However, recent physiologic testing using reenactors found the straight-front corset to be more uncomfortable and constraining than the hourglass styles of the mid-Victorian era.

The shape and construction of the corset changed dramatically over time, but there was no simple progression toward greater ease. Between about 1790 and 1810, the rigid cone-shaped stays of the eighteenth century were temporarily abandoned in favor of a shorter, lighter style, some variants of which resembled a brassiere. However, as high-waisted Empire dresses gave way to lowered waists and fuller skirts, the boned corset reemerged. Now, however, it was shaped more like an hourglass. Over the course of the nineteenth century, technological developments, such as steam molding, contributed toward the fashion for long *cuirasse* corsets. At the turn of the century, the fashionable straight-front corset pushed the pelvis back and the bosom forward, creating the socalled S-silhouette. Yet as women engaged in more sporting activities, such as bicycling, they increasingly adopted flexible elasticized sports corsets. By the 1920s elastic girdles and brassieres had largely supplanted rigid corsets, particularly among the young. In 1939, and again after World War II, fashion showed renewed emphasis on femininity and the corset had a brief resurgence in the form of the "Merry Widow" or *guépière* (waspy).

By the 1960s and 1970s, however, a cultural focus on youth and body exposure resulted in greater reliance on diet and exercise, rather than foundation garments, to create a desirable figure. The corset was, thus, not so much abandoned as it was internalized through diet, exercise, and later, plastic surgery. A minority of corset enthusiasts, both male and female, continue to wear corsets and sometimes tight lace as part of fetishistic, cross-dressing, or sadomasochistic practices.

Beginning in the 1980s, inspired by subcultural fetish styles, avant-garde fashion designers, such as Vivienne Westwood and Jean Paul Gaultier, began to create corset fashions. Madonna famously wore a pink satin corset by Jean Paul Gaultier on her Blonde Ambition tour of 1991. Since then, every few years the fashion press reports on the reappearance of corsets by couturiers such as Christian Lacroix, Alexander McQueen, and Donatella Versace. Although some of these corsets incorporate lacing and (plastic or metal) boning, most are really more like zip-up bustiers than historic corsets. Cheaper versions are popular as club wear for both young men and women.

See also Brassiere; Europe and America: History of Dress (400–1900 C.E); Gender, Dress, and Fashion; Girdle.

Bibliography

Steele, Valerie. *The Corset: A Cultural History*. New Haven, Conn., and London: Yale University Press, 2001.
Summers, Leigh. *Bound to Please*. Oxford: Berg; distributed by New York University Press, 2001.

Valerie Steele and Colleen Gau

Wahgi tribe members. In tribes such as this one in New Guinea, paints are used to portray the varying physical and emotional aspects of their community, both positive and negative. © CHARLES & JOSETTE LENARS/CORBIS. REPRODUCED BY PERMISSION.

COSMETICS, NON-WESTERN

The earliest evidence of the role of cosmetics in human society was found in the remains of artifacts used for eye makeup in Egypt of the fourth millennium B.C.E. Anthropological research also shows that there are several ways used by humans to transform the physical and social appearance of their bodies into cultural manifestations. People use their bodies and faces as objects of aesthetic elaboration or as a medium through which they can project themselves in religious and social life. We can thus identify two distinct, though related, senses of the term "non-Western cosmetic." The first pertains to personal taste and is concerned with the decorative/aesthetic aspect of non-Western cosmetic. The second is more general and is related to ritual and the symbolic essence of body decoration.

The ubiquitous interpretation of non-Western cosmetic in modern society is associated with the aesthetic or decorative. It is concerned with the visual and is related to personal style and denotes what is considered beautiful or fashionable. Non-Western cosmetic, in this case, is used in order to make a fashion statement. It is generally considered an exclusively feminine pursuit, used to aesthetically enhance the beauty of the person. Cosmetic and fashion industries make such physical appearances readily available under the rubric of the ethnic/tribal/oriental look. This look is epitomized by photographic studies of non-Western artistic practices and peoples confined to identifying what may be considered exotic and beautiful to the Western eye (Reifenstahl 1986; Ebin 1979; McCurry 1997).

Products originating from Africa, Asia, and South America and conceptualized in terms of respect for traditional beauty, natural or local ingredients, and non-animal tested products are sold in modern containers. This is meant to bring to mind ideas of purity, health, animal welfare, sunshine, adventure, travel, leisure, serenity, even exoticism and eroticism. Materials used include kaolin, henna, kohl, burnt cork, chalk, clay, and all sorts of vegetable, flower, and plant extracts. The growing demand for an exotic look in fashion has warranted their manufacture on a commercial scale. Production techniques, packaging, and advertising have helped to increase worldwide usage of such products. The best-known leader of this trend is the Body Shop.

The image industry created by advertising agencies mediates the changing aspect of the human body image through fashion and art in glossy magazines and books. This has privileged the aesthetic/decorative and attenuated the transcendent nature of the art of body painting (Baudrillard 1994). Conversely, in tribal and non-Western societies, the aesthetic aspect of body and face decoration often emphasizes the social aspect of the human body (Leach 1966). Non-Western cosmetic can thus be understood by looking into the interpretative properties of cosmetic in terms of rituals and symbols. This is especially helpful for clarifying the meaning of body adornment during festivities, ritual ceremonies, or even everyday occasions. For example, Tilaka is a vermilion mark applied on the forehead by Indian women as a sign of being in wedlock. It is also used by both sexes as a culturally designed communication code, which embodies ritual and sacred symbols. Although red predominates, a variety of other pigments such as yellow, white, gray, saffron, and black are employed. In some cases these pigments are applied on the forearms and the abdomen as well. The origins of these practices are said to lie in a primitive tribal past. This is the case of followers of Shiva, a deity worshiped by proto-Aryan societies in the Indian subcontinent. Even today, the smearing of colors on arms, torso, or face is an essential aspect of the Hindu festival of Holi.

Women and men wear the Tilaka as a sign of belonging to the Hindu religion. Its versatile form, shape, and color also indicate adherence to the various Hindu sects and subsects. Worshipers of the Lord Vishnu apply a "U" sign made of a mixture of red ocher powder (*Sindhura*) and sandalwood paste (*Gandah*). Worshipers of the Lord Shiva prefer to draw three horizontal lines made of ash (*Abhira*). For men the application of Tilaka, made up of their own blood, is an indication of solemn commitment to an oath or a pledge being undertaken (Kelly 2002).

In tribal societies of tropical and equatorial regions the visual and interpretative value of body adornment is used as a schematic representation of values, beliefs, symbols, and myths. Differing pigments and patterns are used for instant recognition of group identity, social status, or age group, while still allowing for gender differences and personal idiosyncrasy. The most elaborate forms of decoration involve lengthy preparation, much care and expense, and hence are generally seen on ceremonial and ritual occasions. Men and women employ a combination of colors and designs in order to make a statement about the nature of a particular occasion. The adornment favored by individuals or group participants is intrinsic to the ceremony and is vital for conveying messages about the community's social and religious values.

The Melpa and Wahgi of Papua New Guinea use body decoration as an essential part of ritual performances and gift exchange ceremonies. During happy occasions men paint their bodies and weapons with white wavy lines intended to represent patterns reflected in water. They adorn their faces with white and red pigments and place similar feathers and flowers in their hair to evoke "brightness." Bright colors symbolize the physical and moral strength, vitality, and well-being of the community. Conversely, war paint is deliberately meant to transform the human body into a terrifying warrior. In times of war, bodies are covered with a deep black charcoal-based pigment, a color associated with poison. Faces and accessories are similarly decorated with dark hues to transmit the message of aggressive power and fierceness. Women in Papua New Guinea wear less brilliant body decoration emphasizing their primarily domestic and agricultural duties. Similarly Australian aborigines paint their body and faces with white clay dots and lines prior to going hunting or war as a protective measure. They also decorate their bodies during initiation ceremonies or when they re-enact stories of their mythical past through music and dancing (Ebin 1979; O'Hanlon 1989, 1992; Strathern and Strathern 1983; Groning, 1996).

In parts of Africa and South America, design and color are used to separate the sexes and invoke magical powers, which are believed to be inherent in nature and the spiritual world. Tchikrin men from Central Brazil paint their bodies white and black; women prefer yellow and red. The Kayapo Indians of Brazil make a connection between the color red and abstract qualities such as heightened sensory sensitivity, energy, and health. They smear red pigments on their faces, hands, and feet, because they associate these parts of the body with swiftness, agility, and sensory contact with the outside world. Black is applied to the torso and signifies the integration of the inner man into social life (Turner 1969). Turning to West Africa, shamans in the Ivory Coast paint their eyes with white clay mixed with herbs and water from "sacred rivers" in order to see into the spirit world. Ghanaian priestesses smear their faces with white clay and paint parallel lines across their foreheads and cheeks. The color white represents the divine nature of the gods, while parallel lines are meant to deflect the attacks of evil mystical beings. Ashanti women from Ghana draw designs on their arms with white clay to invoke mythical protection for themselves and their babies after giving birth (Ebin 1979; Fisher 1984; Groning 1996).

People's preoccupation with rituals and symbols in social life often merges with their purely aesthetic impulses to decorate their bodies. Young Nuba men from the Sudan spend long hours applying elaborate designs all over their bodies to enhance the beauty, elegance, and well-being of their bodies. Their adorned bodies become a field upon which they demonstrate their physical beauty, sexual attractiveness, or personal status. Particular patterns or colors are used to portray in visible terms the individual's progress from infancy through puberty and adulthood or personal status within society. Deep yellow and jet black are only allowed to older age groups. Younger age groups are immediately recognizable by their use of red ocher and simpler hairstyles. The decline in physical strength and attractiveness in old age compels old men to cease to decorate their bodies, shave their heads, and start wearing cloth. Nuba women wear appropriate colors indicating their membership in a particular kinship group (Faris 1972; Brain 1979; Ebin 1979; Strathern and Strathern 1983; Riefenstahl 1986). The above examples of body and face decoration are not merely indicative of our tribal past. They are kept alive in the Western imagination through books on art and photography and their many fashion conscious modern imitators (Thevoz 1984; Vale and Juno 1989; Randall and Polhemus 2000)

See also Cosmetics, Western.

Bibliography

Brain, Robert. *The Decorated Body.* London: Hutchinson, 1979.

Baudrillard, Jean. *Simulacra and Simulation. The Body in Theory: Histories of Cultural Materialism.* Ann Arbor: University of Michigan Press, 1994.

Ebin, Victoria. *The Body Decorated.* London: Thames and Hudson, Inc. 1979.

Faris, James. *Nuba Personal Art.* London: Duckworth, 1972.

Fisher, Angela. *Africa Adorned: A Panorama of Jewelry, Dress, Body Decoration and Hair Style.* New York: Harry N. Abrams, 1984.

Groning, Karl. *Body Decoration: A World Survey of Body Art.* New York: Vendome Press, 1996.

Kelly, Kevin. *Asia Grace.* Cologne, Germany: Taschen GmbH, 2002.

Leach, Edmund. "Ritualisation in Man." *Philosophical Transaction of the Royal Society* 251 (1966).

McCurry, Steve. *Portraits.* Bombay, India: Phaidon Press Ltd., 1997.

O'Hanlon, Michael. *Reading the Skin: Adornment, Display and Society Among the Wahgi.* London: Trustees of the British Museum by British Museum Publications, 1989.

——. "Unstable Images and Second Skins: Artifacts, Exegesis and Assessments in the New Guinea Highlands." *Man* 27, no. 3 (1992): 587–608.

Randall, Housk, and Ted Polhemus. *The Customized Body.* London: Serpent's Tail, 2000.

Riefenstahl, Leni. *The Last of the Nuba.* London: Collins Harvill, 1986.

Strathern, Andrew, and Marilyn Strathern. *Self-Decoration in Mt. Hagen.* Toronto: University of Toronto Press, 1983.

Thevoz, Michel. *The Painted Body.* New York: Skira/Rizzoli International, 1984.

Turner, Terence. "Tchikrin, A Central Brazilian Tribe and Its Symbolic Language of Bodily Adornment." *Natural History* 18, (1969).

Vale, V., and Andrea Juno, eds. *Modern Primitives: An Investigation of Contemporary Body Adornment and Ritual.* San Francisco: RE/Research Publications, 1989.

Paula Heinonen

COSMETICS, WESTERN

In the twenty-first century, cosmetics include a full range of products to protect the skin and improve appearance, from moisturizers to makeup, manufactured by a multibillion-dollar, global cosmetics industry. Before the twentieth century, however, cosmetics were understood differently in Western cultures. In English, the word "cosmetic" referred to skin-improving substances, such as creams and lotions. Cosmetics to mask or color the skin were known as "paint" or, in a theatrical context, "makeup." This fundamental distinction was a legacy of the ancient world, and shaped the early use of cosmetics.

Cosmetics Before 1900

In the seventeenth and eighteenth centuries, European women prepared simple cosmetics from recipes appearing in household manuals and cookbooks or passed on orally from generation to generation. In that period, cosmetics were as much science as art, a branch of self-help therapeutics that women were expected to master. Recipes in early household manuals called for roots, wild-flowers, and other plants to be mixed with water, beer, vinegar, and spices; these produced remedies to clear the complexion, improve color, and remove signs of smallpox. The principles governing these mixtures were based on Galen's theory of the humors, in which the correspondence between internal and external organs, and the balance between hot, cold, dry, and moist qualities, was the key to health and beauty. In addition, belief in the power of nature's cycles and astrology found their way into beauty preparations, in recipes using May dew, the first juice of spring plants, and "virgin milk."

Colonial Americans used similar cosmetic recipes, preparing cold cream, skin lotions, and lip salves from such common substances as wax, lard, nut oils, and sugar. They also incorporated the flowers and herbs of the New World, such as puccoon-root or "Indian paint," prevalent in Algonquin therapeutics. Africans brought to the colonies as slaves similarly adapted native plants into traditional West African techniques of grooming and beautifying, using berries and roots to redden the skin, for example.

In addition to home preparations, a small but significant global trade made exotic herbs, extracts, dyes, and proprietary cosmetics available to the wealthy in the early modern period. French and English court society encouraged the use of enamels, white powder, rouges, and beauty marks to enhance appearance, serve fashion, and cover pockmarks and other disfigurements, and colonial elites followed suit. These paints, powders, and enamels to whiten the skin often contained dangerous substances, such as arsenic and lead, jeopardizing health while creating brilliant effects. Perfumers, hairdressers, and apothecaries in major cities offered fashionable cosmetics to both women and men. Until the early nineteenth century, cosmetics tended to mark rank as much as gender; they connoted gentility, social prestige, and political standing, and were as much a part of high culture as ornamental clothing and tea drinking.

Fashionable cosmetics became a source of controversy, however, in Europe and America. Puritans condemned painting as a mark of vanity and defiance of the divine order; masking the face falsified one's true identity. The American Revolution placed a political perspective on such cosmetics, valuing the plain appearance of republican virtue over the foppery of aristocratic men. In the early nineteenth century, the religious sensibilities and domestic ideals of an emergent middle class in the North emphasized both natural beauty and women's duty to be beautiful, to be achieved through healthful regimens and a moral life. White southern women, especially those on plantations, held onto the earlier ideals of gentility that permitted powder and rouge. Still, the association of cosmetics with prostitution—the "painted woman"— remained a strong one through the 1800s, and women who dared to use cosmetics did so covertly and with a light touch.

Sales of skin creams and lotions grew through the middle of the nineteenth century, but they remained small in scale when compared with such commodities as patent medicines and soaps. According to an 1849 manufacturing census, thirty-nine toiletries firms

produced only $355,000 in merchandise in the United States. Nevertheless, the expansion of the market in this period made formerly rare preparations more available and affordable. Typically pharmacists would use a range of chemicals, herbs, and oils to "put up" skin creams under a house label. Commercial agents also imported goods from around the world, including English patent preparations, French perfumes, Portuguese rouge dishes, and Chinese color boxes, containing color-saturated papers of rouge, pearl powder, and eyebrow blacking.

The most commonly used cosmetics of the nineteenth century, however, were skin whiteners and bleaches. Advertisements claimed they removed tan and freckles and made women look more refined and genteel. These were directed at white, middle-class women, playing on their social aspirations, as well as working-class, immigrant, and black women.

Cosmetics Use and the Beauty Industry

Cosmetics use began to increase in the late nineteenth century, a consequence of several key developments. Embracing photography and the theater, Americans became newly oriented to visual culture and social performances. In retailing, innovative department stores used mirrors, plate glass, and the latest fashions to encourage women to engage in self-scrutiny and display.

Cosmetic counter. Most major cosmetic lines have displays in department stores, complete with beauticians to demonstrate the products and make recommendations to customers. © GREG SMITH/ CORBIS SABA. REPRODUCED BY PERMISSION.

Many cosmetics businesses began as manufacturers of perfume, soap, and patent medicines and initially went into beauty aids as a sideline. Ponds, one of the leading sellers of skin-care products, started out making patent medicines; in an early instance of market research, it discovered a demand for skin-care products in the 1890s. By 1910, Ponds's advertising promoted cleansing cream at night and vanishing cream by day as a regular beauty treatment for women.

Most important, beauty salons and manicure parlors began to spring up in the nation's cities. These popularized a concept of "beauty culture," encouraging women to improve their looks systematically, using proper cosmetics and facial techniques. Emphasizing cleanliness, grooming, and skin care, they also sold tinted face powders, whitening creams, rouge, and lip pomades. Women entrepreneurs pioneered the new beauty culture and some became early leaders of the cosmetics industry. Helena Rubinstein and Elizabeth Arden created their New York salons in the 1910s; each developed a full line of cosmetics for facial treatments and home use. By World War I, each had expanded operations into manufacturing and distribution at the "class" end of the market, selling in exclusive stores, specialty shops, and a growing number of salons. The Parisian fashion for maquillage was slow to be accepted in the United States, although by the 1910s style setters and socialites were purchasing French-made rouge and powder. Helena Rubinstein, Elizabeth Arden, and other women in the beauty business encouraged affluent American women to use makeup and quietly offered applications in their salons.

African American entrepreneurs also found a market for cosmetics within black communities. In the early twentieth century, Anthony Overton developed a "High Brown Face Powder" specifically for women with darker complexions. Although focusing on hair treatments, businesswoman Madam C. J. Walker also expanded her product line to include skin creams and powders for black women. Neither created products for the full range of African American skin tones at this time, but both sought to address black women's dignity and desire for good looks. In contrast, many of the cosmetics sold to African Americans manufactured by white-owned companies relied on blatantly racist appeals to bleach skin and look white. Such products were widely advertised in black newspapers and remained a subject of controversy through the twentieth century.

What is especially striking about cosmetics at this time, however, is the popularity of beauty preparations among workingwomen, including the daughters of immigrants. They embraced powder and paint, along with fashionable clothing, to assert a new sense of individuality. In the early twentieth century, when sexual mores were changing and young women had entered the workforce in large numbers, the "painted woman" could no longer be distinguished as a prostitute. Indeed, by the 1920s, women increasingly used the term "makeup" rather than "paint," thus indicating that cosmetics were not a means of covering up one's looks but rather an integral part of a public persona.

Growing through the 1910s, the cosmetics industry took off after World War I. From 1909 to 1929, the number of American perfume and cosmetics manufacturers nearly doubled; by 1929, Americans were spending $700 million annually for cosmetics and beauty services. The transformation of women's appearance in the 1920s—corsetless and revealing clothing, bobbed hair, a thin body image—went hand-in-hand with the increased consumption of beauty products and makeup.

Still, cosmetics use spread unevenly across the United States and Europe, more popular among the young, employed, and urban women than their mothers or small-town sisters. Surveys of nonurban women's daily regimens in the 1920s showed that most simply washed the face with soap and water, then perhaps applied cold cream or white powder. It was not until the end of the 1930s that farm women's use of cosmetics approximated that of city dwellers.

A number of innovations in cosmetics and packaging appeared in this time. French cosmetics firms had produced finely textured and tinted powders, and American firms followed suit, selling a wider range of shades. These included, in the mid-1920s, powders and rouges to complement suntanned skin, which had become a popular craze. Metal compacts and lipstick tubes emphasized the portability of cosmetics, so that women could touch up throughout the day. Vanishing cream was typically used as a base for powder, but foundations began to appear in the 1930s. Among the most innovative and successful was Max Factor's Pan-Cake, a water-soluble foundation in cake form, invented for use by motion picture actors, then introduced to the general public in 1938.

In the first half of the twentieth century, however, most cosmetics manufacturers followed standard formulas, modifying basic creams, lotions, and other preparations. Firms selling lipstick, rouge, and eye makeup often depended on "private label" manufacturers, who offered similar products with small variations. Scientific discoveries led companies to make new claims for wrinkle removers, and small amounts of vitamins, hormones, and even radium were added to skin creams. By the 1930s, the public paid heightened attention to the composition of cosmetics and the exaggerated claims of advertisers. Consumer advocacy groups highlighted cases where women had been blinded by aniline dyes in mascara or burned by skin bleaches that contained a high percentage of ammoniated mercury, common in whiteners sold to African American women. Such concerns led to the increased regulation of cosmetics in the United States and passage of the Food, Drug, and Cosmetics Act in 1938.

It was advertising and marketing, more than product development, that spurred the expansion of the beauty industry and cosmetics use. Cosmetics and toiletries were heavily advertised in women's magazines, second only to food items, and appeared frequently in general interest magazines, in newspapers, and by the 1930s, on radio. These advertisements invoked aspirational images of beauty, youth, and romance, on the one hand, but also touched anxieties about social competition and failed romance, especially during the Great Depression. Hollywood also played an important role; motion picture actresses established new beauty ideals and endorsed a range of products, including mascara and eye shadow, cosmetics few women wore at the time. Whether sold in department stores or five-and-dimes, cosmetics were often an impulse purchase; retailers set up eyecatching displays in the central aisles of their stores and hired saleswomen to demonstrate beauty techniques and promote specific brands.

Postwar Expansion

By the 1940s, makeup had become accepted as an integral dimension of women's everyday appearance. Home economics courses taught how to use makeup in classes on good grooming; department stores held beauty days for schoolgirls; white-collar personnel offices looked favorably on job candidates with carefully applied lipstick and rouge. Psychologists and other professionals insisted that cosmetics were essential to women's mental health and a mature feminine identity.

During World War II, bright red lipstick became a sign of women's patriotism among the Allies. As women went into industry in record numbers, they continued to use cosmetics to affirm their femininity and boost their morale. When the American government tried to restrict cosmetics as a conservation measure in 1942, it found itself backpedaling six months later. Although discontinuing metal containers and limiting some ingredients, it nevertheless made a wide range of beauty preparations available.

Cosmetics use increased dramatically in the postwar world. Women purchased cosmetics to complement seasonal changes in fashion, buying wardrobes of lipstick and nail polish. As the market for cosmetics matured, the beauty business created distinctive brands intended to appeal to women according to demographics and lifestyle. Maybelline, Revlon, and Noxzema (Noxell)—small-scale firms that before the war had specialized in eye makeup, nail enamel, and skin cream, respectively—became large corporations with extensive product lines. New women entrepreneurs also emerged after World War II, including Estee Lauder and Mary Kay Ash. Home-based selling proved highly successful in this period. Avon, founded in 1886, used door-to-door sales to expand from rural communities and cities into the burgeoning postwar suburbs. Using the multilevel marketing strategy pioneered by earlier black businesswomen, Mary Kay organized home parties for women to learn about and purchase cosmetics.

Postwar youth culture spurred cosmetic firms to market cosmetics especially for teenage girls. Noxzema's Cover Girl offered sheer, medicated foundations and lighter tints as a "clean makeup" that would appeal to both teens and their parents. In the early 1960s, the sale of eye makeup—mascara, eyeliner, and colorful eye shadow—finally took off, an aesthetic trend among young women that coincided with the miniskirt and long hair of the time. Grooming aids, powder, and lip gloss for young girls appeared as early as the 1950s; by the 1970s, toy companies and major cosmetics firms competed for these juvenile consumers.

Market segmentation meant that advertising varied considerably in this period. Compared with their prewar counterparts, however, advertisements in the 1950s and 1960s more boldly accentuated women's sexuality and need to appeal physically to men. Revlon's Fire and Ice campaign in 1952 cast a playful yet erotic and charged aura around a medium-red lipstick. During the "British Invasion" of the 1960s, Mary Quant's Love Cosmetics used phallic packaging and Mod design to tie teen cosmetics to the sexual revolution.

Politics of Cosmetics

By the mid-1960s, the counterculture and a nascent feminist movement attacked these trends in advertising, the commercialization of beauty, and women's sexual objectification in the media. Embracing a "natural" look, some women gave up makeup entirely, while others began to compound their own creams and lotions using herbs, berries, and other organic ingredients. Major cosmetics firms were slow to respond to this challenge. Estee Lauder introduced Clinique in 1968, emphasizing a scientific and hygienic appeal. A number of cosmetics lines appeared that contained natural ingredients and were not tested on animals; these often sold in food coops or other alternative outlets. The Body Shop, founded by Anita Roddick, became highly successful marketing to women sensitive to the environment and influenced by the counterculture.

In the 1960s and 1970s, women of color also protested the narrow images of beauty that appeared in fashion magazines and limited cosmetics lines available to them. African American businesses like Fashion Fair and entrepreneurs from the post-1965 immigrant groups have created niche makeup lines for black, Latina, Asian-American, and other women. Increasingly attuned to American ethnic diversity and the global economy, corporations like Maybelline began to manufacture foundation and other cosmetics for the full range of human skin tones.

The feminist critique of cosmetics continued to be heard in the last decades of the twentieth century, notably in the 1991 best-seller *The Beauty Myth*. That critique, in turn, was challenged in the 1980s and 1990s by postfeminists, postmodernists, lipstick lesbians, and devotees of such subcultural styles as punk. They rejected the "natural" as a measure of authenticity, and held instead to the view that cosmetics use could be a source of play, pleasure, and self-expression. Again, cosmetics companies have picked up on that attitude, marketing lipstick, eye makeup, and nail polish in unusual and extreme colors and such provocative names as Vamp and Juicy.

Developments in the Early 2000s

Western cosmetics became widespread in the global economy in the second half of the twentieth century. Corporations like Unilever and Ponds established subsidiaries, contracted with local import firms, and sold beauty preparations in Latin America, the Middle East, Asia, and Africa. American manufacturers marketed cosmetics in a difficult balancing act, appealing to universal ideals of beauty, promoting the American style of actresses and models, and nodding to national and cultural differences. Avon's success in the international arena depended on native sales agents who understood local customs and concerns even as they projected the image of American beauty, lifestyles, and values. By the 1990s, "Avon calling" could be heard around the world, including post-communist and developing countries.

By the twenty-first century, cosmetics manufacturers had invested heavily in scientific research, working closely with chemists and dermatologists. These new "cosmeceuticals" went beyond the hypoallergenic products available since the 1930s and included creams and ointments containing such ingredients as Retin A, which appears to reduce the effects of aging and improves the skin. These products have increasingly blurred the lines between cosmetics, drugs, and medical specialties. The post-World War II baby-boom generation has fueled the growth of anti-aging research and product development, a trend that is expected to continue.

An important development in cosmetics is the partially successful effort to sell cosmetics to men, beyond the traditional grooming products like aftershave and cologne. Both mass manufacturers and some high-end firms, including Helena Rubinstein, tried unsuccessfully to sell cosmetics to men earlier in the twentieth century. Since 1980, however, a significant number of urban professional men and gay men have begun to use moisturizer, exfoliating liquids, and even bronzers to improve their appearance. Although often similar to women's cosmetics, these products are usually segregated in a separate men's counter in retail stores and appear with different brand names and packaging. Young men in such music and dance subcultures as heavy metal and goth will often wear colorful makeup as performers and audience members. Most makeup remains so deeply associated with femininity and effeminacy, however, that very few men choose to use it in everyday business and social life, and those who do seek a "natural" look.

See also Appearance; Cosmetics, Non-Western.

Bibliography

Allen, Margaret. *Selling Dreams: Inside the Beauty Business.* New York: Simon and Schuster, 1981.

Banner, Lois. *American Beauty*. Chicago: University of Chicago Press, 1983.

De Castlebajac, Kate. *The Face of the Century: 100 Years of Makeup and Style*. New York: Rizzoli International, 1995.

Gunn, Fenja. *The Artificial Face: A History of Cosmetics*. London: David and Charles, 1973.

Koehn, Nancy. "Estee Lauder: Self-Definition and the Modern Cosmetics Market." In *Beauty and Business: Commerce, Gender, and Culture in Modern America*. Edited by Philip Scranton, 217–251. New York: Routledge, 2001.

Manko, Katina L. "A Depression-Proof Business Strategy: The California Perfume Company's Motivational Literature." In *Beauty and Business: Commerce, Gender, and Culture in Modern America*. Edited by Philip Scranton, 142–168. New York: Routledge, 2001.

Peiss, Kathy. *Hope in a Jar: The Making of America's Beauty Culture*. New York: Metropolitan Books, 1998.

Smith, Virginia. "The Popularisation of Medical Knowledge: The Case of Cosmetics." *Society for the Social History of Medicine Bulletin* 36 (1986): 12–15.

Vinikas, Vincent. *Soft Soap, Hard Sell: American Hygiene in an Age of Advertisement*. Ames: Iowa State University Press, 1992.

Wolf, Naomi. *The Beauty Myth*. New York: William Morrow, 1991.

Kathy Peiss

The end of the nineteenth century saw a shift from companies of actors performing a rotating repertoire of plays to stand-alone productions with actors hired specifically for each role. With actors moving from show to show, it didn't make economic sense for producers to maintain a large wardrobe inventory. Simultaneously, a heightened interest in realism called for specialists with the ability to reproduce accurately clothing of the past. Enter the designer.

The First Designers

An article in the *New Idea Women's Magazine* says that by 1906 theatrical costume design firms flourished in most major cities. Some, like Eaves or Van Horn's, in New York and Philadelphia respectively, began as manufacturers of uniforms or regalia and expanded into the theatrical market. By contrast, Mrs. Caroline Siedle and Mrs. Castel-Bert, both in New York, established their ateliers specifically to cater to the growing theater industry.

Producers hired these pioneering designers at their discretion. They were under no obligation to commit to the services of a designer and many preferred to rent existing costumes. For a modern dress show, leading actresses might commission their dressmaker, while minor players raided their closets. Two events changed that.

COSTUME DESIGNER

Costume design as a profession is a twentieth-century phenomenon. Until the end of the nineteenth century, costumes for popular entertainments were assembled piecemeal, either by the director, the actor-manager or by the patron. Repertory companies were the norm in the nineteenth century, and it made sense for a company to maintain a stock of costumes that could be used in multiple productions. Individual actors, working with more than one company, might travel with their own costumes—a practice that continues in the twenty-first century among opera singers.

Exceptions to the piecemeal approach include entertainments devised by artists during the Renaissance and the court masques designed by Inigo Jones in seventeenth-century England, but both are rare examples of a unified vision.

Costumer designers at the Palais Garnier, Paris. Once the concept for a particular production has been agreed upon, the costume designer researches the script and creates sketches of possible garments for each character. © ANNEBICQUE BERNARD/CORBIS. REPRODUCED BY PERMISSION.

The actor's strike of 1919 put an end to the practice of performers providing their own wardrobes. Thereafter, producers were required by contract to supply costumes for everyone. Then, in 1923, the stage designers unionized. As part of the collective bargaining agreement, producers of Broadway and touring productions had to hire a union designer. The first union members were set designers who might also design costumes. By 1936 the union recognized costume designers as a separate specialty.

Film designers also emerged in the 1920s. At first, actresses in contemporary films wore their own clothes, "so ladies with good wardrobes found they got more jobs" (Chierichetti 1976, p. 8). For period films, producers rented costumes.

The industry moved from New York to California in the 1920s and the studio system replaced the independently shot films of the teens. Designers emerged partly because studio heads wanted their films to have a cohesive look but primarily because the shift from black and white to color film, and from silents to talkies, required costumes especially designed for the medium. The early film distorted colors. Blue, on film, appeared white. Red photographed as black. The early microphones were so sensitive to sounds that only soft fabrics could be used. Crisp fabrics rustled, drowning out the dialogue. By the end of the 1920s, every studio had at least one house designer, a support staff of sketch artists and costumers, and a research department and library.

The Process

The costume designer is responsible for the head-to-toe look of everyone who appears on stage or on screen. After reading the script, the designer meets with the director and others to debate their approach to the material. *Hamlet*, for example, has been set in medieval Denmark, in Vietnam, and in contemporary dress. All are valid approaches.

With the production concept agreed on, the designer has an interval for research. He or she develops color sketches for every costume worn in the show. Depending on the medium, a variety of people see and approve these sketches. In the theater, the director, producer, choreographer, and sometimes the star will have approval. For film, the costume designer works with the director, cinematographer, and art director in addition to the stars.

Once approved, the sketches go into the costume shop to be translated into three-dimensional garments. Many regional theater, opera, and ballet companies maintain their own costume shops. All university theater departments do so as well. For other venues, including Broadway and feature films, a range of independent theatrical costume shops submit bids for producing the costumes. Even when contemporary clothes are purchased or come from a rental house, fittings and alterations are performed by the costume shop.

In the Shop

With the sketches in the shop, the costume designer and assistants essentially move in for the length of the build time, which in theater equals the length of the rehearsal period, typically between three and five weeks. The practice differs for film and opera. In a university setting, the designers may do their own fabric and trim shopping. Elsewhere, costume shops have buyers whose job is to scour the market, bringing back swatches for the designer's consideration.

While the buyers are swatching, costume makers are creating custom-made patterns for each costume, which are then made up, usually in muslin. As each is completed, the actor who will wear it is called for the first of several fittings. An important function of the first fitting is to see that the actor can move well in a costume designed before rehearsals began. Once in rehearsal, the director or choreographer may decide that performing a somersault, despite the bustle gown, is integral to the show's concept. This is the designer's moment to learn that vital piece of information and to adapt the design to allow for the movement. For the 1972 Broadway production of *Pippin*, for example, director-choreographer Bob Fosse had insisted that the armor be rigid metal. When his designer, Patricia Zipprodt, saw what the dancers had to do, she realized that only something flexible would satisfy his needs.

At the first fitting, the designer also has a chance to see if the proportions of the garment suit the performer. At the second fitting, the costume has been made up in the actual fabric to be used. Custom underpinnings, shoes, and millinery are included so that both designer and performer can see the total look. At this fitting all the craftspeople have the opportunity to make adjustments that may increase the performer's comfort or that are requested by the designer.

The final fitting is in the completed costume with the expectation that no further work is necessary at this stage. The clothes move out of the shop and into the theater or onto location.

In Performance

Film designers view daily rushes to see how well their costumes work on screen, while a live performance will have one or more dress rehearsals and a series of preview performances before the opening night. The designer attends them all. This is the time when all of the production elements—scenery, lighting, movement, and costumes come together and occasionally what seemed like a good idea in the shop does not work in performance. With an original script, new scenes or musical numbers may be added, requiring new costumes. The designer has only a few days to produce new designs, get them into the shop, select the fabrics, attend fittings, and see the new costumes integrated into the production. The designer's job is finished only when the show opens to the public or when the last scene is filmed.

See also Ballet Costume; Dance Costume; Theatrical Costume; Theatrical Makeup.

Bibliography

Anderson, Cletus, and Barbara Anderson. *Costume Design.* New York: Holt, Rhinehart and Winston, 1984. A good overview of the process.

Anderson, Norah. "Stage Dressmaking and Stage Dressmakers." *New Idea Women's Magazine* (November 1906): 12–16.

Bentley, Toni. *Costumes by Karinska.* New York: Harry N. Abrams, 1995. Especially chapter 5 on the design and construction of costumes for the ballet.

Chierichetti, David. *Hollywood Costume Design.* New York: Harmony Books, 1976. The introduction is good on the origins of film design.

Ingham, Rosemary, and Liz Covey. *The Costume Designer's Handbook: A Complete Guide for Amateur and Professional Costume Designers.* Portsmouth, N.H.: Heineman, 1992. Excellent overview of the profession.

Jones, Robert Edward. *The Dramatic Imagination.* New York: Theatre Arts, 1941. An inspirational classic, especially chapter 5, "Some Thoughts on Stage Costume."

Pecktal, Lynn. *Costume Design: Techniques of Modern Masters.* New York: Backstage Books, 1993. Interviews with

Broadway and feature film designers including training and working methods.

Whitney Blausen

COSTUME JEWELRY

The earliest costume jewelry was simply an imitation of precious jewelry and had little intrinsic value or original style of its own. However, once the French couturiers put their names to costume jewelry it became desirable, acceptable, and expensive. In the early 1910s, couturier Paul Poiret became a proponent of costume jewelry, accessorizing his models with necklaces of silk tassels and semiprecious stones designed by the artist Iribe.

Coco Chanel, Jean Patou, Drécoll, and Premet were also among the first famous couturiers to create costume jewelry along with clothing, which propelled its acceptance. By 1925, the Marshall Field's department store catalog described costume jewelry in positive terms, announcing, "The imitation is no longer a disgrace."

The most ubiquitous jewelry imitation in the 1920s was a pearl necklace. Strands of pearls or colored beads neatly circled the neck or swung to waist, hip, even kneelength, made to move with fast-paced dances like the Charleston. At the end of the period when the little black dress became a daytime standard, shorter strands of light-colored beads and pearls continued as the accessories of choice. Rhinestone jewelry also blazed into prominence, as it was the perfect foil for two fashion innovations: suntans and white evening gowns.

Beginning in the 1920s and continuing throughout the 1930s, fashion and jewelry shared a multitude of influences including Art Deco, the Far East, North Africa, and India. Egyptian motifs were inspired by the discovery of Tutankhamen's tomb in 1922. The Colonial Exhibition in Paris in 1931 and the New York World's Fair in 1939 expanded the vocabulary of foreign influences, and rough, raw, "barbaric" materials (real and imitation), including ivory (and faux versions), bone, amber, wood, and even cork, were used for over-scale jewelry. Chanel's signature necklace in 1939 was a massive East Indian–inspired bib of faux pearls, uncut emeralds, ruby beads, and dangling metal pieces with a cord tie.

In the mid-1930s, fashion's palette turned Technicolor, as plastic was produced in bright colors for the first time and metal jewelry was hand-enameled to add color. Toy-like novelty accessories (both costume and precious jewelry) were wildly popular, inspired by the Surrealists, couturier Elsa Schiaparelli, and Walt Disney's cartoons. The queen of whimsy, Schiaparelli put metal insects and caterpillars on necklaces, and her brooches ranged from miniature musical instruments, roller skates, harlequins, blackamoors, and ostriches. Influenced by the lively antics of cartoons, jewelry also had movable parts: Brooches and necklaces were adorned with "trembler" flowers, hanging plastic fruit, or charms. Clips could be deconstructed into separate pieces. This silly jewelry lightened up the lapels of the fashionable severe and sober, fitted suits.

At the same time, the romantic rococo and Victorian styles flourished, lingering into the 1940s. Rococo jewelry, associated with the Empress Eugenie, was typically frivolous bow-knots, swags and ribbon curves, sparingly ornamented with large, faux-semiprecious cut stones. It was usually plated with real gold (pink, white, yellow) or sterling silver. Victorian styles were copied directly from the originals: lockets, cameos, chokers, even hat pins. Black plastic was the substitute for nineteenth-century jet.

During World War II, imports from Europe were cut off, and many jewelry materials were also restricted. Desperate costume jewelers bought beaded sweaters, evening dresses, and even stage costumes, and harvested their beads, rhinestones, and pearls. They also fashioned jewelry from humble materials that were readily available during wartime: pumpkin seeds, nuts, shells, olive pits, clay, leather, felt, yarn, and even upholstery fabrics. Women wore hand-carved wooden brooches, necklaces of multicolored painted shells, cork, and bits of driftwood. There was little difference between quirky, childish, commercially made jewelry and what the women made themselves following do-it-yourself instructions published in magazines.

Patriotic motifs flourished during wartime, ranging from red, white, and blue to all-American motifs related to California, Hawaii, Native American Indians, and cowboys. Costume jewelry also took on a militaristic theme, and miniature model tanks, airplanes, battleships, jeeps, soldiers, and even hand grenades were made up in metal or wood and worn as brooches, necklaces, and earrings. In the summer of 1940, "V" for victory was a popular design. As Mexico was America's wartime ally, jewelry imported from that country and its imitations was highly fashionable. Two notable Mexican artisans who worked in silver, Rebajes and Spratling, had their sophisticated jewelry featured at top department stores across the country. Patriotic jewelry completely vanished during peacetime.

Postwar fashion succumbed to couturier Christian Dior's highly structured New Look, followed by a series of equally severe styles: the chemise, sheathe, trapeze, and sack dress. The transformation was radical. Clothing concealed most of a woman's body, and only chokers, earrings, bracelets (notably charm bracelets), and brooches were visible. Dresses and suits in heavy, rough-textured fabrics were weighty enough to support the hunky, oversized circles, ovals, snowflake, or starburst-shaped brooches (associated with the atomic bomb), typically three-dimensional. Rhinestones were standard, produced in a rainbow of colors including white, black, pink, blue, yellow, and iridescent, which was an innovation.

Tailored jewelry was the most conservative accessory in the 1950s. Neat and small scale, it was made up in gold or silver metal with little ornamentation. Although clothing concealed their figures, women wore their hair upswept, in a ponytail, or cropped gamine short, to show off hoop, button, and neat pearl earrings. Later in the decade, metal jewelry was thicker, its surface scored, chiseled, or deeply etched, a treatment that lingered into the 1960s.

The distinction between accessories for day and night blurred as casual Italian sportswear became popular. For example, in 1959 actress Elizabeth Taylor was featured in *Life* magazine wearing Dior's black jet choker with a low-cut black sweater. Entertaining at home also created another new fashion category. Theatrical, over-sized chandelier and girandole earrings complemented lounging pajamas, caftans, and floor-length skirts, which remained stylish hostess garb into the 1960s.

Chanel plundered the Renaissance for jewelry inspiration. With her signature suits, in 1957 she showed pendants (notably the Maltese cross), brooches, and chain sautoirs in heavy gold set with baroque pearls, lumpy glass rubies, and emeralds. This style still continues to be identified with Chanel today.

In the 1960s, bold, pop-art graphic "flower power" motifs were fashion favorites. The ubiquitous daisy was produced in every material from plastic to enameled metal, and in a palette of neon bright colors. Daisies were linked into belts, pinned on hats and dresses, and suspended from chains around the neck. Even Chanel and Dior produced flower jewelry, although their brooches, necklaces, and earrings were petaled with fragile poured glass.

Hippies and the counterculture rejected this sophistication in favor of handmade and ethnic jewelry in humble materials: clay and glass beads, yarn, temple bells, papier-mâché, macramé, and feathers. Both men and women pierced their ears, crafted their own headbands, ornamented their clothing with beads and embroidery, strung love beads, or hung a peace sign, ankh, or zodiac symbol on a strip of rawhide around their necks. Singer Janis Joplin typically performed while weighed down with a massive assortment of new and vintage necklaces and bracelets.

Vogue and *Harper's Bazaar* also cultivated this theatrical style. Diana Vreeland, editor-in-chief of *Vogue*, commissioned wildly dramatic, oversized jewelry specifically for the magazine. Usually one of a kind, tenuously held together with wire, thread, and glue, these pieces were too fragile to be worn outside the photo studio. There were breastplates of rhinestones or tiny mirrors, golf-ball-size pearl rings, shoulder-sweeping feather earrings, wrist and armloads of painted papier-mâché bracelets.

Technology also contributed to this fantastical mode. In 1965, plastic pearls were produced for the first time in lightweight, gigantic sizes. They were strung together into multistrand necklaces, bibs, helmets, and even dresses.

Style-wise, costume jewelry was a match for fine jewelry. The so-called beautiful people gleefully mixed costume jeweler Kenneth Jay Lane's $30 rhinestone and enamel panther bracelets (inspired by the Duchess of Windsor's original Cartier models) with their real ones. Lane was well known for his weighty pendant necklaces, shoulder-length chandelier earrings set with gaudy, multicolored fake stones, and enormous cocktail rings. His clients ranged from Babe Paley to Greta Garbo and the Velvet Underground.

Chanel continued to produce Renaissance-style jewelry, notably Maltese crosses and cuff bracelets embellished with large stones, which morphed into a more exaggerated version. Diana Vreeland chose this style as her signature, sporting a pair of bejeweled enamel cuffs reportedly designed by Fulco di Verdura.

At the end of the 1960s and into the 1970s, "space age" style was an alternative to this ornate jewelry. Coolly modern, geometric, it was made up in industrial materials such as transparent plastic and metal hardware. This hard-edged jewelry was a match for clothing ornamented with oversized buckles, zippers, grommets, and nail heads.

Around the same time, punk ruled the streets. The devotees of this style favored leather jackets and jeans that were as aggressive and unisex as their accessories: dog collars and leather armbands bristling with nail heads and spikes, thick chains worn as chokers and around waists. The most notorious punk ornamentation was also the simplest: a safety pin stuck through an ear, nose, lip, or cheek.

Two designers, Elsa Peretti and Robert Lee Morris, heavily influenced costume jewelry during this period. Peretti began designing for Tiffany in 1974, and costume jewelers immediately copied her small-scale, streamlined "lima bean" and "teardrop" pendants, and "diamonds by the yard" of cut stones strung on slender chains.

In New York City, Robert Lee Morris set up his own boutique, Artwear, as a showcase for his handmade gold-bead necklaces, gladiator-size cuffs, metal breastplates, and hefty belt buckles. Fashion designer Donna Karan accessorized her line with Morris's bold and simple creations for several seasons.

In the 1980s, entertainers Cyndi Lauper and Madonna were the female forces that drove style through the new media of music videos, and both mixed lingerie with vintage clothing, and vintage jewelry with cheap new baubles. Madonna wore armloads of rubber bracelets with religious-cross pendants and rosaries. Hip hop and rap music stars sported jewelry in heavy gold or gold-plated look-alikes: nameplate pendants, knuckle rings, ID bracelets. A gold-covered front tooth was a more permanent and extreme ornament.

As the simplified styles of designers Giorgio Armani and Calvin Klein became popular, jewelry gradually shrank in scale until it disappeared. As minimalism ruled fashion, the jewelry business was abysmal. However, costume jewelry came back to glitzy glory in the early 1990s, propelled by the whimsical accessories of Christian Lacroix and Karl Lagerfeld at Chanel. Lagerfeld successfully revived and restyled many of Chanel's signatures, including multistrand pearl necklaces, and Renaissance-style jewelry. He used the "CC" logo as decoration on everything from earrings to pocketbooks.

Entertainers and movie stars steered fashion in 2000, and they wore the real thing, not costume jewelry. Pop music figures Jennifer Lopez and Lil' Kim flashed enormous precious stones on their fingers. Impresario Sean Combs (a.k.a Puff Daddy, P. Diddy) flaunted enormous diamond-stud earrings and monster diamond rings. A long line of movie stars, including Nicole Kidman and Charlize Theron, borrowed jewelry, usually fine antique pieces, from established jewelers such as Harry Winston and Fred Leighton. It was a sign of the times when Chanel launched a line of precious jewelry, and Prada installed precious jewelry from Fred Leighton in their Soho store. Once again, the cycle had turned, and costume jewelry imitated precious jewelry, or "bling bling" as the blinding real thing was called in 2003.

See also Bracelets; Brooches and Pins; Earrings; Jewelry; Necklaces and Pendants.

Bibliography

Becker, Vivienne. *Fabulous Fakes: The History of Fantasy and Fashion Jewellery*. London: Grafton, 1988.

Davidov, Corinne. *The Bakelite Jewelry Book*. New York: Abbeville Press, 1988.

Mulvah, Jane. *Costume Jewelry in Vogue*. London: Thames and Hudson, Inc., 1988.

Nadelhoffer, Hans. *Cartier Jewelers Extraordinary*. New York: Harry N. Abrams, 1984.

Shields, Jody. *All That Glitters: The Glory of Costume Jewelry*. New York: Rizzoli, 1987

Jody Shields

COURRÈGES, ANDRÉ

André Courrèges (1923–) was born in Pau, in the Basque part of France. He studied engineering before pursuing a career in fashion. Courrèges worked first under the illustrious couturier Cristóbal Balenciaga from 1950 until 1961, when he left to open his own house. Balenciaga, whose clients were primarily mature and conservative women of wealth, was paradoxically often years ahead of his time. He produced sculptured garments that served as architecture for the woman's body, and it was from Balenciaga that Courrèges learned a highly disciplined yet innovative approach to design.

Early Career

The London "youthquake" of the early 1960s produced experiments in fashion that glorified young people and sent shock waves all the way to Paris, the capital of haute couture. André Courrèges's success was based on his ability to revitalize and preserve high fashion by injecting elements of the youthquake into haute couture. Along with London-based Mary Quant, Courrèges was a leading figure in the introduction of the miniskirt—the article of clothing most closely associated with youthfulness in its disavowal of traditional social codes and the rules of fashion. The miniskirt offered minimal coverage of the lower body, the better to flaunt the young legs that became so visible in the 1960s. Gone were the days of ladylike propriety, now banished by the emphasis on youth.

Although opinion is divided as to who actually "invented" the miniskirt, Quant or Courrèges, it is generally accepted that Mary Quant was first, although only after "the girls on the street." Courrèges initially showed his miniskirts in the early 1960s, followed by futuristinspired pantsuits, coats, hats, and his trademark white kid boots. *British Vogue* declared 1964 "the year of Courrèges" (Howell, p. 284). The spring–summer collection of 1964 represented a couture version of youth-oriented styles with the invention of the "moon girl" look; the collection ultimately secured for Courrèges the title the designer of the Space Age.

Courrèges's Space Age Design

Courrèges's 1964 Space Age collection unveiled, among other pieces, architecturally-sculpted, double-breasted coats with contrasting trim, well-tailored, sleeveless or short-sleeved minidresses with dropped waistlines and detailed welt seaming, and tunics worn with hipster pants. Vivid shades of pink, orange, green, and navy complemented the designer's bold repeated use of white and silver. Accessories for each ensemble included oversized, white, tennis-ball sunglasses or goggles with narrow eye slits, gloves, helmet-shaped hats and other hats recalling baby bonnets, and square-toed midcalf boots made of soft, white kid leather. Perhaps his most famous contribution to fashion after the miniskirt itself was the "Courrèges boot," originally designed in 1963. The entire 1964 spring collection was a phenomenal success and influenced other designers such as Pierre Cardin and Paco Rabanne to create their own versions of futuristic fashion. It also led ready-to-wear manufacturers, hoping to rake in huge profits, to copy and mass-produce similar designs.

Courrèges's visionary approach to fashion made use of clean geometrical lines and rejected superfluous material. He employed a minimal amount of decorative ornamentation; when he used it at all, it was most often his trademark daisy motif, chosen for its symbolic association with youth. The couturier's love of sharp lines and the angular crispness of his forms reflected his background in engineering. Courrèges's clothing not only emphasized technologically advanced synthetic materials that were evocative of the times, but also pushed fashion further into the future by situating it within modern life. This intellectual component, typical of Parisian design, carried over into Courrèges's work at his studio on the avenue Kléber, where he dressed luminaries from the duchess of Windsor to Jacqueline Kennedy, Lee Radzi-will, and Jane Holzer. The "white" salon, as the studio was known, personified the designer's ideals of functionality and practicality with its modern minimalist decor. André Courrèges created modern clothes for modern women living in modern times.

Courrèges's first official couture collection made its debut in 1965; two years later Prototype, the made-to-order custom line, was introduced. The introduction of luxury prêt-à-porter with Couture Future at the end of the decade marked Courrèges's transition into the 1970s. The new decade saw the establishment of the designer's first fragrance, Empreinte, in 1970 along with a men's ready-to-wear line in 1973. The need to reach a mass-market audience brought with it the lower-priced Hyperbole line in the early 1980s, and the desire to solidify a world-renowned brand name through profitable licensing arrangements led to the sale of the company in 1985 to the Japanese firm Itokin.

Courrèges's Legacy

Along with his contemporaries Paco Rabanne and Pierre Cardin, André Courrèges helped to create an unmistakable style that defined an era. His lasting impact on fashion design was his astute recognition of the revolution launched by the younger generation. The explosion of the "youthquake" onto the scene fundamentally altered the direction of fashion in the 1960s. Fashion now not only celebrated the present but also looked forward to the future. The future was conceivably Courrèges's greatest muse, and the infinite possibilities of tomorrow stimulated his experiments with form.

The mod revival spearheaded in the early 1990s by Miuccia Prada recalled the design principles and iconic looks pioneered by Courrèges three decades earlier. From white, A-line minishift dresses to nylon microfiber accessories, Prada's continual search for innovation is influenced by Courrèges's designs from the 1960s. Furthermore, the fall 2003 collections represented a direct backward glance at youthquake fashion. Designs that evoked the Space Age appeared on catwalks from New York to Paris. White and metallic "lunar" shades with occasional splashes of bright color dominated the palette. Geometrical lines were everywhere. The miniskirt reappeared in full force at Chanel, Marc Jacobs, and Donna Karan, while mid-calf leather boots accessorized mod ensembles at Moschino and Tommy Hilfiger. The focus on youth, the contemporary use of architecturally shaped minimalist designs in bold contrasting colors, and the deliberate application of detailing demonstrates the lasting impact of 1960s fashion. Henceforth, every retro mod fashion will forever be traced back to the work of André Courrèges.

See also Balenciaga, Cristóbal; Cardin, Pierre; High-Tech Fashion; Miniskirt; Prada; Quant, Mary; Rabanne, Paco; Space Age Styles; Techno-Textiles; Youthquake Fashions.

Bibliography

"Balenciaga's Secret." *Women's Wear Daily*, 23 April 1961.

Braddock, Sarah E., and Marie O'Mahony. *Techno Textiles: Revolutionary Fabrics for Fashion and Design*. New York: Thames and Hudson, Inc., 1998.

"Eyeview." *Vogue* (October 1964): 87–89.

Giraud, Françoise. "After Courrèges, What Future for the Haute Couture?" *New York Times Magazine* (12 September 1965): 50–51.

Howell, Georgina. *In Vogue: Six Decades of Fashion*. London: Allen Lane, 1975.

Koski, Lorna. "Courrèges: 60s Encore." *Women's Wear Daily* (26 October 1984).

McDowell, Colin. *Fashion Today*. London: Phaidon Press Ltd., 2000.

Nonkin, Lesly. "Courrèges: Shops Stay in Touch with Customer." *Women's Wear Daily* (12 September 1979).

Sheppard, Eugenia. "Courrèges Back in Action." *World Journal Tribune* (19 March 1967): 8–11.

Steele, Valerie. *Fifty Years of Fashion: New Look to Now*. New Haven, Conn.: Yale University Press, 1997.

Jennifer Park

COURT DRESS

In the increasingly informal society of the early 2000s, in which many social barriers have broken down, it is arresting to read of the rigid code of manners that once determined who was, and who was not, eligible to be received at court, and who was, or was not, therefore part of "Good Society." In Europe, by the seventeenth century, wearing the correct dress on this occasion was quite as important as having the right background.

Within a royal household, officers were appointed to supervise aspects of royal life. The officer, often called a lord chamberlain, who had charge of public and ceremonial events, would usually oversee the regulation of dress and matters of etiquette. By the nineteenth century, as the categories of people eligible for court presentation increased, and the styles of court dress became ever more various and complex, all earlier printed dress instructions were drawn together and published as formal regulations. In Great Britain, "Dress Worn at Court," first published in 1882, was updated and reissued at about five-yearly intervals until 1937. Subsequently, hand-lists have been provided to specific individuals within the Royal Household, Foreign Office, Parliament, and Law Courts where the wearing of court dress may survive.

Until the late eighteenth century, in many European countries, many offices and titles remained as the personal gift of the monarch and members of his family. Both politicians and merchants found it essential to demonstrate to potential supporters that they enjoyed the favor of the court, to see their projects succeed. Even as the political importance of the court began to wane, there was always social advantage to be gained and special efforts continued to be made within the royal household to regulate the numbers and social standing of those attending. It was necessary for any new aspiring attendee to locate someone who had already been presented, to serve as his or her sponsor. In seventeenth-century France, a set of rules called "les honneurs de la cour" were drawn up. A French lady craving admittance had to prove a title of nobility extending back to 1400. Since the eighteenth century, there is evidence that this system could be abused: court officials could be bribed to gain admittance, the services of a sponsor could be bought, and sometimes the monarch himself would override the rules allowing a person of humble birth to attend as "une faveur de choix."

The Spanish court was the earliest to actively promote a distinctive court dress from the sixteenth century. All courtiers, state officials, and those attending court had to wear a doublet and close-fitting knee breeches, made of silk or wool in a somber color, worn with the stiff "gorilla" collar of white linen. Eventually, the practice was adopted throughout the Spanish Empire, in Austria, and certain Catholic German states.

By the mid-seventeenth century, Louis XIV was concerned with promoting himself, the prestige of the French court, French fashion, and culture. In 1661 he devised a system whereby fifty of his closest friends and supporters were allocated by special warrant a specific court dress. It was composed of a blue coat called a "justaucorps a brevet," lined with red and trimmed with gold and silver galloon (braided trimming with scalloped edges), to a degree not allowed within earlier sumptuary legislation. The outfit was completed with a waistcoat, knee breeches, red-heeled shoes, and a sword. When the dauphin reached his majority, a brown coat similarly embellished was devised as the regulation dress for his household.

In about 1670, Louis XIV, perhaps with his brother, Philippe, duc d'Orleans and his wife, established the "grand habit" as a court dress for women. This dress had a stiff-boned bodice with a low, round neckline and cap sleeves trimmed with tiers of ruffles called "engageantes." The skirt was cut full, and pulled back to reveal the petticoat worn beneath. This was often richly decorated. For their first presentation to the French king the "grand habit" had to be black. Subsequently, colored dresses could be worn. By about 1730 the petticoat was worn supported on large side hoops. A train replaced the skirt.

French court dress was adopted with small variations as court dress throughout Europe. By 1700 it had even become the regulation dress at the Spanish court for all but the most formal occasions.

In Great Britain the "grand habit" or "stiff bodied gown" was worn by members of the royal family and their immediate circle for royal weddings and coronations. However, by about 1700, the mantua was the customary dress worn by ladies attending court. It had an unboned bodice and full skirt. The neckline was cut square, and the bodice was closed in front with a separate stomacher. The elbow-length sleeves were finished with tiers of ruffles. The skirt was lifted back to reveal a petticoat worn beneath and by about 1750 served as little more than a train. By 1730 the petticoat was supported with large side hoops.

Ladies attending court in 1750 were generally wearing ostrich feathers as a hair ornament, and in 1762 Horace Walpole notes that they were considered "de rigueur." Lace lappets had also emerged as the enduring trimming.

Men's court dress in Great Britain was also simpler than its French counterpart, comprising a coat, waistcoat, and knee breeches, often made of fine silks and velvet, and frequently lavishly embellished with embroidery.

The "grand habit" saw its demise in 1789 with the French Revolution. However, by 1804 a new official dress had been devised by Jean-Baptiste Isabey for French government officials, as well as Napoleon, his family, and inner circle. For ladies a court train alone was retained, worn over fashionable evening dress.

The second half of the eighteenth century had seen many European courts beginning to devise special uniform liveries to be worn by members of the royal family and royal circle. In France, Louis XV established a green and gold costume as "uniforme des petits chateaux." In 1734 Frederick, Prince of Wales in Great Britain, had devised a blue and buff uniform. His son George III in 1778 was responsible for the introduction of the Windsor uniform with its blue coat and distinctive red facings. It was also in 1778 that Gustavus III of Sweden put together a comprehensive order of court uniforms not only for his family and household, but also encompassing government officials, military officers, legal officials, and even university staff and students. They were of a consciously archaic style having its origin in seventeenth-century fashion, a period associated with Swedish greatness. Small variations in materials and ornament served to differentiate classes of officials. A court dress was also devised for Swedish ladies on similar lines. It was generally black and had a low round neckline trimmed with lace, and distinctive white puffed sleeves trimmed with a lattice of black ribbon.

Isabey's new system of official dress in France included uniforms for almost every office. By 1815 a similar program had been devised in Great Britain, the uniforms based on a pattern used by the French Army. This had a blue coat, embroidered with gold, worn with white knee breeches, silk stockings, flat pumps, a "chapeau bras" and a court sword. As the century progressed, more uniforms were added as new classes of officials were drawn into the system. Typically a uniform would be fashionable at the date of its introduction, but was rarely updated as the years passed. The embroidery would include motifs associated with the nation concerned or those, such as laurel or oak, traditionally associated with valor and steadfastness.

In early nineteenth-century Britain, the cloth court dress, worn by men for whom no uniform was prescribed, maintains the link with eighteenth-century custom. This was replaced in 1869 by "Velvet Court Dress" cut on very similar lines. While a more fashionable option was devised in the 1890s, this style of dress may still be seen worn in the early 2000s.

The French Revolution had comparatively little impact on women's court dress in Great Britain. The mantua continued to be worn, supported with an immense court hoop until 1820 when George IV suggested it should be abandoned. After this date court trains were worn over fashionable evening dress, with ostrich feather headdresses and lace lappets. By 1867 lace lappets were proving increasingly difficult to obtain, and the lord chamberlain permitted the wearing of two silk net streamers instead. In 1912, the lord chamberlain established that the streamers should be no more than forty-five inches long. The great profusion of ostrich feathers included in court headdresses of the early nineteenth century had been reduced to two or three by mid century. In the dress regulations published in 1912, it is noted that there should be three feathers worn after the manner of the Prince of Wales's crest toward the left side of the head. In 1922 the lord chamberlain ordained that the court train was restricted to eighteen inches from the heels of the wearer. The color of ladies' court dress was not prescribed, but it became the convention that the dresses were of a pale hue, particularly for those being presented to the monarch for the first time. Special permission had to be sought to wear black court dress, should the lady being presented be in mourning.

The nineteenth century saw the development in many nations of a distinctive court dress. Some countries such as Russia and Greece followed the Swedish lead and introduced elements of traditional dress into their design. Other countries, as diverse as Venezuela, Norway, and Japan, selected a system of uniforms based on European military patterns. Tailors, in London, Berlin, and Rome in particular, provided a comprehensive service designing as well as manufacturing the garments.

Many of the European courts, where the wearing of court dress had been so enthusiastically promoted, were swept away during World War I. The British court proved more resilient, and in London court dress continued to be worn until the outbreak of World War II in 1939. But Britain emerged from this conflict very changed. The social mores that had underpinned the court system had broken down. Even though court presentation continued until 1958, a special dress was not prescribed.

Court dress is rarely worn in the early 2000s. In most European countries a few particular officials working in the foreign office, parliament, and the law courts may be required to wear it on occasion. In Sweden, Denmark, and Norway since 1988 the wearing of a court dress within the royal family and its immediate circle has been reintroduced for the grandest ceremonial occasions. The new Swedish pattern is based in the eighteenth-century Swedish tradition. The styles in Norway and Denmark are modern creations.

See also Royal and Aristocratic Dress.

Bibliography

Arch, Nigel, and Marschner, Joanna. *Splendour at Court: Dressing for Royal Occasions since 1700.* London: Unwin Hyman, 1987.

Delpierre, Madeleine. *Uniformes civiles ceremonial circonstances.* Paris: Ville de Paris, Musee de la Mode et du Costume, 1982.

de Marly, Diana. *Louis XIV and Versailles.* London: B. T. Bats-ford, Ltd.; New York: Holmes and Meier, 1987.

Mansfield, Alan. *Ceremonial Costume.* London: Adam and Charles Black, 1980.

Rangstrom, Lena, ed. *Hovets Drakter.* Stockholm: Livrust-kammaren/Bra Bocker/Wiken, 1994.

Ribiero, Aileen. *Fashion in the French Revolution.* London: B. T. Batsford, Ltd.; New York: Holmes and Meier, 1988.

——. *Dress in Eighteenth Century Europe 1715–1789.* New Haven, Conn.: Yale University Press, 2002.

Joanna Marschner

CROSS-DRESSING

Cross-dressing occurs for religious reasons, for burlesque, disguise, status gain, even for sexual excitement. It is as old as clothing itself. Mythology and history are full of cross-dressing incidents, mainly of men dressing or acting as women. Women cross-dressing and living as men began to appear in the early Christian Church where there are a number of women saints who were found to be women only upon their death. In fact, women living as men seemed to have been more successful at it in the past three centuries than men living as women, perhaps because their motivations were different. Many of them did so to overcome the barriers that women had to face in terms of economic opportunities and independence in the past.

Anthropologists, impressed by the variety of cultures where cross-dressing and gender change have been found, developed the term "supernumerary gender" to describe individuals who adopt the role and many of the customs of the opposite sex. In American Indian culture, for example, men who took on the roles of women were called berdaches. Berdaches took over special ceremonial rites and did some of the work attributed to women, mixing together much of the behavior, dress, and social roles of women with those of men. Often one can gain status by changing gender identification. Among one group of Blackfeet Indians, there are women known as "manly hearts," who have the character traits associated with men and often adopt the male role and clothing. Some groups such as the Navajo identify three, not two, sexes and designate the nonconformist to the third sex. Several identify more than three genders.

Male cross-dressing is part of religious worship in different Hindu sects. Sakti worshipers consider

Hindu eunuchs. Members of the Sakhībhāava cult emulate women, often to the extent of being castrated, due to their belief that the god Krishnu is the only true male being in the world. © KARAN KAPOOR/CORBIS. REPRODUCED BY PERMISSION.

the godhead be essentially feminine, and men present themselves in women's costumes. In one Hindu cult, the Sakhībhāva, which holds that the god Krishna is the only true male while every other creature in the world was female, male followers dress like women and affect the behavior, movements, and habits of women, including imitating having a menstrual period. Many of them also emasculate themselves, and play the part of women during sexual inter-course, allowing themselves to be penetrated as an act of devotion. The technical term for these men is *hijra* (eunuch or transvestite). Some observers have called them homosexuals, although it is probably better to regard the role as asexual.

Such androgynous beliefs are not confined to Hinduism but exist in sects of other religions as well. In Islamic Oman, the Xanith are regarded by Oman society as neither male nor female but having the characteristics of both. Though they perform women's tasks, are classed as women, and are judged for beauty by women's standards, technically they do not cross-dress. Instead, they feminize their male costume in every way possible. A Xanith, however, can change her or his status in society by marrying and demonstrating his ability to penetrate a woman.

Because Islam is such a sex-segregated society, and public appearances by women limited, many Islamic areas have tolerated and institutionalized female impersonators. In Egypt one groups is called *khāal* ("dancers"). They perform at weddings and other ceremonial occasions, and though technically their costume is not quite like that of women, they do all they can to appear as women, including plucking out hairs on their face.

Though women's roles were not quite so restricted in the West, there were still strong prohibitions. They could not appear on the stage, for example, and women's roles were taken by female impersonators until the seventeenth century. This was also true in Japan, and in other countries as well, including ancient Greece.

The earliest recorded historical woman to dress and act like a man was Hatshepsut, an Egyptian from about the fifteenth century B.C.E. She is even portrayed in statues and carvings wearing a symbolic royal beard. After her death there was an attempt to obliterate her memory, but her record managed to survive. History, however, is less kind to male rulers who cross-dressed. A good example of this is the Assyrian king Sardanapulus (also known as Ashurbanipal) in the fifth century B.C.E., who is said to have spent much of his time in his palace dressed in women's clothing and surrounded by his concubines. When news of this behavior became

widely known, some of his key nobles revolted. Although his cross-dressing was looked down upon because it showed feminine weakness, he fought long and bravely for two years, and before facing defeat, he committed suicide.

Greek literature is full of cross-dressing in both mythological tales and actual events. Greek writers reported that among the Scythians there were groups of individuals known as *Enarées*, who had been cursed with the feminine disease by the god Aphrodite for raiding her temple. Another Greek writer claimed that their cross-dressing was brought on by a temporary impotency caused by spending so much of their time on horseback. Cross-dressing was also part of religious rituals in Greece itself, usually as part of an initiation ceremony emphasizing the essential opposition between the male essence and the female one. Young men at such ceremonies appeared initially in women's clothing and after being initiated into manhood, tossed them aside. Cross-dressing figured prominently in the religious ceremonies associated with the god Dionysus, who according to some legends had been reared as a girl. Other gods and goddesses also required their worshipers to cross-dress at least some of the time. The ubiquity of such festivals might well indicate that the Greek who drew strict lines between sex roles and assigned a restricted role to women, needed periods during which the barriers were removed.

In Sparta, where marriage for men was delayed until they were thirty, men had to live in segregated barracks even after they were married. When they did marry, the young bride (probably a 14-year-old) was dressed in male clothing so that her husband could sneak away and come secretly to her in the night. She was not able to resume her traditional clothing until she had become pregnant, a true sign of womanhood.

Clearly temporary assumption of opposite gender by men was acceptable if the aim was laudable or if the alternatives to the impersonation were considered more socially undesirable than the disguise itself. Hymenaeus, a youth from Argive, disguised himself as a girl to follow the young Athenian maid he loved. Solon is said to have defeated the Megarians by disguising some of his troops as women to infiltrate the enemy forces. Achilles, in order to be protected from potential enemies, was said to have lived the early part of his life as a girl and was finally exposed by Odysseus. The legends are bountiful.

Latin literature, particularly of the imperial period, has a number of stories of cross-dressers. Julius Caesar found a man dressed as a woman at religious ceremonies held in his house who was there to arrange an assignation. The Emperor Nero cross-dressed, and so did the Emperor Elagabalus, who was proclaimed emperor as a fourteen-year-old boy in 218. In both of these cases, however, their cross-dressing was regarded as an indicator of their flawed character.

Christianity was hostile to cross-dressing, as was Judaism from which it derived. But as indicated above, a number of female cross-dressers are known, many of whom became saints. When their true sex was discovered, usually at their death, they were praised for their faithfulness and saintliness, and their ability to rise above female frailties. There were limits, however, on what was acceptable.

A recently discovered Medieval Romance, *Le Roman de Silence*, tells the story of a girl raised as boy in order to preserve the inheritance of her parents. Silence is told by her parents in her early teens that she is really a female; but, though torn by her "feminine desires," she maintains the male role until she is permitted to resume the woman's role by the king. There are other stories as well, but the easiest to document are the male actors who played feminine roles on the stage until they became too old to do so, up to the middle of the seventeenth century. Occasionally a legal case reports a cross-dresser, as did a London city record of a male prostitute who plied his trade as a woman. Even the woman's role in many operas was sung by castrati, a castrated male, until the nineteenth century.

Cross-dressing and impersonation was generally easier for a female to do than a male simply because of the beard problem. This meant that on the stage it was adolescents or young men who usually played the feminine role. Females, for their part, could pass as young men wearing loose clothing until fairly late in their life, and then with a false beard continue to do so. Some young enterprising Dutch girls served as seamen on ships bound for Indonesia, where they settled down. Many women fought as men in most wars and continued to do so until the twentieth century, when pre-induction physicals were established in the American and other armies.

Even the most dedicated transvestite, the Abbé de Choisy (1644–1724), whose memoirs of his life as a woman survive, more or less abandoned his public attempts to pass as a woman as he aged. He continued to cross-dress when the opportunity presented itself, but his identity was no longer a secret. To keep himself entertained he wrote fictional accounts of cross-dressing.

It was in eighteenth-century London where cross-dressing organizations appeared. A number of men's-only clubs were established and some of them became quite notorious. One group, known as the Mohocks, went out at nights regularly seeking lower-class women and girls whom they stood on their heads so that their skirts would fall down, exposing their bare bottoms. Not all clubs of this period, however, were quite so boisterous. One of the more subversive of the male tradition was the Molly club, whose members met in women's clothes to drink and party; Edward Ward, who in 1709 wrote *The Secret History of Clubs*, described their meeting where they dressed as women:

> They adopt all the small vanities natural to the feminine sex to such an extent that they try to speak, walk, chatter, shriek and scold as women do, aping them as well in other aspects. . . . As soon as they arrive, they begin to behave exactly as women do, carrying on light gossip, as is the custom of a merry company of real women. (p. 209)

Whether this club was an organization of homosexuals is not clear, but several historians believe that this was part of an attempt to establish a distinct gay identity.

Certainly there was a growing curiosity about cross-dressing and impersonation in public in both England and France in the eighteenth century. The most notorious cross-dresser was Charles d'Eon, known as the Chevalier d'Eon, who was a member of the personal secret service of the French King Louis XV. D'Eon apparently used his ability to pass as a woman to carry out his spying tasks, and later as he became involved in a struggle with the French government under King Louis XVI, he received a pardon from the King, providing he dressed as a woman that the king believed him to be and lived in exile. When gambling in England over his sex reached a peak, he apparently was involved in a bribery scheme in which two English physicians testified he was a woman, whereby his friends collected some money. For a time he became a sensation in Paris and in London, burlesquing the gestures and mannerisms of women, and when he ran into financial difficulties in England he supported himself by his expertise with the sword. He gave exhibitions and lessons while dressed in proper women's attire. He died in poverty in 1810; as his body was being prepared for burial, he was found to be a male. He might be called the first transvestite to become a media event.

It was not until the last part of the nineteenth century that cross-dressers appeared in ever-increasing numbers. That period in history is when distinctions between male and female domains were strongly entrenched in the upper and middle classes. It was also when there was an increasing emphasis on sports and manliness in these circles. Carried to an extreme, the demands of masculinity could turn to a kind of bullying, as it often did in the English public schools. In America, masculinity, at its worst, was a kind of anti-intellectualism in which music, literature, and all the "finer" things were feminine, and those boys who were interested or excelled in those pursuits were defined by the dominant male group as feminine. Terms such as *queer, fag, fairy,* or even *girlish* were applied to boys who outwardly seemed to express an interest in anything assigned to the women's sphere. This continued on until the rise of the new wave of feminism in the 1960s. In my own studies of cross-dressers carried out in the 1980s, I found that the male cross-dressers who identified themselves as heterosexual had adopted an almost dichotomized personality in their youth. They were well adjusted outwardly to the male world, but in order to express what they regarded as the feminine side of themselves, they felt a need to cross dress. In this way they could express, even temporarily, some of the feminine qualities they felt they had but then safely return to the masculine identity.

The separate-sphere concept tended to make women less understandable and more mysterious to men; the stricter the separation, the more defined the spheres, the more mysterious women were. One result of this was the fetishization of women's apparel. Women spent a good part of their time trying to better understand men's needs as mothers, caregivers, and teachers, but men, rather than attempting to understand women, objectified and eroticized objects identified with the female, such as under-clothes or even outer clothing. In some ways clothing seemed to be the ultimate of being female.

At the same time female clothing was eroticized. The corset is a good example since it was not sold as a waist cincher or form maker but as a preserver of feminine virtue. Corsets also helped rearrange the female figure, emphasizing a narrow waist and resultant hourglass figure that gave prominence to the bust and buttocks. One of the more interesting results of this was the growth of what might be called "corset literature," aimed at a male audience. In this fictional literature adolescent boys are put into corsets to form their

figures and to feminize them. In the late nineteenth and first part of the twentieth century, such literature was widespread. Eroticization of clothing was undoubtedly influenced by the fact that so many of the items of women's apparel were designed to emphasize or bring attention to certain aspects of the female figure, from bras to nylon stockings to high heels. High heels, for example, force the wearer to lean backward, thereby accentuating the buttocks and the breasts. Heels also force women to walk with smaller steps emphasizing their supposed helplessness. It was almost as if clothing made the woman. Men wearing it would often get an orgasm.

A number of plays were written in the last part of the century that included plots in which men had to get into women's clothes. Oscar Wilde's *The Importance of Being Earnest* is just one example. There were so many impersonator parts that some men made a career of playing them, including Ernest Boulton and Frederick William Park. They also dressed as women while offstage and were arrested for soliciting men.

Cross-dressing, in fact, had a significant role in the growing gay community. One way they could come together in public was in the masquerade or cross-dressing balls that began to be held in significant numbers in major urban centers in the late nineteenth century and continued through the twentieth. Not all cross-dressers, however, were homosexual and the phenomenon came under serious study by two pioneering sexologists, Have-lock Ellis and Magnus Hirschfeld.

Ellis called the phenomenon *eonism,* after the Chevalier, while Hirschfeld coined the term "transvestism." Their pioneering studies were neglected by Americans, particularly Hirschfeld, who was not translated into English until the 1990s. The study of cross-dressing received renewed emphasis through the case of Christine Jorgensen, which received international publicity in 1952. Interestingly, the physician involved in the case called her a transvestite, and only gradually was the phenomenon of transvestism distinguished from transsexualism.

Organized transvestism began in the United States in 1959 through the efforts of Virginia Prince, a Los Angeles resident, who began meeting with a group of fellow transvestites she had met in a Hose and Heels club. She quickly emerged as a spokesperson for what she called heterosexual transvestites, to distinguish them from gay queens and transsexuals. The movement spread rapidly around the world so that there are clubs or groups with a variety of names in the majority of the countries of the world. In the United States there are competing national organizations and a lot of local groups that have no affiliation. Coinciding with this growth was the increase of merchants to supply clothes and accessories to would-be cross-dressers, whether gay, straight, or in between.

Interestingly, many of the cross-dressers in the organized groups dress in the style of clothes that were popular when they were young, almost as if there was an imprinting of what a woman should be. They seem to ignore the freedom that women have in clothing, and few of them for example, wear pants even if they lack a fly. One of the objectives of a significant number of transvestites is to appear in public as a woman without being read. This is the ultimate example of a cross-dresser. It is only the most daring of cross dressers who even belong to the organized groups, and it is estimated that there are hundreds of thousands of secret male cross-dressers who are closeted, keeping their clothes in a special suitcase or drawer, to be pulled out when the opportunity arrives. Often the only public indication of their secret life is in buying clothes, through catalogues or getting literature on the topic. Many have wives or significant others who do not know, although in organized transvestism there are wives and other female support groups to help them cope with the cross-dressing activities of the men in their lives.

Though women still impersonate men, it is not the clothing that interests most of them. With the clothing freedom women have, and the increasing breakdown of barriers to job and other economic opportunities for women, cross-dressing, in the sense that the men involved take part in, is almost nonexistent.

See also Fashion and Homosexuality; Fashion, Gender and Dress; Politics and Fashion.

Bibliography

Allen, Mariette Pathy. *Transformations: Crossdressers and Those Who Love Them*. Boston: Dutton, 1990.

Boyd, Helen. *My Husband Betty*. New York: Thunder Mouth Press, 2003.

Bullough, Vern L., and Bonnie Bullough. *Cross Dressing, Sex, and Gender*. Philadelphia: University of Pennsylvania Press, 1993.

——. *Gender Blending: Transgender Issues in Today's World*. Buffalo, N.Y.: Prometheus Books, 1997.

Docter, Richard. *Transvestites and Transsexuals: Toward a Theory of Cross-Gender Behavior*. New York: Plenum, 1988.

Ellis, Havelock. "Eonism." *Studies in the Psychology of Sex*, vol. 2, part 2. Reprinted New York: Random House, [1906], 1936.

Garber, Marjorie. *Vested Interests: Cross Dressing and Sexual Anxiety*. New York: Routledge, 1997.

Hirschfeld, Magnus. *Transvestites*. Translated by Michael Lombardi-Nash, Preface by Vern L. Bullough. Buffalo: Prometheus Books, 1991.

Vera, Veronica. *Miss Vera's Finishing School for Boys Who Want to Be Girls*. New York: Bantam-Doubleday Dell, 1997.

Ward, Edward. *The Secret History of Clubs*. London: 1709, p. 290.

Vern L. Bullough

CUNNINGTON, C. WILLETT AND PHILLIS

C. Willett (1878–1961) and Phillis (1887–1974) Cunnington were medical doctors with a general practice in North London in the 1930s; they were also major dress historians. C. W. Cunnington served in World War I as a captain in the Royal Army Medical Corps after graduating from Cambridge University. He married Phillis in 1918. The Cunningtons amassed a vast collection of English costume between the 1920s and the late 1940s, which they stored in a big shed in the garden of their house in North London.

Together they published on British dress history from the Middle Ages through the 1950s in their five *Handbooks of English Costume*, their *History of Underclothes*, and their *Dictionary of English Costume*, all published between 1951 and 1960. C. W. Cunnington also published his *English Women's Clothing in the Present Century* in 1952, while three of his earlier books, written between 1941 and 1948, elucidated his own theories about dress, fashion, and sexuality. He died in 1961.

The Cunningtons' famous handbooks mapped the development of styles of male and female dress. Each volume was illustrated with quotes from novels and newspapers of the period in question, and was illustrated by small line drawings as well as photographs of paintings. This approach paralleled and extended the work of German and French dress historians of the period as Oskar Fischel, Max von Boehn, and Maurice Leloir.

C. W. Cunnington's medical training influenced his primary interest, which was the psychological motives that he considered responsible for changes in women's dress styles in the late nineteenth century. Born in 1878, he would have been familiar with the bustles of the 1880s, the S-bend of the early 1900s, and the flat-chested boy-girl fashions of the 1920s. His interest in the psychosexual functions of women's dress had been enhanced by the 1930 publication of the psychiatrist John Carl Flügel's study, *The Psychology of Clothes*. James Laver, who was the Keeper of Prints and Drawings at the Victoria & Albert Museum as well as C. W. Cunnington's friendly rival for the leadership of British dress historiography, also took an erudite but more popular approach to similar themes in his book *Taste and Fashion* (1937).

C. W. Cunnington published five books on psychosexual themes in women's dress. His first was *Feminine Attitudes in the Nineteenth Century* (1935), followed by *English Women's Clothing in the Nineteenth Century* (1937), *Why Women Wear Clothes* (1941), and *the Art of English Dress* and *The Perfect Lady* (both 1948). In *Feminine Attitudes* he used the fashionable middle-class Victorian garments he and his wife assiduously collected—which he called his "specimens"—as tools for studying "the psychological background of women," and specifically their sexuality (1935, p. 2). Cunnington added that "we were concerned with mass psychology, not with the psychology of the individual" (Tozer, p. 3).

Cunnington diagnosed "the feminine mind through analysis of a series of 'Attitudes,' . . . That is to say those unconscious postures of mind and body which members of a social group will display as features in common." The attitudes that Cunnington listed included "the Conventional Attitude of those multitudes of mute, inglorious females . . . who never did or said or thought anything that distinguished them from the mass of women of their day." The "Feminine Attitude," on the other hand, was influenced by the element of "sex attraction," while "the Herd Instinct" was defined as "the wish to imitate in appearance and conduct those in the same social group." Thus Cunnington showed that he shared Flügel's view of the centrality of sexuality as a driving motivation in fashion development among women. For example, he saw the development of the 1870s bustle as inspired by the "mating instinct," whereas

that of the 1880s was inspired by the "maternal" instinct. He described the gait of Edwardian women, which he would have seen when he was in his mid-twenties, as "that provocative pelvic roll . . . perhaps the most sensual Attitude of the century" (1935, pp. viii, 254, 306).

The first doubts about the accuracy of Cunnington's opinions surfaced among women dress historians in 1949, when Doris Langley Moore wrote that she "had the strongest doubt that fashion . . . is motivated by sex appeal" (p. 21). Nonetheless, C. W. Cunnington's reputation as a leading dress historian and theorist remained in place for a further thirty-seven years. In 1986, however, his work was subjected to a feminist reconsideration led by Jane Tozer, a curator at the Platt Hall, Manchester, Museum of Costume. While acknowledging the value of the Cunningtons' famous handbooks for their details of style chronology, etiquette, and specific nomenclature, Tozer specifically targeted Cunnington's "dated sexism," denouncing it as a "simplistic and now outdated appraisal of the origins of human sexuality." She also questioned Cunnington's anecdotal approach as well as "his notorious vagueness" in naming sources in his books (pp. 11–12). Cunnington's reputation was undoubtedly damaged.

Phillis Cunnington built on this critique, and later developed a more academic approach to dress history. She produced five meticulously researched specialist studies after her husband's death: *English Costume for Sports and Outdoor Recreation* (1969); *Occupational Costume in England* (1967); *Costume for Births, Marriages and Deaths* (1972); *Costume of Household Servants* (1974); and *Charity Costumes of Children, Scholars, Almsfolk, Pensioners*, published posthumously in 1978.

In addition to their published books, the Cunningtons made a major contribution to the study of fashion history through amassing their dress collection. Put together at a time when almost no one was collecting old garments, let alone late nineteenth-and early twentieth-century middle-class clothing, the Cunningtons' collection has since become one of the most renowned in Britain. They sold it to Manchester City Council in 1947 to form the basis of the Museum of Costume at Platt Hall. The museum's first curator was Anne Buck.

The Cunningtons were medical practitioners. They were not professional museum curators and undertook all their research unpaid if not unrewarded. They were interested in finding examples of "ordinary" people's dress to use as general representations of garment types, which C.W Cunnington then related to his typology of feminine attitudes. He had no interest in the owners of individual garments and felt no need to record their names or to provenance sources. Thus much of this information was lost or never recorded. It was left to Anne Buck and to later generations of curators to put this remarkable collection into order.

While C. W. Cunnington's more theoretical comments have not withstood the passage of time, the handbooks he co-authored with his wife as well as Phillis Cunnington's own work still offer a carefully compiled and useful introduction to the history of English costume. Publishing and collecting through the 1930s to the 1970s, at a time when fashion history still had no academic status and very little standing in museums, the Cunningtons educated the next generation of dress historians and curators who professionalized the field.

See also Clothing, Costume, and Dress; Europe and America: History of Dress (400–1900 C.E.); Fashion, Theories of; Fashion Museums and Collections; Flügel, J. C.

Bibliography

Cunnington, C. W. *Feminine Attitudes in the Nineteenth Century.* London: W. Heinemann, Ltd., 1935.

——. *English Women's Clothing in the Nineteenth Century.* London: Faber and Faber, Ltd., 1937.

——. *Why Women Wear Clothes.* London: Faber and Faber, Ltd., 1941.

——. *The Art of English Dress.* London: Collins, 1948.

——. *The Perfect Lady.* London: Max Parrish, 1948.

——. *English Women's Clothing in the Present Century.* London: Faber and Faber, Ltd., 1952.

——. *Looking Over My Shoulder.* London: Faber and Faber, 1961.

Cunnington, C.W., and Phillis. *History of Underclothes.* London: Faber, 1951.

——. *Handbook of English Mediaeval Costume.* London: Faber and Faber, 1952 and 1973.

——. *Handbook of English Costume in the Sixteenth Century.* London: Faber and Faber, 1954 and 1970.

——. *Handbook of English Costume in the Seventeenth Century.* London: Faber and Faber, 1955.

——. *Handbook of English Costume in the Eighteenth Century.* London: Faber and Faber, 1957.

——. *Handbook of English Costume in the Nineteenth Century.* London: Faber and Faber, 1959.

——. *A Dictionary of English Costume: 900–1900.* London: Adam and Charles Black, 1960.

Cunnington, Phillis. *English Costume for Sports and Outdoor Recreation: From the Sixteenth to the Nineteenth Centuries.* London: Adam and Charles Black, 1967.

——. *Occupational Costume in England: From the Eleventh Century to 1914.* London: Adam and Charles Black, 1967.

——. *Costume for Births, Marriages and Deaths.* London: Adam and Charles Black, 1972.

——. *Costume of Household Servants: From the Middle Ages to 1900.* London: Adam and Charles Black, 1974.

——. *Charity Costumes of Children, Scholars, Almsfolk, Pensioners.* London: Adam and Charles Black, 1978.

Jarvis, Anthea. "An Agreeable Change from Ordinary Medical Diagnosis, the Costume Collection of Drs. C. Willett and Phillis Cunnington." *Costume* 33 (1999): 1–11.

Laver, James. *Taste and Fashion from the French Revolution Until Today.* London: George G. Harrap and Company, Ltd., 1937.

Moore, Doris Langley. *The Woman in Fashion.* London: Batsford, 1949.

Taylor, Lou. *Establishing Dress History.* Manchester, U. K.: Manchester University Press, 2004.

Tozer, Jane. "Cunnington's Interpretation of Dress." *Costume* 20: 1–17.

Lou Taylor

DAHL-WOLFE, LOUISE

Louise Dahl-Wolfe (1895–1989) was born in San Francisco. Aspiring to a career as a painter, she attended the California School of Design (now the San Francisco Art Institute), where she was greatly influenced by Rudolph Schaefer, known for his color expertise.

Dahl-Wolfe's Early Career

After completing her studies, Dahl-Wolfe designed electric signs from 1921 to 1923; in 1924 she began working for a leading decorator. In 1921 she was invited to the studio of photographer Anne Brigman; this meeting prompted her to buy her first camera, an Eastman bellows camera with a reflector made from a Ghirardelli chocolate box. She used her mother as the subject of her first pictures. Early photographic adventures included taking shots of herself and some friends nude on a beach, using the soft-focus style of her mentor. After Dahl-Wolfe befriended another San Francisco photographer, Consuela Kanaga, who taught her to use a 3¼-by-4¼-inch Thornton-Pickard English reflex camera with a Verito soft-focus lens, the two traveled together to Europe in 1927. While in Paris, Dahl-Wolfe bought a Pathé camera; in Germany she purchased a small film pack camera. On an excursion to Africa, she met Meyer (Mike) Wolfe, an artist from Tennessee, whom she subsequently married.

Dahl-Wolfe returned to San Francisco in 1928 and began taking commercial black-and-white photographs. Two years later, she and her husband spent a summer in a rented log cabin in the Great Smoky Mountains of Tennessee, where she began photographing still-life subjects and the local mountain people. She developed her film with a darkroom light powered by the battery of a Model A Ford. After moving with her husband to New York, Dahl-Wolfe was introduced to Frank Crowninshield, then editor of *Vanity Fair*, who decided to publish her work. The documentary pictures of her Tennessee subjects were a sensation when they first appeared in the November 1933 issue of *Vanity Fair*. This success led to the publication of her first black-and-white fashion work in *Harper's Bazaar* in 1936 and her first color work a year later.

Dahl-Wolfe's Work in Color

Dahl-Wolfe was one of the first and most important practitioners of fashion photography in color. Kodachrome film came on the market for the first time in 1935, although the product at that time could not reproduce colors reliably either in the studio or in natural light. A striking aspect of Dahl-Wolfe's work was her color sensibility—a flawless instinct for combinations of colors. This emphasis on the painterly values of tone, line, and color is not surprising, since she had been trained as a painter and strongly influenced by the philosopher of art Clive Bell's theory of significant form. Bell maintained that color is an inherent part of the expressive quality of form and that arrangements of colors carry emotional weight—particularly bright luminous colors, which have a pleasing effect. Dahl-Wolfe's early training in color theory with the painter Rudolph Schaefer also influenced her interest in color photography. In order to achieve the exact effects she desired, she worked with the new eight-inch by ten-inch sheets of Kodachrome because they gave the highest degree of resolution and detail. She often consulted with the printers of the magazines she worked for in order to retain her subtly beautiful effects on the printed page.

Many of Dahl-Wolfe's photographs seem to be built up of colored planes rather than objects. Many of her shots for *Harper's Bazaar* are masterly combinations of compositional lighting, varied textures, repeated patterns, and a broad variety of shades, particularly earth-tone colors. For example, a simple black-and-white suit is seen through a darkened archway leading into a room of exotic warmth; in the room the model is the focal point within the mix of textures, patterns, and colors. The same natural light, here bounced through various screened patterns, is seen in another picture, where it filters through the organdy curtains in a room of lovely femininity and charm. The setting of this photograph was Louise Dahl-Wolfe's own bedroom in her home in Frenchtown, New Jersey, one of her favorite shooting locations. In addition to her pioneering use of color, she was also one of the first fashion photographers to make use of location shots, using architectural backgrounds and exotic locales to add interest to the way the clothing was pictured.

Dahl-Wolfe's Importance

Dahl-Wolfe's style—elegant yet casual, sophisticated yet at ease—was ideally suited for depicting the independent American woman, wearing comfortable ready-to-wear styles by such American designers as Claire McCardell, Hattie Carnegie, and Norman Norell. Both the models and the clothes had a naturalness and authenticity that conveyed a cool and comfortable yet ineffably chic informality. This informality is perhaps the essence of Dahl-Wolfe's style: The models, the clothes, and the way she chose to portray them reflected the relaxed accessibility of a distinctly American fashion sense.

Dahl-Wolfe had a long and productive career as a fashion photographer. She worked for *Harper's Bazaar* for twenty-two years, from 1936 to 1958, leaving shortly after the magazine's editor Carmel Snow and its legendary art director Alexey Brodovitch resigned. Her career included eighty-six *Harper's* covers and over six thousand color photographs as well as thousands of black-and-white pictures. After leaving *Harper's Bazaar*, Dahl-Wolfe worked briefly for *Vogue* before finally retiring from professional photography in 1960.

See also Fashion Magazines; Fashion Photography; McCardell, Claire; Norell, Norman; Vogue; Vreeland, Diana.

Bibliography

Bellafante, Ginia. "What Dahl-Wolfe's Eye Created in a Lens." *New York Times*, 6 June 2000.
Dahl-Wolfe, Louise. *Louise Dahl-Wolfe: A Photographer's Scrapbook*. Preface by Frances McFadden. New York: St. Martin's Press, 1984.
Goldberg, Vicki, and Nan Richardson. *Louise Dahl-Wolfe: A Retrospective*. Foreword by Dorothy Twining Globus. New York: Harry N. Abrams, 2000.
Hall-Duncan, Nancy. *The History of Fashion Photography*. New York: Alpine Book Company, 1979.

Nancy Hall-Duncan

DANCE AND FASHION

The roots of the relationship between Western dance and fashion lay in the Renaissance period, where social dancing reflected the values of society. Dance as a channel of communication was as important as having the appropriate costume for socializing. After the French Revolution in 1789, professional ballet dancers left the Court spectacles in favor of the stage. From the beginning of the nineteenth century, the European ball culture emerged as a social activity and had an enormous impact on fashion and vice versa.

The Waltz Century

The nineteenth century was dedicated to the waltz, which had developed as a bourgeois activity in Europe and America. In *May I Have the Pleasure?*, Belinda Quirey argues that in the wake of political, romantic, and industrial revolutions, the waltz was a completely new dance form that perfectly suited the new conditions of modern life—socially, psychologically, and materially. These nineteenth-century developments in dance were reflected in elaborate dance costumes for lower-and middle-class women, although upper-class ballroom-dance dresses were distinctively splendorous for women. The *danse à deux* activity reinforced the pleasure of watching other people: how they harmonized and what they wore. Ballroom fashion was therefore an enormously important component of acceptance by polite society.

Tango Craze

Modern ballroom dancing began just before World War I, when dance halls flourished in Europe. The Hammer-smith Palais de Danse in London was among the first popular dance halls that provided an up-to-date program for modern ballroom dancing. Although the polka and the quadrille still remained very popular dance forms before the outbreak of World War I, the tango craze started and the fox-trot also became very

ETIQUETTE HINTS FOR THE BALLROOM: DRESSED TO IMPRESS

Hillgrove's Complete Practical Guide to the Art of Dancing (1863) offers a vivid description of the importance of dress in the European ball culture:

> Ladies should remember that men look to the effect of dress in setting off the figure and countenance of a lady, rather than to its cost. Few men form estimates of the value of ladies' dress. This is subject for female criticism. Beauty of person and elegance of manners in woman will always command more admiration from the other sex than costliness of clothing.

In another chapter, Hillgrove recommends that on entering a ballroom, all thought of self should be dismissed: "The pretty ambition of endeavoring to create a sensation by either dress, loud talking, or unusual behavior, is to be condemned." Not only the dress was important; society ladies had to take care of a fashionable hairstyle as well. In 1860, Florence Hartley recommends in The Ladies' Book of Etiquette, and Manual of Politeness that "one has to be very careful, when dressing for a ball, that the hair is firmly fastened, and the coiffure properly adjusted. Nothing is more annoying that to have the hair loosen or the headdress fall off in a crowded ballroom." Accessories played a key role in fashionable dressing for social ballroom events. Henry P. Willis advises in Etiquette, and the Usages of Society (1860) that "ladies should draw on their gloves (white or yellow) in the dressing room, and they should not have them off for one moment in the dancing rooms. However, at supper the gloves can be taken off, because "nothing is more preposterous than to eat in gloves."

---

fashionable. The origins of the tango lie in turn-of-the century Argentina and emerged among European and African immigrants. Since earlier dances did not have the close body contact of the tango, this new dance was considered very risqué at the time. With its sensual rhythm and intense body contact, the tango had a distinctly sexual connotation. In fact, the tango was at first deemed so illicit that it was thought suitable only for prostitutes and their pimps. However, when the tango was legitimized and came to Europe, it was soon taken up by Parisian high society, and ballroom fashion had to be adapted to this new "sexual" dance form. Dance costumes were designed to be more tight-fitting and embellished with shiny paillettes and stones. Soon the tango dress style spread from cabarets and theaters to evening fashion. At the beginning of the twenty-first century, the cinema industry has picked up the tango fashion in scenes of cult films such as Moulin Rouge.

Josephine Baker: A Black Pearl

In her 1920s' performances in "barely there" dresses, Josephine Baker shocked Parisian society with her display of naked skin. In the following decade, she became famous not only for her style of performing but also for her stage costumes: her elaborate headdresses and banana costume received standing ovations at the Folies Bergère. Although her look was considered vulgar, her dresses served as a source of inspiration for fashion in the 1920s and 1930s. Josephine Baker gave shape to a new culture, which liberalized fashion and dance to a new era of evening dresses.

Hollywood Screen Dancing

In the late 1920s, screen dancing became popular, and Hollywood style spread from the screen to day and evening fashion. The lightweight Charleston dress, with its long fringes, became part of the Roaring Twenties lifestyle. Anne Massey describes in Hollywood Beyond the Screen that the films Our Dancing Daughters in 1928, and Our Modern Maidens in 1929, represent the debut of the art deco style reflected in architecture and fashion. In the 1930s, Fred Astaire and Ginger Rogers were the source of inspiration for fashion-oriented cineastes in movies such as Top Hat (1935), and Swing Time (1936). The Hollywood culture and its concept of glamour advanced the Americanization of dance culture, which in turn influenced the fashion scene. During the harrowing Great Depression, dance marathons, with their emphasis on nonstop endurance for the entertainment of the masses, became popular in social dance clubs. Fashion companies advertised at these events to promote club fashion.

Lindy Hop: Swinging Parties

In 1926, the Lindy hop craze started at the Savoy ballroom in Harlem, New York. In the early 1930s, high society was interested in seeing Lindy hop performers entertain at parties. The resulting swing-dance fashion became popular: cotton blouses with fitted waists and puffed sleeves combined with an A-line skirt—sometimes with detachable suspenders to give maximum hold—for female Lindy hoppers, and high-waisted pants with matching fitted vests for their male counterparts. The Savoy style spread quickly over to Europe, and the Lindy hop and its fashions were adopted by the London and Parisian elites.

Broadway Dreams

In the 1940s, the evolution of dance on film had a crucial influence on the whole world of dance. The predominantly working-class audience was getting real Hollywood value for little money in the cinemas of the 1940s. Those who could afford musical theaters enjoyed the pleasure of live performances on Broadway. With the advent of television in the 1950s and movie theater attendance drastically down, financially strapped Hollywood studios turned to film adaptations of successful Broadway shows, as this was a more economical option than developing original screenplays. Film makeup and clothes of Broadway shows had a strong influence on everyday fashion. Department stores such as Bullocks in Los Angeles became the place where both Los Angeles inhabitants and foreign visitors bought their musical dance–inspired wardrobe. Later on, such Broadway shows as *West Side Story* (1957), a modern-day retelling of *Romeo & Juliet*, had a lasting influence on the American teenager, who copied the Broadway look.

From Rock and Roll to Saturday Night Fever

In the 1950s, the postwar generation brought a new form of dance into the nightclubs. Rock and roll—derived from African American rhythm and blues—and stars such as Elvis Presley and Bill Haley immortalized the image of the rebellious teenager and also influenced fashion and hairstyles well into the 1960s. Social dance moved away from couple dancing, and new freedom was expressed in checked shirts and tight-fitting denim jeans for young men, while teenage girls wore petticoats and backcombed their hair. By the end of the 1960s, a particular dance form no longer existed, and young people moved their bodies to the music in whatever way they wanted. The disco scene emerged and exerted a crucial influence on the fashion world. DJs combined records, encouraging dancers to stay on the floor for a

long period. Fashion designers took advantage of the *en vogue* disco style and immortalized dance film stars such as John Travolta in *Saturday Night Fever* (1977). His white disco suit in the movie acquired iconic status, establishing disco as part of mainstream culture until the 1980s, when the public had lost its interest in it, and punk and new wave style challenged its dominance.

Street Style: Hip-hop, Break-Dancing, and Techno

In the early 1980s, hip-hop culture gained a mass appeal when black and Hispanic DJs evolved the use of backbeats in New York City and Los Angeles clubs. Break dancing and hip-hip were very athletic styles, often mimicking robotic movements, and therefore required a more casual clothing style. Sport brands such as Adidas, Nike, and Puma flourished among street-style dancers. During the following decade, the house music style developed from hip-hip and brought alive a new generation of club culture, and club fashion became less casual. In the late 1980s, the rave scene emerged. Rave represented more than a dance party; it illustrated a physical and mental state, unifying the club dancers. Melissa Harrison's *High Society: The Real Voices of Club Culture* offers a detailed description of the rave phenomena. Rave accessories such as glow-in-the-dark-jewelery and clothing with utility bags became very important.

As Seen on Screen: Music Video Style

In the mid-1980s, music stars such as Michael Jackson and Madonna based their performances on dance, and revolutionized the power of music videos. In concept, music videos were based on song, choreography, special effects, and fashion, which was widely copied among club-goers. With the emergence of boy bands, girl bands, and teenage music groups at the beginning of the 1990s and their promotion through videos, a new generation was influenced by the music stars. Mainstream fashion was strongly influenced by performers such as Backstreet Boys, Spice Girls, Take That, Britney Spears, and Justin Timberlake, who pioneered and set up fashion trends, such as tank tops, low-cut jeans, very conspicuous and ostentatious gold jewelry for both male and female teenagers, and "visible" underwear for girls. At the start of the twenty-first century, music performers created a mixture between club style and contemporary dance while using the medium of fashion to create a celebrity style, which became an essential part of the music and dance industry.

See also Dance Costume; Film and Fashion; Music and Fashion; Theatrical Costume.

Bibliography

Dodd, Craig. *The Performing World of the Dancer.* London: Breslich & Foss, 1981.

Driver, Ian. *A Century of Dance: A Hundred Years of Musical Movement, from Waltz to Hip Hop.* London: Hamlyn Octopus Publishing Group Ltd., 2000.

Jonas, Gerald. *Dancing—The Power of Dance Around the World.* BBC Books: London, 1992.

Harrison, Melissa. *High Society: The Real Voices of Club Culture.* London: Judy Piatkus Ltd., 1998.

Hartley, Florence. *The Ladies' Book of Etiquette, and Manual of Politeness.* Boston: 1860.

Hillgrove, Thomas. *A Complete Practical Guide to the Art of Dancing.* New York: Dick & Fitzgerald, 1863.

Massey, Anne. *Hollywood beyond the Screen: Design and Material Culture.* London and New York: Berg Publisher, 2001.

Silvester, Victor. *Modern Ballroom Dancing.* London: Stanley Paul & Co. Ltd., 1993.

Quirey, Belina. *May I Have the Pleasure?: The Story of Popular Dancing.* British Broadcasting Corporation: London, 1976.

Willis, Henry P. *Etiquette, and the Usages of Society.* New York: Dick & Fitzgerald, 1860.

Thomas Hecht

DANCE COSTUME

The relationship between dance and dance costumes is complex and does not simply reflect dance practice in a specific period, but also social behavior and cultural values. Dance costumes can be divided into the following categories: historical, folk or traditional, ballroom, modern, and musical dance costumes. Influence has spread from fashion to dance and back again.

Historical Dance Costumes

From the fifteenth to the eighteenth century, festivities at European courts required highly elaborate dance costumes. The style of court dance costumes tended to be similar to everyday dress of the period, incorporating, for example, laced corsets, puffed and slashed sleeves, farthingales with skirts and applied decoration. In the early twenty-first century, the reproduction of historical dance costumes was evident in the activities of historical dance organizations, such as the Institute for Historical Dance Practice (IHDP) in Ghent, Belgium.

Folk-Dance Costumes

From the fifteenth century onward, folk dance developed steadily in Europe. The field of European folk-dance costumes is very complex, as each of the country's regions has its own dances, dress, and customs. Eastern European folk dances, such as czardas, mazurkas, and polkas, soon spread to England and France. Folk-dance costumes reflected the East European look in the use of bright colors on dark backgrounds. Costumes were often highly decorated with beads, metal, and silk threads. The basic women's dress was a short, light-colored chemise and a petticoat, over which several layers of fabric were worn. A draped headdress indicated the marital status of the wearer (fancy headgear indicated that the girl was unmarried). European folk dance formed the basis for square-dance activities. European settlers who came to America introduced this special type of country dance and its costume first in New England, but before long, square dance started to spread across the

Dancers in unitards. These one-piece garments are typically made from spandex or a similar stretchy, pliable fabric, giving the dancer nearly unlimited range of motion. © Julie Lemberger/Corbis. Reproduced by permission.

country. Evening dress was the standard outfit for dancers: ankle-length hooped skirts for the women and formal jackets for men. During the following two centuries, the cultural mix of European settlers in America has led to a variety of national folk-dance costumes. Farmer and cowboy dance wear were mainly based on components of everyday clothing: shirts, cotton trousers, and cowboy boots for men, and ankle-long cotton gingham dresses for women. The minuet, polka, waltz, and quadrille via France and England brought more elaborated dance costumes to America: tailored long-sleeve shirts and trousers in a Western-cut style for male dancers and full floral-embroidered skirts and blouses for females. Accessories such as Western belts, string ties, or silk kerchiefs completed the square-dance outfit.

In the late 1990s, high-end designers such as Dolce & Gabbana, Roberto Cavalli, and Miu Miu had created an "urban cowboy look" with Western-inspired dress embellished with floral patterns on such articles of clothing as tuxedo shirts and jeans, as well as traditional pointedtoe cowboy boots.

In the early 2000s, amateur and professional female square dancers often wear double-swirl skirts with alternating ruffles in the fabric and wide white lace. The lace is used on bodice and sleeves, and an appliqué and bow are sewn on the fitted midriff. Male square dancers wear cowboy-style shirts with scarf tied around the collar, high-pocket jeans, and sometimes a cowboy hat. Pants cuffs are usually worn inside the cowboy boots. The United Square Dancers of America (USDA) booklet, *Square Dance Attire*, is probably the best resource for the history of square-dance costumes.

Belly-Dance Costumes

Oriental, or belly, dance originates from snakelike movements provided by the sisters of a woman giving birth as they tried to inspire her to deliver the baby. In 1893, belly dance was brought from the Arabic world to the United States on the occasion of the Chicago World's Fair. Exotic-colored fabrics embroidered with semiprecious stones, paillettes, and beads are characteristic of the style. Semitransparent tops with fringes reveal the stomach and navel while brassieres and wraparound skirts swing rhythmically to the beat of Middle Eastern music. Coin belts and hip scarves are an essential part of the belly-dance outfit. Sometimes belly dancers cover their face with a veil, especially when the dance is performed by a male dancer (cross-dressing). Alternatively, shoulder-to-floor-length beaded and sequinned tunics

Greek folk dancers. While traditional Greek costumes vary from island to island, some similarities can be found, such as basic construction, the use of certain fabrics, and head coverings such as those seen here. © GAIL MOONEY/CORBIS. REPRODUCED BY PERMISSION.

over harem pantaloons are worn. Historically, evidence points to the crucial influence of Islamic Orientalism in European fashion during the twentieth century, starting with the French designer Paul Poiret's use of the tunic shape and updating old-fashioned styles with exotic harem pants and veils wrapped around the body in the 1920s. In the 1990s, the prêt-à-porter and haute couture collections of Western European and American designers, such as Miguel Adrover, Jean Paul Gaultier, John Galliano, Alexander McQueen, and Rifat Ozbek, have been influenced by Oriental belly-dance costumes. Nancy Lindis farne-Tapper's *Languages of Dress in the Middle East* is a detailed source about Middle Eastern dress in both the ancient and the modern world.

Ballroom-Dance Costumes

From the early nineteenth century, ballroom dances were taken up by a broad public, and special evening dresses were designed to fit these occasions. The waltz, fox-trot, polka, mazurka, and Viennese waltz required an elegant style. By the twentieth century, dance costumes for the tango, swing and Latin, Charleston, rumba, bolero, cha-cha, mambo, and samba were more erotic.

Modern-Dance Costumes

At the beginning of the twentieth century, Isadora Duncan's natural movements on stage characterized a new era for dance. Duncan's modern dance style has been influenced by Greek art, folk dances, social dances, and athleticism. Free-flowing costumes and loose hair permitted a great freedom of dance movement. After World War I, modern-dance groups emerged with predominantly female dancers. During the following decades, avant-garde choreographers, such as George Balanchine and Martha Graham, and later Merce Cunningham, Paul Taylor, Alvin Ailey, and Pina Bausch, reformed and liberalized traditional dance and its costumes. Moving away from traditional ballet techniques, modern dance gave rise to a new era of costuming. Costumes and makeup took on a unisex look as choreographers felt it less relevant to differentiate female and male dancers. Theater designers experimented with seminude costumes: transparent T-shirts and short black trunks for men and simple bodices and plain tights for women were the standard outfits.

In 1934, neoclassical dance choreographer George Balanchine was the first to dress ballet dancers in rehearsal practice clothes for public performances. The use of noncolors characterized Balanchine's costumes, which were almost always black and white. His sense for minimalism on the stage developed through the revealing of nudity.

Martha Graham was one of the first to promote dance without pointe shoes on stage. In *Diversion of Angels* (1948), she dressed female dancers in draperies, and men were almost naked. Isamu Noguchi–inspired special crowns and hat pins by Graham became particularly famous as part of the modern-dance costume. Newly invented cuts made skirts and dance dress appear like trousers, permitting a great freedom of movement. At the beginning, Graham's dances were performed on a bare stage, which underlined the minimalism she demonstrated in the costumes. Later on,

PROFESSIONAL AND AMATEUR BALLROOM DRESS

Tango dress:

Usually one piece with a tight-fitting top and a swinging bottom slit high to reveal the leg. Stretch materials are used to guarantee a tight silhouette. The dance dress is often highly decorated with rhinestones, beadings, glitter and paillcttes.

Swing and Latin dress:

Very similar to tango dresses, but the much shorter hem-line makes the dress more sexual and can reveal the complete leg. Animal prints such as tiger or leopard intensify the wild connotation of these dresses.

Waltz and fox-trot dress:

Elegant one-piece dress often made in expensive lightweight silks or satins. A wide-swinging, ankle-length style intensifies the soft movements of these dances.

Charleston dress:

The necessary freedom of movement was guaranteed by knee-length shirt-dresses embroidered with glass beads and paillettes. The light weight of the dress and long fringes made it swing rhythmically according to the movements of the dance, which was part of the lifestyle of the Roaring Twenties and

became the most popular American dance in Germany and Europe; thanks in great part to Josephine Baker, who gave performances in 1927 with her Charleston Jazz Band in Berlin.

Polka and mazurka dress:

Folkloric traditional dress with colorful print design and usually a peasant blouse and a wraparound skirt embellished with opulent frills and garlands. During the 1970s, peasant blouses became very fashionable in everyday clothing, and high-end designers such as Emilio Pucci designed ethnic-style garments with embroideries and frills. Floral peasant blouses with soft ruffled hems had a revival in the late 1990s when designer brands such as Yves Saint Laurent, Dolce & Gabbana, Moschino, and Christian Dior created a folkloric fashion theme.

Rumba and samba dress:

With contrasting ruffles on the skirt and sleeves, this dress is often designed in a Caribbean style with bright colors.

Cha-cha dress:

A two-piece dress with a tight-fitting top and a wide offthe-shoulder neckline, while the skirt is full and flounced at the bottom. Rhinestones are usually attached to the fabric to give a glamorous effect.

MEN IN TIGHTS: THE MALE DANCER

In Russia, male dancers are highly regarded, and usually classical ballet training is the basis for a career in dance. Though a growing interest in dance exists among boys in other countries, many are too shy to take dance lessons and be obliged to wear tights, commonly considered a female article of clothing. Therefore, certain dance schools allow young male students to practice in T-shirts and short pants. Under the practice clothes, dancers usually wear suspensories, designed to isolate and support the testicles. Alternatively, a dance belt, specialized underwear, can be worn under tights. In both cases, the pouch in front is triangular, tight, and nearly flat to give support and form during dance moves. The subject of masculinity in dance has received popular treatment in such movies as *The Children of Theatre Street* (1977) and *Billy Elliot* (2000). Ramsay Burt's book *The Male Dancer* explores the subject of masculinity in dance in greater depth.

TAP-DANCE SHOES: FAMOUS SOUNDS

The origins of tap dance, a style of American theatrical dance with percussive footwork, lie in slave dances in the southern states that incorporated African movement and rhythm into European jigs and reels in the early nineteenth century. Tap dance was adopted in theaters from 1840, and clogging in leather-soled shoes became more and more popular. At the fin-desiècle, turn of the century, two different styles of tap-dance shoes had been established: stiff wooden-sole shoes, also called buck-and-wing, made popular by the duo Jimmy Doyle and Harland Dixon, and soft leather-sole shoes popularized by George Primrose. In the 1920s, metal plates (taps) had been attached to leather-sole shoes, which made a loud sharp sound on the floor. In the 1940s and 1950s, dancers such as Fred Astaire, Paul Draper, and Gene Kelly popularized tap shoes to a wider audience through the medium of Hollywood films.

she also replaced the traditional ballet tunics of male dancers and the folk dress and tutus of female dancers with straight, often dark and long shirts or rehearsal leotards. Awarded the Medal of Freedom in October 1976, Martha Graham was the first dancer to receive that distinction.

In the 1950s, costumes of Balanchine-and Graham-oriented contemporary dance choreographers, such as Merce Cunningham and Paul Taylor, tended to continue an emphasis on the seminude style, though prints on leotards personalized the individual contemporary dance style and its costumes. In 1958, the artist Robert Rauschen-berg created shiny silky tights speckled with rainbow dots for Cunningham's *Summerspace*. The designs of choreographer and costume designer Alwin Nikolais influenced the contemporary stage with performances such as *Noumenon Mobilus* (1953) and *Imago* (1963).

Musical-Dance Costumes

Evidence of musical theatres date to the eighteenth century when two forms of this song-and-dance performance emerged in Britain, France, and Germany: ballad operas, such as John Gay's *The Beggar's Opera* (1728), and later on comic operas, such as Michael Balfe's *The Bohemian Girl* (1843). At this time, many plays had short runs, and stage costumes were often based on everyday-dress design. In the late 1880s, comic operas conquered Broadway in New York, and plays, including *Robin Hood*, were designed for popular audiences. From the 1880s until the 1920s, the musical-comedy genre in London emerged, and designers such as Lady Duff-Gordon, known as Lucile, elaborated fashionable costumes for singers and dancers. In the early 1920s, tap-dance techniques were popularized and specially designed tap-dance shoes were available on the open market.

In the fifties, musicals such as *My Fair Lady* (1956) surprised the audiences with numerous costume changes. Costume designer Cecil Beaton had created costumes enhancing the transformation of Eliza, the main character, from a common flower vendor into a society lady. In 1975, Michael Bennett's *A Chorus Line* opened on Broadway, and aerobic and dance outfits became popular on stage and in everyday life. Bright neon shades in pink, green, and yellow dominated the range of colors. Dance tights, leggings, headbands, and wristlets spread from stage to fashion and vice versa. In 1988, the musical *Fame*, inspired by the movie and TV series, opened in London and reflected the fashion of the eighties, showing leotards and shorts. At the beginning of the twenty-first century, A. R. Rahman's Bollywood musical *Bombay Dreams* (2002) opened in London, and its Indian costumes demonstrated the ethnic influence on stage design.

See also Dance and Fashion; Ballet Costume; Music and Fashion; Theatrical Costume.

Bibliography

Balasescu, Alexandre. "Tehran Chic: Islamic Head Scarves, Fashion Designers and New Geographies of Modernity." *Fashion Theory* 7 (2003): 1.

Buonaventura, Wendy, and Ibrahim Farrah. *Serpent of the Nile: Women and Dance in the Arab World*. Northampton, Mass.: Interlink Publishing Group, 1994.

Burt, Ramsay. *The Male Dancer*: Bodies, Spectacle, Sexualities. London and New York: Routledge, 1995.

Carter, Alexandra. *The Routledge Dance Studies Reader*. London and New York: Routledge, 1998.

Dodd, Craig. *The Performing World of the Dancer*. London: Breslich & Foss, 1981.

Lindisfarne-Tapper, Nancy, and Bruce Ingham. *Languages of Dress in the Middle East*. Surrey: Curzon, 1997.

Strong, Roy, Richard Buckle, and Ivor Guest. *Designing for the Dancer*. London: Elron Press Ltd., 1981.

Internet Resources

Education Committee of the United Square Dancers of America, Inc. *USDA Booklet B-018*. USDA Publications, 1997. Available from <http://www.usda.org>.

Institute for Historical Dance Practise (IHDP) 2004. Available from <http://www.historicaldance.com>.

Thomas Hecht

DANDYISM

Walter Benjamin, in his treatise *Charles Baudelaire*, writes: "The dandy is a creation of the English" (p. 96). If dandyism, the style and the practice, is a uniquely English construct, it was the French who defined it in prose and poetry. The French author Jules Barbey D'Aurevilly, in his 1845 essay "Du dandysme et de George Brummell," described it as a nationally characteristic mode of vanity combined with "the force of [an] English originality . . . as profound as her national spirit." The dandy's dandy, George Bryan "Beau" Brummell, captured in the turn of his cuff and the knot of his cravat the studied irony and languor that defined his age. At the height of his popularity, from 1799 to 1810, Brummell, the son of a minor nobleman, held the entire British aristocracy in his sway. Attracted to no one particular feature of character (Brummell was neither great

poet nor eminent thinker), his admirers were ostensibly captivated by his urbane sangfroid and impeccable dress, a clever and consummately constructed package that aimed to "astonish rather than to please" (Walden, p. 52). Essentially Brummell's philosophical stance was to stand for nothing in particular, a posturing that aptly crystallized the uncertainty of a period that witnessed the decline of aristocracy and the early rise of democratic politics. Sartorially, he refined a mode of dress that adopted English country style in a renunciation of the affectations of Francophile fashion (ironically so, if one considers that these very fripperies have become so linked to the dandyism of contemporary imagination). As the dress historian James Laver, writing in 1968, points out, "whatever else it was, [dandyism] was the repudiation of fine feathers" (p. 10).

If Brummell was considered oppositional, it was in the privileging of this country clothing for wholly urban pursuits. Not an innovator (Thomas Coke of Norfolk was the first of the nobility to present himself in court in "sporting" attire over half a century previously), Brummell merely encapsulated and reflected back to society the sentiments of the times. In the early 1800s, the "sporting costume" of the English nobility reflected the increase in time spent supervising their estates; a top hat and tails in sober tones, linen cravats, breeches, and sturdy riding boots were a uniform of practicality and prudence. That Brummell appropriated this style for promenading through London's arcades and holding court at one of the many gentlemen's clubs of which he was a member served a dual purpose—suggesting the validity of entertainment as the "occupation" of the leisured classes while eradicating any immediate visible difference in status between himself and the "working" man.

In his recorded witticisms and his style, Brummell appeared to contemplate no distinction other than taste. His preoccupation with pose and appearance was derided as the last gasp of aristocratic decadence, but in many ways he anticipated the modern era—a world of social mobility in which taste was privileged above birth and wealth. Elevated as a style icon, he presaged the contemporary dominance of fashion and celebrity; clothing is as powerful a tool now as it was two hundred years ago for conveying new social and economic directions. Dedicated to perfection in dress (his lengthy toilette was legendary) and the immaculate presentation of his body, Brummell's total control over his image finds its legacy in twenty-first-century masculine dress styles.

Dandyism in France

Dandyism was a potent cocktail that swiftly endeared itself to England's European neighbor, France (and much later to Russia), privileging a love of beauty in material goods while appearing to nod to the revolutionary sentiment of the times. Most notable of France's dandies was the young Alfred Guillaume Gabriel, count d'Orsay. Only a teenager when dandyism first crossed the seas to Paris, d'Orsay's sartorial power had risen to Brummellian heights by 1845.

Unlike Brummell, however, d'Orsay's pursuit of dandyism was a search for personal fulfillment rather than social power. Already powerful by token of birth, d'Orsay's legacy was of dandyism as fashion plate, and he became known as the original "butterfly dandy." There was also none of Brummell's austerity; the French imagination had already mixed dandyism with English romanticism, as evidenced in d'Orsay's more

Illustration of French author Jules Barbey d'Aureyville. D'Aureyville was a major force in defining dandyism in a positive way, placing more emphasis on the dandy's intellectual pursuits and bohemian spirit than on his clothing. © LEONARD DE SALVA/CORBIS. REPRODUCED BY PERMISSION.

sensual, lavish, and luxurious approach to dress—silk replaced linen, curves replaced stricter lines, gold for silver. That much of France's dandy traditions grew from literary interpretation is important in the context of the development of dandyism into a moral and artistic philosophy.

Dandy Philosophy

Defining dandyism is a complex task, and few writers have done so more successfully than Lord Edward Bulwer-Lytton in his treatise on the dandy of 1828, *Pelham; or, The Adventures of a Gentleman*. Considered at the time to be a manual for the practice of dandyism, it amply demonstrates the growing link between the promotion of the self and promotion through the social ranks. Notable maxims include: "III: Always remember that you dress to fascinate others, not yourself," and "XXIII: He who esteems trifles for themselves is a trifler—he who esteems them for the conclusions to be drawn from them, or the advantage to which they can be put, is a philosopher" (pp. 180–182).

That Bulwer-Lytton associates dandy practice with philosophy was concordant with later literary movements such as Barbey D'Aurevilly's toward enshrining dandyism as intellectual pose rather than fashionable consumption. More immediately, however, *Pelham* inspired a Victorian backlash against dandyism that was to define the 1830s. At around the same time as d'Orsay reached the peak of his influence, back in England William Make-peace Thackeray was releasing the serial of his novel *Vanity Fair*, at the venerable age of thirty-six. Thackeray had contributed significantly to the Victorian approbation of dandyism in the 1830s, epitomized by the views expressed in Thomas Carlyle's *Sartor Resartus* [The tailor retailored] (1838). Thackeray's regular columns and later novels, *Vanity Fair* and *The History of Pendennis*, were vivid representations of the moral and religiously driven belief that dandyism was a shallow and louche behavioral deficiency but they ironically were informed by his association with, and enjoyment of, the company of dandies such as d'Orsay.

It was the French, in particular D'Aurevilly, that were to define dandyism, through literature, as a positive practice and "robust moral philosophy" (Breward, p. 3). D'Aurevilly's *Du dandyisme et de Georges Brummell* had a profound influence on all the texts, British and French, that followed it. Although D'Aurevilly never met Brummell, he formed an intimate friendship with Guillaume-Stanislas Trébutien, a scholar and native of Caen, the provincial French town to which Brummell escaped following his indebtedness and ultimate disgrace in the English court. Trébutien met and befriended William Jesse, a young officer who had in turn met Brummell at a social event in Caen and was impressed with Brummell's "superlative taste." Jesse's accounts of Brummell, relayed to D'Aurevilly through Trébutien, were to form the basis of D'Aurevilly's text. Jesse was to broaden D'Aurevilly's already significant knowledge of dandyism, Regency literature, and the history of the Restoration, which formed the background to the practice by introducing him to more obscure texts that would never have reached the shores of France. D'Aurevilly was a little known author and poet prior to *Dandyisme* and found it hard to find a journal willing to publish his text. Consequently he and Trébutien decided to publish it themselves, further driven by the notion that a book on dandyism should be, anyway, an "eccentric, rare and precious" (Moers, p. 261) object.

D'Aurevilly, for the first time, celebrated dandyism and dedication to pose as a distinction. Dress, while important, was relegated to second place behind D'Aurevilly's emphasis on the "*intellectual* quality" of Brummell's position. As Ellen Moers points out in her seminal text *The Dandy*, "Barbey's originality is to make dandyism available as an intellectual pose. The dandy is equated with the artist; society thus ought to pay him tribute. Brummell is indeed the archetype of all artists, for his art was one with his life" (p. 263).

The understanding of dandyism as an artistic presentation of the body related to the single-minded pursuit of bohemian individuality was developed thoroughly in the writings of Charles Baudelaire. Baudelaire was not that interested in Brummell, but more in the modernity, as he saw it, of the ideas that he expressed. Baudelaire saw in Brummell's dandyism the elevation of the trivial to a position of principle that perfectly mirrored, and offered an ideal framework for, his own beliefs. Baudelaire and D'Aurevilly maintained close contact through the 1850s and 1860s, exchanging letters, books and ideas about the practice. It was primarily through D'Aurevilly's writings that Baudelaire's bohemian dandy philosophy was made clear, although Baudelaire's one essay on the subject *Le peintre de la vie moderne* later came to define Baudelaire's approach to the subject. As Moers suggests, D'Aurevilly's text on Brummell was so definitive as to liberate Baudelaire to "reach for the Dandy whole, as a symbol in the poetic sense" (p. 276).

Baudelaire's view of dandyism as an "aristocracy superiority of [the] mind . . . [a] burning desire to create a personal form of originality" (Benjamin, p. 420), was taken up by the Aesthetic movement as a righteous crusade, a veneration of beauty and abhorrence of vulgarity that was defined by the Oxbridge scholar Walter Pater and, later, the decadent aestheticism of Oscar Wilde. Wilde's earlier interpretation of dandyism took little from Brummell's original aesthetic, influenced as his style was by the material tactility and medieval styling of the period (he later threw off the aesthetic-inspired costume in favor of a more somber style). What appealed to Wilde was the idea of beauty and perfection as expressed through the body and dress—the cultivation of the person as an art form that Baudelaire had crystallized in *La vie moderne*. Like Brummell (and Honoré Balzac, the Victorian-era dandy Benjamin Disraeli, and the Parisian aesthete Count Robert de Montesquiou-Fezensac), Wilde promoted himself and his work through the presentation of his public body and quickly rose to the top of Britain's social circle as a result. The era of decadence was the apogee of dandy performance in a world that was increasingly dominated by "advertising, publicity and showmanship," in front of a far greater audience than Brummell could ever or would have wished to envisage. Wilde's performed individuality and flamboyant costume were shackled to his desire for notoriety.

Like other notable dandies of the period, Aubrey Beardsley, Max Beerbohm, and James McNeill Whistler, Wilde also looked upon dandyism as a refuge from and bulwark against the burgeoning democracy of the times (although the dandyism of the fin de siècle was fueled by new money in a way that the Regency elitists would have decried). Although Wilde believed, hoped, that aestheticism would prevail, he was perhaps more accurate with his comment that London society was "made up of dowdies and dandies—The men are all dowdies and the women are all dandies."

The Female Dandy

The emergence of the female dandy was to coincide with the downfall of Oscar Wilde. In Joe Lucchesi's essay "The Dandy in Me," he cites the American artists Georgia O'Keeffe and Romaine Brooks as notable female dandies of the period along with Brooks's London-based circle of friends—in particular the aristocrat Lady Troubridge, the British artist "Peter" Gluck, and the writer Radclyffe Hall. By the 1900s, dandyism had reached New York, with O'Keeffe and her circle drawing on Baudelaire's dandy philosophy "to make of oneself something original" (Fillin-Yeh, p. 131). Certainly Brooks's adoption of the dandy code was conscious; she noted that "'They [her admirers in her London circle] like the dandy in me and are in no way interested in my inner self or value'" (Fillin-Yeh, p. 153).

Brooks's dandyism was bound up in her lesbian sexuality. The sartorial lexicon of dandy practice offered these women a model for negotiating a social position for themselves that shared signifiers with the dress of the modern woman. Joe Lucchesi writes that "lesbians adopted the signifying dress of the modern woman as a way of expressing their sexuality yet also linking it to a similar but less dangerous figure" (Fillin-Yeh, p. 173).

As Virginia Woolf was to note in *A Room of One's Own* (1929), the woman's position within the sphere of cultural production was still difficult to carve out in what was a male-dominated community. It seems to be no coincidence that Woolf's shape-shifting *Orlando* ultimately takes on masculine form in the character's twentieth-century incarnation. Baudelaire had suggested that lesbians were the "heroines of modernism . . . an erotic ideal . . . who bespeaks hardness and mannishness" (Benjamin, p. 90), and for Brooks and her circle, there was a direct link between the invisibility of the female artist and the invisibility of female homosexuality. The figure of the dandy, certainly following Wilde, united concerns of the self as art form, the feminized homosexual, and the position of the individual within the urban environment.

Inspired by her compatriot and friend James McNeill Whistler, Brooks's dress shared many similarities with his (and de Montesquiou-Fezensac's) gentlemanly elegance and refined creativity. Although the fashions of Brooks's portraits were already thirty years out of date for men, they emerged in parallel with the notion of the modern, heterosexual woman and the modernity of Gabrielle "Coco" Chanel. Masculine dress, within the fashion arena, served to emphasize the sexualized and idealized female physique in the same way that it had always done for the male body. In addition, it offered a means for women like Chanel, who went from country girl to courtesan to milliner to designer to affect a revolution in their social status and representation. Drawing inspiration from masculine, aristocratic sporting clothing, Chanel understood as deftly as Brummell its practical and social value. As Rhonda K. Garelick writes, "By casting off the complicated frill of women's clothing and replacing them with solid colours, simple stripes and straight lines, Chanel added great visual 'speed' to the female form, while granting an increased actual speed to women who could move about more easily than before" (Fillin-Yeh, p. 41).

Contemporary Dandies

The figure of the dandy provides an abundance of material for the subversive and frequently ironic interventions that have come to be associated with British cultural production. Throughout the twentieth century, periods of acute social upheaval have witnessed parallel and intense bursts of dandy behavior. Masculine consumption, and the relationship of material goods to class and status, have played an important role for social and cultural arrivistes from Noel Coward and Cecil Beaton in the 1920s and 1930s to the publisher Tyler Brûlé and the designer Ozwald Boateng in the 1990s. "And," as writer George Walden suggests, "English sensitivities are acutely alive to anything to do with social nuance, whether accent, posture, conduct or clothes" (Walden, p. 29).

The desires of Regency dandyism were amply catered for by a plethora of specialist boutiques that had grown up in and around the streets of London's Mayfair and Piccadilly. The tailors; breeches, boot, and glove makers; milliners; and perfumiers that vied to tend to the immaculate bodies of their dandy customers were sandwiched between numerous specialists catering to the refined tastes of their client's stomach, interior décor, and cultural entertainment and welfare. The consumerism of the Regency dandy makes him a particularly analogous figure to the contemporary British dandies of the late twentieth and twenty-first centuries. Moving beyond the golden triangle to Carnaby Street in the 1960s, and latterly Islington, Spitalfields, and Hoxton Square, the sites of dandy consumption are, for the most part, reassuringly familiar—small, select boutiques, elite tailors, exquisite restaurants and bars, exclusive members clubs, artisan publishers, and celebrity delicatessens still dominate the dandy landscape.

In the twenty-first century, the steady spread of globalization, of branded culture, is once again providing fertile ground for the emergence of the contemporary dandy. The figure of the dandy presents a sartorial and behavioral precedent that allows for the celebration of beauty in material culture while cultivating an aura of superiority to it, and the early twenty-first century has seen a resurgence of interest in the traditional purveyors of material status. London's Savile Row is increasingly populated by filmmakers, recording artists, visual artists, and designers, joining the existing ranks of the traditional British gentleman who is these tailors' staple client. At the same time, brands such as Burberry, Aquascutum, and Pringle, who have traded for decades on their status as suppliers of quality and standing, have seen their customer profile alter to include an international audience in search of distinction as well as a more specific sartorial subculture closer to home—the Terrace Casual.

The early 1980s Casual project was vehemently patriotic. Forays into Europe in the early 1980s showed Britain's football fans in stark contrast to their Italian and French counterparts whose immaculate dress prompted a revolution in British working-class style that saw the football fan become the principle consumer of mostly European luxury sporting brands. Today's Terrace Casual springs from similar terrain. What separates him from his forebears is that the garments he favors are principally British, the upper-class sporting pursuits which with they are associated redolent of the masculine camaraderie and corporeal engagement of club life favored by Brummell and his circle. As with Brummell, the Terrace Casual style is engaged in the positioning of traditional upper-class "country" style in the urban environment, coopting it for the pursuit of leisure rather than the management of rural estates. While adopting the trappings of aristocracy disrupts perceived social status, it acts as a celebration rather than rejection of all the mores and moralities that these garments imply.

Oscar Wilde once said, "One should either be a work of art, or wear a work of art," and Hoxton style is the ultimate expression of the "music/fashion/art" triumvirate that characterizes British street style in the twenty-first century. As Christopher Breward writes, "D'Aurevilly's dandy incorporated a spirit of aggressively bohemian individualism that first inspired Charles Baudelaire and then Joris-Karl Huysmans in their poetic celebrations of a sublime artificiality.... It is possible to see this trajec tory leading forward through the decadent work of Walter Pater and Oscar Wilde to inform.... twentieth century notions of existential 'cool'" (Breward 2003 p. 3). While Wilde's bohemian decadence runs like a seam through the Bloomsbury set; the glam-rock outrage and rebelliousness of Jimi Hendrix, Mick Jagger, and David Bowie; the performativity of Leigh Bowery and Boy George; and the embodiment of life as art in Quentin Crisp, it is the Hoxton Dandy, as epitomized by the singer Jarvis Cocker, who presents

an equally subversive contemporary figure. Originality is as crucial for the Hoxton Dandy as it was for Brummell and Hoxton Square, once a bleak, principally industrial quarter of East London, now at the heart of a trajectory of British bohemianism that began in Soho in Brummell's time. Hoxton has quickly become a hub of new media/graphic/furniture/fashion design style that embraces its gritty urban history of manufacturing. Artisan clothing has often drawn upon dress types more usually associated with the workingman in order to emphasize the masculinity of artistic pursuit, the physical labor involved in its production. This is no less true of the Hoxton style, which is rooted in a flamboyant urban camouflage—a mix of military iconography, "peasant" staples, and industrial work wear, made from high-performance fabrics whose functionality always far outweighs their purpose.

In his time, the modernity of Brummell's monochromatic style marked him out in opposition to more decadent European fashion and made him a hero to writers such as Baudelaire. Modernism in the twentieth century continued to struggle to establish itself as a positive choice in British design culture, yet the periods of flirtation with clean lines and somber formality were intense and passionate, a momentary reprieve from the ludic sensibilities British designers more commonly entertained. The early British Modernists of the 1950s sought to emulate the socially mobile elements of American society. Stylistically, they drew inspiration from the sleek, sharp, and minimal suit favored by the avant-garde musicians of the East Coast jazz movement. Philosophically, early mods saw themselves as "citizens of the world" (Polhemus 1994 p. 51), a world in which it only mattered where you were going, not from where you came. In 2003 clean lines and muted colors once more afforded relief from the riot and parody of postmodernism that had dominated British fashion since the emergence of Vivienne Westwood and, latterly, John Galliano. The Neo-Modernist style draws, as it did in Brummell's day, on established sartorial traditions but subverts them through materials (denim for suits, shirting fabrics for linings), form (tighter, sharper, and leaner than the norm) and, ultimately, function.

Brummell was, in fact, almost puritanical in his approach to style. Max Beerbohm wrote in the mid-twentieth century of "'the utter simplicity of [Brummell's] attire' and 'his fine scorn for accessories,'" which has led contemporary commentators such as Walden to note that "Brummell's idea of sartorial elegance, never showy, became increasingly conservative and restrained"

(Walden, p. 28). Aesthetically, British gentlemanly style is the closest to Brummellian dandyism. As in previous centuries, the gentleman is defined by class and by his relationship to property (rural and urban). This easy, natural association reflects the apparent effortlessness of dress, manners, and social standing. Gentlemanly dress is loaded with expressive, but never ostentatious, clues; as Brummell suggested, "If [the common man] should turn . . . to look at you, you are not too well dressed; but neither too stiff, too tight or too fashionable." Brummell's refusal of finery for a more practical costume can be seen in the contemporary confinement of his own style of cravat, frock coat, and highly polished boots to special-occasion wear. In this, the early twenty-first-century gentlemanly uniform of gray or navy suit, black lace-up shoe, white shirt, and modestly colorful tie more than nods to Brummell's stylistic approach.

See also Benjamin, Walter; Brummell, George (Beau); Europe and America: History of Dress (400–1900 C.E.); Fashion, Historical Studies of; Fashion and Identity; Wilde, Oscar.

Bibliography

Balzac, Honoré de. *Sur le dandysme. Traité de la vie élégante. Par Balzac. Du dandysme et de George Brummell par Barbey D'Aurevilly. La peinture de la vie moderne par Baudelaire. Précédé de Du délire et du rien par Roger Kempf.* Paris: Union générale d'Edition, 1971.

Barbey d'Aurevilly, Jules. In *Du dandysme et de George Brummell.* Edited by Marie-Christine Natta. France: Plein Chant, 1989.

Benjamin, Walter. *Charles Baudelaire: A Lyric Poet in the Era of High Capitalism.* Translated by Harry Zohn. New Left Books, 1973. Reprint, London: Verso, 1997.

Breward, Christopher. *The Hidden Consumer.* Manchester, U.K.: Manchester University Press, 1999.

——. "21st Century Dandy: The Legacy of Beau Brummell." In *21st Century Dandy.* Edited by Alice Cicolini. London: British Council, 2003.

Bruzzi, Stella, and Pamela Church Gibson, eds. *Fashion Cultures.* London: Routledge, 2000.

Evans, Caroline, and Mina Thornton, eds. *Women and Fashion.* London: Quartet, 1989.

Fillin-Yeh, Susan, ed. *Dandies: Fashion and Finesse in Art and Culture.* New York: New York University Press, 2001.

Garelick, Rhonda. *Rising Star: Dandyism, Gender, and Performance in the Fin de Siècle.* Princeton, N.J.: Princeton University Press, 1998.

Laver, James. *Dandies.* London: Weidenfeld and Nicolson, 1968.

Lucchesi, Joe. "The Dandy in Me." In *Dandies: Fashion and Finesse in Art and Culture.* Edited by Susan Fillin-Yeh. New York: New York University Press, 2001.

Lytton, Edward Bulwer. *Pelham; or, Adventures of a Gentleman.* London and New York: G. Routledge and Sons, 1828.

Mason, Phillip. *The English Gentleman: The Rise and Fall of an Ideal.* London: Deutsch, 1982.

Moers, Ellen. *The Dandy: Brummell to Beerbohm.* London: Secker and Warburg, 1960.

Polhemus, Ted. *Street Style.* London: Thames and Hudson, Inc., 1994.

Walden, George. *Who's a Dandy?* London: Gibson Square Press, 2002. Includes a translation of Jules Barbey D'Aurevilly's "Du dandysme et de George Brummell." 1845.

Alice Cicolini

DEBUTANTE DRESS

Once restricted to young women from wealthy families on the social register, the traditional long, white formal dress and opera-length kid gloves of the debutante are more and more frequently also worn by daughters of the middle class. Cultural variations, such as the Hispanic *quinceañera*, not only introduce a young woman into society but also reinforce ethnic identity. While making a debut no longer necessarily signifies that the deb is looking for a husband—the age of a debutante ranges from fifteen to the mid-twenties—it is still a rite of passage denoting adult status socially.

Development of Debuts

The term "debut," to enter into society, is French in origin but became familiar to English speakers during the reign of King George III (1760–1820) when Queen Charlotte began the practice of introducing young aristocratic women at court. From 1837 on, they were called "debutantes," later shortened to "debs." The Lord Chamber-lain's Office developed strict regulations regarding proper dress for court presentations. From 1820 to 1900, ladies wore fashionable evening dresses, a mandatory headdress of veiling and feathers plus a train attached first at the waistline and, in later years, at the shoulders. Long, white kid gloves, bouquets, or fans were often added (Arch and Marschner 1987). In the United States of the early nineteenth century, elite families gave relatively small parties to introduce their marriageable-age daughters to their friends and to single men of appropriate age and status.

After the Civil War and the emergence of new wealth based on industry and railroads, the parties began to grow into lavish balls as old and new wealth vied with one another for status. One party featured an artificial lake with a large papier-mâché swan that exploded on cue, sending hundreds of roses into the air. American debutantes wore full evening dress but did not add the headdresses and trains of their English counterparts. White became standard for English debs by the end of the nineteenth century while American girls could also choose a color, as long as it was a very pale pastel. Male escorts wore formal evening wear, either tails or tuxedos, just as in the early twenty-first century. As an alternative to the private parties, exclusive social clubs, usually all male, were formed in the nineteenth and early twentieth centuries to present a group of their daughters or granddaughters at a cotillion or ball. Social club cotillions are usually more formal than family balls with a master of ceremonies and a grand march or promenade before the dancing begins. All of the girls in the group must wear the same color, almost invariably white, but may choose their own style of dress. Long, white gloves are usually worn with strapless or sleeveless gowns (Post 1937, 1969, 1997). Individual parents may give an additional party sometime within the debutante social season, traditionally the period between Thanksgiving and New Year's when university students are home for the holidays (Mills 1959; Tuckerman and Dunnan 1995).

In the twentieth century, debutante balls, whether given by a family or by one of the exclusive social clubs, gained media attention, and the public began criticizing the lavishness of the events, particularly in the 1930s and 1940s. In the 1950s, subscription dances were organized to raise money for charity through debuts. For an entrance fee, debutantes could be introduced at an annual ball and the proceeds contributed to a charitable cause. One of the largest is the National Debutante Cotillion and Thanksgiving Ball, of Washington, D.C., benefiting the Children's Hospital National Medical Center. In addition to couching the social event within philanthropy, subscription debutante balls allow middle-class parents to give their daughters a debut, as long as they have a

sponsor from the cotillion organization. Financial requirements for balls usually include a participation fee, the purchase of a table for eight, and sometimes the purchase or sale of space in a souvenir book, and, of course, the mandatory dress and gloves. Subscription balls or cotillions vary in prestige and exclusivity, and the costs reflect these differences.

Ethnic and Cultural Debuts

Every year thousands of fifteen-year-olds from a wide variety of Hispanic backgrounds celebrate their birthdays with a *quinceañera*, a unique combination of religion and debut that emphasizes cultural identity. Few young African American women make their debuts through the older social clubs, but many debut through African American organizations. The Van Courtlandt Society in San Antonio, Texas, was founded in 1915 and shortly thereafter began holding balls, and in Savannah, Georgia, the Alpha Phi Alpha fraternity has sponsored the Annual Debutante Presentation and Ball since 1944. Some African American debuts are as expensive and exclusive as those of the white balls, but others, like the Club Les Dames Cotillion of Waterloo, Iowa, are quite inexpensive and focus on the debutantes' social and academic accomplishments. The Chicago chapter of the Kosciuszko Foundation emphasizes scholastic achievement and community service in addition to the debs' Polish heritage. The San Marino Woman's Club of California requires that its debs perform a number of volunteer hours in community projects (Lynch 1999; Salcedo 1997). With the exception of the *quinceañera*, a fashionable white evening gown with long, white kid gloves is the standard dress for all of the above debuts.

Regional Variation

Debutante events vary ethnically and socioeconomically, but the biggest difference in dress is regional. Mardi Gras debutantes in New Orleans wear jeweled gowns and long trains with Medici collars as well as glittering crowns, while Texas debs stray the furthest from classic white formals. For instance, in Laredo, Texas, young women from the oldest families wear elaborate eighteenth-century-style ball gowns with panniers, and middle-class debs wear heavily beaded ultra suede "Native American" costumes in pageants held during the annual George Washington Birthday celebration. During Fiesta in San Antonio, Texas, twenty-four duchesses, a princess, and a queen wear elaborately bejeweled gowns and trains in a faux coronation. The trains are based upon the requirements for English court presentations. The earliest ones were usually of satin and lightly beaded, but soon became the background upon which motifs from such themes as "The Court of Olympus" (1931) or "Court of the Imperial House of Hapsburg" (1987) could be represented in rhinestones and beads. They may weigh up to seventy-five pounds, and up to thirty-five thousand dollars is spent on the handwork. While wearing all of those rhinestones and beads, the young women must perform the royal bow in which they lower their bodies until they are essentially sitting on the floor and then bend forward from the waist until the head almost touches the floor. The bow has been copied all over Texas and is known as the "Texas dip" when it is performed by Texas debs at the International Debutante Ball in New York City (Haynes 1998).

Conclusion

Although many people feared that debuts would disappear in the 1960s when such elitist and ostentatious displays of wealth came under heavy social criticism, debuts have actually become more prevalent. The benefits of debuts have even extended to young men at times. A small number of *quinceañeros* have been given for fifteen-year-old boys in Hispanic communities, and in Dayton, Ohio, the Beautillion Militaire has been held annually since 1968 for African American males. The organizers felt that since debutante events seemed to enhance self-esteem and raise the aspirations of the young women who participated in them, similar benefits might accrue to their young men taking part in

similar events. Now, thousands of daughters (and a few sons) from a wide socioeconomic range become Cinderellas (or Prince Charmings) for a night.

See also Evening Dress; Fancy Dress

Bibliography

Arch, Nigel, and Joanna Marschner. *Splendour at Court*. London: Unwin Hyman, 1987.

Birmingham, Stephen. *America's Secret Aristocracy*. New York: Berkley, 1990.

Haynes, Michaele Thurgood. *Dressing Up Debutantes*. Oxford: Berg, 1998.

Lynch, Annette. *Dress, Gender and Cultural Change*. Oxford: Berg, 1999.

Mills, C. Wright. *The Power Elite*. New York: Oxford University Press, 1959.

Post, Emily. *Etiquette*. New York: Funk and Wagnalls, 1937.

——. *Emily Post's Etiquette*. New York: Funk and Wagnalls, 1969.

Post, Peggy. *Emily Post's Etiquette*. New York: HarperCollins, 1997.

Salcedo, Michele. *Quinceañera!* New York: Henry Holt, 1997.

Tuckerman, Nancy, and Nancy Dunnan. *The Amy Vanderbilt Complete Book of Etiquette*. New York: Doubleday, 1995.

Michaele Haynes

QUINCEAÑERAS: A HISPANIC RITE OF PASSAGE

Quinceañeras (from quince or fifteen) are traditional celebrations of a daughter's fifteenth birthday. Unlike Sweet Sixteen celebrations, they combine religious and social elements. A quinceañera begins with a full Catholic mass followed by a dinner and dance. Most parish priests require attendance at special religious classes before the event. The honoree wears a white or pastel dress with yards of ruffles and lace and is crowned with a tiara by her grandmother at the dance. Ten to fourteen of her closest friends and relatives, who with their escorts make up the court of honor, wear matching bridesmaid-like dresses. A boudoir-style "last doll" is dressed identically to the honoree and symbolizes the end of childhood (Salcedo 1997).

DELAUNAY, SONIA

The artist Sonia Delaunay sought ways to bring modern art out of the confines of traditional easel painting. She carried this out by refashioning everyday objects as tools to explore her theories of color and by infiltrating daily life with art in a way that traditional painting could not. While her involvement in the fashion business spanned less than a decade, her prolific career in textile designs and color studies continues to influence fashion designers.

Sonia Terk was born 14 November 1885 into a poor Jewish family in the Ukrainian village of Gradizhsk and adopted by her well-to-do aunt and uncle in Saint Petersburg at an early age. She studied art periodically in Karlsruhe, Germany, and continued her studies at the Académie de la Palette in Paris, where the intense color palette of artists of the fauvist movement influenced her early development as a painter.

In 1910 she married the painter Robert Delaunay, whose research into the theory of "simultaneity," or "Orphism," served as the basis for her lifelong experiments in color. This new style, which attempted an instantaneous visualization of the experience of modern life in all its complexity, conveyed rhythmic energy and dynamic movement through the creation of color contrasts on the painted surface. Sonia Delaunay's first "simultaneous" paintings include *Contrastes simultanés* (1912) and *Le Bal Bullier* (1913), and she created her first simultaneous dresses in 1913 to match the energy of the new foxtrot and tango at the popular Parisian dance hall Le Bal Bullier. She also collaborated with the poet Blaise Cendrars to design a simultaneous book, *La Prose du Transsibérien et de la Petite Jehanne de France* (1913). In the initial years of her marriage, she integrated the realms of home and art by fashioning her apartment in the simultaneous style, creating blankets, cushion covers, lampshades, goblets, and curtains.

The Russian Revolution of 1917 resulted in the cutting off of Delaunay's substantial family income, so she turned to her marketable designs as a new means of financial support. Living briefly in Spain, she quickly established her public reputation as an innovator in both costume and fashion there by designing costumes for Sergey Diaghilev's *Cléopâtre* (staged in 1918) and showcasing simultaneous dresses, coats, home furnishings, and accessories in her store, Casa Sonia. This exposure earned her interior-decorating commissions from wealthy patrons and the Petit Casino theater (opened 1919).

In 1921 Delaunay returned to Paris and developed a new genre, *robes-poèmes* (poem-dresses), by juxtaposing geometric blocks of color and lines of poetry by Tristan Tzara, Philippe Soupault, and Jacques Delteil onto draped garments. She received a commission for fifty fabric designs by a Lyons silk textiles manufacturer, and over the next thirty years, the Dutch department store Metz and Company purchased nearly two hundred of Delaunay's designs for fashion and home decoration. In 1923 she designed costumes for Tristan Tzara's theater production *La coeur à gaz* (The gas-operated heart) and her first exhibition-style presentation of her textiles and clothing took place at the Grand Bal Travesti-Transmental.

The following year, Delaunay established her own printing workshop, Atelier Simultané, so that she would be able to supervise the design process of her prints. Embroideries in wool and silk combinations,

sometimes accented with dull metal and mixed furs, incorporated a new stitch she invented, *point du jour*, or *point populaire*. Delaunay's meticulously embroidered and appliquéd coats brought commissions from the wives of fashion designers, artists, and architects, and from film and theater actresses including Gloria Swanson, who brought the Atelier much publicity.

Delaunay approached her textile designs in the same manner as her paintings. She incorporated rigorous yet simple geometric shapes, stripes, spirals, zigzags, and disks, crossing and intermingling with the strict discipline typical of constructivism. Colors were limited to four, occasionally five or six, contrasting hues in the same design: deep blues, cherry reds, black, white, yellow, or green, or softer combinations of browns, beiges, greens, and pale yellows. The vibrant synergy of these colors exemplified Delaunay's concept of modernity and the rhythms of an electrified modern city.

At the 1925 Exposition des Arts Décoratifs, Delaunay collaborated with the furrier Jacques Heim in displaying female fashion, accessories, and interior furnishing in her Boutique Simultané. That same year, the Librairie des Arts Décoratifs responded to the positive reception of her work by publishing an album of her fashion plates titled *Sonia Delaunay, ses peintures, ses objets, ses tissus simultanés, ses modes*. Delaunay's success with fashion lay partly in the adoption of the liberating, contemporary silhouette for female clothing that developed during World War I. The stylish, unadorned tunic cuts of the mid-1920s, with straight necklines, no waistlines, and few structural details, served as a blank, two-dimensional canvas for her geometric forms. Shawls, scarves, and flowing wraps for evening gave her additional flat surfaces on which to explore, enabling her to expand her business. She also challenged traditional practices in the fashion industry. In a lecture at the Sorbonne, "The Influence of Painting on Fashion Design," she explained the *tissu patron* (fabric pattern), an inexpensive invention that allowed both the cutting outline for the dress and its corresponding textile design to be printed at the same time.

Financial pressures during the Great Depression, coupled with the 1930s trend toward fabric manipulation and construction details that did not accommodate her designs, led Delaunay to close her couture house in 1931. She foresaw that the future of fashion was in ready-to-wear, not the custom pieces she was creating. While she turned away from fashion design after this point, she continued to take private orders from the couturiers Chanel, Lanvin, and especially Jacques Heim.

Delaunay spent the rest of her life concentrating on painting and continued to apply her theories to a wide range of objects, including tapestries, bookbindings, playing cards, and a children's alphabet. She also became involved in projects with the poet Jacques Damase. Toward the end of her life, she exhibited frequently and was honored in 1967 with a major retrospective exhibition at the Musée National d'Art Moderne in Paris for her contribution to modern art. She died on 5 December 1979 at the age of ninety-four.

Textile and fashion design gave Delaunay the freedom of experimentation and spontaneity that she later transposed into her paintings. She brought art to the streets and made her wearable paintings an integral part of the everyday. Her artistry has had a profound influence on the work of contemporary fashion designers including Marc Bohan for Christian Dior, Perry Ellis, Yves Saint Laurent, and Jean Charles de Castelbajac, all of whom have referenced her work in their collections.

See also Art and Fashion; Chanel, Gabrielle (Coco); Dior, Christian; Fashion Designer; Ellis, Perry; Lanvin, Jeanne; Saint Laurent, Yves.

Bibliography

Baron, Stanley, with Jacques Damase. *Sonia Delaunay: The Life of an Artist.* New York: Harry N. Abrams, 1995. A comprehensive biography of the artist's personal and professional endeavors.

Cohen, Arthur A. *Sonia Delaunay.* New York: Harry N. Abrams, 1975. Provides biographical and visual insight into the artist's overall career.

Damase, Jacques. *Sonia Delaunay, Fashion and Fabrics.* Translated by Shaun Whiteside and Stanley Baron. London and New York: Thames and Hudson, 1991. An extensive collection of the artist's fashion illustrations and textile designs of the 1920s.

Delaunay, Sonia. *Nous irons jusqu'au soleil.* Paris: Editions Robert Laffont, 1978. An autobiography based on journal entries starting from the early 1930s.

Morano, Elizabeth. *Sonia Delaunay: Art into Fashion.* New York: George Braziller, 1986. Explains the artist's impact on the development of modern fashion through a broad collection of fashion plates and textile designs.

Angel Chang

DEMEULEMEESTER, ANN

Ann Demeulemeester (1959–) was born in Courtrai, Belgium. When she presented her first winter collection in Paris in 1987, six years after graduating in fashion design from the Royal Academy of Fine Arts in Antwerp, the press release described her work as "a collection for the conscious woman." The text went on to say, "[her] inspiration sources are neither directly definite nor visual; the clothes are brought about by personal impressions. A logical evolution, that is a result of a purification of ideas, which forms a specific style with its own atmosphere." These words seemed appropriate in the early twenty-first century, as Demeulemeester's work could be read as an interpretation of a very personal universe—one that was not immediately traceable, but could be felt in every article of apparel she designed. At their core lay the study of form and the development of a personal signature, rather than introductions of new trends or fashions or working around seasonal themes. For Demeulemeester, designing was a form of problem-solving. In a rational, almost scientific manner, she sought a solution for each "problem," often over several successive seasons. Cut and pattern were explored until the solution presented itself and perfection was achieved.

The experimental subject in this design laboratory was the designer's own body. Demeulemeester consistently tried out new creations on herself or on a select number of friends. The semiscientific aspect of Demeulemeester's creative process was in stark contrast with her ultimate silhouettes, which bore witness to intense emotion and extensive experience of life. However exhaustively thought out the cut may have been, the result was never sterile. The nonchalance that characterized her style was natural yet profoundly investigated; it was never just a matter of course. This dichotomy in Demeulemeester's creative process distinguished her entire oeuvre. Ann Demeulemeester sought out paradox; she seemed to go along with a certain duality or opposition in order to ultimately undermine it. Her investigation was in fact a study in search of balance, with the underlying thought that perfect balance is unattainable, just as the symmetrical body is in fact nonexistent—and for the designer, perhaps of no interest anyway. The shortcomings, the incompleteness, and the voids are what generate artistic creation. It was this continual search that lay at the root of Ann Demeulemeester's drive and passion—or as the text on a T-shirt and invitation suggested: *Aimer, c'est agir* ("to Love is to act").

Motion and Gravity

Motion was a leitmotif throughout Demeulemeester's work. The challenge of gravity, a force that allows apparel to appear to be in motion even when its wearer is standing still, was technically explored in ever new applications, season after season. One symbol of this investigation was the feathers that reappeared in each new collection in the form of necklaces or jewelry, chosen for their beauty and natural perfection.

We are accustomed to the fact that gravity causes everything to fall, so how does one mislead a law of nature? How does one dislodge the balance of human form into balance, and how does one cut an article of clothing so that it looks as though it is being blown open? How does one summarize the beauty of a T-shirt that just happens to glide off the shoulder? Questions of this nature served as starting points for collections in which the different movements of Demeulemeester's models repeatedly accentuated and revealed different parts of the wearer's body—shoulders, stomach, or hips.

Unforgettable pieces in this context included Demeulemeester's asymmetrically-cut trousers that revealed part of the hips. Whether or not these garments were held up with a subtle ribbon, they looked as though they were just on the verge of sliding to the floor. The movement was subtle yet introduced a hint of danger. Such techniques as drapery and asymmetrical cut as well as ribbons and belts provided the technical tools. When gravity could not be conquered, Demeulemeester made use of ribbons or belts—which had evolved into fetish elements in her collections—to hold the fabric against the wearer's body.

The designer felt a need to find different ways to develop an article of clothing without traditional pattern techniques. Demeulemeester's 1998 winter collection began with a piece of cloth into which she cut holes for her arms. Careful observation of what subsequently happened to the fabric led her to develop a number of wrapping techniques, which in turn produced new forms. In her winter collection for 1999, she pushed this approach even further by applying the wrapping techniques to sheepskin. The result was a most unexpected interpretation of the *mouton-retourné*.

The feeling of motion and nonchalance in Demeulemeester's work found its counterweight in her elegant jackets and pantsuits of the 1990s, which exuded a certain discipline and masculinity. Perfect in cut and shoulder line, here too, it was such details as an asymmetrically-buttoned blouse or the selection of a subtly hanging fabric, for example, that softened the severity of the whole. In her 1997 winter collection, both aspects came together in a jacket that closely hugged the body on one side with the help of a belt, but fell loosely on the other side.

Materials

Alongside Demeulemeester's use of such supple fabrics as rayon, viscose, and silk, she had a passion for leather and fur, two hard-to-control materials that combine such opposites as aggression and tenderness. The tough character of the materials was undermined by the manner in which they were worked into the final pieces. One need think only of her elegantly draped wraparound jackets in fur (autumn–winter 2000–2001) or the jackets with large imposing capes that were produced in the finest leather for her 2002–2003 winter collection. The materials symbolized what the total silhouette demonstrated: the "wild warrior" versus the "fragile innocent girl."

A third noteworthy material was white painter's linen or canvas, which Demeulemeester initially used for invitations, catwalks, the interior of her shop in Antwerp, and a table she designed in 1995—for which she was awarded the first prize in design from the Flemish Community. Demeulemeester first worked this white canvas into her apparel collection in 1999. Since Demeulemeester studied art before going into fashion design, she was especially fascinated by the nude female body and its proportions—a factor that continued to play a central role in her fashion design. Beginning from nothing, from empty space or nudity, in order to then add only the essentials without excess decoration, translated equally strongly into her emphatic choice of black and white, the two extremes of the color spectrum—a choice that is both hard and poetic. In the same way that a black-and-white photograph can embody the essence of an image, Demeulemeester was more interested in nuances, shadows, and forms than in decoration and color.

Gender Issues

Demeulemeester showed her first collection for men in 1996, which was presented together with her collection for women. For Demeulemeester, men and women are not opposites, but rather form a balance around the same extremes. The flow and interchange of masculine and feminine characteristics could be found in the mannequins who modeled her clothes, in the punk singer Patti Smith (her frequently mentioned and quoted muse), but above all in the apparel itself. It is worth noting here that tough-looking shoes or boots more than once formed a symbolic counterpoint within one of Demeulemeester's silhouettes, such as her 1998 shoe, which mounted a man's shoe form on a high heel.

See also Belgian Fashion; Gender, Dress, and Fashion; Margiela, Martin; T-Shirt.

Bibliography

Derycke, Luc, and Sandra van de Veire, eds. *Belgian Fashion Design*. Ghent and Amsterdam: Ludion, 1999.

Kaat Debo and Linda Loppa

DEMIMONDE

Nineteenth-century Paris was acknowledged by contemporaries as the "capital of pleasure" (Rearick, p. 40). Its reputation as a city of diversions and licentiousness was established following the Revolution and Reign of Terror during the period of the Directory (1795–1799), when a heterogeneous, parvenu society indulged itself in a hedonistic lifestyle. Returning émigrés, the newly distinguished, and the recently wealthy, as well as many visiting foreigners, enjoyed the city's luxury shops, restaurants, cafés, dance halls, public gardens, and boulevards. The pleasure-seeking atmosphere that characterized Paris in the Directory set the tone for the next hundred years.

The political upheaval of 1789 created a less rigidly stratified society than that of the *ancien régime*, a society in which birth and wealth no longer dictated access to power. Under Napoleon I and increasingly throughout the nineteenth century, a growing and affluent bourgeoisie claimed its right to the lifestyle and privileges formerly the prerogative of the elite. In this opportunistic culture of burgeoning capitalism and materialism, men and women were on the make. The social mobility, economic expansion, and, to a degree, the political uncertainty of nineteenth-century France gave birth to *le demimonde*.

Coined by Alexandre Dumas fils in 1855 for the title of his play, *Le Demimonde*, the term "demimonde" (literally, half-world) originally designated a class of fallen society women. But the definition came to be much broader, including all women of loose morals who lived at the edge of respectable society and, by extension, the men—royal, aristocratic, bourgeois, and bohemian—who frequented that ambiguous world. Although the demimonde certainly existed prior to the mid-nineteenth century, it was during the Second Empire (1852–1870) and the early Third Republic (1870–1914), that it flourished and that its supreme type, the courtesan, achieved spectacular notoriety.

The Courtesan

In an age of limited career possibilities for women, the courtesan took maximum advantage of one of the oldest professions open to her. Prostitution was widespread in nineteenth-century Paris, but the courtesan was set apart from the anonymous streetwalker by virtue of the wealth and status of her protectors and her own celebrity and visibility on the social scene. In addition to their physical beauty and sexual attractiveness, the most successful courtesans were also personages. In Colette's novella, *Gigi* (1944), Madame Alvarez, a former demimondaine and Gigi's grandmother, sums up a (real-life) leading courtesan: "She is extraordinary. Otherwise she would not be so famous. Successes and celebrity are not a matter of luck" (Colette, p. 24). Accomplished in the arts of gallantry, courtesans were strong-willed and independent women as well as cultivated, entertaining, and witty.

The *cocottes* (literally, hens) and "grand horizontals" of the latter half of the nineteenth and early twentieth century were the culmination in an evolution of women of dubious character. The *grisette* (a reference to her gray work dress) of the First Empire (1804–1814) and Bourbon Restoration (1814–1830) was a tender-hearted, good-natured young woman, toiling in the fashion trades, who formed a relationship—based on love and necessity—with a student, artist, or writer. The more venal *lorette* made her appearance during the July monarchy of the bourgeois king, Louis-Philippe (1830–1848), a time of rapid growth and industrialization in France. In 1841, the French writer Nestor Roqueplan applied the name *lorette* to the kept women who inhabited the newly developed area in the ninth arrondissement, around the parish church, Notre-Dame-de-Lorette. Unlike the *grisette*, the *lorette* did not work for a living; instead, she sold her favors and relied on liaisons (sometimes simultaneous) with men of substantial (though not lavish) means to support her.

The ostentatious lifestyle and moral corruption of the Second Empire produced *la garde*, as the group of about a dozen of the most flamboyant *grandes cocottes* was designated. In fact, the *fête impérial*, or imperial party, has been described both by those who lived through it as well as later historians as the heyday of the demimondaine. Napoleon III himself set the example; among his several mistresses were some of the era's most celebrated courtesans: Marguerite Bellanger, the Countess Castiglione, and Giulia Benini, known as la Barucci.

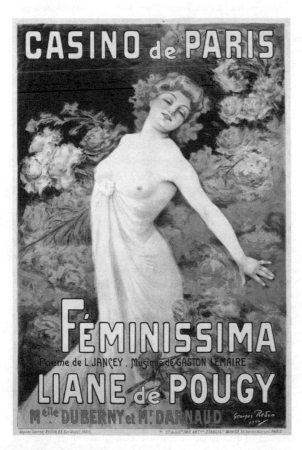

Demimonde poster by Georges Redon, 1904. Liane de Pougy, a star of the Belle Epoque, strikes an uninhibited pose. De Pougy reigned at the top of the social structure of the "grand horizontals," leading an ostentatious and flamboyant lifestyle. © SWIM INK/CORBIS. REPRODUCED BY PERMISSION.

The Belle Epoque, too, contributed its stars to the demimonde firmament. Liane de Pougy, Caroline Otero ("la Belle Otero"), and Emilienne d'Alençon, known as *Les grandes trois*, were the undisputed trio at the apex of the coterié of grand horizontals.

In his essay "The Painter of Modern Life" (1863), the French poet Charles Baudelaire refers to the courtesan (and her alternate type, the actress) as "a creature of show, an object of public pleasure" (p. 36). And indeed the larger-than-life personae of these women not only inspired novels, plays, and paintings (themselves often controversial), but also provided regular fodder for gossip columns in the popular press. Their fabulous gowns, extravagant jewels, lavishly decorated mansions, superb horses and carriages, notable lovers, and outrageous exploits riveted the public's attention. The avariciousness of the courtesans earned them the unflattering neologism of *mangeuses* (eaters—of men and fortunes). Throughout the period, social commentators and writers such as Honoré de Balzac, Emile Zola, and Walter Benjamin linked the courtesan (and prostitution in general) with the rise of capitalism, speculation, commodity exchange, and a culture of consumption, and deplored their degenerative influence on society.

The Courtesan and Fashion

As a signifier of modernity, fashion played an important part in nineteenth-century French society as a whole and for the courtesan in particular, for whom it was the primary vehicle by which she flaunted her power and challenged respectable women of the elite. The rules had changed since the eighteenth century when fashions were set by the court. Adopting a no-holds-barred attitude, the demimondaine used her enormous wealth and status as an outsider to wear the newest, most daring styles. Courtesans became the acknowledged leaders of fashion whose flashy ensembles were reported on, avidly studied, and often copied by upper-and middle-class women.

For the demimondaine, fashion operated on a number of levels. Many courtesans came from a background of poverty and obscurity. As the mistress of a wealthy man, having the means to dress in the height of fashion was surely a gratifying indulgence and a welcome source of attention. But fashion was also a weapon in the battle between the *mondaine* (society lady) and the demimondaine. In the somewhat fluid society of nineteenth-century France, clothing was an all-important tool in the creation of persona. Fashion was unquestionably women's territory, and they were expected to take an active interest in its pursuit. Yet the society woman was confined by strictures of etiquette to maintain respectability in dress. The courtesan, on the other hand, was not bound by these same limitations. In fact, her conspicuous toilettes not only attested to her own originality in taste and sophisticated chic, they also reflected the wealth and generosity of her protector—in all likelihood, a married man. For the demimondaine, fashion was both socially and sexually empowering.

One of the most famous scenes in Emile Zola's novel *Nana* (published in 1880 but set in the Second Empire) illustrates this usurpation of sartorial prestige and supremacy by the courtesan. At the height of her success, Nana attends the Grand Prix de Paris at Longchamp dressed in a strikingly avant-garde and brazenly seductive ensemble. As a courtesan, Nana is prohibited from entering the weighing-in enclosure. However, on the arm of one of her aristocratic lovers, she gains admission to this exclusive preserve, where she walks slowly past the stands in full view of the empress and the wife of another noble lover whom she will eventually ruin. Zola's description of the dresses of the women in the enclosure is intentionally generalized; it is Nana's splendid costume that merits close observation in details of cut and color.

The blurred boundaries between the monde (high society) and the demimonde were nowhere more evident than in the patronage of leading couturiers by courtesans and society women alike. Charles Frederick Worth, considered the father of haute couture, created opulent toilettes for Empress Eugénie and women of the imperial circle. But his other, equally famous clients included Cora Pearl, who counted among her lovers the duc de Morny and Prince Napoleon (respectively half-brother and cousin to Emperor Napoleon III) la Païva, and other demimondaines of the era. At least on one occasion, a socialite and a demimondaine found themselves waiting for a fitting with Worth. Apparently, the couturier gave precedence to the courtesan. At the turn of the twentieth century, Maison Worth as well as more recently established designers such as Jacques Doucet and Jeanne Paquin continued to dress both women of the upper ranks and courtesans and actresses.

The Urban Landscape

Paris of the Second Empire and Third Republic provided the appropriate setting for the demimonde and the courtesan. Under the direction of Baron Georges-Eugène Haussmann, Napoleon III's prefect of the Seine, Paris was transformed from a still largely medieval city with insular neighborhoods of dark, winding streets to a modern metropolis with a more uniform architectural style, straight, broad boulevards, and public parks. In this new urban landscape, arenas of fashionable life multiplied. Already fixtures of the Parisian scene, theaters, restaurants, cafés, and dance halls proliferated, while newer venues such as the *café-concerts* (music halls) became popular toward the end of the century. In Montmartre, the Moulin Rouge and the Folies Bergère drew large audiences from both the moneyed and the plebeian public.

Within Paris itself, the haunts—and breeding ground—of the demimonde were located on the Right Bank. Certain areas such as the Faubourg Saint-Honoré had been known for their luxury shops and *hôtels particuliers* since the eighteenth century. In the first half of the nineteenth century, other fashionable neighborhoods developed north of this older quarter, and by the second half of the century, the epicenter of "le high life" encompassed the Rue de la Paix, the Place Vendôme, the Rue Royale, the Boulevard des Italiens, and the Opera. The most renowned couturiers, jewelers, and silk and lingerie merchants all had their premises here. The well-known Théâtre des Variétés, which figures in the opening scene of *Nana*, and legendary restaurants such as the Café Anglais, the Maison Dorée, and Maxim, the scenes of dazzling parties and amorous intrigue, were also located in this area.

Fashion was an integral part of the demimondaine's public lifestyle and one that required a different toilette for each occasion. Morning, afternoon, and evening dress varied depending on the season and the venue. Carriage dress, appropriate for the obligatory afternoon ride along the Champs-Elysées to the Bois de Boulogne, was deliberately showy. The scene in *Nana* referred to above depicts the fashion contest that took place at Longchamp amid the wide cross-section of society that attended the annual Grand Prix. At theaters catering to an upper-class audience, high fashion was on display both on the stage, as worn by leading actresses, and in the private boxes, where courtesans in décolleté gowns presided in the company of their admirers. Demimondaines of the Second Empire also made their mark at public dance halls such as the Jardin de Mabille, an open-air garden in the Avenue Montaigne patronized as well by Princess Metternich (a Worth client) and members of the exclusive Jockey Club. Since they were constantly on view, it was imperative for leading courtesans to make the most of fashion opportunities in their daily social schedule.

The Demimonde Legacy

World War I brought to an end the rarified lifestyle of the Belle Époque and with it the phenomenon of the demimonde and courtesan. The social, economic, and cultural conditions that permitted the excesses of debauchery and squandering of fortunes were irreversibly changed. The demimondaines who lived beyond the war years were no longer the idolized, public figures they had been. In their old age, many returned to a life of economic deprivation and obscurity.

Nonetheless, the demimonde has left its legacy in the wider world of twentieth-century fashion and celebrity culture. Actresses and performers such as Josephine Baker, Mae West, Marlene Dietrich, and Madonna have capitalized on their erotic appeal as a form of power and a significant aspect of their personae. Madonna in particular, in her collaboration with the French designer Jean Paul Gaultier, has explicitly challenged dress norms, exploiting the implications of both hyperfeminine and androgynous fashions. More than mere sex symbols, these women have an insolence and a flamboyance that derive from the example of the courtesan.

Popular culture of the past century has embraced different elements of the demimonde lifestyle, modes of behavior, and attitude toward fashion. Rock-and-roll musicians and their fans, for example, have carried on the tradition of social and sartorial rebellion and self-creation through clothing that defined the demimondaine. The discotheque and nightclub scene re-creates in a sense the ambiguous and socially mixed terrain of the demimonde with an undercurrent of dangerous glamour. The notoriously public lifestyle of celebrities in the early 2000s (film and sports stars, rock musicians, artists, socialites, and even royals), followed closely in the press, also mirrors that of the late nineteenth century. In these forms, the spirit of the demimonde continues to exert its influence.

See also Balzac, Honoré de; Benjamin, Walter; Fashion and Identity.

Bibliography

Baudelaire, Charles. *The Painter of Modern Life and Other Essays*. Edited and translated by Jonathan Mayne. London: Phaidon Press Ltd., 1964.

Clayson, Hollis. *Painted Love: Prostitution in French Art in the Impressionist Era*. New Haven, Conn.: Yale University Press, 1991.

Colette. *Gigi; Julie de Carneilhan; Chance Acquaintances*. Translated by Roger Senhouse and Patrick Leigh Fermor. New York: Farrar, Straus and Giroux, 1980.

Griffin, Susan. *The Book of the Courtesans: A Catalogue of Their Virtues*. New York: Broadway Books, 2001.

Maneglier, Hervé. *Paris impérial: La vie quotidienne sous le Second Empire*. Paris: Armand Colin, 1990.

Rearick, Charles. *The Pleasures of the Belle Époque: Entertainment and Festivity in Turn-of-the-Century France*. New Haven, Conn.: Yale University Press, 1985.

Richardson, Joanna. *The Courtesans: The Demi-Monde in Nineteenth-Century France*. Cleveland, Ohio: World Publishing, 1967.

Steele, Valerie. *Paris Fashion: A Cultural History*. Oxford: Oxford University Press, 1985.

Zola, Emile. *Nana*. Translated by George Holden. New York: Penguin Books, 1972.

Michele Majer

DEMOREST, MME.

Madame Demorest (1824–1898) created one of the most important and influential fashion empires in the late nineteenth century. She was born Ellen Louise Curtis in Schuylerville, New York, on 15 November 1824. After graduating from Schuylerville Academy at the age of eighteen, Ellen moved to Saratoga Springs, where she opened a millinery shop with the financial help of her father, a hat factory owner. She apparently achieved some success and decided to move to New York City with her business. There she met a widower, William Jennings Demorest, a dry goods merchant who had recently opened Madame Demorest's Emporium of Fashion on Broadway. Ellen Curtis and William Demorest married in 1858. A perfect embodiment of the new Madame Demorest's Emporium, Ellen was pivotal to the expansion and diversification of her husband's business and became one of the most influential arbiters of fashion of her era.

Fashion Innovations

Madame Demorest's entrepreneurial success can be attributed to her astute understanding of the American fashion business as a combination of creativity, marketing, distribution, and brand identity. She claimed a number of innovative products, including a line of comfortable corsets, an affordable hoopskirt, the Imperial Dress-elevators (loop fasteners enabling skirts to be raised), and a sewing machine that could sew backwards; moreover, she developed the Excelsior Dress Model drafting system, a tool for making dress patterns. However, her mass-produced and marketed paper dress patterns remain her most important contribution. Madame Demorest's foray into paper patterns came at a time of great social change, when a growing middle class was clamoring for access to affordable fashions and technical advances like the sewing machine were becoming increasingly common in the home, making these fashion ambitions possible. Madame Demorest's paper patterns reached women across America and Europe, bringing them up-to-date fashions, a feat of no little importance.

Evolution of Patternmaking

A Madame Demorest tissue-paper pattern for a boy's jacket was advertised in Frank Leslie's *Ladies Gazette* as early as March 1854. These early patterns were unsized and sold for twenty-five to fifty cents. Starting first with children's garments, Demorest moved to women's dress. The aim was to sell patterns for separate garments— bodices, sleeves, mantles, basques—that could be used in combination with others. Madame Demorest later made custom patterns by special order available. It was not until the early 1870s (nearly a decade after her archrival Ebenezer Butterick) that Madame Demorest was mass-producing sized patterns. The business burgeoned into an international enterprise within a few short years. In 1876 Madame Demorest sold over 3 million paper patterns throughout America and Europe.

Demorest Publications

Marketing played an enormous role in the success of Madame Demorest's fashion empire. By employing the title "Madame," Demorest imbued her products with the cachet and allure of French fashions, reinforced in the early advertising in fashion journals such as Frank Leslie's *Ladies Gazette* and *Godey's Lady's Book*. Madame Demorest also promoted her products, especially the paper patterns, in the Demorests' own publications, which were generally managed by her husband. In 1860 *Madame Demorest's Mirror of Fashions* began

quarterly circulation. The magazine featured plates of their own dress patterns and included a paper pattern stapled to the inside as an enticement to the reader. In 1864 the magazine was expanded to be *Demorest's Illustrated Monthly Magazine and Madame Demorest's Mirror of Fashions*. In 1865 the name was changed to *Demorest's Monthly Magazine and Demorest's Mirror of Fashions* (commonly referred to as *Demorest's Monthly*) and reached over 100,000 readers. At the peak of her career, Madame Demorest also produced *Madame Demorest's What to Wear and How to Make It* (1877–1884) and quarterly catalogs. She also expanded the *Demorest's Monthly* to London circulation.

Merchandising

In addition to marketing through the magazines, the paper patterns were sold through a nationwide network of shops called "Madame Demorest's Magasins des Modes." In the mid-1870s there were 300 shops employing 1,500 (mainly women) sales agents. In addition to the paper patterns, the Excelsior drafting system was also showcased and sold at these satellite stores, which were located in major cities in the United States, Canada, Europe, and Cuba.

Madame Demorest continued to use the flagship Emporium store on Broadway to merchandise the full array of Demorest products. In the earliest years, Madame Demorest's Emporium of Fashion was located at 375 Broadway near Lord and Taylor and Brooks Brothers; then the business was moved to 473 Broadway in 1860. In 1874 the Emporium moved farther uptown, to 17 East Fourteenth Street, and catered to an increasingly fashionable set. The Emporium provided custom dressmaking services to wealthy clients, as well as ready-made accessories and undergarments; Demorest's unique line of cosmetics and perfumes; and, of course, the monthly magazines and paper patterns. Although it was only a small part of their overall business, the custom dressmaking service at the Emporium lent prestige and luxury to their name, a marketing tool that Madame Demorest was savvy enough to harness.

Madame Demorest's participation in numerous national and international exhibitions cemented her reputation as a fashion arbiter. A frequent exhibitor at London and Paris shows, she is noted as having created a large display at the Philadelphia Centennial Exhibition in 1876 in which she installed several women's and children's fashions; her drafting tool, "Dress Model"; and a huge case filled with paper patterns.

Progressive Causes

In the 1880s Madame Demorest's fashion empire began to decline. Unlike her competitor Ebenezer Butterick, Madame Demorest had never filed patents for her paper patterns and eventually lost out in this arena. The paper pattern business was sold in 1887. In later years both Ellen and her husband, William, turned their attention to social causes that had always been of interest to them. William was deeply committed to the temperance cause, which often found expression in the pages of the *Demorest Monthly* magazine. Ellen increasingly supported women's causes. Both Demorests were strong advocates of abolition and deserve particular recognition for their unusually progressive business policy of hiring African American women agents who were treated equally with their white employees, sharing workplaces and receiving equal pay.

At the height of her career in the 1870s, Madame Demorest could rightly claim to be one of the most influential fashion disseminators of her era. Her paper patterns and fashion magazines reached millions of women in America and Europe, bringing sophisticated yet affordable fashions to the masses. At the same time, Madame Demorest created brand identity through her innovatively named lines of accessories and cosmetic products, while burnishing her reputation for quality through her luxury dressmaking establishment. While it could be said that she appeared at the right place at the right time when a population of women had the inclination and means, via the sewing machine, to make fashions at home, Madame Demorest was singularly astute in her comprehension of women's fashion needs and her ability to market to them through the widely read Demorest publications.

MRS. STRATTON'S WEDDING TROUSSEAU

One of Madame Demorest's most newsworthy custom dressmaking projects was the wedding trousseau she designed for Mrs. Charles Stratton, née Miss Lavinia Warren, in 1863. The Strattons were better known at the time as General and Mrs. Tom Thumb, midgets who toured with P. T. Barnum's circus. After their wedding in New York City, which was attended by 2,000 people, Mr. and Mrs. Stratton headed to Europe on a world tour that included reception at several royal households. The Madame Demorest reception dresses, worn by Mrs. Stratton at these functions, were widely publicized.

See also Godey's Lady's Book; Patterns and Pattern-making; Sewing Machine.

Bibliography

Drachman, Virginia G. *Enterprising Women: 250 Years of American Business.* Chapel Hill: University of North Carolina Press, 2002.

Emery, Joy. "Development of the American Commercial Pattern Industry: The First Generation, 1850–1880." *Costume* 31 (1997): 78–91.

Gamber, Wendy. *The Female Economy: The Millinery and Dressmaking Trades, 1860–1930.* Urbana: University of Illinois Press, 1997.

Kidwell, Claudia Brush. *Cutting a Fashionable Fit: Dressmakers' Drafting Systems in the United States.* Washington, D.C.: Smithsonian Institution Press, 1979.

Milbank, Caroline Rennolds. *New York Fashion: The Evolution of American Style.* New York: Harry N. Abrams, 1989.

Mott, Frank Luther. *A History of American Magazines.* Cambridge, Mass.: Belknap Press of Harvard University Press, 1938.

Ross, Ishbel. *Crusades and Crinolines: The Life and Times of Ellen Curtis Demorest and William Jennings Demorest.* New York: Harper and Row, 1963.

Lauren Whitley

DEPARTMENT STORE

The birthplace of the department store was Paris. The Bon Marché opened in 1852, soon followed by Printemps (1865) and the Samaritaine (1869). Existing shops in the United States—Stewart in New York, Wanamaker in Philadelphia and Marshall Field in Chicago—adopted the format during the 1870s. The department store brought together a series of retail methods tested out in smaller European and American shops earlier in the century, for example, the proto-department stores in industrial cities in the north of Britain (Lancaster, chapter 1). The department store proper was distinctive from previous experiments in its scale, lavishness, and resonance with the society that spawned it. The early Parisian stores were hugely influential models for subsequent stores springing up all over the world. The history of the department store has been largely located in Western

Europe and North America. The arrival of the format in East Asian cities such as Shanghai and Tokyo in the early twentieth century has been associated with westernization, but the stores were often locally owned and managed, creating complex issues surrounding their identity.

The conditions for the rise of the department store lay in late-eighteenth-and early-nineteenth-century industrialization and urbanization, which led to the growth of prosperous, urban, middle-class populations and the ready availability of mass-produced consumer goods, along with an increasingly sophisticated understanding of the pleasurable rather than merely utilitarian possibilities of consuming them. Important department stores were situated in urban centers, on principal shopping streets, working in conjunction with other shops, entertainment venues, and transport networks. However, well-heeled suburbs also had department stores in their high streets. By the late nineteenth century, considered the hey-day of the department store, these shops had become emblematic of metropolitan modernity and were famously made the backdrop of Émile Zola's novel *The Ladies' Paradise*.

The major department stores of each important city—for example, Harrods, Liberty's and Selfridges in London—quickly became urban landmarks and cultural institutions, cited in guide books as tourist attractions. During the early twentieth century, American stores took the lead as innovators, becoming increasingly influential on their European counterparts. During the interwar and early postwar periods, while alternative shopping sites were developing, fashion magazines such as *Vogue* show that the big department stores retained their central position within urban consumption practices in many cities. However, despite stores' attempts to address broader sections of the population, the opening of teen departments and the provision of new buildings, fundamental modernization of the format did not occur. The combined competition from the multiple store and alternative boutique in the urban high street and from the suburban shopping center and out-of-town mall led to a slow decline in the cultural and economic importance of the department store from the 1960s, accelerating during the 1980s. There were several factors that increased a store's chances of survival: possession of an international reputation, such as that of Harrods, London; absorption into a larger group, such as the House of Fraser or the John Lewis Partnership; positioning on a major metropolitan shopping thoroughfare or as the anchor in a shopping center. The

early twenty-first century has witnessed a revival of the metropolitan department store, connected with a renewed focus on luxury goods and designer fashion, prime examples being Selfridges and Liberty in London. The department store has proved to be enduring.

Stock Diversity and New Selling Methods

An important innovation of department stores was their wide variety of merchandise, breaching the boundaries of previously largely trade-specific shop-keeping. Many of the early department stores actually developed from smaller existing shops, most commonly drapers. They grew department by department, taking over neighboring properties to house the expanding businesses, until it was necessary to provide a new building or reface the existing ones to provide coherence. Department store pioneer William Whiteley famously boasted that he sold "everything from a pin to an elephant." The system worked on a basis of low margins and high turnover. The stores were certainly a place for the sale of mass-produced goods and have been associated with the rise of ready-to-wear clothing. However, most stores continued to provide traditional tailoring and drapery well into the twentieth century. The diversity of stock was matched by an array of amenities and entertainments, including banks, restaurants, travel agents, fashion shows and live music, and services such as free delivery and alteration of garments.

Store histories are entwined with those of their owning dynasties, who usually gave their name to their stores, for example, the Wertheims and Schockens in Germany and the Lewises in England. Stores often merged with or were taken over by other stores, for example, the evolving nature of Britain's House of Fraser described by Moss and Turton. The business was organized in a hierarchical, rational, and paternalistic manner. Strict control of the workforce was balanced with benefits such as health-care, pensions, and social clubs. Indeed during the early days many of the employees lived in the upper stories of the building. This practice faded out following several high profile, devastating fires caused by gas lighting and poor fire-proofing of buildings. The stores required vast staffs; for example, Harrods of London had 4,000 employees in 1914. For nineteenth-and early twentieth-century social commentators and novelists, the figure of the young female shop assistant symbolized the dubious respectability, moral ambiguity, and blurring of class boundaries they found so disturbing about the department store. However, until the interwar period, the majority of employees were actually male and lower middle class. Positions were sought after, although salaries were low.

Customers and a New Kind of Shopping

From the beginning, the department store was associated with bourgeois consumers. As Miller has argued, "The department store was . . . a bourgeois celebration, an expression of what its culture stood for and where it had come over the past century" (Miller, p. 3). It was also initially seen as the exclusive province of women. The stores' provision of basic amenities such as lavatories and refreshment rooms made a day trip to town newly accessible for suburban and provincial middle-class women, enabling them to take advantage of improved public transport networks. Early department store owners, such as William Whiteley of Bayswater in London, were vocal in their claims to make shopping in the city a safe and respectable activity for unchaperoned women (Rappaport). However, they also attempted to exploit feminine desires using new ideas about consumer psychology.

The distinctiveness of the department store model lay as much in the presentation of shopping as a pleasurable leisure activity as with the nature or number of goods available. Previously, shopping models had largely favored counter service and the acknowledgment of an obligation to buy once the shop was entered. In the new stores, the role of the retail staff was redefined and a different kind of shopping was encouraged, characterized by window shopping and browsing through displays of goods with fixed and ticketed prices. These practices drew on the cultures of the international exhibitions that followed London's Great Exhibition of 1851. All this, it was believed, would encourage impulse buying.

During the early twentieth century, department stores began to cater to men with dedicated departments. In 1936 Simpson Piccadilly opened in London's West End, claiming to be the first department store entirely for men. The lower ground floor alone was designed to house a barber's shop, soda fountain, gun shop, shoe shop, chemists, florist, fishing shop, wine and spirit shop, luggage shop, snack bar, dog shop, sports shop, cigar and tobacconists, gift shop, saddlery shop, theater agent, and travel agent. During the opening months the aviation department even exhibited full-sized airplanes. The opening of the store coincided with new ideas about masculinity, which allowed for the adoption of shopping methods previously labeled feminine. *The Lady* (7 May 1936) commented on this, "It is amusing to find that the man's shop is designed and set out with all the allure of one devoted to women's luxuries. Shopkeepers, evidently, do not share that masculine theory that a man always knows just what he wants and so is immune from display or advertisement."

Design, Display, and Advertising

Zola called the department stores "cathedrals of commerce" and they were certainly associated with lavish, striking, and fashionable architecture, acting as an advertisement for the goods inside. Famous and innovative architects were often employed: Victor Horta designed Innovation in Brussels (1901), Louis Sullivan designed Carson Pirie Scott in Chicago (1899–1904), and Erich Mendelsohn designed the Schocken store in Stuttgart (1926–1928). The *Scotsman* commented on the opening of Simpson Piccadilly in London designed by the modernist architect Joseph Emberton, "the building is an expression in every way of the modern spirit" (4 May 1936). But the buildings were not just fashionable shells. The latest technological advances were used to assist the retail process. Iron then steel frames created vast uninterrupted expanses of floor space and plate glass technology facilitated story-high bands of display windows flanking the shopping street. Inside, escalators and lifts were installed, helping to sustain a continuous flow of customers between the street and the upper echelons of the building. Pneumatic tube systems were provided for communication and placing orders. Tiers of galleries allowed light from the roof to penetrate the shop floor, assisted by the pioneering use of first gas then electric lighting. Lighting was also used on the facade of the building—floodlighting, lit signage, and window illumination—so that the stores had a nighttime presence in the city, catching the eye of revellers.

Department stores led the way with developments in retail display, with opulent displays of goods inside the stores, in the shop windows, and sometimes spilling onto the streets. Displays were often themed in relation with events being held in the stores or national celebrations. It was the shop window in particular that became emblematic of the department store's contribution to the urban spectacle and seduction of customers. The early department stores had a particularly sophisticated understanding of the power of advertising. To the consternation of traditional smaller-scale retailers, significant amounts were spent on newspaper and magazine advertisements, and on regular publishing of catalogs, the Bon Marché in Paris distributed 1.5 million catalogs. In 1894 (Crossick and Jaumain p. 12). This emphasis on design, display, and advertising was integral to the new kind of shopping promoted in the department store, encouraging consumption through the exploitation of visual pleasures.

See also Boutique; Liberty & Co.; Retailing; Shopping; Window Displays.

Bibliography

Crossick, Geoffrey, and Serge Jaumain, eds. *Cathedrals of Consumption: The European Department Store*. Aldershot, U.K.: Ashgate, 1999. The key text in the field: an excellent and diverse edited collection of essays.

Lancaster, Bill. *The Department Store: A Social History*. London and New York: Leicester University Press, 1995. A comprehensive study of the British department store in social historical terms.

Leach, William. *Land of Desire: Merchants, Power and the Rise of a New American Culture*. New York: Vintage, 1993. A lively account of the American story from the 1890s to the 1930s.

MacPherson, Kerrie L., ed. *Asian Department Stores*. Richmond, Surrey U.K.: Curzon, 1998.

Miller, Michael *The Bon Marché: Bourgeois Culture and the Department Store, 1869–1920*. Princeton, N.J.: Princeton University Press, 1981. A case study of the first department store, highlighting issues of class and business methods.

Moss, Michael, and Alison Turton. *A Legend of Retailing: House of Fraser*. London: Weidenfeld and Nicolson, 1989. A detailed, well-illustrated account of one of Britain's most important department store groups.

Rappaport, Erika Diane. *Shopping for Pleasure: Women and the Making of London's West End*. Princeton, N.J.: Princeton University Press, 2000. A contextual study of the department store in its West End location in the Victorian and Edwardian eras, focusing on issues of gender.

Zola, Émile. *The Ladies' Paradise*. Oxford U.K.: Oxford University Press, 1998. This is a translation of Zola's novel *Au bonheur des dames*, first published in 1883, reputedly based on the Bon Marché.

Bronwen Edwards

DIANA, PRINCESS OF WALES

In 1997 the influential fashion photographer Mario Testino shot a series of seminal images of Princess Diana wearing Gianni Versace for *Vanity Fair* magazine. These photographs have come to define the look and glamour of a woman who became an important fashion icon of the twentieth century. In the early twenty-first century, media interest in her image remained undiminished.

Diana Frances Spencer (1961–1997) was born in Park House on the Queen's estate at Sandringham, the third child of Johnny, eldest son of the seventh earl of Spencer and a member of one of England's most important aristocratic families. In 1969 when Diana's parents were divorced, her father retained custody of the children, and in 1975 when Diana was fourteen, the seventh earl died, and the family moved to their ancestral home, Althorp in Northampton. When she was seventeen, her father bought her an apartment in Kensington, London, where Diana found work as a nanny until the day of her engagement to Prince Charles was announced.

The couple married on 29 July 1981, at St. Paul's Cathedral. Diana's wedding dress, designed by Elizabeth and David Emanuel, was a fairy-tale fantasy showcasing traditional English craftwork. It featured woven silk taffeta by Stephen Walters of Suffolk and historic lace from a flounce of Carrickmacross lace owned by Queen Mary and from the Nottingham Company, Roger Watson. The dress became one of the most famous outfits in the world, and the twenty-five-foot train added a touch of theatricality that would create an enduring image of the event, which was watched on live television by more than one billion people worldwide.

From that moment the princess became an international figure, photographed and documented wherever she went, and she became a global fashion icon. Diana loved clothes; they were a personal passion but also a requirement of her new public life. As one of the most important members of the British royal family, her wardrobe requirements were fixed in a world that required ball gowns and matching hats, shoes, and handbags, items that were not typical of mainstream fashion for young women in the early 1980s.

It is not surprising then that in the early years of her marriage she was steered toward established British fashion designers, including Murray Arbeid, Belville Sassoon, and Gini Fratini, whose traditions of classic tailoring for day and romantic evening wear dated back fifty years. Diana was, however, determined to stamp

Dress worn by Princess Diana. Diana worked within the boundaries of royal tradition to create her own modern style, which was both elegant and youthful, quickly elevating her to fashion icon status. AP/WIDE WORLD PHOTOS. REPRODUCED BY PERMISSION.

a modern and youthful personal style on this public and formal persona, and, more than any other British designer, Catherine Walker helped her to develop an elegant, tailored look that became her own.

From the 1980s Catherine Walker helped Diana create a streamlined modern version of clothes for her public life as the Princess of Wales. After her divorce from Prince Charles, Diana went on to develop a more individual style that reflected her new independence and freedom. Diana understood her role as a fashion icon and that everything she wore—every new accessory and change of hairstyle—would be scrutinized. In the 1990s, in search of a new look, she remained loyal to British designers, notably Jacques Azagury, who encouraged her to wear dresses cut revealingly low and to wear shorter skirts. Increasingly, however, she turned to European designers— the Italian designers Versace and Valentino and to the French couture houses of Dior, Lacroix, and Chanel. Her look became more international with a sophisticated and simple silhouette and an effect that was all in the details. Superb cut and luxurious materials worn with coordinated colored accessories, handbags, jewelry, and shoes became her hallmark. It is this image that defined an enduring fashion look of the late twentieth century.

See also Royal and Aristocratic Dress.

Bibliography

Howell, Georgina. *Diana: Her Life in Fashion.* New York: Rizzoli International, 1998.

Tierney, Tom. *Diana, Princess of Wales, Paper Doll: The Charity Auction Dresses.* New York: Dover Publications, Inc., 1997.

Catherine McDermott

DIOR, CHRISTIAN*

The French couturier Christian Dior (1905–1957) was born in Granville, France. Descendant of a manufacturing family of the Norman bourgeoisie, Dior spent his early childhood in the comfortable surroundings of the family villa, Les Rhumbs, located on the Channel coast in Granville, which now houses a museum dedicated to his memory. At that time the little port was celebrated as a fashionable seaside resort, and in summertime it was transformed into an elegant Paris neighborhood." The family moved to Paris in 1911, to the new bourgeois neighborhood of Passy, near the bois de Boulogne.

Following his father's wishes, Dior registered at the École de Sciences Politiques in Paris after passing his baccalaureate. He eagerly followed Parisian artistic developments and met various writers, painters, and musicians, befriending, among others, Pierre Gaxotte, Maurice Sachs, Jean Ozenne and his cousin Christian Bérard, Max Jacob, and Henri Sauguet. In 1927, after his military service and with his father's support, he opened an art gallery at 34, rue de la Boétie. Because his parents refused to have their name on a commercial sign, the establishment was given the name of his associate, Jacques Bonjean. The gallery exhibited the works of such contemporary artists as Giorgio de Chirico, Maurice Utrillo, Salvador Dalí, Raoul Dufy, Marie Laurencin, Fernand Léger, Jean Lurçat, Pablo Picasso, Ossip Zadkine, Georges Braque, and Aristide Maillol.

Christian Dior's carefree youth soon came to an end: in 1931 his brother was institutionalized, his mother died, and his father was completely ruined financially. "In the face of this accumulation of tragedies," Dior reacted by a "flight to the East." He was "naïvely impelled by a desperate search for a new solution to problems that this crisis of capitalism had made acute," embarking on a study trip to the Soviet Union with a group of architects, only to find on his return that his associate was also ruined. His impoverished family abandoned Paris, retreating first to Normandy and later taking refuge in the village of Callian, near Cannes. Dior stayed behind in Paris, closing his first gallery and later joining the gallery of Pierre Colle on the rue Cambacérès. He thus went from "losses to forced sales while continuing to organize surrealist or abstract exhibitions that drove away the last art lovers." In 1934 he had an attack of tuberculosis, and his friends took up a collection to send him for treatment. The following year he found himself in Paris with no income and no place to live. He survived on the sale of one of his last canvases, *Le plan de Paris* of Raoul Dufy, which the designer Paul Poiret had sold to Dior when he was in similar destitute circumstances.

Couture and Costume

Jean Ozenne, who was designing for couture houses, introduced Dior to the fashion world and to his clientele. At the age of thirty, Dior devoted himself to studying fashion drawing, referring only to what he knew and appreciated of Edward Molyneux, Coco Chanel, Elsa Schiaparelli, and Jeanne Lanvin. He managed to sell his first sketches of hats and then of dresses. His clients were fashionable hat makers and couture houses but he "also sold ideas to foreign buyers." Publication of his drawings in *Le figaro* produced his first public recognition. In 1937 the couturier Robert Piguet selected four of his designs and asked him to produce them for his "half-collection" (midseason collection). Christian Dior was just thirty-two, and these were, he said, the "first dresses that I really created."

In June 1938 Robert Piguet offered him a position as a designer in his couture studio located at the Rond Point of the Champs Élysées. There he designed three collections in a row. The second contained his "first wide dresses," inspired by dresses worn by young heroines of the French second empire children's literature "les petites filles modèles" (well-behaved little girls). They were characterized by a "raised bust, round width starting from the waist, petticoat of English embroidery." As the creator of a successful design called "English coffee," he was introduced to Carmel Snow, editor of *Harper's Bazaar*. In 1939 his last prewar collection for Piguet launched the line of what came to be called "amphora dresses" marking the "beginning of rounded hips." In parallel with his work as a designer, Dior designed theater costumes for individual clients. He dressed, for example, the actress Odette Joyeux in *Captain Smith* by Jean Blanchon (at the théâtre des Mathurins, December 1939) and in *The School for Scandal* by Richard Sheridan (at the same theater, February 1940).

Dior was mobilized at the outbreak of war in 1939 and then joined his family in the unoccupied zone of France after the 1940 armistice. Piguet, still in Paris, asked him to resume his prewar position, but Dior was late in replying and found the position already taken by Antonio del Castillo in the fall of 1941. Dior then went to work for Lucien Lelong, together with another young designer, Pierre Balmain. The two shared design responsibilities throughout the war: "Balmain and I never forgot that Lelong taught us our profession in the midst of the worst restrictions," said Dior. The personality of Lucien Lelong, the clever president of the Chambre syndicate de la couture parisienne (association of haute couture) throughout the German occupation of France, deeply influenced the future couturier. After his study trip to the United States in 1935 and the launch of his Edition line, Dior had developed an interest in foreign markets and high-end ready-to-wear. In contrast, he saw fashion under the German occupation as "appalling" and exclaimed: "With what vengeful joy did I do the opposite later."

It was nonetheless a productive period for him: films (*Le Lit à colonne* by Roland Tual [1942], *Lettre d'amour* [1942] and *Sylvie et le fantôme* [1945] by Claude Autant-Lara, *Échec au roi* by Jean-Paul Paulin [1943], and *Paméla; ou, L'énigme du temple* by Pierre de Hérain [1945]) and Marcel L'Herbier's play *Au petit bonheur* (at the théâtre Gramont, December 1944) gave him the opportunity to escape from the textile rationing that governed ordinary clothing and to conceive, often for Odette Joyeux, historically inspired costumes full of long dresses and extravagant designs.

After the Liberation, Dior's colleague Pierre Balmain opened his own couture house in 1945 on rue François Ier and encouraged Dior to do the same. Marcel Boussac, a major French textile manufacturer and president of the cotton-marketing syndicate, offered Dior the artistic direction of the Gaston firm (formerly called Philippe et Gaston) on rue Saint-Florentin. Considering the business outmoded, Dior suggested instead that he start a couture house "where everything would be new, from the state of mind and the personnel to the furnishings and the premises," in view of the fact "that foreign markets, after the long stagnation of fashion due to the war, were bound to demand really new fashions." Marcel Boussac invested sixty million francs in the project.

The House of Dior

In 1946 Dior chose a private mansion located at 30, avenue Montaigne as the site of his own firm, which was established on 8 October 1946. The enterprise had four models and eighty-five employees, sixty of whom were seamstresses. The management team, in addition to the head couturier, included a financial director (Jacques Rouet), a studio head (Raymonde Zehnacker, who came from Lelong), a head of workshops (Marguerite Carré, who came from Patou), and an artistic adviser and head of high-fashion design (Mitzah Bricard, a designer from Molyneux). The couture house itself included two workshops for dresses and one for suits (whose head was Pierre Cardin, then twenty years old). From the outset, it also had, on the ground floor, a shop selling articles and accessories not requiring fitting. Salons and shops were decorated by Victor Grampierre in tones of white and pearl gray and furnished in neo–Louis XVI style.

The opening was widely publicized: "When the summer 1946 collections came out, everyone was talking about Christian Dior, because an extraordinary rumor was spreading that the financial assistance of Marcel Boussac, the French king of cotton . . . would enable him to create his own house." Even before it was seen, Dior's first collection thus made news, and he won the support of the editors of *Vogue*, *Le figaro*, and *Elle*. The newcomer among couture houses, Christian Dior finally unveiled, at the conclusion of the winter shows, his first collection for spring 1947. Considered the opening shot for the New Look, it immediately gained notoriety for the couturier at the age of forty-two. "The first season was brilliant, even beyond my hopes," he said. The second, in which the couturier carried "the famous New Look line to its extreme," achieved "breathtaking" success and was accompanied by the launch of his first perfume, Miss Dior.

With this impetus, Dior spent the last ten years of his life developing his couture house and extending his influence on world fashion. (In 1955 the Dior firm had one thousand employees in twenty-eight workshops and accounted for half the exports of the French couture industry.) For his first collection, Dior received the Neiman Marcus Award in 1947. From his trip to the United States, he learned, as he put it, that "if I wanted to reach the large number of elegant American women . . . I had to open a luxury ready-to-wear shop in New York." The following year, he set up the subsidiary Christian Dior New York, Inc., at 745 Fifth Avenue. He repeated the process in Caracas in 1953 (Christian Dior Venezuela), in London in 1954 (Christian Dior, Ltd.), and later in Australia, Chile, Mexico, and Cuba. These companies custom-made styles from Paris and

sold accessories. But it was not until 1967 that a real line of ready-to-wear was distributed, under the label Miss Dior.

In 1948 the Christian Dior perfume company was set up, and it launched the second fragrance, Diorama, in 1949, followed by Eau Fraîche (1953) and Diorissimo (1956); the first lipsticks came out in 1955. Dior opened a stocking and glove division in 1951 and established the Christian Dior Delman company, which made shoes designed by Roger Vivier; finally, the Paris shop added a gifts and tableware department in 1954. The range of products with the Dior label was enlarged thanks to a very innovative policy for licenses, the first of which was granted in 1949. By this means, the label was attached to all the accessories of female dress, from girdle to jewelry, but also, and very early on, to totally distinct articles, such as Christian Dior Ties (1950).

The growth of the house was fostered by a simple and effective public relations policy: little direct advertising but excellent relations with the press, which guaranteed great visibility for the fashions as well as for their creator (who was featured on the cover of *Time* on 4 March 1957). The couturier gave many interviews, designed disguises for memorable parties (among them, the Venetian ball of Carlos de Beistegui given at the Palazzo Labia on 3 September 1951), and continued to dress stars, such as Marlene Dietrich in Alfred Hitchcock's *Stage Fright* in 1950 and Henry Koster's *No Highway in the Sky* in 1951 and Ava Gardner in Mark Robson's *The Little Hut* in 1956. In *Christian Dior et moi* (1956), Dior described his career, strewn with Parisian celebrities, pitfalls, coups de théâtre, and palm readers' predictions. In passing, he reassured the reader about the motives for his long-ago trip to the Soviet Union and emphasized his admiration for the entrepreneurial spirit, thus helping to forge the paradoxical myth of the creator of scandals with a reassuring face.

The attention given to the collections was intensified each year by the expectation—followed by the announcement—of a new major change (affecting, notably, the length of skirts). The couturier himself issued descriptive communiqués adopted by the press that frequently took a peremptory tone, such as "No yellow" or "No hats with clean and tailored style," giving force to the new fashion tendency. The collections, each containing approximately two hundred items, unveiled in succession contradictory lines that imposed on fashion a rate of change never seen before: Corolle and 8 (1947), also known as the "New Look collection"; Zig-Zag and Envol, followed by Ailée (1948); Trompe-l'œil and

Milieu de Siècle (1949); Verticale and Oblique (1951); Ovale ou Naturelle and Longue (1951); Sinueuse and Profilée (1952); Tulipe and Vivante (1953); Muguet and H (1954), A and Y (1955); Flèche and Aimant (1956); and Libre and Fuseau (1957).

La Belle Epoque Influences on the New Look

Differing in their lines, his creations were always related to one another through the constancy of certain characteristics. Structurally, the dresses came out of the intention to sculpt the silhouette along predefined lines. Whether it was the New Look, the Shock Look (the English name for the Vivante line), or the Flat Look (the H line), the body was always strongly stylized. The waist was displaced, cinched, or unbelted. The hips swelled or shrank thanks to the choice of materials able to express in shapes the energetic and tense designs of the couturier: shantung, ottoman silk, thick taffetas and satins, velvet, organza, woolen cloth, and cotton piqué generally replaced the customary use of fluid woolen and silk crepes. Originator of a style that used a large quantity of material, artifices, and ornaments, Christian Dior stimulated the growth of a number of parallel industries: corset makers, feather makers, embroiderers, makers of costume jewelry, flower designers, and also illustrators. Thus, the image of the creations of Christian Dior includes the shoes of Roger Vivier, the prints of Brossin de Méré, the tulles of Brivet, the fabrics of Rébé (René Bégué) and Georges Barbier, the jewels of Francis Winter, and the drawings of René Gruau. As for furs and hats, they were manufactured in specialized workshops of the couture house.

Stylistically, Dior's creations were frequently distinguished by ornaments that came directly from pre-1914 fashion. Simulated knots; false pockets; decorative buttons; play with cuffs, collars, basques, and tails; false belts; and bias cuts punctuated his collections with their trompe-l'oeil effects and, from the outset, erased any modernist intentions.

Dior did not specify the origin of his stylistic borrowings. In particular, he expressed only elliptical intentions to justify the inspiration for his New Look: "I have a reactionary temperament, a characteristic that is too often confused with the retrograde; we had barely come out of a deprived, parsimonious era, obsessed with tickets and textile rationing. My dream therefore naturally took on the form of a reaction against

poverty." Hence, it is in the context of the presentation of his shows that we should look for an explicit expression of his historical inspiration. Speaking of the renovation of the mansion on the avenue Montaigne, the couturier asserted that he was striving "to prepare a cradle in the style and the colors of the years of [his] Paris childhood" and described "this neo-Louis XVI, white paneling, lacquered white furniture, gray hangings, glass doors with small beveled panes, bronze wall lamps, and small lamp shades that ruled from 1900 to 1914 in the 'new' houses of Passy." He displayed a "crystal chandelier and a proliferation of palms," while the shop, on the advice of Christian Bérard, was given a hanging of cloth of Jouy "in the tradition of notion shops of the eighteenth century."

In parallel with this nostalgic neo-neo-Louis XVI style, a veritable mirroring of pastiche, Christian Dior seemed throughout his career to draw the material artifice of his pleated, draped, corseted, and decorated effects from the clothing vocabulary of the Belle Époque. "I thank heaven that I lived in Paris during the last years of the belle époque . whatever life has granted me since then, nothing will ever be able to equal the sweet memory of those days," he wrote. But by choosing as his favorite period one in which taste was eclectic, the designer avoided the domination of a single style in order to free himself to adopt all possible reinterpretations of the past.

Neither the structural artifices nor the proliferation of appliquéd ornaments interfered with the readability of the line. Paradoxically, Dior's creations attracted primarily through their sobriety. As evidence of an eclectic sensibility, the ornamental resources derived from turn-of-the-century fashion were effectively deployed with a concern for modernity hostile to the composite. The conception of each model seemed to be guided only by emphasis on a single effect at a time. From one model to the next, one's attention was shifted, for example, from the emphasis of a cut to the shimmering of a pattern or to the luxuriance of the embroidery. The directed gaze, channeled by the erasure of the superfluous—by the notorious choice of uniform and subdued colors when the cut was to be emphasized or, on the contrary, the choice of a simple cut to emphasize the fabric—guaranteed the visual impact of each model and pointed up its strong identity. It thus was beyond the individual model and only in the course of the show that the succession of appearances enabled the presentation of an aesthetic of the whole, both composite and romantic.

The constancy of stylistic borrowings from the past revealed a veritable postmodernist stance on the part of this man who was so admirably ensconced in his century. As Dior himself said:

> It is strange that in 1956 people applied the names avant-garde and aesthetic of the future to the works and the masters that we had admired between the ages of fifteen and twenty and who had already been famous for ten years among the most aware of our elders, guided by Guillaume Apollinaire.

But for Dior, "the new at all costs, even to create the absurd, is no longer the essential area of exploration." Far from the aspirations of prewar surrealism, he confided the origin of his first collections: "After so many years of wandering, weary with consorting with only painters and poets, couture wished to return to the fold and rediscover its original function which is to adorn women and to beautify them." As a result, his haute couture, while remaining a privilege of the wealthy, appeared comprehensible to everyone. Christian Dior thereby gave his signature to the first democratization of taste, if not of fashion.

By conforming the feminine silhouette to design, by dictating the choice of accessories and the circumstances appropriate for every outfit, the couturier left little room for personal expression, risk, and feminine fantasy. On the other hand, the steadiness of his "total look" guaranteed his popularity. It enabled him to satisfy an enormous public, who saw in Christian Dior, whatever their national or individual clothing cultures, the label of a guaranteed elegance. In the end, Dior's conception of a wearable fashion was also that of an exportable fashion.

Christian Dior was, in succession, an avant-garde amateur, an artisan of a kind of return to order, and, finally, a manufacturer of elegance. The first superstar couturier, he died of a heart attack at the age of fifty-two in Bagni di Montecatini, Italy. The financier Marcel Boussac thought at the time of closing the house, but in the face of pressure from license holders, he appointed the young assistant Yves Saint Laurent as artistic director, and in this way the label survived its founder. When Yves Saint Laurent left in 1960, Marc Bohan took his place and held it until Gianfranco Ferré took over in 1989. Their designs upheld the image of a couture distanced from the multiple challenges and manifestos of contemporary fashion. The classicism of Christian Dior was not shaken until the arrival in 1997 of John Galliano, who revived the active media exposure established by Dior himself.

See also Art and Fashion; Balmain, Pierre; Film and Fashion; Galliano, John; Haute Couture; New Look; Perfume; Ready-to-Wear; Saint Laurent, Yves; Theatrical Costume.

Bibliography

Cawthorne, Nigel. *The New Look: The Dior Revolution*. London: Hamlyn, 1996.

Dior, Christian. *Je suis couturier* [I am a dressmaker]. Paris: Éditions du Conquistador, 1951.

——. *Christian Dior et moi* [Christian Dior and me]. Paris: Amiot-Dumont, 1956.

Giroud, Françoise. *Dior*. Paris: Éditions du Regard, 1987.

Golbin, Paméla. *Créateurs de modes*. Paris: Éditions du Chêne, 1999.

Grumbach, Didier. *Histoires de la mode*. Paris: Éditions du Seuil, 1993.

Homage à Christian Dior 1947–1957. Paris: Musée des arts de la mode, Union centrale des arts décoratifs, 1986.

Martin, Richard, and Harold Koda. *Christian Dior*. New York: Metropolitan Museum of Art, 1996.

Milbank, Caroline Rennolds. *Couture: The Great Designers*. New York: Stewart, Tabori and Chang, 1985.

Palmer, Alexandra. *Dior*. London: V&A Publishing, 2009.

Pochna, Marie-France. *Christian Dior*. Paris: Flammarion, 1994.

——. *Dior*. Paris: Assouline, 1996.

Remaury, Bruno, ed. *Dictionnaire de la mode au XXème siècle*. Paris: Éditions du Regard, 1994.

Eric Pujalet-Plaà

DOLCE & GABBANA

Domenico Dolce was born in Polizzi Generosa (near Palermo, Sicily) on 13 September 1958. His family owned a small clothing business, where Domenico worked from childhood. Stefano Gabbana was born in Milan on 14 November 1962. He studied graphics but soon turned to fashion. After a brief period working as assistant designers, they founded the Dolce & Gabbana label, which had its first runway show as part of the New Talent group in Milan in 1985, upon the invitation of Italian fashion promoter Beppe Modenese.

In 1986 they produced their first collection, called "Real Women." In 1987 they launched their knitwear line and in 1989 their beachwear and lingerie lines. Beginning in 1988 they produced their ready-to-wear line in Domenico Dolce's family-owned atelier, located in Legnano, Milan. The first Dolce & Gabbana men's collection appeared in 1990. In 1994 they launched the D&G label, inspired by street style and a more youthful look. The clothes were produced and distributed by Ittierre.

The company launched several fragrances, including Dolce & Gabbana Perfume, By Dolce & Gabbana, and Dolce & Gabbana Men. One of their perfume ads was directed by the Italian film director Giuseppe Tornatore, with whom Dolce and Gabbana developed a close relationship, going on to act in his 1996 film *The Star Maker*. They introduced a line of eyewear under the Dolce & Gabbana and D&G labels and produced music CDs.

In 1996, for their tenth anniversary, they published *Ten Years of Dolce & Gabbana*, which included their most important advertising images and texts. In 1999 D&G Junior was created, their collection for children, which was presented at the children's fashion show Pitti Bimbo in Florence.

In 2003 their newest store, covering three floors, opened in Corso Venezia in Milan, in the former home of Brigatti, perhaps Milan's best-known luxury sportswear store. The store is designed in the round from a central piazza and includes a bar, a traditional barbershop, and an ultramodern spa. The individual stores are illuminated by lamps of Venini glass, made according to designs by Domenico Dolce.

In a 1995 interview Dolce and Gabbana recalled their first professional foray into fashion during the Milan collections as eliciting "one of the strongest emotions we have ever experienced" (Gastel, p. 238). The show marked the occasion of the birth of the Dolce & Gabbana label, which was destined to play a fundamental role in the history of Italian ready-to-wear. The designers showed full-length garments of stretch jersey, silk jackets, and oversize shirts that could be worn with casual sandals. The collection, characterized by fluidity and difference, soon found an enthusiastic public.

Dolce and Gabbana are considered the inventors of a Mediterranean style that draws its inspiration from the Sicily of Luchino Visconti's 1963 film *The Leopard* and the women of Italian realism, sensual and austere like Anna Magnani, to whom they dedicated a collection whose key element was the 1940s slip. At the beginning of their career, the designers also turned to Sophia Loren, Claudia Cardinale, and Stefania Sandrelli for inspiration. The Dolce & Gabbana woman is unbiased and brazen, but fearful of God and devoted to church and family, an attitude typical of southern Italian Catholicism. A woman who simultaneously reveals and conceals brassieres and corsets, lace, lingerie, and veils, and who is disturbing in her impetuous sensuality—a provocative woman proud of her body. The designers' models are soft, round, and full-figured. "Dark girls with dark eyes evoke the women of the south—carnal, provocative, yet austere and proud at the same time" (Sozzani, p. 5). At a time when fashion saw women as executives in two-piece suits with padded shoulders, Dolce & Gabbana's first collection included tulle and angora, twin sets in jersey lace, and soft, wide, extravagant skirts. Their favorite materials were crocheted lace, wool, and silk.

They were not looking for a retro look; however, Dolce & Gabbana turned to the past for innovation. The designers remarked, "We want to use the past to project it into the future" (Sozzani, p. 11). And making it modern involved the creative use of fabrics and colors, and the ability to blend various sources of inspiration, primarily those whose origins could be traced to the heterogeneous world of the Mediterranean.

The elements of Italian culture are reinforced through their meticulous attention to their image, and their publicity campaigns have always been handled by the world's finest photographers. Every shot is organized as if it were a film set. Their first campaign was photographed by their friend, the Sicilian photographer Ferdinando Scianna, who, with Dolce and Gabbana, was just getting started in fashion. Besides Scianna, other photographers who have worked with the label include Fabrizio Ferri, Steven Meisel—famous for his pictures of the Italian film star Monica Bellucci and the supermodel Linda Evangelista—Peter Lindbergh, and Helmut Newton.

The journalist Nicoletta Gasperini of *Donna*, the Italian fashion weekly that gave them their first cover—the model Marpessa photographed by Giovanni Gastel—helped define their image. "We convey to them how we feel and they give us back a mediated image of culture" (Gastel, p. 241).

The turning point in their international success began with their friendship with Madonna. The pop star ordered from their New York showroom a *guêpière* (corset) made of gemstones and a jacket to wear at Cannes to launch her film *Truth or Dare: In Bed with Madonna* by Alek Keshishian (1990). Madonna's participation in the 1992 D&G party and runway show publicized their friendship. Shortly after, the singer asked them to design the fifteen hundred costumes for her 1993 "Girlie Show" tour.

Dolce & Gabbana's Mediterranean style is not a rigid framework but the template of an imaginary world through which they draw inspiration. The collection changes for every season, ranging from the baroque to the plastic, from aristocratic to working class, brazen to bourgeois, from animal prints to a cardinal's cloak. In 1994, for example, after producing corsets, girdles, T-shirts, and styles emphasizing breasts and revealing cleavage, Dolce & Gabbana introduced a "Sapphic chic" masculine style for women characterized by short hair slicked down with brilliantine, which was exemplified by one of their earliest fans, Isabella Rossellini. In 2003 for their Milan men's show, they took their inspiration from contemporary soccer stars. The darlings of the Italian and international press, according to Suzy Menkes, a journalist for the *International Herald Tribune*, the two designers have the ability of being able to mix periods and countries, masculine and feminine looks, fabrics and styles.

Dolce & Gabbana is one of the best examples of the explosion in Italian ready-to-wear that occurred during the mid-1980s. Creativity and versatility, the union of the press and the star system, a range of products and clothing lines, and careful attention to distribution are all elements that contribute to the realization of an integrated system of communication.

See also Italian Fashion; Madonna; Music and Fashion.

Bibliography

Asnaghi, Laura. "Dolce & Gabbana." In *Dizionario della Moda*. Edited by Guido Vergani. Milan: Baldini and Castoldi, 1999.

Gastel, Minnie. *50 anni di moda italiana*. Milan: Vallardi, 1995.

Sozzani, Franca. *Dolce & Gabbana*. Translated by Marguerite Shore. New York: Universe Publishing/Vendome Press, 1998.

Simona Segre Reinach

DRESS CODES

Dress codes may broadly be defined as rules that regulate an individual's appearance. Sociological variables—age, occupation, class, gender, religion, or ethnicity—stipulate what can and cannot be worn. However, most people probably have a narrower, more specifically modern understanding in mind of dress codes. This stricter definition is associated with a massive uniformization of populations that began in the early nineteenth century as workers and students were disciplined to meet the demands of capitalism, industrialization, and national state formation.

Dress codes, whether explicit or implicit, may apply to small groups (for example, school or company) or an entire nation (China's "Mao suit"). Besides mandating what should be worn, dress codes dictate what should not be worn, and they can be better appreciated by conceptualizing a continuum of uniformity, ranging from strict integration into a politico-economic order to being free from its constraints. Some of the variations are as follows:

- highly standardized, group-dominated, clear hierarchy (military uniforms);
- standardized, group-oriented, hierarchy (occupational dress);
- nonstandardized, displays individuality, no hierarchy (casual dress); and
- anti-standardized, overly individualistic, anti-hierarchy (avant-garde fashion).

As an example of how politico-economic institutions regulate daily dress codes, consider how the life cycle of most individuals in Japan is characterized by uniformization, de-uniformization, and re-uniformization. During the first phase (ages 3–18), individuals begin to don school-specific uniforms that have been inspired by European military uniforms. Boys are outfitted in a blue or black jacket with brass buttons and stand-up collar. Girls often wear the *sêrâfuku* ("sailor clothes"), modeled after the traditional English sailor suit. It consists of a sailor-type collar and a pleated skirt. During the second phase of de-uniformization (ages 18–22), the dress code is relaxed as students are allowed to dress casually while at university or other postsecondary schooling institutions. The final phase, re-uniformization (ages from 22), begins after leaving postsecondary schooling and entering the adult workforce.

Inducted into Japan's corporate culture, individuals are required to adopt dress codes that reflect socioeconomic class and gender variables. White-collar male workers, or *sarariman* ("salary man"), are expected to don a white cutter shirt, red necktie, dark blue or gray suit, and black leather shoes. Hair should be short, preferably in the "seven-three part." Facial hair is generally frowned upon. Accessories complete the picture: a briefcase (or shoulder bag or attaché case). Blue-collar workers are seen in uniforms with an open collar, large, functional pockets, and a tag with name or section on the breast pocket. Helmet, boots, work gloves, and safety belt complete the ensemble. Women, who are lower in the corporate pecking order, must adhere to more standardization. OLs ("office ladies") or secretarial staff typically wear a company uniform of white blouse, vest with name tag, skirt (usually 1.9 in, 5 cm, below the knees), and high heels.

At some companies, dress codes are enforced by military-like morning inspections. Besides company loyalty and dedication to work, adhering to dress codes indicates an individual's aspiration to work toward a middle-class lifestyle as well as commitment to Japan's collective project of economic nationalism.

See also Mao Suit; Uniforms, Diplomatic; Uniforms, Military; Uniforms, Occupational; Uniforms, School; Uniforms, Sports.

Bibliography

Davis, Fred. *Fashion, Culture, and Identity.* Chicago: University of Chicago Press, 1992.

Lurie, Alison. *The Language of Clothes.* New York: Random House, 1981.

McVeigh, Brian J. *Wearing Ideology: State, Schooling, and Self-Presentation in Japan.* Oxford: Berg, 2000.

Rubinstein, Ruth P. *Dress Codes: Meanings and Messages in American Culture.* Boulder, Colo.: Westview Press, 1995.

Brian J. McVeigh

DRESS FOR SUCCESS

"Dress for success" is the modern equivalent of "clothes maketh the man"—that is, it articulates the belief that what you wear matters in everyday life. However, in its modern guise, this is a discourse specifically on business dress that proclaims the importance of sartorial presentation in the workplace. Dress for success became popular during the mid-1970s and 1980s in the United States and Europe, but the principles that underpin it stem back much further. The idea that one can dress for success is closely aligned to the more general notion of "impression management," the origins of which go back to the work of sociologist Erving Goffman and his dramaturgical metaphor (the idea that the social world functions like a stage and we, its social actors, are performers). Goffman's work on "the presentation of self in everyday life" demonstrates how mundane features of body management are essential to the ongoing maintenance of a person's identity: Specifically, how our body looks and behaves is often the basis of how others read and judge us (1971). While Goffman's work was concerned with describing social order and interaction, his ideas were popularized outside sociology and have since achieved wide social application. Today "impression management" has become part of mainstream popular psychology and management and business studies, with dress for success a central plank of both. For evidence of the cultural significance of dress for success, one needs look no further than the huge market for books and services offering advice on how to dress effectively at work. Alongside popular "self-help" books, there is a huge industry in "image consultancy" offering all manner of "expert" advice on body presentation, from color analysis to wardrobe and shopping services. More recently, alongside such money-making ventures have sprung not-for-profit, dress-for-success shops offering services to the unemployed.

The Dress-for-Success Manual

The exposition of the "rules" of business dress are laid down in dress manuals, such as the now-classic John T. Molloy's two manuals, *Dress for Success* (first published in the United States in 1975) and *Women: Dress for Success* (published in the United States in 1979). These manuals describe his formula for "successful" dressing. What Molloy calls his "wardrobe engineering" is a (pseudo) "science of clothing" based on quantitative "testing" of the different meanings individuals give to individual garments. What kind of dress did Molloy find was the most "effective" at conveying "one means business"? The dress found to "succeed" is conservative, tailored, and always "smart." However, the way in which men and women should dress for the world of work differs. For men, this means black and gray suits, teamed with not-too-daring ties, and smart, polished shoes. However, while the traditional trousered suit works for men, it does not work for women. Indeed, by the very fact of his writing two manuals on work dress, Molloy points to the way in which dress at work is gendered, both reflecting and reproducing sexual difference. While both manuals have the same goal—the acquisition of status and power at work—men and women must attain it by different means, according to Molloy, and for a woman this means managing her sexuality. While an aspiring professional man need only worry about his dress (which suit to wear and in which color, which briefcase to carry, and so on), his female counterpart must also worry about her body, since her body is sexualized in a way that the male body is not.

The public world of work is a world that demands a clear separation from the erotic, and thus, women's potentially sexual bodies must be covered appropriately. Women, Molloy argues, have to dress for "authority" since their social position, as women, puts them at some disadvantage compared with men at work. The wearing of tailored clothing, namely a smart jacket with tailored knee-high skirt is, according to Molloy, the most "effective" dress. It would seem, therefore, that while suggestive clothes must be avoided, women should aim to look "feminine" at all costs: the wearing of a skirt and the deployment of decorative items, a necktie, brooch, or other accessory, help to soften the severity of the suit. Indeed, Molloy warns career women against trying to "ape" men and claims that his 1980 manual was, in part, a response to those women who had been adopting the garb he had outlined in his first manual. His second stated reason is captured by his story of how, in the mid-1970s, when meeting three businesswomen in a bar, he was unable to spot them. The businesswoman was literally not "visible" as such and was, according to Molloy, in need of a "uniform" that could be relied upon to connote the appropriate status.

The "uniform" that he subsequently helped inaugurate became known as the "power suit" and was a major phenomenon of the 1980s, defining a style of female professional dress that has now become something of a sartorial cliché: tailored skirt suit with shoulder pads, in gray, blue, or navy, accessorized with "token female garb such as bows and discreet jewelry" (Armstrong 1993: 278). These dress-for-success rules arose against the historical backdrop of the women's movement into more prestigious forms of paid employment and addressed the increasing problem of how to rise on the career ladder and break the so-called "glass ceiling." Note that in maintaining the suited torso, the tailored jacket and fitted skirt aimed to separate this female worker from her secretarial counterparts. Power dressing articulated the "career woman" and in doing so gave visible evidence of a new relationship of women to work that had once been the preserve of men (Entwistle 1997, 2001).

That fact that the "power suit" became a major fashion story for women in the 1980s is beside the point for "experts" such as Molloy. The aim of dress for success was to devise techniques that eliminate fashion from the daily process of dressing. The dress-for-success discourse is, in fact, an oblique and sometimes open critique of the fashion system. By virtue of its incessant momentum, fashion keeps the range of choices open, choices left to individuals who run the risk of making the "wrong" one. As individuals come to feel that more is at stake in how they look, especially at work, such a universe of choice is a problem. As a pseudoscience of clothing strategies, dress-for-success formulas, such as Molloy's "wardrobe engineering," offer clearly established guidelines to circumnavigate this precarious world of choice and provide a stable basis upon which to base decisions as to what to wear to work.

Historical Precursors

As it is primarily a "self-help" manual, the modern dress manual sets out to mold and shape the self, calling upon readers to think about themselves and act upon themselves in particular ways. Molloy's manual can therefore be examined as a "technology of the self," to draw on Foucault's concept (1988). "Technologies of the self permit individuals to effect. . . . a certain number of opera tions on their own bodies and souls, thoughts, conduct and way of being so as to transform themselves" (Foucault 1988, p. 18). In this way, dress-for-success strategies encourage particular ways of thinking and acting upon the self, producing the individual as a "reflexive subject" (Giddens 1991); that is, a person who thinks about and calculates body and self, in this case, developing skills and techniques for dressing and presenting the self as a committed career-minded person. The idea that one's dress conveys something of the "self" and that, specifically, one can dress for success at work may seem almost "common sense" today. However, these ideas have arisen out of particular historical circumstances and beliefs about the body and its relationship to personal identity. These are closely related to the emergence of particular forms of modern individualism.

One can trace the circumstances that gave rise to discourses on dress and appearance as far back as the eighteenth century, to the emphasis placed on the "self-made man" under conditions of industrial capitalism and the rise of Romanticism. The eighteenth and nineteenth centuries heralded an era of upward mobility: the new capitalist classes were achieving status and power through their own efforts, not through privileges of the old aristocracy. Individuals could, in other words, rise through the social hierarchy by virtue of their own efforts. This idea of the "enterprising" self reached its apotheosis with the ascendancy of neo-liberalism in the 1970s and 1980s under Reaganomics and Thatcherism; in other words, around the same time as dress-for-success ideas took hold. However, in the history of our modern self, another discourse at variance with capitalism is also important, namely Romanticism, and it underpins the idea of dress for success. Romantic poets, painters, and writers emphasized the idea of the "authentic" self and suggested that one's outward appearance unproblematically reflects the inner self. While up until the eighteenth century public life had allowed a distance between outward appearance and inner self—a clear separation between public and private—under conditions of modern life, according to Richard Sennett (1977), one's public appearance has to be a "true" reflection of the self. This Romantic notion of authenticity has become attached to the public sphere and is the dominant theme permeating discourse on the self at work, suggesting that how you look, from the first day of your job interview, signals your identity and commitment as a worker. Thus, in contemporary society, our bodies are bearers of status and distinction, as the sociologist Pierre Bourdieu (1984) has described in detail. This makes the body, its dress and manners, matters of great import in terms of the "envelope" of the self. As Joanne Finkelstein (1991) notes, increasingly over the nineteenth century appearance comes to stand as an important indicator of inner character and she suggests that the eighteenth-century socialite and "dandy" Beau Brummel exemplifies the wider social movement toward the self-styled or "fashioned" individual, concerned with promoting the self through the careful deployment of clothing. Finkelstein also analyzes the emergence of various "physiognomic" discourses over the nineteenth and twentieth centuries. Such discourses link outward appearance, from the shape of the face and overall body to dress, to inner "self." She points to how, in America over the course of the nineteenth century, there was a movement toward

individual self-promotion through dress: "for upwardly mobile young men how they looked was important not only as a means of business advancement, but also as a measure of self-esteem" (Branner, in Finkelstein 1991, p. 114).

Important to the heightening self-consciousness of body and its outward appearance, and introducing the idea of dress for success, was the dress manual. It is important to note that such manuals are not, therefore, a recent phenomenon and can be seen as closely aligned with other kinds of "self-help" publications which have a longer history (Hilkey 1997). In the eighteenth and nineteenth centuries, as well as in the first half of the twentieth, one can find manuals on "how to dress like a lady" and how to put together a lady's wardrobe on a modest budget. What is different about the manuals on dress that emerged in the 1970s and 1980s was the type of self they addressed and the kind of success sought. A number of commentators (Giddens 1991; Featherstone 1991; Lasch 1979; Sennett 1977) have argued that a new type of self has emerged in the twentieth century and an examination of the dress manual can be seen to indicate this. Featherstone calls this new self "the performing self" which "places greater emphasis upon appearance, display, and the management of impressions" (Featherstone 1991, p. 187) while Lasch (1979) calls it the "narcissistic self." Featherstone (1991) argues that a comparison of self-help manuals of the nineteenth and twentieth centuries provides an insight into the development of this new self and conveys the movement from notions of "character" to "personality." In the earlier self-help manual the self is discussed in terms of character values and virtues—thrift, temperance, self-discipline, and so on—and dress is discussed in terms of such things as thrift and "ladylike" decorum. In the twentieth century we find how "personality" in the self-help manual depends upon how one *appears* as opposed to what one is or should *become*; how, for example, to look and be "magnetic" and "charm" others. In this way, appearance comes to be something malleable, something transmutable. The increasing significance of appearance from the eighteenth century onward meant that people began to be concerned with the control of appearance and clothing. Contemporary Western societies testify to the intensification of these processes with more and more aspects of outward appearance "correctable" through diet, exercise, makeup, and plastic surgery, as well as dress, and with these appearances increasingly linked to identity. All these physiognomic discourses proclaim the notion that achieving the "right" outward appearance will result in greater personal happiness and, of course, success.

Conclusion

It may well seem that the dress-for-success formulas of the 1980s have long since been replaced by more "individuality" and "creativity" in clothing. Indeed, the backlash to all these rules came in the 1990s with "dress down on Friday" introduced in offices both in the United States and United Kingdom. While we may like to think we are "individual" and while dress choice is welcomed by some, the business and professional worlds remain conservative places, even today. Indeed, there has been a swing away from casual Fridays after some offices found that employees dressed far too casually to perform their duties effectively. Meeting a client in jeans or shorts is still taboo in most professions. Only in the "creative industries" are fashion and individuality openly welcomed, indeed, here one finds them essential. The body at work has to fit in with the overall business ethos of the office or sector. In young industries, like popular music, advertising and graphic design, for example, informality rules. However, older professions and industries still prefer the bodies at work to look suitable—that is, in a suit. The dress-for-success idea lives on and a lucrative industry of self-help advice and "experts" maintain the notion that what we wear to work really matters in our overall career "success."

See also Casual Business Dress; Fashion and Identity; Suit, Business.

Bibliography

Armstrong, L. "Working Girls." *Vogue*, October 1993.

Carnegie, Dale. *How to Win Friends and Influence People: How to Stop Worrying and Start Living*. London: Chancellor, 1994.

Entwistle, Joanne. "Power Dressing and the Fashioning of the Career Woman." In *Buy This Book: Studies in Advertising and Consumption*. Edited by M. Nava, I. MacRury, A. Blake, and B. Richards. London: Routledge, 1997.

——. "Fashioning of the Career Woman: Power Dressing as a Strategy of Consumption." In *All the World and Her Husband: Women and Consumption in the Twentieth Century*. Edited by M. Talbot and M. Andrews. London: Cassell, 2001.

Featherstone, Mike. "The Body in Consumer Society." In *The Body: Social Process and Cultural Theory*. Edited by M.

Featherstone, M. Hepworth and B. Turner. London: Sage, 1991.

Finkelstein, Joanne. *The Fashioned Self*. Philadelphia: Temple University Press, 1991.

Foucault, Michel. "Technologies of the Self." In *Technologies of the Self: A Seminar with Michel Foucault*. Edited by L. Martin, H. Gutman and P. Hutton. Amherst: University of Massachusetts Press, 1988.

Giddens, Anthony. *Modernity and Self-Identity: Self and Society in the Late Modern Age*. Stanford, Calif.: Stanford University Press, 1991.

Goffman, Erving. *The Presentation of Self in Everyday Life*. London: The Penguin Press, 1971.

Hilkey, J. *Character is Capital: Success Manuals and Manhood in Gilded Age America*. Chapel Hill: University of Carolina Press, 1997.

Lasch, Christopher. *The Culture of Narcissism*. London: Abacus, 1979.

Molloy, John T. *Dress for Success*. New York: Peter H. Wyden, 1975.

——. *Women: Dress for Success*. New York: Peter H. Wyden, 1980.

Sennett, Richard. *The Fall of Public Man*. New York: W. W. Norton and Company, 1977.

Joanne Entwistle

DRESS REFORM

Over the course of history the emergence of unorthodox clothing styles has revealed much about the social norms governing appearances. New ideologies concerning spirituality, health, hygiene, and gender have not only subverted existing social boundaries but also shaped the trajectory of fashion in the process. Quakerism, Bloomerism, aesthetic dress, and Jaeger dress may be examined as catalysts for both fashion and social change.

Nonconformist Quaker Dress

During the years following the English Civil War of 1642, various influential clothing-reform movements flourished. One of the nonconformist groups that emerged during this time was the Religious Society of Friends, commonly known as Quakers. The group's founder, George Fox, established a set of social practices

that were based on Christian ideologies and utopia-
nism. The main thesis proposed by Fox was simplicity
of appearance and lifestyle. His favor of spirituality over
what he considered to be the unholy virtues of fashion
signaled a radical move within the history of fashion.

The alternative clothing choices embraced by George
Fox and his followers were set in direct opposition to
the fashionable styles of the time. Quakers believed that
the focus on aesthetics within the fashion industry was
immoral. Instead Quakers wore modest, unstructured,
and natural-colored garments that better reflected their
Christian values of humility, piety, and simplicity. The
strict adherence to their faith led Quakers to eschew
contemporary fashions and any decorative clothing.

Both male and female apparel was constructed of
functional, utilitarian fabrics such as calico and flannel. The simple color palette for both sexes consisted of
gray, brown, cream, and pale green tones. Women commonly wore loose-fitting, long-sleeved dresses, aprons,
and bonnets. Men wore unstructured coats, plain hats,
trousers, and buckled shoes. For both sexes, functional garment details were also kept simple. Pockets
were often placed internally, the use of buttons was restricted, and small accessories or jewelry was forbidden.
The commonality of dress between the sexes not only
created group uniformity but also visually reinforced
their detachment from the wider society.

Quaker dress maintained popularity within marginal groups until the 1920s. The Quaker adherence
to plain dress styles was a nonverbal protest against
the aesthetic focus of fashion. "Plain clothing" was adopted by other religious groups as well, such as some
sects of German Pictists. Although the movement only
achieved minority status, it nevertheless succeeded
in challenging the ornamental nature of eighteenth-
century dress.

Dr. Gustav Jaeger

Another revolutionary movement within the history of
fashion involved the promotion of a healthy and rational approach to dress. During the eighteenth century,
various medical professionals gradually began to question the irrational and unhealthy nature of the existing
fashionable garments. Many argued that corsets and
heavily layered undergarments restricted movement,
crippled the spine, and harmed internal organs. As a
consequence, certain medical professionals began to
encourage men and women to turn their attention away
from aesthetics and toward their health.

During the 1880s, Dr. Gustav Jaeger, a German Professor of Physiology and Zoology at the University of
Stuttgart, promoted what he believed to be a healthy
alternative to conventional dress. In 1884 Dr. Jaeger developed a unique system of dress based on the belief
that wearing undyed sheep wool against the skin would
enable skin to breathe freely and prevent perspiration.
Dr. Jaeger recommended avoiding clothing made of
silk, cotton, or linen—or any cloth which had been
dyed. He was also highly critical of the corset.

The nonconformist apparel Dr. Jaeger introduced
was designed to follow the contours of the body closely,
so as to prevent exposure to drafts that he believed
dangerous to the health. Jaeger was best known for undyed woolen undergarments for both sexes, including
chemises, petticoats, and breeches. The range was later
expanded to include other items of clothing such as
jackets and trousers, as well as bedsheets.

The protective properties of woolen undergarments
were widely promoted. Dr. Jaeger was an exhibitor at
the *International Health Exhibition* of London in 1884.
He also published widely and released a book in 1887
titled *Essays on Health Culture.* Although the Jaeger
mode of dress was targeted to all, it initially only acquired a minority and predominately middle-class
following.

As the system gained gradual acceptance however,
London retailer Lewis Tomalin purchased the name
and opened a store on London's Regent St. As public
interest in health and comfort progressed, Lewis Tomalin gained popularity among male and female consumers alike. Competitive retailers gradually became aware
of the changing social consciousness and began producing varied ranges that expanded upon Jaeger's original
ideologies.

By the 1920s, however, the popularity of Dr. Jaeger's
undergarment designs gradually began to wane as fashions became increasingly fitted. Nevertheless, the adoption and persistence of his health-reform movement
illustrates that a portion of society was prepared to
choose clothing primarily on the grounds of supposed
health benefits rather than fashionability.

Bloomerism

In the nineteenth century, as male clothing became increasingly utilitarian, certain women began to feel constrained by the fashionable clothing styles available to
them. The most famous dress-reform movement was
called Bloomerism. The movement was named after

New York resident, Amelia Jenks Bloomer. In 1851 Bloomer published an article in the feminist publication she edited called *The Lily*, stressing the importance of introducing reformed garments for women. The article was later reprinted in popular American press and gained a widespread readership. Later that year, along with her friends Elizabeth Smith Miller and Elizabeth Cady Stanton, she was seen in public dressed in a shortened skirt with Turkish trousers. Although Amelia was not the first woman to wear or invent the garment, the name evolved as a consequence of her association with *The Lily*.

The bloomer costume consisted of loosely fitting, Turkish-style trousers that gathered and frilled at the ankle with an elasticized cuff. The trousers were worn beneath a shortened skirt that fell below the knee, and a fitted bodice. In contrast to the prevailing fashions, the outfit was claimed to be comfortable, convenient, safe, and healthy. Bloomer dress focused not on the way one looked, but rather on the way one felt. The original intention of the garment was thus not to challenge established gender boundaries, but rather to increase mobility and function.

A majority of Victorian society was highly critical of the innovative style of dress. Since trousers were considered to be a traditional symbol of masculinity, female devotees of Bloomerism were subject to ridicule and abuse. For example, satirical caricatures of Bloomers appeared in magazines such as *Punch*. As a consequence, most abandoned the costume after only a few months.

Amelia Bloomer had herself discarded the costume by the mid-1850s. Although the movement was short lived, it exposed entrenched gender stereotypes and challenged the dominant ideals of femininity. As a consequence the innovative costume signaled an advance in the direction of female emancipation.

Rational Dress

The bloomer costume was revived through the establishment of the Rational Dress Society in London during the 1880s. The Society was chaired by Viscountess Haberton and sought to advocate the development of a rational system of clothing. During the late 1880s, the Society started publishing the *Rational Dress Society Gazette* that campaigned against restrictive fashions.

One of the main premises of the Society was the belief that women should forsake heavy undergarments and corsets, as such items restricted movement. In later years members adopted short jackets with bifurcated knee-length skirts, as it was believed such garments enhanced physical mobility. The introduction of new sports such as bicycling and lawn tennis greatly assisted the growing tendency toward functional clothing. In these arenas bifurcated garments became an acceptable mode of sports dress.

Aesthetic Dress

During the same period, the Aesthetic Movement began to emerge out of the field of decorative arts. Aesthetic devotees encouraged women to discard the restrictive garments in vogue and adopt loose-fitting, "artistic" apparel instead.

The style of dress was inspired by the work of Pre-Raphaelite painters such as Rossetti and consisted of loosely draped, medieval-styled robes. The style appealed to a significant number of middle-class women. Oscar Wilde was an avid supporter of the movement. In London, the Liberty Company produced aesthetic dresses.

In the early twentieth century, reform styles influenced the fashions created by avant-garde designers such as Paul Poiret and Mariano Fortuny.

See also Aesthetic Dress; Bloomer Costume; Corset; Gender and Dress; Liberty & Co; Politics and Fashion; Religion and Dress.

Bibliography

Breward, Christopher. *Fashion*. Oxford: Oxford University Press, 2003.

Crane, Diana. *Fashion and its Social Agendas: Gender, Class and Identity in Clothing*. Chicago and London: University of Chicago Press, 2000.

Etten, Henry Van. *George Fox and the Quakers*. London: Long-mans, 1959.

Fischer, Gayle V. *Pantaloons and Power: A Nineteenth-Century Dress Reform in the United States*. Kent, Ohio, and London: Kent State University Press, 2001.

Gattey, Charles Neilson. *The Bloomer Girls*. London: Femina Books, 1967.

Newton, Stella Mary. *Health, Art and Reason: Dress Reformers of the 19th Century*. London: John Murray, 1974.

Kristina Stankovski

E

EARRINGS

Earrings, ornaments decorating the ears, have been one of the principal forms of jewelry throughout recorded history. The term usually refers to ornaments worn attached to the earlobes, though in the late twentieth century it expanded somewhat to include ornaments worn on other parts of the ear, such as ear cuffs, and is used to describe pieces of jewelry in earring form, even when they are worn through piercings in other parts of the body (for example, in the nose). The most common means of attaching earrings to the earlobes has been to pierce holes in the lobes, through which a loop or post may be passed. But a variety of other devices have also been used, including spring clips, tensioning devices such as screw backs, and, for particularly heavy earrings, loops passing over the top of the ear or attaching to the hair or headdress.

In many cultures and contexts, earrings have traditionally been worn as symbols of cultural or tribal identity, as markers of age, marital status, or rank, or because they are believed to have protective or medicinal powers. Even when they have served other purposes, however, the primary function of earrings has been a decorative one. As earrings are so prominently placed near the face, and at the juncture between costume and coiffure, they, perhaps more than any other element of jewelry, have been particularly responsive to changes in fashion; as hairstyles, hats, collars, and necklines have risen and fallen, earrings have correspondingly increased and decreased in size and prominence, and during many periods they have been instrumental in balancing and tying together the desired fashionable appearance.

The Ancient World

In antiquity, earrings were one of the most popular forms of jewelry. The crescent-shaped gold hoops worn by Sumerian women around 2500 B.C.E. are the earliest earrings for which there is archaeological evidence. By 1000 B.C.E., tapered hoop (also known as boat-shaped) earrings, most commonly of gold but also of silver and bronze, had spread throughout the Aegean world and Western Asia. In Crete and Cyprus, earrings were embellished with twisted gold wire, clusters of beads, and pendants stamped out of thin sheet gold.

In Egypt, earrings were introduced about 1500 B.C.E. and were later worn by both men and women. Many Egyptian earrings took the form of thick, mushroom-shaped studs or plugs, which required an enlarged hole to be stretched in the earlobe; these could be of gold, with a decorated front surface, or of humbler materials such as colored glass or carved jasper. Ear studs consisting of two capped tubes that screwed together could be worn alone, but some also had elaborate pendants of gold cornflowers, or falcons with flexible tail feathers inlaid with glass.

In the first millennium B.C.E., Etruscan and Greek goldsmiths brought new refinement and artistry to earrings, which were valued as both an adornment and a sign of wealth. Variations on the hoop were the so-called leech earring, a thick tube secured by a hidden wire, and the Etruscan box-type earring, which encased the earlobe in a wide horizontal cylinder. Disk earrings, with pendants in the form of amphorae (ancient Greek jars), figures of Eros, and decorative beads and chains, were another popular form, joined about 330 B.C.E. by twisted gold hoops with animal-head finials. All of these forms were stamped out of thin sheets of gold and decorated with fine palmettes, scrolls, and flowers in twisted wire and granulation; such earrings were fairly light in weight, but gave an extremely rich effect.

Roman earrings were similar to Etruscan styles until the first century C.E., when new styles with disks and pendants mounted on s-shaped ear hooks appeared. Colored stones and pearls were favored, and earring styles proliferated to satisfy the Roman taste for ostentatious display. At its height, the Roman Empire had the effect of standardizing styles of jewelry over much of the known world; after the center of influence shifted to Byzantium (Constantinople) in C.E. 330, and Roman influence began to decline, local variations once more emerged. Characteristic Byzantine earrings were plain gold hoops with multiple pearl pendants hung on chains, and crescent-shaped earrings of gold filigree.

The Sixteenth to Eighteenth Centuries

In Europe, earrings virtually disappeared between the eleventh and sixteenth centuries, as hairstyles and head-dresses that completely covered the ears, and later high ruff collars, made them impractical. Earrings finally began to revive in the late sixteenth century, as ruffs gave way to standing collars. At first, complex enameled designs were popular, but improved techniques of gem cutting soon shifted the emphasis to faceted diamonds. In the seventeenth century, large, pear-shaped pearl pendants were a favorite earring style, and those who could afford to do so wore two in each ear. It was also fashionable to wear pendant earrings on strings or ribbons threaded through the earlobes and tied in bows, and to tie ribbon bows at the tops of earrings to achieve the same effect. Similar earring styles were also worn by fashionable gentlemen, but usually in one ear only.

By the late seventeenth century, earrings had become an essential element of dress, and larger and more elaborate forms began to develop. Two of these became the dominant styles of the eighteenth century: the gi-randole, in which a single top cluster branches out like a chandelier to support three pear-shaped drops, and the pendeloque, a top cluster with a long single pendant. New sources of diamonds, along with new methods of cutting them, developed early in the eighteenth century, made them the material of choice for jewelry, and high-quality paste imitations were also available. Glittering girandoles and pendeloques, visually tied to the ears by stylized ribbon bows of diamonds set in silver, ef-fectively balanced the high, powdered hairstyles of the period. Despite their refined and delicate appearance, such large earrings were quite heavy; some had addi-tional rings soldered to the tops, permitting the wearer to take some of the weight off of her ears by tying the earrings to her hair.

The Nineteenth Century

When the neoclassical style of dress and simpler hair-styles came into fashion at the end of the eighteenth century, earrings became lighter and simpler. Jewelry of cut steel, seed pearls, Berlin iron, and strongly colored materials such as coral and jet, harmonized well with neoclassical fashions, and classically inspired cameos and intaglios were set in all kinds of jewelry. Heavy gi-randoles gave way to pendant earrings composed of flat, geometric elements connected by light chains. "Top-and-drop" earrings, composed of a small top element attached to the ear wire, from which a larger, often teardrop-shaped element is suspended, also came to the fore around 1800, and remained the most popular ear-ring style throughout the nineteenth century. Matched sets of jewelry, known as parures, assumed new impor-tance in the nineteenth century, and they were available even to women of modest means. These sets usually in-cluded at least a matching necklace or brooch and ear-rings, but could also include bracelets, buckles, and a tiara or tiara-comb.

In the 1810s and 1820s, the trend toward lighter and more delicate jewelry continued, and settings of gold fil-igree or elaborate wirework (known as cannetille) were very popular. In the 1820s, a romantic interest in the past also inspired jewelry designers to revive historical styles from the ancient world to the eighteenth century, and a modified version of the girandole earring returned, along with elaborate gothic tracery and rococo-revival scroll-work. As hairstyles became more elaborate in the 1830s, earrings became more prominent, with small tops and long drops reaching nearly to the shoulders. In spite of their size, these earrings were fairly light in weight, owing to lightweight settings of gold cannetille or of *repoussé* (embossed relief raised from behind with a hammer), which had largely replaced cannetille by the 1840s. Earrings with long, torpedo-shaped drops of carved gemstones with applied gold filigree were also popular, many with detachable drops to allow the tops to be worn alone.

In the late 1840s and through the 1850s, a new hair-style, with hair parted in the middle and gathered to the back of the head in loops that covered the ears, caused a virtual disappearance of earrings. Around 1860, once again owing to a return to upswept hairstyles, long pen-dant earrings made a comeback, and through the 1860s and 1870s they were produced in an astonishing variety of styles. One major theme was historical revival, with Egyptian and Classical styles particularly popular. Some revival earrings, such as those produced by the Castel-lani family in Rome, were fairly faithful reproductions of recent archaeological discoveries; others were fanci-ful pastiches of classical earring forms, architectural elements, and other motifs such as amphorae. Earrings with carved classical reliefs of coral or lava, or Roman glass micro-mosaics, were very fashionable, and were often brought back as souvenirs by travelers to Italy. Other popular styles were naturalistic renditions of leaves, flowers, insects, and birds' nests in gold, enamel, and semiprecious stones; enameled renaissance-revival styles; and, for more precious gems, floral sprays and cascades. A new style in the 1870s was the fringe or tassel earring, with a graduated fringe of pointed drops suspended from a large oval pendant.

In the last two decades of the nineteenth century, large pendant earrings went out of fashion, in part because they were incompatible with the newly fashionable high dress and blouse collars, and with the elaborate "dog collar" necklaces worn for evening, which almost completely covered the neck. Small single-stone and cluster earrings, either firmly mounted to the ear wire or mounted as pendants to move and catch the light, were the most commonly worn style through the early twentieth century. The most fashionable earrings of all were diamond solitaires, which became more available after the opening of the South African diamond fields in the late 1860s. New cutting machines and open-claw settings, both of which increased the amount of light reflected by diamonds and made solitaire earrings more appealing, were developed in the 1870s. To prevent valuable diamond earrings from being lost, catches were added to secure the bottoms of the ear wires. Another innovation, first patented in 1878, was the earring cover, a small hinged sphere of gold, sometimes finished in black enamel, which could be snapped over a diamond earring to protect it from loss or theft. By the end of the century diamond ear studs (also called screws), with a threaded post passing through the ear, and held securely in back by a nut screwed onto the post, were also popular.

The Twentieth Century

By 1900, as earrings declined in size and importance, many women stopped wearing them altogether. Some commentators denounced ear-piercing as barbaric, and women who pierced their ears were considered "fast," or not quite respectable. (In the United States, some of the reaction against pierced ears may be credited to the desire of "native" Americans to distinguish themselves from the large numbers of immigrant women, almost all with pierced ears, who were arriving from Europe at the time.) In spite of piercing's negative image, small screw earrings continued to be worn, and new screw-

back fittings, which could be tightened onto unpierced earlobes, were available for those who did not wish to pierce their ears. Around 1908, pendant earrings were revived, but with light, articulated drops of smaller stones rather than single-stone drops; diamonds, pearls, and stones matching the color of the costume were the most popular materials.

The earring revival continued into the 1910s, aided considerably by a growing acceptance of costume jewelry. Jewelry could now be selected for its decorative value rather than its intrinsic value, and women could afford to own many pairs of earrings to match particular costumes; the rise of costume jewelry also made ear piercing less necessary, as women were less concerned about losing inexpensive earrings. (Many women, as was still true in the early 2000s, also had adverse reactions to the cheaper metals used in costume jewelry, which made pierced earrings seem less practical.) The fashion for the Oriental and exotic inspired by Paul Poiret and the Ballets Russes was reflected in bead necklaces and long drop earrings of Chinese amber, jade, black and red jet (glass), and carved tortoiseshell. Empire-revival fashions also inspired a revival of nineteenth-century jewelry styles and materials, including cut steel and cameos.

By the early 1920s, earrings were again almost universally worn, and the range of exotic styles had expanded to include hoop and pendant earrings of Spanish or Gypsy inspiration, Egyptian styles inspired by the discovery of King Tutankhamen's tomb in 1922, nineteenth-century antiques, and picturesque "peasant" styles from around the world. As reported by the *New York Times* in 1922, in the 1920s earrings could "no longer ... be considered as an article of jewelry; they are *the* article of jewelry." With dress styles now comparatively simple, and many women bobbing their hair, earrings were considered an essential finishing touch—a means both of filling in the area between the ear and shoulder and of expressing the wearer's personality. Bold geometric pendant earrings, made of diamonds and platinum contrasted with strongly colored materials such as onyx and lapis lazuli, were displayed at the Exposition International des Arts Décoratifs in 1925, and this style, which became known as Art Deco, remained popular for both precious and costume earrings for the remainder of the decade.

In the early 1930s, although there was no sudden change in style, earrings began to move closer to the head again, partly in response to smaller, close-fitting hats and the return of high, tied and ruffled collars.

Another major influence was the introduction, in 1931, of clip fastenings for earrings, which made it possible to concentrate ornamentation over the earlobe, and compact designs following the line of the ear soon became popular. Matching earrings, bracelets, and other jewelry made of brightly colored bakelite were another signature 1930s look. For evening, long earrings in Art Deco style were still popular, but earrings with white stones (diamonds or pastes) were now the most popular, and the pendants now added volume by branching out to the sides, in a modern version of the girandole, or "chandelier," style.

In the 1940s, compact clips or screw backs, often made with a matching brooch, were the dominant earring style. Gold, strongly colored stones, and bolder, more sculptural forms were now preferred, in keeping with the padded shoulders and highly structured coiffures of the period. Close-to-the-ear styles, with clip or screw backs, continued to be the most popular in the 1950s, but settings became more delicate, to harmonize with the more deliberately feminine fashions in the years following Christian Dior's 1947 "New Look" collection. An important look of the 1950s was the matched set of choker necklace and button earrings, and these were produced in a wide variety of styles and materials, including newly developed plastics. White and colored rhinestones were popular, as were beads and faux pearls of all kinds, colors, and finishes, often looped in multiple strands around the neck, and fastened with a clasp of clustered beads matching the earrings. Ear piercing, while still not common, began to revive in the early 1950s; in the United States, the trend began as a fad among college girls, and Queen Elizabeth II set an example for many in England when she had her ears pierced in order to be able to wear diamond earrings she received as a wedding present in 1947.

In the 1960s, as in the 1920s, clean-lined dresses and hairstyles, including the long, straight hair popular later in the decade, provided an ideal background for large and decorative earrings. Earrings were again among the most important of accessories, and were often designed to stand alone, rather than as part of a matched set. In both fine and costume jewelry, abstraction was popular, and creative design, visual impact, and wit were often considered more important than the intrinsic value of jewelry. Hoop earrings were one of the signature styles of the decade, and they appeared in designs inspired by tribal jewelry, enormous space-age styles of chrome and plastic, and kinetic designs of concentric, articulated rings. Ethnic styles, particularly from India and

the Near East, were also popular, and delicate dangling earrings helped to propel handcrafted sterling silver jewelry, which had been growing in popularity since the 1940s, into the fashion mainstream.

By the early 1970s, the new fashionable ideal was the "natural look," and large costume earrings disappeared in favor of smaller and more delicate earrings, usually of silver or gold, and almost always worn in pierced ears. In terms of design, earrings remained fairly inconspicuous throughout the decade, though they were given new prominence by the fashion for multiple piercings in the same ear, which began as a teenage fashion around the middle of the decade, and continued into the twenty-first century to be a popular way to wear earrings. Earrings worn in the upper part of the ear, and ear cuffs, which grip the edge of the upper ear, were fashions introduced late in the decade. The 1970s was also when earrings for men returned to fashion after a 300-year absence; earrings had continued to be worn by sailors, by some homosexual men, and by members of groups such as motorcycle gangs, but many more men now began to wear single earrings largely for their decorative value.

Large and flashy earrings, both real and frankly fake, returned in the 1980s, to balance the bolder shapes and colors, padded shoulders, high-volume hairstyles, and dramatic makeup then in fashion. Chunky button earrings covering the lower half of the ear and large pendant hoops were popular styles, and common finishes were shiny gold, bright colors contrasted with black, and a variety of bronzed and iridescent metallic finishes. Even relatively understated earrings tended toward strong shapes, worn close to the earlobe; though most women still had pierced ears, clips were popular because they kept earrings close to the head, and because they distributed the weight of heavier styles.

In the early 1990s, silver, brushed finishes, and simple, elegant earrings began to succeed the shiny gold and jagged shapes of the 1980s, in keeping with the monochromatic and minimalist mood of fashion. At the same time, the trend toward simple, versatile clothes that could be dressed up or down inspired women to use elaborate or unusual earrings to vary the effect of an ensemble, and earring styles proliferated. Since the mid-1990s, there has not been a dominant style in earrings, although historical revivals have been an important trend; the popularity of glamorous "chandelier" earrings inspired the return of girandole and top-and-drop designs from the eighteenth and nineteenth centuries, along with the more familiar kinetic designs of the 1920s and 1960s. Earrings have become a popular form of personal expression, and how and when they are worn, along with their function within an ensemble, became largely a matter of personal choice.

See also Bracelets; Brooches and Pins; Costume Jewelry; Jewelry; Necklaces and Pendants.

Bibliography

Andrews, Carol. *Ancient Egyptian Jewellery*. London: British Museum Publications, 1990.

Bury, Shirley. *Jewellery 1789–1910—The International Era*. 2 vols. Woodbridge, Suffolk, U.K.: Antique Collectors' Club, 1991.

Fales, Martha Gandy. *Jewelry in America 1600–1900*. Woodbridge, Suffolk, U.K.: Antique Collectors' Club, 1995.

"Fashions: Earrings Essential Now for Smart Dressing." *New York Times* (23 July 1922): 80.

Flowers, Margaret. *Victorian Jewellery*. New York: Duell, Sloan and Pearce, 1951.

Mascetti, Daniela, and Amanda Triossi. *Earrings from Antiquity to the Present*. London: Thames and Hudson, Inc., 1990.

Scarisbrick, Diana. *Jewellery*. London: B. T. Batsford, Ltd., 1984.

——. *Tudor and Jacobean Jewellery*. London: Tate Publishing, 1995.

Walters Art Gallery, Baltimore. *Jewelry, Ancient to Modern*. New York: Viking Press, 1979.

Susan Ward

ECCLESIASTICAL DRESS

The term "ecclesiastical" derives from the Greek *ekklesiastikos*, from *ekklesia*, an assembly or meeting called out, which in turn derives from *ekkalein*, to call forth or convoke, *ek*, out, and *kalein*, to call. This assembly often referred to the Christian Church and its clergy. Ecclesiastical dress refers here to garments worn by Christian leaders, including members of monastic orders—as distinct from the laity—from the early Christian era until the present, not only in the West but also in all parts of the world where the Christian religion is practiced.

Historical and Cross-Cultural Examples

The origins of ecclesiastical dress have been debated, with some attributing early forms to garments worn by Jewish religious leaders, while others have argued that these vestments derived from everyday Roman dress worn during the early Christian era. In the early 2000s, the latter explanation prevails. Different forms of ecclesiastical dress have developed with the expansion and elaboration of the Western and Eastern Churches. The forms and meanings of ecclesiastical dress have changed over time and have variously been used to separate the mundane from the spiritual, to emphasize the glory of God through beautiful raiment, to express religious humility and piety, and to identify individuals within the church hierarchy.

Depictions of early Christians in the Catacombs of St. Domitilla in Rome include a painting of the Good Shepherd, wearing a white tunic or *tunica*, a rectangle of white material—made either from linen or wool—with a girdle holding it in place. The secular use of this garment was as an undergarment, covered by a toga. Church leaders adopted the dalmatic, also a tunic-like garment, worn in ancient Rome, by the eighth century as an upper-vestment worn by bishops, deacons, and sub-deacons. The *paenula*, which was worn as an outer garment, was the secular precursor of the chasuble, a term derived from the Latin, *casula*, little house or cottage—a circular piece of cloth with a head opening and sometimes a hood, which protected its wearer like a house. It was formally decreed as an outside garment for clergy in 742 by the Council of Ratisbon. One of the earliest examples of the wearing of these garments by church leaders come from depictions of the chasuble or *paenula*, dalmatic, and *pallium* (a long woven band of white wool, decorated with crosses) in the sixth century mosaic from the Church of St. Apollinaire, in Ravenna.

Ecclesiastical dress in the West and East developed along the same lines until the eleventh century; however, there were differences in the meanings and uses of these garments. In the West, vestments were worn to express Christian beliefs about the sacred and the mundane, as well as to distinguish the roles of clergy within the Church hierarchy. In the Eastern churches, these ideas were also present although the belief that ecclesiastical vestments literally represented the garments of Christ also existed. This belief was visually expressed, for example, in the vestment known as the *sticharion*, a tunic-like garment that had its counterpart in the alb, a white linen tunic used as a vestment in the West by the twelfth century. The *sticharion* had two bands of red ornamentation, known as *clavi*, which referred to the wounds made on Christ's body during the Crucifixion. Similarly, embroidery at the ends of the *sticharion*'s narrow sleeves was meant to represent the manacles with which Christ's wrists were bound. While embroidered pieces known as apparels were used on albs, dalmatics, and tunicles to represent Christ's stigmata when placed at the end of sleeves and at hems, the practice of incorporating this form of ornamentation on vestments was gradually replaced by the use of lace in Western vestments during the sixteenth century.

Vestments used in the Eastern Church include the *phelonion*; the *saccos* (a tunic with wide sleeves, worn by patriarchs); as well as the priestly insignia—the *omophorion*—the Western *pallium*—worn by bishops; two forms of stole—the *epitrachilion* and the *orarion*, worn by priests and deacons, respectively—and the square ceremonial cloth known as the *epigonation*, symbolically representing "the Sword of God," worn only in the Greek and Armenian churches by vested bishops. The *phelonion*, as depicted in medieval frescoes, was a round cloak similar to the medieval bell-shaped chasuble. Initially, it was made from white or colored materials alone, but by the eleventh century it was embroidered with small crosses. The art of Byzantine embroidery of ecclesiastical dress flourished during the period of the Palaeologus Dynasty, from the mid-thirteenth to mid-fifteenth century. Byzantine embroiderers used gold, silver, and silk thread to depict a range of scenes and personages from the Old and New Testaments on silk vestments. Several extant embroidered *sacci* from the fourteenth and early fifteenth century illustrate this Byzantium style of vestment, including two *sacci* associated with the Metropolitan Photius of Moscow (1408–1432). One side of the Grand *Saccus* of Photius includes heavily embroidered portraits of the Grand Prince of Moscow, along with a depiction of the Crucifixion, the Prophets Isaiah and Jeremiah, and three Lithuanian martyrs, all on a blue silk background, with the embroidery outlined with pearls.

The Byzantine or Eastern Orthodox Church also includes the Syrian, Armenian, Nubian, Ethiopian, and the Coptic Churches, with their own traditions of ecclesiastical dress. There was considerable overlap in the vestments of the early Coptic Church with those of the other Byzantine churches. For example, the *sticharion* (tunic), *orarion* (strole), *epitrachelion* (stole),

and *phelonion* (chasuble) were used by both. Later developments, particularly the introduction of the stole-like *ballin* that was worn by priests and bishops during church services, distinguished Coptic practice. Much of what is known of early ecclesiastical dress worn in these churches comes from texts, illuminated manuscripts, and wall paintings.

During the Medieval Period, ecclesiastic dress in the Roman Catholic Church included a range of vestments used in relation to church services: the alb, cassock (an ankle-length garment with sleeves), chasuble, cope (a capelike garment used as outerwear), dalmatic, hood (a hood attached to cope, often nonfunctional), maniple (a folded cloth or narrow strip worn over the left shoulder of bishops, priests, deacons, and subdeacons during Mass), mitre (a cap worn by bishops often with two tabs—lappets—of cloth hanging from the back), stole (a long strip of cloth, worn in particular ways to identify members of priesthood), and surplice (a loose, white, outer ecclesiastical vestment usually of knee length with large open sleeves). It was also during the thirteenth century that the English embroidery of ecclesiastical dress flourished, referred to as Opus Anglicanum. In continental Europe, vestments made of patterned silk velvets with intricately embroidered orphreys, decorative woven bands (used in the forms of crosses, pillars, and simple selvage bands on copes, dalmatics, and chasubles) were also produced at this time. With the separation of the Church of England from Rome in 1534, the embroidery of vestments in England fell into decline, to be resumed there during the nineteenth century Gothic Revival.

Controversies Relating to Ecclesiastical Dress

During periods of religious reform and political change, ecclesiastical dress has often served as a symbol of the old regime, which must be replaced or denigrated by reformers, while those opposing the abandonment of older forms of ecclesiastical dress (and the church doctrine associated with them) have sought to maintain them. One famous example of a controversy was the debate over the white linen surplice, which became a symbol of Roman Catholicism during the Protestant Reformation in sixteenth-century England. With the separation from the Roman Catholic Church made final by an act of Parliament in 1534 and the subsequent establishment of the Church of England during the reign of Queen Elizabeth I (1558–1603), the surplice became the universal vestment of all Anglican clergy in 1563. Yet surplices, along with copes, albs, and chasubles, were seen as remnants of "popish dress" by Protestant religious reformers such as the Puritans, Methodists, and Baptists. Tracts with titles such as "A briefe discourse against the outvvarde apparell and ministring garmentes of the popishe church" written by Robert Crowley in 1578 were published and some Protestant leaders were imprisoned for refusing to wear a surplice during church services. These leaders preferred to wear simple, everyday dress, which did not distinguish them from the laity or from everyday affairs. Nonetheless, Anglican Church leaders preserved distinctive ecclesiastical garments, particularly those that continued to be used for royal services. During the seventeenth century, English Protestant ecclesiastical dress was modeled on contemporary dress fashions—specifically, a simple black suit, including a coast, waistcoat, and knee breeches, and a white neckcloth, while Anglican clergy wore cassocks and gowns. However, during the 1840s, those associated with the Gothic Revival in England sought to reinstate the practices of the Church of England during the reign of King Edward VI. In 1840, the Bishop of Exeter directed Anglican clergy to wear surplices, which led to the Surplice Riots when mobs in Exeter pelted those wearing surplices with rotten eggs and vegetables. The Bishop's order was rescinded, but by the second half of the nineteenth century, ecclesiastical dress—including surplices, copes, and albs— was incorporated into Anglican services, modeled after gothic vestments design, as interpreted by Victorian artists. This revival of the use of vestments coincided with the fluorescence of the Arts and Crafts movement during the nineteenth century in England. One prominent member of this movement, William Morris, who as an Anglo-Catholic, had supplied specially designed vestments to the Roman Catholic Church following the Catholic Emancipation of 1829. In 1854, the Ladies' Ecclesiastical Embroidery Society was organized to produce embroidered replicas of medieval designs (Johnstone 2002, p. 123). Along with these specialized workshops, ecclesiastical dress, which was mass-produced and mass-marketed through catalogs, also became available, in part, due to the increasing demand for such vestments from missionaries working in the British colonies during this period.

Another example in which ecclesiastical dress became the focus of controversy took place in Mexico. Prior to the Mexican Revolution, the wealth and political power of the Roman Catholic Church was evident in ornate cathedrals and ecclesiastical dress. During the second half of the eighteenth century, dalmatics, copes, chasubles, and stoles made with silver and gold threads and elaborately embroidered with the emblem of the Convent of Santa Rosa de Lima, were probably made in the Mexican city of Puebla. While the Church had considerable popular support, its extensive landholding and its association with the political elite contributed to the view that it was an impediment to economic progress and social justice. During the Mexican Revolution that began in 1910, a series of anticlerical measures were taken, culminating with the writing of the Constitution of 1917, which provided for the confiscation of church lands, the replacement of religious holidays with patriotic ones, and the banning of public worship outside of church buildings, including processionals (Purnell 1999, p. 60). While these laws were enacted, they were not always strictly enforced until 1926, when Government leaders sought to further restrict the power of the Church through the Calles Law. This law outlawed Catholic education, closed monasteries and convents, and in Article 130, restricted the wearing of ecclesiastical dress in public. When the Mexican Episcopate ordered the closing of churches in response to the Calles Law, a popular uprising known as the Cristero Rebellion resulted, primarily in central West Mexico, during the period from 1926 to 1929. With the state's agreement to stop its insistence on registering priests and with the restoration of religious services—including the wearing of ecclesiastical dress—the rebellion ceased.

Ecclesiastic dress has also served as a vehicle for expressing anticolonial sentiments in Africa, during the nineteenth and twentieth centuries. However, many early African Christian converts did not reject European styles of vestments, but rather incorporated indigenous elements into ecclesiastical dress as an expression of their discontent. In colonial Nigeria during the first half of the twentieth century, converts who occupied leadership positions in Roman Catholic and orthodox Protestant churches—primarily, Anglican, Methodist, and Baptist—generally wore the tailored garments (cassocks, chasubles, surplices, copes, and mitres) used by home church leaders. These garments distinguished Christian converts from those practicing various forms of indigenous religion, which had their own, often untailored, dress traditions. Yet some early Nigerian Christian leaders sought to assert independence from Orthodox churches over doctrinal disputes, often concerning polygynous marriage. Establishing their own churches, referred to generally as African

Independent Churches, they did not entirely abandon tailored, Western-style vestments. Rather, these leaders developed distinctive ecclesiastical dress forms that identified these new churches and emphasized particular aspects of their doctrine. For example, Bishop J. K. Coker, the founder of the African Church, incorporated indigenous textiles, for example handwoven narrow strip cloths, into ecclesiastical dress. Leaders of the Independent African Churches such as Bishop Coker were the predecessors of nationalist independence leaders who supported secular independent states based on Euro-American models combined with African social and cultural elements.

The controversies surrounding freedom of religious expression have, at times, been moderated through gradual change in ecclesiastical dress, which reflected church leaders' responses to changing political and social contexts. For example, early members of the Marist Brothers apostolic movement, which was founded in France by Father Marcellin Champagnat (1789–1840), wore "a sort of blue coat, . . . black trousers, a cloak, and round hat" garments, which he believed were imbued with spiritual power that protected its wearers from anticlerical attacks. While these vestments helped to attract and visually to distinguish new members during the post-revolutionary period in France, they also gave followers a sense of special protection. However, with the incorporation of the Marist Brothers' Institute as a religious order of the Roman Catholic Church in 1863, Marist ecclesiastical dress came to lose its mystical aspects and shifted to a uniform prescribed by the Church authorities, including a black soutane, white rabat, and a black cloak. With the Second Vatican Council in 1962, Marist Brothers' ecclesiastical dress again changed as a loss in church membership suggested a simpler, less-clerical style—such as a suit—would be more appropriate to modern worship. However, by 1987, some Marist priests returned to wearing the soutane, while others continued to wear secular suits, depending on their preferences and those of their parishioners. This shift from distinctive ecclesiastical dress that identified Catholic orders according to particular configurations and types of garments to current secular dress styles, indistinguishable from contemporary clothing is also evident in Western nuns' garb. Western nuns or Women Religious, whose name as well as dress changed with Vatican II, as of the turn of the twenty-first century wore everyday garments as a way of emphasizing their role in modern society, rather than their separation from it.

Role in Contemporary Society

In the West, this shift back to simplicity in Roman Catholic and Anglican ecclesiastical dress is expressed in simple, fully-cut vestments made from materials using natural fibers, reminiscent of those of the early Christian era. A leading figure in this movement is Sister M. Augustina Fluëler, a Capuchin nun, associated with the Cloisters of St. Klara, in Switzerland. One chasuble that she designed was made of off-white, plain-weave wool, with a stole of plain-weave silk with two embroidered crosses in gold thread. In a simple and elegant wool and silk dalmatic, she used narrow bands of rose and purple as edging, with broader alternating bands of these colors incorporated into the sleeves.

Other expressions of this simplicity of vestment design may be seen in the embroidered works of Beryl Dean Phillips (England), in the handwoven chasubles of Barbara Markey Wallace (United States) and copes and mitres with lappets of Lennart Rodhe (Sweden), in the painted chasubles of Willam Justema (United States) and in the appliquéd chasubles of Henri Matisse (France). While utilizing different techniques—embroidery, handwoven twills, overshot, and tapestry, painting, and appliqué in their production, they share a spareness of patterning—often of crosses or of stylized floral patterns with little background ornamentation—and of natural materials—silk, wool, cotton, and linen. The design and production of these vestments by craftswomen and men underscores the belief that the careful and creative making of objects used in divine service is in itself a form of worship. These vestments convey "a certain splendid sobriety," the essence of the reform of the Roman Catholic Church associated with the *General Instructions* of 1962 that emphasize that the beauty of ecclesiastical vestments derives from "the excellence of their material and the elegance of their cut" (Flannery, p. 197), rather than from their elaborate ornamentation or color. The concept of the simple yet distinctive beauty of vestments coincides with Anglican views of contemporary ecclesiastical dress, the use of which should mark special religious events, but without ostentation.

Ecclesiastical Dress and Globalization

The counterpart to simplicity of ecclesiastical dress produced by vestment makers in the West, which in the Roman Catholic Church was associated with the reforms instituted by Vatican II, is seen in the appearance of individual national churches, whose identities are expressed, in part, through use of local materials in vestments. The basis for the local development of ecclesiastical dress is found in the General Instruction on the Roman Missal:

> 304. Bishops' Conferences may determine and propose to the Holy See any adaptations in the shape or style of vestments, which they consider desirable by reason of local customs or needs.

> 305. Besides the materials traditionally used for making sacred vestments, natural fabrics from each region are admissible, as also artificial fabrics which accord with the dignity of the sacred action and of those who are to wear the vestments. It is for the Bishops' Conference to decide on these matters. (Flannery, p. 197)

The use of local materials may refer to particular techniques—types of weaving, embroidery, or drawnwork—and types of materials—cotton, wool, lurex, among others. In the Philippines, for example, locally made vestments are constructed from handwoven cloth of pineapple (*piña*) and *abaca* (commonly known as Manila hemp) fibers. Abaca fibers are processed from the long plant stalks and the finely spun threads are hand-woven into plain-weave abaca cloth, with designs made through discontinuous supplementary weft patterning (*sinuksok*) and resist-dyed ikat techniques. Abaca cloth made into vestments may also be embellished with a range of decorative techniques including, embroidery, appliqué, beadwork, and cut-and drawn work. Chasubles, copes, stoles, and mitres with lappets made from cloth hand-woven with *piña* fibers are similarly decorated. A new type of vestment was introduced in the Philippines in the 1970s, the chasuble-alb, known in the Philippines as the tunic. This vestment, worn with a stole, serves as both an alb and a chasuble, thus limiting the number of vestments needed by concelebrants and reducing the discomfort of wearing multiple layers of cloth in a tropical climate. However, not all liturgists have agreed with this change and in 1973, the Catholic Bishops of the Philippines restricted its use to particular circumstances.

In Nigeria, there has been a shift from the purchase of ecclesiastical dress, mainly from Great Britain to the production of vestments in Nigeria itself, using locally woven narrow-strip cloth and batik-dyed textiles. Chasubles, mitres, and stoles, machine-embroidered with depictions of scenes and texts from the Old and New Testament as well as with more abstract shapes and symbols, may be produced by individual specialists or by nuns working in convent workshops. One woman, Mrs. Anne Salubi of Ilorin, a university-trained artist, is renowned throughout Nigeria for her chasubles, which have been commissioned by bishops in various Nigerian cities as well as in Ireland. During the recent visit of Pope John Paul II to Nigeria, Mrs. Salubi was commissioned to make the chasuble given to the Pope during his visit. Anglican and Methodist church leaders in Nigeria have also begun to incorporate handwoven cloth strips into ecclesiastical dress, using them mainly as stoles in different colors used for particular church seasons, with simple machine-embroidered design such as crosses. Smaller workshops combine the production of church stoles and choir robes with academic gowns.

The mass-production and mass-marketing of ecclesiastical dress through catalogues reflect the accelerating interdependence of nations and communities in a world system linked through economics, mass media, and modern transportation systems. For example, Mexico-style ecclesiastical vestments are marketed on the website of the Mexican American Cultural Center, of San Antonio, Texas, which includes embroidered chasubles produced by the congregation of Sisters in Guadalajara, Mexico, as well as stoles made with locally handwoven *zarape* cloth strips. The web not only facilitates the marketing of vestments but also serves as a source of materials, such as metallic threads, which might not be available locally. Thus, globalization allows for specialization of local styles of ecclesiastical dress while also expanding the availability of supplies and the marketing of these national or ethnically identified vestment styles to communities outside the immediate homeland.

Conclusion: Main Themes

Several recurrent themes have emerged during the long history of ecclesiastic dress. Early church dress consisted of simple forms, using natural materials, in part due to the persecution of Christians and in part due to a lack of well-defined church doctrine on dress. By the third century, with the acceptance of Christianity by Constantine, there was a shift toward ecclesiastical dress, which both identified wearers as Church leaders and also indicated their rank within the church. These two tendencies—one, toward visually portraying church hierarchy with ever more elaborate ecclesiastical dress, exalting the worship of God and Christ through beautiful vestments; the other toward downplaying distinctions between church leadership and laity through simple, unadorned styles of dress and, in the case of the Protestant Reformation, abandoning ecclesiastical dress entirely—have been expressed in various ways over the centuries. A related theme, uniformity and individualism, has also been expressed in ecclesiastical dress. For example, U.S. "women religious" have abandoned wearing habits, in order to address the contradiction between American social ideals of secular individualism and the religious uniformity that ecclesiastical dress represent, and to function more effectively in the secular world. These themes also reflect the relationship of changes in ecclesiastical dress and political, economic, and social changes, with reformers tending toward simplicity and contemporary secular garments, and with counter-reformers tending toward more elaborated vestments which reflect a nostalgia for past "traditions" in preference to secular "modernity." Contests between church and state have also been reflected in controversies over the wearing of ecclesiastical vestments.

The themes of worldliness and spirituality, unity and individualism, and simplicity and elaboration, have been concerns expressed largely in terms of vestment use in Western and Eastern Churches in Europe and in the United States. The use of ecclesiastical vestments as expressions of anticolonial sentiments and, more generally, to counter assumptions about Western cultural hegemony are themes that emerge in Christian communities in Africa, Asia, and Latin America, where conversion to Christianity has been more recent. European ecclesiastical dress has been viewed as a sign of modernity but also as a symbol of acquiescence to Western power. With national independence and with the later reforms of Vatican II introduced in 1962 and thereafter, African, Asian, and Latin American Roman Catholics began to incorporate locally produced vestments using indigenous materials into religious worship, supporting modern local and Roman Catholic identities simultaneously.

Ecclesiastical dress is especially appropriate for asserting different identities and distinctions among individuals and groups because of the range of materials, colors, embellishments, and styles into which this dress can be shaped. Ecclesiastical dress may also be used to construct new identities that acknowledge cultural distinctiveness, while at the same time emphasizing membership in a universal world church. The continually changing configurations of vestments used in Christian worship attest to this aspiration for unity and distinction. The attempts to find an acceptable balance

of old and new ways, of simplicity and ornamentation, of indigenous and foreign ideas and practices, reflect a striving for the harmonious unity of humankind and at the same time, a need for distinctive identities and beliefs, both expressed through the use of ecclesiastical dress.

See also Religion and Dress.

Bibliography

Innemée, Karel C. *Ecclesiastical Dress in the Medieval Near East*. Leiden, New York: E. J. Brill, 1992.

Mayo, Janet. *A History of Ecclesiastical Dress*. New York: Holmes and Meier Publishers, Inc., 1984.

Elisha P. Renne

ECONOMICS AND CLOTHING

The economics of clothing involve three processes: production, making the clothing; distribution, getting the clothing from the maker to the consumer; and consumption, actually using the clothing. Although consumption drives production and distribution, the three processes are in many ways inseparable. The system is fiercely competitive at all stages, partly but not entirely because clothing is a fashion good. Although some plain utilitarian garments may seem to be little affected by fashion, their production and distribution are highly competitive as well.

In developed nations, fashions in clothing and other goods and services change so rapidly and in so many ways that it's difficult to keep track. People may assume that, in ancient cultures or isolated societies, styles of clothing, dwellings, tools, and customs remained static for generations. Yet scholars discern small incremental changes when they can find sufficient data. Major features of the economics of clothing today have roots in the distant past.

Perhaps in prehistoric times, or on the frontier of pioneer America, isolated family units produced all their own clothing. But in fact, most people probably hunted in groups for large, fur-bearing animals and specialized in doing certain tasks. Production of apparel has always been highly labor-intensive, and evidence of specialization appears early.

Twenty thousand to twenty-six thousand years ago, in the north of what is now Russia, a young man was buried in a shirt and trousers elaborately embroidered with ivory beads. At roughly the same time, in what is now France, craftsmen were carving delicate sewing needles from bone. To shape and drill beads or make needles with the materials and tools available then would require both inherent manual skill and considerable practice. Probably only one person in a settlement or a cluster of settlements mastered the skills for such work; others did tasks such as harvesting and processing fibers or skins and assembling garments. Presumably these specialists bartered what they made for goods and services of other group members. Specialization optimizes use of individuals' time and abilities and makes better quality clothing possible for all. Scientists who uncovered the grave of the youth in the beaded outfit concluded that he was a person of importance—he or his family possessed wealth or power to command a costume of such splendor. Clothing already expressed status, more than 200 centuries ago.

A Global Economy

The apparel economy is truly global. From earliest times, it has extended to the limits of human occupation. In each geographic area, people exploited native plants, animals, and minerals. The Chinese learned the secrets of the silkworm; linen grew in the Nile valley, cotton in the Indus River valley; Mesopotamians raised sheep for their wool. Shellfish found at the eastern end of the Mediterranean sea provided precious purple dye. Polar cultures relied upon the furs and skins of local creatures, both land and sea. Natives of what is now the Pacific coast of Canada used cedar bark garments to shed rain; some peoples made cloaks of grasses.

In time, precious textiles, furs, and ornaments moved by long, difficult overland trade routes or hazardous water voyages. Later, textile centers evolved where people demanded large quantities of luxury fabrics and were willing to pay well for them. Byzantium, as well as Sicily, produced fine silks during the Middle Ages, although they were far from the original sources of silk. Even so, proximity of raw materials gave some geographic areas advantages over others. Certain districts in Italy, Germany, Flanders, and England became textile centers, specializing in locally produced fibers and distinctive techniques. In medieval times, traveling merchants transported fine textiles from production centers to regional trade fairs on a regular basis.

The ramifications of trade in textiles and other apparel materials extended far beyond the obvious. In ancient Mesopotamia, the need to record exchanges of these and other goods stimulated development of counting systems and writing. Eventually, coinage evolved to expedite transactions. Still later, Italians pioneered bookkeeping, banking, and legal systems to facilitate and organize international commerce.

The great plague, the Black Death, which killed as many as one-third of the people in Europe, may have reached Europe from Asia in the middle 1300s, transported by infected fleas on furs carried by caravans along the ancient silk road. As the plague abated, fashion change accelerated because of greater concentration of population in cities, shifts in the distribution of wealth, and growing importance of commercial life. The demand for furs in the sixteenth century, including beaver skins to make fine felt hats, became a major force driving the exploration of North America. Remote Australia and New Zealand were settled largely because sheep could be raised profitably there.

Guilds

In the Middle Ages and Renaissance, members of guilds produced elegant and costly clothing to order for wealthy and high-ranking people on the European continent. Guilds were part civic associations, part trade associations, part labor unions. Guilds specialized in certain crafts ranging from hats to shoes. Membership was strictly controlled; new members served long apprenticeships and had to meet strict criteria for admission. Detailed rules served to uphold quality of production and limit competition. In general, men dominated the guilds; women did certain specialized tasks such as embroidery but had little role in governance. Not until the late 1600s, as guilds were ebbing in power, was the first guild controlled by women, the mantua makers, officially recognized in France.

National Pride and Profit

Nations have long promoted fashions to stimulate demand for their products. In the 1600s, King Louis XIV displayed the beauty of French silks and laces by wearing them and dictating that members of the French nobility also showcase French products. France sent dolls dressed in the latest fashions to other nations to create desire for French goods among the upper classes. According to Mr. Pepys' diary, Charles II of England introduced a subdued style of men's clothing in England in 1666, partly to promote English wool and linen fabrics.

"Demand" is not a quantity; it is the relationship between prices and how much consumers are willing to buy at various prices. If demand for a commodity is great, people will generally buy larger amounts of it at various prices than they will buy if demand is small.

The Origin of Ready-to-Wear

During the reign of Charles II, according to Beverly Lemire, the ready-to-wear clothing industry originated when shipowners or the British navy ordered plain, coarse garments in quantity to outfit crews of English ships heading to sea on voyages lasting months or years. There were as yet no garment or textile factories in the modern sense. Garment production was controlled by (mostly) men who contracted with the government or shipping companies, bought materials in quantity and then hired workers who took the supplies home with them to make the garments by hand. Workers were paid by the unit, and the contractors often cheated them. The system of subcontracting clothing production continues today.

Mechanization of Production

Although production of ready-to-wear clothing began before sewing machines existed, an English clergyman had invented a hand-operated knitting frame near the end of the sixteenth century. Queen Elizabeth I refused to grant him a patent because she feared it would put English hand-knitters, using knitting needles and mostly working at home for contractors, out of work. But by the eighteenth century, England led the

industrial revolution with a stream of inventions that eventually reduced prices of many goods and improved their quality so that ordinary people could afford them. By the later 1700s, English factories were turning out fabric on water- or steam-powered spinning and weaving equipment. Demand for inexpensive clothing gradually increased in England as lower-class people, some of them employed in the new factories, began to have a bit more money to spend, as well as a growing interest in fashionable clothing. London stores began to display appealing merchandise in lighted shop windows and encouraged shopping as recreation. Even low-income people could buy small ribbon ornaments and other accessories (See McKendrick, Brewer, and Plumb).

Meanwhile, clothing styles of English noblemen became simpler and more functional as they supervised agricultural activities on their estates rather than hanging around the royal court, as was the case in France. French noblemen copied English styles when the French Revolution made it dangerous to be seen in public wearing silks and laces.

By the early nineteenth century, workingmen's clothing was being cut and hand-sewn by workers who specialized in specific tasks rather than each making a garment from start to finish. In American coastal cities, workers constructed garments for sailors in lofts where sails were made, from the same sturdy materials. Inventors designed the first sewing machines, but handworkers, who feared losing their jobs, broke up the machines, which didn't work very well anyway. Improved versions soon followed; the 1800s brought numerous apparel-related inventions and discoveries, including shoemaking machinery, vulcanized rubber, artificial cellulosic fibers, and synthetic coal-tar dyes.

Wars such as the American Civil War created demand for large quantities of uniforms. Based on

---

THE CONCEPT OF FASHION

"Fashion" is a complex concept, but economic analyses require simple, operational definitions. Therefore this essay uses definitions based on those stated by Paul Nystrom in his 1928 book, *Economics of Fashion*. He defined "style" as "a characteristic or distinctive mode or method of expression in the field of some art" (p. 3) and "fashion" as "the prevailing style at any given time" (p. 4). A source of confusion is that the word "fashion" can be used to mean either "content" or "process."

In writing or speech, the word "fashion" is often misused as a synonym for women's clothing. Yet most consumer goods and services are subject to the fashion process. Fashion also affects noneconomic matters such as social customs. The economic structure of consumer goods industries reflects the role of fashion, which in turn indirectly affects basic industries. Because "fashion" can involve virtually all aspects of contemporary life, this essay concentrates on the economics of clothing.

measurements of servicemen, standardized sizing of men's clothing evolved. By the later 1800s, men's factory-made clothing of reasonably good quality and fit was being produced in quantity. Although wealthy men still wore custom-made clothing, moderate-income men could dress better than ever before.

The situation for women's clothing differed from that for men's clothing. Styles were relatively simple in the later 1700s and early 1800s, but then outfits became increasingly ornate and complex and remained so for the rest of the nineteenth century. This complexity, plus lack of measurement data for women, delayed large-scale factory production of women's clothing. Late in the century, when separates—shirtwaist and skirt styles and tailored women's suits—became fashionable, it was easier for women to find ready-made clothing to fit. By the end of the 1800s, output of women's factory-made clothing was growing rapidly.

Paris Couture

Although wealthy people still wore custom-made clothing in the 1800s, the guilds were gone by the time Charles Worth, ironically an English immigrant to Paris, opened the first couture house in the mid-nineteenth century. The Paris couture, offering exclusive new styles for women to be made-to-order each season, reached its peak volume in the late 1800s and early 1900s. Only the richest women could afford couture apparel, and volume was never large, but the couturiers were masters of publicity. Actually, the practice of holding well-publicized "showings" of new fashions each season originated in England not with clothing designers but with such enterprising businessmen as Josiah Wedgwood, who in the late eighteenth century invited well-to-do customers to seasonal openings of his latest designs in tableware and decorative ceramics (See McKendrick, Brewer, and Plumb).

Fashion for Everyone

With the help of fashion magazines, which originated in the early 1800s, and paper dress patterns for home sewers, introduced later in the century, seamstresses copied or adapted couture designs for middle-class clientele far from fashion centers. In America, some dressmakers traveled from household to household twice a year, spending a couple of weeks making new clothes for all females in a family. Electric-powered sewing machines were installed in factories, but home sewers and

dressmakers used machines with foot treadles so they were not dependent on electricity.

The first department stores opened in major cities in the United States and Europe in the mid-1800s, with clothing as a major category of merchandise. Instead of bargaining with customers over selling prices, as small shopkeepers did, department stores began putting price tags on their goods. Retail magnates such as B. Altman, John Wanamaker, and Marshall Field built palatial stores to dramatize shopping as recreation. Streetcar transportation, first horse-drawn and later electric-powered, brought customers downtown. Smaller stores specializing in men's or women's apparel, children's clothing, undergarments and lingerie, or shoes, profited from customer traffic attracted to city centers by big stores.

Catalog order firms such as Sears, Roebuck originated in the 1800s as postal service and railroads developed in the United States. Mail order made ready-to-wear clothing available to rural and small-town residents. The first outlying shopping centers opened in the second and third decades of the twentieth century, as automobiles multiplied; Sears, Roebuck opened its first retail store in an early shopping center. After World War II, building of suburban branches of large department stores and major regional shopping centers accelerated, leading to the decline of downtown shopping and the closing of many central city stores. Giant regional shopping centers capitalized on the entertainment aspect of shopping and consumers' seemingly limitless appetite for variety.

Competition for Consumers' Money

Accelerating competitive trends in the apparel business has been the gradual decline of clothing's share of total consumer spending. What limited records survive show that during the Middle Ages and Renaissance in Europe, in the heyday of the guilds, rich people spent huge proportions of their incomes on luxurious clothing for themselves. Furthermore, the nobility outfitted the various ranks in their households, even down to the lowest servant, in appropriate styles and the manor's heraldic colors for specific festivals or occasions.

Once, there were only limited ways to spend money to demonstrate one's wealth—what Thorstein Veblen named "conspicuous consumption." In the past 150 years, factory production has made clothing for ordinary people less expensive, while many appealing new products have become available: phonographs and parlor pianos, household appliances—including sewing machines—motor vehicles, and electronic goods, starting with telephones and radios. All of these impressed people's friends and rivals, competing with clothing for the consumer's money. Of every twenty dollars Americans now spend, only about one goes for clothing. Simultaneously, long-term fashion trends, dating back at least to Charles II of England in the 1600s, have moved toward ever-simpler, less-formal, more casual clothing even for people in the upper ranks of society. As more women work outside the home, fewer of them dress to showcase their husbands' wealth and prosperity, as they might have in Veblen's world. Demand for men's tailored clothing declined in the later twentieth century, as did the number of specialty stores selling men's clothing, as men chose more casual clothing and active sportswear.

Growing Ferocity of Competition

Couture was not profitable after World War I; its client base dwindled further during the Depression of the 1930s. Designers tried to control copying of their designs and sometimes produced lower-priced replicas of their own exclusive models. Design piracy has long been a plague for clothing manufacturers and designers, but no tactics seem to stop it, especially when consumers are eager for the latest fashions at the lowest possible prices. The spending of fickle teenaged customers, anxious to look like popular entertainers, accelerates the pace of fashion change.

For a time after World War II, couture houses licensed their names to other firms to produce lower-priced clothing merchandise and accessories. Some ventured into men's wear, with limited success. In Europe and North America, the number of establishments producing fine custom-made clothing and the number of customers that bought it had declined. Demand continues to shrink for complex and costly custom-made apparel such as elaborately embroidered or beaded garments. To the extent that such clothing is still produced, production moves to India and other Asian countries.

By the late twentieth century, large European corporations, some outside the apparel business, competed to buy Paris couture houses and leading Italian design firms, while other high-end design houses gobbled up each other. Sales of expensive apparel and luxury accessories to wealthy people and entertainers all over the world burgeoned in the 1990s' economic boom. Designer-name firms outdid each other by opening showy retail stores, designed by avant-garde architects, in major cities around the world, but some of these stores attracted more lookers than purchasers and soon closed. Young design-school graduates from England, Belgium, New York, California, and elsewhere started their own small firms; only a lucky few achieved enough recognition or financial backing to stay in business.

A Low-Paid Workforce

Clothing workers have always been poorly paid. Clothing for serfs and servants on medieval estates was produced on-site, usually from materials grown, harvested, and processed by serfs—essentially, slave labor. Slaves made their own clothing on American cotton plantations. Clothing production prospers where cheap labor is plentiful. Although some operations require great skill, most construction tasks are divided into small steps that can be learned quickly. In the past 200 years, garment factories have been among the first large scale manufacturing enterprises to open in developing nations. In nineteenth-century New York, manufacturers crowded hundreds of poorly paid immigrants into high-rise buildings, often in unsafe situations. Contracting and homework were widespread. One group of immigrants after another supplied the labor—German, Irish, Jewish, Italian; in the twentieth century, Puerto Ricans, Chinese, and Blacks joined the list. Even today, "sweatshops" owned by and employing immigrants from Asia flourish in New York City. During the second half of the twentieth century, garment manufacture spread to Hong Kong, then to China and other parts of southeast Asia, not to mention Latin America and African locations that have large numbers of people willing to work for low wages. Although machines facilitate clothing construction, much of the process resists automation. Reading clothing labels is a lesson in geography.

Factoring

A longtime practice in the fashion industry is "factoring," whereby a company takes out short-term loans to buy fabrics and other materials to produce garments for the season, then repays the loans as retailers purchase the goods. The specialized lenders are called "factors." Factoring is not limited to apparel production; it also exists in other industries where fashion changes quickly, such as toys. A plague of the fashion business is that retailers squeeze manufacturers by returning unsold goods or paying less than the agreed-upon price.

Because the garment business is so competitive, profits are low and existence is risky.

The Used Clothing Trade

Trade in secondhand clothing has been important for many centuries. Once wealthy and high-ranking people gave their unwanted clothing to servants. Usually, servants sold the garments—they had no use for them and needed the money. Patrons of theatres such as Shakespeare's Globe donated clothing to actors who could not otherwise afford credible costumes when playing high-ranking characters. Used clothing, including stolen items, was sold by peddlers alongside crude, early ready-to-wear. In the nineteenth century, the first factory-made garments were sometimes introduced by secondhand clothing retailers. Stores selling both used and new clothing (including military surplus) existed until after World War II. Postwar, "yard" and "garage" sales became common, apparently inspired by such sales on military bases, especially when officers' families had to move to totally different climate zones. Consignment shops, operated by charitable organizations or private entrepreneurs, multiplied.

As the quantity of discarded clothing in Europe and North America exceeded the capacity of welfare agencies to distribute it to the poor, large quantities of used clothing have been shipped to developing nations. In Africa, inexpensive used clothing can displace traditional apparel and compete with local industries. At the other extreme, "vintage" clothing—used couture or high-fashion women's clothing—has become so popular and acceptable that leading Hollywood actresses may wear old designer gowns to the Academy Awards ceremonies. Exclusive auction houses sell vintage designer clothing for high prices; retail stores in New York and Los Angeles specialize in such clothing.

Continuing Change

The garment business consists of all sizes of firms from giant to tiny. Although the trend is giant companies, these are not assured of success. Large corporations manufacture clothing under many labels. Some famous brand names produce different qualities of clothing for different types of retailers, contracting out production of some merchandise lines to other corporations. Major producers can go bankrupt unexpectedly; failure lurks just around the corner due to shifting customer tastes and a variety of other uncertainties. International trade regulations, tariffs, and quota systems engage the services of a corps of lawyers and other specialists.

Everything changes quickly in the apparel world. Cities of developed nations are littered with abandoned factories, empty retail stores, defunct design houses, and wreckage of supporting industries. Once-famous department stores are now history; Montgomery Ward is nearly forgotten; Sears Roebuck slips in importance. Someday Wal-Mart may fade away. As more shopping centers and big-box stores open, downtowns and old shopping centers die. Everyone in the business knows that there is too much retail space, yet they keep building stores. Change is the only certainty.

The next phase in clothing distribution may be the Web, whether goods are sold by conventional retail stores, catalog retailers, Web-based retailers, or something completely different. Auction sites such as eBay offer vintage clothing and also help manufacturers and retailers trade large quantities of materials and clothing among themselves.

See also Department Store; Fashion Industry; Globalization; Labor Unions; Mantua; Ready-to-Wear; Retailing; Secondhand Clothes, Anthropology of; Secondhand Clothes, History of; Sewing Machine; Sweatshops.

Bibliography

Benson, Susan Porter. *Counter Cultures: Saleswomen, Managers, and Customers in American Department Stores, 1890–1940.* Champaign: University of Illinois Press, 1988.

Cobrin, Harry A. *The Men's Clothing Industry: Colonial Through Modern Times.* New York: Fairchild Publications, 1970.

Cooper, Grace Rogers. *The Sewing Machine: Its Invention and Development,* 2nd ed. Washington, D.C.: Smithsonian Press for the National Museum of History and Technology, 1976.

Cray, Ed. *Levi's.* Boston: Houghton Mifflin, 1978.

Danish, Max D. *The World of David Dubinsky.* Cleveland: The World Publishing Co., 1957.

DeMarly, Diana. *The History of Haute Couture, 1850–1950.* New York: Holmes & Meier, 1980.

Frick, Carole Collier. *Dressing Renaissance Florence—Families, Fortunes, and Fine Clothing.* Baltimore: Johns Hopkins University Press, 2002.

Hansen, Karen Tranberg. *Salula: The World of Secondhand Clothing and Zambia.* Chicago: University of Chicago Press, 2000.

Helfgott, Roy B. "Women's and Children's Apparel." In *Made in New York: Case Studies in Metropolitan Manufacturing.* Edited by Max Hall. Cambridge: Harvard University Press, 1959.

Hendrickson, Robert. *The Grand Emporiums.* New York: Stein and Day, 1979.

Kirke, Betty. *Madeleine Vionnet.* San Francisco: Chronicle Books, 1998.

Lemire, Beverly. *Dress, Culture and Commerce: The English Clothing Trade Before the Factory, 1660–1800.* New York: St. Martin's Press, 1997.

Lockwood, Lisa. "Mega-Merger Mania: The New Blueprints of Five Ravenous Firms." *WWD* 186, no. 36 (2003): 1, 6–7.

McKendrick, Neil, John Brewer, and J. H. Plumb. *The Birth of a Consumer Society: The Commercialization of Eighteenth-Century England.* Bloomington: Indiana University Press, 1982.

Nystrom, Paul H. *Economics of Fashion.* New York: The Ronald Press Company, 1928.

Rexford, Nancy E. *Women's Shoes in America, 1795–1930.* Kent, Ohio: Kent State University Press, 2000.

Sandars, N. K. *Prehistoric Art in Europe,* 2nd ed. New York: Viking Penguin, 1985, pp. 49–50.

Spufford, Peter. *Power and Profit: The Merchant in Medieval Europe.* New York: Thames & Hudson, Inc., 2003.

Veblen, Thorstein. *The Theory of the Leisure Class.* New York: Macmillan, 1899. Reprint, New York: The Modern Library, 1934.

Walker, Richard. *Savile Row: An Illustrated History.* New York: Rizzoli International, 1989.

Winakor, Geitel. "The Decline in Expenditures for Clothing Relative to Total Consumer Spending, 1929–1986." *Home Economics Research Journal* 17 (1989): 195–215.

Geitel Winakor

EMPIRE STYLE

In its broadest sense as a term in contemporary fashion, "empire style" (sometimes called simply "Empire" with the French pronunciation, "om-peer") refers to a woman's dress silhouette in which the waistline is considerably raised above the natural level, and the skirt is usually slim and columnar. The reference is to fashions of France's First Empire, which in political terms lasted from 1804 when Napoleon Bonaparte crowned himself Emperor, to his final defeat at the Battle of Waterloo in 1815. It should be noted that the styles of this period, when referring specifically to English or American fashions or examples, may be termed "Regency" (referring to the Regency of the Prince of Wales, 1811–1820) or "Federal" (referring to the decades immediately following the American Revolution).

None of these terms, whose boundaries are defined by political milestones, accurately encompasses the time frame in which "empire style" fashions are found, which date from the late 1790s to about 1820, after which skirts widened and the waistline lowered to an extent no longer identifiable as "empire style."

The Empire style in its purest form is characterized by: the columnar silhouette—without gathers in front, some fullness over the hips, and a concentration of gathers aligned with the 3–4" wide center back bodice panel; a raised waistline, which at its extreme could be at armpit-level, dependent on new forms of corsetry with small bust gussets, cording under the breasts, and shoulder straps to keep the bust high; soft materials, especially imported Indian white muslin (the softest, sheerest of which is called "mull"), often pre-embroidered with white cotton thread; and neoclassical influence in overall style (the silhouette imitating Classical statuary) and in accessories and trim.

Neoclassical references included sandals; bonnets, hairstyles, and headdresses copied from Greek statues and vases; and motifs found in ancient architecture and decorative arts, such as the Greek key, and oak and laurel leaves. The use of purely neoclassical references was at its peak from about 1798 to just after 1800; after that, they were succeeded by other influences.

The adoption of these references has been linked with France's Revolution and adoption of Greek and Roman democratic and republican principles, and certainly the French consciously sought to make these connections both at the height of their Revolution, and under Napoleon, who was eager to link himself to the great Roman emperors.

Applying this political reference to America is more problematic. The extremely revealing versions of the style were seldom seen in America, where conservatism and ambivalence about letting Europe dictate American fashions ran deep. However, Americans did adopt the general look of the period, and plenty of dresses survive to testify that fashionable young women did wear the sheer white muslin style. Moreover, there is ample evidence that women of every class, even on the frontiers, had some access to information on current fashions, and usually possessed, if not for everyday use, modified versions of them.

The origins of the neoclassical influence are visible in the later eighteenth century. White linen, and later, cotton, dresses were the standard uniform for infants, toddlers, and young girls, and entered adult fashion about 1780. During the 1780s and early 1790s, women's silhouettes gradually became slimmer, and the waistline crept up, the effect heightened by the addition of wide sashes, whose upper edge approached the level that waistlines would in another decade. After 1795, waistlines rose dramatically and the skirt circumference was further reduced, the fullness no longer equally distributed but confined to the sides and back. By 1798, fashion plates in England and France show the form-clinging high-waisted neoclassical style, with England lagging a little behind in its adoption of the extreme of the new look.

As England and France were at war for nearly all of this period, English styles sometimes took their own direction, showing a fluctuating waistline level (which should not be taken literally, as garments from this period show remarkably little deviation from a norm) and numerous decorative details borrowed from peasant or "cottage" styles, historic references, especially medieval and "Tudor," and regional references such as Russian, Polish, German, or Spanish. Often, contemporary events inspired fashions, such as the state visit of allies in the Napoleonic wars; military uniforms also inspired trim and accessories in women's fashions during these years.

Several myths persist about the styles of this period, including the idea that the style was invented by Josephine Bonaparte to conceal her pregnancy, and that ladies of fashion dampened their petticoats to achieve the clinging-muslin effects seen in classical statues. Fashions can rarely be attributed to one person (although a hundred years earlier, a pregnancy at the French court did inspire the invention of a style) and the most cursory glance at fashions of the 1780s and 1790s shows a clear progress of internal change in fashion.

The dampened petticoat myth may have arisen from some early historians', and historical novelists', misunderstanding of some comments on the new style. Compared to the heavier fabrics and stylized body shapes (created by heavily-boned, conical-shaped corsets and side-hoops) that immediately preceded them, the new sheer muslins, worn over one slip or even, by some European ladies, a knitted, tubular body stocking, would have revealed the contours of the natural body to an extent not seen in centuries. Several contemporaries and early fashion historians wrote that women looked *as if* they had dampened their skirts. However, no evidence, including scathing denunciations of the indecent new style, as well as gleeful social satirists' commentary and caricatures, exists to document that this was ever done.

The Empire style has seen numerous revivals, although modern eyes must sometimes look closely for the reference, as it is always used in tandem with the silhouette and body shape fashionable at the time. Tea gowns of the 1880s and 1890s are sometimes described as "empire style." Reform dress often borrowed the high waist and slender skirt of the Empire period, perhaps finding the relatively simple construction notably different from the styles it rejected, the high waist providing freedom from the era's constrictive corsets. By about 1908, "empire style" dresses were a large segment of fashionable offerings. The 1930s saw another minor revival, as did the 1970s. The release in the late 1990s of several film and television adaptations of Jane Austen's novels, all set during the Empire period, inspired another revival.

See also Dress Reform; Maternity Dress; Tea Gown.

Bibliography

Ashelford, Jane. *The Art of Dress: Clothes and Society 1500–1914*. Great Britain: The National Trust. Distributed in the United States by Harry N. Abrams, New York, 1996.

Bourhis, Kate, ed. *The Age of Napoleon: Costume from Revolution to Empire, 1789–1815*. New York: Metropolitan Museum of Art and Harry N. Abrams, 1989.

Cunnington, C. Willet. *English Womens' Clothing in the Nineteenth Century*. London: Faber and Faber, Ltd., 1937. Reprint, New York: Dover Publications, 1990.

Ribeiero, Aileen. *Fashion in the French Revolution*. New York: Holmes and Meier, 1988.

——. *The Art of Dress: Fashion in England and France 1750–1820*. New Haven, Conn.: Yale University Press, 1995.

Alden O'Brien

EQUESTRIAN COSTUME

Comfort, practicality, and protection from the elements are central qualities of riding attire, though it has always been considered stylish. Distinctive accessories marked equestrian costume from streetwear: sturdy knee-high boots with a heel and sometimes spurs for both men and women, a crop, whip or cane, gloves to spare the wearer from the chafing of leather reins, and most importantly a hat for style and later a helmet for safety. Contemporary riding dress still emphasizes comfort and protection but modern materials are used in its construction, including cotton-lycra fabrics for breeches, polystyrene-filled helmets, and Gore-Tex jackets, bringing it in line with high-technology clothing used in other sports.

Construction and Materials

The materials worn for riding from the mid-seventeenth to the early twentieth centuries were easily distinguished from the silks, muslins, and velvets of fashionable evening dress. Equestrian activities required sturdy and often weatherproof fabrics such as woolen broadcloth, camlet (a silk and wool or hair mixture), melton wool, and gabardine for colder weather and linen or cotton twill for summer or the tropics. In the eighteenth and early nineteenth centuries, habits were frequently adorned with gold, silver, or later woolen braiding, often imitating the frogging on Hussar or other military uniforms.

For example, in Wright of Derby's double portrait of Mr. and Mrs. Coltman exhibited in 1771, both wear stylish riding dress. Thomas Coltman's dress consists of a deep blue waistcoat trimmed with silver braid, a loosely fitting frock coat, high boots, and buckskin breeches fitted so tight that the outline of a coin is visible in his right-hand pocket. British styles of equestrian dress strongly influenced civilian fashions in other countries. In particular, French Anglophiles imitated British modes as early as the eighteenth century. The British frock coat became known as the *redingote* in France, a corruption of the word "riding-coat." Equestrian influence has subtly shaped men's dress to the present day, and vestiges of it remain in the single back vent of coats and suit jackets, which derive from the need to sit comfortably astride a horse and wick off the rain. Mary Coltman sits sidesaddle and wears a habit in one of the most fashionable colors for women in the eighteenth century when red, claret, and rose were in vogue. Her light waistcoat is trimmed with gold braid and she sports a jaunty plumed hat. Other portraits that feature eighteenth-century riding dress include Sir Joshua Reynolds's portrait of Lady Worsley and George Stubbs's double portrait of the Sheriff of Nottingham and his wife, Sophia Musters.

In the nineteenth century, riding dress became more subdued in style and hue for both sexes. The early nineteenth-century gentleman wore a single-breasted tail-coat, sloping in front with a single-breasted waistcoat and cravat or stock. On horseback, he wore the same garments on his upper body but his coat might have distinctive gilt buttons. His legs required more specialized garments: breeches made from buckskin were typically worn and for "dress" riding trousers or pantaloons with a strap to keep them from riding up. If he wore shoes rather than boots, he could use knee-gaiters to protect his legs.

Because of their practicality, lack of decorative detail, and allowance for mobility, women wore riding habits not only on horseback but also as visiting, travelling, and walking costumes during the day. For women, the upper half of riding habits often differed little from the clothing worn by their male counterparts, with the addition of darts and shaping for the bust. The bottom half of the horsewoman's costume expressed her femininity. Because ladies were expected to ride sidesaddle from the fifteenth to the early twentieth centuries, they wore skirts specially designed for the purpose. This contrast between the masculine upper half and feminine lower half led one early eighteenth-century writer to call it "the Hermaphroditical." While skirts tended to be relatively simple in cut and construction and quite voluminous in the early modern period, the Victorian habit-skirt was a masterwork of tailoring. Because the skirt could catch on the saddle in the event of a fall, injuring or killing the rider, many "safety skirts" were designed and patented by British firms like Harvey Nicholl and Busvine. These asymmetrical shorter skirts took many forms, including the apron-skirt, a false front that covered the legs when mounted and could be buttoned at the back when the rider dismounted.

Emerald green habits with short spencer jackets were popular in the early decades of the nineteenth century and during the 1830s followed the fashions for leg o'-mutton sleeves. During the Victorian period, as men's dress became more somber, so did women's riding habits. This is because riding habits were made by tailors rather than dressmakers and cut and fashioned with the same techniques from the same selection of fabrics. By the end of the century, black was the most appropriate color for women's riding dress. As riding became a popular leisure activity for the middle classes, etiquette and equitation manuals aimed at those who had no experience of riding flourished, and these often included strict advice about dress. As Mrs. Power O'Donoghue wrote in *Ladies on Horseback* (1889):

> A plainness, amounting even to severity, is to be preferred before any outward show. Ribbons, and coloured veils, and yellow gloves, and showy flowers are alike objectionable. A gaudy "get-up" (to make use of an expressive common-place) is highly to be condemned, and at once stamps the wearer as a person of inferior taste. Therefore avoid it.

The Victorian period introduced breeches and riding trousers for women. This garment prevented chafing and was concealed under the skirt. Tailors and breeches-makers often advertised a lady assistant to measure a woman's inseam, and the resulting breeches were made from dark wool to match the habit and remained invisible if the skirt should fly up.

Colonialism, female emancipation, and increased participation in a wide variety of sports, especially bicycling, changed women's relationship with the riding costume. On their travels, women used horses for practical transportation and exploration and these animals were not always broken to ride sidesaddle. For safety and comfort, women had to ride astride and new habits with breeches or "zouave" trousers and jackets with long skirts were devised. Jodhpurs, named after a district in Rajasthan, were based on a style of Indian trousers that ballooned over the thighs and were cut tightly below the knees. These became popular for both men and women on horseback. "Ride astride" habits began to become acceptable in the first decades of the twentieth century, though many women continued to ride sidesaddle until mid-century. A 1924 illustration in American *Vogue* shows both a more formal black sidesaddle habit worn with cutaway coat and top hat and a tweed ride-astride habit worn with jodhpurs and a floppy-brimmed hat. Tweeds were standard for informal riding wear such as "hacking jackets." In the second half of the twentieth century riding had evolved in the directions of both recreation and competitive sport and specialized clothing with higher safety standards had become the norm, and less expensive materials like rubber replaced leather boots while polar fleece, Gore-Tex, and down jackets were used for warmth and waterproofing.

Different types of equitation demanded variations in dress and etiquette. While horses were often the most practical means of transportation in the eighteenth century, the advent of rail travel increased the popularity of riding as a leisure activity. The degree of formality in dress depended on whether the activity was an informal country hack, an aristocratic foxhunt, or a ride in an urban park. The most fashionable urban sites for riding were Rotten Row in London and the Bois de Boulogne in the west of Paris.

Functional clothing worn for work with horses included the carrick or greatcoat of the coachman with triple capes to keep off rain and snow. Each equestrian profession, from the groom to the liveried postillion, had a distinctive form of dress. Those who worked in agricultural contexts around the world developed specialized attire, such as the leather or suede chaps worn by the American cowboy, the sheepskins worn by herders in the French marshes of the Camargue, or the poncho worn by gauchos in South America.

Hunting clothing was often regular riding clothing adapted for convenience and protection from the elements. In the eighteenth century some hunts adopted specific colors and emblems, though the red coat was by no means universal and green, dark blue, and brown were popular. Red woolen frock coats or "hunting pinks" with black velvet collars were the mark of the experienced fox-hunter.

Racing developed its own specialized clothing as well. In contrast with the thick and waterproof garments worn on the hunt, the jockey's clothing had to be light and streamlined, fitting the body very tightly. By the early eighteenth century, jockeys were wearing attire that is recognizable in the early-twenty-first century: tight jackets cut to the waist, white breeches, short top-boots, and peaked cap with a bow in front. At that time, the cap was black; but the bright and highly visible, often striped or checked "colored silk" livery of the jacket made the owner's identity clear. Satin weaves gave these silks their glossy sheen. Because of its sexual appeal and bright coloring, jockey suits were often copied in women's fashions by nineteenth-century couturiers like Charles Worth.

For example, in Zola's novel *Nana*, the eponymous heroine, a Parisian courtesan, goes to the races dressed in a jockey-inspired outfit:

> She wore the colours of the De Vandeuvres stable, blue and white, intermingled in a most extraordinary costume. The little body and the

tunic, in blue silk, were very tight fitting, and raised behind in an enormous puff . . . the skirt and sleeves were in white satin, as well as a sash that passed over the shoulder, and the whole was trimmed with silver braid which sparkled in the sunshine. Whilst, the more to resemble a jockey, she had placed a flat blue cap, ornamented with a feather, on the top of her chignon, from which a long switch of her golden hair hung down in the middle of her back like an enormous tail. (pp. 289–290)

Manufacture and Retail

Because of its traditions of equestrian sport, Britain has led the Western world in making riding costumes. Men could go to their habitual tailors who specialized in sporting dress.

The fabric used for making women's habits could be very expensive and because of the amount of cloth needed, it often cost substantially more than an evening gown. Like men's suits, riding habits were expected to last several years and to stand up to intensive use. Despite its elite connotations, ready-made habits were available in the eighteenth century from mercers and haberdashers' shops, and in the nineteenth century from department stores and working-class men's clothiers and outfitting firms trying to move upmarket by advertising "ladies' habit rooms." At the upper end of the market, firms offered luxury services to their clientele. In the 1880s, British tailoring firms such as Creeds opened branches in Paris. The suites of the British women's tailor and couturier Redfern in Paris, situated on the rue de Rivoli, were celebrated as "the rendez-vous of all the sportswomen whom the foreign and Parisian aristocracy count among their number." Redfern proposed stuffed block horses of several colors so that his clients could choose their habits in a tone that matched the hide (robe) of their favorite mount. The word for the hue of a horses' hide and woman's dress were the same in French.

Riding attire has always symbolized grace and leisured elegance. It implied that its wearer belonged or aspired to belong to the horse-owning classes. Wearers often used it to challenge formal social mores in dress, deportment, and gender roles. Its rustic simplicity and informality connoted youth, ease, and sometimes impudence. For example, the dandy George Bryan Brummell made riding dress fashionable in the salons of Regency Britain, bringing "rural" modes into an urban

setting. For horsewomen, etiquette was more stringent. Any woman who wore gaudy or overly ornate habits or who made a spectacle of herself was in danger of being branded a "pretty horsebreaker" or "fast woman" rather than a "fair equestrienne" in the Victorian period. Contemporary fashion designers continue to recycle traditional equestrian motifs and fabrics in haute couture and prêt-àporter collections. In this context riding costume is most often used to connote country elegance and traditional elite English style.

See also Boots; Breeches; Brummell, George (Beau); Protective Clothing.

Bibliography

Arnold, Janet. "Dashing Amazons: The Development of Women's Riding Dress, c. 1500–1900." In *Defining Dress: Dress as Object, Meaning and Identity*. Edited by Amy de la Haye and Elizabeth Wilson, 10–29. Manchester U.K.: Manchester University Press, 1999.

Chenoune, Farid. *A History of Men's Fashion*. Paris: Flammarion, 1993.

Cunnington, Phillis, and A. Mansfield. *English Costume for Sports and Outdoor Recreation: From the Sixteenth to the Nineteenth Centuries*. London: Adam and Charles Black, 1969.

David, Alison Matthews. "Elegant Amazons: Victorian Riding Habits and the Fashionable Horsewoman." *Victorian Literature and Culture* 30, no. 1 (2002): 179–210.

O'Donoghue, Power [Nannie]. *Ladies On Horseback: Learning, Park-Riding and Hunting, With Hints Upon Costume, and Numerous Anecdotes*. London: W. H. Allen, 1889.

Zola, Émile. *Nana*. London: Vizetelly and Company, 1884.

Alison Matthews David

ETHICAL FASHION AND ECOFASHION

The textile and clothing industries occupy a powerful position both economically and in sociocultural terms. Although the fashion industry is fast-moving and often dismissed as frivolous and unimportant, it represents one of the major economic players on the global stage. Fashion is one of the few remaining craft-based industries, relying on skilled manual labor for manufacturing across its wide spectrum of levels, from couture to mass production, which raises particular issues for production.

The production and consumption of fashion represent two extremes of a long, fragmented, and complex supply chain that transforms fiber into yarn and fabrics, which are then mediated by designers, manufacturers, and buyers into the clothing offered in retail outlets. The complexity of the fashion industry has made the concept of environment ally and economically sustainable, ethically sound clothing extremely difficult for the industry to address. This "fashion paradox" as defined by designer and academic Sandy Black articulates the contradictions between fashion's economic and sociocultural importance and its inbuilt obsolescence and wastefulness in the context of sustainability. There is an urgent need to reconcile ethical, environmental, social, and personal agendas through future product development and manufacturing cycles in the fashion industry, with an increasingly important role for the designer in making and influencing choices. Within fashion, economic imperatives and the transience of passing trends fuel a continuous cycle of production, consumption, and obsolescence, stimulated by desire and aspiration and far removed from basic clothing needs. Fashion (in its widest sense incorporating textiles, apparel, and accessories) is, however, one of the major global industries upon which millions depend for their livelihoods around the world, from cotton farmers and garment workers to retail-shop staff.

Since the early 1990s, fashion has become both faster and cheaper. The chain of supply and demand, previously tied to a rigid pattern of biannual seasonal fashion cycles, has largely broken down, and fashion has become pluralistic, with any number of looks simultaneously in vogue. Factors such as the spread of global communication technologies and sophisticated marketing, together with greater competition and the growth of "offshore" manufacturing for Western markets, have increased the availability of cheaper clothing. This in turn has fueled demand and heightened consumer expectations for constant novelty, resulting in faster and faster fashion cycles, especially evident in the United Kingdom and Europe. Here, new business models, focused on demand-led supply-chain management, have reduced the time needed from fabric to garments in the store. Exemplified by the retail labels Zara (part of the Spanish conglomerate Inditex) and Top Shop (part of the United Kingdom Arcadia Group), these models stimulated further competition by introducing new merchandise into stores every six weeks or

less. The breakdown of the traditional fashion "seasons" into a greater number of shorter cycles has reached its physical production limits and represents an unsustainable model for the long term. In the United Kingdom, a shift has occurred in the way clothing and fashions are sold, with the rise of low-priced "value fashion" available in supermarkets together with the weekly groceries or in high-street stores such as Primark and Matelan that sell specifically on low price. In the twenty-first century, clothes are far cheaper relative to incomes than they were a few decades ago; however, spending has increased. Cheap fashion has translated into disposable fashion of lower quality, worn perhaps once or twice, which has in turn encouraged higher consumption and the devaluation of clothing in real terms. In the United Kingdom, the amount of clothes purchased per capita increased 37 percent between 2001 and 2005, at the same time as prices dropped 14 percent, whereas housing, transport, and food prices all increased (Allwood et al. 2006, 12).

Although new trends continue to be launched by the major design houses at the twice-yearly shows, in the twenty-first century "fast fashion" introduces new styles to the high street every month, closely following designer fashion (often before designer collections are in stores). Reorders are not a feature of fast fashion—once a style has sold out, it is not restocked, and sourcing new fashions takes place "in season" as well as ahead of season as in traditional cycles. This strategy keeps customers coming back regularly for new fashions, perpetuating the faster system of production and increasing expectations and competition. Thus, fast fashion works in decreasing circles, squeezing the production loops tighter. However, competition is fierce at all levels, and aggressive expansion of luxury and designer marketing have also played their part in stimulating demand and driving down prices. This has put all but the most exclusive designer brands in reach of more people, a democratization of fashion.

As more fashion companies have followed suit in shortening their production cycles, fast fashion has put increased pressure on clothing manufacturers to produce goods in less time, impacting most on those at the bottom of the supply chain who actually sew the garments. Campaigns by nongovernmental organizations (NGOs), such as War on Want, and investigative journalists have given prominent media coverage to labor issues in the fashion industry, exposing inequities in working conditions in developing countries such as Bangladesh and Cambodia. However, for those living below the poverty line in countries such as these, jobs in clothing factories often offer a better alternative to living by subsistence farming, even if wages may be no more than the bare local minimum. Complex ethical issues are therefore hidden behind all fashion-purchasing decisions, which, as consumers become more aware of them, create personal dilemmas within the shopping experience. This has stimulated demand for more information, accountability, and transparency in clothing manufacture and supply.

The early years of the twenty-first century saw the convergence of a number of high-profile initiatives in the United Kingdom and Europe, on both ethical and environmental issues, such as Make Poverty History, Forum for the Future, The Clean Clothes Campaign, and Labour Behind the Label (LBL). The European landfill directive and legislation on waste electrical and electronic goods came into force to deal with the end of life of consumer products. Reports from NGOs including the World Health Organization, Pesticide Action Network (PAN), and the Environmental Justice Foundation have highlighted serious welfare and environmental issues in cotton growing in developing countries. In the United States, the films *An Inconvenient Truth* (2006), by politician Al Gore, and the *11th Hour* (2007), produced by film actor Leonardo di Caprio, raised the popular, media, business, and economic profile of environmental sustainability through the key issue of climate change. The British government-commissioned Stern Report exposed the serious economic impact of global warming. Sustainability and environmental concerns rose to the top of business and media agendas. Since 2004, publications across the entire spectrum of consumer and trade magazines, newspapers, and journals including *Vanity Fair*, *Business Week*, and *Time* have produced a "Green Issue" highlighting issues of corporate and consumer responsibility.

Increased environmental awareness has stimulated closer consumer scrutiny of manufacturing and service industries, from transportation and electrical goods to food and fashion. Demand for transparency in the provenance and manufacturing of products has grown exponentially. Although European legislation banning certain chemical dyestuffs came into force from the mid-1990s and more recent directives on landfill and waste are in place, the fashion industry had largely avoided the issues of ethical and sustainable production of fashion and clothing, being preoccupied with speed to market and production. However, serious attempts to create more ecological clothing have increased rapidly as the mainstream fashion industry becomes greener, following the lead of a number of relatively small but pioneering companies such as Patagonia, Katharine Hamnett, Gossypium, and Edun. There has been a fundamental shift as a new era of ethical and conscientious consumption develops.

Issues Within The Fashion Supply Chain

Fashion is a truly global business, in which the different functions such as fiber and fabric production, design, manufacturing, and selling are physically separated in many different parts of the world, with companies often subcontracting several levels and in several geographic places along the stages of the supply chain. This is one of the key factors making traceability very difficult, for buyers as much as for consumers. The complexity of the subcontracting networks means that retail buyers have little or no knowledge of operations and circumstances at the end of their supply chain.

The commercial fashion process commences with textile sourcing and development by design teams and textile manufacturers, fashion collection design and sample garment development, followed by range planning and garment specification, sales to the retail trade, bulk textile sourcing, and mass garment manufacturing according to wholesale orders, then distribution, merchandising, and retail sales, and finally consumer purchase and statistical feedback, which may in turn trigger fast repeat orders for best-selling lines.

Environmental and ethical issues arise at each stage of the textile and fashion production process, before the customer purchases, wears, washes or cleans, and finally throws away the items. These issues, which are systemic within the industry, include constantly shifting global sourcing of manufacturing; working conditions and employment practices in garment factories; the environmental impact of textile raw materials and processing, both natural and synthetic; intensive agriculture and use of nonrenewable resources; choice of materials, dyes, and processes and their impact on a garment's life cycle; end-of-life recycling and disposal of footwear and clothing; and pay and conditions for retail staff. In the postconsumer phase, the impact of laundry, dry cleaning, and disposal of clothing and footwear is ecologically significant, generating both high energy usage and high volumes of waste, the vast majority of which is not recovered or recycled and remains in landfills, contributing to methane and carbon emissions and global warming.

Contemporary consumers want to know more about how, where, and under what conditions their clothes are made. In her seminal book *No Logo* published in 2000, journalist Naomi Klein exposed a largely unaware consuming public to the realities of global production and the working conditions found behind U.S. global brands including Gap, Nike, Walmart, and McDonalds. Since the late 1990s, a dramatic turnaround in corporate social responsibility on the part of textile, dyeing, and clothing-manufacturing businesses has taken place. Companies that were previously seen as a major part of the problem became part of the solution as each developed policies on sustainability and ethical trading. In response to public and media pressure, global companies including Nike, Gap, and H&M have became advocates of ethically and ecologically sound clothing, having been forced to examine and reassess their supply-chain systems and purchasing functions.

One example of a growing number of initiatives for change within the fashion industry is the Ethical Trading Initiative (ETI), a tripartite UK-based organization consisting of national and global fashion and food retailers, NGOs, and trade unions. The formation of the ETI responded to increasing pressure from the media and campaign groups to act on behalf of garment workers' rights globally. ETI members agree to a nine-point base code of practice comprising minimum standards governing ethical trade and international labor practices, including guidance on levels of pay and conditions for garment workers. Many well-known names are part of this initiative including Asda (Wal-mart), Gap, Marks & Spencer, Primark (joined in 2007), Tesco (a founding member), Inditex (Zara), Jaeger, Next, Monsoon, and New Look.

The effective implementation of codes of practice, however, remains a challenge for the industry as a whole, requiring significant commitment of time and resources to monitor operations in situ in factories around the world. The UK campaign group LBL, which is affiliated with the European Clean Clothes Campaign (which is not one of the NGOs in the ETI), highlighted issues in the fashion industry in two reports: " Wearing Thin: The State of Pay in the Fashion Industry " (2000) and " Let's Clean Up Fashion: The State of Pay behind the UK High Street " (2006). Much of the debate on garment workers' conditions rests on definitions and local interpretations of "living wage," "legal minimum wage," and industry benchmark standards for pay. The notorious "sweat-shops" still exist, although the second report acknowledges "a few glimmers of hope." In particular, LBL highlighted the fact that too much reliance is placed on audits, which are "not the panacea that many companies believe them to be, frequently failing to pick up serious problems" (LBL 2006, 3). They also found that companies' good intentions cannot be guaranteed to translate to action on the ground. Major retailers were graded by LBL, and two companies, Gap and Next, were considered to be seriously engaging with the issues.

A report produced by the charity War on Want in December 2006, " Fashion Victims: The True Cost of Cheap Clothes at Pri-mark, Asda, and Tesco," had great media impact. Based on interviews with sixty workers at six garment factories in Bangladesh, the report criticized working conditions and actual wages paid as below minimums, despite the ETI base code, and called for immediate action. Reports such as this and continued media exposés demonstrate the gap to be bridged between good intentions and practice on the factory floor of the garment industry.

Globalization And International Sourcing

The resurgence of interest in fashion and sustainability in the early twenty-first century is due to the convergence of many environmental and commercial factors, together with changing cultural and social norms. Fashion has always been a global affair; people have sought out the unusual or the exotic from faraway places for its rarity and prestige since the first trade routes were opened between Eastern and Western empires. Globalization has come to have negative connotations since the mid-1990s, following the great commercial impetus of worldwide communication technology. The demise of domestic manufacturing and the migration of production to countries with cheaper labor, seen in the United Kingdom and the United States, has been evident since the 1970s, with a further sharp decline in domestic manufacturing in the 1990s. However, the steep increase in overseas manufacturing, particularly in China and India, is a direct result of the changes in international trade agreements that occurred in January 2005, when the Multifiber Arrangement (MFA) and General Agreement on Trade and Tariffs (GATT), which had previously regulated import and export quotas between countries, came to an end. Until then, individual markets were protected to varying degrees from competing cheap imports (into the United Kingdom from China, for example). The end of regulation enabled cheaper goods to flood the market, disrupting the previous status quo. As a consequence, many developing countries such as Bangladesh and Cambodia entered the garment-manufacturing trade, becoming significant elements of the fashion-supply and outsourcing system.

As production moved significantly offshore and from formerly established areas such as South Korea and the Philippines to new countries, the complex chains of responsibility within fashion manufacturing became longer and more difficult to control directly. As sales volumes increased and prices became more competitive in a saturated market, the results, as exposed by Klein, could be increased exploitation. An extract from the Gap Inc. "2005–2006, Social Responsibility Report" states:

> we've come to see that some of the everyday business practices in our industry—from decisions about where to source products to last-minute changes to product orders, to poor production planning on the part of factories— can have a significant impact on working conditions in factories. . . .

The report summarizes research published in 2003 by Women Working Worldwide (an NGO) entitled "Bridging the Gap," and it states that this report "found that inefficient purchasing practices are endemic throughout the garment industry, and that the situation is not unique to Gap Inc." (p. 29).

The report goes on to acknowledge three problem areas: delays with materials or approval of samples; changes to production orders very close to production, such as fit, details, or quantity; and poor production planning in the factory, leading to quality issues and unauthorized subcontracting. All are typical problems of many fashion companies.

The Ethics Of Textile Production And The Evolution Of Ecofashion

Debates about textiles and sustainability have been vigorous with regard to the ethical and environmental issues of cotton production, which is highly significant in the textile and fashion industries, particularly for the production of the ubiquitous denim jeans and cotton T-shirts. Cotton is the most important nonfood agricultural commodity worldwide and accounts for over

half of all clothing textile production. The campaign groups PAN and the Environmental Justice Foundation together with the World Health Organization have succeeded in raising awareness of serious health risks, environmental pollution, high water usage, and intensive farming methods involved in the conventional cotton industry. The U.S.-based Organic Textiles Association and PAN-UK advocate a change to organic cotton growing, especially in Africa and other developing countries. Organic cotton production is growing rapidly at approximately 50 percent a year but represents only a tiny fraction—less than 2 percent—of the total cotton produced worldwide. Detractors believe it is not feasible to grow enough organic cotton to meet demand due to land requirements. The conventional cotton-growing industry in the United States, represented by Cotton Incorporated, has countered the criticisms made against it by stating that it has reduced its use of agrochemicals and water compared to 1996 and claims its modern growing methods are sustainable.

The buying and production power of large fashion companies means that even a small percentage shift toward ethical manufacturing and ecological fabric sourcing (such as including a proportion of organic cotton in the fabric or eliminating certain dyes) can make a significant difference. Nike in the United States announced its intention to use up to 10 percent organic cotton in all its cotton products by 2010, and Marks & Spencer in the United Kingdom made commitments in 2007 on many aspects of sustainability, including the use of recycled polyester and the introduction of organic fibers into basic clothing ranges.

Given the multiple interpretations associated with fashion as a hybrid cultural, economic, and social phenomenon and its importance economically, the concept of ecofashion can be seen as contradictory—itself an oxymoron. Fashion appears directly opposed to sustainability. However, significant improvements have been made by companies aiming to minimize their environmental impact.

The ecofashion movement first appeared as part of the hippie revolution in the mid-1970s, when it was anti-establishment and consequently antifashion. The movement was characterized by its participants as "opting out" of mainstream commercial activities and setting up "alternative" lifestyles that aimed at self-sufficiency; homemade, handcrafted "ethnic" fabrics (for example, handwoven Indian cloths) and clothes were the norm. This ecofashion philosophy embraced fabrics such as hemp and natural dyeing, eschewing chemicals and synthetic materials; a contemporary incarnation can be found in "new-age traveler" communities and other alternative lifestyles.

The second important wave of ecofashion appeared within commercial fashion in the 1990s. Pioneering companies including Esprit, Katharine Hamnett, Patagonia, and Conscious Earthwear questioned the environmental standards and ethics of the textile and fashion industries and found systemic problems with the business of clothing manufacture. One of ecofashion's most prominent champions was the U.S. fashion company Esprit, an environmentally aware retail and manufacturing company established in San Francisco in the 1960s (the cradle of alternative culture and environmentalism). In 1994, Esprit launched a range of ecological clothing, the Ecollection, designed by Lynda Grose, using criteria covering both sustainable materials and the ethics of production. At this time, there was a substantial amount of ecoactivism in California, and the outdoor clothing companies Patagonia and J. Crew had already started to develop environmentally sensitive ranges of specialist clothing for outdoor wear, utilizing materials such as organic cotton and recycled polyester. Although the Ecollection principles were intended to be rolled out within Esprit's mainstream ranges, the line closed in 1995 leaving little visible legacy in the contemporary business.

A prominent fashion designer in the 1980s, Katharine Hamnett later aimed to create a clothing line that was produced in an ethically sound and environmentally conscious manner. Unusually for a fashion-design company, Hamnett went back to the fiber-sourcing stage for her textiles and personally developed organic cottons, wool, and all the associated materials such as thread and zip tape, finally launching her ethical Katharine E Hamnett line in 2006. Hamnett, known for her outspokenness about her political views, figures as a champion in a number of organic cotton and hemp campaigns.

California-based Patagonia started as a company supplying equipment for mountain climbers and began to innovate in clothing design and materials for enhanced functionality. Patagonia, like Hamnett, commissioned a survey of natural and synthetic textiles to assess their environmental impact and, as a result, changed from conventional cotton to organic cotton and developed innovative recycled polyester fabric and clothing in collaboration with Malden Mills.

Conscious Earthwear was a small, design-led fashion label based in London that pioneered the use of reclaimed and recycled materials in the early 1990s, such as old sweaters, sleeping bags, and denim, which were redesigned into a fashion context for a style-conscious market. Ciel, the company's incarnation in the early twenty-first century, continues to source environmentally friendly materials such as hemp blends and Peruvian cotton and works directly with small groups of artisan printers and embroiderers in India.

In order to meet the objective of a sustainable future, ecofashion is required to satisfy consumers' personal, symbolic, and fashion needs while simultaneously transforming their relationship with clothes. This requires a paradigm shift toward consumption of fewer clothes while maintaining economic value. Influenced by the wishes of the new conscientious consumer and cognizant of the ecopioneers, large fashion companies (Gap, Nike, American Apparel, and Marks & Spencer, for example) are addressing the ecological and ethical issues within fashion by adopting more holistic systems-based strategies. In 2000, American Apparel set up a business model in which design and production were completely integrated in its factory in Los Angeles, rather than outsourcing production. New ecofashion labels are continually emerging. The increase in ethical awards and fashion shows held in Paris, New York, London, and Los Angeles since 2004 is a testament to the consciousness-raising activities of small eco-companies, celebrities, and campaigning groups such as the project Fashioning an Ethical Industry in the United Kingdom, part of the LBL campaign. Transparency within the supply chain is a key tenet of ethical fashion. New partnerships have been formed directly between producers and consumers, breaking down barriers between traditionally separated groups. The model of fair trade adopted in food production in developing countries has been applied to cotton growing, although its application to clothing requires significant further development due to the numerous stages of production.

In tandem with accessories—footwear, bags, jewelry, and eyewear—that represent substantial earning power in fashion, the cosmetics sector is a major part of the fashion-related industries. Here, consumption is strongly linked to self-perception, appearance, and identity. In addition, in a similar manner to the food industry, concern about the ingredients that go into cosmetic and personal-care products such as shampoos and sun-screens has grown steadily since the 1970s. Entrepreneur Anita Roddick, founder of The Body Shop empire, built her business on products made from fairly traded natural ingredients that she personally sourced from small producer groups around the globe. These were not tested on animals—unlike common practice in the cosmetics and personal-care industry—a stance that became a major marketing platform; many other companies have followed this lead. Currently, "natural" rather than "chemical" (that is, synthetic ingredients) are gaining momentum within both luxury and mainstream brands, leading to industry and media debates on the validity of the use of the terms *natural* and *organic* in the labeling of cosmetics. Unlike organic food products, personal-care product ingredients are unregulated, and there are no accepted international standards about the minimum percentage of organic ingredients that must be used in products labeled as organic. Certain chemical ingredients, such as phthalates, are banned in Europe due to potential health risks but still used in the United States and Canada. Consumer campaigns and industry initiatives to develop codes and standards have begun in the United States, while new product ranges are continually being offered to consumers. In Europe, designer Stella McCartney, well known for her antifur and antileather ethical stance on animal by-products in her fashion collections, launched an organic plant-based range of skin-care products in 2008, as did the much smaller ecofashion company Ciel, which markets a range of "paraben-free" products (paraben is a synthetic fragrance and preservative ingredient). As packaging of cosmetics is a major part of their marketing and consumer appeal, issues also arise around the environmental impact of packaging materials, volume, and types.

Ecofashion Strategies, Standards, And Labeling

Ecofashion companies adopt many varied strategies for moving toward sustainability. Some, like Hamnett, Gossypium, and Noir, work directly with cotton growers in Africa and India to create demand and develop markets for organic or sustainable fibers; others, such as People Tree, in collaboration with aid organizations such as Aid for Artisans, work directly with small, often disadvantaged producer groups making jewelry, embroideries, and clothing by hand to create new markets for these products, capitalizing on indigenous craft skills. New models of business are being developed in order to allow environmental benefits to be traced. For example, the "1% for the Planet" scheme takes a levy from the profits of its company members to reinvest in environmental projects. The Netherlands-based garment-labeling scheme Made-By aims to make each garment sold by its members completely traceable through the supply chain by providing Internet-based information on who made the clothes and where in the world, using a number coding on garment labels.

A focus on materials is an ecofashion strategy pursued by many fashion companies. This may take the form of using existing preor postconsumer waste materials and refashioning them into new products—using clothing diverted from the waste stream via charity collections (for example, Junky Styling or TRAID) or factory surplus (for example, Stewart and Brown or From Somewhere). Innovative accessories are also made in this way: jewelry made from reclaimed computer keyboard buttons (Secco), purses made from duct tape, and bags from recycled grain and food sacks or canvas sails (Reiter8). UK company Terra Plana makes shoes using a diverse range of reclaimed materials, including postal sacks, blankets, bicycle tires, and waste fabrics, and developed a project to compare the environmental footprint of producing the same shoe in three different countries. Nike in the United States has instigated a scheme to recycle parts of its used trainers as surfaces for playgrounds by grinding down the soles.

Alternative fabrics made from sustainable or renewable materials are increasingly being utilized by fashion designers. Materials include hemp, lyocell (Tencel) made from wood pulp, natural polymer from cornstarch (Ingeo), soy, and bamboo. U.S. designer Linda Loudermilk promotes a wide range of sustainable fabrics in a style-led luxury ecobrand and has devised an accreditation scheme for her own and other fashion products. Anyone can set up a system such as this, without any external verification, which is typical of the mix between marketing and consumer information that has created confusion for the retail customer.

Consumers and designers face a bewildering array of labeling and terminology—for example, sustainable, organic, green, fair trade, ethical, eco-, bio-, or environmental—and need information that helps in making comparisons and informed choices. There has been a proliferation of individual standards and labels set up to certify the environmental credentials of fibers, dyes, and fabrics in different countries around the world; however, no recognized system exists for labeling the provenance of clothing at the retail level. Most textile standards are established by private organizations, some long-established and well-recognized (e.g., the Soil Association) and others more recently established. Some are organic standards, such as the EKO label by Control Union or the U.S. Organic Trade Association's mark for cotton; others are safety standards against hazardous chemicals—for example, the European Union Oeko-Tex standard. Others such as the Fairtrade mark are concerned with trade in agricultural products (coffee, bananas, and more recently cotton) in developing countries. Four organizations across Europe, the United States, and Japan have collaborated to devise the Global Organic Textile Standards, implemented in 2006. There is some progress toward harmonization, but ultimately legislation by publicly accountable bodies and governments is needed to regulate this proliferation of standards. Consumer labeling for fabrics and clothing is being developed by the United Nations Better Cotton program, one of the first certifications to cover material, production, and labor.

Footwear has been the subject of similar scrutiny to clothing. Shoes, in particular, trainers, are highly complex products with many component parts entailing high energy use and labor input; a major proportion of the world's shoes are made in China. The U.S. company Timberland devised a program of green labeling, trialed in 2007, which told the consumer the provenance, materials, and carbon footprint of a range of its shoes.

In the United Kingdom, the group Reducing the Impact of Textiles on the Environment was formed in 2006 to bring stakeholders from the textile and retail industries together with academics and NGOs, with one of its aims to create shared standards. Responsibility for fundamental changes in the fashion and textile industries is therefore diffused in a pattern of individual and collective actions by governments, NGOs, charities, educational establishments, manufacturers, designers, buyers, and retailers, together with individual consumer responses.

Consumer Behavior

Fashion-purchasing decisions in mature markets are based on desire and aspiration rather than basic need. Although reports show a movement toward ethical consumption, radical shifts in consumer behavior and industry practice would be required to engender sufficient impact to slow down environmental degradation. It is widely accepted that stringent measures through government regulation and taxation will be required to effect such major change by manufacturers and consumers. Sustainably and aesthetically designed products will be increasingly important throughout the fashion and clothing industry, where purchases are based on visual and fashion appeal or price, not on ecocredentials.

The concept of life-cycle analysis, measuring energy use and environmental impact, has been applied to textiles and clothing in a number of studies (Franklin Associates 1993; Laursen 1997; Blackburn and Payne 2004). These show that for basic everyday clothing such as T-shirts and jeans, the greatest environmental impact occurs during the consumer-use phase, due to the high energy consumption of laundering clothes. This, however, varies for different types of garments: For outerwear such as coats, which are cleaned far less frequently, the environmental impact of manufacturing and materials may be highest. Social evolution regarding hygiene during the twentieth century has resulted in more frequent washing of clothes than was practiced by earlier generations, another aspect of changing consumer behavior. Eco-fashion design takes account of the entire "cradle to grave" impact and life-cycle stages of clothing, from materials and design to disposal. In parallel with European legislation for other consumer goods, fashion and clothing retail responsibility may be extended to the end of a garment's life as clothing, which is unlikely to be the end of its useful life, as it may then be used, for example, in a quilt or other item. Innovative take-back schemes have been implemented, for example, by Patagonia, to recycle polyester garments; the retail store Takashimaya in Japan has piloted the collection of unwanted clothes. New initiatives such as these are required to divert reusable clothing from the waste stream, as only a small fraction of used clothing is recycled. As clothing has become cheaper, its secondhand value in developed markets has eroded; therefore, the majority of discarded clothing is re-sold to developing countries. William McDonough and Michael Braungart, whose radical "cradle to cradle" concept for rethinking design has been influential in manufacturing sectors including interior textiles and engineering, have argued that "the best way to reduce any environmental impact is not to recycle more, but to produce and dispose of less."

It is widely accepted that the rate of human consumption and depletion of natural resources by transportation, travel, and manufacturing (including fashion) must be drastically reduced in the short term. A new intelligence about design and ways of reframing, defining, and approaching problems are needed to generate solutions with the wider social, ecological, and sustainability contexts in mind. A number of strategies working simultaneously with certain changes in behavior and expectations have been suggested by design theorists and practitioners. These might include the following.

Design and Systems.

+ Designing for longer life and ease of disassembly of component parts, with regard to the future life of the materials.
+ Simplifying use of materials in a product, perhaps to a single fiber type, for ease of recycling.
+ Designers and manufacturers choosing materials and developing processes that are "closed loop," aiming to eliminate waste materials, or that produce only waste products that can be source materials for other processes.
+ Harnessing new technologies for innovation; examining existing technologies and processes for ways to increase efficiency and reduce environmental impact.
+ Rethinking the way fashion is designed, made, and distributed speculatively and involving the customer in codesigning the end product through personalized services to meet a wider range of needs.

Production.

+ Reducing obsolescence and overall consumption through companies creating higher-quality clothes with longer life expectancy and high design values.
+ Reusing and recycling both pre- and postconsumer waste materials in innovative ways, creating a significant saving of energy and raw materials compared with use of new materials.
+ Slowing down fashion cycles and simultaneously increasing the price per item to reflect true value in human, environmental, social, and economic terms.

Consumption.

+ Creating new services such as renting, sharing, remodeling, and repairing, which prolong the useful life of clothing and accessories.
+ Buying fewer clothes but enjoying what is bought—ensuring each garment is wanted (a substantial proportion of clothes bought are never worn as they are "impulse buys").

+ Purchasing recycled or reclaimed products that preferably have been designed and created with an aesthetic value equal to or higher than that of the original elements.

End of Life.

+ Creating infrastructure for new types of recycling to encourage more reuse of waste materials and diversion from landfills.

Ethical and sustainability awareness have become a fundamental part of everyday life in twenty-first-century society, engendering significant changes in behavior. Therefore, radical strategies need to be adopted at a deep level of design and production, so that consumers can, without conscious decisions, make a difference through their purchasing—because the innovative design thinking for sustainability has already been built in. Fashion companies, manufacturers, and retailers can apply many approaches to the complex ethical issues and environmental concerns of contemporary society. Information at the consumer level, standards and labeling, and transparency throughout the supply chain are key areas to be addressed in order for ecofashion to become mainstream. Shifts in consumer behavior toward lower consumption and sustainably designed fashion can change the balance between the many factors in operation in the market, allowing clothes to regain their previous value, to satisfy longer and therefore be less disposable, reducing the high volume of fashion waste. To counter the environmental impact of clothes care, low maintenance needs to become a reality.

Consumers have developed a powerful lobbying voice and can significantly influence retail companies through their spending choices. It is increasingly important for brands to develop customer trust and loyalty in a fickle and constantly changing social and retail climate. Displaying ethical credentials has become a tool for competitive advantage that has been criticized as "green-washing." However, the pressure for, and evidence of, fundamental change and reexamination of the endemic problems in the complex fashion system of design, manufacturing, and supply is incontrovertible in the early twenty-first century. Ecofashion and ethical fashion are spreading beyond niche markets to the mainstream. Coupled with necessary social and cultural changes in consumer behavior through "sustainability literacy," ecofashion can attempt to meet the requirements of a sustainable future while satisfying economic and aesthetic needs through innovation and delight.

See also Globalization and Dress.

References and Further Reading

Allwood, Julian M., Søren E. Laursen, Cecilia Malvido de Rodriguez, and Nancy M. P. Bocken. *Well Dressed? The Present and Future Sustainability of Clothing and Textiles in the UK*. Cambridge: University of Cambridge Institute for Manufacturing, 2006.

Black, Sandy. " Interrogating Fashion: Practice Process and Presentation. New Paradigms for Fashion Design in the 21st Century." In *Designing for the 21st Century, Interdisciplinary Questions and Insights*, edited by Tom Inns, 299-314. London: Gower, 2007.

Black, Sandy. *Eco Chic: The Fashion Paradox*. London: Black Dog Publishing, 2008.

Blackburn, Richard, and John Payne. " Lifecycle Analysis of Cotton Towels: Impact of Domestic Laundering." *Green Chemistry* 6 (2004): G59-61.

Cotton Incorporated. " Sustainable Cotton Production." July 2006. http://www.cottoninc.com/sustainability (accessed 8 October 2007).

Environmental Justice Foundation. *White Gold, the True Cost of Cotton*. London: Environmental Justice Foundation, 2005.

Fletcher, Kate. *Sustainable Fashion and Textiles*. London: Earthscan, 2008.

Frankel, Susannah. " The Real Cost of Fashion." *The Independent*, 16 November 2007. http://news.independent.co.uk/uk/this_britain/article3167610 (accessed 2 December 2007).

Franklin Associates. *Resource and Environmental Profile Analysis of a Manufactured Apparel Product: Woman's Knit Polyester Blouse*. Washington, DC: American Fiber Manufacturers Association, 1993.

GAP Inc. " 2005-2006, Social Responsibility Report." http://www.gapinc.com/public/SocialResponsibility/socialres.shtml (accessed 8 August 2008).

Hansen, Karen. *Salaula: The World of Secondhand Clothing and Zambia*. Chicago: Chicago University Press, 2000.

Klein, Naomi. *No Logo*. London: Flamingo, 2000.

Laursen, Søren E., and J. Hansen. *Environmental Assessment of Textiles*. Copenhagen: Danish Environmental Protection Agency, 1997.

Maycumber, S. Gray. " Facts on Cotton: Another Side of the Pesticide Debate." *Textiles Intelligence*, January 2007, 10.

McDonough, William, and Michael Braungart. *Cradle to Cradle: Rethinking the Way We Make Things*. New York: North Point Press, 2002.

McVeigh, Karen. " High Price Paid for Cheap UK Clothes." *The Guardian*, 16 July 2007, 2.

PAN-UK. *The Deadly Chemicals in Cotton*. London: Pesticide Action Network UK, 2007. Porritt, Jonathon. *Capitalism: As if the World Matters*. London: Earth-scan, 2007.

Stern, Nicholas. *Review on the Economics of Climate Change*. Cambridge: Cambridge University Press, 2006.

UK Government's Dept. of Environment, Food and Rural Affairs, Strategy and Legislation. " EU Landfill Directive." http://www.defra.gov.uk/environment/waste/topics/landfill-dir (accessed 8 April 2009).

Sandy Black

ETHNIC DRESS

Ethnic dress ranges from a single piece to a whole ensemble of items that identify an individual with a specific ethnic group. An ethnic group refers to people who share a cultural heritage or historical tradition, usually connected to a geographical location or a language background; it may sometimes overlap religious or occupational groups. Ethnicity refers to the common heritage of an ethnic group. Members of an ethnic group often distinguish themselves from others by using items of dress to symbolize their ethnicity and display group solidarity. The words "ethnic" and "ethnicity" come from the Greek word *ethnos*, meaning "people." Many anthropologists prefer to use the inclusive term "ethnic group" instead of "tribe," because the latter is often employed as shorthand for "other people" as opposed to "us." Sometimes the term "folk dress" is used instead of ethnic dress when discussing examples of ethnic dress in Europe and not elsewhere in the world. "Folk" and folk dress ordinarily distinguish European rural dwellers and peasants and their dress from wealthy landowners, nobility, or royalty and their apparel. Ethnic dress, however, is a neutral term that applies to distinctive cultural dress of people living anywhere in the world who share an ethnic background.

Ethnic Dress and Change

The readily identifiable aspect of ethnic dress arises from a garment characteristic (such as its silhouette), a garment part (such as a collar or sleeve), accessories, or a textile pattern, any of which stems from the group's cultural heritage. Many people believe that ethnic dress does not change. In point of fact, however, change in dress does occur, because as human beings come into contact with other human beings, they borrow, exchange, and modify many cultural items, including items of dress. In addition, human beings create and conceive of new ways of making or decorating garments or accessories, and modifying their bodies. Even though changes occur and are apparent when garments and ensembles are viewed over time, many aspects of ethnic dress do remain stable, allowing them to be identifiable. In many parts of the world, ethnic dress is not worn on a daily basis; instead items are brought out for specific occasions, particularly holiday or ritual events, when a display of ethnic identity is a priority and a source of pride. When worn only in this way, ethnic dress may easily be viewed as ethnic costume, since it is not an aspect of everyday identity.

Ethnic Dress and Gender

Across the contemporary world as well as historically, gender differences exist in all types of dress, including ethnic dress. Thus, ethnic dress and gender become intertwined. Sometimes women retain the items of dress identified as ethnic while men wear items of dress and accessories that come from the Western world, especially in urban areas. For example, in India, many women commonly wear a sari or *salwar* and *kameez*, but many men wear trousers and a shirt or a business suit. One explanation is that those who work in industrial and professional jobs connected with or stemming from Westernized occupations begin to wear types of tailored clothing that have arisen from Europe and the Americas. Another explanation for the continued wearing of ethnic styles is that a widely shared cultural aesthetic in dress may influence preferences for particular garments. For example, the soft lines of the sari in India, and the shapely but body-covering sarong and blouse (*kain-kebaya*) in Indonesia, reflect the cultural ideal of femininity in those countries.

Selected Examples of Ethnic Dress

Garments and accessories for ethnic dress are fashioned from a wide variety of materials, often thought to be made by hand. In today's world, however, many are manufactured by machine. Textiles of many types are most frequently used for garments, although in some locations, people wear furs, skins, bark cloth, and other fibers. Particularly in tropical and subtropical areas in Africa, Asia, and the Pacific, examples of ethnic dress include wrapped garments, such as the wrapper, also called *lappa*, the sari, sarong, and pareo. In moderate and cold climates on all continents, tailored or pre-shaped clothing is cut and sewn to fit the body closely to provide warmth.

Asia and the Pacific

On the Asian continent, where the climate extends from tropical to Arctic, garment types range from wrapped to cut-and-sewn examples. Throughout India, women wrap six to nine yards of unstitched fabric in specific styles to fashion the wrapped garment called the sari, which is ordinarily worn with a blouse (called a *choli*). Many styles of wrapping the sari exist that distinguish different ethnic backgrounds within India. Indian men wrap from two to four yards of fabric to fashion garments called *lungi* and *dhoti* that they wear around their lower body. Among the Hill Tribes of Thailand, Hmong women wear a blouse and skirt with an elaborate silver necklace, an apron, a turban-type head covering, and wrapped leg coverings. In the steppe lands of Asia (for example, Mongolia), tailored garments of jacket and trousers are worn with caps and boots. In China, types of dress have changed over time, in relationship to contact with other peoples. Turks, Mongols, Manchus, and other peoples of China's Central Asian and northern borderlands sometimes influenced the cut and style of tailored garments in China itself. The fitted, one-piece women's garment with mandarin collar and side-slit skirt known as a cheongsam, or *qipao*, was invented in Shanghai in the 1920s as a garment that was acceptably both "Chinese" and "modern." Its use declined in the People's Republic of China after the late 1950s, but it continued to be worn in Chinese communities outside the mainland and is widely regarded as the "ethnic dress" of Chinese women. In Japan, variations of the garment known as kimono are cut and sewn, as well as wrapped. The kimono's body and sleeves are formed by stitching textiles together, but the body of the garment wraps around the human form and is secured by a sash known as the obi. The Korean ensemble called a *hanbok* includes a skirt for women and pants for men that are cut and sewn, but the top garment, a jacket for both men and women, is called *chogori* and wraps across the breast.

In Indonesia, cloth (*kain*) is wrapped around the lower body for both women and men, and is worn with a blouse (*kebaya*) or a shirt (*baju*). Another option for clothing the lower body is the sarong, cloth sewn to make a tubular garment. (This word was borrowed by Hollywood to refer to the wrapped garment worn by Hedy Lamarr and Dorothy Lamour that also covers the breasts. Among many of the peoples of Indonesia, the latter style is regarded as highly informal, worn for example by women on their way to the bathing pool.) Bare feet or various types of sandals and slippers are worn with these garments.

On many of the islands of the Pacific, such as Samoa and Hawaii, the wrapped garment is called a pareo. The long, shapeless dress called a muumuu, or *robe mission* ("mission dress"), introduced by missionaries to clothe women who traditionally were only lightly dressed, is now widely accepted as a form of ethnic dress throughout the Pacific islands. Elaborate feathered headdresses are worn in many parts of New Guinea with few other body coverings. At the time of European arrival in Australia, Aborigine dress consisted of animal skin cloaks, belts, and headbands along with body piercings, scarification, and body paint. Tattooing various parts of the body has been common among many groups in the Pacific, such as the Maori people of New Zealand and some groups of Japanese.

Because of extensive colonization in Asia and the Pacific, Europeans influenced garments and accessories of indigenous people. In return, the colonizers were influenced by exposure to Asian types of dress and borrowed or modified Asian garments, such as the cummerbund, the pajama, and bandannas, into both everyday and formal dress, thus culturally authenticating them.

Africa

The African continent extends from the Mediterranean Sea to the Cape of Good Hope and from the Atlantic Ocean to the Indian Ocean, providing a wide variation in climate, temperature, and terrain. A majority of indigenous garments include wrapped textiles. Both men and women in West Africa wear wrappers that cover the lower body and a shirt or blouse on the upper body. African women's head ties also exemplify a wrapped textile. In Ghana, some men's garments wrap the body with a large rectangle of cloth pulled over one shoulder that extends to the feet, similar to the Roman toga. Many indigenous people wrap blankets and skins around their bodies in South Africa, and in East Africa ethnic groups like the Maasai and Somali wear variations of

garments wrapped around the torso and over one shoulder to below the knees, exposing bare legs and sandals. Distinctive printed textiles that evolved from Dutch influence in Indonesia are highly visible in African ethnic dress, but the patterns and motifs are now specifically African and often manufactured on the African continent. In North Africa, Islamic influence in dress exists that ties some of this region of Africa to other countries that are primarily Islamic in the Middle East with such examples as the gowns called caftan, djellaba, and *jilbab*. Tailored fashions with European influence also prevail across the continent, particularly in cosmopolitan cities, where the frequency of Africans wearing ethnic dress is particularly diminished. Many Africans have traveled elsewhere in the world, are exposed to mass media such as television, cinema, magazines, and newspapers, and also share knowledge of fashions from Europe and the Americas based on their colonial past. Schoolchildren frequently wear Western-style school uniforms. The secondhand market of clothing from Europe and America has also affected what Africans wear in many countries. Alterations change the garments into local fashions. In comparison to the higher prices of readymade or tailor-made garments, the lower cost makes secondhand clothing highly desirable. Europeans and Americans who have visited or lived in African countries borrowed items and styles of dress that became incorporated into their wardrobes. Examples are the dashiki, the Yoruba shirt adopted by returning Peace Corps volunteers who served in West Africa during the 1960s, African women's head ties and hairstyles (such as cornrowing) worn by African American women, and children, and garments made from the striped Ghanaian textile called *kente*.

Europe and Eurasia

Ethnic dress in Europe and Eurasia consists primarily of ensembles, often called folk dress that relate to garments generally from the eighteenth century on. Many such examples can be found in folk museums, such as the Benaki Museum in Athens or the Nordiskmuseet in Stockholm. Sometimes the distinctive aspect of ethnic dress appears minimally to be one item, such as the plaid or tartan kilt of men in Scotland or the elaborate lace headdress of women in Brittany that is known as the *coiffe*. Such items become romanticized as ethnic dress, worn for special events and holidays. A strong argument has arisen that indeed the tartan is a relatively recent invention that arose for clan distinction in

Scotland. Among most European countries, from as far north as Norway and as far south as Greece, smaller geographic areas are often identified with a specific ethnic group that initially occupied the area. The members of these groups may vary their ensembles or particularly distinct dress items only minimally to set themselves apart from other groups within that country as in the examples of both Norwegian and Greek ethnic dress. The Saami (formerly known as Lapplanders) who live in northern Norway, Sweden, and Finland wear a distinctive tunic-suit, sedge-grass boots, and the "four-winds" hat with four corners that allow the storage of items. For those coming from the ethnic backgrounds known as Czech and Slovak, a large linen shawl and a matron's cap surface as ethnic social indicators.

The Americas

The enslaved Africans arrived with few examples of garments or their traditions remaining from their past, except for the African women's tradition of wearing a wrapped piece of cloth on her head. In the northern part of North America, the Inuit people (formerly known as Eskimo) fashioned furs to keep their bodies snugly warm from frigid winter temperatures. The many examples of indigenous people across the two continents often called Indians (also known as Native Americans or Native Peoples, depending on government policy and idiomatic expressions) had traditions that stemmed from various weaving and embroidery practices in Central and South America. Many weaving traditions continue from earlier times that first set apart the garments of indigenous people from the Spaniards and Portuguese who encroached upon their land and wore European-types of clothing. In such cases, it is tempting to call only the indigenous examples "ethnic dress," yet the Argentine gaucho ensemble that arose from the work traditions of Argentinean cowboys can equally be called ethnic.

See also Caftan; Clothing, Costume, and Dress; Dashiki; Jilbab; Kente; Qipao; Sari; Sarong.

Bibliography

Baizerman, S., J. B. Eicher, and C. Cerny. "Eurocentrism in the Study of Ethnic Dress." *Dress* 20 (1993): 19–32.
Barnes, R., and J. B. Eicher, eds. *Dress and Gender: Making and Meaning in Cultural Context.* Oxford and Providence, R.I.: Berg, 1992.
Boulanger, C. *Saris: An Illustrated Guide to the Indian Art of Draping.* New York: Shakti Press, 1997.
Chapman, Malcolm. "Freezing the Frame: Dress and Ethnicity in Brittany and Gaelic Scotland." In *Dress and Ethnicity: Change across Space and Time.* Edited by J. B. Eicher. Oxford and Washington, D.C.: Berg, 1995.
Eicher, J. B., ed. *Dress and Ethnicity: Change across Space and Time.* Oxford and Washington, D.C.: Berg, 1995.
Hansen, Karen Tranberg. *The World of Secondhand Clothing and Zambia.* Chicago: University of Chicago Press, 2000.
Hobsbawn, E., and T. Ranger, eds. *The Invention of Tradition.* Cambridge, U.K.: Cambridge University Press, 1983.
Kennet, F. *World Dress.* New York: Checkmark Books, 1995.
Tarlo, E. *Clothing Matters: Dress and Identity in India.* Chicago: University of Chicago Press, 1996.
Van der Plas, Els, and Marlous Willemsen, eds. *The Art of African Fashion.* Trenton, N.J., and Asmara, Eritrea: Africa World Press, 1998.
Welters, L., ed. *Folk Dress in Europe and Anatolia.* Oxford and New York: Berg, 1999.

Joanne B. Eicher

ETHNIC STYLE IN FASHION

During the 1990s and the first years of the new millennium, ethnic style has been one of the strongest influences in fashion. Designers such as Christian Lacroix, Dries van Noten, John Galliano, Kenzo, Vivienne Tam, Yeohlee and many others have taken their inspiration from a variety of Asian, African, Arctic, Native American and several other dress forms and aesthetic styles and created colorful, syncretic styles evocative of the past or faraway lands. They have also found sources for ethnic fashion within the West, for example in the folk traditions of Northern and Eastern Europe. The fantasy element is strong in ethnic fashion; even when based on detailed research, designs are typically given a twist so they appear contemporary.

For many Western designers, non-Western aesthetics have provided a fertile subject matter, which has enabled them to develop creatively. This ability to break conventions is associated with a way of seeing, rather than faithful adherence to any particular ethnic style. The overall eclecticism of ethnic fashion is expressed, for example, by Dries van Noten, as noted in *Touches d'exotisme, xive–xxe siècles*:

For me, exoticism is the elsewhere, the other, the difference. It is generally associated with distant countries. But for me, it is rather everything that reroutes us from the ordinary . . . from our habits, our certainties and from the everyday to plunge us into a world that is amazing, hospitable and warm. (p. 203)

Fashion theory has been informed by the distinction between fashion—modern, changeable, and emanating from Western urban centers—and ethnic clothing—stable, oriented toward tradition, and belonging in the periphery. This distinction has not always been precise; however, it has had a profound influence on how society thinks about fashion. Many accounts of ethnic fashion thus tend to overemphasize the original reworking of exotic designs on the part of Western creators, just as they exaggerate the fixity of non-Western dress. In this respect, the ongoing impact of ethnic styles on Western fashion has been marginalized.

Historically, luxury has been associated with foreign origins. It is therefore impossible to date the starting point of ethnic style in Western consumption modes; in ancient times, novel and sumptuous goods arrived through trade routes from Persia, Egypt, and Central Asia, and later from India, China, Japan, Colombia, Mexico, and elsewhere. Designs and production methods of these imports were imitated, and whole industries—such as Italian and French silk production—were founded to cater for what had initially been a demand for exoticism. The taste for the foreign was also evident in the initial popularity of the cashmere shawl as a fashion item among European and American women from 1800 to 1870. Materials such as silk and cashmere are now fully naturalized in Western fashion, but from time to time their foreign origins are rearticulated in the context of ethnic fashion, for example in the recent trend for *luxe povera*.

Looking at clothes design in a stricter sense, ethnic styles were an important element in the intense experimentation with female dress in the first decades of the twentieth century. Paul Poiret adapted the lines and silhouette of the Japanese kimono to contemporary dresses, and a few years later, he picked Middle Eastern inspiration to a sultan-and-harem mode of loose garments and bold color combinations. Mariano Fortuny combined inspiration from contemporary Middle Eastern clothing and European art, especially Italian renaissance, in pleated dresses that follow the lines of the body. His artistic dresses connote both

timelessness—they are not made for special occasions or age brackets and are beyond the seasonal changes of fashion—and femininity that comes "from within," in the sense that it is less formal and less manifestly visible than the conventional gender code.

The second wave of ethnic fashion came in the late 1960s with such representatives in haute couture as Yves Saint Laurent, Kenzo, and Sonia Rykiel. Also in this period, ethnic style was associated with transcendence of conventions, thereby allowing perceived deeper sensual qualities to be expressed. The philosopher Hélène Cixous said about a jacket by Sonia Rykiel, and by implication about ethnic fashion as such: "A garment which is not a noisy manifestation of the street, but a fine manifestation of the world" (p. 97). She adds, "The dress doesn't separate the inside from the outside, it translates, sheltering" (p. 98).

In the 1960s and 1970s, ethnic style provided a rich field for fashion without designers: Palestinian scarves, Latin American skirts, Indonesian batik sarongs, Moroccan djellabas, Chinese jackets, rattan baskets, embroidered purses, leather sandals, and tribal jewelry, bought either in special third-world import stores or on long-distance travels, were worn in combination with ordinary clothes. Ethnic style thus became a highly personal as well as cosmopolitan way of dressing, sometimes associated with a political attitude.

An important issue is the position of non-Western fashion designers. When Japanese avant-garde designers, including Issey Miyake, Yohji Yamamoto, and Rei Kawakubo (of Comme des Garçons), presented the most sought-after collections in Paris in the 1980s, the international fashion press wrote them off as a mere exotic—in the pejorative sense of passing—influence. There was a tendency to interpret their designs in the light of traditional Japanese aesthetics, rather than acknowledge them as innovative designers working with a minimalism that self-consciously fused elements of East and West with very few overt ethnic references. In this respect, the Western fashion world has pushed non-Western designers towards self-exoticization. While some Asian fashion designers find it stimulating to apply their creative skills to their cultural backgrounds, others experience the demand for exoticization as devaluation of their talents and skills in the highly globalized fashion business.

In some markets, especially in the United States, there has been considerable recognition of non-Western designers; however, they have tended to remain identified with a particular ethnic style as aesthetic exponents of multiculturalism. A key example is Vivienne Tam: born in China, educated in Hong Kong, resident of New York City in the early 2000s. She incorporates Chinese motifs in her designs, but highly eclectically, so that her clothes have included both Buddhist and Maoist imagery. In contrast to Western designers, whose engagement with ethnic styles tends to be superficial, Tam's consistent work with Chinese aesthetics has led to a deep involvement with cultural tradition, including spiritualism, architecture, medicine, art, and performance.

There are also minority niche markets where diaspora women in the West find their *salwar-kameez*, the socalled Punjabi suit, or their Vietnamese *ao dai*. These markets are typically operated by women entrepreneurs without any formal training in fashion design. They tend to keep in touch with the styles current in the homeland; however, this does not stop them from influencing dynamics of fashion in the West, as was the case with the Punjabi suit in the late 1990s.

Ethnic style in fashion is an important, yet somewhat neglected, area of fashion studies. As fashion continues adjusting to the multicultural condition, both within each Western nation and at the transnational level, ethnic style provides a particularly rich and diverse field of study—one that is likely to produce major future developments in fashion theory.

See also Fads; Folklore Look; Galliano, John; Miyake, Issey; Saint Laurent, Yves; Yamamoto, Yohji.

Bibliography

Bhachu, Parminder. "Designing Diasporic Markets: Asian Fashion Entrepreneurs in London." In *Re-Orientating Fashion: The Globalisation of Asian Dress*. Edited by Sandra Niessen, Ann Marie Leshkowich, and Carla Jones. London: Berg, 2003.

Cixous, Hélène. "Sonia Rykiel in Translation." In *On Fashion*. Edited by Shari Benstock and Suzanne Ferriss. New Brunswick, N.J.: Rutgers University Press, 1994.

Kondo, Dorinne. *About Face: Performing Race in Fashion and Theatre*. New York: Routledge, 1997.

Legrand-Rossi, Sylvie, et al. *Touches d'exotisme, xive–xxe siècles*. Union centrale des arts decoratifs. Paris: Musée de la mode et du textile, 1998.

Leshkowich, Ann Marie. "The *Ao Dai* Goes Global: How International Influences and Female Entrepreneurs Have Shaped Vietnam's 'National Costume.'" In *Re-Orientating Fashion*. Edited by Sandra Niessen, Ann Marie Leshkowich, and Carla Jones. London: Berg, 2003.

Skov, Lise. "Fashion-Nation: A Japanese Globalization Experience and a Hong Kong Dilemma." In *Re-Orientating Fashion*. Edited by Sandra Niessen, Ann Marie Leshkowich, and Carla Jones. London: Berg, 2003.

Steele, Valerie, and John Major. *China Chic: East Meets West*. New Haven, Conn.: Yale University Press, 1999.

Tam, Vivienne, with Martha Huang. *China Chic*. New York: Regan Books, 2000.

Lise Skov

EVENING DRESS

Simply put, evening dress is the prevailing style prescribed by fashion to be worn in the evening. Though straightforward in its basic definition, there are surprisingly complex expectations related to appropriateness of fashionable dress for evening. Regardless of the era, evening dress is intricately connected to fashions of the day, with specific characteristics that distinguishes it from everyday dress. An evening gown is a special form of dress that amplifies a woman's femininity and often proclaims her desirability. In general, necklines are low, bodices are tightly fitted, arms are bared, and skirts are extravagantly designed. Fabric surfaces vary from reflective to matte, textured to smooth, and soft to rigid. Gowns may be bouffant or hug the body, emphasizing every curve and swell. Regardless of these distinctions, there tends to be an overall emphasis on the woman's body and in many instances on the gown itself. Through the decades, undergarments have played a critical role in reshaping the body into the desired silhouette, from corsets and petticoats of the nineteenth century to control-top panty hose and padded Wonderbras of the twenty-first century.

Historical Overview

Although formal court dress has existed for centuries, there is consensus among dress historians that evening dress materialized as a discrete category in the mid-1820s. It is probably not coincidental that this form of dress emerged at roughly the same time the Romantic Movement in art and literature surfaced as an influence in European and American cultures. Romantics accentuated passion and sentiment, placing a greater emphasis on love rather than on duty. Other cultural factors such as increased fabric production, a thriving textile industry, and an expanding ready-made clothing industry resulted in greater access to resources. By the 1820s, fashion had been fairly democratized. Additionally, Parisian and American fashion magazines experienced a burgeoning popularity among women in the United States and Europe. Dresses of the 1820s were frequently identified in *Godey's Lady's Book* and *Peterson's Magazine* according to explicit activities or time of day. Women viewed fashion plates with captions like morning dress, day dress, walking dress, promenade dress, carriage dress, seaside dress, dinner dress, evening dress, or ball dress. From these labels, it seems the evening dress was born.

1820 to 1899

During the last eighty years of the nineteenth century, women's fashions evolved from an X-shaped silhouette (1820s) to the introduction of the cage crinoline (1850) through the bustle period (1870–1890) and ended with an hourglass silhouette (1890s), and in each era evening dress took its profile from current styles of the day. However, evening dress was discernible by its use of opulent and supple gauze and satin fabrics, the cut of the neckline—typically low or off-the-shoulder—short sleeves, and by the lavishness of surface embellishment. Skirts were especially complex in ornamentation— with layers of swags and puffs and such trim details as artificial flowers, ribbons, rosettes, and lace. During the bustle period and the 1890s, trains were frequently attached to full-length skirts.

1900 to 1945

The early years of the twentieth century included a progression in women's fashions from an S-shaped silhouette to a revival of Empire styles to the flapper style of the 1920s to the bias-cut fashions of the 1930s. With the exception of the latter part of this time-period, evening dress followed the conventions of daytime dress. Necklines tended to be deep and wide, sleeves were short or were mere straps on the shoulder, skirt lengths varied according to fashions and frequently involved complex floating panels, draping, or layers. Fabrics were extravagantly pliant chiffons and satins and luxuriant velvets and taffetas. Pleating, embroidery, lace, beading, fringe, braid, and ruffles decorated the surfaces.

During the 1930s, evening dress made an uncharacteristic split from daytime styles, remaining floor-length while daywear fluctuated in length from mid-calf to ankle. Evening gowns were designed in bias-cut styles and were usually constructed with an open back, with fabric skimming the body to the hips and flaring out and to the floor.

1945 to 2003

The late 1940s through the early 1960s saw the last of a singular identifiable fashion for evening. Dior's New Look—with a rounded shoulder line, a nipped waist, and either an exceptionally full skirt or a pencil-slim skirt—defined the style of the day. Evening dress generally paired strapless bodices with full rather than narrow skirts and it was not unusual for skirts to be floor-length.

By the 1960s, a plethora of options in evening wear emerged. Mini-skirted straight dresses were made from metallic fabrics or brilliantly patterned fabrics, and surfaces may have been trimmed with sequins, beads, or plastic bits. By the late 1960s, evening dresses had returned to floor length. Pantsuits with full-legged trousers and palazzo pants paired with a coordinating top also became viable options. In the mid-1970s, fashionable evening dress was typically long and made from fabrics that were soft, clinging, and often knitted. In the 1980s, the glamour of evening dress contrasted with professional dress for career women and integrated bright and vibrant colors with plenty of glitter, embroidery, sequins, and beading. Lacroix introduced a gown with a short wide puffy skirt, nicknamed *Le Pouf*, which was eagerly copied and made available to the masses. Wide-skirted, short styles called mini-crinolines were also popular. By the late 1980s, evening dresses made from elasticized fabrics hugged the body were short, and were strapless or had tiny shoulder straps. In the early 1990s, basic slip dresses made from soft crepe fabrics became popular. By the mid-1990s, full-skirted, short, strapless evening gowns reemerged. Also fashionable were lace or elaborately decorated bustiers and fitted evening gowns and black was the color of choice.

Contemporary Use of Evening Dress

Today, evening dress is limited to such formal or semi-formal events as balls, high school proms, gala fundraisers, pageants, and awards ceremonies. While men's dress tends to be quite typical (usually a standard dark-colored suit or tuxedo), women's gowns vary drastically from demure black garments to revealing objets d'art, as might be seen on celebrities at the Academy Awards. Despite the range of possibilities for contemporary evening dress for women, a gown will undoubtedly include a lowcut neckline, a constricting bodice, bared arms, and lavish skirts. Evening dress draws attention to a woman's body and serves to define her gender, establishing her as an object to be gazed upon by her audience.

See also Ball Dress; Cocktail Dress.

Bibliography

Boucher, François. *20,000 Years of Fashion: The History of Costume and Personal Adornment*. New York: Harry N. Abrams, 1987.

Laver, James. *Costume and Fashion: A Concise History*. London: Thames and Hudson, Inc., 1982.

Lobenthal, Joel. *Radical Rags: Fashions of the Sixties*. New York: Abbeville Press, 1990.

Milbank, Caroline Rennolds. *New York Fashion: The Evolution of American Style*. New York: Harry N. Abrams, 1989.

Mulvey, Kate, and Melissa Richards. *Decades of Beauty: The Changing Image of Women 1890s–1990s*. New York: Octopus, 1998.

Payne, Blanche, Geitel Winakor, and Jane Farrell-Beck. *The History of Costume*. 2nd ed. New York: HarperCollins Publishers, Inc., 1992.

Russell, Douglas A. *Costume History and Style*. Englewood Cliffs, N.J.: Prentice-Hall, 1983.

Steele, Valerie. *Women of Fashion: Twentieth-Century Designers*. New York: Rizzoli International, 1991.

——. *Fifty Years of Fashion*. New Haven, Conn., and London: Yale University Press, 2000.

——. *The Corset*. New Haven, Conn., and London: Yale University Press, 2001.

Tortora, Phyllis, and Keith Eubank. *Survey of Historic Costume*. 3rd ed. New York: Fairchild Publications, 1998.

Watson, Linda. *Vogue: Twentieth Century Fashion*. London: Carlton Books Ltd., 1999.

Jane E. Hegland

F

FADS

Here today, gone tomorrow. It is hard to identify a fad until it has fizzled. Fashion cycles, more generally, vary in speed; fads are those particular fashion cycles that "take us by surprise, but also fade very quickly" (van Ginneken, p. 161). The term "fashion" implies "strong norms" (Crane, p. 1), and although this criterion may also apply to fads, these norms are of shorter duration and within a more limited population. Fred Davis goes so far as to say that fashion itself "somehow manage[s] on first viewing to startle, captivate, offend," but ultimately "engage[s] the sensibilities of some culturally preponderant public, in America the so-called middle mass" (p. 15). By implication, a fad represents a temporary and limited divergence from a more general path of fashionability; the "so-called middle mass" may never approve.

A perusal of academic books in fashion studies over the last decade reveals that the term "fad" itself may have fallen out of style. Even Arthur Berger's text *Ads, Fads, and Consumer Culture* includes little mention of fads. Still, popular media feature lists of "what's hot" versus "what's not." Why aren't these called fads? Perhaps the time-space nexus associated with contemporary fashion cycles is at issue: Influencing the rapidity and scope of "what's hot" are factors such as a global economy, rapid technological change and media influence, "fast fashion" (or speed-to-market production), and a fashion system that combines branded commodities with stylistic diversity among consumers.

Nevertheless, a case can be made for interpreting the concept of fad for its historical, heuristic, and analytical significance. Issues of time, identity, stylistic detail, expression, and emotion all come into play in contemporary life, regardless of what we call the phenomenon in question. Historically, the term has been used to characterize collective behavior that may range from an article of clothing or an accessory (or how it is worn) to a hair-style or other way of grooming. Or, it may describe toys or gadgets, or even activities or practices that do not require consumer purchase. Fads tend to be: (1) of a strikingly new or revolutionary quality that sets them apart from current fashion; (2) short-lived, with a rapid growth in popularity and demise; (3) accepted only in, and intensely popular within, small groups or subcultures; and (4) often "nonessential," "mostly for amusement," or a "passing fancy."

The concept of a fad seems to relate almost as much to who participates as it does to time. According to the *Oxford English Dictionary* the term is related to the earlier concept of fidfad (short for fiddle-faddle). A fidfad, dating back to 1754, was a person who gave "fussy attention to trifles." In the mid-nineteenth century, the terms "fad" and "faddish" were used to refer to shallow or unpredictable patterns of behavior or people.

It is interesting to note that the *Oxford English Dictionary* has not added new entries for the concept since its 1989 edition. However, it has generated related concepts that deserve careful attention: namely, "trendy" and "fashion victim." Trendiness implies the state of being fashionable and up to date; it also connotes following the latest trend ("sometimes dismissively"). Since the early 1960s, "trendy" and "trendiness" have begun to displace the concept of fad linguistically. By the 1980s, the concept of trendy had become well-entrenched in everyday speech. The connotation of being shallow or narrowly focused persisted; the term still does not describe individuals who are immersed in the larger, "mainstream" issues of the day. Dating back to the eighteenth and nineteenth centuries, the concept of a trend implied divergence from the mainstream—initially in the context of physical or geological manifestations (for example, streams, currents, or valleys). By the 1960s, the idea of trend analysis had taken hold in the social context as well. The idea of a fad was morphing into a "trend."

Aside from issues of intensified speed, media saturation, and identities and intentions, there is the question of who benefits from fads or trends, and how.

Accordingly, Marx and McAdam made an analytical distinction between "spontaneous" and "sponsored" fads. The former appear and spread without the involvement (at least initially) of an entrepreneur or business. Usually a spontaneous fad can be pursued without an extensive monetary commitment; it tends to be behavioral in nature. Examples might include goldfish swallowing in the 1920s or "streaking" (running naked) in the 1970s; both of these fads spread and deceased rapidly as trends on college campuses. In contrast, a sponsored fad tends to be consciously promoted; this is probably most obvious when applied to toys or gadgets (for example, the "pet rock" fad of the mid-1970s or the Pog craze of the early 1990s).

Although there may be heuristic reasons for making distinctions between spontaneity and sponsorship in fads (just as there might be similar reasons for distinguishing fads from fashions), the two often become inextricably intertwined, especially in a commodified, branded, and celebrity-oriented consumer culture. First, it is difficult to ascertain in advance what will endure. Second, most fads or trends seem to include a commodity in some way, even (maybe especially) if it is somewhat affordable. Third, what may begin as a spontaneous fad (using the materials one has on hand to modify one's appearance, for example) can quickly become appropriated commercially. The phenomenon of trend spotters, or later, "cool hunters," took hold in the latter part of the twentieth century. Apparently, some analysts were able to spot or hunt trends so as to capitalize on them in some way.

Subcultural style, in particular, is open to such appropriation. In the mid-1970s, British working-class youth experimented with safety pins as accessories, with the use of Vaseline to spike their hair, and with ways of ripping their clothes. These looks were soon appropriated by top fashion designers and the apparel and beauty industries. Similarly, the hip-hop styles of inner-city (often African American) youth in the United States in the late 1970s became mainstream even in the suburbs of white, middle-class youth populations. Both of these examples were innovated by limited segments of society and then became more mainstream. But the time factor does not quite fit the classic definition of a fad. For example, the "sagging" trend associated with hip-hop male pants styles is still a way some young men of various ethnic backgrounds continue to wear their pants at the time of this writing. Whereas some adults might describe this look as a fad, younger people might simply characterize it as a

longer-lasting fashion that resonates with some individuals and groups their age.

The approximately 250-year-old concept of fidfad reminds us that a fad is likely to be in the eye of the beholder. For example, when does the tendency to be trendy (or faddish) merge into that of becoming a fashion victim? Not surprisingly, the concept of fashion victim is usually used in a diminutive or depreciative way. The implication is that a fashion victim is susceptible to change, without devoting "serious" thought (as might a connoisseur) to the meaning of that change.

Michelle Lee's 2003 book *Fashion Victim*, intimates that fashion victim is an inclusive concept—not one confined to certain, limited groups within the population: "The Fashion Victim is all around us. The Hollywood startlet who's personally dressed by Donatella Versace is no less a Fashion Victim than the small-town salesgirl who hops on every fad at her local JC Penney" (p. xi). She goes on to say that a fashion victim is "anyone who has ever looked back at old pictures and cringed" (p. xii).

Fiddle faddle. The concept of a fad is frustrating and difficult to distinguish from fashion in general. Issues of time, identity, fun, commodification, appropriation, looking back, and moving forward all relate to the concept of fad as it has been used historically and analytically. None of these issues is without its own ambiguities. Still, fads, by any name or duration, are likely to remain a part of how we live and change.

See also Fashion Advertising; Trendsetters.

Bibliography

Agins, Teri. *The End of Fashion: The Mass Marketing of the Clothing Business.* New York: William Morrow and Company, 1999.

Berger, Arthur Asa. *Ads, Fads, and Consumer Culture: Advertising's Impact on American Character and Society.* 2nd ed. Lanham, Md.: Rowman and Littlefield Publishers, Inc., 2004.

Crane, Diana. *Fashion and Its Social Agendas: Class, Gender, and Identity in Clothing.* Chicago: University of Chicago Press, 2000.

Davis, Fred. *Fashion, Culture, and Identity.* Chicago: University of Chicago Press, 1992.

George, Nelson. *Hip Hop America.* New York: Penguin Books, 1999.

Hebdige, Dick. *Subculture: The Meaning of Style*. New York: Routledge, 1979.

Hoffman, Frank W., and William G. Bailey. *Fashion and Merchandising Fads*. New York: Harrington Park Press, 1994.

Kaiser, Susan B., Richard H. Nagasawa, and Sandra S. Hutton. "Fashion, Postmodernity, and Personal Appearance: A Symbolic Interactionist Formulation." *Symbolic Interaction* 14, no. 2 (1991): 165–185.

——. "Construction of an SI Theory of Fashion: Part 1. Ambivalence and Change." *Clothing and Textiles Research Journal* 13, no. 3 (1995): 172–183.

Lee, Michelle. *Fashion Victim: Our Love-Hate Relationship with Dressing, Shopping, and the Cost of Style*. New York: Broadway Books, 2002.

Marx, Gary T., and Douglas McAdam. *Collective Behavior and Social Movements: Process and Structure*. Englewood Cliffs, N.J.: Prentice-Hall, 1994.

Meyersohn, R., and E. Katz. "Notes on a Natural History of Fads." *American Journal of Sociology* 62 (1957): 594–601.

More, Booth. "Going Von Dutch." *Los Angeles Times*, 2 January 2004.

Nystrom, Paul H. *Economics of Fashion*. New York: Ronald Press, 1928.

Sproles, George B., and Leslie D. Burns. *Changing Appearances*. New York: Fairchild, 1994.

Van Ginneken, Jaap. *Collective Behavior and Public Opinion: Rapid Shifts in Opinion and Communication*. London: Lawrence Erlbaum Associates, 2003.

Susan B. Kaiser, Joyce Heckman,
and Denise Kastrinakis

FANCY DRESS

Celebrating festivals by wearing masks and disguises has been customary in Europe for many centuries. The eighteenth-century masquerade, forerunner of the fancy dress balls and parties of the nineteenth and twentieth centuries, owes its origin to the Venetian pre-Lent Carnival, developed in the seventeenth century. This was a public, open-air event in which all classes participated in dancing, feasting, and practical jokes. The revelers wore masks and either fanciful decorative costumes or all-concealing dark cloaks called dominoes, to enjoy flirtations and intrigue incognito.

Masquerading, or masking, was introduced as a public entertainment in London in 1710, held first in theaters and from the 1730s at the public pleasure gardens at Ranelagh and Vauxhall. In 1772, the Pantheon was built in Oxford Street to provide a winter indoor venue. Many masqueraders wore a mask and domino over fashionable evening dress, but others chose very diverse costumes. The dress of the commedia dell'arte characters Harlequin, Columbine, Punchinello, and Pantaloon was popular, as were nuns' and monks' habits (worn with subversive intent) and comic Scotsmen, sailors, and savages. Turkish dress for men and women, admired for its exoticism, appeared frequently at masquerades, and elements of *turquerie* were adopted in fashionable dress. Most outfits were probably hired, as advertisements show the existence of several London "habit-warehouses" engaged in this trade.

Romanticism

The morally questionable masquerade became unfashionable by 1820, but European society's love of fancy dress continued. To accord with the new mood of decorum, fancy balls became the fashion, given either in private houses or as large-scale civic fundraising events. Masks disappeared, and costumes were based on historical characters (many from Shakespeare's plays or Sir Walter Scott's novels), Turkish and Greek dress inspired by Byron's poems, or the peasant dress of Spain, Italy, and Switzerland. The most admired romantic heroine was Mary, Queen of Scots, whose story combined legendary beauty, doomed love, and a tragic death; her popularity ensured that the "Marie Stuart" cap entered mainstream fashion in the 1830s.

Large civic balls were reported in detail in the press, with lists of costumes worn. Many women wore "a fancy dress," meaning fashionable evening dress with fanciful trimmings, particularly feathers. Local dressmakers or even the ballgoer herself created these outfits. Ladies' periodicals, especially *The World of Fashion* (first published 1828), included plates of historical or foreign dresses for inspiration. For more elaborate costumes and for men's dress, firms specializing in making and hiring fancy costumes advertised widely. London firms (including Nathan's, which still existed in the early 2000s), rented temporary premises in provincial towns where a ball was planned.

Watteau evening dress designed by Vivienne Westwood, from her 1996 Spring/Summer collection *Les Femmes ne Connaissent pas toute leur Coquetterie*. Westwood was inspired by eighteenth century French paintings and made direct reference to the art of Antoine Watteau to create this contemporary take on a sack-back gown. Photograph © Niall McInerney.

Coat designed by Jean Patou, ca. 1928. This fashion illustration is typical of the period, emphasizing the clean lines and streamlined look of Art Deco fashion. ©Mary Evans Picture Library.

A model wearing a design by Belgium designer Ann Demeulemeester for her ready-to-wear Autumn–Winter 2010–2011 fashion show, Paris, January 2010. Demeulemeester's creations are often only in black and white, as she prefers to explore the form of different fabrics and how they hang on the body. FRANCOIS GUILLOT/AFP/Getty Images.

A participant at the International Tattoo Convention displays his face piercings and tattoos, London 2009. Leon Neal/AFP/Getty Images.

A model walks the runway at the Burberry Prorsum Fall–Winter 2010–2011 menswear collection, Milan, 2010. In 2001 Christopher Bailey became creative director of the British clothes manufacturer and has since successfully transformed the traditional, old fashioned look of Burberry into a very desirable modern brand. Damien Meyer/AFP/Getty Images.

A model showcases a camouflage skirt at the Christian Dior Spring/Summer 2001 fashion presentation, Paris, 2000. In the 1960s camouflage cloth appeared in civilian clothing as an ironic response to the Vietnam War, and many designers have since used this patterned cloth in their collections. Petit & Hel/Prestige/Newsmakers/Getty Images.

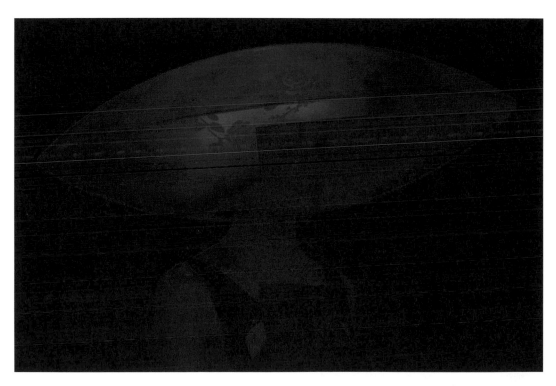

A model wearing a Hussein Chalayan creation during the Autumn/Winter 2007/2008 ready-to-wear collection show, Paris, 2007. FRANCOIS GUILLOT/AFP/Getty Images.

Elizabeth Hurley wearing a black Versace dress held together with safety pins, at the post-premiere party of the film *Four Weddings and a Funeral*, London, 1994. By wearing this now-famous cocktail dress, Hurley became a household name overnight. Dave Benett/Hulton Archive/Getty Images.

Titian, Emperor Karl V and dog ("Ulmer Dogge"), 1533. The codpiece was worn as a symbol of wealth and power until the late sixteenth century. Imagno/Getty Images.

An experimental creation from Kawakubo incorporating hexagonal shapes, at the Comme Des Garcons Spring/Summer 2009 collection at Paris Fashion Week, 2008. Chris Moore/Catwalking/Getty Images.

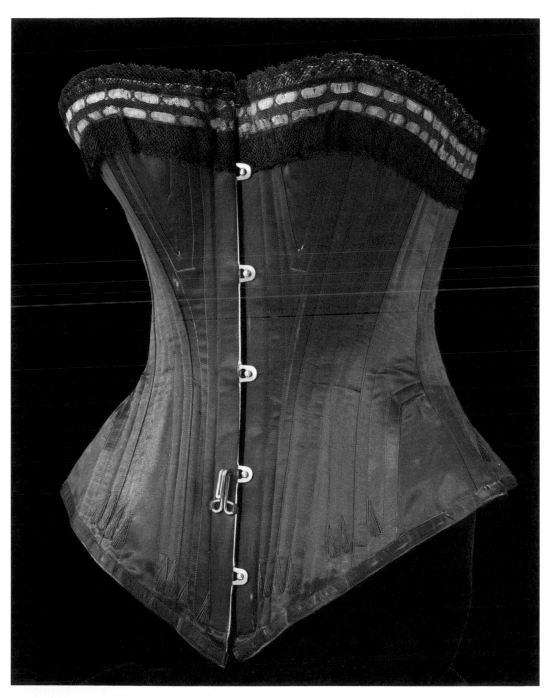

Pink satin corset with hand-made bobbin lace, Great Britain, early 1890s. For 400 years, up until the early twentieth century, the corset was an essential item in a fashionable woman's wardrobe. Photo © Victoria and Albert Museum, London.

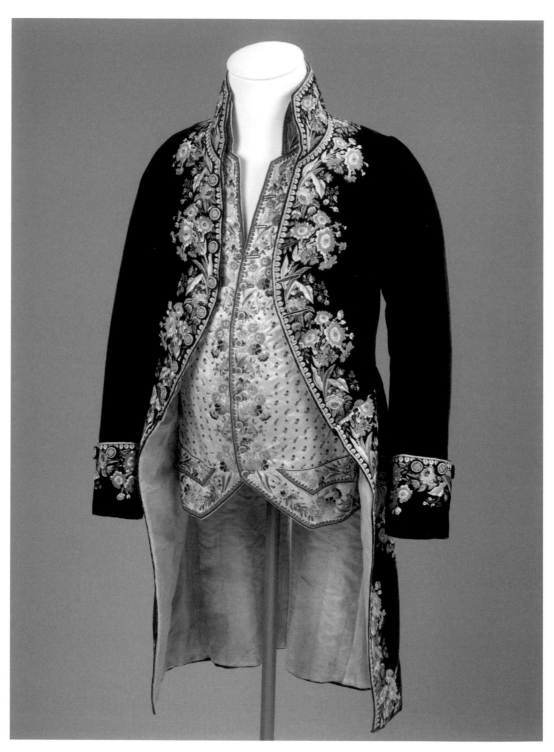

A man's coat and waistcoat richly embroidered in silk, England or Scotland, ca.1800. This court suit is typical of the most formal style of dress worn at the time. Photo © Victoria and Albert Museum, London.

Models for Dior outside the Cathedral of the Dormition, Moscow. In 1959 the Soviet Union officially allowed fashion shows and Dior took the opportunity to showcase his haute couture collection in Moscow. Howard Sochurek/Time & Life Pictures/Getty Images.

A model wearing a Fath dress, 1956. Jacques Fath's designs combined a clean and tailored look with dramatic features. Hulton Archive/ Getty Images.

A model displaying an example of fetishism in fashion at the John Galliano Spring/Summer 2005 men's ready-to-wear collection, Paris, 2004. Pierre Verdy/AFP/Getty Images

John Galliano is considered to be one of the most innovative and influential fashion designers of the early twenty-first century. Here a model presents one of his creations for the Christian Dior Haute-Couture Fall/Winter 2000–2001 collection in Paris. Jean-Pierre Muller/ AFP/Getty Images.

A model presents a Jean Paul Gaultier creation for his spring–summer 2010 haute couture collection in Paris. FRANCOIS GUILLOT/AFP/
Getty Images.

"Grecian" evening dress made from silk jersey, designed by Madame Alix Grès, France, 1945. Made to enhance the female body without physically restricting its movement, the 'Grecian' dress is perhaps one of the most famous and recognizable designs of Grès. ©The Museum at FIT.

Kate Moss behind the scenes at the Isaac Mizrahi show, Spring Fashion Week, 1994. In the 1990s, models such as Moss were chosen for their emaciated and gaunt look. Fashion shoots held in run-down, seedy settings, with the models using certain gestures and facial expressions to imply drug use, reinforced this look and led to the term "heroin chic." Rose Hartman/WireImage/Getty Images.

Italian high-heeled shoes with bevel-carved wood heels covered in red leather and silk embroidered uppers, 1700–1720. Copyright © 2010 Bata Shoe Museum, Toronto.

Roger Vivier high-heeled shoes c.1950s. Known as the "Fabergé of shoes," Vivier is credited with creating the first stiletto heels in 1956. Copyright © 2010 Bata Shoe Museum, Toronto.

Crêpe silk kimono with paste-resist decoration (*yuzen*) of pine trees and clouds, Japan ca. 1830–1880. Photo © Victoria and Albert Museum, London.

A model wears a design by Karl Lagerfeld as part of the Chanel spring/summer 2009 ready-to-wear collection, Paris, 2008. FRANCOIS GUILLOT/AFP/Getty Images.

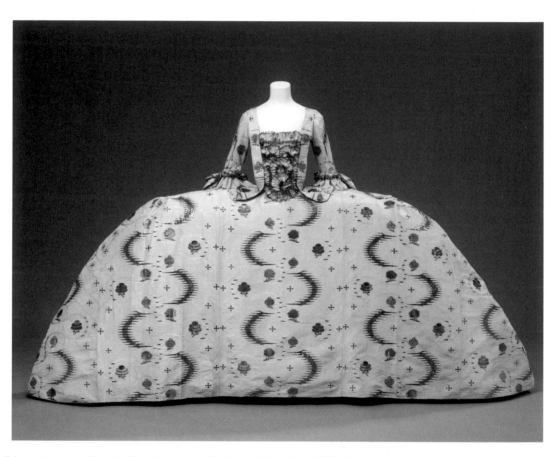

English court mantua of French silk and brocaded with silver gilt threads ca. 1760s. Photo © Victoria and Albert Museum, London.

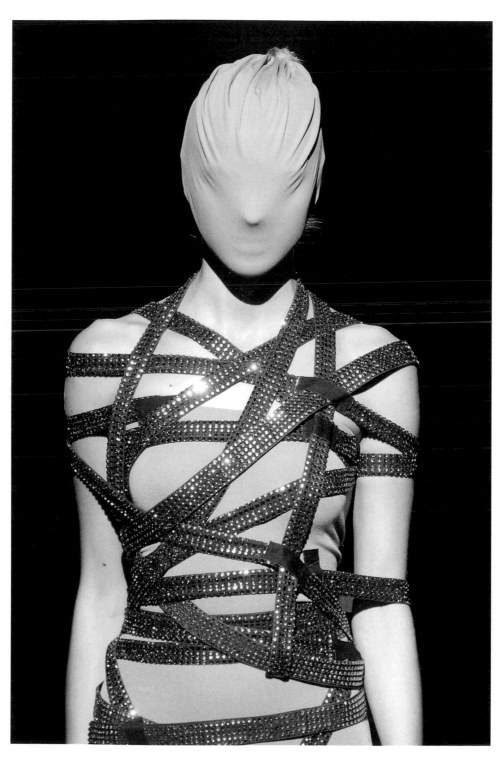

A model presents a creation by the Belgian designer Martin Margiela for his Spring/Summer 2009 collection during Paris Fashion Week, 2008. Karl Prouse/Catwalking/Getty Images.

A model wearing a design by Alexander McQueen as part of his ready-to-wear Autumn/Winter 2009 collection during Paris Fashion Week, 2009. Dominique Charriau/WireImage/Getty Images.

Originating from designs by André Courrèges and Mary Quant, miniskirts made their debut in the 1960s. They were quickly adopted by young fashionable women, and became one of the defining fashions of "swinging London." Duffy/Getty Images, 1966.

Emilio Pucci standing with models wearing his designs, ca. 1968. Pucci was known for his bold designs and vivid colour combinations. Bill Eppridge/Time Life Pictures/Getty Images.

Detail of a pink fitted jacket designed by Elsa Schiaparelli. Featuring a repeat pattern of blue rearing horses and handmade cast metal buttons in the shape of playful acrobats, this jacket formed part of Schiaparelli's Circus collection of 1938. Photo © Victoria and Albert Museum, London.

Models wearing "space-age styles" from the 1968 fashion collection by André Courrèges, Paris, France. Bill Ray/Time Life Pictures/Getty Images.

Michelle Obama brought the work of Isabel Toledo into the public eye by choosing to wear this ensemble at the inauguration of Barack Obama in Washington, DC, 2009. Described as a "designer's designer" Isabel Toledo has been creating fashion garments since the mid 1980s, using a variety of experimental techniques. Chip Somodevilla/Getty Images.

A model wearing a Yohji Yamamoto design for his Autumn/Winter collection, Beijing, 2008. Yamamoto is famed for his deconstructed creations and frequent use of a monochrome palette in his garments. Liu Jin/AFP/Getty Images.

In France the masquerade was a fashionable way to celebrate state occasions. Louis XV attended the bal masqué at Versailles, celebrating the marriage of the Dauphin in February 1745, as one of a group of topiary trees.

Imperial Pageants

From the 1860s onward, fancy dress opportunities multiplied. Society papers listed columns of private balls, often celebrating comings-of-age and housewarmings, as well as public balls hosted by lord mayors, children's parties, and clubs' and works' Christmas parties. Such was the demand for ideas for costumes that women's periodicals, especially *The Queen*, published regular articles and correspondence columns, and from 1879, books were also available; Ardern Holt, *The Queen*'s columnist, produced *Fancy Dresses Described*, which ran to six editions by 1896. Popular costumes included "Vandyke" and rococo dress, Japanese dress (inspired by *The Mikado*, 1885), European peasant dress, and allegorical costumes such as Night, Winter, or Folly. By the 1880s, there was a demand for novel and inventive ideas (such as "The Front Hall" and "Oysters and Champagne"), and originality was important. As well as private dressmakers, the newly established department stores in London and provincial cities made fancy dresses for customers.

Queen Victoria's 1897 Diamond Jubilee inspired two of the most lavish fancy dress balls of the century: the Devonshire House Ball given in London by the duchess of Devonshire and attended by royalty and the cream of London society, and the Victorian Era Ball, given in Toronto by the governor general of Canada, Lord Aberdeen, and Lady Aberdeen. At Devonshire House, the guests dressed as famous people from history or fable; the hostess represented Zenobia, queen of Palmyra, and the countess of Warwick was Queen Marie Antoinette. Many of the costumes were couture creations, several by Jean-Philippe Worth (son of Charles). For the Canadian ball, the theme was the British Empire, and many costumes were allegorical: the Aberdeens' daughter represented "The Forests of Canada," and other ballgoers dressed as "Electricity," "Postal Progress," and "Sports and Pastimes."

Bright Young Things

Fancy dress fitted the mood of 1920s party-going perfectly. Young people turned the social world topsy-turvy with all-night parties, jazz, cocktails, and exhibitionist behavior. Masks were reintroduced, and the most admired outfits were outrageous or bizarre, with good taste out-of-date. Theme parties became popular: Greek parties, baby parties, Wild West parties, and circus parties were held in London during the 1920s. The commedia dell'arte characters enjoyed a revival, especially Harlequin and Pierrot, given a contemporary twist. Fancy dress balls became annual events at universities and colleges and a popular feature of holiday cruises.

The press called the fancy dress ball given by Carlos de Beistegui, a Mexican millionaire, in the Palazzo Labia, Venice, in September 1951, the "Party of the Twentieth Century." The cream of international society dressed in sumptuous eighteenth-century costumes, many by French and Italian couturiers. In decline since the 1950s, fancy dress returned to fashion from the 1980s. Favorite characters in the 2000s include perennials such as monks, nuns, clowns, devils, joined by topical characters from films and TV. Themed parties are popular; Prince William of Wales celebrated his twenty-first birthday in June 2003 with an "Out of Africa" ball at Windsor Castle.

Children's Fancy Dress

Nineteenth-century children's costumes, apart from some nursery-rhyme characters, were usually miniature versions of adult dress, reflecting the mother's taste more than the child's. By the 1920s and 1930s, however, with more occasions for fancy dress, including pageants and street carnivals, and wider social participation, children's outfits were enormously varied, based on cartoon characters and cinema heroes, animals, storybook characters, even advertisements. Many were home-made: the paper pattern firm Weldon's produced catalogs of fancy dress patterns, and magazines suggested how to contrive costumes from everyday clothes or household furnishings.

In the early twenty-first century, dressing up is part of everyday play for three- to six-year-olds. Outfits

"I arrived at the Sutherlands' ball impenetrably disguised as a repulsive baby boy in rompers with a flaxen wig and a ghoulish baby-face mask, then I dashed home and returned as a Sylphide in white tulle with a wreath of gardenias."

Loelia, duchess of Westminster, 1927

are on sale in all toyshops and chain stores, to turn children into princesses, knights, nurses, policemen, Disney characters, or the popular fiction hero Harry Potter.

See also Ball Dress; Masquerade and Masked Balls.

Bibliography

Cooper, Cynthia. *Magnificent Entertainments: Fancy Dress Balls of Canada's Governors General, 1876–1898.* New Brunswick, Canada: Goose Lane Editions and Canadian Museum of Civilization, 1997.

Finkel, Alicia. "Le Bal Costumé: History and Spectacle in the Court of Queen Victoria." *Dress* 10 (1984): 64–72.

Holt, Ardern. *Fancy Dresses Described, or What to Wear at Fancy Balls.* 5th ed. London, Debenham and Freebody, 1887, 6th ed., 1896.

Jarvis, Anthea. "'There was a Young Man from Bengal...': The Vogue for Fancy Dress, 1830–1950." *Costume* 16 (1982): 33–46.

Jarvis, Anthea, and Patricia Raine. *Fancy Dress.* Aylesbury, U.K.: Shire Publications Ltd., 1984.

Ribiero, Aileen. "The Exotic Diversion: The Dress Worn at Masquerades in Eighteenth-Century London." *Connoisseur* (January 1978): 3–13.

Stevenson, Sara, and Helen Bennet. *Van Dyck in Check Trousers: Fancy Dress in Art and Life, 1700–1900.* Edinburgh: Scottish National Portrait Gallery, 1978.

Westminster (Duchess of), Loelia. *Grace and Favour: The Memoirs of Loelia, Duchess of Westminster.* London: Weidenfeld and Nicolson, 1961.

Anthea Jarvis

FASCIST AND NAZI DRESS

Already in the decade preceding the Third Reich, female fashion had become a locus of contentious debate in Germany. In reaction to the "Garçonne" style that had become popular in the post-World War I years, conservative critics railed against "degenerate" cosmetics and clothing, which they described as "jewified," "masculinized," "French-dominated," and "poisonous." They also castigated the trend mongers who pushed such tasteless, unbecoming fashions onto unsuspecting female consumers. Short hair, shorter hemlines, pants, and visible makeup—all of these were purportedly causing the moral degradation of German women.

Vituperative commentaries claimed that French fashions were unhealthy for German women, both morally and physically, and that it was imperative for German designers to establish complete independence from the nefarious French influence on female fashion. Also denounced was the dangerous American vamp or Hollywood image that young German women were foolishly imitating with penciled eyebrows, darkly lined eyes, painted red mouths, and provocative clothing. Additionally, by the mid-1920s, Berlin had become an acclaimed world center of fashion, especially for ready-to-wear women's apparel and outerwear. Highly exaggerating the percentage of Jews in the German fashion industry, diatribes in pro-Nazi publications polemicized against the "crushing" Jewish presence, which was blamed for both ruining economic opportunities for the Aryan middle class and conspiring to destroy feminine dignity by producing immoral, whorish fashions for German women. This downward spiral in female appearance, critics asserted, could be halted only with the creation of a "unique German fashion." That term, however, was never fully defined.

Fashion Ideology and Policy

Such reactionary, anti-Semitic, and rabidly nationalistic messages were repeated on countless occasions throughout the 1920s and early 1930s, so that by the time the Nazi Party came to power in 1933 the argument was clear. Only German clothing, specifically Aryan-designed and manufactured, was good enough for females in the Third Reich. Racially appropriate clothing depended upon the elimination of French and, especially, Jewish influences from the German fashion industry.

To that end, an Aryanization organization named the *Arbeitsgemeinschaft deutsch-arischer Fabrikanten der Bekleidungsindustrie* (or Adefa), was established in May 1933 by several longtime German clothing manufacturers and producers. The group's aim was to systematically purge the Jews from all areas of the fashion industry. Through a combination of massive pressure, boycotts, economic sanctions, illegal buy-outs, forced liquidations, and the systematic exclusion and persecution of countless Jews, Adefa succeeded by January 1939 in ousting all Jews from the German fashion world. The *Deutsches Mode-Institut* (German Fashion Institute) was also founded in 1933, with strong backing from the Ministry of Propaganda and several other governmental agencies. Its mission was to attain fashion independence from French influence, to unify the various facets of fashion creation and fashion production in the German clothing industry, and to create a "unique German fashion" that would garner the Third Reich international acclaim and monetary rewards via its designs. Beset with internal conflicts throughout its existence and given little actual power, the German Fashion Institute never succeeded in fulfilling any of its goals.

Additionally, the Nazi state attempted to construct a female appearance that would mirror official ideology, uphold the government's autarkic economic policies, and create feelings of national belonging. This proposed female image would need to correlate to the Nazis' gender ideology, which urged women to return to their authentic role of wife and mother. Women's natural maternal instincts would thereby be satisfied, while also allowing them to fulfill the honorable duties of childbearer for the nation, significant consumer, and loyal citizen that Nazi Germany had bestowed upon them. As "mothers of the German *Volk*," women were assigned to correct the nation's sinking birthrate, guarantee the racial purity of future generations, and strengthen the economy by purchasing only German-made products. These were important tasks that required an image befitting the propaganda. For the ideal German woman, devoted to her family's well being, beauty stemmed not from cosmetics or trendy fashions, but from an inner happiness derived from her devotion to her children, her husband, her home, and her country.

The two images most often proposed and put into visual forms of propaganda were the farmer's wife in folk costume, usually referred to as *Tracht* or dirndl, and the young woman in organizational uniform. The rhetoric surrounding these two proposals advanced the "natural look" for women and condemned cosmetics and other "unhealthy vices," such as smoking and drinking, as unfeminine and unGerman. Stress was placed on physical fitness and a healthy lifestyle, both of which would facilitate a higher birthrate. Moreover, while the folk costume looked to the past and promoted an image that illuminated the Nazis' "blood and soil" ideology, and the female uniform spoke to the present and exemplified the idea of conformity over individuality, both

images signified a rejection of international trends, again, as unGerman. Both proposals also fit the state's anti-Semitic and anti-French agendas, as well as its "made-in-Germany" autarkic policy.

The Dirndl Fashion

The farmer's wife, labeled "Mother Germany," was offered as one female ideal. She was the link between the bonds of German blood and soil. Her natural looks, unsullied by cosmetics, her physical strength and moral fortitude, her willingness to bear hard work and to bear many children, and her traditional dress that recalled a mythical, untarnished German past, were deified through countless exhibits, paintings, and essays. In propaganda photos, rural women usually were shown with their hair braided or pinned up in a bun, no cosmetics, surrounded by children, and beaming with an inner glow that gave no hint of the difficult work that filled their days. And what was the ideal farmer's wife wearing? According to Nazi propaganda, she should dress herself in *Trachtenkleidung*, a folk costume that reflected Germany's rich cultural heritage. Promoted as an expression of the true German-Aryan character, the age-old *Trachtendirndl*—generally comprising a dress with tight bodice and full, long skirt, a white blouse with puffed and gathered sleeves, a heavily embroidered or crocheted collar, an embellished apron, and a variety of head pieces or hats—was viewed as the most suitable example of racially pure clothing and held up as a significant symbolic metaphor for pride in the German homeland.

To promote the resurrection of the folk costume, state-sponsored *Tracht* gatherings and folk festivals cropped up everywhere, even occasionally in metropolitan areas. Girls and women were told to proudly wear dirndls for Nazi Party-sponsored occasions and historic celebrations. And, farm women were encouraged to rediscover the many attributes of *Tracht*. They were also urged to sew their dirndls from fabric they had woven themselves, while caring for their flock of children and helping with the harvest. The problem was that most of them had ceased wearing anything resembling *Tracht* on a regular basis by this time, due to its impracticality and the difficult economic straits in which so many rural families found themselves. Farm women had long ago turned to dark fabrics that showed little dirt, looser clothes that allowed for greater movement, and sleeves that did not encumber them at their work. Except for the rare special occasion

German schoolgirls in peasant costume. The Nazi Party urged women to embrace their cultural heritage by adopting traditional German dress, but most found such clothing impractical and continued to wear modern fashions. © Hulton-Deutsch Collection/Corbis. Reproduced by permission.

or celebration, rural women had not regularly worn the traditional dirndl for decades. Also problematic, the Nazis' extensive *Tracht* propaganda did not succeed in convincing urban women to embrace the folk costume. While dressing in dirndls for certain events was considered fun, the majority of women living in large cities, such as Hamburg and Berlin, continued clothing themselves according to the latest international styles shown in German magazines, despite arduous efforts by some Nazis to convince them to dress otherwise.

The Female in Uniform

As an urban alternative to the farmer's wife in *Tracht*, the Nazis offered another female ideal: that of the young German woman in uniform, a reflection of the Party's attraction to organization and militarization. Much like *Trachtenkleidung*, the uniform offered yet another visible sign of inclusion into the Nazi-constructed German racial community. It also represented order and accommodation, as well as a rejection of international trends and individuality.

As organizations quickly proliferated in the Third Reich, so did female uniforms. Whether for girls, young women, female youths in the labor service, or female auxiliary units, once World War II began, each group had a distinct uniform or, minimally, different insignia, badges, and armbands that specified rank or branch of

service. Hair was to be kept neat and away from the face, preferably in braids for young girls and a bun for adult females. Cosmetics were shunned as unnatural and unnecessary for these young women who glowed from health and love of country. Physical fitness, self-sacrifice, obedience, and loyalty to the Nazi regime and its tenets were the most important components of all organizations, whose overriding purpose was to groom a generation of racially pure, healthy, ideologically sound females to become future "mothers of the *Volk*." No individual touches, no embellishments, nothing was allowed that might detract from the symbolic significance of the requisite clothing. The uniform sartorially expressed the Third Reich's demand for unity, uniformity, conformity, and community.

Clothing females in organizational uniforms, while fairly popular when the nation was at peace, became a political problem for the government once the conflict broadened throughout Europe and additional women were needed as war-essential auxiliaries. Uniforming increasing numbers of females and placing them in positions that had been designated as "male only," obviously upended the Nazi Party's "separate spheres" propaganda and its gender-specific work policies of the prewar years. The state's other concern was that extensive female uniforming would make clearly visible to the home population that the war was not going well. Furthermore, as the conflict continued and drastic textile shortages developed, some auxiliaries, who were only issued armbands indicating service affiliation in order to save material, openly complained and privately resented that they could not wear the full uniform others wore. Female auxiliaries stationed inside as well as outside of the Reich wanted, at the least, to look official as they risked their lives for the nation.

Popular Female Fashions

The image most widely embraced by German women not only competed with these two state-sanctioned offerings, but also often glaringly conflicted with either the Party's rhetoric or its policies. While "the natural look" was the beauty slogan pushed by Nazi stalwarts, and a "unique German fashion" was relentlessly advocated, neither was enthusiastically adopted by most women in the Third Reich. Instead, they bought the latest cosmetics, tried the newest hairstyles, and wore variations of the same fashions being worn by women in France, England, and America.

Reflecting the interests of their readership, popular magazines published articles that illustrated makeup techniques, advertised face creams, tanning lotions, and hair dyes, and offered tips on replicating the looks of Hollywood stars, such as Greta Garbo, Jean Harlow, and Katharine Hepburn. Photos in fashion journals depicted the newest styles by Parisian and American couturiers next to elegantly fashionable creations by Berlin's best designers. Well-known German fashion schools, such as the *Deutsches Meisterschule für Mode* in Munich and the *Frankfurter Modeamt* in Frankfurt, eschewed the dirndl image in favor of international influences and female consumer desires, much to the dismay of Nazi hard-liners. And for those women who did not have the means to purchase their clothing from dress salons or department stores, sewing patterns, with which to recreate popular fashions, were widely available and affordable.

Wartime Fashions and Rationing

On 14 November 1939, two months after the onset of World War II, the government issued the first *Reichs-kleiderkarte* (or Reich Clothing Card). This rationing system was designed to ensure an equitable means by which to supply the civilian population with sufficient shoes, clothing, and textiles during the war. German Jews, deemed unworthy of receiving even minimal support, received no clothing coupons beginning in 1940. The clothing card was based on a point system, from which a recipient could not use more than 25 points in the time span of two months. Numerous other restrictions also applied. Hats were "points-free," which meant they could be acquired without ration vouchers or clothing cards and so would become the major fashion item of the war years. Once hat supplies were depleted, and thus unobtainable for purchase, women created their own turbans and hats from fabric remnants, lace scraps, netting, and felt pieces.

The first clothing card, good for one year, allotted 100 points, but severe shortages rapidly developed in several areas, particularly shoes and cloth. Because textile and leather production increasingly was geared toward the needs of the German army, many stores were soon emptied of their reserves. Consequently, material remnants replaced leather shoe uppers, and soles were often made from cork or wood. Additionally, the government quickly discovered that its autarkic economic policy had, in part, resulted in an unsuccessful scramble for a wide variety of viable synthetics that were urgently needed to keep Germans, military and civilian, clothed.

Many of the textile and leather substitutes were of poor quality and disintegrated when washed or ironed.

The second clothing card, issued in the late fall of 1940, was worth 150 points, but the additional 50 points had no real value since, by then, extreme clothing and footwear shortages had developed in several major German cities. Widely circulated government brochures urged women to "make new from old," but a dearth of available sewing goods, such as thread and yarn, contradicted the state's catchy mottos. Despite admonishments by those who viewed pants as unfeminine and unacceptable female attire, women increasingly wore trousers as the war dragged on and shortages continued to mount. Pants were warmer than skirts, especially once supplies of stockings and socks had been exhausted. They were far more practical for women to wear as work attire in war-related factories. And, often, they were the only clothes item in the household still in plentiful supply, with so many absent husbands and brothers serving in the armed forces.

By 1943, drastic garment and shoe shortages rendered the clothing card virtually useless in some areas of Germany. In response, civilians turned ever more frequently to the burgeoning black market, even though this was a highly punishable offense. The inability of the regime to provide adequate clothing provisions throughout the war years was met with growing resentment and overtly expressed discontent, which belied the Nazis' depiction of a harmonious, supportive national community.

Summary

During the Third Reich, female fashion became a topic of much discussion and dispute. Instead of a unified view of what "German fashion" meant and a singular, consistently touted public image of the female, incongruities abounded. Additionally, no cohesive national fashion program was ever implemented successfully, despite tireless attempts by some officials. Women's fashion, which the Nazis had hoped would be a sartorial sign of inclusion into the national community, the *Volksgemeinschaft*, instead became a signifier of disjunction. Female appearance could and did circumvent Nazi ideological tenets and state regulations, sometimes flagrantly. Concurrently, ambiguous directives laid bare the government's obvious fear of losing both women's support on the home front and a lucrative fashion market abroad. In the end, fashion proved to be an unsuccessful tool in defining German womanhood and citizenship, partially through the dictates of clothing and appearance. This failure exposed the limits of state power in a highly visible manner. What was propagandized in the sphere of women's fashion had only a slight correlation to reality in Nazi Germany.

See also Politics and Fashion.

Bibliography

Bundesarchiv R3101/8646 (regarding the papers of the aryanization organization "Adefa").

Bundesarchiv R55/692, R55/795, and other less voluminous files (regarding "German Fashion Institute").

Die Dame. One of the longest-running top contemporary German fashion magazines.

Deicke-Mönninghoff, Maren. "Und sie rauchten doch. Deutsche Moden 1933–1945.

Der deutsche Volkswirt and *Die deutsche Volkswirtschaft.* Contemporary trade journals filled with anti-Semitic essays regarding the role of Jews in the German economy.

Guenther, Irene. "Nazi 'Chic'? German Politics and Women's Fashions, 1915–1945." *Fashion Theory: The Journal of Dress, Body and Culture* 1, no. 1 (March 1997): 29–58. Overview of the subject of German fashion, with particular emphasis on the Nazi period and World War II.

——. *Nazi "Chic"?: Fashioning Women in the Third Reich.* Oxford: Berg, 2004. The only comprehensive English-language study of German fashion and the German fashion industry from World War I through the end of the Third Reich. All of the information quoted and summarized throughout this encyclopedia essay can be found in this source.

Jacobeit, Sigrid. "Clothing in Nazi Germany." In *Marxist Historiography in Transformation: New Orientations in Recent East German History.* Edited by Georg Iggers, 227–245. Translated by Bruce Little. Oxford: Berg, 1991. Translated overview of women's clothing developments and relevant state policies during the Third Reich. Jacobeit has published several German-language essays pertaining to fashion in the Nazi period, which include the issue of folk costume or *Tracht.*

Koonz, Claudia. *Mothers in the Fatherland: Women, the Family, and Nazi Politics.* New York: St. Martin's Press, 1987. Comprehensive study of Nazi gender ideology and policies, and the role of women as "mothers of the German Volk."

Die Mode. High fashion German magazine begun in 1941, two years after the onset of the war. Because of wartime paper shortages, the journal ceased publication in 1943, along with all other fashion magazines.

Das Schwarze Korps. Newspaper of the Nazi SS, excellent source for condemnations of female fashions and cosmetics, as well as for anti-Semitic polemics.

Semmelroth, Ellen, and Renate von Stieda, eds. *N.S. Frauenbuch.* Munich: J. F. Lehmanns Verlag, 1934. Early Nazi anthology, the essays' themes pertain to the role of women in Nazi ideology and policy, fashion, autarky, and consumption.

Stephenson, Jill. "Propaganda, Autarky, and the German Housewife." In *Nazi Propaganda* 117–142: *The Power and the Limitations.* Edited by David Welch, London: Croom, Helm, 1983. In-depth essay about the Nazis' efforts to promote and implement the state's policy of autarky as it pertained to German women.

Sultano, Gloria. *Wie geistiges Kokain . . . Mode unterm Hakenkreuz.* Vienna: Verlag für Gesellschaftskritik, 1995. Excellent study of fashion during the Nazi period; however, sources are mostly Austrian-based, so study is focused more on Austria than on Germany.

Völkischer Beobachter. Pro-Nazi newspaper, excellent source for early diatribes against women's fashions.

Westphal, Uwe. *Berliner Konfektion und Mode: Die Zerstörung einer Tradition, 1836–1939.* 2d ed. Berlin: Edition Hentrich, 1986; 1992. Excellent examination of the early, important role of Jews in the German fashion world, and their persecution and exclusion from the fashion industry during the Third Reich.

"*Zeitmagazin,* supplement to *Die Zeit*" 19 (6 May 1983): 30–40. Interesting German-language article about fashion in the Nazi period, with particular emphasis on the obvious contradictions between Nazi fashion rhetoric and reality.

Irene Guenther

FASHION ADVERTISING

Fashion advertisements have their own stylistic modes and spheres of production and consumption, involving the interrelationship of word and image among other things. Yet, technological and social changes in clothing and retailing, and the impact of class, gender, and race politics, also have to be taken into account. Early forms of fashion promotion that originated in the eighteenth century, for example, overlapped with the rise of urban culture and shopping and embraced diverse forms of promotion, some of which we might not strictly recognize today as advertising. In the first instance, the majority of retailers regarded the creation of an enticing shop façade and interior as sufficient means for attracting and establishing a suitable clientele. This would subsequently be complemented by the circulation of handbills and trade cards, and to a lesser extent by press advertising, all of which were used to reinforce the reputation of the shop in question rather than to publicize the sale of particular wares. In the *London Evening Post* for 24 April 1741, for example, the haberdasher John Stanton placed an advertisement, not to tell the public about the goods he sold but to inform them of a change of trading address. Otherwise, newspaper advertisements were occasionally used by large-scale retailers and manufacturers to promote both new and second-hand goods at fixed prices, and from the 1760s tailors also began to advertise different items of male and female clothing. The emphasis of such publicity was the printed word and the general format was the list, enumerating the items on offer and how much they cost. By contrast, more alluring pictorial representations of the latest fashions were available as engraved or etched plates, displayed for sale in print sellers' windows and also incorporated into such volumes as Heidelhoff's *Gallery of Fashion* (1794–1802) and intermittently in magazines like the *Lady's Magazine*.

During the late eighteenth and early nineteenth centuries, the nexus between what Roland Barthes refers to as image-clothing and written clothing in *The Fashion System* became more evident in French and British publications, such as the *Cabinet des Modes*, *La Belle Assemblée*, and Ackermann's *Repository of Arts*, where illustrations were accompanied by captions and editorials concerning changes in the styles of fashion. These titles were the fore-runners of such popular illustrated weeklies as the *Illustrated London News* (ILN), *Graphic*, *Lady's Pictorial*, and *Ladies' Home Journal*, which had sprung up by the mid-nineteenth century on both sides of the Atlantic to cater to middle-class readers and in which the first distinctly recognizable alpha-pictorial advertisements for clothing retailers appeared. Many of these promotions, however, were similar in approach to the "reason why" format of their antecedents since they consisted of straightforward wood-engraved illustrations of women—and men—wearing the garments alongside text that relates the cost of the clothing represented and where it could be purchased. Occasionally more suggestive or atmospheric forms of advertising,

in which the product appeared in a situational context, cropped up. Thus press promotions during the 1880s and 1890s in *Lady's Pictorial* and *Graphic* for "My Queen" Vel-Vel, a velvet for dressmaking, resorted to the trope of Queen Victoria as consumer. In them, she is embodied in a domestic setting as a saleswoman unfurls the fabric before her. Yet, Victoria's detached gaze and demeanor transcend the material situation, and it is rather her majestic aura that symbolically bestows favor on the fabric and invests it with value.

By the turn of the century, the color lithographic poster, pioneered by Jules Chéret in France, had also become a popular form of advertising internationally, although there are few extant examples relating directly or exclusively to fashion promotion. In 1900, for instance, H. G. Gray produced a poster to publicize the latest fashions on sale at the Parisian department store Prix Unique. Publicity for some manufacturers also tended to a form of double symbolism; hence an 1885 poster for the American company New Home Sewing Machine, representing a mother painting and a daughter playing with a cat in their new clothes, not only represented the products that such domestic technologies enabled but the leisure time that they also afforded middle-class women.

The seeds for a modern, atmospheric form of fashion advertising, therefore, were sown by the late nineteenth century. Not until the twentieth century, and especially the interwar period, did an evident quantitative and qualitative shift take place in the promotion of fashion and clothing for women and men. This was due in no small measure to the expansion of the ready-to-wear and bespoke markets, as well as the professionalization of the advertising industry itself, which had begun to get involved more systematically with market segmentation and to probe what made different types of consumers tick in terms of sex, age, and class. At the same time, the impact of modernist aesthetics, the role of the copywriter, and the deployment of avant-garde designers and photographers also greatly transformed fashion advertising.

Prussian-born Hans Schleger (alias Zéró) was probably the most renowned of this new breed of commercial artists, and he worked both in Europe and America. Between 1925 and 1929, he was hired by outfitters Weber and Heilbroner of New York to transform their advertising campaigns. To this end he devised press advertisements that dynamically conveyed a sense of rhythm and proportion, such that the layout of asymmetric or expressive typeforms into wave or wedge formations was complemented by the shape and directional thrust of the illustrations or photographs. In 1929, he struck up an association with the pioneering British advertising agency W. S. Crawford (founded 1914), which held accounts for Wolsey hosiery and Jaeger amongst others. Working in collaboration with the copywriter G. H. Saxon Mills, he created imaginative promotions for Charnaux corsets that appeared in *Vogue* during the 1930s and that used sporting metaphors to emphasize the idea of health and freedom in the design and wearing of undergarments.

America took the lead in pioneering the evolution of photographic advertising during the early 1920s, with Clarence White, who had founded a school of photography in New York in his own name in 1914 and the Art Center in 1921, becoming one of the first apologists for its application. The modern style he advocated was based on sharp focus, simple geometry, and oblique perspectives, and manifested itself in the photography of the school's most well-known graduates, Edward Steichen and Paul Outerbridge. The former promulgated the idea of straight photography in advertising campaigns for Realsilk hosiery in *Ladies' Home Journal* between 1927 and 1937, and the former in his campaign for the Ide Shirt Collar, which was photographed in stark isolation against a checkerboard and published in *Vanity Fair* in November 1922. In Europe, similar ideas had taken root during the 1920s with the advent of the Neue Sachlichkeit (New Objectivity). Thus, László Moholy-Nagy, in "How Photography Revolutionizes Vision" (1933), espoused a battery of different techniques, including photomontage and the photogram, and a range of different stylistic approaches to the object, such as the introduction of the greatest contrasts, the use of texture and structure, and the use of different or unfamiliar perspectives that offered "new experiences of space." All of these formal concerns are evident in an advertisement in *Punch* in 1933 for Austin Reed shirts featuring a color photograph of bales of material, which invites us to contemplate everyday objects from a fresh vantage point.

The photographic forms of fashion advertising that had begun to supplant the use of hand-drawn illustrations during the 1930s continued unabated after World War II. By the mid-1950s the market for teenage and youth fashions had also influenced the sexual iconography of many advertisements. A common motif in press promotions during the 1960s for designers as diverse as Mary Quant and Dior, and garments from miniskirts to coats and trousers to tights, was the woman-child,

represented clowning in playful poses or pouting provocatively. Between 1961 and 1963, photographs by David Olins of "the girl" wearing a man's shirt were also deployed in poster and press ads to promote the Tootal brand. At the same time, the male consumer was drawn into this ornamental realm of desire and in promotions for Newman Clothing during the 1960s was depicted as the object of the adoring female admirers who surrounded him. But it would be erroneous to argue that men had not been objectified in this way before; in poster advertisements for Pope and Bradley in 1911–1912 and in many of those by Tom Purvis for Austin Reed during the 1930s, as well as press advertisements for multiple tailors like the Fifty Shilling Tailors, the fashionable peacock was connoted as someone who could turn women's heads.

Since the 1960s it is probably more casual forms of dress, and jeans in particular, that have made an appeal on television and in the press to both men and women in terms of sexual desire. As competition between brands and designer labels heated up in the late 1970s and early 1980s, advertisers began to fetishize the contour-hugging nature of denim. Thus press ads for Calvin Klein, featuring Brooke Shields, and for Jordache traded on closeups of pert buttocks clad in jeans. In this vein, the retro British television campaign for Levi 501's (masterminded by Bartle, Bogle and Hegarty and screened in 1985–1986), which featured Nick Kamen stripping down to his boxer shorts in a launderette, initiated a more subtle and ambiguous form of sexual objectification.

Interestingly, although Levi's are sold across the world, publicity for the brand has not been orchestrated on a multinational basis. In comparison with the retrostyled British television and press campaigns of the 1980s, for instance, in America the "501 Blues" television advertisements traded on the idea of nonconformity by associating the product with contemporary street-smart individuals and blues music, while press advertisements tended to foreground the idea of jeans as leisure wear on a more conventional or "reason-why" level with images of men playing pool or dressing down for the weekend. At the same time, in Japan, the retro association of Levi's and the 1950s was symbolized by images of James Dean.

One company that has promoted itself on a multinational basis is Benetton, and in doing so, it has transformed the way that clothing can be publicized. Under the banner "United Colors of Benetton," the company's artistic director Oliviero Toscani mobilized fashion advertising to promote historical and ideological consciousness of issues as wide as race and national identities, religion, and HIV/AIDS. Between 1985 and 1991, he juxtaposed young people of disparate ethnic origins in the hope of encouraging racial tolerance, and since that time he has manipulated existing news photographs, such as a man shot dead by the Mafia, or created politicized images, such as his photograph of blood-stained garments worn by a dead militant in the Serbo-Croat conflict, to connote a similar message of national and international harmony. Such events have little or nothing to do with Benetton per se, whose exploitative production methods have themselves been subject to moral scrutiny, and it is debatable whether they draw more attention to the company rather than raising awareness of the issues with which they purport to be concerned. Nonetheless Benetton advertising remains at the cutting edge artistically and ideologically, and not least in the way that it has encouraged other fashion advertisers to deal with the ambiguities of sexual and racial identities.

The leitmotiv of many promotions for clothing at the turn of the millennium, therefore, has been the queering of femininities and masculinities, such that the normative dynamics of spectatorial pleasure and the gaze are leitmotiv problematized (much as they had been earlier in the twentieth century in the homoerotic advertisements designed by J. C. Leyendecker for the Arrow Shirt Collar). Key examples of this kind of promotion since the 1990s include advertisements for Versace, Calvin Klein, Dolce & Gabbana, Diesel, Ben Sherman, Northwave Shoes, and Miss Sixty, all of which exploit the tension between straight and gay identities for men and women, and white and nonwhite spectators alike. At the same time, some designers like Vivienne Westwood and Yves Saint Laurent, and companies like Diesel have made post-modern intertextual references between well-known works of art or the cult of media celebrity and their own products not only to deconstruct the meaning of personal identities but also to undermine the distinction between the representation and reality of fashion itself.

See also Art and Fashion; Economics and Clothing; Fashion Magazines; Fashion and Homosexuality; Retailing.

Bibliography

Goffman, Erwin. *Gender Advertisements*. London: Macmillan, 1979.

Loeb, Lori-Anne. *Consuming Angels: Advertising and Victorian Women*. New York: Oxford University Press, 1994.
Moholy-Nagy, László. "How Photography Revolutionizes Vision." *The Listener* (November 1933): 688–690.
Mort, Frank. *Cultures of Consumption: Masculinities and Social Space in Late Twentieth-Century Britain*. London: Routledge, 1996.

Paul Jobling

FASHION AND HOMOSEXUALITY

Throughout the twentieth century, clothing has been used by lesbians and gay men as a means of expressing self-identity and of signaling to one another.

Male Cross-Dressing

Even before the twentieth century, transvestism and cross-dressing among men were associated with the act of sodomy. By the eighteenth century, many cities in Europe had developed small but secret homosexual subcultures. London's homosexual subculture was based around inns and public houses where "mollies" congregated. Many of the mollies wore women's clothing as both a form of self-identification and as a means of attracting sexual partners. They wore "gowns, petticoats, head-cloths, fine laced shoes, furbelowed scarves, and masks; [and] some had riding hoods; some were dressed like milk maids, others like shepherdesses with green hats, waistcoats, and petticoats; and others had their faces patched and painted" (Trumbach, p. 138).

Male homosexuals continued to cross-dress in both public and private spaces throughout the nineteenth century. In the 1920s, the Harlem drag balls offered a safe space for gay men (and lesbians) to cross-dress. Similarly the Arts Balls of the 1950s in London offered an opportunity denied in everyday life. Cross-dressing performers, commonly known as drag queens, used women's clothes to parody straight society and create a gay humor. One of the greatest American drag performers was Charles Pierce, who began his career in the 1950s, and was best known for his impersonations of film stars such as Bette Davis and Joan Crawford. The tradition has been carried on by gay drag performers such as American performers Divine and RuPaul and British television star Lily Savage.

Una, Lady Troubridge, 1924. The period between the two world wars saw a rise in the visibility of lesbians. This oil-on-canvas portait by artist Romaine Brooks typifies the masculinized lesbian dress of the period. Note the wing collar, monocle, and men's jacket. © Smithsonian American Art Museum, Washington, DC/Art Resource, NY. Reproduced by permission.

Effeminacy

Overt gay men, who did not want to go so far as to cross-dress, sometimes adopted the most obvious signifiers of female mannerisms and dress: plucked eyebrows, rouge, eye makeup, peroxide blond hair, high-heeled shoes, women's blouses. In America it was illegal for men (and women) to cross dress unless attending a masquerade. At least three items of clothing had to be appropriate to the gender. Adopting such an appearance was dangerous, for it was risky to be overtly homosexual. In his autobiography, *The Naked Civil Servant* (1968), Quentin Crisp recalls being stopped a number of times by police because of his effeminate appearance. However, the risks were worthwhile for many. Dressing as a "flaming queen" was a means of entering into the subculture of gay society. Also, by adopting female characteristics and by adhering to strict gendered rules of sexual behavior,

queens could attract allegedly "normal," straight sexual partners. The adoption of effeminate dress codes began to wane with the rise of gay liberation, but has continued to play a role in gay life.

Masculinity and Lesbian Dress

In the late nineteenth and early twentieth centuries, the adoption of male dress was a means for many women, including many lesbians, to protest the status of women and the roles assigned them by patriarchal societies. Cross-dressing had been and continued to be utilized by women to allow them to "pass" as men and be accepted. Some, like writer George Sand and painter Rosa Bonheur utilized the methods in order to have their professional work be taken seriously. The period between the two World Wars saw a rise in lesbian visibility. The typical masculinized lesbian dress of the period is typified by the wing collar, monocle, and man's jacket worn by Lady Una Troubridge (lover of Radclyffe Hall, author of *The Well of Loneliness*) in her portrait by Romain Brooks. In America, lesbian performers such as Ma Rainey and Gladys Bentley wore men's top hat and tails to express their identity, while bisexual film stars Greta Garbo and Marlene Dietrich wore masculine clothes both on-and offscreen.

Until the 1970s, the public image of lesbians was very much centered on masculinity. As a means of asserting difference and signaling to other lesbians, many women-loving women adopted certain "masculine" markers, such as a collar and tie or trousers. In America, it was illegal for women to dress completely in men's clothes, and they were required to wear "three pieces of women's clothing" (Nestle, p. 100). Public reaction was not sympathetic to "butch" lesbians. American lesbian writer and activist Joan Nestle "walked the streets looking so butch that straight teenagers called [her a] bulldyke" (Nestle, p. 100).

Not all lesbian women felt drawn to the adoption of male clothing, preferring instead more conventional female attire: makeup, high-heeled shoes, and skirts. Many accounts of lesbian bar life note the prevalence of "butch" and "femme" identities and behavior, where butch lesbians were expected to form relationships only with femme lesbians, and lesbians were expected to identify with one role or the other.

Subtle Signifiers

The illegality of homosexuality and the moral disapproval that it attracted forced gay men and lesbians to live virtually invisible lives in the first part of the twentieth century. Up until the gay liberation movement of the late 1960s, the most important criterion of dressing in public, for the mass of gay men and lesbians, was to be able to "pass" as heterosexual. Despite this need, many were aware of the dress codes and items that could be used to signal sexual orientation. These symbols of identity often took the form of a specific type or color of accessory and, like other secret symbols, developed and changed over time. The primary signifier at the time of the Oscar Wilde trials in the 1890s was the green carnation. Indeed, the color green had been associated with the effeminate and sometimes sodomitical macaronis of the 1770s and continued to have gay associations in clothing through the first part of the twentieth century. George Chauncey notes that in 1930s New York City, green suits were the badge of open "pansies." Other signifiers for gay men included a red necktie (worn in New York City before World War II) and suede shoes (one of the most international and enduring gay signifiers). Lesbian signifiers included accessories such as ties and cufflinks, short haircuts (particularly the "Eton crop" of the 1920s), and the color violet.

Menswear Revolution

During the "menswear revolution" of the 1960s, the association of fashion and homosexuality began to diminish. With the rise in subcultural fashions and the dissemination of Carnaby Street fashions around the world, it was suddenly acceptable for young men to be interested in fashion, and to spend time and money on clothes and appearance. Carnaby Street fashions were initially sold to a gay "theatrical and artistic" clientele by a former physique photographer by the name of Vince from a shop near Carnaby Street. John Stephen, who was later to be known as the "King of Carnaby Street," had worked at Vince's shop and produced the clothes faster, cheaper, and for a younger market. In America, too, a close-fitting "European style," worn primarily by gay men, was sold from "boutiques" in Greenwich Village, New York, and West Hollywood in Los Angeles.

Gay Men and Masculinity

By the late 1960s, lesbians and gay men throughout the Western world had begun to question their position as second-class citizens and their stereotype as effeminate "queens" or "butch dykes." Along with the demands for equality and recognition, lesbians and gay men began

to address their appearance. There had always been gay men who dressed in a conventionally masculine style, but in the early 1970s, gay men in New York and San Francisco looked to the epitomes of American masculinity—the cowboy, the lumberjack, the construction worker—for inspiration for a new dress style. The clones, as they were known, adopted the most masculine dress signifiers they could find—work boots, tight Levi's, plaid shirts, short haircuts, and moustaches. Their clothes were chosen to reveal and celebrate the contours of the male body.

Some clones also developed their sexual tastes by experimenting with sadomasochism. Consequently, they sometimes adopted a "leatherman" appearance and lifestyle, which involved a strict codification of dress and a new system of signifiers, most notably colored handkerchiefs in a back pocket, specifying particular sexual interests. The hypermasculine image has continued to be important even after the supposed death of the clone in the late 1980s, when the image became associated with an older generation of pre-AIDS gay men. Gay men have interpreted and demonstrated their masculine looks through the celebration of muscular "gym" bodies and clothing that shows off those bodies, as well as the emergence of other masculine subcultural styles such as the shaven-headed, boots and braces wearing, but not necessarily racist skinhead.

Post-Liberation Lesbian Style

The advent of both the women's and gay-rights movements led to a questioning of the stereotyped dress choices previously available to lesbians. Trousers had become increasingly acceptable for women from the 1950s, and during the 1960s it became more difficult to identify lesbians on the grounds of trouser-wearing. "Androgyny" became a key word in fashion, and this manifested itself in various ways. Initially, the move was toward a feminine look for men, but the radical lesbian and gay community rejected this in favor of a more masculine look for both men and women.

The rise of radical feminism saw a rejection of fashion-forced femininity. Flat shoes, baggy trousers, unshaved legs, and faces bare of makeup made a strong statement about not dressing for men. Radical feminist politics during the 1970s took this to an extreme as a new stereotype was born—that of the dungaree-wearing, crew-cut lesbian feminist.

The 1980s and 1990s saw a new diversification in lesbian dress. The breakdown of the old butch and femme divides, the changes instigated in women's dress by feminism and punk, and the increasing visibility in public life of lesbians opened up the debate about what lesbians could and should wear. One of the most significant developments was the appearance of the lipstick lesbian (also known as glamour or designer dyke). Dress styles signaled a move away from the traditional butch or radical-feminist styles and allowed out gay women to develop a fashionable urban look that combined signifiers of lesbianism or masculinity with fashionable women's dress. However, critics accused lipstick lesbians of hiding behind a mask of heterosexuality.

The Fashion Industry

The large proportion of gay men who have worked in creative fields of fashion and the theater and service industries, such as catering, has been well documented by historians such as Ross Higgins, whose study highlighted the involvement of gay men at all levels of the fashion industry in Montreal.

Throughout the twentieth century, many of the top couture fashion designs were gay, even though social pressure called for them to keep their sexuality quiet if not secret. Indeed, many of the greatest names in twentieth-century fashion were gay or bisexual, including such figures as Christian Dior, Cristobal Balenciaga, Yves Saint Laurent, Norman Hartnell, Halston, Rudi Gernreich (who was one of the founding members of the first American homophile organization, the Mattachine society), Calvin Klein, and Gianni Versace.

As designers took over from traditional tailors and gentleman's outfitters in men's fashion, a new gay influence became evident. Because gay men were often more willing to experiment with new ideas, styles, and fabrics in clothing, designers such as Jean-Paul Gaultier began to look at what was happening at street level and in gay clubs for ideas for their men's collections. Moreover, gay men bought clothes that were influenced by and styled toward a gay aesthetic, so their taste influenced fashion in both obvious and subtle ways.

The advent of the "new man" (as a media icon) in the 1980s was a result of men's reaction to major social changes brought about by a second wave of feminism. As a consequence, it became acceptable for straight men to be interested in their appearance, clothes, and grooming products. New magazines aimed at a wider, heterosexual male consumer were published, but even here a gay influence could be perceived. It was not just that gay designers were creating the looks, but gay stylists,

Homosexual men in cowboy clothing. In the 1970s, gay men began to look to traditional icons of masculinity for fashion inspiration, donning rugged clothing that showed off the physique. Photo by Leonard Fink, Lesbian, Gay, Bisexual & Transgender Community Center. Reproduced by permission.

hairdressers, and photographers all exerted a fashion influence. For example, stylist Ray Petri (featured in *The Face*, *i-D*, and *Arena* magazines) drew on looks that he saw in gay clubs to create a whole new style known as Buffalo. Buffalo style dressed black and white, gay and straight models in an unlikely mix of elements such as cycling shorts, flight jackets, skirts, hats, and boots.

The early 1990s saw the advent of "lesbian chic" in the fashion world. This manifested itself most visibly in a series of photographs in *Vanity Fair* in 1993, including a cover that featured lesbian singer k. d. lang cavorting with supermodel Cindy Crawford.

Today it is perfectly acceptable for straight men to be interested in fashion and to be obvious consumers of clothes, grooming products, and fashion or "lifestyle" magazines. Popular figures, such as soccer player David Beckham, are avid consumers of clothes and even acknowledge their debt to gay men's influence on fashion. In an age where homosexuality is tolerated and to a great extent accepted in major urban centers, it has become increasingly difficult to distinguish gay and straight men, and lesbians and straight women, on the basis of their dress. Acknowledging this, Elizabeth Wilson poses the following question: "Throughout the queer century we have disguised and revealed our deviant desires in dress, masquerade, disguise. Now that everyone's caught on in a postmodern world, what do we have to do to invent new [gay and] dyke style?" (Wilson, 177)

See also Fashion and Identity; Gender, Dress, and Fashion.

Bibliography

Ainley, Rosa. *What is She Like: Lesbian Identities from the 1950s to the 1990s*, London: Cassell Academic Publishing, 1995.

Blackman, Inge, and Kathryn Perry. "Skirting the Issue: Lesbian Fashion for the 1990s." *Feminist Review* 34 (Spring 1990): 67–78.

Chauncey, George. *Gay New York: Gender, Urban Culture and the Making of the Gay Male World, 1890–1940*. New York: Basic Books, 1994.

Cole, Shaun. *Don We Now Our Gay Apparel: Gay Men's Dress in the Twentieth Century*. Oxford: Berg, 2000.

Fischer, Hal. *Gay Semiotics*. San Francisco: NSF Press, 1977.

Higgins, Ross. "A la Mode: Fashioning Gay Community in Montreal." In *Consuming Fashion: Adorning the Transnational Body*. Edited by Anne Bryden and Sandra Nieman Oxford: Berg, 1998.

Levine, Martin P. *Gay Macho: The Life and Death of the Homosexual Clone*. New York and London: New York University Press, 1998.

Nestle, Joan. *A Restricted Country: Essays and Short Stories*. London: Sheba, 1988.

Schuyf, Judith. "'Trousers with Flies!': The Clothing and Subculture of Lesbians." *Textile History* 24, no. 1 (1993): 61–73.

Trumbach, Randolph. "The Birth of the Queen: Sodomy and the Emergence of Gender Equality in Modern Culture, 1660–1750." In *Hidden From History: Reclaiming the Gay and Lesbian Past*. Edited by Martin Baum Duberman, Martha Vicanus, and George Chauncey Jr. London: Penguin, 1991.

Wilson, Elizabeth. "Dyke Style or Lesbians Make an Appearance." In *Stonewall 25: The Making of the Lesbian and Gay Community in Britain*. Edited by Emma Healey and Angela Mason. London: Virago, 1994.

Shaun Cole

FASHION DESIGNER

A fashion designer is responsible for creating the specific look of individual garments—including a garment's shape, color, fabric, trimmings, and other aspects of the whole. The fashion designer begins with an idea of how a garment should look, turns that idea into a design (such as a sketch), and specifies how that design should be made into an actual piece of clothing by other workers (from patternmakers to finishers). The category of fashion designer includes people at different levels of the fashion business, from well-known couturiers, to anonymous designers working for commercial ready-to-wear houses, to stylists who might make only small modifications in existing designs. Fashion designers hold a special place in the world. Their talent and vision not only play a major role in how people look, but they have also made important contributions to the cultural and social environment.

The Origin of Fashion Designers

Charles Frederick Worth is considered the father of haute couture. An Englishman, he opened his couture house in Paris in 1846. Along with Worth, the Callot sisters, Jeanne Paquin, Jacques Doucet, and Jeanne Lanvin are considered to be among the first modern fashion designers, as compared with the dressmakers of earlier generations. Paris was the center of international fashion for more than one hundred years, with French couturiers setting the trends for Europe and the Western world. But the position of Paris as the undisputed leader of fashion was disrupted by World War II.

During that war, with Paris occupied by the Nazis, American designers and manufacturers were cut off from the fashion leadership of Paris. As a result, American designers began to receive more serious recognition. Claire McCardell, known as the creator of the "American Look," drew some of her inspiration from the vernacular clothing of industrial and rural workers as inspiration. Other American designers such as Hattie Carnegie, Vera Maxwell, Bonnie Cashin, Anne Klein, and Tina Leser had flourishing careers; they helped shape the development of sportswear that reflected the casual American lifestyle.

In the postwar economy, as fashion became big business, the role of the designer changed. Increasingly, especially in the United States, fashion designers worked closely with store buyers to identify customers' preferences and lifestyle needs. Customer demographics influenced designers to create fashions targeted to specific customer profiles. Through sales events known as "trunk shows," designers traveled to stores with their latest collection in a trunk. This simple and inexpensive marketing technique allowed customers to preview and respond to the designer's new collection, and to buy clothes. Bill Blass was one of many designers who used trunk shows to gain customers, profits, and a growing reputation.

The Role of the Fashion Designer

From the 1950s through the 1980s, the design room in the United States became the equivalent of the European atelier. With a staff of assistant designers, sketchers, patternmakers, drapers, finishers, and sample makers, American designers worked in their design rooms to create a collection each season. "First samples" were produced in the design room and later shown in a fashion show or in the company showroom. Design rooms are extremely costly to maintain and have been downsized due to the fact that most manufacturing is now done offshore. In the early 2000s, most designers work with an assistant and a technical designer to create tech packs. A tech pack contains a designer's original idea, which is then resketched by the technical designer whose responsibility is to detail all garment specifications and construction information. Tech packs are sent directly to factories in China, Hong Kong, India, or other countries where labor costs are low and where, increasingly, first samples are made and production takes place.

As the apparel industry grew, fashion schools were established to train designers and other industry professionals. Design schools in New York City include Parsons (1896) and Fashion Institute of Technology, or FIT (1944). These schools train students in specializations like children's wear, sportswear, evening wear, knitwear, intimate apparel, and activewear, for both the men's and women's market. Design schools have been established in Paris, London, Antwerp, and throughout Italy. Some American institutions have partnerships with other design schools in China, India, and elsewhere around the world.

Although designers in the twenty-first century are to some extent still responsible for creating trends, the notion of designers dictating fashion has been replaced with lifestyle designing. Each season, designers follow a process of identifying trends and searching for inspiration, researching fabrics and colors. They then focus on creating a collection that will appeal to their specific target customers' lifestyle. Although fashion trends continue to emanate from Europe, many designers look to the street for inspiration. Fashion designers, working in tandem with the film and music industries, have launched or helped popularize such fashion trends as mod, punk, grunge, hip-hop, and cholo. Fashion designers are both creators and trend trackers. Much of what they now design is a response to street styles.

With the help of marketing and advertising, designers promote themselves to the world. Some designers market their look through runway shows, as well as maintaining their own retail stores. The concept of lending their name to other licensed products is yet another vehicle to expand their brand identity. Many celebrity designers actually do very little designing of the collections that bear their name.

A major trend in the fashion business is the iconic use of sports and music idols to sell product. With the hope of increasing sales, manufacturers hire anonymous designers to create apparel bearing celebrity names. Television, the Internet, personal appearances, film, print ads, and editorial coverage used as marketing tools for fashion, have become as important, if not more so, than the clothing itself. New entrepreneurial designers rely on editorial coverage to launch collections while established companies spend millions of dollars each year on advertising, marketing, and promotion.

Mass retailers and manufacturers enlist the services of market-research firms to predict consumers' changing tastes so as to make appropriate product. Fashion designers utilize data for design purposes that is collected from focus groups and consumer behavior studies. The business of fashion has morphed into the science of fashion.

The Future of the Fashion Designer

Designers in the twenty-first century are beginning to adopt new technologies such as body-scanning for custom fit, along with seamless and whole garment knitting technologies, which can manufacture garments with the push of a button. Both are forerunners in a movement toward automation that will once again revolutionize the fashion industry. Just as the sewing machine changed the face of fashion in the past, technology will change it in the future. Designers of the future, as they have in the past, will continue to serve their customer's needs but will do so utilizing new resources and tools.

To create new product lines, designers in the future will utilize high-tech textiles, including those that possess healing, sun protection, and other unique qualities. Designing clothes in the future may have more to do with function than with fancy, in response to new consumer demands and preferences.

See also Callot Sisters; Color in Dress; Fashion Advertising; Haute Couture; Ready-to-Wear; Worth, Charles Frederick.

Bibliography

Baudot, Francois. *Fashion: The Twentieth Century.* New York: Universe Publishing, 1999.

Frings Stephens, Gini. *Fashion: From Concept to Consumer.* 7th ed. Englewood Cliffs, N.J.: Prentice-Hall, 2001.

Payne, Blanche, Jane Farrell-Beck, and Geitel Winaker. *The History of Costume.* 2nd ed. New York: Harper Collins, 1992.

Francesca Sterlacci

FASHION EDITORS

The title "fashion editor" evokes images of fashionable women, those arbiters of style and taste, who pronounce and decree what's new and what's next. They've appeared on stage and screen—from the indecisive Liza Elliot of *Lady in the Dark* ("the circus cover or the Easter cover?") to the very decisive Maggie Prescott of *Funny Face* ("Think pink!").

With the advent of the fashion magazine, the fashion editor emerged as the tastemaker in the early twentieth century. The first and most enduring of these women was Edna Woolman Chase of Conde Nast's *Vogue*, who rose from assistant in the circulation department in 1895, three years after *Vogue* was founded, to editor in chief in 1914. She remained in that venerable position until retirement in 1952. Through the 1940s and 1950s, the most visible of her fashion editors was the tasteful and talented Bettina Ballard. An earlier colleague, Carmel White (later Snow) had left *Vogue* to head Hearst's *Harper's Bazaar.* Her longtime fashion editor was a flamboyant eccentric (her outrageous column *Why Don't You . . .?* was notorious) named Diana Vreeland, who in 1963 was tapped by

Conde Nast's new owners to become editor in chief of their flagship, *Vogue.*

These grandes dames of fashion publishing were there at the creation. At first they filled their pages with news of what fashionable and wealthy women were wearing and doing. Actually, they were covering and reflecting their own worlds, as each had come from, or married into, families of wealth and society; and most of their staffers served in their low-paying but prestigious jobs as stop-offs between finishing school and marriage. Coverage of the Paris couture, the wellspring of fashion, and of the emerging American designers established these two magazines as the ultimate authorities—the innovators of fashion and fantasy.

They also discovered and encouraged such talents as Richard Avedon, Irving Penn, Martin Munkacsi, Edward Steichen, Louise Dahl-Wolfe, art director Alexey Brodovitch, Cecil Beaton, and more. The arts were covered, distinguished writers wrote for every issue, and an environment for fashion was carefully integrated.

By the mid-1950s, a new breed of editor was being sought. The competition coming from the newer, younger fashion magazines devoted to the emerging working woman, the post-war suburbanite, and the "youth market" of the sixties, brought into the editors' chairs a more pragmatic, reality-based editor. *Vogue* had tapped its merchandising editor, Jessica Daves, to succeed Mrs. Chase. Diana Vreeland followed as editor in chief, after being passed over at *Bazaar.* Those qualities ultimately did her in at *Vogue,* when she was replaced by her assistant, Grace Mirabella, a down-to-earth market-trained fashion editor. Mrs. Snow's niece, Nancy White, who'd been editor at Hearst's service magazine, *Good Housekeeping,* followed her at *Bazaar.*

Of the booming "younger" books, *Mademoiselle,* edited first by Betsy Blackwell, then Edie Raymond Locke, was the first to "merchandise" each fashion shown, informing the reader of its price and where to buy it. *Charm, Glamour,* and *Mademoiselle* mounted promotions with editors making appearances in retail stores, as the link between the editorial and advertising departments grew stronger. A fashion editor, covering her assigned market, learned to dutifully cover the advertisers' "lines." She even collaborated with designers and manufacturers, developing ideas for new looks for her readers.

Fashion was beginning to reverse itself—starting on the streets and then inspiring designers—so it was important to keep an eye on a magazine's younger staff and the streets of New York, Paris, Milan, and

Saint-Tropez to spot the trends. Paris couture (made-to-order for private customers) no longer dominated; ready-to-wear (prêt-a-porter), started in 1969 in Paris and later in Milan, was manufactured for and sold directly to American and European retailers. These collections became the trendsetters. American fashion editors sat side by side with store executives in the front rows of the overcrowded showings, their photographers jockeying for position along the runways, shooting the photos for the next issue, while space was being held until the last minute before deadline.

The fashion editor's job was to report the news, making choices from the season's offerings, whether from Europe or America; to play a major role in the selection of the photographers and models for each "portfolio," or series of pages; and often to oversee the "sitting" in the studio or the "shoot" on location. High-profile "stars" were Polly Mellen of *Vogue* and Carrie Donovan of the *New York Times*.

New media brought new opportunities, and in the 1980s Elsa Klensch, a former *Vogue* and *Harper's Bazaar* fashion editor, convinced CNN that women the world over would be eager to view the designers' collections within weeks of their showings. Her viewers numbered in the millions, but CNN canceled *Style* in 2000. Successors include *Full Frontal Fashion* and cover not just the collections but the "fashionistas" and front-row celebrities attending.

The technology of the information age has made all things possible on demand. Fashion editors can now view the collections online (not the same as being there in the tents of New York, Milan, London, and Paris); they over-see the selections for their own magazine's popular Web sites, such as *Vogue*'s Style.com.

Communicating with and serving the reader are duties of today's fashion editors, who have a whole new world of titles such as "fashion news editor," "fashion market editor," "editor-at-large," "stylist," and more. Many appear regularly on TV "what's in" and "how to" segments. They still watch the streets, but mostly they watch the New York and Los Angeles clubs, music videos, and the red carpets to spot the trends. Perhaps the first star of the 2000s is Anna Wintour of *Vogue*, who, in the tradition of earlier grandes dames, pronounces and decrees what's new and what's next.

See also Fashion Journalism; Fashion Magazines; Fashion Online; Fashion Television; Vogue; Vreeland, Diana.

Bibliography

Ballard, Bettina. *In My Fashion*. New York: David McKay, 1960.

Chase, Edna Woolman, and Ilka Chase. *Always in Vogue*. New York: Doubleday, 1954.

Esten, John, and Katherine Betts. *Diana Vreeland: The Bazaar Years*. New York: Universe Books, 2001.

Mirabella, Grace, and Judith Warner. *In and Out of Vogue*. New York: Doubleday, 1995.

Snow, Carmel, and Mary Louise Aswell. *The World of Carmel Snow*. New York: McGraw-Hill 1962.

Lenore Benson

FASHION ICONS

The term "fashion icon" has recently replaced the slightly antiquated notion of "fashion leaders." During the second half of the twentieth century, fashion became less hierarchical, more meritocratic, and media-dominated. Indeed, the media itself created its own icons of style, while scrutinizing those proffered up by journalists, stylists, and others involved in the professional process of promoting fashion. The "trickle-down," designer-led fashions of the past were joined by the concept of "bubble-up," where fashions are created on the streets and fed upward through the fashion system. "Style is not fashion until it has reached the street," is a statement popularly attributed to Coco Chanel, herself a leader; she was also part of the democratization of fashion.

The "fashion leaders" of past generations were those in the very highest society—royalty, aristocrats, and their wives and mistresses. The Bourbon courts of pre-Revolutionary France were famous for their fashion excesses, while in the 1790s Napoleon's wife, Josephine, embraced the new "Empire-line dresses," which quickly crossed the Channel. In England, at precisely the same moment in history, the Prince Regent, who gave his name to an architectural style, was consorting with the dandies of the day, including the famous Beau Brummel.

At the start of the twentieth century, magazine journalism had been enlivened by still photographs, and cinema was in its infancy. Much of the newsreel footage from the first decade of the new century showed King

Edward VII and his elegant wife, Alexandra; many of his mistresses were also fashion leaders, such as Madame Standish of Paris, who was the first to wear the new "tailor-mades" by Creed to the Paris racecourse; and Lillie Langtry, the music-hall actress, who was a favorite of the popular press. It was her amply curved figure that was the fashionable silhouette, as seen in the popular illustrations of the "Gibson Girls," created by the American, Charles Dana Gibson.

Chanel set up her fashion business before World War I and, in its aftermath, a radically altered society found her designs suited its new needs. During the War, many women had experienced the freedom of wearing trousers for manual work—and freedom of movement was Chanel's aim. She liked wearing men's sweaters and put women in soft jersey and fluid garments. She popularized costume jewelry, the little black dress—and the suntan. She was emulated in every way, and when she came back from the Riviera to display her suntan at the Opera, a new craze began.

The war annihilated a generation of young men; the women who survived wanted to forget, rather than to mourn. Economic independence and changing mores meant new fashion icons were needed for the 1920s—the "Bright Young Things" of London and the stars who personified the Jazz Age: Clara Bow, the "It Girl" of cinema; and the idol of Paris, singer Josephine Baker. In the Roaring Twenties, too, stage actresses—such as Gertrude Lawrence—were still relevant; they, too, had shingled hair, short skirts, and cigarette holders.

There was still a role for royalty—men and women were fascinated by the dress of Edward, Prince of Wales, and his Oxford bags, plus fours, and Argyle sweaters were widely copied. He even had a fabric pattern named after him—Prince-of-Wales check. His long-term mistress, Freda Dudley Ward, embodied the flapper look of the 1920s, but in the following decade he abandoned her to marry the stylish American divorcée, Wallis Simpson. It was she who formulated the fashion dictum, "A woman can never be too rich or too thin." Although the public was distressed by his abdication, they nevertheless bought mass-market copies of her Molyneux wedding dress.

Technological changes now meant that fashions could be copied at moderate prices, and, at last, ordinary women could copy their icons. This was the decade when Hollywood moguls allowed women to imitate the dresses of their favorite stars, as well as their makeup—Adrian's outfits for Joan Crawford were highly influential, and Travis Banton's dressing of Marlene Dietrich

made trousers seem sexy rather than merely functional. Joan Crawford's famous puff-sleeved dress, created by Adrian for the film *Letty Lynton* in 1932, was instantly copied, and inspired young girls' party dresses for the next ten years. Dietrich in *Morocco* (1930) was the first woman to don men's evening wear, and created a sensation when she appeared on screen in her tuxedo and top hat.

World War II meant fashion was curbed—and economic recovery was slow in the postwar period of shortages and rationing. The most famous couture collection ever was Dior's New Look of 1947, with its long skirts and nostalgic elegance—it filtered down to high-street level and was popular well into the 1950s with Hollywood costume designers. Edith Head dressed leading stars Grace Kelly, Audrey Hepburn, and the young Elizabeth Taylor in outfits inspired by the New Look.

The 1950s saw a sea change with the advent of youth-oriented fashions, linked to music and to the newly discovered and largest consumer group, the "teenagers." Economic power meant that young people wanted their own fashions and music, and their own icons. Marlon Brando created a particular look with his T-shirt in *A Streetcar Named Desire* (1951) and his leather jacket in *The Wild One* (1953). James Dean put the two together—as did Elvis Presley. The changing mood was reflected by the antifashion look of Brigitte Bardot in *And God Created Woman* (1956)—with untidy hair, short cotton dresses, and bare feet, she was the antithesis of groomed Hollywood glamour.

Jackie Kennedy presented a very different fashion picture in the early 1960s; copies of her suits, dress-and-coat outfits, and pillbox hats were very popular. But taste had changed—and fashion became, for the first time, completely youth-led, with London at the epicenter of the "youthquake." Models such as Jean Shrimpton and Twiggy, film stars like Julie Christie and, above all, musicians, were the new icons. Whether dressed in sharp suits, like the Beatles, or wearing their own eclectic mix of clothes, like Jimi Hendrix and Keith Richards of the Rolling Stones—whatever they did was picked up immediately. Designer Ossie Clark famously dressed Mick Jagger in a white tunic and trousers in 1969, and in the 1970s the male stars of "glamrock" wore makeup.

The economic difficulties of the 1970s produced the hedonism of Studio 54—where Bianca Jagger appeared, attired by Halston—and the confrontational androgyny of punk. In 1977, the Sex Pistols wore clothes designed by Vivienne Westwood—torn, provocative, and fetishistic.

JACKIE KENNEDY

Jacqueline Lee Bouvier was born into a wealthy family and raised to a life of privilege. Her 1953 marriage to Senator Jack Kennedy at the wealthy enclave of Newport, Rhode Island, was one of the most glittering social events of the decade. Mrs. Kennedy became a popular figure during the 1960 presidential campaign; after her husband's election, her beauty, love of clothes, and sense of style set her apart from her rather plain predecessors as First Lady, Bess Truman and Mamie Eisenhower. Criticized in some quarters for wearing European fashions, she patronized American designers, particularly Oleg Cassini (whose designs, however, owed much to European originals). Her inauguration outfit of a fawn-colored woolen coat with matching pillbox hat was instantly copied by thousands of women; a red dress (by Chez Ninon after a Marc Bohan for Dior original) that she wore for a televised tour of the White House became another iconic "Jackie Look."

In 1968, five years after her husband's assassination, Mrs. Kennedy married wealthy Greek shipowner Aristotle Onassis; after his death in 1975 she returned to New York City and lived there until her death in 1994. Throughout those years she dressed with elegance and style; but her time as a true fashion icon came during her brief years in "Camelot," the Kennedy White House.

In the 1980s, as economic prosperity returned, so did conventional icons, like the young Princess Diana, and more glamorous icons; the "supermodels" were dressed and lionized by Gianni Versace. Rap stars, like Run-DMC, made active sportswear fashionable; designers copied their look. In the 1990s, there was a need for less "glitzy" icons; fashion followed music into "grunge," photographers like Corinne Day created "waifs" such as Kate Moss, and sports stars became emblems of style. In 2003, there is no shortage of icons—"celebrity culture" has provided, perhaps, too many. This could mean that the notion of a "fashion icon," like that of a "fashion leader," needs to be redefined.

See also Actors and Actresses, Impact on Fashion; Celebrities; Fashion Models.

Bibliography

Bailey, David, and Peter Evans. *Goodbye Baby and Amen.* London: Conde Nast, 1969.

Beaton, Cecil. *The Glass of Fashion* London: Weidenfeld and Nicholson, 1954.

Bruzzi, Stella, and Pamela Church Gibson. *Fashion Cultures: Theories, Explorations, Analysis.* London: Routledge: 2000.

Garland, Madge. *The Changing Face of Fashion.* London: Dent and Sons, 1970.

Pamela Church Gibson

FASHION ILLUSTRATORS

Fashion illustration, although often considered quaint and recherché, cannot, in fact, be separated from the development of printing technologies and the growth of fashion journalism.

The appearance of the first costume books (records of regional and ethnic dress) in the sixteenth century, is linked, as Alice Mackrell confirms in her book, *An Illustrated History of Fashion*, to: "The invention of movable printing types by Johannes Guttenberg in Munich in 1454" (p. 14). The development of engraving techniques further propagated the distribution of fashion art, even as the computer is doing today.

The advent of fashion photography, however, has had as great an impact on fashion illustration as any printing technologies. Today, illustration exists in a symbiotic, and secondary, relationship to the lens, where once it was king.

Photography—no matter how altered or retouched—has become irrevocably equated with what is real and true. The photographic image is seen to provide a "customer service"—to show the clothes, just as the fashion plate once did. In contrast, in the twentieth century, fashion illustration has become more and more expressive, conveying an idea or an attitude, the fragrance of a look, as it were.

In some ways the predominance of photography is very logical. During a time of fashion dictatorship (through the 1950s) fashion illustration existed alongside photography as a sort of couture art form that mirrored in many ways the production, presentation, and style of the clothes. The 1960s' emphasis on youth and street influences was well suited to the immediacy of photography and its bynow iconic pioneers, like the rough-and-tumble David Bailey–type parodied in Michelangelo Antonioni's *Blow-Up*. Illustrators, in contrast, are mostly anonymous, working as they do, alone.

The all-star list of fashion artists might be topped by the seventeenth-century artists Jacques Callot (1592–1635) and Abraham Bosse (1602–1676), both of whom exploited improving engraving techniques to produce realistic details of the clothes and costumes of their times. A litany of fashion magazines appeared between the seventeenth and nineteenth centuries in France and England—among them *Le Mecure Gallant, The Lady's Magazine, La Gallerie des Modes, Le Cabinet des Modes,* and *Le Journal des dames et des modes*—all of which propelled the fashion plate to its nineteenth-century efflorescence.

The fashion plate, which captured trend-driven information as well as provided general dressmaking instruction, came into its own in the eighteenth century, flourishing, finally, in *fin de siècle* Paris. A shining example of this flowering is Horace Venet's *Incroyables et Merveilleuses,* a series of watercolor drawings by Venet of fashions under Napoleon I, engraved by Georges-Jacques Gatine as a series of fashion plates. France's position as the arbiter of fashion insured that there was a constant demand, at home and abroad, for fashion illustration. This demand was met by such talented artists as the Colin sisters and Mme. Florensa de Closménil.

The focus of nineteenth-century illustrators was on accuracy and details. They conformed to static, iconographic conventions in order to provide information and instruction to their viewers. In contrast, contemporary fashion illustration, which dates to the turn of the twentieth century, is highly graphic and focuses more on the artist's individual filter of the world. For example, Charles Dana Gibson's (1867–1944) scratchy renderings of the modern American woman, with upswept hair and shirt-waist, defined a type as well as provided a humorous, sometimes satirical, commentary on contemporary American life.

In Paris, Paul Poiret was commissioning limited edition albums by artists like Paul Iribe (1883–1935), known for his jeweled-tone palette and clean graphic line, as pure artwork. In this way Poiret aligned his new uncorseted and exotic silhouettes with the elite and exclusive world of art.

Iribe was part of a cabal of fashion illustrators who contributed to the celebrated *La gazette du bon ton,* which was published from 1912–1925 and included work by such greats as: Charles Martin (1848–1934); Eduardo Garcia Benito (1892–1953); Georges Barbier (1882–1932); Georges Lepape (1887–1971); and Umberto Brunelleschi (1879–1949). The now highly collectible plates they produced for the gazette show the influence of Japanese wood-block prints as well as the new sleek geometry of Deco styling.

Vogue and *Harper's Bazaar* magazines also kept the art of fashion illustration alive, featuring from about 1892 through the 1950s the work of fashion illustrators like Christian Berard (1902–1949), Eric [Carl Erickson] (1891–1958), Erté [Romain de Tirtoff] (1892–1990), Marcel Vértes (1895–1961), Rene Bouché (1906–1963), and René Gruau (1908–). Berard and Vértes in particular are famous for their friendships and collaborations with designers such as Coco (Gabrielle) Chanel and Elsa Schiaparelli, who also worked with fine artists like Jean Cocteau and Salvador Dalí (who illustrated several *Vogue* covers). Both Berard and Vértes had a soft line, similar to that of Andy Warhol's fashion illustrations. René Gruau, on the other hand, is famous for his work for Christian Dior. His bold calligraphic style is among the most distinguished of the first half of the twentieth century.

One illustrator dominated the century's second half: Puerto Rican-born Antonio Lopez (1943–1987). Inspired as much by the street as by experiments with art historical styles (Deco, Op, etc.) his sensual renderings of personalities from friends like Pat Cleveland and Jerry Hall to urban break-dancers, all drawn from life, had relevance and resonance even in a photographic age. "When Antonio died," says fellow illustrator Tobie Giddio, "it's as if he took illustration with him."

Indeed, in spite of the contributions of artists like Jeffrey Fulvimari, Joe Eula, Lorenzo Mattotti (1954–), Mats Gustafson (1951–), Thierry Perez, and Tony Viramontes (1960–1988), the métier was not to see a revival of any scale until the 1990s. However, *Vanity,* a short-lived illustrated magazine founded in Milan by Anna Piaggi (for which François Berthoud [1961–] illustrated most of the covers), deserves mention.

Credit for a renewed interest in illustration at the turn of the twenty-first century goes to Barneys New York for their 1993–1996 advertising campaign. Conceived of by Ronnie Cooke Newhouse, with copy by Glenn O'Brien and squiggly, indeterminate—yet bitingly satirical illustrations—by Jean-Philippe Delhomme (1959–), these bizarre advertisements stood in direct, and effective, contrast to the aesthetics of the time, especially the super-model phenomenon and the penchant for the grungy, often androgynous "heroin chic" look.

The next blip in the history of contemporary fashion illustration came via a lifestyle—not a fashion—book: Tyler Brulé's *Wallpaper*.* In *Wallpaper** illustration was considered an extension of design, and the magazine's out-sized pages were given over to such talents as Anja Kroenke, Liselotte Watkins, and the magazine's illustrative mascot of sorts, Jordi Labanda. Fashion magazines, with the notable exception of *Vogue Italia*, which often features the work of Mats Gustafson, the Swedish-born master of minimalism, continue to relegate illustration to spots—often on cooking or horoscope pages. *Vogue Nippon*, founded in 2000, also proves an exception to the rule, favoring the work of such artists as Ruben Toledo and Piet Paris.

Most recently, illustration has come into vogue through collaborations between designers and illustrators/artists. Marc Jacobs at Louis Vuitton has partnered with Julie Verhoeven and Takashi Murakami, and Stella McCartney with David Remfy.

At the turn of the twenty-first century, illustration is being revolutionized by technology—again—this time via the computer. While the late nineties saw the rise of slick computer-based drawing by such pioneers as Ed Tsuwaki, Graham Rounthwaite, Jason Brooks, and Kristian Russell, there has been a backlash in favor of work that is, or looks like it is, hand-drawn. Charles Anaste's realistic, biographical illustrations are much in demand, but so are the hyperrealist work of René Habermacher, the surreal stylings of Richard Gray, and Julie Verhoeven's erotic fashion drawings. Mixed media work is also popular, as virtual collages are made possible by new technology.

Technology's greatest impact, though, is on the actual production of artwork. What fashion illustration is, must be reconsidered. It is a strange, strange irony, too, that the fashion plate, an early form of fashion illustration, was mechanically produced and hand-colored, whereas contemporary illustration usually starts with a hand sketch and is finished—and colored—by hand. "I am curious about what is going to happen," muses Habermacher, whose work fully exploits digital processes. "In recent years," he said, "I have realized that the direction of my work is different from what you can describe as classical fashion illustration. Continuing on that road will necessarily lead to a new definition."

However difficult a definition of fashion illustration might be, its existence, and importance, is without question. The world has need of what art director Davis Schneider refers to as "visual luxuries"—illustrated fashion art.

See also Barbier, Georges; Fashion Plates; Fashion Magazines; Fashion Models; Fashion Photography; Iribe, Paul.

Bibliography

Borrelli, Laird. *Fashion Illustration Now*. London: Thames & Hudson, Inc., 2000.

Holland, Vyvyan. *Hand Coloured Fashion Plates: 1770–1889*. London: B. T. Batsford, Ltd., 1955.

Mackrell, Alice. *An Illustrated History of Fashion: 500 Years of Fashion Illustration*. New York: Quite Specific Media Group Ltd., 1997.

Packer, William. *Fashion Drawing in Vogue*. London: Thames & Hudson, Inc., 1989.

Steele, Valerie. *Paris Fashion*. New York: Oxford University Press, 1988.

Weill, Alain. *Paris Fashion: La gazette du bon ton: 1912–1925*. Paris: Bibliotèque de l'image, 2000.

Laird Borrelli

FASHION INDUSTRY

The fashion industry is unique from other fields of manufacturing in that it is ruled largely by the same intention as its end product: change.

What defines the fashion industry is largely based on the functions of the individuals who comprise it—designers, stores, factory workers, seamstresses, tailors, technically skilled embroiderers, the press, publicists, salespersons (or "garmentos"), fit models, runway models, couture models, textile manufacturers, pattern makers, and sketch artists. In simplest terms, the fashion industry could be described as the business of making clothes, but that would omit the important distinction between fashion and apparel. Apparel is functional clothing, one of humanity's basic needs, but fashion incorporates its own prejudices of style, individual taste, and cultural evolution.

The notion of fashion as solely fulfilling a need is past, as the modern apparel industry finds its purpose in the conception, production, promotion, and marketing of style on the basis of desire. It reflects the changing wants of consumers to be defined by their attire, or more commonly to be accepted, which has precipitated change throughout fashion history—from iconic silhouettes referred to in the patronizing language of the early twentieth century, the Gibson Girls and Floradora Girls, to the enlightened New Look (a term coined by

Carmel Snow, the editor of *Harper's Bazaar*, in 1947) and evolving right on through an ever-changing lexicon of haberdashery. Changing styles always necessitate change through industry, notably in the ever-specialized fields of manufacturing and merchandising, as well as through the promotion of designs and designers, expanding their scope into what are known in the early 2000s as "lifestyle brands," encompassing more than just fashion—incorporating the vernacular of fragrance, accessories, home furnishings, automobiles, jewelry, and writing instruments as well.

Even limited to the business of making clothes, its components have continually adapted to the changes of fashion and prevailing consumer demands, whether for casual clothes or formal suits, American sportswear, or celebrity-endorsed street wear. Over the decades, crinoline makers have become bra manufacturers, suit makers have adapted to the rise of separates, and textile mills have discovered the comfort of stretch. Meanwhile, new advancements in fabric development, manufacturing, and information management have become as important commodities as cotton and wool in the ever more complicated and competitive field. Throughout it all, the industry has developed classifications of pricing and style to facilitate its basic functions of designing and selling clothes along the traditional dividing line of wholesale and retail, one that has become much less distinct in recent years.

Following the traditional view of fashion's infrastructure, as referenced in the textbook *The Dynamics of Fashion*, there are four levels of the fashion industry: the primary level of textile production, including mills and yarn makers; the secondary level of designers, manufacturers, wholesalers, and vendors; the retail level, which includes all types of stores and distribution points of sale; and also a fourth level—the auxiliary level—which connects each of the other levels via the press, advertising, research agencies, consultants, and fashion forecasters who play a part in the merchandise's progression to the end consumer. While the relationship between the levels is more or less symbiotic—they need one another to survive—historically, the competitive spirit of capitalism has also created a tension between retailer and manufacturer, where the balance of power is usually tipped to one side in the race to capture profits and margins. The degree to which each side benefits financially from the sale of apparel has changed gradually over the decades, subject to many factors from social advancements to economic swings to cults of designer personalities to wars—both between countries

and conglomerates. Over the century, the retailer, in many cases, has taken on the role of the manufacturer, and manufacturers have become retailers of their own designs.

The mass production of clothing began roughly in the mid-nineteenth century, when some manufacturers began to produce garments that did not require fitting, but fashion did not become an established industry in the institution sense of the word until the twentieth century, when networks of neighborhood tailors casually evolved into manufacturing businesses, factories grew from necessity during the world wars, and the ensuing social and cultural changes signified the dawn of less restrictive and unilateral codes of dress. Changes in the business of fashion, and the establishment of designers as arbiters of taste, began to take shape in the early part of the century, although largely led by European houses. As the French designer Paul Poiret said during a presentation at the Horace Mann School in 1913, "Elegance and fashion have been the pastime of our ancestors, but now they take on the importance of a science" (quoted in *Women's Wear Daily* in its ninetieth anniversary issue, 16 July 2001).

Just as French couture houses were beginning to gain an international reputation in the late nineteenth century, following the styles introduced by Charles Worth, Jeanne Lanvin, Paquin, and Poiret, the fast rise of garment factories, meanwhile, was largely an American phenomenon. It was most visible as an industry in New York City, where more than 18,000 workers were employed in the manufacture of blouses by 1900 at the time of the founding of the International Ladies Garment Workers Union (ILGWU), a precursor to the modern-day apparel union UNITE (Union of Needletrades, Industrial and Textile Employees), formed in 1995 with the merger of the Amalgamated Clothing and Textile Workers Union. The rapid shift of custom-made to ready-made clothes during the industrial revolution was stimulated by the growth of the middle class and a large increase in foreign labor, mostly Jewish and Italian immigrants who brought their tailoring skills from Europe and first organized themselves in tenements on the Lower East Side. However, the immigrant connection and overcrowded conditions generally associated with the industry led to zoning restrictions that quickly pushed production from apartment buildings into lofts and away from increasingly sophisticated showrooms. For twenty years, manufacturers continued to migrate north and west, often driven by law, such as when the Save New York Committee campaigned to move apparel factories out of the neighborhood known as Madison Square—where Broadway and East 23rd Street converge—because of fears that the factories would be a detriment to the atmosphere of nearby Fifth Avenue, known as the Ladies' Mile.

Working conditions declined as manufacturers took advantage of the increasing pools of immigrants, influencing the rise of sweatshop labor as well as the move to unionize workers. The industry grew exponentially—by 1915, apparel was the third largest in America, after steel and oil. The Triangle Shirtwaist fire of 1911, in which 146 workers were killed, had finally led to the regulation and scrutiny of garment industry working conditions.

The industry moved again beginning in 1920, when two sites along Seventh Avenue between 36th and 38th Streets were developed by the Garment Center Realty Co., an association of thirty-eight of the largest women's clothing makers, sparking the first influx of apparel businesses in a neighborhood that has become the early twenty-first-century home to New York's garment district. Yet change is still occurring, as most production has moved offshore to factories in cheaper locales and many designers have moved their offices to more "refined" neighborhoods away from the bustle of rolling racks and button shops.

In the 1930s, though, as the unified center for garment production, and the most highly concentrated apparel manufacturing capital in the world by this point, Seventh Avenue from 30th to 42nds Streets began to reflect the need for categorization within fashion. Although the industry can broadly be divided into two primary functions—wholesale and retail—the growing prevalence of department stores necessitated further distinctions. Certain buildings, in a tradition that continues in the early 2000s, house bridal firms, and others specialize in furriers, dress vendors, or coat companies, and within those categories grew distinctions of price or targeted demographic. The modern industry divides its pricing into four general categories of moderate, better, bridge, or designer apparel, from the least to most expensive, and within those categories are even more specialized distinctions, such as the relatively new silver and gold ranges (for prices that are too high to be considered bridge or too low to be called designer). There are also categories geared toward types of customers, such as juniors (a more generic classification for sportswear in the 1960s that is used to define teen-oriented labels), contemporary (geared toward young women and relating commonly to smaller sizes),

and urban (reflecting the growing market for street wear).

For much of the twentieth century, the industry continued its evolution along familial lines, as the descendants of poor immigrants who had once operated those small factories along Orchard and Mulberry Streets on the Lower East Side began to establish serious businesses on Seventh Avenue, along with impressive fortunes behind companies with names that were for the large part inventions. Apart from the few pioneers of the first half of the century—Adrian, Bonnie Cashin, and Claire McCardell among them—the personalities behind the American fashion industry operated largely in anonymity compared with their counterparts in Paris, where Coco Chanel, Alix Grès, and Madeleine Vionnet had already become celebrities of international acclaim. Until World War II, it was common for American manufacturers to travel to the seasonal Paris shows, where they would pay a fee known as a caution to view the collections, usually with a minimum purchase of a few styles. They were legally permitted to copy these styles in the United States, where department stores began a tradition of lavishly presenting their copied collections with their own runway shows.

In the 1950s and 1960s, however, a growing number of entrepreneurial designers—many striking out in the business following their service in the war—began to make their way out of the backrooms to feature their own names on their labels, a development facilitated in part by the curiosity of the press and also by the ambitions of manufacturers to capitalize on designer personalities. Licensing a designer name into other categories became a common practice, and by the 1980s, propelled by an economic boom, designers had become celebrities—led by such ambitious and charismatic personalities as Oscar de la Renta, Bill Blass, Calvin Klein, and Halston. Meanwhile, the advent of the modern designer business stood in stark contrast to the overall industry, which remained largely characterized by independent companies, with as many as 5,000 businesses then making women's dresses, helmed by a prosperous but aging second generation. Since the 1980s, the apparel industry has come to be defined by consolidation, globalization, and the economics of publicly traded companies, where the biggest news stories have been the rush of many designers to Wall Street and the retail industry's continual merging into only a handful of remaining department store companies—giants encompassing the majority of retail nameplates.

Change continues to come. The fashion industry of the early 2000s is global, with luxury conglomerates taking stakes in American businesses and production constantly moving to countries that offer the most inexpensive labor. Garments are conceived, illustrated, and laser-cut by computers, and replenished automatically by a store's data system alerts. Designers compete directly with their biggest customers by opening flagships around the world, and stores compete with designers by sourcing and producing their own private label collections, often based on the prevailing runway looks. Magazine editors and stylists have gone on to become designers, while Hollywood actors and pop stars have gone from wearing designer clothes to creating them. At the outset of the twenty-first century, what defines the fashion industry has little to do with the artisan's craft of a century ago, but would be better described as the pursuit of profitable styles by multinational conglomerates with competitive technology and the most efficient delivery of timely merchandise.

But change in fashion—or the fashion industry—is nothing new. It seems fitting to refer to the opening line on page 1 of the first issue of *Women's Wear Daily*, which was founded as *Women's Wear* in June 1910, in response to the rise of the women's apparel industry: "There is probably no other line of human endeavor in which there is so much change as in the product that womankind wears."

See also Economics and Clothing; Fashion Education; Fashion Marketing and Merchandising; Globalization.

Bibliography

Friedman, Arthur. "New York's Lucky Seventh." *WWD Century, Women's Wear Daily Special Edition* (September 1998): 162.

——. "Garment Town's Rise to Fashion Avenue." *WWD Ninety, Women's Wear Daily Special Edition* (16 July 2001): 226.

Stone, Elaine. *The Dynamics of Fashion.* 2nd ed. New York: Fairchild Publications, 2004.

Stegemeyer, Anne. *Who's Who in Fashion.* 3rd ed. New York: Fairchild Publications, 1996.

Wilson, Eric. "The Early Years." *WWD Ninety, Women's Wear Daily Special Edition* (16 July 2001): 58–60.

Eric Wilson

FASHION JOURNALISM

Until Virginia Pope of the *New York Times* made fashion the topic of serious newspaper coverage with the attendant responsibilities for accuracy, objectivity, and fairness, the words "fashion journalism" were an oxymoron.

During her tenure at the *Times* (1925–1955), she raised the bar not only for fashion journalism, reporting on the Paris haute couture collections beginning in 1934 in addition to her regular New York coverage, she also introduced the idea of live theatrical fashion presentations, which she produced for the public each fall under the auspices of the *Times*.

Many other U.S. papers of that era ran occasional photos of the latest Paris creations and counted on their society editors to report on who-wore-what to the local charity ball. There was little or no regard for the business of fashion, its sociological implications, or news from designers.

In 1943, the New York fashion publicist Eleanor Lambert, who represented many New York designers of that era, initiated "press weeks," inviting fashion editors from newspapers throughout the country to attend capsule presentations of her clients' collections—showings that took place in New York hotel meeting rooms months after those same collections had opened to buyers in Seventh Avenue showrooms. Similar "press weeks" were held in Los Angeles, sponsored by the California Fashion Creators, a loose coalition of designers there.

The general tenor of the fashion writing in the 1940s and early 1950s was a labored accounting of skirt lengths, jacket cuts, color choices, and fabric descriptions. In 1956, Eleanor Nangle of the *Chicago Tribune*, together with fashion editors from the *Milwaukee Journal* (now the *Milwaukee Journal Sentinel*), the *Buffalo News*, and the *Fort Worth Star-Telegram* decided that fashion should be covered as sports are covered—at the time the games are played, in this case, at the time the seasonal collections opened to buyers, and not from hotel suites months later. (New York papers had "always" covered the showroom openings, but the out-of-town press had not, as few newspapers considered fashion an important enough subject to justify the expense of a week in New York.)

Lambert's press weeks continued, but more and more fashion editors from metropolitan newspapers began to attend the buyer openings and report, on the spot, from New York. And as they came, their competitors followed. A few—the *New York Times*, the *New York Times Magazine*, the *New York Herald-Tribune*, the *Chicago Tribune*, the *Washington Post*, the *Boston Globe*, the *Chicago Sun-Times*, and the *Los Angeles Times*—also reported on the Paris haute couture openings, as did the trade publication *Women's Wear Daily*.

Eugenia Sheppard, then at the *New York Herald-Tribune* and later at the *New York Post* and *Women's Wear Daily*, was one of the first to make fashion writing entertaining. She also proved her resourcefulness as a journalist by once sneaking into a Balenciaga show as a buyer in order to get immediate coverage. (Balenciaga and Hubert de Givenchy showed one month after the other couturiers and put embargos on news coverage for a month after their openings.) Her coverage got her banned from the next season's show, but she managed to cover that one, and others from which she would eventually be barred, by interviewing buyers who were in attendance. Such ingenuity also made her one of the first to be a fashion journalist celebrity.

By 1969, Paris ready-to-wear was becoming more and more important to American retailers, and newspaper fashion editors gradually started reporting on these twice-yearly events, later expanding that coverage to include Florence, Milan, and London. One editor, Nina Hyde of the *Washington Post*, made an exceptional contribution to fashion journalism by her efforts to discover new talent.

Bill Cunningham, first a columnist for *Women's Wear Daily* and later a freelance contributor to the *Chicago Tribune*, *Los Angeles Times*, and *Details* magazine, was the first fashion photojournalist to point out design copying. His photos of original designs juxtaposed with his photos of the copies left readers of *Details*, the *Los Angeles Times*, and the *Chicago Tribune* with little doubt of the design's provenance, and his witty texts became classroom examples of how to make fashion writing interesting. Cunningham's photo essays of the New York fashion scene for the *New York Times* are a weekly documentary of what real people really wear on the streets and in the social arena.

That so much fashion coverage in the 1970s, 1980s, and 1990s centered on the seasonal shows in Europe was a reflection of the Eurocentric nature of fashion at that time. The news—the trends that set the scene for the direction of fashion—was, for the most part, coming from Paris, Milan, or London. Americans were generally known as fashion marketers or stylists. Europeans, especially Paris designers, were the *créateurs*. As some have said: Americans make clothes; Europeans make fashion.

Increasingly aware that a lot of the fashion space they usually garnered was being taken by the European coverage, New York designers began to join the trend to more theatrical shows by leaving their showrooms in favor of larger hotel venues. Many upgraded their presentations from models instructed to bring their own shoes and the announcing of style numbers to buyers seated in rented-for-the-day little gold chairs to choreographed shows with music, never-seen-before, never-worn-before accessories crafted especially for the collection, hair and makeup professionals creating beauty looks, backstage booze, and, eventually, "supermodels."

In 1980, television fashion coverage, which until then had been limited to an occasional fashion "special," makeovers, and sixty seconds or so at the end of a morning show during collection openings, got its biggest boost when Elsa Klensch went on the air for CNN, her shows televised around the world. Given her international audience and her interviewing style—always respectful, never critical—Klensch was able to attract all the top designers for interviews and to gain access to their shows. For the first time, a viewer could watch the runway shows of all the major fashion players in New York, Tokyo, Paris, Milan, London, and Klensch's native Australia. *Style with Elsa Klensch* truly brought fashion to the masses. When the show was discontinued in 2000, it had an estimated 120 million viewers in 210 countries. *Edie Raymond Locke's Show* was another groundbreaking TV show from that time (1981–1986). The show was hosted by Edie Raymond Locke, who brought the magazine format she had pioneered as editor-in-chief of *Mademoiselle* magazine to USA Network. Her half-hour weekly shows concentrated on fashion, beauty, decorating, finances for women, makeovers, and model of the month. In the early 1990s, Geoffrey Beene became the first American designer to forsake the runway for the stage—first a mise-en-scène at Lincoln Center, then Broadway-type shows at the Equitable Building with elaborate stage sets, music created just for the show, and models interspersed with ballet dancers.

By 1993 the Council of Fashion Designers of America (CFDA) decided to try to compete with the European cities as a fashion capital by creating 7th on Sixth (7th on Sixth was the CFDA's way of saying Seventh Avenue—typically known as Fashion Avenue—had moved over a block to Sixth Avenue where Bryant Park is located) and producing shows under tents in Bryant Park. As the showmanship increased, fashion coverage increased, and designers attracted movie and rock stars to sit front row, some exchanging clothes for appearances. Journalists from Europe and Japan attended, providing a global audience for New York designers, a few of whom had begun to sell to European stores and open their own boutiques there. Madonna became a regular. Barbra Streisand, Whitney Houston, David Bowie, Mariah Carey, Lenny Kravitz—all brought their star power to the tents, juicing the entertainment element and thereby increasing newspaper readership and television viewers. The Bryant Park shows inspired a television show, *Full Frontal Fashion*, which went on the air with New York's Metro Channel in 1998, featuring footage taken during the shows and designer interviews, many of them with the show's founder, Judy Licht. Producer John Filimon says the object of the show, which was being broadcast on the WE channel in the early 2000s, was, and is, to make the designer the star.

During the 1980s and 1990s, most newspaper fashion editors had a laissez-faire approach to their coverage, writing about trends rather than critiquing individual collections. The exceptions, notably Eugenia Sheppard, Hebe Dorsey of the *International Herald Tribune* and her replacement Suzy Menkes, and Amy Spindler and Cathy Horyn, the first and second fashion critics at the *New York Times*, treated (and treat) the subject of fashion, especially the openings, as critics covering other fields would do—with opinions as well as facts.

The role of fashion journalism has obviously changed with the times. It also changes with the type of medium involved. Most magazine fashion editors do not write. They cover markets, making recommendations to the top editors for specific garments for specific shoots, and they style photography. The oldest fashion magazines, *Vogue* and *Harper's Bazaar*, have traditionally defined their fashion coverage not only by their audience demographics—upper-income adults—but also by their conviction that fashion begins in Europe and is homogenized in America. By encouraging American designers to "adapt" the designs of Cristóbal Balenciaga, Jacques Fath, and Christian Dior, for example, editors in the 1930s, 1940s, and 1950s discouraged design innovation in America, effectively relegating the New York designer to the backrooms of Seventh Avenue. And until the mid-1980s and 1990s, before it joined Paris, Milan, and London as a fashion capital, New York was generally considered a digester of fashion, not a feeder. The media

effect of those two magazines, plus the editorial slant of *Women's Wear Daily* during the years John Fairchild was publisher, was to place Europe at the top of the fashion chain and to convince many American designers that their role was to assimilate, not innovate.

In many respects, Fairchild revolutionized the way fashion was covered—with great irreverence. He and his staff mixed fact with opinion, encouraged controversy, baited designers, followed them, scared them, coined phrases ("the lunch bunch" was code for rich socialites), made some of them heroes and destroyed others. *WWD*, as it is known, even created a new syntax, using . . . as a way of separating thoughts instead of as an ellipse to indicate an omission.

Like magazine fashion coverage, television fashion coverage is more subject-friendly than confrontational or critical. The entertainment element is fundamental.

In many ways, the advent of television fashion coverage has influenced fashion in a way few predicted. As Malcolm McLaren was quoted as saying in the May 1995 issue of *W Magazine*: "Fashion is a television spectacle now. But at the same time, it has become voyeuristic. Because if people watch it enough, and read about it enough, to some extent they don't have to wear it. They've already consumed the idea." This raises the question: Is the widely circulated immediate coverage of the seasonal openings giving people too much advance knowledge of the season and thereby making the clothes look old by the time they reach the stores?

The Internet's biggest impact on fashion journalism in the early twenty-first century is to enable users to see images of the collections here and abroad and read capsule reviews within hours after the runway show. For manufacturers inclined to copy, this is a great service. For designers eager to see what their competition is doing, it is far more valuable than an occasional photograph in a newspaper or trade publication. For consumers eager to see for themselves what lies ahead, and thereby help them plan their seasonal purchases, it is a boon. For someone hoping to see the season synthesized and trended, it is a boondoggle. For journalists who cover the shows and for stylists who will be responsible for accessorizing the clothes with the point of view of their magazine or their advertising client, it is a quick reference for planning future stories or avoiding the seasonal clichés. For magazine editors accustomed to making their own runway sketches as notes, it is a great backup.

With the beginning of fashion on television, some, like McLaren, were concerned with its potential long-term impact on the subject. The same questions are being asked now about the Internet. Fashion can now be conveyed in a variety of ways, from print to live satellite feeds to video conferencing with designers.

The question now remains: Why does a fashion journalist have to be there—wherever *there* is—to get the story?

See also Fashion Advertising; Fashion Designer; Fashion Magazines; Fashion Models; Fashion Online; Fashion Shows; Fashion Television.

Bibliography

Wood, Dana. "Modus McClaren." *W* (May 1995): 49.

Marylou Luther

FASHION MARKETING AND MERCHANDISING

The goal of fashion marketing and merchandising, for both manufacturers and retailers, is to sell merchandise at a profit. This requires careful planning and coordination.

In ancient times, people "shopped" in open-air markets and bazaars, finding not only necessities but also products that were unique and gave excitement to their everyday lives. Today, we shop and buy in much the same way, but open-air markets and bazaars have evolved into department and specialty stores, discount outlets, and huge malls that continue to excite and entice the shopper. The difference is that fashion marketing and fashion merchandising are now the watchwords of successful fashion businesses. In the early twenty-first century, the customer has become the most important ingredient in successful fashion retailing. Determining the needs and wants of the targeted customer has become very important, and this challenge has led to the creation of specific goods and stores for specific categories of customers.

For many years, fashion producers were concerned only with what was economical and easy for them to produce. They would spend considerable time and money trying to convince the consumer that what they produced was what the consumer wanted. The fashion producer had little or no interest in the needs and wants of the consumer. However, marketing proved so successful in the growth of consumer goods such as automobiles, packaged foods, and health and beauty aids that it was eventually adopted by the fashion businesses. Under the classic definition of marketing, the key task of the organization is to determine the needs and wants of target markets and adapt the organization to deliver the desired satisfactions more effectively and efficiently to the ultimate customer.

Through the use of sophisticated marketing techniques such as focus groups, surveys, data mining, and market segmentation along with systematic approaches such as electronic data information (EDI), inventory tracking, and constant evaluation of advertising results for determining consumer tastes, the industry's awareness of the importance of pleasing the target customer has greatly increased. Every step—design, production, distribution, promotion—is geared to consumer demand.

"Fashion marketing" includes all of the activities involved from conceiving a product to directing the flow of goods from producer to the ultimate customer. Activities of marketing include product development, pricing, promotion, and distribution. If a fashion retailer or manufacturer is to make a profit, the firm must have a product that consumers perceive as desirable, and the product must be presented to potential customers in a way that makes them want to buy it.

The first step in a fashion marketing approach is to define the company's target customers, those persons the company most wants to attract as customers. Fashion marketers determine their target customer's needs and wants by examining various market segments, identified by geographics, demographics, psychographics, and behavioral studies. Fashion marketers also track trends in population growth and diversity. Changing patterns of immigration bring with them new influences from different parts of the world. Products that will meet the needs and desires of these customers are then developed or selected. Most fashion manufacturers and retailers recognize that following a consumer-marketing approach leads to a profitable business.

"Fashion merchandising" is defined as the buying and selling of goods for the purpose of making a profit. Merchandising is the planning involved in marketing the *right* merchandise at the *right* price at the *right* time in the *right* place and in the *right* quantities. Commonly known as the 5Rs, merchandising is concerned with all the activities necessary to provide customers with the merchandise they want to buy, when and where they want to buy it, and at prices they can afford and are willing to pay. This includes making buying plans, understanding the customer, selecting the merchandise, and promoting and selling the goods to the consumer.

Fashion merchandising is practiced by both manufacturers and retailers. For manufacturers, merchandising begins with estimating consumer demand in terms of styles, sizes, colors, quantity, and price. Merchandising also involves designing the goods and selecting the fabrics and findings, designing the packaging, pricing, advertising, and other sales promotion activities.

For fashion retailers, merchandising also begins with forecasting the needs and wants of their target customer. The retailer must first project sales in terms of dollars and units of merchandise. Just as the manufacturer must anticipate the needs of the retailer, the retailer must also anticipate the needs of the consumer by reviewing past sales, keeping up on trends, and knowing where on the fashion cycle their customer falls. The retailer must also know what colors, sizes, styles, and prices of merchandise that their target customers want to purchase. After planning what and how much to buy, merchandising for the fashion retailer includes determining resources from which to purchase, selecting from their assortments, and purchasing the goods for sale to the consumer. Another factor of merchandising is presenting the merchandise attractively and effectively to the consumer and promoting the merchandise so that the target customer will want to buy it.

In the early 2000s, technology has been a major factor in helping fashion manufacturers and retailers to successfully satisfy the needs and wants of the targeted customer, with body scanning being just one example. Body scanning software customizes patterns for an individual's body. This results in the kind of fit previously available only to couture customers. As technology continues to improve and become less costly, scanning of the entire body will become more common, resulting in the kind of fit previously available only in expensive made-to-measure fashion products.

The development of fashion marketing and merchandising as distinct professions with their own expertise, insights, and techniques, has made them the cornerstone of the modern world of fashion. The use of sophisticated marketing and merchandising methods and techniques has given rise to some of the most exciting and innovative strategies: among them are entertainment-oriented shopping malls, themed environments, designer and manufacturer retail flagship stores, brands, off-site retailing and e-tailing and packaging, now viewed as the science of temptation.

Fashion marketing and merchandising present a unique problem because of the ever-changing nature of fashion and the difficulty of predicting consumer demand. The fashion world is famous for its fast-moving, do-or-die success or failure rate. With a need to respond quickly to consumer purchasing, sophisticated processes are required for quick decision making that will support the fashion marketers and merchandisers in satisfying the customer.

See also Fashion Industry; Retailing.

Bibliography

Harris, Louis. *Merchant Princes*. New York: Harper and Row, 1979.

Kotler, Philip, and Gary Armstrong. *Principles of Marketing*. 9th ed. Upper Saddle River, N.J.: Prentice Hall, 2001.

Stone, Elaine. *The Dynamics of Fashion*. New York: Fairchild Publications, 2004.

Traub, Marvin. *The Bloomingdales' Legend and the Revolution of American Marketing*. New York: Random House, 1993.

Elaine Stone

FASHION MODELS

In the nineteenth century, the first living mannequins, or "manikins," took their name from the static dummy or lay figure they were soon to replace as the principal form of display in the dress-maker's salon. While the word "mannequin"—in French, *le mannequin*—described the woman, the word "model"—*le modèle*—designated the gown she exhibited in the salon. The model gown was a one-off that did not go into production; it was thus both an exclusive dress for sale to an individual client, and a prototype (hence the term model) sold to a fashion buyer for adaptation to the mass market. Both model gowns and model women were at the heart of the commercial development of the French couture industry and its global markets, and there was always some confusion in the terminology. The dual meaning of the word "model" also signals the ambivalent status of the earliest fashion models, hovering uneasily between subject- and object-hood. They invoked both admiration and disapproval, disconcerting their critics precisely because they wore fashionable dress in public for money rather than for its own sake.

Origins

Charles Frederick Worth is generally thought to be the first couturier to use live models. However, many nineteenth-century dressmakers had a young woman available to put on a dress for a client, although their primary mode of display was a wooden or wicker dummy. Indeed, Worth met his future wife, Marie, while she was employed to model shawls to customers on the shop floor of their mutual employer, the mercer Gagelin et Opigez. The couple set up their first *maison de couture* in 1858, and Marie modeled in the Worth salons until the 1870s, after which she remained responsible for training the house mannequins. Maison Worth's real innovation was thus to institutionalize the profession within the increasingly bureaucratic structure of a couture house, having several trained house mannequins, rather than using the occasional *petit main*, or seamstress, as a model.

The Early Twentieth Century

Lady Duff Gordon, trading as Lucile, claimed to have started the first mannequin parades in London in the late 1890s. She trained her mannequins in carriage and deportment and gave them stage names such as Hebe, Gamela, and Dolores. Often six feet tall, they struck dramatic poses during the parades but barely smiled and never spoke. When Lucile opened in New York in 1910 and then Paris in 1911, she took with her four of her London mannequins whose glamour was widely reported in the press of both continents. Dolores later joined the Ziegfeld Follies, and there are many parallels between the fashion model and the chorus girl.

In the same period, fashion magazines began to use photography alongside fashion illustrations, but the women in these photographs were often actresses and, later, society women, rather than professional mannequins, and, with some notable exceptions, the two career paths—photographic and catwalk models—remained separate until well into the 1960s.

Catwalk modeling was always a specialist option. Mannequins were full-time employees of the house and sometimes even lived in. In Paris, both Paquin and

Poiret were in the vanguard in showing their fashions on live mannequins, but between 1900 and 1910 most couture houses had their *cabine*, or studio, of mannequins. Although poorly paid and barely respectable, they were also considered exceptionally glamorous. From behind the scenes, they would be summoned several times a day to model gowns for private customers and professional buyers alike, under the direction of the *vendeuse*. Until approximately 1907, they wore a high-necked and long-sleeved black satin sheath, or *fourrure*, beneath the luxury gowns; although generally believed to designate their lack of respectability, the *fourrure* must also have facilitated the rapid costume changes required.

The appearance of three paid mannequins with an unnamed couturier at the Auteil racecourse in 1908 caused outrage, but the practice rapidly became common. In 1910, Poiret made a film of a mannequin parade, and in 1911 he toured Europe with a troupe of uniformed mannequins. In 1913, both he and Paquin undertook mannequin tours of the United States; in one town, the host department store responded to Paquin's mannequins with a matching parade of American male mannequins. Department stores in the United States were, if anything, ahead of Parisian couturiers in pioneering the use of models in dramatic fashion shows. In 1924, Jean Patou traveled to New York to recruit six American mannequins to model in Paris for his American customers whose physique, he claimed, was longer and leaner than that of the "rounded French Venus." Paquin, Poiret, and Patou understood the importance of showing on live models in the marketing of modern fashion. All were able to harness innovative publicity techniques to the early twentieth-century desire to see fashion in motion.

The Mid-Twentieth Century

John Powers opened the first American model agency in 1923; the Ford modeling agency was founded in 1946. By contrast, the first French model agency opened only in 1959, perhaps because French fashion houses had always employed their own models. In New York in the 1920s, there was also a mannequins' school dedicated to teaching fashion modeling techniques.

By the 1920s, fashion journalists were beginning to report not only on the seasonal fashions, but equally on individual mannequins from the Paris "openings." Captain Molyneux's principal mannequin, Sumurun (Vera Ashby), was well known; in the 1930s, the in-house mannequins of the London department store Selfridges were popular figures, while Schiaparelli's mannequin Lud was reputed to be married to a lion-tamer.

After World War II, the profession of model acquired some respectability, perhaps due to cinematic representations of models in films such as *Cover Girl* (1944), *Funny Face* (1957), and *Blowup* (1966). The social status of models improved as several married into the aristocracy.

Modeling styles changed. From the early twentieth-century the mannequin had been required to move sedately in the salon, notwithstanding the risqué connotations of Lucile's "goddesses" and Poiret's undulating mannequins. By contrast, when, in 1947, Christian Dior showed his "New Look," he encouraged his models to do theatrical turns, knocking over ashtrays in the audience as their coats swung round. However, in general modeling styles remained staid and the 1950s' model was required to look haughty and disdainful. Paris fashion houses maintained a *cabine* of fourteen to eighteen models, and there tended to be a "house style" of modeling, although each model was a different physical type to represent the range of clients' looks. It was therefore, revolutionary when, in the late 1950s, the British designer Mary Quant first showed on photographic mannequins who danced frenetically to jazz music and then froze in graphic, static poses on the catwalk.

The 1960s to the Early 2000s

Quant laid the path for the innovations of the 1960s when the development of ready-to-wear required a different kind of presentation. Now models were required to dance, act, and clown on the catwalk. In Courrèges's futurist collection of 1965, grinning models danced in experimental kinetic movement to *musique concrète*. Marie Helvin recalled that haute couture modeling in the 1960s and 1970s was about contact with hand-made, one-off clothes, whereas showstopping modeling techniques, photogenic beauty, and the showgirl instinct were the prerequisites of the ready-to-wear show.

Until then, models had been poorly paid, but their compensation went rocketing up in this period; top models could command $1,000 for a one-hour show in Milan and even a little more for one in Paris. The strict separation between house mannequins and photographic models began to be eroded and the proliferation of media images of the young, beautiful, and fashionable in the 1960s ensured that photographic

models like Jean Shrimpton ("the Shrimp") and Twiggy became iconic figures of their times.

The rise of the supermodel in the early 1990s was followed by a fashion for more waiflike models with slighter frames and quirkier looks. Their salaries, however, did not shrink correspondingly. By the end of the twentieth century, models were firmly established as the new celebrities. Feted in gossip columns and highly compensated, they were far removed from their early twentieth-century predecessors with their dubious status and poor pay. Nevertheless, and despite the high visibility of the black model Naomi Campbell, models of color continue to be underrepresented in the industry at the beginning of the twenty-first century.

See also Mannequins; Patou, Jean; Quant, Mary; Twiggy; Worth, Charles Frederick.

Bibliography

Ballard, Bettina. *In My Fashion*. London: Secker and Warburg; New York: David McKay Company, 1960.

Balmain, Pierre. *My Years and Seasons*. Translated by Edward Lanchberry with Gordon Young. London: Cassell, 1964.

Bertin, Célia. *Paris à la Mode*. Translated by Marjorie Deans, London: V. Gollancz, 1956.

Castle, Charles. *Model Girl*. Newton Abott, U.K.: David and Charles, 1977.

De Marly, Diana. *Worth: Father of Haute Couture*. London: Elm Tree Books, 1980.

Evans, Caroline. "Living Dolls: Mannequins, Models and Modernity." In *The Body Politic*. Edited by Julian Stair, 103–116. London: Crafts Council, 2000.

——. "The Enchanted Spectacle." *Fashion Theory* 5, no. 3 (2001): 271–310.

Etherington-Smith, Meredith, and Jeremy Pilcher. *The "It" Girls*. London: Hamish Hamilton, 1986.

Gordon, Lucy Wallace Duff, Lady. *Discretions and Indiscretions*. London: Jarrolds, 1932.

Gross, Michael. *Model: The Ugly Business of Beautiful Women*. London and New York: Bantam, 1995.

Helvin, Marie. *Catwalk*. London: Pavilion Books, 1985.

Kaplan, Joel H., and Sheila Stowell. *Theatre and Fashion: From Oscar Wilde to the Suffragettes*. Cambridge, U.K.: Cambridge University Press, 1994.

Keenan, Bridget. *The Women We Wanted to Look Like*. London: Macmillan, 1977.

Leach, William. *Land of Desire: Merchants, Power, and the Rise of a New American Culture*. New York: Vintage Books, 1994.

Liaut, Jean-Noël. *Cover Girls and Supermodels 1945–1965*. Translated by Robin Buss. London and New York: Marion Boyars, 1996.

Poiret, Paul. *My First Fifty Years*. Translated by Stephen Hayden Guest. London: V. Gollancz, 1931.

Seebohm, Caroline. *The Man Who Was Vogue: The Life and Times of Condé Nast*. London: Weidenfeld and Nicolson, 1982.

Caroline Evans

FASHION PHOTOGRAPHY

A fashion photograph is, simply, a photograph made specifically to show (or, in some cases, to allude to) clothing or accessories, usually with the intent of documenting or selling the fashion. Photographs of fashionable dress, in existence since the invention of photography in 1839, are not fashion photography. The distinguishing feature—and the common denominator in the enormous diversity of style, approach, and content—is the fashion photograph's intent to convey fashion or a "fashionable" lifestyle. At the end of the twentieth century, the Calvin Klein advertisement featuring only Calvin's portrait changed the very definition of a fashion photograph from a picture of the featured clothing to the selling of a glamorous lifestyle identified with a specific logo.

Fashion photography has sometimes been called ephemeral, commercial, and frivolous, and its importance has been called into question. That fashion photography has a commercial intent implies to some that it lacks photographic and artistic integrity. In reality, it has produced some of the most creative, interesting, and socially revealing documents and revealed the attitudes, conventions, aspirations, and taste of the time. It also reflects women's image of themselves, including their dreams and desires, self-image, values, sexuality, and interests.

The psychology behind a fashion photograph as a selling device is the viewer's willingness to believe in it. No matter how artificial the setting, a fashion photograph must persuade individuals that if they wear these clothes, use this product, or accessorize in such a way, the reality of the photograph will be theirs. The fashion photograph can offer a vision of a certain lifestyle (from glamorous to grunge), sex, or social acceptance (via the most current, the most expensive, or the most highly unattainable), but it is the viewer's buy-in that makes the photograph successful.

Early Fashion Photography

The earliest fashion photographs were made, probably in the 1850s and 1860s, to document fashion for Parisian fashion houses. Reproduction in fashion journals occurred much later, between 1881 (with the invention of the halftone printing process by Frederic Eugene Ives) and 1886 (when the refinement of the process made it financially practicable). This breakthrough made it possible to reproduce photographs and sell to a large audience through the medium of the printed page.

In the late nineteenth and early twentieth centuries, distinctions between fashion photography, portraiture, and theater photography were often blurred. The idea of using professional models was initially considered shocking, and it thus became fashionable in the early years of the century for society celebrities, such as Gertrude Vanderbilt Whitney, to model. The result was that fashion photographs were strikingly similar to society portraits. The idea of using an actress such as Sarah Bernhardt is not unlike the vogue in the early 2000s for using Gwyneth Paltrow or Madonna or the tennis stars Venus and Serena Williams to model current fashion.

That nineteenth-century fashion photography did not exist is a misconception. Many believe that Americans were first in this field, perhaps based on Edward Steichen's claim that he was the first fashion photographer. This has obscured the contributions of such important Parisian fashion photographers as Maison Reutlinger, Talbot, Felix, Henri Manuel, and Boissonnas et Taponnier as early as 1881. They worked in the studio, but charming outdoor fashion photography was also shot on the Parisian boulevards and at the races by the Seeberger Frères in the first decade of the twentieth century.

American Fashion Photography, 1900–1930

The first important American photographer of fashion was European-born Baron Adolf de Meyer, who had entered fashionable London society through his marriage to Donna Olga Alberta Caracciolo (the daughter of the duchess of Castelluccio and reputed to be the illegitimate daughter of King Edward VII) and was knighted by the king of Saxony. De Meyer changed fashion photography by disintegrating form and bathing his pictures in a limpid atmosphere and shimmering light, creating what *Vogue* in 1914 termed "artistic" photography. This approach changed the idea of what a fashion photograph should be, from an exacting depiction of a garment's detail to an evocation of mood.

In 1924, Edward Steichen replaced the soft-focus effects of de Meyer's style with the clean geometric lines of photographic modernism. Steichen rejected the rococo backdrops used by de Meyer in favor of unadorned, sleek settings and showed modern woman in the sports clothes that reflected a new, liberated sense of herself and her freedom from the corset. Many of Steichen's most important photographs featured his signature model Marion Morehouse, who epitomized the look of the "contemporary" woman, the flapper. Other important photographers who benefited from and were influenced by Steichen's innovations were George Hoyningen-Huene, known for his extraordinary use of

Photograph of model at Lincoln Memorial. The true fashion photograph is not one that simply records a clothing design, but one that conveys a desirable lifestyle suggested by that design. PHOTOGRAPH BY TONY TINSELL. THE LIBRARY OF CONGRESS. REPRODUCED BY PERMISSION.

negative space and passion for the Greek ideal, and his student Horst P. Horst, who used theatrical lighting and trompe l'oeil effects to great advantage.

Realism and Surrealism

Another startling change—and one that would have profound impact on future fashion photography—was the 1933 introduction of out-of-door realism by the Hungarian sports photographer Martin Munkacsi. Munkacsi's *Harper's Bazaar* photograph of the model Lucile Brokaw running down the beach—blurred, in motion, and possessing the naturalness of amateur snapshots—changed the course of fashion photography. The spontaneity was revolutionary, particularly when contrasted to Steichen's posed and static style that preceded it. Realistic fashion photography offered the modern woman a vision that she could apply to her own life. Munkacsi's snapshotlike realism influenced a long line of photographers, including Toni Frissell, Herman Landshoff, and Richard Avedon.

The artistic ferment of Paris in the 1930s, particularly the fantastic, mysterious, and dreamlike aspects of surrealism, had a profound influence on fashion photography. The painter and photographer Man Ray produced fashion photography as a way of earning money that enabled him to pursue "serious" painting and experimental photography. He was able to chart a new direction for fashion photography because he disregarded the conventions of fashion depiction, instead producing elongations, double exposures, and a "fashion rayograph" that simulated what a fashion would look like when radioed from Paris to New York. Other fashion photographers who incorporated surrealist-influenced ideas in their work were Peter Rose-Pulham, André Durst, George Platt Lynes, and Cecil Beaton.

Constant experimentation and technical virtuosity marks the fashion work of Erwin Blumenfeld, who used solarization, overprinting, combinations of negative and positive images, sandwiching of color transparencies, and even drying the wet negatives in the refrigerator, resulting in crystallization, to achieve his extraordinary effects. Also important in the 1930s was the appearance of Kodachrome, which arrived on the market in 1935. Louise Dahl-Wolfe was one of the first and most important practitioners of color in fashion photography, creating striking photographs of American fashion with the new color technology.

Fashion Photography after World War II

Fashion photography was severely affected at the outbreak of World War II in 1939, not only because of the lack of materials, models, and safe locations, but also because of a demoralization in attitude toward the medium: because fashion was seen as a frivolous and unnecessary form of luxury, fashion magazines stressed women's role in the war, rationalized fashion as morale building, published war reports instead of society columns, and featured the tailored, plain, and often drab clothing more suitable for a world subjected to daily reports of death and destruction. Studio photography with its complicated props and setups was almost eliminated. In general, photographers such as Lee Miller in Paris and Cecil Beaton in London turned to a straightforward documentary approach. Louise Dahl-Wolfe produced some of the most important American fashion photography of the 1940s using a clear, straightforward style.

With the end of the war, New York replaced Paris as the mecca of fashion photography. America's fashion design and ready-to-wear industry achieved its first international success in the postwar period. The time was thus ripe for the emergence of two young American talents who would dominate fashion photography for many years to come: Richard Avedon and Irving Penn.

The charming ease of Richard Avedon's fashion style of the 1950s was perfectly suited to a war-weary society. In this decade, Avedon staged his models as glamorous but "real" girls whose carefree exuberance was both sophisticated and appealing. Each was an actress of sorts, creating both a fashion look and a dialogue of emotions. By the 1960s, Avedon's fashion work had moved from the outdoor locations and softly beautiful natural light of this early work to his signature style of models running and jumping across a plain white background, illuminated with the harsh, raking light of the strobe.

The other major fashion leader whose work started in the 1940s is Irving Penn. Penn's work has no rival in terms of formal complexity, in the rich beauty of constructed shape, elegance of silhouette, and abstract interplay of line and volume. Compared with the white-hot moment of immediacy of Avedon's photographs, Penn's work aimed at the values of monumentality, formal clarity, and quiet truth. Perhaps his most extraordinary shots are those done in collaboration with his wife, the model Lisa Fonssagrives-Penn.

Both Avedon and Penn have each sustained careers over a period of five decades, a record of remarkable range and consistency. Avedon's ability to take inventive risks and his creative inspiration, with its kaleidoscope of techniques and ideas, are unequaled in the field of fashion photography. He always captures the "look" of the moment, in part because of his choice of the model who best epitomizes the time, from Dorian Leigh, Dovima, and Suzy Parker to Verushka, Twiggy, Jean Shrimpton, Brooke Shields, and Nastassja Kinski.

Fashion Photography in the 1960s

Fashion photography in the 1960s yielded to more socially oriented and exotic themes. In part this was due to the fact that fashion design began to show the influence of many diverse sources, from peasant and "street" styles to the women's liberation movement, the space program, and pop art. There was a break with convention, both in social mores and fashion itself: outrageous, seemingly unwearable outfits were designed, models reflected a new diversity of "look" and race, and fashion was redefined toward a defiant market dominated by the youth culture.

The 1960s was also a time when certain fashion photographers, including Bert Stern and David Bailey, enjoyed high-voltage lifestyles, skyrocketing fees, and lavish studio setups. At the opposite extreme, the influence of Penn and Avedon continued to attract serious young photographers from the world over to New York. Yasuhiro Wakabayashi, known professionally as Hiro, developed a monumental, clear, and memorably vivid style while Bob Richardson's work flirted with social concerns such as lesbianism. Other photographers working in the field of fashion in the 1960s included William Klein, Art Kane, and Diane Arbus, whose photography for the *New York Times Magazine* was among the most disturbing and uncharacteristic children's fashion images ever published.

Fashion Photography in the 1970s

In the 1970s, the tide again turned: Diana Vreeland resigned from her influential reign as editor-in-chief of *Vogue*, and in January 1977, American *Vogue* reduced the actual trim size of the publication. Meanwhile, French *Vogue* took the creative lead in fashion photography in this decade and offered their two leading photographers, Helmut Newton and Guy Bourdin, complete creative autonomy. Deborah Turbeville produced work that reflected psychological dislocation in the modern world, in part through her slouching and stylized poses. She was the first to use overweight and "ugly" models, pioneering a more diverse standard of model. Her "bathhouse" photographs published in *Vogue* (May 1975) created a furor by evoking the grisly aura of a concentration camp or the frightening vacuousness of drugged stupor.

Fashion Photography in the 1980s

Some of the most important editorial and advertising fashion photography of the 1980s continued to be done by Richard Avedon. His brilliant advertising campaign "The Diors," a story spun weekly in the pages of the *New York Times Magazine*, created the enduring vogue for narrative in fashion photography. Avedon's shot of Nastassja Kinski, her nude form sensuously entwined with a gigantic snake, has become a classic. Women's strength and independence was emphasized, from sporty and athletic to domineering and brutalizing. Numerous photographers, including Denis Piel, Bruce Weber, and Bert Stern pictured women threatening men with everything from pocketbooks to knives and chains. Fashion itself, particularly in the work of such designers as Jean Paul Gaultier, Azzedine Alaïa, and Issey Miyake (whose work was notably photographed by Penn), helped form the look of the decade's photography

Fashion Photography in the 1990s

In the last decade of the century, Herb Ritts, Steven Meisel, and Bruce Weber continued to produce some of the most interesting and innovative work, including Weber's hilarious hip-hop version of a black Snow White and the Seven Dwarfs and his seminal spread dealing with the impact of grunge on fashion in the 1990s (including the first post-punk nose ring in a *Vogue* fashion spread). Two of the greats of fashion photography, Irving Penn and Helmut Newton, continued to dominate the field. Ellen von Unwerth's romantic individualism and Sheila Metzner's spare but sumptuous style were also widely evident. Models were increasingly racially diverse, with a number of black models, such as Iman, Naomi Campbell, and Karen Alexander, achieving the status of celebrity superstars. As to the early years of the twenty-first century, one must await the knowledge of hindsight to assess the importance of very recent fashion photography as well as the development of such young talents as Christophe Kutner, Glen Luchford, Javier Vallhonrat, and Craig McDean. What

seems certain is that fashion photography—whether published in *Vogue*, *W*, *Dazed and Confused*, or *Sleaze Nation*—will continue to reflect the society and the times in which it was made.

See also Actors and Actresses, Impact on Fashion; Art and Fashion; Avedon, Richard; Beaton, Cecil; Hartnell, Norman; Hoyningen-Heune, George; Newton, Helmut.

Bibliography

Brooke-Adler, Isabel. "Baron von Meyer." *Art Journal* (1899): 270–272.

Chase, Edna Woolman, and Ilka Chase. *Always in Vogue*. Garden City, N.Y.: Doubleday and Company, 1954.

Edwards, Owen. "Blow-Out: The Decline and Fall of the Fashion Photographer." *New York* 6, no. 22 (28 May 1973): 49–56.

Ewing, William A., and Nancy Hall-Duncan. *Horst*. New York: International Center of Photography, 1984.

Frenzel, H. K. *Hoyningen-Huené: Meisterbildenisse*. Berlin: Verlag Dietrich Reineer, 1932.

Garner, Philippe, and David Alan Mellor. *Cecil Beaton, 1920–1970*. New York: Stuart, Tabori and Chang, 1995.

Goldberg, Vicki, and Nan Richardson. *Louise Dahl-Wolfe*. Foreword by Dorothy Twining Globus. New York: Harry N. Abrams, 2000.

Hall-Duncan, Nancy. *The History of Fashion Photography*. New York: Alpine Press, 1978.

Harrison, Martin. *Appearance: Fashion Photography since 1945*. New York: Rizzoli International, 1991.

Hayden-Guest, Anthony. "The Return of Guy Bourdin." *New Yorker* 70, no. 36 (7 November 1994): 13–46.

Kramer, Hilton. "The Dubious Art of Fashion Photography." *New York Times*, 28 December 1975.

Lehmann, Ulrich. *ChicClicks: Creativity and Commerce in Contemporary Fashion Photography*. Boston: The Institute of Contemporary Art in collaboration with Hatje Cantz Publishers, 2002.

Liberman, Alexander. *The Art and Technique of Color Photography: A Treasury of Color Photographs by the Staff Photographers of Vogue, House and Garden, and Glamour*. New York: Simon and Schuster, 1951.

Ray, Man. *Self-Portrait: Man Ray*. London: Andre Deutsch, 1963.

Sargeant, Winthrop. "Profiles: Richard Avedon." *New Yorker* 34 (8 November 1958): 49–50.

Steichen, Edward. *A Life in Photography*. New York: Doubleday and Company, 1963.

Thornton, Gene. "Turbeville Gives Fashion a Torture Treatment." *New York Times*, 24 January 1977.

Nancy Hall-Duncan

FASHION PLATES

Fashion plates are small printed images, often hand-colored, of people wearing the latest fashions and depicted in conventional minimally narrative social contexts. They flourished from the late eighteenth to the early twentieth centuries, and were usually distributed with fashion magazines either as integral parts of the editorial content or as supplementary plates. The poet Charles Beaudelaire, in his essay *The Painter of Modern Life*, described fashion plates as an image of the "ideal self" and thus a reflection of the artistic, historical, moral, and aesthetic feeling of their time. He wrote in 1863, when fashion plates were reaching a peak in their development. Although the basic purpose of the fashion plate was to illustrate new styles and sell more clothes, their charm gives them an established place among the minor graphic arts. Sadly for the student, fashion plates are often removed from the magazines in which they appeared and sold as collectors' pieces; divorced from their original context they lose much value as historic sources.

Origins

People attractively or unusually dressed have been popular graphic subjects at least since the sixteenth century, when the *Costume Book* or *Trachtenbuch* brought them into popular publishing. By the middle of the seventeenth century, the graphic artist Vaclav Hollar had given such illustrations new artistic status and Bosse, Callot, and de Hooghe began to group their fashionables in suitable settings.

Not until the last quarter of the seventeenth century did the series of popular prints (usually termed *Les Modes*) of fashions and fashionable people appear. Published by the Paris print sellers, the Bonnarts, with plates by Saint Aubin, Bérain, and Arnoult, they promoted French taste to a wide international market. Nevertheless, such illustrations did not take on a commercial role as advertisements until Jean Donneau de Vizé introduced them into the *Mercure Extraordinaire*

and the *Mercure Galant* of 1678 and 1681, noting suppliers as well as garments.

The Eighteenth Century

Thereafter the fashion plate fell into disuse until the 1750s, reappearing in ladies pocketbooks, diaries, almanacs, and magazines. Occasionally credited to dressmakers, they were popular as fashion guides. The small monochrome plates were often by well-known artists and engravers.

By the last quarter of the eighteenth century, the ending of French Guild restrictions in 1777 made fashionable clothing available to many more consumers, and so opened the market to a flood of illustrated fashion material. The best known, an anthology of some 200 to 400 colored fashion plates compiled from several sources by the publishers Esnaut and Rapilly between 1778 and 1787, is the *Galerie des Modes et Costumes Francais*, illustrated most notably by Watteau le Jeune and Desrais. The fine *Suite d'Estampes pour servir à l'Histoire des Moeurs et du Costume* (1778), drawn by J. M. Moreau, had as its stated aim the promotion of French taste. Though often regarded as the quintessence of French fashion, it is more a complete guide to the world of fashionable people in their material context.

The Nineteenth Century

The publishing boom of the late eighteenth and early nineteenth centuries stimulated the flow of fashion illustrations. Despite the Revolution and the Napoleonic wars, French plates continued to dominate the market, though equally fine examples were produced in England and Germany. Le Brun Tossa in the *Le Cabinet des Modes*, 1785–1789, and La Mésangère in *Le Journal des Dames et des Modes*, 1797–1839, featured high-quality plates by excellent artists, as did John Bell in the English *La Belle Assemblée* 1806–1832, but Bell's illustrations were often pirated and adapted to local taste.

La Mésangère extended the range of his artist illustrators by publishing them in a series of fashion and genre prints, such as Debucourt's *Modes et Manières du Jour*, 1810, and the Vernets' *Incroyables et Merveilleuses* and *Le Bon Genre*, 1818. They are a precedent for the more intimate picture series by Gavarni and Deveria, whose fashion plates were such a feature of the periodicals of the 1830s and 1840s. A successful formula, it was followed by the *pochoir* fashion illustrators of the twentieth century, most notably George Barbier.

The most prestigious early nineteenth-century British contribution to the art of the fashion plate was *Heideloff's Gallery of Fashion*, 30 aquatint plates, 1797–1801, published by subscription to an aristocratic clientele. Focused on fashions worn by anonymous noble ladies, it also included the creations of named dressmakers. With the aquatint plates of British popular venues crowded with fashionable men, women, and children, published by London tailor Benjamin Read between the 1820s and 1840s, the fashion plate was decisively democratized. Prints and full-scale patterns were sold through Read's establishments in London and New York, where American versions soon appeared.

By the mid-nineteenth century, with the expansion of popular and pictorial publishing as well as the clothing trade, the fashion plate proliferated. To satisfy demand, engraving establishments, especially in Britain and Germany, provided type images easily grouped and amended for the cheaper fashion and advertising market. The male fashion figure largely disappeared from fashion plates at this time; however arranged and accessorized, he lacked the vivacity of fashionable men as drawn by Paul Gavarni and the Vernets.

Quality fashion plates remained available through large-scale French publishers and agents for publications abroad, such as Goubaud and Mariton. The best documented and most prolific artists during the middle of the nineteenth century were the Colin sisters—Heloise Leloir, Anais Toudouze, and Laure Noel—who, together with their rival Jules David, were skillful in showing the requisite dress detail in conventional evocative settings. American fashion plates, sometimes modified from French originals, as in *Godey's Ladies' Book* and the publications of Mme Demorest, could be more practical, even featuring domestic appliances.

The Artist and the Photographer

By the end of the century, the earlier romanticizing tradition was challenged by avant-garde black-and-white work, dramatic rather than representational. An idealized realism also became fashionable, and A. Sandoz, especially for the House of Worth, produced Tissot-like groupings set in the wider world of the modern woman of the twentieth century.

His source material probably included photographs from the house archives, but although promotional photographs had been occasionally used in fashion publications since the 1860s, and press pictures of fashionable scenes, such as those by the Seeberger brothers, were popular, the detailed color reproduction expected by the quality market was expensive. Retouching was easy but the photographs from *Les Modes*, their speciality, illustrate the problems. Idealization, the core of fashion illustration, was problematic, and fashion artists were available, adaptable, quicker, and cheaper.

Confronted by advances in printing and photographic technology and the easy availability of the conventional graphic image, in the early twentieth century the artistic avant-garde retreated to the craft technique of *pochoir* (stencil) printing and hand coloring, producing formal, modernist, *faux naives* fashion plates in exotic or romantic settings reminiscent of the early nineteenth century. The genre was pioneered by Paul Iribe for Poiret's 1909 collection in *Les Robes de Paul Poiret*, 1909, and by Georges LePape in *Les Choses de Paul Poiret*, 1911. Their work and others of the group, such as Charles Martin and George Barbier, was brought to a wider public by the publisher Lucien Vogel, who launched the elitist *Gazette du Bon Ton* in 1911, the precursor of several similar art and fashion magazines. The general public became aware of the style and technique through prestige advertising, such as *Art Gout Beauté*, 1920–1936, published by the textile firm Albert Godde Bedin.

In general the advertising agencies were very open to modern trends. Not without reference to the cinema, by the early 1930s they had revived the male fashion image illustrating active realistic men in glamorized everyday settings. *Esquire* adopted this style in 1933 and subsequent men's fashion advertisements and magazines would continue it well into the 1960s.

By 1923, the *Gazette du Bon Ton* and its artists had been taken over by *Vogue*. Fashion narrative illustrations were not part of *Vogue's* format, and the work of the *Bon Ton* artists, like that of established *Vogue* artists such as Helen Dryden and Douglas Sutherland, was confined to the elegantly decorative covers. By the late 1920s and 1930s, a new generation of fashion artist, Eric (Carl Erickson), H. Bouet Willaumez, Bouché, and Christian Bérard had begun to convey the essence of style, scene, and above all movement, in vivid and impressionist plates, though occasionally their lack of detail was deplored.

It is the ability to convey the soul of the garment as well as the seams, the ambience and the dynamic of fashion, and the essence of its modernity, which keeps the fashion plate an element of publishing in the early twenty-first century.

See also Fashion Illustrators; Vogue.

Bibliography

Cornu, Paul, ed. and preface. *Galeries des Modes et Costumes Francais, dessinés d'après nature, 1778–1787.* New, collected edition. Paris: E. Lévy, 1911–1914.

Gaudriault, Raymond. *La Gravure de Mode Feminine de France.* Paris: les editions de l'amateur, 1988.

Ginsburg, Madeleine. *An Introduction to Fashion Illustration.* London: V & A/Compton/Pitman, 1980.

Hay, Susan. "Paris to Providence: French Couture and the Tirocci Shop." In *From Paris to Providence.* Edited by Susan Hay. Providence: Museum of Art, Rhode Island School of Design, 2000. An admirable study that illustrates the practical use of fashion illustrations.

Packer, William. *Fashion Drawing in Vogue.* New York: Coward McCann, 1983.

Steele, Valerie. *Paris Fashion: A Cultural History.* Oxford: Berg, 1998.

Madeleine Ginsberg

FASHION SHOWS

The fashion show has evolved from an exclusive in-house presentation of haute couture held for a private clientele, to a biannual spectacle of both couture and ready-to-wear clothing that is seen by a vast cross-section of consumers, the mass media, and the fashion industry. A number of cultural and social forces are responsible for this evolution, including the increased consumer awareness of Parisian couture, the rise of the ready-to-wear industry after World War II, the growth of the modeling profession, and the increasing attention paid to the runway by the popular press. While the fashion show today is different from its early-twentieth-century incarnation, it does retain links to its origins in theatrical display and the couture salon shows of that period.

Origins

In nineteenth-century Paris, it was common practice for dressmaker houses to use their assistants or

Model backstage at a fashion show. Since their inception in the early 1900s, fashion shows have evolved from relatively simple in-house events to highly publicized worldwide spectacles. © Langevin Jacques/Corbis Sygma. Reproduced by permission.

saleswomen (*desmoiselles du magasin*) to wear the designer's creations while working at the shop. To reach a broader clientele, many couturiers extended this display to the public arena as well, with figures such as Charles Frederick Worth dressing his wife in the latest styles to promenade in socially important areas of the city such as the Bois du Boulogne. In the late nineteenth and early twentieth centuries in London and Paris, the custom-dressmaking trade also maintained important and effective links to the world of theater and advertised its wares by dressing famous actresses both on and off the stage. The couture houses of Doucet and Paquin, for example, were very successful promoters through this medium and their clientele included such popular stars as Sarah Bernhardt, Réjane, and Cecile Sorel. The theater, particularly in France and England, became a place to see the most avant-garde styles and eventually a "fashion play" genre developed that revolved around the presentation of the latest couture creations. Dressing members of the fashionable demimonde and house mannequins (the term for models in this period) for the races, opera, and theater premieres, and resort areas were another means of advertising up-to-the-minute designs.

In the first decade of the century, social display was supplemented by organized shows at a fixed time in the couture house. Although a number of designers and fashion personalities claim responsibility for the first fashion show, it was not one person who started the trend, but rather a gradual evolution toward more formal presentations of seasonal clothing lines. By the mid-1910s many designers, including Paul Poiret, Lucile, and Paquin, were using the fashion show as a promotional vehicle. In 1910 Lucile promoted the opening of her New York branch with a spectacular fashion show in a city theater. The presentation had an Arabian Nights theme inspired by vaudeville revues. Lucile was one of the first to promote her mannequins as public personalities, giving them exotic names such as Dinarzade and Sumurun, and training them to walk with a distinctive gait.

For Paris haute couture, the shows were first presented in Paris or London and then sometimes traveled to America on well-publicized tours. Paul Poiret followed this pattern, organizing a tour in 1911 in which he and his mannequins showed his exotic creations in venues such as charity bazaars, theaters, and department stores throughout Europe. In 1913 he also conducted a heavily promoted tour of the United States with his mannequins, and other designers followed suit, including Jeanne Paquin in 1914 and Jean Patou in 1924. Another innovative mode of presentation in the 1910s was the organization of a *thé dansant*, a popular pastime that showcased new dances such as the tango and the fox-trot. Designers including Lucile and Paquin showed their new designs in such a context, often using theaters as a show venue.

In America, department stores, such as Wanamakers in Philadelphia, started holding regular fashion shows in 1910 and gradually broadened the audience for such fashion display. The advent of the fashion newsreel in the same period also served to bring the fashion show to a wider clothes-buying public. Beginning in 1910, a number of French, English, and American film companies began to show fashion reels as part of their weekly newsreel production. In 1913 a New York–based film company started documenting the biannual fashion shows in New York that now took place in February for the spring–summer collections and July for fall–winter collections. At this point, modeling was not an evolved routine and both film and fashion magazines often used actresses, opera singers, and dancers as mannequins.

In the United States during World War I, a number of fashion shows were organized to benefit the war effort and toured across the country. In 1914, a Fashion Fête was organized by Edna Woolman Chase, the editor of *Vogue*, to showcase New York designers. Also in that year a number of couture houses banded together to form Le Syndicat de defense de la grand couture francaise with Paul Poiret as president. In an effort to fight design piracy, the organization charged a standard copyright fee for business customers who wished to reproduce couture designs. The syndicate also placed more stringent rules on who could attend the couture shows and wholesalers and retailers were barred from couture showings unless they were invited.

By 1918 the couture industry had fixed dates for two major shows per year for the foreign buyers that were coming to Paris. The shows were becoming organized presentations using in-house mannequins and by the 1920s, the House of Patou, for example, was employing 32 mannequins to model 450 dresses at each showing. Other contemporary references document between 7 and 15 mannequins regularly employed in the couture houses at this time. One 1920s commentator wrote that the mannequins were still considered "demimondaine" but they did have paid salaries, bonuses, and some had season contracts. In 1923 John Robert Powers established the first modeling agency in New York, which served to professionalize the industry and positioned modeling as a more socially acceptable career. In the 1920s designers also had a set routine and started by showing sports and day clothes, then evening wear.

In the 1930s Elsa Schiaparelli was the first to create themed collections, including "Circus," "Commedia dell'Arte," and "Astrology," among others. These themes added a theatrical flair to her shows between 1936 and 1939 by incorporating music, special lighting, and dance into the presentation. Her 1938 "Circus" collection, for example, included circus performers who jumped, skipped, and flipped all over the couture house.

The Postwar Era

An increasingly formal presentation style marked the postwar era and at this point the show evolved into the essential organization that is still associated with it in the early 2000s. The show took place in the couture salon, the crowded audience consisted of invited buyers with important journalists at the front, and there was a specific sequence for the type of dress shown (for example, the wedding dress at the end). Fashion shows often lasted seventy-five minutes and approximately sixty ensembles were presented on between eight and ten models. This period also witnessed the association of particular mannequins with specific couture houses. Mannequins, such as Bettina at Jacques Fath or Praline at Pierre Balmain, with their distinctive saunters, visually represented the designer's philosophy and often acted as the designer's muse. While Paris had successfully reestablished itself as the style leader in the postwar era, countries such as the United States, England, and Italy also held regular fashion shows.

It was still common practice to hold fashion shows in department stores and hotels and the *Vogue* editor Edna Woolman Chase recorded in her 1954 memoirs:

> Now that fashion shows have become a way of life, now that a lady is hard put to it to lunch, or sip a cocktail, in any smart hotel or store from New York to Dallas to San Francisco without having lissome young things in the most recent models, swaying down a runway six inches above her nose—it is difficult to visualize that dark age when fashion shows did not exist. (Chase and Chase 1954, p. 119)

By the mid-1950s, fashion shows were common in urban centers in semiannual department store displays and, at the local level, they were often incorporated into charity events.

Ready-to-Wear Market

In the late 1950s the rise of the ready-to-wear market had a significant impact on the organization, number, and scale of fashion shows. In 1959 Pierre Cardin showed his ready-to-wear collection in the *Printemps* department store in Paris and by the mid-1960s, ready-to-wear was regularly included in the fashion calendar. The growth of the ready-to-wear market was also related to the decline in interest in haute couture by the younger generation, who did not want to follow the fashion dictates of Paris. New designers responded to this cultural phenomenon by adding a youthful energy to their fashion shows. The English designer Mary Quant, for example, presented her mod ready-to-wear designs to jazz music and her mannequins skipped and danced down the runway. Quant opted to use print models rather than runway models because she liked the way they moved and the fast pace allowed her to show forty garments in fourteen minutes. The distinction between the runway and photography model was on the wane.

This growth of the ready-to-wear market eventually changed the function of the haute couture fashion show, shifting its targeted audience from private clientele to one consisting mainly of press and buyers. The 1960s also mark the beginnings of the use of the fashion show as a marketing tool to promote the licensed products associated with the house.

Fashion Show as Spectacle

In the 1970s and 1980s the public visibility and magnitude of fashion shows increased dramatically. In 1973 the designer Kenzo presented a large-scale ready-to-wear show on a stage rather than a runway, indicating a break with haute couture tradition and the increasing emphasis on spectacle. In the 1980s Thierry Mugler and Claude Montana staged theatrical events that further removed the fashion show from the couture salon. Mugler hired a rock impresario to stage his fashion show, an audience of six thousand people attended, and half of the show's tickets were available for purchase by the public. This was the first time that the public was allowed to attend a couture show and marks a trend toward the fashion show as mass entertainment. In the mid-1980s the regular broadcasting of the ready-to-wear shows on cable television further broadened the viewing public. The increased public awareness of the catwalk shows led to the promotion of "supermodels" in the early 1990s. By this time, modeling had long been a socially acceptable profession and the increasing cult of personality in various cultural arenas served to promote models as celebrities on a par with movie actors.

While the majority of fashion designers hold traditional runway shows during the fashion weeks in Paris, London, New York, and other cities, many now have specific themes, mood music, and special lighting and other effects. In the 1990s there were a number of designers, including John Galliano and Alexander McQueen, who became renowned for producing extravagant shows in unusual spaces with narratives and fictional characters. These theatrical stagings have pushed the fashion show beyond the garment and into the realm of the conceptual fantasy. These types of shows function primarily to promote brand recognition and to sell the ready-to-wear lines and the licensed products.

See also Department Store; Fashion Designer; Fashion Models.

Bibliography

Bertin, Célia. *Paris à la Mode: A Voyage of Discovery*. Translated by Marjorie Deans. London: Victor Gollancz Ltd., 1956.

Castle, Charles. *Model Girl*. Newton Abbott, U.K.: David and Charles, 1977.

Chase, Edna Woolman, and Ilka Chase. *Always in Vogue*. New York: Doubleday, 1954.

Evans, Caroline. "The Enchanted Spectacle." *Fashion Theory* 5, no. 3 (September 2001): 270–310.

Michelle Tolini Finamore

FASHION, ATTACKS ON

While fashions in furniture and architecture have not generally been perceived as a problem, fashionable dress has been frequently criticized by clergy, philosophers, moralists, and academics for centuries. The condemnations have been numerous and varying; fashionable clothes are attacked for encouraging vanity, loose sexual morality, conspicuous consumption, and effeminacy (in men), and thus blamed for all manner of social breakdown and sexual and gender confusion. Further, the very idea of discarding clothes once they are no longer fashionable (rather than "worn out") has been seen by some as wasteful, frivolous, and irrational. The reasons fashion has been singled out for such condemnation are important and illustrative of the way in which fashionable dress intersects with wider social debates concerning gender, class, and sexuality. Perhaps the problem has to do with the close relationship of dress to the body, which bears the weight of considerable social, moral, sexual pressure, and prohibition (see Barcan 2004 and Ribeiro 2003). Further, given the close cultural associations between a woman's identity and her body, it is no surprise that fashion is subjected to such an onslaught of criticism: As feminists have argued, the things associated with women are likely to carry a lower social status than the things of men. This is not to say that men are exempt from criticisms concerning fashionable dress (indeed, they sometimes are), but such criticisms are less frequent in history and when they occur, it is the inappropriate nature of male interest in clothes, and fears about masculinity, that prompt such attacks.

Gender, Sexuality, and Morality

Understanding the historical condemnations of fashionable dress therefore necessitates an examination of attitudes toward gender, sexuality, and clothes. At the same time that women have long been associated with the making of clothes, with textiles, and with consumption, there has existed also a metaphorical association of femininity and the very idea of fashion. According to Jones (1996, p. 35), "women had for centuries been associated with inconstancy and change," characteristics that also describe fashion. It is also the case that as Breward (1994) and Tseëlon (1997) note, up until the eighteenth century, fashion had been considered a sign of the weakness and moral laxity of "wicked" women. Tseëlon (1997) examines how ancient myths about femininity have informed Western attitudes toward women. She points out (1997, p. 12) that between them, archetypal figures, such as Eve, inform Western moral attitudes toward women. Within Judeo-Christian teachings, from the tales of the Old Testament through the writings of the apostle St. Paul, woman has been associated with temptations of the flesh and decoration. At the heart of this attitude toward women was a fear of the body that, in Christian teachings, is the location of desires and "wicked" temptations to be disavowed for the sake of the soul. Thus the decorated (female) body is inherently problematic to Judeo-Christian morality, as Ribieiro has also argued. So too, however, is the naked or unadorned body. As Tseëlon (1997, p. 14) notes, in Judeo-Christian teachings, nakedness became a shameful thing after the Fall and, since the Fall is blamed on woman, then "the links between sin, the body, woman, and clothes are easily forged" (see also Barcan 2004).

Given its associations with sexuality and sin, it is not surprising that female clothing is the subject of heated debate amongst moralists and clergy, and that feminine dress is the object of quite vitriolic attacks. One can find particularly misogynistic diatribes on femininity and dress in the medieval writings of clergymen, as well as in the writings of later moralists of the seventeenth and eighteenth centuries. For example, Edward Cooke in 1678 wrote,

> a double crime for a woman to be fashion'd after the mode of this world, and so to bring her innocence into disrepute through her immodest nakedness; because she her self not only sins against shame, but causes others to sin against purity, and at the same time, renders her self suspect. (Tseëlon 1997, p. 635)

To counter fears as to female sexuality and dress, Christianity produced "a discourse of modesty and chastity in dress" which became encoded into female sexuality (Tseëlon 1997, p. 12). Christian teachings held that redemption lay in the renunciation of decoration and modesty in dress, a moral duty born of Eve's guilt. Thus, while men's fashions were often highly erotic, it was women's immodest display that was the focus of religious and moral condemnation. Only a woman could be accused of seduction in dress. While such ideas may seem almost quaint by contemporary standards, where it seems all bodies can "shamelessly" flaunt bottoms, breasts, and bellies, in fact, evidence of the continuing associations between women, seduction, and morality today can be found in contemporary culture. In rape cases, for example, women are still implicitly and explicitly criticized for wearing "sexually revealing" clothes and what a woman wore at the time of attack can be given as evidence of her desires for sex and used as male defense in the form of "she was asking for it." The ghost of the temptress Eve still haunts contemporary culture.

Class, Morality, and Social Order

While sumptuary laws remained in place, fears about the breakdown of class distinctions were another source of anxiety for moral and social writers, particularly over the course of the eighteenth century. Here again, women's fashion exemplifies these concerns about class, along with familiar fears about female sexuality. Sumptuary laws attempted to regulate status but, in the case of women, they also attempted to differentiate between the good, gentile wealthy woman and her "fallen" sister, the prostitute. As Emberley (1998, p. 8) notes, the hierarchy of furs and social positions created by these regulatory acts also influenced notions of sexual propriety among different classes of women. At certain times prostitutes were forbidden to wear fur to differentiate them from "respectable women." However, it was not just sexual morality that was at stake in discourses on women and fashion. Women's supposed love of fashion, and all that glitters and shines, has been seen as problematic to the general social and moral order. This was true in the seventeenth and early eighteenth centuries when particular fears about the spread of luxury sometimes focused on women's supposed insatiable desires for such consumption and the threats they posed to the family, as this tract from 1740 illustrates: "although her children may be dying of hunger, she will take food from their bellies to feed her own insatiable desire for luxury, she will have her silk fashions at any cost" (Jones 1996, p. 37). Thus moral discourse gave way to other kinds of rhetoric: "sartorial offence moved from being defined as a moral transgression to being defined as a social transgression" (Tseëlon 1997, p. 16). While the former was considered indicative of character flaw, the latter indicates a lack of gentility and education and civility. Thus, while moral transgression through clothing was a matter for both sexes, a woman might transgress moral codes in more ways than a man. By being too highly decorated she might be seen to have fallen prey to the sin of vanity (Jones 1996, p. 36).

Masculinity and Morality

While men of aristocratic birth were at least as equally decorated as women, for much of the early modern period right through to the eighteenth century (and indeed, beyond, if one includes military dress), this simple fact did not dilute the association of fashion with femininity. Indeed, when male peacocks were criticized it was often on the grounds of "effeminacy," for showing too great an interest in fashion was deemed "inappropriate" to masculinity. Sometimes this criticism was leveled on the grounds that male interest in fashion transgressed the rightful division of the genders. At other times, effeminacy was seen as problematic to the image of a nation. The equation of effeminacy in male attire with the diminution of national interests can be seen in Elizabethan England: In the sermon "Homily Against Excess," which Queen Elizabeth I ordered to be read out in churches, such associations are described as follows, "yea, many men are become so effeminate, that they care not what they spend in disguising themselves, ever desiring new toys, and inventing new fashions. . . . Thus with our fantastical devices we make ourselves laughing-stocks to other nations" (Garber 1992, p. 27).

As Garber notes, effeminacy here does not mean homosexuality (as it often does) but "self-indulgent" or "voluptuous" and therefore close to "womanly" things. Criticism is leveled at the money, time, and energy devoted by the effeminate man to the "feminine" and "trivial" frivolities of fashion. Similar criticism was directed at the "Macaroni" style (as in the rhyme "Yankee Doodle Dandy") that was popular among young aristocratic men of the eighteenth century. Macaronis appeared in the English lexicon of 1764 to describe ultra-fashionable young men of noble birth. It was a rather "foppish" style, Italianate and Frenchified, and was criticized on the grounds that this gentleman had "become so effeminate and weak, he became unable to resist foreign threats and might even admire European tyranny" (Steele 1988,

p. 31). Men have, therefore, not been immune to sartorial criticism, because it was thought that they should
be "above" fashion. However, while moralists and clergymen might hope to dissuade men from decoration,
historical evidence illustrates that they, too, have been
under the sway of fashion.

Fashion as Irrational

Over the nineteenth century, as fashionable clothing
became more widespread, moving from the aristocracy
to the new bourgeois classes as part of a more general
opening up of consumption, other problems associated
with fashion were singled out for criticism. For some,
fashionable clothing was indicative of wastefulness
associated with new forms of consumption. One key
figure in this line of attack is Thorstein Veblen, whose
Theory of the Leisure Class, first published in 1899, has
remained a classic study of fashionable dress in late
Victorian times and whose central theoretical tenants
are still very much alive in contemporary critiques of
consumption. Veblen argues that the newly emerging
bourgeoisie express their wealth through conspicuous
consumption, conspicuous waste, and conspicuous leisure. Dress is a supreme example of the expression of
pecuniary culture, since "our apparel is always in evidence and affords an indication of our pecuniary standing to all observers at the first glance" (Veblen 1953,
p. 119). Fluctuating fashions demonstrate one's wealth
and transcendence from the realm of necessity. However, what motivates fashion change is that wastefulness is innately offensive and this makes the futility
and expense of fashion abhorrent and ugly. He suggests
that new fashions are adopted in our attempt to escape
this futility and ugliness, with each new style welcomed
as relief from the previous aberration until that too is
rejected. According to Veblen, women's dress displays
these dynamics more than men's since the only role of
the bourgeois lady of the house is to demonstrate her
master's ability to pay, his pecuniary strength to remove
her entirely from the sphere of work. The Victorian
woman's dress was also an important indicator of vi-
carious leisure since she wore clothes that made her
obviously incapable of work—elaborate bonnets, heavy
and elaborate skirts, delicate shoes, and constraining
corsets—testimony to her distance from productive
work. Veblen condemns all these traits of fashionable dress, not just because they characterize women
as men's chattel, but also because this fashionablity is

inherently irrational and wasteful. He calls for dress
that is based on rational, utilitarian principles, and his
ideas are closely aligned to the principles of many dress
reformers (Newton 1974).

Ugly, Futile, and Irrational: The Dress Reform Critiques of Fashion

Veblen was not alone in his condemnation of the fashions of his day. Numerous dress-reform movements
emerged in the nineteenth century attacking fashionable dress. These movements were diverse and motivated by different concerns—social, political, medical,
moral, and artistic—with some more progressive than
others (Newton 1974; Steele 1985). For feminist dress
reformers, the way in which narrow shoulders, tight
waists, and expansive and awkward petticoats constrained the locomotion of the female body was a real
political problem. However, more conservative medical
discourses similarly attacked the corset for the way it
constrained the reproductive organs, thus damaging
women's reproductive capacities and preventing her
from performing her "natural" duties. Indeed, the corset has excited considerable controversy, stimulating
intense debate and outright condemnation: For some
it is an instrument of physical oppression and sexual
objectification (Roberts 1977; Veblen 1953 {1899}), for
others, it is a garment asserting sexual power (Kunzle
1982; see also Steele 1988).

While women's dress, in particular, was singled out
for criticism by these reform movements, men's dress,
with its tight collars, fitted waistcoats and jackets, was
also criticized by those, such as Flügel, associated with
the men's dress reform movement. The dress of both
men and women was seen by some to be "irrational" in
that it contorted the body into "unnatural" shapes and
was driven by the "crazy" rhythms of fashion considered
to be not just archaic to a scientific age, but wasteful
and unnecessary. For example, "aesthetic" dress of the
late nineteenth century challenged the artificial constrictions of the fashions of the day with a new kind
of dress for men and women that was free flowing and
more "natural." At the same time health and hygiene
campaigns often singled out women's dress as unhealthy or unhygienic: It was said that corsets damaged
the spleen and internal organs, particularly the reproductive organs, and the long petticoats picked up the
mud, debris, and horse manure that were a constant

feature of city streets in the nineteenth century (Newton 1974).

While fashion may be subject to much less criticism today, and no equivalents to the health and hygiene campaigns of the nineteenth century can be found, remnants of some criticisms linger in contemporary commentaries. For example, fashionable dress is still sometimes considered irrational and ugly, especially among intellectuals. Like Veblen, the contemporary philosopher Jean Baudrillard (1981, p. 79) condemns fashion as irrational and ugly, arguing that

> Beauty ("in itself") has nothing to do with the fashion cycle. In fact, it is inadmissible. Truly beautiful, definitely beautiful clothing would put an end to fashion. . . . Thus, fashion continually fabricates the "beautiful" on the basis of a radical denial of beauty, by reducing beauty to the logical equivalent of ugliness. It can impose the most eccentric, dysfunctional, ridiculous traits as eminently distinctive.

Wilson (1987) takes issue with Veblen and Baudrillard's account of fashion as wasteful and futile since both assume the world should be organized around utilitarian values; "there is no place for the irrational or the nonutilitarian; it was a wholly rational realm" (Wilson 1987, p. 52). A further problem with Veblen's and Baudrillard's accounts, according to Wilson, concerns their causal account of fashion change. The idea that fashion is constantly changing in an attempt to get away from ugliness and find beauty is reductive and over-deterministic. Both fail to acknowledge its ambivalent and contradictory nature, as well as the pleasures it affords, and their critique "grants no role to contradiction, nor for that matter to pleasure" (1987, p. 53).

Conclusion

Dress is still, perhaps, accorded less status than furniture, architecture, and other decorative commodities, which are similarly driven by fashion. There is something so intimate, sexual, and moral about what we hang at the margins of our bodies that makes dress susceptible to a kind of criticism that does not accompany the other objects we use. However, despite the fact that men and women wear fashionable dress, it is not considered a matter of equal male and female concern. Associations of fashion with femininity linger, and women's supposed "natural" disposition

to decorate is still considered "trivial" and "silly," thus leaving women open to greater moral condemnation. While such ideas seem to be less obvious today, the lower status accorded to fashionable dress is evident in the sorts of criticism leveled at women, such as "mutton dressed up as lamb" (of which there is no equivalent term for men), and "fashion victim," (usually denoting the woman who is a "slave" to her wardrobe). As these phrases suggest, fashion still comes in for moral judgment and criticism.

See also Dress Reform; Gender, Dress, and Fashion; Politics and Fashion.

Bibliography

Barcan, R. *Nudity: A Cultural Anatomy.* Oxford, U.K. and New York: Berg, 2004.

Baudrillard, J. *For a Critique of the Political Economy of the Sign.* St. Louis, Mo.: Telos, 1981.

Breward, C. *The Culture of Fashion.* Manchester, U.K.: Manchester University Press, 1994.

Garber, M. *Vested Interests: Cross Dressing and Cultural Anxiety.* London: Penguin, 1992.

Jones, J. "Coquettes and Grisettes: Women Buying and Selling in Ancien Regime Paris." In *The Sex of Things: Gender and Consumption in Historical Perspective.* Edited by V. de Grazia and E. Furlough. Berkeley: University of California Press, 1996.

Kunzle, D. *Fashion and Fetishism: A Social History of the Corset, Tight-Lacing and Other Forms of Body-Sculpture in the West.* Totowa, N.J.: Rowan and Littlefield, 1982.

Newton, S. M. *Health, Art and Reason: Dress Reformers of the 19th Century.* London: John Murray Ltd., 1974.

Roberts, H. "The Exquisite Slave: The Role of Clothes in the Making of the Victorian Woman." *Signs* 2, no. 3 (1977): 554–569.

Steele, V. *Paris Fashion: A Cultural History.* Oxford, U.K.: Oxford University Press, 1988.

Tseëlon, E. *The Masque of Femininity.* London: Sage, 1997.

Veblen, Thorstein. *The Theory of the Leisure Class: An Economic Study of Institutions,* (1899). New York: Mentor, 1953.

Wilson, E. *Adorned in Dreams: Fashion and Modernity.* London: Virago, 1985. Reprint, Piscataway, N.J.: Rutgers University Press, 2003.

Joanne Entwistle

FASHION, HEALTH, AND DISEASE

The relationship between fashion and health is a complex one, with fashion sometimes being shaped by current beliefs about health and disease and, at other times, acting as the cause of illness.

Early Beliefs

For many centuries, those in the Western world believed that human illness was primarily related to the disposition of "humors," vapors coming from deep inside the body and released at the skin surface (Renbourn and Rees 1972, p. 401). The ancient Greeks believed that a damp, cold environment prevented these humors from passing out through the skin, being turned back instead toward the internal organs. There, they caused inflammation and every imaginable disease. The belief that damp cold was almost solely responsible for most human illness persisted until the middle of the nineteenth century, when the science of bacteriology began to link disease to the spread of infectious organisms.

The fear of damp cold led to multiple theories about dressing for health. There was, of course, the fear that the very clothing worn to protect the body from damp cold, could itself block the passage of humors outward. Arguments were made in favor of each of the natural fibers as being the most healthy to be worn, with wool being believed by many to be the most healthy because it was found to be the greatest absorber of water.

The human body does actually release vapors from the skin surface in a continual drying out of the skin called insensible perspiration. Research in the mid-1800s established for the first time that wool had the ability to absorb insensible perspiration and later condense it under cooler conditions, sending the resulting heat from condensation back toward the body (Renbourn and Rees, p. 40). Cotton and linen appeared to have no such capacity to produce heat; they continued to cool until dry, leading to a dangerous chilling of the body.

These findings caused many health practitioners to advocate wool in the years that followed. One, a German physiology professor named Jaeger, touted his all-woolen system of dress as the key to revolutionizing the health of all ages in all climates (Renbourn and Rees, p. 46). Many believed that wool also served as a "filter" to prevent impurities from reaching the body. Wool later was discovered to have another prized quality—it

retained an electric charge. In the middle of the eighteenth century, many believed that a strong positive electrical charge led to male virility (Renbourn and Rees 1972, p. 33). During the nineteenth century, electric and magnetic garments were in vogue, and statically charged undergarments were credited with having powers from curing rheumatism to affecting the bowels (Renbourn and Rees, p. 39).

Wool, however, had its detractors, particularly among those who worked and lived in the tropics. A number of physicians in the seventeenth and eighteenth centuries noted that because wool was not easy to clean, it housed and propagated fleas, lice, and other carriers of disease. Excessive swaddling of infants in wool in the tropics by British nurses working there was thought to be one cause of infant mortality. Many believed cotton to be healthier than wool in warm climates because it provided more continual cooling and was more easily cleanable and less irritating to the skin.

From the seventeenth to nineteenth centuries, an almost irrational fear of exposure to drafts existed in many countries. Exposure to air currents was believed to be responsible for a wide range of conditions, including head colds, sore throats, and rheumatism. This concern contributed to excessive coverage of the body, even in warmer weather. During the French Revolution, when women ignored traditional admonitions for body coverage, the supposed link between diseases like consumption and revealing garments made of the sheer muslins of the time even led to new labels, such as "muslin disease" and "pneumonia blouses" (Renbourn and Rees, p. 34).

Color was believed to have had magical properties that affected human health. Various colors have been thought to best intercept dangerous rays of the sun or attract or repel toxins. While there has been considerable debate about the importance of specific hues in protecting the body, many cultures that exist in desert climates have long accepted that most whites and lighter colors reflect more sunlight than most blacks and darker colors. The white robes of desert dwellers, for example, offer thermal protection by reflecting the radiant heat of the sun away from the body.

Fashion as Detriment to Health

One of the main reasons early fashion was detrimental to health was that dressing in many layers and bathing infrequently combined to make clothing a breeding ground for infectious organisms and vermin. Some fashions also seemed to attract infected refuse. A medical paper of 1900 reported on a bacteriological examination of the trailing voluminous skirts of the time in which the author "found large colonies of germs, including those of tuberculosis, typhoid, tetanus, influenza" (Rudofsky 1947, p. 181).

Fashion has often involved modification of the body. The professed reasons for this range from ceremonial to practical, among them: influencing the morality of a wearer's behavior, communicating social status, increasing sexual allure, and establishing an aesthetic ideal. Harold Koda states that "Shoes have been the most persistent example of fashion's imposition of an idealized form on the natural anatomy" (2001, p. 140). He notes that the portion of the shoe that contained the toes has rarely, if ever, reflected the shape of the human foot but that the shape of a shoe, "consistently worn eventually molds the foot" (p. 140).

There has been much controversy about the health effects of modified feet. The most extreme example of foot modification is the Chinese bound, or lotus, foot. Dorothy Ko states that while Chinese footbinding shifted the placement of the bones of the foot, it broke no bones. It simply shortened the length of the foot and changed the locus of its support of body weight (p. 60). Many lotus shoes were designed to allow the axis of support of body weight to pass through the heel alone, alleviating any painful pressure on the folded toes (p. 152). Koda states that the spiked heel that was first made popular in the 1950s has acted to place the foot of its wearer in almost the same vertical position as the lotus foot. (2001, p. 159). In addition to precipitating ankle injury, the "tiptoe" stance of the foot in high heels "has been known to shorten the leg muscles, and in creating a destabilized stance, it can precipitate problems at the small of the back" (p. 163).

In the nineteenth century, physicians argued that the "wasp waist" of the corseted woman was detrimental to health, producing various conditions such as fainting, cracked ribs, miscarriage, difficulties in breathing, and abnormally functioning internal organs (Renbourn and Rees 1972, p. 11). More recent research on the effects of the corset have found few, if any, permanent health effects for adult women once a corset is removed (Steele 2001). However, Steele acknowledges that because corsets interfered with respiration, they did create "a disincentive" for Victorian women to exercise (p. 71). Indeed, one of fashion's primary negative effects on health in the past may have been limiting the types of activities in which individuals have felt able to participate.

Current Approaches

The belief that cold, damp weather and exposure to drafts are responsible for the common cold and flu has persisted to modern times, despite the assertions of clothing physiologists that "cold stress" is only one of dozens of stresses of modern life that lead to these illnesses.

During the second half of the twentieth century, dressing to protect the body from thermal conditions in the environment generally involved one of two approaches: using clothing to insulate the body against sudden heat loss or using it to shield the body from excessive heat gain. While much has been made of the healthful effects of specific fibers, it is well accepted that the fiber used in garments is only one factor in the ability of clothing to provide thermal balance. Watkins cites multiple factors: the fiber, yarn type, fabric construction, fabric finish, garment design, and the way of wearing a garment (1995, p. 26). Even when the same garments are worn in a different layering order, or freed or tucked in differently, the thermal balance of the wearer can be greatly affected.

New processing methods for fibers and fabrics have markedly improved insulation materials, and a variety of methods of protecting insulations from wind and water have emerged. The development of a material with micropores, Gore-Tex, in the mid-twentieth century brought the advent of waterproof materials that "breathe." These fabrics exclude liquid water, but allow vapor such as insensible perspiration to migrate out of an ensemble. Supple aluminized coatings on materials enable the reflection of radiant heat from the sun, fires, or high-heat industrial settings.

Despite technological advances that have created the potential for healthy clothing, some cultural norms may still dictate the use of garments that negatively affect health. Muslim women continue to wear the chador, the heavy, full-length veil that has been said to have caused fainting and serious long-term health problems such as osteoporosis. Western men continue to wear improperly sized business shirts with collars that cut off proper blood flow, leading to a variety of conditions from fainting to decreased visual acuity (Langan and Watkins 1987).

Other cultural norms focus on what is believed to be healthier approaches to dressing. Some Western professionals wearing high fashion walk to the office in running shoes, donning fashionable footwear only for meetings. Elderly women in nursing home wheelchairs are increasingly seen, not in the socially acceptable dresses from their pasts, but in nonbinding jogging suits.

The growing interest in alternative medicine has also revived a number of clothing practices that have met with great skepticism in the past. Experiments with the effect of color on the immune system continue. Proponents believe that magnetic clothing items may relieve pain and cure a number of different conditions. Citing new evidence relating copper to the body's enzyme production, proponents have revived interest in copper jewelry as a cure for arthritis.

The Future

Clothing has been designed to shield the body from all sorts of hazards of modern life. During the Gulf War in 1991, it was not unusual to see Israeli civilians of all ages carrying gas masks as constant accessories. Filtration masks to prevent the spread of respiratory diseases or protect asthmatics from pollution have become familiar sights. The U.S. Occupational Safety and Health and Administration (OSHA) has established educational programs to teach laborers who work with toxic chemicals the dangers of exposing the skin and respiratory system to those hazards and help them select appropriate protective suits and respirators. Space suits have been miniaturized to allow immune-deficient patients to venture into the world. Sheer, supple stainless-steel undergarments have been marketed particularly to pregnant women who work at computers, to protect them from electromagnetic radiation. There are few occupational hazards for which health-protective apparel has not been developed. Many of these have been reshaped into fashionable forms; others themselves establish a new fashion aesthetic.

All of these approaches to protection are essentially passive design concepts, working to shield the body somehow from the environment. Advances in technology are making it increasingly possible to use active approaches to protection, where clothing contributes to thermal balance or other forms of protection. For example, electrically heated and water-cooled systems have existed for decades, but the increasing miniaturization of power sources will make these more available and easily incorporated into everyday clothing. Clothing fibers have been impregnated with chemicals that absorb body heat when the wearer is warm and release it when the body begins to cool. These advances allow clothing to serve not just as a barrier, but as an active

provider of thermal balance without an external power source.

Some proposed clothing designs incorporate mechanisms that will massage and stimulate blood flow to an ailing body part or trigger an automatically inflated airbag should the wearer start to fall. Others, for example a wristband worn to prevent seasickness, simply help the body heal itself, operating on centuries-old knowledge based on alternative treatments such as acupuncture.

Garments have been impregnated with bacteria-deterring agents to actively fight organisms that attempt to make their way toward a wearer. Undergarments have been developed that monitor multiple aspects of body function and send signals that stimulate medical devices or trigger the release of medications into the body. Many of these have been connected to computerized body-monitoring systems allowing clothing to respond automatically to each individual's needs. These garments allow patients formerly tied to hospital beds to move into the world. Many are wireless, so that doctors can monitor a patient's health at a distance and make adjustments in treatment accordingly. As the body's most intimate environment, clothing has enormous potential to help individuals meet the health challenges of the future.

See also Color in Dress; Corset; Footbinding; High Heels.

Bibliography

Ko, Dorothy. *Every Step a Lotus.* Berkeley: University of California Press, 2001.

Koda, Harold. *Extreme Beauty.* New York: Metropolitan Museum of Art, 2001.

Langan, Leonora, and Susan Watkins. "Pressure of Menswear on the Neck in Relation to Visual Performance." In *Human Factors* 29 no. 1 (1987): 67–72.

Renbourn, E. T., and W. H. Rees. *Materials and Clothing in Health and Disease.* London: H. K. Lewis and Company, 1972.

Rudofsky, Bernard W. H. *Are Clothes Modern?* Chicago: Paul Theobold, 1947.

Steele, Valerie. *The Corset.* New Haven, Conn.: Yale University Press, 2001.

Watkins, Susan. *Clothing: The Portable Environment.* Ames: Iowa State University Press, 1995.

Susan M. Watkins

FASHION, HISTORICAL STUDIES OF

The earliest books on fashion history published in Europe date back to the Renaissance and the early modern period. Between 1520 and 1610, over two hundred books on dress were published in Germany, Italy, France, and Holland. These little books, designed for wealthy consumers, contained wood-engraved plates and minimal text, often in Latin and were focused on contemporary clothing. Curiosity about the foreign and the strange was as intense as ignorance was rife and publications contained fantasized images of the noble savage (the Peruvian, the Florida Indian, the African) set against plates of the fashionable clothes of European aristocracy and the dress of merchants, peasantry, and tradesmen. Between 1760 and 1820 interest in fashion and dress from wealthy consumers encouraged the publication of large folio-size costume books featuring hand-colored, etched copper plates and the new color printing technique of aquatint and, from the 1830s, lithography. Romanticism suffused all these luxury publications, with their emphasis on illustration with brief text, now no longer in Latin. Thomas Jefferys's ambitious four volumes, *Collection of the Dresses of Different Nations, Ancient and Modern* (1757 and 1772), covered dress of the entire known world, including "Old English Dresse after the Designs of Holbein, Vandyke, Hollar and Others." His view of women's fashions was that they were simply "a Decoration of Beauty, and an encitement to Desire."

"Antiquarian" Research into Fashions

A widening fascination with classical dress of ancient Greece and Rome in France led to Michel-François Dandré Bardon's *Costume des anciens peuples* of 1772 and André Lens's *Costume des peuples de l'antiquité* in 1776. These helped to fuel the eventual development of neoclassical fashions. The Gothic Revival too encouraged a wave of European interest in medieval dress history. These books provided "authentic" details of "Gothic" dress for dressmakers as well as artists, architects, and enthusiasts of fancy dress. Interest lasted into the nineteenth century and indeed beyond. The central dress historian of this period in England was Joseph Strutt, an artist and antiquarian. His major work was *A Complete View of the Manners, Customs, Arms, Habits etc. of the Inhabitants of England* (1774, 1775, and 1776) and *Complete View of the Dress and Habits of the People of England*, 1796 and 1799, which covered the Middle Ages through to the seventeenth century, using literary sources, and medieval manuscripts and monuments.

Dress of the Orient

The passion for an exotic, fantasy "Orient" encompassed Turkey, Arabia, India, China, and finally Japan, and fueled the imaginations of the makers of fashions and fancy dress throughout the eighteenth and nineteenth centuries. The vogue for Chinese decoration and chinoiserie infiltrated deeply into court and middling circles in Europe from 1680 to 1780 and much artistic and fashion inspiration was drawn from costume books of the period. Jean Baptiste Joseph Breton de la Martiniere's *La Chine en minature, . . . costumes, arts et métiers de cet empire*, with its seventy-four plates, was published in Paris, in 1811–1812. William Miller's *The Costume of China* of 1800 was reprinted in 1805, but with new plates drawn by William Alexander, official draftsman to the embassy of Earl Macarthy from 1792 to 1794 to China.

The elitist fashion vogue for *Turquerie* styles drew on plates from costume books such as William Miller's *The Costume of Turkey* of 1804 and, in 1814, on Jean Baptiste Joseph Breton de la Martiniere's *L'Egypt, et la Syrie au moeurs, usages, costumes et monuments des egyptians, des arabs, et des syriens*. Indian women became exoticized and sexualized, while modified Indian styling also filtered in to European fashionable dress. François Baltasar Solvyns's *Costumes of Indostan* was published in Calcutta in 1798–1799 and in London in 1804. Books with plates of Japanese dress were disseminated from the early nineteenth century. Thus, well before the tidal wave of publications of the 1880s and 1890s, Breton de la Martiniere's *Le Japon, ou moeurs, usages, et costumes des habitons de cet empire d'après les relations récentes de Krusenstern, Landsdorf, Titzing* was published in Paris by A. Nepveu in 1818.

Rural Europe

From the early nineteenth century a wave of descriptive books on the dress of European peasantry also exerted an influence on fashionable and fancy dress. Utopian notions and Romanticism turned to visions of a rural Europe peopled by a healthy peasantry in picturesque clothing. These costume books are informative and charming but also reveal period imperialist, gender, and stereotypic race and class prejudice. *The Costumes of the Hereditary States of the House of Austria* of 1804, for example, contains both sweet images of romanticized peasant women from all over central, southern, and eastern Europe set against textural and visual anti-Semitism in coverage of Polish Jewish dress. Twenty-three major French works were published between 1810 and 1830 on Breton peasant dress alone, such was the interest.

Books of Historical Dress for Theater and Fancy Dress

The role of historians undertaking research for theater costume and fancy dress purposes has been central to the development of fashion history since the eighteenth century. Thomas Hope's *Costumes of the Ancients* in 1809 was planned as a designer's dictionary, for "the theatrical performer, the ornamental architect and every other artist to whom the knowledge of classical costume is necessary." James Robinson Planché, the major early nineteenth-century British costume historian, not only republished volumes of Strutt but made the first attempt to design historically accurate costumes for a Shakespearean play in 1823. His 1834 *History of British Costume* became the first really popular costume history book, republished in cheaper versions in 1849 and in 1893.

Nineteenth-Century French Histories

In France, Camille Bonnard's *Costume historique des XIIe, XIIIe, XIVe et XVe siecles*, published in Paris by A. Levy fils in 1829–1830, became an important Pre-Raphaelite costume source book. Paris produced, too, Le Comte Horace de Viel-Castel's *Collection des costumes, armes, et meubles*, in four volumes, 1827–1845. Paul Lacroix's long list of publications includes his ten-volume *Costumes historiques de France* published from 1852. Laver declared that Raphael Jacquemin's *Iconographie du costume du IVe–XIXe siècle*, produced in three folio volumes in Paris between 1863 and 1869, was "superb and scholarly." In 1881, Augustin Challamel produced his *Histoire de la mode en France* translated into English and published in 1882 by Sampson Low, Marston, Searle and Rivington. In 1888, Firmin Didot published Auguste Racinet's famous and expensively produced six-volume *Le costume historique*.

Fashion, Sociology, and Psychology

While these early generations of descriptive dress history studies, all by male writers, laid the foundation stones of fashion history, it took Thorstein Veblen's *Theory of the Leisure Class* (1899) and George Simmel's *Philosophie der Mode* (1905) to launch lasting theoretical debate about the cultural meanings behind fashion development and the causes of variation in consumption patterns. Interestingly, however, their theories made virtually no impact on fashion history until at least sixty years after their publication. A selection drawn from the many new dress history books of the 1900 to 1930 period, including George Clinch's book *English Costume, from Prehistoric Times to the End of the Eighteenth Century*, for example, of 1909, showed little change from established antiquarian approaches. *Modes and Manners of the Nineteenth Century* by Oscar Fischel and Max von Boehn is a four-volume German study of fashion from the 1790s onward, first published in 1909, which used a lively choice of cartoons as well as the usual fashion plates. Hilaire Hiler's *From Nudity to Raiment* in 1929 took a painter's interest in the field. With M. Meyer, he produced one of two meticulous costume bibliographies of the 1930s. Theirs was a *Bibliography of Costume*, published by H. W. Wilson in 1939. This followed René Colas's *Bibliographie genérale du costume et la mode* of 1933. These carefully researched books were basically descriptive with little detailed study of garments.

Early Object-Centered Dress History

Elisabeth McClellan's unusually progressive study of 1904, however, *Historic Dress in America*, took markedly different approaches. It examined clothing worn in Spanish, French, English, Dutch, Swedish, and German settlements in early North America. This study, little discussed in the early 2000s, is remarkable on several counts. First it was written by a woman; and second, the author worked from a strongly object-based approach, declaring that "some relics of by-gone days have been preserved intact and placed in our hands for the preparation of this book—veritable documents of history on the subject of dress in America" (McClellan 1904, p. 5). Exceptional for studies of this period, hers took care to include everyday working clothes, such as her "Woman in Typical Working Dress 1790–1800" drawn from an original garment from the Stenton house in Philadelphia.

The second, major object-focused study is now a forgotten book by the painter Talbot Hughes, whose dress collection was accepted by the Victoria and Albert Museum in 1913. In that same year, interested in dress history for his own genre paintings, he published his *Dress Design—an account of Costume for Artists and Dressmakers—Illustrated by the author from old examples*. The book is illustrated with little line drawings, photographs, and even cutting patterns of surviving clothes from the mid-sixteenth century through the 1870s (Taylor, *Establishing Dress History*, pp. 47–49). Thalassa Cruso, the first costume curator at the Museum of London, basically a social history museum, also pioneered object-based fashion history. Her ideas were published in the museum's first dress catalog in 1933. She was probably the first woman costume curator to fuse theories related to issues of fashion production and consumption with close garment study.

The Psychology of Dress

The psychology of dress opened up further debates about the functions of dress and fashion. These debates were taken up by Frank Alvah Parsons in New York, whose study of that name was published in 1920, by J. C. Flügel, in his study *The Psychology of Clothes* of 1930, and in the work in England of the dress historians C. W. Cunnington and James Laver from the 1930s.

Thus by 1933, three diverging approaches to the study of fashion were in place—the descriptive, somewhat social history–oriented methods; object-focused research conducted largely but not exclusively by women curators; and the more detached, theoretical approaches developed by male specialists. These divisions remained firmly in place for another fifty years.

The Men Dress Historians

Drawing on Flügel, Dr. C. W. Cunnington, a medical doctor, and James Laver, Keeper of Prints and Drawings at the Victoria and Albert Museum, both took a deep interest in fashion history and in issues of women, style and sexuality, and fashion. Between 1931 and the late 1960s, they published books that successfully opened dress history to a wider popular audience. James Laver produced over fifty books dealing with art, prints, social, theater, and dress history. He understood well the problem of explaining the ephemeral character of fashion to those who still continued to dismiss the field as culturally worthless, defining fashion as "a spear

head of taste, or rather it is a kind of psychic weathercock which shows which way the wind blows" (J. Laver 1945, p. 211). Laver's very real understanding of the creative and commercial processes of fashion were coupled with a detailed interest in social history and a profound knowledge of dress history. He died in 1975. By then, through lectures and radio and TV appearances, he had become the popular, articulate public face of British dress history. The Cunningtons' most lasting work was based on object analysis, though C. W. Cunnington also wrote up his own theories on women's motivation for wearing fashionable dress, now considered outdated (Taylor, *Establishing Dress History*, pp. 51–57).

The Women Fashion Historians

It is in this period too that women historians finally make their mark. It is significant within the history of the development of feminine approaches that they chose object-based approaches, much like those of Elizabeth McClellan and Thalassa Cruso. Directional, object-centered publications in the 1940s by Doris Langley Moore and from the 1950s onward by Anne Buck created methodological approaches that have remained lastingly valid.

Doris Langley Moore, whose personal costume collection formed the basis of the now famous Museum of Costume in Bath, published two much-neglected books: *The Woman in Fashion* of 1949 and *The Child in Fashion* of 1953. Using her own collection, these explored fashionable dress from 1800 on photographed on live models, (her famous actress and theater friends and their children) with carefully correct period hairstyles and in period settings. While this method of illustration is no longer used because of the danger to the garments, both her books contain directional debate that sought to explode popular sartorial myths, such that Regency dress was transparent and that Victorian women had tiny waists. Attacking Flügel and C. W. Cunnington for an overemphasis on women's sexuality as the most significant motivation for wearing fashionable dress, Langley Moore addressed the social and cultural codes hidden within fashionable dress, avoiding the trap of class generalization that Fischel and von Boehn and Cunnington fell into.

C. W. Cunnington's wife, Phillis, also a doctor, who had worked with him on the famous *Handbook* series, began, after his death in 1961, to collaborate with new researchers. Thus, she began producing a now-famous and well-reputed series of dealing with specialist dress histories, including her seminal study *Costume for Births, Marriages and Deaths.*

Anne Buck, as the first Keeper of the Gallery of English Costume at Platt Hall, from 1947 to 1972 quickly established an object-based approach that emphasized both the social function of dress and professional museological methods of conservation and display of clothing artifacts. This exerted a seminal influence in the dress history world after the 1950s. Her meticulously researched publications fused close analysis of clothing examples with archival study and are classic examples of "good practice." Her range of special interests included smocks and English lace making. In 1961 she published her *Victorian Costume and Costume Accessories* and in 1965, *Children's Costume in England from the Fourteenth to the end of the Nineteenth Centuries* (republished in 1996) and *Dress in Eighteenth Century England* of 1979. Once retired and with more time for archival research, she published a series of articles that incorporated new consumption approaches. That Buck centered her work on object-based approaches was rare enough, but rarer still is that her enthusiasms and expertise embraced the clothes of all levels of society.

Another group of women fashion historians developed the work of Talbot Hughes, studying surviving clothing through analysis of the cut and making up garments and specializing in producing cutting patterns of period clothing. Nora Waugh taught theater wardrobe design at the Central School of Arts and Crafts in London. She published *Corsets and Crinolines* in 1954, *The Cut of Men's Clothes* in 1964, and *The Cut of Women's Clothes* in 1969. Based on patterns drawn up from surviving garments, Waugh added details of style history and making up details but was vague on many sources.

This methodology was further developed by Janet Arnold and explained in her *Handbook of Costume* of 1973. Arnold spent a lifetime exploring dress history through meticulous analysis of the cut of male and female fashionable dress. She was frequently called on by museums on both sides of the Atlantic to advise on dating reconstructing damaged period clothing and often advised on film and theater productions.

New Approaches from the 1980s

From the 1980s, a great range of more open-minded theoretical approaches, derived from other academic fields, transformed the entire field of fashion history study These included analysis of the semiotics of fashion, new approaches to the coded body (fashionable, subcultural, and male/female, and gay/lesbian). Elizabeth Wilson's work is cited by many as seminal to the acceptance of "fashion" as a legitimate field of study. Wilson's *Adorned in Dreams* of 1985 (revised in 2003), which included a celebration of the enjoyment that women can derive on their own terms from fashionable dress, was a turning point. From the 1980s, interest in fashion history blossomed through new critical approaches flowing out from the developing fields of cultural and gender studies. These have had a dramatic impact on fashion history research as reflected since 1997 in the pages of *Fashion Theory: The Journal of Dress, Body and Culture*, founded and edited by Valerie Steele.

Object-Focused Study

Older, established fashion history methodologies have had to respond to these fresh approaches and have held their ground. Naomi Tarrant, of the Royal Museums of Scotland, Edinburgh, in her 1994 book, *The Development of Costume* stressed her conviction that artifact-based approaches remained a vital counterweight to theoretical analysis. Museum fashion history exhibitions in North America and across Europe spawned significantly new types of glossy yet informative and critical shows and catalogs, such as Richard Martin's and Harold Koda's study of orientalism and fashion at the Costume Institute of the Metropolitan Museum of Art in 1994. *Radical Fashion*, curated by Claire Wilcox at the Victoria and Albert Museum in London, placed contemporary radical couture and conceptual dress in front of the British public for the first time. Other "designer" exhibitions and catalogs have sparked debate about an overly close relationship between museums and global fashion companies through muchneeded financial sponsorship. Some suggest that as the fashion world itself relies more and more on celebrity product endorsement, fashion history too must respond to the commercial and cultural realities that surround the fashion world in the early 2000s.

Studies on Fashion Designers

The history of the haute couture industry is thus subject to more intensive debate than ever before and studies now move far beyond the usual coffee-table books. Alexandra Palmer's *Couture and Commerce*, for example, is a seminal example of these new approaches. This beautifully illustrated study details the processes of the designing, making, and retailing of

Paris couture clothes, as well as their social consumption and cultural meanings to Toronto society in the 1950s.

Conceptual Fashion

The advent of conceptual fashion has triggered new analytical debate in studies by, for example, Caroline Evans, Jennifer Craik, Richard Martin, Joanne Entwhistle, and Christopher Breward. The journal *Fashion Theory*, too, has been at the forefront of these developments. Breward writes that "the self constructed role of radical fashion design seems to be to present a very specialized commentary on the vicissitudes of contemporary taste and aesthetics, everything to do with internal fashion culture debate about genre, hierarchy, presentation and style" to be "showcased rather than sold" (Breward 2003, p. 229). Finally, Caroline Evans's seminal 2003 study *Fashion at the Edge* debates conceptual and couture fashion from the 1990s, using fashion development as a tool through which to "pathologize contemporary culture" and to examine its characteristics of "alienation and nihilism." She discusses conceptual and couture fashion as "a form of catharsis, perhaps a form of mourning and a coping stratagem. . . [It is] the dark side of a free market economy, the loosening of social controls, the rise of risk and uncertainty as key elements of 'modernity' and 'globalization.' She writes, "The dark history of twentieth century seems finally to have caught up with fashion design" (Evans 2003, p. 308–309).

Thus, fashion studies and fashion history are fields that positively incorporate critical approaches built around anthropology, psychology, history of technology, business, sociology, material culture, and cultural studies. The best examples of good practice are also finally filled with impressive color plates and intelligently fuse object and theory. It is serious debates such as these that confirm the fundamental and central cultural place of fashion within society and that clarify the future directions for the field of fashion history and fashion studies.

See also Ancient World: History of Dress; Appearance; Fashion, Theories of.

Bibliography

The sections on the history of fashion publications are drawn from chapters 1 and 2 of Lou Taylor, *Establishing Dress History*, 2004, Manchester University Press, with their kind permission.

Arnold, Janet. *A Handbook of Costume*. London: Macmillan, 1973.

Bertin, Célia. *Paris à la Mode: A Voyage of Discovery*. London: Gollancz, 1956.

Breward, Christopher. *The Hidden Consumer: Masculinities, Fashion and City Life 1860–1914*. Manchester, U.K.: Manchester University Press, 1999.

——. *Fashion*. Oxford: Oxford University Press, 2003.

Buck, Anne. *Victorian Costume and Costume Accessories*. London: Jenkins, 1961.

——. *Thomas Lester, His Lace and the East Midlands Industry 1820–1905*. Bedford: Ruth Bean, 1981.

Craik, Jennifer. *The Face of Fashion: Cultural Studies in Fashion*. London and New York: Routledge, 1994.

Cunnington, Cecil Willett. *English Women's Clothing in the Nineteenth Century*. London: Faber, 1937.

——. *Handbook of English Costume in the Eighteenth Century*. London: Faber, 1957.

——. *Handbook of English Costume in the Nineteenth Century*. London: Faber, 1959.

Cunnington, Phillis. *Costume for Births, Marriages and Deaths*. London: Adam and Charles Black, 1972.

Entwistle, Joanne, and Elizabeth Wilson, eds. *Body Dressing*. Oxford: Berg, 2001.

Evans, Caroline. *Fashion at the Edge: Spectacle, Modernity and Deathliness*. New Haven, Conn., and London: Yale University Press, 2003.

Evans, Caroline, and Minna Thornton. *Women and Fashion: A New Look*. London: Quartet, 1989.

Davis, Fred. *Fashion Culture and Identity*. Chicago: University of Chicago Press, 1994.

Flügel, John Carl. *The Psychology of Clothes*. London: Hogarth Press Institute of Psycho-Analysis, 1930.

Habitus Praecipuorum Populorum tam Virorum quam Feminarum Singulari Arte Depicti. Nuremberg, Germany: Hans Weigel, 1577.

Langley Moore, Doris. *The Woman in Fashion*. London: B. T. Batsford, Ltd., 1949.

——. *The Child in Fashion*. London: B. T. Batsford, Ltd., 1953.

Laver, James. *Taste and Fashion*. London: Harrap, London, 1937. Reprint, London: G. G. Harrap, 1945.

——. *Costume and Fashion: A Concise History*. London: Thames and Hudson, Inc., 1982. Reprint, New York: Thames and Hudson, Inc., 1995.

Martin, Richard, and Harold Koda. *Orientalism and Fashion: Visions of the East in Western Dress*. New York: Metropolitan Museum of Art, 1994.

McClellan, Elisabeth. *Historic Dress in America, 1607–1800*. Philadelphia: George W. Jacobs and Company, 1904.

Palmer, Alexandra. *Couture and Commerce: The Transatlantic Fashion Trade in the 1950s*. Vancouver, Canada: University of British Columbia Press, 2001.

Parsons, Frank Alvah. *The Psychology of Dress*. New York: Doubleday, Page; London: B. T. Batsford, Ltd., 1920.

Planché, J. R. *History of British Costume*. London: George Bell, 1893.

Steele, Valerie. *Paris Fashion: A Cultural History*. New York and Oxford: Oxford University Press, 1988.

——. *The Corset: A Cultural History*. New Haven, Conn., and London: Yale University Press, 2001.

Strutt, Joseph. *A Complete View of the Manners, Customs, Arms, Habits etc. of the Inhabitants of England* (1774, 1775, and 1776) and *Complete View of the Dress and Habits of the People of England*, 1796 and 1799.

Tarrant, Naomi. *The Development of Costume*. London: Routledge, 1994.

Taylor, Lou. *The Study of Dress History*. Manchester, U.K.: Manchester University Press, 2002.

Troy, Nancy. *Couture Culture: A Study in Modern Art and Fashion*. Cambridge, Mass., and London: MIT Press, 2002.

Veblen, Thorstein. *Theory of the Leisure Class*. New York: Macmillan, 1899.

Wilcox, Claire. *Radical Fashion*. London: Victoria and Albert Museum, 2001.

Wilson, Elizabeth. *Adorned in Dreams: Fashion and Modernity*. New ed. London: I. B. Tauris, 2003.

Lou Taylor

FASHION, THEORIES OF

Fashion involves change, novelty, and the context of time, place, and wearer. Blumer (1969) describes fashion influence as a process of "collective selection" whereby the formation of taste derives from a group of people responding collectively to the zeitgeist or "spirit of the times." The simultaneous introduction and display of many new styles, the selections made by the innovative consumer, and the notion of the expression of the spirit of the times provide impetus for fashion. Central to any definition of fashion is the relationship between the designed product and how it is distributed and consumed.

Fashion systems model. The study of fashion in the twentieth century has been framed in terms of a fashion systems model with a distinct center from which innovations and modifications radiate outward (Davis 1992). Designers work from the premise of one look, one image for all, with rules about hem lengths and what to wear with what. In this model, the fashion-consuming public develops from an innovative central core, surrounded by receptive bands of fashion consumers radiating outward from the center.

Within this system innovation can originate from a select grouping of designers, such as Christian Dior who introduced the "New Look" in 1947. Influential factors can range from individual tastes, to current events, to marketing and sales promotions. The ultimate qualifier of the fashion systems model is the scope of influence, urging, even demanding, one look for all. The element of conformity is instrumental.

Populist model. An alternative model to the fashion systems model is the "populist" model. This model is characterized as polycentric, where groups based upon differences of age, socioeconomic status, location, and culture create their own fashion. Such groups might include teenagers in a certain school or senior citizens in a retirement community. Polhemus (1994) describes "styletribes" as a distinct cultural segment that generates a distinctive style of dress and decoration. Such "styletribes" may create their own looks from combining existing garments, creating their own custom colors by tie-dyeing or painting, mixing and matching from previously worn and recycled clothing available in thrift shops and vintage markets. They are not so concerned with one style of dressing as with expressing themselves, though there is an element of conformity that derives from the processes used and the resulting social behavior. Polhemus reflects that such "styletribes" have flourished at "precisely that time in history when individuality and personal freedom have come to be seen as the defining features of our age" (p.14).

The Flow of Fashion

The distribution of fashion has been described as a movement, a flow, or trickle from one element of society to another. The diffusion of influences from center to periphery may be conceived of in hierarchical or in horizontal terms, such as the trickle-down, trickle-across, or trickle-up theories.

Trickle down. The oldest theory of distribution is the trickle-down theory described by Veblen in 1899. To function, this trickle-down movement depends upon a hierarchical society and a striving for upward mobility among the various social strata. In this model, a style is first offered and adopted by people at the top strata of society and gradually becomes accepted by those lower in the strata (Veblen; Simmel; Laver). This distribution model assumes a social hierarchy in which people seek to identify with the affluent and those at the top seek both distinction and, eventually, distance from those socially below them. Fashion is considered a vehicle of conspicuous consumption and upward mobility for those seeking to copy styles of dress. Once the fashion is adopted by those below, the affluent reject that look for another.

Trickle across. Proponents of the trickle-across theory claim that fashion moves horizontally between groups on similar social levels (King; Robinson). In the trickle-across model, there is little lag time between adoption from one group to another. Evidence for this theory occurs when designers show a look simultaneously at prices ranging from the high end to lower end ready-to-wear. Robinson (1958) supports the trickle-across theory when he states that any social group takes its cue from contiguous groups in the social stratum. King (1963) cited reasons for this pattern of distribution, such as rapid mass communications, promotional efforts of manufacturers and retailers, and exposure of a look to all fashion leaders.

Trickle up. The trickle-up or bubble-up pattern is the newest of the fashion movement theories. In this theory the innovation is initiated from the street, so to speak, and adopted from lower income groups. The innovation eventually flows to upper-income groups; thus the movement is from the bottom up.

Examples of the trickle-up theory of fashion distribution include a very early proponent, Chanel, who believed fashion ideas originated from the streets and then were adopted by couture designers. Many of the ideas she pursued were motivated by her perception of the needs of women for functional and comfortable dress. Following World War II the young discovered Army/Navy surplus stores and began to wear pea jackets and khaki pants. Another category of clothing, the T-shirt, initially worn by laborers as a functional and practical undergarment, has since been adopted universally as a casual outer garment and a message board.

Thus how a fashionable look permeates a given society depends upon its origins, what it looks like, the extent of its influence, and the motivations of those adopting the look. The source of the look may originate in the upper levels of a society, or the street, but regardless of origin, fashion requires an innovative, new look.

Product Innovation

A new look may be the result of innovations in the products of dress, the way they are put together, or the type of behavior elicited by the manner of dressing. A fashionable look involves the form of clothing on the human body and its potential for meaning (DeLong 1998). Meaning can derive from the product, but meaning can also develop from ways of wearing the product, or from the body itself (Entwistle 2000). Fashionable dress embodies the latest aesthetic and what is defined as desirable at a given moment.

Lehmann (2000) describes fashion as a random creation that dies as an innovation is born. He views fashion as contradictory, both defining the ancient and contemporary by randomly quoting from the past as well as representing the present. Robinson (1958) defines fashion as pursuing novelty for its own sake. Lipovetsky (1994) claims that determining factors in fashion are the quest for novelty and the excitement of aesthetic play, while Roche (1994) describes fashion as dynamic change.

Though fashion implies continual change, certain products have persisted over long periods of time, such as blue jeans, which were made a staple of dressing in the United States in the twentieth century. Though blue jeans are a recognizable form, there is the potential for great variety in the product details, including stone washing, dyeing, painting, tearing, and fraying. Blue jeans epitomize the growth of casual fashion and endure because they can change to resonate with the times.

The way products are combined can define a fashionable look. For example, the idea of buying "separates" to mix and match instead of buying complete ensembles has increased the separate purchases of jackets, trousers, shirts, or blouses. The advent of the concept of separates coincided with the advent of the desired casual look. Mass production of sizes began to reflect a "one size fits all" model of fitting; more consumers could be fitted by choosing among the separate parts than would occur with the purchase of an ensemble with head-to-toe sizing requirements. Acceptance of separates and the growth of leisure was accompanied by a profound change, reflecting the restructuring of consumer societies and an increase in non-work lifestyles (Craik, p. 217).

The Fashion Life Cycle

An innovation is perceived as having a life cycle, that is, it is born, matures, and dies. Rogers's (1983) classic writing spells out rate of change, including characteristics of the product, the market, or audience, the distribution cycle, and those characteristics of individuals and societies where innovation takes place.

Diffusion of innovations. Diffusion is the spread of an innovation within and across social systems. Rogers (1983) defines an innovation as a design or product perceived as new by an individual. New styles are offered each season and whether an innovation is accepted depends upon the presence of five characteristics:

1. Relative advantage is the degree an innovation is seen as better than previous alternatives, in areas such as function, cost, social prestige, or more satisfying aesthetics.
2. Compatibility is the degree to which an innovation is consistent with the existing norms and values of the potential adopters. An innovation is less likely to be adopted that requires a change in values.
3. Complexity concerns how difficult it is to learn about and understand the innovation. An innovation has a greater chance of acceptance if easily learned and experienced.
4. Trialability is the extent to which an innovation may be tested with a limited commitment, that is, easily and inexpensively tried without too much risk.
5. Observability is the ease with which an innovation may be communicated to others.

The individual's role. The fashion adoption process results from individuals making a decision to purchase and wear a new fashion. Rogers (1983) suggests that this process involves five basic stages: awareness, interest, evaluation, trial, and adoption. The individual becomes aware of the fashion, takes an interest in it, and evaluates it as having some relative advantage that could range from a new fabric technology or simply as being consistent with self concept or what one's friends are wearing. If the individual evaluates the fashion positively, the process proceeds to trial and adoption.

The study of the pattern of consumers' adoption of a fashion is often represented by a bell-shaped curve. The life cycle of a specific fashion represented graphically indicates duration, rate of adoption, and level of acceptance. The graph depicts the rate and time involved in the diffusion process, with the horizontal axis indicating the time and the vertical axis indicating the number of adopters or users (Sproles and Burns 1994). Such graphically portrayed data can be used to calculate the level of acceptance for a fashion. For example, the curve for a fashion that is rapidly adopted but also rapidly declines will show early growth and quick recession. The curve resulting from plotting the data in this way leads to characteristic patterns of fashion adoption, applicable for fads or classics. The graph is also useful to identify type of consumer in terms of when each adopts a fashion within its life cycle. The consumer who adopts the fashion at the beginning of the curve is an innovator or opinion leader; at the peak, a mass-market consumer; after the peak, a laggard or isolate.

Fashion leaders and followers. Theories of fashion distribution all have in common the identification of leaders and followers. The fashion leader often transmits a particular look by first adopting it and then communicating it to others. Fashion followers include large numbers of consumers who accept and wear the merchandise that has been visually communicated to them.

A distinction exists between the role of the innovator and leader. The leader is not necessarily creator of the fashion or the first to wear it. The leader seeks distinction and dares to be different by wearing what the innovator presents as new. By adopting the look, the leader influences the flow or distribution of fashion. But the innovator within a group is also influential in serving as the visual communicator of the style. Historically the leader has been influential in some desirable way and possible leaders include athletes, movie stars, royalty, presidents, or fashion models.

Characteristics and Influencing Factors

Basic tensions addressed by fashion in Western culture are status, gender, occasion, the body, and social regulation. Craik (1994) suggests potential fashion instabilities, such as youth versus age; masculinity versus femininity; androgyny versus singularity; inclusiveness versus exclusiveness; and work versus play (p. 204). Fashion systems generally establish means for self-formation through dress, decoration, and gesture that attempt to regulate such tensions, conflicts, and ambiguities.

Social change and fashion. Social change is defined as a succession of events that replace existing societal patterns with new ones over time. This process is pervasive and can modify roles of men and women, lifestyles, family structures, and functions. Fashion theorists believe that fashion is a reflection of social, economic, political, and cultural changes, but also that fashion expresses modernity and symbolizes the spirit of the times (Lehmann, 2000; Blumer 1969; Laver 1937). Fashion both reflects and expresses the specific time in history.

The tension of youth versus age has influenced dress in the twentieth century. The trend has been toward separate fashionable images for the younger and older consumer, especially with the burgeoning baby population that followed World War II. Fashions for the young have tended to take on a life of their own, especially with the parade of retro looks of the last decades of the twentieth century that increasingly borrow images of recent time periods. Roach-Higgins (1995) reasons that because fashionable dress requires an awareness of change in the forms of dress within one's lifetime, the older consumer who has experienced that look before may choose not to participate (Roach-Higgins, Eicher, and Johnson, p. 395).

How one dresses for work and play has changed over time. A persistent trend of the twentieth century has been toward coveting leisure time coupled with an increasing need to look leisurely. Wearing casual clothing and leisurewear increased in the 1950s because families moved to the suburbs and engaged in many outdoor activities and sports. Clothing for spectator sports has increased, as has clothing for participation in many sports, such as tennis, golf, jogging, cycling, skiing, and rock climbing. In the 1970s the number of women who adopted pantsuits encouraged the trend to more casual dressing. In the 1990s the workplace was infiltrated by casual dress on Fridays. The formal-informal nature of dress reflects how much importance is placed on dress for work and play, but also the ambiguity and tension involved.

Appearance and identity. Clothes are fundamental to the modern consumer's sense of identity. That criticism of one's clothing and appearance is taken more personally and intensely than criticism of one's car or house suggests a high correlation between appearance and personal identity (Craik, p. 206).

People may buy a new product to identify with a particular group or to express their own personality. Simmel (1904) explained this dual tendency of conformity and individuality, reasoning that the individual found pleasure in dressing for self-expression, but at the same time gained support from dressing similarly to others. Flügel (1930) interpreted paradox using the idea of superior and inferior, that is, an individual strives to be like others when they seem superior but unlike them when they seem inferior. In this way fashion can provide identity, both as an emblem of hierarchy and equalizer of appearance.

Whether or not fashion and the way products are combined upon the body can be considered as a visual language has been a source of discussion in recent years. Barthes (1983) insists that fashion be perceived as a system, a network of relationships. Davis (1992) concludes that it is better to consider fashion as a code and not as a language, but a code that includes expression of such fundamental aspects of an individual as age, sex, status, occupation, and interest in fashion.

Culture, observer, and wearer. Fashion favors the critical gaze of the knowing observer, or the one "in the know," and the wearer who arranges the body for his own delight and enjoyment. Perceptions of the observer and wearer of fashion are sharpened based upon the many potential variations in lines, shapes, textures, and colors. For example, clothing of French inspiration and origin emphasized contour and cut of dress historically. Fashion changes occurred in the layout of the garment, which in turn focused attention on the silhouette and details, such as bias cutting and shaping (DeLong 1998). In contrast, societies where traditional dress has been worn, Korea, for example, fashion in traditional dress has derived more from the colors, motifs, and patterns adorning the surfaces, with the layout of the garments holding relatively constant. Thus subtle meaning derives not from the proportions of the *chogore* and *chima*, but from the variations found in the treatment of the surfaces (Geum and DeLong 1992).

Dress, agency, and popular culture. Popular culture can be defined loosely as those elements of entertainment that run alongside, within, and often counter to the elite structures of society. In the seventeenth century civilizing agents of aristocratic society included courtly entertainment, tournament, masque ball, and opera. But at the same time, popular culture became subject to increasing entrepreneurial control and commodification, with widening appeal to the urban merchant class (Breward 1995, p.97).

A new conception of popular culture was pertinent to the potential of dress as a communicator of social distinction and belonging. This movement preceded and contributed to the consumer and technological revolutions of the eighteenth century. Today popular culture is enhanced by the influence of mass media, and the medium has become the message, in many ways. According to Wilson (1985), fashion has become the connective tissue of the cultural organism and is essential to the world of mass communication, spectacle, and modernity.

Pursuit of modernity. Fashion is an accessible and flexible means of expressing modernity. The fashionable body has been associated with the city as a locus of social interaction and display (Breward, p. 35; Steele 1998). In the nineteenth century fashion was identified with a sense of contradiction of old and new. Modernity resulted in part from new technologies and a sense of the modern resulting from new ideas of design and consumption. Tensions from a growing commodification of fashionable trends emphasized the worldly and metropolitan. In the twentieth century modernity was identified through various but subtle means, from the way the dress contoured the body, to obvious product branding.

As a means of expressing modernity, Western fashions have been adopted by non-Western societies. In some societies where traditional styles of dress were prevalent, the men were quick to adopt Western business suits. Women have been slower to adopt Western dress in favor of traditional styles that express historical continuity. This creates an ambivalent message related to gender: Are women excluded from the modern world or are they simply the purveyors of tradition? Traditional dress in South Korea is more often seen on older women on occasions of celebration (Geum and DeLong). Both Chinese men and women have been encouraged recently to adopt Western styles of dress (Wilson 1985).

Gender and dress. A tension exists when women have been assigned the dual role of being fashionable as well as the subordinate gender (Breward 1995). In the last two centuries fashion has been primarily assigned to women, and it follows that fashionable dress and the beautification of the self could be perceived as expressions of subordination. Male dress has been somewhat overlooked. Veblen (1899) in the nineteenth century described separate spheres of the male and female, with feminine sartorial dress as a symbol of enforced leisure and masculine dress a symbol of power. Display and appearance of the body were considered innately feminine pursuits and thus the model was constructed in which overt interest in clothing appearance implied a tendency toward unmanliness and effeminacy. This gave rise to ultra-conservative, non-expressive male dress codes that prioritized the uniformity of the city suit as the model for respectable middle classes for males in most of the nineteenth and twentieth centuries (Breward, p. 170). This model does not entirely explain the way men consumed fashion, for example, the aesthete of the 1880s and dandy of the 1890s.

Such expressions of difference in gender roles and fashionable appearances of men and women also occur in other historical periods. Within medieval culture, the display of masculinity and femininity varied according to class, age, wealth, and nationality. Clothing, fashionably cut, moved toward overt display of the body and its sexual characteristics (Breward, p. 32). Interpretations of a male and female ideal permeated visual and literary interpretations of the human body. The male ideal focused upon proportion, strength, nobility, and grace; the female ideal included diminutive size, delicacy, and heightened color.

In medieval society, concepts of femininity included monopoly on production and maintenance of textiles, clothing, and accessories and the display of patriarchal wealth and status. When the monopoly of women was broken, production of clothing moved from the home to the public sphere. Male-dominated systems of apprenticeships emerged for weavers, cloth cutters, and tailors; the mass production and marketing system was born.

Market Forces and Momentum

The fashion industry has led the way, or followed, depending upon the nature of the fashion and its origins (Wilson 1985). Fashions serve as a reflection of their time and place and can be determined by society, culture, history, economy, lifestyle, and the marketing system. The market for fashion ranges from the world of couture to mass-produced clothing called ready-to-wear.

The couture fashion system and the couturier, who regularly presents a collection of clothing, originated in Paris, France. The couturier caters to the handmade, made-to-measure, exquisite product. In some ways the couturier functions as an artist, but when the product fails that designer ceases to exist. In this way the couturier walks a fine line between artist and industrialist (Baudot, p.11). The dominance of Paris as an international center depends as much on its sophistication as a fashion center as on the superiority of its clothing (Steele 1998).

Other countries beside France have taken on fashion leadership—notably, Italy, the United Kingdom, and the United States—and each country has placed its unique stamp on fashion (Agins 1999). For example, Milan, the hub of the Italian fashion industry is close to the country's leading textile mills in the Lake Como region. The Italians not only produce beautiful fabrics, they also design beautiful clothes as exemplified by such notable talents as Giorgio Armani and Krizia.

Though some may consider fashion frivolous, it is also considered a serious, lucrative business in capitalist society. The United States has been a leader in the technologies required for mass production and mass marketing of apparel, making fashion a democratic possibility, available to all.

Mass production and democratization of clothing. To provide clothing at moderate cost for all citizens took two primary developments, mass production and mass distribution (Kidwell and Christman 1974). Mass production required developing the technology for middle-quality clothing that could be made available for the majority. Mass distribution required the retailing of ready-made clothing and innovations in salesmanship and advertising. Department stores sprang up in every city following the Civil War and by the end of the century, mail-order houses were developed sufficiently to reach all citizens in the United States.

The clothing revolution that occurred in the twentieth century in the United States was a double revolution. The first was the making of clothing, from the homemade and custom-made to the ready-made or factory-made; the second was the wearing of clothing, from clothing of class display where clothing was worn as a sign of social class and occupation, to the clothing of democracy where all could dress alike. According to Kidwell and Christman (1974), in the eighteenth century anyone walking in Philadelphia or Boston could easily have distinguished towns people from country folk by the striking differences in their clothing. Clothing was distinctive because of differences in textiles and clothing construction. America was dependent upon England's textile industry so the rich purchased fine-quality silks, woolens, and cottons while others had limited access to fabrics that were coarse and middle to low grade. The tailor and dressmaker made clothing for the rich and the amateur made clothing for the average person.

In the nineteenth century, the industrial revolution brought the machine, the factory, and new sources of power. A series of great inventions mechanized the making of yarn and cloth. By 1850 machines included the invention and distribution of a practical sewing machine that was quickly adopted for men's shirts and collars and women's cloaks, crinolines, and hoopskirts. By the end of the nineteenth century, machine cutting was standard; pressing became more efficient. Men began to look and dress alike, and the sameness of their dress made multiple production by machine entirely possible.

Ready-made clothing for women lagged behind what was available for men. In 1860 ready-mades for women included only cloaks and mantillas, and dressmakers continued to supply women's fashions. Women of limited income made their own clothing, thus saving their clothing dollars for male family members. The department store and mail order were established means of distribution in the latter half of the nineteenth century.

In the early twentieth century, the mass-manufacturing process was organized and capable of producing clothing for both men and women. Thus was born an industry of industries, each with a system of organization to create ready-made clothing for everyone (Kidwell and Christman 1974). Though fashion always was an identifier of person, mass production equalized every person's opportunity to identify.

Marketing and distribution systems. Entwistle (2000) describes fashion as the product of a chain of activities that includes industrial, economic, cultural, and aesthetic. Changes in production and marketing strategies allowed for the expansion in consumer activity during the second half of the eighteenth century that led to increased consumption and the speeding up of the fashion cycle. This led to an increase in fashions that could be selected to reflect specific and individual circumstances.

In the twentieth century consumer choice was affected by means of mass distribution including chain stores, mail order, and Internet shopping. Chain stores have made fashion accessible within a relatively short drive for most consumers. Mail order has enabled a consumer in a remote area to follow fashion trends, select an appropriate garment, and place an order for ready-made clothing. Internet shopping relies on a person's access to a computer. Chain stores, mail order, and Internet shopping have extended the reach of fashion and created new consumer groups.

A Historical Perspective

Fashion is viewed broadly as a chronology of changing forms and a critique of wider cultural influences and their historical interpretation (Carter 2003; Johnson, Tortore, and Eicher 2003). The history of fashion reveals the importance of changes in appearance, but also the way fashion is conceived, who participates, and for what and how many occasions. The middle years of the fourteenth century have been identified as the first period of significant fashion change, generally related to the rise of mercantile capitalism in European cities (Lipovetsky 1994; Roche 1994; Breward 1995; Tortore and Eubank 1998). At that time, fashion became a practice of prestigious imitation among social groups and changes in tastes occurred often and were extensive enough for people to gain an appetite for new fashions in dress (Lipovetsky 1994; Roche 1994; Breward 1995). With class distinctions on the wane and an accelerated rate of stylistic change, the specific character of dress was associated with gender and the circumstance of different lifestyles. In the history of fashion, modern cultural meanings and values, especially those that elevate newness and the expression of human individuality to positions of dignity have allowed the fashion system to come into being and establish itself (Lipovetsky, p. 5).

The rise of fashion is associated with "the civilizing process" in Europe. The medieval woman engaged in what became the feminine pursuits of weaving, textile work, and fashion. Fashion in medieval society had a direct impact on the emerging of the individual, on self-knowledge, and understanding one's place in the world (Breward, p. 34). The body provided a principal means of expression through clothing; for example, to throw down one's glove was an act of defiance that committed a person to certain actions. The deliberate manipulation of the social meanings attached to clothing helped initiate a heightened sense of the significance of fashion.

Though fashion was first created for the privileged few, in the late nineteenth and twentieth century mass production made fashion accessible to the majority. In the nineteenth century the distinguishing feature of fashion was its imposition of an overall standard that nevertheless left room for the display of personal taste.

Fashion change accelerated with major apparel changes occurring in twenty-year intervals.

The twentieth century is characterized as the age of mass production, mass consumption, and mass media. Mass fashion became a form of popular aesthetics and a means of self-enhancement and self-expression. Advances in technology and materials used for clothing production provided more comfortable, cheaper, and more attractive items to a larger proportion of the population. In the early twentieth century, mass consumption of fashionable dress increased within the sphere of fashion promotion and advertising, leading to unlimited diversification. The fashion industry became more complex and fashion intervals shortened to ten years (Tortore and Eubank 1998).

Mass media has allowed for wide dissemination of fashion information and opportunities for the stimulation of a more homogeneous public imagination. The fashion magazine and the Hollywood film brought fashionable models to a hugely expanded audience from the 1920s onward. Examples of fashionable dress were often made available through the expansion of chain stores and mail-order companies. At the same time, a reorganization of business practices, of marketing and advertising, prioritized certain strands of society as fashion leaders. A cult of the designer, revolving around ideals of couture and high fashion or strong subcultural identities, ensured the survival of hierarchies based on notions of quality, style, and individuality (Breward, p. 183).

Steele (2000) surmised that in 1947 when Christian Dior launched his "New Look," it was still possible for a fashion designer to transform the way a woman dressed. The postwar transformation was remarkable, from the war years of boxy shoulders, rectangular torso, and short skirts to the postwar look of narrow shoulders, nippedin waist, padded hips, and long, full, flowing skirts. You could like it or hate it, but the look was the fashion, regardless (Steele 2000, p. 7).

Today major fashion changes occur frequently, but the choices and selections have increased so that mainstream fashion is one choice among many, including recycled clothing, vintage clothing, and wearable art. Also the easily recognizable rules of fashion, such as rigid proportions, hem lengths, and silhouettes now relate more to the particular look of one group than to a fashionable look for all. Agins (1999) has declared the end of fashion, but only as it has been known historically.

See also Fashion, Historical Studies of; Trickle-Down.

Bibliography

Agins, T. *The End of Fashion*. New York: William Morrow, 1999.

Barthes, R. *The Fashion System*. New York: Hill and Wang; Farrar, Straus, and Giroux, 1983.

Baudot, F. *Fashion, The Twentieth Century*. New York: Universe, 1999.

Benedict, R. "Dress." *Encyclopedia of the Social Sciences*. New York: Macmillan, 1931.

Blumer, H. "Fashion: From Class Differentiation to Collective Selection." *The Sociological Quarterly* 10, no. 3 (1969): 275–291.

Brannon, E. *Fashion Forecasting*. New York: Fairchild Publications, 2000.

Breward, C. *The Culture of Fashion*. Manchester, U.K.: Manchester University Press, 1995.

Carter, M. *Fashion Classics: From Carlyle to Barthes*. Oxford: Berg, 2003.

Craik, J. *The Face of Fashion*. New York: Routledge, 1994.

Davis, F. *Fashion, Culture, and Identity*. Chicago: University of Chicago Press, 1992.

DeLong, M. *The Way We Look, Dress and Aesthetics*. 2nd ed. New York: Fairchild Publications, 1998.

Entwistle, J. *The Fashioned Body, Fashion, Dress and Modern Social Theory*. Cambridge, Mass.: Polity Press, 2000.

Flügel, J. *The Psychology of Clothes*. London: Hogarth Press, 1930.

Geum, K., and M. DeLong. "Korean Traditional Dress as an Expression of Heritage." *Dress* 19 (1992): 57–68.

Johnson, K., S. Tortore, and J. Eicher. *Fashion Foundations: Early Writings on Fashion and Dress*. Oxford: Berg, 2003.

Kidwell, C., and M. Christman. *Suiting Everyone: The Democratization of Clothing in America*. Washington, D.C.: Smithsonian Institution Press, 1974.

King, C. "Fashion Adoption: A Rebuttal to the 'Trickle Down' Theory." In *Toward Scientific Marketing*. Edited by S. Greyser. Chicago: American Marketing Association, 1963.

Laver, J. *The Concise History of Costume and Fashion*. New York: Harry N. Abrams, 1969.

Lehmann, U. *Tigersprung: Fashion in Modernity*. Cambridge, Mass.: MIT Press, 2000.

Lipovetsky, G. *The Empire of Fashion*. Princeton, N.J.: Princeton University Press, 1994.

McCracken, G. "Meaning Manufacture and Movement in the World of Goods." In *Culture and Consumption*. Bloomington: Indiana University Press, 1988.

Nystrom, P. *Economics of Fashion*. New York: Ronald Press, 1928.

Polhemus, T. *Streetstyle: From Sidewalk to Catwalk*. London: Thames and Hudson, Inc., 1994.

Roach-Higgins, M. E. "Awareness: Requisite to Fashion." In *Dress and Identity*. Edited by M. E. Roach-Higgins, J. Eicher, and K. Johnson. New York: Fairchild Publications, 1995.

Robinson, D. "The Rules of Fashion Cycles." *Harvard Business Review* (November–December 1958).

——. "Style Changes: Cyclical, Inexorable, and Foreseeable." *Harvard Business Review* 53 (November–December 1975): 121–131.

Roche, D. *The Culture of Clothing*. Translated by J. Birrell. Cambridge, U.K.: Cambridge University Press, 1994.

Rogers, E. *Diffusion of Innovations*. 4th ed. New York: Free Press, 1995.

Simmel, G. "Fashion." *International Quarterly* 10 (1904): 130–155.

Sproles, G., and L. Burns. *Changing Appearances*. New York: Fairchild Publications, 1994.

Steele, V. *Paris Fashion: A Cultural History*. Rev. ed. Oxford: Berg, 1998.

——. "Fashion: Yesterday, Today and Tomorrow." In *The Fashion Business*. Edited by N. White and I. Griffiths. Oxford: Berg, 2000.

Tortore, P., and K. Eubank. *Survey of Historic Costume*. 3rd ed. New York: Fairchild Publications, 1998.

Veblen, T. *The Theory of the Leisure Class*. New York: Macmillan, 1899.

Wilson, E. *Adorned in Dreams: Fashion and Modernity*. London: Virago Press, 1985.

Marilyn Revell DeLong

FATH, JACQUES

A key figure in the revival of the Paris fashion industry after World War II, Jacques Fath (1912–1954) created colorful and inventive designs catering to a young and sophisticated international clientele who identified with the vitality of his label. Though Fath was regarded as one of the "big three" Paris designers in the early 1950s—along with Christian Dior and Pierre Balmain—his untimely death at the age of forty-two meant that the impact and importance of his work was often overlooked in comparison to that of his contemporaries. While Fath's designs were right on the mark of the glamorous postwar look, it was his attitude toward business and his understanding of the power of publicity and marketing that helped to place this charismatic and flamboyant designer apart from his peers.

Fath was born just outside Paris into an artistic family in 1912. His grandfather was a successful artist named René-Jacques Fath. Although Fath's great-grandmother had also been an artist who occasionally worked in fashion illustration, the designer did little to suppress the rumor that she had been a couturière to the Empress Eugénie. Encouraged by his family to enter the business world, Fath worked for a stockbroker for two years upon finishing his education. After completing a required year of military service, however, he realized that a more creative career lay in store. He spent some time in drama school and also took evening courses in drawing and pattern cutting. During this period Fath met Geneviève Boucher de la Bruyère, a photographer's model and fellow drama student, who became his wife in 1939. She modeled many of Fath's early creations and came to epitomize the elegantly finished style of the Jacques Fath woman.

At the end of 1936, Fath established a couture house in the rue de la Boetie and showed his first collection of just twenty garments in the spring of 1937. The collection was well received and enabled Fath to build up a steady clientele, although he still had something of a hand-to-mouth existence in the 1930s. Guillaune notes that in later years Fath recalled how he often used the money from a deposit on a garment to purchase the fabric to make it.

Fath served in the French Army during World War II. After he was demobilized following the fall of France to the Germans in 1940, however, he continued to run his house on a small scale. Having already moved once, Fath secured a permanent home for his label in an imposing eighteenth-century building on the avenue Pierre Premier de Serbie. In 1945 he created four designs for the Théâtre de la Mode, a traveling exhibition of fashion dolls that showcased the work of the top Parisian couturiers.

An astute businessman, Fath decided to add a line of perfumes to his fashions. He launched his first perfume, Chasuble, in 1945 and his second, Iris Gris, a year later. Recognizing the incredible potential to expand his business in the United States, he signed a contract with the New York manufacturer Joseph Halpert in 1948. Fath contracted to provide two collections a year, each comprising about twenty models to be marketed in large department stores throughout the United States. His popularity in America was further increased when Rita Hayward chose him to design her wedding dress and trousseau for her marriage to Prince Aly Khan in 1949. Fath had a loyal following in Hollywood, and designed the costumes for several movies both in the United States and Europe. His costumes for Moira Shearer in the celebrated film *The Red Shoes* (1948) were considered classics.

An attractive and gregarious person, Fath recognized the importance of associating his label with fantasy and marketing images of a lavish lifestyle that his clients could share. He was often photographed with his beautiful wife at evening events in Paris or basking in the sun on the Riviera. He threw large, sumptuous, themed costume parties at his château, inviting an international mix of socialites, actors, and fellow couturiers—which ensured maximum publicity in the press.

The year 1950 was eventful for the designer, with both the launch of his perfume Canasta and the opening of his boutique. Fath's boutique offered more affordable items, such as accessories, scarves, ties, and stockings. He was also chosen by the Chambre Syndicale de la Haute Couture to become one of five designers, alongside Carven, Desses, Paquin and Piguet, to make up a group of associated couturiers. Later that same year he set up a separate company, Parfums Jacques Fath, to market his growing line of scents. In 1953, preempting similar moves from other designers to target a larger market, Fath made the decision to launch a ready-to-wear collection. The Jacques Fath Université range was inspired by the fast and efficient mass-production methods that the designer had seen in the United States.

Fath's love of the dramatic was evident in his clothes. He drew much of his inspiration from historic costume, the theater, and the ballet. These influences are apparent in his use of the bustle and corsetry as recurring motifs, and in his playful and undulating lines. He perfected a clean and tailored hourglass shape, enhancing it with plunging necklines, sharp pocket details, or dramatic pleats. Fath experimented with asymmetry, pleating, and volume, designing huge voluminous skirts for both day and evening attire. These skirts cascaded from beneath his signature constricted waistline, or appeared as explosions of fabric under large enveloping coats and jackets. Fath's clever use of color ran from discreet juxtapositions of soft colors to loud prints in strong shades. His designs often featured a tartan patterned fabric and a plain fabric combined in one garment and he was unafraid to use bold modern prints to add an extra dimension to the controlled lines of his tailored garments.

Fath's collections of 1948 were notable for rejecting the full New Look silhouette in favor of severe tubular skirts and dresses cut along diagonal lines. His spring collection of 1950 caused a sensation when it was displayed, with dresses featuring a plunging décolletage accompanied by starched wing collars fastened with a bow tie—a suggestive look that later became identified with Playboy bunnies. Fath was extremely fond of fine wool tweed and jersey fabrics for daywear, often draping these materials directly onto a mannequin to create a new design. Rich satins, taffetas, and fine chiffons were his fabrics of choice for evening gowns, and he often used fur, both in trimmings and as full garments, to dramatic effect.

In 1954 Jacques Fath died tragically early at the age of forty-two. He left behind him a fashion empire at the height of its success, with over six hundred employees. Geneviève Fath valiantly took over the business for a few years, but closed the clothing line in 1957. The Fath name continued as a perfume label until 1992, when it was acquired by a succession of different companies. The most recent owner of the Fath label was the France Luxury Group, who resurrected the clothing line in 2002 in an attempt to restore the success of this once great house.

See also Fashion Marketing and Merchandising; Film and Fashion; Haute Couture; New Look; Paris Fashion; Perfume; Tartan; Theatrical Costume.

Bibliography

Balmain, Pierre. *My Years and Seasons*. London: Cassell and Co.,1964.

Charles-Roux, Edmonde, et al. *Théâtre de la Mode: Fashion Dolls: The Survival of Haute Couture*. Portland, Ore.: Palmer-Pletsch Associates, 2002.

Guillaume, Valérie. *Jacques Fath*. Paris: Adam Biro et Paris Musées, 1993.

Lynam, Ruth, ed. *Paris Fashion, The Great Designers and Their Creations*. London: Michael Joseph, 1972.

Millbank, Caroline Rennolds. *Couture: The Great Fashion Designers*. London: Thames and Hudson, 1985.

Steele, Valerie. *Paris Fashion: A Cultural History*. 2d ed. Oxford, New York, and Tokyo: Berg/Oxford International Publishers, 1998.

Watson, Linda. *Vogue: Twentieth Century Fashion*. London: Carlton Books, 2000.

Oriole Cullen

FENDI

Fendi is a synonym of fur and revolution, two apparently contradictory concepts. Having accepted the idea of mass consumption, Fendi attempted to provide furs for women of every social position, or nearly so, demystifying the luxury connotations that have always characterized this type of garment.

The story begins at the corner of the Piazza Venezia in Rome in 1925, where there was a small Fendi boutique and, next door to it, a fur and leather workshop, owned by Edoardo and Adele Fendi. By the 1930s they had expanded the business considerably. But the true protagonists of Fendi's success are their daughters—Paola (b. 1931), Anna (b. 1933), Franca (b. 1935), Carla (b. 1937), and Alda (b. 1940)—who made the Fendi label famous throughout the world. All five daughters began working in the family business at an early age—between fifteen and eighteen—assuming different responsibilities as required. In 1964 they opened the office on the via Borgognona in Rome, with a large picture of their mother, Adele, in the entrance. In 1965 they began their collaboration with Karl Lagerfeld, the designer who, together with the Fendi sisters, helped develop a renewed interest in furs. During this time, the famous black and brown double "F," one of the first company logos, was created.

During the second half of the 1950s, ownership of a fur garment was the dream of many women, but following the social changes that occurred in the 1960s and 1970s, fur came to be seen as old-fashioned and bourgeois. An illustration by the well-known painter Giuseppe Novello, outstanding illustrator of Italy's postwar bourgeoisie, shows a woman at two different stages of her life. In the first image she is young and thin and wears a fitted coat. In the second she is weighted down by the years and stuffed into a large fur. The caption reads "When I first started wanting a fur coat . . . and when I finally had one" (Novello, p. 32).

Lagerfeld, under the sisters' direction, experimented with materials, patterns, finishes, weight, tanning methods, and colors, so that furs would be seen as something completely new, supported by advanced technological craftsmanship, suited to the needs of a public that wanted more accessible and wearable fashion. In 1966 he scandalized the fashion world by introducing color as a design element: "A colorful fur coat that was not precious but original" (Aragono, p. 92).

One of the characteristics of the Fendi label is the company's unusual way of working with traditional skins. Fendi designers were continually experimenting on furs and in 1969, with the introduction of their Pret à Porter line, besides the exclusively artisan manufacturing, Fendi succeeded in producing a product accessible to the ordinary consumer: beautiful furs at a limited price.

Fendi used furs that were considered to be of "poor" quality, which the company then reworked and reinterpreted, and expensive skins, such as fox, ermine, mink, and astrakhan, which it transformed using different finishes and colors, so that they no longer were seen as stiff and conservative but as fashionable outerwear.

The same approach was used in the treatment of leather, especially handbags, which although they were luxury items, were made more versatile through the addition of printed patterns, unusual colors, and new designs. In 1968 Classic Canvas was launched, an alternative to leather; then striped colored rubber—beige and black—that became Fendi's classic colors.

In 1977 Fendi introduced a line of ready-to-wear, known as "365—a dress for every day of the year, for a woman who wants her fur and purse to match her dress." (Villa). In 1978 they brought out a line of shoes, produced by Diego Della Valle. In the 1970s Fendi also launched new artisan-made lines: Giano, Astrologia, Pasta, and Selleria, all in limited edition and numbered.

When Adele died in 1978, each of the five Fendi children took over a different part of the business: Paola was primarily interested in furs; Anna, in leather goods. Franca handled customer relations, Carla coordinated the business, and Alda was responsible for sales. In the 1980s, as was the case with many Italian fashion houses, Fendi underwent a period of considerable expansion, involving product diversification and especially licensing. A wide range of products now bore the Fendi label—sweaters, suits, jeans, umbrellas, clocks, ceramics, and household decorations. Stores and boutiques were opened around the world. In 1985 Fendi even produced the uniforms for the Rome police department. That same year they launched their first perfume. In 1987 they introduced the Fendissime line, conceived by the third generation of the Fendi family: Silvia, Maria Teresa, Federica, and Maria Ilaria Fendi. The new line included sportswear, furs, and accessories for younger buyers. In 1989 they opened their first store in the United States, located on Fifth Avenue in New York City. The following year

they introduced a men's perfume and ready-to-wear line.

In 1997 they began making a series of handbags that quickly became cult objects. The most famous is the Fendi "Baguette," inspired by the shape of French bread, and conceived by Silvia Venturini Fendi. A small, minimalist jewel produced in a wide range of materials from horsehide to pearls, in six hundred different versions, it was an extraordinary success, chosen by Madonna, Julia Roberts, Naomi Campbell, and Gwyneth Paltrow. A special baguette called Lision was produced in limited edition, embroidered with an eighteenth-century loom at the speed of only five centimeters per day. The Rollbag, which was wrapped in a transparent case, followed in 1999. The Ostrik bag appeared in 2002 and the Biga Bag, favored by Sharon Stone, in 2003.

Silvia Venturini Fendi, together with Karl Lagerfeld, pursued the Fendi tradition of research in furs. For their Winter 2003–2004 collection they launched, among other furs, the "Vacuum Persian Fur," that is, a fur put into a PVC packaging, a fox fur cut into small stripes and then reassembled with small rubber bands, and depilated mink coats.

Meanwhile a number of licenses that had weakened the company's image were sold and Fendi focused on its core business, leather and fur. The Dark Store is the Fendi concept store based on the company's realignment. Dark Stores could be found in Paris, on rue François 1er and in the Galeries Lafayette on boulevard Haussmann, and on Sloane Street in London in the early 2000s.

Also in the early 2000s Silvia Venturini Fendi, Anna's daughter, was in charge of the style department as creative director of accessories and Man's Line.

In 2001, after considerable legal maneuvering associated with the mergers and acquisitions that typified the fashion world early in the twenty-first century, Fendi became part of the LVMH group, a giant in the world of luxury goods.

Over the years Fendi has designed costumes for both cinema and theater and has worked with a number of directors, including Luchino Visconti (*Gruppo di Famiglia in un Interno* 1975, *L'Innocente* 1976), Mauro Bolognini (*La Dame aux camélias* 1980), Franco Zeffirelli (*La Traviata* 1983), Sergio Leone (*C'era una Volta in America* 1983), Lina Wertmuller (*Scherzo*), Marco Ferreri (*Futuro di Donna* 1984), Dino Risi (*Le bon roi dagobert* 1984), Liliana Cavani (*Interno Berlinese* 1985), Francis Ford Coppola (*The Godfather III* 1999), Martin Scorsese (*The Age of Innocence* 1993, a film that won the Oscar for costumes, in which Michelle Pfeiffer was wearing Fendi furs designed by the costumist Gabriella Pascucci), and Alan Parker (*Evita* 1996, starring Madonna). Wes Anderson's *Royal Tenenbaums* (2001) featured a fur coat worn by Gwyneth Paltrow, that became popular.

See also Fur; Lagerfeld, Karl; Leather and Suede; Tanning of Leather.

Bibliography

Aragono, Bonizza Giordani, ed. *Moda Italia: Creativity and Technology in the Italian Fashion System.* Milan: Editoriale Domus, 1988.

Bianchino, Gloria, ed. *La moda Italiana.* Milan: Electa, 1987.

Laurenzi, Laura. "Fendi." In *Dizionario della moda 2004.* Edited by Vergani Guido and Gabriella Gregorietti. Milan: Baldini and Castoldi, 2003.

Novello, Giuseppe. *Sempre più difficile.* Milan: Mondadori, 1957.

Villa, Nora. *Le regine della moda.* Milan: Rizzoli International, 1985.

Simona Segre Reinach

FETISH FASHION

Fetishism is a term with a long and complicated history, encompassing religious, anthropological, economic, and sexual meanings. Missionary tracts with titles such as *Fetishism and Fetish Worshippers* denounced the "barbarous" religions of "primitive" people who worshiped "idols of wood or clay." The term fetish was then extended to refer not only to objects allegedly possessing magic powers, but also to anything that was irrationally worshiped. Karl Marx famously coined the term "commodity fetishism" to describe the way objects produced through human labor acquired an exaggerated exchange value. Sexologists and psychiatrists traditionally described fetishism as a sexual "perversion." Today, fetishism is usually characterized as a type of variant sexuality, in which arousal is associated with a (nongenital) part of the body, such as hair, or an inanimate object, such as a shoe.

Experts tend to agree that the majority of sexual fetishists are men. Indeed, the psychiatrist Robert Stoller argued, "fetishizing is the norm for males, not for females." However, the subject of female fetishism is of interest to cultural theorists. There are also thought to be degrees of fetishism. Many men may be sexually aroused by high-heeled shoes, for example, but only a minority require the presence of such shoes for sexual arousal—and even fewer women have such a directly sexual relationship with shoes. Fetishism has also been associated with sadomasochism and transvestism. Leather fetishists, for example, may be involved in sadomasochistic sexuality. Sigmund Freud argued that fetishism was caused by castration anxiety, but this theory is not widely accepted today.

High-heeled shoes, so-called "kinky" boots, corsets, lingerie, and garments made of leather or rubber are among the most common clothing fetishes. Sometimes individual clothing fetishes are combined; thus, a black leather corset might be worn with high-heeled boots and long rubber gloves. Fetishes are associated with particular sexual fantasies. Or as Stoller put it: "A fetish is a story masquerading as an object." In the nineteenth and early twentieth centuries, fetish clothing was utilized in secret sexual scenarios; for example, in brothels or the staging of pornographic imagery. Since the 1970s, however, clothing fetishes have played an increasingly important role in fashion and popular culture. As early as the 1960s, the television program *The Avengers* featured a character, Mrs. Peel, who wore a black leather catsuit that was modeled on an authentic fetish costume. Mrs. Peel's costume was a precursor of Michelle Pfeiffer's latex catsuit and mask in the film *Batman Returns*.

Fetishism moved from the sexual underground into mainstream popular culture via subcultural groups such as punks and leathermen. A youth subculture associated with bands like the Sex Pistols, the punks appropriated fetish clothing as part of their own "style in revolt." The fashion designer Vivienne Westwood, herself a punk, opened a shop in London called Sex, where she sold bondage trousers, rubber stockings, corsets, and extreme shoes to a clientele divided between real fetishists and young people attracted by the idea of breaking taboos. Westwood herself wore "total S&M as fashion" in the early 1970s, not just in private or at clubs, but on the street, as a way of subverting accepted social values.

The 1970s saw the spread of sexual liberation, women's liberation, and gay liberation—all movements that provided a context for the emergence of fetish fashion. Although many feminists regard fetish fashion as exploitative and misogynistic, the iconography of sexual fetishism unquestionably focused on images of powerful women. The image of the dominatrix or phallic woman was especially pronounced in the work of Helmut Newton, a very influential fashion photographer of the 1970s. As a result of his controversial pictures in magazines such as the French edition of *Vogue*, Newton is often credited with having made fetishism "chic." One of his fashion photographs of 1977, for example, was titled "Woman or Superwoman?" It showed a woman wearing a leather trench coat by French designer Claude Montana, accessorized with riding boots to convey the image of an Amazon, a subcategory of the dominatrix.

Jean Paul Gaultier is another designer who pioneered fetish fashion in the 1980s. Gaultier has told interviewers that, as a child, his grandmother's flesh-colored corsets fascinated him, and he describes the process of lacing a corset as ritualistic. Many of his designs for both men and women have featured corset-style lacing. He is probably most famous for the corset that he designed for Madonna's Blonde Ambition tour, which helped launch the trend for underwear-as-outerwear. Lingerie, of course, has become a ubiquitous influence on fashion

Perhaps even more than Gaultier, Thierry Mugler has focused on corsetry and on fetishized materials such as rubber and leather to create costumes that evoke the image of "the phallic woman." One of his couture ensembles was entirely handcrafted of leather, including a leather neck-corset. It resembled the carapace of an insect. Other hard-bodied styles include metal corsets and entire ensembles made of metal and plastic, which transform the wearer into a kind of armored cyborg. Indeed, there is virtually no fetish ensemble—from the clothing of the equestrienne to the military uniform—that has not appeared on Mugler's runways.

Leather is the material most often utilized in fetish fashion. Claude Montana was among the first to become known for fetish leather, to be followed in the 1990s by the Italian designer Gianni Versace, who caused a sensation with his leather fashions. Is it "chic or cruel?" asked *The New York Times*. Similar styles had been pioneered by sadomasochists, especially gay leathermen. Designers such as Thierry Mugler and John Galliano for Dior have also incorporated other second-skin materials, such as latex, into high fashion. All of the designers mentioned are also known for their "kinky" shoes and boots, which are the most important accessories in the wardrobe of fetish fashion. Fetish shoes typically feature extremely high heels and sometimes also high platforms and ankle straps or lacing that allude to bondage. Fetish boots tend to be either very high (to mid-thigh) or overtly aggressive-looking.

See also Fashion and Homosexuality; Film and Fashion; Galliano, John; Gaultier, Jean-Paul; Madonna; Mugler, Thierry; Versace, Gianni and Donatella; Westwood, Vivienne.

Bibliography

Gammon, Lorraine and Merja Makinen. *Female Fetishism.* New York: New York University Press, 1994.

Kunzle, David. *Fashion and Fetishism.* Totowa, N.J.: Rowman & Littlefield, 1982.

Lafosse-Dauvergne, Geneviève. *Mode et fétichisme.* Paris: Éditions Alternatives, 2002.

Steele, Valerie. *Fetish: Fashion, Sex & Power.* New York: Oxford University Press, 1996.

Stoller, Robert. *Observing the Erotic Imagination.* New Haven, Conn.: Yale University Press, 1985.

Valerie Steele

FILM AND FASHION

The couturier and designer of surreal hats, Elsa Schiaparelli once declared, "The film fashions of today are your fashions of tomorrow" (Prichard 1981, p. 370). Besides planning haute couture collections, Schiaparelli also designed costumes for such stars as Mae West (*Every Day's a Holiday* [1937]) and the British stars Margaret Lockwood and Anna Neagle (*The Beloved Vagabond* [1936], *Limelight* [1936]). Since then, the interrelationship between film and fashion has become more complex. Schiaparelli's belief in the direct influence of the "dream factory" on what ordinary people wore is borne out by a number of examples from the classical Hollywood period: one of Adrian's robes for Joan Crawford in *Letty Lynton* (1932) was widely copied, as was Edith Head's white party dress for Elizabeth Taylor in *A Place in the Sun* (1951). However, since then various factors have enriched and diversified fashion's interaction with film. First, there was—in the wake of Audrey Hepburn's successful collaboration with the then young and relatively unknown Paris couturier Hubert de Givenchy from *Sabrina* (1954) onward—the growing use of fashion as opposed to costume design on a number of key movies. Second, alongside this industrial shift and commensurate with the expansion within the couture industry into prêt-à-porter, there was an escalation of fashion's influence over film as well as the other way round. Third (and a far more contemporary factor) is the rise in celebrity culture and a burgeoning interest in movie stars, what they wear both on and off the screen.

From the 1920s through the 1940s, relatively few fashion designers demeaned themselves by working for moving pictures. The most notable Parisian export was Coco Chanel who, in 1931, was lured to Hollywood by Sam Goldwyn for $1 million, only to find that Hollywood costume design—because she was too meticulous, too precise—was not for her. When she returned to France, Chanel did return to costume designing, working on the films *Les Amants* (1958) and *L'année dernière à Marienbad* (1961). Despite the phenomenal impact on cinema as well as fashion of his New Look in 1947, Christian Dior lent his designs to a relatively small and eclectic series of films: René Clair's *Le silence est d'or* (1946), for example, some of the costumes for Jean-Pierre Melville's *Les enfants terribles* (1950), and Marlene Dietrich's costumes for Alfred Hitchcock's *Stage Fright* (1950). It was Givenchy's collaboration with Hepburn that changed everything.

Called in reputedly at Hepburn's behest, Givenchy's first film costumes were the ball gowns in *Sabrina*. The details of this story are muddled because Givenchy's account of his input in the film at times directly contradicts the version proffered by the film's overall costume designer, Edith Head. Head, who had designed the costumes for Hepburn's Oscar-winning role as the princess in *Roman Holiday* just the previous year, was clearly hurt by the star's—and director's—decision to acquire an actual Paris wardrobe for Sabrina. In *The Dress Doctor*, Head comments: "I had to console myself with the dress, whose boat neckline was tied on each shoulder"—widely known and copied as 'the *Sabrina* neckline'" (Head and Ardmore 1959, p. 119). Elsewhere, Givenchy queried Head's claim to the *bateau* neckline design. Certainly it is a more eyecatchingly cut than one might expect from Head who, having found her so-called breadline, rationing-conscious costumes of World War II made to look démodé by the immediate impact of Dior's opulent New Look, declared herself to be a "fence-sitter" who would follow rather than lead

fashion. This claim by Head that she intentionally occupied the middle of the road crystallizes the difference between the couturier and the straightforward costume designer. While the couturier might be more expressive and daring when designing for the screen, costume designers opted for safer styles that remained secondary to character and narrative and never, as the Hollywood director George Cukor commented, "knocked your eye out" (Gaines and Herzog 1990, p. 195). The inherently spectacular quality of Givenchy's designs for Hepburn is frequently accentuated by the nature of the narratives the costumes serve. In both *Sabrina* and later *Funny Face*, the story revolves around the Hepburn characters' Cinderella-esque rags-to-riches tales, transformed from a chauffeur's daughter to a millionaire's wife in one, bookshop assistant to an icon of glamour and sophistication in the other. The joke in *Funny Face*—in which Hepburn's character models clothes on a Paris catwalk—is ultimately that, for all the appeal of high fashion, Hepburn is happiest (and most iconic) when dressing down in black leggings, turtleneck, and flats.

There have been other significant collaborations between stars and designers—Adrian's partnerships with Greta Garbo and Joan Crawford, or Jean Louis's designs for Doris Day's comedies of the late 1950s and early 1960s—and following these, couturiers contributed more regularly to film costume design. Hardy Amies (Queen Elizabeth's favorite fashion designer) designed the wardrobe for films such as *The Grass Is Greener* (Stanley Donen, 1960) and *2001: A Space Odyssey* (Stanley Kubrick, 1968). Giorgio Armani later became the most prolific couturier costume designer, working on a number of films, ranging from *American Gigolo* (1980) to the remake of *The Italian Job* (2003). However, the way in which Armani has approached costume design—and this holds for several classic designers such as Nino Cerruti, Yves Saint Laurent, Donna Karan, Calvin Klein—is in a likewise classic way. His costumes occupy a traditional, servile role in relation to the narratives and characters they serve; they remain stylishly unobtrusive and do not "knock your eye out," as arguably Givenchy's extravagant ball gowns for Hepburn do. Cinema's most popular couturier costume designers, it seems, are those who follow the underpinning conventions of costume design.

From the 1970s onward, a schism has become increasingly apparent between the classic and the spectacular look in film. Peter Wollen has argued that only the latter kind of extrovert costume design (such as those in William Klein's 1966 film *Qui êtes-vous, Polly*

Maggoo?) can be considered art, thus echoing Saint Laurent's belief that "Art is probably too big a word for fashion. Fashion is a craft, a poetic craft" (Saint Laurent 1988, p. 20). The "art" of fashion in film would be exemplified by the film work of Jean Paul Gaultier, who has designed costumes for various art-house movies including *The Cook, the Thief, His Wife and Her Lover* (1989) and *Kika* (1993). In both, exaggerated versions of Gaultier's signature styles—his cone bras, his use of corsetry as outer clothing, his asymmetrical cutting, his persistent predilection for classic tailoring alongside much more radical designs—are evident with a pervasive, more nebulous interest in creating outlandish costumes in their own right. Gaultier's designs are intrinsically fashionable and extend the boundaries of costume and style (as Chanel once explained, there is an essential distinction to be drawn between "fashion," which is ephemeral, and "style," which endures). Although Gaultier trained with Pierre Cardin and Jean Patou (thereby explaining his residual interest in traditional tailoring), in *The Cook, the Thief* alone one can find a string of witty, audacious juxtapositions—there are echoes of Courrèges's space-age costumes (far more outlandish than Amies's designs for *2001*), the influence of the effete cavaliers and more than a whiff of seventeenth-century cardinals. In *Kika*, the smooth surface of classicism—exemplified by Victoria Abril's black bias-cut dress—is ruptured by radical flourishes, such as the prosthetic breasts bursting out of it.

The creation of self-consciously spectacular costumes (less "over the top" than drawing attention to themselves in whatever way) has persisted through a variety of eclectic movies. Gaultier's own wardrobe for Luc Besson's *The Fifth Element* (1997) is incontrovertibly spectacular; the clothes are ostentatious, wildly colorful, eclectic and, again, overtly sexual, as in Leeloo's artful stretch-bondage gear. Once more, these costumes flagrantly come in the way of character identification as one cannot help but notice them, and in their very styles (asymmetric, clashing) and man-made fabrics, they proclaim their ephemerality. This is only one, obvious, use of the spectacular; other more subtle examples from within contemporary film of costumes that draw attention to themselves and so intrude upon the seamlessness of the classical narrative form would be *The Talented Mr. Ripley* (1999), *Far from Heaven* (2002), and *Dolls* (2002). Like Luis Buñuel's *Belle de jour* (1967) before them, *Ripley* and *Far from Heaven* in particular make use of costumes that are only slightly out of the ordinary. The cardigan trimmed with thick, swirling braid

that Cate Blanchett is wearing when she bumps into the only slightly less ostentatiously dressed Paltrow is a further example of a costume's overt fashionableness being used to prevent the spectator's unthinking identification with the characters and the scene. Fashion (and it is important that the character Blanchett plays here is a textiles heiress) creates an alternative dialogue between text and spectator.

However, it is perhaps not altogether surprising that the dominant tendency in cinema has been to follow the Armani route, using fashion to denote stylishness and class but not to be too spectacular and so interrupt the flow or balance of a scene. For *The Italian Job* (2003), Armani's costumes are used, very traditionally, as a means of interpreting character. Essential differences between the principal characters are signaled through costume, in much the same way as Edith Head created a shorthand for understanding her characters through dress (a high-buttoned neckline for a repressed woman, a shimmering décolleté dress for a more sexually available one). So, Donald Sutherland's sensuous, unstructured wool coat and warm turtleneck sweater serve as coded references to his innate charm and old-school heist-master values (he has had enough of the criminal life and the "job" at the start of the film is meant to be his last before going straight), while Mark Wahlberg's tighter-fitting, slightly spivvy black leather jacket quickly makes him out to be eager and on the make. Armani had used a similar system of typage for the four protagonists in *The Untouchables* (1987)—the friendly father-figure in chunky knits, the nerd in a coat slightly too big, the cop from the wrong side of the tracks in his rather-too-jazzy brown leather jacket, and the dependable leader (again) in his flowing Armani coat and tailored three-piece.

The dressing of Gwyneth Paltrow in many of her films conforms to a similar pattern. Apart from her period films (*Emma*) and latterly *The Royal Tenenbaums* (2001), in which she appears to be signaling her desire to break free of her previous typecasting, Paltrow has exemplified a certain well-groomed, affluent but slightly frigid and repressed look, given to her in films such as *Sliding Doors* (1998) or Alfonso Cuarón's modern-day *Great Expectations* (1998) by the elegant but unexceptional designs of Calvin Klein and Donna Karan respectively. These designers, like Ralph Lauren before them, exemplify a specific kind of safe but sophisticated New York fashion. Like costumes in Hollywood's heyday, the clothes in these films accomplish the easy, unobtrusive creation of Paltrow's characters' social identity.

The straight lines, modern fabrics, and neutral colors do more than suggest the characters' fashionableness, they mark them out as coming from a specific milieu, in much the same way as Head's costumes for Grace Kelly in her Hitchcock films of the 1950s (*Rear Window, Dial M for Murder, To Catch a Thief*) had done.

The refined, slightly aloof elegance of Grace Kelly could perhaps have been expected to make a bigger impact on fashion itself than it did. The relationship between fashion and film is a two-way process: fashion designers get involved in films in part to showcase their designs and perhaps influence fashion outside cinema along the way. Armani, for example, has denied that his film designs are product placement, although the association with movies is a tidy way of giving his designs exposure. Films, even the less clearly fashionable ones, have frequently influenced fashion. There are multiple examples throughout cinema history of items of clothing in films making a significant intervention into fashion on the street. Some films (such as Michelangelo Antonioni's quintessentially 1960s' *Blowup*) are notable as "time capsules" of the fashions of their times, while others might add a look, a garment, or accessory to the contemporary fashion scene. The latter are more intriguing, as they are actively rather than passively engaged with fashion. Sometimes, though, the precise reason for a film having a significant impact on fashion might remain elusive; it simply captures the zeitgeist.

An early example of a single garment changing the course of fashion occurs in *It Happened One Night* (1934) in which Clark Gable takes off his shirt to reveal that he is not wearing an undershirt underneath (reputedly because he felt that taking off another shirt would prove ungainly). Undershirt sales in the United States plummeted by 30 percent. Male underwear sales went up again in the 1950s when the white T-shirt became a fashionable item of male clothing, with Marlon Brando sporting one in *The Wild One* (1953) and James Dean another in *Rebel without a Cause* (1955). Later examples of films directly impacting on fashion are *Annie Hall* (1977) and *Out of Africa* (1985). Just months after the respective releases of both films, the pages of American and British *Vogue* were awash with derivative images. The distinctive, ditsy look Ralph Lauren created for Diane Keaton as Annie Hall was swiftly mimicked in fashion magazines and in department stores as women were urged to mix up masculine and feminine styles as Annie had done—a big tweed jacket over a feminine shirt, or a waistcoat and tie over peg-top trousers to accentuate rather than obscure the feminine form. In

the wake of *Out of Africa*, both in the pages of glossy magazines and on the street, the safari look dominated women's and men's fashions alike. Fashion shoots had safari settings and ensembles featuring billowing linen, cotton shirts, wide skirts, breeches, and leather riding boots. A clear reason for the fashion success of both these films was that their looks were easily attainable; the British store Top Shop tempted shoppers to its *Out of Africa*–inspired collection with the tag line "Out of Oxford Circus, into Top Shop." Likewise, women and girls could achieve the androgynous Annie Hall look by simply raiding the wardrobes of their older, more traditional male relatives or by visiting thrift shops.

Two issues emerge from the impact a film such as *Out of Africa* had on fashion: that it still, despite being a period film, exerted considerable influence on contemporary fashion and that its wardrobe manifestly illustrated the importance of accessibility and democratization when it comes to film's influence on fashion. Few costume films have influenced fashion—although Edward Maeder makes a case for the 1933 version of *Little Women* leading to the popularization of such items as the gingham pinafore, and John Fairchild, publisher of *Women's Wear Daily*, waged a personal crusade in the late 1960s to have hemlines drop after enjoying *The Damned* (1962), *Doctor Zhivago* (1965), and *Bonnie and Clyde* (1967) (Prichard, 216). It is tempting to presume that any period piece that influences fashion must contain elements of inauthenticity: Julie Christie's "swinging sixties" makeup and hair in *Far from the Madding Crowd* (1967) or the anachronistically colorful gowns Michelle Pfeiffer wears in *The Age of Innocence* (Hollander 1993). If such period films have affected contemporary fashion, there has tended to be a manifest overlap between the fashions of the historical period and the fashion trends at the time the film is made. This mutuality was evident in the safari clothes of *Out of Africa* and was logically the reason for *Moulin Rouge*, with its basques and retro-new romantic styles, having been readily emulated in shop windows. While costume films have indirectly influenced designers (Kubrick's *Barry Lyndon* [1975] has been cited more than once as an inspiration by modern couturiers), the films rarely impact upon clothes styles as a whole.

The accessibility of film fashion has become a hugely significant factor in their appeal. In the 1970s and 1980s, fashion had become about what people wear, not what they might fantasize about wearing, a transition that altered the relationship with film. Quentin Tarantino's *Reservoir Dogs* (1992), which inspired London department store windows and led to an increase in the wearing of dark suits and shades amongst younger men, is just such an example of film's democratization of fashion; the costume designer Betsy Heimann had bought the suits cheaply. As *Reservoir Dogs* became successful as a movie, however, so did the clean-silhouetted French gangster look (Tarantino readily admitted to having emulated the look created by the French director Jean-Pierre Melville for his gangsters). By the time Tarantino came to make his second film, *Pulp Fiction* (1994), the idea that his films were trendy was cemented, and this time he bought suits for Samuel L. Jackson and John Travolta and Uma Thurman's black trousers and white shirt duo at *Agnès b.* Audiences now somewhat randomly scavenge films for fashion ideas, so Thurman's Chanel Rouge Noir nail polish in *Pulp Fiction* was much in demand, as earlier Tom Cruise's sunglasses from *Top Gun* (1986) had been. The overall attractiveness of the film is only partly responsible for its potential impact on fashion; sometimes just a single garment or accessory becomes popular, such as Keanu Reeves's mobile phone and long black coat in *The Matrix* (1999) or Nicole Kidman's half-fitted, half-loose teddy in *Eyes Wide Shut* (1999), which sold out everywhere. As Schiaparelli noted back in the 1930s, cinema is inevitably going to influence fashion. Since then, a more fluid, flexible interaction has emerged—sometimes fashion borrows from film, but often the exchange is reversed. Film actors are inevitably dressing up, and this use of clothes as fantasy comes out in audiences' acquisitions of particular on-screen looks, whether this be women using patterns to make up their favorite costume designs in the 1940s or their granddaughters going to Agnès b. in the 1990s to find Uma Thurman's trousers. Likewise, as Jean Paul Gaultier has remarked, film lets the designer's imagination run riot in a way fashion, because of its commercial constraints, does not. In the early twenty-first century, there is the added dimension of what stars wear off-screen becoming as important in influencing cinema audiences. Film and fashion will continue to serve each other.

See also Actors and Actresses, Impact on Fashion; Celebrities; Hollywood Style.

Bibliography

Bruzzi, Stella. *Undressing Cinema: Clothing and Identity in the Movies.* London and New York: Routledge, 1997.

Gaines, Jane. "Costume and Narrative: How Dress Tells the Woman's Story." In *Fabrications: Costume and the Female Body,* 180–211. London and New York: Routledge, 1990.

Gaines, Jane, and Charlotte Herzog, eds. *Fabrications: Costume and the Female Body.* London and New York: Routledge, 1990.

Head, Edith, and Jane Kesner Ardmore. *The Dress Doctor.* Boston and Toronto: Little Brown and Company, 1959.

Hollander, Anne. *Seeing Through Clothes.* Berkeley: University of California Press, 1993.

Maeder, Edward, ed. *Hollywood and History: Costume Design in Film.* Los Angeles: Thames and Hudson, Inc., 1987.

Prichard, Susan Perez. *Film Costume: An Annotated Bibliography.* Metuchen, N.J., and London: Scarecrow Press, 1981.

Saint Laurent, Yves. *Yves Saint Laurent: Images of Design.* With an introduction by Marguerite Duras. London: Ebury Press, 1988.

Wollen, Peter. "Strike a Pose." *Sight and Sound* 5, no. 3 (March 1995): 10–15.

Stella Bruzzi

FIRST LADIES' GOWNS*

For over one hundred years, one of the Smithsonian Institution's most visited exhibitions has been a display of gowns worn by the First Ladies of the United States. An unofficial title, "first lady" has been in popular use since the 1860s to refer to the president's official hostess who is usually, but not always, the president's wife.

Many people think of the first family as the United States' version of royalty who are expected to fulfill ambiguous and evolving ideals of how to act and look. New first ladies have often discovered that they will have to learn how to dress to belong in this national spotlight. If a first lady fails to achieve this elusive goal, she is vulnerable to the political consequences of media criticism; but when a first lady does succeed, she may popularize a fashion.

Political Implications

While Americans want their first lady to look as if she represents an affluent and powerful country, citizens do not want her to look too regal—spending excessive amounts on high-fashion clothing. For example, in the early 1860s the southerner Mary Todd Lincoln was severely criticized for her extravagant fashions and entertainment as the nation dealt with the horrors of the Civil War. A hundred years later, Jacqueline Kennedy's love of expensive clothes, particularly French couture, became a political liability during the 1960 presidential campaign between her husband and Richard Nixon. To avoid these hazards, attractive Pat Nixon restrained herself from buying anything too special. The fur coats she purchased in the past did not support the public persona of a "good Republican woman in a cloth coat."

Some presidents' wives have only slightly refined their wardrobe for their public role. For example, in 1998, self-assured Barbara Bush had no intention of becoming more concerned with her appearance while first lady; but she came to appreciate her American designers, Arnold Scaasi and Bill Blass. They transformed her into a glamorous grandmother who felt pretty even as she endured treatments for Graves disease.

As the first president's wife to have been born after World War II, Hillary Rodham Clinton was part of a generation who paid more attention to their achievements than to their appearance. She eschewed the fashionable trappings of traditional "well-bred" ladies and focused on her education and professional career. Mrs. Clinton was first criticized for this lack of attention to her appearance and then judged for all the "fine tuning" she attempted, particularly changes in hairstyles. When a first lady's appearance is continually criticized, it seems more likely that she is being attacked because she acts different rather than just because she looks different. Never was this truer than for Mrs. Clinton—a lawyer, a public servant, and a new kind of first lady.

Two significant additions were made to the collection of First Ladies' Gowns in 2009: Michelle Obama's lemongrass-yellow inauguration outfit by Isabel Toledo; and her white evening dress by Jason Wu. Michelle Obama has been widely praised for her patronage of independent American designers.

Fashion Popularizer

Although a successfully dressed first lady is not a fashion innovator, a favorite color—Mamie (Eisenhower) pink—or accessory—Barbara Bush's three-strand imitation pearl necklace—or even a single dress style could become more popular because of her well-publicized role in the White House. In 1993, Mrs. Clinton wore to her first official White House event a Donna Karan turtleneck, long-sleeved, long black dress with cutouts that bared her shoulders. This glamorous dress was not a new style; it had already been seen on celebrities such as Liza Minnelli and Candice Bergen. Nevertheless, within a week of Mrs. Clinton's stunning appearance, manufacturers copied it by the thousands for the mass market.

Dolley Madison and Jacqueline Kennedy were two first ladies who popularized more than a dress style. They each embodied a unique way of dressing that influenced women in their own time. In the early nineteenth century, Dolley Madison's love of French fashions and elegant furnishings encouraged conservative American women to more fully embrace the latest foreign fashions. The popularity of the lively Mrs. Madison blunted the effect of the critics who accused her of aristocratic behavior unsuitable for the first lady of a republic. In contrast, two months before the election in 1960, Jacqueline Kennedy was directed by her husband's advisers to stop buying French couture. Taking into account the best of French fashions, she crafted a simple, youthful, made-in-America glamour. She exemplified a new, and soon-to-become classic, American look.

Collection and Exhibition

In the early twentieth century, the Smithsonian Institution, along with other museums presenting American history, celebrated the accomplishments of notable people, most of whom were important white men. Intended as a way to educate the public in the values of hard work and good citizenship, the focus was on traditional masculine achievements. As Edith Mayo, curator emeritus First Ladies Collection, reported in her 1996 publication, *The Smithsonian Book of the First Ladies*, a volunteer supporter of the Smithsonian, Mrs. Cassie Myers James "introduced the idea of women as historical role models by building a collection of clothing that showed 'the fashions of the women of the United States from colonial times . . . and their sphere in home life'" (p. 279).

The inspiration to acquire and exhibit dresses of the first ladies came about when a descendant of President James Monroe, Mrs. Rose Gouverneur Hoes, was invited to contribute to the collection. In 1912 the success of this effort was assured when Mrs. William Howard Taft, the current first lady, and descendants of five other presidents, promised gowns for the collection. By 1915 the display of dresses in rows of cases was called "Historical Costumes, Including those of the Mistresses of the White House."

These collections and the exhibition were radical innovations. For the first time, women were made visible in the nation's museum, creating a precedent for future collections about women. Over time, the Smithsonian's pre-

Smithsonian exhibit of First Ladies. First Ladies often walk a fine line when choosing their dress, as the public wants them to look sophisticated and elegant, but not extravagantly so. © RICHARD T. NOWITZ. REPRODUCED BY PERMISSION.

sentation of the first ladies has changed. In the 1950s the dressed mannequins were reinstalled in elaborate room settings resembling public spaces in the White House during different periods. In March 1992 a new exhibition, "First Ladies: Political Role and Public Image" opened. In a break with tradition, the first ladies are rein-terpreted as historical agents in their own right within the context of the American presidency and the history of women in America. The continued popularity of the Smithsonian's First Ladies Hall demonstrates both the American fascination with first ladies and the power of dress to evoke the personality and life experiences of the wearers.

See also Blass, Bill; Celebrities; Fashion Icons.

BIBLIOGRAPHY

Mayo, Edith, ed. *The Smithsonian Book of the First Ladies: Their Lives, Times, and Issues.* New York: Henry Holt, 1996.

Claudia Kidwell

FLAPPERS

The flapper was an important figure in the popular culture of the 1920s and helped to define the new, modern woman of the twentieth century. She was the embodiment of the youthful exuberance of the jazz age. Although she defied many of society's taboos, she was also seen by many as the ideal young woman and was described by author F. Scott Fitzgerald as "lovely, expensive and about nineteen."

It is commonly assumed that the term "flapper" originated in the 1920s and refers to the fashion trend for unfastened rubber galoshes that "flapped" when walking, an attribution reinforced by the image of the free-wheeling flapper in popular culture. Despite this potent imagery, the word has its origins in sixteenth-century British slang. Deriving from the colloquial "flap," the word indicated a young female prostitute and likely referred to the awkward flapping of a young bird's wings when learning to fly. By the nineteenth century the term had lost most of its lewd connotations and instead was used to describe a flighty or hoydenish adolescent girl. In the years following World War I, the word was increasingly used to describe a fashionably dressed, impulsive young woman and by the 1920s, it was used to describe "modern" young women who broke traditional rules of both appearance and behavior.

The "fast living" ethos of the 1920s was widely perceived to be a direct consequence of World War I. During wartime, many young women experienced freedoms previously unheard of, such as taking jobs, shortening skirts, driving cars, and cutting their hair. Competition for male attention was paramount since the pool of eligible men had been depleted during the war, and this probably contributed to the flashier fashions and aggressive behavior of many young women. Outrageous behavior and dress was seen as an investment against spinsterhood or, at the very least, boredom.

The Flapper Image

The common perception of the flapper had as much to do with behavior as it did with appearance. Flappers displayed a carefree disregard for authority and morality. They drank heavily in defiance of Prohibition, smoked, embraced new shocking dances like the Charleston, the Shimmy, and the Black Bottom, used slang, drove fast, and freely took lovers and jobs. Posture and motion were important elements of the flapper persona. The fast, jerky motions characterized by these popular dances emphasized bare arms, backs, and legs. The posture of the flapper was an affected "debutante slouch," often with hand on hip. This limp, listless pose was not possible on a traditionally corseted body and was meant to imply the aftereffects of the previous night's debauchery.

Accordingly, flapper styles blatantly disregarded established fashions in exchange for the new and daring. Popular styles of the 1920s focused on the display of the slim, youthful body through the use of short skirts and dropped waists. Gabrielle "Coco" Chanel and Jean Patou were particularly known for this youthful, sporty style. The flapper took this fashionable ideal to the extreme and wore the shortest skirts possible, low cloches, and negligible underwear. Evening dresses were sleeveless, flashy, and frequently featured slit skirts meant to enable active dancing. She bobbed her hair, wore obvious makeup, and sunbathed in skimpy, one-piece bathing suits.

A common element of the flapper style was the tendency to misuse clothing and accessories—a way of thumbing noses at high fashion and polite society. Examples of this phenomenon were the rolling of stockings below the knees, the wearing of unhooked rubber galoshes that "flapped" when walking, evening shoes worn with daywear, and occasionally even the natural waist worn in defiance of the dictates of high fashion. Flappers were also rumored to rouge their knees, and this is a part of the greater emphasis on legs crucial to the flapper persona. Besides the previously mentioned galoshes and rolled stockings, flappers were associated with elaborate garters and anklets. A daring minority rejected stockings altogether when the weather was warm, but many opted for stockings in fashionable "suntan" shades. Accessories that flaunted outrageous behavior, like the jeweled cigarette holder and ornate compact, were also popular.

The Rise and Fall of the Flapper

The creation of the flapper image is largely credited to the writings of F. Scott Fitzgerald and the drawings of John Held Jr., which frequently featured skinny, stylized flappers in comical situations. Fitzgerald's writings focused on the fast pace of modern life, but when he was given the credit for popularizing the movement, he responded, "I was the spark that lit up Flaming Youth and Colleen Moore was the torch. What little things we are to have caused that trouble."

Fitzgerald shrewdly understood the power of the motion picture to spread the flapper image to a mass audience. Colleen Moore, Joan Crawford, Anita Page, and Clara Bow were some of the many actresses who specialized in flapper roles during this period. The flapper had been a popular screen type since the 1910s, and by the mid-1920s, films featured titles like *Flapper Fever*, *The Painted Flapper*, *Flapper Wives*, *The Perfect Flapper*, and *The Flapper and the Cowboy*.

Although viewers were unlikely to adopt the fast living and flamboyant dress seen on screen, it is quite likely that they incorporated elements into their lives. The 1928 film *Our Dancing Daughters*, which starred Joan Crawford and Anita Page, was particularly influential. The film was mentioned repeatedly in the Payne Fund Studies commissioned to determine the effects of film on the youth of the United States. One respondent claimed that after seeing *Our Dancing Daughters*, "I wanted a dress exactly like one she had worn in a certain scene. It was a very 'flapper' type of dress, and I don't usually go in for that sort of thing" (Massey, p. 30).

As early as 1922, it was suggested that the term "flapper" be divided into three levels: the semi-flapper, the flapper, the superflapper. By the end of the decade, most young women could easily be classed as a semi-flapper since flapper styles and behaviors were gradually being adopted into mainstream life. Bobbed hair, lipstick, and short skirts no longer were the sign of a flapper, just that of a modern fashionable woman.

With the stock market crash of 1929, the frivolity and excess characterized by the flapper and the jazz age were replaced with frugality and a return to a more traditional view of feminine behavior and dress. Although the stock market crash signaled the flapper's demise, she remains a potent symbol of flaming youth.

See also Chanel, Gabrielle (Coco); Patou, Jean; Subcultures.

Bibliography

Evans, Mike, ed. *Decades of Beauty*. New York: Reed Consumer Books Limited, 1998.

Hall, Lee. *Common Threads: A Parade of American Clothing*. Boston: Little, Brown and Company, 1992.

Hatton, Jackie. "Flappers" In *St. James Encyclopedia of Popular Culture* Vol. 2: E–J. Edited by Tom Pendergast and Sara Pendergast. Detroit: St. James Press, 2000.

Latham, Angela J. *Posing a Threat: Flappers, Chorus Girls, and Other Brazen Performers of the American 1920s*. Hanover, Conn.: Wesleyan University Press, 2000.

Massey, Anne. *Hollywood Beyond the Screen: Design and Material Culture*. Oxford: Berg, 2000.

Rosen, Marjorie. *Popcorn Venus: Women, Movies and the American Dream*. New York: Avon Books, 1974.

Clare Sauro

FLÜGEL, J. C.

John Carl Flügel (1874–1955) was an English academic psychologist, a prominent member of the British Psychoanalytical Society, and a leading figure in the movement for liberal social reform between the two world wars (1918–1939). A member of the Men's Dress Reform Party, in 1930 he published *The Psychology of Clothes*, the first Freudian-inspired analysis of dress

and fashion. In this work he advances the idea that clothing is a "compromise-formation" that mediates between the desire of children to exhibit their naked bodies and the later social prohibition that the body be covered for the sake of modesty. For Flügel the story of clothing is the story of the relative strength of these two forces.

Freud, Flügel, and Politics

Flügel makes little use of Freud's ideas of clothing as either fetish objects or as sexual symbols in dreams. Central to his analysis of clothing is the sociopolitical interpretation he gives to Freud's model of the human psyche. Freud argues for a three-part division of the mind into id, superego, and ego. The id is the dimension of primitive instinct and the ultimate propelling force of the organism. The superego is an equally primitive inhibitory mechanism that operates as a crude controller of the desires of the id. The ego has the difficult task of establishing a compromise between the demands of the id, the superego, and the outside world so that the individual can exist as a functioning entity. Flügel assigns a general political value to each of these dimensions of the mind. He relates his program of reform to lessening of the power of an overbearing superego, which he regards as the driving force of authoritarian conservatism. As he comments, "The troubles that we experience in adjusting ourselves to civilized social life seem to be due, not merely, as earlier moralists had supposed, to the strength of our a-social instincts [the id], but also, in no inconsiderable degree to the power of the primitive moral factors embodied in the superego" (Flügel 1934, p. 296).

Clothing, for Flügel, comes into being so as to reconcile the demands that these opposing forces place upon the human body and psyche. Dress, therefore, is a prime area of dispute between political liberals and conservatives over what sort, and how much, clothing is appropriate in civilized society.

The Psychology of Clothes

Flügel's theory of clothing attempts to answer two questions. First, why do human beings wear clothes at all? Second, why do the ways in which human beings dress vary so greatly?

The conventional answer given by European thinkers to the first question proposed the existence of three "fundamental motives" out of which clothing was thought to have arisen—bodily protection, modesty, and decoration. Flügel concentrates on the motives of modesty and decoration. Using a version of Freud's model of how the child becomes a socialized adult, he argues that we are born in a condition of narcissistic self-love. The consequence is a "tendency to admire one's own body and display it to others, so that others can share in the admiration. It finds natural expression in the showing off of the naked body and in the demonstration of its powers, and can be observed in many children" (Flügel 1930, p. 86).

This state of idyllic infantile nudity ceases with the arrival of the somatic prohibitions associated with the forces of modesty. The infant relinquishes its pleasurable self-absorption. The body is covered, and shame is triggered when too much of it is inappropriately revealed. However, neither of these tendencies is ever able fully to cancel out the other. As Flügel observes:

> The exhibitionistic instinct originally relates to the naked body, but in the course of individual development it inevitably (in civilised races) becomes displaced, to a greater or lesser extent onto clothes. Clothes are, however, exquisitely ambivalent, in as much as they both cover the body and thus subserve the inhibiting tendencies that we call "modesty," and at the same time afford a new and highly efficient means of gratifying exhibitionism on a new level.
>
> (Flügel 1932, p. 120)

Clothes simultaneously both hide and draw attention to the body.

Variations of Dress

Flügel realizes that while all humans are dressed, the manner in which this is achieved varies greatly with time and place. His explanation of this is the following:

> to understand the motives that lead to different kinds of clothing, to changes in our clothing and to the changes in our whole attitude towards clothes, we shall have to be constantly on the look out for changes in the manifestations of these two fundamental conflicting tendencies, the one proudly to exhibit the body, the other modestly to hide it. (Flügel 1928)

The most striking of these dress variations, certainly to Flügel and his contemporaries, are those between men and women. Indeed, contemporary European clothing presented Flügel with an added complication, in that it seemed to run against the "normal" situation encountered in nature as well as the evidence of "primitive peoples." There the man "is more ornamental than the female" and almost always the most "adventurous and decorative" in his appearance. In explaining this anomaly, Flügel argues that a profound reorganization of masculinity took place during the political and economic revolutions of the late eighteenth and nineteenth centuries. The tendency to modesty increased at the expense of "male sartorial decorativeness," and the result was a set of simplified garments, less colorful and with a greater degree of uniformity than had existed in previous historical epochs. Flügel named this dramatic shift "The Great Masculine Renunciation" (Flügel 1930, p. 110ff). Against this, he greatly approved of the development taken by European female dress. Beginning with the extremely modest clothing styles of the Middle Ages, female dress had gradually reformed itself. Flügel claimed that female clothing now exhibited a more rational integration of the antagonistic forces operating on dress than was the case in male dress. Indeed, it was his respect for what he saw as the positive mental benefits provided by contemporary forms of female dress that lead him to advocate the reform of men's clothing.

The Nude Future

Near the end of his book *The Psychology of Clothes*, Flügel speculates about a future in which clothing could become obsolete. He argues that, the three main reasons for wearing clothes—bodily protection, modesty, and adornment—will all be surpassed as humans evolve a more "developed" and "rational" way of life. The need for protection will diminish as the control of the environment—for example, by the heating engineer—increases (Flügel 1930, p. 235). The urge to cover our bodies out of a sense of modesty will evaporate once we understand how irrational our fears of nakedness are. Finally, decorative modification and alteration of our bodies would cease as we become reconciled more and more to the natural human form (Flügel 1930, p. 235). As a species we will achieve a "complete reconciliation with the body [which] would mean that the aesthetic variations, emendations, and aggrandizements of the body . . . produced by clothes would no longer felt [to be] necessary" (Flügel 1930, p. 235). Clothing would just fade away.

See also Fashion, Theories of; Nudity.

Bibliography

Burman, B. "Better and Brighter Clothes: The Men's Dress Reform Party, 1929–1940." *Journal of Design History* 8, no. 4 (1995): 275–290. A fascinating account of the men's dress reform movement, in which Flügel was an important participant.

Carter, Michael. "J. C. Flügel and the Nude Future." In *Fashion Classics from Carlyle to Barthes*. Oxford and New York: Berg, 2003. An examination of Flügel's ideas on clothing, particularly as they pertain to his liberal social beliefs.

Flügel, John C. Unpublished transcript of a talk given by Flügel on BBC Radio, 26 June 1928.

——. *The Psychology of Clothes*. London: Hogarth Press, 1930.

——. *An Introduction to Psycho-Analysis*. London: Victor Gollancz, 1932.

——. "A Psychology for Progressives—How Can They Become Effective?" In *Manifesto: Being the Book of the Federation of Progressive Societies and Individuals*. Edited by C. E. M. Joad. London: George Allen and Unwin, 1934.

Michael Carter

FONTANA SISTERS

Zoe (1911–1979), Micol (b. 1913), and Giovanna (b. 1915) Fontana were born in Traversetolo, near Parma, Italy. They learned sewing and tailoring from their mother, Amabile Fontana, who opened her own tailor shop in 1907. The three sisters became apprentices as soon as they were old enough to handle needles and scissors. Legend has it that the work was hard and unpaid and that the sisters worked Saturdays and Sundays. Despite the long hours, the sisters' memories of childhood are happy ones, and they look back with fondness on the years spent in the large, quiet house surrounded by greenery. Micol writes often of her childhood experiences in her memoir, *Specchio a tre luci.* "We were never alone, but always accompanied by our mother's love" (p. 20).

Apprenticeships

In the 1930s Zoe, the eldest of the three, left Traversetolo to become an apprentice in Milan. Micol joined her there, while Giovanna remained in the countryside. Shortly after her marriage in 1934, Zoe moved with her husband to Paris, where she continued her apprenticeship in an atelier. After returning to Italy in 1936, Zoe, excited by her experiences in Paris, moved to Rome. In her memoirs she treats this major turning point in her life casually: "I took the first train that arrived. . . . It could have gone north or south. It happened to be going south, to Rome" (2001, p. 14). After her sisters joined her in Rome, Zoe went to work for Zecca and Micol for Battilocchi; Giovanna sewed garments at home. Based on their experiences in Milan and Paris, the sisters felt they were ready to go into business for themselves. Although French fashions were still dominant in the world of haute couture, the sisters opened their own workshop in Rome in 1943, changing the name from "Fontana" to "Sorelle Fontana" and leading members of the Italian aristocracy soon began patronizing it.

International Fame

However, their Roman clientele would not have been sufficient to cement the Fontana sisters' reputation if Hollywood had not discovered Italy and *la dolce vita romana* in the 1950s. One of the events that helped secure their international reputation was the marriage of the Hollywood actors Tyrone Power and Linda Christian, whose wedding gown the Fontana sisters designed. The ceremony was held in the basilica of Santa Francesca Romana in Rome in 1949. The gown was constructed of white satin, with a five-yard train, and was covered with embroidery; it resembled a dress that might have been worn by a fairy tale princess. The international press covered the event, and photographs of the ceremony and a radiant Linda Christian appeared in papers around the world. A magazine published for foreign tourists in the 1950s proclaimed, "Rome? Twenty minutes in St. Peter's, twenty in the Coliseum, and at least two days in the Fontana sisters' studio" (Soli, p. 75).

In 1951 the Fontana sisters participated in the first fashion show held in Florence, which was organized by Giovanni Battista Giorgini, the promoter of Italian fashion and organizer of catwalk shows at Sala Bianca, Palazzo Pitti. That same year Micol Fontana left for Hollywood, arriving in the United States as the guest and personal friend of Tyrone Power and Linda Christian. Power organized a show for her because he wanted to introduce other members of the Hollywood community to the Fontana sisters' designs. From that moment on, the Fontana sisters began designing for many of Hollywood's best-known stars, from Ava Gardner to Elizabeth Taylor, and started developing a varied international following as well. Margaret Trujillo (the Santo Domingo dictator's wife who ordered Sorelle Fontana's atelier 150 dress), Grace Kelly, Margaret Truman (President Harry S. Truman's daughter), Jackie Kennedy, Soraya Esfandiary, Marella Agnelli (of the family that runs the Fiat), and Maria Pia di Savoia, (one of the daughters of last king of Italy, Umberto of Savoia) were some of their regular customers. From Linda Christian Marriage, they also specialized in celebrities' wedding dress: Margaret Truman (1956), Janet Auchincloss, Jacqueline Kennedy's sister (1966), Maria Pia di Savoia (1955), whose dress is now shown at the Museum of Art and Costume in Venice, and Angelita Trujillo, the daughter of the Santo Domingo dictator (1955), are some examples.

In 1957 the Fontana sisters were received by Pope Pius XII to mark fifty years of tailoring begun by their mother, Amabile. In 1958 they were invited to the White House as Italy's representatives to the Fashion around the World conference. In 1960, at the request of American customers, they introduced a line of ready-to-wear. This product launch was followed by a line of furs, umbrellas, scarves, costume jewelry, and table linen. Because of the careful division of labor among them, the three sisters were invincible: Micol traveled around the world—Japan, Europe, and ninety-four trips to the United States, Zoe handled public relations, and Giovanna monitored work in the studio.

In 1972, while continuing their work in couture and ready-to-wear, the sisters withdrew from most of the official fashion shows. In 1992 the Fontana label and the company itself were sold to an Italian financial group. In 1994 Micol created the Micol Fontana Foundation, the mission of which is to promote fashion and the training of talented newcomers.

Inspiration for Designs

The Fontanas' designs, although they referred to French models, were inspired by eighteenth-century modes of dress, which were based on designs of the early Renaissance. The sisters were able to navigate between Parisian haute couture, an essential reference point, and the originality of the Italian fashions with which American women had become enamored. The sisters' designs

were known for craftsmanship and intuition. Embroidery, lace, and impeccable tailoring were characteristic of their garments. They specialized in formal wear and evening gowns and used the most precious materials, including silk and velvet. Their ideas came from a wide variety of sources, but their designs, for the most part, were Italian in inspiration. Quintavalle remarked that the Fontana sisters "redeemed the Italian culture that Fascism had disfigured, restricting it within the confines of a local culture" (Bianchino, p. 43).

Innovations

The sisters' love for America continued to deepen. In her diary Micol writes that she felt more at home in America than in Italy and that public relations was not the only reason she traveled. Micol was a close observer of the way Americans dressed, and she tried to determine exactly what they wanted to wear. The sisters' relations with the international jet set, and especially with Hollywood and the film industry, were one of their strengths; in fact, Nicola White remarks that it is unlikely they would have been able to achieve such fame without their connection to Ava Gardner, as well as to other stars like Myrna Loy, Grace Kelly, Audrey Hepburn, and Kim Novak. However, their skill as couturiers, which allowed them to compete with Dior's Paris, cannot be overlooked. The clothing they created was designed for the individual client. Zoe, known as the "golden scissors," could cut and drape as well as the best designers in Paris.

Renato Balestra and Alain Reynaud, the creators of Biki, are among the designers who had worked with Sorelle Fontana. By presenting some of their designs in newspapers—an innovation resulting from their ability to intuit future developments in fashion—they took another step in consolidating their fame, completely altering their relationship with the public. Unlike other designers, their relations with their clients did not develop through frequent customer visits to their studio, which had typified the role of the designer until then. Most of their clients learned of them through the media and wanted to meet the sisters so they would design something for them. In this sense they helped lay the foundations for the star designers of the future.

Italian cinema put the atelier of the Sorelle Fontana under the spotlights when it became the set for the film *Le ragazze di piazza di Spagna* by Luciano Emmer (1953). The Fontana sisters also designed the costumes for Ava Gardner in *The Barefoot Contessa*, a film released in 1954. One of their designs, the "cassock dress," which was made for Gardner in 1956, was used by the costume designer Danilo Donati for Anita Ekberg in Federico Fellini's film *La dolce vita*. The Fontana sisters' work has been presented in several exhibitions and designs are exposed in the museums internationally: the Metropolitan Museum of Art in New York, the Metropolitan Museum of Art in San Francisco, the Museo d'Arte e Costume in Venice, and the private library of Harry Truman.

See also Evening Dress; Haute Couture; Wedding Costume.

Bibliography

Bianchino, Gloria. *Moda dalla fiaba al design*. Novara, Italy: De Agostini, 1989.

Fontana, Micol. *Specchio a tre luci*. Roma: Rai Radiotelevisione Italiana, 1992.

Gastel, Minnie. *50 anni di moda italiana*. Milan: Vallardi, 1995.

Giordani Aragno, Bonizza. *900 Il Secolo Di Moda: Sorelle Fontana*. Roma: Fondazione Micol Fontana, 2001.

———, ed. *Storia di un atelier: Sorelle Fontana 1907–1992*. Rome: Logart Press, 1992.

Pisa, Paola. "Sorelle Fontana." In *Dizionario della moda*. Edited by Guido Vergani. Milan: Baldini and Castoldi, 1999.

Soli, Pia. *Il genio antipatico*. Milan: Arnoldo Mondadori, 1984.

White, Nicola. *Reconstructing Italian Fashion*. London, New York: Berg, 2000.

Simona Segre Reinach

FOOTBINDING

Footbinding was specific to and unique to traditional Chinese culture. Its various names conveyed its multifaceted image in Chinese eyes: *chanzu* (binding feet) called attention to the mundane action of swaddling the body with a piece of cloth; *gongwan* (curved arch) described a desired shape of the foot similar to that of a ballerina in pointe shoe; *jinlian* (golden lotus, also gilded lilies) evoked a utopian image of the body that was the subject of fantastical transformation. A related poetic expression of *lianbu* (lotus steps) suggested that foot-binding was intended to enhance the grace of the body in motion, not to cripple the woman.

Body Modification

The much-maligned practice has often been compared to corsetry as evidence that women were oppressed in cultures East and West, modern and traditional. The comparison is apt albeit for different reasons. The goal of both practices was to modify the female figure with strips of carefully designed and precisely positioned fabric, and in so doing alter the way the wearer projected herself into the world. During its millennium-long history, footbinding acquired various cultural meanings: as a sign of status, civility, Han Chinese ethnicity, and femininity. But at its core it was a means of body modification, hence its history should be sought from the foundational garments of binding cloth, socks, and soft-heeled slippers.

The materials needed for binding feet were specialized articles made by women (binding cloth, socks, and shoes) together with sewing implements readily available in the boudoir (scissors, needle, and thread). Alum and medicinal powder were sprinkled between the toes as an astringent. Women often wove the cotton binding cloth; its average width was three inches, and its length ranged from seven to ten inches. Skillful wrapping of the cloth allowed the woman to reshape the foot into desirable shapes in accordance to footwear fashion. The method and style of binding feet varied greatly with geography, age, and occasion. A moderate way involved compressing the four digits into a pointy and narrow tip; an extreme regiment required both the folding of the digits and the bending of the foot at midpoint into an arch. The tendons and extensors of the toes were stretched to the point of breakage, but the breakage did not, at least in theory, require fracturing the bones. The binding of feet altered the shape of the foot and the woman's gait. Slender slippers and dainty steps signified class and desirability.

Similar to tattooing, footbinding bespeaks an attitude that viewed the body as a canvas or a template—a surface or "social skin" on which cultural meanings could be inscribed. Yet the effect of binding was more than skin deep. It signaled an extreme form of self-improvement and mastery; the contemporary body-piercer's motto of "no pain, no gain" is equally apt for Chinese women.

Unlike tattooing and body-piercing, however, foot-binding was only practiced by females, and its connections with the female handicraft traditions of textile, embroidery, and shoemaking rendered it a quintessential sign of feminine identity. It is paradoxical that footbinding, supposedly a signal of the woman's family status as "conspicuous leisure," was in itself a result and expression of a strenuous form of female labor.

Early Beginnings

The earliest material evidence for the binding of feet is several pairs of shoes from twelfth- to thirteenth-century tombs in south-central China. Scholar Zhang Bangji (fl. 1147) provided the first known textual reference to foot-binding as an actual practice: "Women's footbinding began in the recent times; it was not mentioned in any books from the previous eras." By the twelfth century, foot-binding was a common but by no means mandatory practice among the wives and daughters of high-status men, as well as courtesans and actresses who entertained this same group of privileged scholar-officials.

Song-dynasty China (960–1279) enjoyed a prosperous commercialized economy. The Northern Song capital of Kaifeng and the Southern Song capital of Hangzhou, with populations of over a million each, were the largest cities in the world at the time. Indeed, historians have suggested that the beginnings of Chinese modernity can be traced back to the Song. A taste for novelty, together with status-anxiety—the same factors that gave rise to fashion in early modern Europe—also facilitated the birth of footbinding. Adoration for small feet ran deep in Chinese culture: the story of Ye Xian, China's Cinderella, appeared in a ninth-century story collection *Youyang zazu* (Ko, pp. 26–27), and poets eulogized dainty steps and fancy footwear from the sixth to tenth centuries. But these fantasies gave rise to the actual practice of binding feet only in the urban culture that emerged after the fall of the Tang aristocratic empire.

The style of women's shoes from the twelfth to fifteenth centuries conforms to two subtypes: one is long and narrow with pointy toes, like a kayak; the other, with turned-up toes, is like a canoe with a high stem. These shoes are made of monochrome silk and decorated with embroidered abstract floral or cloud patterns. The length of archaeological specimens ranges from 5.9 inches to 9.4 inches (15 to 24 cm). Both styles feature flat fabric soles, suggesting that in this early stage women swaddled their four digits together with a binding cloth to achieve a sleek, pointy look.

Paintings show these pointy toes or the more dramatic upturned toes peeking out from long, flowing silk trousers, creating an aesthetic of subdued feminine elegance. The most credible origin myth attributes footbinding to Yaoniang, a dancer in the court of the last ruler Li Yu (r. 969–975) of the Southern Tang kingdom, who beguiled Li with her graceful dance and shoes that "curl up like the new moon." In the beginning, footbinding was not meant to cripple.

The Cult of the Golden Lotus

A more extreme regime of beauty arose around the sixteenth century with the invention of high heels. One type of shoes was elevated on a cylindrical heel; another featured a curved sole supported by a piece of silk-covered wood from the heel area to the instep. Not only did heels afford an optical illusion of smallness, they also enabled an extreme way of binding that pushed the base of the metatarsal bones and the adjoining cuneiforms upward, forming a bulge on the top of the foot. A crevice was formed on the sole due to the compression of the fifth metatarsal bone toward the calcaneus or heel bone. The high heel redirected the wearer's body weight into a tripod-like area consisting of the tip of the big toe, the bent toes, and the back of the heel. However unsteadily, heeled footwear provided better support for the triangular foot than flats.

This strenuous regimen bespeaks heightened female competition in a fashion-conscious society. In the sixteenth century, the Ming Empire (1368–1644) enjoyed the largest trade surplus in the world. Buoyed by a net inflow of New World silver, the money economy spread to the countryside. In a world of material abundance and social fluidity, there was intense pressure on women to display the status of their fathers and husbands. The incessant drive for small feet and their attendant eroticization in this atmosphere gave rise to a cult of the golden lotus.

Female footwear—often store-bought—became fanciful. Some women hired famous carpenters to carve their heels, often of fragrant wood. Floral cutouts were made on the surface of hollowed heels; perfumed powder inside the heels would leave traces of blossoms on the floor as the wearer shifted her steps. The shoe uppers were fashioned from red, white, or green silk with increasingly elaborate embroidered motifs of auspicious symbols. The earlier flat socks evolved into contoured and footed soft "sleeping slippers" which women wore to bed on top of the binding cloth. The erotic appeal of the golden lotus was wrought of layered footwear as instruments of concealment.

Even at the heyday of the cult, many women did not have bound feet. Footbinding was more a privilege than a requirement. Women of Manchu descent, an ethnic minority group, eschewed footbinding, as did Hakka women, who shouldered back-breaking manual labor. After the Manchus became the rulers of China in 1644, they issued prohibition edicts that only served to make foot-binding more popular among the subjugated Han Chinese majority.

The Anti-Footbinding Movement

The decline of footbinding can be attributed to internal and external factors. Domestically, it became a victim of its own success. As footbinding spread geographically outward and socially downward during the Qing dynasty (1644–1911), it lost its raison d'être and ceased to be a sign of exclusivity. Externally, Christian missionaries and merchants brought an imported concept of the natural God-given body as well as a new sartorial regime in the second half of the nineteenth century. Footbinding became so dated that it was synonymous with "feudal and backward China" in the Republican period (1912–1949). Although coastal women gave up the practice in the early decades of the twentieth century, girls in the remote southwestern province of Yunnan were forced to stop by the Communist regime only in the 1950s.

Ironically, on the eve of footbinding's decline, the paraphernalia of footbinding reached the height of its glory, surpassing previous centuries in rapidity of stylistic changes and ornamental techniques. Each region developed its own distinct footwear styles. New

---

THE FETISHISM OF BOUND FEET AND TINY SHOES

William Rossi has suggested the bound foot was "the organ of ultimate sexual pleasure"; the soft fleshy cleavage on the underside of the foot was "the equivalent of the labia" for men (pp. 29–30). Although this view is corroborated by Chinese erotic paintings from the nineteenth and twentieth centuries, no premodern Chinese sources depict footbinding in this light.

Novels, poetry, and prose by premodern Chinese male scholars suggest that embroidered slippers and partially undressed, but still concealed, feet served as the locus of their erotic imagination. The first credible connoisseur of bound feet was the Yuan dynasty scholar-poet Yang Weizhen (also known as Yang Tieya, 1296–1370), who in his later years retired from the court and dallied in the garden city of Suzhou. To add to the merry-making, Yang drank from wine cups fashioned from courtesans' tiny shoes. Brothel drinking games involving the tiny shoe persisted and became more fanciful, as evinced by the connoisseur Fang Xuan's (probably a pseudonym) treatises first published in the last decade of the Qing dynasty (Levy, pp. 107–120).

The connoisseur Li Yu (c. 1610–1680)—no relation to the Southern Tang ruler—described the sexual appeal of the bound foot in both visual and tactile terms. In a bedroom scene in Li's erotic novel The Carnal Prayer Mat, the protagonist Vesperus removed all the clothes of Jade Scent but left her leggings on, because "in the last resort tiny feet need a pair of dainty little leggings above them if they are going to appeal" (p. 50). Li recounted his own experience of removing courtesans' stockings to fondle feet so soft that they feel "boneless" in an essay collection, Casual Expressions of Idle Feeling. Presumably the binding cloth was not removed. Li added: "Lying in bed with them, it is hard to stop fondling their golden lotus. No other pleasures of dallying with courtesans can surpass this experience" (Hanan, p. 68).

The most vivid Chinese account of the fetishism of shoes and feet during the height of the cult of the golden lotus is the erotic novel The Plum in the Golden Vase, first published in 1618. Presiding over a polygynist household, the protagonist Simen Qing is the paragon of male privileges and excesses. Females vie to get his attention, hence their heart's desires, by a parade of tiny shoes they designed and assembled. Simen was partial to red sleeping slippers; his love for them—and their wearer—was transference for his own desire to wear red shoes (chapter 28). Simen, a merchant, personifies the commodity culture that enabled new economies of pleasure and desire in seventeenth-century China.

Chinese fetishism assumes different meanings than that which crystallized in Europe in the second half of the nineteenth century, in part because the association of pleasure and guilt is absent in Confucian morality. But in China as in Europe, the fetishism of the foot found its most graphic expression in the spectacular details lavished onto high heel shoes. As a vessel for wine, plaything, or token of exchange, embroidered slippers were receptacles of boundless fantasy.

The very subject of footbinding has been fetishized in the West. As a stand-in for the exotic and erotic Orient, footbinding has continued to fascinate modern observers and collectors after its demise in China as a social practice.

---

genres of patterns, snow clogs, and rain boots served the growing number of working-class women with bound feet. Footwear innovation continued into the 1920s and 30s, when women with bound feet updated their wardrobes with such Western styles as the Mary Jane, fastened with buttons and flesh-colored silk stockings.

In sum, there is not one footbinding but many. During each stage of its development the way of binding, shoe styles, social background of the women and their incentives are different; the regional diversities are also pronounced. But in the final analysis, the binding of feet was always motivated by a utopian impulse to overcome the body and to elevate one's status in the world.

See also China: History of Dress; Fetish Fashion.

Bibliography

Feng, Jicai. *Three-Inch Golden Lotus*. Translated by David Wakefield. Honolulu: University of Hawaii Press, 1994. A realistic novella that explores the complex female psychology during the anti-footbinding period.

Hanan, Patrick. *The Invention of Li Yu*. Cambridge, Mass., and London: Harvard University Press, 1988. An introduction to the life and times of Li Yu, maverick writer and connoisseur of bound feet.

Ko, Dorothy. *Every Step a Lotus: Shoes for Bound Feet*. Berkeley and Los Angeles: University of California Press, 2001. Includes an illustrated chart of regional footwear styles and a discussion of shoemaking tools.

Levy, Howard S. *Chinese Footbinding: The History of a Curious Erotic Custom*. Taipei: Nantian shuju, 1984. A convenient summary of the six-volume *Caifei lu*, a Chinese encyclopedia on foot-binding, and early Japanese scholarship on the subject.

Li Yu. *The Carnal Prayer Mat*. Translated by Patrick Hanan. Honolulu: University of Hawaii Press, 1990.

The Plum in the Golden Vase, or *Chin P'ing Mei*. Volume 2: *The Rivals*. Translated by David Tod Roy. Princeton, N.J.: Princeton University Press, 2001.

Rossi, William A. *The Sex Life of the Foot and Shoe*. Ware, Hertfordshire, U.K.: Wordsworth Editions, 1989.

Steele, Valerie. *Fetish: Fashion, Sex and Power*. New York and Oxford: Oxford University Press, 1996.

Wang, Ping. *Aching for Beauty*. Minneapolis: University of Minnesota Press, 2000. A Chinese woman's poetic evocation of the male and female desires that sustained the thousand-year custom.

Zhang, Bangji. *Mozhuang manlü*. In *Congshu jicheng chubian*, nos. 2864–2866. Changsha: Shangwu, 1939.

Dorothy Ko

FORD, TOM*

In his role as creative director for the Gucci Group, designing collections for both Gucci and Yves Saint Laurent, Tom Ford was central to early twenty-first-century fashion. Under Ford's direction, creativity and innovation shared equal value with marketing and promotion in the positioning of the brands.

Born in 1962 and raised in San Marcos, Texas, and Santa Fe, New Mexico, Ford first began his career as a model for television advertisements before studying interior design at Parsons School of Design in New York City. In his final year of school, he changed his focus to fashion design. As a freelance designer on Seventh Avenue, he first worked for Cathy Hardwick and then in 1988 in the jeans department of Perry Ellis, under the short-lived direction of Marc Jacobs.

In 1990, the company's worst year financially, Ford was appointed womenswear designer at Gucci. Because of loss of strategic and creative direction and in-house family feuding, the company was losing 340 billion lire annually. In 1992 Ford was appointed design director, and in 1994, creative director; by the first six months of 1995, the company's revenues had increased by 87 percent. This financial turnaround was largely achieved by a consolidation of the company's product range, editing out weak licenses for vulgarly branded goods and redesigning core items, typified by the reappearance of the classic Gucci loafer in rainbow hues (1991) and the success of the Gucci platform snaffle clog (1992).

The international recognition of Gucci as a producer of prêt-à-porter collections was crystallized by the autumn/winter season of 1995–1996. From the prevailing aesthetic of pared-down minimalism and understated luxury, Ford presented a sleek, retro-inspired collection evoking a somewhat louche sexuality. The look was defined by velvet hipster trousers with a kick at the heel and a narrowly cut silk shirt, accessorized with a large, unstructured shoulder bag and matching platform court shoes in patent leather with a metallic shine normally associated with car chassis.

The collection was pivotal, as it established a trend for the consumption of seasonal fashion defined not so much by a total look as by how the look could be attained through buying the "must-have" accessory. As Ford later suggested, "You have to get the product right, it's the most important aspect." Much of this success was achieved through the advertising campaigns the company produced with fashion photographer Mario Testino, where the glamorous proposition of the dressed models was matched on the opposite side of the spread by an isolated close-up of the accessory. The close relation between the image of Gucci and its advertising campaigns eventually produced a lapse in confidence, when for the spring/summer collections in 2003 the company ran an image of a model who had her pubic hair shaved into the Gucci "G." The image was widely criticized for being too blatantly sexual and in dubious taste. Meanwhile, the Gucci Group had acquired the Yves Saint Laurent (YSL) brand after the legendary designer retired from the couture. From an uncelebrated opening collection (largely due to the French press berating an American ready-to-wear designer for having the audacity to step into the most hallowed of shoes), the brand developed consistently and confidently, particularly from Ford's gaining access to the YSL archive.

Through his close relation to Domenico de Sole, CEO of the Gucci Group, Tom Ford was central to the increasing dominance of the company in the designer fashion and luxury goods market, as Gucci acquired stakes in Balenciaga, Alexander McQueen, Stella McCartney, Bottega Veneta, and Sergio Rossi. The unexpected 2003 announcement of Ford's departure from the Gucci group, effective in April 2004, shook the fashion world. In 2007, Ford opened his own store on Madison Avenue, featuring upscale menswear, fragrances, and accessories. He is scheduled to re-launch his own menswear line in 2010. Meanwhile, he made a surprisingly successful debut as a film director with "A Single Man," which premiered in 2009.

See also Gucci; Saint Laurent, Yves; Shoes.

Bibliography

Ford, Tom, for Gucci. *Light*. *Visionaire* 24. New York: Visionaire Publishing, 1998. Unique, multiformat album of fashion and fine art published three times yearly in numbered, limited editions. Artists are given freedom to develop a theme. In issue 24 *Visionaire* and Tom Ford created the first such publication that is battery-operated. Only 3,300 copies were made.

——. *Tom Ford*. New York: Rizzoli, 2008.

Forden, Sara Gay. *The House of Gucci: A Sensational Story of Murder, Madness, Glamour, and Greed*. New York: Perennial, 2001.

Alistair O'Neill

FORMAL WEAR, MEN'S

The quintessence of uniform elegance in men's wear must surely be those nearly unchanging garments described as "formal." The exact opposite of "casual" clothes, men's formal garments are as curiously elevating and ennobling as they are utilitarian and leveling. This might seem a contradiction in terms at first, but one has only to think of a "black-tie" event to realize that at least en masse, the uniform nature of the clothes—coded and easily recognizable globally—places all men in the same category, much like a uniform does for the army, navy, or air force. But like the armed forces, which have panoplies of different ranks, a tangible difference in provenance can be evinced in evening or formal clothes. Is this suit custom-made? Is that rented? Is that a hand-me-down? Is this a lucky find in a vintage market?

A black-tie event is a sea of ebony and ivory—all men, although from different ranks in society, at least visually and superficially are united by convention. Formal wear not only functions as a social leveling device for the men at a gathering, but it also provides a uniform backdrop (or perhaps, "black-drop") for the female guests who are of course, not restricted to the color black for their gowns. Formal clothes have an air of assured authority and confidence about them and are generally resistant to fashion, although of course some designers attempt to play with their strictures from collection to collection. But customers always seem to revert to the history, tradition, and timeless style of the unshakable classics.

The most recognizable formal wear costume is the black-tie—in the United States, usually referred to as the tuxedo and frequently shortened to "tux." In 1896, a mischievous, iconoclastic dandy, Griswold Lorillard, wore a shorter, black formal jacket (without tails) to a country club in Tuxedo Park, New York—and the name was established. The jacket part of the black-tie ensemble is sometimes referred to as a "dinner jacket," though that appellation is too limiting to encompass all its myriad social functions. Essentially, the terms all refer to the same costume, though some contend that the classic tuxedo jacket must have a shawl collar rather than peaked lapels, and many would permit no color other than black (some will allow cream). But these distinctions have more to do with the wearer's upbringing and taste as opposed to the outfit itself.

There are generally five styles to choose from: single-breasted, double-breasted, peaked lapels (usually double-breasted) and single-or double-breasted shawl collared. Basically, it is a black suit but ennobled by a silk or grosgrain facing on the lapels, the better to provide a suggestion of luxury and attention to detail. And black-tie is, and should only ever be, black—or perhaps midnight blue, which the late royal couturier Sir Hardy Amies always maintained looked blacker than black itself, under artificial light. A corresponding black silk or grosgrain stripe runs down the sides of the trouser—again echoing uniform pants.

The shirt is always white. It can be made in anything from the finest zephyr cotton to polyester—but it must always be white. Pearl buttons or studs are the norm and a wing collar a matter of choice and taste, although if one is sported it should be buttoned on or studded through—not ready-made. And the bow tie is not considered one if it is not hand-tied. Aficionados frown upon the ready-made examples with elastic and hooks. Cummerbunds are reserved for the most formal of occasions, but they do have a small function which rescues them from being pure items of conspicuous consumption; in their pleats is concealed a tiny pocket for small essentials.

While the basic elements of formal wear are conveniently precise, the wearer is able to exert his individuality through the sporting of discreet (or not so discreet) items of jewelry—these for the most part being concealed by the jacket cuff in the form of links or by the jacket itself if a spirited watch chain or fob is attached to a waistcoat.

The luxe de luxe of formal wear is white-tie, an ensemble that includes tails, wing-collared shirt, hand-tied white bow tie usually in a cotton pique or fine grosgrain, and corresponding white waistcoat—traditionally three buttoned and cut low to expose maximum shirt front. For the feet, nothing but glacé, glossy pumps will suffice, topped off with a pair of silk, decorative bows. And at the other end of the body, a top hat—in glossy black silk—is the point finale. This look was established as a sartorial must by the early 1920s. Whether formal

or extremely formal, the basic sonorous quality of the ensemble is the color black As the costume historian James Laver has pointed out, since the eighteenth century, all attempts to introduce color to male formal attire have failed or have been derided. A shiny, colorful, patterned male evening ensemble is unthinkable; such is the continuing power and influence of tradition.

Formal daywear is now found primarily in the world of sports, and especially of horse racing and boat racing. Royal Ascot, Goodwood, and Henley are social institutions where formal clothes are demanded and specific dress code requirements are imposed on all who attend. Formal wear for Royal Ascot would be full morning dress (dove gray or black); the groom or the bride's father at a formal daytime wedding would wear the same ensemble. The coat is sometimes referred to as a cutaway coat (being a frock coat with the corners removed), not to be confused with a tailcoat, which is cut to the waist in the front, and sports a pair of tails behind. A gray, buff, or for the more fashion conscious, brightly colored and patterned silk waistcoat, is worn beneath and teamed with a tie, cravat, or some other individualistic neck wear—but never a bow.

The origin of formal wear is open to discussion and challenge, but one name forever associated with formality, uniformity, and simplicity was Beau Brummell—king of the dandies and a one-time favorite of King George IV. He is often referred to as the "father of modern male formal costume" as he eschewed the brightly hued silken finery and powdered wigs generally worn at court for a sober suit of midnight blue-black with minimal jewelry (a signet ring was permissible), no wig, no perfume but plenty of shaving and washing—a well-scrubbed appearance being the natural partner to formal dress.

It is the Beau whom many think invented or at least popularized the under-the-foot strapped pantaloon (from the French—*Pend en talon*—to the heel) and set the standard for what would become the ubiquitous tailcoat. Brummell was belligerently exact when it came to matters of formal and what came to be "court dress." To a would-be dandy seeking sartorial approval he snapped, "Do you call that *thing* a coat?" Brummell made formality look simple—challenging the brightly colored costumes in feminine fabrics like silk and velvet for the sharp masculinity of well-cut wool and flannel. Thus formal wear showed and still does show its class by line, not content.

In the twenty-first century, the reduction of occasions on which to wear formal clothes has curiously thrown a

Men's formal wear. Formal attire for men has seen little change since the nineteenth century. These men are modeling the fashions of 1932, ranging from the highly formal tuxedo on the right to less formal business attire at left. © Bettmann/Corbis. Reproduced by permission.

sharper light on these style stalwarts. Not even a hundred years ago, BBC radio announcers were required to wear black-tie—the premise being that the stiff formality of the shirt, bow tie, and exact-fit jacket aided the gravitas of the voice and the assurance of the delivery. At weddings and funerals, formal clothes were obligatory and many other social situations demanded this "civilian uniform" as a means of maintaining a required ambiance, from balls and tea dances to memorials and visits to the opera. Just a hundred years ago, dressing for dinner in one's own home could have meant having to wear full formal dress—even if it was just with family members. A visit to almost any vintage clothing fair or market will reveal several yesteryear formal garments for men—a clue as to how vital they were and perhaps how few the occasions for which they are needed in the early 2000s.

In the mid-1950s, everyone who could afford to have at least one formal outfit owned one, which would most often be mothballed until needed. Those who did not own formal wear relied on borrowing from relatives or renting. The formal rental market is still hugely successful with providing formal wear for weddings to royal garden parties and theatrical opening nights. The respect that formal wear lends to the occasion is thus implied—even if not required or requested—and many will opt for formality to suggest this. Those who have chosen casual attire will be thrown into sharp contrast. Perhaps formal wear represents the last bastion of constancy in clothing with a conspiratorial nod to time, not trend.

See also Brummell, George (Beau); Tuxedo.

Bibliography

Curtis, Bryan, and John Bridges. *A Gentleman Gets Dressed Up: Knowing What to Wear, How to Wear It, and When to Wear It.* New York: Rutledge Hill Press, 2003.

Flusser, Alan. *Dressing the Man: Mastering the Art of Permanent Fashion.* New York: HarperCollins Publisher's Inc., 2002.

Hollander, Anne. *Sex and Suits: The Evolution of Modern Dress.* Tokyo and New York: Kodansha International, 1995.

Robin Dutt

FORTUNY, MARIANO

Although Mariano Fortuny considered himself a painter, he pursued various critical and aesthetic interests. He is primarily remembered for remarkable layers of dyed and patterned fabrics, which he created between 1906 and 1949. Born in Granada, Spain, to an upper-class family of distinguished painters, Mariano Fortuny y Madrazo (1871–1949) is more often associated with the city of Venice, Italy, where he lived and worked most of his life.

As a child, Fortuny was surrounded by eclectic assemblages of ephemera: antique textile remnants, carpets, costumes, vestments, furniture, armor, and implements of war collected as art objects. Following the untimely death of his father, the painter Mariano Fortuny y Marsal, in 1874, young Mariano, his mother, and his sister moved to Paris in 1875. Although he considered himself self-taught, he was guided toward the arts by his uncle Raymundo, a painter, and informally by the sculptor Auguste Rodin. He later expanded his education in Germany, where he studied physics and chemistry. In 1889 the Fortuny family traveled to Venice; finding it a romantic and artistic center, they moved there permanently in 1890.

Business Innovations

Fortuny's garments and textiles fuse history, anthropology, and art. By blending various dyes he achieved luminous, unique colors. Resurrecting the ancient craft of pleating fabric, artistically symbolizing a reflection of the sun's rays, Fortuny developed his own interpretation of this craft and registered his heated pleating device in 1909. Between 1901 and 1933 he registered twenty-two patents, all of which related to garments and printing methods. Prolific in artistic pursuits, he printed etchings, invented a type of photography paper, designed lamps and furniture, bound books, and maintained an extensive, private reference library. He displayed his own artistic creations in the ground floor showroom of his residential palazzo.

An interest in Richard Wagner's operatic productions drew Fortuny to Bayreuth, Germany, in 1892. Fascinated by the dramatic spectacle unfolding before him, he developed a revolutionary, indirect lighting system that transformed cumbersome stage scenery and obsolete gas lamps, significantly changing the atmosphere onstage. Commissioned by an art patron, he constructed two enormous, vaulted quarter spheres of cloth, expanded over a collapsible metal frame, which amplified color and sound. The spheres were 225 square meters (269 square yards) in area and 7 meters (7.6 yards) high. His first theatrical costume was a figure-enveloping, border-printed scarf titled the Knossos, presented in a private theater in 1907. Isadora Duncan was the first to wear the Knossos scarf. At the home of his patron Cotesse de Bearn in 1906 in Paris, his stage lighting system first appeared as well as his first textile creation printed with geometric motifs. This theatrical endeavor transformed his awareness and appreciation of materials into a tactile form, quite separated from his representational works.

Fortuny preferred working alone to avoid conflict, illustrating his theory that an artist must control all aspects of the creative act, but he did allow collections of his fabrics, gowns, and accessories to be sold in a Paris boutique operated by Paul Poiret. His gowns were also available at Liberty of London and his shops in Paris, London, and New York.

Personal Image and Acknowledgments

Throughout his life Fortuny maintained a striking figure, dressing in artistic combinations, even regional and ethnic dress. He married Henriette Negrin, an accomplished French seamstress who designed patterns for his garments. Together, they developed methods and practices in the atelier of their Palazzo Orfei residence. Driven by spirited curiosity rather than training as a couturier, Fortuny depended on ancient and regional

styles that became the foundation of his modern and comfortable styles for women, costumes for the theater, and yardage for interiors.

In an atmosphere of antiquated splendor, Fortuny dressed Venice's artistic community at the turn of the century, where Americans and Europeans—including the actress Sarah Bernhardt, the dancer Isadora Duncan, and the poet Gabriele D'Annunzio—were among those who sought cultural legitimacy with the notion that the classical and the beautiful were one. Artists of the theater and American travelers were the first to wear his gowns in public.

Artistic Hallmarks

Among the garments viewed in museum collections, the loosely twisted, pleated gowns labeled Delphos and Peplos, of Greek origin, are exhibited more frequently than any others. His diagrams of the Delphos and the wooden structure fitted with ceramic tubes that heat-set his signature pleats are also popular museum exhibits. Similar avant-garde dresses, referred to as tea gowns, enhanced Fortuny's popularity with the wave of orientalism that dominated the arts in the years before World War I.

Echoing his knowledge of textile history, Fortuny produced his imaginative manipulations through printed and applied methods, freeing him to experiment. His vertical pleating and undulating silk and cotton yardage yielded natural elasticity, flowing effortlessly over the contours of female forms. Delicate Murano glass beads were laced onto silk cording and hand-stitched along hems, seams, and necklines, giving weight to an even edge, similar to the ancient Greek method of weighting fabric with metal. His method was to piece-dye cut lengths, frequently layering natural and, later, aniline dyes and occasionally incorporating agents to resist previously applied colors, which resulted in random, transparent irregularity. Clients were required to return the garment to the island factory of La Giudecca in order to clean and pleat the material.

For his imported silk, cotton, and velvet surfaces, Fortuny studied Japanese and Southeast Asian methods of hand-printing, including the *pochoir* method, for precise color transfer to cloth. Block printing and silk screening, positioned on seams in central areas of a garment and along edges, provided striking effects. Fortuny combined metal powder with pigments to simulate shimmering metallic thread, inspired by sixteenth-century velvets. On occasion, more than a dozen processes—including paintbrushes, sponges, and decolorization—were implemented on each unique length. The paintbrushes and sponges were used to create a marbled effect, already a method known in Lyon, to create the same effect of patchiness. Artisans were directed to incorporate various methods to correct or retouch the yardage. Textile patterns and motifs reflected his studies in the art museums of Venice, where he made note of the dress depicted in canvases. When he adapted the traditional practice of goffering, realizing a relief in velvet pile, he may have used block-printing methods and silk screening. His pattern adaptations of regional dress, hand-stitched with one of three labels (Mariano Fortuny Venise, Fabriqué en Italie, or Fortuny de Pose), can be identified as variations inspired by ancient Greek dress for men or women, dress of the Renaissance and the Middle Ages, the Moroccan djellaba, North African *bournous*, Arabic *abaia* (a kind of caftan), Japanese kimono, Coptic tunic, and Indian sari.

Fortuny in the Twenty-first Century

In 1922 Fortuny, Inc., was established in collaboration with the American interior designer Elsie Lee McNeill, later Countess Gozzi. Henriette remained in the palazzo to oversee the production of silk and velvet garments, while Fortuny moved production to a factory on the island of La Giudecca. After his death in 1949, garments were no longer produced. Gozzi continued to promote the mysteries of his textiles for almost forty years, until she sold her rights to printing yardage to her friend and attorney, Maged Riad, in 1998. In the early twenty-first century, Riad's children became responsible for the firm in New York, and his brother took over as the artistic director of production on La Giudecca. Appointments for research in the Palazzo Fortuny are limited, though the building is frequently the venue for art exhibitions, managed by the city of Venice.

The company's contemporary collection of yardage contains approximately 260 original patterns and color combinations printed on silk, velvet, and Egyptian cotton, including irregular application by artisans, who give each length an aged and artistic patina. Antique textile dealers and international specialists represent original yardage.

Since Fortuny creations were originally an attraction for travelers, interpretations of his artistry have been faithfully recovered by Venetia Studium, directed by Lino Lando and available to the visitor to Venice.

Connoisseurs, collectors, historians, and antique dealers agree that Mariano Fortuny achieved an elegant, impressive balance, fusing art and science. His legacy proves his relevance.

See also Art and Fashion; Clothing, Costume, and Dress; Orientalism; Proust, Marcel.

Bibliography

Deschodt, Anne-Marie, and Doretta Davanzo Poli. *Fortuny.* Translated by Anthony Roberts. New York: Harry N. Abrams, 2001.

D'Osma, Guillermo. *Fortuny: Mario Fortuny, His Life and Work.* New York: Rizzoli International, 1980.

Fortuny, Mariano. *Fortuny.* New York: Fashion Institute of Technology, 1981. Published in conjunction with the exhibition *Fortuny*, shown at the Fashion Institute of Technology and the Art Institute of Chicago.

Fuso, Silvio. "Fortuny the Magician." *FMR* 120 (February/March 2003).

Steele, Valerie. *Paris Fashion: A Cultural History.* 2nd rev. ed. New York: Berg, 1998.

Gillion Carrara

FUR

Fur garments occupy a long and significant place in European history. From the fourteenth to seventeenth century, the kings and queens of England, for example, issued royal proclamations in order to regulate furs and fur apparel and, especially, to reserve the more exclusive furs of marten, fox, gray squirrel, and ermine for the aristocratic and clerical elite. These royal proclamations became part of what is known as "sumptuary legislation" in which everyday practices involving clothing, drinking, and eating were subject to public governance and scrutiny. Thus, from very early on furs and fur garments were regulated, not only in order to establish a hierarchy of desirable fur, but also to create recognizable codes of social status in the wearer of fur. While by law the most exclusive furs were reserved for the higher nobility, the middle class wore less costly furs such as beaver, otter, hare, and fox, and the peasantry wore the hardier, rougher furs of wolf, goat, and sheepskin.

Very little appears to have changed in six hundred years. In the global economy of the twenty-first century, the luxurious full-length fur coat is subject to various processes of identification, as a commodity and sign of elite standing and material wealth from England to Japan. What is markedly different at the turn of the twenty-first century, is that fur garments, especially those worn by women, now come under intense scrutiny for the dangers and risks they pose to the planet's ecological stability. Politics and fur fashions have become so intertwined in the contemporary setting that it is impossible to discuss fur fashions without reference to ecological struggles, not to mention the challenges faced by indigenous peoples in Canada, Greenland, and Alaska whose very livelihood, in some cases, still depends on the fur trade initially created by Europe's early modern industrial economy and mercantile trade.

Class, Gender, and Sex Distinctions

In the Middle Ages the exclusivity of some furs meant that they were used sparingly. The practice of "purfling" was invented in which the more expensive furs were reserved for decorative trim, while cheaper furs were used to finish the lining. There are some examples of excessive expenditures on the part of nobles such as Charles VI of France who apparently used 20,000 squirrel pelts to line a garment. It was not until the fur trade was established in the sixteenth century between France, and then England, and the New World (what is now Canada), that furs were available to European consumers in newer and larger supplies. Beaver fur was especially important to this new trade initiative and, in fact, became the primary economic unit from the mid-sixteenth century to the 1870s. In England, the technologically innovative process of felting beaver fur was used to produce the broad-brimmed beaver hats worn by the opposing religious and political groups of the seventeenth century, the Puritans and Cavaliers. One of the most significant promoters of the cavalier style of beaver hat was Charles II. With his restoration to the throne in 1660, the beaver hat emerged as a dominant fashion article supported no less than by Charles II's incorporation of the Hudson's Bay Company by royal charter. Thus, the English fur trade was firmly established and once again fur circulated in abundance among the nobility as well as among a rising mercantile class of consumers as a distinctive sign of class and imperial wealth.

In Russia, similar motivations to expand colonial governance and mercantile wealth were carried out through fur trading. From the mid-eighteenth century and throughout the nineteenth century, Russian frontier merchants traded in sea otter pelts from northern Pacific waters to fulfill the clothing demands of the Chinese elite. Competition from China and eventually the United States and Britain led to various economic and territorial accommodations that resulted in a treaty with the United States and the formation of the Russian-American company in 1824, and between the latter and the Hudson's Bay Company in 1839.

The history of the fur trade and fur garments is in many ways a history of imperial class distinctions but one that is also marked by gender and cultural differences. Influenced by the Russian fur market, in the earlier period in England the fur coat was worn both by men and women. The fur was mostly on the inside, visible as trim on the collar and cuffs. But during the late nineteenth century and throughout the twentieth century, fur became increasingly identified with elite women's fashions and the fur coat was "reversed" in the sense that fur was now worn almost exclusively on the outside.

The 1920s saw the image of the fur-clad woman emerge as a sign of unevenly distributed economic wealth. From debates in the British House of Commons in February of 1926 over the benefits of socialism in providing women with practical and affordable cloth coats against the excesses of capitalism represented by a luxury fur coat, to G. W. Pabst's brilliant silent film *Joyless Streets* (*Die Freudlose Gasse*, 1925) in which Greta Garbo plays the heroine who is offered a fur coat in exchange for her sexual services, the image of the fur-clad bourgeois woman not only signified material wealth; it also came to represent, in contradictory fashion, feminine passivity and female sexual power.

Political Protests and Fur Fashion Design

The symbolic power associated with the fur garment in the Middle Ages ensured its value for contemporary fashion as a mark of distinction in the making of luxury commodities. Since the late nineteenth century and the publication of Leopold von Sacher-Masoch's novel, *Venus in Furs*, the fur coat's value increased with its strong identification with sexual fetishism. However, by the 1970s the fur coat was transformed from desirable female commodity to a symbol for animal rights' activism. Efforts to ensure that the international trade in specimens of wild animals, including fur by-products, did not threaten their survival resulted in the national and international legislation of the Endangered Species Act (1973) in the United States and the Convention on International Trade in Endangered Species of Wild Fauna and Flora (1975). The antisealing campaigns off the coast of Labrador in Canada in the 1970s anticipated the antifur protests of the 1980s and 1990s, headed by organizations such as People for the Ethical Treatment of Animals (PETA) in the United States and LYNX in England, which were successful, momentarily, in diminishing fur sales. More recently, the European Union tried to introduced a ban on the import of wild fur from countries using the leg-hold trap. The ban was temporarily postponed pending an international agreement on humane trapping standards among Canada, the United States, Russia, and the European Union. In response to the global politicization of fur garments, fur manufacturers developed new dyeing and tailoring techniques in order to change the conventional image of the elite fur-clad woman as well as to "disguise" fur, although the Federal Fur Products Labeling Act requires that all fur products bear a label indicating, among other things, whether the fur product was artificially colored. The fashion for fur knitting, popularized in the 1960s, was rejuvenated as a result of these new design strategies. The synthetic textile manufacturers benefited from the antifur media campaigns and developed "fake fur" alternatives. In an interesting twist on the environmental implications of natural fur products, the Montréal-based fashion designer Mariouche Gagné recycled fur into fashion accessories, arguing that fur was a biodegradable product and, therefore, more ecologically friendly than the synthetic alternatives offered by the "green" marketplace.

INUIT DRESS AND SOCIAL CLASS

Inuit now use combinations of traditional and southern-style garments to convey group affiliation, gender, age, role, status, social organization, interaction with neighboring groups, and changing technology. . . . Contemporary Inuit clothing provides an intriguing unwritten essay reflecting the social, economic, and technological changes to which Inuit have adapted over the last generation.

Judy Hall, Jill Oakes, and Sally Qimmiu'naaq Webster, eds., *Sanatujut, Pride in Women's Work: Copper and Caribou Inuit Clothing Traditions.*

In the early 1990s more established fashion designers such as Jean Paul Gaultier and Isaac Mizrahi tried to give their turn on fur fashion an edge of political correctness by creating designs that incorporated Inuit and First Nations motifs and images. First Nations and Inuit communities responded to this politics of appropriation, as well as to the economic devastation of their participation in the contemporary fur trade, by forming their own political organizations, for example, Indigenous Survival International. They also made use of public institutions—the British Museum in London, and the Canadian Museum of Civilization in Ottawa—to exhibit traditional as well as contemporary fur fashions in an effort to educate the general public about the symbolic and practical dimensions of fur in northern societies and economies.

See also Muffs.

Bibliography

Emberley, Julia. *The Cultural Politics of Fur.* Ithaca, N.Y.: Cornell University Press, 1997. Comprehensive historical and cultural overview of the history of fur and fashion.

Hall, Judy, Jill Oakes, and Sally Qimmiu'naaq Webster, eds., *Sanatujut, Pride in Women's Work: Copper and Caribou Inuit Clothing Traditions.* Hull, Quebec: Canadian Museum of Civilization, 1994. Excellent book on fur, clothing, and Inuit culture and society.

Pelts: Politics of the Fur Trade. Dir. Nigel Markham. Videocassette. National Film Board of Canada, 1989. An example of the environmental movement's critique of fur fashion industry.

Steele, Valerie. *Fetish: Fashion, Sex, and Power.* New York: Oxford University Press, 1996. Authoritative text on fetishism and fashion, including fur fetishes.

Julia Emberley

FUTURE OF FASHION

Predicting the future of fashion can be as analytical as market research and statistical analysis allow, or as speculative as the predictions William Norwich of the *New York Times* received when in April 2003 he playfully asked the fashion world's favorite psychic the question, "Where is the future of fashion?" Attempts to influence the future of fashion—made at times by dress reform-ers, moralists, and social thinkers—have invariably had little effect. Actual influences on fashion have typically stemmed from changing technologies, political events, and the creativity of certain individuals.

The manufacturing of clothes has always been af-fected by technological advances. The sewing machine revolutionized the clothing industry in the nineteenth century, and zippers altered clothing construction when they were perfected for use in the 1930s. In the early 2000s, technological innovations in fabrics influence how designers think about clothing, with textiles being developed that have properties unheard of in natural fi-bers. The abilities of these high-tech fabrics to stretch to over-whelming sizes or change their structure according to temperatures inspire clothing designers and blur the lines between fashion and industrial design. The Ital-ian firm Corpo Nove designed a shirt woven with tita-nium that reacts to shifts in temperature. Wrinkles in the fabric are released when the shirt is exposed to hot air. Another item from the firm is a nylon jacket with a cooling system. The changing face of communications is also influencing styles of the future. A nylon jacket, manufactured by Industrial Clothing Design, a venture of Philips Electronics and Levi Strauss and Company, features a "fully integrated communications and enter-tainment system" (Lupton, p. 153).

Designers are also looking at ways of incorporat-ing clothing with other functions of daily life. The C.P. Company has produced jackets that transform into chairs, tents or sleeping mattresses. Ixilab, a Japanese firm, designed plastic shorts with a cushion in the rear that inflates for the wearer to have a place to sit. New ideas for multifunctional clothing are also coming from industrial designers. A class called Weaving Mate-rial and Habitation at Harvard's Graduate School of Design "has been experimenting with Lycra-spandex type materials that can stretch out to four times their original size. A poncho or sweater might expand into a 7-foot-by-4-foot tarp" (Stevenson, p. 28).

Throughout fashion history, shifts in styles have been attributed to political and historical events. Amer-ica's war with Iraq has elicited reactions from fashion designers ranging from antiwar sentiments to milita-ristic overtones. Proponents of various political and social issues attempt to influence what people wear and how clothes are produced. Antifur organizations frequently disrupt fashions shows featuring animal fur. The exploitation of labor is another controversial issue. Some politically minded consumers boycott clothes produced in factories and countries considered to have unfair labor practices. For some designers, these issues resonate; Katharine Hamnett has said that her goal is "the hope of making clothing that is environmentally friendly" (Jones and Mair, p. 209).

Primarily the fashion designers, in their roles as cre-ators, determine the course of fashion. As a result, cloth-ing designers are often asked to look into the future. Over time, their ideas and themes relating to these pre-dictions remain almost constant. In 1968, André Cour-règes described the future of fashion: "Women have become liberated little by little through thought, work, and clothes. I cannot imagine that they will ever turn back. Perhaps they will continue to suffer occasionally to be beautiful, but more than ever they seek to be both beautiful and free" (*Fashion, Art, and Beauty*, p. 140). He might have said the same in the early 2000s.

In her 1982 book *Fashion 2001*, Lucille Khornak asked fashion designers to each select a garment that would reflect fashions in 2001, and she interviewed them about how fashions would change by 2001. Many of the predictions made were unlikely to be achieved in that short period: "Paco Rabonne predicts that the clothes of the future will be premolded, bound or welded—no longer will they be sewn" (Khornak, p. 7). Issey Miyake is one designer rethinking how to make clothes for the future. Miyake's A-POC (A Piece of Cloth) features knitted tubes of fabric with markings for an outfit. When purchased, the fabric is cut by the wearer to make different articles of clothing. But ideas such as these are beyond the realm of mainstream fash-ion in the early twenty-first century.

One of the ongoing influences on fashion is the shift in women's roles in society. Fashion designers look at these changes from various angles and possibilities: the approach of unisex or androgynous clothing; the work-ing woman's wardrobe as compared with men's wear; or the validity of femininity now that women are suppos-edly equal. The result is a spectrum of styles that caters to a diverse group of women, yet retains many stereo-types. Fashion continues to represent female sexuality as both demure, with pleats and bows and flowing chif-fon, and as aggressive, with leather, corsetry, and body-revealing shapes. This dichotomy was featured in a 20 July 2003 *New York Times Magazine* fashion edito-rial of "good girl/bad girl" clothing.

The human body plays as integral a role as the clothes for many fashion designers working in the early 2000s. The idea of clothing as a "second skin" is often discussed when designers speak of the future of clothing. This concept has yet to be achieved with the wearing of only body stockings, or as Jean Paul Gaultier predicted in 1982 that we "spray on a latex body suit" (Khornak, p. 62). Yet this idea of a second skin continues to interest Gaultier and other designers. For his Fall 2003 collection, Gaultier created patterned bodysuits, worn under clothes, including one outlining the body's arteries. More often fashion designers attempt to mold the body into other shapes. While the concept differs little from bustles of the nineteenth century, the results found in the early twenty-first century differ greatly. As Walter van Beirendonck, the Belgian designer for Wild and Lethal Trash, said, "the body of the future will be different" (Lupton, p. 187).

How fashion designers will manifest their ideas depends partly on the changing structure of the fashion industry and the evolving needs, and demands, of consumers. There remains the ongoing question regarding the demise of French couture and the stimulus to fashion from street styles. In *The End of Fashion*, Teri Agins argues that street style, consumer demands, and profit making have changed and will continue to alter the fashion industry. "In today's high-strung, competitive marketplace, those who will survive the end of fashion will reinvent themselves enough times and with enough flexibility and resources to anticipate, not manipulate, the twenty-first century customer" (Agins, p. 16). While Agins's theories apply to the marketplace, fashion in the twenty-first century still belongs to the elusive world of luxury, status, sex, and glamour. While fashion is known to be fleeting, many predictions about its future are slow to arrive.

See also Fashion, Historical Studies of; Fashion Designer; Fashion Industry; Gaultier, Jean-Paul; Miyake, Issey.

Bibliography

Agins, Teri. *The End of Fashion*. New York: HarperCollins, 1999.
Braddock, E. Sarah, and Marie O'Mahony. *Techno Textiles: Fabrics for Fashion and Design*. New York: Thames and Hudson, Inc., 1999. Reprint 2001.
Breward, Christopher. *The Culture of Fashion*. Manchester, U.K.: Manchester University Press, 1995. *Fashion, Art, and Beauty. Metropolitan Museum of Art Bulletin* 26, no. 3 (November 1967).
Jones, Terry, and Avril Mair, eds. *Fashion Now*. Köln, Germany: Taschen, 2003.
Khornak, Lucille. *Fashion 2001*. New York: Viking Press, 1982.
Lupton, Ellen. *Skin: Surface, Substance + Design*. New York: Princeton Architectural Press, 2002.
Norwich, William. "Change Your Life, Boost Your Aura." *New York Times Magazine*, 27 April 2003, 63–67.
——. "The Mirror Has Two Faces." *New York Times Magazine*, 20 July 2003, 48–54.
Stevenson, Seth. "Gimme Temporary Shelter." *New York Times Magazine*, 18 May 2003, 26–30.

Donna Ghelerter

FUTURIST FASHION, ITALIAN

Futurism in fashion is not limited to the artistic movement alone. The pervasive conceptual and visual influence of futurist art at the beginning of the twentieth century accounts for the fact that the term "futurism" continues to be applied—in the case of fashion to designs that are made from unorthodox materials, demonstrate new technologies and shapes, and display colorful dynamism. Futurism as a modernist movement was born on 20 February 1909 when Filippo Tommaso Marinetti published his manifesto "Manifeste du Futurisme" in the Paris daily *Le Figaro*. His aim was to extol the shock of the new (as cubism had done previously). However, whereas the provocation had previously been limited to museums or books, Marinetti wanted to extend it to social and political life. While futurist paintings mixed stylistic idioms from cubism and divisionism, its poetry, music, photography, film, and drama expanded along more abstract principles like speed, novelty, violence, technology, nationalism, and urbanity, which were often expressed according to prior formulated declarations. For fashion the programs were written by Giacomo Balla in the form of the "Futurist Manifesto of Men's Clothing" of 1914, followed by his "The Anti-Neutral Clothing: Futurist Manifesto" of the same year; in 1920 the "Manifesto of Futurist Women's Fashion" by Volt (pseudonym of Vincenzo Fanni); 1932 saw the "Manifesto to Change Men's Fashion" by the brothers Ernesto and Ruggero Michahelles; then Marinetti collaborated with Enrico Prampolini and a couple of second-generation futurists on "Futurist Manifesto: The Italian Hat," and in 1933 the "Futurist Manifesto: The Italian Tie" was formulated by Renato di Bosso and Ignazio Scurto.

The trajectory of these various programs can be constructed parallel to changes in futurist art from the avantgarde protest of its first generation, through the drama of World War I and sobriety of the time after the conflict, and the decorative subjectivism of the interwar years, to the rise in nationalist culture that would lead to the close association in the early 1930s between futurism and fascist Italy. The manifestos about fashion accordingly move from the direct intervention into culture by transforming the appearance of man—and to a lesser extent woman—in the street, where it was hoped that manners and mores would follow radical alterations in the bourgeois dress code, via a utilitarian attitude to dress as expression of communal principles, and the design of decorative and colorful costumes, to the fervent declaration of a nationalist dress. These various attitudes are not dissimilar to those that other art movements displayed vis-à-vis fashion, for example, aesthetic dress in Vienna or Proletkult clothing in 1920s U.S.S.R. Only futurism, however, ran through the entire range of oppositional clothing, from radical individualism to collective uniform, from decadent subjectivity of sartorial expression to formal invention in the construction of clothes.

Despite the founding role of poetry (with its onomatopoetic "parole in libertà") futurist aesthetics were disseminated markedly through painting. This implies a leaning toward decorative rather than structural solutions. And it favors the alteration of visual appearances and style (artistic, mode of living) rather than changing the sociopolitical foundation of artistic production proper. Similarly, fashion in futurism was often conceived as decorated surfaces of fabrics and textiles, where the introduction of color functioned as a novel element. An actual change in the cut and construction of clothes was comparatively rare.

From its very beginning futurism had a strong performative quality. Through the primacy of speed and dynamics, the representation of objects in movement became paramount. This was demonstrated not only through actual performances—although the poetry readings, musical soirées, and theater pieces, as well as demonstrative excursion in the motorcar, initiated an early concept of "performance art." Significantly, futurist photographs and canvases aimed at showing successive stages of an object moving through space. This in turn accounts for the early significance of fashion, as an aesthetic expression that is directly—and

almost exclusively—applicable to the active and activated body. Futurists like Balla and Fortunato Depero, who both designed costumes for the Ballets Russes in Paris, realized the opportunity of playing with volumes, density of material, and animated objects. Balla's early designs between 1912 and 1914 show the attempt to break the surface of the body into fractions and lend movement to even heavy and static cloth. He hoped that the painted "speedlines" and colorful beams on the fabric would render even the most conservative and immovable individual a model of dynamism. Balla himself sported his designs well into the 1930s and conceived a rapid manner of walking and moving appropriate for the aesthetic principles of his dress. In contrast Marinetti, Depero, and others favored more staid sartorial expressions, wherein brightly colored waistcoats or ties offered the habitual outlet for individualism (1920s). Whereas men's bourgeois suits, as the somber constructed mainstay of modernity, offered the most obvious target for a futurist reform of the dress-code, women's fashion with its seasonal changes and decorated surfaces did not appear to require the same reformist zeal. Thus the futurist contribution to female dress is to be found outside Italy, in the "simultaneous" dresses by Sonia Delaunay created in Paris in the 1920s and the cubo-futurist costumes by Alexandra Exter and Liubov Popova made in Moscow from 1915 onward.

Balla had attempted to provide new patterns for the cut of shirts and suits that were based on geometric principles of nonobjective paintings, but it took Ernesto Michahelles, who worked under the pseudonym Thayaht, to innovate a utilitarian and unisex dress that was based on the progressive notion that form and volume were to follow only inherent constructive principles. His "Tuta" of 1918 was designed as a cheap and uniform overall that due to its simple pattern could be tailored at home from a variety of fabrics. The aim was to provide "sportswear" that maximized freedom of movement for the body and directed an active lifestyle and corporeal ideal that would feed later into the fascist glorification of athleticism. In the early 2000s "tuta" is used in Italy to denote a track-suit and Thayaht, who went on to illustrate haute couture for Madeleine Vionnet, thus designed a template for the emancipation of the body in the time between the wars. More decorative solutions for the embellishment of dress came from Depero, whose contribution lies in the commercial viability of his designs for fashion boutiques, posters, and the theater, from Tullio Crali who continued Balla's efforts to redesign the jacket and suit, and from Pippo Rizzo's textiles.

Balla's first Manifesto of 1914 had proclaimed: "We must invent futurist clothes, hap-hap-hap-hap-happy clothes, daring clothes with brilliant colors and dynamic lines. They must be simple, and above all they must be made to last for a short time only in order to encourage industrial activity and to provide constant and novel enjoyment for our bodies." It was a sartorial call to arms that mixed progressive aesthetics in dress with a shrewd understanding of its commercial and industrial basis, thus perfectly fitting as a credo for the artist engaging in modernity.

See also Art and Fashion; Theatrical Costume.

Bibliography

Balla, Giacomo. "Futurist Manifesto of Men's Clothing." In *Futurist Manifestos*. Edited by Umberto Apollonio. London: Thames and Hudson, Inc., 1973.

Crispolti, Enrico. *Il Futurismo e la moda*. Venice: Marsilio, 1986.

Fiorentini Capitani, Aurora. "Tra arte e moda." *Imago Moda* no. 1, Florence 1989.

Hulten, Pontus, ed. *Futurism & Futurisms*. London: Thames and Hudson, Inc., 1987.

Lapini, Lia, ed. *Abiti e costumi futuristi*. Pistoia, Italy: Edizioni del Comune, 1985.

Lista, Giovanni. *Balla*. Modena, Italy: Galleria Fonte d'Abisso, 1982.

——. "La Mode Futuriste." In *Europe 1910–1939*. Edited by Valérie Guillaume. Paris: Les Musées de la Ville de Paris, 1996.

Ruta, Anna-Maria. *Arreddi Futuristi*. Palermo, Italy: Il labirinto, 1985.

Scudiero, Maurizio. *Fortunato Depero*. Trento, Italy: Il Castello, 1995.

Stern, Radu. *Against Fashion*. Cambridge, Mass., and London: MIT Press, 2003.

Ulrich Lehmann

G

GALLIANO, JOHN*

John Galliano (1960–) is widely considered one of the most innovative and influential fashion designers of the early twenty-first century. Known for a relentless stream of historical and ethnic appropriations, he mingled his references in often surprising juxtapositions to create extravagant yet intricately engineered and meticulously tailored clothes. His continual interest in presenting fashion shows as highly theatricalized spectacles, with models as characters in a drama and clothes at times verging on costumes, won him applause as well as criticism. With his respective appointments at Givenchy and Christian Dior, Galliano rose to international celebrity status as the first British designer since Charles Frederick Worth to front a French couture house. He has been a member of France's Chambre Syndicale de la Haute Couture since 1993 and is the winner of many prestigious awards, most notably British Designer of the Year in 1987, 1994, 1995, and 1997, and International Designer of the Year in 1997.

Education and Early Career

Galliano, christened Juan Carlos Antonio, was born in Gibraltar in 1960. He moved to Streatham, South London, with his Gibraltan father and Spanish mother at the age of six. Galliano had a brief period of work experience with Tommy Nutter, the Savile Row tailor, during his studies at St. Martins School of Art in London (since renamed Central St. Martin's), as well as a part-time position as a dresser at the National Theatre. He graduated from St. Martins with first class honors in fashion design in 1984. His hugely successful final collection, Les Incroyables, was based on fashion motifs of the French Revolution and was immediately bought by the London boutique Browns, where it was featured in the entire window display. Galliano launched his label in the same year and has designed in his own name ever since.

Despite Galliano's rapid securing of a cult following and critical acclaim with such collections as Afghanistan Repudiates Western Ideals, The Ludic Game, Fallen Angels, or Forgotten Innocents, the business part of his early design career was most challenging. With inadequate and unstable financial backing—the Danish businessmen Johan Brun and Peder Bertelsen were among his first backers—Galliano had to produce several collections on a limited budget; some seasons he was not able to show at all. Galliano's shows of this period sometimes relied on last-minute improvisations for the final effect—as in his Fallen Angels show when he splashed buckets of cold water over the models just before the finale. Galliano began to work with the stylist Amanda Harlech, who worked closely with him until 1997. Other long-term associates include the DJ Jeremy Healy, the milliner Stephen Jones, and the shoemaker Manolo Blahnik.

In 1990 Galliano designed the costumes for Ashley Page's ballet Currulao, performed by the Rambert Dance Company. In 1991 he launched two less expensive, youth-oriented diffusion lines, Galliano's Girl and Galliano Genes. By the early 1990s, Galliano had become firmly rooted in London's club scene. This, combined with his first-hand knowledge of the theater, channeled his interests toward experimentation and rarefied eccentricity, while it also fed the self-styled re-inventions of his personal image. Both remain Galliano trademarks.

From London to Paris

Galliano moved to Paris in 1990, hoping for better work prospects. His acclaimed 1994 spring–summer collection, inspired by his personalized fairy-tale version of Princess Lucretia's escape from Russia, opened with models rushing down the catwalk, tripping over their giant crinolines supported by collapsible telephone cables. Thanks to the support of (U.S.) Vogue's creative director Anna Wintour and the fashion editor Andre Leon Talley, Galliano's breakthrough 1994–1995 autumn–winter collection was staged in an *hôtel particulier*, the eighteenth-century mansion of the Portuguese socialite São Schlumberger. The show recreated the intimate mood of a couture salon, with models walking through different rooms in the house that held small groups of guests. The interior of the house was transformed into a film set, evoking an aura of romantic decadence, with unmade beds and rose petals scattered about. Despite being composed of a mere seventeen outfits, the show used choreography and its exotic location to mark a momentous mid-1990s shift toward fashion shows as spectacles. A comparable mode of presentation was developed by Martin Margiela and Alexander McQueen around the same time.

In 1995 the president of the French luxury conglomerate LVMH, Bernard Arnault, appointed Galliano as Hubert de Givenchy's replacement as principal designer at Givenchy. Here Galliano had an excellent opportunity to study the archives of a major Parisian couture house. He developed his skill for merging—within one collection or a single outfit—traditional feminine glamour with a distinctly contemporary element of playfulness. He was also able to do justice to the breadth of his vision as one of fashion's most spectacular showmen. During and after Galliano's brief tenure at Givenchy, the house acquired an air of "Cool Britannia," and received unparalleled publicity. Alexander McQueen took over at Givenchy in 1996, while Galliano was installed as chief designer at another LVMH label, Christian Dior, as Gianfranco Ferré's successor. Four years later, Galliano's creative control over Dior's clothes was extended to the house's accessories, shop design, and advertising. Meanwhile, Galliano has continued to design under his own label. In 2003 he opened his first flagship store on the corner of the rue Duphot and the rue du Faubourg-Saint Honoré in Paris. The building's interior was designed by the architect Jean-Michel Wilmotte. Galliano launched his first signature men's wear collection since 1986 for autumn–winter 2004.

Galliano creates eclectic clothes, which are based on sources from fashion, film, art, and popular culture, and modernizes his borrowings to varying degrees. Inspired by extensive travel experiences as well as thorough research in libraries, museum exhibitions, and archives, Galliano interprets not only exotic and historical looks but also construction techniques—most significantly the body-flattering elastic bias cut

popularized by Madeleine Vionnet in the 1920s. His approach has been described variously as magpie-like, history-book-plundering, romantic escapism, and postmodern pastiche. Galliano's first haute couture Dior collection for spring–summer 1997, which coincided with Dior's fiftieth anniversary, juxtaposed quasi-Masai jewelery and quasi-Dinka beaded corsets with hourglass silhouettes reminiscent of the Edwardian era and Dior's own New Look. In the same collection, innocent white leather doily-like dresses and hats were shown alongside 1920s Chinese-inspired dresses styled with a menacing edge.

Unlike the androgynous creatures who paraded avant-garde shapes in Galliano's London shows of the 1980s, the heroines of his 1990s Paris period were luxurious icy divas by day and exotic opium-fueled seductresses by night—as represented in his Haute Bohemia collection for spring–summer 1998. For most of the decade he found inspiration in mysterious and sexually ambiguous women, ranging from real historical aristocrats, showgirls, and actresses to imagined characters and female stereotypes: Indian princess Pocahontas, Lolita (stemming from Vladimir Nabokov's fictional character), Edwardian demimondaines, the actress Theda Bara as Cleopatra, the artist and model Kiki de Montparnasse, the Russian princess Anastasia Nicholaevna, the Duchess of Windsor, the film character Suzie Wong, other prostitutes, and trapeze artists. Galliano's real clients in this period included Béatrice de Rothschild, Madonna, Nicole Kidman, and Cate Blanchett.

Since around 2000, in addition to Galliano's multicultural cross-referencing, he has placed new emphasis on shaking up the high and low of fashion. He has returned to the excesses of his earlier work and "dirtied" traditional elegance with over-the-top chaotic mixes of street culture and spoof of "rock n' roll chic." While the designer maximized the concepts of couture and ready-to-wear alike as a masquerade and "laboratory of ideas," with clothes as "showpieces," he has reinforced the identity of the House of Dior as a leading luxury brand with a tongue-in-cheek twist. The creative identity of his own label, which makes up for two of the six collections he produces yearly, has been closely linked to that of Dior.

See also Blahnik, Manolo; Dior, Christian; Givenchy, Hubert de; Grunge; London Fashion; Margiela, Martin; McQueen, Alexander; Paris Fashion; Punk; Vionnet, Madeleine.

Bibliography

Arnold, Rebecca. *Fashion, Desire and Anxiety: Image and Morality in the Twentieth Century.* London and New York: I. B. Tauris, 2001.

Barley, Nick, Stephen Coates, Marcus Field, and Caroline Roux, eds. *Lost and Found: Critical Voices in New British Design.* Basel, Boston, and Berlin: Birkhäuser Verlag AG and The British Council, 1999.

Bradberry, Grace. "From Streatham to Dior." *The Times* (London), 15 October 1997.

Breward, Christopher. *Fashion.* Oxford: Oxford University Press, 2003.

Evans, Caroline. *Fashion at the Edge: Spectacle, Modernity, and Deathliness.* New Haven, Conn., and London: Yale University Press, 2003.

Frankel, Susannah. *Visionaries: Interviews with Fashion Designers.* London: V and A Publications, 2001.

McDowell, Colin. *Galliano.* London: Weidenfeld and Nicolson, 1997.

Menkes, Suzy. "Dior's Aggression Misses the New Romantic Beat." *International Herald Tribune*, 10 October 2001.

Tucker, Andrew. *The London Fashion Book.* London: Thames and Hudson, Inc., 1998.

Marketa Uhlirova

GARMENTS, INTERNATIONAL TRADE IN

Garments have been perhaps the most international of consumer products dating back to the late 1800s when Paris couturiers—led by the House of Worth—dictated the styles that affluent women around the world wore. Those garments were composed of rich, imported fabrics and trimmings: silks from China, woolens and velvets from England, damasks and lace from Italy. Back then, representatives from the first department stores in the United States, Chicago's Marshall Field's, R. H. Macy's in New York, and John Wanamaker in Philadelphia, voyaged to Paris in order to purchase haute couture samples, that their workrooms translated into styles suitable for America's growing consumer society.

In the 1980s, the fashion boom popularized designer jeans and athletic shoes and accelerated the globalization of fashion, as licensing became a lifeline to the fashion business, especially couture fashion houses. In fashion licensing, a design house collects a royalty payment between 3 percent to 10 percent of wholesale volume, from an outside manufacturer who produces and markets the merchandise. Licensing enabled designers to put their trademarks on clothes, handbags, jewelry, shoes, and perfume quickly and relatively painlessly. Licensing turned designers like Pierre Cardin and Calvin Klein into household names as they built billion dollar empires marketing sofas, bedsheets, clocks, and even frying pans to an international marketplace.

Modern fashion houses have no national borders. For example, an outfit that carries an Italian fashion label might have well been created in Milan, by a team of British, French, and American designers, and manufactured by contractors from countries in China, Korea, and Mexico.

This shift toward globalization is evident in trade statistics. In 1999, the five leading exporters of clothing were China ($30.08 billion), Italy ($11.78 billion), Hong Kong ($9.57 billion), the United States ($8.27 billion), and Germany ($7.44 billion). The five largest importers of clothing were the United States ($58.79 billion), Germany ($20.77 billion), Japan ($16.40 billion), the United Kingdom ($12.53 billion), and France ($11.58 billion). France, despite the continuing prominence of Paris in the world of fashion design, had only $5.69 billion in clothing exports in 1999 (International Trade Centre, World Trade Organization, 2001).

Like McDonald's and Starbucks, fashion marketers have been forced to think globally in order to cater to a cross section of international shoppers whom they now serve directly. No longer do consumers have to travel abroad to find the top brands, as Giorgio Armani, Valentino, and Polo Ralph Lauren have blanketed the world with boutiques from Buenos Aires to Tokyo.

Thanks to the Internet, Hollywood, and cable television, there is not much difference between consumers in Spain and those in the United States, who are all exposed to the same trends, celebrity role models, and popular music simultaneously. Furthermore, globalization has leveled the playing field, enabling retailers from the Gap to Zara to Target to compete in the multibillion-dollar fashion game, as these discount chains have learned to master the mechanics of delivering fast fashion at rock bottom prices.

Fashion entered a new era in the 1990s, as the world's buoyant high-tech industries broke the pattern for formal dress codes. Jeans, khakis, and knitwear replaced suits as the new corporate uniform. Seeking higher ground, the high fashion industry could no longer bank on dress-up clothes. Marketers thus found a new hook to captivate consumers: accessories like handbags, shoes, and watches, which could be plastered with showy designer logos and coordinated with casual clothes. Furthermore, accessories delivered higher profit margins than apparel, making them even more attractive to fashion marketers.

Luxury accessories thus became the focal point of such European conglomerates as Gucci, Prada, and LVMH Moët Hennessy Louis Vuitton, which scooped up dozens of faded fashion brands like Givenchy, Yves Saint Laurent, and Fendi. By owning a roster of fashion brands, these clothing giants have benefited from economies of scale. The luxury fashion boom began in the late 1990s as women began collecting status trinkets, the $1,000 Fendi baguette handbags, for example, that they wore to dress up their casual clothes. The accessories boom underscored how international fashion trends have become as shoppers in Tokyo, Paris, and New York all flocked to buy the hot designer handbags of the season.

Industry experts agree the next frontier is the Internet, which takes globalization to new heights. With the click of a mouse from their laptop computers, the world's consumers can conveniently shop the shelves of Harrods in London, L.L. Bean in Maine, Neiman Marcus in Texas, as well as Ebay, the auction Web site that features fashion merchandise offered by millions of individuals from around the world.

More than anything, the Internet has exposed the world's consumers to an infinite range of choices at all price ranges. It is the ultimate example of globalization, built on the back of rapidly changing media, which has further democratized fashion, shrinking the world into a single, accessible marketplace.

See also Fashion Industry; Globalization.

Bibliography

Dickerson, Kitty G. *Textiles and Apparel in the Global Economy*. 3rd ed. Englewood Cliffs, N.J.: Prentice Hall, 1998.

Hyvarinen, Antero. "The Changing Pattern of International Trade in Textiles and Clothing." Geneva: International Trade Centre, World Trade Organization, 2001.

Teri Agins

GAULTIER, JEAN-PAUL

Jean-Paul Gaultier was born in 1952 in the Paris suburb of Arcueil. An autodidact, he discovered fashion at a very early age. In childhood and adolescence, television and fashion magazines fed his imagination; he was particularly fascinated by the fashion features in *Elle*. He served his apprenticeship as a designer from 1970 to 1975 in the most innovative couture houses of the time: Pierre Cardin, Jacques Esterel, Jean Patou, and Angelo Tarlazzi. He soon struck out on his own and presented his first show of women's fashion in 1976.

Noticed and financed at first by the Japanese consortium Kashiyama, Gaultier established his own business in 1982, the success of which was continuous into the early 2000s. He developed a men's fashion line in 1984 and attracted a broader clientele through his Junior Gaultier collections, replaced in 1994 by a new JPG line. In 1992 he introduced Gaultier Jean's creations, and accessories and perfumes completed the lightning-fast rise of his business. Gaultier's fashion consecration arrived with his first haute couture collection in 1997. Investment support from Maison Hermès in 1999 enabled him to increase his reputation and his distribution, notably with the establishment of a network of boutiques bearing his name.

A Parisian designer, Gaultier was deeply attached to his city, which provided the backdrop to his inspirations. Neighborhoods such as Pigalle and Saint-Germain, monuments like the Eiffel Tower and the Moulin Rouge, and the most emblematic Parisians, from Toulouse-Lautrec to Juliette Greco, fueled his imagination. In the tradition of Chanel and Saint Laurent, his clothing has made it possible for women to assert their independence in an emancipated city.

From the beginning of his fashion career, London was Gaultier's second city. It very early became an immense source of inspiration, with the punk and ska movements, the allure of James Bond, and especially the flea markets and the eccentricities of Londoners. He felt a deep and enthusiastic admiration for his elder, Vivienne Westwood. The street fascinated him, providing him with the means of attaching fashion to the present and amplifying the echoes of the world around him. He has reinterpreted and made his own uses of the wardrobe of the past and its legacy in order to provide clothing for the future.

The Gaultier style of the 1980s was identifiable by the famous silhouette of broad and sloping shoulders and narrow hips that emphasized stockinged legs. In the 1990s his palette of colors and materials was enriched by contact with many cultural worlds. The silhouette became more balanced, and comfort and protection took on added importance. His shows, with their exuberant and provocative staging, long obscured the fact that his clothes are designed to be worn. At the beginning of the millennium, he attained a certain classicism without renouncing the original image of his talent as the enfant terrible of fashion.

Gaultier's work has been characterized by a stylistic consistency since 1976: jacket and pants constitute the basic link between male and female wardrobes. The masculinity of double-breasted jacket, fitted coat, leather jacket, overalls, trench coat, smock, and down jacket is inflected by the femininity of corset, stockings, and garters, or is enriched by Eastern touches, by the influence of caftans and djellabas.

Mixtures and superimpositions make lingerie an item of clothing in itself, so that hybrid costumes like chemise-jackets and pants-skirts make up an unexpected wardrobe. Some accessories, such as ties and leotards, sewn together, become new textile materials. While women have adopted masculine attire, men are not far behind, and in Gaultier's shows they have worn skirts, corsets, and dresses with trains, increasing their masculinity. Gaultier has brought great care to textiles and employed the most luxurious materials; wool, taffeta, and velvet, for example, are blended with rayon, latex, imitation leather, and synthetic tulle. Lycra blended with traditional materials provides comfort in his designs. His designs often give fabrics a worn, faded look, as though they had already been worn. Knitwear in every form, always present, season after season, has been one of his distinctive signs. Precious fabrics enhance work clothes or military uniforms, and denim flourishes in evening dresses.

Navy blue, khaki, brown, red, and deep purple—Gaultier's original colors—have in the course of time been joined by salmon and powder pink, orange, turquoise, beige, and bronze. His motifs make up a distinctive repertoire: astrology, including the bull's head from his own sign; tattoos, writing, escutcheons, Celtic symbols, and faces; and religious themes like the cross, the star of David, and the hand of Fatima, all appear in a variety of forms on his fabrics, and are printed or sewn on accessories, particularly on jewelry. Stripes, plaids, and polka dots have been fetish designs for Gaultier. Certain details are trademarks, such as fastenings for his clothes: his designs feature distinctive zippers, laces,

hooks, tortoiseshell buttons, or buttons with an anchor design.

A creator of images and atmospheres, Jean-Paul Gaultier could not avoid the cinema. He has created costumes for films of Peter Greenaway, Jean-Pierre Jeunet, Pedro Almodóvar, and Luc Besson. He has made stage costumes for Madonna and the dancer and choreographer Régine Chopinot. In 1993 he hosted a television show on Channel 5 in England.

Jean-Paul Gaultier's strong personality and his multifaceted universe have for decades influenced the worlds of both fashion and street clothes. He has enabled people to think about the place of clothing in contemporary society. Breaking the last taboos of the late twentieth century, his designs have exalted the theme of androgyny, brought men and women closer, moved to put an end to the prejudice against age, given sublime expression to the encounter between worlds and cultures, and associated memory with the strictly contemporary.

See also Caftan; Corset; Djellaba; Extreme Fashions; Hermès; Punk; Unisex Clothing.

Bibliography

Chenoune, Farid. *Jean-Paul Gaultier.* New York: Universe Publishers, 1998.

McDowell, Colin. *Jean-Paul Gaultier.* New York: Viking Press, 2001.

Xavier Chaumette

GERNREICH, RUDI

Rudi Gernreich was born on 8 August 1922 in Vienna and died in 1985. Gernreich's family came from the nonreligious Jewish middle class and had ties to the Social Democrats. One of his mother's sisters ran a fashion salon in Vienna where the newest French designs were translated with high-quality craftsmanship.

In 1933 Austria, having affiliated itself with Nazi Germany, became the scene of rampant anti-Semitic violence. Rudi Gernreich and his mother were able to flee to Los Angeles. Gernreich studied art for a few semesters and quickly made a connection in Los Angeles with The Modern Dance Studio of Lester Horton, whose

Rudy Gernreich on the cover of *Time* magazine, December 1, 1967. Born in Vienna, Austria, Gernreich was well known for using provocative fashion designs, such as the "monokini," to express the 1950s and 1960s generations' desire for freedom. TIME LIFE PICTURES/GETTY IMAGES. REPRODUCED BY PERMISSION.

choreography was concerned with antifascist themes and racial discrimination. In the mid-1940s, his first sketches for dance costumes appeared. For a few years, Gernreich was a fashion designer for Adrian and others before developing his first small collection in 1948. In the late 1940s he worked for a short time in the garment district of New York's Seventh Avenue, returning eventually to California. Around 1950 he developed a collection of sportswear for Morris Nagel, which featured interchangeable pieces. Hattie Carnegie engaged Gernreich for a few months during which he provided her with design sketches. In 1950 he met Harry Hay (1912–2002), who was a member of the California Communist Party and an activist union organizer. Hay and Gernreich founded the secret Mattachine Society, one of the first organizations to agitate for homosexual rights.

In 1952 Gernreich began work for Walter Bass, and his first designs were an immediate success. The

newly founded Beverly Hills boutique, JAX, as well as department stores like Lord and Taylor in New York and Joseph Magnin in San Francisco, sold Gernreich's sportswear. Gernreich developed jersey tube dresses and printed nylon stockings and used synthetic materials. Starting in 1955 Gernreich also designed knitted bathing suits. In 1954 he met Oreste Pucciani, the future chairman of the UCLA French department, and began a relationship that would last until Gernreich's death in 1985. Finally in 1960, Gernreich established his own company: Rudi Gernreich Incorporated. In 1964, the monokini, or topless bathing suit, brought the name Gernreich into the headlines. In 1968 Gernreich closed his company but continued his work as a designer.

From the beginning of his career, Gernreich also designed costumes for various film productions, such as Eva Marie Saint's wardrobe in Otto Preminger's 1960 film *Exodus*. In 1970 he designed "Dress Codes" of the new decade for the January issue of *Life* magazine. Gernreich's fashion concept of the future was "unisex." In 1971 he presented an ironic military collection: jersey pieces in uniform colors, mounted pockets, and models armed with guns. In 1972 Gernreich developed a perfume, which came in a bottle shaped like a chemical laboratory beaker. Gernreich never thought of his activity as a designer as limited to fashion alone; clothing was only one possible expression of a freely chosen lifestyle.

Gernreich's 1950s bathing suits were influenced by the work of the American designer Claire McCardell. Gernreich's suits, conceived as an expression of a new body consciousness, were unstructured and emphasized the body's natural form. In 1965, Gernreich accessorized his bathing suits with visors, over-the-knee vinyl boots, and even fishnet stockings. In 1961 Gernreich's bathing suits and clothes featured cutouts, and in 1968 he used transparent vinyl inserts, which integrated the skin and silhouette of the wearer into the clothing.

The monokini, or topless bathing suit, first presented in 1964, finally made Gernreich internationally famous. Gernreich's monokini consisted of a rib-cage-height bottom, held up with shoulder straps. Gernreich had wanted to liberate the bosom from its status as something that had to be kept concealed. He also used this idea in his underwear collection "No." The bras from the collection, the "no bra," the "maybe bra," or, later, the "almost bra," were distinguished by their transparency and lightness. The thong, presented in 1974, is part of the standard repertoire of clothing in the early 2000s.

Gernreich used patterns—bold animal skins or graphic decorations—in clothing, accessories, and even underwear. The body became, in the Total Look, an abstract, aesthetic element, and clothing became a conscious field of aesthetic experimentation, like architecture or furniture design. The fall collection of 1964 featured a suit of a top and skirt and matching stockings, with dark-blue and gray (oyster) vertical stripes, completed by garish green patent-leather pumps. In 1966, three models, Peggy Moffit, Léon Bing, and Ellen Harth, appeared in William Claxton's short film *Basic Black*, which focused on Rudi Gernreich's fashions. All three mannequins wore suede suits, with dalmatian, giraffe, and tiger-skin patterns complete with matching patterned accessories: caps, gloves, pumps, stockings, and even underwear.

Gernreich's collections often featured uncommon color combinations, such as black and white, orange and yellow, or red and purple, and the juxtaposition of differing graphic motifs, such as stripes with polka dots, checks with diagonal stripes, zigzags with cubes. On the one hand, the influence of the Vienna Workshops is apparent, on the other hand, Gernreich was responding to the antifashion of the 1960s and 1970s, whose signals and messages he transformed. "Real T-shirts are worn with slogans or Mickey Mouse figures or letters. All of these deliver messages. I have abstracted these signals into symbols, conveying them by various inserts: panels, stripes, or circles" (*Topeka State Journal*, 23 February 1972). Instead of extravagant tucks, folds, or piping, Gernreich accentuated and molded particular body parts through the optical effect of colors and patterns. With refined trompe l'oeil effects, the illusion of a multiple-piece suit was created.

Gernreich's collections often included elements of folklore, quoted and freshly adapted: the pattern mixture of Austrian dirndl, the hussar's uniform with embroidery on black vinyl, or elements of Chinese and Japanese clothing, such as obis or colorfully patterned silks. The 1968 collection was criticized by the press at the time as not contemporary enough and seemed to many to even contradict Gernreich's modernism. But the designer had not intended to offer romantic dress-up as an escape from reality, but rather as a medium for a continual self-exploration or role-play. According to Gernreich, such a repertoire of historical and national style elements could only be successfully introduced in a free society whose members were capable of personal exploration and experimentation with a confident mastery of existing dress codes.

Gernreich always advocated the interchangeability of men's and women's clothes. In the Unisex Project

of 1970, for example, Gernreich arranged for a woman and a man to be shaved completely of body hair. Then the pair modeled identical clothing: both in bikinis or miniskirts, both topless. In the conception of his unisex-style, Gernreich chose abstract, unromantic, democratic clothing which was intended to be available to all—in Gernreich's words: "an anonymous sort of uniform of an indefinite revolutionary cast" (*Michigan News*, 15 July 1971).

"We have to take this terrible world and make fun of it with fun clothes, functional clothes" (*Los Angeles Herald Examiner*, 29 September 1966). Already in 1954 Gernreich had used white vinyl for an evening dress. He tried to break through the traditional boundaries of clothing manufacture by using new materials. He was not only interested in the aesthetic characteristics of synthetic materials, but also in their manufacturing possibilities. He hoped to produce seamless clothing, but was frustrated due to the inability, at the time, to overcome technical problems. In addition to synthetic materials, Gernreich favored mechanical elements like zippers or metal fasteners, and he incorporated elements of both motorcycle clothes and dance leotards in his designs. He designed overalls with detachable pants legs, sleeves, or skirts, which could be altered at will.

"I consider designing today more a matter of editing than designing," said Gernreich describing his aesthetic method (*Los Angeles Times*, 30 January 1972). During the course of his career Gernreich utilized various styles, drawing upon austere secessionist patterns for casual slacks, reworking the simple cut of a sleeveless dress, season after season, with new materials and color combinations, introducing industrial materials like vinyl, or historical costumes for greater social flexibility. The exclusivity of expensive craftsmanship, the value of a particular material, or the refined solution to a particular technical sewing problem—be it sleeve holes or folds—would not have harmonized with Gernreich's design intentions. He reduced clothing to an inventory of functional pieces, which could be infinitely varied with colors, materials, or patterns.

Fashion magazines ignored, for the most part, his taboo-breaking, subversive fashion strategies. Gernreich, however, always saw his fashion concepts as carriers of a total, aesthetically formulated worldview. With the monokini he succeeded in pushing the fashion envelope. He utilized the success and fame awarded by his first collections in the 1950s to introduce his new aesthetic concepts about contemporary and futuristic clothing theory to the public eye. Art and fashion, thus, were never separated worlds for him. In the 1950s and 1960s, Gernreich was accepted in artistic circles because he had utilized fashion to radically question societal conventions. He rejected the idea of fashion as a corset of socially relegated hierarchy and rigid gender polarization. He used ironically provocative concepts such as the monokini, topless, unisex, and the Total Look to articulate a generation's desire for freedom as program.

See also Ethnic Style in Fashion; McCardell, Clare; Unisex Clothing.

Bibliography

Faure, Jacques, ed. *Rudi Gernreich. A Retrospective.* Los Angeles: Fashion Group Foundation, Inc., 1985.

Felderer, Brigitte, ed. *Rudi Gernreich: Fashion Will Go Out of Fashion.* Catalog for eponymous exhibition from Oct. 7 to Nov. 26, 2000. Künstlerhaus Graz, Cologne: Dumont, 2000.

Lobenthal, Joel. *Radical Rags: Fashions of the Sixties.* New York: Abbeville Publishers, 1990.

Moffitt, Peggy. *The Rudi Gernreich Book.* New York: Rizzoli, 1991. Photography by William Claxton. Essay by Marylou Luther.

Brigitte Felderer

GIGLI, ROMEO*

The designer Romeo Gigli was born in 1949 in Castelbolognese, near Faenza, Italy, into a family of antiquarian booksellers with a collection of more than twenty thousand volumes from the fifteenth and sixteenth centuries. The region of Faenza has a rich cultural and historical heritage. It was there, in the Byzantine mosaics of Ravenna and in the rare books in his family's library, that Gigli found the initial inspiration for his future art.

Gigli studied architecture in Florence. At the end of the 1970s, after ten years spent traveling around the world, during which time he collected objects, fabrics, and clothing, he began to take an interest in fashion. In 1979 he went to New York, where Pietro Dimitri, a tailor who made custom clothing for men, asked Gigli to design a line of women's clothing. It was a defining moment for Gigli, who, after returning to Italy and settling in Milan, decided to enter fashion on a full-time basis. In 1983 he launched the Romeo Gigli label, which was produced by Zamasport beginning in 1985.

Gigli broke with existing conventions, revolutionizing the approach to women's fashion common in the 1980s. During a period characterized by padded shoulders and aggressive sexuality, Gigli introduced a new look for women—one that was romantic and intimate. He turned away from the hard-edged contours that were then prevalent and based his designs on classic proportions, which he updated, sometimes radically. He made use of contrast and asymmetry and combined simplicity with luxurious fabrics, sometimes pairing smaller, microlength designs with long, full garments. He made use of unusual combinations of colors, such as sand and pink, dark blues, verdigris, saffron, red, and gold, and of fabrics, such as stretch linen, silk, chiffon, cotton gauze, wool, and cashmere. And he was one of the first designers to use Lycra.

The Gigli woman is ethereal and silent, fragile and poetic; her conical silhouette, with its long, narrow sleeves and layered overcoats, jackets, and scarves, emphasizes the sensuality of a woman's arms and shoulders, her gestures and bearing. Even Gigli's men's collection, begun in 1986, broke with the traditional schema and returned to classical proportions and uncommon pairings of materials. He reintroduced the three-button jacket and the natural, or Neapolitan, shoulder; his pants were narrow and his shirts colorful. The Gigli man is neither aggressive nor a dandy; he is an intellectual, casual in appearance only, careful in his choice of colors and fabrics.

In 1987 Gigli signed an agreement with Takashimara—the Japanese department store specializing in luxury and quality goods—for the exclusive production and distribution of the women's ready-to-wear collection and men's and women's accessories.

For several years Gigli showed his clothes in Paris, where he was received with considerable enthusiasm. In Milan his showrooms at 10 corso Como, Spazio Romeo Gigli, which opened in 1988 in a former automobile repair shop in the working-class Garibaldi neighborhood, have become a place of cult worship for intellectuals and fashion rebels, for whom Gigli is the undisputed leader.

One of his women's perfumes, Romeo di Romeo Gigli, received the International prize Accademia del Profumo for the best packaging of 1989 and the award of the American Fragrance Foundation for the best packaging of 1991.

In 1990, he launched the G Gigli line, produced by Stefanel for a younger market. From 1987 to 1996 he designed Callaghan for Zamasport, a collection of richly decorated ethnic clothing. In 1993 he started a cooperation with Christopher Farr's Handmade rugs for the carrying out of carpets in a limited edition.

Because of disagreements with his associates, Gigli decided to completely redefine his activity. To begin with, he continued as the artistic director of Gigli Spa, a part of IT Holding. Then, in 2004, a dispute with IT Holding left Gigli without the rights to his own name. In 2009 he launched his new fashion company, "io ipse idem" (meaning approximately, "I am myself"). Romeo Gigli, considered Italy's poet-designer, has been a forerunner of minimalism and understatement in modern clothing design. His stylistic and conceptual innovations have been widely imitated.

See also Elastomers; Ethnic Style in Fashion; Italian Fashion.

Bibliography

Borioli, G. "Gigli." In *Dizionario della moda*. Edited by Guido Vergani. Milan: Baldini and Castoldi, 1999.

Giordani Aragno, Bonizza. *Callaghan: 1966. La nascita del prêt-à-porter italiano*. Milan: Mazzotta, 1997.

Simona Segre Reinach

GIRDLE

Mary Brooks Picken defined girdle as a "flexible, lightweight shaped corset, made partly or entirely of elastic. Worn to confine the figure, especially through the hip line." *Merriam-Webster's Collegiate Dictionary* offered: "A woman's close-fitting undergarment often boned and usu. [sic] elasticized that extends from the waist to below the hips." Neither definition does full justice to the undergarment that changed shape, materials, and functions through its six decades of prominence in women's wardrobes, from the 1910s through the 1960s. Girdles evolved continuously to take advantage of new fibers and fabric structures and to respond to each new silhouette in women's outerwear. Pantie girdles came on the scene when substantial numbers of women began to wear pants. Initially, girdles appealed to younger

women and teen girls, but women of all ages eventually wore some type of girdle, before control-top panty hose supplanted the girdle's functions for all but the most conservative women.

The modern girdle's origin may be traced to the short hip-confiners worn over corsets during the early 1900s, but the term itself began to assume its contemporary meaning in the mid-1910s. Treo, an early manufacturer, applied the term girdle to its flexible Para rubber corsets without laces. Competing terms to describe girdles included the French ceinture, belt, and sash. In 1916, Stanford Mail Order Company, New York, marketed girdles to "Misses and Small Women." At the outset, girdles were associated with youth and informality, in part because their light control suited the figures and activities of a younger clientele. However, rubber "reducing girdles" were sold to weight-conscious women of all ages.

Flappers and Girdles

In the famously unconstrained 1920s, teens and young women, collectively termed flappers, generally abhorred the heavy corsets on which their mothers depended for figure control. Fashionable young women often rolled their stockings and limited underwear to a wispy bandeau and step-in panties. By the mid-1920s, as a contoured silhouette began gradually to return to women's fashions, flappers and other fashionables accepted garter belts and light girdles. The advertising agency J. Walter Thompson reported the views of a Manhattan department store buyer thus: "widely talked of abandon [sic] of corsets was a myth. Even flappers wear something, if it's only a garter belt or corselette." Girdles of the 1920s usually extended from natural waistline to hipline, came in white or peach-tone knit elastic, and were worn over step-ins. More conservative girdles included woven brocade panels over the tummy and derriere. Generally priced from $1 to $6 dollars, girdles appealed to the budgets of young women.

Thriving During the Depression

In the 1930s, technology and fashion converged to produce styles of girdles that sold by the millions, despite the persistence of the business depression. Unit sales of girdles topped 20.6 million in 1935 alone ("The Corset," *Fortune*, March 1938). Technological innovation arrived in the form of Lastex, an extruded (spun) rubber latex yarn covered by mercerized cotton. Put on the market in autumn 1931, Lastex made possible the lightweight twoway stretch girdles that gained wide appeal, especially with young customers, for their ability to move with the body. Lastex hand-washed easily and provided control without boning, though some girdles added a few bones and often had panels of woven fabric to tame front and rear bulges.

Warner made knitted Lastex girdles, whereas Kops Brothers specialized in woven two-way stretch fabrics. By the end of the 1930s, makers had devised tubular, seamless knitted girdles and knits of differential density and tension for molding different parts of the wearer's anatomy.

Fashion also contributed to the survival of girdles. Throughout the 1930s, dress silhouettes gradually became fuller in the bust, slimmer and higher in the waist, and gently curved and elongated in the hips. Compared with the changes in bust contours and bras, where aggressive uplift held sway by 1939, girdle shapes altered only subtly. Fashion's overall trimness of line meant that all but the very young and slender needed a girdle (or corselette) to wear a chic dress well.

Fashionable women's 1930s wardrobes began to include pants, primarily for active sports, gardening, and strictly informal social events. Enter the pantie girdle. Beginning about 1934, pantie girdles constituted a staple in the lines of many manufacturers. Most panties had garters, because stockings continued to be worn under pants, but a few styles featured removable garters or special leg bands to hold down the girdle when socks were worn or the woman went barelegged. Regular girdles were marketed for all purposes, from housework to evening parties, and at prices that ranged from 59 cents to $15 dollars.

Like bras, girdles sold mainly in peach (like present-day nude) or white, but by 1939 at least a couple of makers offered black girdles. "Talon slide fasteners"—zippers—appeared in slightly heavier or fancier girdles. Talon argued that roll-on girdles caused frustrating tugging matches. A girdle could be as short as eight inches—like a glorified garter belt—but most came in ten-, twelve-, fourteen- and sixteen-inch lengths, varying with both the height of the wearer and her need for control at the hip and waist.

Girdle manufacturing was widely dispersed during the 1930s, with many of the 240 corset companies ("The Corset," *Fortune*, March 1938) producing some type of girdle. Some stores featured private-brand girdles, but generally the industry divided between prestige-brand makers and small, marginal firms. Even the better-known companies split between those grounded in corset-making, such as Maidenform and Formfit, and those derived from knit underwear makers, including Carter, Kayser, and Munsingwear.

Wartime Retrenchment and Postwar Expansion

New fibers and innovative marketing might have constituted the core of the girdle story in the 1940s but for the hiatus of World War II. Nylon, introduced for hosiery in 1939, was offered in girdles in 1940; Formfit and other companies marketed all-nylon and blended-fiber girdles by that autumn. Nylon and Lastex created strong, light powernet, so effective in girdles for the junior market. Latex film Playtex all-way-stretch girdles offered another route to smooth control.

As war approached, the U.S. government took possession of strategic textiles, including nylon and latex. Regulation L90 stipulated allowable amounts of elastic in girdles and other undergarments; however, neither Lastex nor nylon wholly disappeared from girdles or bras. Small sections of elastic provided some relief from rigidity. Knitted fabrications helped too, but wartime girdles often looked and felt dowdy to young customers. Pantie girdle sales held up well, because women working in armaments factories often wore pants or coveralls, which looked better over a pantie girdle. Slim and fit girls just wore garter belts or inexpensive briefs with garters.

Late in the war, synthetic rubber neoprene appeared in girdles, but was overshadowed by the newly plentiful nylon and Lastex. With wartime seriousness forgotten, pink, blue, rose, black, and plaid girdles gladdened consumers' hearts. Embroidered touches, including custom sorority emblems from the new Olga Company, lent glamour to formerly stodgy foundations. The biggest news, however, came from the outerwear silhouette. American dress and girdle styles were moving tentatively toward fuller hips and smaller waists as early as fall 1945, but the 1947 French New Look took the trend much further, faster. Girdles rose in the waistline, swelled in the hip, and even returned to selective lacing to achieve the newly desired hourglass effect. American brands pursued a more moderate line, in order not to alienate customers—especially the all-important teenagers, who demanded comfort, easy care, and flexibility in their girdles.

Far longer-lasting than the New Look was the new marketing, presaged before the war by Playtex's packaging of its Living Girdles in tubes for self-service. Other girdle and bra makers followed suit after 1945, and the old tradition of corsetieres fitting customers began a slow decline.

1950s' Heyday

Sheath dresses, popular periodically through most of the 1950s, kept various types of girdle in adult women's wardrobes. Many girdles sported waists as much as four inches above the natural line, supported by boning, wires, and Lastex reinforcements. Snug pants, a fashion of the mid- to late 1950s, augmented the need for long-legged pantie girdles. However, as early as 1952, hints of eased fit in some dress and suit styles foretold the coming of shift dresses in the 1960s. Blousons, Empire-waisted dresses, and the ill-fated chemise of 1957–1958 offered women escape from the stifling embrace of the sheath and its confining foundations.

During the 1950s, very short girdles and pantie girdles proliferated, designed for informal wear and appealing to older teens and young adults. Some merited the nickname "postage stamp" that Jantzen applied to its 1952 style. Some makers featured girdles proportioned for tall women. Companies tried to serve varied customers, though some, including Jantzen, Olga, and Hollywood Vassarette, specialized in a young clientele.

Young or mature, women made their complaints about girdles known, because companies repeatedly trumpeted improvements in comfort. Several firms began to cut the lower front edge in a high upward curve to reduce discomfort in walking. Sarong famously brought out a crisscrossed lower front to move with the wearer's stride. Legs of panties were redesigned for ease in wearing, and both top and bottom of the rear of the girdle were engineered to prevent riding up—a major lament. Removable, even disposable, crotches remedied the panties' laundry problems.

Throughout the decade, manufacturers trumpeted their girdles' lightness, at no sacrifice of shaping power. Girdles, like their wearers, seemed to be on a diet. Nylon in Powernet and woven materials subtracted ounces. Openwork fishnet improved ventilation—crucial in selling girdles for warm-weather wear. By 1954, Dacron polyester appeared in girdles, alone and in blends with cotton. Less-clammy textured nylon came to market under the brand names of Helanca and Ban-lon. Most successful of the weight-reducing textiles, however, was Dupont's Fiber K, which in 1959 produced a two-ounce girdle! Spandex was born.

Comfort alone did not suffice; beauty was also required. Colors proliferated—from subtle almond and pale gray to vibrant red, purple, and salmon. Individual styles came in as many as eight colors by 1957. Embroidery, lace, and appliqués gratified the desire for luxury. All of this cost money. Although $2.95 could purchase a down-market girdle, typical prices ranged from $5 to $25 dollars.

Girdles reportedly contributed 39 percent to total 1956 sales dollars in foundation departments, but those sales were highly seasonal, peaking in April, September, and December, and hitting troughs in January, July, and August (*Merchants Trade Journal*, January 1957; *Merchants Trade Journal*, September 1955). Despite blandishments about comfort, women lost interest in girdles in hot weather.

Surviving the 1960s

Like the 1920s, the 1960s had an exaggerated image of uncorseted, braless freedom. In fact, the early 1960s produced waist-hugging dresses and tight pants that drove some women to retain their girdles. Constraint was achieved by machine-washable powernets of Fiber K, christened Lycra in 1960, and joined by rivals Vyrene and Numa in the 1960s. Every girdle company used proprietary shaping in front and side panels to tame tummies and thighs. Derrieres, however, came into fashion, and girdles that uplifted the gluteus maximus moved from racy Frederick's of Hollywood into mainstream companies in the mid-1960s.

Other aspects of girdle shape evolved through the decade. Snug waists in the early 1960s were gradually replaced by dipped waists. By 1962, so-called "hip-hangers" or "hipbone pants" came into fashion, producing lowslung panty girdles. As skirts rose, girdles shortened, ending the decade at crotch level. Tights and panty hose drove girdle makers to promote their products as panty-hose mates. Taste ran to riotous colors in outerwear, and innerwear followed suit: Floral swirls, polka dots, checks, butterflies, and leopard prints enlivened girdles and coordinating innerwear.

Frantic pursuit of fashion and novelty availed little. A 1963 report showed that girdles constituted only 23.6 percent of foundation-department sales, compared with 71.8 percent for bras. Fashion reportage stressed the nude look, and played up Yves Saint Laurent's statement "underwear is dead." Despite howls from the trade press, girdles seemed to be in terminal decline. By 1970, a mere scattering of ads for panty-sized "smoothers" appeared. But fashion has taken many turns through the years, and in 2003 at least a few companies still produced nylon and spandex "body slimmers." Under such euphemisms, the girdle lives.

See also Brassiere; Corset; Petticoat; Underwear.

Bibliography

"The Corset." *Fortune* (March 1938): 95–99, 110, 113, 114.

Corset and Underwear Review, various issues, 1916–1969.

Dry Goods Merchants Trade Journal (title varies), various issues, 1929–1959.

Field Sales Guide. 1 May 1963. Maidenform Archives, Box 27, Folder 3. National Museum of American History.

"Girdles Contributed 39 Percent to 1956 Foundation Sales." *Merchants Trade Journal* (January 1957): 90.

Harper's Baza(a)r, various issues, 1935–1968.

"How Do Your Bra and Girdle Sales Compare?" *Merchants Trade Journal* (September 1944): 104.

Kops Brothers Account Record; transcript of Interview No. 6. J. Walter Thompson Archives, John Special Collections, Duke University.

Mademoiselle, various issues, 1940–1975.

Maiden Form Mirror, various issues, 1931–1966.

Picken, Mary Brooks. *The Fashion Dictionary*. New York: Funk and Wagnalls, 1957, p. 149.

Vogue, various issues, 1935–1975.

Merriam-Webster's Collegiate Dictionary. 10th ed. Springfield, Mass.: Merriam-Webster, Inc. 1980.

Jane Farrell-Beck

GIVENCHY, HUBERT DE*

Hubert de Givenchy was born on 21 February 1927 in Beauvais, France. The son of a prosperous family, he attended college at Beauvais and then moved to Paris. In 1944 he took a position as an apprentice designer at the couture house of Jacques Fath while studying at the École des Beaux-Arts in Paris. In the late 1940s and early 1950s he took a series of jobs as an assistant designer—first with Fath, then with Lucien Lelong, Robert Piguet, and Elsa Schiaparelli. Givenchy's years as an assistant designer encompassed the period of the New Look and perhaps instilled in him a sense of romanticism that was to characterize his work for over four decades.

Givenchy opened his own couture house in 1951 and made an immediate mark with his design of the "Bettina blouse," a simple white cotton shirting blouse named for Fath's favorite model, Bettina Graziani. Givenchy was quickly recognized as an innovative talent for his system of designing his creations—including evening gowns—as compositions of separate and interchangeable elements. In 1953 he met Cristóbal Balenciaga, who quickly became his mentor and lifelong friend. Givenchy moved his business in 1955 to 3, avenue George V, across the street from Balenciaga's atelier, and the two men were in almost daily contact thereafter. In 1954 Givenchy opened his fragrance business, Société des Parfums Givenchy. He designed his first outfits for the actress Audrey Hepburn that same year. She quickly became his most famous model and muse and looked so enchanting in his creations in a series of films—beginning with *Sabrina* in 1954 and continuing with *Funny Face* (1957), *Breakfast at Tiffany's* (1961), *My Fair Lady* (1964), and others—that she made Givenchy a household name. The designer was generous in acknowledging Hepburn's role in his career, remarking that "often ideas would come to me when I had her on my mind. She always knew what she wanted and what she was aiming for. It was like that from the very start." Givenchy also became known as one of Jacqueline Kennedy's favorite designers; he designed the dress that she wore to President Kennedy's funeral.

Givenchy's style was characterized by bright cheerful colors and a youthful femininity. Yet his simple tailleurs, cocktail dresses, and evening dresses were also the height of chic, emphasizing line more than decoration. "You have to know when to stop," he once said. "That is wisdom."

Givenchy expanded his business in the late 1960s and into the 1970s to include women's ready-to-wear clothing as well as a line of menswear. He sold his company to the French luxury conglomerate LVMH in 1988 but continued to serve as head designer until his retirement in 1995. His first successor was John Galliano, who departed in 1996 and was replaced by Alexander McQueen. McQueen in turn left the company in 2001 and was succeeded as artistic director by Julien McDonald. In 2005, Riccardo Tisci was appointed as creative director of Givenchy.

See also Balenciaga, Cristóbal; Fath, Jacques; Galliano, John; McQueen, Alexander; New Look; Paris Fashion; Perfume; Schiaparelli, Elsa.

Bibliography

Benbow-Pfalzgraf, Taryn, ed. *Contemporary Fashion*. 2nd ed. Farmington Hills, Mich.: St. James Press, 2002.

Buxbaum, Gerda, ed. *Icons of Fashion: The 20th Century*. Munich, London, and New York: Prestel Verlag, 1999.

Join-Diéterle, Catherine, Susan Train, and Marie-José Lepicard. *Givenchy: 40 Years of Creation*. Paris: Musée de la Mode et du Costume, 1991.

Milbank, Caroline Rennolds. *Couture: The Great Designers*. New York: Stewart, Tabori and Chang, 1985.

Mohrt, Françoise. *The Givenchy Style*. New York: Vendome Press, 1998.

John S. Major

GLOBALIZATION

In a certain sense, the Western economy has been "global" since the sixteenth century. After all, the African slave trade, colonialism, and the intercontinental trade in sugar and coffee made capitalism possible. But since the early 1980s, transnational corporations, cyber technology, and electronic mass media have spawned a web of tightly linked networks that cover the globe. Taken together, these forces have profoundly restructured the world economy, global culture, and individual daily lives. Nowhere are these changes more dramatic than in the ways dress and fashion are produced, marketed, sold, bought, worn, and thrown away.

For consumers in dominant Western countries, globalization means an abundance of fashions sold by giant retailers who can update inventory, make transnational trade deals, and coordinate worldwide distribution of goods at the click of a computer. It means that what people are consuming is less the clothing itself than the corporate brand or logo such as Nike, Victoria's Secret, or Abercrombie & Fitch. Consumers are purchasing the fantasy images of sexual power, athleticism, cool attitude, or carefree joy these brands disseminate in lavish, ubiquitous, hyper-visible marketing on high-tech electronic media. But much less visible is the effect of globalization on the production of fashion.

As fashion images in magazines, music videos, films, the Internet and television speed their way around the world, they create a "global style" (Kaiser 1999) across borders and cultures. Blue jeans, T-shirts, athletic shoes and base ball caps adorn bodies everywhere from Manhattan to villages in Africa. Asian, African and Western fashion systems borrow style and textile elements from each other. Large shopping malls in wealthy countries house all these styles under one roof. Like high-tech global bazaars, they cater to consumers of every age, gender, ethnicity, profession, and subculture.

According to Susan Kaiser, "This tendency toward both increased variety within geographic locations and a homogenizing effect across locations represents a global paradox" (Kaiser 1999, p. 110). On the one hand, shopping malls in every city have the same stores, and sell the same fashion items. Yet if we take the example of jeans, we find a seemingly infinite and often baffling array of cuts and fits: from stretched tight to billowing baggy, from at-the-waist to almost-below-the-hip; from bell-bottom to tapered at the ankle; from long enough to wear with stiletto heels to cropped below the calf. While a somewhat baggy, "relaxed" cut can signify dignified middle-aged femininity, a baggy cut taken to excess can signify hyper-masculine ghetto street smarts. Each variation takes its turn as an ephemeral and arbitrary signifier of shifting identities based on age, gender, ethnicity, or subculture.

While marketing campaigns encourage us to associate fashion consumption with pleasure, power, personal creativity, and individual fulfillment, business economists and corporate finance officers have a different view. Contrary to fashion magazines, business organs like *The Wall Street Journal* anxiously watch over consumer behavior as minutely measured by the Consumer Confidence Index managed at the University of Michigan (Weiss 2003). In this view, consumption is neither personal nor individual, but necessary for upholding a vast, intricate global capitalist economy. Dependent on massive fashion consumption in the wealthier countries, this economy depends equally on massive amounts of cheap labor in poorer countries.

The Global Assembly Line

No longer manufactured by the company whose label it bears, clothing from large retailers is manufactured through a network of contractors and subcontractors. Pioneered by Nike, the largest retailer of athletic shoes and fashions, the outsourcing or subcontracting system was quickly taken up by giant retail chains like Express and The Gap, and big-box stores such as Wal-Mart. These companies do not manufacture their own goods, but rather source and marketing goods produced on

Employees making shoes at a Reebok factory, 1996.
Since the early 1980s, globalization has become an increasingly
dominant force in the production of fashion goods. In the early
twenty-first century, to take advantage of costs, fashion corporations outsourced much of their manufacturing to factories in countries such as China, Thailand, Mexico, and Vietnam. © Michael S.
Yamashita/Corbis. Reproduced by permission.

contract in low-wage environments. Because they make
large profits, they can force manufacturers to contract
with them at lower and lower prices. To reduce their
costs, manufacturers subcontract much of the sewing, and even the cutting, to sweatshops in countries
such as Mexico, China, Thailand, Romania, and Vietnam, where poverty is high and wages can be as low as
23 cents per hour. Manufacturers can also subcontract
to sweatshops in the vast underground economies of
immigrant communities in cities like Los Angeles, New
York, or London. There is a huge contrast, but a tight
relation, between production in sweatshops, where
young women workers are often subjected to physical and sexual abuse, and consumption in retail chains
filled with glamorous images. Jobs come without even
the most basic worker safeguards and benefits.

Since retailers can lower their prices to consumers
by lowering their labor costs, consumers have unwit-
tingly participated in intensifying a system of competition among manufacturers that drives wages and
working conditions downward. According to the World
Bank, one of the most powerful institutions of globalization, "the competitive intensity of the U.S. retailing
industry has increased significantly" (Biggs et al., p. 1).
As a consequence, it says, "new emerging retail strategies" include "the drive to offer more value-oriented,
low-priced goods to their customers, utilizing a global

sourcing network that increasingly favors low wage,
quota free countries," and the "liberalization of labor
regulations" (Biggs, p. 2). This "liberalization" means
relaxing worker protections for health and safety, lowering and also enforcing less stringently the minimum
wage, and prohibiting workers from organizing for better wages and working conditions.

Immigrant Labor

By contrast to the World Bank's optimism about globalization, in 1998, the California Labor Commissioner
said: "Global competition results in a feeding frenzy
in which local producers compete against one another
and against foreign factories in a brutal race to the bottom" (Rabine, p. 118). Referring to one among countless examples of production on the global assembly
line, he was speaking on the occasion of the closure of
a garment factory in Los Angeles that owed its workers $200,000 in unpaid wages. To meet a contract for
T-shirts from the Disney Corporation, it had to reduce
its profit margin and keep accelerating its production
schedule in a downward spiral to closure.

One effect of globalization is increased immigration from third-world countries to all the countries of
the world. Immigrants to the United States provide a
labor pool for local versions of third-world sweatshops.
In 1997, Southern California came to lead the nation in
garment production. By 1999, hourly wages for garment
workers in Los Angeles had dropped below minimum
wage of $5.75 to as little as $3.00. Often workers were
not paid at all. The California Labor Commissioner estimated in 1999, right before a new anti-sweat-shop law
was passed, that the industry accumulated $72,620,000
in unpaid wages to mostly immigrant garment workers.

Responses to the Global Assembly Line

Until 1997, CEOs of the giant retailers, such as Philip
Knight of Nike, claimed that they had no responsibility
for the working conditions in the sweatshops because the
owners were independent contractors. But by this time
consumer groups, religious groups, and student groups,
including the National Labor Committee in New York,
Global Exchange in San Francisco, the Los Angeles
Jewish Commission on Sweatshops, the national organizations of United Students Against Sweatshops and
Sweatshop Watch, as well as garment workers' unions
like Unite, began campaigning for reforms. By bringing

publicity to the practices of the giant retailers, these groups persuaded corporations to pledge themselves to accept fair labor standards and to have independent monitors in the factories that supply their fashions. These groups have also promoted legislation in California and New York that aims to hold the retailers responsible for the wages and working conditions of the workers who produce the products they sell.

Informal Global Networks

While the global assembly line and mass consumption form the dominant circuits of globalized fashion, other, less visible circuits span the globe. These shadow networks concern fashion production and consumption in third-world countries. The global economy of high-tech, large-scale networks also works by exclusion. In third-world countries, globalization has resulted in the destabilizing and dismantling of official economies, massive unemployment, and the rise of informal or underground economies. As part of the restructuring and deregulation of global capital, the World Bank and International Monetary Fund have imposed on debtor nations in the third world Structural Adjustment Programs. These programs dismantled state economic controls on basic necessities and social programs for health, education, housing, and sanitation, in favor of free-market strategies, austerity programs, and privatization of basic utilities like electricity and water. These measures have resulted in a disintegration of formal institutions of the government and economy. Out of desperation, people have devised means of surviving in informal economic networks. In Africa and Latin America, this has had two effects on fashion.

One is that the numbers of artisanal producers, especially tailors, dyers, weavers, and jewelry makers, have increased dramatically. In an alternative global network, suitcase vendors sell to tourists, or they travel to diasporic communities in Europe and the United States, where they sell their fashions in people's homes, at ethnic festivals, or on the street. They also sell in the boutiques and on the Web sites of nonprofit organizations dedicated to helping third-word artisans.

A second effect concerns global networks of used-clothing dealers and consumers. Large wholesalers buy masses of used clothing from charity thrift shops such as Goodwill in the United States, Canada, and Europe. In giant warehouses, dealers sort the clothes, bale them, and send them by container to smaller wholesalers in countries of Asia, Africa, and Latin America. Small retailers then sell the clothes for affordable prices at open-air stalls in cities and tiny rural towns. Jeans, T-shirts, and athletic shoes thus become the most visible symbol of globalization in virtually every corner of the world.

See also Sweatshops; Textiles and International Trade.

Bibliography

Anderson, Sarah, John Cavanagh, and Thea Lee. *Field Guide to the Global Economy*. New York: New Press and the Institute for Policy Studies, 2000.

Biggs, Tyler, Gail R. Moody, Jan-Henfrik van Leeuwen, and E. Diane White. *Africa Can Compete!: Export Opportunities and Challenges for Garments and Home Products in the U.S. Market*. World Bank Discussion Papers, no. 242. Washington, D.C.: The World Bank, 1994.

Bonacich, Edna, and Richard Appelbaum. *Behind the Label: Inequality in the Los Angeles Apparel Industry*. Berkeley: University of California Press, 2000.

Brydon, Anne, and Sandra Niessen, eds. *Consuming Fashion: Adorning the Transnational Body*. Oxford: Berg, 1998.

Hansen, Karen Tranberg. *Salaula: The World of Secondhand Clothing and Zambia*. Chicago: University of Chicago Press, 2000.

Kaiser, Susan. "Identity, Postmodernity, and the Global Apparel Marketplace." In *Meanings of Dress*, edited by M. L. Damhorst, K. Miller, and S. Michelman. New York: Fairchild, 1999.

Rabine, Leslie W. *The Global Circulation of African Fashion*. Oxford: Berg, 2002.

Ross, Andrew, ed. *No Sweat: Fashion, Free Trade, and the Rights of Garment Workers*. New York: Verso, 1997.

Stiglitz, Joseph E. *Globalization and Its Discontents*. New York: W. W. Norton and Company, 2002.

Internet Resources

Global Exchange. Available from <http://www.globalexchange.org/campaigns/sweatshops.htm>.

Los Angeles Jewish Commission on Sweatshops. Available from <http://www.pjalliance.org/SweatrshopReport.pdf>.

National Labor Committee. Available from <http://www.nlcnet.org.htm>.

Sweatshop Watch. Available from <http://swatch.igc.org/swatch/industry/cal/.htm>.

United Students Against Sweatshops. Available from <http://www.studentsagainstsweatshops.org>.

Leslie W. Rabine

GODEY'S LADY'S BOOK

Godey's Lady's Book, first published in Philadelphia in 1830 as *Godey's Ladies' Handbook*, was the leading women's magazine in mid-nineteenth-century America. Similar publications had been produced in Europe since the late eighteenth century and *Godey's* was closely patterned after its English and French counterparts. Several variations of the periodical's name occurred over time, including *Godey's Magazine and Lady's Book*, but the magazine is generally known by its most familiar title, *Godey's Lady's Book*.

The magazine's founder and first publisher, Louis Antoine Godey (1804–1878), provided his female audience with a wide range of articles designed to educate and entertain. *Godey's* topics included fashion, travel notes, exercise regimens, practical advice for the housewife on home decoration, recipes, gardening, and crafts, plus fiction, poetry and essays by celebrated nineteenth-century authors, such as Harriet Beecher

Fashion plate from *Godey's Lady's Book*, October 1852. Founded by Louis Antoine Godey in 1830, *Godey's* was the leading women's magazine in mid-nineteenth-century America. It ceased publication in 1898. PUBLIC DOMAIN.

Stowe, Edgar Allan Poe, and Nathaniel Hawthorne. In the 1850s, *Godey's* had the highest circulation of any American women's magazine, reaching a peak of 150,000 subscriptions by the early 1860s. The periodical's success during these years was largely due to Sarah Josepha Hale (1788–1879), *Godey's* editor from 1837 to 1877. Before coming to *Godey's*, Hale edited her own literary journal, an experience that influenced her work at Godey's and strengthened the magazine's content, making it more appealing than its competitors.

Fashion illustrations were part of *Godey's* from its first number. Single hand-colored fashion plates were issued until 1861, when folded double-page plates were introduced. The magazine also included descriptions of the outfits in the fashion plates, detailing fabrics, trims, and accessories. Additional uncolored plates illustrating accessories or individual garments were also found in most issues, along with needlework and craft projects, and occasionally, patterns.

Godey's was not the first American publication to use hand-colored fashion plates—that distinction goes to a competitor started in 1826, *Graham's American Monthly Magazine of Literature, Art and Fashion*. The fashion plates in American magazines through the 1840s were generally inferior copies of designs that initially appeared in English or French periodicals. By the 1850s, the quality of the images improved because some of the metal engraving plates used in French publications were imported to the United States. The original captions on these plates were removed and new ones, such as "The Latest Fashions, only to be found in Godey's Lady's Book," were substituted. While tactics like these obviously resulted in illustrated fashions some months behind the latest European modes, they did give *Godey's* subscribers direct contact with such styles.

Although homemakers were *Godey's* targeted audience, the magazine's fashion information and illustrations were invaluable tools for professional dressmakers in determining what was stylish and for tips in achieving the newest look. The resulting garments, however, were generally much less elaborate than those in the fashion plates. Beginning in 1870s, *Godey's* fashion influence was eclipsed by new publications like the high-style fashion magazine *Harper's Bazaar*, or others with a practical focus, such as *What to Wear and How to Make It: Madame Demorest's Semi-Annual Book of Instructions on Dress and Dressmaking*. It was also in the 1870s that Godey sold the magazine and Hale retired, accelerating *Godey's* decline as a quality publication. After passing through several owners, *Godey's Lady's Book* ceased publication in 1898.

See also Fashion Illustrators; Fashion Magazines; Fashion Plates.

Bibliography

Finley, Ruth Elbright. *The Lady of Godey's, Sarah Josepha Hale*. Philadelphia and London: J. B. Lippincott, 1931. Laudatory biography of the remarkable life of *Godey's* edited by Sarah Josepha Hale.

Godey's Lady's Book, 1830–1898. A full run of this title can be found at the Library of Congress.

Holland, Vyvyan. *Hand Colored Fashion Plates, 1770 to 1899*. London: B. T. Batsford Ltd., 1955. A history of hand-colored fashion plates that details the uncredited use of European plates in American magazines.

Kunciov, Robert, ed. *Mr. Godey's Ladies: Being a Mosaic of Fashions and Fancies*. New York: Bonanza Books, 1971. A compendium of fashion illustrations and quotations from *Godey's Lady's Book* issues from 1830 to 1879, with an introductory history of the magazine.

Mott, Frank Luther. *A History of American Magazines*. 6 vols. Cambridge, Mass.: Harvard University Press, 1938–1968. Comprehensive history of American magazines.

Colleen R. Callahan

GOTHS

Having emerged in the wake of punk during the 1980s, the contemporary goth scene has existed for more than two decades, as a visually spectacular form of youth culture, whose members are most immediately identified by the dark forms of glamour displayed in their appearance.

Goth or Gothic Revival?

Extensive links are sometimes drawn between goth style and various "gothic" movements and individuals throughout history associated with themes such as elegance, decadence, and death. Gavin Baddeley has detailed a linear progression of gothic culture that ends with present-day goths, having journeyed through twentieth century horror genres in television and cinema, through various examples of literature and fashion from the preceding two hundred years and finally back to the "grotesque" art and sculpture credited to the original fourth century goths. The notion that what is known as goth fashion in the early 2000s is merely the latest revival of a coherent centuries-old tradition has undoubted appeal and convenience, even to some enthusiasts for the sub-culture. The reality, though, is that they owe a greater debt to post-1960s developments in popular music culture than to literary, artistic, or cinematic traditions.

Origins

A selection of British bands that appeared prior to, during, and after the late 1970s punk era set the tone for the goth subculture that was to emerge. Crucial ingredients were provided by the deep-voiced feminine glamour of David Bowie, the disturbing intensity and eclecticism of late 1970s Iggy Pop, and the somber angst-ridden despair of Joy Division. The key direct founders of goth, though, were former punks Siouxsie and the Banshees, whose style began to take on a decidedly sinister tone toward the early 1980s, and Bauhaus, whose self-conscious emphasis upon funereal, macabre sounds and imagery was epitomized in the now legendary record "Bela Lugosi's Dead." As the dark, feminine appearance and imagery associated with such bands began to be taken up by their fans, the new "scene" received extensive coverage in the music press. By the mid-1980s, the deep vocals, jangling guitars, and somber base lines of The Sisters of Mercy alongside black clothes, long coats, and dark shades, had established them as the archetypal "goth rock" band. A period of chart success for the Sisters, alongside The Mission, Fields of the Nephilim, The Cure, and Siouxsie and the Banshees, would ensure that toward the end of the 1980s goth enjoyed significant international exposure. Through the 1990s, however, the subculture existed in a rather more underground form, with occasional moments of mass exposure provided by high-profile artists such as Marilyn Manson and through the borrowing of goth style by emerging metal genres and, intermittently, by major fashion labels.

Horror Fiction

Consistent with this emphasis upon sounds and appearances emerging from the music industry, the goth scene has consistently been focused, first and foremost, around a blend of music, fashion, pubs, and nightclubs. As such, it would be more usefully seen in the context of punk, glam, skate, and other contemporary style subcultures, than that of ancient tribes or nineteenth-century poets. Yet this should not be taken to imply that previous "gothic" movements are somehow irrelevant here. Most notably, it is clear that goth musicians and fans have drawn—sometimes "ironically," sometimes not—upon imagery associated with horror fiction in both literary and cinematic forms. Beyond a general emphasis upon black hair and clothing, this has manifested itself, for both males and females, in the form of ghostly white faces offset by thick dark eyeliner and lipstick. As if the vampire link were not clear enough, some have sported even more overt signifiers, from crosses to bats, to plastic fangs. For others, there has been a tendency to adapt elements of the traditional bourgeois fashions associated with vampire fiction, something often mediated through the wardrobes of such cinema blockbusters as *Bram Stoker's Dracula* (1992) and *Interview with the Vampire* (1994). Obvious examples here would include corsets, bodices, and lacy or velvet tops and dresses. Furthermore, although it is seldom regarded as pivotal to subcultural participation, many goths enjoy directly consuming and discussing horror fiction in both its literary and cinematic forms.

Contemporary Influences

Yet there is more to goth fashion than this. The subculture's emphasis upon the somber and the macabre has been accompanied by consistent evidence of other themes that fit rather less neatly with the notion of a linear long-term history of gothic. For example, an emphasis upon particular forms of femininity, for both sexes, goes far beyond the macabre angst and romanticism associated with vampire fiction. Notably, for some years, PVC skirts, tops, corsets, and collars have been among the most popular styles of clothing for goths of both genders, something that borrows more from the contemporary fetish scene than it does from traditional gothic fiction. Links with fetishism, punk, and rock culture more generally can also be demonstrated by the consistent display of facial piercing, tattoos, dyed hair, and combat pants by goths. Indeed, one of the most popular types of clothing among goths has consistently been T-shirts displaying band logos, something distinctive to the goth scene in the specific artist

name and design, but otherwise comparable with other music cultures. During the course of the 1990s, another contemporary influence from music culture established itself as central to the evolving goth style, particularly in Europe. In search of new directions in which to take a well-established set of looks and sounds, bands and their fans increasingly began to appropriate and adapt elements of dance culture into the goth sound and appearance. In addition to the incorporation of mechanical dance beats and electronic sequences into otherwise gloom-ridden, sinister forms of music, "cybergoth" involved the juxtaposition of more established elements of goth fashion with reflective or ultraviolet-sensitive clothing, fluorescent makeup, and braided hair extensions.

Distinctiveness and Identity

In spite of its variety of influences, goth fashion is a contemporary style in its own right, which has retained significant levels of consistency and distinctiveness for over two decades. Put simply, since the mid 1980s, goths have always been easily recognized as such, both by one another and by many outsiders to their subculture. Attempts to interpret their distinctive appearance as communicating a morbid state of mind or a disturbed psychological makeup are usually misplaced. What *is* symbolized, though, is a defiant sense of collective identity, based upon a celebration of shared aesthetic tastes relating primarily to music, fashion, and nightlife (Hodkinson 2002).

See also Occult Dress; Punk; Street Style; Subcultures.

Bibliography

Baddeley, Gavin. *Goth Chic: A Connoisseur's Guide to Dark Culture*. London: Plexus, 2002.

Hodkinson, Paul. *Goth: Identity, Style and Subculture*. Oxford: Berg, 2002.

Mercer, Mick. *Gothic Rock Black Book*. London: Omnibus Press, 1988.

——. *Gothic Rock: Everything You Wanted to Know but Were Too Gormless to Ask*. Birmingham: Pegasus, 1991.

Thompson, Dave. *The Dark Reign of Gothic Rock*. London: Helter Skelter, 2002.

Paul Hodkinson

GRÈS, MME.*

Madame Alix Grès is widely regarded as one of the most brilliant couturiers of the twentieth century. She employed innovative construction techniques in the service of a classical aesthetic, creating her hallmark "Grecian" gowns as well as a wide range of simple and geometrically cut designs based on ethnic costume. Her garments are noted for their three-dimensional, sculptural quality.

Mme. Grès's life, like the creation of her gowns, was unconventional. Born Germaine Emilie Krebs on 30 November 1903 in Paris, France, she became a couturier after her bourgeois Catholic parents discouraged her desire to pursue a career first as a professional dancer and then as a sculptor. Around 1933, during a brief apprenticeship of three months at the couture house of Premet, she learned the basics of dressmaking and changed her first name to Alix. That same period she began to work for a couturier named Julie Barton, who renamed her house Alix to reflect the astounding success of her assistant.

On 15 April 1937 Grès married a Russian-born painter, Serge Anatolievitch Czerefkow. It was then that she became Alix Grès, Grès being an anagram of her husband's first name, which he used to sign his paintings. In August 1939 their only child, Anne, was born. Months earlier, however, Serge had left France and relocated to Tahiti.

In the spring of 1940 the Nazis occupied Paris. After a falling out with Barton, Grès fled the city, like many other Parisians, and moved south with her infant daughter. The one enduring legacy of her exile was the donning of a turban; she took to wearing the headdress initially because she could not go to a hairdresser. It became her personal trademark.

In 1941 Grès returned to Paris and opened her own salon. After refusing to accommodate the Nazi's insistence that she reveal her trade secrets and adhere to the regime's fabric restrictions, she was forced to close the shop in January 1944. Finally, in the early summer of 1944, she was authorized to resume her business in time to show a final collection before the liberation of Paris. This now legendary group of garments was made using only the red, white, and blue of the French flag.

The most famous and recognizable design of Mme. Grès was her classically inspired floor-length, pleated gown. In the 1930s these "Grecian" garments were primarily white in color, made from uncut lengths of double-width matte silk jersey, most often sleeveless, and cut to enhance the female body without physically restricting its movement. By the onset of World War II, because of textile restrictions, Grès focused on the manipulation of the bodices, sleeves, and necklines of much shorter garments.

In the late 1940s Grès resumed the use of larger quantities of fabric as well as a tighter and finer style of pleating. She also employed inner reinforcement or corseting. By the 1970s Grès has eliminated the corset and, simultaneously, cut away portions of the bodice, thus exposing large areas of the nude torso.

In the 1950s and 1960s Mme. Grès's business and her designs thrived. She engaged in several licensing agreements, the most successful of which was her perfume, Cabochard, released in 1959. Literally meaning "pigheaded," it describes the tenacity of the couturier. Madame Grès's ethnic-inspired garments were an important part of her oeuvre during this time. Non-Western art was a major source of inspiration to her beginning in the 1930s, with the proliferation of exhibitions and expositions that displayed the products of France's colonies. Although her output of such garments was to drop off significantly during the 1940s and 1950s, she responded to a strong revival of ethnic influences during the mid-1960s, creating caftans, capes, and pajamas for "couture hippies." These gowns were different from her prewar creations in that Grès relied on construction techniques she observed in non-Western dress. This change occurred after a 1959 trip to India, where Grès studied ethnic costume and took note of Eastern cultures' aversion to the cutting of textiles. She also experimented with fabrics, using faille and brocaded silks as well as more pliable materials such as fine wool knits and djersakasha, a cashmere jersey that could be woven as a tube, eliminating the need for seams.

In 1972 Mme. Grès was unanimously elected president of the Chambre Syndicale de la Couture. Four years later she became the first recipient of the Dé d'Or (Golden Thimble award), the highest honor given by the Chambre Syndicale. By the mid-1980s, however, the house of Grès had fallen into decline. After entrusting both her business and her trademark to a businessman-cum-politician named Bernard Tapie, Grès lost both. In April 1986 Maison Grès was expelled from the Chambre Syndicale for nonpayment of dues. Difficulties continued until the official retirement of Madame Grès, after the presentation of her 1988 spring/summer collection. The exit of one of the greatest figures in the world of haute couture took place quietly, with no official press release from the house of Grès. She died in the south of France on 13 December 1994.

No figure in French couture used the elements of classicism so completely or so poetically as Madame Grès, who used this aesthetic in her creation of seemingly limitless construction variations on a theme. Often referred to as the great "sculptress" of haute couture, Grès used the draping method to create her most dramatic designs, often consisting of puffed, molded, and three-dimensionally shaped elements that billowed and fell away from the body. Examples included capes made with yards of heavy wool manipulated into deep folds, taffeta cocktail dresses that combine finely pleated bodices balanced with full balloon-shaped skirts puffed sleeves, and evening gowns with enormous circular sleeves and trains that could rise like sails. Although volumetric, her sculpted garments are supple and pliable and have no reinforcement such as an attached inner facing. The end result was sensual fashions that stood away from the body rather than falling next to it.

See also Ethnic Style in Fashion; Haute Couture.

Bibliography

Aillaud, Charlotte. "Legend: Madame Grès." *Architectural Digest* (August 1988).

Ardisson, Thierry, and Jean Luc Maitre. "The Greatness of Grès." *Interview* (February 1981).

Brantley, Ben. "Mme. Grès on Finely Chiseled Couture." *Women's Wear Daily* 7 (November 1979).

Charles-Roux, Edmond. "Madame Grès, a Romantic View without Nostalgia." *Vogue* (September 1964).

Cooper, Arlene. "How Madame Grès Sculpts with Fabric." *Threads Magazine* (April/May 1987).

Hata, Sahoko, ed. *L'Art de Madame Grès.* Tokyo: Bunka Publishing Bureau, 1980.

Hollander, Anne. "A Sculptor in Fabric." *Connoisseur* (August 1982).

"Madame Grès, Hellène de Paris." *Jardins des Modes* (December 1980–January 1981).

Mears, Patricia. *Madame Grès: Sphinx of Fashion.* New York and London: Yale University Press, 2008.

Nemy, Enid. "Timeless Styles by Madame Grès." *New York Times* (10 October 1979).

Villiers le Moy, Pascale. "The Timeless Fashions of Madame Grès." *Connoisseur* (August 1982).

Patricia Mears

GRUNGE

The term "grunge" is used to define a specific moment in twentieth-century music and fashion. Hailing from the northwest United States in the 1980s, grunge went on to have global implications for alternative bands and do-it-yourself (DIY) dressing. While grunge music and style were absorbed by a large youth following, its status as a self-conscious subculture is debatable. People who listened to grunge music did not refer to themselves as "grungers" in the same way as "punks" or "hippies." However, like these subcultures, grunge was co-opted by the music and fashion industries through its promotion by the media.

Grunge Music

The word "grunge" dates from 1972, but did not enter popular terminology until the birth of the Seattle sound, a mix of heavy-metal, punk, and good old-fashioned rock and roll, in the late 1980s. Many musicians associated with grunge credit their exposure to early punk bands as one of their most important influences.

Like San Francisco in the 1960s, Seattle in the 1980s was a breeding ground for music that spoke to its youth. The independent record label Sub Pop recorded many of the Seattle bands inexpensively and was partly responsible for their garage sound. Many of these bands went on to receive international acclaim and major record label representation, most notably The Melvins, Mudhoney, Green River, Soundgarden, Malfunkshun, TAD, and Nirvana. Nirvana's second album, *Nevermind*, was released in 1991, making Nirvana the first of this growing scene to go multiplatinum and Kurt Cobain, Nirvana's lead singer, the reluctant voice of his generation.

(Sub)Cultural Context

The youth movements most often associated and compared to grunge—hippie and punk—were driven both by music and politics. Punks and hippies used music and fashion to make strong statements about the world and are often referred to as "movements" due to this political component. While the youth of 1980s Seattle were aware of politics, grunge was fueled more by self-expression—sadness, disenchantment, disconnectedness, loneliness, frustration—and perhaps was an unintentional movement of sorts. There does not appear to have been a common grunge goal, such as punk's "anarchy" or the hippies' "peace." Despite this lack of unifying intentionality, grunge gave voice to a bored, lost, emotionally neglected, post-punk generation—Generation X.

Grunge Fashion

If punk's antifashion stance can be interpreted as "against fashion," then that of grunge can be seen as "nonfashion." The grunge youth, born of hippies and raised on punk, reinterpreted these components through their own post-hippie, post-punk, West Coast aesthetic. Grunge was essentially a slovenly, thoughtless, uncoordinated look, but with an edge. Iconic items for men and women were ripped and faded jeans, flannel shirts or wool Pendletons layered over dirty T-shirts with outdated logos, and black combat-style boots such as Dr. Martens. Because the temperature in Seattle can swing by 20 degrees in the same day, it is convenient to have a wool long-sleeved button-down shirt that can be easily removed and tied around one's waist. The style for plaid flannel shirts and wool Pendletons is regional, having been a long-time staple for local lumberjacks and logging-industry employees—it was less a fashion choice than a utilitarian necessity.

The low-budget antimaterialist philosophy brought on by the recession made shopping at thrift stores and army surplus outlets common, adding various elements to the grunge sartorial lexicon, including beanies for warmth and unkempt hair, long underwear worn under shorts (in defiance of the changeable weather), and cargo pants. Thrift-store finds, such as vintage floral-print dresses and baby-doll nightgowns, were worn with over-sized sweaters and holey cardigans. Grunge was dressing down at its most extreme, taking casualness and comfort dressing to an entirely new level.

Grunge Chic

The first mention of grunge in the fashion industry was in *Women's Wear Daily* on 17 August 1992: "Three hot looks—Rave, Hip Hop and Grunge—have hit the street and stores here, each spawned by the music that's popular among the under-21 set." The style that had begun on the streets of Seattle had finally hit New York and was heading across the Atlantic. Later that same year, Grace Coddington (editor) and Steven Meisel

(fashion photographer) did an eight-page article and layout for *Vogue* with the help of a Sub Pop cofounder and owner Jonathan Poneman: "Flannels, ratty tour shirts, boots, and baseball caps have become a uniform for those in the know, and their legions are growing" (p. 254). The fashion machine was drawn to the utilitarian aspects of grunge as well as the juxtapositions of textures and the old against the new. Marc Jacobs is credited with bringing grunge to the runway with his spring 1993 collection for Perry Ellis. He was later followed by such designers as Calvin Klein, Christian Francis Roth, Armani, Dolce & Gabbana, Anna Sui, and Versace who all came out with layered and vintage looks made out of luxury fabrics.

Ultimately, grunge failed as a high-fashion trend because its vitality came from the unique and personal art of combining clothes and accessories from wildly disparate and idiosyncratic sources. Grunge was not easily repackaged and sold to the people who related to it because it was out of their price range and the upscale consumer was not taking the bait. Where grunge worked well was at low to moderate price points as middle-class kids across America were buying pre-ripped jeans, beanies, and flannels all the while dancing to Nirvana.

Post-Grunge World

Repackaging was also the fate of grunge music as every major record label tried to find the next Nirvana, and bands like Pearl Jam and Bush filled stadiums but paid little homage to grunge's punk roots. Nevertheless, grunge ultimately managed to revive rock and roll, redefine the music of the 1990s by bringing the focus back to the guitar, and make the word "alternative" meaningless in the twenty-first century as alternative music is now the music of the masses.

What grunge did for music it also did for fashion. Grunge opened the door to recycled clothes for everyone as a fashionable, and even a chic, choice. Grunge defined a new approach to dressing that included layering and juxtapositions of patterns and textures. The DIY approach to dress has become the norm, giving the consumer the freedom to choose, to not be a slave to one look or designer, and the confidence to create personal ensembles with the goal of self-expression through style.

See also Hip-hop Fashion; Hippie Style; Punk; Street Style; Subcultures.

Bibliography

Coddington, Grace. "Grunge and Glory." *Vogue* (December 1992): 254–263.

de la Haye, Amy, and Cathie Dingwall. *Surfers, Soulies, Skinheads, and Skaters: Subcultural Style from the Forties to the Nineties.* London: V&A Publications, 1996.

Polhemus, Ted. *Street Style: From Sidewalk to Catwalk.* London: Thames and Hudson, Inc., 1994.

Sims, Joshua. *Rock/Fashion.* London: Omnibus Press, 1999.

Steele, Valerie. *Fifty Years of Fashion: New Look to Now.* New Haven, Conn., and London: Yale University Press, 1997.

Shannon Bell Price

G-STRING AND THONG

The G-string, or thong, a panty front with a half- to one-inch strip of fabric at the back that sits between the buttocks, became one of the most popular forms of female underwear in the early twenty-first century. Its sources are manifold; the thong bikini designed by Rudi Gernreich in 1974, launched with a matching Vidal Sassoon hairstyle, is one which in turn spawned the more popular Brazilian string bikini brief, or tanga, of the late 1970s. This tiny bikini—dubbed the *fio denta*, or dental floss—ensured that the buttocks achieved maximum exposure to the sun and openly displayed an erogenous zone that was a particular favorite in Latino culture.

The stripper's G-string is another influence and has been an important part of the striptease artist's—or, more latterly, lap dancer's—wardrobe since the 1950s, when the taboo of displaying the vagina or any degree of pubic hair was paramount. The G-string was comprised of an elastic string that went around the waist and up between the buttocks and is popularly believed to have been originally added to the stripper's accoutrements on the occasion of the 1939 World's Fair in New York when Mayor Fiorello La Guardia demanded that the city's nude dancers cover themselves as a mark of respect for the thousands of visitors thronging the city. However, these types of coverings could be described as derivations of male underwear or garments associated with sports, such as jockstraps, which tend to reveal the muscle power of the legs and buttocks. Posing pouches worn by nude models in life classes since the Renaissance and in the nineteenth and early twentieth century

in magazines promoting "health culture" and featuring body builders could be seen as types of G-string in that they have a front part that covers the genitals and a string at the back that exposes the bottom.

The thong was incorporated into the vocabulary of women's underwear in the 1980s in response to tighter and tighter trousers, especially jeans worn by women to display more of their gym-honed bodies in an era that emphasized muscled body shape. Women demanded underwear that would remain invisible under outerwear and combat what became known as VPL, or Visible Panty Line. Frederick Mellinger, of popular underwear manufacturer Frederick's of Hollywood, realized the potential of this form of underwear; Frederick's began to mass-market the thong, at first known as the "scanty panty," as an erotic item alongside crotchless or edible underwear. By the mid-1980s, however, the thong began to be appreciated as a practical garment in its own right. By 2003, it had become the fastest growing segment of women's underwear, making "full-bottomed" panties almost obsolete. In order to persuade the few reluctant women left to wear the thong, a "training" garment was invented called the Rio, or "starter" thong, which rose more sedately up the sides to expose less of the buttocks.

In the 1990s, the thong became a garment of folkloric proportions after the White House intern Monica Lewinsky's affair with U.S. president Bill Clinton was outlined in the Starr Report. Lewinsky admitted initiating her liaison with Clinton by flirtatiously lifting the back of her formal suit jacket to reveal the straps of her thong underwear. This indicated the irony of the thong for, in its original incarnation as underwear, it was designed to remain invisible so as to reveal the contours of a shapely bottom under the tightest of trousers. By the early 2000s, it became fashionable to wear low-cut hipster jeans that revealed the back of the thong, which became a focal point reinforced by diamanté-covered straps by such designers as Agent Provocateur and Frost French and the manufacturers Gossard. This fad, believed to be initiated by glamour model Jordan in England and singers Britney Spears and Mariah Carey in the United States, also showed a cultural shift in the sexual zoning of women's bodies. The prominent, fleshy bottom mythologized in African American culture by songs such as "The Thong Song" by American rhythm and blues star Sisqó, who exhorted, "Let me see that thong," and eulogized in the shape of actress and singer Jennifer Lopez, began to take over from the breasts as the primary erogenous zone. The popularity of the thong spread across all ages and sexes (although the man in the thong is mainly popular in certain gay circles), and by 2003, a moral panic had ensued as parents and the media saw the thong as responsible for sexualizing girls at too young an age. According to provisional figures compiled by manufacturers' sales of thongs to *tweenage* girls, the marketing definition of twelve- to fourteen-year-olds, jumped 33 percent from 2002 to 2003 in the United Kingdom. In 2003, an estimated ten million thongs worth about sixty-five million pounds were sold in the United Kingdom. The British shop Tammy Girl came under particular fire for marketing thongs to pre-teenaged girls with logos such as "Cupid Rules" and "Talent" printed on them. A further attack on the thong came in 2002, when the authorities at Daytona Beach, Florida, using anti-nudity laws to dissuade the use of the thong, threatened to arrest anyone displaying more than a third of their buttocks in public.

See also Lingerie; Underwear.

Bibliography

Cox, Caroline. *Lingerie: A Lexicon of Style.* London: Scriptum Editions, 2001.
Craik, Jennifer. *The Face of Fashion: Cultural Studies in Fashion.* London: Routledge, 1994.

Caroline Cox

GUCCI*

From modest beginnings at the end of the nineteenth century, the Gucci company became one of the world's most successful manufacturers of high-end leather goods, clothing, and other fashion products. As an immigrant in Paris and then London, working in exclusive hotels, young Guccio Gucci (1881–1953) was impressed with the luxurious luggage he saw sophisticated guests bring with them. Upon returning to his birthplace of Florence, a city distinguished for high-quality materials and skilled artisans, he established a shop in 1920 that sold fine leather goods with classic styling. Although Gucci organized his workrooms for industrial methods of production, he maintained traditional aspects of fabrication. Initially Gucci employed skilled workers

in basic Florentine leather crafts, attentive to finishing. With expansion, machine stitching was a production method that supported construction.

Together with three of his sons, Aldo, Vasco, and Rodolfo, Gucci expanded the company to include stores in Milan and Rome as well as additional shops in Florence. Gucci's stores featured such finely crafted leather accessories as handbags, shoes, and his iconic ornamented loafer as well as silks and knitwear in a signature pattern. The Gucci loafer is the only shoe in the collection of the Museum of Modern Art in New York.

The company made handbags of cotton canvas rather than leather during World War II as a result of material shortages. The canvas, however, was distinguished by a signature double-G symbol combined with prominent red and green bands. After the war, the Gucci crest, which showed a shield and armored knight surrounded by a ribbon inscribed with the family name, became synonymous with the city of Florence.

Aldo and Rodolfo Gucci further expanded the company's horizons in 1953 by establishing offices in New York City. Film stars and jet-set travelers to Italy during the 1950s and 1960s brought their glamour to Florence, turning Gucci's merchandise into international status symbols. Movie stars posed in Gucci's clothing, accessories, and footwear for lifestyle magazines around the world, contributing to the company's growing reputation.

Gucci clothing and accessories for sale. The Gucci company, which began as a single Italian leather goods shop founded in 1920, expanded to become one of the most successful international purveyors of fashion © Jacques M. Chenet/Corbis. Reproduced by permission.

Gucci's distinctive lines made its products among the most frequently copied in the world in the early 2000s. Pigskin, calf, and imported exotic animal skins were subjected to various methods of fabrication. Waterproof canvas and satin were used for evening bags. Bamboo was first used to make handbag handles by a process of heating and molding in 1947, and purses made with a shoulder strap and snaffle-bit decoration were introduced in 1960. In 1964 Gucci's lush butterfly pattern was custom-created for silk foulards, followed by equally luxuriant floral patterns. The original Gucci loafer was updated by a distinctive snaffle-bit ornament in 1966, while the "Rolls-Royce" luggage set was introduced in 1970. Watches, jewelry, ties, and eyewear were then added to the company's product lines. A particularly iconic touch, introduced in 1964, was the use of the double-G logo for belt buckles and other accessory decorations.

The company prospered through the 1970s, but the 1980s were marked by internal family disputes that brought Gucci to the brink of disaster. Rodolfo's son Maurizio took over the company's direction after his father's death in 1983, and dismissed his uncle Aldo—who eventually served a prison term for tax evasion. Maurizio proved to be an unsuccessful president; he was compelled to sell the family-owned company to Investcorp, a Bahrain-based company, in 1988. Maurizio disposed of his remaining stock in 1993. Tragically, Maurizio was murdered in Milan in 1995, and his former wife, Patrizia Reggiani, was convicted of hiring his killers. Meanwhile, the new investors promoted the American-educated Domenico De Sole from the position of family attorney to president of Gucci America in 1994 and chief executive in 1995.

The company had previously brought in Dawn Mello in 1989 as editor and ready-to-wear designer in order to reestablish its reputation. Well aware of Gucci's tarnished image and the value of its name brand, Mello hired Tom Ford in 1990 to design a ready-to-wear line. He was promoted to the position of creative director in 1994. Before Mello returned to her post as president of the American retailer Bergdorf Goodman, she initiated the return of Gucci's headquarters from the business center of Milan to Florence, where its craft traditions were rooted. There she and Ford reduced the number of Gucci products from twenty thousand to a more reasonable five thousand.

Tom Ford came to the foundering company with vision and style. Having the strong support of Dominico De Sole, Ford wished to maintain a sense of the company's history while updating Gucci's trademarks. In 1994 Ford became responsible for creative direction, and by 1996 he directed all aspects of the company—including ready-to-wear clothing, visual merchandising, packaging, interior design, and advertising. Ford and De Sole struggled to restore the former reputation of Gucci, while redirecting the growing brand to a new level for the market of the late 1990s.

There were seventy-six Gucci stores around the world in 1997, along with numerous licensing agreements. Ford was instrumental in the process of decisionmaking with De Sole when the Gucci Group acquired Yves Saint Laurent Rive Gauche, Bottega Veneta, Boucheron, Sergio Rossi, and, in part-ownership with Stella McCartney, Alexander McQueen and Balenciaga. By 2001 Ford and De Sole shared the responsibility for major business decisions, while Ford concurrently directed design at Yves Saint Laurent as well as at Gucci.

The French conglomerate Pinault-Printemps-Redouté, however, gained ownership of 60 percent of the Gucci Group's stock in 2003. *Women's Wear Daily* then announced the departure of both Domenico De Sole and Tom Ford from the Gucci Group when their contracts expired in April 2004. The last spring collection under the direction of Ford and De Sole was a critical and commercial success. Amid widespread speculation in the fashion press about Ford's heir, the company announced in March 2004 that he would be replaced by a team of younger designers promoted from the ranks of the company's staff. Fridi Giannini became artistic director for womenswear in 2005, and was promoted to creative director for all Gucci lines in 2006.

See also Brands and Labels; Ford, Tom; Italian Fashion; Leather and Suede; Saint Laurent, Yves; Shoes.

Bibliography

Bianchino, Gloria, et al., eds. *Italian Fashion*. Vol. 1, *The Origins of High Fashion and Knitwear*. Milan: Electa SpA, 1987.

Forden, Sara Gay. *The House of Gucci: A Sensational Story of Murder, Madness, Glamour, and Greed*. New York: William Morrow, 2000.

Horyn, Cathy. "Tom Ford Goes Out with a Roar." *New York Times*, 26 February 2004.

Steele, Valerie. *Fashion, Italian Style*. New Haven, Conn.: Yale University Press, 2003.

Gillion Carrara

HAIRDRESSERS

Hairdressers seem to appear with civilization itself. Comparatively little is known about history's earliest coiffeurs, those who curled the beards of Sumerian princes and built the fabulous headdresses of Egyptian princesses, except that the Egyptian deities included a barber god. The market squares of ancient Greek cities included barbershops, where people could laze and gossip. Roman towns also contained hairdressing salons, visited mostly by the middle classes, while slaves dressed the heads of upper-class women. These practices survived in the Byzantine east, long after they had been destroyed in the Latin half of the empire.

The Viking hordes and Arthurian nobility of the Dark Ages doubtless continued to cut their hair and trim their beards, but hairdressers as such disappeared along with the cities where they had always practiced their trade. They return to recorded history with the revival of urban life and fashion in the Middle Ages. Medieval towns organized guilds of barber-surgeons who, in addition to shaving clients, lanced boils and pulled teeth. The hairdressing profession continued to develop during the Renaissance, particularly as women's headdresses became more popular and elaborate. More often than not, the ladies' hairdresser was principally a wig maker.

The modern era of splendid hairdos and celebrity coiffeurs, like "Champagne," who opened the first beauty salon in Paris, emerged with the development of court society in the seventeenth century. The courts of Charles II and Louis XIV were among the last places where men's coiffures were as important as women's, but as the elaborate headdresses of the era depended on the skills of wig makers—the French court contained more than forty of them in 1656—barbers became superfluous.

The eighteenth century belonged even more decidedly to the wig makers. While men's wigs generally took on more modest proportions, by the middle of the 1700s women's headdresses reached unprecedented dimensions and raised their architects to a new level of prominence. Léonard became the most famous of his peers, under the patronage of Marie-Antoinette. So much confidence did the queen place in her coiffeur that in 1791, as the royal family tried to flee Revolutionary France, she sent him ahead to Brussels with a collection of crown jewels—although she and the king were arrested before they could reach him there. The French Revolution hurt hairdressers by repressing extravagant coiffures and the taste for wigs and by hastening the destruction of the guilds that had protected barbers' monopoly on shaving and bleeding.

The fashions for clean-shaven faces for men and long, natural hair for women, made the century of industrialization and urbanization an unspectacular one for hairdressers. Barbers sunk to being among the poorest and worst paid of tradesmen. The appearance of King Gillette's remarkable safety razor in 1903 threatened them with the loss of much of their remaining business. As for ladies' hairdressers, the mass of working women in cities and on farms had neither need nor money for their services. Society dames might call on a hairdresser artiste for a very special occasion, but most of the daily work of arranging hair fell to their ladies' maids.

It was only near the end of the century, with the appearance of the "marcel" wave, that the hairdressing profession began to take on its contemporary shape. The beautiful, long-lasting waves that Marcel and his imitators created attracted women to beauty salons in unparalleled numbers and gave hairdressers a huge new source of revenue. The success of "marcelling" also reflected important social changes, in particular women's growing independence and the expansion of the market for fashionable things among the popular classes, especially among young women. Ladies' hairdressers became pioneers on the frontier of mass-consumer society.

World War I further revolutionized the hairdressers' trade. First, by adding to women's economic and personal autonomy, it increased the market for hairdressers' services. Second, by pulling men out of the salons, it set in motion a process that feminized what had always been a predominantly male trade. The vogue for women's short hairstyles that swept through Western societies in the 1920s accelerated these developments. The majority of ladies' hairdressers initially rejected what they considered a threat to their "art," but they soon came to embrace the radical new fashion for the revenue it brought. For short hair was not only cut, it was shampooed, "permed," and often colored, making salons more profitable even as they became more numerous. As the fashion for short hair spread beyond Europe and America, modern hairdressing salons began to open in Shanghai, Tokyo, and other major non-Western cities.

Although most shops remained very small, the number of large, chic salons multiplied. These usually belonged to the profession's luminaries and often were established in the more fashionable department stores. Antoine, the most luminous of all, expanded his operations to the United States through an agreement with Saks Fifth Avenue, which also sold a line of beauty products bearing his name.

In an era when new fashions and products gave ladies' hairdressers fresh business and artistic opportunities, barbers' fortunes continued to decline. Men's conservative haircuts proved barren ground for the sort of value-added services that fueled ladies' hairdressing, while, at least before the 1960s, the ethic of maleness sharply limited the market for cologne and cosmetics.

The consumer revolution that followed World War II carried more women than ever into the hairdressing salons. At the top of the profession, a host of new stars, led by Alexandre, the Duchess of Windsor's protégé, joined Antoine in the hairdressers' pantheon. Yet even as the trade became increasingly feminized, few women rose to the summit. The Carita sisters and Rose Evansky are rare exceptions.

In the 1950s, the modish styles of Vidal Sassoon and the "poodle cut" of the campy Raymond made London the second capital of hairdressing. Beginning with Jacques Dessange in 1976, the best-known coiffeurs began to attach their names not only to products but to salons, as well. In the 1980s and 1990s the practice spread rapidly, and in the early 2000s franchises bearing the names of Jean-Louis David, Jean-Claude Biguine, and others control a large portion of the hairdressing business all over the world.

Other fashion capitals turned out their own prodigies, who performed in international competitions and opened chic salons far from home in what by the end of the millennium had become an international society of hair fashion.

See also Barbers; Hair Accessories; Hairstyles.

Bibliography

Cooper, Wendy. *Hair: Sex, Society, Symbolism*. New York: Stein and Day, 1971.

Corson, Richard. *Fashions in Hair: The First Five Thousand Years*. London: Peter Owen, 1965.

Cox, Caroline. *Good Hair Days: A History of British Hairstyling*. London: Quartet Books, 1999.

Graves, Charles. *Devotion to Beauty: The Antoine Story*. London: Jarrold's, 1962.

Willet, Julie T. *Permanent Waves: The Making of the American Beauty Shop*. New York: New York University Press, 2000.

Steve Zdatny

HAIRSTYLES

Standards of beauty have varied enormously according to time and place. Yet as long as people have ordered their social relations, hairdressing has had a role in the struggle for status and reproduction. "Humans," writes Robin Bryer, "are unique in two aspects of their behavior: wearing clothes and having their hair cut voluntarily" (p. 9). Hairdressing is part of the human condition.

One presumes that the first hairdos were long, scraggly, and filthy. Even given the general squalor atop primitive heads, however, it is likely that some hair was considered more attractive and admirable than others. What is certain is that wherever primitive society congealed into civilization, it produced a culture of hairdressing.

Archaeological evidence suggests that the early Egyptians wore their natural hair in tight braids. That changed with the discovery of the art of wig making. Hair was then cut short or shaved. Young boys retained their queues, but adults who could afford them wore wigs, especially for special occasions. Specialists made up elaborate headdresses filled with jewels and expensive accessories and splashed with oils and perfumes. The Mesopotamian civilizations preferred

In Fashions in Hair: The First Five Thousand Years, the author Richard Corson quotes a seventeenth-century source describing a teenage noblewoman attempting to turn her hair blonde. After exposing it to the hot sun for hours and anointing it with a coloring substance that seemed to produce the effect, she was afflicted with a near-daily nosebleed and being desirous to stop the Blood by the pressing of her Nostrils, not farr from her right Eye toward her Temple, through a pore, as it were by a hole made with a needles point, the Blood burst out abundantly, and . . . she was diseased by the obstruction of her courses (p. 173).

heavy beards and long hair, often frizzed or waved. At Knossos, Cretan women wore elaborate coiffures, with golden hairpins, and lots of makeup. As always, different codes distinguished elites—kings, nobles, priests—from commoners.

The ancient Greeks invented the beauty salon, where women had their cheeks blanched with white lead and their naturally blonde hair artistically dressed. Sometimes it was dyed red or blue. Spartan brides cropped their hair; Athenians wore veils over their dressed hair. They cut it as a sign of mourning. Beginning in the fifth century B.C.E., Greek men began to wear their hair short. It was Alexander the Great who insisted that his soldiers shave their beards in order to deprive their foes of a handle during combat.

Typically, the Romans at first copied the Greeks and then developed more elaborate hairstyles to match the imperial ethic. Men often wore their hair short, in what came to be called the "Titus," after the Emperor. Attended to by the barbers who worked at the marketplaces and public baths, or by their slaves (who were shaved bald), both men and women curled their hair and dyed it red. They applied costly oils and pomatums or wore expensive wigs. The most extravagant powdered their hair with gold dust. In the East, Byzantine hairstyles blended Greco-Roman culture with oriental. Men wore moderately short hair, mustaches, and beards. Feminine coiffures incorporated pearls and precious metals, which were also used for ecclesiastical costumes. Sometimes the fashion was for bare heads, sometimes for ribbons or ornamented turbans. Turbans became standard in Moorish culture—although the Islamic injunction against "graven images," like that of the Jewish religion, means that documentation of Islamic hairstyles remains sparse before the Christian Middle Ages.

The paintings of the Pre-Raphaelites have provided a certain image of Arthurian damsels and knights. A small amount of evidence suggests that the period between the departure of the Romans and the arrival of the Normans in England favored flowing locks and facial hair for men. But, in fact, very little documentation about hairstyles during the Dark Ages survives.

The revival of European culture in the Middle Ages also brought back something like international fashion, of which coiffures were a part. Hairstyles differed between northern and southern Europe. And if the return of fashion meant anything, it was that coiffures popular at one moment became démodées in the next—although the fashionable "moment" in the Middle Ages could be rather long by later standards. The bobbed styles for men of the twelfth century were still around in the fifteenth, when smart Venetian gentlemen were also sporting yellow silk wigs. Depending on the time and place, women wore long braids or huge, horned headdresses. Or they packed their hair into a variety of bonnets and bags, often adorned with jewels and expensive knickknacks. The expanding middle class ordinarily adopted "quieter" versions of these noble styles. Poorer women wore their hair long and enclosed. Their men folk cut theirs short or shoulder length, while beards and mustaches came and went.

By the Renaissance, whatever the particular arrangement, hairstyles had become one of those idioms of international art that allowed fashion to circulate across the continent. Variety and inventiveness were the rules. Hair was frizzed, or not. Some women plucked or shaved their foreheads—thus becoming "highbrow," in the manner of Elizabeth I, who was also reputed to own a hundred perukes. Blonde was the hair color of choice, and women bleached their hair by sitting in the sun and using saffron or medicated sulphur. Blonde wigs became the vogue in France and Italy, and nobles—Marguerite de Valois, most notably—would engage blonde maids in order to command their hair for wigs. Mary, Queen of Scots possessed many beautiful curled wigs and adorned her head with lace. Other ladies used pads and wire frames to give their coiffures volume.

Contemporary illustrations of the early sixteenth century depict Englishmen with long hair and clean chins. Beards were more popular on the Continent. By the end of the century, English courtiers had cut their hair and adopted stylish beards with precious names such as the "swallowtail" and the "spade."

The portraits of the great Flemish painter Sir Anthony Van Dyke capture the Cavalier style that reached its height in the 1630s and 1640s, with men sporting long hair and neat, pointed beards under wide-brimmed hats. Hair became politicized briefly, during the English Civil War, when the more austere Protestant Roundheads battled the more elegantly coiffed forces of the English king, Charles I. The Pilgrims of the Colony of New Plymouth condemned long hair for men as prideful.

The Puritan position on hair must have softened, for later portraits of Cromwell depict him with longer hair, although not nearly as long as the styles coming out of the French court and brought back to England with the Restoration of Charles II in 1660. This was the great age of periwigs for men. Indeed, the French court imported so much blonde hair that Louis XIV's finance minister Colbert tried to ban wig making in France so as to stem the outflow of French gold.

The most popular women's styles of the period were the "hurluberlu"—unevenly cut and crimped, with two long curls over the shoulders—worn by Louis's favorite, Madame de Maintenon, and the "Fontange"—with its high curls secured by ribbon and bow—invented by the king's new mistress, the Duchess de Fontange. The fashions of Versailles traveled to all the other courts of Europe, and from there to the modish classes of every country.

In the eighteenth century, women's hair became the principal focus of art and conspicuous consumption. The massive headdresses of the middle decades serve as both the symbol of the Old Regime and the classic image of excess in fashion. It was in the 1770s that coiffures reached their most exaggerated form. Wendy Cooper describes "a certain Madame de Lauzun," whose "enormously high headdress," stuffed with the usual assortment of trash, was topped with "modeled ducks swimming in a stormy sea, scenes of hunting and shooting, a mill with a miller's wife flirting with a priest, and a miller leading an ass by its halter" (p. 95). Coiffures grew so immense that doorways had to be enlarged, and in two instances ladies were killed when their headdresses were set on fire by chandeliers. Men of weight and fashion in the Enlightenment wore modest, powdered wigs, although George III made enemies of English wig makers when he took to powdering his own natural hair.

The powdered look disappeared altogether in England when the Younger Pitt imposed a one-guinea tax on hair powder. Events in France had an even more revolutionary effect on hairstyles, as the fall of Louis XVI swept aside the fashion habits of the Old Regime. An era that admired the civic virtues of classical antiquity found men and women wearing their hair à la Titus. Those with a sharper sense of political irony adopted the mode à la victime, with their hair pulled up off the neck in imitation of those about to be guillotined. In the aftermath of the Terror, women wore their hair long and loose over diaphanous dresses. No one in Revolutionary France wanted to look like an aristocrat.

In the nineteenth century, men's hairstyles tended to the short and simple. Common in one decade, facial hair vanished in the next, only to return thereafter. In mid-century Naples, the government so objected to mustaches that it instructed police to shave them off offenders. While men's hair became increasingly tame and standardized, women's coiffures retained their complexity, if not their old proportions. The early part of the century saw a vogue for concatenations of natural hair adorned with feathers, rich combs, and other items. Other moments featured puffs of curls or ringlets. Powder reappeared briefly on the hair of fashionable dames under the Second Empire. Chignons vanished in the 1870s; jeweled pins became popular in the 1880s. In general, the pace of fashion quickened, and intricate coiffures made ladies more dependent than ever on their hair-dressers, even though the daily work of brushing and arranging a lady's hair fell to her lady's maid.

Wigs no longer played the dominant role in coiffure, as they had in the past. Still, the century admired long, luxurious hair, and since most women did not possess hair of sufficient quality or quantity, they made generous use of false hair. In fact, the taste for postiches (bits of false hair) drove the international market in hair to new heights. By the turn of the twentieth century, the United States was importing more than half a million tons of hair per year—a $3 million business. Most of this stuff came from European peasant women in the poorer rural areas, who used their long tresses as a sort of cash crop.

The wheel of hair fashion took its next dramatic turn in the mid-1880s, when Marcel Grateau, a hitherto unknown hairdresser in Paris, perfected a technique for giving hair soft, beautiful, durable waves and thereby launched the modern era of hairdressing. Replacing the nests of postiches and fancy bijoux, the "marcel" wave radically simplified ladies' hairstyles. Many of the most celebrated coiffeurs hated the "marcel" for precisely this reason, but women loved it. An insatiable popular demand soon forced its opponents to capitulate, and the "marcel" wave became the basis of a fashionable coiffure for the next twenty-five years—although, to be sure, enterprising hairdressers found ways to dress "marceled" hair with the traditional assortment of feathers, flowers, and pricey doodads. The "négligé" styles of the Belle Epoque, often colored with henna or dusted with white or gray powder, featured ribbons, enameled combs, and big chignons.

When the dean of French coiffeurs, Emile Long, complained about the cheap waves he saw on the *midinettes* (working girls) on the streets of Paris, he was pointing to the fact that the stunning success of "marceling" depended on a fundamental change in the social contours of fashion. It coincided with the early stages of a big expansion in the market for fashionable things in Western society.

In effect, three developments combined to create the modern beauty salon and the culture associated with it. First, rising wages gave women more disposable income, while greater autonomy freed them to spend it as they pleased. Second, a loosening of social constraints made it more acceptable for women to move in public spaces, that is, to take their toilettes out of the boudoir and into the hairdressing salon. Third, a critical series of technological developments expanded the services available in the salon.

New sensibilities about hygiene, combined with water heaters and hair dryers, encouraged women to have their hair shampooed. Non-toxic dyes helped dissolve old taboos about hair coloring. Most critically, the invention of the permanent-wave machine enabled women to alter their hair dramatically, while it brought hairdressers a huge new source of revenue. For a few hours hooked up to this contraption, a woman would pay anywhere from ten to fifty times the cost of an ordinary haircut. These new consumer habits were nourished by the growing number of magazines aimed at middle- and working-class women, and especially by the movie stars who were coming to dominate popular ideas of beauty and fashion.

All of this paved the way for the "bob," which proved to be a seminal moment both for coiffure and for Western society more generally. From the lacquered "garçonne" of Josephine Baker to the more fluid "Eton crop," the bob had many incarnations. Some of them had appeared on some stylish young heads before World War I, especially in the United States. But the vogue took off only in the 1920s, when it became part of the aesthetic turnabout associated with "flappers." As the "androgynous" clothes of Coco Chanel surpassed the curvaceous styles of the great Edwardian couturiers, so the bob became the badge of the so-called Modern Woman.

No other hairstyle in history provoked so much comment and controversy. Cultural conservatives hated it for its challenge to inherited gender verities. Stories abound of outraged men locking up, even murdering, their newly shorn wives and daughters. On the other side, women endorsed it by the millions. Observers generally saw the short hairstyles and women's spontaneous taste for them as evidence of a significant "emancipation" of women. It is true that the bob provided some relief from the arduous regimes of Edwardian coiffures. At the same time—permed, dyed, in need of frequent retouching, and often requiring a postiche for evening wear—it was hardly carefree or cheap.

At the end of the day, however, the bob was more fashion than political statement, and by the close of the Roaring Twenties, women had begun to tire of it. The hairstyles of the 1930s, created by such international stars as Antoine and Guillaume, were longer and more "feminine," although there was no return to the massive, superfluous hairdos of the pre-bob era. The Platinum Blonde, curvy and sexy, defined the new "New Woman" of the depression decade. Men in the period between the wars continued to favor short, neat haircuts, accompanied sometimes by a thin moustache (never by a beard) in the manner of Rudolph Valentino or Clark Gable.

The war years, rich in misery, were poor in new hair fashions. *Haute coiffure* survived mostly in Hollywood, where, for example, Veronica Lake became famous for the silky blonde hair that fell across half her face in the "bad-girl" style that alarmed some moralists. More commonly, millions of women involved in the war effort tucked their short, simple hairdos under military caps or hard hats. If the war brought the world one distinctive hairstyle, however, it would have to be the shaved heads belonging to camp survivors and "horizontal" collaborators.

The consumer revolution, born out of the ashes of war, once again transformed hairdressing. Stylistically, the postwar years promoted the so-called petite tête, the compact hairdos that fit so well with Christian Dior's fashion revolution, the New Look. Long styles made a partial comeback in the 1950s, led by the "artichoke" cut that Jacques Dessange created for the nubile Brigitte Bardot. The clear trend, however, was toward more compact coiffures. In the United States, ponytails became the classic expression of 1950s adolescence.

In the end, the 1950s may be less important for stylistic innovation than for the changes in the structures of consumption that occurred. While disposable incomes rose steadily, a growing mass media of movies, television, women's magazines, and broadcast images of beauty and stimulated the demand for fashionable commodities. More and more women indulged themselves in a weekly visit to the beauty parlor. In the United States, this became one of the defining rituals of middle-class femininity and an important communal event. At the same time, new hair care products—"cold" perms, do-it-yourself hair coloring, and setting—allowed women to exercise much of their expanding beauty regimen at home.

Men continued to provide a much poorer field for art and profit. Their haircuts became, if anything, plainer in the 1950s. Yet change was in the air. Rebellious teenagers began to turn away from crew cuts and flattops by wearing the "duck ass" cut associated with the likes of James Dean, Elvis Presley, and Johnny Halliday. In France, George Hardy achieved a small breakthrough in 1956 when he introduced the razor cut. Beards and mustaches turned up on the chins and lips of "beatniks" and other nonconformist types.

"Anti-fashion" hair spread over the next few decades, following the prominence of rock stars and hippies. Blacks in America and Europe put aside the hair-relaxing agents they associated with self-loathing and began to sport voluminous Afros. In the 1970s, "Mohicans," dread-locks, and the sinister skinhead became the protest hair-styles of choice. Throughout, sales of personal grooming products for men increased, and the men who visited the new "unisex" hair salons paid more than the proverbial "two bits." But hairdressing remained an overwhelmingly female preoccupation.

The "beehive," made possible by the invention of lacquered hairspray and the copious use of false hair, carried the 1950s ideal of femininity into the sixties. However, that raucous decade really belonged to the geometrical cuts that Vidal Sassoon created to fit the latest styles of Mary Quant, creator of the miniskirt. *Haute coiffure* survived, as the profession's contemporary stars coiffed movie stars, society dames, and runway models. But the rule for the last quarter of the twentieth century was variety and innovation. Hairstyles were long or short, flowing or spiked, natural or tinted, straight or permed.

The diversity of coiffures also reflected a critical change in the trajectory of fashion. In the days of Marie Antoinette or Marcel, a small, privileged elite made the laws that ruled taste. In the twentieth century, the masses gained a larger and larger say in the success of this vogue or that. By the end, masses of women were not merely endorsing (or not) the choices made by a select group of the fashionable. "The street" produced its own styles, which then permeated the formal structures of fashion.

The ceaseless evolution of hairstyles has produced a lot of speculation, both casual and academic, on their etiology and meaning. Numerous speculations have linked coiffures, not coincidentally but organically, to their historical moment. The many observers who attributed the popularity of the bob to women's emancipation provide the most pointed example of this. Others have gone further and tried to find the deeper meaning of forms. The French critic Roland Barthes offered an entire science, semiotics, dedicated to deconstructing those forms.

Hairstyles can unquestionably supply important clues about the societies that produce them. Once again, the bob is the perfect illustration. Permed, tinted, created in commercial establishments with electricity and hot running water, and consumed by millions of women spending considerable sums of money, it has a lot to say about Western civilization in the 1920s. Sometimes the meaning of coiffures is not hidden at all, but openly proclaimed, as it might be in a punk band, a neo-Nazi rally, a hippies' commune, or a lesbian rights parade.

Yet, in many ways, those who assert the free-flowing nature of fashionable "signifiers" have the stronger argument. After all, "liberated" women of the 1960s often sported long, straight hair, while the sainted defender of a medieval French king, Joan of Arc, wore a bob. It seems fair to say that in a historical world where

Charles II and Cher look alike from behind, the forms of fashion obey an elusive logic of their own.

See also Afro Hairstyle; Barbers; Hair Accessories; Hair-dressers.

Bibliography

Asser, Joyce. *Historic Hairdressing*. Bath: Pittman Publishing, 1966.

Bryer, Robin. *The History of Hair: Fashion and Fantasy Down the Ages*. London: Philip Wilson, 2000.

Cooper, Wendy. *Hair: Sex, Society, Symbolism*. New York: Stein and Day, 1971.

Corson, Richard. *Fashions in Hair: The First Five Thousand Years*. London: Peter Owen, 1965.

Cox, Caroline. *Good Hair Days: A History of British Hairstyling*. London: Quartet Books, 1999.

Keyes, Jean. *A History of Women's Hairstyles, 1500–1965*. London: Methuen, 1967.

Louis, M. *Six Thousand Years of Hair Styling*. New York: M. Louis, 1939.

McKracken, Grant. *Big Hair: A Journey into the Transformation of the Self*. Woodstock, N.Y.: The Overlook Press, 1995.

Rambaud, Rene. *Les fugitives. Precis anecdotique et historique des coiffures feminines a travers les ages, des Egyptiens a 1945*. Paris: Rene Rambaud, 1947.

Reynolds, Reginald. *Beards: Their Social Standing, Religious Involvements, Decorative Possibilities and Value in Offense and Defense through the Ages*. New York: Doubleday and Co., 1949.

Severn, Bill. *The Long and the Short of It: Five Thousand Years of Fun and Fury over Hair*. New York: David McKay and Co., 1971.

Trasko, Mary. *Daring Do's: A History of Extraordinary Hair*. New York: Flammarion, 1994.

Willet, Julie T. *Permanent Waves: The Making of the American Beauty Shop*. New York: New York University Press, 2000.

Steve Zdatny

HALSTON*

The designer Roy Halston Frowick (1932–1990) was born in Des Moines, Iowa, and began his career as a milliner. He subsequently rose to become one of the most important American designers of the 1970s, whose influence was still being felt into the twenty-first century.

Biography

While studying fashion illustration at the Art Institute of Chicago in 1952, Halston began designing hats in his spare time. Eventually, he started to sell his designs at André Basil's hair salon at the Ambassador Hotel. Halston moved to New York City in 1958 to design hats for the legendary milliner Lilly Daché and then began working in the custom millinery salon of the prestigious retailer Bergdorf Goodman in 1959. While there, he designed the famous pillbox hat worn by the First Lady Jacqueline Kennedy for the 1961 presidential inauguration of her husband, John F. Kennedy.

Moving beyond hats, Halston went on to design his first clothing collection for Bergdorf Goodman in June 1966. Two years later he left the retailer to form his own company, Halston Ltd. In December of 1968 Halston showed his first namesake collection in his new Angelo Donghia–designed showroom at 33 East Sixty-Eighth Street in New York City. As his business grew, Halston took over the entire building, creating a retail boutique in 1972 that took up three floors of the building, with each floor selling a different collection (and at a different price point). Later that year a ready-to-wear company, Halston Originals, was formed with two partners and headquartered on New York's Seventh Avenue.

In a first-of-its-kind deal for a fashion designer, Halston and his partners sold both the Halston businesses and the Halston trademark to Norton Simon Industries (NSI), a large multibrand corporation, in 1973. Halston's success soared during the mid-1970s, and so did his fame. An article in *Esquire* magazine asked the question: "Will Halston take over the world?" (p. 69).

As the success continued, NSI started signing a multitude of licensees—thirty existed at one point. In 1978 the company moved its design studio to a spacious venue on the twenty-first floor of the Olympic Tower at Fifty-first Street and Fifth Avenue. With the bigger space once again came an increased workload. Eventually, Halston was designing four ready-to-wear, four sportswear, and two made-to-order collections per year. All this was in addition to furs, shoes, swimwear, robes, intimate apparel, men's wear, luggage, and uniforms for both Avis Rent A Car System and Braniff Airline employees. Halston also continued to design costumes for his celebrity friends, including the performer Liza Minnelli, and for Martha Graham's dance company.

By the early 1980s, however, Halston's influence was waning, and his social life began to garner more attention than his fashions. The beginning of the end, according to many, came when, in 1982, Halston signed a multimillion dollar deal with the J. C. Penney discount chain to create products under the Halston label. Many prestigious retailers voiced concern about the deal, and Bergdorf Goodman dropped the designer's ready-to-wear line from their store.

Before signing the deal with Penney's, things had started to unravel for the designer. Many cite the pressure of his workload and his inability to delegate responsibility as major faults. Others noted that as he spent more time socializing, allegedly using drugs, and as his increasingly difficult temperament became apparent, his business started to fail. In 1984, with tension mounting between the designer and NSI, Halston took a two-week vacation and never returned to Halston Enterprises. Until 1988 he kept trying to buy back a part of the company that bore his name from the various owners of the trademark, but he was unsuccessful. While negotiating one such buyback with Revlon, the owners of the trademark, in 1988, Halston tested positive for HIV. He died of complications from AIDS on 26 March 1990.

Mr. Clean

Halston was known for his minimalistic approach to fashion, and his signature looks were spare, fluid, and often deceptively simple. He married the ease and comfort of sportswear with ready-to-wear and then raised the bar with luxurious fabrics and his distinct eye for cut and proportion. Halston has been credited with creating a unique new look, an original American way of dressing. His clothes were a representation of his own pared-down lifestyle. Many say that his life and his work were one and the same. In simplifying fashion for modern lifestyles without sacrificing glamour and luxury, he influenced many other designers. "Halston was one of the most influential designers of our time," said Donna Karan, quoted in Gross and Rottman (p. 225). "I say that on a personal level, because when I was young, he was the designer I aspired to be like. He understood luxury, glamour, simplicity, fit and the importance of uniform. To me, he represented all that was modern and pure. What more could a designer hope to be?" Narciso Rodriguez, also a fan, said, "Halston changed the face of fashion and the way women dressed with a clean and pure look. Within its purity there was extreme femininity and sexiness. His slink dress as well as his double faced coats both maintained his clean, sensual line with brevity of construction. He is one of my heroes!" (Gross and Rottman, p. 225.)

In her book *The Fashion Makers*, Bernadine Morris wrote, "A nod from Halston and a fashion is flashed around the world" (p. 90). After Halston fell in love with Ultrasuede in 1971, he went on to use the fabric in everything from suits and coats to his famous shirtdress. As a result, Ultrasuede became as famous as Halston himself.

When he tied a sweater around his models' shoulders, the look was adopted by fashionable women everywhere. Other designs also became Halston trademarks: the strapless dress, dresses made of draped rayon matte jersey, cashmere knits, caftans, one-shoulder and halter dresses, and asymmetrical necklines. He was well known for his love of the bias cut and his single-seamed spiral and wrapped dresses. In 1976 the designer created his first perfume, the enormously successful Halston. The Elsa Peretti–designed tear-shaped bottle was so recognizable that Halston insisted that it not be stamped with his name. The only branding was a small paper band with the name "Halston" that was wrapped around the neck. It broke off when the bottle was opened.

There have been a number of attempts to re-launch the Halston brand in the twenty years since his death, but these attempts have led to creative instability and a revolving door of designers.

See also Dance and Fashion; Flocking; Hats, Women's; Ready-to-Wear; Retailing; Sportswear.

HALSTON'S CLIENTELE

Halston's most famous saying was "You're only as good as the people you dress." If that is true, he was better than good. He was good enough, in fact, to win five coveted Coty Fashion Critics Awards, the Oscars of the fashion industry. Halston's clientele list reads like a who's who of celebrities and socialites: Lauren Bacall, Marisa Berenson, Candice Bergen, Princess Grace of Monaco, Katherine Graham, Margaux Hemingway, Bianca Jagger, Liza Minnelli, Jackie Kennedy Onassis, Elsa Peretti, Barbara Cushing "Babe" Paley, Lee Radziwill, Elizabeth Taylor, and Barbara Walters.

Bibliography

Berkin, Lisa. "The Prisoner of 7th Avenue." *New York Times Magazine*, 15 March 1987.

Bowles, Jerry. "Will Halston Take Over the World?" *Esquire*, August 1975, p. 69.

Gross, Elaine, and Fred Rottman. *Halston: An American Original*. New York: HarperCollins Publishers, Inc., 1999.

Herald, Jacqueline. *Fashions of a Decade: The 1970's*. New York: Facts on File, 1990.

Milbank, Caroline Rennolds. *Couture: The Great Designers*. New York: Stewart, Tabori and Chang, 1985.

Morris, Bernadine. *The Fashion Makers*. New York: Random House, 1978.

Fred Rottman

HARTNELL, NORMAN

Norman Hartnell (1901–1979) was Britain's most successful and distinguished mid-twentieth-century couturier. He was the first in a wave of London-based designers to emerge in the 1920s and 1930s who offered wealthy British women an alternative to patronizing a court dressmaker or purchasing a Paris-designed model. His graceful, feminine designs, which combined dreamy nostalgia with fairy-tale glamour, appealed to English sensibilities. He excelled at making dresses for grand entrances and was equally at ease designing court-presentation dresses for debutantes and stage costumes for actresses. The latter were sophisticated and sexy as well as glamorous, but Hartnell is remembered for the romantic, quintessentially English gowns that he designed for the upper classes and the royal family. His role as dressmaker to Queen Elizabeth, consort of King George VI, and Queen Elizabeth II won him international recognition and honors. He was nominated an *officier d'académie* by the Institut de l'education nationale de France in 1939 and was given a Neiman Marcus Award for contemporary influence on fashion in 1947. In 1977 he became the first fashion designer to be knighted.

The theater, ballet, fine art, and the natural world inspired Hartnell. As an undergraduate at Cambridge University, he neglected his architectural studies to design for the university's amateur dramatic societies and then dropped out of school to try his luck as a dress designer. After working briefly as a sketch artist, he set up on his own in 1923 and in 1934 moved to 26 Bruton Street. He made his name designing for debutantes, society weddings, and charity galas, many of which required fancy dress and Hartnell's talents as a stage designer. In 1942 he was a founding member of

> Commenting on how the creative impulse is evoked, Hartnell remarked, "Who can say exactly . . .? A wax-white magnolia in the moonlight is a debutante dancing at Hurlingham. Swans on the lake may turn into a young woman in white arriving to cut the cake at Queen Charlotte's Ball, and a farmyard is redolent of sporting tweeds." (Hartnell, p. 82)

the Incorporated Society of London Fashion Designers and was named president several times. After World War II, Hartnell was the largest couture house in London, employing a staff of 385.

Hartnell designed clothing for members of the royal family from 1935. His most legendary commission was the all-white wardrobe he designed for Queen Elizabeth for her 1938 state visit to France, when she was still in mourning for her mother. Hartnell and the photographer Cecil Beaton created a lasting image for the queen that was fresh and feminine but unmistakably regal. In 1947 he designed Princess Elizabeth's wedding dress and, six years later, her coronation robes. Hartnell relished the symbolism and pageantry of British ceremonial and found embroidery, which had already become his signature, the perfect medium for conveying the gravity and glamour of monarchy.

Drama, color, and light suffused Hartnell's designs. He enjoyed working with soft, floating fabrics, particularly tulle and chiffon, and with plain, lustrous silks, which provided the perfect foil for his spectacular, eye-catching embroideries. He was the master of the special-occasion dress that flatters and dignifies both wearer and occasion with consummate tact. His legacy to the future lay in his Englishness, in his creative and romantic engagement with history and tradition, and in his love of spectacle.

See also Court Dress; Embroidery; Fancy Dress; Royal and Aristocratic Dress; Theatrical Costume; Wedding Costume.

Bibliography

Brighton Art Gallery and Museums and the Museum of Costume. *Norman Hartnell*. Haslemere, U.K.: South Leigh Press, 1985. Well-illustrated and an excellent overview of Hartnell's career.

Hartnell, Norman. *Silver and Gold*. London: Evans Brothers, 1955.

McDowell, Colin. *A Hundred Years of Royal Style*. London: Muller, Blond and White, 1985.

Edwina Ehrman

HAUTE COUTURE

Historically, aristocratic and upper-class women's fashionable Western dress was created by an intimate negotiation between the client and her dressmaker. The investment in the design was principally in the cost of the luxurious textile itself, not in its fabrication. The origins of the haute couture system were laid by the late seventeenth century as France became the European center for richly produced and innovative luxury silk textiles. Thus the preeminent position of France's luxury textile industry served as basis and direct link to the development of its haute couture system. The prestigious social and economic value of an identifiable couturier, or designer's name, is a development of the late nineteenth and early twentieth centuries.

Beginning in the mid-nineteenth century, the Paris-based haute couture created a unique fashion system that validated the couturier, a fashion designer, as an artist and established his or her "name" as an international authority for the design of luxurious, original clothing. Couturiers were no longer merely skilled artisans, but creative artists with identifiable names printed or woven into a petersham waist tape that was sewn discreetly into the dress or bodice. This was the beginning of designer labels in fashion. The client was required to visit the couture house where a garment was made to measure to high-quality dressmaking and tailoring standards.

The couture house workrooms are carefully distributed according to sewing techniques. The sewing staff are divided between two areas: dressmaking (*flou*), for dresses and draped garments based upon feminine dressmaking techniques, or tailoring (*tailleur*), for suits and coats utilizing male tailoring techniques of construction. The staff work according to a hierarchy of skills ranging from the *première*, head dressmaker or tailor, to apprentices. The selling areas, salons, are equally controlled and run by the *vendeuse*, saleswoman, who sells the designs to clients and negotiates the fabrication and fittings with the workrooms.

The British-trained tailor and dressmaker Charles Frederick Worth is commonly credited as being the "father" of haute couture. What was radical in the mid-nineteenth century was that a male was creating women's fashion, a situation that required intimacy between a dressmaker and client, and had previously been a female-dominated profession. Worth's designs also commanded high prices that were a substantial investment in the garment itself and his associated and recognizable design style. This significant shift established the profession of fashion designer of women's garments as a suitable and profitable one for men. Worth worked directly with the French silk weaving industry to access and promote the original, luxury textiles that were a signature of his production. His clientele included the nobility of European courts as well as the new haute bourgeoises who followed his advice on appropriate dress for day to evening wear. Worth and his contemporaries, particularly Doucet, introduced innovations that have become standards for haute couture establishments. They created luxurious Paris salons to which wealthy clients came rather than the couturier visiting his patrons at their homes; they created artistic designs from which clients could select and that were made to measure; they also employed live mannequins who modeled the designs for private individuals. Thus the haute couture system of luxury dressmaking production was created.

In 1868, Worth instigated a new group called *La Chambre Syndicale de la confection et de la couture pour dames et fillettes*. This body, an outgrowth of the medieval guild system, was formed as a collective or type of union that could lobby and deal with issues related to labor, taxes, administration, and production for dressmakers. At this time there was little distinction between *couture*, clothing made to measure, and *confection*, ready-made clothing. In 1910, the two activities were clearly divided and the nomenclature *la haute couture* was strictly reserved for couture salons that produced collections for private clients, not solely for professional buyers. The newly named *Chambre Syndicale de la haute couture parisienne* outlined specific rules for membership that evaluated the creativity of designs and the quality of fabrication that had to be made to measure for the client, and also instituted regulations concerning the sale of designs and reproductions. The issue of copying and design piracy was of constant concern to the haute couture industry that relied upon exclusivity to retain design supremacy and its resultant high prices. The creation of PAIS (*L'Association de protection des industries artistiques saisonnières*) in 1921 by Madeleine Vionnet aimed to protect individual haute couture designs. Designs were photographed on a mannequin, front, back and side, and these documentary design records were registered with PAIS, thereby intending to discourage piracy and could be used as evidence if required. Allegations of design piracy were dealt with under the French penal code. This service was later taken over by the *Chambre Syndicale* in 1943. By 1930, the *Chambre Syndicale* established a formal calendar of fashion shows that were coordinated, consecutive, not concurrent, and able to accommodate the increasing numbers of foreign buyers and journalists to the collections.

In 1929, the *Chambre Syndicale de la haute couture parisienne* established vocational sewing and design training in its associated schools under the Ministry of National Education. The school offered an apprenticeship of three years that began with practical sewing skills in the first year, garment construction techniques in the second, and women's tailoring and draping in the third year. Two more years were available to a select few thought capable of working as first hands within a couture salon and who could train heads of workrooms and potentially be creative designers. These schools and courses continue to operate in the early 2000s.

In 1939, there were seventy haute couture salons. However, World War II (1939–1945) and particularly the German Occupation of Paris, created a crisis in the industry. The Nazis wanted to move the Paris haute couture industry to Berlin or Vienna, but the president of the *Chambre Syndicale*, the couturier Lucien Lelong, successfully negotiated to keep it in operating in Paris. After the Liberation of Paris the haute couture industry needed to recapture the North American buyers and manufacturers in order to reinstate France's historical position as the center of fashion design and also in order to rebuild a fragile economy and industry. Even before the war, the principal client was no longer the private client, but the commercial buyer and the attendant fashion press, and this situation was heightened after the war. This was clearly reflected in the schedule of showings of the collections set by the *Chambre Syndicale* that showed to the North American commercial buyers, then the European buyers, and finally to private clients. Postwar recognition of the importance of the Paris haute couture for fashion design leadership was internationally recognized after 1947 with the acclaim of the new house of Christian Dior (founded in 1945) by Carmel Snow in the American fashion magazine *Harper's Bazaar*.

In 1945, the *Chambre Syndicale* introduced more rigorous regulations intended to further control the quality and prestige of the haute couture industry in the difficult immediate postwar years. Haute couture was divided into two classes: *Couture*, and the more prestigious *Couture-Création*. An haute couture house had to apply for membership that was reviewed annually. The application made by a couturier for the classification *Couture-Création* covered several areas: at least twenty-five designs had to be created in-house, spring and fall, and made up on a live mannequin. The collection was then to be presented on live mannequins, and in an "appropriate" setting in the haute couture house located in Paris. The rules also covered the technical execution of the original models, the repetitions to be made in-house to clients' measurements, the number of fittings required and at what stage in the making, and the sales of the designs.

The 1950s were years of huge profits and press and the continuation and emergence of new haute couture salons. The most important, and largest, houses in terms of production were those of Christian Dior, Pierre Balmain, and Jacques Fath. The postwar years continued and consolidated the prewar situation that was shifting the economic basis of the houses from private sales to the commercial buyers. The large market for haute couture was as a design source. Couture was copied and adapted to limited editions, or line for line copies, a process that began in the 1930s, as well as for mass-market fashions. Haute couture houses sold the original models as well as *toiles* (muslins) and paper patterns, all of which was regulated by the *Chambre Syndicale*.

This situation stimulated many new initiatives from the Paris couture to control their designs and for the design houses to directly profit from them. Christian Dior began his own licensing arrangements with Christian Dior, New York, and Jacques Fath entered into the American ready-to-wear market with Joseph Halpert.

THE USE OF TOILE

A couturier's design was usually first created in inexpensive muslin, called a toile, so as to perfect the design, cut, and fit. These toiles record the exact cut and sewing techniques, and include samples of the inter-linings, linings, and fabric required in the final garment. Paper patterns were also used to replicate designs.

Increasingly couturiers opened boutiques within their couture salons in order to sell less expensive versions of their haute couture lines as well as accessories, a development begun by Paul Poiret in the early twentieth century. The society *Les Couturiers associés*, founded in 1950 by Jacques Fath, Robert Piguet, Jean-Marc Paquin, Marie-Louise Carven, and Jean Dessès, was a precursor to the creation of prêt-à-porter designed by couturiers who sold readymade designs to French department stores. A similar initiative, *Le Prêt-à-porter Création* (1958–1962) was directly aimed at international buyers and press. It ceased as ready-to-wear collections by couture houses became firmly established. However, the successful governance of the *Chambre Syndicale* over the couture houses, and its huge success during the 1950s is reflected in prosperity of the haute couture that in 1959 exported garments worth 20 million francs, and 3,000 workers were employed on a full-time basis, totaling 100,000 hours per week for most of the year.

The Paris haute couture system was such a successful formula for attracting sales, prestigious clients, commercial buyers, and international press that all other couture organizations were based upon this French model. In 1942, the Incorporated Society of London Fashion Designers was formed in England; in Spain during World War II the Cooperativa de Alta Costura was formed in Barcelona; the first Italian couture collective was shown in Florence in 1951; and the Association of Canadian Couturiers was founded in 1954. However, no other nation managed to create a haute couture industry that was as prestigious or economically important as Paris. The French system was historically based on its luxury textile industry and its ancillary industries of beading, embroidery, ribbons, and lace as well as its highly skilled artisans

The craft base of haute couture was financially difficult to maintain in an increasingly industrialized society. The numbers of couture house fell from 106 in 1946 to 19 by 1970. The establishment of quotas and high custom duties resulted in radical declines of haute couture exports and served to intensify the commercialization of rights for reproduction and licensing agreements. In 1953–1954, Pierre Cardin presented his first prêt-àporter collection and made it a separate department within the house in 1963. In 1966, Yves Saint Laurent created Saint Laurent Rive Gauche, the first freestanding couture boutique. Sociocultural shifts and an emphasis on youthful fashion instead of designs for mature women caused the breakdown of uniformity in the women's wear market, and resulted

in the haute couture's departure as the only or leading source for international fashion design. The more profitable ready-to-wear market necessitated new initiatives for the haute couture houses, which began to create new, less expensive noncouture lines marketed with labels associated with the prestige of the haute couture house.

The 1970s and 1980s were years of crisis and reconstruction for the haute couture, as the United States was no longer the primary market that it had been since the 1930s. In 1973 the *Chambre Syndicale de la couture parisienne* joined with the Prêt-à-porter federation, and became *La Fédération français de la couture, du prêt-à-porter des couturiers et des créateurs de mode*, and in 1975 joined with the *Fedération de l'union nationale des artisanale de la couture et des activités connexes*. In the early 2000s the organization has approximately 500 members and promotes French fashion at home and abroad. The consortium of French luxury products led by the group LVMH (Louis Vuitton Moët Hennessy) created by Bernard Arnault, bought out the leading names of the haute couture. In the early 1980s, Christian Lacroix renewed the 1930s house of Jean Patou, where he was artistic director from 1981 to 1987, and Parisienne haute couture was front-page fashion news as it had been in the 1950s and early 1960s. Karl Lagerfeld designed for Chloé and resuscitated the house of Chanel by cleverly employing all the Chanel hallmarks of design (logo, chains, cardigan suit jacket, loose tweeds, and so forth) and updating them for a younger market. The designer signature and logo became ubiquitous and familiar on an enormous range of products from fashion to home furnishings. Once again haute couture was worn and promoted by international celebrities and equally famous and highly paid super models. In 1987, Arnault invested millions in the new haute couture house of Christian Lacroix, which had a similar impact on the revitalization and public interest in the haute couture industry that Marcel Boussac's investment in the opening of the house of Christian Dior had immediately after World War II in 1946. During the 1990s, LVMH purchased Dior, Lacroix, Givenchy, Celine, Kenzo in a restructuring aimed at reclaiming French fashion design leadership, which had been overtaken by Italian and Japanese high-end ready-to-wear fashions. Celebrity designers were selected to design the Paris haute collections. Claude Montana worked for the house of Jeanne Lanvin from 1990 to 1992, and young, radical, Brits John Galliano and Alexander McQueen designed for Givenchy. In

1996, Galliano was placed as the chief haute couture designer for the most prestigious house of Christian Dior as a replacement for Gianfranco Ferre. Few couture houses have kept their independence in an increasingly global and conglomerate economy. The houses of Pierre Cardin, André Courrèges, Patou, and Phillipe Venet all ceased haute couture production, leaving only eighteen haute couture establishments by 1996. The 2002 retirement of Yves Saint Laurent closed one more establishment, but the new couture collection of Jean Paul Gaultier resulted from success as a ready-to-wear designer, a twenty-first-century inversion of the couture tradition.

In the early 2000s the business of haute couture is viewed as a costly and luxurious design laboratory that attests to and sustains France's international cultural position as a taste leader. Though haute couture posts enormous financial losses and produces less than 10 percent of the French clothing industry, the salons garner fantastic international press and prestige for the house name, which fuels lucrative licensing agreements for ready-to-wear collections, perfumes, accessories, and domestic products.

See also Balmain, Pierre; Cardin, Pierre; Courrèges, André; Dior, Christian; Doucet, Jacques; Lagerfeld, Karl; McQueen, Alexander; Patou, Jean; Worth, Charles Frederick.

Bibliography

Antoine-Dariaux, Geneviève. *Elegance: A Complete Guide for Every Woman Who Wants to Be Well and Properly Dressed on All Occasions*. Garden City, N.Y.: Doubleday, 1964.

Dior, Christian. *Dior by Dior*. Translated by Antonia Fraser. London: Weidenfeld and Nicolson, 1957.

Fraser-Cavassoni, Natasha, and Jennifer Jackson Alfano. "Couture's Big Spenders." *Harper's Bazaar*, October 2002, pp. 88ff.

Grumbach, Didier. *Histoires de la Mode*. Paris: Seuil, 1993.

Lynam, Ruth, ed. *Couture: An Illustrated History of the Great Paris Designers and Their Creations*. New York: Doubleday, 1972.

Palmer, Alexandra. *Couture and Commerce: The Transatlantic Fashion Trade in the 1950s*. Vancouver: University of British Columbia Press, 2001.

Picken, Mary Brooks. *Dressmakers of France: The Who, Why and How of French Couture*. New York: Harper and Brothers, 1956.

Steele, Valerie. *Paris Fashion: A Cultural History*. New York and Oxford: Oxford University Press, 1988.

Troy, Nancy J. *Couture Culture: A Study in Modern Art and Fashion*. Cambridge, Mass.: MIT Press, 2003.

Veillon, Dominique. *La mode sous L'Occupation: Débrouillardise et coquetteries dans la France en guerre (1939–1945)*. Paris: Payot, 1990.

Alexandra Palmer

HAWES, ELIZABETH

Elizabeth Hawes (1901–1971) belonged to the first generation of American designers who succeeded in making a name for themselves as individuals outside the sphere of the Parisian couture. In 1925 Hawes graduated from Vassar College, where she was an economics major sympathetic to socialism, but she pursued an interest in fashion by participating in school theatricals and making her own clothes. By graduation she had decided to go to Paris and learn fashion design. Hawes spent the next three years in various positions within the couture business: as a design copyist, journalist, and assistant designer. During this time she wrote a fashion column for *The New Yorker*, using the pen name "Parisite." She also worked briefly for Nicole Groult, the sister of the designer Paul Poiret. Her life in Paris was divided between socializing with her wealthy Vassar friends and engaging in the bohemian life; she spent much of her time with an artistic crowd, including the sculptors Alexander Calder and Isamo Noguchi.

Hawes's Vassar education gave her the critical faculty to dissect the couture industry and the fashion press, while her social connections and her exposure to couture at the highest levels left her ambivalent about fashion, a feeling that grew all the stronger for her love of its creative potential. In 1928 Hawes returned to New York and started her own custom dressmaking business with a Vassar classmate, Rosemary Harden. Harden left the business one year later, and Hawes decided to continue on her own as Hawes, Inc. Advertising, for which Hawes herself wrote the copy, helped business pick up significantly. Calder and Noguchi designed decorative objects for her New York showroom and influenced Hawes's own work. In 1930 Hawes married the artist Ralph Jester, whom she had known in Paris; they divorced in 1934.

Fashion and Politics

In 1932 Hawes and two other young American designers were promoted by the Lord and Taylor department store. This was one of the earliest attempts (if not the first) to prove that there was homegrown talent worthy of the public's notice. Hawes fully understood the power of publicity and exploited it. The ensembles in her collections were named according to themes: Spring/Summer 1933 was political, and the collection included such ensembles as "The Five Year Plan," a cotton nightgown and bed jacket; "the Yellow Peril," a silk afternoon dress; and "Disarmament," an embroidered evening dress. Her work was characterized by a bold use of fabrics—wide strips and large prints were used in simple, comfortable silhouettes. Hawes was an early advocate of trousers for women and wore them often herself.

In 1935 Hawes traveled to the Soviet Union to explore her growing interest in mass-produced clothing; as part of this trip, she showed some of her designs to members of the Soviet State Clothing Production Board, known as the Soviet Dress Trust. During her trip to the Soviet Union, she was accompanied by the theatrical director Joseph Losey, whom she married in 1937. The next year brought the birth of their son, Gavrick, and the publication of her first major work as an author: *Fashion Is Spinach*. This was Hawes's manifesto, and in it she expounds on the difference between "style" and "fashion" and how women are manipulated by the fashion industry:

> Style . . . gives you the fundamental feeling of a certain period in history. Style doesn't change every month or every year. . . . Fashion is that horrid little man with an evil eye who tells you that last winter's coat may be in perfect physical condition, but you can't wear it. (pp. 5–6)

Hawes's criticism was not limited to women's clothing; she maintained that men needed to be freed from their conservative attitudes toward clothing. She staged an all-male fashion show in 1937, showing brightly colored clothes of her own design. This led to her next book, *Men Can Take It*, published in 1939. She could be considered the Dorothy Parker of fashion criticism, with her snappy tone and tell-it-straight attitude.

Career Change

Hawes, Inc., closed early in January 1940. The onset of World War II had firmly awakened Hawes's social conscience, and she felt that being a fashion designer was not an appropriate career for her at that time. She became committed to her career as a writer, becoming involved in writing for the new left-wing paper, *PM*. In 1943 she took a job in a munitions factory for three months and then relocated to Detroit to work for the United Auto Worker's Union, where she also wrote for the *Detroit Free Press*. The result of her war work was her fifth book, *Why Women Cry; or, Wenches with Wrenches* (1943).

In 1948 Hawes made a last attempt at the fashion business and reopened Hawes, Inc., for eleven months. To demonstrate the timelessness of her designs, she played a game at the inaugural show, making guests guess which designs were new and which were from 1930s collections. Hawes settled in Southern California in the early 1950s. While she experimented with the production of knitwear, creating simple shapes decorated with abstract patterns, she spent the majority of her time writing. Her most rewarding experience during this period was her association with the young designer Rudi Gernriech, in whom she found a kindred spirit. In 1967 a retrospective of their work was mounted at the Fashion Institute of Technology.

Hawes moved back to New York in 1967 and lived in the Chelsea Hotel until her death on 6 September 1971. In total, she published nine books on fashion and culture as well as numerous articles in journals ranging from the left-leaning *PM* to the *Ladies' Home Journal*. In reality, her clothes did not appear radical for their time; it was her outspoken philosophy that set her apart.

See also Fashion Designer; Fashion Journalism; Paris Fashion; Politics and Fashion.

Bibliography

Berch, Bettina. *Radical by Design: The Life and Style of Elizabeth Hawes*. New York: E. P. Dutton, 1988.

Hawes, Elizabeth. "The American Designer Has Not Yet Been Born." *Magazine of Art* April 1937.

——. *Fashion Is Spinach*. New York: Random House, 1938.

Mahoney, Patrick. "In and Out of Style." *Vassar Quarterly* 82, no. 2 (Spring 1986): 8–10.

Steele, Valerie. *Women of Fashion: Twentieth-Century Designers*. New York: Rizzoli International, 1991.

Melinda Watt

HEAD, EDITH

Edith Head (1897–1981) was born in San Bernardino, California. In 1923, after a brief career as a schoolteacher, Head answered an advertisement for a sketch artist at Famous Players–Lasky (soon to be renamed Paramount Studios). Although she had very little artistic training, her versatility impressed Howard Greer, the chief costume designer, who hired her immediately. When Greer left Paramount in 1927, he was replaced by his assistant designer, Travis Banton. As chief designer, Banton costumed the stars at Paramount, while Head, who had been promoted to assistant designer, costumed the B-movie players and extras. When Banton left the studio in 1938, Paramount named Edith Head chief designer; she remained at the studio in this capacity until 1967. That same year she received a contract with Universal Studios, where she worked until her death in 1981. From the 1950s on, Head became a media personality through her regular appearances on the television show *Art Linkletter's House Party*. She also published two books: *The Dress Doctor* (1959) and *How to Dress for Success* (1967).

During her fifty-eight-year career, Head received more than one thousand screen credits, garnered thirty-five Oscar nominations, and won the Academy Award for costume design an unprecedented eight times. She was legendary for her ability to please difficult personalities and to camouflage figure problems. She was considered particularly skilled at defining character through costume, and her "character" costumes were among her most successful, including those for *Double Indemnity* (1944), *The Heiress* (1949), and *Sunset Boulevard* (1950). Head was especially proud of her work on *The Heiress*, for which she had traveled to the Brooklyn Museum of Art to conduct period research, winning her the first of her many Academy Awards. Her collaborations with the director Alfred Hitchcock were renowned, since Head shrewdly understood the importance of costume to Hitchcock's creative vision in his films *Rear Window* (1954), *To Catch a Thief* (1955), and *Vertigo* (1958).

Head's designs were also occasionally responsible for influencing popular fashions. Her costumes for the Mae West film *She Done Him Wrong* (1933) reputedly set off a flurry of Gay Nineties–inspired fashions, while the sarong worn by Dorothy Lamour in the film *The Jungle Princess* (1936) continued to influence styles well into the next decade. Her costumes for Barbara Stanwyck in *The Lady Eve* (1941), which featured bare midriffs and fringed bolero jackets, are said to have popularized Latin American styles. Her most influential design by far was the lilac-strewn gown worn by Elizabeth Taylor in *A Place in the Sun* (1951). The dress was a sensation in the teen market, and thousands of copies were sold.

Throughout her career, Head was criticized for taking credit for costumes she did not design and for exaggerating her influence on popular fashion. Despite these flaws, Head was undeniably one of the hardest-working talents in costume design and certainly one of the most versatile. Her intelligence and dedication secured her position both in the Hollywood studio system and in the history of fashion.

See also Costume Designer; Film and Fashion.

Bibliography

Chierichetti, David. *Edith Head: The Life and Times of Hollywood's Celebrated Costume Designer*. New York: HarperCollins Publishers, Inc., 2003.

Epstein, Beryl Williams. "Edith Head." In *Fashion Is Our Business*. Philadelphia: J. B. Lippincott, 1945.

Head, Edith, and Jane Kesner Ardmore. *The Dress Doctor*. Boston: Little, Brown and Company, 1959.

Head, Edith, with Joe Hyams. *How to Dress for Success*. New York: Random House, 1967.

LaVine, W. Robert. *In a Glamorous Fashion: The Fabulous Years of Hollywood Costume Design*. New York: Charles Scribner's Sons, 1980.

Clare Sauro

HEADDRESS

Headdress is an elaborate, ornamental, or practical covering for the head, as differentiated from the hat, which has a crown, and includes many varieties such as the hairnet, headband, head wrap, wreath or chaplet, mantilla, turban, crown, and others. Headdresses incorporate complex meanings including religious symbolism, political power and affiliation, social status or rank, and fashion consciousness. Made of numerous materials, designs, shapes, and embellishments, headdresses can also serve practical purposes—protecting the head against natural elements, carrying objects like weapons, baskets, or water pots—and are often associated with ceremonies, particularly rites of passage.

Hairnets

Hairnets may be the oldest headdresses worn by humans. A mammoth-ivory figurine dated circa 36,000 B.C.E. and found at Brassempouy (Las Landes), France, shows a human face with hair possibly braided and covered with what appears to be a netting. Bronze Age second millennium B.C.E. hairnets of horsehair using the sprang or twisted-thread technique were found in Borum Eshøj, Denmark, and are preserved in the National Museum, Copenhagen. Complementing long, unfitted robes, a fashionable silk hairnet, known as a crespine, was worn with head and chin bands by upper-class women during the late thirteenth century C.E. in medieval Europe. By the 1500s, as Renaissance styles spread from Italy to northern Europe, ornate gold cord mesh, pearl-studded nets called cauls became fashionable. A modern version of the Renaissance-style silk-knobbed hairnet, Goyesca, which cascades down to a tassel is still worn at Spanish festivals. It commemorates Francisco Goya (1746–1828) who painted celebrating peasants of both sexes wearing tasseled hairnets. By the 1920s, new cropped and wavy hairstyles on European and American women led to the mass production and marketing of fine human hairnets, particularly for outdoor wear. Within a few years, international designers such as Elsa Schiaparelli (1930s) and Sally Victor (1940s) popularized the "snood" style hairnet, often made of chenille, cord, or ribbon and attached to a hat.

Headband Bandeau

Modern headbands, originally made of knitted wool, cotton, and later of natural and synthetic fiber mixtures, have many functions besides holding the hair in place. Athletes such as marathon runners, skiers, basketball, and tennis players wear them across the forehead to absorb perspiration. Political advocates use them like earlier hatbands to make public statements. In 1893, native Hawaiians in Western clothing appeared on Honolulu streets wearing hatbands with the words Aloha Aina ("Love of Country") indicating their loyalty to Queen Liliuokalani and opposing U.S. annexation. World War II Japanese kamikaze pilots wore white samurai headbands (hachi-make), with a red rising-sun emblem and the words "Absolute Victory" in black Japanese calligraphy, while participating in rituals before flying off

on suicide missions against U.S. targets; and in 2003, exiled protesters demonstrating against their country's ruling military dictatorship wore red headbands with white stars, symbolizing the Burmese peoples, outside Burma's Embassy in Bangkok, Thailand.

Aesthetically, headbands are part of many ethnic costumes. On the Indonesian islands of Bali and Sulawesi, men wear cotton batikked headbands (formed from a folded square of cloth) for everyday, ornamented brocades for festivals. Reflecting social rank, lace-edged cotton headbands were part of a maid's uniform in Europe and America, representing nineteenth- and twentieth-century middle-class gentrification, a carryover from earlier aristocratic livery customs.

Metal headbands worn across the top of the head hold earmuffs in place. Over centuries, in cold climates, earflaps on fur hats could be tied over the head or let down as desired. By the early twentieth century, with outdoor recreational sports gaining popularity, mass-produced metal-headband fur earmuffs came to be marketed for adults and children. The industrial revolution had another impact on ear protection, namely, against noise. By the 1920s, pilots flew open-cockpit planes wearing cloth "helmet" caps designed with inner pockets over the ears to hold noise-absorbent material. More recently, responding to concerns for worker safety, industrial earmuffs were introduced for preventing hearing loss caused by loud machinery noises. In the early 2000s, there are noise-reduction, liquid-foam filled cushioned earmuffs, cap-mounted earmuffs, a Velcro-adjustable type, and three-position version (over-the-head, behind-the-head, and under-the-chin). Most contemporary flight or fire-fighting helmets are additionally equipped with wired earmuffs allowing communication between the wearer and coworkers. Cyclers, hunters, and other sports enthusiasts can enjoy musical CDs, tapes, and radio broadcasts through ear covers, computer designed for lightweight comfort, portability, and noise attenuation.

Kerchief and Head Wrap

The kerchief, a cloth covering the head, from the French couvrir (to cover) and chief (head), is usually worn by women. Traditionally, European peasants wore a small cloth tied under the chin while working outside; thus, the kerchief became associated with rural women and later with lower-class city residents. As late as the 1950s, a domestic servant girl in Madrid, Spain, was considered breaking social barriers by wearing a hat rather than the kerchief assigned her class. Also called a bandanna, the kerchief did become a practical middle-class head cover used for riding in open automobiles.

The head wrap, a kerchief worn by tying over the forehead, is believed to have traveled with women from Senegal and Gambia (West Africa) along the slave trade routes to Caribbean Islands and ports in North and South America. The falla, a strip of cotton cloth tied around the head in eighteenth-century Gambia, may be the precursor to the head wrap later identified with adult female slaves. Imported into New Orleans possibly by way of the French colonies Martinique and St. Dominique, the head wrap when worn by free women of color, became a nineteenth-century fashion called Tignon, created from brightly-colored madras, occasionally adorned with jewels and feathers.

Spanish Mantilla

Usually black or white, the mantilla may derive from *manton* (mantle or cape) worn both indoors and outdoors during the Muslim rule of Spain. Mantillas (small capes) were originally head coverings of handmade silk lace, often imported from Chantilly, France, and worn by aristocratic women, as documented in portraits by Velasquez (c. 1625) and Goya (1792). By the nineteenth century, a popular hairstyle, the chignon, provided suitable positioning for high, decorative combs (tortoiseshell, silver, ivory) to support larger mantillas—some measuring 7 × 3 feet—which drape over the shoulders. This style is commonly worn for special events such as Holy Week processions and community fiestas. Redsilk knobbed mantillas are occasionally worn by unmarried young women to bullfights. Romantic myths transported to Spanish colonies in Latin America (Mexico) and the Philippines depict señoritas in white mantillas on balconies listening to guitar-playing suitors. Because of their cost, mantillas are often passed down from mother to daughter as family heirlooms. The lace mantilla, without a comb, was a French fashion during the 1920s and 1930s.

Royal Headdresses

Since antiquity, rulers have worn impressive and costly headdresses, visible symbols of their power and claims to divinity. Prehistoric peoples stressed survival; their practical head coverings were made of animal skins in northern regions, twisted straws in warm climes. With the evolution of complex population centers, textile production and class stratification emerged in Mesopotamia, which resulted in Sumerian turbans and head wraps (3000 B.C.E.), and later splendid regal twisted hair and headbands during the Akkadian era (2250 B.C.E.). Egyptian royal ceremonial headdresses of the New Kingdom (c. 1580–1085 B.C.E.) were extremely precious, some made of gold decorated with inlaid carnelian, colored glass, and ostrich feathers.

The Ancient Greek korone (crown), a golden circlet or gold wreath, symbolized political and military power during the fourth century B.C.E. Macedonian era, while Olympic champions were crowned with nature cult head-pieces: laurel, olive, pine, or celery wreaths. Adopting Greek depictions of gods, especially Apollo, many Roman emperors were portrayed on coins wearing the laurel wreath. Christian monarchs since Charlemagne have worn bejeweled crowns with a cross symbolizing their power as God-given.

Gigantic turbans, three to four times the head size, usually wrapped around a tall hat, adorned the heads of Ottoman sultans including Süleyman I in early sixteenth-century Istanbul. For public occasions, Manchu royalty in China wore ornate cone-shaped, silkcovered head-pieces, with imperial insignia above a tall gold finial intricately decorated with dragons, Buddhas, and pearls. But the nonofficial headdress worn by the Empress Dowager Cixi and her courtiers (1903) was more striking. Bat-wing shapes of false hair and black satin were arranged over a wide frame with large artificial flowers and long silk tassels dangling from the sides.

For centuries, Japanese emperors have worn the black lacquered ceremonial headpiece (kanmuri) with a birdlike tail made of fine horsehair, associated with Shinto priests and courtiers. Because of his role as intermediary between humans and gods, only the emperor wore the tail vertically.

Glass beads, cowrie shells, and feathers are the precious materials used for elaborate headdresses of many African chieftains. A Yoruba king in Nigeria, who represents the collective destiny of his people, wears a tall conical beaded headdress asserting his authority in social, political, and religious matters. Numerous strands of beads hang from the royal headdress hiding his face, which is considered powerful and dangerous. The headdress, which represents the king, must be given reverence in his absence.

A 46-inch-high Aztec headdress (kopilli ketzalli), popularly called "Montezuma's Crown" and adorned with over 400 Quetzal bird feathers, is exhibited at Vienna's Hofburg Museum of Ethnology in the early

2000s. For Aztecs, the number 400 represented eternity; only the highest-ranking ruler could wear 400 feathers of this sacred bird, associated with wisdom, peace, and freedom. The headdress supposedly was taken by Spanish invaders under Cortez and sent in 1524 as a present to Hapsburg ruler Charles V, then Holy Roman Emperor and king of Spain. Since the early 1990s, Yankuikanahuak, an association fostering revival of native Indian cultures supported by the Mexican government, has been lobbying the United Nations and the Austrian government to return this sacred relic to its rightful homeland. Similar efforts have taken place in the United States. Under the Native American Graves Protection and Repatriation Act, an eight-foot-long war bonnet, made of thirty-five sacred bald and golden eagle feathers each measuring one foot, and claimed to have belonged to the renowned nineteenth-century Apache Chief Geronimo, came under government protection for return to tribal ownership.

Wedding Headdresses

In many cultures and religious traditions, elaborate wedding headdresses become ritual objects. The Mien mountain tribal peoples of Laos and Thailand in the Golden Triangle emphasize a complex structure on the bride's head. Her hair, coated with beeswax, is pulled through a tube projecting from a large board on her head above which a vault (like a roof truss) is created from bamboo sticks. A red-embroidered patterned fabric covers the whole ensemble. After two days of ceremonies, the headdress is removed indicating the bride's acceptance as a full member of the groom's household.

For festivals, including weddings, Hmong (Miao) women in China's Yunnan Province wear an elaborate black scarf measuring to 35 feet long that is wrapped around the head creating a plate shape. The headdress features an embroidered belt with dangling tassels or coins around its edge. Decorations include amuletic symbols: a spiral motif representing family; triangular patterns as "sacred mountains" protecting against evil spirits.

Traditional Japanese brides wear an elaborate hairstyle called Bunkin-Shimada. Hair decorations include a comb (*kushi*) and gold or silver multithreaded string folded in back in an elaborate shape. Hand-painted, lacquered floral-motif hairpins (*kanzashi*) may depict good-luck symbols such as pine trees for durability. Matching comb-and-hairpin sets are sold or rented in bridal stores. A white brocade band or hood (*tsuno-kakushi*), matching a white kimono, covers the elaborate

bridal-adorned coiffure. White symbolizes the bride's willingness to "color herself as the husband wishes." The term "tsuno-kakushi" combines the words for "horn" and "concealer." It is said the white hood hides horns of jealousy or hatred the wife might have toward her husband, in-laws, or neighbors. At ceremony's end, the bride removes the white headdress signifying she has left her family and adopted his.

In imitation of Ming empress crowns, Chinese brides wear an ornate phoenix headdress made of tiny gilded silver butterflies, flowers, and fruits dangling from wires, with inlaid kingfisher feathers (fertility and good-luck symbols) and embellished with strings of pearls hiding the bride's face. A large red veil completely covers the bride's head. Symbolism of the phoenix headdress and dragon motif on her robe associates the couple with the royal family, suggesting they are "emperor and empress" for the day.

Jewish wedding headgear incorporates local ethnic variations. One ornate example is the Yemenite bridal gargush, or hood, with its elaborate metallic ornamentation. Everyday gargushes are black cotton or velvet with a band of jewelry pendants (*agrat*), tiny silver rings, discs, and balls dangling over the forehead. Costly bridal gargushes are crafted from gold brocade decorated with golden agrats, golden chains (*khneishe, salsa*), valuable coins, and fine filigree pins (*koubleh*) of geometric shapes.

Crowns, wreaths, and veils are wedding head wear popularly used for Christian rituals. In Russian Orthodox ceremonies, ornate royal-style crowns with Christ and the Virgin icons are held over the bride and groom's heads. The couple is recognized as ruling a new kingdom, the home, where they are urged to live together as moral Christians.

Throughout Europe, peasants held spring flower festivals (Christian substitutes for earlier pagan fertility rites) and some groups adopted them for wedding celebrations. The white lace veil with orange blossom wreath became a classic after Queen Victoria's attire worn at her 1840 wedding to Prince Albert.

In the twenty-first century, Greek Orthodox couples wear wreaths of real, fabric, or artificial flowers joined together by a long ribbon representing their marital union. A similar practice of combining wedding headpieces is used by Buddhist couples in Thailand, where round white "Circles of Eternity" are joined by long strings.

See also Crowns and Tiaras; Hats, Men's; Hats, Women's; Helmet; Turban; Veils.

Bibliography

Arnoldi, Mary Jo, and Christine Mullen Kreamer. *Crowning Achievements: African Arts of Dressing the Head*. Los Angeles: Fowler Museum of Cultural History, University of California, 1995.

Biebuyck, Daniel P., and Nelly Van den Abbeele. *The Power of Headdresses*. Brussels, Belgium: Tendi, 1984.

Boucher, François. *20,000 Years of Fashion: A History of Costume and Personal Adornment*. New York: Harry N. Abrams, 1967.

Cocuzza, Dominique. "The Dress of Free Women of Color in New Orleans, 1780-1840." *Dress* 27, (2000): 78–87.

Foster, Helen Bradley. *New Raiments of Self and African American: Clothing in the Antebellum South*. Oxford and New York: Berg, 1997.

Garrett, Valery M. *Chinese Clothing, an Illustrated Guide*. Hong Kong: Oxford University Press, 1994.

Kilgour, Ruth Edwards. *A Pageant of Hats, Ancient and Modern*. New York: Robert M. McBride, 1958.

Lewis, Paul and Elaine. *Peoples of the Golden Triangle*. London: Thames and Hudson, Inc., 1984.

Rubens, Alfred. *A History of Jewish Costume*. New York: Crown Publishers, 1973.

Wilcox, R. Turner. *The Mode in Hats and Headdress*. New York: Charles Scribner's Sons, 1959.

Beverly Chico

HELMET

A helmet—a defensive covering for the head—is made of hard materials for resisting blows so as to protect ears, neck, eyes, and face. Helmets have been worn over centuries for military combat and ceremonies, later for hazardous occupations, and recently for sports. Helmet design fluctuated with changes in warfare and technology.

Ancient Helmets

Prehistoric peoples probably wore woven basketry or hide head protectors; ancient Ethiopians used horse skulls, manes, and tails. Archaeological evidence reveals that rawhide caps and copper helmets, protecting ears and neck nape—with chin straps and padded wool or leather lining—were worn by Sumerian, Babylonian, and Assyrian warriors during the third to first millennia B.C.E. Early Greek helmets were usually bronze hemispherical crowns. The Corinthian version incorporated a movable face mask; the Attic style had cheek guards (mentioned by Homer). Romans used Greek designs, including elaborate horsetail plumes; crested gladiator helmets were made of hammered bronze.

Middle Ages

European medieval helmets evolved from the seventh to seventeenth centuries as part of body armor, beginning with a boiled leather conical casque (*spangenhelm*) worn by tribal warriors over a hood of mail. During the feudal era, a large, heavy iron pot (*heaume*) protected the head from lances in chivalry tournaments, and the towering steel snouted visor (*basinet*) was worn in battle. Archers and pikemen used lighter, more flexible helmets with neck guards during the Hundred Years' War (c. 1337–1453).

By 1550, the Italian-invented *armet*, with its thin laminated iron or steel plates and joints providing ease of movement, was adopted by many armies in Europe. The crescent-shaped morion, copied from Moorish designs, protected sixteenth-century Spanish conquistadores in the New World against Indian bows and arrows.

Armor and helmet production reached its artistic zenith for knights and nobles during the sixteenth and seventeenth centuries; ornamental parade pieces often had embossed relief decorations reflecting Renaissance-style, Biblical, and mythological motifs, along with ostrich or peacock panaches. By the eighteenth and nineteenth centuries, when the ultimate weapon was a cannon, metal helmets were displaced by lighter, felt tricorne hats, lamb's fur busbys, and beaver-with-leather shakos.

Another head protector came into widespread use after the 1850s mutinies in Bengal, India, where British troops encountered light, strong helmets made from the dried pith of the solah or sponge wood plant. Subsequently, the "pith sun helmet" was adopted by England and other countries for overseas military campaigns and sports.

Modern Military

World War I technologically revolutionized warfare and weaponry. Shallow-crowned, felt-padded steel helmets protected combatants in trenches against automatic machine guns, replacing earlier spiked and plumed headgear. M-1 steel helmets of World War II infantry were more comfortable with an internal sweatband liner that rested lightly on the soldier's head. Serving multiple functions for the troops, helmets were used as washbasins, eating bowls, and cooking pans. Throughout the twentieth century, at military funerals, a soldier's helmet often sits atop a rifle symbolizing personal heroism and patriotism.

From 1970 to 1997, the U.S. Army Natick Research, Development, and Engineering Center in Massachusetts developed the standard Personnel Armor System Ground Troops (PASGT) helmet; its shell is a one-piece composite molded structure made of multiple levels of Kevlar aramid fiber. Inside is a cradle-type suspension providing space between the helmet and head for ventilation and deformation during impact. Cotton and nylon twill camouflage reversible covers reflect different environments: woodlands, snow, and daylight desert.

Continuing innovation, the twenty-first-century U.S. Army incorporates the most advanced high-tech features in its standard bulletproof Integrated Helmet Assembly Subsystem (IHAS). Its attachments, including night-vision goggles, allow for viewing the battlefield via digitized maps, messages, and sensor imagery generated from a personal computer and weapon sights, while receiving audio communications through a computer/radio subsystem composed of components embedded into the ballistic helmet shell. Defensively, the headgear also includes a chemical/biological protection mask and ballistic/laser eye protection.

Occupation Helmets

With nineteenth-century urban growth, larger police and fire units wearing military-style uniforms and helmets including chin straps, badges, and spikes encouraged esprit de corps. In 1863, London's Metropolitan Police began wearing the high-crowned dark serge-covered cork helmet (called "bobby hat" after the Tory prime minister Robert Peel, founder of the Metropolitan Police), similar to the lightweight pith helmet. Around 1900, a more practical, modern peaked hat was adopted in many countries, complemented decades later by titanium or plastic helmets with transparent anti-riot shields. Despite the changes, the English bobby hat survived.

Parisian fire brigades in the 1830s were outfitted with metal, gendarmerie cavalry visor casques. Wide-brimmed leather fire helmets, which (unlike metal) resisted retaining heat, were first used in New York (1740s) and spread to many areas over the next century. By 1959, U.S. government safety regulations began requiring the use of polycarbonate-plastic helmets that are impact, penetration, and water resistant, insulated against electrical charges, and self-extinguishing. Fire helmets of 2004 have transparent plastic face masks.

Coal and ore mining, which grew exponentially during the nineteenth century, gave little attention to head protection for workers. Leather or cloth caps had dangerous oil wick lamps attached for lighting. They were replaced by tin and fiber-compound helmets with carbide lamp attachments, which sometimes still caused explosions. The safest contemporary helmets have battery-powered electric lamps. The U.S. Department of Labor's Occupational Safety and Health Administration (OSHA) establishes regulations for industrial workers' hard hats, which come in varying types for use in construction, welding, electrical work, and mining, with appropriate accessories.

Sports Helmets

Protective helmets for sports were largely introduced in the twentieth-century Western world. Earlier, horseracing jockeys, polo players, and fencers wore head protectors. Advertisements for English bicycle manufacturers in the 1880s show cyclers wearing dark pith helmets. By 1915, bicycle racers wore heavy, round leather helmets, similar to those of aviators and American football players, although recreational cyclists went bareheaded. After World War II, the "hairnet" made of leather strips attached to a round base became popular for racers; its style was later incorporated into Styrofoam and plastic headgear providing increased comfort and protection.

As bicycle technology and design produced faster, more efficient vehicles and the number of cyclers grew to the millions, issues related to safety came to public attention. Beginning in 1957, the nonprofit Snell Memorial Foundation promoted helmet safety after the head-injury death of internationally renowned car racer Pete Snell the previous year. This foundation developed car racing helmet standards and later bicycle helmet criteria, which are used complementing rules set by the American National Standards Institute (A.N.S.I.). Legislation followed that mandated government-approved, laboratory-tested, head-protecting helmets, effective since the 1990s in many countries including Australia, New Zealand, Canada, and the United States

Also in the 1990s, participants in other individual sports, such as motorcycling, skateboarding, and snowboarding, began adopting helmets. Ski helmet use proliferated in 1998 after the accidental deaths of the celebrities Sonny Bono and Michael Kennedy.

Design and durability for recreation sport helmets is usually classified by motorized and nonmotorized sports, including specifications for adults, children, and toddlers. Car racing helmets have neck braces, like those designed for pilots. Rollerblading helmets have ear covers but an open aerodynamic design for air circulation. Helmets for the more dangerous sport of skateboarding incorporate additional padding and snug fit, and bicycle helmets vary according to use—road racing, mountain biking, or touring.

Many ski helmets incorporate a plastic shell over an inner Styrofoam liner with venting system for thermal protection. A few are made from lighter carbon or platinum materials. In the early 2000s ski racer, hockey, and football helmets have large extending chin protectors. Accessories include headphones or built-in speakers for radio communication, CDs, tapes, MP3 or mini disc listening, and cameras. Appealing to youth, helmet manufacturers produce a wide range of helmet colors and novelty decals.

Space Helmets

The most complex helmets ever created are for National Air and Space Administration (NASA) astronauts. They protect the wearer in alien environments against extreme temperatures (250° F to 250° below zero); micrometeoroids traveling up to 64,000 miles per hour; solar ultra-violet, infrared, and light radiation from the sun; and zero gravity conditions. The pressure helmet consists of a transparent polycarbonate (plastic) shell with aluminum neck ring that fits into and locks with the space suit neck ring. The helmet left side contains a feed port where water and food enter, and a purge valve. A vent port of synthetic elastomer foam is bonded in back with a ventilation opening. The helmet functions as an integral part of the astronaut's life-support system. Oxygen, warmed to avoid fogging the visor, enters the helmet rear and travels over the head downward to the front. Carbon dioxide exits, via a fan and tubing, along with respiration- and perspiration-caused humidity. These are also integrated with the Feed-water and Liquid Transport Systems, which cool the astronaut, and radio transmitter/receivers. Recent "micro display" technology provides a visual image inside the

helmet allowing technical diagrams to be beamed the astronaut.

See also Hats, Men's; Hats, Women's; Headdress; Military Style; Protective Clothing.

Bibliography

Alderson, Frederick. *Bicycling, a History*. New York: Praeger Publishers, 1992.

Howell, Edgar M. *United States Army Headgear to 1854*. Vol. I (1969); *United States Army Headgear 1855–1902*. Vol. II (1976). Washington, D.C.: Smithsonian Institution Press.

Les casques de combat: du monde entier de 1915 à nos jours. Paris: Lavauzelle, Vol. I, 1984. (Paolo Marzetti, *Combat Helmets of the World*, 3 vols.)

Nickel, Helmut, Stuart W. Pyhrr, and Leonid Tarassuk. *The Art of Chivalry, European Arms and Armor from the Metropolitan Museum of Art*. New York: American Federation of Arts, 1982.

Reynosa, Mark A. *The Personnel Armor System Ground Troops (PASGT) Helmet*. Atglen, Pa.: Schiffer Publishing Ltd., 1999.

Beverly Chico

HERMÈS

The world's most acclaimed maker and purveyor of status goods, Hermès has evolved from its days supplying harnesses to coach builders. The firm has been in family hands since it was begun in 1837, when Thierry Hermès (1801–1878), who had moved to France from Prussia in 1821, established his wholesale business near the old city wall on the rue Basse du Rempart in Paris.

In 1879 his son Émile-Charles Hermès (1835–1919) acquired the current flagship building at 24, rue du Faubourg Saint-Honoré and expanded the business into retailing by manufacturing and selling saddles along with related equestrian accoutrements. At the time the phrase "carriage trade" connoted the uppermost level of the haute monde: those who could afford to commission, equip, and maintain exquisite horse-drawn carriages, not to mention stables of purebred horses. Thus the Hermès clientele came to be composed of the upper crust of international society.

Somewhat unusually for a company associated with the stately past, Hermès adapted astutely to a rapidly changing world as the early twentieth century witnessed enormous changes in modes of transportation. Émile-Maurice Hermès (1870–1951), understood that people's preferred methods of travel had increasingly become an expression of their personae and position in society. Thus the company developed luggage, folding portable furniture, and other articles made specifically for travel by ocean liner, airplane, safari, or automobile. Nor was the world of the horse ignored, as riding became even more glamorous as a sport than it had been as a means of transportation.

Émile-Maurice's son-in-law Robert Dumas (1905–1978) was the next director of the company. Robert was succeeded by one of his sons, Jean-Louis Dumas (1938–), who held the reins after 1978. Numerous Hermès family members continued to be closely involved with the company, and the fact that it remained a family-run firm made all the difference in its continuing reputation for superb quality. At Hermès tradition and innovation were almost paradoxically intertwined; what might have seemed like mechanical precision was achieved by carefully nurtured and trained artisans working entirely by hand. Besides a level of quality against which all other quality goods were measured, Hermès came to be best known for several of its products that progressed from practical items to best-sellers to classics to cultural icons.

Hermès Handbags

Few articles of women's attire carried the significance of a Hermès handbag in the early 2000s. The Hermès Kelly and Birkin bags entered modern consciousness as icons laden with status. As a plot element in Diane Johnson's novel Le Divorce, the Kelly bag was instantly recognizable to those conversant in the language of status and society as a sign that the American-in-Paris Isabel Walker had acquired a well-heeled older lover. And Martha Stewart's carrying two Birkin bags—not just a black bag but a brown one as well—received international attention at her 2004 trial and might have contributed to the distance the jurors perceived between her lifestyle and theirs.

The haphazard path of the Kelly bag's journey to icon status was part of its appeal. Originally a large bag for holding a saddle when it was introduced around 1892, the prototype of the Kelly bag was known as the Haut à Courroies, indicating that it had a high handle.

During the 1930s the Haut à Courroies joined the Mallette and Bollide as roomy Hermès travel bags. An early depiction in the July 1937 issue of the French high-fashion magazine Femina showed two women waiting as a curved aerodynamic train pulled into the station. Both women were dressed in typically chic travel clothes of the period—sober and tailored. One carried a light-colored Mallette bag; the other, a dark and soft rather than stiff Kelly bag in dark leather. Both handbags represented a departure from the dominant purse of the 1930s, which was a simple flat small envelope.

The boxy Kelly bag got its nickname, famously, when Princess Grace of Monaco was shown on the cover of Life magazine in 1956 shielding her stomach with her handbag so as to ward off rumors (which would have been front-page news the world over) of her first pregnancy. In the 1950s Princess Grace was more than a fascinatingly beautiful style-setting woman; she was romance incarnate. She represented two types of American aristocracy—East Coast upper-class families and Hollywood celebrities—married to European royalty. Sales of the Kelly bag took off; it began to be used as a town bag, appropriate to wear with a tailored dress or suit.

Thirty or so years later, Jean-Louis Dumas chanced to sit next to the actress Jane Birkin on an airplane. Dismayed by the unkempt appearance of her straw carry-all, Dumas asked Birkin if she would help develop a new tote for the company. The much-coveted result was introduced in 1984. Like the Kelly, the Birkin bag had its origins in the world of luggage. An early version of the bag had appeared in a 1963 advertisement on top of a stack of small Hermès suitcases. That women of the early twenty-first century required the equivalent of antique luggage to help contain a day's necessities spoke volumes about their lives having become more rather than less complicated.

Many of the hundreds of Hermès handbags became classics, including Jacqueline Kennedy Onassis's favorites—the casual Trim, the more formal Constance with its large H-shaped clasp, and the Mangeoire, made like a horse's feed bucket with holes through which a scarf could be threaded. The Bollide, however, deserves special mention for its use of zippers. While in Canada during World War I, Émile-Maurice Hermès was intrigued by the sliding fastener used to close the top of his Cadillac convertible. Although Elsa Schiaparelli usually gets the credit for having discovered zippers, Hermès used them throughout the 1920s for all sorts of sports clothes, luggage, and purses, including the zippered and padlocked precursors of the Bollide and Plume handbags.

Hermès Scarves

The famous Hermès scarf, known as a silk carré or square, was launched in an advertisement in December 1936 as a coming attraction of 1937. Called "*Jeu des omnibus et dames blanches*," its pattern was based on a woodcut of an eighteenth-century game. Hermès scarves of the 1930s tended toward modernist geometric patterns. By designing a large square of silk printed with boldly scaled figural scenes, Hermès invented a whole new genre of fashion accessory, one that maintained its popularity for more than seventy years. Although all sorts of patterns came later—the stable of designs hovered around a thousand in the early 2000s—the typically bold scale of the patterns never wavered, and also influenced the design of high-fashion prints during the late 1980s. Besides the patterns, many based on Hermès's private museum holdings of art and antique objects, what made the scarves instantly recognizable as Hermès products was the quality of the crisp silk twill, woven in Lyons from raw silk from China, and the precision printing. Each scarf design made use of as many as forty-five screens and 75,000 tones, resulting in unparalleled brilliance of color.

Hermès Ties

The first Hermès ties for men were dark, with discreet geometric designs, and made their debut in 1953. After the 1960s Hermès ties were designed by Henri d'Origny. They typically featured small repeated equestrian or sailing-inspired patterns in dazzling colors not usually associated with menswear. Hermès ties were steadily popular for more than forty years, no small feat in the fickle world of fashion.

Hermès Fashions

At the turn of the twenty-first century, the global brand conglomerates that dominated the market for luxury goods vacillated between emphasizing star designers and brand names. Hermès had offered clothes for sport, both custom-made and ready-to-wear, since the 1920s, but the firm's typical style was better known than the contribution of any particular designer. Since the 1980s, the names of designers associated with Hermès included Eric Bergère and Martin Margiela—whose most lasting contribution may have been an accessory rather than a line of clothing, namely a double-wrapped watch strap. Jean Paul Gaultier, who presented his first collection for Hermès in the fall of 2004, tapped a mien conspicuously lacking from contemporary fashion—the insouciance of the aristocrat born with a good seat. Designs in this mood included fringed cashmere coats fitted like horse blankets that had been thrown around the shoulders and belted, and a leather corset reminiscent of a saddle fastened with the famous Hermès padlock in the style of a chastity belt.

See also Celebrities; Gaultier, Jean-Paul; Handbags and Purses; Leather and Suede; Margiela, Martin; Scarf; Schiaparelli, Elsa; Silk.

Bibliography

Nadelson, Reggie. "Out of the Box." *Departures* (May–June 2002): 142–178.

Remaury, Bruno, ed. *Dictionnaire de la mode au XXe siècle.* Paris: Editions du Regard, 1994.

Reynolds, C. P. "Hermès." *Gourmet*, February 1987, 42–122.

Caroline Rennolds Milbank

THE ORANGE BOX

Appropriately for a firm that can be said to have invented the nonprecious status object, the Hermès box itself became a coveted item, decorating glamorous foyers and boudoirs, and being auctioned off on Internet websites. The box's distinctive color and texture were originally designed to resemble pigskin, one of the most popular sporty materials used for Hermès products of the 1920s and 1930s.

HEROIN CHIC

At the U.S. Conference of Mayors on 21 May 1997, President Bill Clinton triggered a media furor on both sides of the Atlantic with his comments about the dangers of so–called heroin chic in contemporary fashion imagery. "You do not need to glamorize addiction to sell clothes," he asserted. "The glorification of heroin is not creative, it's destructive. It's not beautiful, it's ugly"

(White House Briefing Room p.1). The photographs in question showed emaciated models, eyes half-closed, skin pale and clammy, heads twisted in apparent abandon against a backdrop of seedy, anonymous hotel rooms and dirty apartments. Clinton's fears had been heightened by fashion photographer Davide Sorrenti's death at twenty-one, from a drug overdose on 4 February 1997. The gap between image-makers' and models' real lives and constructed fashion photographs blurred. Since the 1970s fashion designers' struggles with drug addiction, for example, Yves Saint Laurent and Roy Halston, had been related alongside discussions of their work and influences. In the 1990s media coverage merged actual drug abuse and fashion scenarios created to suggest decadent and nihilistic rejections of conventional notions of beauty. Clinton decried what he saw as fashion's glamorization of heroin use, and his words were reinforced by fashion journalists such as Amy Spindler of the *New York Times*, who felt that fashion insiders were irresponsible, that they ignored drug use by models and photographers, and that they made images that spoke of dark addictions in order to promote clothing and fashion ideals.

The ensuing media debate was further fueled by revelations of heroin abuse within the fashion industry. It is notable, though, that heroin chic existed only at the level of representation, in photographs and in styling for cat-walk shows, rather than in actual clothing. It was a conjuring of signifiers that were frequently intended to evoke a more realistic idea of beauty and which its creators felt linked to their everyday lives in a way that more traditional fashion photographs, which relied upon sanitized visions of artificially enhanced perfection, never could.

This realist aesthetic had evolved since the early 1990s, with the London-based photographers Corinne Day and David Sims, and German-born Juergen Teller highly influential in its formation. They worked with like-minded stylists, most importantly Melanie Ward (with Day) and Venetia Scott (with Teller), who sought out secondhand clothes to mix with designer and high street garments to create a mood or atmosphere that related to their own experiences. Their work responded to post-rave youth culture, disenchantment with politics, and the impact of the global recession. It drew upon the intensity and fluidity of the rave scene and the darker obsessions and sense of alienation of rock bands such as Nirvana.

They were influenced by 1960s and 1970s fashion photographers who had experimented with notions of morality and acceptability, such as Bob Richardson and Guy Bourdin, and combined their images' often jarring, filmic quality with the raw emotion and intimate expositions of Larry Clark and Nan Goldin. In the 1990s, fashion photographers locked into a tradition of documentary photography that drew significance from traces of the everyday and sought to express the intensity of the moment. Goldin and Clark had both photographed real scenes of sex and drug use. They used the camera as a visual record, an external memory of their lives, and that is what 1990s photographers—Sorrenti, Teller, and Day—integrated into their own work.

They mainly worked for style magazines such as *The Face*, *Dazed and Confused*, and *i-D* in London, and therefore drew a young audience that responded to the stripped-down settings and light touch of Ward's and Scott's styling, which created outfits that seemed to have been thrown together from old favorites rather than crisp, new clothes. The models they chose, Emma Balfour, Rosemary Ferguson, and Kate Moss among them, were skinny and androgynous, and embodied a challenge to the more Amazonian physiques of previous models. However, their thinness at times seemed acute, and their glazed, Vaseline-lidded eyes and pale faces were jarring among glossier beauty ideals shown in advertisements in the same magazines.

Although other areas of culture were equally preoccupied by images of youthful rebellion, through drugs and partying, the models' fragile bodies appeared bruised and vulnerable. Their delicate features seemed blurred by smudged makeup and incongruous in the context of dirty rooms or overgrown countryside. They recalled the emaciated style shown in the 1981 cult film, *Christiane F.*, which depicted the life of a teenage heroin addict. Models were often shown lying prone, perhaps asleep, perhaps passed out.

Irvine Welsh wrote about heroin addiction in *Trainspotting*. Films, such as the one inspired by his book made in 1996; *Drugstore Cowboy*, 1989; *Pulp Fiction*, 1994; and *The Basketball Diaries*, 1995, were all far more graphic in their scenes of drug abuse; they were also able to show their protagonists' suffering and turmoil. Fashion images, however, presented snapshots that covered perhaps eight magazine pages, a mini-narrative that was ambiguous, with drugs never actually explicit but implied to some onlookers by gestures, settings, and facial expressions.

By the time Clinton spoke out about so-called heroin chic, a term that had been circulating, along with "junkie chic," in the press for the past year, many felt the style was over, and fashion had moved on. It had been a strand within fashion that had grown up over the previous years, coming to fruition in 1993, as evidenced by, for example, fashion shoots for *The Face* of that year, and it gradually shifted, into more straightforward documentary work for Day and Teller, into a darker, more erotic fantasy for photographers such as Sean Ellis, or into more explicit imagery for Terry Richardson. Camilla Nickerson and Neville Wakefield's book, *Fashion, Photography of the Nineties* (1996), brought together many of the key images of the period and showed the breadth of the realist style, of which heroin chic was only a part. The outcry came as mainstream labels appropriated the aesthetic, Calvin Klein included, adding an edge to their brand. As it shifted context, and therefore reached a wider audience, heroin chic's suggestions of internalized violence and illicit pleasures became increasingly controversial. Heroin chic was a symptom of cultural anxiety, and fashion's contradictory position within Western culture meant that its exploration of uncomfortable themes of alienation, deathliness, and beauty were problematic, especially at a time when representations of reality and fiction were ever more blurred.

See also Extreme Fashions; Fashion Photography.

Bibliography

Arnold, Rebecca. "Heroin Chic." *Fashion Theory, The Journal of Dress, Body and Culture* 3, no. 3 (September 1999): 279–295.

——. *Fashion Desire and Anxiety: Image and Morality in the 20th Century.* New Brunswick, N. J.: Rutgers University Press, 2001.

Nickerson, Camilla, and Neville Wakefield, eds. *Fashion: Photography of the Nineties.* Zurich, Berlin, and New York: Scalo, 1996.

Internet Resource

White House Briefing Room. "White House Press Release: Remarks by the President at the U.S. Conference of Mayors." Available from <http://www.treatment.org/news/mayors.html>.

Rebecca Arnold

HIGH HEELS

High-heeled shoes, perhaps more than any other item of clothing, are seen as the ultimate fashion symbol of being a woman. Little girls, who raid their mother's closets for dressing-up props, gravitate toward them. A first pair of high heels was often a rite of passage into womanhood.

To be so fashionably shod is often detrimental to one's feet, but a high-heeled shoe is widely perceived as the sexiest, most feminine shoe a woman can wear. High heels have the ability to change radically the wearer's posture and appearance. Heels make the leg look longer, slimming calves and ankles. A woman's silhouette changes. Her breasts are thrust forward and her bottom pushed out to create a seductive S-shape that helps to create that sexy walk. These physical changes influence how a woman feels and often how she is perceived, so creating the paradox of wearing heels. On the one hand, high heels are all powerful. A woman becomes taller, striking a defiant pose that signifies sexuality and power. In heels she can take on the world. Yet, high heels can also create a helpless woman, teetering and unsteady, unable to run for the bus, passive and weak.

High heels have had a long association with sexual fetishism—from the dominatrix in black leather high-heeled boots to the submissive in bondage shoes.

Origins

Heels were first introduced in the 1590s. In the 1660s Louis XIV of France made high heels fashionable for men. As a relatively short man he coupled high heels with tall wigs to create an illusion of height. Royal customization gave rise to red heels, a symbol of status and power, initially only worn by those in the royal court. High red heels continued to be fashionable into the 1770s.

The Eighteenth Century

The French fashion of the 1770s and 1780s saw high heels placed under the heel arch of the foot, causing the wearer's toes to be crushed in the upturned pointed toe, yet tilting the wearer forward in a provocative manner. The resulting pain was worth it for the very fashionable look. A satirical poem of the time says it all: "Mount on French heels/When you go to a ball/'Tis the fashion to totter/and show you can fall!" Toward the end of the eighteenth century, heels became lower or wedged, disappearing altogether by around 1810.

The Nineteenth Century

From the 1850s women's heels began to make a comeback, and by the 1860s fashionable heels could measure 2.5 inches. In June 1868 the *Ladies Treasury* told its readers: "High-heel boots are universal, notwithstanding that medical men have been writing very severely against them. They say the fashion causes corns, cramps, lameness at an early age, lessens the size of the calf and thus makes it lose its symmetry" (Swann, p. 48). From 1867 there was also the introduction of a straight, slender high heel known as the Pined PINET, after the French shoemaker Francois Pinet.

In the 1890s some courtesans wore a style known as the Cromwell shoe, based on the Victorians' rather fanciful ideas of the shoes worn by Oliver Cromwell and his followers; this style had a heel of up to 6.5 inches.

Early heels were carved from wood and covered with leather or fabric used for the upper shoe. To strengthen the area between the sole and the heel the leather sole often ran down the heel breast.

The Twentieth Century

The Cuban heel with straight sides appeared in 1904. It was usually constructed using pieces of leather stacked to create its height. The bar shoe was the classic style of the 1920s, sporting a high Louis or Cuban heel. Jewelled heels decorated with paste, diamante, and enamels were featured on evening shoes.

A significant development in the history of high heels came on the wave of Christian Dior's New Look in 1947. This style required a correspondingly slim and elegant high heel. Previously high slim heels were prone to breaking. The problem was solved when a steel rod was inserted through a molded plastic heel. Stilettos were first mentioned in the *Daily Telegraph* on 23 September 1953. Initially high fashion, made popular by the French shoe designer Roger Vivier, all women were soon wearing them until the early 1960s. Stilettos caused many practical problems, including the pitting of wooden floors and getting caught in street gratings.

It was also in the 1960s that for the first time since the 1720s, the high heel was reclaimed by men in the form of the Cuban heel on what were known as Beatle boots, a style made popular by the the Beatles. In the 1980s high stiletto heels made a comeback, as power dressing for women at work became de rigueur. Coupled with a shoulder-padded masculine tailored suit and red lipstick, the high heel symbolized sexual power and dominance, a "don't mess with me" visual attitude.

Since then the high heel has never really disappeared. Its resurgence in the early 2000s was reflected in the popularity of Manolo Blahnik's shoes in the TV show *Sex and the City*. Some women only wear high heels for special occasions as formal wear, while others wear them all the time. Whatever the preference is, the high heel will never go away.

See also Blahnik, Manolo; Boots; Shoes; Shoes, Women's.

Bibliography

McDowell, Colin. *Shoes: Fashion and Fantasy*. London: Thames and Hudson Inc., 1989.

Pattison, Angela, and Nigel Cawthorne. *Shoes: A Century of Style*. London: The Apple Press, 1998.

Pratt, Lucy, and Linda Woolley. *Shoes*. London: V&A Publications, 1999.

Swann, June. *Shoes*. London: B.T. Batsford, Ltd., 1982. Excellent historical overview.

Rebecca Shawcross

HIJAB

Equating the terms *hijab* and "veil" is a common error. "Veil" is an easy, familiar word used when referring to Arab women's head, face, and body covers. *Hijab* is not the Arabic equivalent of veil—it is a complex and multilayered phenomenon.

"Veil" has no single word equivalent in Arabic. Instead many different terms refer to diverse articles of women's and men's clothing that vary by region, era, lifestyle, social stratum, stage in the life cycle, and gender. Adding to this complexity is the fact that some covers and wraps worn by both sexes have multiple usages and are manipulated flexibly to cover the face when socially required. For example, women use head covers or large sleeves to hide the face in ways that can communicate kinship, distance, or social stratum of a person they encounter. Men, as well, can use their head covers in the same way.

"Dress" is a more inclusive word and has an Arabic equivalent, *libas*, that in Arab-Islamic culture connotes meanings beyond material form and function. *Libas* extends conceptualization to notions of family and gender implying haven-shelter-sanctuary—a protective shield, as it were. Dress is integral to Islam's sacred beginnings and explicit Qur'an references reveal a role for *libas* (dress) in Islam's conceptualizations.

Dress in Arab and Islamic culture can be viewed in two ways: the traditional-secular dress (clothing adopted through customary practices over time without religious connotation) and religious dress (clothing forms justified or believed to be justified or prescribed by religious sources or authorities). The Christian example of the latter would be the nun's habit. The Afghan burqa, the object of scrutiny and attack by some feminists preceding the Afghan invasion by the United States, exemplifies the traditional or secular form of dress. Hijab is the religious kind of cover in an Islamic context. The English word "veil" can apply to either secular or religious kind of cover. Hijab is more culturally specific than veil, but embodies multiple cultural levels of meaning and is better understood when embedded in wider sociocultural and sociopolitical contexts. Muslims use Qur'anic references to support their adoption of practices or in taking positions regarding related issues, and there are indeed some references to hijab in the Qur'an.

Qur'anic References

In the Qur'an (considered the primary and divinely revealed source), but mostly according to the *Hadith* (Prophetic Narrative, a secondary worldly source), evidence suggests that the Prophet Muhammad had paid much attention to dress style and manner for Muslims in the emerging community, gradually developing a dress code. There was a specific focus on Muslim men's clothing and bodily modesty particularly during prayer, but reference to women's body cover is negligible.

Within the Qur'an's references to hijab, only one concerns women's clothing. Muslim men and women who argue in the early 2000s for the Islamic dress and behavioral code usually cite two chapters in support of modesty for women and for an Islamic basis for wearing the hijab.

As Islam gradually established itself in the Madina community, after it had been chased out of its place of origin in Makka, the interpretation of "seclusion" for Muhammad's wives originated from sura (chapter) 33, ayah (verse) 53 in which hijab is mentioned:

O believers, enter not the dwellings of the Prophet, unless invited. . . . And when you ask of his wives any thing, ask from behind a hijab. That is purer for your hearts and for their hearts. (33:53)

Evidence suggests that this sura is ultimately about privacy of the Prophet's home and family and the special status of his wives in two ways—as Prophet's wives and as leaders with access to Islamic information and wisdom who are increasingly sought by community members. There was a need to protect their privacy by regulating the flow of visitors and the comportment of the men who entered upon the women's quarters. Here "hijab" refers not to women's clothing, but to its use as partition or curtain to provide privacy for women.

Sura al-Ahzab (33), ayah 59 enjoins the Prophet's wives, daughters, and all Muslim women to don their *jilbab* for easy recognition and protection from molestation or harassment:

O Prophet tell your wives, daughters and believing women to put on their *jilbabs* so they are recognized and thus not harmed (33:59).

Jilbab refers to a long, loose shirtdress, and does not connote head or face cover. This verse distinguishes the status of the Prophet's wives from the rest of the believers, and the other (33:53) protects their privacy from growing intrusions by male visitors.

Sura 24 refers to *khimar* (head cover) in the general context of public behavior and comportment by both sexes. In it ayah 31 (24:31) has been widely cited in scholarly works, often in isolation from the rest of the verse, distorting the meaning, implying that women are singled out for "reserve" and "restraint." Preceding it, ayah 30 addresses men first:

Tell the believing men to lower their gaze and conceal their genitals; for that is purer for them, God knoweth what they do.

Ayah 31 follows, continuing the same theme:

And tell the believing women to lower their gaze and conceal their genitals, and not reveal their beauty, except what does show, and to draw their *khimar* over their bosoms, and not to reveal their beauty except to . . . etc. (emphasis added).

Evidence from the usage of hijab in the Qur'an, from early Islamic discourse, and subjected to anthropological analysis, supports the notion of hijab as referring to a sacred divide or separation between two worlds or two spaces: deity and mortals, good and evil, light and dark, believers and nonbelievers, or aristocracy and commoners. The phrase *"min wara' al-hijab"* (from behind the *hijab*) emphasizes the element of separation and partition.

When referring to women's clothing, the terms often used are *jilbab* (long, loose-fitting shirtdress) and *khimar* (head cover). Neither hijab nor *niqab* are mentioned. *Niqab* and *lithma* are terms that unambiguously refer to face cover. Hijab, which only refers to head (shoulder) cover and to the general Islamic attire, is not mentioned in these two suras either. In other references to comportment and modest way of dressing appropriate to the new status of the Prophet's wives, hijab is not mentioned either. When it is used in other suras, the word conveys more the sense of separation than veiling or covering.

The Qur'an and the contemporary Islamic movement make clear that Muslim men and women are to carry themselves in public with a sense of reserve and restraint. Exhibitionist public comportment, through behavior, dress, voice, or body movement, is frowned upon, and becomes associated with *Jahiliyya* (pre-Islamic era) that is not confined to a historical moment, but rather becomes a state and a condition of society that can occur at any time when social and moral controls are abandoned. But overall the contemporary

movement is not simply about clothing but about a renewal of a cultural identity and traditional ideals and values.

Etymology and Meaning

The cultural and linguistic roots of "hijab" are integral to Islamic (and Arab) culture. "Hijab" translates as cover, wrap, curtain, veil, screen, partition. The same word is used to refer to amulets carried on one's person (particularly for children or persons in a vulnerable state) to protect against harm.

By the nineteenth century, upper-class urban Muslim and Christian women in Egypt wore the *habarah*, which consisted of a long skirt, a head cover, and a *burqa*, a long rectangular cloth of white transparent muslin placed below the eyes, covering the lower nose and the mouth and falling to the chest. When veiling entered feminist nationalist discourse during British colonial occupation, "hijab" was the term used by feminists and nationalists and secularists. The phrase used for the removal of urban women's face and head cover was *raf'* (lifting) *al-hijab* (not *al-habarah*: the term used for cloak or veil among upper-class Egyptian women up to the early 1900s).

Three Arab Feminisms

Muslim and Christian women of the upper and middle classes described the Egyptian feminist movement at the turn of the century as a secular movement. Some observers linked European colonialism and feminism, distinguishing two feminist trajectories: a Westward-looking feminism and a more local one. In neither form have women made veiling or unveiling the central issue. Rather, some prominent men advocated feminist programs and called for reform centering on women's veiling. Removing the veil was not part of the official feminist agenda of the Egyptian Feminist Union. Importantly, when the most prominent Arab feminist, Huda Sha'rawi, "lifted the hijab" as the famous public gesture came to be described, she had only removed the face cover (*burqa* or *yashmik*), which was worn by upper-class women at the turn of the century, but kept the head covering. Technically, therefore, Huda Sha'rawi never "lifted the hijab," since "hijab" refers broadly to the whole attire, but more commonly to the head covering. Some attribute her success in feminist nationalist leadership, compared with other contemporaries, to the fact that she had respect for the traditional attire.

Hijab. The *hijab* is used as women's headcover in the Islamic world. Although it is commonly, and mistakenly, referred to simply as a veil, it serves the higher purpose of representing Islamic identity and morality. © JULIE PLASENCIA/SAN FRANCISCO CHRONICLE/CORBIS. REPRODUCED BY PERMISSION.

In her memoirs she mentions being congratulated for "my success in . . . lifting the hijab . . . but wearing the *hijab shar'i* (lawful or Islamic hijab)" (Sha'rawi 1981, p. 291). This distinction is important and assumes special significance because the other prominent feminist, Malak Hifni Nasif, opposed mandatory unveiling for women. Her agenda in early 1900 stressed two elements absent in Sha'rawi's feminist agenda: the opening of all fields of higher education to women and demanding space accommodation for public prayer by women in mosques. These local elements contrast to French-influenced agendas by other feminists. A third movement developed through the seeds sown since 1908 calling for the importance of Islam and the wearing of the hijab, formed under the initiative of Zaynab al-Ghazali in the 1970s espousing Islamic ideals and supporting family values. None of the three feminisms espoused calling for abandoning the hijab.

Contemporary Movement

Beginning in the 1970s in Egypt an Islamic movement emerged. The Islamic movement reasserted a cultural historical identity and stood for resisting hegemonic colonial occupation. It centered initially on youth and college-level young adults and broadened across generations and social strata and spread throughout the region. The public appearance of an innovative form of dress for men and women without exact historical precedent characterized the movement. This new style was not a return to any traditional dress form, and had no tangible model to emulate, and no industry behind it—not one store in Egypt carried the new garb in the 1970s. In the early 2000s there are many stores that sell this outfit throughout the region, on the Internet, in Europe, and in the United States. The dress was referred to as "the Islamic dress," in Arabic called *al-ziyy al-Islami* or *al-ziyy al-Shar'i*, or more commonly *al-hijab*.

This new fashion seemed incomprehensible and bewildering to observers. The strong, visible appearance of young Egyptian women going to college dressed in a manner unfamiliar to their own parents, completely "veiled" from head to toe, sometimes covering the face and hands as well, disturbed many. Some young women had switched almost overnight from wearing sleeveless dresses and miniskirts to becoming a "veiled" doctor, engineer, or pharmacist. Confused observers speculated about the cause. Was it an identity crisis, a version of America's hippie movement, a fad, a youth protest, an ideological vacuum, an individual psychic disturbance, a life-crisis, a social dislocation, or protest against authority?

Dress Code

The contemporary dress code translates materially this way: men and women wear full-length *gallabiyyas*, loose-fitting to conceal body form, in solid or otherwise austere colors made out of opaque fabric. The wearers lower their gaze in cross-sex public encounters and refrain from body or dress adornment that draws attention to their bodies. The dress code for men consists of sandals, baggy trousers with loose-top shirts in off-white or, alternatively (and preferably) a long, loose white *gallabiyya* and a white or red-checkered *kufiyya*. They grew a *lihya* (full beard trimmed short). Women wear the hijab, which consists of *al-jilbab* (ankle-length, long-sleeved, loose-fitted dress) and *al-khimar*, a head covering that covers the hair and extends low to the forehead, comes under the chin to conceal the neck and falls down over the chest and back. During the first decade of the movement, women wore solid colors such as beige, brown, navy, burgundy, or black. The *muhajjabat* (women wearing hijab) engaged fully in daily affairs and public life. That is, austerity in dress and reserve in public behavior are not accompanied by withdrawal or seclusion and neither communicates deference nor sexual shame. Modern hijab is about sanctity, reserve, and privacy.

Colonialism and Resistance

The role of the veil in liberating Algeria from French colonial occupation is popularly known. When the French landed in Algeria in 1830 most inhabitants were Arabic-speaking Sunni Muslims, with a large Berber population that was by then bilingual Berber Arabic speaking. Administratively, Algeria was a France populated by "the Muslims"—a majority of second-class citizens. France began a gallicization process on many fronts: French law was imposed on Islamic law, French social plan was imposed on local custom, French education substituted for Arab education, and the French language replaced Arabic. Many Algerians were excluded from education altogether. The French conquest of Algeria represented a deformation of the social, moral, legal, and cultural order. Economically the French monopolized the best land and the top jobs, exploited labor, harnessed local energies, and cultivated crops for French consumption (grapes for wine) while violating Islamic morality. Another strategy was to assimilate upper-class Algerians by gallicizing the woman and uprooting her from her culture. The target of the colonial strategy became to persuade the Muslim woman to unveil. Thus, Arabs and Muslims often link the deveiling of Muslim women with a colonial strategy to undermine and destroy their culture. The effect was the opposite: it strengthened the attachment to the veil as a national and cultural symbol, and gave it a new vitality.

Since 1948 Palestinian women who were uprooted from their homeland, particularly the older ones, wore a dress and head covering that communicated their rural origins and their contemporary status in refugee camps. After the 1967 Six-Day War, women wore white or black shawls (*shasha*) and had no access to their traditional fabrics and tools to embroider their clothing. In the late 1970s, as militant Islamic consciousness began to arise, Palestinians attempted to restore the hijab. Women affiliated with the movement began wearing long, tailored overcoats and head covers now known as *shari'a* or Islamic dress. As in Egypt, the Islamic dress had no precedent in indigenous Palestinian sartorial history, but is an innovative tradition in form and meaning.

Conclusion

The hijab worn by Muslim women in Arab, Muslim, European, or United States society is largely about identity, about privacy of space and body. In specific social settings, veiling communicates exclusivity of rank and nuances in kinship, status, and behavior and also symbolizes an element of power and autonomy and functions as a vehicle for resistance.

Hijab in the early twenty-first century is politically charged in France and Belgium, countries that are taking measures to ban the wearing of headscarves (hijab) to schools purportedly for maintaining the integrity of secularism, but the issue is considered to be fraught with anti-Islamic implications. To many young women the hijab represents an identity of choice and a freedom of expression they do not want to lose.

See also Burqa; Djellaba; Islamic Dress, Contemporary; Jilbab; Kaffiyeh; Middle East: History of Islamic Dress.

Bibliography

Sha'rawi, Huda. *Huda Sharawi: Muthakkirat Ta'idat al-Mar'a al-Arabiyya al-Hadith* (Memoirs of Huda Shawari, Leader of Modern Arab Women). Introduction by Amina al-Said. Kitab al-Hilal, Silsial Shahriyya. Cairo: Dar al-Hillal, 1981. In Arabic.

Fadwa El Guindi

HIP-HOP FASHION

Hip-hop is both the voice of alienated, frustrated youth and a multibillion-dollar cultural industry packaged and marketed on a global scale. Hip-hop is also a multifaceted subculture that transcends many of the popular characterizations used to describe other music-led youth cultures. One of the important considerations about hip-hop is that since its conception in the early 1970s, hip-hop has arguably become more potent and efficient in galvanizing black social identity than the civil rights movement of the 1960s.

The evolution of hip-hop has developed from a self-conscious rumination of words and music to an obstinate expression of contemporary urban life through corporal gestures and apparel. From the beginning, hip-hop fashion has been on a trajectory of relentless flowering. Developments have been primarily in the men's wear sector; early clothes were functional and included conventional items—multicolored appliqué leather jackets, sheepskin coats, car coats, straight leg corduroy or denim jeans, hooded sweatshirts, athletic warm-up pants, mock turtlenecks, and sneakers and caps. Less functional items included designer jeans and moniker belts, gold jewelry, Kangol caps, Pumas with fat laces, basketball shoes, and oversized spectacles by Cazal.

Baggy apparel shapes that disguise the contours of the body were introduced in the 1980s. During the early 2000s, the archetypal hip-hop look consisted of baseball caps emblazoned with insignia from the Negro leagues and football teams and well-known fashion designers. Woolen beanie hats and bandannas were worn singularly or together. Goose down jackets or other foul-weather outerwear teamed with hooded sweatshirts. During the late 1990s the ubiquitous oversized white T-shirt, basketball vests, and hockey shirts became staples of the expression. Baggy denim jeans or camouflage cargo pants worn in a low-slung manner, backpacks, combat- or hiking-styled boots or sports shoes were complemented with tattoos and shaved, plaited, or dreadlocked hairstyles.

Initially hip-hop women's wear consisted of inconsequential looks that reflected contemporary women's wear and were accompanied with items such as Gloria Vanderbilt jeans, bamboo earrings, Fendi and Louis Vuitton handbags, name chains, midriff tops, bra tops, short skirts, tight jeans, high boots, straight hair weaves and braids, tattoos, and false fingernails and oversized gold jewelry. In addition, some women wore apparel that consisted of items similar to those worn by men during the 1990s. Female rappers such as Lil' Kim and Foxy Brown displayed provocative apparel and outlandish sexual gesturing that would eventually become a raison d'être for hip-hop women's wear.

From within the postindustrial environment, hip-hop has emerged as an articulation of an affirmative "otherness," which is at times unpopular and misunderstood by politically conservative and socially moralistic groups, and especially by those who regard the modernist, anti-pluralist perspective to be sacrosanct.

Consequently, hip-hop tends to be unpopular with establishment agencies who wish to censor the expression and supervise the conduct and morals of the young; however, hip-hop is understood by mass media agencies and is exploited as a symptom of the volatility between the pull of materialism and the stagnancy of the urban underclass. The precarious state of this condition forces hip-hop to become a project concerned with the mastery of urban survival, and therefore has a global appeal that is demonstrated in hip-hop from New Zealand, Japan, Africa, France, and Great Britain.

A centrifugal force, hip-hop has contributed to the conceptualization of an alternative perspective in the wider society; this includes materialism, manners, morals, gender politics, language, gesture, music, dance, art, and fashion. Hip-hop music and fashion have attained an essential position in culture, though they oscillate on the periphery of conformity and general acceptability, but because of the notion of outsider status, and building upon the popularity of rock music, hip-hop has been admired and emulated by teenagers of most ethnicities and social classes.

Where Hip-hop Began

Hip-hop has at times become synonymous with a constellation of products in the luxury goods market, though such a situation would have been absurd at hip-hop's genesis. Hip-hop was formed in the culture of the basement parties that took place in the Bronx in New York City. These parties became formalized when the DJs Kool Herc, Grandmaster Flash, and DJ Starski began to play at impromptu parties in parks, streets, and community centers. Jamaican DJ Kool Herc, the credited founder of hip-hop break-beats based his Herculords discotheque system on the Jamaican reggae sound systems that played in Jamaica and New York. The art form of rapping emerged as the way of communicating narrative to the audience. Rapping is similar to "toasting," a long-established feature of reggae music.

Toasting and rapping are delivered in the style of the African oral tradition. The DJ, or toaster in Dance-hall, and the MC, or rapper, in hip-hop are the progeny of the African griot (storyteller), each offering a narration of everyday events.

It is from rap and music video that followers are able to determine and validate their assumptions about their lifestyle decisions, including apparel expressions. Followers of hip-hop have created apparel expressions that are comparable to the utterances of hip-hop music. Hip-hop fashions reflect the energy and resonance of the urban experience while omitting illusory signs that demonstrate the metamorphosis of the subaltern individual into street luminary.

Influence on Other Styles

"B-boy" and "Flyboy" were designations used to differentiate those focused on music and dance, and those who were focused on fashion. B-boys and B-girls were the former, and Flyboys and Flygirls the latter. B-boys have derived their designation from break-dancing. Break dancers dressed in sportswear like Puma sneakers, Adidas track pants, T-shirts, and padded nylon or leather jackets. They specialized in making poetic, gravity-defying acrobatic and explosive body-popping movements to the accompaniment of the interrupted, repeated, and over-laid phrasing of break-beat recordings.

The subtrends that followed break-dancing became the forerunners to rap-influenced fashion. For example, there are direct correlations to the fashion associated with hardcore rap, gangsta rap, and Afrocentric/cultural rap.

The B-boy expression has successfully crossed the subcultural divide. Skate boarders, who are predominantly white, also embraced much of the B-boy expression and have adapted it for their lifestyles. The Daisy Agers were exemplified by rappers De La Soul, who drew on the Afrocentric characteristics demonstrated by various black consciousness movements since the

A NEW YORK HOME BOY IN THE MID-1990s

The wearer is dressed in iconic mainstream American classics, a white T-shirt, and Levi's 501 jeans. Either he is ignorant of that or his other clothes and the way he wears them are chosen to offset their status: Kangol golf hat, Nike sneakers, and the ubiquitous boxer shorts.

However, the key device of the display is achieved in wearing boxer shorts with jeans in a manner that the elastic edge of the boxer shorts peeps over the jeans waist causing the designer branded elastic to be visible. As a consequence the jeans are restructured, to the extent that the form of the pants begins to affect the wearer's stride. Bundles of fabric collect around the lower legs, causing bulk and restrictive movement. This precarious way of wearing jeans creates the foundation for the expression.

1960s. Neo-Panthers, Afrocentrics, Sportifs, and Gangstas represent developments that enjoyed widespread followings. Indeed these characterizations contain apparel objects that demonstrate complicity in virtually every diaspora expression since hip-hop defined itself during the early 1980s. Many of the fashion objects utilized by the 1980s B-boy were affirmations of the pre-1980s. Much of the gangsta expression borrowed from the 1970s pimp style, while the mid-1980s look of the archetypal B-boy fused a Black Panther aesthetic with a sportswear look flavored by Jamaican Rude *Bwoys*. B-boys and Flyboys have succeeded as a result of the intercultural exchange between "the cultural imperatives of African-American and Caribbean history and identity" (Rose p. 21).

During the mid-1980s and early 1990s, hip-hop fashion gathered importance as hip-hop music became successful around the world. As a consequence, B-boys are no longer black and working class.

The genesis of fashion hip-hop had been skillfully articulated by the B-boys of the 1970s who created a path for subsequent hip-hop groupings (Daisy Agers, New Jacks, Sportifs, Nationalist [neo-Panthers]), who all added their own unique expressions to the fashion. As unofficial designers, such groups breached and corrupted many of the extant propositions about fashion and provided the template that a new generation of hip-hop fashion wearers should have committed. Like hip-hop music, hip-hop fashion edits, samples, repeats, unites, and creates new fashions—sometimes from

nonsense and sometimes from deep-felt sentiment that defines the bona fide experiences of hip-hop wearers. In many instances B-boys are found to have enthusiasm for mainstream fashion labels. A feature of hip-hop fashion expressions is a predilection for American, Italian, and English designer labels such as Tommy Hilfiger, Ralph Lauren, Gucci, and Burberry. For the B-boy, consumption of clothes is part of a rite of consumption and exhibition which reaffirms the formula, "I am = what I have and what I consume" (Fromm p. 36).

The overstated stylization of the B-boy is articulated in humorous, exaggerated, and outlandish clothes that are sometimes similar to an animated cartoon character. This visual aesthetic replaces and dispels any idea that alienation renders individuals invisible. The "standardized" version of hip-hop fashions has become locked into parody. During the 1980s, fashion labels became ensconced in hip-hop culture. The adoption of counterfeit Gucci and Fendi apparel and bona fide Nikes and Timberlands represented attempts to create fashion that has resonance beyond the context of hip-hop community.

During the 1980s, the Harlem store Dapper Dan became renowned for the idea of exalting "exotic" conspicuous fashion labels such as Fendi and Gucci. Much of the appeal to consumers was in the distillation of the logotypes of these high fashion brands on to *their* clothing and on to the streets of Harlem. Typically, fabric printed with the logotypes of these brands would be made into apparel that would not be found in the bona fide collections of Fendi or Gucci. Ultimately Dapper Dan was a postmodern project that included the development of hip-hop fashion.

Designers and Producers

In part, hip-hop fashion came about by default. Designers of active sportswear and sports shoes did not target the streets, nightclubs, or music videos as the primary location for their products. In particular, branded sportswear such as Adidas, Reebok, Nike, and British Knights had been appropriated by hip-hop and became precursors to the dedicated fashion sportswear hip-hop brands of Troop, Cross Colors, Mecca, Walker Wear, and Karl Kani. However, apparel companies have never surpassed the preeminence of the sportswear shoe brand. Nike and Adidas sneakers are indicators of hip-hop's distance from the mainstream; for many wearers the sneaker and the Nike Swoosh were potent objects in the urban rite of passage. Nike Air Force 1s and Air

Jordans became iconic and fetishistic. The Nike logo-type has been worn as jewelry, cut into hair, and tat-tooed onto skin.

Hip-hop has created its own trends and consump-tion patterns, with cultural networks that mutate at an intimidating rate. Its collusion with mainstream fash-ion is well established. Many of the raps by major hip-hop stars exalt the importance of wearing Gucci, Prada, Versace, Tommy, Earl, Burberry, Timberland, Coogi, and Coach. Such raps are usually arrogant brags con-doning one-upmanship such as Lil' Kim's request on her song "Drugs" on the album *Hardcore*, "Call us the Gabbana girls, we dangerous, bitches pay a fee just to hang with us" or "Yes indeed, flows first class and yours is coach like the bag, the Prada mama."

Motifs, fabrics, color, and the drama of wearing ap-parel dramatically altered during 1998 when hip-hop leaders began to recognize the mainstream fashion quartet of Versace, Prada, Dolce & Gabbana, and Gucci as the ultimate in fashion expression. The materialist focus set by the hip-hop gangstas, players, and hip-hop celebrities populated the idea of "ghetto fabulousness" (the juxtaposition of "fabulously" expensive objects placed in the context of the impoverished ghetto) as a replacement for hip-hop fashions that did not rely upon endorsements of glamorous and expensive mainstream fashion brands.

Such new inflections prompted another revision of hip-hop fashion. Although branded performance sportswear was initially popular in hip-hop culture, its displacement was prompted when Lil' Kim—among other hip-hop stars—used important designer labels to create an image of privilege and status. Ordinary hip-hop fans and fashion companies alike understood this idea. The raps of Lil' Kim and other rappers have injected retail, advertising, and promotion strategies of fashion companies with a new thematic source and a previously unexploited marketplace. Hip-hop fashion represents a subversive discourse; fashion companies recognize this standpoint as being favorable if they wish to affect values and attitudes that are urban and therefore cool. However, some companies fail in this ambition and have all suffered from "myths" about con-sumers that are "in-compatible" with the companies branding.

In their attempts to achieve postmodern relevance, fashion companies such as Asprey, Puma, Versace, and Iceberg have used the formal recommendation of-fered in strategies of cross-marketing. This can range from a celebrity appearing in an advertising campaign or just sitting in the front row of a designer's runway show.

To counter this, a number of hip-hop music moguls—Russell Simmons, P. Diddy, and Master P—have all have owned apparel companies. Their com-panies produce creative fashion collections that are syn-chronized with the musical output of their recording enterprises. These companies separate into those that follow an accurate rendition of hip-hop fashion and those companies that seek to cross over and produce designs that have broad mass fashion appeal rather than a specialist hip-hop appeal.

In attempting to model the direction and content of hip-hop fashion, hip-hop's moguls have disregarded the life experiences, economic means, and self-creative tendencies of hip-hop followers in favor of a personal ideology.

How Hip-hop Crosses Boundaries

In the early 1990s, a group of Brooklyn hip-hop follow-ers began to reuse Ralph Lauren garment labels, and to sew them on apparel not made by Ralph Lauren. The action of the Lo-lifer subculture was to challenge the commercially aggressive opposition of Ralph Lau-ren and to counteract the "antagonism" of the fashion label. The deconstruction of the fashion company's well-maintained branded image creates a reversal in hierarchy. When Ralph Lauren's Polo label is hand-painted onto a wall, or even a towel, as the Lo-lifers did, a question is asked about commercial branding and the mythological representation of the fashion logotype.

A characteristic of hip-hop fashion is the multiple themes that are filtered through the aspirations of wearers and designers alike. The American mainstream designer Tommy Hilfiger has successfully captured an understanding of hip-hop culture and has produced very specific fashion items, which fit the market place without being apologetic.

During the mid-1990s, new cuts of Hilfiger's jeans were given titles such as "Uptown," which refer to the geographical placements of Harlem and the Bronx, two New York districts with large African American popu-lations. The Uptown cut of the jeans are ostensibly the same as extra-baggy, low-slung jeans manufactured by any other hip-hop designer or popular mainstream manufacturer addressing the hip-hop marketplace;

however, the degree of hip-hop enthusiasm for Hilfiger made the brand very popular.

Hip-hop fashion is regarded as a delineator of "cool." Indeed aspects of hip-hop have become the characterization of dissonance; that is why British royal princes William and Harry were happy to adopt homeboy gestures while wearing baseball caps. Probably having never met a real live B-boy, cool gesturing postures are no doubt gleaned from music videos.

In one of the most informative studies of the cool expression, Majors and Billson suggest that cool adds value to the disenfranchisement of the individual. Its practice is constructed through attitude and implies status for the wearer through an attributed importance of fashion objects. The phenomenon of cool emerges as the compelling ingredient to hip-hop life; it is effected by the attachments of self. Cool, or to use other evocations, "fly" or—in Britain—"styling it out" is a creative procedure of stealth serving as a badge of belonging, though it allows wearers the scope to make minor adjustments to their apparel configuration.

See also Hilfiger, Tommy; Lauren, Ralph; Music and Fashion.

Bibliography

Fricke, Jim, and Ahearn Charlie. *Yes, Yes, Y'all: The Experience Music Project Oral History of Hip-Hop's First Decade.* Cambridge, Mass., Da Capo Press, 2002.

Fromm, Erich. *To Have or to Be?* New York: HarperCollins Publishers, Inc., 1976.

Lil' Kim. "Drugs." *Hardcore.* (Sound recording.) New York: Undeas/Big Beat, 1996.

Lusane, Clarence. "Rap, Race and Politics." *Race and Class: A Journal for Black and Third World Liberation* 35, no. 1 (July–September 1993): 41–56.

Majors, Richard, and Janet Mancini Billson. *Cool Pose: The Dilemmas of Black Manhood in America.* New York: Touchstone Books, 1993.

Perkins, William Eric, ed. *Droppin' Science: Critical Essays on Rap Music and Hip Hop Culture.* Philadelphia: Temple University Press, 1995.

Rose, Tricia. *Black Noise: Rap Music and Black Culture in Contemporary America.* Middletown, Conn.: Wesleyan University Press, 1994.

Van Dyk Lewis

HIPPIE STYLE

In the mid-1960s, the hippies—the rebels and dropouts of the Haight-Ashbury community of San Francisco—generated one of the most influential of history's dress reform movements. Their style was so outrageous and anomalous that it alone could have made the hippie movement impossible to ignore. As did their lifestyles, their fashion built upon San Francisco and California's tradition of iconoclasm; important, too, was the precedent provided by the young ready-to-wear designers of London, whose international impact began in the late 1950s.

The hippies' protest against capitalist society informed their impunity to all received strictures or etiquettes about clothes. They coordinated garments so that harmonies and homogeneity were fractured. Mad, anarchic mélanges resulted. They simulated acid phantasmagoria in their color schemes and paraded recycled old clothes, proclaiming them not as cast-off rags but proudly worn pedigree. They disguised and revealed themselves in costumes that were avatars of theatrical or historical or mythological identities, rather than the easily legible roles recognized by contemporary society. Their clothes were a paean to sexuality and sensuality: texture and tactility were foregrounded in their favorite fabrics, which ranged from slinky satin and stretch to all variety of embroidered and figured surfaces. Sometimes their fashion became not a second skin, but the exposure of their own nude bodies, painted and patterned in tribal fashion; this was a celebration of instinctual expression that they believed had been obliterated by industrialization.

Ecological Fashion

The hippies built on the generic silhouettes that prevailed during the 1960s—the miniskirt, the pantsuit—but they transmogrified Mod fashion at the decade's midpoint by the way they put their clothes together, by their choices of fabric, and by the way they accessorized. Folkloric motifs, style, and fabrics were ubiquitous in hippie fashion. Their adoption of long peasant skirts helped move fashion back to longer hemlines. The generally loose and unconstructed silhouette of the 1960s became even more flowing with the adoption of mideastern tent shapes. The hippies' infatuation with the ensembles of Native Americans demonstrated solidarity with their plight as well as well an aesthetic appreciation.

Another prong of hippie fashion likewise proclaimed common cause with the workers of the world: this was the utilitarian fare that came to be known as "anti-fashion." It was fashion at its least overly decorative, most rugged, and basic: blue jeans worn with T-shirts, work shirts, and other commonplace attire. Decorative appeal was provided instead by the contours outlined by these body-clinging garments. Thus the youthful counterculture promulgated an allure that could not be achieved by expenditure alone.

The hippies generated an ecological consciousness of fashion by their recycling of vintage clothes as well as their cannibalizing of old fabrics and hangings, out of which they cut new garments. They drew attention to the way that all clothes costume the wearer into roles, some—businessman, housewife—so integrated into the warp of society that they were no longer recognized as constructed characterization. Their pacific appropriation of military uniform likewise showed a determination to mock and denature the pieties vented by the opposite side of the ideological divide.

Los Angeles, New York, and London also became important citadels for hippie fashion. On Los Angeles's Sunset Boulevard and in New York's Greenwich Village were clustered constellations of independent boutiques. London's contribution to hippie fashion was indebted to the art and crafts movement of a century earlier. More than San Francisco, the city's secondhand clothes stores and bazaars were more likely to be filled with heirloom couture. London raided its storage vaults, disgorging into the city's auction house fabulous caches of vintage clothing as well as theatrical and ballet costumes.

The Rich Hippies

"We got pretty scathing about store-bought hip that didn't come from the soul," said Linda Gravenites (interview with the author, November 1986), who made clothes for many residents in the Haight-Ashbury community and the rock bands based there. Nevertheless the purists or the ideologues were powerless to stop the inevitable co-opting, the proliferation of hippie fashion within the mainstream fashion industry. From 1967 to 1971, the hippie's fashion was grist for the couture and upscale ready-to-wear mills. The "rich hippie" look upgraded hippie style into fabrics that were largely well beyond the economic reaches of the financially marginal denizens of Haight-Ashbury.

The fashion of the hippies was as much threat as influence to the fashion establishment. The hippie's open-ended pluralism threw down the gauntlet to the seasonable revisions proffered to women by the mainstream fashion industry. Savoring vintage garments established a continuum between past and present, a rejoinder to the forced amnesia of customers told that each year marked a tabula rasa of consumption.

Perhaps what above all made hippie fashion so subversive to the mainstream industry was its tacit message that the time had come to abolish the fashion designer. It resonated as well with the burgeoning women's liberation movement: women would no longer be told what to wear by a designer, who was usually male. After Rudi Gernreich decided to close his ready-to-wear business in 1968, he told reporters that he was now disenchanted by clothes that bore the imprint of the individual designer. The very act of designing, in fact, seemed to him to be an a priori dictate that no longer fit the needs and aspirations of the clothes-wearing public.

With every question of identity in Western civilization of the late 1960s being debated, fashion exploded with costume and fantasy, thanks in large part to the inspiration provided by the hippies. "Today nothing is out, because everything is in," Marshall McLuhan wrote in 1968. "Every costume from every era is now available to everyone." (*Harper's Bazaar*, April 1968, p. 164)

Hippie fashion continued to steep throughout fashion during the 1970s. Even as fashion retreated from the utopian threshold advanced during the late 1960s, the hippies' ideas were disseminated to many more people than they had been during the 1960s. By the end of the decade, it seemed to have become exhausted. But since the mid-1980s, hippie style has enthralled designers and the public again and again, becoming a recurrent influence in every echelon of fashion.

See also Music and Fashion; Politics and Fashion; Social Class and Clothing.

Bibliography

Lobenthal, Joel. *Radical Rags: Fashions of the Sixties*. New York: Abbeville Press, 1990.

Reich, Charles A. *The Greening of America: How the Youth Revolution Is Trying to Make America Livable*. New York: Random House, 1970.

Joel Lobenthal

HISTORICISM AND HISTORICAL REVIVAL

Prior to the rise of the bourgeoisie, historical revivals in dress were the preserve of the aristocratic classes, principally employed as costume either for masquerade and pageantry, portraiture or professional function (courtly and legal uniform), and always as a distinguishing mark of timelessness and status—of both power and beauty.

From the sixteenth to eighteenth centuries, fashions in the choice of historical focus were mainly informed by divisions between town (the urban powerful) and country (the Arcadian idyllic), and received ideas of morality and immorality. The meaning and embodiment of the latter coupling shifted most frequently—morality at some stages implied by Anglo-Saxon mythologies of status and structure. The body coverings most frequently represented by fashions were crinolines, hoops, bustles, and corsetry for women, and armor and padded upper bodies for men. In turn, however, the looser costume of Greco-Roman mythology and the reverence for the ideal physique, and the beauty of nature that they represented, were also held up as archetypes of morality in different periods—although they were usually quite swiftly decried for their immorality in openly revealing the female body. As with all the revivals to follow, these trends were rarely based on historical accuracy, relying primarily on a nostalgic imagination and secondhand source material.

Gothic

The original fifteenth-century Gothic dress for women combined thirteenth-century ideals of fitness for purpose and an ecclesiastical sensibility (headdresses in particular bore direct reference to the wimple) with beauty of line and sumptuous fabrics (velvets and brocades). Gothic revivalism was already taking place in the mid-seventeenth century (the Puritans drew on the religious overtones of the Gothic in the face of Royalist decadence), and was popularized again in the mid-eighteenth century as a decorative and architectural movement (Gothick), its leading proponents including Batty Langley (1696–1751) and Horace Walpole, whose Strawberry Hill project (1750–1770) came to epitomize the period. The eighteenth-century revival was a movement driven by romance, and one that stood against the perceived rigidity and rules of the classical style; the medieval appeared more natural, fantastical, and foreign

compared to the worlds of Greece or Rome. In dress, its expression was principally neomedieval, somber in tone and concentrated on flat, embroidered pattern on sleeve and bodice panels. It was notoriously inaccurate and widely ridiculed until the 1830s when A.W. N. Pugin (1812–1852) proposed an accurate and faithful return to Gothic style as a nationalist, moral, and spiritual bulwark in the face of advancing industrialization. Pugin's work heavily influenced the Victorian aesthetic and later, the flat printed pattern of William Morris (1834–1896) and the Arts and Crafts movement. In the late twentieth century, the Gothic style returned again as an addendum to punk, drawing on but darkening the punk movement's oppositional stance and twisting the spiritual meaning of Gothic style to embody older, more mystical religions (such as Wicca, paganism, and Buddhism). But, as with previous Gothic revivals, 1980s' goths embraced the romanticism of the movement, combining the PVC and rubber of punk with the velvets and brocades of their eighteenth- and nineteenth-century predecessors.

Neoclassicism

The taste for what became known as neoclassical style has its roots in the 1750s, emerging in opposition to the exoticism and opulence of the rococo (promoted by the launch of the Dilettanti Society in 1734 and the Society of Arts in 1754). Much of the literature (Rousseau) and painting (Gainsborough, Reynolds, and Hogarth) in the decades leading up to the neoclassical movement was directed toward proposing a romanticized classicism as a moral tendency linking the purity of nature with purity of spirit. It was possible for both the neoclassical and the Gothic to exist in much the same space, due both to the opening up of society to fashion and to the shared beliefs of each movement.

The movement achieved prominence in the 1780s and is most closely associated with Thomas Hope (1769–1831), whose Costumes of the Ancients (1809) and Designs of Modern Costumes (1812) were pivotal to popularizing the looser, unstructured Greco-Roman dress styles. Dresses were made principally from muslin with waistlines rising to the bust, which was still firmly secured by stays and highlighted by a sash and knotted scarf. The effect was naïve and childlike, best expressed in the popular 1880s' illustrations of Kate Greenaway. In keeping with antique statuary and notions of the ideal physique for men, tightly fitting breeches and cutaway jackets revealed more of the body.

Hope was also an exoticist and hosted Turkish-inspired parties at his home, similar to those favored by the Parisian designer Paul Poiret (1879–1944) in the early twentieth century. Poiret and two other designers of the period, Madeleine Vionnet (1876–1975) and Mariano Fortuny (1871–1949), were the principle players in the revival of the neoclassical in the 1920s and 1930s (also known as vogue regency).

The Aesthetic Movement

As with neoclassicism, the aesthetic movement studied and celebrated beauty. The movement took hold in the United Kingdom in the 1870s. Its proponents in the decorative arts (William Morris), literature (Walter Pater, Charles Baudelaire, Oscar Wilde), and fine arts (James McNeill Whistler, Aubrey Beardsley, and the Pre-Raphaelite painters) proposed elegance in everything. Nature (flora, fauna, and the athletic human body) was eulogized in all its glory as the epitome of beauty, a manifestation of God on Earth. What separated Gothic and aesthetic was the latter's belief of "art for art's sake" as shifts in understanding over the nature of morality gave rise to an intense dispute between the Philistines (art as a medium for social and moral purpose) and aesthetics (art as beauty and truth) that raged throughout the 1860s and 1870s.

The proponents of grace, athleticism, and activity for women had to wait for the Rational Dress Society, launched in 1881, to put forward their case. The Healthy and Artistic Dress Union swiftly followed it in 1889 pronouncing Victorian restraint unhygienic and spiritually detrimental. Women's clothing became looser, more opulent in texture and heavily influenced by medieval styling, folklore, fairytale, and Arthurian legend. The figure of woman as represented in painting was most commonly sleeping—a state of innocence and purity that also implied the awakening, or liberation (sartorial and sexual), into womanhood that was to follow in the fin de siècle era of decadence. The legacy of the aesthetic movement is most clearly seen in the artistic circles of the Bloomsbury Set in the early twentieth century and the hippie movement of the 1960s.

Neo-Edwardianism

The Teddy boy (derived from the nickname of Edward VII) grew out of a sensibility fostered in post–World War II Britain that the shared hardships of war and rationing would result in a more egalitarian society (Polhemus,

p. 34). The expectations of the young working class were manifested in the reworking of a neo-Edwardian style that had been pioneered by London's Savile Row tailors for their upper-class clients—single-breasted, long, and fitted jackets with velvet collars were worn with drainpipe trousers and brocaded waistcoats. Young men from the East End paired similar clothing with a cowboy's tie and the extravagant sentiments of American East Coast, black Zoot style. The adoption of these specific signifiers served to ally Britain's working classes simultaneously with the American Dream, and the outsiders who challenged it. In doing so, the Teds presented a challenge to establishment British society, particularly by subverting aristocratic dress codes, and this subcultural style served as blueprint for all the street style that followed in the latter half of the twentieth century.

Retro

The fashion for retro styling had often left the industry open to accusations of moribund nostalgia. Both at street level—the Teds by the Edwardians, the mods by the Italians, glam-rock by the aesthetics, the casuals by the mods, the goths by the punks—and at the level of high design, the speed and influence of revivalism has increased incrementally over the last forty years, to the point that even futurism is retro. But critics ignore the importance of sociopolitical and cultural context in the process of selection. This is particularly apparent in high design. Walter Benjamin, in *Theses on the Philosophy of History*, speaks of the creative "tiger's leap" into the past, the aggressive and specific selection of historical reference to serve contemporary comment. Historical revivalism is most often used as a tool to create a pervasive, and recognizable, environment for fashion that responds very pertinently to the times in which it is created. Arguably, there is nothing new to create, only creative ways of reinterpreting the past. As the designer John Galliano points out, "What's modern? . . . Gucci? Or Prada? That's just their interpretation of modern but it's still an historical take. . . . I think reinterpreting things with today's influences, today's fabric technology is what it's all about" (Frankel, p. 176).

See also Aesthetic Dress; Goths; Retro Style.

Bibliography

Burman Baines, Barbara. *Fashion Revivalism: From the Elizabethan Age to the Present Day*. London: B. T. Batsford, Ltd., 1981.

Frankel, Susannah. *Visionaries: Interviews with Fashion Designers*. London: V and A Publications, 2001.

Lambourne, Lionel. *The Aesthetic Movement*. London: Phaidon Press Ltd., 1996.

Polhemus, Ted. *Fashion and Anti-Fashion: An Anthropology of Clothing and Adornment*. London: Thames and Hudson, Inc., 1978.

Internet Resource

Benjamin, Walter. "Theses on the Concept of History." Available from <http://www.tasc.ac.uk/depart/media/staff/ls/WBenjamim/CONCEPT2.html>.

Alice Cicolini

HOLLYWOOD STYLE

In 1974, Diana Vreeland organized an exhibition at the Metropolitan Museum of Art, devoted to studio designs. The exhibition's title, *Romantic and Glamorous: Hollywood Style*, sums up perfectly the way in which traditional "Hollywood style" is perceived. It is seen as synonymous with glamour and opulence. Vreeland emphasized this in the exhibition's catalog: "Everything was larger than life. The diamonds were bigger, the furs were thicker and more luxurious . . . silks, satins, velvets and chiffons, miles and miles of ostrich feathers . . . everything was an exaggeration" (p. 5).

Certainly this is true of archetypal "Hollywood style." But, arguably, there is another important factor—the way in which cinema can be used to sell most products and, in particular, to disseminate new fashions. As Charles Eckert argues, Hollywood gave consumerism its "distinctive bent"—it influenced the way men and women wanted to look, as well as the cars they chose to drive, and the cigarettes they decided to smoke. Gradually, this influence became globalized.

This potential power was not immediately perceived. However, as early as 1907 there was widespread public interest in the rumored disappearance of Florence Lawrence, the "Biograph Girl." A desire to know about the private lives and off-screen activities of the first identifiable stars was apparent at an early stage.

With the identification and growing popularity of stars such as Mary Pickford, Gloria Swanson, and Irene Castle before, during, and after World War I, women began to see the star "image" as something to emulate. During the radical sartorial changes that took place in the 1920s, Hollywood was a vital part of the process through which it became both desirable and socially acceptable for women to wear makeup, after a century of taboo. The carbon lighting of early films meant makeup was a necessity—pink cheeks became gray and skin bleached. Max Factor, a makeup artist for the Moscow State Theatre, arrived in Los Angeles in 1908, and by 1914 he had perfected a product called Supreme Grease-paint for all the studios, along with newly developed eye shadows and pencil liners. This product was packaged in a compact tube and manufactured in several colors, and in a very short time he was selling directly to the public, for it was the faces of the stars that had the most impact on the public at this early stage.

Clara Bow was the first star that women set out to imitate, copying her "Cupid's bow" mouth and penciled brows. Furthermore, her bobbed hair made the new cuts desirable. Bow portrayed the sort of girl who, although unusually pretty, was not too far removed from the world of her female fans.

This kind of popularity with a female fan base meant that a star could popularize not one, but several fashions. Just as in the next decade Garbo would make berets, trench coats, and men's pajamas simultaneously desirable, so Clara Bow persuaded women to shorten their skirts, bare their legs, and adopt the cloche hat, which had been in fashion for some time. And in 1928 Jean Harlow, the "Platinum Blonde," prompted many women to experiment with peroxide; hence, safe home hair dyes were swiftly produced. Harlow also made a Paris fashion popular—the backless, bias-cut dress she wore in *Dinner at Eight* (1933) was instantly copied.

Retailing Tie-ins

Hollywood studios were beginning to appreciate their power. The studio system, which lasted until the 1950s, meant that stars and costume designers were under contract to a particular studio, which could profit from their work. The studios owned distribution rights in cinemas across America, and it was easy to export Hollywood films, first to Europe and later worldwide, despite the existence of national cinemas elsewhere. In the early 2000s, despite the vast size of the Hindi film industry, American cinema was still dominant.

The fashion industry had been swift to recognize the commercial possibilities of the cinema—in 1923

Salvatore Ferragamo, founder of the firm, provided every single pair of sandals for *The Ten Commandments*. Couture designers became involved—Paul Poiret designed the clothes worn by Sarah Bernhardt in *Elizabeth I* (1912) and Sam Goldwyn lured Chanel to Hollywood. Meanwhile, the studios, becoming aware of the appeal of the costumes designed by Adrian and his peers, worked speedily to prevent unauthorized copying and to maximize profit.

In 1930 the Movie Merchandising Bureau was established, and Macy's had a Cinema Shop. During the 1930s different studios would issue their own licenses, so that by the end of the decade there were various different retail outlets within department stores across America. This was the age of the "tie-in," when promotional campaigns linked to particular films were highly successful—window displays featured not only clothes and accessories from a particular film but also other themed goods. *Queen Christina* (1933), for example, was used to promote "hostess gowns" and Swedish flatware.

The fan magazines were at the height of their popularity—and discussions raged in their pages. Dorothy Lamour conducted a dialogue with her fans as to whether or not she should make another "sarong" film. In fact, she would always be associated with this garment, designed for her by Edith Head—and now a wardrobe staple. At the same time, glossy magazines were debating the question of whether Hollywood could lead fashion, or merely follow Paris.

Gone with the Wind (1939) influenced bridal wear for decades—and it was suggested that Dior had the popularity of the film's costumes in mind when he created the New Look. The decade had also made lingerie an enormously profitable business through the slips, negligees, and marabou slippers seen on screen.

The Postwar Period

The influence of Hollywood did not end in 1939—and included body shape. The busty stars of the 1950s meant enormous profits for the underwear industry, and Marilyn Monroe was arguably the most influential star of all time, as women sought the different components of her "look."

With the emulation of Marlon Brando and James Dean in the 1950s, and the gym culture, which resulted from the sight of well-muscled male bodies in the action pictures popular from the 1980s onward, it seems that men in the postwar period have been more influenced by Hollywood than ever before. Men's wear designers responded quickly, and continue to remain heavily involved. Ralph Lauren's designs for Robert Redford in *The Great Gatsby* (1974) were not as heavily covered in the press as his women's wear for Diane Keaton in *Annie Hall* (1977). However, it had been clearly demonstrated that a mainstream Hollywood film could be used to showcase clothes not unlike those in the designer's current ready-to-wear range, and Armani was the first to manipulate this opportunity by dressing Richard Gere for *American Gigolo* (1980); Cerruti followed his lead by dressing Michael Douglas for a number of influential films in the 1980s, including *Wall Street* (1988). Much of what we wear is a legacy of Hollywood—trousers for women, tennis shoes for everyday, leather jackets, jeans, and T-shirts. Yet some designers were never convinced—Elsa Schiaparelli complained that Joan Crawford's shoulder pads were copied from her collections and that Adrian had simply stolen the concept. Vivienne Westwood's one foray into cinema—she designed the collection supposedly produced by Richard E. Grant in the box-office debacle *Prêt-à-Porter* (1995)—has obviously made some other designers wary of involvement. But attempts to use film as a way of presenting new ideas continue; Uma Thurman's yellow trainers for *Kill Bill* (2003) did not impress audiences, but Samuel L. Jackson's Kangol beret in the same hue, worn in *Jackie Brown* (1997) meant that their already buoyant sales figures virtually doubled.

See also Actors and Actresses, Impact on Fashion; Film and Fashion.

Bibliography

Bruzzi, Stella. *Undressing Cinema: Clothing and Identity in the Movies*. London: Routledge, 1997.

Eckert, Charles. "The Carole Lombard in Macy's Window." In *Fabrications: Costume and the Female Body*. Edited by Jane Gaines and Charlotte Herzog. London: Routledge, 1990.

Fox, Patty. *Star Style: Hollywood Legends as Fashion Icons*. Santa Monica: Calif.: Angel City Press, 1999.

Maeder, Edward. "Hollywood and Seventh Avenue." In his *Hollywood and History: Costume Design in Film*. Los Angeles: Thames and Hudson, Inc., 1987.

Pamela Church Gibson

HORST, HORST P.

Horst Paul Albert Bohrmann (1906–1999) was one of the most creative and prolific fashion photographers of the twentieth century. (He took the name of Horst P. Horst during World War II and was known professionally simply as Horst.) From the beginning of his career in 1931 until 1992, when failing eyesight forced him to abandon his work, his photographs graced the pages of American, French, British, German, Spanish, and Italian editions of *Vogue, Vanity Fair, House and Garden*, and a host of photography magazines, books, and catalogs. Horst came to prominence in the 1930s, by which time the power unique to the medium of photography was dramatically apparent to promoters of fashion. He is appreciated in the twenty-first century not only for the spare elegance and refined glamour of his fashion work, which produced icons of the genre, but also for his myriad portraits, male and female nudes, flower studies, and pictures of homes and gardens.

Early Life and Training

Horst Bohrmann was born in Weissenfels-an-der-Saale, Thuringia, in 1906, the second son of prosperous, middle-class, Protestant parents. The family suffered financial hardships as a result of World War I but eventually recovered in the 1920s, enabling Horst to attend the Hamburg School of Applied Art, where he studied furniture making and carpentry. Exposure to Bauhaus principles and personalities led him to seek an apprenticeship in Paris with Le Corbusier. However, Horst was disappointed both with the projects and the great architect himself and soon quit. Wandering about Paris in search of something more vital, he encountered the fashion photographer George Hoyningen-Huene, by then well-established at Condé Nast. Soon Horst was a familiar figure at the studio, helping his older friend arrange sets and lighting, as well as serving as a male model for some of Huene's most striking swimwear images, and even starring in a short film with Natasha Paley (now sadly lost).

First Photographic Assignments

In the spring of 1931 Horst was given a sudden chance to try his own hand at the métier. Dr. Mehemed Agha, American *Vogue*'s celebrated art director, was then visiting Paris and thought Horst might have the required talents. Horst passed his initial tests, which required still lifes of accessories and jewelry, with flying colors, these first photographs being published in the November and December issues of *Vogue*. An invitation to work from American *Vogue* soon followed, but the engagement was short-lived: he was sent back to Europe for insubordination. When Hoyningen-Huene later left Paris for an assignment for *Vanity Fair* in Hollywood, Horst shouldered his work, and when his friend and mentor left *Vogue* for good in 1935, it was Horst who inherited the mantle as photographer-in-chief. Almost immediately, Condé Nast recalled him to New York, though he was allowed to continue to photograph the Paris collections each season. By 1937 he was firmly established in New York.

In 1942 Horst volunteered to serve in the United States Army, and despite being initially classed as an enemy alien, he was called up in July 1943 as a photographer. His assignments, however, remained on American soil. At war's end he was invited to the White House for a portrait commission of President Truman.

Postwar Life and Work

The postwar decades were filled with fashion and portrait assignments on both sides of the Atlantic, as well as trips to Mexico, Syria, Iran, and the new state of Israel.

Horst P. Horst. One of the most prolific and inventive fashion photographers of the twentieth century, Horst P. Horst first came to prominence in the 1930s. During a sixty-year career in photography, his photographs appeared in numerous magazines, including *Vanity Fair* and *Vogue*. COURTESY OF FAHEY/KLEIN GALLERY, LOS ANGELES, @ WWW.FAHEYKLEINGALLERY.COM. REPRODUCED BY PERMISSION.

Moreover, he moved in the same circles as luminaries such as the film director Luchino Visconti, the artist Leonor Fini, Coco Chanel, Salvador Dali, Marlene Dietrich, Gertrude Stein, President and Mrs. Eisenhower, Gore Vidal, Yves St. Laurent, and Jacqueline Bouvier. He became close friends with a number of these people.

In 1952 Horst began to fall out of favor at *Vogue*, whose new editor, Jessica Davies, imposed rigid rules on the photographers. His fortunes were restored in 1962, however, when the much more supportive Diana Vreeland arrived to head the magazine. In 1971, on the latter's departure from *Vogue*, Horst gravitated to *House and Garden*, where he had occasionally worked beginning in 1947. He returned to Europe for an extensive cruise-wear assignment with French *Vogue*, which led to renewed work for the magazine.

Notable Exhibitions and Publications

From the early 1930s Horst exhibited both his professional and personal work, at first in European galleries, then more gradually in museums, most of which were hesitant to accept fashion photography as a legitimate domain of art. Significant group exhibitions include *Fashion 1900–1939* at the Victoria and Albert Museum, London, 1975; *Fashion Photography* and *Fleeting Gestures*, at the International Center of Photography, New York, in 1977 and 1984, respectively; *Lichtbildnisse: Das Porträt in der Fotografie*, at the Rheinisches Landesmuseum in Bonn in 1982; and *Das Akfoto*, at the Fotomuseum in Munich in 1985. Major gallery exhibitions were held at the Galerie la Plume d'Or, Paris, in 1932; at the Germain Seligman Gallery, New York, in 1938; at the Sonnabend Gallery, New York, in 1974 and 1980; at Hamilton's Gallery, London, in 1986 and 1999; at the Staley-Wise Gallery, New York, in 1984; and at the Galerie Thierry, Paris, in 1999.

Horst's major retrospective of his fashion work was organized by the International Center of Photography, New York, in 1984; it then traveled to the Fortuny Palace, Venice, in 1985. A retrospective look at his fashion photography was held at the Musée des Arts de la Mode, the Louvre, Paris, in 1991. A major retrospective of his portraits was shown at the National Gallery, London, in 2001.

Horst's own books include *Photographs of a Decade*, 1944; *Patterns from Nature*, 1946; *Salute to the Thirties*, 1971; *Return Engagement: Faces to Remember—Then and Now* (with writer James Watters), 1984; and *Horst: Images of Elegance*, 1993.

Horst's Legacy

Most critics consider Horst's prewar fashion photographs, together with a select number of portraits from the same era, to be his finest work. His style, consistent across the various genres he explored, was characterized by a high degree of eclecticism. There are manifold references to art history, and he made liberal use of classical, baroque, and surrealist props and decor along with witty trompe l'oeil effects. Appreciative of historical precedents, he was as able to fabricate pictorial images in the style of Baron de Meyer as easily as he could cool modernist pictures in the style of Edward Steichen and Hoyningen-Huene. Horst's women subjects, in fashion studies or in portraits, project the power of their sex rather than the power of sex; they are bold, poised, and serene. Horst saw the body in architectonic terms, so that appendages of the body could be severed and reassembled to striking effect. Above all, he is known for his exquisite compositional sense, prompting an early admirer, Janet Flanner, to characterize his work as "a linear romance." His work influenced many younger photographers of fashion, portraiture, flowers, and the nude, including Robert Mapplethorpe, Bruce Weber, and Herb Ritts.

See also Fashion Photography; Hoyningen-Huene, George; Vogue; Vreeland, Diana.

Bibliography

Deal, Joe. "Horst on Fashion Photography." *Image* 18 (September 1975): 1–11.

Ewing, William A. *The Photographic Art of Hoyningen-Huene.* New York: Rizzoli International, 1986.

Flood, Richard. "Horst." *Artforum* (October 1980): 81.

Hall-Duncan, Nancy. *The History of Fashion Photography.* New York: Alpine Book Company, 1979. This publication gives an overall context for Horst's contribution to fashion photography.

Horst, Horst P. *Photographs of a Decade.* New York: J. J. Augustin, 1944.

——. *Patterns from Nature.* New York: J. J. Augustin, 1946.

——. *Salute to the Thirties.* New York: Viking Press, 1971.

Lawford, Valentine. *Horst: His Work and His World.* New York: Alfred A. Knopf, 1984.

Liberman, Alexander. *The Art and Technique of Color Photography.* New York: Simon and Schuster, 1951.

Pepper, Terence. *Horst Portraits: 60 Years of Style.* New York: Harry N. Abrams, 2001. An exhibition catalog. This publication, accompanying the retrospective exhibition of Horst's photographs, *Horst Portraits: Sixty Years of Style*, includes a detailed chronology of Horst's life by Robin Muir.

Rose, Barbara. "Horst in Fashion." *Vogue*, May 1976, 175–176, 208.

William Ewing

HOYNINGEN-HUENE, GEORGE

George Hoyningen-Huene (1900–1968) is remembered as one of the finest fashion photographers of the 1920s and 1930s. He was born in St. Petersburg, Russia, to a Baltic nobleman, the chief equerry to Tsar Alexander III, and an American mother whose own father had been the United States Minister Plenipotentiary and Envoy Extraordinary to the Russian court. Huene's early upbringing was one of privilege, though the revolution brought those advantages to an abrupt end: the family's properties were confiscated, and they were forced to flee for their lives.

Huene settled in Paris. Dreaming at first of reclaiming his rightful heritage, he participated briefly in the British Expeditionary Force's disastrous campaign against the Reds in 1918. However, the fiasco taught him that there was no turning back the historical clock and that he would have to forge a new life for himself in the West.

While the family chose exile in London, Huene settled in Paris, where he supported himself with a series of odd jobs, the most interesting being the role of an extra in cinema. Delighted to be in a city that so valued art, for which he had long harbored a passion, Huene decided to pursue drawing and painting, signing up for classes with the famed cubist instructor André Lohte. Huene was instinctively attracted to the world of couture, which he saw as another manifestation of art, and he was quick to grasp that a topflight fashion illustrator like Georges Lepape or Edouard Benito could command a high salary. Huene first put his drawing talents to work for Yteb, his sister Betty's dressmaking business, and by 1925 he had expanded his clientele considerably, selling illustrations to *Harper's Bazaar*, *Women's Wear*, and *Le Jardin des modes*.

Never one to be chained to a desk, Huene teamed up with his new friend, the photographer Man Ray, to produce a portfolio of "the most beautiful women in Paris."

Huene's role had only been to recruit the women, but *Vogue*'s Main Bocher (later the couturier Main-bocher) was impressed with the ambitious project, and while he didn't accept it for *Vogue*, he took it upon himself to introduce the young man to Edna Chase, the editor-in-chief of the magazine. This led to his "first real job," as he put it, as an illustrator, though Huene always suspected that Chase's decision had more to do with Huene's access to the world of glamorous women than it did with his drawing skills.

Huene fell into photography literally by chance, though in retrospect he seems to have been slowly gravitating toward the métier. He took every opportunity at the *Vogue* studio to help photographers with their sets and lighting, and when one of the photographers did not appear one morning in 1926, Huene stepped in. Thus begun a ten-year photographic collaboration with *Vogue*.

Huene brought a neoclassical style, lightly inflected by cubism, to the magazine, a mix perfectly attuned to the zeitgeist. H. K. Frenzel's introduction to a slim volume of Huene's portraits, published in 1932, notes how

> Ionic columns rose alongside factory smokestacks, Greek temples alongside railroad tunnels and depots . . . and the ladies and gentlemen of Paris, London, New York and Biarritz enjoyed the sunshine among pedestals from which the gods of ancient Greece looked down in naked silence, between snorting stallions and muscular heroes.

Greek columns, temples, and statuary were common motifs in Huene's imagery; thus enobling the clothes. Not surprisingly, he admired the couture of Madame Grès ("fluid, harmonious and sculptural"), Madame Vionnet ("Her clothes were built like great architecture"), and Coco Chanel, whom he appreciated for her "absolute assurance of her own talent, competence and authority."

At *Vogue* Huene had the chance to study the contributions of his predecessors, and in the case of Edward Steichen—then chief photographer at *Vogue*—even to watch him work. From Baron de Meyer's early twentieth-century fashion photography he learned the power of suggestion, "the mysterious air of making every woman look like a vision in a dream," and from Steichen he learned the importance of psychology:

> In addition to directing the activities of his assistants the photographer plays the clown, the

enthusiast, the flatterer. He acts and talks about other things while his mind is watching the building up of the picture—its lights, shadows and lines; its essential fashion photograph requirements—distinction, elegance, and chic.

Huene also absorbed a great deal from painters, and two friends made particularly strong impressions: the painter and fellow Russian Pavel Tchelitchev, who accepted commissions for magazine covers in addition to his own personal art work and could be as enthusiastic about workman's clothes and army surplus gear as he was about haute couture; and Christian Bérard, an artist famed for his Dionysian temperament that was poles apart from Huene's own more own Apollonian sensibilities.

Huene also followed developments in cinema and photography. He rubbed shoulders with personalities as diverse as the French photographer Henri Cartier-Bresson, the American dancer Josephine Baker, and the Armenian mystic G. I. Gurdjieff. He played bit roles in movies and even tried his hand at making three films, all of which were subsequently lost. Although his fashion work has long been given its due, his exquisite portraiture has not received the attention it deserves. His photographs of his great friend and fellow photographer Horst P. Horst, the authors Jean Cocteau and Janet Flanner, the composer Igor Stravinsky, the photographers Baron de Meyer and Cecil Beaton, the actor Johnny Weismuller, the painter and sculptor Alexander Calder, Coco Chanel, and dozens of other celebrities of the day, never resort to formulaic poses or superficial flattery but always find a way of signifying their subjects' originality.

The second significant period of Huene's fashion photography (though it could never match his Paris output) was spent at *Harper's Bazaar* in New York, where he arrived in 1935. Although Huene continued to innovate, the magazine's art director, Alexey Brodovitch's, penchant for bleeding photographs off the page and over-laying graphic elements on the image undermined the integrity of Huene's exquisitely balanced compositions. Gradually he began to lose interest in his photographic work. American fashions could never match their French counterparts; the problem solving that had once given him so much pleasure no longer did so, and the business-is-everything climate of New York was increasingly discouraging.

Huene escaped, temporarily, to the ancient world of the Middle East, looking for spiritual renewal. He found solace on grand voyages across Africa and Arabia. One beautifully written book, *African Mirage, the Record of a Journey* (1938), came of his travels, and other journeys resulted in equally fine photographic albums (*Hellas* in 1943; *Egypt* in 1943; *Mexican Heritage* in 1943; and *Baalbek/Palmyra* in 1946).

In the mid-1940s Huene abandoned fashion photography, leaving it to a new generation less committed to his prewar ideal of elegance. He famously greeted the young Richard Avedon, just beginning his own career in photography, with the words, "Too bad, Too late!" His mind was increasingly set on travel—especially spiritual explorations—and he was willing to try new ways of earning a living. He taught photography at the Art Center School in Pasadena, California, experimented briefly with drugs under the guidance of Aldous Huxley, and served as a color coordinator for several filmmakers such as Jean Negulesco, Michael Kidd, Michael Curtiz, and most notably, George Cukor, who became a great friend.

Hoyningen-Huene first exhibited in a Parisian group show in 1928, in the *Premier Salon indépendant de la photographie*, and was invited to show several works at the seminal *Film und Foto* exhibition in Stuttgart in 1929. He did not show his work again until 1963, when he was selected for Cologne's influential *Photokina* exhibition. However, it was only after his death that he was acknowledged by two important collective exhibitions: *Fashion Photography: Six Decades*, shown at the Emily Lowe Gallery at Hofstra University, Hempstead, New York in 1975, and *History of Fashion Photography*, held at the International Museum of Photography in Rochester, New York, in 1979, and with a full retrospective, *Eye for Elegance*, at the International Center of Photography in New York. In the interim, fashion photography had been treated as a minor commercial vein, and books and exhibitions rare, though one exception should be noted: *Glamor Portraits*, held at the Museum of Modern Art in 1965.

George Hoyningen-Huene died of a heart attack at his home in Los Angeles in 1968. His outstanding contribution to fashion photography is unquestioned, and he broadened this field with his erudition and his flair. In the final analysis the full range of his photography must be considered in any appreciation. His legacy is as a coherent system of images, chiefly of fashion and portrait studies, which were characterized by precision, economy of means, harmony, elegance, and psychological acuity.

See also Fashion Photography; Film and Fashion.

Bibliography

Beaton, Cecil. *The Magic Image: The Genius of Photography from 1839 to the Present Day*. Boston: Little Brown, 1975.

Chase, Edna Wollman, and Ilka Chase. *Always in Vogue*. New York: Doubleday, 1954

Devlin, Polly. *Vogue Book of Fashion Photography 1919-1979*. New York: Simon and Schuster, 1979.

Ewing, William. *Eye for Elegance: George Hoyningen-Huene* (exhibition catalog). New York: Congreve Press; International Center of Photography, 1980

———. *The Photographic Art of Hoyningen-Huene*. London and New York: Thames and Hudson, Inc.; Rizzoli International 1986

Frenzel, H. K.. *Hoyningen-Huene: Meisterbildenisse*. Berlin: Verlag Dietrich Reineer, 1932

Harrison, Martin. *Appearances: Fashion Photography since 1945*. London: Jonathan Cape, 1991.

Horst, Horst P. *Salute to the Thirties*, foreword by Janet Flanner. New York: Viking Press, 1971

Maloney, Tom. "Hoyningen-Huene." *U.S. Camera Annual*, 1950

Pepper, Terence. *Horst Portraits, London, Paris, New York*. London: National Portrait Gallery, 2001

Pucciani, Oreste, ed. *Hoyningen-Huene* (exhibition catalog). Los Angeles: Los Angeles University Press, 1970

William Ewing

HUGO BOSS

At the start of the twenty-first century Hugo Boss AG was among the biggest companies producing menswear in Germany and, in the last decade of the twentieth century, dominated the German menswear designer market through the distribution of various lines and licenses. In 1923 Hugo Boss founded the clothing company in Metzingen, near Stuttgart in the south of Germany. At first the company specialized in the production of work clothes, overalls, raincoats, and uniforms. From 1933 onward it made uniforms for German storm troopers, Wehrmacht, and Hitler Youth. Boss brought forced laborers from Poland and France to his factory to boost output in the following years. When Boss died in 1948, the factory returned to making uniforms for postal and police workers. In 1953 it produced its first men's suits.

By the early 1970s, after several changes in the management and ownership since the founding of the company, Jochen and Uwe Holy, the grandchildren of Boss, took over work-wear manufacturing, and the duo started to manufacture fashion-conscious men's suits and sportswear. In the following years the new owners turned Hugo Boss from a work-wear manufacturer into a stylish clothes company for formal men's wear. Hugo Boss was the first German company to construct a brand identity within the men's wear sector.

After the relaunch of the Boss brand in the early 1970s, the company developed steadily into an international fashion designer house. In the 1980s, Hugo Boss constructed a high degree of brand awareness through the distribution of licenses and brand extension in fragrances, dress shirts, sportswear, knits, and leatherwear. Boss went public in Germany in 1985. Their formal menswear, in particular, became strongly associated with the Yuppie.

Family control ended in 1992, and since 1993 Mazzotto S.p.A. in Valdagno, Italy, has held majority control of Hugo Boss AG. The company operates in more than ninety countries with a product range including body-wear, cosmetics, evening wear, eyewear, fine clothing, formal wear, fragrances, hosiery, leisurewear, shoes, and watches. Since control by Mazzotto began, Hugo Boss AG has applied a three-brand strategy for the men's wear market under the labels Boss Hugo Boss, Hugo, and Baldessarini. Boss Man, the company's core brand is divided into three subsidiary labels—Black Label (business and leisure wear), Orange Label (urban sportswear), and Green Label (outdoor activewear).

The Hugo brand encompasses an avant-garde collection, which is designed for business and leisure, and which combines unconventional details with new materials. The Baldessarini brand is the most sophisticated label, featuring the finest Italian fabrics and hand stitching. As a traditional men's wear manufacturer, Hugo Boss made an unsuccessful attempt to start a women's wear line in 1987. Eleven years later Hugo Boss successfully launched the female counterpart to the male Hugo label. In 2000 the designer brand introduced Boss Woman, designed for the sophisticated female business-woman. The Hugo Boss brand is clearly defined by a dynamic design with an emphasis on functionality, clean lines, and attention to details.

The Hugo Boss collections are distributed on the international market through selected specialty stores and Hugo Boss monobrand shops. The collections are designed and managed according to a standardized concept that reflects the clean, stylish brand image applied at monobrand shops worldwide. Nevertheless, the company opened a 20,000-square-foot store in New York City in 2001 that presented all brands and collections under one roof for the first time.

See also Formal Wear, Men's; Suit, Business; Uniforms, Military; Uniforms, Occupational.

Bibliography

Clark, Andrew. "Dressed for Success." *Guardian*, 24 February 2001. Available from <http://guardian.co.uk>. Interview with Werner Baldessarini, the chairman of Hugo Boss.

Givhan, Robin. "Fashion Firm Discovers Its Holocaust History: Clothier Hugo Boss Supplied Nazi Uniforms with Forced Labour." *Washington Post*, 14 August 1997.

Thomas Hecht

IRIBE, PAUL

Paul Iribe (1883–1935) was born in Angoulême, France. He started his career in illustration and design as a newspaper typographer and magazine illustrator at numerous Parisian journals and daily papers, including *Le temps* and *Le rire*. In 1906 Iribe collaborated with a number of avant-garde artists to create the satirical journal *Le témoin*, and his illustrations in this journal attracted the attention of the fashion designer Paul Poiret. Poiret commissioned Iribe to illustrate his first major dress collection in a 1908 portfolio entitled *Les robes de Paul Poiret racontées par Paul Iribe*. This limited edition publication (250 copies) was innovative in its use of vivid fauvist colors and the simplified lines and flattened planes of Japanese prints. To create the plates, Iribe utilized a hand-coloring process called *pochoir*, in which bronze or zinc stencils are used to build up layers of color gradually. This publication, and others that followed, anticipated a revival of the fashion plate in a modernist style to reflect a newer, more streamlined fashionable silhouette. In 1911 the couturier Jeanne Paquin also hired Iribe, along with the illustrators Georges Lepape and Georges Barbier, to create a similar portfolio of her designs, entitled *L'Eventail et la fourrure chez Paquin*.

Throughout the 1910s Iribe became further involved in fashion and added design for theater, interiors, and jewelry to his repertoire. He continued to illustrate fashion, opened a store of decorative art on the rue du Faubourg St.-Honoré in Paris, and created textiles for the firm Bianchini Ferier and for designer André Groult. His association with the theater resulted in several publications related to the renowned dancer Vaslav Nijinsky, including the album *Prélude à l'aprés-midi d'un faune*, which captured Nijinsky's choreography for the Claude Debussy composition in photography by Adolph de Meyer.

Iribe is perhaps best recognized for his contributions to the *Gazette du bon ton*. Started in 1912 by the publisher Lucien Vogel, the fashion journal featured the creations of the top couture houses illustrated by the leading visual artists of the day, including Iribe, Georges Barbier, Georges Lepape, A. E. Marty, and Charles Martin. Like Iribe's earlier work, the magazine was a deluxe limited-edition journal. The publication included between eight and ten *pochoir* plates in each issue and helped position fashion graphics as a modern medium. While the *Gazette du bon ton* slowed its publication during World War I, it resumed putting out monthly editions from the end of the war until 1925, and a total of sixty-nine issues were printed. In 1925, the publisher Condé Nast purchased the *Gazette* and it merged with *Vogue*.

In 1919 Iribe moved to New York, and his art deco style was further disseminated to the American fashion-buying public through his continued work in fashion illustration and interior design. His work was published in seven issues of American *Vogue*, and he also opened a store on Fifth Avenue called Paul Iribe Designs New York–Paris. Iribe was one of the first French fashion figures to work in Hollywood. Cecil B. DeMille commissioned him to create clothing for Gloria Swanson in the 1919 film *Male and Female*. This film marked the beginning of a six-year collaboration with the Hollywood studio, during which Iribe acted as artistic director for eight DeMille films.

Iribe moved back to France in 1930 and became involved in numerous design projects, including the publication of *Choix*, a book that showcased his designs for furniture, decorative arts, and jewelry. He continued to design jewelry, working with Coco Chanel in 1932 to create a line that her couture house produced. In 1933 Iribe was awarded *la Légion d'honneur* for his work as an artist-illustrator. He died of a heart attack in 1935 at Chanel's villa in Roquebrune Cap Martin, France.

See also Art and Fashion; Art Nouveau and Art Deco; Dance and Fashion; Fashion Illustrators; Fashion Magazines.

Bibliography

Lelieur, Anne-Claude. *Paul Iribe: Précurseur de l'art déco*. Paris: Bibliothèque Forney, 1983.

Mackrell, Alice. *An Illustrated History of Fashion: 500 Years of Fashion Illustration*. New York: Costume and Fashion Press, 1997.

Robinson, Julian. *The Golden Age of Style: Art Deco Fashion Illustration*. New York: Harcourt Brace Jovanovich, 1976.

Michelle Tolini Finamore

ITALIAN FASHION

During the Renaissance, Italian city-states such as Florence were centers of fashion innovation. For centuries thereafter, however, Paris dominated the world of fashion. Of course, fashions were produced in Italy during that time, but they were usually derivative of French styles. Only since the 1950s has Italy achieved its own independent identity as a source of fashionable clothing for the rest of the world.

The emergence of the "Italian look" drew on important historical advantages, such as the existence of fine craft traditions in textile production, luxury leather goods, high-quality tailoring, and other trades crucial to the fashion system. The artistic textiles and garments of Mariano Fortuny were well known internationally in the decades before World War II, as were the superb men's woolen suiting fabrics woven by Ermenegildo Zegna and fine accessories made by Ferragamo and Gucci. Still, it is symbolic of Italy's relative invisibility on the international fashion scene that Italy's most famous prewar designer, Elsa Schiaparelli, was based in Paris.

Modern Italian fashion first came to international prominence with the rapid post-World War II war reconstruction of the textile industry and the rise of ready-to-wear clothing production, as Nicola White documents in her important book *Reconstructing Italian Fashion*. The postwar rise of Italian fashion was not accidental. A number of Italian manufacturers, with the support of the Italian government, made a systematic effort to create an export-oriented fashion industry that would play a significant role in Italy's postwar economic reconstruction. Beginning in 1949 fashion shows designed to emphasize Italy's heritage of art and culture were staged to capture the attention of foreign journalists. In July 1951 a pivotal fashion show in Florence attracted almost two hundred American buyers and journalists, along with another hundred from Italy and elsewhere in Europe. Soon journalists and department store buyers attending the Paris fashion shows began to take the train down to Florence. There, fashion presentations were conceived, in part, to cater to the demand for creatively constructed, well-made ready-to-wear combining distinction and informality, adapted to the American fondness for sunny weather and colorful, affordably priced garments. Originally, the Italian *alta mode* (couture) houses also showed in Florence, but soon the couturiers for a variety of reasons began to show instead in Rome, where many of them were members of Roman society. There they organized and presented their own singular creations for *la dolce vita*.

American journalists enthusiastically promoted "the Italian Look," identifying it with casual yet aristocratic elegance. Italian designers were said to have a special knack for resort wear; capri pants, sandals, gold jewelry, and chic sunglasses were essential elements of Italian style. Italian fashion offered an appealing (and less expensive) alternative to the more formal Paris couture.

The commercial and cultural relationship between Italy and America played an important role in the postwar development of Italian fashion. One manifestation of this was the close connection between the worlds of film and fashion. For example, the Fontana Sisters, who had opened their couture house in Rome in 1944, became closely associated with Hollywood glamour. Ava Gardner wore Fontana dresses in the 1953 film *The Barefoot Contessa*. Other film stars, including Audrey Hepburn, Elizabeth Taylor, and Kim Novak, wore Fontana Sisters evening dresses, and Margaret Truman was married in a Fontana Sisters wedding dress in 1956. Also important in the glamorous world of film was Emilio Schuberth, who was born in Naples in 1904 and opened a couture house in Rome in 1938. Among his clients were Gina Lollobrigida and Sophia Loren.

Emilio Pucci entered the fashion business in 1948 and quickly became known for his kaleidoscopic textile designs, which were made up into "featherweight" jersey scarves, shirts, and other separates. Pucci helped establish the reputation of Italian designers for easy, comfortable, body-conscious clothing. His brightly colored fashions were part of a broader range of Italian products, such as Vespa motor scooters and Olivetti typewriters, that became icons of modern style. By the early 1960s, it was clear that Italy had changed the way the world looked; the word "Italian" had become synonymous with "good design."

Another important Italian designer was Roberto Capucci, born in 1930, who opened his own atelier in Rome in 1950 and quickly gained a reputation as a master of both silhouette and color. Capucci approached his work as an artist, pleating and manipulating fabric into fluid, sculptural forms. Probably the single most important and successful Italian designer to emerge during the 1960s was Valentino. Valentino Gavarni studied couture in Paris before opening his own *alta moda* house in Rome in 1960; his career now spans more than four decades. He designs both ready-to-wear and couture, and is known for his fondness for brilliant red fabrics. His opulent gowns have appealed to many celebrities, from Sophia Loren to Gwyneth Paltrow, but his most famous client was Jacqueline Kennedy, who wore a lace-trimmed Valentino dress for her marriage to Aristotle Onassis.

The Italian Look that had such a profound impact on women's fashions extended to men's wear as well. Even before World War II, Italy had an international reputation for the highest quality bespoke shirts and men's accessories. By the 1950s, tailoring firms such as Brioni created the "Continental look" in menswear. Italian tailors created luxurious, body-conscious suits that offered a clear alternative to the dominant Ivy League look of American men's wear and the traditional styles of London's Savile Row.

The persistent, unresolved competition between Florence and Rome, each with its own schedule of fashion shows, contributed to the rise of Milan, which emerged in the 1970s as the center of Italian fashion for both men and women. Some of the most innovative Italian houses, including Krizia and Missoni, shifted their collections to Milan, as did the influential stylist Walter Albini, who designed for several different firms that showed in Milan, as well as producing clothing for his own label.

A northern Italian industrial city, Milan lacked the historic allure of Rome and Florence, but was able to draw on the established Italian tradition of fine textiles. Textile producers in northern Italy provided financial backing to Italian clothing manufacturers who showed in Milan. Moreover, Milan was known for modern product design, and *Vogue Italia* had been published there beginning in 1961. The rise of a ready-to-wear clothing industry was a natural consequence of these circumstances. Two designers in particular rose to

prominence and worldwide fame in this milieu: Giorgio Armani and Gianni Versace.

Armani revolutionized men's wear in the 1970s, creating unstructured jackets that were as comfortable as sweaters and that radiated an air of seductive elegance. Armani's clothes were prominently featured in the 1980 film *American Gigolo*; by 1982 his picture was on the cover of *Time* magazine. His women's wear was also characterized by an easy elegance and luxurious minimalism. Meanwhile other Italian firms long known for fine fabrics and superb workmanship, such as Ermenegildo Zegna, also benefited from the rise of Italian tailoring to a position of world leadership from the 1970s onward.

Very different from Armani was Gianni Versace, who founded his own label in 1978. Where Armani emphasized understated luxury, his rival Versace grounded his designs in an aesthetic of flamboyance and display; he produced, for both men and women, some of the most sexually expressive clothing ever made within the mainstream of fashion. After Gianni Versace was murdered in 1997 in Miami, his sister Donatella became the company's head designer. Having collaborated closely with her brother for many years, she was able to build on his aesthetic, while also making her own contributions to the Versace style. Popular music, for example, had always been a passion of Gianni's, but became even more central to Donatella's style. Her body-revealing and consciously outrageous dresses, worn by top singers and actresses, became by the early 2000s an eagerly awaited feature of the annual Oscar and other entertainment business award ceremonies.

Franco Moschino was overshadowed commercially by Armani and Versace, but his witty send-ups of the fashion system were popular with women who wanted to be seen as stylish but not as "fashion victims." Other important Italian designers of the late twentieth and early twenty-first centuries include Romeo Gigli; Gianfranco Ferré; knitwear designer Laura Biagiotti; and Renzo Rosso, founder of the irreverent sportswear firm Diesel.

Among the most remarkable success stories of Italian fashion in the late twentieth century are the revival of Gucci under the direction of the American Tom Ford, the rise of the firm of Prada, and the impact of Dolce & Gabbana. After Miuccia Prada took charge of her grand-father's small, respected leatherwear firm in the 1980s, it burgeoned into an international phenomenon in accessories, shoes, and clothing. Her first big success was a black nylon backpack with a triangular silver label that became a must-have cult item among fashion-conscious women. By the mid-1990s, Prada bags and shoes were setting the international standard for cool. Meanwhile, Gucci, founded in the 1920s as a leather-goods firm, and famous among jet-setters in the 1960s, had lost prestige until its reinvention in the 1990s as a source of ultrasexy fashions and accessories. Domenico Dolce and Stefano Gabbana founded Dolce & Gabbana in 1982, and skyrocketed to fame with fashions that recall the sex-bomb stars of 1950s Italian cinema.

Italy's success as a center of modern fashion derives in large part from a uniquely Italian model of the fashion industry, quite different from that in other countries. It is immediately apparent, for example, that the family unit remains an important feature of the Italian fashion system. Craft traditions also remain strong. At the same time, the most up-to-date technology is readily available. While a handful of star designers from Milan and Rome attract public attention, hundreds of anonymous but highly trained creative talents work at family firms and large companies throughout the country. A skilled workforce is available both for factory employment and in small-scale production by independent contractors. Florence, Rome, and later Milan have all been important fashion centers, but the geography of Italian fashion is widely dispersed, and different regions of Italy specialize in different materials and goods. In addition to the regional segmentation of production in specific geographic areas known as "the Districts," the Italian fashion system is also characterized by the vertical integration of production from fiber to finished product.

The Italian fashion system in the early 2000s integrates state-of-the-art production of modern apparel, relaxed tailoring, luxury leather goods and knitwear, and research into new modes of design and production together with thread, yarn, and fabric innovations. Italian style is characterized by understated luxury and modernism, as well as glamour and sensuality. Fashion designers in Italy are not considered "artists" so much as skilled workers within an industrial system. One of the dominant characteristics of the Italian fashion industry is its interdisciplinary nature: the seamless blend of product development, new materials and technology, new communications methods, celebrity, tradition, and art.

Since the Biennale di Firenze in 1997, which included a city-wide exhibition that posed the relationship between art and fashion, further opportunities of this kind of convergence have been created; for example, the Fondazione Prada in Milan has an exhibition policy of promoting contemporary art. Nothing could be more representative of a designer's aesthetic spirit than a flagship store. In 2000, Prada Group hired the eminent architect Rem Koolhaas to conceive of new and technologically innovative retail spaces for the presentation of products in new and ultra-modern ways. And, as Guy Trebay wrote in the *New York Times*, Carla Sozzani, proprietor of Corso Como 10 in Milan, presents Italian and international luxury brands in a "true theater of commerce."

Italian fashion has evolved to supply the market with styles based on both the latest technology and traditional craftsmanship. Designers concur that imagination, research and experimentation are the basis for the Italian Look.

See also Armani, Giorgio; Capucci, Roberto; Dolce & Gabbana; Moschino, Franco; Prada; Pucci, Emilio; Valentino; Versace, Gianni and Donatella.

Bibliography

Bianchino, Gloria, et al. *Italian Fashion*. Milan: Electa, 1987.

Gastel, M. *50 anni di moda italiana*. Milan: Vallardi, 1995.

Giacomoni, Silvia. *The Italian Look Reflected*. Milan: Mazzotta, 1984.

Malossi, Gino, ed. *Il Motore della moda*. Florence: Monacelli Press, 1998.

Menkes, Susy. "Are Italian Designer Brands Having an Identity Crisis?" *International Herald Tribune*, 1 March 2000.

Steele, Valerie. *Fashion: Italian Style*. New Haven, Conn., and London: Yale University Press, 2003.

Trebay, Guy. "Fashion Diary; A Model and Her Traitorous Stilettos." *The New York Times*, 5 March 2002.

White, Nicola. *Reconstructing Italian Fashion: America and the Development of the Italian Fashion Industry*. Oxford: Berg, 2000.

Valerie Steele and Gillion Carrara

J

JAMES, CHARLES

Charles Wilson Brega James was born 18 July 1906, in Camberley, Surrey, England. He was described by a friend, Sir Francis Rose, as temperamental, artistic, and blessed even in childhood with the ability to escape the mundane chores of life like a trapeze artist. His mother's family was socially prominent in Chicago and his father was a British military officer, so young Charles experienced an international upbringing. He was educated at Harrow, a British public school, where he met the fellow fashion enthusiast and fashion photographer Cecil Beaton, whose images later defined James's work.

While still in his teens James initiated his design career in Chicago, where friends of his mother supported him. He began by making patterned scarves that he modeled and sold from his office desk at the architectural division of a utilities company, where he was employed. When he was fired from his job, he turned to millinery. He sculpted hats directly on the heads of clients in the shop he had named after a school friend, Charles Boucheron. In 1928 James left Chicago in a swirl of financial confusion and relocated in New York City. He was there long enough for Diana Vreeland to observe and comment on his hats, to have his hats merchandised through a prominent department store of the time, and to begin designing dresses before heading to London in 1929. For the next ten years he divided his time between London and Paris, with brief promotional journeys to Chicago and New York. During this period he opened his first salon in London, located in Mayfair, but he quickly declared bankruptcy. In 1933 he reopened the business.

James, who was never afraid to try new materials, spiraled a zipper around the torso in 1929, thus designing his famous taxi dress. The taxi dress and several other of his designs were licensed in the early 1930s so that manufacturers in both England and the United States could copy them. Marketed in famous department stores of the day—most notably Best and Company, Marshall Field's, and Fortnum and Mason— these garments gave his designs, if not his name, wide visibility. Friends of James's mother on both sides of the Atlantic were counted among his most enthusiastic clients for his increasing output of couture garments, at least until her death in 1944. Additionally, his designs intrigued actresses such as Gertrude Lawrence and women with artistic leanings such as Anne, countess of Rosse, and Marit Guinness Aschan. By this time, however, the twin nemeses of James's career were obvious: his desire to receive outsized financial rewards for his designs, coupled with perfectionism and his insistence on total control, eventually destroyed him.

The late 1930s were a period of great and lasting creativity for James. He produced the Corselette or L'Sylphide evening dress (1937); the two-pattern piece halter gown (1937); La Sirène evening dress with a pleated front panel (1938); a raised, pouf-fronted gown (1939); and the Figure-8 wrapped skirt (1939). In 1937 James held his first showing in Paris; included among the garments were striking wraps made of old silk ribbons from the firm of Colcombet. For the remainder of his design career, James produced variants of the ribbon gowns he first fashioned for this Paris show. The gowns were initially in two pieces, bodice and skirt, with the winglike skirt featuring tapering tips of ribbon ending in infinity at the waistline; later examples featured one-piece skirts constructed of cut fabric terminating in a much less graceful manner. Indeed, James continually reused many of the designs that he first created in the 1930s. For example, the garment made for Austine Hearst that James himself identified as his thesis in dressmaking, the 1953 Clover Leaf or Abstract gown, actually evolved from a trilobed, skirted gown created in 1938 and a cloverleaf crown hat designed in 1948. Excluding mass-produced designs of the 1930s, for which no records are known to exist, James created just over one thousand designs during his career. Only a few of James's designs are titled; those that generally identify a unique cut rather than a single garment.

Because of various financial escapades that skirted the limits of legality, James found himself in 1939 no longer welcome in England. The next year he opened Charles James, Incorporated, at 64 East Fifty-seventh Street, New York City. Virtually ignoring wartime rationing, he began designing collections for Elizabeth Arden and redesigning her couture collection in 1944; their relationship was severed in 1945 because of financial overruns. However, the Arden-James partnership spawned a Cecil Beaton drawing of several of James's greatest designs, including a variant of the Sirène gown, which is associated with the collaboration.

Following his year-long stint at Arden, James established himself at 699 Madison Avenue, the address where he remained longer than any other in his career. One observer quipped that it was James's perpetual house of torture, not couture. The majority of extant James couture creations came from the Madison Avenue workrooms. James did not let go of his creations easily. He made his clients pay, sometimes twice for the same gown, and sometimes for a garment he had also promised another client. He was notorious for not having garments delivered on time. He was known to cut completed garments off of clients because he was unhappy with either the product or the client. Despite his volatile and often outrageous behavior, his clients acknowledged his genius for cut and color, and many of them supported him financially until the end of his career.

James was obsessed with understanding exactly how clothes worked on the body. He spent thousands of dollars in 1950 and 1951 trying to understand how a sleeve worked. The result was an arced sleeve that drew an editorial observation that James's interest in a sleeve was equivalent to an engineer's interest in a bridge. The writer had it right, for James worked not only with tools associated with dressmaking but also construction tools like calipers, a compass, and a plumb line, among others. During his later years James tried teaching his theories, which related to the proportion of the female figure and how it intersected with apparel construction. In the end, some of his clients found his clothes a joy to wear, while others were tortured. One even bought two opera seat tickets, one for the skirt of her "Butterfly" gown, the other for its sweeping, layered tulle back panel.

So sure was James of the cut of his garments that only rarely does one find him using either patterned fabrics or surface embellishment. Indeed, one of the joys of looking at a James creation is following the flow of seams, seams that seem to go in previously unexplored directions. He made this indulgence easy by selecting contrasting fabrics, such as silk jersey, satin, and taffeta or velvet, organdy, and satin to meld in skirts of black, garnet, and tobacco brown or rose red, white, and ruby. He enjoyed blending cool celadon and celery greens, as well as contrasting warm moss and cool bottle greens. When combinations of purple, pink, and green were all the rage in the mid-1940s, James never blended such colors; rather, he would meld dusty rose and pale gold; mustard and maroon; and oranges and blacks in different materials. On a garment's surface he treated the two sides of the fabric equally, playing the color and texture of the one against the other.

For roughly a decade, from 1947 to 1954, James achieved success and recognition. His garments were acquired by many of the fabled socialites of the period, including Mrs. William (Babe) Paley, Mrs. William Randolph (Austine) Hearst Jr., Mrs. Harrison (Mona) Williams, Mrs. Cornelius Vanderbilt Whitney, Mme. Arturo Lopez-Willshaw; by fabled theatrical personalities such as Gypsy Rose Lee and Lily Pons; and by notable collectors of art such as Dominique de Menil. But the most important client of his career was Millicent Huddleston Rogers, a Standard Oil heiress. In her he found a perfect figure to dress, a client with whom he could discuss art and design. Moreover, she was able to pay his inflated prices. She arranged an exhibition of James's work at the Brooklyn Museum in 1948; the show featured the garments he had made for her during the previous ten years. These formed the nucleus of the unequaled collection of Charles James material at this institution, which includes not just garments but half and full toiles and card patterns. Of all James's clients, Rogers is the only one with whom he is known to have codesigned a garment, an eighteenth-century inspired, open-robe gown.

Even while the manager Kate Peil was keeping his dress salon on an even keel, James was becoming restless and demanding more recognition of his talents as well as increased financial reward. To this end he rapidly entered into contractual arrangements with a variety of manufacturers. In 1951 he began by working with the Cavanaugh Form Company, a mannequin manufacturer, to produce his uniquely proportioned, papier-mâché dress form that he called Jenny. In 1952 he began designing collections of dresses and separates for Seventh Avenue's Samuel Winston and suits and coats for William Popper that were retailed by Lord and Taylor. In 1953 James designed furs for Gunther Jaeckel and belts for Bruno Belt based on his "floating line" principle—that is, the waist is not a true oval but has depth as well as dimension. In 1954 he added a line of jewelry to be manufactured by Albert Weiss and agreed to design for another Seventh Avenue concern, Dressmaker Casuals. By the time this last contract was signed, however, previously signed agreements were unraveling due to James's inability to deliver designs on time and his convoluted business practices. Two Coty awards in 1950 and 1954 for "great mystery of color and artistry of draping" and "giving new life to an industry through his sculpturesque ready-to-wear coats designed for Dressmaker Casuals" did nothing for the ensuing courtroom battles that effectively ended the most productive and potentially profitable period in James's career.

He tried in 1956 to design a line of Borgana synthetic fur coats with Albrecht Furs as well as a coat for off-the-rack distribution by E. J. Korvette. Most astonishingly, he designed a line of infant wear to be manufactured by Alexis Corporation of Atlanta. James married Nancy Lee Gregory in 1954 and soon had a young family. His success with the baby garments surely lay in the fact that once again he had at his disposal a live model on which to experiment, his son, Charles Junior. As with so many other early designs that evolved over the years, James transformed some of the baby clothes into adult attire.

By 1958 James was a beaten man, unwelcome on Seventh Avenue, and mentally, physically, and financially drained. His marriage ended in 1961, and in 1964 he moved into New York's bohemian hotel, the Chelsea. Here he worked with the illustrator Antonio to document his career. Old clients joined with his protégé Halston in 1969 in a bravely attempted salute to his career. James attempted to document the creations of a lifetime, whether they were in public or private holdings. He accomplished some design work with Elsa Peretti and Elizabeth de Cuevas. Above all, during those final years of his life, Charles James was fanatical about securing his proper place in the history of twentieth-century fashion.

His fellow fashion designers, potentially his most severe critics, left no question regarding their assessment of his talent. Poiret passed his mantle to James, and Schiaparelli and Chanel dressed in his clothes. Dior praised him for being the inspiration for the New Look, and Balenciaga saw James as the greatest and best American couturier; moreover, he believed that James was the only couturier who had raised dressmaking from an applied to a pure art form.

See also Art and Fashion; Halston; Milliners.

Bibliography

Coleman, Elizabeth A. *The Genius of Charles James*. New York: Holt, Rinehart and Winston, 1982.
Martin, Richard. *Charles James*. London: Thames and Hudson, 1997.

Elizabeth Ann Coleman

JAPANESE FASHION*

The appearance of Western clothing and fashion during the Meiji era (1868–1912) represents one of the most remarkable transformations in Japanese history. Since the United States' 1854 treaty allowing commerce, negotiated by Commodore Matthew Perry, the Japanese have enthusiastically and effectively borrowed and adapted styles and practices from Western countries. Until then, Japan had isolated itself economically, politically, and culturally from the West as well as neighboring countries for two hundred years. The new Meiji era heralded hope for the future, and government officials felt change necessary for the system to quickly convert Japan into a modern state. Emperor Meiji instituted a parliamentary form of government and introduced modern Western educational and technological practices. The Japanese were then exposed widely to Western influences, and its impact on people's lives has been impressive.

This new modern phenomenon encouraged and expedited the spread of Western clothing among ordinary people, and it became a desirable symbol of modernization. It was first adopted for men's military uniforms, with French- and British-style uniforms designed for the army and navy, as this style was what Westerners wore when they first arrived in Japan. Similarly, starting in 1870, government workers, such as policemen, railroad workers, and postal carriers, were required to wear Western male suits. Even in the court of the emperor, the mandate to dress in Western clothing was passed for men in 1872 and for women in 1886. The emperor and empress, as public role models, took the lead and also adopted Western clothing and hairstyles when attending official events, and Japanese socialites were also participating in lavish balls in Western-style evening gowns and tuxedos.

By the 1880s, both men and women had more or less adopted Western fashions. By 1890, men were wearing

Western suits although it was still not the norm, and Western-style attire for women was still limited to the high nobility and wives of diplomats. Kimonos continued to dominate in the early Meiji period, and men and women combined Japanese kimonos with Western accessories. For instance, for formal occasions, men wore Western-style hats with *haori*, a traditional waistcoat, *hakama*, an outer garment worn over the kimono that is either split like pants between the legs or nonsplit like a skirt.

Conversely, there was also a trend for Japanese goods in the West. The opening of Japan's doors to the West enabled the West to significantly come into contact with Japanese culture for the first time. New trade agreements beginning in the 1850s resulted in an unprecedented flow of travelers and goods between the two cultures. By the end of the nineteenth century, Japan was everywhere, such as in fashion, interior design, and art, and this trend was called *Japonisme*, a term coined by Philip Burty, a French art critic. Western appreciation for Japanese art and objects quickly intensified, and World Fairs played a major role in the spread of the taste for Japanese things. In an age before the media, these fairs were influential forums for the cultural exchange of ideas: London in 1862, Philadelphia in 1876, and Paris in 1867, 1878, and 1889.

Fashion after World War II

During the Taisho period (1912–1926), wearing Western clothing continued to be a symbol of sophistication and an expression of modernity. It was in this period that working women such as bus conductors, nurses, and typists started wearing Western clothes in everyday life. By the beginning of the Showa period (1926–1989), men's clothing had become largely Western, and by this time, the business suit was gradually becoming standard apparel for company employees. It took about a century for Western clothing to completely infiltrate Japanese culture and for people to adopt it, although women were slower to change.

After World War II, the strong influence from the United States caused Japanese ways of dressing to undergo a major transition, and people began to more readily follow the trends from the West. Japanese women were starting to replace the loose-fitting trousers called *monpe*, required wear for war-related work, with Western-style skirts. By the early 2000s, the kimono had virtually disappeared from everyday life in Japan. Kimonos were worn only by some elderly women,

Western-style clothing for sale in Japan. In the mid-nineteenth century, Japanese dress began to be influenced by the West, and by the late twentieth and early twenty-first centuries, most urban Japanese only wore traditional clothing on special occasions. © Michael S. Yamashita/Corbis. Reproduced by permission.

waitresses in certain traditional Japanese restaurants, and those who teach traditional Japanese arts, such as Japanese dance, the tea ceremony, or flower arrangement. Furthermore, special events at which women wear kimonos included *hatsumode* (the new year's visit to shrines or temples), *seijinshiki* (ceremonies celebrating young people's reaching the age of twenty), university graduation ceremonies, weddings, and other important celebrations and formal parties.

Fashion information from Europe, such as Christian Dior's New Look, was disseminated by way of the United States. The new trends and fashion were generated primarily from the American and European movies shown to the Japanese public. For instance, when the English film *The Red Shoes* was first screened in Japan in 1950, red shoes became fashionable among young people. Similarly, when the film *Sabrina*, starring Audrey Hepburn, was shown in 1954, young Japanese women became fond of tight-fitted Sabrina pants, and flat low-heel Sabrina sandals became trendy. After the mid-1960s, Japanese men adopted the new "Ivy Style," which paid homage to the fashions of American Ivy League university students. This style supposedly came from the traditional fashions of America's elite class and spread from young students to middle-aged Japanese men.

As Japan's economy prospered in the 1980s, the Japanese fashion and apparel industries expanded rapidly

TABLE 1
JAPANESE DESIGNERS' YEAR OF FIRST COLLECTION IN PARIS

Japanese Designers	First Collection in Paris
Kenzo	1970
Issey Miyake	1973
Kansai Yamamoto*	1974
Yuki Torii	1975
Hanae Mori	1977
Junko Koshino	1977
Yohji Yamamoto	1981
Comme des Garçons by Rei Kawakubo	1981
Junko Shimada	1981
Hiroko Koshino*	1982
Zucca by Akira Onozuka	1988
Mitsuhiro Matsuda*	1990
Trace Koji Tatsuno	1990
Atsuro Tayama	1990
Yoshiki Hishinuma	1992
Masaki Matsushita	1992
Junya Watanabe	1993
Shinichiro Arakawa	1993
Naoki Takizawa**	1994
Koji Nihonmatsu	1995
Miki Mialy	1996
Junji Tsuchiya	1996
Yoichi Nagasawa	1997
Keita Maruyama	1997
Oh!Ya? By Hiroaki Ohya	1997
Gomme by Hiroshige Maki	1997
Hiromichi Nakano	1998
Yuji Yamada	1999
Undercover by Jun Takahashi	2002

*Hiroko Koshino, Kansai Yamamoto, and Mitsuhiro Matusda are no longer showing their collections in Paris but continue to design in Japan.
**Takizawa started designing for Issey Miyake's menswear in 1994 and, after Miyake withdrew from his women's wear in 1999, Takizawa took over the collection.

and became very profitable as consumers were becoming fashion-conscious. A new fashion movement called the "DC Burando" was focused on brands of clothing with insignia or with clearly identified styling of specific fashion designers. Famous brands, such as Isao Kaneko, Bigi by Takeo Kikuchi, and Nicole by Hiromitsu Matsuda, among many others, had cult-like followings. Some of the women's fashion trends diffused during this decade were *bodikon* (body-conscious) style, emphasizing the natural lines of the body, and *shibukaji* (Shibuya casual), originating among high school and college students who frequented the boutiques of Tokyo's Shibuya Ward shopping streets.

While Japanese create their own unique trends, they are at the same time voracious followers of Western fashion. They are eager to dress themselves in the latest designs from such names as Chanel, Yves Saint Laurent, Christian Dior, and Gucci. Even in the traditional corporate world, many companies implemented the trend "Casual Friday" that originated in the United States, allowing workers to wear casual clothing on Fridays.

Japanese Youth Fashion

In Japanese society of the early twenty-first century, the uncontested arbiters of fashion, street fashion in particular, were high school and junior high school students. Among them, loose, baggy white knee socks deliberately pushed down to the ankles like leg warmers were all the rage. Fashion-conscious girls have took the lead in setting fashion trends. Young Japanese embraced Western fashion in a unique Japanese way. While Japan produced its own distinctive fashion, it drew on a mix of the latest trends from the United States and Europe. They became the new breed of young Japanese who were not afraid to break and challenge the traditional values and norms.

In the early twenty-first century, it became common on the streets of Tokyo to see groups of young girls with

"The widespread popularity of the 'Japanese fashion' in the 1980s was a decisive factor in placing Tokyo on the list of international fashion capitals. A number of Japanese designers . . . established the Tokyo Designers' Council in the early 1980s to handle the inflow of foreign editors covering the local collections."

Lise Skov, in "Fashion Trends, Japonisme and Postmodernism."

long, dyed-brown hair, tanned skin, and miniskirts or short pants that flare out at the bottom. Their natural black hair was often replaced with hues of bleached-blond and red. It became fashionable to have a light suntan with heavy makeup. Many of them wore thick-soled mules in the summer and white boots with towering platform soles in winter. As in the West, tattoos were also part of the latest fashion. Previously, tattoos held a connection to the Yakuza, the Japanese mafia, who adorned themselves with elaborate tattoos as a badge of membership.

As Japan faced the worst economic recession in history, the younger generation's value system had become changed—the result of a deliberate move away from traditional ideology and ways of life. The previous generation's Japanese values, such as selfless devotion to their employers, respect for seniors, and perseverance, were breaking down. The decline of traditional way of thinking had accelerated in the teenage generation. Attending cram schools after their regular school hours was no longer the norm. The Japanese shifted from deeply disciplined, industrial attitudes to much freer consumerist ways. The doctrine of long study hours and single-minded focus on exams and careers that helped build Japan were disappearing and evaporating. The Japanese youth post–World War II became more hedonistic and wanted to have fun and live moment to moment, and their attitude was reflected in their norm-breaking fashion and styles.

Designers and Their Influence

As Japanese began to consume Western fashion, Japanese designers were becoming prominent in the West, especially in Paris. They are said to have created the Japanese fashion phenomenon and influenced many Western designers. Kenzo in 1970, Issey Miyake in 1973, Hanae Mori in 1977, Rei Kawakubo of Comme des Garçons and Yohji Yamamoto in 1981, first appeared in the Western fashion world and have since solidified their positions. Fashion professionals recognize and accept their achievements because of their "Japaneseness" reflected on their designs, and many called it "the Japanese fashion" only because these clothes were definitely not Western in regard to constructions, silhouettes, shapes, prints, and combination of fabrics. The Japanese public is reminded of its racial and ethnic heritage every fashion season with the references to Japanese cultural products and artifacts. Fashion journalists and critics in the West used everyday Japanese vocabulary familiar to Westerners to describe their designs. The source of their design inspiration undoubtedly came from symbols of Japanese culture, such as Kabuki, Mount Fuji, the geisha, and cherry blossoms, but their uniqueness lies in the ways they deconstructed existing rules of clothing and reconstructed their own interpretation of what fashion is and what fashion can be. These Japanese first proved to Paris, and then to the world, that they were masters of fashion design, prompting Western societies to reassess the concept of clothing and fashion and also the universalism of beauty. They shocked fashion professionals in the West by showing something none of them had seen before.

The Japanese designers were the key players in the redefinition of clothing and fashion, and some even destroyed the Western definition of the clothing system. Rather than being isolated as deviant and left outside the French fashion establishment, they were labeled as creative and innovative and were given the status and privilege that, until then, only Western designers have acquired. These Japanese managed to stay within the territory that is under the authorization of the system and the fashion gatekeepers.

After the first generation Japanese designers, other Japanese were flocking to Paris one after another. The second, the third, and the fourth generations were emerging in Paris. There were formal and informal connections among almost all the Japanese designers in Paris, some through school networks and others through professional networks. They can be traced back directly or indirectly to Kenzo, Miyake, Yamamoto, Kawakubo, and Mori as they have learned the mechanism of the fashion system in France.

These Japanese acquired the means to enter the French fashion system and at the same time used their ethnic affinity as a strategy. They achieved insider status in the realms where artistic power is concentrated and where gatekeepers, such as editors and critics, participate. The line between inside and outside the

"When I first began working in Japan, I had to confront the Japanese people's excessive worship of things foreign and fixed idea of what clothes ought to be. I began . . . to change the rigid formula for clothing that the Japanese followed."

Issey Miyake, quoted in *Issey Miyake: Bodyworks.*

system is an issue about status and legitimacy, and the inside bound-aries provide privilege and status whose boundaries in the world of fashion can be expanded and manipulated through style experiments and innovation. Fashion professionals accept and welcome designers who push and test the boundaries, signs of creativity. Once the designers are acknowledged as insiders, although recognition is never permanent, they slowly gain worldwide attention. Fashion design is an occupation where prestige necessarily antedates financial success. Prestige, image, and name bring financial resources. Until designers reach that stage, they struggle to achieve it; once it is achieved, they struggle to maintain it.

Due to the structural weaknesses of the fashion system in Japan, Japanese designers have continued to mobilize in Paris, permanently or temporarily, to take part during the Paris Collection. Though Kenzo's appearance in Paris in 1970 through Yamamoto's and Kawakubo's in 1981 had some impact, in the early 2000s Tokyo still fell far behind Paris in the production of "fashion"—that is, setting the fashion trends, creating designers' reputation, and spreading their names worldwide. Tokyo as a fashion city lacked the kind of structural strength and effectiveness that the French system had. Thus, lack of institutionalization and of the centralized fashion establishment in Japan forced designers to come to Paris, the battlefield for designers, where only the most ambitious can compete and survive.

Acceptance of the new Japanese styles led to the success of a group of Belgian designers, who also utilized the French fashion system to their advantage. From the mid-1980s to the early 1990s, a group of radical Belgian designers trained at the Royal Academy of Fine Arts in Antwerp followed the path that the Japanese had taken: Dirk Bikkembergs in 1986, Martin Margiela in 1988, Dries Van Noten in 1991, and Ann Demeulemeester in 1992, among others. By tracing the success of new designers, such as the Japanese and the Belgians, in Paris, one can see whether they are promoting and reinforcing the existence of the French fashion authority and the system, or are impeding the stability of the system and proposing the emergence of a new institutional system.

Influence in Western Fashion

Exhibitions such as *Orientalism* at the Costume Institute of the Metropolitan Museum in 1994, *Japonisme et Mode* at the Palais Galliéra costume museum in 1996, *Touches d'Exotisme* at the Art Museum of Fashion and

Textile in Paris in 1998, and *Japonisme* at the Brooklyn Museum of Art in 1998, show that Western designers have long been inspired by the Eastern textiles, designs, construction, and utility, including Japanese kimonos. For instance, Jeanne Lanvin's dress with its bolero jacket in the 1930s simulated kimono sleeves. Similarly, in the beginning of the twentieth century, as boning and corsetry were reduced to a minimum, a loose fitting kimono sleeve of Paul Poiret came in, and the high-neck collar was abandoned for an open V-neck resembling a kimono. Chrysanthemum prints or the exotic fabrics were used by many couturiers, such as Charles Worth and Coco Chanel. Those fascinated by the kimono's geometry, such as Madeleine Vionnet, cut dresses in flat panels and decorated only with wave-seaming, a Japanese hand-stitching technique. The East remained a fashion influence through World War I. Western designers incorporated Japanese elements into Western clothing with Western interpretation while remaining within the normative definitions of clothing and fashion.

There has been continued interest in Japanese fashion, with a major exhibition from the Kyoto Costume Institute at the Barbican Gallery in London in 2010, and another separate exhibition in the same year, "Japan Fashion Now," at the Museum at the Fashion Institute of Technology in New York, the latter including major brands such as Comme des Garçons, Yohji Yamato, and Issey Miyake, but also newer brands such as Undercover by Jun Takahashi as well as street styles like "Gothic Lolita" created by designers such as h.NAOTO.

See also Japanese Traditional Dress and Adornment; Kimono; Miyake, Issey; Mori, Hanae; Yamamoto, Yohji.

Bibliography

Dalby, Liza. *Kimono: Fashioning Culture*. New Haven, Conn.: Yale University Press, 1993.

Kawamura Yuniya. *The Japanese Revolution in Paris Fashion*. Oxford: Berg Publishers, 2004.

Kenzo. Tokyo: Bunka Publishing, 1995.

Mendes, Valerie, and Amy de la Haye. *20th Century Fashion*. London: Thames and Hudson, 1999.

Modem. Collections femme printemps-été, 1999 (Women's Spring–Summer Collection, 1999), 1998.

——. Collections femme automne-hiver 1999–2000 (Women's Fall-Winter Collection, 1999–2000), 1999.

Mori Hanae. *Hanae Mori Style*. Tokyo: Kodansha International, 2001.

Skov, Lise. "Fashion Trends, Japonisme and Postmodernism." *Theory, Culture and Society* 13, no. 3 (August 1996): 129–151.

Steele, Valerie. *Women of Fashion: Twentieth-Century Designers*. New York: Rizzoli International, 1991.

Sudjic, Deyan. *Rei Kawakubo and Comme des Garçons*. New York: Rizzoli International, 1990.

Tsurumoto Shozo, ed. *Issey Miyake: Bodyworks*. Tokyo: Shogakkan Publishing Co., 1983.

Wichmann, Siegfried. *Japonisme: The Japanese Influence on Western Art since 1858*. London: Thames and Hudson, Inc., 1981.

Yuniya Kawamura

JAPONISME

Prior to the 1800s, Japan was a nation isolated from the West. The arrival of its wares in Europe and America in the second half of the nineteenth century precipitated a new creative surge in art and design that became known as *Japonisme*. While many scholars have studied the influence of Japonisme, or the assimilation of Japanese aesthetic principles on European painting and decorative arts, few have addressed its influence on Western dress. And yet fashion, which differs from traditional dress in that it stresses urbanity and constant change, eagerly absorbed the principles of Japanese design.

In the mid-nineteenth century, European and American garments were ornamented with Japanese motifs or made of fabrics exported from Japan while conforming to fashionable Western silhouettes. Later, in the early twentieth century, some costume items, ranging from tea gowns to opera coats, were constructed with elements adapted from the construction of kimonos. More recently, some of the world's most influential designers have emerged from Japan to redefine contemporary fashion.

Although some Japanese objects had been arriving in Europe since the 1600s, it was not until after the American commodore Matthew Perry opened this island nation to international trade in 1854 that Japonisme began in earnest. Its popularity accelerated when many Europeans and Americans saw Japanese artworks and design objects for the first time at the world's fairs of 1862 in London, 1867 in Paris, and 1876 in Philadelphia. These expositions exerted a profound influence on innumerable nineteenth-century artists, artisans, designers, and manufacturers. Everything from paintings to porcelain began to be produced in the Japanese manner. In the 1870s and 1880s, such designs—then considered avant-garde—developed into a distinctive style that came to be associated with the aesthetic movement.

While nineteenth-century critics had reservations about artists' adopting Japanese conventions in paintings and prints, this was not true in the arena of fashion. French textile designers in the 1890s, for example, readily appropriated new and "exotic" floral motifs from Japan, and these fabrics were readily used by couturiers like Charles Frederick Worth. The most popular item of dress exported to the West in the late nineteenth century was a modified version of the kimono, worn as a dressing gown. Both fully finished garments and unsewn components were sold at small boutiques and at large firms such as Liberty of London. Kimonos for export were often constructed with elements to suit the European market; these might include a set-in box pleat to accommodate the bustle; a collar lining instead of an under kimono; the addition of a knotted and tasseled trim; and a variety of sleeve styles.

In the decade prior to World War I, the construction of women's garments began to change dramatically. As early as 1908, revolutionary couturiers, such as Marie Callot Gerber and Paul Poiret, took inspiration from the drapery-like quality of kimonos. Loosely cut sleeves and crossed bodices were incorporated into evening dresses, while opera coats swathed the body like batwinged cocoons.

One of the twentieth century's greatest couturiers, Madeleine Vionnet was inspired by the kimono, with its reliance on uncut lengths of fabric, and raised dressmaking to an art form. From the onset of World War I to the late 1920s, she abandoned the traditional practice of tailoring body-fitted fashions from numerous, complex pattern pieces, and minimized the cutting of fabric. A "minimalist" with strict aesthetic principles who rarely employed patterned fabrics or embroidery, Vionnet relied instead on surface ornamentation through manipulation of the fabric itself. For example, the wavy parallel folds of a pin-tucked crepe dress evoked the abstracted image of a raked Zen rock garden, itself a metaphor for the waves of the sea.

Although the influence of the kimono on the construction of garments was extremely important in the 1910s and 1920s, surface ornamentation remained a vital force. During the art moderne, or art deco, era, French textiles in the Japanese style developed a more sophisticated use of both abstract motifs and recognizable images. Examples range from metallic lamé dresses that replicate the appearance of black lacquer inlaid with gold particles, to garments of brocaded silk woven with a pattern of crashing waves and fish scales. Also appropriated was the *mon*, or family crest. While the *mon* is usually an abstracted image drawn from nature, such as a bird or flower, it can also represent a man-made object, such as the *nara bi-ya*, or parallel rows of arrows; or celestial bodies such as the *mitsuboshi*, an abstraction symbolizing the three stars of Orion's belt.

The influence of "exotic" cultures on fashion began to diminish in the late 1930s. Instead, American and European designers created modern versions of historical Western dress, and this trend dominated fashion from the late 1930s through the 1950s. The revival of historical styles offered an escape from the pressures of the Great Depression of the 1930s and helped assert the growing sense of nationalism in Europe at that time. Also a factor in the United States was strong anti-Japanese sentiment during and after the war. Nonetheless, some of this country's most innovative designers remained open to Japanese influence. One of the best was Elizabeth Hawes, who designed a variety of Asian-inspired garments in the late 1930s and early 1940s using modern Japanese kimono fabric.

The use of Japanese elements became the cornerstone for another revolutionary American ready-to-wear designer, Bonnie Cashin. Born in California in 1915, Cashin was one of a handful of female American designers who made clothes for the modern and active woman. By using the loose construction of the *naka-juban*, or informal kimono worn by peasants, and discarding Western tailoring, Cashin created functional fashions that fit a broad range of sizes and later seemed decades ahead of their time. Not only were her garments in sharp contrast to the couture creations of her French contemporaries, they had little in common with the designs of her American counterparts. Cashin's use of indigenous Japanese textiles, like double *ikat* silks with their subtle geometric designs, did much to advance the notion of modern luxury in American fashion.

Although by 2004 Japonisme was no longer a major force in fashion, the influence of Japanese design and aesthetics continued to be important. One of the main reasons was the dramatic impact of creators such as Issey Miyake, Rei Kawakubo, and Yohji Yamamoto. Born just before and during World War II, they became some of the most important fashion figures to chart a new course since the 1970s. Their use of oversized silhouettes, cutting-edge textiles, and the appropriation of Japanese aesthetic principle like *sabi/wabi* have made them leaders of the avant-garde.

See also Asia, East: History of Dress; Cashin, Bonnie; Europe and America: History of Dress (400–1900 C.E.); Kimono; Vionnet, Madeleine.

Bibliography

Evett, Elisa. *The Critical Reception of Japanese Art in Late Nineteenth Century Europe.* Ann Arbor, Mich.: UMI Research Press, 1982.

Fukai, Akiko, and Jun Kanai. *Japonism in Fashion.* Kyoto, Japan: Kyoto Costume Institute, 1996.

Grand, France. *Comme des Garçons.* New York: Universe Publishing, 1998.

Hiesinger, Kathryn B., and Felice Fisher. *Japanese Design: A Survey Since 1950.* New York: Harry N. Abrams, 1995.

Issey Miyake: Ten Sen Men. Hiroshima: Hiroshima City Museum of Contemporary Art, 1990.

Kirke, Betty. *Madeleine Vionnet.* San Francisco: Chronicle Press, 1998.

Kondo, Dorinne. *About Face: Performing Race in Fashion and Theater.* New York: Routledge, 1997.

Koren, Leonard. *New Fashion Japan.* Tokyo: Kodansha International, 1984.

——. *Wabi Sabi for Artists, Designers, Poets and Philosophers.* Berkeley, Calif.: Stone Bridge Press, 1994.

Martin, Richard, and Harold Koda. *Orientalism.* New York: Metropolitan Museum of Art, 1994.

Martin, Richard, Harold Koda, and Laura Sinderbrand. *Three Women: Madeleine Vionnet, Claire McCardell, and Rei Kawakubo.* New York: Fashion Institute of Technology, 1987.

Sudjic, Deyan. *Rei Kawakubo and Comme des Garçons.* New York: Rizzoli International, 1990.

Vreeland, Diana, and Irving Penn. *Inventive Paris Clothes: 1909–1939.* New York: Viking Press, 1977.

Wichmann, Siegfried. *Japonisme: The Japanese Influence on Western Art in the 19th and 20th Centuries.* English translation. New York: Harmony Books, 1981.

Patricia Mears

JEANS

"Blue jeans" are the archetypal garment of the twentieth century. They are traditionally ankle-length, slim-fitting trousers made of blue denim worn for labor and casual dress. The term "jeans," or "blue jeans," has been in widespread usage since the mid-twentieth century.

The word "jeans" comes from the word *Génes*, the French word for Genoa, Italy, where sailors were known to wear sturdy pants of fustian, a sturdy twill of cotton, linen, or wool blend. By the sixteenth century, the fabric was being referred to as "Jene Fustyan." By the eighteenth century, jean fabric was made entirely of cotton and was being used to make work clothes. Jean was available in many colors, but often dyed with indigo. Pants made from jean were often referred to as "jean pants," the origin of the contemporary jeans.

Jeans, however, are made of denim. Denim is also a sturdy cotton twill, similar to jean, but even stronger. Denim is traditionally yarn-dyed and woven with an indigo-blue face and a gray or unbleached fill. This method of manufacture enables denim to develop distinctive areas of fading and wear with usage. It is commonly believed that the name "denim" is an Anglicised name for *serge de nîmes*, a French fabric dating back to the seventeenth century. While this attribution has been popular and widely disseminated, it has recently been called into question. *Serge de nîmes* and a second French textile known simply as "nim" were mainly wool, not cotton. The sturdy cotton twill now recognized as denim was originally given the name "denim" in eighteenth-century England. It has been theorized that the French name was given to an English product to add prestige.

To confuse the matter even further, jeans are sometimes referred to as dungarees. This term refers to a coarse calico fabric that was often dyed blue and used to make work pants. The word "dungaree" would later describe the pants as well.

Miners and the Workingman

The first true "jeans" were created in 1873 by Jacob Davis, a Nevada tailor, who went in with Levi Strauss, a San Francisco merchant, for the patent. The pair received a patent for the addition of copper rivets at the pocket joinings of work pants to prevent tearing—a boon to the many California miners and laborers. The first jeans Levi-Strauss and Co. produced were available in brown cotton duck and blue denim and were known as waist overalls (the name jeans not adopted until the mid-1900s). In the late nineteenth century, Levi's (as they became known) began to acquire their hallmarks: the leather "Two Horse Brand" patch, lot numbers, and back patch pockets with distinctive stitching. The Levi's "501," which originated in 1890, is considered by many to be the archetypal pair of blue jeans.

Levi-Strauss had cornered the market with their denim pants, but competitors moved quickly. Companies manufacturing similarly styled denim work pants entered the market. These included OshKosh B'Gosh in 1895 and Blue Bell in 1904, which later became Wrangler. The Lee Mercantile began production of their waist overalls in 1911 and enjoyed their first great success with the Lee Union-All in 1913. During World War I, Union-Alls were standard issue for all war workers, and the design was modified for the doughboy uniform.

Hollywood, Cowboys, and Wartime

During the 1920s and into the 1930s, the image of the waist overall was given a glamorous spin by handsome cowboy movie stars like Tom Mix, John Wayne, and Gary Cooper. In 1924 H. D. Lee Mercantile Co. introduced their 101 cowboy pants, which were designed to meet the needs of cowboys, rodeo riders and others looking for authentic western garb. The 101 cowboy pant was given a facelift in 1941 when Sallie Rand, the wife of famous rodeo champion Turk Greenough, recut them for a tighter fit. These new and improved cowboy pants were then called Lee Riders. The romanticized view of the cowboy life seen onscreen brought about an enthusiasm for dude-ranch vacations, and tourists brought back comfortable waist over-alls as souvenirs. This glamorous new image was reinforced by publicity photos featuring actresses like Ginger Rogers and Carole Lombard wearing the humble waist overalls while camping and fishing. Through these glamorous associations, the waist overall became associated with leisure and rugged individualism rather than manual labor. Young people began to adopt them into their casual dress, wearing them rolled up and baggy.

World War II would change the image of the waist overall forever. Raw materials were restricted for the war effort, and the general silhouette was slimmed down to reduce fabric consumption. As a result of these restrictions, Levi's lost their back cinch and copper crotch rivet while the stitching on the back pocket was painted on to conserve thread. Denim began to be used as a fashion fabric by fashion designers like Claire McCardell, whose denim wrap dress, the "popover," sold in the thousands.

American GIs brought jeans overseas with them to wear while off-duty. This had an important impact on the international reputation of jeans; they became associated with American leisure and abundance, especially in countries devastated by the war. To many, blue jeans were an important symbol of freedom and wealth.

Post-World War II Leisure and Rebellion

Blue jeans would continue to be associated with leisure in the post–World War II period. The term "jeans" became widely adopted during this time, and jeans began to be marketed specifically to the youth market. In 1947, Wrangler introduced the slim "body fit" jeans, which emphasized fit and appearance over traditional qualities like durability. In 1949, Levi Strauss and Co. opened an outlet in New York, and began nationwide promotion of their waist overalls, which they grudgingly began to call "jeans" in 1960. In 1953, H. D. Lee (formerly Lee Mercantile Co.) began an advertising campaign aimed at teenagers. Lee Riders were transformed into a slimmer "drainpipe" style popular with teens.

Once again, Hollywood films had an important role in the reinvigoration of the image of the utilitarian waist overall. While young children continued to idolize the cowboy, teenagers found new denim-clad idols in Marlon Brando (*The Wild One*, 1953) and James Dean (*Rebel Without a Cause*, 1955). Denim now had a dangerous element and a healthy dose of sex appeal. Exciting new rock'n'roll musicians like Eddie Cochran, a Levi's devotee, also played a role in the popularization of denim. This rebellious association caused jeans to be banned from many high schools throughout the 1950s, but this only strengthened their popularity.

The 1960s saw an explosion of the production and acceptance of jeans as leisure wear. Denim as a fashion fabric also became widely accepted, and the important contribution denim jeans had made to fashion and popular culture began to be acknowledged. In 1964, it was boldly stated in *American Fabrics* magazine:

> Throughout the industrialized world denim has become a symbol of the young, active, informal, American way of life. It is equally symbolic of America's achievements in mass production,

for denim of uniform quality and superior performance is turned out by the mile in some of America's . . . most modern mills. (American Fabrics, No, 65, 1964, p. 30)

With this mass acceptance came the need for distinction. Early in the 1960s, slim-fitting styles dominated but were superceded by the well-worn bell-bottom styles popularized by the hippie movement. The wearing of jeans was both a political and social statement and the baby boomers embraced the aesthetic of customized decorated denim. Embroidery, paint, and appliqué on faded bell-bottom jeans became a powerful symbol of anti-establishment ideals around the world.

Designer Jeans

Since jeans and denim-inspired fashions were everywhere in the 1970s, this period has been called "the golden age of denim." The customization of jeans continued and reached its pinnacle with Levi's Denim Art Contest of 1973. Mass-produced jeans echoing the earthy styles worn by political activists and rock stars, and the traditional workingman's garb, the overall, became popular.

Increasingly though, denim jeans reflected a new sophistication. Early inroads were made by the Italian company Fiorucci with their Buffalo 70 jeans. Buffalo 70 jeans were skintight and dark, the opposite of the faded bell-bottoms worn by most consumers. Since they were also expensive and difficult to find, they became a status symbol among the Studio 54 set. Their success paved the way for the high-end designer jean market of the early 1980s. American socialite Gloria Vanderbilt introduced her jeans in 1979. Similar in styling to the Fiorucci Buffalo 70 jeans, they also featured dark denim, a slim fit that emphasized a woman's curves and a bold designer logo on the rear pockets. They were significantly more expensive than other jeans and were promoted as being "high fashion." The jeans used the glamour and celebrity of socialite Gloria Vanderbilt to promote them, rather than emphasizing their practicality or styling.

This type of marketing strategy would become increasingly important during the 1980s, since there soon was a deluge of similarly styled "designer" jeans on the market. Advertising had the ability to make or a break a brand's success, and this trend has continued. Designer jeans lines from this period included Jordache, Sassoon, Sergio Valente, and the legendary Calvin Klein Jeans. In

Advertisement featuring Brooke Shields in Calvin Klein jeans. In 1976, designer Calvin Klein became the first fashion designer to showcase blue jeans on the runway. AP/WIDE WORLD PHOTOS. REPRODUCED BY PERMISSION.

1980, Calvin Klein Jeans embarked on a now-legendary ad campaign featuring fifteen-year-old model Brooke Shields, who cooed provocatively, "Nothing comes between me and my Calvins." The public outcry was great, but Calvin Klein Jeans sales rose from $25 million to $180 million in the span of one year. During the next decade, sexy marketing campaigns became standard. Some of the most successful were advertisements for Guess? Jeans that featured sultry models like Claudia Schiffer in seductive poses.

The jeans market grew increasingly fragmented during the 1980s. What had been the uniform of youthful rebellion and social protest during the 1950s and 1960s was now seen as a wardrobe basic and worn by all age groups. The many different styles offered included pinstriped, acid-washed, stonewashed, cigarette cut, twotoned, stretch, and pre-ripped. With this focus on innovation and novelty, many traditional denim manufacturers languished. The designer denim movement continued into the 1990s when well-established fashion houses like Versace, Dolce & Gabbana, and Donna Karan branched out into denim.

Vintage Denim and Retro Styling

After more than a decade of designer jeans of various finishes, denim saw a return to classic styles, dark denim, and dangerous rebellion. Dark denim returned to mainstream popularity during the 1990s, a dramatic change from the pale, fluffy denim being produced throughout the 1970s and 1980s. Dark denim

was stiff and was often worn with cuffed hems in the style of a 1950s bobby-soxer. Dark denim was seen as intellectual and ironic, a deliberate throwback to the essential elements of mid-century jeans. Traditionally styled dark denim was given an additional boost by the popularity of hip-hop. The hip-hop styles of the early 1990s were characterized by oversized, low-slung baggy jeans, associated with convicts forced to turn in their belts. Manufacturers like Ben Davis and Carhartt prospered since their no-frills, dark denim work clothes appealed to this hard-edged prison aesthetic and were prominently featured in music videos and lyrics by artists such as Dr. Dre and Snoop Dogg. Based on styles popularized by the hip-hop community, urban sportswear labels like FUBU, Rocawear, and Phat Farm emerged. Mainstream labels like Tommy Hilfiger and Polo Jeans were also appropriated in this style.

At the same time, vintage denim was experiencing a renaissance. By the late 1980s, the simple garment of the mid-century had been bastardized by the glut of fashion jeans on the market. To many consumers, vintage denim symbolized strength and integrity, a direct challenge to the perceived corruption of the 1980s. Increasingly the wearing of vintage denim became popular, and prices for original Levi's, Wranglers, and Lees soared. Others turned to faithful modern renditions of vintage denim. Evis Jeans, a Japanese company, made their name during the early 1990s by producing modern versions of classic denim, like the Levis 501 and the Lee 101 with a twist. In 1999, Levi Strauss and Co. launched the "Red" line, a successful series of high-priced reproductions of vintage styles. Likewise, Lee jeans produced a replica of their highly collectible "hair on hide" cowboy pants for the Japanese market. Jeans, at least for the moment, had returned to their roots.

During the 1980s, smaller, higher-priced lines began to experiment with vintage-styled denim, paving the way for the vintage-inspired denim explosion of the 1990s. Adriano Goldschmied, founder of the influential "genius group" of denim innovators, was an early proponent of sandblasted knees and painted on "cat's whiskers" (the wear pattern at the crotch of vintage jeans). The genius group would become hugely influential, spawning many denim labels, such as Diesel and replay, whose higher priced lines provided finishes that the coveted striations and fading that characterized vintage denim. By the mid-1990s this aesthetic had gone mainstream as seen by success of "Dirty Denim" produced by designers such as Helmut Lang and Calvin

Klein. The denim craze has continued into the twenty-first century with cult denim lines like Mavi, Paper Denim and Cloth, Seven, and Blue Cult all competing in the marketplace with perfectly faded, whiskered, and creased jeans.

Jeans, the ubiquitous twentieth-century garment, will undoubtedly continue to have a permanent place in twenty-first-century wardrobes around the world. Their iconic status will remain intact, largely since they will be reinterpreted by each passing generation. In 1983, legendary French couturier Yves Saint Laurent told *New York Magazine*, "I have often said that I wish I had invented blue jeans. They have expression, modesty, sex appeal, simplicity—all that I hope for in my clothes" (*New York Magazine*, November 28, 1983, p. 53).

See also Denim; Klein, Calvin; Strauss, Levi.

Bibliography

Downey, Lynn, et al. *This Is a Pair of Levi's Jeans: The Official History of the Levi's Brand*. San Francisco: Levi Strauss and Co. Publishing, 1997.

Finlayson, Iain. *Denim: An American Legend*. New York: Simon and Schuster Inc., 1990.

"The Genius of Yves Saint Laurent." *New York Magazine* (28 November 1983): 53.

Gordon, Beverly. "American Denim: Blue Jeans and Their Multiple Layers of Meaning." In *Dress and Popular Culture*. Edited by Patricia A. Cunningham and Susan Voso Lab. Bowling Green, Ohio: Bowling Green State University Popular Press, 1991.

Hall, Lee. *Common Threads: A Parade of American Clothing*. Boston: Little, Brown and Company, 1992.

Harris, Alice. *The Blue Jean*. New York: Powerhouse Books, 2002.

Hay, Ethan. "Jeans." In *St. James Encyclopedia of Popular Culture*, vol. 2: E–J. Edited by Tom Pendergast and Sara Pendergast. Detroit: St. James Press, 2000.

Marsh, Graham, and Paul Trynka. *Denim: From Cowboys to Catwalks: A Visual History of the World's Most Legendary Fabric*. London: Aurum Press Limited, 2002.

Musées de la Ville de Paris. *Histoires du jeans de 1750 à 1994*. Paris: Paris Musées, 1994.

"Stretch Denim: Bright Star in the Modern Family of Stretch Fabrics" (Special merchandizing insert). *American Fabrics*, no. 65 (Fall 1964): 30.

Clare Sauro

JEWELRY

Jewelry is often associated with treasure—gold, gemstones, valuable materials—and is considered to be objects of intrinsic beauty, though the early beginnings were very different. In prehistoric times, long before humans worked metals, jewelry was made of non-precious materials. Burials of 30,000 B.C.E. in Europe show that at the time people used local materials available to them, such as shells and pebbles, and, in hunting societies, also animal teeth and claws, to make jewelry. Existing examples reveal that pieces were engraved with intricate geometric patterns and, later, zoomorphic images. Thus, jewelry was an early form of decorative art. The study of some primitive cultures gives evidence that organic materials, which have since disintegrated, would have also undoubtedly been utilized in the past. It was not until a later stage of human development that people chose precious and possibly scarce materials from far-away for jewelry.

Jewelry is as old as humankind. Whether coming from a primitive culture or modern civilization of the West or East, and regardless of material and style, humans of both genders and all age groups have the need for self-adornment. The significance of jewelry transcends time limits and geographic boundaries; similarities in the use of jewelry for personal adornment become apparent in the study of various cultures.

In prehistoric times, as well as in contemporary cultures, jewelry is not only ornamentation for the body, but also a means of communication. Hierarchy, prestige, and power are expressed through jewelry, which can affirm the status of an individual in society. What initially appears to be an ornament can mark allegiance to a society or individual. Men and women can impress each other through jewelry. Yet possibly the most powerful qualities attributed to jewelry are the amuletic and talismanic functions of warding off evil or giving luck. These properties go back to the origins of jewelry and continue well into the nineteenth century. Even in contemporary cultures people carry good-luck charms. Jewelry also played an important role in protecting against the dangers of life, and was given in burials for the afterlife of the deceased. In addition, jewelry was also worn as a sign of personal affection and fidelity, and marked special occasions in life, such as coming of age, association to a religion through communion or confirmation, nubility, marital status, and motherhood. Jewels in their aesthetic expression are not only signs of wealth and taste, but also reflect—and communicate—the personal character and temperament of the wearer.

Throughout its history until about the mid-twentieth century, when jewelry experienced a radical change, it had been dependent on the fashions of the day, with the exception of finger rings. Varying necklines, sleeve lengths, hemlines, and fabrics determined the type of jewelry worn, while the choice of materials and symbolism determined its function and usage. The creativity of the goldsmith is boundless, as are the types and styles of wearable objects for the body.

If not passed on as a family heirloom or given for the person's afterlife and found in excavations of burials, many types of jewels that are known to have existed have not survived. Jewelry made of precious materials, regardless of century or culture, have been destined to be dismantled, the gemstones reused and the metals such as silver and gold melted down for bullion, either to become a financial resource or to be remodelled in a new fashion. Jewels with enamel have withstood this destiny, as it was too complicated and costly to remove the enamel, whereas golden chains with a considerable weight in metal were the first to be melted down. Few images of jewelry types and how they were worn survive from antiquity. Mummy masks and wall paintings of the ancient Egyptian era, ancient Greek statues of gods and vase painting, Etruscan tomb sculpture, Roman tombstones, and the informative mummy portraits of Fayum from the Roman period all give valuable evidence. In the Middle Ages, tomb effigies and even religious paintings of the Virgin Mary and saints illustrate jewelry of the time. More importantly, the development of portrait painting and the depiction of the individual from the fifteenth century onwards (supplemented after the mid-nineteenth century by photography) enables a comprehensive study of jewelry, and makes possible the reconstruction of many types that are no longer in existence.

In prehistoric times people chose materials from their immediate environment. A statuette dating back to 20,000 B.C.E., the so-called "Venus of Willendorf," shows a fertility statue wearing a bracelet, and burials give evidence of the use of necklaces made of snails and shells—both fertility symbols and a sign of motherhood. Men wore animal teeth and claws to signify their strength over the animal kingdom and their ability to hunt and, in turn, feed and protect their families. Such objects would possibly have marked their position within the community. In its early stages, jewelry was predominantly amuletic—its function was to guard its wearers in a life of hardships.

Until recently, and even to a limited extent in the early 2000s, among traditional peoples who managed to resist the impact of Western religion and culture, it is possible to discern elements of these more traditional attitudes toward personal adornment. Tattoos, makeup, and jewelry were in many cases, in such societies, not simply matters of personal adornment, but also conveyed specific messages about social and gender roles; they were used to ward off disease and other evils, and sometimes also to work magic against opponents; and as acts and signs of prayer and devotion to divinities. A widespread, if attenuated, example of the magical power of jewelry can be found throughout the Middle East and in parts of Africa, where the wearing of blue glass beads as a means of warding off the "evil eye" is very common.

In some societies, Western-style jewelry has still not completely effaced the wearing of more traditional forms of jewelry. The use of natural materials in jewelry in ways that probably preserve a very long continuous tradition of craftsmanship can be found, for example, among the highland peoples of New Guinea, where shell, bird-of-paradise feathers, boar tusks, and other animal products are commonly employed in personal adornment. Until the second half of the twentieth century these elements of jewelry were ubiquitous in the absence of alternative materials (for example, metal objects); in the early twenty-first century their continued use represents a choice among a wide range of possibilities.

In other contemporary non-Western societies, jewelry can still be seen as fulfilling another of its ancient functions, that is, it acts as a repository of wealth while also retaining its amuletic properties. Among pastoral nomadic peoples in the steppelands of Asia, throughout the Middle East, and in North Africa, women commonly wear very heavy silver jewelry, including headdress ornaments, earrings, necklaces, bracelets, belts, and frontlets, sometimes including actual silver coins (of many eras and many countries) worked into the jewelry. These coins also had an amuletic function, because their jingling sound was believed to ward off evil. Such jewelry not only displays the status of the family to which the woman belongs, but also acts as a highly portable form of wealth that can be converted to monetary use at any time it is needed. Likewise, in cities and agricultural regions of the Middle East, India, and Southeast Asia, gold jewelry acts as a repository of wealth as well as being beautiful and prestigious. In many Indian communities, for example, the conspicuous wearing of gold jewelry by a bride is an essential element of a wedding ceremony.

Jewelry found in western Asia in the cradle of civilization from about 5000 to 2500 B.C.E. illustrates a society with a taste for refined and decorative jewelry, as well as a trade network in supplying rare materials for their goldsmiths and differing local traditions. The earliest examples were necklaces made of obsidian from Turkey and cowrie shells with red stain from the nearby coastal areas. The most splendid jewels found in the area were from the royal graves of the Sumerian city of Ur in southern Mesopotamia, where the king and queen lay buried accompanied by their soldiers and attendants. Men wore beads to keep their headdress in place, whereas women's jewelry was more elaborate with dress pins, headdresses, and necklaces made of embossed and repousée gold, probably from the areas currently known as Iran and Turkey. The motifs were stylized flowers and foliage, interspersed with beads in varying geometric shapes cut from lapis lazuli imported from Afghanistan and carnelian from India. The designs are intricate with signs of inlay, filigree, and the use of alternating colors.

Like the Sumerians, the ancient Egyptians from 3100 B.C.E. till the Graeco-Roman period in the first century B.C.E. showed a preference for lapis lazuli and carnelian, and typically, in Egyptian jewelry, turquoise is added to this combination. The resources in the area were vast and the choice of materials for the Egyptian jewelry-maker amazing as they also included a variety of organic materials. Gold and many other metals were found in the surrounding areas as were agates, amethysts, garnets, jaspers, malachite, and steatite, to name but a few. Glazed faience, and glass imitations in substitution, were applied to achieve colorful compositions, forming a contrast to the rather plain clothing the Egyptians wore, which was essentially made of white linen. Pectorals and necklaces were the most popular of jewelry types, but bracelets and head ornaments of all sorts are characteristic for the culture. The motifs ranged from the animal world (including fish and lions), the magical scarab, sphinxes, the udjat eye, and deities, either signifying rank or serving an amuletic purpose. Other designs are of a more decorative nature with vivid color combinations achieved through varied bead shapes and stones. Pharaohs, princesses, peasants, and artisans alike wore jewelry in life and in death, many surviving types were in fact funerary objects. The jewelry-making techniques were most sophisticated, such as inlaying in cloisons and granulation, and we even have pictorial records of craftsmen from ancient Egypt demonstrating technical processes in their workshops.

In the eastern Mediterranean of about 2500 B.C.E. there was the Minoan culture in Crete, which was taken over by the Mycenaeans in about 1450 B.C.E. The jewelry of that period and area is characterized by an abundance of gold; their styles were greatly influenced by the jewelry of the Babylonians and Egyptians. The Phoenicians were traders who colonized the eastern and western Mediterranean from Syria to Spain, and their choice of jewelry was influenced by the ancient Egyptians. Near Eastern designs also had influence on the later Greeks, as seen in the Orientalizing style of the Archaic period (700–480 B.C.E.), and in Etruscan jewelry (seventh to fifth centuries B.C.E.). The Etruscans were known for their technical perfection in goldsmithing and most of all for their outstanding technique of granulation with almost pulverized granules of gold. By the seventh century B.C.E., however, forms and decorative elements in jewelry were dominated by Greek designs and symbols.

Greek goldsmiths of the classical to Hellenistic periods were renowned for their technical skills and fine craftsmanship mainly in gold—a reputation that would be retained in future centuries. Greece was not rich in gold resources until its empire was extended as far as Persia in the fourth century B.C.E. In the classical period, from the Crimea to as far west as Sicily, Greek men wore more jewelry in some areas than others. In certain places it was even considered to be effeminate. Jewelry were gifts presented at birth, birthdays, and weddings, or even as votive offerings to cult statues. Rings and hair wreaths adorned men, both men and women wore rings, and the main forms of adornment for women were necklaces, earrings, bracelets on their upper arms or thighs, and diadems or golden nets in their hair. Fibulae were widespread and not only a decorative feature, but functional in as much as they held the drapery of the chiton on the shoulder. As the iconography of Greek jewelry confirms, it was intended for women, mainly to attract the opposite sex. This may explain the numerous images of Aphrodite, the goddess of love, in gold, as three-dimensional figures suspended from necklaces or earrings, possibly given at the birth of a child. Eros, symbolic of desire, was equally popular and given as a token of love. Deities such as Athena or Dionysus or other figures from mythology referred to religious beliefs and the power of the deities during life. Bracelets worn in pairs on the upper arm or rings with elaborately coiling snakes functioned as amulets, calling on the sacred creatures of the underworld to protect against evil. Antelopes and goats would attract the opposite sex, whereas lions were worn as emblems of fertility and royal power. These decorative motifs were all rendered in a naturalistic manner in gold sheet metal with intricate filigree wires and granulation, as were the interspersed motifs from nature such as seeds, nuts, and different shapes of foliage. Enamels, garnets, emeralds, and glass pastes became fashionable during the Hellenistic period as beads or inlay to add color to the previously predominantly gold jewelry.

With the loss of Greek independence and the victory of the Romans over Macedonia in 168 B.C.E., Rome became a strong military and political power. The wealth of the new empire attracted many Greek craftsmen to come to the capital, where they were most successful. Essentially the Romans followed Greek styles until about the first century B.C.E., when the aesthetics of their jewelry began to change. The jewelry became unpretentious, the gold techniques less elaborate, the designs simplified, and more emphasis was laid on the choice of stones and the use of color—a new taste had developed, it was the beauty of the material to which one aspired. Regional differences are evident: jet was fashionable in Britain, where it was found in Whitby, and amber from the Baltic Sea was cut in Aquileia in Roman Italy. Emeralds from the newly discovered mines in Egypt—what was then recently acquired Roman territory—became fashionable and their abundance led to the natural hexagonal crystal shapes being drilled, strung on thread, or connected with simple gold links to be worn as necklaces. Garnets were imported from the Middle East, and sapphires from Sri Lanka. Pearls were considered to be an expression of luxury and indulgence. Apart from the Romans showing a preference for gemstones, each has a special significance, described in the *Historia naturalis* by Pliny the Elder (23–79 B.C.E.). Specific gemstones were chosen for certain images, such as Bacchus on amethyst as a safeguard against drunkenness; the Sun god Sol is depicted on heliotrope; and Demeter, goddess of crops, on green jasper to symbolize growth and abundance.

Trade was flourishing in the vast empire with far-reaching provinces, and jewelry was being produced in Rome, Alexandria, and Antioch. Roman goldsmiths had guilds and rules existed about who could wear certain types of jewelry, but these soon diminished. During the Republic gold jewelry was reserved for the aristocracy, but by the first century C.E. its significance soon depreciated and by the second century gold was worn by those who could afford it. With adornment becoming socially acceptable for a wider public, even slaves were permitted to wear jewelry made of iron—it was mass produced, and thus plenty has survived from the Roman period. With a thriving economy by the second century, Roman jewelry became more elaborate, even heavy and gaudy—a sign of wealth and status—yet at the same time the iconography suggests the jewelry was full of symbolism and personal messages for the wearer. Deities became symbols of wealth and good fortune, the gorgon Medusa destroyed evil powers, the phallus was a popular good luck charm, and cupids with Venus or cupids riding on dolphins tokens of love. Images of clasped right hands or husband and wife facing each other alluded to the marriage vows, and Latin inscriptions served as charms to protect life. Other types of jewelry such as the brooch were more decorative in character and, in fact, served a functional purpose of holding the drapery together.

By the fourth century the Roman Empire was in decline. With Christianity having been recognized by Constantine the Great, the iconography found in jewelry was relevant to the new religion, but often coded to protect the owner from being persecuted. The early Christians appear to have worn finger rings as a sign of their allegiance, and engraved on the bezels are symbols and ciphers of Christ the Saviour. In the fourth century the empire transferred to East Byzantium with its capital in Constantinople, which continued as an ecclesiastical and successful trading power until 1453 when the city fell to the Ottoman Turks. Greek goldsmiths were active there, and with their influence, despite the style being a continuation of late Roman jewelry with a love for gemstones and color, there was a greater emphasis on intricate gold-work with enamel or niello decoration. Except for bronze gilt or gold rings, the laws were strict about who could wear jewelry. Emeralds, pearls, and sapphires were reserved for the emperor, and all the splendor of their richly embroidered and bejeweled fabrics is documented in the mosaics of the churches in Ravenna, northern Italy, as are the elaborate necklaces, earrings, and brooches. Nevertheless, the iconography was religious and the cult of saints is confirmed by the use of pectoral crosses with their images and relic inserts.

Mutual artistic influence between the Byzantine world and the expanding world of Islam is evident from the mid-seventh century onward. Byzantine and Islamic influence can also be seen in the jewelry of the Germanic tribes that occupied much of Europe after the fall of the western Roman Empire. Germanic tribesmen acquired gold from Byzantium. The jewelry of these nomadic tribes tended to be restricted to basic types and was more functional in its application, but nonetheless the jewels were a statement of status. Men wore belts, buckles, and sword harnesses; both men and women needed clasps for their dress, and these are found in the form of disc brooches or fibulae. The tribes show distinctive styles in their goldsmiths' work, but even they had many common elements, such as sophistication in the applied goldsmithing techniques, the lavish engraving, the use of garnet inlays, and the intricacy of patterns, including stylized animal themes.

During the Middle Ages cities were enlarging, the merchant classes were gaining prominence and becoming a new economic force, and with the church losing power, society became more worldly. With the rise of the middle classes and increase in wealth, sumptuary laws became necessary to restrict who was allowed to wear jewelry. Fashions determined the types of jewelry worn: with the sleeves becoming wider and more lavish, bracelets were unnecessary; high collars did not allow for earrings; cape-like coats required brooches; and the high waistlines of women's dresses made fancy belts necessary. Rings with signets or love messages were very popular.

By the twelfth and thirteenth centuries an international style in jewelry had evolved. Shapes of stone settings, designs, and decorations showed astonishing similarities in England, France, Denmark, Germany, and Italy. This phenomenon presumably can be explained by the trade routes and import of gemstones from the Near and Far East. Paris was trend-setting in the manufacturing of jewelry, whereas the ports of Venice and Genoa were influential in trade. The inscriptions on jewelry were mostly in Latin or French, the international language of the courts. The pointed arches and tracery of Gothic architecture, naturalistic rendering of foliage in sculpture, and the colors of stained glass were mirrored in the jewelry designs of the time. Devotional and secular iconography were often interlocked, gemstones in cabochon were amuletic or reflected divinity, and the images of saints had protective and healing powers, as did the emerging use of the bones of saints in reliquary pendants. Flowers and animals decorate medieval jewels as a symbol of faith, and classical gems were given Christian interpretations. Medieval jewelry was largely heraldic, religious, or expressive of courtly love.

In Europe the transition to the Renaissance period differed according to country, beginning with Italy in the fifteenth century and spreading throughout Europe by the sixteenth century. Italy, with its discoveries of ancient monuments and sculpture, was all-important in the rebirth of the cultures of ancient Greece and Rome, whereas in northern Europe Gothic styles continued much longer. With an explosion of economic trade, in particular wool and banking, many wealthy families in Italy became patrons of the arts. Goldsmiths became known as individuals by name. In the fifteenth century, Florence and the Burgundian Courts established trends in dress and jewelry; by the sixteenth and seventeenth centuries Spain became a major European power with colonies all over the world, leading to a dominant Spanish style in dress and jewelry. Religious wars raged in Europe and, often due to the circumstances, artisans traveled from one country to another—at the same time following the wealth of emerging courts in Europe. Jewelry again developed into an international style with less regional distinctions. Another factor that led to this phenomenon was the newly discovered art of printing. Artists made ornamental drawings that were printed and distributed throughout Europe, and even as far as the Spanish colonies, where jewelry was made in the style of the day for trade with Europe.

Men, in fact, showed more adornment than women. However, the function of jewels was display, as the abundance of portraits of that period document. The merchant classes were following fashions of the aristocracy, the materials used, though, were usually less precious. The heavy and dark velvets or brocades with gold embroidery were covered with jewelry, either sewn on the fabric as ornaments, or worn on the body. Pendants were fashionable for all genders, and the images were either religious or from classical mythology; exotic birds, flowers, or marine themes were also displayed as symbols of status and new wealth. Gemstones were in open settings when on the body, so that the amuletic qualities would be more effective. Heavy gold chains worn by both men and women on the breast or across the shoulder and cascading in multiple strands were undoubtedly a sign of social ranking. Men wore hat jewels, belts with sword harnesses, and jeweled buttons. The custom of wearing bracelets in pairs was revived from antiquity, as was the fashion for earrings. Decorative chains encompassed ladies' waists, often from which pomanders or pendants were suspended. Dress studs ornamented the already elaborate fabrics. To add to the display of color, Renaissance jewels often had polychrome enamels in combination with gemstones, such as rubies from Burma, emeralds from the New World, pearls off the coast of Venezuela, and diamonds from India. In contrast to the cabochon cuts of the Middle Ages, during the Renaissance table cuts were common. With the renewal of classical traditions the art of cameo cutting was revived and northern Italy was an important source for this form of lapidary arts.

In the second half of the seventeenth century while Spain was in decline, France became the most important economic and cultural center. All luxury industries flourished in the France of Louis XIV. French silks from Lyon and dress fashions were exported and, with these, styles for jewelry. It was also a period when women were playing an increasingly significant role in society. For their dress, heavyweight brocades had been replaced by light silks in various pastel shades. The splendor and bright colors of the fabrics required a decrease of color in jewelry. Portraits of the period illustrate a passion for pearls, strung as necklaces or worn as pearl drops suspended from earrings, or from brooches worn on the breast, sleeve, or in the hair. Pearls were very valuable, and while pearls often were ostentatiously displayed, it is likely that most of them were fake; fake pearls are known to have been produced since about 1400. Diamonds were favored. French-style enamelled settings and decorations were equally subdued in their color scheme: opaque white enamel was outlined with black, and pale pink or turquoise enamel was applied as highlights of the decoration. A source for the naturalistic floral designs of enamel decorations was the study of botany, a new science. Jewelry had the tendency of being less figural and more decorative with bows and clusters of gemstones. However, the Thirty Years War that ravaged Europe between 1618 and 1648, as well as the plague, resulted in a new type of jewelry, *memento mori*. The wearer was reminded of his or her transience and mortality, and skull's heads and skeletons were featured in all types of jewelry, which lived on in mourning jewelry of the eighteenth and nineteenth centuries with funerary ornaments and weeping maidens as motifs.

Designs in jewelry were in general more playful by the eighteenth century and the grand elegant court style of Louis XV of France was to influence the whole of Europe, even as far as Russia. The compositions of the jewelry were more naturalistic, and thus asymmetrical; flower sprays and baskets were gem-studded, as were feathers, ribbons, and bows. Eighteenth-century jewelry moved from monochrome to polychrome; metal

foils placed under the gemstones enhanced their color. Indian diamond mines had been exhausted, but with new mines found by the Portuguese in Brazil the fashion continued, and by 1720 the rose-cut diamond had been developed, allowing more light reflections. Other fashionable stones were agates, mossagate, and marcasite. Pearl strands with ornate clasps were worn like chokers; large stomachers were attached to the narrow bodices, and aigrettes to the hair; and shoe buckles were also bejewelled. With the Industrial Revolution in its beginnings towards the end of the eighteenth century, new materials for jewelry had been discovered, including cut steel. This hard metal was facetted to look like diamonds. The industrialist, Josiah Wedgewood (1730–1795), the founder of Wedgewood pottery, designed porcelain cameos to be inserted into jewelry. A special formula for making glass paste was named after Georges Frédéric Strass (1701–1773). After Marie Antoinette of France wore strass at court, it became socially acceptable to wear paste jewelry, which would have shimmered splendidly in candlelight.

In 1789 the French Revolution had dramatic effects not only in the politics and life of France, but also on Europe as a whole. Outside France the market was flooded by the jewels and gemstones of those who managed to escape, and prices fell radically. In France anybody owning jewels of aristocratic origin faced death by guillotine; only jewelry made of base metals was permitted, and this jewelry had political and patriotic inscriptions or symbols.

Luxury was revived in France with Napoleon when he proclaimed his empire in 1804. His wife Josephine was a trend-setter and wore Greek fashion, which was reflected in jewelry. Cameos, the Greek key pattern, laurel wreaths, and filigree work were reminiscent of antiquity. However the Napoleonic Wars led to quite a different and innovative type of jewelry known as Berlin iron, first developed when ladies gave their golden jewelry to finance the wars and received iron jewelry in return. The fashion spread from Germany to Austria and France; the style of this jewelry was antique or Gothic, typical of the nineteenth century with its eclectic styles.

The effects of the Industrial Revolution and the rise of the middle class became particularly evident in Britain. The middle class imitated the jewelry of the aristocracy, but instead of diamonds, rubies, sapphires, and emeralds, gemstones such as amethyst, chrysoprase, tourmaline, turquoise, and many other colourful substitutes were applied. Seed pearls were labour intensive, but as an inexpensive material replaced opulent pearl jewelry. As in dress fashions, evening and day jewelry was differentiated, the full parure consisting of necklace, bracelets, brooch, and earrings was intended for the evening, whereas the demi-parure, a brooch with matching earrings, for daytime wear. Sentimental jewelry was extremely popular: gifts with love or messages of friendship, and souvenirs of hair of the beloved or deceased were integrated in jewels. The newly acquired wealth of the middle class enabled travel, and souvenir jewelry was invented soon after, such as *pietra dura* work from Florence, coral from Naples, micromosaics from Rome, and the archaeological styles from Egypt, Assyria, and the Celtic lands. Not only were archaeological and exotic cultures rein-terpreted, but so were the Middle Ages and Renaissance. By the second half of the nineteenth century the famous jewelry houses of today opened branches in the capital cities of Europe; jewelry became global.

The path to modernism in jewelry began around the turn of the twentieth century, during the *belle époque* when there was a mood for renewal and individually crafted luxury items. Paris with its exhibition of 1900 was predominant in the new aesthetic movement. The jewelry expressed emotions, and winged women were symbolic of emancipation; nature was metaphorically interpreted: themes such as birth, death, and rebirth were expressed through plants in varying stages of their life. René Lalique laid the foundation for artists' jewelry of the twentieth century and introduced novel material combinations, such as precious gold with non-precious glass. Diamonds were applied sparingly, *plique-à-jour* enamel allowed light to shine through, opals gave iridescence, and materials appeared to almost dematerialize. In contrast, silver with enamel and a few gemstones defined the Jugendstil in Germany and the Viennese Secession in Austria, both reducing nature to stylized geometric forms. Liberty of London chose Celtic inspirations, and Georg Jensen in Denmark a more sculptural rendering of nature. By 1910 platinum jewelry in the Louis XVI style with bows, tassels, and garlands enabled thin, almost invisible settings and linear designs. The costumes of the Ballets Russes in Paris were immensely inspirational for vivid color combinations in jewelry, such as emeralds with sapphires, turquoises, and coral.

Decisive innovations in jewelry were brutally interrupted by World War I. Many widows were obliged to gain employment to survive; dress and hair fashions became casual, and so did jewelry. In the golden twenties elegant lifestyle and lavish luxury prevailed again, mirrored in the jewels of the epoch. Diamonds and gemstones form stylized compositions in contrasting colors that are reminiscent of such art movements as Cubism, de Stijl and Futurism. The exoticism of Africa and Egypt attracted jewelers as well. Germany, struggling with political and economical concerns and following the artistic philosophies of the Bauhaus school of design, developed jewelry made of non-precious materials such as chrome-plated brass. Events such as the stock market crash on Wall Street in 1929 had a global economic effect in Europe, as did World War II, when materials for jewelry were scarce, but the desire for jewelry never ceased.

In the aftermath of the wars in the twentieth century, jewelry experienced a departure from its traditional values due to radical changes in society: housewives could no longer afford staff, and young people learned to be self-sufficient. Like fashion, jewelry designs followed the movements of youth culture. Women became more independent, and began buying their own jewelry rather than traditionally having it given to them by their husbands as had been traditional. Never before had jewelry been so diverse and so independent of dress fashions.

In the 1950s and 1960s the desire for luxury was epitomized by Hollywood with its make-believe world, mink stoles, and diamonds galore. During this time jewelers in Europe were experimenting with gold surfaces, designing unconventional settings, and, thus, transforming jewelry into a free art form. After the 1960s jewelry took an almost revolutionary turn with the freelance artist jewelers in their studios boldly setting out on the path of the fine arts—by the 1980s they broke existing boundaries of dimensions and materials and used materials from gold to rubber to paper.

More than any other time in its history, by the early twenty-first century, jewelry reflected the wearers' moods and feelings, favorite colors, taste, understanding of the arts, and last, but not least, their individuality.

See also Brooches and Pins; Earrings; Necklaces and Pendants; Rings.

Bibliography

Andrews, Carol. *Ancient Egyptian Jewelry*. New York: Harry N. Abrams, 1991.

Bury, Shirley. *Jewellery 1789–1910: The International Era*. 2 vols. Woodbridge, Suffolk, England: Antique Collectors' Club, 1991.

Daniëls, Ger. *Folk Jewelry of the World*. New York: Rizzoli, 1989.

Dormer, Peter, and Ralph Turner. *The New Jewelry: Trends and Traditions*. Revised edition. New York: Thames and Hudson, 1994.

Lightbown, Ronald W. *Mediaeval European Jewellery: With a Catalogue of the Collection in the Victoria and Albert Museum*. London: Victoria and Albert Museum, 1992.

Mack, John, ed. *Ethnic Jewelry*. New York: Abrams, 1988.

Phillips, Clare. *Jewelry: From Antiquity to the Present*. New York: Thames and Hudson, 1996.

Princely Magnificence: Court Jewels of the Renaissance, 1500–1630. London: Victoria and Albert Museum, 1980. An exhibition catalog.

Tait, Hugh, ed. *Seven Thousand Years of Jewellery*. London: British Museum Publications, 1986.

Williams, Dyfri, and Jack Ogden. *Greek Gold: Jewelry of the Classical World*. New York: Abrams, 1994.

Anna Beatriz Chadour-Sampson

JEWISH DRESS

Although no specific costume was ever mandated by Jewish law, and no universal Jewish costume ever evolved, certain dress codes have been clearly identified with the Jewish people throughout the ages. In addition to the influence of Jewish law and custom on the development of these dress codes, these codes were impacted by the geography and historical setting in which the costume developed, and the extent of integration in the wider, gentile community.

Several principal factors have determined Jewish dress throughout the ages:

1. Halachah: the whole legal system of Judaism which embraces all laws and observances, from the Bible henceforth, as well as codes of conduct and customs.
2. Restrictive decrees and edicts by non-Jewish authorities in countries where Jews lived, as well as Jewish inner-communal regulations.
3. Prevailing local sartorial styles and dress codes.

Halachah

Halachah, the code of Jewish law, is based mainly on biblical precepts, which are considered the primary and most authoritative source for all Jewish laws. Since biblical precepts concerning dress are few, they determine only several aspects of Jewish costume. Later halakhic rulings regulated dress codes and interpreted the biblical injunctions.

The explicit biblical precepts refer to attaching fringes to men's dress and the prohibition of wearing a garment made of a mixture of wool and linen. Some rabbinical authorities and scholars deduce that the covering of women's hair and *peoth*—sidelocks (Leviticus 19:27) worn by Jews, which are today distinctive features of the Jewish male external appearance, were also biblical precepts. One should also mention the *tefillin*—philacteries: these are small leather boxes containing holy and protective texts which are attached to the forehead and the left arm during morning prayer (see Exodus 13:9, 16, and Deuteronomy 6:8; 11:18). Today these are ritual accessories to which utmost importance is attributed, but in Talmudic times some scholars wore them throughout the day.

Tzitzith. In biblical times, fringes were attached to outer garments, which were probably a kind of sheetlike wraps, which had four corners. In time, when dress styles changed, two separate ritual garments evolved to fulfill this precept. The *tallith*, the prayer shawl, is a rectangular fringed shawl worn for prayer and important events in the Jewish life cycle. The *tzitzith*, which literally means fringe, or *tallith katan* (literally "small tallith"), is a poncholike undershirt worn at all times by orthodox Jewish men. According to the Torah, one tassel should be blue (Numbers 15:18), but as the process of production of the blue extracted from the *murex purpura* (a snail used for dying blue and purple in the Mediterranean) was lost, the fringes were usually white. The fringes consist of four cords folded to produce eight ends, knotted in differing numerical combinations, equivalent to the numerical value of the letters of names of God. The religious, mystic-symbolic meaning attributed to these garments imbued them also with protective and magical powers.

Sha'atnez. Because it is not outwardly visible, *sha'atnez*, though kept to this day by certain observant Jews, is not a distinctive mark of Jewish dress. With mass-produced clothing, special laboratories are required to determine whether a particular garment contains the forbidden mixture. In the past, in many communities, tailoring became a prevalent Jewish occupation in order to be able to control the combination of fibers and textiles of clothes.

Two major tendencies direct halakhic rulings concerning dress. One is segregation from the gentile environment: "Nor shall you follow their laws" (Leviticus 18:3), as is stated generally in the Bible. More specifically relating to dress, Maimonides, the renowned medieval Jewish scholar, stated: "One must not follow in the ways of those who worship the stars nor imitate them either in dress or hairstyle" (*Mishneh Thorah, Hilkhot Avodat Kokhavim* 11:1).

Modesty

Another major concern of halakhic rulings regarding dress are various issues of modesty—for instance, the requirement to be decently dressed and covered during prayer (Tosefta Brachot 2:14, second century C.E.). This attitude was later interpreted as the separation between the upper part of the body, considered spiritual and pure, from the lower part, considered mundane and impure. Among the Hasidim of Eastern Europe (from the eighteenth century on) this division of the body acquired a rich symbolical meaning and is fulfilled by the *gartle*, a belt donned ritually before prayer.

The equivalent item among women was the apron, the purpose of which was to cover and protect their reproductive organs. These aprons, worn either under or above the skirt or both, were considered a symbol of modesty and magically protective. The wearing of aprons persisted among Eastern European Jewish women and after having almost vanished, made a comeback among some of the ultraorthodox women who wear them while lighting Shabbat candles and during festive occasions. They regard them as charms that will bring them well-mannered children.

Head covering for women. The practice of women covering their heads became pervasive and universal throughout the Jewish world. In some communities, it became customary to cut the hair or even shave it shortly before or after the wedding. Some women attempt to leave no hair uncovered while others allow some parts to be seen as is customary in each community. The custom of wearing *sheytl*s, wigs, was adapted by Jewish women in Europe in the sixteenth century, when it was fashionable for both men and women, and it has lasted as an option for head covering among some Jewish orthodox groups into the twenty-first century. In several places in Morocco, in Bukhara and Georgia, Jewish women's coifs incorporated false hair that served as partial wigs. Such is the elaborate *mahdour* headgear

of the Jewish women of the Sous region on the southern coast of Morocco. This is an intricate work of silver interwoven with the hair of a horse's tail, two locks of which frame the woman's forehead.

The wearing of wigs even in the twenty-first century is a highly controversial issue among the different orthodox groups. Some claim that the display of hair, even false hair, does not abide with the prohibition to conceal it, since the showing of any hair is considered erotic, and therefore immodest.

With the passing of time, both the manner and style of the head covering have taken many forms and differ immensely from place to place. In the past, prior to modernization, women's head covering attested both to her marital status as well as to her socio-economic status, her place of residence, and communal affiliation. In Sana'a, Yemenite Jewish women wore the distinctive *gargush*, a hoodlike headgear that concealed the hair, the forehead, and the neck. It identified the Jewish woman from the Muslim woman and the Jewish woman of San'a from Jewish women of other localities. Every woman had several hoods, the most sumptuous was the *gargush mezahhar merassaf* (the full golden hood), decorated with gilt, silver filigree pieces, and with several coins. All these riches formed part of the woman's dowry, which she received from her father and were used as her cash reserve.

In the early twenty-first century the distinction is less geographic and attests to religious group affiliation and degree of religiosity. Szatmar Hasidic women in New York and Jerusalem wear similar head coverings—a scarf covering their hair entirely, sometimes with a padding under it or a small piece of synthetic wig in front, or a synthetic wig worn under the scarf.

The women of the Neturei Karta, and the most extreme groups, shave their hair, and cover their head with a tight black scarf. Whereas the Belz Hasidic women wear a wig and a small cap on top of it, Sephardi-Oriental women in Israel do not wear wigs but fashionable hats and scarves.

Head covering for men. Unlike women's hair covering, men's head covering has only become obligatory in the last centuries. It is not mentioned in the Torah, and in the Babylonian Talmud it is only a custom practiced by certain people—Torah scholars—and at certain times, such as during prayers and benedictions. It is conceived as a sign of religious submission and respect to higher authorities and before God.

In the sixteenth century, when the Shulhan Aruch, the Code of Jewish Law, was written and accepted by all

Jewish communities, men's head covering was not yet universal or compulsory. The code stated that covering the head was a sign of a God-fearing Jew and especially important during study and prayer (*Orakh khayyim* 2,2; 151.6). In Christian countries, the Jewish covering of the head in the synagogue evolved as contrary to the practice of uncovering one's head as a sign of reverence, while in the Muslim world, Jews were no exception to the general practice of covering their heads. In both Christian and Muslim lands, Jews were required to wear a hat, the shape and color of which would serve to identify them as Jews.

Well known in its time was the *Judenhut*, the medieval pointed Jewish hat by which Jews were identified, and which are clearly seen in both Jewish and Christian depictions of Jewish life. The wearing of a double head covering—a *kippah* or yarmulke (skullcap) and hat—among the ultraorthodox, or a scullcap only, by orthodox Jews, evolved in nineteenth-century Europe and became part of the controversy between reformists and traditionalist groups. Among some of the reformists, the skullcap is worn during prayer and other ceremonial occasions. As for the ultraorthdox, in order to express their opposition to the reform, they started to wear a skullcap and a hat on top of it. In the early twenty-first century, especially in Israeli society, covering of the head or not distinguishes between secular and observant Jews. The type of covering indicates socio-religious and ideological, even political affiliation. For instance the *kippah srugah*, a crocheted skullcap, has become an identity mark of the National Religious community and political party.

Restrictive Decrees and Edicts

Apart from the inner Halakhic rules, Jewish costume was determined by restrictive decrees issued by the gentile authorities in the countries in which Jews lived in the diaspora. These laws required Jews to wear special garment items, prohibited them from wearing particular fabrics and colors, and obliged them to mark their dress with badges.

In Muslim lands, the edicts began with the Laws of Omar (in the eighth century) that required that all non-Muslims be distinguished by their external appearance, by their clothing, the external manifestation of their lower legal status as "infidels." This distinction had far-reaching legal and social implications, and it served as a tool for keeping ethno-religious hierarchies and boundaries. These laws were the conceptual guidelines

for practical restrictions imposed by different rulers. The decrees did not deal with entire outfits, but pertained mainly to the colors and quality of fabrics, and sometimes to particular components of dress such as head gear or footwear. In Bukhara, the Jews had to wear ropelike belts as a distinction mark.

Infidels were supposed to wear dark colors such as black or dark blue (some places had specific colors for Jews and others for Christians). Green was reserved for Muslims because it is the holy color of Islam. Jews were not allowed to use luxurious fabrics, as were enumerated in the edicts. There were restrictions pertaining to the cut and size of the garment. In Turkey, the size of the turban was of great significance—the larger the turban, the higher the rank of its wearer—thus the edicts restricted the length of the turban fabric and the width of the cloak permitted to Jews. In Afghanistan in the first half of the twentieth century, Jewish men could only wear gray turbans.

Similar restrictions were imposed in medieval Europe by the church councils. In 1215, the Lateran Council issued the well-known dress restriction as a reaction to the forbidden mingling of Christians with Jews and Muslims:

> . . . [T]hey may not . . . resort to excusing themselves . . . for the excesses of such accursed intercourse, we decree that such [Jews and Saracens] . . . in every Christian province and at all times shall be distinguished in the eyes of the public from other peoples by the character of their dress. (Rubens, 1973, p. 81)

These decrees also included the wearing of a badge. The badge differed in shape and color as well as in the place where it should be displayed, either on the right shoulder or on the hat. In the duchies of Italy, a yellow patch was worn. In England, its shape was of the Tablets of the Law, and in Germany, the badge was a ring-shaped sign. The Jews were also obliged to purchase these badges from the government. "Every Jew above the age of seven must wear a yellow or red and white badge. The royal tax collectors will collect the fee for the purchase of the badge" (France, 1217–1284).

These edicts and restrictions were intended to mark the Jewish population and set them apart from others, thereby aiming at degrading and humiliating them. The spirit of this distinction did not disappear altogether and was revived by Nazi Germany by imposing the yellow badge as a race discriminator. The reaction of the Jewish population to these laws took different forms. In many cases, as can be expected, it was resented, but in some instances, it was accepted positively as described by a traveler to the Ottoman empire in the seventeenth century: "As in religion they differ from others so they do in habit: in Christendom enforcedly, here in the Turkie voluntarily" (Sandys, p. 115).

Though this may not be accurate, it does acknowledge different reactions to the humiliating restrictions. These differentiating restrictions were accepted positively, as they met with the Halakha and the desire to differentiate themselves from others by their clothing. In some cases, these restrictions were given different explanations and an inner symbolic interpretation. For example, Moroccan and Tunisian Jews and the Jews of Sana'a in Yemen held that the wearing of black, adapted by the Jews themselves, was considered as a sign of mourning commemorating the destruction of the Temple. (There are several other signs commemorating the destruction that, according to Jewish law, one has to keep).

These restrictions were at times corroborated by inner communal regulations and sumptuary laws called *takkanot*. These regulations issued by Jewish communities referred mainly to women's attire, instructing them to refrain from wearing luxurious clothes—especially with gold decorations and opulent jewelery—mainly in the public domain. Their purposes were twofold: the first, to avoid arousing jealousy among non-Jews, as it was feared that excess finery in Jewish dress might bring about additional edicts by the authorities; the second, to avoid internal tensions between rich and poor families within Jewish communities. These regulations limited excessive finery in weddings and other festive occasions but allowed some exceptions.

Such rules and regulations provide very important historical sources for a meticulous study of dress codes in each community.

> We have unanimously decided that from this day forward . . . no woman, young or old, shall wear arm bracelets, or chains, or gold bracelets, or gold hoops, or gold rings, or any gold ornament . . . or pearl necklaces, or nose rings . . . [A woman] cannot wear any garment made of wool or silk, and [she] certainly [cannot wear] gold or silver embroidery, even if the lining is inside out, except for a head covering, which is all she is allowed to wear . . . and as for children and infants, neither boys nor girls may [dress] themselves [in articles made] either of gold or of silver

or of silk. (From regulations pronounced by the rabbis of the community of Fez, Morocco, 1613)

> Velvet for dresses, even for linings, is forbidden to women and girls, with the exception of black velvet. The bride may wear any kind of velvet under the canopy during her wedding . . . any type of skirt which is stiffened with a hope of wire or . . . other devices is forbidden to married and single women . . . even small children. . . . From today until further notice, no silk dresses of two colors should be made for women, with the exception of dark grey and brown. (Fine: 20 thalers). Whoever offends openly or in secret will be excommunicated and treated as someone who has sinned against God. (From the Jewish regulations for clothing and weddings, Hamburg, Germany, 1715)

Sartorial Styles and Dress Codes

The great variety of Jewish traditional attire prior to modernization, attests to the marked influence of the surrounding culture on each Jewish community. One can safely say that the attire of the Jews resembled more that of their surrounding culture than that of Jews living in other places, notwithstanding the distinction marks imposed on them.

Yet costume was not only conceived as marking ethno-religious boundaries, but also as defining group identity within the Jewish communities; one example is the "great dress," worn as a bridal and festive dress by urban Spanish Jewish women (descendants of the Jews expelled from Spain in 1492) in Morocco. This sumptuous outfit made of metal thread–embroidered velvet, was strikingly different from the local Muslim costumes. It strongly resembled Spanish costume of the sixteenth century and preserved many of its stylistic traits. In Morocco, this dress became an identity mark of the urban Spanish Jews vis-à-vis the local rural Jews; it was one of the symbols of the preservation of the Spanish heritage, which was a source of pride to this group. However, it is not certain that this dress was worn by Jews in Spain. Within Morocco, there were also variations of this dress each belonging to a certain town, Fez, Rabat, Mogador, and others.

This rare example of the preservation of sartorial styles by an immigrant group for over 400 years leads to another feature thought to be typical or recurring in Jewish costume in different places. It has been observed that Jews in many communities had a tendency to re-tain dress styles long after they have been abandoned by the gentile society. After some time, these anachronistic clothes or items of dress were appropriated by the Jews and considered later to be exclusive to them and even an identifying trait. The best known example of this phenomenon is the Hassidic or ultraorthodox costume, derived from the Polish eighteenth-century dress of nobleman and appropriated and preserved by the Jews, which became a distinctive attire exclusive to them. Another example is the sheetlike wrap-and-veil street wear worn by Jewish women in Baghdad until 1952. The custom of veiling was a norm in Muslim society. Jewish women adhered to that norm. Veiling was the prerogative of Muslim women and was not imposed on low-status women such as servants and non-Muslims. Non-Muslim women are not re-quired to veil themselves. The Bagdadi wrap covered the whole body, while the face was hidden by a square black veil. In this period, Baghdadi Jewish women's *izar*, veils, were made of pastel-colored silk interwoven with metal thread. Prevalent among Muslim women in former times, such dress came to be considered a distinctively Jewish outfit in the early twentieth cen-tury when the customary Muslim attire changed to a plain black wrap.

The conflict between the will to integrate and the will to isolate Jewish society from the gentile surround-ing cultures was strongest in Europe in the period of emancipation and modernization during the nine-teenth century. As European society enabled the Jews to become equal citizens, some of the Jews wanted to assimilate and not to be distinguished by their dress, while others saw this assimilation as a great danger to Jewish religion and culture. The reform Jews changed their traditional garb to fashionable modern costume. This change was accompanied by debates over head covering and other matters. These changes and reforms caused a strong reaction among some of the East Euro-pean Jews centered in Hungary, who preached to cling more strongly to tradition. Every domain of life and dress was considered a central aspect of this tradition (under the *halachic* precept that anything new is forbid-den by the Torah).

The wearing of better clinging traditional attire down to the minutest detail has turned the dress of the ultraorthodox Jews into a kind of uniform by which they are recognized. It is also considered a protective mechanism against sin.

Since there are few common features of Jewish cos-tume across time and place, it is fundamental to study it in relation to surrounding historical and cultural setting. Yet, in the confines of a given society and the bounds of limited time, Jews could still be identified by certain particularities of their dress, which were often a combination of local dress with one or two sartorial ele-ments that they carried with them throughout time.

See also Religion and Dress.

Bibliography

Bar'am, Ben Yossef No'am. *Brides and Betrothals: Jewish Wed-ding Rituals in Afghanistan.* Jerusalem: The Israel Mu-seum, 1998.

Carrel, Goldman Barbara. "Women's Head-Coverings: A Feminised System of Hasidic Distinction." In *Religion and Dress and the Body.* Edited by Linda Boynton Arthur. Oxford: Berg, 1999, pp. 163–180.

Frankel, Giza. "Notes on the Costume of the Jewish Woman in Eastern Europe." *Journal of Jewish Art* 7 (1980): 50–57.

Goitein, Shlomo Dov. *A Mediterranean Society.* Berkeley: University of California Press, 1983, pp. 150–200.

Juhasz, Esther. *Sephardi Jews in the Ottoman Empire: Aspects of Material Culture.* Jerusalem: The Israel Museum, 1989.

Krauss, Samuel. "The Jewish Rite of Covering the Head." In *Beauty in Holiness.* Edited by Joseph Gutman. Hebrew Union College Annual XIX, 1946. Reprint, Hoboken, N.J.: Katv Publishing, 1970, pp. 420–467.

Muller-Lancet, Aviva. "Jewish Ethnographic Costume." In *En-cyclopedia of Jewish History.* Israel: Masada, 1986.

——. *La vie juive au Maroc.* Jerusalem: The Israel Museum, 1973.

Rubens, Alfred. *A History of Jewish Costume.* London: We-idenfeld and Nicolson, 1967, 1973.

Sandys, George. *Travels Containing an History of the Origi-nal and Present State of the Turkish Empire.* London: Rob. Clavell, 1673.

Schwartz-Be'eri, Ora. *The Jews of Kurdistan: Daily Life, Customs, Arts and Crafts.* Jerusalem: The Israel Museum, 2000.

Slapak, Orpa, ed. *The Jews of India: A Story of Three Commu-nities.* Jerusalem: The Israel Museum, 1995.

Stillman, Yedida K. "The Costume of the Moroccan Jewish Woman." In *Studies in Jewish Folklore.* Edited by F. Tal-mage. Cambridge, Mass.: Association for Jewish Studies, 1981.

Orpa Slapak and Esther Juhasz

K

KILT

The kilt has come to signify a natural and unmistakable masculinity, but it has a long history of outside intervention and deliberate reinvention. From its origins as the basic garb of the Highlander, Scotsmen and non-Scotsmen alike have embraced it as uniform, formal and semiformal wear, and casual, everyday wear. The kilt's ability to remain recognizable while responding to changing circumstances and consumer demands has been instrumental in maintaining its popularity through successive generations and, increasingly, throughout the world.

Form and Evolution

The kilt as we know it today originated in the first quarter of the eighteenth century. Known to the Gaelic-speaking Highlander as the "little wrap" (*feileadh beag*), it evolved from the "big wrap" (*feileadh mor*), or belted plaid, the first identifiably "Scottish" costume that emerged in the late sixteenth century. Earlier, the Scottish Gaels had worn the same clothes as their Irish counterparts, namely a shirt known in Gaelic as the *léine* and a semicircular mantle known in Gaelic as the *brat*.

The belted plaid consisted of a four- to six-yard length of woolen cloth about two yards wide. In *Highland Costume* (1977), John Telfer Dunbar explains how the belted plaid was arranged on the body. It was laid out on the ground and gathered in folds with a plain section left at each side. The man lay down on it with one selvage at about knee level, and fastened it with a belt. When he stood up, the lower part was like a kilt, and the upper part could be draped around the body in a variety of different styles. Several dress historians, however, have discounted this method on the grounds of impracticality. They propose that the most pragmatic and time-effective method was to gather the pleats in the hand, pass the plaid around the body, secure it

loosely with the belt, and then tighten it after a final adjustment of the pleats.

The kilt as worn in the early 2000s is the lower half of the belted plaid with the back pleats stitched up. Its invention is credited to Thomas Rawlinson, an English ironmaster who employed Highlanders to work his furnaces in Glengarry near Inverness. Finding the belted plaid cumbersome, he conceived of the "little kilt" on the grounds of efficiency and practicality, a means of bringing the Highlanders "out of the heather and into the factory" (Trevor-Roper 1983, p. 22). However, as Dorothy K. Burnham asserts in *Cut My Cote* (1973), it is more likely that the transformation came about as the natural result of a change from the warp-weighted loom to the horizontal loom with its narrower width.

Romanticism: The Kilt as National Dress

Not long after the kilt's invention, the Diskilting Act was passed in the wake of the Jacobite Uprising of 1745. This rebellion, organized by Prince Charles Edward Stuart (Bonnie Prince Charlie), marked the final attempt by the Jacobites to regain the British throne. As in the previous Jacobite risings, the "Young Pretender" sought and won the support of many Highland chiefs and their clans. When the Jacobites were defeated at the Battle of Culloden (1746) by the duke of Cumberland and his troops, a campaign of "pacification" of the Highlands was undertaken "beginning with fire and the sword, and leading on into social engineering of various kinds" (Chapman 1992, p. 125). The latter included the proscription of Highland costume, which was seen as a symbol of rebellion and primitive savagery.

The Diskilting Act made an exception for those serving in the armed forces. Originally, the Highland regiments were dressed in the belted plaid, but in order to conform to the other regiments of the British Army they wore a red coat cut away at the skirts to allow for its voluminous folds. Other distinctive Highland features of the uniform included a round blue bonnet, a small leather sporran, red and white knee-length hose, and black buckled shoes. By about 1810, however, the Highland regiments had replaced the belted plaid with the little kilt. At the same time, the small, practical leather sporran developed into a large, hairy, decorative affair. This early-nineteenth-century military style was to have a lasting impact on civilian dress. Several dress historians have claimed that Highland costume would not have survived in civilian form had the Highland regiments not been raised and uniformed in elements of their native dress.

In 1782, through the efforts of the Highland Society of London, the Diskilting Act was repealed. By the time of the repeal, the kilt had fallen out of use as an item of ordinary dress, allowing for what Malcolm Chapman in *The Celts: The Construction of a Myth* (1992) calls the "romantic rehabilitation of Highland dress." The romantic gaze was a reaction against the urban and the industrial and a celebration of the untamed wilderness. No longer the threat from the North, the image of the Highlands could represent this wilderness within the bustling economy of the "new" Britain. Rather than dangerous, bare-legged barbarians, the Highlanders became admirable, a kilted version of the noble savage.

The romantic rehabilitation of the kilt reached its apotheosis with King George IV's carefully stage-managed state visit to Edinburgh in 1822, during which he disported himself in full Highland dress. This "publicity stunt" promoted the kilt as fashionable wear among the Scottish nobility and, in so doing, helped establish the kilt as the national dress of Scotland. However, the king's clothes, like those worn by Scottish noblemen, were far removed from those worn by the Highlanders of the previous century. Given the fact that they were largely designed for the levee, assembly, and ballroom, the emphasis was on the dramatic and spectacular. As Hugh Cheape points out in *Tartan* (1991), "'Highland dress' turned into 'tartan costume.' A practical dress with style became . . . a fashionable dress with little regard for function" (Cheape 1991, p. 52).

Throughout the nineteenth century, aristocratic patronage continued to provide cachet for this new urban-based national style, which began to have "correct" items and styles of wear for day and evening. From the 1840s, it was given new impetus through Queen Victoria's cult of the Highlands. Queen Victoria shared King George IV's romantic vision of Scotland, and in 1852 Prince Albert bought Balmoral Castle in Aberdeenshire. Parts of the interior, most notably the queen's private suites, were decorated with tartan. Queen Victoria herself wore dresses made from "Dress Stewart" or "Victoria" tartan, sparking a trend for tartan fashions worldwide. It was not until the twentieth century, however, that women embraced the kilt as fashionable attire. After World War II, a simplified version of the kilt emerged in the form of a pleated, wrap-around skirt belted at the waist and secured near the hem with a large pin. Popular with middle- and upper-class women, it also formed a component of the uniforms of private girls' schools in England and America, thus maintaining the kilt's connotations of wealth and class privilege.

Re-contextualization

As Scotland gained a new level of cultural and political confidence toward the end of the twentieth century, "a new generation of [young] radical Scots . . . reclaimed the wearing of the kilt from the embrace of nearly two hundred years of establishment, commodified gentrification" (Taylor 2002, p. 220). The Victorian styles of day wear and evening wear gave way to contemporary usage. Many younger Scotsmen began to wear their kilts for everyday use with a T-shirt or sweater, a denim or leather jacket, sneakers or chunky, heavy-soled boots, and woolly socks falling around the ankles. As Lou Taylor observes in *The Study of Dress History* (2002), "Now young Scotsmen wear their kilts according to their own cultural codes and on their own national identity terms" (Taylor 2002, p. 220).

Recently, the kilt has become increasingly popular among non-Scotsmen wishing to project a self-confidently fashionable image. This can be attributed, at least in part, to the immense success of such films as *Rob Roy* (1995) and *Braveheart* (1995). In the tradition of the Romantic movement of the late eighteenth and early nineteenth centuries, these films portray the Highlander as "warrior hero," embodying timeless, masculine values. This image has been reinforced in the arena of sport, most obviously through the Highland Games, now broadcast around the world. In putting the shot, tossing the caber, and throwing the weight, men of obvious stamina are shown competing in kilts. Most recently, however, Scottish football supporters have promoted the Highlander as a beau ideal. Their tribal antics and kilted uniforms received widespread publicity in France during the World Cup in the summer of 1998. Through such images, the kilt has come to represent a ready access to Highland male sexuality. For non-Scotsmen, it provides the means of asserting a self-consciously yet unambiguously masculine persona.

Contemporary designers have drawn heavily on the kilt's hypermasculine connotations in their attempts to appeal to the young fashion-conscious male. At the same time, various designers have attempted to blur the lines between the "kilt" and a "skirt" by reworking elements of the kilt's design. Most typically they have focused their efforts on foregrounding the cut over the culturally specific tartan, employing nontraditional "street" materials like denim or leather, and even adapting its cut, length, and construction. These "skirt-kilts" offer men a means of expressing a frank masculinity while simultaneously projecting a self-confidently unconventional persona. As such, they have proved particularly successful among youth and countercultural movements such as punks in the 1970s and new romantics in the 1980s. Since the early 1990s, kilts and skirt-kilts have entered the lexicon of gay fashion. Worn by gay men as an expression of hypermasculinity and a flaunting of perceived femininity, the kilt has become a standard item in the masculinized gay wardrobe.

See also Europe and America: History of Dress (400–1900 C.E.); Gender, Dress, and Fashion; Tartan; Uniforms, Military.

Bibliography

Burnham, Dorothy, K. *Cut My Cote*. Toronto: Royal Ontario Museum, 1973.

Chapman, Malcolm. *The Celts: The Construction of a Myth*. London: Macmillan, 1992.

Cheape, Hugh. *Tartan: The Highland Habit*. Edinburgh, U.K.: Weatherhill, 1991.

Dunbar, John Telfer. *Highland Costume*. Edinburgh, U.K.: Laurier Books Ltd., 1977.

———. *The Costume of Scotland*. London: B. T. Batsford, Ltd., 1981.

Scarlett, James D. *Scotland's Clans and Tartans*. Guildford, U.K.: Lutterworth Press, 1975.

Taylor, Lou. *The Study of Dress History*. Manchester, U.K.: Manchester University Press, 2002.

Trevor-Roper, Hugh. "The Invention of Tradition: The Highland Tradition of Scotland." In *The Invention of Tradition*. Edited by Eric Hobsbawm and Terence Ranger. Cambridge, U.K.: Cambridge University Press, 1983.

Andrew Bolton

KIMONO

Around the world, the kimono is recognized as the national dress of Japan. Made from a single, long fourteen-inch-wide bolt of silk, the kimono has an over-all T-shape, with its component parts joined mostly in straight, vertical seams. In contrast to typical Western garb, the kimono is flat rather than three-dimensional, and angular, not form-fitting. It is more an expression of surface design by means of dyed and/or embroidered patterns than a product of tailoring and weave.

The term "kimono" was coined during Japan's first era of modernization, the Meiji Period (1868–1912), in response to the heightened awareness of the Japanese to Western clothing, customs, and ideas. Japan had recently emerged from an enforced period of isolation with feelings of self-consciousness in regard to their dress as compared to that of occidentals. A dichotomy was established distinguishing Western clothing (*yōfuku*) from native dress (*wafuku*).

Kimono, the best-known article of traditional clothing, takes its name from the verb *kiru*, meaning "to wear," and *mono*, meaning "thing." In its narrowest sense, the kimono is the descendant of the *kosode*, a former undergarment that emerged prior to the Edo period (1603–1868) as the principal article of dress most sensitive to changes in styles and fashion. More broadly, kimono can refer to any traditional Japanese T-shaped garment, whether worn by men or women in any context—sacred or secular, for weddings or funerals, onstage or at festivals, or simply for relaxing at home.

Kosode/Kimono Parameters

The kosode takes its name from the adjective *ko*, meaning "small," and *sode*, for "sleeve." In that a kosode/kimono sleeve has the appearance of a large pouch, it is difficult to consider the kosode sleeve as being small. In fact, what is small relative to the overall sleeve size is the opening through which the hand passes. The kosode sleeve opening is so-named in contrast to the *ōsode* sleeve, which is entirely open and unsewn.

The kosode took precedence over the ōsode as the primary vehicle for fashion, while the ōsode was relegated to conservative milieux such as court rites, religious rituals, and the no theater. Other variations in construction include the absence or presence of a lining, wide lapels that overlap or narrow ones that abut, a flat collar, and the occasional use of padding. When the front panels of the robe are wide enough to overlap, the left front panel is always closed over the right side. The obi is a sash used to secure the robe around the body.

Distinctions existed among kosode of the past, some of which are still current in kimonos. One type of kosode, the *furisode* (literally, "swinging sleeves") has sleeves especially long in their vertical dimension. The furisode is reserved for unmarried girls. The *katabira*, for which the nearest modern descendant is the *yukata*, was unlined and not made of silk, but rather of a bast fiber (usually hemp or ramie). Two other types of kosode, called *koshimaki* and *uchikake*, were worn as outer robes on top of another kosode. The koshimaki was densely embroidered with small auspicious motifs and draped around the hips while held in place by an obi. It became obsolete; however, the uchikake, worn like a cape and not fastened at the waist, had a thickly padded hem and was still being worn at marriage ceremonies in the early 2000s.

Early Styles

After the kosode ceased to be the plain, unpatterned silk garment worn next to the skin under layers of voluminous robes, as in the Heian Period (794–1185), it served as outerwear, initially for the lower classes and eventually for the samurai class and the aristocracy.

One of the first discernible styles in kosode, *nuihaku*, featured decoration in embroidery (*nui*) and metallic foil (*haku*). In some examples, the robe's markedly contrasting sections differ in both motifs and color schemes. Another early style, known by the poetic name *tsujigahana* (literally "flowers at the crossroads"), was technically exacting, involving careful tie-dyeing, delicate ink painting, and, occasionally, embroidery and applied metallic foil. Some kosode patterned in this fashion were only decorated at the shoulders and hem, with the midsection left empty.

Kanbun Style

The earliest style for which there is considerable pictorial and written documentation, as well as extant garments, is known as Kanbun (1661–1673) after the Japanese era of that name. Order books from the Kariganeya clothing atelier in Kyoto, which catered to samurai class and aristocratic clients, reveal an exuberant asymmetrical style often featuring large-scale motifs in a sweeping composition extending from the shoulders to the hem, with the left body panel (as viewed from the back) mostly free of decoration in its midsection. The broad, flat expanse of surface area and the T-shape, two characteristics inherent in *kosode* construction, are exploited to their full design potential in such robes.

In Kanbun kosode, tiny tie-dye spots were used extensively in the creation of individual motifs, and in combination with embroidery in polychrome silk threads and gold and silver threads. Occasionally, written characters in a flowing script were incorporated into the design scheme, adding a literary aspect and creating deeper levels of meaning in the pattern by combining words with individual design motifs.

The two most elite (and, eventually, most conservative) levels of society, the aristocracy and the samurai class, were patrons of this bold and innovative style. The earliest published kosode design books (*hinagata-bon*), printed from wood blocks to allow for wide dissemination, also featured the Kanbun style, indicating there was also a popular audience for this new fashion. Members of the nouveaux riche merchant class had the money to afford such expensive robes, although they were at the bottom of the social scale, below farmers and artisans.

Kosode design books allowed a larger public to keep pace with changing fashions. A client would select a design from such a book, then choose colors from an album of dyed fabric swatches; after which a kosode maker, in collaboration with a dyer, would produce the finished product. The concept of ready-to-wear clothes for both Western-style garments and kimono did not have an impact in Japan until after World War II. Even as late as the early twenty-first century, most finer kimonos were still made to order, like haute couture in the West.

Genroku and Yōzen Styles

The next dominant style is named for the Genroku years (1688–1704). During this time women's obi grew wider, and therefore more prominent as a fashion accessory. Many different methods were invented for tying the obi, adding another element to the repertory of styles available to fashionable women. The obi was now usually knotted at the back.

As the obi widened, the sleeves of the furisode-type kosode lengthened even more and its unpatterned space diminished, although the shoulder-to-hem Kanbun-style sweeping design composition was more-or-less preserved. The overall effect was one of opulence, as the design filled up more space and the wider obi added a further expanse of decoration.

The Kabuki theater, a new and raucous form of popular entertainment, enjoyed a wide audience in the urban centers where the merchant class was based. Since women were banned from the Kabuki stage, male actors also played the female roles. They launched fashion trends in women's kosode, particularly by popularizing certain shades of colors and individual design motifs. Woodblock print publishers had eager urbanites lining up to buy the latest images of Kabuki stars, and also of geisha, who were the female trendsetters of the moment. By this time, men's kosode were no longer interchangeable with women's dress, except within the Kabuki and brothel demimonde.

Another style that emerged during the Genroku years was named after a Kyoto painter, Yōzensai Miyazaki, and is simply referred to as *Yōzen*. He is believed to have popularized a technique that combined freehand painting and paste-resist dyeing using a wide variety of colors and allowing for the production of highly pictorial imagery and unusual shading effects on kosode.

Yōzen kosode represented a uniquely Japanese achievement in the costume arts. Whereas technological advances in textile production had previously been initiated on the Asian mainland (especially in China) and were later copied and refined by the Japanese, a new means of decoration involving the skill of the dyer and the hand of the painter had been created in Japan itself. The nearest equivalent to Yōzen in textiles outside of Japan is Indian chintz, which, however, utilizes cotton fabric rather than silk and makes less use of freehand painting and shading effects. Yōzen remains a popular technique for the decoration of kimono in the early 2000s.

Late Edo–Period Styles

Extravagance in Genroku and Yōzen-style kosode led the Tokugawa authorities to enact sumptuary laws from time to time, leading to restrictions on the use of certain colors for the lower classes and to controls on some of the more costly textile techniques. Apart from the sumptuary laws, which were randomly enforced, a reaction against flamboyance and excess became the underlying basis for a new style.

Esthetic terms such as *iki* and *shibui* were used by trendsetters who dressed in kosode with a simple striped pattern in subdued colors, or who chose a quiet ikatpatterned fabric for their robes. Other kosode were decorated only along the hem, with the remainder of the garment devoid of design except for traditional family crests arrayed across the shoulders. Subtlety, with a touch of luxury, could be conveyed by wearing a plain kosode with a richly decorated lining.

Excess was not completely forgotten during the late Edo period. The Bunka-Bunsei years (1804–1830) saw the production of many densely embroidered kosode rich Yo in gold thread and that were often chosen by brides for their weddings. Even Buddhist monks commissioned extravagantly woven ritual robes during this period.

A trend in kosode of the Samurai class played on the juxtaposition of certain design motifs alluding to literary works from Japan's medieval period. Another style, which continued into Japan's modern era, was based on the work of the Shijō-Maruyama school of painting, whose artists were influenced by Western painting techniques such as the use of perspective. Several of these painters were recruited to work on kosode designs, and were able to successfully adapt their landscape, bird, and flower themes to the T-shaped garment.

Meiji Period (1868–1912)

In the 1850s, Japan was forced to end its policy of isolation when militarily superior Western powers demanded trading concessions. China, which had historically been the fount of culture for Japan, as ancient Greece and Rome had been for the rest of Europe, was then under the yoke of Western imperialism and was no longer considered to be a suitable role model for the Japanese.

When power was assumed by the Meiji emperor in 1868 after the shogunate collapsed, the elite of Japan embarked upon a serious program of studying and emulating Western technology and customs, including dress. In 1887, the Meiji empress issued a statement denouncing the wearing of kimono as harmful to the female body and advocated the Western blouse and skirt as a more practical form of women's wear.

However, only wealthy women who moved in international circles felt the need and had the means to dress Western style. The long kimono and its wide, tightly bound obi made chair sitting a challenge. In the traditional Japanese home, kimono-clad women sat on a tatami mat–covered floor with their lower legs folded under their thighs. Most women continued to wear kimonos, as they did not lead public lives and had no occasion to experience Western-style interior decor. The daughters of Meiji women did, however, improvise a sort of Western two-piece outfit to serve as school dress. They wore their kimonos tucked into *hakama*, the traditional skirtlike trousers, which had most recently served as part of formal dress for samurai-class men during the Edo period.

For urban men, whose lives were led in public while their wives stayed home, uniforms based on European models were worn in the exercise of certain professions. If a man had the means, he could visit a tailor and be fitted for a suit, which would invariably be made of wool, a fiber Japan itself never produced. Otherwise, at least a token article of Western dress would be worn in public, such as the bowler hat.

Meanwhile, in the West, kimonos appealed to certain sophisticates who developed a passion for things Japanese. Numerous portraits were painted of Western women in kimono during the latter part of the nineteenth century. The kimono could add both an exotic and an erotic flavor to a painting. Puccini's *Madame Butterfly* and Gilbert and Sullivan's *The Mikado* put the kimono on stage in front of large audiences in Europe and the Americas. Fashion designers such as the Callot sisters and Paul Poiret were inspired by the kimono shape.

Taishō Period (1912–1926)

Japan continued to modernize and prosper during this period. When a major earthquake seriously damaged Tokyo in 1923, much of the city was rebuilt in a more Western style, making Western attire more practical in the new modern interiors. The kimono and other traditional dress for women were further marginalized as female students started to wear blouses and skirts instead of kimono tucked into *hakama* (although such an outfit can still be seen at graduation ceremonies), and as more women entered the workforce.

Shōwa Period (1926–1989)

Militarism came to the fore in 1930s Japan, eventually leading to the disaster and devastation of World War II. Rampant nationalism did not bring about a revival of the kimono. Women were needed to fill jobs abandoned by men in the armed forces, and kimonos were impractical as work clothes. Fabric was rationed, and the kimono was seen as wasteful, requiring more material than Western-style clothes. During the occupation period following Japan's defeat, many families were forced to sell or barter heirloom kimonos for daily

necessities, causing yet another setback to the tradition of kimono wearing.

However, economic recovery and prosperity created a large middle class in Japan, resulting in an increase in disposable income and leisure time. Housewives now sought to cultivate themselves by engaging in traditional arts such as flower arranging and tea ceremony, for which kimono was the appropriate dress.

Department stores became major retailers of kimonos, which were still made to order from narrow bolts of silk. Brides continued to dress in kimonos for weddings (but would also change into a Western-style wedding dress for a portion of the ceremony), and might even enroll in a school at which the proper choosing and wearing of the kimono and obi were taught. Traditional annual events, such as New Year festivals and coming-of-age ceremonies, were further occasion for kimono wearing, although primarily for women and children.

Colors and patterns in kimono did change from year to year, but the burst of creativity in surface design and dyeing of the Edo period has yet to be equaled. The modern kimono represented a middle-class rediscovery of a traditional garment. Its role is minor, or nonexistent, in the lives of Japanese women in the early twenty-first century, with the exception of the geisha, who continued to wear kimono with a sense of style while entertaining men.

However, kimonos did experience another incarnation in postwar Japan as art objects. Certain artisans who continued to practice traditional crafts, including textiles, were designated "Living National Treasures" by the Ministry of Culture. Two of the best-known Treasures in the field of textiles, Kako Moriguchi and Keisuke Serizawa, had some of their fabric production made into kimonos, which were subsequently shown at exhibitions and collected as works of art. Their work, and that of other artists of their caliber, has extended the creative life of the kimono.

The Art-to-Wear Movement led to kimono-inspired artistic production in the West. Such pieces have been worn as clothing or displayed on walls, illustrating that the scope of the kimono has broadened well beyond that of a national costume.

See also Japanese Traditional Dress and Adornment.

Bibliography

Asian Art Museum of San Francisco. *Four Centuries of Fashion: Classical Kimono from the Kyoto National Museum.* San Francisco: Asian Art Museum, 1997.

Dalby, Liza Crihfield. *Kimono: Fashioning Culture.* New Haven, Conn.: Yale University Press, 1993.

Gluckman, Dale Carolyn, and Sharon Sadako Takeda. *When Art Became Fashion: Kosode in Edo-Period Japan.* New York: Weatherhill, 1992.

Ishimura, Hayao, and Nobuhiko Maruyama. *Robes of Elegance: Japanese Kimono of the 16th–20th Centuries.* Raleigh: North Carolina Museum of Art, 1988.

Kennedy, Alan. *Japanese Costume: History and Tradition.* Paris: Editions Adam Biro, 1990.

Kyoto National Museum. *Kyoto Style: Trends in 16th–19th Century Kimono.* Kyoto: Kyoto National Museum, 1999.

Liddell, Jill. *The Story of the Kimono.* New York: E. P. Dutton, 1989.

Peebles, Merrily A. *Dressed in Splendor: Japanese Costume 1700–1926.* Santa Barbara, Calif.: Santa Barbara Museum of Art, 1987.

Stevens, Rebecca A. T., and Yoshiko Iwamoto Wada, eds. *The Kimono Inspiration: Art and Art-to-Wear in America.* Washington, D.C.: The Textile Museum, 1996.

Stinchecum, Amanda Mayer. *Kosode: Sixteenth–Nineteenth Century Textiles from the Nomura Collection.* New York: Japan Society and Kodansha International, 1984.

Alan Kennedy

KLEIN, CALVIN*

Calvin Klein was born in the Bronx, New York, on 19 November 1942. He attended the High School of Industrial Arts and the Fashion Institute of Technology in New York, where he studied fashion design.

Klein's first major position in the fashion industry was with Dan Millstein, a Seventh Avenue coat and suit manufacturer. He worked there from 1962 to 1964, starting as a pattern cutter and advancing to a full-fledged designer. Klein's second position was with Halldon, Ltd., where he began to be recognized in the press for his designs.

Klein soon became frustrated by the design restrictions of moderate-priced fashion manufacturers. Encouraged by his parents and financed by his boyhood friend Barry Schwartz, Klein developed a collection of coats and suits under his own label.

Klein's first line was discovered by a buyer from Bonwit Teller, who was so impressed by the collection of finely tailored coats in fresh colors that he sent Klein to meet with Mildred Custin, then president of Bonwit Teller. Custin placed a large order with Klein, giving a jumpstart to the newly formed Calvin Klein Limited.

Early on, the savvy Klein developed relationships with fashion insiders, including the designer Chester Weinberg and *Vogue* fashion editor Nicolas de Gunzburg. The publicity agent Eleanor Lambert took Klein on as a client and was instrumental in guiding his early career. Klein's first *Vogue* cover was in September 1969, with his classically cut outerwear featured prominently in the New York fall preview editorial inside. Throughout the 1970s, Klein's designs were noted for their sportswear influence, muted pastel color palettes, and simplicity of design. Looks that are considered classic Klein were introduced at this time: the pea coat, the trench coat, the shirtdress, and the wrap blouse. Klein was also an early advocate of all-occasion or "day into night" dressing, with evening pajamas being his preferred form of formal wear.

As the decade wore on, Klein eased up his tailoring for a relaxed, sexy look. Klein also began to incorporate looks from active sportswear into his collection—swimwear and tennis outfits that could be used off the beaches and tennis courts by pairing them with wrap skirts or pants. Corduroy cargo pants, flannel shirts, and elegant fur-trimmed parkas were shown on Klein's 1970s fall runways. For all his innovations, Calvin Klein won his first Coty American Fashion Critic's Winnie Award—as the youngest recipient ever—in 1973. He won again in 1974, and in 1975 he was inducted into the Coty Hall of Fame. In 1978 Klein began designing a menswear collection that was licensed to Maurice Biderman.

The most groundbreaking piece of sportswear Klein showed on the runway first appeared in spring 1976: a slim-cut pair of jeans with his name embroidered on the back pocket. Although the idea of logo-emblazoned jeans was not brand-new, this was the first time that jeans had shown up on a designer runway. By 1978, with Puritan Fashions as manufacturer, Klein was selling 2 million pairs of jeans per month. The phenomenal success that Klein had with his jeans line was due in no small way to a brilliant and controversial advertising campaign starring a young Brooke Shields.

The 1980s

Klein's designs, even in the excessive 1980s, continued to evoke a minimalist aesthetic, with a relatively restrained use of embellishment and color. The core of the collection was, as always, made up of timeless pieces in good fabrics. The Council of Fashion Designers of America (CDFA) recognized Klein when he won designer of the year awards in 1982 and 1983 for his women's collection. Klein won a CFDA award in 1986 for both his men's and women's collections, the first time a designer had won both awards in the same year.

In 1982 Calvin Klein launched a men's underwear line. The collection revolved around a standard men's brief, with Klein's name stamped on the waistband. Bold black-and-white photography on the packaging and an advertising campaign featuring celebrity models Antonio Sabato Jr. and Marky Mark in suggestive poses helped make the product appealing to both straight and gay men. The underwear line became a phenomenon when Klein took the same briefs and modified and marketed them for women. Warnaco purchased the underwear division in 1994.

By 1983 Calvin Klein, whose eponymous fragrance had produced a lukewarm reception four years earlier, was ready to give perfume another try. The result was Obsession and, again, with brilliant advertising—television ads directed by Richard Avedon and print ads shot by Bruce Weber—Obsession was a success. In 1986 Klein married Kelly Rector, one of his design assistants. The marriage, as well as the mid-1980s "return to family values" mood, inspired the designer's next fragrance, Eternity. A shared-gender fragrance, cK One, was launched in 1994.

The 1990s

In the 1990s Calvin Klein's worldwide expansion into Asia, Europe, and the Middle East markets brought his name international consumer recognition. The decade also saw Klein revamp the jeans/sport division of the company, creating the cK collection, made to appeal to a younger, hipper customer. Klein had been farsighted enough to realize the importance of archiving his work, so a constant recall of his roots was readily available. The cK line, largely inspired by these vintage collection pieces, was recognized by the CFDA with an award in 1993.

Klein surrounds himself with people who share his aesthetic, and he is known in the fashion world for his intensely collaborative relationships with those who work with him. Most noteworthy is Zack Carr, who was Klein's creative doppelgänger for almost thirty years. Jeffrey Banks, Isaac Mizrahi, and Narciso Rodriguez are also notable Calvin Klein alums.

The twenty-first century began with litigation between Klein and Warnaco over underwear and jeans distribution. The case was eventually settled out of court. Klein and his partner Barry Schwartz sold Calvin Klein, Inc., to Phillips–Van Heusen in December 2002. Since that time Klein has stepped down as creative head of the company that bears his name and has assumed a consultant role. In 2004, Francisco Costa took over as Creative Director.

The name Calvin Klein represents so many different things—controversial advertising campaigns, the leading name in the designer-jeans phenomenon, stylish boyish underwear for women, and brilliant and ruthless business practices. So much of what Klein designed has become fundamentally what Americans wear that his clothing can rightly be called an American uniform.

See also Avedon, Richard; Brands and Labels; Vogue.

Bibliography

Carr, George. *Zack Carr*. New York: Power House Books, 2002.

Gaines, Steven, and Sharon Churcher. *Obsession: The Lives and Times of Calvin Klein*. New York: Carol Publishing Group, 1994.

Horyn, Cathy. "The Calvinist Ethic." *New York Times Magazine*, 14 September 2003, 64–69.

Marsh, Lisa. *House of Klein: Fashion, Controversy, and a Business Obsession*. Hoboken, N.J.: John Wiley and Sons, 2003.

Plaskin, Glenn. "Calvin Klein: The Playboy Interview." *Playboy*, May 1984.

Reed, Julia. "Calvin's Clean Sweep." *Vogue*, August 1994, 236–241.

Gretchen Fenston and Beth Dincuff Charleston

"I didn't think I was doing anything different from what *Vogue* did when it used Brooke as a model. . . . *Vogue* put $3,000 dresses on her, but it wasn't expecting to sell those dresses to 15-year-olds. It was using her as a model and I was using her as an actress" (Quoted in Plaskin, p. 4).

With the Brooke Shields ads, Calvin Klein forever changed television commercials. Klein spent an unprecedented $5 million on marketing that year. Feminists were enraged by the jeans ads and felt that, rather than sales, the commercials—with slogans such as "You know what comes between me and my Calvin's? Nothing"—would provoke violence against women (Plaskin, p. 62).

LACROIX, CHRISTIAN*

The creations of Christian Lacroix embody in spectacular combinations his Provençal roots, his passion for folklore, and his fascination with the history of clothing. His artfully unexpected mixtures express a new form of luxury, simultaneously youthful, baroque, and sophisticated. Lacroix mingles bright tones and extravagant materials in creations that express a refined blending of different cultures; distant and forgotten costumes form the basis, if not the raison d'être, for his work.

Christian Marie Marc Lacroix was born in 1951 in Arles, France. In early childhood Lacroix showed a flair for design by putting together little albums on theater and opera, collages assembling family portraits, and reproductions by Christian Bérard. He left his native Arles to study the history of art in Montpellier, and then enrolled at the Sorbonne in Paris in 1973. He wrote a master's thesis on French costume in the paintings of the seventeenth century while at the same time taking courses at the École du Louvre to become a museum curator. It was at this time that he met his future wife, Françoise Rosensthiel; they married in 1974.

With the encouragement of his wife, he soon turned to fashion design. In 1978 he joined Hermès, where he learned the technical aspects of the profession. Two years later he was an assistant to Guy Paulin and then succeeded Roy Gonzales as a designer for Jean Patou in 1981. In 1986 he received the Golden Thimble award for dresses designed in honor of his native region of Camargue. In December 1986 Lacroix met Bernard Arnault, chief executive officer of the multinational luxury firm Louis Vuitton Moët Hennessy (LVMH), who offered him the financial support needed to open his own couture house.

The Christian Lacroix house was inaugurated in 1987 at 73, rue du Faubourg Saint-Honoré in Paris. On 26 July 1987 Lacroix presented his first collection under his own name, and that year the Council of Fashion Designers of America awarded him the prize for Most Influential Foreign Designer. Inspired by dresses in the style of the 1880s, he designed an off-the-shoulder dress with a high waist, the miniskirt of which became the emblematic "pouf." Completed by a short bolero jacket, the ensemble was cut in highly colored and decorative fabrics inspired by Provence. Folk and traditional elements were set off by a certain French grandeur, coquettishness, and whimsy that reflected the desires of a new generation hungry for luxury. Lacroix's style thus confirmed the taste for a typically southern opulence, instilling new life into French haute couture, which had been stigmatized as a dying art. *France Soir* described Christian Lacroix as the "Messiah," and *Time* featured him on its cover. In 1988 the profession awarded him a second Golden Thimble. The dream collapsed with the stock market crash. The pouf soon became a metaphor for the excesses of the 1980s, which gave way to the minimalism of the 1990s.

In his designs, Lacroix nevertheless remained faithful to his roots and his history in a clothing collection where east meets west, the north basks in the southern sun, and the past blends with the future. The 1980s had allowed him to define and focus these influences, and over the years he continued to quote from and vary his sources of inspiration, as he developed and refined them.

Lacroix also carried on using a glittering palette of colors. "Colors I have always liked, so much so that when I was a child, I dreamed of swallowing tubes of yellow and vermilion paint," he said (de Bure, p. 129). His designs became more abstract and the dresses more simplified, their architecture more apparent. Previously, the decoration had been designed before the dress; now it came into play only after the dress had been constructed. "In reality, I love only what veers off course, has a defect, is heterogeneous, transitory," he said. "I think I love everything and its opposite. That is probably the key" (du Bure, p. 130).

Lacroix has turned his fashion world into a stage, designing for more than twenty ballets, operas, and plays. In 1996 he was awarded the Molière for best costume design for the Comédie Française production of *Phèdre*. In 2000 he signed a new contract with LVMH, the owner of his couture house. He divides his time between his responsibilities as artistic director of this couture house and his own company, XCLX. The list of his projects is long and varied and his commissions ever more spectacular. Among his extravagant designs are eight carriages of the TGV Méditerranée (a high-speed French train), which he "dressed" and presented as haute couture creations. "This is what now interests me: going beyond fashion to participate in ways of living, in our global environment, with uniforms [for Air France], seats for the TGV, stage costumes. Each of these areas—clothing, theater, design . . . helps me to express a facet of my personality" (Brébant, p. 61). Spectacle is inherent to his vision: "The Lacroix woman is staged in a theatrical fashion. She is not afraid of being noticed; for her one can imagine nothing that is bland (Alessandrini, p. 22).

In 2002 Lacroix was named artistic director of the Florence ready-to-wear house Emilio Pucci. That year he was awarded the medal of Chevalier of the Légion d'Honneur. Lacroix describes French haute couture as "eternally dying and paradoxically constantly being reborn from its ashes" (Sausson, p. 6). A great defender of couture, Lacroix does not conceive of it as an art but rather as a service rendered to his clientele: "Art is something made for love. Art is what makes life more beautiful. Something that motivates and inspires. My work has a purpose; it is not just made for the sake of it" (Lowthorpe, p. 14). His creations, brought into being by a wide range of craftsmen, knitters, corsetieres, painters, and embroiderers, overwhelm and plunge the spectator into a world located between dream and reality, where fantastic textures rival embroidered materials in elegance, where fluid fabrics wedded to richly colored costumes speak in a flamboyant vocabulary signed Christian Lacroix.

In May 2009, Christian Lacroix declared insolvency and ceased trading.

See also Art and Fashion; Ballet Costume; Haute Couture; Paris Fashion; Pucci, Emilio; Theatrical Costume.

Bibliography

Alessandrini, Marjorie. "Christian Lacroix: La mode est un théâtre." *Le nouvel observateur.* 12–18 July 2001, p. 22.

Brébant, Frédéric. "Christian Lacroix relance la Puccicmania." *Weekend le Vif/L'Express*, 28 February 2003, p. 61.

de Bure, Gilles. "Christian Lacroix, l'homme qui comble." *Technikart* 28 (December 1998): 129.

Lowthorpe, Rebecca. "Christian Lacroix." *Independent on Sunday*, 1 July 2001.

Sausson, Damien. "Christian Lacroix, au-delà de la beauté." *L'œil*, September 2000, p. 6.

Pamela Golbin

LAGERFELD, KARL

Karl Lagerfeld was born on 10 September 1938 to a wealthy family in Hamburg, Germany. He moved to Paris in 1952 and first came to the attention of the fashion world two years later when he won a competition prize for his design of a woolen coat. In 1954 he was hired as a design assistant by Pierre Balmain, one of the premier couture houses of the early postwar period. In 1958 he parted ways with Balmain and became art director at the House of Patou, where he remained until 1962. For most of the next fifteen years he designed for a number of companies and under a variety of contractual and freelance agreements.

He was associated especially with Chloë (1963–1983), where he created styles that simultaneously were elegant and focused on the young. Many of his most striking designs for Chloë had an art deco flavor, being very streamlined and body conscious. He also utilized prints to excellent effect. At the same time, he worked as a freelance designer for Krizia, Valentino, Ballantyne, and other companies. Beginning in 1965 he designed furs for Fendi. His ability to design simultaneously for several different houses has been a defining characteristic of his career; Lagerfeld became known as a man who was never content to do just one thing at a time.

In 1975 Lagerfeld formed his own company and in 1983 became artistic director of the House of Chanel. While continuing his responsibilities at Chanel and at Fendi, he formed Karl Lagerfeld S.A. and KL to market his own ready-to-wear lines. Karl Lagerfeld S.A. was acquired by Dunhill (the parent company of Chloë) in 1992, and Lagerfeld returned to Chloë at that time and held the post of chief designer until 1997, when he was replaced by Stella McCartney. When he left Chloë, he regained control of the company bearing his own name; in the early 2000s Lagerfeld was designing for Karl

Lagerfeld/KL, Chanel, and Fendi. He has also designed costumes for many films and theatrical productions.

Lagerfeld probably is most admired for his work at Chanel, where in 1982–1983 he took over responsibility for a company that had become somnolent, if not moribund, and very quickly made it exciting again. Taking the basic vocabulary established by Coco Chanel, he modernized it, introducing new materials, including denim, and exaggerating such details as the "double C" logo. Remarkably, his work for Chanel has remained as vital in the twenty-first century as it was in the mid-1980s.

Karl Lagerfeld has had a wide-ranging career in the arts, achieving considerable success as a writer and photographer. Over the years he has produced many fashion photography spreads for his collections at Chanel and for his own labels and has published several books of his photographs. He also is well known as an aesthete and connoisseur of art and antiques. In 2000 he sold part of his antique furniture and art collection at auction for more than $20 million. With his signature silver-white hair and newly slim figure, he is a familiar and iconic presence on the European fashion scene.

See also Balmain, Pierre; Chanel, Gabrielle (Coco); Paris Fashion; Patou, Jean.

Bibliography

Buxbaum, Gerda, ed. *Icons of Fashion: The Twentieth Century.* New York: Prestel, 1999.
Lagerfeld, Karl. *Karl Lagerfeld: Off the Record.* Göttingen, Germany: Steidl, 1994.
——. *Dreams.* New York: Te Neues, 2002.
Milbank, Caroline Rennolds. *Couture: The Great Designers.* New York: Stewart, Tabori, and Chang, 1985.

John S. Major

LANVIN, JEANNE*

Jeanne Lanvin (1867–1946) was born in Paris, France, and spent much of her youth as a seamstress and millinery apprentice. In 1883 she was employed to trim hats in the workshop of Madame Felix at 15, rue du Faubourg Saint-Honoré. Lanvin established her own millinery workshop at the age of eighteen in 1885. With just

forty francs in cash and three hundred francs in credit, Madame Lanvin opened her millinery house in a modest apartment at 16, rue Boissy-d'Anglas in 1889.

Lanvin married the Italian aristocrat Emilio di Pietro in 1895. Although their marriage was brief, ending in 1903, the union produced a single child, Marguerite Marie-Blanche, who was born in 1897. This child inspired and supported one of the greatest design careers of the twentieth century. In 1907 Lanvin married Xavier Melet, a journalist. Lanvin's daughter married for the second time in 1925; her husband was the comte Jean de Polignac, and she became known as Marie-Blanche, comtesse de Polignac.

History of the House

In 1908 Lanvin opened a children's clothing department in the millinery shop, inspired by the wardrobe created for her own daughter, and just one year later she opened departments for ladies and girls as well. Becoming a full-fledged *couturière*, she joined the Syndicat de la Couture, the ruling body of the haute-couture industry. Her first dress designs followed the lines of the chemise frock, a long, slender, empire-waist design that offered ease of movement. By 1910, a mere two years after opening her children's department, her designs appeared in *Les modes*, a French fashion periodical.

By 1925 twenty-three ateliers operating under the Lanvin name employed up to eight hundred people. That year, branches of Lanvin were opened in Cannes and Le Touquet. Through the years the house continued to grow, with several other boutiques opening in foreign locales: In 1927 alone, additional shops were opened in Deauville, Biarritz, Barcelona, and Buenos Aires. Lanvin created departments for menswear, furs, and lingerie in 1926 and then launched several successful fragrance lines, including Arpège (1927), Scandal (1933), and Rumeur (1934).

When Jeanne Lavin died in 1946, her daughter, Marie-Blanche, became the chairman and managing director of Lanvin and Lanvin parfums; she remained at the helm of the businesses until her death in 1958.

In 1950 Marie-Blanche invited Antonio Canovas del Castillo to design the haute-couture collection. This position passed to Jules-François Crahay in 1963; to Maryll Lanvin, the wife of Jeanne Lanvin's nephew, in 1985; and, finally, to Claude Montana in 1990. He presented five haute-couture collections, two of which won the Golden Thimble Award from the Chambre Syndicale de la haute couture parisienne. By 1993 the House of Lanvin had withdrawn from haute couture to concentrate on their image as a luxury goods house.

The design career of Madame Lanvin survived sixty-one successful and productive years. Lanvin is the oldest surviving couture house in continuous existence, from 1909 to 1993. In the early 2000s, Lanvin continues to focus on ladies' ready-to-wear clothes and luxury accessories. Collections for men and made-to-measure sportswear are also produced. Fragrance remains part of the Lanvin offerings, releasing Oxygene to the masses. L'Oreal, the parent company, sold Lanvin to an unidentified Chinese owner in 2001 who focused on finding a designer who could put a modern edge on the historic, antiquated company; among designers employed during this period were Ocimar Versal Oto and Christine Ortiz. In 2003, Alber Elbaz began designing the luxury collection and has had great success in reviving the Lanvin name, gaining a more youthful clientele of fashion editors, models, celebrities.

Social Life

For the sole purpose of advertisement and publicity, Madame Lanvin employed the innovative technique of dressing the highly social demimondaines and actresses. Informally modeling the latest creations of the couture house, they created great interest among the social set. Demimondaines were a less respectable group of women who had lost their social standing—although they were highly social and extremely fashionable—due to sexual promiscuity or other ethically questionable activities (such as prostitution). Their male companions gave them the money to buy the finest fashions and accessories; in fact, demimondaines were notably the most fashionable women in town.

Unlike her successful contemporaries, Madame Lanvin shunned the spotlight. She avoided large social settings, preferring her small, creative circle of artists, musicians, designers, and writers. On rare occasions Madame Lanvin could be seen at horse races for the sole purpose of research. Her attendance at these events enabled her to see what women were wearing, what looked good and what did not, how fabrics moved, how silhouettes looked, what was cumbersome, and what was ridiculous. In addition, by observing what the women were wearing, she could deduce what they would next be desiring to add to their wardrobes. Lanvin downplayed her image and personality, maintained a discreet background position, and rarely socialized with her clients. These habits contributed to her anonymity in the years following her death.

Jeanne Lanvin et sa fille, 1907. This photograph was the inspiration for the Lanvin insignia. PATRIMOINE LANVIN, DROITS RÉSERVÉS. REPRODUCED BY PERMISSION.

Inspiration

The originality of Lanvin garments, constructed in such a masterly fashion, lay in their surface detail and embellishment. Madame Lanvin extracted inspiration from various objects to be translated into viable, modern, functional design. For example, her signature color, "Lanvin blue," was inspired by the fifteenth-century Italian frescoes of Fra Angelico. Her desire to create the perfect colors for her designs prompted her to establish her own dye factories in Nanterre in 1923. This shrewd move ensured the originality and exclusivity of her colors, and, indeed, competitors who tried could never successfully duplicate them.

The beading and embroidery patterns on her designs were inspired by various exotic elements and destinations. Lanvin was an avid traveler and methodical collector of objects from various cultures around the globe; they later served as a personal library of inspiration.

Versatility

The House of Lanvin was a fashion leader and innovator in the 1920s, utilizing extraordinary beading techniques; and in the 1930s, with technically innovative surface treatment ensuring the singularity of her creations. Versatility contributed to the longevity of the couture house, as the Lanvin image was clearly defined and redefined from season to season. Marie-Blanche was her mother's muse and lent her youthful perspective to the designer's creative ideas. Consequently, the House of Lanvin forever maintained its image of youth, femininity, and beauty.

Clientele

Lanvin women typically began their association with the house as debutantes and maintained their loyalty through their weddings, motherhood, and widowhood. The youthful silhouette of the *robe de style*, synonymous with Lanvin, experienced great success, as it was offered in every collection. It flattered every figure at every age for all occasions. The *robe de style* was inspired by eighteenth-century fashions and consisted of a quasi two-dimensional silhouette created by the use of a pannier, or basket-like structure on either hip. This silhouette achieved great success during the 1920s as an option to the slender, cylindrical silhouettes promoted by other couturiers.

Madame Lanvin successfully combined romanticism and historicism in the most modern way. "Modern clothes need a certain romantic feel," she remarked (*Vogue*, 1 June 1942, p. 66). The youthful, elongated torso and romantic full skirts created a large surface that served as a canvas for any tasteful combination of beading, embroidery, or appliqué.

While the success of the vast Lanvin empire was a substantial accomplishment in itself, Madame Lanvin applied her skills to other creative areas as well. Pooling her talents with Armand Albert Rateau, a great French architect, in 1922, she completed several interior design projects, including her own homes, shops, and the Théâtre Daunou. She also opened her first interior decoration store, Lanvin Décoration. In addition, she shouldered the enormous responsibility of organizing and executing the couture exhibits at many of the great world expositions. For these efforts she was created chevalier of the Légion d'honneur on 9 January 1926. In 1938 Madame Lanvin was made an Officier of the Légion d'honneur.

> "The longevity of this couture house may be attributed to the untiring force and determination of a woman driven by the relentless need to create, succeed, and excel within her chosen field among many worthy, predominantly male, contemporaries."
>
> *Dean L. Merceron*

Lanvin's legacy to the world of fashion is youth, beauty, and feminity—modernity softened with romance; beautiful colors in feminine silhouettes that blur the lines of age. The *robe de style* was a dress that could be worn literally by everyone. Lanvin was primarily an artist, and a businessperson second. She was guided by her artistic sensibility and supported by her fair sense of business and strong work ethic. She was an innovator and a leader, working for the industry as a whole, not just for the house of Lanvin. As one who "had it all," she was a role model for women: She started her own business, married, and had a child. Even as a single mother, she continued to run her empire and raised her daughter to be an inspirational success.

See also Color in Dress; Dyeing; Twentieth-Century Fashion.

Bibliography

Barillé, Élisabeth. *Lanvin.* London: Thames and Hudson, Inc., 1997.

Merceron, Dean. *Lanvin.* New York: Rizzoli, 2007.

Picon, Jérôme. *Jeanne Lanvin.* Paris: Flammarion, 2002.

Vial, Franck Olivier, and François Rateau. *Armand Albert Rateau: Un baroque chez les modernes.* Paris: Éditions de L'Amateur, 1992.

Dean L. Merceron

LATIN AMERICAN FASHION

Latin American dress and fashion refers to the dress, body, and culture of a large and heterogeneous world culture region that includes Mexico, Central America, the Caribbean, and South America. Given that the nature of dress in Latin America is highly diversified, one can look to overlapping socio-historical influences that have shaped the pursuit of elegance and transformed the dynamics of everyday life to elucidate some general characteristics.

When Christopher Columbus claimed the islands of Cuba as well as the Dominican Republic and Haiti for Spain in 1492, he initiated the conquest of the indigenous populations living in the region that came to be known as Latin America and the Caribbean. The first images and accounts of American natives that circulated throughout Europe reveal much about a sense of awe experienced by the first colonizers. They view the natives' nakedness with bewilderment and marvel at the presence of material goods such as cotton cloth, intricate feather work, and weavings. This "New World" would provide Europe with material goods as varied as silver, gold, sugar, chocolate, textiles, and dye. Portugal, involved in its own push for colonial power, would successfully challenge Spain for the region that makes up the country of Brazil. As Spain and Portugal quickly established colonial governments, the native populations suffered the effects of brutal conquest, incurable disease, and forced conversion to Christianity. Friar Bartolomé de Las Casas harshly condemned the exploitative practices of conquistadors and settlers who had turned to slavery and other forms of systematic violence to establish ranches, mines, and textile industries.

To maintain a sense of hierarchy and respond to increasing *mestizaje*, or racial mixing, a caste system was established throughout the region. Prior to colonization, dress and textiles had often served as indicators of social and religious identity and as a medium of exchange. The caste system forced natives and African slaves to wear Western styles of dress, thereby reinforcing the authority of the Spanish and Portuguese, and over time, their Creole descendants. Some indigenous communities gave voice to their history and religious beliefs with the help of intricate color-coding systems, as found in woven textiles or compilations of strings. In this way, the *huipil* of Guatemala and the highlands of Mexico placed deities of the sun and the underworld in dialogue with the Christian faith. Still worn today, this traditional blouse component of the Mayan *traje*, or dress, reveals information about a woman's village, status, heritage, and personal beliefs. Recent excavations in Argentina and Brazil point to the African as well as Islamic origins of some pieces of jewelry found near the sites of plantations and urban mansions, suggesting that accessories may not have been censored by colonial authorities in the same way as dress. As court records indicate, one could wear almost any design

provided that it was gender specific. The selection of fabric, however, was a highly serious matter. Depending on her social status, a Mexican woman of the eighteenth century would have purchased either a silk or cotton *rebozo*, or scarf. Decrees prohibited the use of certain textiles by those who the caste system deemed as inferiors, thus leading to the prohibition of velvet or taffeta for specially fashioned Incan *unku*s, or tunics, in the Andean region.

By the early nineteenth century, the region experienced several calls for independence from Spain and Portugal that deeply affected the way people consumed fashion. For Cuba and Puerto Rico, this struggle for independence would not materialize until the end of the nineteenth century, although the description of fashion and dance in several literary works began to plot the demise of Spanish rule and to construct alternate political identities. In the visual imaginary of this period, Creole leaders such as Simón Bolívar (Venezuela) and José de San Martín (Argentina) appear in wind-swept capes and uniforms of their own design. Many women found themselves called upon to sew the accessories of war, their products in view and their identities concealed. A few, among them Juana Azurduy de Padilla (Bolivia) and Josefa Tenorio (Argentina), took on male uniforms in order to fight on the battlefield, later arguing that they merited equal status in postcolonial society. Distancing themselves from the customs of Spain, fashionable women of Buenos Aires transformed the Spanish *peineta*, or hair comb, into the three-foot-by-three-foot Argentine *peinetón* in order to assert their presence and at times obstruct the very public sphere that professed independence from oppression but which, ironically, had not yet granted all the privilege of citizenship. In satirical caricatures from the period, the enlarged crests of women's combs take to downtown Buenos Aires and quickly overpower the top hats of men.

Following the retreat of Spanish colonialism, the rhetoric of fashion provided a forum for discussions on the configuration of national identity. In some cases, fashion writing allowed intellectuals to disseminate important political agendas and evade censors. In the Southern Cone region, the regime of Juan Manuel de Rosas sought to eliminate the political opposition by requiring a scarlet insignia on a *chaleco*, or men's vest, of all citizens. In a violent push toward homogeneity, a decree prohibited light blue, the identifying color of the opposition, and green, a well-known symbol of hope. In this challenging climate, socialites introduced a secret language of fans, coded inserts for top hats, and message-revealing gloves, to state what was on a wearer's mind. Appropriating metaphors from the realm of fashion, in 1837, a group of Argentine intellectuals founded a fashion magazine, entitled *La Moda* after the audacious *La Mode* that had served as a force of violent opposition in revolutionary France. Using female pseudonyms and taking advantage of the fact that few associated fashion writing with politics, these founding fathers of modern Argentina asserted their urban, democratic ideals before seeking exile in neighboring Chile and Uruguay to avoid persecution. In an exploration of the dynamics of civilization and barbarism in his native country, Domingo Faustino Sarmiento, one of *La Moda*'s founders and a future Argentinean president (1868–1874), advocated a consolidation process that shed the nation of its traditional rural values, epitomized by the lawless poncho-clad gaucho who had long upheld Rosas's power; Sarmiento's goal was for the country to embrace an urban, and therefore more "civilized," lifestyle more conducive to the government's goals for economic growth and modernization. Economic booms at the end of the nineteenth century would earn Argentina the reputation of the Paris of South America, as its cityscape stood transformed into an allusion of luxury, consumerism, and international capitalism.

With the massive influx of European immigrants to Latin American cities at the turn of the century, luxury took on a fraudulent role. Members of the nouveaux riches and new arrivals began to imitate the styles of the upper classes in order to find work, holding in high esteem the novelties of Paris. With the emergence of the fashion lithograph, *modistas*, or tailors, copied European designs (sometimes appropriating styles for the climate of a particular region) and then commissioned seamstresses who, enduring miserable working conditions, pieced garments together with the help of sewing machines. While women's dress had become a bit more flexible, it still incorporated the corset and layered skirts and trains that required bustles. As sewing machines became more affordable, many women opted to purchase ready-made clothing or to fashion their own, more comfortable, styles at home. Encouraging readers to consider individualized designs and the prospect of female emancipation, Juana Manuela Gorriti (Argentina) and Clorinda Matto de Turner (Peru) used the language of fantasy and self-transformation, or fashion writing, to enter a public debate on materialism and female economic autonomy.

During the twentieth century, Latin American dress would inspire several fashions in Europe and the United States, from the blouse with lace ruffles inspired by the Afro-Cuban rumba, to the well-known Mexican *huaraches*, or woven leather sandals, to the straw Panama hat actually created in Ecuador. *Vogue* and *Look* turned attention to trendsetting Latin American women whose visions of haute couture, as in the case of Eva Perón (Argentina), and native designs, bringing to mind the surrealist painter Frida Kahlo (Mexico) who incorporated folkloric *china poblana* costume in bright colors and with a full skirt in her self-portraits and in real life, would continue to resonate in the popular imaginary until the present day. Other, more contemporary, fashion statements have tended to revisit the past for a retro effect, such as the young Cuban American donning the *guayabera*, a lightweight, embroidered cotton shirt worn untucked throughout the Caribbean; or the Chicano zoot-suiter, whose wartime appropriations of his father's suits inspired ethnic pride in the face of racism and brutality; or the teenage club kid wearing Inca-techno styles while discotheque dancing.

The latter part of the twentieth century witnessed a horrifying backlash against democratic values when countries such as Argentina, Chile, and Uruguay installed military governments. Strict gender codes imposed clean-cut looks for men and feminine styles for women. Responding to human-rights abuses and the plight of the "disappeared" (which refers to the tens of thousands of victims who were killed or whose whereabouts still remain unknown), the Mothers of the Plaza de Mayo in Argentina began to protest near important national monuments in their morning robes and house slippers, as if to state visually that they had no one at home to care for, as the regime had taken away their sons and daughters. The Mothers wear a white scarf, embroidered with the names of their missing loved ones, during their weekly marches. Serving as living monuments for the victims of repression, mother's groups in El Salvador and throughout the world have appropriated this same white scarf in their struggles against social injustice.

The revolutionary movements of Cuba (1959–) and Nicaragua (1979–1990) signaled a turn toward socialist antifashion, which associated the elitist pursuit of luxury with the kind of capitalist domination that created dependencies on foreign goods and exploited the working classes. Indeed, much of Latin America had experienced uneven economic development throughout the twentieth century. In the garment industry, multinationals relied on the cheap labor of native workers for the weaving, assembly, and sewing of garments. But in more recent years, even revolutionary Fidel Castro (Cuba) occasionally shed his camouflage for the sartorial pleasures of a dark-blue designer suit. A heightened awareness of the sweatshop conditions of the *maquiladora*, the export-processing zones established in 1960s that continue to operate under the North American Free Trade Agreement (NAFTA), sometimes led consumers to boycott specific collections and push for a more socially conscious fashion system. Some designers, such as Carlos Miele (Brazil), have worked with women of the *favelas*, or shantytowns, and various indigenous communities to establish cooperatives that will ensure fair-trade wages for their creations.

Responding to the possibilities offered by a global marketplace and Internet connections, Hispanic designers Carolina Herrera (Venezuela), Oscar de la Renta (Dominican Republic), together with Beth Sobol (United States) and Victoria Puig de Lange (Ecuador), formed the Council of Latin American Fashion Designers in 1999. An affiliated Fashion Week of the Americas established an international platform for Latin American fashion and culture. In newspapers, a new word surfaced in popular culture that combined *fashion* and the Spanish suffix *-ista* (implying, with a tinge of sarcasm, a devotee). The dress-conscious *fashionista* scoured the ever-expanding style pages of newspapers and e-zines for information about new talents like Narciso Rodríguez (United States), the famed designer of Carolyn Bessette Kennedy's bridal gown, and faced the proliferation of fashionable identities with gusto. In the urban centers of São Paulo, Buenos Aires, and Bogotá, supermodels such as Gisele Bündchen (Brazil) and Valeria Mazza (Argentina) promoted national fashion events with international appeal. At the same time, free-trade agreements between countries, such as the Mercosur block of the Southern cone region, have enabled fashion designers to create transnational organizations, such as *Identidades Latinas*, to tap into new markets. Among others, the houses of Laurencio Adot (Argentina), Alexandre Herchcovitch (Brazil), Ronaldo Fraga (Brazil), Rubén Campos (Chile), Silvia Tcherassi (Colombia), Sitka Semsch (Peru), and Angel Sánchez (Venezuela) earned strong reputations in the category of women's wear. Lina Cantillo and Ricardo Pava (both of Colombia) seemed best known for their men's collections. Fraga and Sylma Cabrera (Puerto Rico) were noted in fashion circles for their attention to children's wear. Into the twenty-first century, the reputation of

Latin American fashion designers continued to rise on the world fashion stage.

See also Latino Style.

Bibliography

Bauer, Arnold J. *Goods, Power, History: Latin America's Material Culture*. Cambridge and New York: Cambridge University Press, 2001.

Holland, Norman. "Fashioning Cuba." In *Nationalisms and Sexualities*. Edited by Andrew Parker, Mary Russo, Doris Sommer, and Patricia Yeager. New York: Routledge, 1992.

Masiello, Francine. *Between Civilization and Barbarism: Women, Nation, and Literary Culture in Modern Argentina*. Lincoln and London: University of Nebraska Press, 1992.

Meléndez, Mariselle. "La vestimenta como retórica del poder y símbolo de producción cultural en la América colonial: De Colón a El lazarillo de ciegos caminantes." *Revista de Estudios Hispánicos* 29 (1995): 411–439.

Root, Regina A. "Tailoring the Nation: Fashion Writing in Nineteenth-Century Argentina." In *Fashioning the Body Politic*. Edited by Wendy Parkins. Oxford: Berg, 2002.

——, ed. *Latin American Fashion*. Oxford: Berg, 2004.

Regina A. Root

LAUREN, RALPH

An argument can be made that Ralph Lauren is the most successful and influential designer of his time, though he is known less for the creativity of his designs than for being an astute marketer and image maker. His fascination with style began in early childhood. He was born Ralph Lifshitz in the Bronx, New York, in 1939, the fourth and last child of Frank and Frieda Lifshitz, both Jewish refugees from Eastern Europe. He was educated in both public schools and strict yeshivas and raised with high expectations.

Early Interest in Fashion

Even as a boy Lauren loved to dress well and was always a sartorial step ahead of his peers. He liked to try on his dapper father's jaunty hats, and he wore his older brothers' hand-me-downs with a notable sense of style.

Even if his clothes were not expensive, he distinguished them with an unusual drape or combination. He knew how to tie a Shetland sweater around his shoulders just so and rolled the cuffs of his jeans in a particular and unique way. When he fantasized about being a teacher, he imagined himself wearing a tweed jacket with suede elbow patches. Ralph and his brother Jerry often went shopping together where they discovered thrift-shop clothing. The memories of those hunting expeditions still inform Lauren's collections: it was in thrift shops that he discovered the joys of rugged military clothes, the integrity of British tweed suits, the thrilling transformation that could take place when a socially backward Jewish kid donned a cowboy shirt and a pair of jeans and imagined himself at home on the range.

Early Career

Once out of school he became a furnishings buyer for Allied Stores, and then (having changed his surname to Lauren) a tie salesman at Brooks Brothers. After a brief stint as a supply clerk in the U.S. Army, Lauren spent the 1960s pounding the New York pavement selling gloves, men's fragrance, and ties. More importantly, however, he was refining his personal style, designing his own custom-made suits, haunting great men's stores like Paul Stuart, and gaining inspiration from custom-made suit makers like Roland Meledandri.

Lauren grew frustrated with his conservative bosses in the tie business, since they seemed unaware of the oncoming peacock revolution in men's fashion. Secretly, he designed a line of wide ties, inspired by ones made in England by the brand Mr. Fish. He sought out a backer to finance the line and others to produce it. In 1967 he launched Polo as a division of the tie-maker Beau Brummel. Soon Bloomingdale's, then America's most cutting-edge department store, discovered Ralph Lauren. Thus began an intense and mutually advantageous relationship that still thrived in the early 2000s.

Polo Brand

In 1968 Lauren left Beau Brummel, taking the name Polo with him, and went into business with the suit maker Norman Hilton. Lauren began expanding, first into a full range of clothing and furnishings for men, and then, in 1971, into women's fashions. Even in those early days, he displayed characteristics that defined his career: an innate understanding of branding (he embroidered his polo player logo on the cuffs of his

first women's shirts, creating one of the most singular brand identities in the history of marketing); a fearless refusal to be reined in by finances or expectations; and a recklessness (doing too much too soon with insufficient capital and staff) that soon led to the first of several financial crises. Later crises were caused by Lauren's fierce—but never entirely realized—desire to be as successful in women's fashions as he was, almost immediately, in men's wear. Still, he produced iconic clothing for both sexes after those first wide ties: his famous polo and oxford shirts, khakis, perfect Shetlands, prairie skirts, Navajo blanket coats, and men's wear–inspired women's suits. Over the years, despite nagging fit and delivery problems caused by his insistence on dressing only a certain body type and an almost paralyzing uncertainty over what to include in his lines, those styles won him a grudging respect. Clothing from his collections, which appeared in two acclaimed films from the 1970s—*The Great Gatsby* and *Annie Hall*—helped promote his name.

Print Advertising

In the late 1970s, when Lauren formed a fragrance company with Warner Communications, money began pouring in, earning him serious commercial power and financing his next and perhaps greatest innovation. In partnership with the photographer Bruce Weber, who also worked for Calvin Klein, Polo began producing extraordinary print advertisements that served as mini-movies, advertising the myriad, linked product categories Lauren produced. More significantly, they hammered home Polo's most potent product, the idea that clothes not only make the man and woman, but make them whatever they want to be, whether that is a New England patrician or a Colorado cowgirl.

Retailing Legacy

In the late 1980s Lauren and his creative services department unveiled the extensive renovation and preservation project that is the Rhinelander Mansion, long one of New York's architectural treasures, and now the backdrop to Lauren's ultimate Polo retail store. It has forever redefined fashion retailing. He had become, as a biographer called him, the personification of "the commodification of status, of the democratization of symbols of the haute monde, of the perfection of luxury merchandising and the rise of 'lifestyle' marketing, and of the globalization of branding and the simultaneous

Americanization of international fashion" (Gross, 2003).

Though Lauren still did not always receive the approbation of fashion editors and his peers in the fashion design world, he went on to win every award that could be bestowed on designers, as well as worldwide fame and enormous wealth. Polo grew so large that in June 1997 it became a public corporation, listed on the New York Stock Exchange.

At age sixty-five Lauren, one of the greatest businessmen-designers in fashion history, remained driven and unsatisfied, still struggling to prove himself. His attempt to reposition Polo as a premium luxury brand was a troubled one. In 2004 Polo's stock price still languished below the highs it hit the day it was first offered to the public, and investors and financiers remained skeptical not just of Polo's position in the market, but also of its future. As head of a company heavily dependent upon his design and marketing skills, his style intuition, and his personality, Ralph Lauren showed no signs, however, of climbing off his polo pony.

See also Fashion Advertising; Fashion Marketing and Merchandising; Perfume.

Bibliography

Gross, Michael. *Genuine Authentic: The Real Life of Ralph Lauren.* New York: HarperCollins, 2003.

McDowell, Colin. *Ralph Lauren: The Man, the Vision, the Style.* New York: Rizzoli International, 2003.

Trachtenberg, Jeffrey A. *Ralph Lauren: The Man Behind the Mystique.* Boston: Little, Brown, 1988.

Michael Gross

LAVER, JAMES

Born in Liverpool, England in 1899, James Laver was a dress historian who worked at the Victoria and Albert Museum in London as a curator from 1922 to 1959. His initial interest in dress grew out of the need to date accurately the pictures in his care. His instrumental relationship to costume quickly changed, and, as he writes in his autobiography, "Having studied the What and the When, I began to wonder about the How and the Why" (1963, p. 240). Laver became one of the most

prolific authors in the English-speaking world to write on the history of dress and fashion as well as on the sociology of those topics. Not only did he recast the conventional narratives of European high fashion, but he also wrote about nonfashionable forms of attire, such as school and military uniforms, children's dress, and sporting clothes. He died in 1975.

Dress and Time

Laver was fascinated by the effects that the passing of time has upon people and their works. He was greatly influenced in his theory of time by a notion of *zeitgeist*, or "time spirit," a concept taken from nineteenth-century German philosophy. Zeitgeist proposes the existence of a collective psychological, or spiritual, entity that imparts a distinctive pattern of aims and emphases to a culture, nation, or historical epoch. Drawing on this idea of cultural unity, Laver concluded that every aspect of social life is permeated by the emotional and intellectual dispositions lodged within the zeitgeist. He broadened the scope of the original idea of the "time spirit" by aligning it to a theory of modernity, arguing that all things human are increasingly subject to dictates of "time consciousness." Clothing is one of the things most sensitive to changes in the zeitgeist. In dress is found an immediate physical manifestation of the patterns of the time spirit (style), while in their rapid changes (fashion) can be observed the ever widening influence of the modern form of time. As Laver observes, "Nothing illustrates the Triumph of Time more clearly than the growing dominance of fashion" (1933, p. 132).

Clothes and Style

Laver's approach to the forms of clothing was based upon his belief that there are "no accidents in the history of dress" and that "all clothes are inevitable" (1949, p.6). He explains this assertion so:

> In every period costume has some essential line, and . . . [when examining previous fashions] . . . we can see quite plainly what it is, and can see . . . that the forms of dresses, apparently so haphazard, so dependent on the whim of the designer, have an extraordinary relevance to the spirit of the age (1945, p. 250).

The task is to understand the meanings of this "essential line" as it insinuates itself into the dress styles of a culture or epoch. Some of Laver's most controversial assertions are to be found in the connections he makes between the social and political structures of an age and in the details of its dress, as indicated in *Taste and Fashion from the French Revolution until To-day*:

> The aristocratic stiffness of the old regime in France is completely mirrored in the brocaded gowns of the eighteenth century. . . .Victorian modesty expressed itself in the multiplicity of petticoats; the emancipation of the post-War flapper in short hair and short skirts (1937, p. 250).

Laver wrote a book about the French physician and astrologer Nostradamus (1942) and also *A Letter to a Young Girl on the Future of Clothes* (1946). At times, he came close to seeing the interpretation of clothing and its changes as being akin to clairvoyance. He names this apparent ability of clothing to anticipate the future "the wisdom of forms." When, later in life, he became a media personality, he would shock audiences by asserting that links exist between the fluctuations of the stock market index and a propensity for women to abandon corsets. In his book *Style in Costume* (1949), Laver describes his method for drawing these conclusions as "to take some dominant shape of dress—a hat, a trouserleg, or whatever it may be—and to place it beside some form of architecture or interior decoration of the same epoch, and to note the parallelism, if such exists, between them" (p. 7).

Clothes and Fashion

Laver stressed that in modern life things are increasingly subject to change, and the existence of dress fashions is evidence of the extent to which *time* has displaced *place* as the major influence on clothing. He saw the process of fashion as having two aspects. There are the broad, objective rhythms of style change in dress and the subjective, but shared, aesthetic dispositions (taste) that incline groups to prefer one type of clothing to another. Laver was convinced that neither of these sorts of change is accidental or arbitrary, and in his book *Taste and Fashion: From the French Revolution to the Present Day* (1945), he attempted to describe and explain the regularities he noticed in both these areas.

Laver's approach to taste is novel because, rather than focusing on why certain types of clothing are deemed fashionable, he instead asks the question: How can it be that what was thought of as fashionable becomes grotesque and can then start to appear charming

---

> Laver wrote or edited seventy books between 1921 and 1972, at least twenty-seven of which had to do with dress or costume. He explored a variety of topics, from poetry to art to the theatre. He was also the author or coauthor of seven plays.
>
> Contemporary Authors Online

---

as time passes? The answer is his list of the stages (*Taste and Fashion*, p. 258) undergone in the decay of chic.

Indecent: 10 years before its time
Shameless: 5 years before its time
Outré (daring): 1 year before its time
Smart
Dowdy: 1 year after its time
Hideous: 10 years after its time
Ridiculous: 20 years after its time
Amusing: 30 years after its time
Quaint: 50 years after its time
Charming: 70 years after its time
Romantic: 100 years after its time

Laver encountered more serious intellectual difficulties in explaining the objective shifts in dress styles. As he investigated forms of attire such as uniforms and professional dress, he realized that not all clothing changed at the same rate. To explain these different rates of change or, in some cases, their complete absence, he began to supplement his ideas about the relation between zeitgeist and dress with those of Thorstein Veblen and J. C. Flügel.

When Laver published his book *Dress* in 1950, he explained changes in dress styles using a version of the "three motives" model of the nineteenth century. Laver argued that clothing both expresses and is shaped by three fundamental principles: the hierarchical principle, the attraction or seduction principle, and the utility principle. The seduction principle plays the most significant role in fashion change, particularly as it affects women's clothes. Laver theorizes that the seduction principle is the most important because "our clothes are dictated by the fundamental desires of the opposite sex." (1950, p. 15). He goes on, "Men still choose their mates by their physical allure; that is why women's clothes follow what might be called the Attraction Principle; they are designed to make their wearers as physically attractive as possible" (1950, p. 15).

Women, according to Laver, have to compete with one another through their appearance, and wherever there is sartorial competition there will also, he argued, be fashion.

See also Fashion, Historical Studies of; Fashion Museums and Collections; Flügel, J. C.; Veblen, Thorstein.

Bibliography

Works by James Laver

"Triumph of Time." In *Contemporary Essays: 1933*. Edited by Sylva Norman. London: Elkin Mathews and Marrot, 1933.

Nostradamus; or, The Future Foretold. London: Collins, 1942.

Taste and Fashion from the French Revolution until To-day. London: G. G. Harrap and Company, Ltd., 1937. New revised edition titled *Taste and Fashion from the French Revolution to the Present Day*, 1945.

A Letter to a Girl on the Future of Clothes. London: Home and Van Thal, 1946.

Style in Costume. London: Oxford University Press, 1949.

Dress: How and Why Fashions in Men's and Women's Clothes Have Changed during the Past Two Hundred Years. London: John Murray, 1950.

Museum Piece; or, The Education of an Iconographer. London: Andre Deutsch, 1963.

Works about James Laver

Carter, Michael. "James Laver: The Reluctant Expert." In *Fashion Classics from Carlyle to Barthes*. New York and Oxford: Berg, 2003.

Michael Carter

LESAGE, FRANÇOIS

François Lesage, a French embroiderer born in Chaville in 1929, is the son of Albert Lesage (1888–1949), founder of Albert Lesage and Company in 1924, and of Marie-Louise Favot, known as Yo, a designer for Madeleine Vionnet. After an apprenticeship in the family firm in Paris, François Lesage went to the United States in 1948 and opened a shop on Sunset Boulevard, Los Angeles, where he embroidered for dressmakers and Hollywood studios, but the death of his father the following year put an end to his American adventure. François Lesage returned to Paris to assist his mother in managing the renowned company.

History

At the time of his father's death, the embroidery house that Lesage inherited was among the most important and prestigious specialty companies of its type in the world. In 1924 his father, Albert, had taken over the business of the embroiderer Michonet. Michonet's venerable firm, which was founded in 1858, had supplied the great names of couture of the belle epoque (Charles Frederick Worth, John Redfern, Jacques Doucet, Callot Soeurs) with beautiful embroidery to decorate their creations. The firm had also supplied the imperial court of Napoleon III with embroidery and had succeeded in establishing new connections with the talented generation of couturiers between World War I and World War II. François Lesage was thus familiar from a very young age with the technical and aesthetic feats accomplished by his parents for the original collections of Madeleine Vionnet and Elsa Schiaparelli, among others.

When he took charge of the firm, which possessed tens of thousands of samples, the young François continued the craft tradition and created his own collections of samples, which were immediately admired by such designers as Pierre Balmain, Cristóbal Balenciaga, Robert Piguet, Jacques Griffe, and Jean Dessès. For the *jolie Madame* (the trade name of Pierre Balmain), full of grace and delicacy expressed in muted tones, he updated the rococo ribbon. The artificial flowers, straw spangles, and planished sequins to be found in the work of several couturiers of the time are early examples of the style of the young Lesage, a subtle mixture of tradition, novelty, and a bold approach to every challenge.

Innovations

François Lesage freed himself from the weight of tradition in the 1960s. He successfully experimented with new materials, including patterns of plasticine and cellophane, bold treatments of classic materials, and uncommon arrangements that revealed a different approach to relief. Embroidery had become fabric, and fashionable dresses, cut straight and not fitted to the body, offered an ideal setting for Lesage's graphic compositions, which covered the entire surface of the design. Lesage acquired new clients, including such stellar names as Lanvin, Givenchy, Dior, Grès, Patou, and Yves Saint Laurent.

Work with Haute Couture

In the 1970s Lesage designs returned to the thematic collections that had been favored by Schiaparelli. Yves Saint Laurent was the first designer to recognize the aesthetic potential of this change. The entire industry, stimulated by lavish orders from Arab princesses, followed Saint Laurent's lead and kept the embroidery workshops operating overtime. Lesage developed embroidery on jersey and new techniques, such as precut designs attached by thermoplastic films to fabrics. In 1977 he embroidered the court dress of the wife of Jean Bedel Bokassa, which was ordered from Lanvin on the occasion of the coronation of Bokassa to the office of emperor of the Central African Empire.

In 1982 Lesage began to collaborate with the American designers Calvin Klein, Bill Blass, Geoffrey Beene, and Oscar de la Renta. Throughout the decade thematic collections provided opportunities for creation and innovation. Lesage established fruitful dialogues with Yves Saint Laurent; as well as with Karl Lagerfeld, the new artistic director of Chanel and Christian Lacroix, with whom he collaborated from the opening of his couture house in 1987. While Lacroix was still at the house of Patou, he met Lesage, whom he considered his "godfather in fashion." For all these designers, who competed with one another in erudition and historical references, Lesage revisited the entire history of art, producing masterpieces for each of them that required hundreds of hours of work. Among the most famous of his productions transposed Van Gogh's irises and sunflowers onto Yves Saint Laurent jackets in 1988, a feat requiring no fewer than six hundred hours per jacket.

Accessory Line

Encouraged by this infatuation with the magic of embroidery, Lesage launched a line of embroidered accessories in 1987, created by Gérard Trémolet and sold in the Lesage boutique opened that year on the Place Vendome on the former site of Schiaparelli's business. After the shop closed in 1992, the accessories were sold in department stores around the world.

Legacy

In 1990 Lesage joined the Comité Colbert; in 1992, in order to perpetuate his art and transmit his skill, he opened the Lesage School of Embroidery at the address of his workshop, 13 rue de la Grange Batelière in Paris.

Having attained the summit of his art, Lesage became the subject of several one-man shows: at the Fashion Institute of Technology in New York (1987), at the Musée de la mode et du costume Palais Galleria in Paris (1989), at the Fashion Foundation Hanae Mori of Tokyo (1989), and at the Los Angeles County Museum of Art (1991).

With the 1990s came an influx of new orders from creators such as Thierry Mugler and Jean Paul Gaultier, who launched their own haute couture activities. But also, paradoxically, orders for ready-to-wear clothes from houses and designers such as Chanel, Dior, and Yves Saint Laurent added to the work of the embroiderers working under Lesage.

In addition to the work done for designers, Lesage has carried out many special orders. For example, on the occasion of the World Youth Days in Paris (1997), he embroidered the chasuble and miter of Pope John Paul II. Additionally, he embroidered the costumes of Erik Orsenna and Roman Polanski for their entry into the Académie française (1999) and costumes for the new revue at the Moulin Rouge (1999). Lesage followed the long tradition of the house in working for royalty when he collaborated with Moroccan craftsmen and designed costumes for the trousseau of the bride of Mohammed VI in 2001. In 2002 the Lesage company was acquired by Chanel as part of its Paraffection group, bringing together craftsmen of elegance who possess exceptional skill.

See also Beads; Embroidery; Spangles.

Bibliography

Kamitsis, Lydia. *Lesage*. (Paris: Editions Assouline; New York: Universe/Vendome, 2000).

White, Palmer. *The Master Touch of Lesage: Embroidery for French Fashion*. Paris: Chene, 1987.

———. *Haute Couture Embroidery: The Art of Lesage.* New York: Vendome Press, 1988.

Lydia Kamitsis

LEVI STRAUSS & CO.

The name Levi Strauss is indelibly linked with a quintessential American fashion—blue jeans. The original riveted work pants, called "waist overalls," were patented by Levi Strauss in 1873 and became staples of quality, durable workingmen's garments for more than fifty years. In the 1950s blue jeans, particularly Levi Strauss classic riveted "501's" emerged as fashion statements, anticipating the skyrocketing popularity of denims worldwide in the following decades. The dominance of Levi's in this fashion phenomena transformed Levi Strauss & Co. from a successful regional company into one of the world's largest clothing brands, with $4.1 billion in total sales in 2002.

While Levi Strauss & Co. has aligned itself more closely with style and fashion in the twenty-first century, its origins were humble and rooted in the dry goods trade. Its founder, Levi Strauss, was born "Loeb" Strauss in Buttenheim, Bavaria, in 1829, one of seven children of Hirsch Strauss. In 1847, Loeb Strauss emigrated to the United States to join his stepbrothers, Jonas and Louis, owners of a dry-goods business in New York City. Loeb quickly learned the family trade and by 1850 he had changed his name to Levi.

The discovery of gold in California and the subsequent Gold Rush of 1849 brought throngs of fortune hunters west in the hopes of striking it rich. In 1853, Levi Strauss headed to San Francisco, too, not to pan for gold, but to establish his own dry-goods business catering to this new workforce.

Levi Strauss set up his wholesale business selling bolts of cloth, linens, and clothing at 90 Sacramento Street, close to the waterfront for convenient access to goods coming off ships. In the late 1850s and early 1860s, his enterprise, known merely as "Levi Strauss," profited, and its steady expansion forced him to relocate several times to other waterfront addresses. In 1863 his brother-in-law, David Stern, joined his firm, and the company was officially renamed Levi Strauss & Co. By this time, Levi Strauss was in his thirties and the firm was a profitable entity providing a variety of goods. The

next decade, however, would assure Levi Strauss his place in fashion history.

In 1872, Levi Strauss was contacted by one of his customers, Jacob Davis, a tailor in Reno, Nevada. Davis had discovered a practical and ingenious way to make work pants stronger by adding metal rivets to the weak points at the pocket corners and the base of the fly. Davis's rivets proved successful and his new reinforced work pants became popular among his local clients. Fearful that his idea would be copied, Davis wanted to secure a patent, but did not possess the $68 necessary to file for a patent. Instead, he turned to Levi Strauss, a successful wholesale goods purveyor from whom he often purchased fabric, and offered to share the patent if Levi Strauss & Co. would underwrite the expense.

Levi Strauss recognized the potential in this endeavor and agreed to share the patent. In 1873, Davis and Strauss received patent #139,121 from the U.S. Patent and Trademark Office for an "Improvement in Fastening Pocket-Openings." The riveted "waist overalls" (as work pants were then known) quickly achieved a reputation for strength, quality, and durability among working men. For twenty years Levis Strauss & Co. held the patent on riveted waist overalls, thereby curbing competition from other manufacturers. In 1890 the lot number 501 (which it would thereafter retain) was first used to designate the riveted waist overall. The following year, the patent expired and went into the public domain, where riveted waist overalls were quickly copied by other firms. However, the demand for Levi's waist overalls continued to grow, forcing Levi Strauss & Co. to open several manufacturing plants of its own in San Francisco.

By the turn of the century, Levi Strauss was in his early seventies and highly regarded as a successful businessman and philanthropist. He died in September 1902, a lifelong bachelor, leaving the bulk of his $6 million estate to relatives and to his favorite charities. With his four nephews running the company, Levi Strauss & Co. continued to thrive and became one of the leading companies producing work pants in the 1920s.

The company's market, however, was still restricted to predominantly western states and to the niche of work clothing. In the 1930s and 1940s, Levi Strauss & Co.'s sphere of influence got a boost from Hollywood through western movies. Popular westerns mythologized cowboys and cowboy dress, including the waist overalls. It was during this period that denims became associated with the ideals of honesty, integrity, and rugged American individualism.

After World War II, Americans enjoyed a level of prosperity marked by greater leisure time. Denims, including Levi's, began to lose their connection with manual labor and emerged as appropriate casual dress. Pivotal to the acceptance of denims was their adoption by teenagers, an increasingly vocal and important market group. When the actor James Dean wore blue jeans in the film *Rebel Without a Cause*, denims attained a completely new status as cool fashion. By this time, the term "waist overalls" was no longer used; denims were known as jean pants or simply as "Levi's."

In the 1960s denims continued their evolution as acceptable leisure wear. As a result, denim producers such as Levi Strauss & Co. and Lee (another former working-pant manufacturer) continued to expand. The 1960s was an important decade for fashion—one which witnessed challenges to the traditional haute couture system and the rising popularity of more democratic, street-inspired fashions. Denims emerged as a symbol of individualism and anti-establishment fashion, much to the benefit of Levi Strauss and its competitors. During the height of the hippie era, Levi Strauss & Co. even sponsored a competition to promote the personalized decoration of Levi's jeans.

Founder Levi Strauss could never have foreseen the meteoric rise of Levi Strauss & Co. in subsequent decades. As tastes changed in the 1970s, denims were transformed from leisure wear to high fashion at the hands of designers such as Calvin Klein. Denims now became acceptable dress for all occasions. In the 1970s and the 1980s, Levi Strauss & Co. dominated the market for blue jeans, which became a de facto uniform for youth in America and abroad. Demand for American Levi's in Europe and around the globe was widespread. In Eastern block countries American Levi's jeans even attained the status of black-market cash in the early 1980s.

The importance of the Levi Strauss brand name in the denim market has been enormous. Through clever marketing and hip advertisements, Levi's capitalized on the revival in popularity of the "classic" 501 button-fly jeans in the mid 1980s. By 1990, Levi Strauss & Co. was an international manufacturer with a global market, selling under the brands Levi's, Dockers, and Slates. Only in the late 1990s and early years of the twenty-first century has Levi Strauss & Co. seen a slight reversal of fortune. Changes in taste, from traditional blue to other colors and the revival of retro-1970s flared leg and baggy, hip-hop silhouettes has worked against Levi's

classic-cut jeans in favor of trendy styles marketed by new competitors such as Tommy Hilfiger and Guess. Since the 1990s, Levi Strauss & Co. has been forced to restructure its company to remain competitive. Ironically, Levi's "classic" denims are no longer manufactured in the United States, the production having been entirely shifted to overseas manufacturers with cheaper labor.

Despite competition from the Gap, Tommy Hilfiger, and Guess jeans, Levi Strauss & Co. remains the standard bearer in the denim world. With roots in the settling of America's west, Levi Strauss & Co. has come full circle achieving (and retaining) iconic status as the maker of the quintessential American garment, still popular throughout the world.

See also Cowboy Clothing; Denim; Jeans; Klein, Calvin.

Bibliography

Cray, Ed. *Levi's*. Boston: Houghton Mifflin, 1978.
"Custom Fit." *W Magazine* (December 2003): 54–62.
Hambleton, Ronald. *The Branding of America: From Levi Strauss to Chrysler, from Westinghouse to Gillette: The Forgotten Fathers of America's Best Known Brand Names*. Dublin, N.H.: Yankee Books, 1987.

Internet Resources

Downey, Lynn. "Invention of Levi's 501 Jeans." About L S & Co. Available from <http://www.levistrauss.com/about/history/jeans.htm>.
"Founder Biography." About L S & Co. Available from <http://www.levistrauss.com/about/history/founder.htm>.

Lauren D. Whitley

LIBERTY & CO.

In 1875, Liberty & Co.'s first small shop opened on Regent Street in London's emergent West End. It grew into a showcase for cosmopolitan goods, and the company became synonymous with exotic and avant-garde design. In particular, Liberty garments were associated with the Aesthetic movement.

Arthur Lasenby Liberty (1843–1917), the company's founder, was the son of a small provincial draper. From 1862 his formative business and aesthetic experiences were at Farmer and Rogers' Oriental Warehouse, Regent Street, specializing in fashionable Kashmir shawls and oriental goods.

At Liberty's, Middle Eastern and Asian goods determined the character of the store. Sympathetic to Arts and Crafts ideals, which rejected factory production in favor of hand craft and sought to beautify everyday things, Lasenby Liberty's ambition became the reform of dress and home furnishings along "artistic" lines. As an entrepreneur, he found ways of supplying an expanding market with exotic, handmade goods in a retail environment evoking an oriental *souk* rather than a conventional department store.

Textiles

Liberty's early catalogs, published from 1881, featured silks remarkable for their variety of color, print, and weight. By the 1880s Liberty's name had become a trademark. "Liberty Art Fabrics" were sensuous and subtly colored, widely admired and imitated. Fashionable aniline dyes were rejected in favor of natural colorings; lack of chemical adulteration, antiquity of design, and irregularity of weave, indicating hand production, were also emphasized.

Initially, dyed and printed silks were imported from India; later, silks were dyed and hand-printed in England, often by Thomas Wardle. Other companies used by Liberty include G. P. and J. Baker; David Barbour; Arthur H. Lee and Sons; Alexander Morton and Co; Turnbull and Stockdale; and Warner and Sons. Leading designers were used anonymously by Liberty. Textile printing was done increasingly by Edmund Littler at Merton, just upstream from Morris and Co.'s workshops. In 1904 Liberty bought the business; until the 1960s, the emphasis was on hand printing with wooden blocks.

Early Liberty textiles were inspired by the Middle East and Asia; by the 1890s, they had a more contemporary look. Although Lasenby Liberty expressed dislike for its more extreme forms, Art Nouveau was dubbed *Stile Liberty* in Italy. "Oriental" designs continued to sell well in the 1920s and 1930s, when small floral patterns also became associated with Liberty fabrics, which then included a huge variety of natural and synthetic materials.

Cloth and Costume

Liberty fabrics were renowned for their softness. Artists appreciated their draping qualities, and Liberty's early dress designs exploited this tendency to follow the contours of the body. This could be perceived as a challenge to propriety, particularly when used in at-home garments such as the tea gown, pioneered by Liberty and others. Early catalogs are illustrated with vignettes of women in exotic or classical costumes. Some assistants in the shop wore unusual dress; even in the 1930s, shopwalkers wore medievally inspired velvet gowns. Liberty's "artistic" styles were imitated and caricatured, notably by the cartoonist George du Maurier.

A Costume Department was established in 1884 to design and make garments suited to the fabrics; eclecticism predominated over fashionable dress. It reflected Lasenby Liberty's determination to control the entire process of design, production, and retailing. The architect E. W. Godwin was consultant designer until his death in 1886. While his earlier designs were notably Japoniste, classical models and the principles of dress reform inspired Godwin's later ideas about dress.

Liberty resisted the dominance of Paris-led styles, although a successful branch was maintained there from 1890 to 1932. Instead, the company pioneered the unstructured cut of Asian clothing as a means of liberating women from their corsets. *Tokado* was described in the company's 1884 catalog as a "Japanese robe arranged as a tea gown." Other popular garments included the *burnous* cloak, derived from North Africa, and the Greek-inspired tea gown (*Hera*, 1901–1909) was an example of Liberty's attempt to promote classical "Greek" dress well after Godwin's death. As fashion absorbed dress-reform principles, Liberty designs appeared less eccentric. By 1925, a "kimono" style floral-print coat, reminiscent of designs by the French couturier Paul Poiret, appeared highly fashionable. Poiret even used Liberty fabrics in his couture business and, following its demise, designed four collections for Liberty in the 1930s. From the 1880s, Liberty also promoted "Artistic Dress for Children," inspired by the drawings of Kate Greenaway; the "Liberty Smock" was a notable example.

The Liberty Home

Liberty also developed a reputation for furnishing fabrics, curtains, bedspreads, and upholstery. A furniture department, supported by its own workshops, opened in 1880 under the direction of Leonard F. Wyburd. At first Liberty imported goods from countries seen as "exotic" and pre-industrial, producing handmade, but relatively inexpensive, furniture and artifacts. Lasenby Liberty traveled widely, notably to Japan, to observe their production firsthand. Shrewd business instincts drove him to innovate however, and he had no scruples about modifying designs for the home market, developing hybrid, Anglo-oriental artifacts and other ersatz styles, incorporating Arts and Crafts, "Celtic," "Tudor," Art Nouveau, and oriental elements. He also invested substantially in small companies producing ceramics, metalwork, and jewelry.

During the 1920s and 1930s, Liberty goods changed little, although after both World Wars, traditional, "English" values were favored. In the 1950s and early 1960s, the company redefined itself as contemporary and European, commissioning work from world-class designers. From 1962, Bernard Nevill directed a new era of distinguished textile design; dress reflected the exuberance of the fabrics. When "ethnic" and revivalist styles became fashionable in the late 1960s and 1970s, Liberty acknowledged the exotic and Art Nouveau heritage it had earlier rejected.

The company remained in family ownership until 2000. Subsequently, the store was modernized, and fabrics and oriental goods became less prominent, while greater emphasis was placed on luxury accessories, furnishing, and "idiosyncratic" fashion by international designers.

See also London Fashion.

Bibliography

Adburgham, Alison. *Liberty's: A Biography of a Shop*. London: Allen and Unwin, 1975. Commissioned by the company for its centenary.

Ashmore, Sonia. "Liberty's Orient: Taste and Trade in the Decorative Arts in Late Victorian and Edwardian Britain, 1875–1914." Ph.D. diss., The London Institute/The Open University, 2001.

Calloway, Stephen, ed. *The House of Liberty: Masters of Style and Decoration*. London: Thames and Hudson, 1992.

Morris, Barbara. *Liberty Design: 1874–1914*. London: Pyramid Books, 1989.

Okabe, Masayuki et al., eds. *The Liberty Style*. Tokyo: Japan Art and Culture Association, 1999.

Victoria and Albert Museum. *Liberty's 1875–1975*. London: V & A Publications, 1975. Exhibition catalog.

Sonia Ashmore

LINGERIE

The term "lingerie" is derived from the French *linge*, or linen, and thus makes direct reference to the material from which underwear was traditionally made. By the late nineteenth century, lingerie had become a generic term commonly used to describe underwear that had moved beyond practical function to become a tool of erotic pleasure used for the display of the body during sexual play. The notion that women, other than prostitutes, could use underwear to designate specific occasions as sexual was particularly popularized during the Edwardian era. Under the relatively austere "tailor-made" suit, women were prepared to wear sensual camisoles and petticoats of lace, chiffon, and crepe de chine, offsetting the accusations of "mannishness" directed by the conservative press at the New Woman, a product of the suffragette movement. Lingerie was a symptom of conflicting gender relations at the turn of the century, on the one hand, the suffragette movement promoted a sea change in sexual politics, while lingerie evoked a more traditional brand of femininity, which objectified the female body. Underwear became deliberately branded as either male or female, feminine or masculine, determined by the use of delicate fabrics and applied decoration for women and practical wool and cotton for men. However, as the twentieth century progressed, the increase in the popularity and use of lingerie mirrored women's gradual freedom from the constraints of Victorian morality and notions of what constituted an appropriate femininity as they emerged as more sexually and socially independent beings. Lingerie was also set apart from the rationalist and unashamedly moralistic undergarments advocated by the Victorian Dr. Jaeger, who espoused the use of wool next to the skin for reasons of hygiene and health—lingerie was unashamedly erotic. However, caution was advocated at first: Lingerie should only be used by women within the confines of a happily married life. One female fashion journalist wrote in 1902, "'Lovely lingerie' does not belong only to the fast. . . . dainty undergarments are not necessarily [sic] a sign of depravity. The most virtuous of us are now allowed to possess pretty undergarments, without being looked upon as suspicious characters" (Steele, p. 194).

At first, handmade lingerie was a sign of social status, afforded only by the very few. Of note were those designed by English couturiere known as Lucile (Lady Duff-Gordon), who fashioned camisoles, peignoirs, and petticoats using lace, chiffon, and crepe de chine—materials that mirrored the feel of idealized flesh, deliberately appealing to the sense of touch, and evoking a new sensuality for the twentieth-century woman. Although artificial fibers such as rayon were marketed in the 1920s as a luxury fabric through the use of the name "artificial silk," their development led to a democratization of lingerie. The more body-conscious fashions of that decade also led to a new item of lingerie, the teddy, named after its inventor Theodore Baer, who combined a chemise with a short slip or attached panties. The camisole, originally derived from a decorative waist-length garment with an embroidered and pleated front and shoulder straps that were worn over the corset for warmth and modesty, became a staple garment of lingerie, eventually becoming an item of outerwear by the 1970s. Similarly the slip, a standard piece of lingerie from the 1950s and produced by the company La Perla, founded by Ada Masotti, in 1954, was used by a number of fashion designers as outerwear in the 1990s, most notably John Galliano, Dolce & Gabbana.

Sales of lingerie declined in the 1960s as the new silhouette defined by the miniskirt needed a more practical combination of matching polyester bra and panties with tights to replace stockings and suspenders. In the 1970s, however, a lingerie revival was lead by the English designer Janet Reger, whose company became one of the most renowned lingerie names of the late twentieth century. Reger was even the object of an essay by the English journalist and cultural commentator Angela Carter, who described her ranges of lingerie as "part of the 'fantasy courtesan' syndrome of the sexy exec, a syndrome reflected admirably in the pages of *Cosmopolitan* magazine. Working women regain the femininity they have lost behind the office desk by parading about like *grande horizontale* from early Colette in the privacy of their flats, even if there is nobody there to see" (Carter, p. 97). Carter was prescient in her comments, as with the rise of women entering the executive arena in the 1980s came an exponential rise in the sales of lingerie and the power suit with a lacy camisole peeping through the jacket became the staple of many a working wardrobe. In the 1990s, a lingerie revival, attracting both male and female consumers, was led by Californian companies Victoria's Secret and Frederick's of Hollywood. Victoria's Secret was estimated in 2000 to be selling six hundred items of lingerie per minute while the simple Egyptian cotton camisole made by the Swiss firm Hanro and worn by Nicole Kidman in Stanley Kubrick's film *Eyes Wide Shut* (1999) was a major lingerie bestseller. The British company Agent Provocateur, founded by Joseph Corres and Serena Rees in 1994, has successfully integrated the glamour of 1950s underwear with the catwalk, recreating seminal garments like the baby-doll nightie and matching puff panties worn by Carroll Baker in the 1956 film *Baby Doll*. Sourcing vintage undergarments and amalgamating them with new fabrics, such as Lycra, and high-fashion design concepts, they have redefined lingerie as a luxury item with a strong appeal for a young fashion-oriented consumer. Dorothy Parker's well-known remark, "Brevity is the soul of lingerie," invokes the appeal of these most personal of undergarments.

See also Embroidery; Lace; Lucile; Pajamas.

Bibliography

Carter, Angela. "The Bridled Sweeties." In *Nothing Sacred: Selected Writings*. London: Virago, 1982.

Saint Laurent, Cecil. *The Great Book of Lingerie*. London: Academy Editions, 1986.

Steele, Valerie. *Fashion and Eroticism: Ideals of Feminine Beauty from the Victorian Era to the Jazz Age*. New York: Oxford University Press, 1985.

Caroline Cox

LITTLE BLACK DRESS

At once demure and daring, the little black dress conjures up a host of images and associations. Consistently a symbol of elegance and chic, it is an international fashion icon capable of being interpreted in myriad different styles. Since the late 1920s, some of the world's most elegant women, including Audrey Hepburn, Marlene Dietrich, Maria Callas, and Edith Piaf, have been photographed wearing a version of the little black dress. Coco Chanel claimed to have "invented" the little black dress, and that claim has found its way into fashion mythology. But although Chanel greatly influenced the status of the little black dress as a classic fashion item, beginning with her 1926 introduction of a simple black jersey day dress, many other designers were experimenting with the same look at the same time, and black as a fashion color has a long history.

Historically, black has been associated with mourning and asceticism. By the fourteenth century, however, black was being used to create a dramatic effect in one's appearance. In the fifteenth century, Philip the Good, duke of Burgundy, dressed exclusively in black. He was second to none in the luxury of his dress, but in black this magnificence was conveyed with much greater discretion. Black, expensive to produce with natural dyes and thought to convey an air of refinement, became the color of choice for the fifteenth-century Spanish aristocracy, and connoted wealth and social status among the Dutch commercial middle class.

By the eighteenth century black clothing was considered respectable, even dowdy, as it was associated with mourning and the dress of the clergy. Black was revived as the color of elegance, especially for men, by the dandies of the early nineteenth century. The introduction of aniline dyes later in the nineteenth century created a new vogue for bright colors for fashionable women's clothing; black clothing for women signified mourning, or was a badge of middle-class respectability. When fashionable women did wear black it was to make a statement. One of the most memorable, if controversial, examples of this was John Singer Sargent's 1884 portrait of "Madame X," Virginie Gautreau, dressed in a form-fitting black evening gown. Conventional portraiture employed colorful frilly, even demure dress that all but obscured the subject. That Mme. Gautreau, a socialite of the day whose improprieties were hardly secret, appeared in a seductively form-fitting black gown

with deep décolletage was quite a departure, underscoring the subject's decision to play by a different set of rules.

In the early 1900s, black "widow's weeds" were still being sold in department stores, but black was beginning to make appearances on other occasions as well. Paul Poiret made vivid colors fashionable between 1908 and 1914. Chanel claimed to be "nauseated" by Poiret's colors and favored instead black, beige, and navy blue. Her 1926 showing of the little black dress was a milestone in the creation of this fashion icon. However, she was hardly alone. The House of Premet had already had a great success with a little black dress. Indeed, the terrible death toll in World War I had resulted in a plethora of fashionable black dresses.

The little black dress was the ideal mix of elements. It was easy, versatile, and practical; it was also chic, elegant, and sophisticated. Capable of embodying many meanings, the little black dress's chameleon-like quality enabled it to evolve with the trends, but never to be beholden to them.

Of the little black dress, *Vogue* declared in 1944, "Ten out of ten women have one" (MacDonell Smith, 2003, p. 14). Fashion magazines everywhere featured the new phenomenon. By 1948 Christian Dior's ground-breaking New Look was calling for hem- and necklines to drop and skirts to be fuller. The little black dress obliged. As Dior said in 1954, "You can wear black at any time. You can wear black at any age. You may wear it on almost any occasion. A little black frock is essential to a woman's wardrobe" (MacDonell Smith, 2003, p. 14).

The little black dress's versatility ensured its immortality. Parisian Left Bank intellectuals wore it for its associations with creativity and rebellion. Paired with black tights and black eyeliner, it was the uniform of the beatnik generation. Audrey Hepburn wore black in *Funny Face*, and a little black dress by Givenchy in *Breakfast at Tiffany's*.

The 1960s marked a low point in the life of the little black dress. Not only did one of its masters, Cristóbal Balenciaga, retire in 1968, but it was an era focused on a youthful sense of color and fun rather than sophistication and elegance. But a decade later, a new generation of designers began to make it once again the uniform of the modern woman. From Claude Montana's versions in leather to Azzedine Alaia's in stretch fabric, the little black dress took on a more aggressive edge during the late 1970s and 1980s. Showcased at the groundbreaking New York store Charivari, the status of the little black dress was underscored by Helmut Newton, the German-born, Australian photographer, known for his blatantly provocative erotic, sometimes violent images of women. The evolution continued and by the early 1980s a new breed of Japanese designers led by Rei Kawakubo and Yohji Yamamoto reinterpreted the little black dress according to new somber, intellectual criteria.

At the turn of the twenty-first century, the little black dress remains a mainstay of the clothing industry and a must in the wardrobe of every woman. At once impervious to and accommodating of the vicissitudes of fashion, the little black dress has become a lens through which to view the evolution of fashion and dress, since at least the late 1920's.

See also Balenciaga, Cristóbal; Chanel, Gabrielle (Coco).

Bibliography

Hollander, Anne. *Seeing Through Clothes* New York: Viking Press, 1978.

Ludot, Didier. *The Little Black Dress: Vintage Treasure*. New York: Assouline Publishing, 2001.

MacDonell Smith, Nancy. *The Classic Ten: The True Story of the Little Black Dress and Nine Other Fashion Favorites.* New York: Penguin Books, 2003.

Mendes, Valerie. *Black in Fashion*. London: Victoria and Albert Museum Publications, 1999.

Liz Gessner

LOGOS

The logo (logotype) is the emblem or device used to identify a particular company or organization. The design of a logo may be based around the name or initials of a company using a distinctive letter form, such as Coca-Cola (first used in 1887). It may also be a visual symbol of abstract or figurative design, such as the Nike swoosh (designed 1971). In order to function effectively a logo must be easily recognized in a variety of forms—on products, packaging, and advertising.

The logo is the modern equivalent of the maker's stamp; the hallmark or trademark that indicates the authenticity of a product. Logos, like monograms, heraldic devices, flags, and crests, are forms of graphical devices that have been used to indicate the origin, ownership, and status of property and people.

Law protects modern logos, so that the form, color, shape, and graphical detail of any mark cannot be copied or closely imitated without legal redress. This legislation was put into place in the mid-nineteenth century in Europe and America, and is now effective across national borders.

The logo is central to any company's concept of its brand. As the graphic designer Milton Glaser once said, "The logo is the point of entry to the brand" and is used to encapsulate all that a brand may stand for. A logo with a high recognition factor can be a major financial asset to any business, and therefore it sits at the heart of any corporate identity policy. A manufacturer's product range may change from season to season, but successful logos are rarely tampered with and, when design changes are made, they are usually subtle rather than radical. Logos also need to be adaptable to a variety of uses. The interlocking CC logo of Chanel, like many logos used by the garment industry, work well as both a repeat pattern on fabric and as an embossed button on a coat or jacket. The "Medusa head" logo used by Versace was adapted from a classical architectural motif. It can be used in print or relief, and appears on stationery, packaging, buttons, cosmetics containers, and tableware.

The use of the logo as a decorative element was traditionally the preserve of the luxury goods sector (rather than the clothing industry). Leather goods (luggage and saddlery) companies have exploited the familiarity of their logos and signature patterns as they compete in the high-fashion market. The French luggage company Louis Vuitton (founded 1854) first used its monogram in a repeat-patterned canvas in 1896, and the monogram fabric has been a staple of its collections ever since. The monogram pattern has been reinterpreted by a succession of designers from the mid-1990s, including Marc Jacobs and Stephen Sprouse. Gucci's monogrammed fabric, using the GG logo adopted in the 1960s, appeared for many years on handbags and as linings before being used for clothing.

One key factor in the development of fashion branding has been the shift of the "signature" or logo from the inside to the outside of the garment. Conventionally, the designer or manufacturer's label would be sewn inside a garment, originally to guard against the illegal copying of fashion house models. In the field of sportswear, logos began to be more prominent in the 1940s, when the brand named after the tennis star Fred Perry borrowed the idea of the team or club crest, displayed on the breast of shirts and sweaters. In the 1970s, when sportswear was worn increasingly off pitch, court, or course as leisurewear, brands such as Lacoste and Fred Perry used their logos to brand generic garments like the polo shirt. This first wave of fashion sports brands was eclipsed by the phenomenal rise of global sports corporations such as Nike in the 1980s and 1990s.

The "designer decade" of the 1980s introduced many more designer logos to the mass market, where they became adopted as part of street culture. Logos associated with status and expense, such as BMW and Mercedes car mascots in the shape of corporate logos, were worn as jewelry by American rap artists. Heavily branded sportswear by Nike and Tommy Hilfiger (where the logos became increasingly prominent) was worn with a brash, competitive attitude and an emphasis on "box-fresh" products. Between 1995 and 2000, several high-fashion brands including Gucci, Fendi, Dior, and Louis Vuitton produced collections almost entirely focused on the repeat use of the logo (dubbed "logomania" by the style press).

Reaction to this visibly over-branded culture has been strong. One economic and legal side effect has been the flourishing of a counterfeit trade in clothes and accessories where fake logos are applied to unlicensed and inferior goods. The other effect is cultural and political. Global brands have come under attack by the so-called "No Logo" generation (named after Naomi Klein's 1999 book of that title), who reject overtly branded goods as symbols of late capitalist economic exploitation and social inequality.

See also Brands and Labels.

Bibliography

Clifton, Rita, and John Simmons, eds. *Brands and Branding.* Princeton, N.J.: Bloomberg Press, 2004.

Jane Pavitt

LONDON FASHION*

In the twenty-first century London ranks highly amongst the world's cities as a distinctive fashion center. Its characteristic products and sense of style compete with and complement the fashion values of other global fashion capitals including Paris, New York, Milan, and Tokyo. In the popular imagination, which is fed by the stereotyping tendencies of fashion journalism, London has become most associated with the traditional handcrafts of tailoring, shirtmaking, hatmaking, and shoemaking that underpin the image of the English gentleman, a vibrant subcultural club and street scene, and the nurturing of eccentric and innovative design talent in its famous art schools. These are largely phenomena that blossomed during the twentieth century, but London's fashion history is as old as the city itself and closely related to its economic, social, and cultural development over time.

With its thriving docks and strong mercantile economy, London operated as a natural hub for trade and cultural exchange in the late medieval period, building on a heritage that stretched back to its status as an important port on the western fringes of the Roman Empire. By the fifteenth century, it was already one of the largest cities in the world, though it could not compete with smaller European centers such as Paris, Florence, and Rome as a focus for the production and display of fashionable commodities. London operated more as a transit point in an international fashion system, exporting primary or unfinished products like wool and metal and importing luxuries such as fur and embroideries. But in a national context, the city began to exert a formidable political and cultural pressure over the rest of the country as parliament, law courts, and the crown established permanent bases there. This process drew the rich and influential into London and helped to ensure that fashionable trends originated in its streets, markets, and great houses. The palaces of Henry VIII, Elizabeth I, and Charles I at Hampton Court, Greenwich, and Whitehall thus operated as forcing houses for a very English sense of sartorial style, which nevertheless still relied largely on the pattern books, fabrics, and craftsmanship of Spain, France, and Italy for its luxurious impact.

By the early eighteenth century, the political stability afforded by the accession of the Hanoverian line of monarchs and a prosperous professional class, together with the increased income that attended London's rise as the capital of a widening network of colonies, meant that the city entered a new phase of development during which its growing confidence and urbane sophistication produced the distinctive sartorial identity that would influence world trends for the next three centuries. After the Great Fire of 1666, London's developers and architects had shifted their attention westward and the arising geography of graceful squares and parks encouraged the aristocracy to base their domestic and business affairs in the West End during those periods of the year (later known as the Season) when Parliament was sitting or the royal family was in residence. The flurry of social activity that followed, with its balls, theater visits, and court presentations, offered great incentives to entrepreneurs in the clothing trades, and it was on this basis, from the 1740s on, that the craftsmen of Savile Row, Jermyn Street, and St. James's established themselves as producers of a home-grown masculine style of dressing, replete with the genteel codes and sporting influences that have bracketed the idea of London with the identity of the dandy. The methods of tailoring developed in Savile Row in the eighteenth century also went on to inform the design of women's wear in the capital, producing the severe "tailor-mades" of the late nineteenth century and the artfully restrained creations of Norman Hartnell, Hardy Amies, and Victor Stiebel in the mid-twentieth century.

Through the nineteenth century the range and organization of the clothing industries in London expanded considerably, augmented by successive waves of immigration. As the West End became increasingly associated with the consumption of high quality, locally produced bespoke goods, so the East End or working-class districts of Aldgate and Bethnal Green played host to other, less prestigious forms of manufacturing. In the eighteenth and early nineteenth centuries, the French Huguenot community had woven high-quality figured silks for gowns, waistcoats, and ribbons in the upper floors of their tall Spitalfields houses, but by the 1870s, when the fashion for brocades had passed, the sewing of shirts and ready-made suits provided one of the few opportunities for employment in an area bedeviled by poverty and overcrowding. Even then, the infamous practice of sweating ensured that clothing production was a profession of poor pay and low esteem, associated with the exploited labor of women and Jews.

Some aspects of Victorian London's fashion scene maintained a positive gloss. In line with the city's entrepreneurial spirit, the capital witnessed several pioneering inventions such as William Perkin's discovery of synthetic (aniline) dyes in the late 1850s or Thomas Burberry's experiments with waterproofing later in the century. Perhaps the most lasting innovations to come out of London in the period were in the realm of fashion retailing. By the 1830s the West End had been transformed by the architectural renewal set in place by the Prince Regent and John Nash. The new arcades leading off of Piccadilly and the majestic sweep of Regent Street offered a fresh conception of shopping as a modish leisure activity for the middle and upper classes, where emphasis was placed on spectacular display, comfort, and escapism. Unsurprisingly the first great couturier Charles Worth learned his trade in a Regent Street emporium, and two decades later in the 1870s and 1880s Arthur Liberty perfected the selling of a lifestyle nearby, in a store that provided all the exotic accoutrements for the aesthetic movement. Napoleon's dismissive take on the English as a nation of shopkeepers would find further resonance in the development of the great London department stores such as Harrods, Selfridges, and Harvey Nichols from the Edwardian period on, and the emergence of the "happening" fashion boutique in Chelsea and West Soho in the 1950s and 1960s.

These London traits of tradition, innovation, and a certain sense of theatricality continued to inform the development of fashionable style in the city in the twentieth century. In the late 1940s and 1950s young men from chic Mayfair and working-class South and East London, with seemingly little else in common than a passionate interest in style as a means of subverting the stultifying status quo, resurrected Edwardian notions of elegance in a shocking manner of dressing that soon became associated with the "Teddy Boy" craze. Their velvet-trimmed draped jackets, drainpipe trousers, and extravagantly combed hairstyles presaged a succession of teenage poses whose influence was felt worldwide. The Mods of 1960s Carnaby Street and the Punks of 1970s King's Road all earned London a certain notoriety as the breeding ground for revolutionary acts of sartorial rebellion.

Various London designers have found their inspiration in this street-level creativity. In the 1960s Mary Quant, Barbara Hulanicki (of Biba), and Ossie Clarke were closely associated with the phenomenon of "Swinging London," famously promoted to America by *Time* magazine in 1966; while in the 1970s Zandra Rhodes and Vivienne Westwood offered a more astringent and eccentric take on contemporary mores. By the 1980s and 1990s a generation brought up in the hedonistic, post-punk environment of neo-romanticism and the commercial club scene, seemed more adept at selling their London-honed individuality abroad. Central Saint Martins–trained John Galliano, Stella McCartney, and Alexander McQueen, and the Royal College protégé Julien McDonald have thus famously risen to supplant local talent at the creative helms of the great

Parisian fashion houses. But behind the famous names, the studios and warehouses of London continue to support an active and influential local economy of young independent designers, stylists, photographers, publishers, and journalists (London has nurtured a wide-range of edgy fashion magazines including *The Face*, *i-D*, *Sleaze Nation*, and *Dazed and Confused*). Though there has been little concrete state support for the growth of a British fashion industry, the sheer size, diversity, and chaotic energy of the British capital still seems to foster a productive and adventurous sartorial spirit in the early twenty-first century. In recent years Gareth Pugh has been acclaimed as London's latest rising star.

See also Amies, Hardy; Biba; Clark, Ossie; Europe and America: History of Dress (400–1900 C.E.); Galliano, John; Hartnell, Norman; McQueen, Alexander; Paris Fashion; Rhodes, Zandra; Royal and Aristocratic Dress; Westwood, Vivienne.

Bibliography

Breward, Christopher. *Fashioning London: Clothing and the Modern Metropolis*. Oxford: Berg, 2004.

Breward, Christopher, Edwina Ehrman, and Caroline Evans. *The London Look*. New Haven, Conn., and London: Yale University Press, 2004.

Tucker, Andrew. *The London Fashion Book*. London: Thames and Hudson, Inc., 1998.

Christopher Breward

LUCILE

Although many of Lady Duff-Gordon's claims to originality and innovation are now discredited, her high-end dressmaking firm Lucile remains a potent example of early British couture. Although at the forefront of designing and merchanting clothes for society women at the turn of the twentieth century, these skills were eclipsed by her talent for literary biography demonstrated by the entertaining autobiography *Discretions and Indiscretions* (1932) that was intended to cement her reputation with a light, literary style of prose.

Divorced from an alcoholic husband and with little formal education, Lady Duff-Gordon persuaded her mother in 1889 to save her reputation by financially backing her as a dressmaker, capitalizing on her only practical skill of sewing. Her first design was based on a tea gown, inspired by a dress worn by an actress on stage. It became her calling card for society ladies and was worn by the Hon. Mrs Arthur Brand on the occasion of her staying with a society hostess.

The tea gown originated as a garment worn by society women when in the country, after they had derobed from their shooting tweeds and before donning evening dress for dinner. This practice is considered to have followed on from them being solely worn for the purpose of taking tea. Set between function and formality the loose and uncorseted style of the garment implied, if not a state of undress, then at least a private and introspective state on the part of the wearer. Duff-Gordon seized on the risqué potential of the tea gown as a way of challenging late Victorian London's views on modesty and morality in women's dress, while championing her own cause for notoriety. This led her to be accused of peddling the cult of immoral dressing (Etherington-Smith 1986, p. 73).

The association of the tea gown with refreshment and sociability between women became actively embedded in the business, most notably at Maison Lucile, her Hanover Square shop at no. 17 opened in 1897 (no. 23 opened in 1901).

Duff-Gordon's belief that "nobody had thought of developing the social side of choosing clothes, of serving tea and imitating the setting of a drawing-room" informed her idea of a commercial space for the selling of clothing appearing as a space of leisure and, to some degree, domesticity. However, it was her skill in innovative sales techniques that helped to establish a glamorous cult of personality for both the designer and her committed clients.

Lucile's business was unusual in that it also was well known for designing theatrical dress for the stage. Many of the features of dress design that Lucile became renowned for, such as the delicate layering of fabrics, fusions of color, and use of filigree and trim, were very much learned from the traditions of theatrical dress design that were engineered to catch the floodlights and project the performer.

Yet it was in her efforts to create a theatrical setting in her own salon for the presentation of her latest designs for the fashionable woman that Duff-Gordon excelled. From a small stage hung with olive-colored chiffon curtains, she presented collections on models that she personally trained in deportment, each one bearing a dress with a literary title rather than a number. Duff-Gordon termed them "Gowns of Emotion," also referred to at the time as personality dresses. This oddity began in her wish to promote the idea that the clothes she made in her early career were individual to each client. As a working practice, this went against the model of practice for a couturier established by Worth, who always decided the blueprint of what all fashionable woman should wear. Duff-Gordon's approach suggested that the inspiration of what could be termed fashionable was drawn from the innate quality of each of her clients individually; a dress that could suit their personality rather than their needs.

Lucile's Gowns of Emotions were given titles such as The Captain's Whiskers, The Sighing Sound of Lips Unsatisfied, and Twilight and Memories. In associating the appearance of a dress with an inner state of mind, the disassociation of dress from social hierarchy and towards signifying a psychological state began.

What is also notable about Lucile's titles is their similarity to the themes of love found in the salacious novels written by Duff-Gordon's sister, Elinor Glyn, who also wore her sister's designs. Many of Glyn's fashionable works featured well-dressed women with descriptions that faithfully aped the latest designs of Maison Lucile. Duff-Gordon's last epic was not to be literary invention. In 1912 she survived the inaugural trip of the *Titanic*. For her husband, who also survived after joining her in a rescue boat intended for women and children only, it led to the end of his reputation. For Duff-Gordon it was the final chapter in a sensationalized career. To distance herself from the tragedy of the *Titanic*, Lady Duff-Gordon moved her career to New York where her models came to the attention of Florenz Ziegfeld in 1916. Ziegfeld persuaded Duff-Gordon to let her models wear her creations in his current Follies. She designed the costumes until 1920.

See also Haute Couture; Tea Gown; Theatrical Costume.

Bibliography

Beaton, Cecil. *The Glass of Fashion*. London: Weidenfeld and Nicolson, 1954.

Duff-Gordon, Lady. *Discretions and Indiscretions*. London: Jarrolds, 1932.

Etherington-Smith, Meredith, and Jeremy Pilcher. *The It Girls: Lucy, Lady Duff Gordon, the Couturière 'Lucile' and Elinor Glyn, Romantic Novelist*. London: Hamilton, 1986.

Glyn, Elinor. *Three Weeks*. London: Duckworth and Company, 1907.

Alistair O'Neill

M

MACARONI DRESS

"Macaroni" was a topical term connoting ultra-fashionable dressing in England circa 1760–1780. First use of the term appears within David Garrick's play *The Male-Coquette* (1757) that includes the foppish character the Marchese di Macaroni. Although used occasionally to refer to women noted for their conspicuous gambling—described, like fashion, as a form of ephemeral expenditure—the term generally referred to the styling of men. The famous observer of manners Horace Walpole makes numerous reference to these figures. In the first relevant letter, dated February 1764, Walpole discussed gambling losses amongst the sons of foreign aristocrats at the "Maccaroni [*sic*] club, which is composed of all the traveled young men who wear long curls and spying-glasses" (Lewis 1937, p. 306). The "Macaroni Club," was probably the Whig venue Almack's in St. James's, the court end of London.

Macaroni dress was not restricted to members of the aristocracy and gentry, but included men of the artisan and servant classes who wore examples or cheaper versions of this visually lavish clothing with a distinctive cut. To wear macaroni dress was to wear the contemporary continental court fashion of the male suit, or *habit à la française*, which consisted of a tight-sleeved coat with short skirts, waistcoat, and knee breeches. At a time when English dress generally consisted of more sober cuts and the use of monochrome broadcloth, macaronis emphasized pastel color, pattern, and textile ornamentation which included brocaded and embroidered silks and velvets, some encrusted with chenille threads and metallic sequins. Fashionable men in the late 1760s and 1770s replaced the small scratch-wig of the older generation with elaborate hairstyles that matched the towering heights of the contemporary female coiffure. For men, a tall toupée rising in front and a club of hair behind required extensive dressing with pomade and white powder. This wig was garnished with a large black satin wig-bag trimmed with bows. The use of a pigtail and wig-bag was viewed as a Francophile affectation; so much so that the visual shorthand for Frenchmen in caricature imagery was this device.

Macaroni men deployed a number of accessories that characterized court society. These included the hanger sword, which was traditionally the preserve of the nobility, and which in England was fading from general usage. Other Macaroni features include red-heeled and slipper-like leather shoes with decorative buckles of diamond, paste, or polished steel; a tiny *nivernais* or *nivernois* hat named after the French ambassador resident in London; large floral corsages or nosegays; chatelaines or hanging watches, and seals suspended around the waist; decorative neoclassical metal snuffboxes; and eyeglasses feature in descriptions of macaronies. These objects contributed to an emphasizing of courtly artifice in posture, gesture, and speech further underlined by the use of cosmetics such as face-whiteners and rouge. According to contemporary reports, there was even a highly mannered macaroni accent and idiom, captured in popular ditties of the period. Colors particularly associated with the macaroni include those used in the contemporaneous interior design of Robert Adam: pea green, pink, and deep orange. Striped or spotted fabrics on stockings, waistcoats, and breeches appear to have been popular fashions, sometimes worn in contrasting arrangements.

Macaroni Motives

Macaroni identity was not a peripheral incident in eighteenth-century culture but a lively topic of debate in the periodical press. Motives for retaining elaborate dress requisite at court but not necessary in the streets of commercial London was various, inflected by the class interests and personal motivations of the wearers. Macaroni status was attributed to such famous figures as the Whig politician Charles James Fox (1749–1806), "the Original Macaroni;" the botanist and South Sea explorer Sir Joseph Banks (1743–1820), the "Fly

Catching Macaroni;" the renowned miniature painter Richard Cosway (1742–1821); the famed landscape garden–designer Humphrey Repton (1752–1818); the St. Martin's Lane luxury upholsterer John Cobb; Julius "Soubise," the freed slave of the duchess of Queensbury, the "Mungo Macaroni;" and the Reverend William Dodd (1729–1777), the extravagantly-dressed Chaplain to George III. Aristocratic Whig adherents emphasized a version of ultra-fashionable court-dress in order to assert their preeminent wealth and privilege in the face of Tories, the English court, and its more modest Hanoverian monarchy. French and Italian goods and manners had added appeal in that travel to the Continent had not been possible and the importation of French textiles had been banned during the Seven Years War (1756–1763). Alleged macaroni status was used to attack the professional credentials of Joseph Banks within the scientific community; Cosway was similarly ridiculed as an absurd-looking parvenu. Dodd, the "Macaroni Parson," in becoming the subject of a forgery trial resulting in his execution, further highlighted the potency of the macaroni label.

Historiography

Macaroni dress was lampooned as excessive and bizarre in numerous caricature prints, plays, and satirical texts. The macaronies form the largest subset within the English graphical social satires produced in abundance from the early 1770s. The catalogers of the British Museum caricature collection, Frederic George Stephens in 1883 and Dorothy George in 1935, published a wealth of primary material relating to macaronis that has formed the basis of all further studies. Aileen Ribeiro wrote the first article devoted to them in 1978, and has included them in subsequent studies of eighteenth-century costume, where they are discussed as an amusing episode in the sartorial folly of young men. In 1985 they formed the subject of an article by Valerie Steele that broadened awareness of their social and political influence and helped lift them from the taint of triviality. Diana Donald's study of caricature indicates that a reading of the macaroni type provides important insights into eighteenth-century English society. She highlights their role in defining the English character as sane and measured in contrast to the reign of folly experienced across the Channel. Represented in a wide range of verbal and visual sources, from the press to the theater, the macaronis provided the perfect frame for critique regarding consumption and emulation, as they suggested wild expenditure, the spread of fashionability, and even the cult of gambling in late-eighteenth-century English society.

The commonly held explanation for the title "macaroni," that it was derived from a fondness for that Italian dish, may be supplemented in that "macaronic" refers also to a type of mixed language poetry known for its wit, a hallmark of the macaroni stereotype. "Macaroni" thus also suggested the world of the medieval carnival, burlesque, carousing, and excessive food. The macaroni was regularly connected with a slavish and shallow love of things continental and Catholic. The amused suspicion of the English toward these supposedly uncritical followers of fashion is linked to a hostility toward fashionable dress that had colored British life since at least the seventeenth century. This censure had generally been more strongly directed at women, and the macaroni episode shifted much of this attention toward a redefinition of effeminate men. In occasional prints, plays, and satires the macaroni was cast as an indeterminate figure who did not fit normative stereotypes of gender and sexuality. Sometimes the macaroni stereotype took on sodomitical suggestion. Fictional descriptions of "Lord Dimple," "Sir William Whiffle," and "Marjorie Pattypan" deployed the notion of a neutral or unnatural gender in which

---

HISTORICAL DEFINITION

"Maccaroni [sic], An Italian paste made of flour and eggs; also, a fop; which name arose from a club, called the Maccaroni [sic] Club, instituted by some of the most dressy travelled gentlemen about town, who led the fashions. . ."

Pierce Egan. *Grose's Classical Dictionary of the Vulgar Tongue.* Revised and corrected, with the addition of numerous slang phrases, collected from tried authorities. London, for the Editor, 1823 [revised ed. of work published 1785], n.p.

"Such a figure, essenced and perfumed, with a bunch of lace sticking out under its chin, puzzles the common passenger to determine the thing's sex; and many a time an honest labouring porter has said, by your leave, madam, without intending to give offence."

"Character of a Macaroni." *The Town and Country Magazine* vol. IV, May 1772, p. 243

"inappropriate" feminine attributes were grafted onto male appearance, dress, and behavior. The attributes of the Regency dandy (circa 1800)—deviant masculine consumption, nonreproductive irresponsibility, a rejection of middle-class gendering, a creation of the male body and home into a work of art—are firmly evinced in the macaroni type. As a foppish type, the macaroni also shares characteristics with the precursor, the seventeenth-century Restoration fop. The macaroni fashion preferences, however, were quite different and the two should not be conflated. The macaroni remains commemorated within the song *Yankee Doodle* (1767)—"Yankee Doodle Came to Town/Riding on a Pony./Stuck a feather in his cap/And called it Macaroni"—in which the appearance and masculine identity of the American troops is ridiculed within the theater of war.

See also Dandyism; Europe and America: History of Dress (400–1900 C.E.); Fashion, Historical Studies of.

Bibliography

Donald, Diana. *The Age of Caricature: Satirical Prints in the Reign of George III.* New Haven, Conn., and London: Yale University Press, 1996.

George, Mary Dorothy. *Catalogue of Political and Personal Satires Preserved in the Department of Prints and Drawings in the British Museum.* Vol. 5, 1771–1783, London: Trustees of the British Museum, 1935.

Lewis, Wilmarth S. *The Yale Edition of Horace Walpole's Correspondence.* Vol. 38. New Haven, Conn.: Yale University Press, 1937.

McNeil, Peter. "'That Doubtful Gender': Macaroni Dress and Male Sexualities." *Fashion Theory. The Journal of Dress, Body & Culture* 3, no. 4 (1999): 411–447.

Ribeiro, Aileen. "The Macaronis." *History Today* 28, no. 7 (1978): 463–468.

——. *Dress in Eighteenth-Century Europe, 1715–1789,* London: B. T. Batsford, Ltd., 1984.

Steele, Valerie. "The Social and Political Significance of Macaroni Fashion." *Costume,* no. 19 (1985): 94–109.

Stephens, Frederic George, and Edward Hawkins. *Catalogue of Prints and Drawings in the British Museum. Division I. Political and Personal Satires.* Vol. 14, A.D. 1761–A.D. 1770, London: Trustees of the British Museum, 1883.

Peter McNeil

MAINBOCHER

Main (after his mother's Scottish maiden name and pronounced like the New England state) Rousseau Bocher (his French Huguenot surname was pronounced Bocker) was born in 1891 on Chicago's West Side. Artistically inclined from childhood, he attended the Chicago Academy of Fine Arts and had moved to New York City by 1909 to study at the Art Student's League. Broadening his pursuits to include classical voice training as well, he departed for Paris and Munich, where he celebrated his twenty-first birthday. While studying music, he began sketching dresses for fashion designers to help support his mother and sister, who had joined him abroad. They returned to America at the onset of World War I in 1914, but not before three of Main Bocher's drawings were included in an exhibition at the Paris *Salon des artistes decorateurs.* In New York he financed his studies with the career-building vocal coach Frank LaForge through the sale of his sketches to another Chicago transplant, ready-to-wear manufacturer Edward L. Mayer. This marked the true beginning of his fashion career.

Editing Career

Back abroad in 1917 with a volunteer hospital unit, Bocher enlisted in the United States Army in the Intelligence Corps. Demobilized in France in 1918, he remained there and returned to singing. A vocal failure during a pivotal audition finally forced him to abandon his operatic aspirations and to focus all of his creative attentions on fashion. He applied to the Paris office of *Harper's Bazaar* as a sketcher, then joined French *Vogue* in 1923 as the Paris fashion editor, became editor-in-chief in 1927, and resigned over a salary dispute in late 1929. With the financial backing of a discreet group of compatriots that included Mrs. Gilbert Miller, daughter of the American banker and art collector Jules Bache, he now turned his seasoned eye and editing skills toward the realization of his own fashion vision.

Paris Salon

At a time when American designers had yet to establish credibility on their native soil, Mainbocher, his name now contracted in the manner of Paris-based couturiers Louiseboulanger and Augustabernard, opened his salon at 12, avenue George V. The impeccable designs and pristine dressmaking of this American-in-Paris proved irresistible, especially to the coterie of international hostess and taste arbiter Elsie de Wolfe. Through her influence Mainbocher was introduced to the most celebrated client of his young career, Mrs. Wallis Warfield Spencer Simpson. The international publicity surrounding the austerely classic dress he devised for her Château de Cande wedding to the Duke of Windsor in June 1937 catapulted him to celebrity status, spawning a frenzy for "Wally" dress copies and the color "Wallis blue." His couture models were imported into the United States by elite establishments, including Hattie Carnegie, I. Magnin California, Saks Fifth Avenue's Salon Moderne, and Jay Thorpe. By decade's end Mainbocher had become a pillar of the world of couture and in the process secured the adoration of a clientele who followed him back across the Atlantic upon his departure from occupied Paris in 1939.

World War II

The fashion press celebrated the opening of Mainbocher's reincarnated salon at 6 East Fifty-seventh Street and his first American-designed collection late in 1940. The November 1941 *Harper's Bazaar* applauded his rigorous attention to maintaining all the traditions of his Paris house. Innovating ingeniously around daunting governmental restrictions (his invoices stating that his designs met with L-85 standards), his work remained fresh and appealing throughout the balance of

World War II. During this period he featured glamour belts, aprons, and overskirts to vary the look of concise short or long black evening dresses. He launched a sensation for plunge-backed evening gowns and "Venus pink" with his Grecian designs for the 1943 Broadway production of *One Touch of Venus* starring Mary Martin. His surprising English cashmere sweaters, lined either in fur or coordinating silk, or jeweled, elegantly addressed wartime fuel conservation.

Trademark Vision

The steadfast loyalty of his patrons and press withstood the challenge of the postwar return of French fashion and Christian Dior's triumphant "New Look" (a silhouette Mainbocher himself had presaged with his 1939 Victorian cinch-waist.) Mainbocher was as passionate about fabric as he was fastidious about craftsmanship and design. The opulent simplicity of his clothes weathered the ephemeral. His silhouettes nodded to trends yet remained true to Mainbocher. His archetypal vision of pedigreed, meticulous clothing was as readily transcribed into his polished 1950s designs as it was interpreted in architectural fabrics to relate his minimalist eloquence to the space-aged spirit of the 1960s.

Famous Clients

Mainbocher's society client list included Daisy Fellowes, Diana Vreeland, Millicent Rogers, the Duchess of Windsor, Barbara Paley, C. Z. Guest, and Gloria Vanderbilt. He designed on and offstage wardrobes for Mary Martin, Katharine Cornell, Ethel Merman, Rosalind Russell, and Ruth Gordon.

Mainbocher closed the doors of his salon at 609 Fifth Avenue in 1971. Returning to Europe, he alternated his final years between Paris and Munich, where he died in 1976.

Innovations

Although a self-described quiet innovator, Mainbocher succeeded in incrementally altering the complexion of contemporary fashion. As a fashion editor he initiated the "Vogue's Eye View" feature and introduced the terms *spectator-sports clothes* and *off-white*. As a couturier he promoted the nontraditional use of cotton gingham and lingerie crepe and glamorized cloth coats for evening use. His was the first strapless evening dress, which he executed in black satin in 1934. His wartime

---

DESIGN PHILOSOPHY

Throughout his forty-year career, Mainbocher's beliefs regarding the purpose and nature of clothing were inseparable from his work and were routinely incorporated into press coverage, providing a running philosophical commentary on his collections:

Between the beautiful classical that has proved its worth and some new stunt, I always choose the tried and true. I like persuasive dresses that have manners and I hate aggressive ill-bred concoctions (Bocher, 1938, p. 102).

A woman who has to remember to arrange any part of what she is wearing, simply cannot be smart. A well-dressed woman always appears to have forgotten what she is wearing. . . . To me, repose and natural ease are among the inimitable and essential attributes of the well-dressed woman (Bocher, 1950, p. 1).

---

civilian and military contributions included "day length" evening dresses and adorned sweaters as well as uniform designs for the WAVES, the women's auxiliary of the Marine Corps, and the American Red Cross. In 1948 he designed the intermediate Girl Scout uniform.

See also Evening Dress; Fashion Magazines; Uniforms, Military; Windsor, Duke and Duchess of.

Bibliography

Bocher, Main, "Mainbocher by Main Bocher," *Harper's Bazaar*, January 1938, 102–103.

Carter, Ernestine. *Magic Names of Fashion*. Englewood Cliffs, NJ: Prentice-Hall, 1980.

Lambert, Eleanor. *Quips and Quotes about Fashion: Two Hundred Years of Comments on the American Fashion Scene*. New York: Pilot Books, 1978.

Lee, Sarah Tomerlin. *American Fashion: The Life and Lines of Adrian, Mainbocher, McCardell, Norell, and Trigère*. New York: Quadrangle/New York Times Book Company, 1975.

Milbank, Caroline Rennolds. *Couture: The Great Designers*. New York: Stewart, Tabori and Chang, 1985.

——. *New York Fashion: The Evolution of American Style*. New York: Harry N. Abrams, 1989.

Morris, Bernadine, "Mainbocher, Fashion Designer for Notables Since the 1930's, Is Dead in Munich at 85," *New York Times*, 29 December 1976, sec. A, p. 14.

Phyllis Magidson

MAKEUP ARTISTS

In the media industries of fashion, film, television, and theater, an increasing number of runway shows, photographic shoots, and film and theater productions rely on the specialized skills of the makeup artist to communicate style and image.

When Maurice Levy designed the first retractable lipstick in 1915, no one could have guessed how popular cosmetics would become or how significant the role of the makeup artist would be in such emerging new fields as fashion photography and cinema production. Indeed, the concept of "makeup artist" hardly existed at the time. Until well into the twentieth century, theatrical performers were expected to do their own makeup, as they were expected to supply their own stage costumes. The professional makeup artist, like the theatrical or cinematic costume designer, is a modern phenomenon.

For much of the twentieth century, the role of the makeup artist remained a largely anonymous one, as audiences focused on the face of the model or actor rather than the makeup techniques that enhanced it. But makeup artists in fact have a great deal to do with how an actor or model looks in any given performance or production. The looks created evoke a theme, and it is important that the makeup be correct or else the artistic theme will be obscured or inaccurate, particularly when the makeup artist's task is to evoke a particular historical era or setting. While the image created by the makeup will always be paramount, by the early twenty-first century the makeup artist's expertise was receiving greater cultural recognition, and the role of the professional makeup artist had become a more conspicuous one.

Spaces where the made-up face is viewed include theaters, films, and photographs; the makeup artist's workplace is the dressing room, the film set, and the photographer's studio. The techniques of makeup used in these spaces are quite different from those of cosmetic makeup, and the professional makeup artist's skills are typically acquired over the course of a long period of training and practice. The heavy greasepaint and panstick used for theatrical makeup require special techniques for effective use. They are designed to work in harmony with strong lighting, which the makeup artist must anticipate while doing the makeup under weaker light. What might appear exaggerated and excessive in normal lighting will appear natural to a theatrical audience watching a performance on a lit stage. The applied shading and highlighting may be deliberately overemphasized by the makeup artist to increase the impact of the designed look for stage, screen, or catwalk.

Makeup artists build on their training, technical skills, and personal experience to develop an individual style. For example, Serge Lutens, who worked for many years with the Japanese cosmetics company Shiseido, prefers to be acknowledged as an artist who uses makeup. His style has been inspired by the cultures of China and Japan, and particularly by the highly artificial makeup of the Japanese *geisha*. He is famous for creating a geisha-like oval facial effect on the models he uses for photographic shoots. Lutens dramatically changes the faces of his models, and it is often impossible to recognize even the most famous models when he has made them up. Topolino is also recognized as an innovator in professional fashion makeup. Since the 1980s his work has broken the mold of established practice in fashion makeup, and he is known for his ability to create new looks every season for designers. Another makeup artist who has raised the prestige and visibility of the profession is Sarah Monzani, who designed the looks for the 1996 film *Evita*, starring Madonna. Some makeup artists have achieved star quality in their own right; some, such as Laura Mercier, have built upon their artistic success to become entrepreneurs in the cosmetics business. These successes have helped to establish a healthy reputation for expertise and creativity for the profession of makeup artist as a whole.

Makeup artists in the fashion industry have used conventions and techniques drawn from theater and film to expand their individual styles. The result has been a change in the face of fashion, on catwalks, in magazine editorial content, and in advertising. Prosthetic and special-effects products are used to adorn the face and the body. Feathers and crystals are used to morph the body from its human form and recreate it in statuesque or animal proportions. Makeup artists create ghostly or ghoulish looks that reference the horror film genre, and film noir is a fertile source used to create the femme fatale often seen in the pages of monthly fashion magazines.

The makeup artist today is not bound by traditional materials, styles, and conventions, but is able to call upon a wide range of techniques to create innovative effects. While new materials and techniques expand the range of possibilities available to the makeup specialist, the success of performed roles in theater, film, and fashion will continue to depend heavily on the skill and artistic vision of makeup artists.

See also Cosmetics, Non-Western; Cosmetics, Western; Theatrical Makeup.

Bibliography

Aucoin, Kevin. *Making Faces*. New York: Little, Brown, 1999.

Delamar, Penny. *The Complete Make-up Artist: Working in Film, Television, and Theater*. 2nd edition. Evanston, Ill.: Northwestern University Press, 2002.

Kehoe, Vincent. *The Technique of the Professional Make-up Artist*. New York: Focal Press, 1995.

Elizabeth McLafferty

MANNEQUINS

There are several historical strands that led to the development of the modern female fashion-display mannequin. From the fifteenth century, the miniature fashion doll (known as a "milliners' mannequin") was sent by dressmakers to wealthy customers, or exhibited for money by dressmakers to customers who wanted to copy the fashions. Other precursors of the fashion-display mannequin include artists' lay figures (life-sized wooden dolls used by artists); anatomical wax models, used for teaching medicine; and, finally, tailors' dummies. These examples utilized expertise in modeling representations of the human figure in wood, cane, papier-mâché, and/or wax.

The first wickerwork mannequins appeared in the mid-to late-eighteenth century and were made to order. In 1835 a Parisian ironmonger introduced a wirework model, and it was in France in the mid-nineteenth century that the first fashion mannequins were developed. Among the first mannequins to be patented were those designed by Professor Lavigne. He had begun manufacturing tailor's dummies, but won a medal in 1848 for his patented trunk mannequin, and opened a mannequin house in France in the 1850s. He went on, together with a student of his, Fred Stockman (who founded Stockman Brothers in 1869, later Siegel and Stockman's) to develop mannequins with legs and realistic heads and hands made from wax, improving on the earlier and cruder papiermâché ones. When clothed, these wax mannequins appeared strangely lifelike, with features detailed down to individual hairs and glass eyes. The market for fashion mannequins quickly opened up with the department stores built in Paris in the 1850s and soon after that in America and Britain.

The Fashioned Body

It was Paris that defined fashion from the mid-nineteenth until the mid-twentieth century, and the French mannequin manufacturers were able to exploit this reputation. Not only were French mannequins technologically advanced—fueled by the investment in shops and display in France—but notions of what was fashionable at any one point were centered on France, so French mannequins were considered the apex of fashion. Their new designs were also regularly exhibited at the international expositions, with French models usually winning prizes, thus enhancing their fame and desirability.

The arrival of electricity was important to the appearance of the mannequin, as the faces of wax models would suffer in the heat of the window. It was imperative that new materials be found. In the 1920s, the French firm of Pierre Iman's perfected a lighter and heat-resistant material, "Carnasine," a plaster composite which would take the mannequin into a new, faster phase of change and mass production. By 1927 the French firm of Siégel and Stockman had some 67 factories in New York City, Sydney, Stockholm, and Amsterdam and had acquired agents in other parts of the world. They also employed the architect-designer René Herbst as an artistic advisor, and under his aegis the mannequin became an icon of the moderne style.

Mannequin in Indian clothing store. As department stores opened in France, Britain, and the United States in the late nineteenth century before expanding worldwide, the fashion mannequin saw a rise in popularity. © DAVID H. WELLS/CORBIS. REPRODUCED BY PERMISSION.

The Artistic Body

At the end of the nineteenth century, the female mannequin had become a silent muse for artists and photographers who were appropriating mass culture as subject matter. The photographer Eugene Atget photographed shop windows, and later Erwin Blumenfeld photographed mannequins as though they were human. These images resonated with the Surrealists who would use mannequins as subjects: from Man Ray's photograph of a Siégel mannequin at the 1925 Paris Exposition des Arts Décoratifs, published in the *Révolution Surréaliste* magazine, to the sixteen mannequins dressed by different artists and writers (including Salvador Dali, André Masson, and Eileen Agar) that were used as the central motif in a room at the Parisian Exposition Internationale du Surréalisme in 1938. The mannequin even became the subject of a film, *L'Inhumaine*, designed by artist Fernand Léger in 1924.

On the other hand, mannequin designers drew on ideas in works by artists such as Pablo Picasso, Marcel Duchamp, and Jean Cocteau, modeling mannequins with abstracted features and dislocated figures. The aesthetic that these extreme mannequins, usually French in origin, represented was one which appealed in particular to the elite boutiques, and it began to look outdated, as a new popular aesthetic swept in from America.

The Iconic Body

In the 1920s and 1930s the American film industry was providing an international visual language that would influence both the design of window displays and the appearance of mannequins. By the 1930s American mannequin designer Lester Gaba had produced mannequins of the film stars Marlene Dietrich and Greta Garbo, and a Shirley Temple mannequin produced by Pierre Iman's was sold on both sides of the Atlantic. Film stars imparted glamour to the window display, which was itself looking more like a film set than ever. While World War II halted mannequin production in Europe, in America production increased, and mannequins continued to reflect the American mass aesthetic. In their expansion, American firms like D.G. Williams and Lillian Greneker were aided by a material new to mannequin production—plastic.

In the 1950s, mannequins represented a sophisticated and grown-up glamour. It wasn't until 1966, when mannequin designer Adel Rootstein produced models of Twiggy and Sandie Shaw, that the emergent youth culture was reflected in shop windows.

Mannequins Now

In the late-twentieth century, supermodels and television stars served as models for fashion mannequins. Conversely, the mannequin again became a subject for artists as fashion photographer Deborah Turbeville featured mannequins extensively in her work, and fashion illustrator Ruben Toledo designed a plus-sized mannequin for manufacturer Pucci. Mannequins have also captured the interest of designers like Alexander McQueen, whose innovative shop windows provide alternatives to the ubiquitous visual merchandising of the large fashion chains.

See also Fashion Advertising; Fashion Dolls.

Bibliography

Adburgham, Alison. *Shops and Shopping: 1800–1914*. London: Allen and Unwin, 1964.

Gronberg, Tag. *Designs on Modernity: Exhibiting the City in 1920s Paris*. Manchester: Manchester University Press, 1998.

Parrot, Nicole. *Mannequins*. New York: St. Martin's Press, 1982.

Jane Audas

MANTUA

The following definition of mantua was published in a book that recorded symbols for coats of arms and was compiled in 1688 by Randle Holme, a third-generation craftsman in that field. It is the earliest known definition of the style:

> A Mantua is a kind of loose Coat without any stays in it, the body part and sleeves are of as many fashions as I have mentioned in the Gown Body; but the skirt is sometime no longer than the Knees, others have them down to the Heels. The short skirt is open before, and behind to the middle: this is called a Semmer, or Semare: have a loose Body, and four side laps or skirts; which

extend to the knee, the sleeves short not to the Elbow turned up and faced.

The mantua style was introduced in the 1670s and remained fashionable until the beginning of the eighteenth century. Distinctive features of the mantua are its loose-fitting unboned bodice and the fact that it was cut in one length instead of cutting the bodice and skirt as two separate pieces. The loose-fitting over robe with a train was draped up and pulled back to reveal the petticoat. It was unboned but worn with a corset. The mantua is thought to have originated as informal dress to provide relief from the heavily boned bodices of the *grand habit* that was the style at court. The mantua had a kimono-like construction inspired by imported Indian robes worn as dressing gowns in Europe. In its earliest form, the mantua was constructed of two long pieces of fabric that ran from the front hem over the shoulders and down the back to the hem of the train. The textile was cut only minimally—at the neck and under the arm to the waist. It was recognized that styles would change and it was advantageous to have as much fabric available to convert it to the new style. Its one-piece construction formed the basis of much of women's clothing in the eighteenth century. Sack gowns of the early eighteenth century directly evolved from the mantua style.

Its loose fit and reference to dressing gowns gave the mantua an air of undress that Louis XIV considered too informal to be worn at French court functions. The mantua was supposed to be worn only in one's own chamber or at specific country residences of the court. Despite royal disapproval of the style, the mantua was the height of fashion in town and became the dominant fashionable garment for women through the beginning of the eighteenth century. Another important distinction from the *grand habit* of the court was that the mantua covered the shoulders. Ladies appreciated the warmer, more comfortable style over the off-the-shoulder cut of the *grand habit* which had to be worn no matter what the temperature.

As the mantua evolved it became more formalized and was accepted at court. The loose folds of the bodice were stitched down into pleats for a closer-fitting shape. Eventually it was allowed for all but the most formal occasions at court, and even crystalized in varied forms as court dress in England through the eighteenth century.

The overall appearance, textile, trimmings, and accessories of a mantua were far more important than the fineness of its construction. The largest portion of the cost of any new garment in that period was the fabric. Careful consideration was given to the cutting of the textile and placement of dominant motifs, but the inside stitching was sometimes quite coarse and uneven. Distinctive brocaded silk damasks now known as *bizarre* silks, fashionable from circa 1695 to 1720, were often used for the mantua. Characterized by elongated, asymmetrical patterns that combined natural and abstract motifs, bizarre silks used bold color combinations and textured gold and silver metallic threads. The combination of textures and colors of these textiles created spectacular effects in a mantua's flowing appearance. The surface of gold and silk threads change with movement, casting light and dark within the free folds of the draped train.

The interest in scientific and technical experimentation, and the influence of exoticism from imported goods from the East, coupled with the increasing demand for luxury and change of the late seventeenth century, came together to create free and dazzling bizarre silk designs. The vertical lines of the mantua complemented the long, flowing lines and large repeats of the bizarre silks. An average vertical repeat of a bizarre silk at the height of the movement was nearly 27 inches, 10 across (69 centimeters and 26 centimeters across). Commonly, the design repeated across the width of the textile twice.

Mantua makers used a combination of flat cutting and draping. First, the pieces of the garment were cut from the fabric according to measurements taken from the client. Second, the long center back seam was sewn with close stitches in the bodice, and long loose stitches below the waist. The bodice area that fits more closely and takes more stress with movement than the lower parts requires closer stitching. Side gore pieces would have been added to the sides of the main panel to make the dress wider below the waist. These seams were sewn in two different ways depending on whether the mantua was of the lined or unlined style. If the mantua was lined, the seams were sewn in the conventional manner of placing the right sides together leaving the outside with a clean finish. If the robe was unlined these seams would have been sewn wrong sides together so that the seam allowances were on the outside of the dress. The draping back of the front edge of the mantua positions the inside of the mantua to the outside in this area. Fabrics that were attractive on both sides were joined with special mantua-makers seams giving both sides a clean finish for the draped arrangement of the skirt of the mantua.

See also Coat; Europe and America, History of Dress (400–1900 C.E.).

Bibliography

De Marly, Diana. *Louis XIV and Versailles*. New York: Holmes and Meier Publishers, Inc., 1988.

Dennita Sewell

MAO SUIT

This suit comprises a front-fastening jacket, buttoned to the neck, and a pair of trousers in matching material. Its main association is with communist China. It is named in English after Mao Zedong (1893–1976), the leader of the People's Republic of China from 1949 to 1976. Its salient features are a high, turned-down collar that fits the neck closely, and four patch pockets, two large ones at waist level and two smaller ones on the breast. A classic Mao suit has expandable lower pockets, and both the top and bottom pockets close with a buttoned-down flap. The trousers have a waistband, with a fly-front fastening for men and a side fastening for women. The suit can be made from a variety of materials with cotton, polyester, or a mix of the two being the most usual. It is almost always blue, though within that spectrum the colors range from pale gray to dark blue-black. The suit is often teamed with a matching worker's cap. Mao suits can either be purchased off-the-rack or tailor-made.

Despite its name, Mao was not the first person to wear such a suit. Its precise origins are hard to pin down. In the early years of the twentieth century, as an alternative to both the long gown and the western suit with collar and tie, several different styles, similar to the Mao suit but with a high-standing collar and no patch pockets, began to be worn by Chinese men. These have been viewed as precursors of the Mao suit and are called student suits because they were first adopted in Japan by Chinese studying there. The student suit, which had derived from European, probably Prussian, military dress, became linked with those urging political and economic reform for China. Another famous Chinese leader, Sun Yat-sen (1866–1925), revered by Chinese the world over as the "Father of the Nation" for his part in creating a Chinese Republic in 1911, is credited with making adaptations to the student suit, although it still did not look like the Mao suit we know today. It was in the 1920s that Sun himself appeared in what we now perceive as a fully fledged version of the Mao suit with patch pockets. This followed on a more overt link with Soviet communist advisors, who also wore this type of suit.

See also China: History of Dress; Politics and Fashion.

Bibliography

Roberts, Claire, ed. *Evolution and Revolution: Chinese Dress, 1700s–1900s.* Sydney: Powerhouse Publishing, 1997.
Steele, Valerie, and John S. Major, eds. *China Chic: East Meets West.* New Haven, Conn.: Yale University Press, 1999.

Verity Wilson

MARGIELA, MARTIN*

Martin Margiela (1957–) was born in Hasselt, Belgium. He studied fashion design at the Royal Academy of Fine Arts in Antwerp—at the same time as Ann Demeulemeester—followed by a three-year apprenticeship with Jean-Paul Gaultier (1984–1987). He established the Maison Martin Margiela in Paris in 1988, together with Jenny Meirens, a boutique owner. Margiela was categorized more than once as the deconstructivist par excellence in a period when the term was applied indiscriminately to designers whether or not it was appropriate. Margiela was probably one of the few designers in the early 2000s whose work could be fairly described as deconstructivist. His investigation into the different aspects underlying any article of clothing, such as form, material, structure, and technique, were central to his entire body of work. His work was deconstructivist because he took not only the garment itself into consideration, but also the system that produced it. Ideas about haute couture, tailoring, high or low fashion, innovation, and commercialism do not arise from any apolitical standpoint, nor are they formulated as criticisms of established fashion assumptions. Margiela's work began from a set of analyses questioning the established theories of what already exists in order to search for alternatives that can be brought to life, both within and outside the system.

Margiela's attention to tailoring often exposed the production process behind the clothing, or revealed techniques that traditionally remain hidden in its production. The experimental aspect of his clothes in fact did not take place at the expense of ease in wear or aesthetic considerations. Margiela's summer collection for 2004 included blouses and dresses whose forms were no longer determined by classic lines or cut, but rather by small black stitches that stood out sharply against the fabrics he selected. The pleating and folding techniques that formed the starting point for his 2002 and 2003 collections were further developed in the 2004 garments. The tiny stitches were applied with surgical precision in order to achieve the correct fit. The result was elegant, slightly aggressive, yet simultaneously a tribute to the work of the many professionals in the field of fashion who remain literally unseen.

The study of form was equally central to Margiela's 1998 summer collection, which was a series of "flat garments." When the pieces are not being worn, they seem to preserve the two-dimensional structure of the paper pattern. The armholes were not placed at the sides of these garments, but rather cut out of the front section. Only when the flat garments are put on does their actual three-dimensional form appear. A second collection worthy of note in this regard was Margiela's summer 1999 collection. The basic idea was to reproduce a series of doll clothes enlarged to human size. The designer retained the disproportions and finishing details, however, resulting in rather alienating pieces with giant buttons and zippers.

In 1997 Margiela based two successive semi-couture collections on an old Stockman tailor's dummy. Various elements that pointed to subsequent stages of the production process, such as the sections of a toile, for example, were permanently pinned to the bust as part of a jacket. Other jackets assumed a masculine shoulder line, with the inside of the prototype replaced with a second structure and with a feminine shoulder line. Removing the sleeves revealed both the masculine and the feminine tailoring. Shoulder pads were sometimes placed on the outside of the garment or used as a separate accessory: the inside became the outside.

This process of reversal also applied to other aspects of the designer's work. The use of recycled materials was particularly evident in Margiela's early collections. In his first winter collection, displayed in 1988, shards from broken plates were worked into shirts. Plastic shopping bags were cut to form tee-shirts and held together with brown cellophane tape. In the summer 1991 collection, secondhand ball gowns from the 1950s were dyed gray and given new life as waistcoats; old jeans and denim jackets were reworked to become elegant, full-length coats.

Margiela's reversals were more frequently a source of confusion. In his 1996 summer collection, photographs of garments, knitted goods, sequined evening wear and different fabrics were printed onto lightweight cloth with a subtle fall, which was in turn worked into simply cut designs. The very realistic printing created a trompe'oeil effect or optical illusion and suggested tailoring that the actual pieces did not have. The models wore cotton voile during the show to cover their faces and hair. Hiding the physical features that make a person unique increases the desire for identity and uniqueness evoked by the clothing itself.

The most noteworthy detail in Margiela's clothing was the nameless, somewhat oversized white label, identifiable on the outside of the garment by four white stitches attaching its corners. The label itself carried neither brand identification nor size indication, and therefore seemed utterly extraneous. The conspicuousness of the white stitches increased the visibility of something that at first did not seem intended to attract attention. The phenomenon of merchandise branding was thus referenced in all its complexities and ambiguities. Margiela's refusal to supply his designs with a brand name produced the opposite effect, a select in-crowd who recognized his "brand." In similar fashion, Margiela the designer wished to disappear behind his work in a decade characterized by extreme narcissism, in which other designers attained superstar status. No photographs of the designer were distributed. Communications concerning the collections consistently took place only through Maison Margiela. Interviews were allowed only by fax, and were always answered in the first person plural. This created an ambiguous result as well. Margiela's refusal to appear in person resulted in the creation of a personality myth.

Maison Margiela seemed to rebel against the rhythm of production that the economic system imposes on designers, not by radically rejecting the system but by filling it in with its own table of contents. In the strictest sense, the house's collections and its various sideline activities are not bound to trends or seasons. Consequently, the tabi boot—a Japanese-inspired shoe in the form of a hoof—reappeared with each new season, albeit in slightly modified form. Moreover, not only were existing garments reworked into new creations, but also the "success items"—or favorite pieces from previous collections—were repeated. This method led to the evolution of different lines, each of which was given a number that referred to differences in content, working method, and technique. All the lines except 1—the main line for women—bore labels printed with a line of numbers from 0 to 23 and the relevant number was circled.

Margiela was engaged in 1997 as the in-house designer for Hermès, one of the greatest luxury houses of France, with an established reputation for quality and finishing. Here, too, Margiela succeeded in further developing the achievements of his characteristic investigations into tailoring, although he worked entirely within the Hermès atmosphere and tradition. The interpretation that Margiela contributed to Hermès was a guarantee of absolute quality and excellence in luxury productions in leather and cashmere. No busy prints were to be found, but rather a return to the article's essence, and the core of true luxury, that is, the stripping away of everything that is not essential.

Where the inside was brought outside in more experimental fashion in Margiela's own collections, the inside was also central to flawless finishing in his work for Hermès. Maison Margiela introduced line 4 in 2004, which appeared to be an in-between collection that bridged Margiela's work for his own house and his work for Hermès. Collection 4 represented a reworking of a number of pieces from line 1, with inside finishing placed on the outside of the garment but now executed in more traditional and luxurious form, as was customary in the Hermès tradition. Only the neck and shoulders of these garments were provided with a lining. Margiela left Hermès after the 2004 spring–summer collection. The Martin Margiela company was bought by Diesel in 2002, and Margiela withdrew from active participation in the company in 2009, leaving his design team to carry on.

See also Belgian Fashion; Brands and Labels; Demeulemeester, Ann; Gaultier, Jean-Paul; Grunge; Hermès; Recycled Textiles.

Bibliography

Evans, Caroline. "The Golden Dustman: A Critical Evaluation of the Work of Martin Margiela and a Review of *Martin Margiela: Exhibition (9/4/1615)." Fashion Theory* 2 (1998): 73–93.

Gill, Alison. "Deconstruction Fashion: The Making of Unfinished, Decomposing and Reassembled Clothes." *Fashion Theory* 2 (1998): 25–49.

Maison Martin Margiela, *Maison Martin Margiela.* New York: Rizzoli, 2008.

Street Editorial Office. *Maison Martin Margiela Street Special Edition.* Vols. 1 and 2. Tokyo, Japan: 1999.

Te Duits, Thimo, ed. *La Maison Martin Margiela: (9/4/1615).* Rotterdam, Netherlands: Museum Boijmans Van Beuningen, 1997.

Vinken, Barbara. "Mannekin, Statue, Fetisch." *Kunstforum International* 141 (Juli–September 1998): 144–153.

Kaat Debo and Linda Loppa

MASQUERADE AND MASKED BALLS

Masquerades and masked balls are linked to the celebration of Carnival and *mardi gras*. Originally part of a cycle of pagan festivities celebrating the advent of the spring planting season, in the Middle Ages, Carnival began after the winter solstice as part of the Feast of Fools, for which the congregation elected abbots and bishops from among the junior clergy who masked and dressed in women's clothes and performed a mock Mass that ended with dancing in the church and streets, and the coronation of an Abbot of Misrule. With the Reformation, Protestant countries banned Carnival, while the Feast of Fools moved into the street. The result was that in Catholic countries, Carnival revelry and masking took over the streets of towns and cities between Twelfth Night and Ash Wednesday, in anticipation of giving up all *carne*—meat and sex—for Lent. Carnival thrived in Paris, Venice, and Rome, among other cities. The last six days of Carnival were called *les jours gras* (fat days) lasting from *feudi gras*, the Thursday before Ash Wednesday through the night of *mardi gras*. *Les jours gras* were celebrated with masked balls, obscene dancing, and eating, drinking, and sex. On the morning of Ash Wednesday, this orgiastic explosion ended in a parade of exhausted, masked revelers.

Masquerades also existed in eighteenth-century London, but it is Parisian Carnival and its masked balls in the nineteenth century that have produced the most commentary, gossip, and visual images. Many European and American observers published memoirs describing their experiences at the masked balls in Paris, while lithographs of the masked balls at the opera and at other Parisian theaters and dance halls proliferated during the nineteenth century, producing countless imitations. Indeed, in popular culture masked balls and the French were so closely linked that an early American silent movie (1908) is titled *At the French Ball*—the story, of course, of adultery at a masked ball.

Court theatricals with masks and a ballet were initially introduced at the French and English courts in the seventeenth century. By the early eighteenth century, masquerades and *bals masqués* (the French term for masked balls) were attracting large crowds at the newly opened public dance halls in London and Paris, at the aristocratic balls at the Paris opera (as of 1715), and in private Parisian mansions that welcomed the masked public during Carnival. During the eighteenth century, the masked balls in public dance halls were the height of English fashion, while the French celebration of Carnival was increasingly politicized and used to attack the monarchy. In this world turned upside down, women dressed as men, frequently as soldiers, sailors, or stevedores; men as women; the poor disguised themselves as bishops, lawyers, and aristocrats; and the rich disguised themselves as beggars, peasants, fishmongers, in Oriental masquerade, and *in domino*, the classic Venetian costume of a hooded black cape and mask. Regardless of a persons gender and class, sexual license was tolerated at masked balls so that men and women were free to indulge their sexual proclivities with persons of whatever sex and class they chose. With the French Revolution, Carnival and masking were temporarily banned, while in England such permissiveness died. In 1800 Napoleon reintroduced Carnival, although by 1830 Parisian Carnival was said to be a thing of the past.

Nonetheless, from a mere three authorized public masked balls during Carnival in 1830, by 1831 Parisian Carnival exploded in the aftermath of the July Revolution (1830). The combination of a new revolutionary generation disaffected with the conservative government of the July Monarchy and the spread of romanticism infused new life into Parisian Carnival. The fashion press and the new satirical dailies, benefiting from the introduction of cheap lithographs illustrating the masked balls at the opera and at other theaters. The introduction of gossip columns and cheap newspapers, paid for by advertising instead of subscription, provided Parisians and readers everywhere a blow-by-blow account of the masked balls during Carnival after 1830. The satirical daily *Le Charivari* coined the catchwords of Carnival, "Down with the Carnival of our ancestors! Hooray for the carnival of romanticism and politics," and published lithographs by Honore Daumier and Paul Gavarni depicting the Carnival masked balls in all their glory. Hundreds of pamphlets, satires, illustrations, and fashion magazines supplied a running commentary on the pleasures to be found at the Carnival masked balls at their height in the 1830s and 1840s, including the masked balls that took place in the middle of the Revolution of 1848. It is not surprising, then, that although these balls continued until the end of the century, it was this period in the 1830s and 1840s that was mythic and that was depicted in Edouard Manet's famous painting *Le Bal masqué de l'Opéra* (1873).

What made this Carnival and its masked balls so remarkable was the confluence of political discontent and the emergence of a consumer society that fanned the flames of pleasure and desire. Many of the costumes reflected a rejection of traditional roles and a yearning for the exotic, suggesting a widespread ambivalence about the values of emerging capitalist society and its imposition of middle-class culture and domesticity. The most chic costumes of the moment worn to masked balls in eighteenth-century London were Oriental masquerades, while in nineteenth-century Paris, Spanish dancers, or couples dressed as stevedores were the most fashionable. None of these fashions lasted beyond their moment, although designers in the early twenty-first century have looked at illustrations from the masked balls of nineteenth-century Paris as an inspiration for clothes.

However, what is significant about Parisian masked balls in the nineteenth century are the technological inventions that made the balls fashionable and accessible to an expanding literate public. The introduction of the lithographic process and the rotary press made it possible for newspapers and magazines to print more newspapers with cheap illustrations, while advertising, a new capitalist invention, reduced their cost. The preeminence of Paris fashion, made more accessible through beautifully illustrated fashion magazines and the introduction of department stores and costume warehouses, offered this new consuming public fashionable disguises and cheaper clothes. Serialized novels in newspapers and gossip columns fed the aspirations and desires of increasing populations and an expanding middle class, especially the women, who now had more money to spend and places to spend it, including the masked balls during Carnival. Most of these elements already existed in England in the eighteenth century, when masquerades were the height of fashion. Missing was the French genius for publicity and seduction, which made the special pleasures and intensity of Parisian masked balls legendary and guaranteed their immortality in print and visual culture, both high and low.

See also Carnival Dress; Ceremonial and Festival Costumes; Masks.

Bibliography

Alter, Ann Ilan. "Pursuing Pleasure at the Masked Balls at the Opera during the July Monarchy." *Laurels: The Magazine of the American Society of the French Legion of Honor* 60, no. 2 (1989): 101–118.

——. "Parisian Women at the Opera Balls." In *Masquerade and Identities: Essays on Gender, Sexuality and Marginality.* Edited by Efrat Tseëlon. London: Routledge, 2001.

Burke, Peter. *Popular Culture in Early Modern Europe.* New York: New York University Press, 1978.

Castle, Terry. *Masquerade and Civilization: The Carnivalesque in Eighteenth-Century English Culture and Fiction*, Stanford, Calif.: Stanford University Press, 1996.

Cohen, Sarah R. "Masquerade as Mode in the French Fashion Print." In *The Clothes That Wear Us: Essays on Dressing and Transgressing in Eighteenth-Century Culture.* Edited by Jessica Munns and Penny Richards. Newark: University of Delaware Press, 1999.

Flaubert, Gustave. *L'Éducation Sentimentale.* Paris: Éditions Garnier, 1984.

Ann Ilan Alter

MATERNITY DRESS

Throughout most of history, all over the world, women's attire has of necessity been designed to adapt to the needs of pregnancy and breast-feeding, which were likely to take up a large percentage of women's lives between puberty and menopause. Before the industrial revolution, the making of fabric and clothing was labor-intensive enough to preclude the making of garments exclusive to pregnancy.

Thus, in Western Europe since medieval times, regular dress of all classes has been easily adapted for pregnancy. Laced bodices, frequently involving center panels to cover expanding waistlines, were prevalent. Petticoats, separate or integral with bodices, were tied at both sides, equally adaptable. Women appeared not to mind the rising hemline in front that resulted from the use of a normal wardrobe during pregnancy.

Beginning in the sixteenth century, styles became more restrictive. Bodices were reinforced with boning, but they were still most often laced. Writers scolded women for wearing these styles during pregnancy, accusing them of putting vanity above the health of their unborn child. But it is possible to rest the bodice or corset on the pregnant belly without constricting it, and this was probably common. Women did not abandon corsets during pregnancy, at least in public. Women of all classes wore corsets during pregnancy, tilted across their stomachs, aprons worn high to conceal the gap at the bodice's front.

Some women did contrive garments specifically for pregnancy, as a surviving set of eighteenth-century quilted garments in the collection at Colonial Williamsburg attests, in which a waistcoat expands over the belly to cover the gap in the jacket front. Possibly this sort of individualized contrivance occurred more often, at least among members of the upper class who could afford it, than surviving examples can document.

Privately, fashionable women in the seventeenth and eighteenth centuries could wear loose "wrapping gowns," popular at-home wear, worn by both sexes. Women of all classes also donned unboned sleeveless bodices, quilted or corded to support the belly and breasts. Working-class women had the added choice of loose, unconstructed jackets called "bed gowns" over a petticoat.

The sack or sacque gown, introduced in the early eighteenth century, can apparently be credited to the marquise de Montespan, mistress of Louis XIV, who strove to conceal her pregnancy to remain longer at court. This was reported at the time and may be credited more than most such anecdotes deserve. Falling loose both front and back, the sacque later became fitted in front, and thus no more suited to pregnancy than other styles.

At the turn of the nineteenth century, high-waisted styles were well suited both to pregnancy and breast-feeding. Not until waists returned to their normal level in the 1830s did pregnancy require more careful wardrobe planning.

By 1830, most dresses hooked in back; center front openings, and a "drop-front" skirt, were still occasionally used, suggesting wear during pregnancy. In the 1840s and 1850s, the "fan pleated" bodice was popular, partly because it was easily adapted. In surviving examples, gathers beginning at the shoulders extend to the waist and are gathered on drawstrings, allowing expansion and access for breast-feeding and gradual tightening as the body returned to pre-partum shape. Other innovations also existed, such as expansion of the gathers found in the era's ample skirts. Some nineteenth-century maternity garments contain linings intended to lace over the belly, providing support without constricting it, since the period's more curvilinear corsets were likelier to cause harm than earlier styles. Less constrictive corsets—less boned, or with expandable lacings over the belly—were also available.

Victorian women did not, as popular myth says, stay at home during pregnancy. Fashion magazines, with typical reticence, fail to identify maternity styles, but they can be detected by careful reading: pregnancy corsets are called "abdominal corsets," and phrases such as "for the young matron," "for the recently married lady," reveal maternity styles. An alert modern reader can easily find them, although pregnant figures are not depicted.

The 1860s brought the use of separates to aid pregnant women. For the rest of the nineteenth century, both at-home and fashionable dress offered styles that worked during pregnancy. Boxy jackets and amply gathered center bodice panels, for example, seen in the 1880s and 1890s, are among the obvious styles to choose.

In the twentieth century, the ready-to-wear industry strove to cater more to women by adapting current fashions to pregnancy. When catalogs finally identify maternity fashions (about 1910), they still refrain from depicting the pregnant form, revealing old discomfort with the issue but suggesting that the styles were the same as others of the time, albeit with specialized construction. Often this meant a series of fasteners at the sides, so that the dress need not be any larger than necessary in the earlier stages of pregnancy.

After World War II, specific maternity styles developed more markedly. Designers made pencil-thin skirts with elastic panels to cover a pregnant belly. Still, the tops often were made unnecessarily full, unlike regular fashions. Typical of postwar maternity fashion were oversized collars and buttons, an infantalizing effect possibly meant to balance the scale of the garment, although one may see in them a condescending attitude to women. Lucille Ball, star of *I Love Lucy*, exemplified the maternity fashions of the early 1950s, and at the time influenced many women during her 1952–1953 televised pregnancy, seen weekly by millions.

In the early 1980s, Diana, Princess of Wales' two pregnancies influenced maternity styles. Dropped-waist dresses, then in fashion, were well suited to pregnancy and a favorite of Diana's. Dresses dropping straight from the yoke with no waist at all, one of the styles favored in the 1950s and 1960s, were also worn. Long tunics and sweaters over stretchy leggings became a popular casual choice.

In the 1980s, styles for working pregnant women also emerged as a category of fashion, as garment makers, and would-be mothers, struggled to find styles apt for women in the workplace. Styles based on men's business suits still dominated, suggesting unease with the notion of women in business; pregnancy required even more cover-up. Maternity versions of masculine business suits resulted, with boxier jackets and expanded skirts. Since then, both office wear and maternity wear have developed away from closely copying men's business wear.

The 1990s saw an end to the customary attempt to conceal pregnancy. The emphasis on fit, athletic bodies, and the culture's comfort with revealing the human form, have led to adopting clinging maternity styles in place of centuries of draping and concealment, and even bare-midriff shirts are worn by pregnant women. Feminism and a body-conscious culture have taken maternity fashion in new directions.

See also Empire Style.

Bibliography

Baumgarten, Linda. "Dressing for Pregnancy: A Maternity Gown of 1780–1795." *Dress: The Journal of the Costume Society of America* 23 (1996).

Hoffert, Sylvia D. *Private Matters: American Attitudes Toward Childbearing and Infant Nurture in the Urban North, 1800–1860* (Women in American History). Urbana: University of Illinois Press, 1989.

Leavitt, Judith Walzer. *Brought to Bed: Childbearing in America 1750–1950*. Oxford and London: Oxford University Press, 1986.

Poli, Doretta Davanzo. *Maternity Fashion*. Drama Publishers, 1997.

Alden O'Brien

McCARDELL, CLAIRE

Claire McCardell was one of the most influential women's sportswear designers of the twentieth century. Best known for her contributions to the "American look," she was inspired by the active lifestyle of American women. Known for casual sportswear, shirtwaist dresses, and wool jersey sheaths, as well as practical leisure clothing and swimwear, which she liked to refer to as "playclothes," McCardell designed for working women who wanted stylish, well-made clothing in washable fabrics that were easily cared for.

McCardell was born in Frederick, Maryland, in 1905, where she attended Hood College for two years in the mid-1920s before earning a degree in fashion design at the Parsons School of Design in New York City in 1928. In the course of her studies she spent one year in Paris. Working after graduation as a fit model for B. Altman and Company, McCardell later obtained a job as a salesperson and design assistant with Emmet Joyce, an exclusive, made-to-order salon on Fifth Avenue. Within a matter of months, she was lured away by the knitwear manufacturer Sol Pollack to design and oversee his Seventh Avenue cutting room, where she stayed for less than a year. By late 1929 McCardell was working as a design assistant to Robert Turk, an independent designer and dressmaker, who later took her along with him when he was employed as chief designer at Townley Frocks in the early 1930s.

Turk died unexpectedly in a boating accident in 1932, and McCardell was promoted to chief designer at Townley. McCardell remained with Townley throughout her career, with the exception of a brief hiatus in the early 1940s, and eventually became a partner. During the time that Townley's partners restructured their business, McCardell worked at Hattie Carnegie; however, Townley soon rehired her as their head designer.

Innovation

While most of McCardell's contemporaries followed the long-standing tradition of copying Paris fashion, McCardell looked instead to the lives of American women for her inspiration. Insisting that "clothes should be useful," McCardell became one of the first designers to successfully translate high-styled, reasonably priced, impeccably cut clothing into the mass-production arena. Proudly American and rebelliously innovative, McCardell (who, as a student in Paris, had admired the work of Vionnet, Chanel, and Madame Grès) turned her back on the expensive, handmade confections of the haute couture and instead promoted American mass production, readily available materials, and the form-follows-function approach to design. Insisting that heavily decorated, padded, and corseted French fashions often sacrificed comfort to style, McCardell designed clean-lined, comfortable clothes that proved such a sacrifice was not only unacceptable; it was also unnecessary.

The retail magnate Stanley Marcus once described McCardell as "the master of the line, never a slave to the sequins . . . one of the few truly creative designers this country has ever produced." Shunning shoulder pads, back zippers, boning, and heavily constructed looks, McCardell became known for her self-tailoring, wrap-and-tie styles, backless halters, hook-and-eye closures, coordinated separates, racy bathing suits, and boldly printed, cotton plaid, shirtwaist dresses cut from men's shirting fabrics. Often referred to as "America's most American designer," McCardell's fresh, youthful designs were founded on logic, informed by comfort, and replete with a common sense, entirely undecorated look. As the veteran fashion model Suzy Parker once described them, McCardell's designs were "refreshingly 'unFrench.'" McCardell's

American Swimwear, 1946. Models showcase Claire McCardell's "Pantung Loincloth" (left) and Joset Walker's "Hug Me Tights" (right) swimsuits. Crafted to show off the female body, these styles were considered racy during their time. © GENEVIEVE NAYLOR/CORBIS. REPRODUCED BY PERMISSION.

first commercial hit came in 1938 with the "Monastic" dress, an unfitted, waistless shift, cut on the bias, that hung straight from the waist and was belted in any way the wearer chose. The Monastic was so resoundingly popular that it was copied by competitors into the next decade and remained in her own line in updated versions for almost twenty years. Another McCardell success story was "capsule dressing," or four- and five-piece, mix-and-match separates groups in supple wool jersey, cotton, denim, and even taffeta. These stylish, well-edited groupings offered women a convenient travel wardrobe that sold altogether for about one hundred dollars and could be tucked into a handbag. An avid champion of pants and wool jersey for both day and evening wear, McCardell's forward-looking designs and fabric sensibility provided American women with multiseasonal clothing that was easily cared for, comfortable, and stylish, but never conspicuously chic.

The "American Look"

McCardell's pared-down, casual American style was the hallmark of what came to be hailed as the "American look," the name under which the work of McCardell and several of her like-minded contemporaries, such as Tina Leser and Tom Brigance, was marketed at Lord and Taylor during the late 1930s and early 1940s. During World War II, McCardell's designs earned further credibility, as they reflected an acute awareness of the evolving roles of mid-century American women. Offering sportswear and daywear that were at once appropriate for the office, cocktail hour, and leisure, McCardell eliminated the fuss, decoration, and strict categorization so often encountered in women's apparel of the time. Answering practical needs, McCardell's 1942 blue denim "Popover" dress, which sold for only $6.95, was made specifically for at-home domestic work or gardening and even included an attached oven mitt. True to her problem-solving approach to fashion design, McCardell used humble fabrics such as cotton calico, denim, jersey, and even synthetics, effectively ennobling everyday materials by way of thoughtful design and deftly executed construction. And while restrained and disciplined, McCardell's work was hardly devoid of details: Her signature, even idiosyncratic, "McCardellisms" included severe, asymmetrical, wrap necklines, yards-long sashes, spaghetti-string ties, double-needle top stitching, metal hook-and-eye closures, and even studded leather cuffs. With their sleek lines and "no-price look," McCardell's clothes became a mainstay in the wardrobe of college girls, working women, and housewives alike.

Claire McCardell achieved international fame during her lifetime, appearing on the cover of *Time* magazine and authoring a book on her fashion philosophy, *What Shall I Wear?* in 1957. In 1943 she married the architect Irving Drought Harris. McCardell was diagnosed with cancer in 1958, at the height of her success. The disease claimed her life that same year.

Looking at her own life as a starting point for her line, McCardell's casually elegant, pared-down minimalism and lifestyle-driven sportswear of the late 1930s and 1940s helped forge and define what came to be known as the "American look" and heralded the beginning of a new appreciation for American fashion. As fashion historian Valerie Steele points out in *Women of Fashion*, "without McCardell it is simply impossible to imagine a Donna Karan, Calvin Klein or a Marc Jacobs."

See also Casual Business Dress; Ready-to-Wear; Sportswear.

Bibliography

Kirkland, Sally. "Claire McCardell." In *American Fashion: The Life and Lines of Adrian, Mainbocher, McCardell, Norell, Trigère.* Edited by Sarah Tomerlin Lee for the Fashion Institute of Technology. New York: Quadrangle/New York Times Books, 1975.

McCardell, Claire. *What Shall I Wear?* New York: Simon and Schuster, 1956.

Milbank, Caroline Rennolds. *New York Fashion: The Evolution of American Style.* New York: Abrams, 1989.

Steele, Valerie. *Women of Fashion: Twentieth Century Designers.* New York: Rizzoli International, 1991.

Yohannan, Kohle, and Nancy Nolf. *Claire McCardell: Redefining Modernism.* New York: Harry N. Abrams, 1998.

Kohle Yohannan

McQUEEN, ALEXANDER*

Born Lee McQueen in the East End of London in 1969, Alexander McQueen was the youngest of six children to a taxi driver and a social history teacher.

He left school at the age of sixteen and started an apprenticeship with the Savile Row tailors Anderson and Sheppard. From there McQueen moved to the tailors Gieves and Hawkes, the theatrical costumers Bermans and Nathans, the designer Koji Tatsuno in London, and (at age twenty) to Romeo Gigli in Milan. Returning to London in 1990, he sought employment teaching pattern-cutting at Central Saint Martins College of Art and Design; instead, despite his lack of formal fashion training, he was offered a place in the fashion design course as a graduate student. He was awarded the master of arts degree in 1992. After leaving college, McQueen claimed unemployed social security benefits and feared criminal prosecution if caught working for money. He then began designing under the name of Alexander McQueen, continuing to claim benefits as Lee McQueen. His graduate collection was bought in its entirety by the influential stylist Isabella Blow, at that time a *Vogue* fashion editor, who went on to promote and encourage his work over several years.

As Alexander McQueen he immediately started his own label, first showing in autumn-winter 1993. His early collections, such as Nihilism (spring-summer 1994) and Highland Rape (autumn-winter 1995) relied on shock tactics rather than wearability, a strategy that helped him establish a strong identity. With their harsh styling, the designs in these collections explored variations on the themes of abuse and victimization. They frequently featured slashed, stabbed, and torn cloth, as well as McQueen's brutally sharp style of tailoring. He introduced extraordinary narrative and aesthetic content to his runway shows. Styling, showmanship, and dramatic presentation became as important as the design of the clothes; models walked on water, were drenched in "golden showers" on an ink-flooded catwalk, or were surrounded by rings of flame. The shows were put together on minimal budgets, assisted by models, makeup artists, stylists, and producers prepared to work for nothing. His creative director, Katy England, played an important role in both the development of

> "He takes ideas from the past and sabotages them with his cut to make them thoroughly new and in the context of today. . . . He is like a Peeping Tom in the way he slits and stabs at fabric to explore all the erogenous zones of the body."
>
> Isabella Blow, quoted in Sarajane Hoare, "God Save McQueen." *Harper's Bazaar* 30 (June 1996): 148.

his aesthetic and the design and styling of his shows. At this stage McQueen began collaborations with designers such as Dai Rees and the jewelers Shaun Leane and Naomi Filmer, whose accessories and jewelry he used in his shows. Besides these activities, he also worked with innovative film, video, and pop producers.

McQueen played up to his bad-boy reputation, opening himself to accusations of misogyny in his Highland Rape collection, which featured apparently bruised and battered models staggering along an apocalyptic, heather-strewn runway, and baring his backside to the buyers at the New York version of his Dante show (autumn-winter 1996). His commercial sense, however, was as sharp as his tailoring, and his antics and anecdotes were always to a purpose, be it to attract press, buyers, or backers. The Dante show in New York, for example, elicited an order from Bergdorf Goodman. From the start McQueen understood the commercial value of shock tactics in the British fashion industry, which had almost no infrastructure despite its reputation for innovation. After he had acquired his first backer, he toned down, while not entirely losing, the outrageous content of the shows. Other important developments for McQueen occurred in 1996. Late in that year he changed his backer to the Japanese corporate giant Onward Kashiyama, one of the world's biggest clothing production houses; it also backed Helmut Lang and Paul Smith. Its subsidiary, Gibo, produced the McQueen line. In October he was appointed designer in chief at Givenchy in Paris, replacing John Galliano, who went to Christian Dior. Also in 1996 McQueen was named the British Designer of the Year—a success he repeated in 1997 and 2001.

McQueen and Galliano thus spearheaded an assault on Paris-based fashion by young British designers in the 1990s, and their iconoclastic imagery and show techniques did much to boost a flagging French business. The appointment to Givenchy brought with it the backing of the conglomerate LVMH (Moët Hennessy Louis Vuitton), which allowed McQueen to continue his uncompromising design style for his own label. While he toned down the rougher edges of his style for Givenchy, in both the Givenchy and McQueen collections he continued to develop themes that had been with him since graduation. Darkly romantic, with a harsh vision of history and politics, McQueen's approach differed from the more straightforwardly romantic output of Galliano or Vivienne Westwood. His inspirations were as likely to be cult films by Stanley Kubrick, Pier Paolo Pasolini, or Alfred Hitchcock; seventeenth-century anatomical plates; or the photographs of Joel-Peter Witkin, as his predecessors in the pantheon of fashion design. His early designs included the low-slung and cleavage-revealing "bumster" trousers; he maintained a fascination with highly structured corsets and tailoring, as well as with historical cut and detailing. However, in the late 1990s the victimized look of his early models gave way to an Amazonian version of female glamour as a form of terror. Growing up with an older sister who was a victim of domestic violence, McQueen has said that as a designer he aimed to create a vision of a woman so powerful that no one would dare to lay a hand on her.

In tandem with his commercial work, McQueen continued to collaborate with photographers such as Nick Knight and Norbert Schoerner in publishing projects, and to work with those outside the fashion world, such as the artist Sam Taylor-Wood and the musician Björk. Whereas his sharp tailoring was sold in shops, his dramatic, unique showpieces that never went into production were in demand from art galleries and exhibitions across the world.

McQueen sold a controlling share in his business to Gucci in December 2000 and left Givenchy early in 2001, continuing to show under his own name in Paris rather than London. His role as creative director of the company permitted him to retain creative freedom as a designer, while the backing of Gucci—owner of Yves Saint Laurent, Stella McCartney, and Balenciaga—facilitated the transition of his business from a small-scale London label to a global luxury brand. In March 2001 he launched his custom-made menswear line in collaboration with the Savile Row tailors Huntsman. That year McQueen also opened a flagship store in New York and, in 2003, two more in London and Milan. He launched his perfume, Kingdom, in 2003 as well, the same year that the Council of Fashion Designers of America named him International Designer of the Year and that Britain awarded him a CBE (Commander of the British Empire) for his services to the fashion industry. Recently, McQueen explored new ways of making runway shows available on the Internet. His very theatrical Webcast show with a hologram of Kate Moss attracted tremendous attention, as did his live streaming of his runway shows. On February 11, 2010, McQueen, at the age of forty and reportedly in despair at the recent death of his mother, took his own life, sending waves of shock and sorrow through the international world of fashion.

See also Fashion Shows; London Fashion.

Bibliography

Arnold, Rebecca. *Fashion, Desire, and Anxiety: Image and Morality in the Twentieth Century*. London and New York: I. B. Tauris, 2001.

Barley, Nick, ed. *Lost and Found: Critical Voices in New British Design*. Basel, Switzerland: Birkhäuser, 1999.

Evans, Caroline. *Fashion at the Edge: Spectacle, Modernity and Deathliness*. New Haven, Conn.: Yale University Press, 2003.

Frankel, Susannah. *Visionaries: Interviews with Fashion Designers*. London: V & A Publications, 2001.

Tucker, Andrew. *The London Fashion Book*. London: Thames and Hudson, 1998.

Wilcox, Claire, ed. *Radical Fashion*. London: V & A Publications, 2001.

Caroline Evans

MILITARY STYLE

"Uniforms are the sportswear of the twentieth century," Diana Vreeland said once. Strolling through the streets of any cities in the world, one may add that military dress will be an important part of the twentieth-first-century look as well.

Teenagers in cargo pants, men in flight jackets and hooded parkas, and women in safari jackets and sailor pants are common sights on the everyday scene. Fashion runways have featured seasonal flurries of camouflage: print chiffon evening gowns, multipocket vests in bright satin, white leather cinched trench coats, and armies of military cashmere greatcoats with gilded buttons where the initials of famous fashion designers and the logos of powerful brands have taken the place of the insignia of royal families, dictators, and military empires. In the distant aftermath of the great wars, as real soldiers begin to look more and more like civilians—consider the Hollywood icon of the American soldier in plain khaki shirt, tie, and pants—"the imitation of the military uniform has triumphed over the original prototype." This was the comment of Holly Brubach in the *New York Times* on the decision of the American Navy to eliminate the bell-bottomed sailor trousers just when the fashion designers and the club kids were eager to wear them again.

The formal and technological evolution of uniforms lies at the origin of modern dress; standard military issue consists of a system of industrially produced garments in different sizes and qualities, which change according to social and weather conditions, and communicate belonging or rejection values. We may say that military uniforms are the first ready-to-wear garments, with standardized sizes and proportions to adapt to men and women with different physiques.

In a continuous process of osmosis, military uniforms and civilian dress have influenced each other over the years. An early documented case of this is, after the French Revolution, when the leg-wear of the *sans-culottes*, in revolt against the monarchy, became the model for the practical, clinging trousers worn by Napoleon and his army. The same thing happens with the new fashions of the century: the practicality of civilian clothing is continuously incorporated into military uniforms. And the garments perfected and idealized in military iconography make a triumphant return in everyday civilian dress.

The hunting dress of English country gentlemen—the Norfolk suit—is the prototype for combat gear, the fatigue jacket with deep convenient pockets and a reversible collar. The khaki color—from the Persian word *khak*, meaning dust, earth or mud—of uniforms all over the world, was borrowed from the personal wardrobe of Indian soldiers who dyed their clothing with natural pigments to disguise dirt. Perhaps the most telling of all examples is the continuous and repeated passage of the trench coat from the military to the civil sphere. Created in England, probably by the manufacturer Burberry as a garment for shepherds, farmers, and country gentlemen for protection from rain and wind, this coat became such a common feature among soldiers in the rainy trenches during War World I that it took the name "trench coat" and became a standard garment in the uniforms of many armies around the world. The practicality of this belted raincoat in certain weather conditions justified its utilization even before it became a part of the uniform. Then, between the two world wars, the trench coat returned to everyday closets and became the uniform of adventurers, spies, and rebels without a country, perfectly worn by Humphrey Bogart in *Casablanca* (1942). After being worn again by generals and colonels during World War II, the trench coat returned as the uniforms of intellectuals, writers, and journalists all over the world. It later wound up, on and off, in fashion shows, from Yves Saint Laurent to Giorgio Armani, down to the monogrammed GG,

LV, and DG—Gucci, Louis Vuitton and Dolce & Gabbana—versions of recent seasons.

Dozens of familiar, common items in our everyday wardrobe have shared a similar fate: the wool pea coat of sailors, the leather flight jacket of pilots, the fur-edged hooded parka of explorers, safari jackets and cargo pants, multipocket vests, and backpacks.

The short coat known as an Eisenhower jacket is a perfect example of the way national borders become useless against the power of fashion. This garment—Wool Field Jacket M1944—was originally a combat jacket cut short at the waist for comfort and to save on fabric. First worn by the English troops during World War II, was so admired by General Eisenhower, the head of the Allied Forces in Europe and future president of the United States, and so popular among American soldiers that it became Eisenhower's most famous outfit, the most known uniform of the U.S. Army and the most common piece of sportswear in the male wardrobe. In the modern version, the buttons have been replaced by zippers, and a designer logo has taken the place of the decorations, but the proportions remain the same: wide around the chest and narrow at the waist with broad shoulders.

Soldiers in every war have come back from the front with new experiences and terrifying tales, but also with military garments that silently became a part of everyday dress. The functional quality and the comfort tested in combat, the technology used to create new, more resistant fibers and fabrics, and the economy of resources and materials represented a legacy, which the clothing industry ably transferred from military to civilian production.

While the more theatrical characteristics of uniforms are just a memory in the technologically advanced equipment issued to modern soldier, the 1990s and 2000s have seen an increase and refinement of the political, revolutionary, or conservative use of those same details. In the uniforms from the 1930s, as in the outfits of rock stars or runway models fringed epaulettes on capes, silver buckles on shiny high boots, hussar braiding on riding jackets, coats of arms, decorations, metal eagles, and gold buttons are all defining elements. Freed from their practical function—the epaulette was created as protection against blows of the sword—these elements have assumed a symbolic and at times ideological value, but increasingly serve just a decorative purpose. Such elements include the Armani eagle, the Versace medusa head, and the crossed C's of Chanel.

See also Camouflage Cloth; Uniforms, Military; Unisex Clothing.

Bibliography

Brubach, Holly. "Running a Fever." *New York Times Magazine*, 13 July 1997: 45.

Edwards, T. *Men in the Mirror: Men's Fashion, Masculinity and Consumer Society*. London: Cassel, 1997.

Greco, L. *Homo Militaris: Antropologia e letteratura della vita militare*. Milan: Angeli, 1999.

Finkelstein, J. *The Fashioned Self*. Cambridge, U.K.: Polity Press, 1991.

Nathan, J. *Uniforms and Non-Uniforms: Communication through Clothing*. New York: Greenwood Press, 1986.

Stefano Tonchi

MILLINERS

Milliners create hats for women; hat makers make hats for men. This is the nineteenth- and twentieth-century differentiation of the two trades, which, although related, require very different technical skills and working practices.

The term "millinery" is derived from "Millaners," merchants from the Italian city of Milan, who traveled to northern Europe trading in silks, ribbons, braids, ornaments, and general finery. First chronicled in the early sixteenth century, these traveling haberdashers were received by noble aristocratic households, passing on news of the latest fashions as well as selling their wear. News of the latest styles and variations on dress was as important to men as it was to women, and milliners often acted as much sought-after fashion advisers to nobility all over Europe. One such milliner is mentioned by William Shakespeare in the historical drama *Henry IV* part 1, written in 1597, when the gallant warrior Hotspur refers to his encounter with a "trimly dress'd lord" as:

> Fresh as a bridegroom; and his chin reap'd
> Show'd like a stubble-land at harvest-home;
> He was perfumed like a milliner;
> And 'twixt his finger and his thumb he held
> A pouncet-box.

Milliners would also have traded in fine Florentine straw hats, a trade that might have been the reason for some of them to settle down as hat makers. Creating extravagant hats as well as having a flair for fashion and finery were, and still are, the trademarks of successful milliners.

The first celebrated "Marchande de Mode," or "modiste" as they were later called in France, was Rose Bertin (1744–1813). Her name is linked with Queen Marie-Antoinette of France, the most extravagant and illfated fashion icon of the eighteenth century. It could be argued that Marie-Antoinette and her "Ministre de Modes," Rose Bertin established haute couture in Paris and thus made it the capital of fine fashion. Elaborate hats, demure straw bonnets, and extravagant headdresses, called "poufs" were the height of fashion in the last quarter of the eighteenth century. Rose Bertin's witty creations were perched high up on the coiffure and featured rising suns, miniature olive trees, and, most famously, a ship in full sail. Her fame was enhanced by her notoriety and attracted an array of ladies of European nobility. Her salon survived the French Revolution but sadly all her hats, just like her famous clients, have disappeared and can only be traced in copies of the *Journal des modes*, which according to the custom of the period, never mentioned or credited the designer or creator of model hats.

The fashion for straw bonnets spread to the newly independent America and with it the millinery trade. Betsy Metcalf of Providence, Rhode Island, was one of the first milliners in the United States. She is said to have invented a special way of splitting locally grown oat straw, which she bleached in sulfur fumes, plaited, and sewed in spirals, creating straw bonnets intersected with fine lace and lined with silk. Having started to make hats at the age of twelve, she set the trend for new straw weaving techniques and became the founder of American millinery. The production of straw hats became an important home industry and rivaled the expensive imports of Florentine (Leghorn) straw from Italy. A bonnet that is said to be one of Betsy Metcalf's is in the collection of Rhode Island's Literary and Historical Society.

During the nineteenth century, bonnets and hats were not only fashionable, but essential in any woman's wardrobe. Bonnets were romantic and coquettish and thus the perfect accessory for women of the era. Millinery flourished, led by a strong force of Parisian "modistes," who set the tone for high fashion and demanded to be addressed reverently as "Madame." Famous names were Madame Herbault, Madame Guerin, and Madame Victorine, who created Queen Victoria's bonnets. Society ladies expected milliners to create unique

Portrait of a lady in a gown and elaborate straw hat, 1796. Straw bonnets were popular fashion accessories throughout the eighteenth century. © HISTORICAL PICTURE ARCHIVE/CORBIS. REPRODUCED BY PERMISSION.

Milliner Frederick Fox, March 9, 1993. This famous hatmaker, shown in his studio, was a royal milliner for Queen Elizabeth II. Based in London, Fox's career peaked during the 1970s and 1980s. © TIM GRAHAM/CORBIS. REPRODUCED BY PERMISSION.

models and jealously kept their sources secret. Sadly, not many hats survived, as they were often restyled or the trimmings reused. Testimony of some exquisite creations can only be found in illustrations and pictures without the mention of the relevant designer or maker. However, as millinery thrived on both sides of the Atlantic, millinery designers established their personal creed and reputation.

Caroline Reboux, at the Maison Virot, was the first legendary Parisian couture modiste, making hats for the French Empress Eugénie in 1868. She reputedly created individual designs by cutting and folding felt or fabric directly on the customer's head. Her famous salon in the rue Saint Honoré survived until the 1920s. Her pupil Madame Agnes became equally sought after for her experimental surrealistic styles. Elsa Schiaparelli, the Italian-born couture designer and friend of Salvador Dali, also created surreal hats in the 1930s. She unleashed her artistic talents by creating hats using newspapers, seashells, and birdcages with singing canaries. Her Shoe Hat designs of 1937, famously worn by Daisy Fellowes, editor of *Harper's Bazaar*, made headlines on both sides of the Atlantic.

Gabrielle (Coco) Chanel was a milliner before she started her couture career. She established her first salon in the elegant apartment of her lover in Paris in 1910. An avant-garde fashion trend leader of her time, she created simple shapes and decorated sparingly to compliment her vision of modern dress. She is credited with the creation of the cloche hat, which, pulled down low over the new short hairstyles, was to become an all-time classic.

Other famous Parisian modistes of the 1930s and 1940s included Maria Guy, Rose Valois, Suzanne Talbot, Rose Descart, Louise Bourbon, and Jeanne Lanvin, who like Chanel expanded her millinery salon into haute couture. Most couture houses, like Dior, Jean Patou, or Nina Ricci, had their own millinery ateliers, all headed by a "Premiere" (Designer), a "Seconde" (Head of Workroom), with several workrooms full of "Petites Mains" (workers). Millinery hierarchy had strict rules of etiquette, with La Premiere and La Seconde always addressed as "Madame" and the inferior workers given diminutive names like Mimi, Gigi, and Flo-Flo. Milliners working in couture houses considered themselves superior to their dressmaking colleagues. The girls had a reputation for being pretty and coquettish, were always meticulously groomed, and spent more money on lipsticks and powder than on food and rent. The industry had economic importance, with top ateliers employing up to 300 milliners each.

Parisian milliners not only created hats for a selective private clientele, they also supplied a thriving wholesale export business to many stores in the United States. Lilly Daché, a Viennese-born, Parisian-trained milliner, settled in New York and led the way for talented American designers. Having opened her first tiny studio in 1926, Lilly Daché built a millinery emporium, taking over a whole building of seven floors, with a silver room for her blonde clients and a gold one for brunettes. Her devotees included the Hollywood stars Carmen Miranda, Betty Grable, and Marlene Dietrich, who all loved her chic toques, demure snoods, and stylish "profile hats," which were her trademark.

Sally Victor and Mr. John of New York later took over the reign of Lilly Daché and maintained the importance of American millinery design. Mr. John had been in partnership with Frederic Hirst since 1928 and established his own business in 1948. His famous clients included Marilyn Monroe, Lauren Bacall, and Mrs. Simpson, the future Duchess of Windsor. Toward the end of his career Mr. John of N.Y. collaborated with Cecil Beaton on the extravagant costumes for Audrey Hepburn in *My Fair Lady*.

In Europe, the most notable milliner of the interwar years was Adele List in Vienna, whose hats were an expression of aesthetics and art. She was a highly disciplined, austere-looking figure and created hats with masterly craftsmanship. Using felt, straws, silks, and feathers, she combined shape, proportion, and texture in a unique harmonious way, which never looked dated. Some of her intricate pieces took over fifty hours to make and had detachable necklaces built into the shapes. One devoted client collected and preserved 248 model hats created by Adele List, all preserved in individual hat-boxes. After her death, the collection was donated to the Museum of Applied Art in Vienna, Austria, in 1983.

Aage Thaarup was a Danish milliner established in London and the first in a line of male milliners who were to dominate the second half of the twentieth century. He was self-taught and broke the established French rules of apprenticeship and gradual mastery of millinery. Having charmed the core of his high-society clientele on a voyage to India, his reputation spread quickly, and drew in ladies of the British Royal family, including the duchess of York and her daughters, Elizabeth and Margaret. When the duchess became queen of England in 1936, Aage Thaarup was officially "appointed by Her Royal Highness" and later created hats for the young Queen Elizabeth as well as for the Queen Mother.

Paris still dominated the millinery scene until the 1960s, when London took the lead with Otto Lucas, who established a most successful model wholesale business in Bond Street. His designers and ideas still came from Paris, but his flair for style created a chic, modern look much praised by millinery buyers on both sides of the Atlantic. Madame Paulette, his favorite designer, was the last of the *grandes modistes* of the Parisian school. With Claude Saint-Cyr, Jean Barthet, and Jean-Charles Brosseau, she was part of an era sadly in decline during the 1970s. At the height of her career Paulette had reigned over a much admired hat salon, with workrooms of 125 milliners and 8 *vendeuses mondaines*, society ladies with personal relations to important clients. Paulette created twice-yearly collections of 120 hats, presented to powerful foreign buyers as well as to her distinguished high-society clientele. Paulette's trademark was *le chapeau mou*, her draped soft turban, a sophisticated headwear for "bad hair days," popular during the 1940s and 1950s. Few of her clients knew that Algerian soldiers had inspired Paulette's original turban design during the liberation parade on the Champs Elysées in 1944.

Youth culture and the social liberation during the 1960s and 1970s brought a demise in the fashion for hats and with it a steep decline in business for milliners. The 1980s heralded a brief revival, which was partly due to Princess Diana, a fashion leader and icon of the British hat industry. London held on to its lead in millinery design, supported by royal patronage and social summer events like horse racing at Royal Ascot and Garden Parties at Buckingham Palace. John Boyd, Graham Smith, and the royal milliners Frederick Fox and Philip Somerville, a quartet of hat designers during the 1970s and 1980s, managed very successful model millinery as well as wholesale businesses in London. Small factories in Luton, Bedfordshire, U.K. supported manufacture, which, historically had been the center for straw hat production in the nineteenth century. Some factories, millinery supply businesses, and block makers are left in the early 2000s, but a museum has a rich collection documenting the importance of the hat trade in the past.

During the 1980s, a new generation of millinery designers graduated from London's Fashion and Art Colleges, creating hats as pieces of art. David Shilling was the first, gaining notoriety and much press coverage with striking Ascot creations he designed and made for his mother. Mrs. Gertrude Shilling's entrance, wearing yet another extraordinary hat, was much anticipated and celebrated every year at Royal Ascot.

Patricia Underwood was a star milliner in New York during the 1980s and 1990s, with her unmistakable style of pure shape and simplicity. New York also had Eric Javits, a very successful millinery designer, who built a multimillion-dollar business and was voted Hat Designer of the Year by the Millinery Institute of America. Millinery has also declined in the United States, but the Headwear Information Bureau (HIB) founded in New York in 1989, promotes millinery with public relations and competitions for young designers.

Stephen Jones, a New Romantic of the 1980s, included men among his devoted clients, and created hats for the pop stars Boy George and Steve Strange, as well as for the Spandau Ballet. His hat salon in London's Covent Garden district was designed to be full of fun, wit, and unexpected details. Stephen Jones is a rebel with a romantic streak and designs an eclectic mix of very wearable fabric hats, which reflect his original training as a tailor. Apart from creating diffusion ranges under the label "Miss Jones" and "Jonesboy," Stephen Jones works with many of the new top designers, such as Jean-Paul Gaultier, Claude Montana, and John Galliano, creating headpieces for cutting-edge catwalk shows.

Philip Treacy, an internationally awarded accessory designer, graduated from London's Royal College of Art in 1990 and immediately hit the headlines with his flamboyant and unmistakable hat creations, lifting millinery to an even higher level of art and design. The meteoric rise of the Irish-born young designer was also much celebrated at Parisian catwalk shows, staged by top couture houses like Dior, Chanel, and Givenchy. Philip Treacy even created his own millinery show in 1993, when supermodels paraded wearing show-stopping creations, acclaimed by the fashion press. One of his famous, much-photographed pieces was a hat with a black sailing ship, which might have been inspired by Rose Bertin's design in the late eighteenth century. A true and devoted lover of his craft, Philip Treacy personally makes many of his masterpieces. His label has become a status symbol and some of his celebrated hats are collector's pieces, treasured by museums, like the Victoria and Albert Museum in London.

During the twentieth century, women's lives changed drastically and imposed a fast-living lifestyle not compatible with the ethos of beautiful hat creations. The twenty-first century has become a bare-headed era and glamorous hats have become "special occasion wear," only worn for weddings and high-society horse races.

However, it is conceivable that the next generation of young designers might reinvent millinery with a new concept and purpose.

See also Chanel, Gabrielle (Coco); Hats, Men's; Hats, Women's; Lanvin, Jeanne; Schiaparelli, Elsa; Treacy, Philip.

Bibliography

Buxbaum, Gerda. *Die Hute der Adele List*. New York: Prestel Munchen, 1995.

Ginsburg, Madeleine. *The Hat, Trends and Traditions*. London: Studio Editions, Ltd., 1990.

Hopkins, Susie. *The Century of Hats*. London: Aurum Press, 1999.

McDowell, Colin. *Hats, Status, Style and Glamour*. London: Thames and Hudson, Inc., 1992.

Muller, Florence, and Lydia Kamitsis. *Les chapeaux, une histoire de tête*. Paris: Syros Alternatives, 1993.

Susie Hopkins

MINISKIRT

The debut of the miniskirt in the early 1960s can be compared to the birth of rock'n'roll music. When rock'n'roll took hold in the 1950s, parents and clergy were up in arms, railing against it. They were hopeful that it was a fad that would play itself out and fade away. Neither the miniskirt nor rock'n'roll has faded away. They have both endured and continue to serve as chief symbols of youthful rebellion.

Fashion history is characterized by the shifting focus on one female "erogenous zone" of the body to another. The fashionable Victorian silhouette focused attention on the waist, bosom, and hips through the use of corsetry. By the beginning of the twentieth century, the "mono-bosom" was prominent. During the 1920s, the flapper-style dress, which was based on a loose tunic or tubular shift, dared to reveal more of the female leg than ever before in modern Western history. However, fashion reverted to longer hemlines by the 1930s. Just as Art Deco set the stage for modern art, so did the fashions of the Jazz Age pave the way for the miniskirt.

While the decade of the 1950s embraced prescribed rules of dressing for special occasions and time of day, there was a new freedom in the area of casual clothing. The ideal fashionable woman was a statuesque adult, and young women were expected to imitate adult styles when it came to dressing. Teenagers tended to wear grown-up versions of clothing, except for casual wear. But rumblings of change were in the air.

Mary Quant

American teenagers of the 1950s and 1960s, later dubbed baby boomers, were taking note of each other on television dance party shows spawned by Dick Clark's "American Bandstand" in Philadelphia, especially after it went nationwide in 1957. Great Britain, which lagged behind the United States in recovering from World War II, was also giving birth to its own baby boomers. Among them was the intrepid Mary Quant, whose name is forever linked with the creation of the miniskirt.

Quant was part of the restless youth culture in the Chelsea section of London. Along with her friends Alexander Plunkett Green (who later became her husband) and Archie McNair, Quant felt that clothing for her age group did not really exist, so they opened their own shop called *Bazaar* in 1955. Quant infused her designs with a fresh, youthful energy, and even appeared at Buckingham Palace in a miniskirt to receive the Order of the British Empire in 1966. Along with the Beatles, Quant reinvigorated British culture, helping to launch the phenomenon known as "swinging London." Quant once noted, "London led the way to changing the focus of fashion from the Establishment to the young. As a country we were aware of the great potential of these clothes long before the Americans and the French."

Short skirts were incompatible with garters and stockings, making tights a vital new option. Already in the early 1940s, American designer Claire McCardell had presented her tunic-jumpers with dance leotards. However, the relatively high cost of producing tights kept them a novelty until the 1960s, when colored tights diffused some of the overt sex appeal of the miniskirt. Soon panty hose had largely replaced stockings and garter belts.

André Courrèges

By 1960, more than half of the world's population was under the age of 25, but it took some time before the

Paris haute couture recognized the emergence of youth style. By the early sixties, however, even couture-trained designers, such as Pierre Cardin and André Courrèges, began designing youthful styles.

When Courrèges presented his autumn 1964 collection, it affected fashion as dramatically as Christian Dior's "New Look" had done in 1947. Courrèges' 1964 collection included stark, modern designs that were futuristic and electrifying. In addition to carefully sculpted tunics and trousers made out of heavy wool crepe, Courrèges created his version of the miniskirt. He paired his shorter skirts with white or colored leather, calf-high boots that added a confident flair to the ensemble. This look became one of the most important fashion developments of the decade and was widely copied. Scores of other designers embraced the miniskirt concept and strove to adapt the look for clients of various ages.

While the miniskirt did not always complement each and every figure, almost every Western woman eventually tried some version of the style during the 1960s. Young women were the first to embrace it, despite resistance from parents and school administrators. The miniskirt became a symbol of the sexual revolution, as the contemporaneous invention of the birth control pill liberated women from the specter of unplanned pregnancies.

Whereas during the early twentieth century short hemlines were associated with prostitutes and theatrical performers, by the 1960s short hemlines were also adopted by "respectable" women. The miniskirt was synonymous with Mod style. By 1969 the miniskirt evolved into the "micro-mini." As Mods gave way to hippies, however, subcultural styles increasingly emphasized long, romantic skirts. By 1970, the fashion industry had launched "midi" and "maxi" skirts, which dominated the following decade.

In the early 1980s, the miniskirt made a comeback, linked again with the power of music and the rise of MTV. Music videos promoted highly charged, sensual images of female performers wearing skimpy clothing. Rap and hiphop performers have promoted their music by using mini-clad women in their videos. The miniskirt, first unleashed by Mary Quant and André Courrèges, has come and gone every few seasons on the fashion runways, but it has become a mainstay of popular culture.

See also Courrèges, André; Quant, Mary; Youthquake Fashions.

Bibliography

Bond, David. *The Guinness Superlatives Guide: 20th Century Fashion*. Middlesex: Guiness Superlatives Limited, 1981.

Buxbaum, Gerda, ed. *Icons of Fashion: The 20th Century*. Munich, London and NewYork: Prestel, 1999.

Ewing, Elizabeth. *History of 20th Century Fashion*. 3rd ed. Lanham: Barnes and Noble Books, 1992.

Glynn, Prudence. *Skin to Skin: Eroticism in Dress*. New York: Oxford University Press, 1982.

Lehnert, Gertrud. *A History of Fashion in the 20th Century*. Cologne: Köneman, 2000.

Lobenthal, Joe. *Radical Rags: Fashions of the Sixties*. New York: Abbeville Press Publishers, 1990.

Myra Walker

MIYAKE, ISSEY*

Issey Miyake was born in Hiroshima, in the southern part of Japan, in 1938. In 1965 he graduated from Tama Art University in Tokyo, where he majored in graphic design. Following graduation, he went to Paris just three months after Kenzo Takada, the first Japanese designer to became successful in France, arrived there. Miyake and Kenzo had known each other in Tokyo, and they studied together at a tailoring and dressmaking school, l'Ecole de la chambre syndicale de la couture. In 1966 Miyake worked as an apprentice under the French couturier Guy Laroche, and two years later he apprenticed at Givenchy.

He then went to New York to work with the American designer Geoffrey Beene before returning to Tokyo, where he founded the Miyake Design Studio in 1970. One of Miyake's New York friends took some of his design samples to *Vogue* magazine and a major department store, Bloomingdale's. Both *Vogue* and Bloomingdale's were enthusiastic about his work, and Bloomingdale's was so impressed that Miyake got a small section in the store. His first small collection in New York included T-shirts dyed with Japanese tattoo designs and *sashiko*-embroidered coats (*Sashiko* is a Japanese sewing technique that gives strength to the fabrics used in clothing designed for workers). In 1973, when French ready-to-wear was institutionalized for the first time as prêt-à-porter, Miyake was invited to Paris to join a group show with such other young designers as Sonia Rykiel and

Founded Japanese Avant-Garde

Miyake laid the foundation in Paris for avant-garde designers worldwide, the Japanese ones in particular. He was showing in Paris long before other Japanese designers, and his presence was further pronounced by the emergence of two influential, norm-breaking designers. Rei Kawakubo, working under the label Comme des Garçons, and Yohji Yamamoto began to present their collections in Paris in 1981 along with the already-established Miyake, who is considered the founding father of the new fashion trend. These three effectively started a new school of Japanese avant-garde fashion, although it was never their intention to classify themselves as such. Kawakubo said in an interview with Olivier Séguret in *Madame Air France*, "We certainly have no desire to create a fashion threesome, but each of us has a strong urge to design new, individual clothes which are recognizably ours" (pp. 140–141). Similarly, Miyake is quoted in Dana Wood's article in *Women's Wear Daily* as follows: "In the Eighties, Japanese fashion designers brought a new type of creativity; they brought something Europe didn't have. There was a bit of a shock effect, but it probably helped the Europeans wake up to a new value" (p. 32).

Miyake was the first to redefine sartorial conventions. His clothing patterns were very different from the Western styles in that he restructured the conventional construction of a garment. As the *Time* magazine writer Jay Cocks observed:

> "Issey," asks one of his friends, standing in the middle of a bustling hotel lobby, "how do I work this?" . . . "I made it like this," says the designer . . . He unbuttons a half-cape that spans the sleeves, and puts the loose ends around his friend's neck. (p. 46)

A student who worked as a dresser backstage at one of Miyake's show in the late 1980s recalled the intricate construction of his garment:

> There was a garment that was totally out of shape and had four holes. You could hardly tell which holes are supposed to be for the arms to go in or the neck to go in. During the rehearsal, Issey's patternmakers would be going around the dressers making sure we knew which hole was for which part of the body. Models usually come running back from the stage to get

changed to the next outfit, and it is our job to help them get dressed as quickly as possible with the right shoes, the right accessories and so on. It's a mad house at the back during the show. At that point, you have no time to think which hole goes where! Some dressers couldn't match the neck to the right hole. It was totally wrong. But who can tell?

In other words, it is up to the wearer to be creative and decide how to wear it. Miyake claims that simplicity is often the key to wearing his clothes, which are versatile enough to be worn in a variety of ways.

Western female clothes have historically been fitted to expose the contours of the body, but Miyake introduced large, loose-fitting garments, such as jackets with no traditional construction and a minimum of detail or buttons. His dresses often have a straight, simple shape, and his large coats with sweepingly oversized proportions can be worn by both men and women. He challenged not only the conventions of garment construction, but also the normative concept of fashion. All of this came at a time when women's clothes by most traditional Western designers were moving in the opposite direction, toward a tighter fit and greater formality. The avant-garde Japanese view of fashion was opposed to the conventional Western fashion. It was not Miyake's intention to reproduce Western fashion, as he pointed out in his speech at the Japan Society in San Francisco in 1984:

> I realized that my very disadvantage, lack of western heritage, would also be my advantage. I was free of Western tradition or convention . . . The lack of western tradition was the very thing I needed to create contemporary and universal fashion.

Sculptor of Fabric

Miyake is best known for his original fabrics. He collaborates with his textile director, Makiko Minagawa, who interprets his abstract ideas. With Minagawa and the Japanese textile mills, he introduced his most commercially successful collection, Pleats Please, in 1993. Traditionally, pleats are permanently pressed before a garment is cut, but he did it the other way round. He cut and assembled a garment two-and-a-half to three times its proper size. Then he folded, ironed, and oversewed the material so that the straight lines remained in place. Finally the garment was placed in a press between two sheets of paper, from which it emerged with permanent pleats (Sato 1998, p. 23).

As early as 1976 Miyake began his concept of APiece-of-Cloth (A-POC), or clothes made out of a single piece of cloth that entirely cover the body. He introduced the line, which evolved from his earlier concept, in 1999. The A-POC clothes consist of a long tube of jersey from which individuals can cut without wasting any material. A large variety of different clothes can be made in this manner; the tubes are manufactured with an old knitting machine controlled by a computer and can be made in large quantities. His objective was to minimize waste by using all leftover material. These garments allow the buyer to size and cut out a small hat, gloves, socks, a skirt, or a dress. Depending on the way the dress is cut, it may appear in two or three pieces. In addition to Miyake's APOC project, new techniques of sewing garments, such as heat taping and cutting by ultrasound, were also featured in his Making Things exhibition at the Fondation Cartier pour l'art contemporain in Paris in 1999.

Place in History

No history of fashion is complete without the mention of Issey Miyake, as he has made a major contribution to the world of fashion. Miyake retired from the Paris fashion scene in 1999, when Kenzo also decided to withdraw from his own brand. In 1999, Naoki Takizawa became head designer of womenswear (as well as of menswear, which he had been designing since

> "I am neither a writer nor a theorist. For a person who creates things to utter too many words means to regulate himself, a frightening prospect."
>
> Issey Miyake quoted in *Issey Miyake Bodyworks* 1983, p. 99.

> "When I first began working in Japan, I had to confront the Japanese people's excessive worship for foreign goods and the fixed idea of what clothes ought to be. I wanted to change the rigid formula of clothing that the Japanese followed."
>
> Issey Miyake quoted in *Issey Miyake Bodyworks* 1983, p.103.

Issey Miyake and Dai Fujiwara exhibit in Berlin, 2001. Japanese designers Issey Miyake and Dai Fujiwara show their A-Pieceof-Cloth (A-POC) designs at the Vitra Design Museum in Berlin, Germany. Each garment item is fashioned from one single piece of fabric. © SEIMONEIT RONALD/CORBIS SYGMA. REPRODUCED BY PERMISSION.

1983). In 2007 Takizawa launched his own brand with the support of Issey Miyake, and was replaced as head designer for Issey Miyake by Daj Fujiwara.

Miyake has said, "I do not create a fashionable aesthetic . . . I create a style based on life" (Mendes and de la Haye 1999, p. 233). He is opposed to the words "haute couture," "mode," and "fashion," because they imply a quest for novelty; over the course of his career he stretched the boundaries of fashion, reshaped the symmetry of clothes, let wrapped garments respond to the body's shape and movement, and destroyed all previous definition of clothing and fashion. It was Miyake who set the stage for the Japanese look in the fashion establishment.

See also Japanese Fashion; Trendsetters.

Bibliography

Cocks, Jay. "A Change of Clothes: Designer Issey Miyake Shapes New Forms into Fashion for Tomorrow." *Time*, January 27, 1986, 46–52.

Holborn, Mark. *Issey Miyake*. Cologne, Germany: Taschen, 1995.

Koike, Kazuko, ed. *Issey Miyake, East Meets West*. Tokyo, Japan: 1978.

Mendes, Valerie, and Amy de la Haye. *20th Century Fashion*. London, New York: Thames and Hudson, Inc., 1999.

Miyake, Issey. Speech delivered at Japan Today Conference in San Francisco, September, 1984.

——. *Issey Miyake and Miyake Design Studio: 1970–1985*. Tokyo, Japan: Oubunnsha, 1985.

Sato, Kazuko. "Clothes Beyond the Reach of Time." *Issey Miyake: Making Things*. Paris: Fondation Cartier pour l'art contemporain 1998, 18–62. An exhibition catalog.

Séguret, Olivier. "Les Japonais." *Madame Air France* no. 5 (1988): 140–141.

Tsurumoto, Shogo, ed. *Issey Miyake Bodyworks*. Tokyo, Japan: Shogakkan, 1983.

Wood, Dana. "Miyake's Lust for Life." *Women's Wear Daily*, December 18, 1996, p. 32.

Yuniya Kawamura

MODERN PRIMITIVES

The Modern Primitive subculture exists primarily in North America and Europe. Members are known for their use of body modifications, such as blackwork tattoos (i.e., heavy black ink applied and reapplied until the color of the skin is completely obscured), three-dimensional implants, scarification, and brands. Utilizing both modern and ancient technology, members often participate in culturally authenticated rituals to achieve the desired body modifications. The subculture's basic ideology is to return to a simpler way of life, which they believe they can achieve through their body modifications.

Modern Primitive History

Modern Primitive subculture members were first evident in the latter half of the 1960s. A self-proclaimed Modern Primitive and body artist, Fakir Musafar, originally named this subculture "Modern Primitive" because "modern" represents this subculture's connection to and place in the contemporary (urban) world, and "primitive" represents the primary or initial (non-Western) cultural groups.

Fakir Musafar is one of the most recognized and publicized members of the Modern Primitive subculture. Naming himself after a nineteenth-century Sufi who wandered through India for nearly two decades with heavy metal objects hanging from his torso's flesh as a spiritual sacrifice, Musafar has numerous body modifications, such as septum, ear, and chest piercings, and blackwork tattoos. Articles in *National Geographic* and other such ethnographies about non-Western cultures, as well as personal visions, inspired many of his body modifications.

Body Modification Technology

Modern Primitive subculture members have distinct appearances because of their extreme body modifications, achieved by a variety of both modern and ancient methods. Not only do members research the design, but some also research the techniques and tools to be used for their body modification. Steve Haworth invented instruments and techniques to insert transdermally or subdermally three-dimensional Teflon and surgical steel implants (for example capture jewelry).

Body Modification Rituals

Some Modern Primitives acquire body modifications by participating in rituals, often inspired by non-Western cultures. For example, Musafar has acquired some of his most notable body modifications from participating in rituals, such as the Kavandi-bearing ceremony, where spears of Siva are placed through the skin to achieve spiritual transcendence; the Hindu Ball Dance, a ritual in which a Sadhu (i.e., an Indian holy man) is pierced by weight-bearing hooks as proof of religious fervor; and the Sun Dance, a Native American ceremony in which a participant is bodily hung from chest piercings as a token of personal sacrifice and endurance. Often the chosen rituals are modified to utilize a chosen technology, to incorporate the participant's spirituality and ideology, and to create the desired body modification. The result is a unique Modern Primitive body modification ritual.

Ideology

Modern Primitives acquire body modifications as rites of passage, spiritual transcendence, and autonomy. Members of this subculture wear their body modifications as evidence of their experiences, often in an attempt to mimic non-Western cultures. Some subculture members claim that participation in these rituals allows spiritual transcendence via enduring the associated pain. Modern Primitives believe that pain is the key to connecting the real truth and the self in the modern world. Body modifications are the link between the contemporary world and the desired "tribal," "pagan," or "primitive."

See also Branding; Goths; Punk; Scarification; Street Style; Tattoos.

Bibliography

Mercury, M. *Pagan Fleshworks: The Alchemy of Body Modification*. Rochester, Vt: Park Street Press, 2000.

Musafar, Fakir. "Body Play: State of Grace of Sickness?" In *Bodies Under Siege: Self-Mutilation and Body Modification in Culture and Psychiatry*. Edited by A. R. Favazza, M.D. Maryland: Johns Hopkins University Press, 1996.

Vale, V. and Juno, A. *Re/Search: Modern Primitives*. Hong Kong: Re/Search Publishers, 1989.

Winge, T. M. "Constructing 'Neo-Tribal' Identities through Dress: Modern Primitives Body Modifications." In *The Post-Subcultures Reader*. Edited by D. Muggleton and R. Wienzeirl. Oxford: Berg, 2003.

Theresa M. Winge

MOORE, DORIS LANGLEY

Doris Langley Moore was one of the foremost scholars and collectors of historic dress in the twentieth century, a cofounder of the Costume Society, and the founder of the Museum of Costume, Bath. Born in Liverpool, England in 1902, Doris Elizabeth Langley Levy spent her youth in Johannesburg, South Africa, where her father worked as a newspaper editor. She returned to England in the early 1920s and published her first book in 1926, the same year in which she married Robin Sugden Moore.

In addition to her significant work in the field of historic clothing, Moore had a long and varied career. She was a successful designer for stage and film; a television commentator; a well-known author of fiction and non-fiction, including biography; and a Byron scholar (in 1962 at Bowood House, Wiltshire, she discovered the Albanian ensemble worn by the romantic writer in a portrait of 1814 by Thomas Phillips). Moore's many achievements were recognized during her lifetime. She was made a Member of the Order of the British Empire in 1971; a Fellow of the Royal Society of Literature in 1973; and she was awarded the Rose Mary Crawshay Prize by the British Academy in 1975. Moore died in London in 1989.

Moore's enduring contributions to the field of costume history include her outstanding collection of men's, women's, and children's dress and accessories, primarily English and Continental, dating from the sixteenth through the mid-twentieth century, and amassed over four decades beginning around 1930; her numerous books, articles, and related publications both on her collection and on the wider subject of dress; and her establishment of the Museum of Costume in 1963, and of the Costume and Fashion Research Centre (a part of the museum) in 1974. At the time of its opening, the Museum had the largest collection of fashionable historic dress on view in Britain. Both the museum and the Research Centre remain important educational and study facilities for scholars, students, and the general public.

Moore's impressive and rigorous connoisseurship encompassed all aspects of dress history, including surviving garments, visual and literary source material, display, and fashion theory. *The Woman in Fashion* (1949) and *The Child in Fashion* (1953), in particular, attest to her detailed knowledge of the silhouette and its evolution, acquired by years of close observation of objects in her own and other collections. Beyond clothing itself, Moore's expertise included the mechanics of the fashion industry and representations of costume in portraits, prints, and fashion plates. In *Fashion through Fashion Plates* (1971), Moore examined both the history of the fashion press and the nature of the plate as an idealized image.

Although she would later change her mind about the appropriateness of using live models for historic dress (as she did in *The Woman in Fashion* and *The*

Child in Fashion), Moore felt strongly about presenting the totality of a given period silhouette, without which she felt the main garment would be meaningless and misunderstood. Her displays at the museum in Bath featured realistic, fully accessorized mannequins, complete with real or simulated hair, set in lively vignettes.

Moore was a pioneer in the study of costume history and instrumental in bringing appreciation of the subject to a popular audience. The perceptive, inquiring, and farranging approach of her scholarship laid the foundation for future dress historians. Moore's publications are still considered important sources of information, and her exemplary costume collection constitutes one of the most important in public institutions worldwide.

See also Fashion, Historical Studies of; Fashion Museums and Collections.

Bibliography

Byrde, Penelope. "Doris Langley Moore, 1902–1989." *Costume* 24 (1990): 149–151.

Moore, Doris Langley. *The Woman in Fashion.* London: B. T. Batsford, 1949.

——. *The Child in Fashion.* London: B. T. Batsford, 1953.

——. *The Museum of Costume Assembly Rooms, Bath: Guide to the Exhibition and a Commentary on the Trends of Fashion.* Bath: Museum of Costume, [1969?].

——. *Fashion through Fashion Plates, 1771–1970.* London: Ward Lock, 1971.

Taylor, Lou. *The Study of Dress History.* Manchester: Manchester University Press, 2002.

Michele Majer

MOURNING DRESS

In the twenty-first century, when family funerals are private and black is worn as a fashion color, it is rarely possible to recognize that a person is in mourning. But in the past, family bereavement involved a series of highly visible public rituals. The use of mourning ceremonial and dress was originally a privilege of the royal courts of Europe from the Middle Ages and was regulated by court protocol through sumptuary laws. Over a period of five hundred years, however, the use of mourning dress spread outward to the rest of society.

Court and National Mourning

At royal funerals, the hearse was accompanied for burial by a vast procession of representatives of the nation's power: the bereaved family, the aristocracy, military, church, and merchants—their mourning dress carefully coded to indicate their gender and social rank. The highest in the land, both men and women, wore the longest mourning trains and hoods in expensive dull black wool, with black or white crape or linen trimmings. Lengths of mourning and details of the requisite dress followed strict royal protocol. Widows, always deeply veiled in public, wore mourning for the longest periods.

National mourning was declared on the death of a sovereign or key political figure. This indicated that black clothing had to be worn for a specific period by established society on formal occasions and whenever royalty was present. In the eighteenth century, this could be as long as a year. After the death of Queen Elizabeth the Queen Mother, on 30 March 2002, Buckingham Palace announced ten days of national mourning in Britain.

Eighteenth Century

Efforts to restrict the use of mourning dress to court use had to be abandoned from the late seventeenth century because wealthy European merchant families, determined to copy aristocratic etiquette, defied sumptuary restrictions, paid any fines imposed, and wore versions of court mourning dress as they pleased. Mourning dress for the wealthy became increasingly fashionably styled, with black coats and breeches for men and mantua dresses for women, in black and half-mourning mauve.

The use of mourning dress, also for reasons of social ambition, next spread slowly to the growing middle classes. Demand across Europe thus expanded and was met through the extensive manufacture of dull black mourning wools, black and white silk mourning crapes, and jewelry. Mourning dress was made up by court and private dressmakers and tailors to suit the specific styles required by these widening consumer groups.

Mourning Dress 1850–1914

By the middle of the nineteenth century, the correct fulfillment of the minutiae of family mourning became a coded and very public sign of middle-class respectability. Etiquette rules escalated. Queen Victoria, widowed at the age of 45 in 1861, wore mourning until her death in 1901. Many other widows and families followed her example, including those of the rising industrial middle classes of Europe and North America.

The weight of participation still fell heavily on widows. A respectable widow wore mourning dress for at least two and a half years after her husband died, while a widower was required only to do so for three months. Other family bereavements were mourned for specific, graduated periods.

Widening the Market

Another reason for this rising tide of mourning wear was its successful commercial exploitation by astute manufacturers who produced etiquette-coded goods priced to suit a wide range of consumers. Thus, from the 1840s, family-mourning dress was provided by couture salons, private dressmakers working at every social level, new department stores, wholesale ready-to-wear manufacturers, and by homemade provision. Speed of supply was essential, encouraging new and well-organized wholesale manufacturing and delivery methods. Advertising struck a balance between enticing wealthy clients and encouraging the less well off. Thus, *Myra's Journal* of March 1876 reassured middle-class customers that "these extremely cheap clothes will look and wear well, a consideration for those whose means are not unlimited." This heavily feminized cult reached a peak between 1880 and 1900.

Commodification Processes

The vast array of products included widow's weeds (crapeladen bodice, skirt, and cape, with black outdoor bonnet and crape veil), indoor caps, fans, underwear, gloves, black-edged handkerchiefs, and a huge array of mourning jewelry, including black jet and "in memoriam" rings, brooches, and lockets. All of these came in three styles for use in first, second, ordinary, and half mourning. The complexities are epitomized by the finesse of descriptions for half-mourning mauve—"violet," "pansy," "scabious," and "heliotrope," none of which were to be confused with the bright purple fashion shade of "Parma violet." For wealthy women, all mourning dress also had to follow the seasonal shifts of fashion set by Paris. Styles thus went rapidly out of date and had to be replaced.

Etiquette Anxieties and Errors

Advice on all of this was offered to the anxious through books and magazines. *Sylvia's Home Journal* in 1881 advised, for example, that mothers should wear black without crape for six weeks after the death of the mothersor fathers-in-law of their married children. Aristocratic families were advised always to travel with complete sets of mourning clothes, because they might be required to wear complementary court mourning if a death occurred in any European royal family. This practice is still maintained by the British royal family.

Altering and Making Do

At the other end of society, from the 1840s, many women purchased simpler and secondhand mourning dress. Many dyed and altered garments. Styles were modified in conformity with the less fashionable expectations of local communities. By 1900, through the growth of ready-to-wear production of women's woolen costumes, black clothing was also directed at the better-off working-class consumer. For the poorest the provision of any sort of mourning dress remained a trauma. Many, unable to afford it, even had to rely on the help of neighbors to avoid the public disgrace of a pauper funeral.

Decline of Mourning Dress

The use of black mourning crape declined steadily from the 1880s, and by the 1930s, widows' veils were already out of use except in Catholic countries and royal circles. After World War II, the provision of mourning dress was no longer a specific branch of the ready-to-wear industry. By the early 2000s family funerals had become so discreet that death barely interrupted the routine of life for both women and men alike. There are no longer "norms" of mourning dress—even among royalty. In 2002, Princess Anne's break with correct royal funeral etiquette was extreme and is so far unique. Taking on a male rather than a female role at her grandmother's funeral, she strode in the funeral procession behind the coffin, alongside the male royal mourners, wearing male military uniform complete with trousers and sword.

Conclusion

The cultural functions of mourning dress as well as the styles thus varied across society. Although Fred Davis writes that "the democratization of fashion was furthered, of course, by major technical advances in the late nineteenth and early twentieth centuries in clothing manufacture" (p. 139), the widening commodification of mourning dress by 1900 in fact reenforced existing social differences through the provision of different qualities of mourning garments and the inability of the poor to afford them at all.

Mourning dress did, however, significantly influence modern processes of garment manufacture, retailing, and consumption. The need for a rapidity of supply helped found department stores and encouraged the wholesale manufacture of women's wear. It enhanced the commercial implementation of the use of sewing machines and early forms of mail order. Mourning etiquette also contributed to the development of early forms of plastic used in imitation of jet jewelry, and finally, the careful niche marketing of mourning dress contributed to the development of modern mass-advertising techniques.

See also Royal and Aristocratic Dress.

Bibliography

Davis, Fred. *Fashion Culture and Identity*. Chicago: University of Chicago Press, 1992.

Mercier, Louis. *Le Deuil, sons observation dans tout les temps et dans tous les pays comparée a son observation nos jours*. London: P. Douvet, 1877.

Taylor, Lou. *Mourning Dress: A Costume and Social History*. London: Allen and Unwin, 1983.

Lou Taylor

COURT MOURNING, FRANCE, FROM *ORDRE CHRONOLOGIQUE DES DEUILS DE LA COUR*, 1765

Widower for wife: total 6 months: first 6 weeks in black wool suit with deep weepers on cuffs; 6 weeks in black suit with silver buckles.

Widow for husband: total 1 year and 6 weeks; first 6 months in black wool trained robe with white trimmings; 6 months in black silk with white crape trimmings, 6 weeks in black and white.

First cousin: total 8 days of ordinary mourning—5 in black and 3 in white.

Translation from Mercier, 1877.

FAMILY MOURNING, FRANCE, 1876

Widower for wife: total 3 months: black suit with black trimmings.

Widow for husband: total 2.5 years: 1 year and 1 day, black wool and crape; 9 months in black wool with less crape; 3 months in black silk; 6 months in half mourning.

First Cousin: total 6 weeks to 6 months: 3 weeks to 3 months in black silk; 6 weeks to 3 months in half mourning.

Translation from Mercier, 1877

MUFFS

The muff, a cylindrical accessory, usually furred, into which the wearer's hands are placed on either side, was called *manchon* in French, *mouffe* in Flemish, and *manicone* in Italian, and was first called snuffkin, skimskyn, and snoskyn in England. Francis Weiss cites the first mention of a snuffkin in 1483 but the earliest image is in the illustration of L'Angloyse in *Receuil de la diversite des habits*, 1567, a small tube attached to the girdle by a cord. Furs per se were not fashionable in the English or French courts in the last thirty years of the sixteenth century, but imported skins for trims and accessories had cachet, and the muff was to prove a popular means of displaying furs and status; in 1583 a skinner named Adam Blande trimmed a velvet snuffkin with five "genette skins." Imported from Africa via Italy, the genet was exotic and expensive. The quantities of skins used suggest that the snuffkins were furred inside and out.

The rich source of fur-bearing animals inhabiting colonized Newfoundland, Canada, and North America provided quantities of beaver for hats and marten, mink, lynx, otter, and fox for dress and what were, by 1601, called muffs (also a double entendre for the female genitalia). Furs provided decoration and interest, contrasting with the undecorated silks worn following sumptuary legislation controlling the use of gold decoration in fabric. In Wenceslaus Hollar's *Winter*, 1641–1644, an English lady of fashion carries a sable or marten fur muff as befits her station, decorated with a ribbon to tie at the waist: "The cold not cruelty makes her weare/In Winter, furs and Wild beasts haire/For a smoother skinn at night/Embraceth her with more delight." Not all muffs were fur, but this contrast between smooth and hairy skins belies the notion of function over fashion and the frisson of sex; Hollar's later studies of muffs show an almost fetishistic interest in the look and feel of furs. Antoine Furetiere in his *Dictionnaire universel*, 1690, defined a muff as a fur object, "originally used only by women; at present, however, men also carry them. The finest muffs are of marten, the less expensive ones of squirrel. The muffs for horsemen are of otter or tiger." Ladies would also carry lapdogs in their *manchons*. The engravings of Bonnard and Jean de St. Jean show men of fashion carrying large muffs in lynx and otter furs suspended from the waist on a belt.

The Hudson's Bay Company was formed in 1670 and provided a supply of furs to a burgeoning middle-class consumer base. In *Mundus Muliebris*, the lady has "three Muffs of Sable, Ermine, Grey (squirrel)," from the most expensive to a cheaper but pretty fur. The rococo period saw delicate muffs in sable, skunk, squirrel, and sea otter, small and barrel-shaped or large and bag-like; in 1765 William Cole noted with disapproval that in Paris "all the world got into Muffs, some ridiculously large and unwieldy." The *Gallerie des modes et costumes français* showed large muffs worn by men and women of fashion in the 1780s, one style, worn to the opera, 1784, called "*d'agitation momentanee.*" More prosaic is Thomas Gainsborough's portrait of the actress Mrs. Siddons depicting a large fox muff, matching the trim of her silk mantle. As a supporter of Charles James Fox, Siddons is showing her political affiliations—as well as being fashionable. The wearers of the light dress fabrics of the revolutionary and early nineteenth century required warm muffs and fashion plates depict ones made from bearskins. By the 1820s and the Romantic period, faux medieval muffs in ermine or the more luxurious chinchilla were imported from Chile and Peru. In the 1860s, the fur coat, the ultimate in conspicuous consumption, became fashionable and muffs were less prominent. Muffs enjoyed revivals in the early twentieth century, when Revillon stocked over a million muffs in their shops and *Vogue* wrote of chinchilla, sable, leopard, mole, ocelot, and monkey muffs (Sears and Roebuck advertised coney, meaning rabbit); but muffs were less of a focus. The all-important fur item, because fur now meant status, was the coat. During World War II, there was a brief return of the accessory, which added a touch of glamour, often reworked from an old fur. American *Vogue* described muffs in 1940, being in skunk, Persian lamb, blue fox, broadtail, mink, and leopard. The muff, however, did not survive the war. They were unsuited to modern women who drove cars, traveled on planes, lived in heated houses, and earned their own living.

See also Europe and America: History of Dress (400–1900 C.E.); Fetish Fashion; Fur.

Bibliography

De Monvel, Boutet. "What's in a Muff?" *Vogue*, 1 November 1916.

Evelyn, Mary. *Mundus Muliebris, or The Ladies Dressing Room Unlock'd.* London: J. Costume Society, 1977. Published privately in 1690.

Ribeiro, Aileen. "Furs in Fashion, the Eighteenth and Nineteenth Centuries." *The Connoisseur*, December 1979.

Uzanne, Octave. *L' Ombrelle, Le Gant, Le Manchon.* Paris: A. Quantin, 1883.

Weiss, Francis. "Furred Serpents, Snuffskins and Stomachers." *Costume* (1973).

Judith Watt

MUIR, JEAN

Born in London, England, in 1928, Miss Muir (as she liked to be called) started her career at Liberty in Regent Street. She worked in sales and as a sketcher (1950–1954) at Liberty, followed by a brief spell at Jacqmar, before joining Jaeger, Ltd., as a designer (1956–1962). She was then invited to design a range of garments in woolen jersey for David Barnes, a collection that was so successful that he formed the company Jane and Jane for her (1962–1966). With her husband, Harry Leuckert, whom she married in 1955, she launched Jean Muir, Ltd., at 22 Bruton Street, London, in 1966. She described herself as a "dressmaker" and acknowledged no influences.

From its inception, the Jean Muir label became associated with virtually timeless designs that flattered but never dominated the wearer. The collections evolved subtly but remained true to Muir's basic ethos: to create clothing that was feminine without being fussy, and classic but devoid of nostalgia. In a 1985 article in British *Vogue*, Muir stated that her style of dressmaking had been developed through an adherence to the anatomy and techniques of dressmaking:

> On that, one diverts, exaggerates, pares down the lines to make the kind of shape and movement

one wants. Then it's a natural eye in terms of shape and colour, a sense of evolving while never losing sight of the structure (p. 118).

Muir's signature fabrics were matte wool crepe and jersey, buttery-soft suede, and ultrasoft leather, which was invariably punched with small holes in decorative borders. Her fluid jersey garments were accented with precise rows of stitched or pin tucks, pleats, smocking, and shirring. Hemlines were determined by proportion rather than fashion. Although she was best known for her dark and neutral palettes, Muir was also a superb colorist. She adored beautiful buttons; for example, her tubular Perspex buttons, which were dyed to match the fabric of the garment they adorned and featured notched sides, were exquisitely restrained.

In addition to her mainline collections, Muir presented "JM in Cotton" from 1978 until about 1985 and "JM in Wool" from 1978 to 1995. In 1986 she launched her lower-priced Jean Muir Studio line, and within this, from the early 1990s, she introduced a capsule collection of well-priced separates in washable jersey called "Jean Muir Essentials." She was an ardent supporter of the United Kingdom's clothing industry.

Muir shared her knowledge of fashion and design by teaching and was a vocal spokesperson for the need to raise standards in education, training, manufacture, and design. Not surprisingly, her contribution to the catalog that accompanied a 1980 traveling exhibition of her designs was an entirely practical essay aimed at students, outlining every stage of the production process. Her many honors include the following: Royal Designer for Industry (1972), Fellow of the Royal Society of Arts (1973), and Fellow, Chartered Society of Designers (1978). She was appointed a Member of the Design Council in 1983; made a Commander, Order of the British Empire in 1984; and received a British Fashion Council Award for Services to Industry in 1985. Muir was inducted into the British Fashion Council's Hall of Fame in 1994.

Following Muir's death in 1995, the company amalgamated the Main and Studio lines under the Jean Muir label. The label's design team, in the early twenty-first century—Sinty Stemp, Joyce Fenton, Angela Gill, and Caroline Angell—jointly have some forty year's experience working with Miss Muir. Since the founder's death they have continued to evolve the line while retaining Miss Muir's signature.

See also Jersey; Leather and Suede.

Bibliography

Bleichroeder, Ingrid. "A Certain Style: Jean Muir." *Vogue* (U.K.), August 1995, 118–119.

Miller, Beatrix. "Obituary: Jean Muir." *Vogue* (U.K.), August 1995, 98–101.

Muir, Jean. *Jean Muir*. Leeds, England: Leeds Art Galleries, 1980. An exhibition catalog.

Amy de la Haye

MUSIC AND FASHION

The relationship between fashion and popular music is one of abundant and mutual creativity. Reciprocal influences have resulted in some of the most dynamic apparel visualizations ever created in popular culture. Some exist as memorable creations for the stage and music video; others become long-lasting fashion trends, which settle in the culture to become noteworthy, referential, and lasting.

Three collaborations exist. One is when fashion designers and entertainment celebrities engineer fashion to fit a declared project. Another collaboration occurs when youth subcultures articulate themselves through fashion. The third is when the fashion industry interprets a musicled theme or trend.

Music celebrities and designer collaborations have altered the course of fashion, though good examples of this relationship are few. The affects of these unions have been very significant. Outcomes include Jean Paul Gaultier's whirlpool corset dress worn by Madonna on her 1990 Blonde Ambition tour, which subsequently contributed to the trend for wearing bra tops and less clothing. Grace Jones's collaborations with the art director Jean-Paul Goude, who in the 1980s rendered Grace Jones's body a fashion object, made groundbreaking music videos and advertisements for various products. However, Grace Jones's haircut became a major trend; it became known as a "high top" when copied by young black youth.

Both Madonna and Grace Jones acted as muses for creative designers; their musical representations became reference points for widespread interpretations. The images produced by these collaborations were decisive, especially in the way they altered conceptions of traditional beauty and gestures.

The outcome of many associations of the performer and the designer or stylist is usually a confirmation of the extant youth subcultural fashion. Rather new perspectives, new methods, and new resonances of fashion are made when fashion and music are linked to subcultural expression.

Consider the partnerships of Kurt Cobain and Grunge, Marilyn Manson and Goth, and Avril Lavigne and Skater. Designer interpretations of performer and subculture expression include Jean Paul Gaultier's facsimile Marilyn Mason (Summer 2003) and Belgian designer Raf Simons's continual referencing of music-led subcultures. Simons's collections have included T-shirts emblazoned with images of the missing Manic Street Preachers guitarist Richey Edwards and a joint effort with Peter Saville, the graphic designer of Factory Records.

This article non-chronologically highlights the main collaborations since the inception of popular music. It is not a comprehensive review; Goth, Skinheads, Northern Soul, Funk, Independent Music, Rock, Grunge, Soul, Dance, and Drum & Bass cultures and collaborations are not considered. Nevertheless, it does demonstrate how innovative music and fashion expression are rooted.

Music's Influence on Fashion

Bobby-soxers. With the birth of rock'n'roll in 1951, youth culture and popular culture gained impetus. In the 1940s, American teenage girls known as bobby-soxers, became famous not only for their fashions, but for their fanatical adulation of male crooners such as Frank Sinatra. Bobby-soxers wore ankle socks, hair ribbons, denim rolled-up jeans, felt poodle skirts with an embroidered and appliquéd French poodle, and blouses with small flounced edging, sloppy sweaters, and saddle shoes. Bobby-soxers were rare in music fashion cultures because males usually led most innovations.

Mods. The idea of intra- and inter-group identification was also important to the Mods, who formed in Britain around 1965 and had a resonant influence on fashion and menswear. They sited themselves in an urban backdrop of espresso bars, Vespa scooters, the mini motorcar, and an image backdrop of Perry Como and the French look, which was influenced by the movie *Shoot the Pianist* (1960). They wore American army parkas over imported American shirts and their suits were tailored. A small number of Mods altered off-the-peg suits or tailored their own suits. Much of the allure of Mod was that fashion designers such as Mary Quant

and Pierre Cardin had the term applied to their work. Graphics symbols such as targets, Union Jacks, horizontal color stripes, and cycling images were appealing to the Mods, fashion designers, and artists. Although Mods were a fusion of teenage groups that had different interests, they were sound sophisticates who had rejected the wooliness and unhewn skiffle and trad music for the poise of modern jazz, and later rhythm and blues, blues, and bluebeat. Mods were fanatical stylist who understood that nodes of change already existed and if they connected them they would become distinct from the rest of society.

In the 1980s, the new wave band the Jam illustrated the divergence of old and new Mod. The music became trashy and aggressive while the look drew on the stereotypical apparel items that already had been diluted by other Mod bands.

During the 1980s and 1990s the legacy of Mod continued in bands such as the Style Council, Blur, and Oasis though the fashion trend had begun to assume cross-cultural references. Sojourns to Ibiza and Morocco, references to Northern soul, and 1970s Regency Mod provided the visual vitality for bands such as the James Taylor Quartet, Brand New Heavies, D'Influence, and Galliano, whose clothes fused with the "ethnicity" of Mod. The new guise, Acid Jazz, became synonymous with the urban modern menswear that included formal and sportswear items.

Retro-Futurism and Neoclassicism

The German band Kraftwerk had underwritten the creative disposition for a number of British bands and the musical styles of Electro, Techno, and Rave. Kraftwerk were influenced by Stockhausen and Italian futurism. Their music encapsulated a metronomic electronic minimalism. Its austere, almost uniformed and metered beats defined a musical soundscape that challenged the conception of music in the way John Cage's ideas about music, noise, and silence did.

During the early 1980s Gianni Versace, Thierry Mugler, and Claude Montana used motifs that included asymmetry, stark bicoloration, and monochromatic uniformity. Fashion shops such as PX and Plaza in London were good examples of how fashion synchronizes with music. Designer Anthony Price's close-fitting uniforms worn by Kraftwerk were indivisible from Price's menswear. Price's London shop, Plaza, was one of the most innovative retail concepts of its day. Price clearly referenced the Retro-Futuristic trend. From outside, neon signage was juxtaposed onto a stark white storefront, and a waist-up view of two android-like shop dummies standing behind the shop window.

These were references to Retro-Futurism and Neoclassicism that were the zeitgeists of that period. Album covers by New Order, Joy Division, and Roxy Music referenced Neoclassicism. Artists such as Gary Numan, Ultravox, and David Bowie were influenced by Kraftwerk and styled themselves in celebration of the Futurist, the Suprematist, and German and Russian Modernist.

The fashions worn by these artists varied from Numan's asymmetric all-in-one uniforms, to Bowie's mid-1970s foray in to monochromatic plain black pants and white shirt, his loose peasant shirts, pants tucked into riding boots, and exceptionally broad leather belt. Ultra-vox's Midge Ure captured a romantic kitsch-heroic characterization that was suitable for inclusion in a Tyrolese peasant painting by Franz von Defregger.

Rave

Techno music was an inheritor of Kratfwerk's music. Techno became a cornerstone of British Rave in the late 1980s. Rave, a loose symbiosis of Chicago House, Electro, and Balearic Beat, started as Acid House in Manchester during 1987, which became known as the second "summer of love." The label was applied to a frenetic period that ushered in the drug Ecstasy (MDMA),

the ascendant of the band the Stone Roses, and Manchester's Hacienda Club, which had become acknowledged as the center of British club culture.

Known for impromptu "happenings" at motorway service stations and on farmland, raves were notorious for the popularization of the drug Ecstasy, which became the essential accompaniment to the movement.

Techno's hypnotic digitized bleeps and sampled hooks drew diverse followers from across the social and racial spectrum. Despite an indefinable constituency, Rave began to define itself as a fashion expression.

Girls wore tight leather or denim pants, waistcoats, fitted T-shirts, and long-sleeved jerkins. Accessories included large silver rings often worn on the thumb and index finger, masses of silver bracelets, and friendship bracelets and leather wristbands like those that hippies wore. Long, lank hair became de rigueur.

Boys were less definable, though many wore fashions by leading designers such as C. P Company, Stone Island, Paul Smith, John Richmond, Nick Coleman, and Armand Basi. Their clothes consisted of Polo shirts, T-shirts, jeans, anoraks, and reflected the current mood of menswear. Certainly, the "clubwear" designer label came of age between 1987 and 1993. However, these labels tended to be cheap, poorly made clothes, although they were perfect for Rave followers who were accustomed to wearing different clothes to "party" in each weekend. Rave personalities, such as Keith of the band Prodigy, communicated a visual sensibility that the second phase (mid-1990s onward) of Rave in Europe, America, and Britain continued. Rave's second phase improved on the intense colorations, silly costumes, and computer graphics that had featured Rave's first phase. Events like Berlin's annual Love Parade, which started in 1992, and designer Walter van Beirendonck's W&LT collection demonstrate how Rave has evolved into a lifestyle form.

Hip-hop and Rastafarians

Occasionally fashion draws directly on music culture for inspiration. Rastafarian music has provided popular culture with an aesthetic that is applicable in a number of forms. Fashion has been a consistent interpreter of Rastafari's fashion iconography. Fashion companies like Complice, Jean Paul Gaultier, and Rifat Ozbek have used the Rastafarian iconography such as the red, gold and green symbolism of Rastafarianism, dredlocked hair, and khaki uniforms, in what the fashion press had called "international ethno-chic." This term could also

Grace Jones's "hightop," 1983. A designer's "muse" and fashion trendsetter, musician Grace Jones displays her "hightop" haircut while being interviewed by nighttime television host David Letterman. © Corbis. Reproduced by permission.

be applied to the collections of Owen Gaster and John Galliano who in 2000 appropriated Jamaican Dancehall and America Fly Girls as the themes for their respective collections.

The summer 2000 advertisements by the Italian fashion label "Versace Jeans Couture," show white models wearing multiple heavy, gold neck chains, a male model wearing a stocking hat, a gold tooth, and low-slung jeans. Here the grittiness of hip-hop fashion is reconstituted, sanitized, and made accessible for the mainstream.

New Romantics

In his 2003 spring/summer runway presentation for Dior, John Galliano referenced New Romantic personalities such as Leigh Bowery and Trojan.

The New Romantics were the most outré fashion-obsessed youth subculture London had ever witnessed. Youth subcultures tend to be motivated by class conflict and evolve fashions to counteract their position; the New Romantics lacked those anxieties. They were "Posers" who did not accept the limited propensity of glamour offered by the Punk movement. The New Romantics were led by Rusty Egan and Steve Strange, who in the late 1970s ran Billy's—A Club for Heroes—, and later Blitz, a wine bar in London's Covent Garden, where they danced to Roxy Music, David Bowie, and Kraftwerk. They developed a series of looks based on romantic themes; in fact, almost any theme was possible if the wearer made the appropriate changes to create an outlandish and weird look. Dressing themes included Russian constructivism, Incroyables, Bonny Prince Charlie, Pirates, 1930s Berlin cabaret, and Hollywood starlet, puritans, and clowns, all heavily and inventively made-up. This alternative fashion expression became tangible and important once designers such as Vivienne Westwood, Stephan Linard, Helen Robinson, Richard Torry, Melissa Kaplan, Bell and Khan, and Rachel Auburn took notice. There were no references for this type of dressing, and no magazines except for *i-D*, *The Face*, and *Blitz*, which featured a review of what people wore in the clubs three months ago. The subculture became the catalyst for a number of new bands. In 1982 two new bands emerged, looking distinctly less weird than many diehard New Romantics. Spandau Ballet and Duran Duran commercially crossed and became accepted by the radio stations, newspapers, and television as the palatable faces and sounds of New Romanticism.

Fashion's Influence on Music

When the British band Wham wore Katherine Hamnett's "Choose Life" T-shirts—a prompt for self-preservation in the middle of the 1980s AIDS crisis—a subtext of protest was being enacted. This call to "revolt into style" was analogous to the Hepcat's bewilderment about society's ordinariness (Cosgrove 1984, pp. 77–91).

African American youth were the first to wear zoot suits and to adopt a number of bodily gestures appropriate to the wearing of a suit, which took five yards of cloth to make. The idea of the revolt into style in youth culture is well founded (Melly 1970). Interpreters of the zoot suit were the early rock'n'roll fans from America, the Caribbean, and Europe. The drape shape of the zoot suit transferred in Britain via photographs of American rock'n'roll stars on albums and other publicity, and through the West Indian migrants who arrived at London's Tilbury Docks in 1948. West Indian migrants to Britain were mainly young people who were influenced by American movies, music, and fashion. They wore clothes that were more vivid in shape and color than anything the British had been accustomed to. Fashion and music melded together in attempts to disengage its participants from the procession of tradition. A small number of Savile Row tailors had reintroduced the Edwardian look in 1948; it became popular with young upper-class men Londoners called Guardees. Subsequently, working-class youth groups, the Cosh boys and late in the 1950s the Teddy Boys, began to indicate their discontent with society's norms by adopting dandies narcissistic tendencies. They copied the style of the Guardees by wearing long jackets that were cut in a drape shape with velvet collars and cuffs, bright ankle socks, slim ties, and drainpipe trousers that were similar to those worn at the time of Edward VII (1901–1910). The clothes of early American rock stars such as Bill Haley, Gene Vincent, Little Richard, and Elvis Presley drew from and exaggerated the prevailing fashion aesthetic of black America, the drape silhouette. Also from the Mississippi riverboat gambler, blue-collar worker styles that included youth culture's omnipresent blue denim jeans with rolled cuffs, leather biker jackets, biker boots, a chain, and a white T-shirt were evident. Detractors labeled the status of the rock'n'roll musicians to being outside of the mainstream and to label the fashion adoptions, music and dance moves as being aligned to "the devil."

Punk

Punk rock was of the most influential and stimulating collaborations of fashion and music. It served as a pivotal catalyst for the way people in the 2000s think, create, and comment on fashion, music, and design.

Punk started in London during the 1970s and almost simultaneously became a musical genre, a fashion expression, and a way of life. Although bands such as the Slits, the Dammed, the Clash, and the Banshees were important, the Sex Pistols became the preeminent band of the genre. The fashions and the attitude of punk were on display in Malcom Maclaren's Kings Road store called Sex, and later, Seditionaries. Maclaren and his partner, Vivienne Westwood, sold clothing that was dislocated from the accepted idea of what fashion should be. The spectacle of the punk was attained by using forthright images out of context, thereby creating a distortion. Consequently, punk fashions shocked and intimidated. Punk's iconic fashion items included Maclaren and Westwood's replica of the Cambridge rapist mask, T-shirts emblazoned with corny playing card pin-up girls, homosexual cowboys, shirts with a Nazi swastika, and T-shirts of the Queen of England's face corrupted with a safety pin through her nose. All of the punk bands wore similar clothes with images that were taboo; this included torn clothes, fetish clothes, and even clothes with simulated bloodstains.

Hippies

Punk was a reaction against the hippie culture, which became accepted as the pinnacle of youth rebellion.

The hippies were a 1960s folk- and rock-led movement that propagated an alternative perspective for living. According to one hippie commentator, "Hippy fashions originated from used-clothes bins, army/navy stores, and handmade clothes from scraps. In other words, whatever was cheap and available. . ." (New York Sun: 25, July, 2002). Clothes also originated from the Hippie trail, which passed through Turkey, Iran, Afghanistan, and Pakistan to India and Nepal.

During the 1980s and the 2000s, mainstream fashion design and rock music youth cultures adopted the hippie look. In the 1980s, the Italian designer Romeo Gigli used rich Indian embroideries and delicate prints and handwork to create soft and romantic themes that are seen in hippie dress. Marni, another Italian design company, has used the hippie theme exclusively in a brand that is elite and expensive and is therefore the antithesis of hippie ideology.

Fashion Catalysts

Music offers fashion more than a theme or a movement. Occasionally, a performer possesses fashion awareness that directly influences fashion.

As catalysts of fashion change (1973–1980s), David Bowie and Bryan Ferry experimented with new themes, beliefs, and values. Bowie's alter ego, Ziggy Stardust, wore elaborate costumes designed by avant-garde designer Kansai Yamamoto. The garments were not made exclusively for Bowie; they were simply part of Yamamoto's ready-to-wear collection. Bowie's fans reinterpreted the Ziggy look by wearing street clothes of the period. The ensemble consisted of high-waist pants, platform shoes, and brightly colored shirts and tank tops, which were occasionally bought from women's stores for their colors and tight fit. Ferry's various costumes included a Cosmic rocker look of a metallic leopard-skin bomber jacket and black silk trousers; the 1950s Rocker with black pants, dark blue T-shirt, and neck chain; and the lounge lizard clad in a white tuxedo, black bow tie, white shirt, and red cummerbund. He also dressed as an Army G.I., wearing khaki shirt and pants; a Neoclassic storm trooper; a gaucho, complete with gaucho pantaloons, a vest and shirt with wide sleeves and a black hat; and a 1960s soul singer, wearing a three-buttoned suit in various colors and materials, including leather and shark-skin. In many ways, 1970s disco provided exception of a music-led movement that

---

REBELLIOUS FASHION

In 2001 the Belgian designer Raf Simons paid homage to the Welsh band the Manic Street Preachers. The menswear collection feature oversized shirts and sweaters adorned with marxist slogans. The manics were not the first music group to wear political iconography (the Sex Pistols wore Lenin) but Simons's adoration of the Manics and of the politics of rebellion was a first in high fashion. (Porter, 2001)

comprehensively affected fashion. Existing at the same time as glam rock, disco had spread through much of the West. In America and Britain it had achieved the alliteration of a spectacle that fluently contorted across the age gap and from stage to the discothèque to the street.

Fashion and music proficiently and often independently create similar themes, yet the dynamic interaction between them motivates reactions that might not have otherwise occurred. The mistlike phenomenon of sub-cultural fashion holds apparel and popular music in totemic significance, creating fantastic fashion objects and moments from these restless forms. Formalized fashion is bound by an emphatic trepidation and terror. Its praxis and natural impulse is to conduct the activity of objectifying popular music, youth subcultures, and other "sexy" forms. This is why developments away from orthodox or formalized fashion customs can only be made when the agenda is no longer centered on the commerce of fashion, but is concerned with the irreverence and irrationality of making fashion images.

See also Hippie Style; London Fashion; Punk.

Bibliography

Conrad, Peter. "Tommy, We Can Hear You." *Independent On Sunday.* (30 March 1997).

Cosgrove, Stuart. "The Zoot-Suit and Style Warfare." *History Workshop Journal.* 18 (Autumn 1984): 77–91.

de La Haye, Amy and Cathie Dingwall. *Surfers, Soulies, Skinheads, and Skaters: Street Styles from the Forties to the Nineties.* Woodstock, N.Y.: Overlook Press, 1996.

Graev, Nicole. "What's Next: MTA-Chic? Talks to the True Originators of Today's Fashions." *New York Sun,* (25 July 2002).

Haug, W. F. *Commodity Aesthetics, Ideology and Culture.* International General, 1987.

Lusane, Clarence. "Rap, Race, and Politics." *Race and Class: A Journal for Black and Third World Liberation* 35, no. 1 (July-September 1993): 41–56.

Melly, George. *Revolt into Style: The Pop Arts.* Doubleday and Company, 1971.

Polhemus, Ted, and Lynn Procter. *Pop Styles.* London: Vermilion, 1984.

Porter, Charlie. "What a Riot." *The Guardian,* (6 July 2001).

Van Dyk Lewis

N

NAIL ART

Beautiful nails are considered to be a precious gift to be treasured and cared for. In Greek mythology Eros is identified as the first manicurist. He cut the goddess Aphrodite's fingernails while she was sleeping and scattered them on the beaches of the earth. Seeing what had transpired, the fates collected the clippings and turned them into the semiprecious stone onyx—that is Greek for fingernail. In fact, human nails—the convex, hard horny plates covering the dorsal aspect of the fingertips and toes—have evolved from the primeval claw. In folkloric beliefs, the nails are often said to continue growing after death, temporarily evading mortal decay. Thus, long nails are characteristic of vampires, revenants, and others of "undead" status. The phenomenon is in fact due to the dehydration of the corpse which causes the skin around the nails to retract and shrink back, but the alarming effect of this particular aspect of decomposition has inspired countless morbid horror stories where sorry individuals who have been buried alive attempt to scratch their way out of the tomb. Nails, along with bones, hair, and teeth of the dead were, as Sir Thomas Browne noted in the seventeenth century, "the treasures of Old Sorcerers" and one of the oldest forms of poisoning was grated nail, which was slipped into an unsuspecting victim's food or wine. Even today people take care to disinfect a human scratch, perhaps because nails actually do contain a small percentage of arsenic.

The Origins of Manicuring

The practice of manicuring is itself extremely ancient. There is evidence that as far back as 4,000 years ago, manicures took place in southern Babylonia, and manicure instruments have been found in Egypt's royal tombs. The Romans painted their nails with a mixture of sheep fat and blood. Turkish women created a pink tint for the nails from boiled rose petals. Women in biblical times not only dyed their hair but also painted their fingernails and toenails as well as hands and feet with henna juice (as mentioned in the Song of Solomon), a practice that still forms part of Middle Eastern culture today. The custom of growing long nails relates to status, since it can preclude certain forms of manual labor. Chinese noblemen and women of the Ming Dynasty (1368–1644) were well known for their extraordinarily long fingernails, which were sometimes protected with gold and jewel-encrusted nail guards. Servants were required to feed, dress, and perform other personal chores for them so that they did not break a nail. The Chinese also used nail polish made from egg whites, beeswax, vegetable dyes, and Arabic gum.

In the Western Hemisphere colored nail polish was uncommon until the twentieth century. Instead, unstained hands with white and regularly formed nails were esteemed as part of a dominant aesthetic linking physical hygiene and moral purity. Etiquette guides from the 1800s recommend a little lemon juice or vinegar and water to whiten the nail tips and commercial products available at this time included nail polishers or buffers, crystal stones, emery boards, hand and cuticle creams, pearly white liquid, and several kinds of bleaching powders for the hands and nails. This apparent lack of adornment was an obvious indicator of wealth and enforced leisure. Emma Bovary's nails for instance are "scrubbed cleaner than Dieppe ivory and cut almond shape." Such fastidious treatment of the nails was in keeping with the anti-cosmetics stance, which professed a belief in the transparency of inner beauty and continued well into the early 1900s.

The Innovation of Nail Polish

Hollywood film did more than any other visual medium to popularize the wearing of nail polish in the West. Film actresses of the 1920s looked exotic, symbolized modernity, and flaunted nails that were painted with colorful glossy enamel that soon became commercially available. In a literal sense, the new

Cutex brand advertisement. This "cute tomato" poster advertises a red nail color by Cutex. AP/WIDE WORLD PHOTOS. REPRODUCED BY PERMISSION.

lacquer was derived from the movies since cinematic film and nail polish originate from the same primary ingredient—nitrocellulose. One early method of making nail polish was to mix cleaned scraps of film with alcohol and castor oil and leave the mixture to soak overnight. The first tinted nail lacquers were produced in subtle shades of pink and had names like "rose," "ruby," "coral," and "natural" in an attempt both to downplay the chemical origins of the product and to overcome the monochrome format of contemporary advertising. Deep color polishes like cardinal red were unavailable until the 1930s, when Charles Revson and his partners developed a method to add opaque pigments (rather than dyes) to polish so that it would coat the nails evenly.

Their company, Revlon Inc., still one of the leading producers of nail polish, became particularly famous for its legendary 1950s "Fire and Ice" advertising campaign. These ads for a range of matching nail enamels and lipsticks were groundbreaking in their use of dramatic

visuals and clever text and are considered to be among the first to overtly link cosmetics with sexuality. A typical headline ran "For you who love to flirt with fire . . . Who dare to skate on thin ice." Like much cosmetic advertising of the period, Revlon's marketing exploited a range of connotations of nail decoration. Painted nails were part of the self-scrutinizing feminine masquerade that was dependent on male approbation, but they were also associated with increasingly liberal ideas about a pleasure-seeking modern woman.

Nail Art Today

The last few decades have seen further innovations and fashions in Western nail art. Manufacturers have created quick-drying polishes targeted at women with active lifestyles, and the range of colors available has multiplied. From the 1980s onward brightly colored polish has been available in unusual colors ranging from ice-cream pastels to gunmetal gray, along with polishes that contain built-in decorations such as glitter or tiny metallic stars. In 1995 Chanel brought these colors firmly into the mainstream when it launched a deep black-red polish. "Vamp" continued the Hollywood connection when the actress Uma Thurman in the film *Pulp Fiction* wore it that same year. Priced at $15 a bottle, Chanel's polish helped to create a market for high-priced nail products and paved the way for the success of companies like Urban Decay and Hard Candy—which made huge profits from manufacturing odd experimental colors for nails. In 1998 the American Jenai Lane created "mood nail polish" which is designed to change color according to body temperature—in reflection of one's mood.

Over $6 billion is spent on services in American nail salons every year and the art of the manicurist has become increasingly prized worldwide. Men as well as women are now regular clients since well-kept hands are considered to be an important part of a professional image. New technologies have also resulted in more realistic-looking acrylic nails and nail extensions, which are attached with glue adhesives and glue tabs. At the fantasy end of the market, fingernails and toenails have become a natural canvas for the expression of creative imagination. Nail art is often stunningly elaborate—nails can be sculpted, stenciled, pierced, and of course painted with intricate designs. Competitions such as the Nail Olympics held annually in Las Vegas honor the art of the manicurist—as a latter-day miniaturist painter—and indicate the growing professionalization of the industry. In Britain and the United States, contemporary nail art resonates particularly with black culture. In this context elaborately painted nails are seen to offer a highly decorative alternative to Eurocentric ideals of beauty.

See also Cosmetics, Western; Cosmetics, Non-Western.

Bibliography

Blackmore, Colin, and Sheila Jennett. *The Oxford Companion to the Body.* Oxford: Oxford University Press, 2001.

Browne, Thomas. *Urne Buriall and The Garden of Cyrus.* Edited by John Carter. London and New York: Cambridge University Press, 1958 (originally published in 1658).

Corson, Richard. *Fashions in Makeup from Ancient to Modern Times.* London: Peter Owen, 1972.

Flaubert, Gustave. *Madame Bovary.* London: Penguin Books, 1985 (originally published in French, 1856).

Mulvey, Kate, and Melissa Richards. *Decades of Beauty: The Changing Image of Women 1890s–1990s.* London: Hamlyn, 1998.

Peiss, Kathy. *Hope in a Jar: The Making of America's Beauty Culture.* New York: Henry Holt and Company, Inc., 1998.

Sherrow, Victoria. *For Appearance's Sake: The Historical Encyclopaedia of Good Looks, Beauty and Grooming.* Westport, Conn.: Oryx Press, 2001.

Tobias, Andrew. *Fire and Ice: The Story of Charles Revson—The Man Who Built the Revlon Empire.* New York: William Morrow and Company, Inc., 1976.

Katherine Forde

NAUTICAL STYLE

Nautical refers to the sea and to ships. There is a romantic image of life on the sea reflected in a navy jacket with brass buttons, a crisp white sailor's uniform, a sou'wester hat and yellow slicker, or a fisherman's sweater. All sailors and those whose occupation depends on the sea deal with the unpredictable nature and allure of the sea. Protection from the salt water, wind, and sun is a primary consideration along with allowing the mobility needed to perform the duties of their job on a ship among the ropes, nets, and sails. Historic traditions in nautical dress continue to influence modern nautical apparel.

Occupational Sailing

The "Jack-tar" describes a sailor of sixteenth century Europe who wore a waist-length tarred leather jacket and hat for water protection. To facilitate movement on the ships, loose breeches called "slops" and tunics of canvas or coarse linen were worn. The slops were often striped or red in color. In addition, a tar-coated canvas petticoat called a tarpaulin was often worn over the slops during rough weather. A neckerchief and knitted woolen cap provided additional protection for the head. The tarred jacket has evolved into the classic pea coat of today, while the tarpaulin remained prevalent with fishermen through the nineteenth century.

With the birth of an official Navy uniform in England during the mid-eighteenth century, there was a more noticeable distinction between the occupational dress of a sailor and a fisherman. Blue and white with gold and silver trim for officers was the designated color palette for the Navy. This was the origination of the term "navy blue." Later in the century, American-tar wore a short blue or black-tarred jacket, cropped trousers with a knitted striped shirt, and neckerchief. Sailor hats were now made of oilcloth, a recent innovation in waterproofing that treated cotton or linen with boiled linseed oil. The oilcloth was also used in bib trousers and jackets, their yellow color serving as a safety feature for sailors who were blown overboard. A knitted wool gansey or jersey became popular during the mid-eighteenth century. These tightly knitted sweaters button on one shoulder and were patterned to represent the town of the sailor. Solid colors were reserved for naval officers, while the sailors wore stripes. The jerseys were often embroidered by the sailors with the name of the ship on the front chest.

Naval uniforms continued to evolve during the nineteenth century with the use of the sailor collar and black neckerchief that mimicked the wide collar points and black cravat worn by fashionable gentlemen. Sailors maintained variations of the blue waist-length jacket and white trousers while officers wore a gold-trimmed coat that was short in the front with tails in the back. Twenty-first-century naval officers have a white dress uniform of jacket and trousers with brass buttons and epaulets, while their service uniform is built of a navy blue jacket and pants with white shirt and black tie. The enlisted sailor wears white trousers and a tunic with a sailor collar and black tie. It is affectionately referred to as a "monkey suit" (Wilcox 1963, p. 82). Present-day commercial fishermen consider function and safety with their use of insulated layers of fleece and waterproof hooded-jackets and pants. Orange and yellow gear provides good visibility in case of a water rescue.

Recreational and Competitive Sailing

Traditional sailing garments have had a large influence on recreational and sport sailing apparel. Sailing as a competitive sport is marked by the first international yachting event, the Hundred Guineas Cup, in 1851, and its Olympic debut in 1896. The term yacht evolved from the Dutch "jaghtschiffs," which were boats designed to chase pirates. Yacht clubs developed to encourage and support the sport of sailing. Dress for most active recreational sailors needs to provide the same function and mobility required of professional sailors. Navy blue, white, red, and yellow are garment colors associated with both professional and recreational sailors. Navy jackets with brass buttons are a popular image, borrowed from the Navy, for the more social yacht-club member.

Traditional sailing garments have also been a popular influence for generations of children's garments. Sailor suits are a classic design for both boys and girls that began during the mid-nineteenth century when Queen Victoria began dressing her children in the style. It spread quickly through Europe and America, continuing to be a classic children's style in the twenty-first century along with the middy blouse.

Women in Sailing

Women have historically been on shore professionally until 1942 when the U.S. Navy began to allow women to serve in positions on ships. Their uniforms were similar in style to the men's with the addition of a skirt. A 1931 *Vogue* cover shows a woman in full bell-bottom navy slacks with a red, white, and blue striped top designed for lounging rather than rough seas. A later 1956 image shows a woman on a small dinghy wearing cropped denim jeans, a white "sloppy joe," white deck shoes, and red bandanna on her head. This outfit is intended to be comfortable and functional, but designed only for good sailing conditions. Women have dramatically increased their skill and participation in competitive sailing. Dawn Riley led the first all-women's America's Cup team in 1995 and was the first female member of the winning America 3 team in 1992.

New Developments in Sailing

The garments worn by competitive sailors in the twenty-first century have the same requirements of protection from the elements and good mobility. However, innovative fiber and textile developments can now better protect the body, increase health and safety, and improve the wearer's sailing efficiency. Though wool has traditionally been the fiber used for insulation and water protection, apparel-layering systems take advantage of new fiber technology to help maintain the body's thermal balance. The first layer uses olefin to wick away moisture from the skin, while polyester fleece acts as an insulating layer to trap body heat. The outer-layer fabrics, such as Gore-Tex, provide a waterproof, yet breathable barrier from water and wind. The use of spandex, a fiber with stretch, in the first two layers allows for garments that fit closer to the body while allowing a greater freedom of mobility.

See also Jacket; Military Style; Rainwear.

Bibliography

Cunnington, Phillis, and Catherine Lucas. *Occupational Costume in England from the Eleventh Century to 1914*. New York: Barnes and Noble, 1967.

Lee-Potter, Charlie. *Sportswear in Vogue since 1910*. New York: Abbeville Press, 1984.

Wilcox, R. T. *Five Centuries of American Costume*. New York: Charles Scribner's Sons, 1963.

Internet Resources

Naval Influences on Boys' Clothing. Naval Uniforms and Boys' Clothing. Available from <http://histclo.hispeed.com/youth/mil-navy.html>.

Olympic History: Sailing. Available from <http://cbs.sportsline.com/u/olympics/2000/history/sailing.htm>.

Elizabeth K. Bye

NECKTIES AND NECKWEAR

Though the origins of wearing cloth tied around the neck lie embedded in antiquity (Chaille 2001), most scholars concur that it was the Thirty Years' War (1618–1648) that cemented the practice within European cultures. Fought between Sweden and France on one side and the Hapsburg Empire on the other, the conflict introduced French soldiers to the loose-tied neckerchiefs of Croatian soldiers, which some continued to wear once they had returned home.

Nevertheless, disagreement shrouds the etymology of the word "cravat," a derivative of the French *cravate*, which denotes modern neckties, men's scarves, and neckbows. While some sources—including the Oxford English Dictionary—make a direct link between *cravate* and *croate*, others are more circumspect, looking instead to the Turkish *kyrabàc*, the Hungarian *korbàcs*, and the French *cravache*, all of which relate to long, slender or whiplike objects (Mosconi and Villarosa 1985).

Linguistic roots aside, there is consensus that 1650 was the key point at which neckwear became a distinctive feature of western men's dress. It has been suggested that its popularity was further enhanced by a climatic factor known as the "Maunder minimum," which saw temperatures dip especially low between 1645 and 1705 (Chaille 1994).

The Battle of Steinkirk in 1692 introduced the "Steinkirk" to fashionable Europeans. Consisting of a long scarflike cravat with ends of fringe or lace that were looped through the buttonhole of the jacket (Fink and Mao 1999), it was also popular with women who would sew buttonholes into their gowns to accommodate the loose ends, or simply tuck them into the laces of their corsets (Chaille 1994). The Steinkirk had a continuing presence in portraiture long after its real-life popularity had waned, for artists such as Joshua Reynolds and Thomas Gainsborough often painted their subjects wearing the attire of their predecessors (Gibbings 1990).

By the early eighteenth century the soft flamboyance of the Steinkirk was replaced by yet another style with military origins. Popularized by French and German foot soldiers at the end of the seventeenth century, by 1700 the stock had been adopted by civilians (Colle 1974). Originally consisting of a piece of white muslin folded into a narrow band, wound once or twice around the neck and fastened at the neck with tapes, buttons, or a detachable buckle (Hart 1998), the stock developed into a simple high collar stiffened with horsehair, whalebone, pig bristle, card, or even wood covered in cloth (Gibbings 1990). While it did impart a stiff, formal posture, it was ultimately an uncomfortable and unhealthy style because it restricted the throat (Gibbings 1990). However, stylistic formality evolved into a softer, more decorative style when black ribbons used to tie the hair

back were brought to the front and tied in a bow known as a solitaire, creating a contrast with the white stock beneath it (Fink and Mao 1999).

The next significant development came in the 1770s, championed by a group of young English aristocrats dubbed the Macoronis. Influenced by styles they had seen while travelling in Italy, they took to wearing white cravats with voluminous bows (Chaille 1994). In France, in the 1790s, young men known as the *Incroyables* (or Unbelievables) displayed their contempt for sartorial conventions by wearing clothing with exaggerated proportions, including huge cravats consisting of fabric wound around the neck up to ten times (Fink and Mao 1999).

The extravagance of the late 1700s gave way to a quest for simple elegance in the early nineteenth century, exemplified by dandyism in general and George Bryan Brummell (1778–1840) in particular. The key to "Beau" Brummell's style lay in understatement. Though decidedly middle-class in origin, he attained an aristocratic air through an obsessive emphasis on the cut, detail, and refinement of his clothing. Immaculate, starched cravats were central to his self-presentation and he is said to have spent hours perfecting the art of knotting, pleating, folding, and arranging them (Gibbings 1990). The popularity of cravats at this time gave rise to publications that detailed ways of tying them. Published in 1818, *Neck-clothitania* presented 12 styles, *L'Art de se mettre sa cravate* described 32, and *L'Art de la toilette* outlined 72.

Around the time of Brummell's death in 1840, cravats became politicized as proponents of white cravats—affiliated with traditionalism—took on those who favored black cravats, which were associated with liberal politics (Chaille 1994). Ultimately, it was the black stock and cravat, made popular by the English monarch George IV (who reigned from 1820 to 30) that triumphed, although red ones—briefly fashionable with French and German revolutionaries in 1848— never gained much of a following in English society (Chaille 1994).

As the nineteenth century progressed, high-buttoned jackets became popular, making large, complicated cravats difficult to accommodate. Moreover, as increasing numbers of men joined the office-based workforce, few had the time to spend on the knotting and arranging of neckwear. While ready-made neckwear may have offered convenience, the higher echelons of English society remained disdainful of such practices (Hart 1998). Yet the growing diversification of the workforce, prompted by the industrial revolution, fostered a proliferation of neckwear styles by the late 1800s.

Ultimately, the cravat of the nineteenth century gave rise to four main styles: the bow tie, scarves and neckerchiefs, the Ascot, and the four-in-hand or long tie (Hart 1998). Developments in photography since the mid-nineteenth century have allowed costume historians to examine neckwear from this period onward in detail, and nineteenth-century visiting cards—often showing just the head and shoulders—have proved an invaluable resource to researchers (Ettinger 1998).

Evolving from some of the popular Regency styles, the bow-tie diminished in size so that by the end of the nineteenth century, two dominant shapes were recognizable: the butterfly and the bat's wing (Fink and Mao 1999), both of which have an ongoing presence in men's attire even today, but especially in the context of formal wear.

Scarves and neckerchiefs, by contrast, tend to be associated with the working classes who originally wore them out of necessity. Popular with both men and women and typified by a square shape folded into a triangle, scarves may be knotted in dozens of ways to protect and decorate the throat (Mosconi and Villarosa 1985).

Similar to the Gordian cravat of the early nineteenth century, the Ascot became popular in the 1880s when the upper middle classes of English society started to wear it to the Royal Ascot race and other outdoor events (Hart 1998). Initially made of plain silk, the Ascot had square-ended blades that were crossed over the shirtfront and held in place with a cravat pin. Many were sold readymade in very bright colors (Gibbings 1990).

The long tie or vertical tie originated as young men's sporting attire in the 1850s, but became widespread within a decade (Fink and Mao 1999). More than one explanation is given for its alternative name, the four-in-hand. Some believe it to be a reference to the Four-in-Hand Club, a London gentlemen's club whose members tied their neckwear using the four-in-hand knot (Fink and Mao 1999), while others suggest that its knot and trailing ends resembled the reins of four-horse carriages driven by members of the English aristocracy (Chaille 1994). Early versions of this style of tie were simple rectangular strips of material with identical square ends that reached no lower than the sternum as waistcoats were usually worn (Chaille 1994). Practical because it neither impeded movement nor came undone, it was adopted both by workers and by the leisure classes as high, stiff collars gave way to soft, turned-down ones.

As the Victorian middle class grew and male attire became increasingly homogenous (dark, somber coat and jacket and trousers in a limited range of cuts), ties became a signpost of social status (Gibbings 1990). Evolution of the club, school, and regimental ties meant that those in the know were able to identify a man's social ranking based primarily on the color and pattern of the tie they wore. Even in the twenty-first century, some sectors of British society still believe that the stripes on one's tie define an individual to himself and to others (Sells 1998), and the expression "old school tie" persists, reflecting membership of a specific, privileged class.

Although women had worn cravats and scarves in various forms alongside their male contemporaries primarily out of coquetry (Chaille 1994), it was in the late nineteenth and early twentieth century that neckwear took on a politicized significance. The evolution of Rational Dress encouraged women to adopt attire that not only allowed greater freedom of movement but also was essentially more masculine in appearance (Gibbings 1990). As the women's suffrage movement gained momentum, the tie—when worn by women—became a symbol of independence and feminist convictions (Chaille 1994).

Already established as the most popular form of men's neckwear in the early part of the twentieth century, the four-in-hand's success was cemented commercially by an American named Jesse Langsdorf. He improved the drape, elasticity, and wear of ties by cutting them diagonally (at 45 degrees) on the bias instead of cutting the fabric conventionally in an up-and-down direction. The process of constructing a tie from three separate pieces of material, known as Resilient Construction, was patented by Langsdorf's company, Resilio, in 1924 (Ettinger 1998). Though knitted ties, or Derbys, attained a degree of popularity in the early part of the twentieth century, Resilient Construction essentially brought the evolution of the modern necktie to a halt (Chaille 1994). Since then tie widths have fluctuated from two to five inches, although the usual width continues to be three to three-and-a-half inches (Fink and Mao 1999).

With shape and dimension more or less fixed since the 1920s, mass-production methods ensured that ties were readily available to men from all socioeconomic groups. With the onset of the Great Depression in the United States during the late 1920s and early 1930s, business slowed down; however, the widespread popularity of cinema contributed to a boom in tie sales as

Americans sought to emulate their film idols (Ettinger 1998). Images of actresses such as Marlene Dietrich and Katharine Hepburn wearing ties remain some of the most iconic and memorable in cinematic history, demonstrating the potent impact of a woman wearing what had become a quintessentially male item (König 2001). In the United Kingdom, meanwhile, society figures such as the Duke of Windsor were influential, and the Windsor Knot became a popular method of tie-knotting (Chaille 1994).

As the twentieth century unfolded, variety in neckwear continued primarily through the changing use of fabric and color. Developments in textile technology, particularly throughout the 1930s and 1940s, meant that traditional fibers such as silk, wool, and cotton gave way to synthetic yarns including rayon, nylon, and polyester as they were cheaper and therefore well-suited for mass production (Goldberg 1997). Yet tie aficionados would argue that woven silk, possibly blended with wool, continues to be the most suitable fabric for a tie because of the "hand" that it gives (Chaille 2001).

Though wartime rationing in Europe during and after World War II (1939–1945) put a hold on nonessential manufacturing, in the United States, the tie market flourished with stripes, plaids, and other patterns making an appearance (Ettinger 1998). In the postwar years, however, men on both sides of the Atlantic sought flamboyance, leading to a proliferation of brightly colored ties known as the Bold Look (Goldberg 1997). Popular designs in the 1950s included those with an Art Deco influence, flower and leaf prints, wildlife themes, and "Wild West" designs (Ettinger 1998).

In the latter half of the twentieth century, ties ceased to be an essential component of everyday menswear, and were no longer seen as the definitive signifier of respectability. As youth culture liberated young men from the sartorial conventions of their parents, the tie became an occasional item to be worn at school (by girls as well as boys), work, and formal events (Chaille 2001). Having said this, distinctive styles, such as skinny "mod" ties and wide "kipper" ties of the 1960s, have earned their place in fashion history, complementing the stylistic characteristics of the suits they accompanied (Goldberg 1997). Despite a global drift toward casual dress, it seems likely that neckwear, and specifically the tie, will continue to have a presence in men's dress.

See also Dandyism; Europe and America: History of Dress (400–1900 C.E.); Military Style; Sports Jacket.

Bibliography

Chaille, François. *The Book of Ties*. Paris: Flammarion, 1994.
——. *The Little Book of Ties*. Paris: Flammarion, 2001.
Colle, Doriece. *Collars, Stocks, Cravats: A History and Costume Dating Guide to Civilian Men's Neckpieces, 1655–1900*. London: White Lion Publishers Ltd., 1974.
Ettinger, Roseann. *20th Century Neckties: Pre-1955*. Atglen: Schiffer Publishing Ltd., 1998.
Fink, Thomas, and Yong Mao. *The 85 Ways to Tie a Tie: The Science and Aesthetics of Tie Knots*. London: Fourth Estate, 1999.
Gibbings, Sarah. *The Tie: Trends and Traditions*. London: Studio Editions, 1990.
Goldberg, Michael Jay. *The Ties That Bind: Neckties, 1945–1975*. Atglen: Schiffer Publishing Ltd., 1997.
Hart, Avril. *Ties*. London: V&A Publications, 1998.
König, Anna. "Tie Me Up, Tie Me Down." *The Guardian* 31 (August 2001).
Mosconi, Davide, and Riccardo Villarosa. *The Book of Ties*. London: Tie Rack Ltd., 1985.
Sells, Christopher. *Ties of Distinction*. Atglen: Schiffer Publishing Ltd., 1998.

Anna König

NEHRU JACKET

The Nehru jacket worn by men in the United Kingdom, United States, and Europe differs from the upper-body garments worn by Jawaharlal Nehru, independent India's first Prime Minister (1947–1964), after whom the Western garment is named. The Nehru jacket is similar to a Western man's tailored suit jacket, but with a difference. The collar and lapels are replaced by a front-button closure rising to a high, round neckline surmounted by a narrow stand-up collar. The stand-up collar may be cut with a slight curve to set it into a well-cut neckline, evidencing the transformative effect of Western tailoring on the Indian men's collar from which it is derived. When popular in the late 1960s and early 1970s, the Nehru jacket was paired with trousers and one of several choices for shirts—turtleneck, mock turtleneck, or tunic. The design of the jacket facilitated the display of bead necklaces, a new element in the dress of male youth in that period.

The eponymous upper-body garments worn by Nehru during his public life are three in number: a *kurta* (tunic), and worn over it a *bundi* (vest) in summer or an *achkan* in winter, variously also called *jama* in Indian languages, and in Colonial English, *Pharsi-fashion coat*, or long coat (Ghurye 1996, pp. 168, 176, 188). Each of the three sports a stand-up collar atop a front-button closure, though kurta collars are optional.

In most other respects Nehru's Indian garments differed significantly from the Nehru jacket of Western men's fashion that they inspired. The kurta is a cotton or silk shirt with a broad flowing A-line silhouette, side slits, uniquely Indian inseam side pockets, inset long sleeves, stand-up collar, and a front-buttoned placket that reaches down to the wearer's lower chest. Nehru wore his kurta at below-knee length, ensembling it with *churidar payjama*—a bias cut, drawstring waist pant cut narrowly over the leg from knee down to ankle, with additional length added to the garment so that the fabric forms gathers at the ankle, mimicking the narrow *churi* glass bracelets that Indian women wear on their wrists. The churidar payjama is the ancestor of jodhpur riding pants.

Nehru's Indian bundi is a front-buttoned, high hip-length sleeveless vest with stand-up collar and three front pockets—two below and one above. It is made from cotton, silk, or wool *khadi* (homespun) fabrics. Nehru wore his bundi with a knee-length kurta and churidar payjamas.

Nehru's long coat extends below the knee, and has a front opening down through the hem but closed with buttons only from neck to waist; stand-up collar; and inset long sleeves with straight hem at the top of the hand. Unlike the aristocrats of pre-Nationalist Indian society, Nehru made his long coats from khadi fabrics, abstaining from the luxurious silk and gold brocades (*kinkhabs*) from which the Indian nobility usually made theirs. The long coat is worn with a kurta and churidar payjamas, with all its buttons closed, presenting a very finished look.

The manner in which the Western men's garment gave up its lapels and took on the stand-up collar and "Nehru jacket" name is a history of global dimensions in fashion and politics that begins before Nehru was born. Both the long coat and the kurta gained their style of inset sleeves and the kurta gained its front-button placket under European and British colonial influence. Long coats also became more tailored under the British, both during the early colonial era and, after a hiatus of rejection of western dress influence during the independence struggle, as the public officials of the new nation took their places on the global political stage.

Nehru came into public consciousness in Britain from the early decades of the twentieth century during India's long political struggle. In the United States, popular attention focused on Nehru from the mid-twentieth century, when in 1962 China attacked newly independent India. U.S. leaders courted Nehru and Pakistani leaders as allies against the spread of communism. Nehru visited Presidents Truman, Eisenhower, and Kennedy in 1949, 1956, and 1961, respectively. Jacqueline Kennedy visited Nehru in 1962. As Americans watched the first lady's dress, they also learned what Nehru wore.

Experimentation with and rejection of suit dressing for men (Bennett-England 1967) was occurring in Western fashion during this same political period. Cinema idols, such as Marlon Brando, appearing in T-shirts and black leather jackets, popularized nonsuit dressing and valorized the classes of men who could ill afford the expense of suit dressing. Inspired by advances in space travel, Pierre Cardin offered his Space Age line in 1964. The most influential piece was his collarless, lapel-free suit jacket (McDowell 1997, pp.144–145). It buttoned all the way up the front ending in an unadorned round neckline that revealed the collar of a dress shirt. Though not widely accepted, Cardin's garment found favor with the Beatles and other early 1960s British rock groups who wished to remain respectable through suit dressing, but wanted to cut an independent image. While collarless suits gained only limited popularity, Cardin's rejection of vestigial aspects of men's dress encouraged further experimentation with the suit jacket, such as the use of innovative fabrics like denim and velvet, or bright colors and prints for men's suits. A general narrowing of the entire men's suit—leg, torso, sleeve, lapel, and its accompanying necktie—also occurred. This fashion threatened to make parts of the suit disappear. It simultaneously made the suit even more uncomfortable to wear. Formal dressing in tunics à la Yves Saint Laurent and others provided nonsuit alternatives for formal male attire. After the release of the Beatles' *Sgt. Pepper's Lonely Hearts Club Band* album, stand-up collar military uniforms as featured on the album cover—with or without gold braid—as well as second hand navy pea jackets (double-breasted with lapels) became an additional popular alternative to suit dressing for youth. Within this climate of broad attack on and experimentation with suit dressing, a new type of designer arose in Britain to serve the youth who were its primary proponents in dress practice. These British boutique designers offered innovative clothing in successions of quick fads popular among youth.

The Nehru jacket appeared as one of these brief fads after George Harrison and the Beatles went to India in 1966 to learn meditation and music. They brought into fashion not only Ravi Shankar's sitar music and incense, but also paisley prints, bead necklaces (originally Indian meditation beads) for both men and women, Kolhapuri sandals, white-on-white Lucknow *Chikan* embroidered cotton kurtas, and the stand-up collar of the Nehru jacket. Whether worn on a vest or jacket, the stand-up collar joined in the general experimentation with men's suit dressing. Marly (1985, p. 134) reports Simpson's of the United Kingdom offered a velvet lapel-free suit with Indian style stand-up collar in anticipation of a popular market they forecast with the opening of the movie *The Guru*, in 1969.

American youth were not as cognizant as British youth of Nehru and India, but they were very involved in British popular music. The Nehru jacket crossed the Atlantic and was briefly worn in the United States, too. Several entertainers, including Johnny Carson and Sammy Davis, Jr., made it a regular part of their wardrobe. However, military-style stand-up collar jackets were also redesigned and worn by youth in this period. Not all stand-up collar jackets from this period strictly trace their origins back to India via Nehru or the Beatles.

Though considered a short-lived fad on both sides of the Atlantic among sectors of Western society deriving from European roots, the Nehru jacket has achieved classic status in those sectors of global society—especially British Commonwealth countries—with significant Indian diasporas. Their tuxedo-rental agencies now routinely provide Nehru jackets with matching suit trousers as one of their options for formal attire. Conversely, the several garments that Nehru wore remain in fashion among urban upper- and upper-middle classes in India for bridal and special occasion wear. The humbler versions of these garments also continue in use in the regions of rural India whence they originated.

See also India: Clothing and Adornment; Sports Jacket.

Bibliography

Bennett-England, Rodney Charles. *Dress Optional: The Revolution in Menswear*. London: Peter Owen, 1967.

Ghurye, G. S. *Indian Costume*. 2nd ed. Bombay, India: Popular Prakashan, 1966.

Marly, Diana de. *Fashions for Men: An Illustrated History*. New York: Holmes and Meier, 1985.

McDowell, Colin. *The Man of Fashion: Peacock Males and Perfect Gentlemen*. New York: Thames and Hudson, Inc., 1997.

Hazel Lutz

NEW LOOK

The New Look was the name given to a style of women's clothing launched by Christian Dior in his first haute couture collection presented in Paris on 12 February 1947. The styles that made up the look corresponded, according to the show's program, to the shapes "8" and "Corolla," respectively described as "clear, rounded, bust emphasized, waist indented, hips accentuated," and "dancing, very full-skirted, tight-fitting bust, and narrow waist" (Musée, p. 131).

At the end of the show, Carmel Snow, editor in chief of *Harper's Bazaar*, is said to have inadvertently named the style by saying to Christian Dior: "Your dresses have such a new look" (Cawthorne, p. 109). The English term was then adopted without translation by the designer himself and by many commentators in the form "New Look" or "New-Look." Christian Dior used it to define his own style between 1947 and 1952: "1952 began in solemnity . . . the euphoria of the New Look was finished" (Dior, p. 178–179). However, the term is more broadly applicable to all the creations inspired by Christian Dior's first collections, both his own and those of his famous or anonymous imitators. This is true regardless of the date. The New Look, a watchword in the 1950s, particularly in haute couture, had striking stylistic repercussions at least into the 1960s. It was not until 1970 that Yves Saint-Laurent dismissed the style as a thing of the past with his fall-winter 1970–1971 "Liberation" haute couture collection that celebrated the aesthetic of the World War II years that the New Look had fought against. There after considered a historical style, it still inspires contemporary work that periodically quotes it (Jean-Paul Gaultier in particular) or pays it true homage (Yohji Yamamoto, "homage to French couture" collection for spring-summer 1997).

The New Look had multiple origins: the collections of the period immediately before World War II already hinted at a return to fullness in Balenciaga, Mainbocher, Lelong, and Piguet, which returned beginning in 1946; theater and film during the war revealed a clear taste for the Belle Époque and long dresses in general. The basque created by Marcel Rochas in 1942 finally opened the way to emphatic stylization of the torso. But Christian Dior was responsible for the formal, structural, and stylistic definition of the New Look, and for its economic and social impact.

In terms of form, the New Look was constructed with reference to the individual garment as a reaction against wartime style. The voluminous and composite hats in fashion in Paris under the Occupation were supplanted by those with a "deliberately simple" silhouette (Musée, p. 131). Broad shoulders were replaced during the day by the sloping profile of raglan sleeves, and in the evening by bustiers. The loose-fitting style was rejected in order to reveal the structure of the breasts.

The waist remained fitted, very often belted, to emphasize the contrast between the new width of the hips and the flare of the skirts that, "definitely lengthened" (Musée, p. 131) in the spring of 1947, and by the following fall "reached unlikely dimensions and this time went down to the ankles" (Dior, p. 49). From the spring 1947 collection, the history of fashion has preserved the styles of the "Bar" suit and the "Corolla" dress as manifestos of the New Look, reminding us that the style affected suits constructed by tailors as well as looser garments draped by dressmakers.

For the wardrobe, the New Look marked the triumphal return of the long evening dress, which the war had replaced with short formal dresses. By restoring very visible gradations between daytime clothing and evening dress, the spotlight thrown on evening gowns lastingly reestablished the fashionable dress code.

Structurally, the New Look was built on choices of material and technical procedures aimed at sculpting contours: "I wanted my dresses to be 'constructed,' shaped on the curves of the feminine body and stylizing those curves" (Dior, p. 35). Fabrics were chosen for their solidity, accentuated by lining them with percale or taffeta. In 1952, for example, Harper's Bazaar saw the "Cigale" style as "a masterpiece of construction" and described its watered ottoman fabric as "so heavy that it looks like pliant metal" (Martin, p. 107). Dresses were conceived as multilayered compositions supported by underpinnings, including underwired bustiers and tulle and horse-hair skirts. The body itself was, if necessary, artificially shaped by the use of girdles and basques, or by recourse to flattering padding. These artifices, modifying shape as well as bearing, characterized the fashion of the 1950s with an ultra-feminine and affected aesthetic.

In counterpoint to the tendency toward simplification and lightening, which sums up the evolution of fashion from the 1910s to the 1940s, the New Look seemed in 1947 to be an anachronism. Of his second collection (fall-winter 1947–48), even more emblematic than the first, Christian Dior conceded that the "sumptuous fabrics, velvet and brocade, were heavy, but who cared!. . . Abundance was still too much of a novelty for people to reinvent a snobbism of poverty" (Dior, p. 49).

Considered backward-looking and extravagant, the New Look offended popular sensibility in the immediate postwar period. While the French press was indifferent or favorable to the style, it found enthusiastic support in the United States (Life, Vogue, Harper's Bazaar). For his very first collection, its creator was given the Neiman Marcus Award, indicating the serious commercial involvement of American buyers. A segment of the Anglo-American press, however, conducted a kind of populist anti–New Look campaign. Leagues were established in the United States against the lengthening of skirts, such as WAWS (women at war against the style) and the "little below the knee club." In England, the opposition took on a political flavor: "The long skirt is a caprice of the idle rich" (Braddock, Bessie, quoted in Steele, p. 20). These unexpected repercussions of the New Look testify to the rigor of clothing restrictions during the war. Imposed more or less drastically as part of the war effort on the American and English populations in order to contribute to victory, privations were experienced in France as despoilment by the occupying forces and had nothing of the character of patriotic sacrifice. The postwar period saw the victory of the independence of the New Look over the morality of the allies. Both liberating and respectful of custom, the style surprised and comforted bourgeois conventions. Thus, it quickly made headway in all social circles in Latin and Anglo-Saxon countries to become an international style, the popular interpretation of which was summed up in the ensemble of pleated skirt, belt, and blouse. Its diffusion was then the consensual expression of the construction of a new transatlantic social order on the ruins of European urbanity: "If I dare to refer to the style of 1947, which was called the New Look, it was successful only because it fit in with a time that was trying to escape from the inhuman in order to redis-cover tradition" (Musée, p. 14).

See also Dior, Christian; Haute Couture; Paris Fashion.

Bibliography

Cawthorne, Nigel. *Le New-look / la révolution Dior*. Paris: Celiv, 1997.

Dior, Christian, ed. *Christian Dior et moi*. Paris: Amiot-Dumont, 1956.

Martin, Richard, and Harold Koda. *Christian Dior*. New York: Metropolitan Museum of Art, 1996.

Musée des Arts de la mode. *Hommage à Christian Dior 1947–1957*. Paris: Union centrale des Arts décoratifs, 1986.

Remaury, Bruno. *Dictionnaire de la mode au XXème siècle*. Paris: Éditions du Regard, 1994.

Steele, Valérie. *Se vêtir au XXème siècle*. Paris: Adam Biro, 1998.

Veillon, Dominique. *La Mode sous l'Occupation*. Paris: Payot, 1990.

Eric Pujalet-Plaà

NEWTON, HELMUT

Helmut Newton (1920–2004) was arguably the single most inventive and influential photographer working in the realm of fashion in the second half of the twentieth century. Yet it would be selling him short to label him a fashion photographer. While he proved himself a master at this métier, his talents went far beyond the eloquent depiction of fashionable clothes. Newton's oeuvre constitutes a richly layered document of social and cultural history, intensely personal, often auto-biographical, but always engaged with the world as he saw and knew it. Newton's curiosity was wide-ranging and insatiable. Within the sphere of fashion, he was in-strumental in greatly extending the possibilities of what a magazine editorial photograph might be, as he wove into the equation the subtexts of his endless fascination with women and the way they lived, with status and power, and with the environments and protocols of the rich and sophisticated people who were his principal subject matter. And of course he injected sex into the

mix, exploring the often-perverse erotic codes and nar-ratives that are as integral to the processes of fashion as to life itself.

Photographic Style

Helmut Newton became an exceptional social anthro-pologist, constructing images that were always based on his close observations. His was a documentary project that involved reconstructing the essence of what he had seen, and doing so with the mordant wit of a satirist. While his pictures can have a theatrical extravagance of gesture or context, their incisiveness, credibility, and substance derive from their being always grounded in the realities of the worlds that he illustrated. Newton was not happy working in a studio. Like the photojournal-ists or documentary photographers he admired, like his heroes Dr. Erich Salomon or Brassaï, he found energy and inspiration in the world around him, on the streets, in hotels, in parks, on trains. He greatly respected the paparazzi, valuing the immediacy and energy in their way of working. Newton created a unique meld of cool, polished stylishness with authentic frontline reporting. His pictures are carefully prepared, minutely controlled and crafted, with every detail of hair, makeup, props, and accessories meticulously overseen, but they work because, however contrived and extreme, they are ulti-mately believable.

Early Experiences and Influences

Helmut Newton was born in Berlin into a Jewish family that enjoyed the prosperity generated by their button-manufacturing business. The pampered child of loving parents, Newton enjoyed a charmed childhood, from which date his tastes for grand cars and hotels, for elegant fashions and other symbols of the privileged lifestyle of the old European bourgeoisie. His youthful passions were swimming, girls, and photography; he single-mindedly turned these interests into a way of life. He had little interest in academic studies and even-tually persuaded his parents to allow him to abandon school in favor of an apprenticeship in the portrait and fashion studio of the Berlin photographer Yva (Elsa Simon). Newton's idyllic Berlin years were undermined by the rise of the Nazi party and the incremental per-secution of Jews. In due course he had no option but to flee. Leaving his family and home in December 1938, he sailed for the Far East. He spent time in Singapore where he worked briefly, but unsuccessfully, as a photographer on the *Straits Times* and lived self-indulgently as a gigolo. In 1940 he made his way to Australia. After the war Newton set up a studio in Melbourne and worked hard towards his ambition to live by his photography. In 1948 he married June Browne, an actress he met when she visited his studio looking for modeling work. June played a crucial role in Newton's life through more than fifty years, supporting, encouraging, editing, and protecting her husband.

Occasional assignments for the Australian supplement to British *Vogue* led to an invitation in 1957 to work for a year in London. Newton was unhappy there and found Paris far more to his liking. Work for *Jardin des modes* provided his first involvement with the world of Paris fashion. He returned to Melbourne to work for Australian *Vogue*, but he knew his destiny was to work in Europe. The big opportunity came with the offer of a contract from French *Vogue* in 1961, and his return to Europe at this date marks the beginning of his mature career. This relationship between Newton and French *Vogue* lasted until 1983. "For twenty-three years," he has said, "I did my best work for French *Vogue*." He created some of his most celebrated and admired images—such icons as the androgynous model in a Saint Laurent trouser suit in the rue Aubriot at night (1975), *Sie kommen*, naked and dressed (1981), or the first *Big Nudes* (1980)—for this magazine. Newton lived to work, and he made fashion pictures at every opportunity for numerous other magazines besides French *Vogue*, including *Elle*, *Queen*, *Nova*, *Marie-Claire*, and *Stern*.

Mature Work

If the 1961 French *Vogue* contract was a turning point, so too was an unanticipated trauma ten years later. In 1971 Newton suffered a major heart attack on the street in New York. Medical assistance was close by and he recovered, but he was severely shaken by this brush with death and determined from that moment not to waste a single day of his life. He knew he must abandon any inhibitions and concentrate on making only the pictures that he wanted to make, pushing his ideas and instincts to the limit. From this time on, he extended his range to include what he at first called his *portraits mondains* and his *sujets érotiques*. He proved himself immensely skilled in probing the boundaries of acceptability and in creating the strange mood of disquiet that pervades his pictures. Newton drew on his memories of the Weimar Berlin of his childhood and on his nostalgia for prewar Europe. He flirted with the pornographic, challenged conventions, and created a provocative, hybrid photography that embraced fashion, erotica, portrait, and documentary elements, producing a highly stylized exposé of elegant and decadent ways of life. Newton turned his attention to making powerful, confrontational nudes. He conceived witty, erotic picture stories for the American magazine *Oui*, and he gave his unique twist to the creation of pictures for *Playboy*.

Newton's portraits of celebrities became an evermore important aspect of his work, and while these were at first mostly related to the worlds of fashion, over the years he broadened his portfolio to include countless people who intrigued him—artists, actors, film directors, politicians, industrial magnates, the powerful and the charismatic from all spheres. Many of these photos were published through the 1980s in *Vanity Fair*.

Newton staged his first one-man exhibition in Paris in 1975. The following year he published his first book, *White Women*. Over the next twenty-five years he worked steadily and productively, publishing a series of books and creating countless exhibitions, the most impressive of which was surely the large-scale celebration of his career at the Neue National Galerie in Berlin on the occasion of his eightieth birthday in 2000, accompanied by the simply titled book, *Work*. His last major project before his death in 2004 was the planning of a foundation devoted to preserving and promoting his archive and that of his wife in his native Berlin.

See also Fashion Magazines; Fashion Photography; Vogue.

Bibliography

Blonsky, Marshall. *Helmut Newton: Private Portraits*. Shirmer/ Mosel, 2004

Felix, Zdenek, ed. *The Best of Helmunt Newton*. New York: Thunder's Mouth Press, 1996.

Newton, Helmut. Autobiography. New York: Nan A. Talese/ Doubleday, 2003.

——. *Helmut Newton's Illustrated: No. 1–No. 4*. New York: Thunder's Mouth Press, 2000.

Philippe Garner

NUDISM

Nudism is the practice of nonsexual social nudity, usually in mixed-sex groups, often at specially defined locations, such as nude beaches or nudist clubs. Nudism can be differentiated from the practice of spontaneous or private nude bathing ("skinny-dipping") in that it is an ongoing, self-conscious and systematic philosophy or lifestyle choice, rather than a spontaneous decision to disrobe. Nudists believe in the naturalness of the naked body, and in the medicinal, therapeutic, or relaxing properties of unself-conscious social nudity. They believe that modesty and shame are socially imposed restrictions on the freedom of the naked body, and that eroticism is not a necessary condition of nakedness. They frequently emphasize the importance of *total* nudity, arguing that partial concealment is more sexual than total exposure.

Early Nudism

Nudism arose in Germany at the turn of the twentieth century, and spread through Europe, the United States, and Australia. The so-called "father of nudism" was the German Heinrich Pudor (real name Heinrich Scham), who coined the term *Nacktkultur* ("naked culture") and whose book *Nackende Menschen* (Naked man [1894]) was probably the first book on nudism. Richard Ungewitter (author of *Die Nacktheit* [1906]) is more widely known as the founder of nudism, his reputation having survived Pudor's accusations of plagiarism.

Nudism flourished in Germany, France, England, elsewhere in Europe, and in the United States, but its advocates often had to fend off legal challenges or accusations of depravity. While nudism had distinctive national flavors, and there was occasionally some rivalry (especially between the French and the Germans), there was also considerable communication, influence, and overlap between nudist cultures. Nudism was known by many names: in Germany, as *Nacktkultur*, *Freikörperkultur* (free-body culture), or *Lichtkultur* (light culture); in France as *nudisme*, *naturisme*, or *libre-culture* (free culture), and in England as Gymnosophy or naturism.

Germanic nudism was a proletarian movement, mostly communitarian and ascetic in style. Its constituency was largely the unemployed and the working poor. By and large however, nudism was a movement endorsed and organized by educated people—physicians,

scientists, lawyers, clergy, and, in France especially, occasionally by members of the aristocracy. Nudism produced an extensive proselytizing literature. Key nudist figures or writers of the 1920s and 1930s included: in Germany, Adolf Koch, Paul Zimmerman, and Hans Surén; in France, Marcel Kienné de Mongeot, the Durville brothers, and Pierre Vachet; in the United States, Maurice Parmelee and Frances and Mason Merrill; and in England, the Reverend Clarence Norwood, John Langdon-Davies, and William Welby. Nudists often met with religious opposition, but there were also many openly Christian nudists, who argued that it was time for Christianity to rid itself of superstition.

Early nudism was a medical, philosophical, and political movement. Its key contentions were the therapeutic benefit of unhindered access to sun and air, and the psychological benefit of an open relation to the naked body. Nudist writing commonly begins with cross-cultural and historical examples demonstrating the relativity of shame and modesty, before proceeding to expound the psychological, moral, social, and physical benefits of nudity. Clothing was considered to be both an instrument of class oppression and a major cause of ill health. Nudists claimed that an excess of shame and modesty bred psychological complexes, unhealthy relations between the sexes, and produced bodies that were both unhealthy and an affront to beauty.

The contribution of nudism to the aesthetics of the race was regularly cited as one of its benefits. Maurice Parmelee, for example, argued that nudism would contribute to a more "beautiful mankind" (p. 179). Some nudist clubs banned the disabled and the corpulent as a punishment for unhygienic lifestyles, but other nudists were troubled by too strong an emphasis on the aesthetic:

> While extreme cases of deformity and mutilation can be so distressing and painful to view that there may be some justification for such exclusion, it is of supreme importance that the gymnosophy movement be maintained on a lofty humanitarian plane (*Parmelee*, pp. 179–180)

The relation between nudism and eugenics was complex, and use of an aesthetic discourse is no simple marker of eugenic thought or of fascism. Although Pudor, for example, was overtly anti-Semitic, Karl Toepfer warns that there was no "deep, inherent connection" between Germanic body culture and Nazism (p. 9).

Nudism was neither simply reactionary nor progressive. On the one hand, it was a trenchant critique of modernity. Nudist physicians lamented the soot-choked air of industrial cities and the lack of exposure to fresh air and sunlight of most working people. Socialist accounts argued that this physical malaise was compounded by the role of clothing in effecting oppressive social stratification; clothes were seen as masking the innate equality of all people. Some nudist writing is characterized by a romantic and nostalgic evocation of nature, a conception no doubt aided by the use in England and France of the euphemistic alternative "naturism" (a term that, incidentally, appears to be gaining some favor in contemporary nudism as a more "acceptable" term than nudism). For many writers, however, nudism was emphatically *not* a return to nature. As Parmelee put it, the idea that nudists want to discard anything artificial or man-made was "manifest folly" (p. 15). Scientists and physicians saw nudism not as a return to Eden (although this trope certainly occurred in nudist writing), but as a path forward to a shining new modernity in which science, rather than superstition, would lead the way.

Nudism was thus not (only) nostalgic but also saw itself as *modern* and *rational*. Nudist writing intersected with a raft of other modern discourses—heliotherapy (sun-cure), sexology, socialism, feminism, and eugenics. Caleb Saleeby, for example, was a fervent advocate of nudism, heliotherapy, and eugenics (he was Chairman of the National Birthrate Commission and author of a number of books on eugenics). Sexologist Havelock Ellis considered nudism to be an extension of the dress reform movement for women, and Maurice Parmelee saw it as a powerful adjunct to feminism. Ennemond Boniface was a socialist nudist, who fervently believed that nudism was an alternative to bloody socialist revolution, and would bring about a new naturist era in which all would be equal under the sun (see sidebar). For many, nudism was not just a therapeutic practice; it was a revolutionary plan for an egalitarian utopia.

Contemporary Nudism

There are a number of forms of contemporary organized nudism, each with a somewhat distinct culture: nude beaches, nudist resorts, nudist clubs, and swimnights. "Clothes optional" resorts are becoming more common in some countries, as part of the growth of naturist tourism.

The utopian and political underpinning of early nudism has largely disappeared. Nudism has remained

---

NUDISM AND CAPITALISM

The French socialist Ennemond Boniface predicted that nudism would bring about the end of capitalism:

> "[T]here will be an exodus . . . from the cities, and the willing return . . . to the good nourishing earth. Little by little, men will desert the monstrous, nauseating agglomerations [of our] towns, in order to found . . . new and increasingly numerous naturist towns. Then . . . the factories, those places of hard labor where decent folk are imprisoned, will progressively become empty. The ferocious reign of the industrialist and his accomplice the banker will be over." (Salardenne, p. 93)

---

a minor practice, and it has by and large mutated into a "lifestyle" chosen by individuals rather than either a medical practice or a program for social reform. Contemporary nudists tend to be more private and less evangelical about their practice, and they are unlikely to see it as connected to any form of radical philosophy or politics. The major benefits are, they believe, a relaxed lifestyle and a healthy body image.

Body image is, in fact, the one social issue around which nudists are likely to be united in their opinion. Whereas for the early nudists, one of the prime benefits of nudism was that it would promote healthy, beautiful bodies and, by social selection, contribute to the elimination of unhygienic or unappealing bodies, contemporary nudists see nudism as a way of escaping the debilitating effects of the modern obsession with the body beautiful. They believe that nudism teaches one to be comfortable with one's body, whatever it looks like.

See also Nudity.

Bibliography

Barcan, Ruth. *Nudity: A Cultural Anatomy.* Oxford: Berg 2004.

——— "'The Moral Bath of Bodily Unconsciousness': Female Nudism, Bodily Exposure and the Gaze." *Continuum: Journal of Media and Cultural Studies* 15.3 (2001): 305–319. On contemporary female nudists' accounts of the benefits of nudism.

Clapham, Adam, and Robin Constable. *As Nature Intended: A Pictorial History of the Nudists.* Los Angeles: Elysium Growth Press, 1982. Useful history.

Clarke, Magnus. *Nudism in Australia: A First Study.* Victoria: Deakin University Press, 1982. A comprehensive study.

Merrill, Frances, and Mason, Merrill. *Nudism Comes to America*. New York: Alfred A. Knopf, 1932.

Norwood, C. E. (Rev). *Nudism in England*. London: Noel Douglas, 1933.

Parmelee, Maurice. *Nudism in Modern Life: The New Gymnosophy*. London: Noel Douglas, 1929. An account of the benefits of nudism by a nudist physician, with an introduction by Havelock Ellis.

Pudor, Heinrich [Heinrich Scham]. *Naked People: A Triumph-Shout of the Future*. Translation by Kenneth Romanes. Peterborough: Reason Books, 1998 [1894]. Earliest nudist text; little read.

Salardenne, Roger. *Le nu intégrale chez les nudistes français: Reportage dans les principaux centres*. Paris: Prima, 1931.

Saleeby, C. W. *Sunlight and Health*. London: Nisbit and Company, 1923. A eugenic view.

Toepfer, Karl. *Empire of Ecstasy: Nudity and Movement in German Body Culture, 1910–1935*. Berkeley: University of California Press, 1997.

Ruth Barcan

NUDITY

Nudity is paradoxical—a bodily state that is seen as so banal or matter of fact that it is rarely given sustained conceptual or academic treatment, while all the while most societies subject it to intense regulation via customs, taboos, and laws. Nudity is customarily imagined as a "natural" state—since we are all born naked—and yet its powerful social and cultural regulation means that it is anything but simple or natural.

Nudity might seem so uncomplicated as to need no definition; it is simply the state of being without clothes. But this is too simple. In the past, the word *naked* could mean clad only in an undergarment. In fine art, the term "nude" almost always includes semiclad or lightly draped bodies. So too, in some legal jurisdictions, the erect penis is legally "nude" even when covered in an opaque fabric. Conversely, some uncovered parts of the body—an elbow, a nose, a wrist, a face—are unlikely to be considered naked. Definitions of nudity, which are subject to historical and cultural variation, rely on assumptions about what counts as clothing. Defining nudity can also be an ideological or political matter. Are ornamentation, tattooing, feathers, skins, jewelry, or even hairstyles forms of clothing? This can

matter greatly, as in the colonial context, where nudity was often seen as a sign of savagery.

Nakedness versus Clothing

Nakedness and clothing help define each other. They can function as "nuclei" of humans' "sense of order" (Clark, p. 4), as in the following sample list of fundamental sense-making oppositions in the Western tradition:

nakedness vs. clothing
natural vs. cultural
unchanging vs. changeable
invisible vs. visible
truth vs. lies
pure vs. corrupt
human nature vs. human society
pre-, non-, anti-social vs. social

These terms are valued according to context, blurry at their edges, and occasionally reversible. Thus, nakedness has been able to be imagined as both an indecent state needing to be covered by "culture" (clothing) and a pure state far superior to the indecent cultural masquerade of clothing. The nakedness of "savages," for example, has been imagined as evidence of their inferior humanness—but it has also been subject to romanticization (the "naturalness" of the "noble savage").

Metaphorical Meanings of Nudity

In the Western tradition, nudity can, broadly speaking, attract both positive and negative metaphorical meanings. Mario Perniola has argued that these opposing meanings arise from the different metaphysics underlying the Greek and the Judaic traditions. In the Platonic tradition, he argues, truth was understood as something to be unveiled. Nudity, therefore, accrued metaphorical meanings of truth, authenticity, and innocence. Moreover, in sculptural and athletic practice, the ideal human figure was naked. In the Judaic tradition, however, in which the Godhead was imagined as gloriously *veiled*, nakedness was more likely to signify degradation, humiliation, or loss of personhood. It is important to stress that this is a simplification; there was internal complexity within, and interchange between, the two systems of meaning. In any case, metaphorical meanings and lived practice did not always match up; nor were the idealized meanings of nudity open to all types of naked bodies (for example, those of women, older men, or slaves).

The Naked and the Nude

English has two major terms for the state of undress: nakedness and nudity. Nakedness is the older word, coming from the Germanic family of languages. Nude is of Latin origin, entering the language in late Middle English. The original connotations of these terms persist—nakedness tends to suggest a raw, natural state, while nudity suggests a state of undress refined by culture into an aesthetic state.

Within fine arts, this etymological nuance has been elaborated into a full-fledged aesthetic distinction between the naked and the nude, a distinction most famously articulated by Kenneth Clark. Put simply, Clark's opposition is this: nakedness is the "raw" human body, the human body without clothes. Nudity results when the artist works on that raw material. Thus, the nude is not a subject of art but a form of art (p. 3). John Berger glosses it thus: nakedness is a starting point and the nude is "a way of seeing" (p. 53). Nakedness is imperfect and individual; the nude is ideal and universal. Nakedness is nature; nudity, culture. The artist's work de-particularizes the model's nakedness, lifting it into ideality.

Conceptually, the difference relies on the myth of an unmediated original bodily state—as though there were in the first place some raw "nature" untouched by culture. The opposition also depends on underlying value judgments that have made it politically unpalatable to some. Some feminists, for example, have seen much to criticize in Clark's denigration of the naked as a pitiful state. We are, says Clark, "disturbed" by the natural imperfection of the naked body, and we admire the classical scheme that eliminates flaws, wrinkles, and signs of organic process: "A mass of naked figures does not move us to empathy, but to disillusion and dismay. We do not wish to imitate; we wish to perfect" (p. 4). For many feminists, such unabashed idealism is not only conceptually untenable, it is politically suspect, since it denigrates the (traditionally feminized) body.

Clearly, the idealizing processes Clark describes are not limited to classical art. They are the backbone of the glamorizing tendencies of contemporary consumer

> "It is widely supposed that the naked human body is in itself an object upon which the eye dwells with pleasure and which we are glad to see depicted. But anyone who has frequented art schools and seen the shapeless, pitiful model which the students are industriously drawing will know that this is an illusion" (Clark, p. 3).

> "[I]n our Diogenes search for physical beauty, our instinctive desire is not to imitate but to perfect. This is part of our Greek inheritance . . . 'Art,'[Aristotle] says, 'completes what nature cannot bring to a finish'" (Clark, p. 9).

culture, as critics such as John Berger first pointed out. Contemporary advertising favors smoothed, youthful surfaces, and it employs its own techniques, including image manipulation, to ensure that bodily ideals do not "disturb" us with signs of imperfection. It is not hard to see why feminists have by and large been less than enthusiastic about the distinction between the naked and the nude, since they are critical of the pressures that such idealization puts on women, especially, and argue that dissatisfaction with the "natural" body is a major cause of psychological and cultural malaise.

See also Nudism.

Bibliography

Barcan, Ruth. *Nudity: A Cultural Anatomy*. Oxford: Berg, 2004.

——. "Female Exposure and the Protesting Woman." *Cultural Studies Review* 8 no. 2 (2002): 62–82.

Berger, John. *Ways of Seeing*. London: BBC; Harmondsworth: Penguin, 1972. Explores the naked/nude distinction in art and advertising.

Clark, Kenneth. *The Nude: A Study of Ideal Art*. Harmondsworth: Penguin, 1956. Classic discussion; source of naked/nude distinction.

Hollander, Anne. *Seeing through Clothes*. Berkeley: University of California Press, 1993.

Miles, Margaret R. *Carnal Knowing: Female Nakedness and Religious Meaning in the Christian West*. Boston: Beacon Press, 1989.

Nead, Lynda. *The Female Nude: Art, Obscenity, and Sexuality*. London: Routledge, 1992. Feminist text that includes an extended critique of the naked/nude distinction.

Perniola, Mario. "Between Clothing and Nudity." Translated by Roger Friedman. In *Fragments for a History of the Human Body. Part Two*, pp. 236–265. Edited by Michel Feher, with Ramona Naddaff and Nadia Tazi. New York: Zone, 1989. Outline of nakedness in Greek and Judaic traditions.

Ruth Barcan

O

OCCULT DRESS

Occultism is any nonmainstream Western system of spirituality that uses magic, the definition of magic being the way in which internal thoughts are used to effect changes in the outside world. Occultists, such as northern European Pagans (e.g., Wiccans, Druids, and witches) and ceremonial magicians (Cabalists, hermetics, and the like) practice magic as part of their religions. Occult dress is used when participating in magic rites, rituals, or ceremonies. Western occult dress has three primary functions: (1) to psychologically place the wearer in an extraordinary sense of reality; (2) to identify the status of the wearer within a social group; and (3) to indicate the beliefs of the wearer.

Clothing

Occult beliefs promote nudity as occult dress, because clothing is believed to impede the flow of magical energies through the body from the surrounding environment. Wicca practitioners and witches have traditionally performed rites in the nude to show their devotion to the Wiccan goddess. Due to modesty or weather, some occultists wear robes or tunics with bare feet and no undergarments. This latter dress is believed to still allow the flow of magical energies. Many covens and magical groups have set occult dress guidelines, using tradition or personal tastes as a basis for these guidelines. Occult dress, especially nudity, is not a common Western mode of dress, therefore it psychologically alerts and reinforces the awareness of special occasions and presence of magic for occultists. Each magical group sets the guidelines for occult dress. There is not a specific literature, although a magical group may draw inspiration from books, movies, or even more mainstream cultural practices.

Some occult groups don garments symbolically colored according to a ceremony or rite. For example, a Northern European Pagan coven may don white clothes to celebrate Yule rites and green clothes to celebrate Beltane festivals. Ceremonial magic groups, such as the Hermetic Order of the Golden Dawn, have an extensive magical color symbolism, and thus certain colored clothing is worn for a specific ritual. This is done in order to mentally link the practitioner to the rites being performed, raising awareness and effectiveness of the spiritual ritual.

Occult dress is also used to indicate status within a group. Wiccan high priestesses of Alexandrian lineages indicate status to other initiates by a colored leg garter. Also, a waist cord may be worn in the same group to indicate the wearer having taken oaths pertaining to a level of initiation. Other occult groups, such as the Order of Bards, Ovates, and Druids, who originated in England, wear colored robes denoting rank during some occult ceremonies.

Cultural disposition is another motivation for specific occult dress. For example, Asatru practitioners may don tunics and mantles of historic Germanic styles to denote their affiliation to the ancient Teutonic religion. Celtic knotwork designs on clothing and jewelry may be worn to show an affiliation to Druidism and other ancient Celtic spiritualities.

Western occult dress tends to be self-manufactured (sewn by the practitioner or by a fellow occult member), or if technical skills are lacking, utilizes existing everyday clothing for a magical purpose such as a silk bathrobe purchased at a department store that could be worn in ritual as magical raiment.

Jewelry

Jewelry is used to indicate occult status or beliefs. A Wiccan priestess may don a silver tiara or crown emblazoned with moon-phase symbols, while a Wiccan practitioner or a Witch may wear a necklace with a moon or feminine symbol. Both silver metal and the moon symbolize the Goddess and feminine energies. A Wiccan priest may wear a headdress of antlers to symbolize fertility, fecundity, and the God of Wicca. A high priest or other practitioner may wear a necklace or torc decorated with appropriate spiritual symbols.

The pentacle, a disk emblazoned with a five-pointed star known as a pentagram, is commonly worn by many occultists as a token of affiliation to a nature-based pagan religion. The pentagram's points symbolize the elements of air, earth, wind, fire, and spirit, important concepts in northern European paganism. Another common indicator of a belief in a nature-based religion, especially witchcraft, is the Egyptian ankh pendant, worn as a symbol of eternal life.

Practitioners of Teutonic religions may wear an upside-down T-shaped "Thor's hammer." This symbol is used as an overall indicator of Asatru, a name sometimes used for the Teutonic pantheon-based religion.

Tattoos

Tattoos may be used to indicate Pagan spiritual beliefs. Celtic knotwork and swirls are common designs employed as indicators of a nature-based religion. Tattoos can be utilized as proof of initiation or devotion. For example, some worshippers of Odin may get a tattoo of three interlocking triangles as a sign of their devotion to that Teutonic deity.

Contemporary Occult Stereotypes

The media generally depicts occultists wearing all-black clothing, especially black robes or cloaks, and having pentacles as jewelry. This stereotypical dress perpetuates the erroneous belief that the occultist is sinful or "evil."

"Witch" stereotype. The "witch" is an enduring stereotype of female occult dress, exemplified by the Wicked Witch of the West from *The Wizard of Oz* and the witch antagonist from various Grimm's fairy tales. The witch stereotype consists of ragged, all-black clothing, cape, conical wide-brimmed hat, and facial deformities. This stereotype originated in medieval Christianity's attempt to denigrate practitioners of Western Pagan religions. The color black and physical deformities are associated with the concepts of evil and sin, hence the witch stereo-type is "covered" in sin—black clothing and warts. Around the turn of the twenty-first century, the popularity of the *Harry Potter* book series by J. K. Rowling helped to alter the stereotype of the witch, replacing it with more diversified images and connotations.

Warlock/Satanist stereotype. The "warlock/Satanist" from cinema, such as those in the 1970s' *Hammer* horror films, is another Western occult dress stereotype. The male and female Satanist stereotypes typically wear pentacle jewelry, black robes, black hair, and black eyeliner; similar dress is used for the (male) warlock. Since Western cinema has historically dressed the villain archetype in all-black clothing, dressing the occultist in black visually communicates a sinister character to the audience.

Influences on Contemporary Dress

In the late twentieth century, some occultists wishing to be recognized in mainstream religious and cultural arenas adopted stereotypical occult dress—black robes, pentacle jewelry, black hair, and black eyeliner. While controversial among occult communities, they visually publicized and communicated occult membership and beliefs by wearing this type of dress.

Occult dress has also influenced subcultures. The dark-romantic Goths, some heavy metal music fans "headbangers," and a variety of vampire subcultures utilize elements of occult dress, especially stereotypical components, such as black clothing and pentacles. Occult dress styles are more commonly worn by these subcultures as a symbol of subculture affiliation, rather than as an indicator of religious or spiritual beliefs and practices.

See also Ceremonial and Festival Costumes; Religion and Dress.

Bibliography

Buckland, Raymond. *Buckland's Complete Book of Witchcraft.* St. Paul, Minn.: Llewellyn Publications, 1998.
——. *The Tree: The Complete Book of Saxon Witchcraft.* York Beach, Me.: Samuel Weiser, 1985.
Campanelli, Pauline. *Rites of Passage.* St. Paul, Minn.: Llewellyn Publications, 1995.
Fitch, Ed. *The Rites of Odin.* St. Paul, Minn.: Llewellyn Publications, 2002.
Raven Wolf, Silver. *Solitary Witch: The Ultimate Book of Shadows for the New Generation.* St. Paul, Minn.: Llewellyn Publications, 2003.

Thomas A. Bilstad and Theresa M. Winge

Women wearing dresses by Japanese designer Chiyo Tanaka. After World War II, the West showed a reemergence of interest in other cultures, and Asian designers began to make an impact in the fashion world. © Bettmann/Corbis. Reproduced by permission.

ORIENTALISM

The Orient has been a source of inspiration for fashion designers since the seventeenth century, when goods of India, China, and Turkey were first widely seen in Western Europe. While the use of the term "Orientalism" has changed over time, it generally refers to the appropriation by western designers of exotic stylistic conventions from diverse cultures spanning the Asian continent.

Though luxury goods have been filtering into Europe from countries like China since ancient times, it was not until the great age of exploration that a wider array of merchandise from cultures throughout Asia found their way to the west. For example, the importation of Chinese ceramics exploded in the seventeenth century. Not only did these wares remain popular for centuries, they also inspired the creation of stellar ceramic companies like Sevres in France and Meissen in Germany. Even plants, like the legendary flower from Turkey that led to the "tulipmania" craze in Holland and the brewed leaf that became the status drink of the well-to-do and evolved into the ritualized "high tea," fueled the love of all things from Asia.

It was in the realm of fashion that the impact of "Orientalism" could also be profoundly felt. Platform shoes from central Asia led to the creation of the Venetian chopine in the sixteenth century. Textiles from all over Asia, primarily China, India, and Turkey, inspired the creation of fashions like the *robe á la turquerie* in the eighteenth century. This was a more extraordinary phenomenon since the fear of Turkish Islamic invaders was a constant and imminent threat. Coupled with the threat of an invasion was a diametrically opposed view: the romantic notion of a far-distant land, such as Cathay (or China), filled with genteel philosophers and lovers of art. This idealized impression of China would continue until the rise of the industrial revolution and European colonialism in the early nineteenth century. The gritty reality of ever-increasing business transactions between East and West, as well as the ever-encroaching military dominance by European powers in Asia was firmly cemented by the middle 1800s.

As Queen Victoria ascended the throne of England 1837, then the most powerful empire in the world, she oversaw an eclectic art style that would come to dominate the remainder of the nineteenth century. The Victorian era brought together many historical European styles of the past, Gothic and Rococo for example, which were sometimes surprisingly combined with elements from cultures like Japan. The end result of one amalgamation, Gothic and Japanese, led to the creation of the Aesthetic Movement. Fashion gowns reflected this blend: smocked robes like medieval chemises were embroidered with asymmetrically placed floral motifs of chrysanthemums, two distinctly Japanese design elements.

The influence of Orientalism on fashion could be seen in many other ways, both frivolous and profound. For example, the fad for harem pants from Turkey appeared in the form of fancy dress costume at balls, just as the Zouave costume of North Africa found its way into the wardrobes of some Southern soldiers fighting in the American Civil War and the closets of European ladies. On the other hand, items of dress from Asia would become essential for women through the mid-nineteenth century. Kashmiri shawls, originally woven in India then exported to the west in the late eighteenth century, became a ubiquitous part of the neoclassical costume. The shawl was often paired with a white columnar dress made of diaphanous, finely woven Indian cotton. Its popularity inspired many weaving companies in Europe to create their version of this essential nineteenth-century wrap, later known as the paisley shawl.

The Orientalism trend reached an apex in the early twentieth century, and the sources for this mania for "all things oriental" ranged from nostalgia for the legends of Persia and Arabia, as popularized by "A Thousand and One Nights," to the Paris debut of Sergei Diaghilev's Ballets Russes in 1909. This burst of Orient-inspired creativity in the realm of fashion also had lesser-known sources, including the avant-garde art movement Fauvism and Japanese kimonos made expressly for the western market.

French couturiers, such as Paul Poiret and Jeanne Paquin, were inspired by the Ballet Russes' performances of "Cléopatre," "Schéhérazade," and "Le Dieu Bleu." This Russian dance company took Paris by storm with their revolutionary choreography, music, and costume and set designs by the Russian artist Leon Bakst (1866–1924). In addition to these fantastic costume shapes and opulent decorative elements, couturiers incorporated the vibrant color palette of Fauve artists such as Henri Matisse. Not only did designers create garments with Orientalist influences, so did the modistes: turbans topped with aigrette or ostrich plumes and secured with jeweled ornaments were paired with either neoclassic columnar gowns or fantastical lampshade tunics.

Clothing created more in the realm of craft by artists such as Mariano Fortuny and Monica Monaci Gallenga also fused historical European and Asian styles into cohesive aesthetic statements. Using silk velvet as a base, both Fortuny and Gallenga precisely incorporated textile patterns from East Asia and the Islamic world for their creations. The importance of craft also fueled the European and American fad for batik cloth. Both the technique for making resist-dyed fabrics like batik and the motifs perfected in cultures like Indonesia were created by artisans on both sides of the Atlantic Ocean in the 1920s.

Marie Callot Gerber (1895–1937), the venerable head of the leading couture house Callot Soeurs, was another innovator who readily embraced Orientalism. She was inspired by the kimono and created some of the earliest versions of harem pants. From 1910 to the out-break of World War I, acclaimed beauty and woman of style, Rita de Acosta Lydig, worked with Gerber to create versions of Oriental costumes that were composed of vests made from seventeenth-century needle lace that

topped trousers or one-pieced garments that were full and loose over the lower part of the torso before tapering over the calves. Often called the tango dress, after the dance craze imported from Argentina, this style was popularized by couturiers like Lucile (Lady Duff Gordon, 1863–1935) and by fashion illustrators. The house of Callot would go on to lead the 1920s trend for embellishing the columnar dresses of the era with rich embroideries that readily copied Persian and Chinese design elements.

Also influential were exhibitions and expositions geared specifically to exhibit products of France's colonies. One of the first was a major exhibition of Moroccan art installed at the Pavillion de Marsan in March, 1917. The exhibition also forecasted far larger things to come: the Exposition Coloniales, held in Marseilles in 1922 and in Paris nine years later. These shows not only generated public interest in non-Western cultures, but also projected France's commitment to imperialism. According to art historian Kenneth Silver in his publication *Esprit de Corps*, the exposition of 1922 expressed a "less than covert sense of racism." The French were still recovering from the devastating effects of World War I as late as 1925, and there is little doubt that these exhibitions and expositions allowed them to publicly display not only their high position in the modern world, but also their dominance over a vast array of Third World cultures.

Many of the centuries most noted couturiers in France were readily absorbing the influences of the Colonial Expositions of 1922 and 1931. It was the first time that many had direct access to art from such remote countries. This exposure to ethnic dress gave them a far more profound understanding of non-Western dress, primarily objects from Asia. This understanding would enable a few enlightened couturiers to create both new fashion silhouettes as well as imbue their designs with a fundamentally different construction that emphasized the textile rather than complex tailoring.

Marcel Rochas, for example, was directly inspired by dance costumes from the Balinese court, as seen in his broad-shouldered garments of the season immediately following the 1931 Exposition. His "robe Bali," a black silk dress with a broad and square collar trimmed in white pique, is interesting in that it follows the silhouette of a non-Western garment but uses typical European colors and fabrics. Madame Alix Grès also created her version of a Balinese costume in 1937. Jacques Heim designed a sarong-style bathing suit inspired by the Tahitian exhibits in the 1931 Exposition. These sarong suits, in a radical departure from contemporary bathing-suit construction, were made not of knitted wool but with draped woven cotton. *Harper's Bazaar* made mention of these sarongs and his *pareos* from later collections. By the mid-1930s, Hollywood costumer Edith Head designed a version of the sarong for actress Dorothy Lamour in a series of comedic films starring Bob Hope and Bing Crosby. As noted earlier, all these designers' ethnic-inspired work of this period was not based on non-Western construction techniques, but rather their inspirations came from overall cultural impressions.

The output of "ethnic" garments by fashion designers was to drop off significantly during the 1940s and 1950s as the influence of exotic cultures on fashion had already begun to diminish around 1934. Inspired by the play "The Barrets of Wimpole Street" and the Hollywood film version, couturiers like Madeleine Vionnet, to cite but one of many examples, began to create modern versions of nineteenth-century Western dress. This trend dominated fashion from the late 1930s through the 1950s. The revival of historical styles offered an escape from the pressures of the Great Depression of the 1930s and helped assert the growing sense of nationalism in Europe at that time. Also a factor in the United States was strong anti-Japanese sentiment during and after World War II.

Fashion periodicals of the 1940s, 1950s, and early 1960s seem to indicate only a minimal interest in foreign dress for most designers, as compared with earlier decades. However, a strong revival of ethnic influences arose during the mid-1960s, as the fashion world responded to the purposeful rejection of standard, mass-produced fashion by young people. The young people known as "hippies" ushered in a style noted for its free-form mix of fashion elements from around the world, particularly the Middle East, India, and Native American cultures. Coupled with this renewed interest in non-Western cultures was the emergence of Asian designers. For the first time, Japanese creators like Hanae Mori not only made fashion, they began to influence the work of western designers.

After World War II, other Asian garments began to find their way into the fashion mainstream. One example is the quintessential twentieth-century Chinese dress—the *qipao* or *cheongsam*. This figure-revealing garment worn by a range of urban Chinese women since the mid-1920s has become known in the Western world as the "Suzie Wong" dress, deriving its nickname from the infamous, fictional prostitute in Richard Mason's novel, *The World of Suzie Wong*, published in 1959. Born in the tumultuous years of early Republic China, the *qipao* (meaning "banner gown" in Mandarin) or *cheongsam* (meaning "long dress" in Cantonese) is a true fashion hybrid that fused the elements of traditional Qing Dynasty court dress, Han Chinese costume, and the modern European silhouette. Despite its respectable status in China, Taiwan, and Hong Kong, the *qipao* came to represent in the Occidental mind a two-pronged, stereotypical view of Asian women—subservient, obedient, traditional, on the one hand, and exotic, sexual, even menacing, on the other. Films such as *Love Is a Many Splendored Thing* (1955) and *The World of Suzie Wong* (1960) are tales filled with textual excess whose narratives featuring Asian-Caucasian sexual liaisons use the *qipao* to uphold and sometimes subvert culturally accepted notions of race.

Perhaps it is those provocative elements of the *qipao* that have made contemporary reinterpretations of it so prevalent in the early twenty-first century. European or American designers, along with Chinese transplants like the New York–based Hong Kong native Vivienne Tam, have been creating their popular versions of Chinese-inspired fashions since the late 1990s. Examples range from the lavishly embroidered Neo-Chinoiserie gowns by John Galliano for Dior, Miuccia Prada's minimalist remake of the Mao jacket, and the body-revealing corseted mini *qipaos* by Roberto Cavalli. It is clear that the continued fascination with Orientalism continues into the twenty-first century.

See also Japanisme; Qipao.

Bibliography

Ames, Frank. *Kashmir Shawl and Its Indo-French Influence.* Woodbridge, U.K.: Antique Collectors Club, 1988.

Barbera, Annie. Interview by author, Musee de la Mode et du Costume, Palais Galliera: Paris. January 1992.

Battersby, Martin. *Art Deco Fashion: French Designers 1908–1925.* New York: St. Martin's Press, 1974.

Beer, Alice Baldwin. *Trade Goods: A Study of Indian Chintz.* Washington, D.C.: Smithsonian Institution Press, 1970.

Burnham, Dorothy. *Cut My Cote.* Toronto: Royal Ontario Museum, 1974.

de Osma, Guillermo. *Mariano Fortuny: His Life and Work.* New York: Rizzoli, 1980.

Druesedow, Jean. Interview by author, Costume Institute, Metropolitan Museum of Art, New York. 18 December 1991.

Garnier, Guillaume, et al. *Paris Couture Années Trente.* Paris: Musée de la Mode et du Costume, 1987.

Jon, Paulette. Interview by author. Paris: January 1992.

Kirke, Betty. *Madeleine Vionnet.* San Francisco: Chronicle Books, 1998.

Koda, Harold. Interview by author, Fashion Institute of Technology, New York. January 1991.

Levi-Strauss, Monique. *The Cashmere Shawl.* New York: Harry N. Abrams, 1987.

Martin, Richard, and Harold Koda. *Orientalism.* New York: Harry N. Abrams, 1994.

Poix, Marie-Helene. Interview by author, Musee des Arts de la Mode: Paris. January 1992.

Steele, Valerie, and John S. Major. *China Chic: East Meets West.* New Haven: Yale University Press, 1999.

Tiel, Vicki. Interview by author: Paris. January 1992.

White, Palmer. *Poiret.* New York: Studio Vista, 1973.

Wichmann, Siegfried. *Japonisme: The Japanese Influence on Western Art in the 19th and 20th Centuries.* New York: Harmony Books, 1981.

Patricia Mears

P

PAPER DRESSES

The paper dress enjoyed a brief but lively vogue in the late 1960s as a novelty fashion item. A simple, above-the-knee length chemise, constructed from nonwoven cellulose tissue reinforced with rayon or nylon, the inexpensive "paper" garment featured bold printed designs and was meant to be discarded after a few wearings.

Individual paper clothes and accessories existed as early as the nineteenth century, when paper was especially popular for masquerade costumes. The first modern paper dress is credited to the Scott Paper Company of Philadelphia, which introduced it as a 1966 mail-in promotion. Consumers were invited to send in a coupon from a Scott product, along with $1.25, in order to receive a "Paper Caper" dress made of Dura-Weve, a material the company had patented in 1958. The dress boasted either a striking black-and-white Op Art pattern or a red bandanna print. Scott's sales pitch underscored its transience: "Won't last forever . . . who cares? Wear it for kicks—then give it the air."

The campaign was unexpectedly successful, generating 500,000 shipments and stimulating other manufacturers to promote paper garments. Within a year of Scott's promotion, paper fashions were on sale in major department stores. Some, such as Abraham & Strauss and I. Magnin, created entire paper clothing boutiques. At the height of the craze, Mars Hosiery of Asheville, N.C., was reportedly manufacturing 100,000 dresses a week.

A big factor in the appeal of the dresses was their eye-catching patterns—daisies, zigzags, animal prints, stripes—that suggested Pop Art. Some imagery made the dresses akin to walking billboards, showcasing ads for *Time* magazine, Campbell's Soup cans, political candidates, and poster-sized photographs. Fun and fashion-forward, the dresses could be hemmed with scissors or colored with crayons. And, at about $8 apiece they were affordable, inspiring *Mademoiselle* magazine editors to exclaim in June 1967: "The paper dress is the ultimate smart-money fashion" (p. 99).

Modern, whimsical, and disposable, paper garments captured the 1960s zeitgeist. It was a time when new industrial materials like plastics and metallic fibers were making inroads, Rudi Gernreich and Paco Rabanne were pushing the limits of clothing design, and the post-World War II baby boomers were in the throes of a vibrant youth culture centered on fashion and music. Consumers accepted the notion of cheap, throwaway clothing as they embraced disposable cutlery, plates, razors, napkins, lighters, and pens. The fashion press even predicted that paper garments might take over the marketplace.

Instead, by 1968 paper dresses had lost their currency. Wearers found they could be ill-fitting and uncomfortable, the printed surfaces could rub off, and there were concerns about flammability and excessive post-consumer waste. Plus, they had simply lost their cutting-edge appeal due to overexposure.

However, the dresses' paperlike cellulose fabric was adapted as a practical and lightweight material for disposable garments for hospital and factory workers. And the legacy of the 1960s paper dress continues to inspire contemporary fashion designers like Yeohlee and Vivienne Tam, whose spring 1999 collection featured a line of clothes constructed from DuPont Tyvek, the reinforced paper used in overnight mail envelopes.

See also Fads; Gernreich, Rudi; Rabanne, Paco.

Bibliography

Palmer, Alexandra. "Paper Clothes: Not Just a Fad," In *Dress and Popular Culture*. Ohio: Bowling Green State University Popular Press, 1991, pp. 85–105.

"Paper Profits." *Mademoiselle* June 1967, 99–101.

Szabo, Julia. "Pulp Fashion Continues to Inspire," *New York Daily News*, May 30, 1999.

Internet Resources

"Paper Dress, 1966." Available from <http://www.consumer
reports.org>.

Kimberly-Clark. "1966, The Paper Caper Dress." Available
from <http://www.kimberly-clark.com/aboutus/paper_
dresses.asp>.

Kathleen Paton

PAQUIN, JEANNE

Jeanne Paquin (1869–1936) was the first woman to gain
international celebrity in the fashion business. Her design
career spanned the three decades from 1891 to 1920.
She was born Jeanne Marie Charlotte Beckers in l'Ile
Saint-Denis, on the outskirts of Paris. As a young girl
she was employed at a local dressmaker's shop and then
became a seamstress at the distinguished Parisian firm
of Maison Rouff. In February 1891 she married Isidore
Rene Jacob *dit* Paquin (legally changed to Paquin in
1899), a former banker and businessman. One month
before their marriage he founded the House of Paquin
at 3, rue de la Paix, where for two years prior he was a
partner in a couture business under the name of Paquin
Lalanne et Cie. Creating a new business model, with
Madame as head designer and her husband as business
administrator, the couple built a couture business whose
worldwide scope and stylistic influence were unparalleled
during the early years of the twentieth century.
Their innovative approaches to marketing and youthful
yet sumptuous design aesthetic attracted fashionable
women of the world who were poised for a new fashion
image at the end of the Victorian era. The diverse and
prestigious client list included famous actresses and
courtesans, European royals, and the wives of American
business tycoons such as Rockefeller, Astor, Vanderbilt,
Ballantine, and Wannamaker. At its height the house
employed more than two thousand workers, surpassing
even the house of Worth. In 1907 Isidore Paquin died
suddenly, leaving Jeanne Paquin to head their fashion
empire alone. Her half brother, Henri Joire, and his
wife, Suzanne, joined her as partners in 1911. She retired
in 1920 and eleven years later married Jean-Baptiste
Noulens, a French diplomat. The House of Paquin remained
open under a series of designers, until it merged
with Worth in 1954. Worth-Paquin closed in 1956.

Business Innovations

Astute and inventive in their approaches to doing business,
the Paquins originated practices that later became
standard operating procedures in the fashion world.
Most sweeping was the concept of international expansion
through opening foreign branches. In 1896 the
house opened a full-scale branch in London, the first of
its kind, where designs from the Paris house were produced
in ateliers on the local premises. A branch in Buenos
Aires and a fur establishment in New York followed
in 1912, and a final branch opened in Madrid in 1914.

The Paquins also took bold initiatives in the areas
of client relations and marketing. From the very beginning,
in contrast to the aloof approach of their contemporaries,
the Paquins developed personal relationships
with their clients that addressed their individual personalities
and scheduling needs. Harnessing from the
outset the power of glamour and entertainment to promote
clothing, they sent beautiful young actresses to
the opera and the races dressed in their newest models,
several often wearing the same dress. Later, Madame
introduced all-white ballet finales at her fashion shows,
and in 1913 produced "dress parades" of dresses designed
specifically for dancing the tango at the popular "Tango
Teas" held on Monday afternoons at the palace in London.
In 1914 she sent her entire spring collection on an
American tour, which included New York, Philadelphia,
Boston, Pittsburgh, and Chicago. The fashions
were modeled by Paquin's own mannequins who astonished
the public by wearing mauve and pink wigs on
the street.

Personal Image and Acknowledgments

Beautiful, chic, intelligent, and charismatic, Paquin was
herself the best publicist for her own style. She always
wore her own designs, and, widely admired by the public,
was the first woman to become a fashion icon, establishing
the precedent for Gabrielle Chanel. Equally
acclaimed for her business skills, she received numerous
awards and appointments, all firsts for a woman in
her time. In 1900 her fellow couturiers selected her to
head their first collective public display of couture at
the great Paris Universal Exposition. She was awarded
the Order of Leopold II of Belgium in 1910 and the
prestigious Légion d'honneur in the field of commerce
in 1913, and was elected president of the Chambre syndicale
de la couture, the official organization of Parisian
couturiers, in 1917.

> [Sometimes] . . . it is the material that inspires me. But I get inspiration everywhere. When I am travelling or walking in the street, when I see a sunset with beautiful blendings of colour, I often get an inspiration that helps me to evolve new combinations. . . . Our work in some respects resembles that of the painter.
>
> Jeanne Paquin in *Designs and Publicite*, 1913.

Clothing Designs and Artistic Hallmarks

The house offered a full range of garments that included fashions for all occasions—chic *tailleurs* (suits) for day wear; extravagant outerwear, especially evening wraps; and sporting clothes, which were sold in a special department opened in 1912 at the London branch. Opulent furs and fur-trimmed garments were always a specialty. Paquin clothes were renowned for their imaginative design, superb craftsmanship, and incomparable artistry. A brilliant artist and colorist, Paquin created breathtaking visual effects with color, light, texture, and tonal nuance that ranged from an ethereal luminescence in the filmy, pastel dresses fashionable from 1900 to 1910, to a bold vibrancy in the Oriental-inspired creations that followed. Extant examples of these clothes are some of the most stunning works of art in fabric ever created. Signature techniques to achieve these effects, especially in the earlier pieces, included layering, blending, and veiling filmy and textural materials of subtly varying hues; orchestrating the play of light on a garment's surface by juxtaposing trims and fabrics having differing light-reflective qualities, often outlining them with contrasting piping or chenille; and building up surface design motifs with dense encrustations of the smallest possible decorative elements, paying minute attention to size gradation and variation of placement. Endless varieties of gleaming paillettes, beads, and sequins; finely worked shirring and ruching box-pleated ribbon trim; padded appliqué; silk-wound beads; and spotted net were some of the favorite materials used to imbue the gowns with the uniquely Paquin visual quality. Other hallmarks were unorthodox combinations of materials, such as chiffon with serge in a tailored suit and strips of fur on a filmy, pastel evening gown. Always seeking novelty and individualism for her designs, Paquin frequently incorporated elements from other eras and cultures into her contemporary designs, as in a 1912 opera coat fashioned from fabric derived from the eighteenth century and draped like a Roman toga. Her signature accent color was a brilliant pink, and she was famous for her dramatic use of black, both as an accent and as a chic color in its own right. Neoclassicism was a favorite design motif.

While her artistry in visual effects and composition was unsurpassed, Paquin also designed for function and comfort. Through her promotion of these principles, she was a significant force in moving fashion towards the modern style that took hold in the 1920s. She herself frequently wore a practical, ankle-length, blue serge suit for work. By 1905 she was already aggressively promoting the more natural and less restrictive empire line that established the context for Paul Poiret's radical versions of 1908. Between 1912 and 1920 she designed clothes for the active woman, such as a gown that combined tailoring with draping, so that it could appropriately be worn from day into evening, and a version of the hobble skirt that kept the narrow line but allowed for ease of movement with the invention of hidden pleats.

Paquin's contributions in the areas of business, public persona, art, and design firmly establish her place in fashion history as the first great woman couturier.

See also Fashion Designer; Paris Fashion; Spangles; Worth, Charles Frederick.

Bibliography

Buxbaum, Gerda, ed. *Icons of Fashion: The Twentieth Century.* Munich, London, and New York: Prestel Verlag, 1999.

McAlpin, W. L. "Mme. Paquin Honoured. A Famous Dressmaker and Her Methods." In *Designs and Publicite.* By Jeanne Paquin. Volume 336. Unpublished scrapbook, 1913.

Reeder, Jan Glier. "The House of Paquin." *Textile and Text* 12 (1990): 10–18.

——. "Historical and Cultural References in Clothes from the House of Paquin." *Textile and Text* 13 (1991): 15–22.

Sirop, Dominique. *Paquin.* Paris: Adam Biro, 1989.

Steele, Valerie. *Women of Fashion: Twentieth-Century Designers.* New York: Rizzoli International, 1991.

Troy, Nancy J. *Couture Culture: A Study in Modern Art and Fashion.* Cambridge, Mass.: The MIT Press, 2003.

Jan Glier Reeder

PATOU, JEAN

Jean Patou (1880–1936) was born in Normandy in northwestern France in 1880. His father was a prosperous tanner who dyed the very finest leathers for bookbinding, and his uncle, with whom he went to work in 1907, sold furs. In 1910 Patou opened a dressmaking and fur establishment that foundered, reportedly due to insufficient funding, although he was able to open a tailoring business in Paris the following year. In 1912 he opened Maison Parry, a small salon located at 4, Rond-Point des Champs-Elysées, which offered dressmaking, tailoring, and furs. Patou's designs were striking for their simplicity in comparison to the prevailing fashions, although his biographer quoted him as stating that this change was the result of ignorance rather than any great fashion instinct. In 1913 a major New York City buyer known as the elder Lichtenstein praised Patou as an innovator and purchased the designer's entire collection, presaging his future popularity in the United States.

Early Career

In 1914 Patou established a couture house at 7, rue St. Florentin, near the rue de la Paix. Although his first collection was prepared, it was never shown, as he went to serve as a captain in a French Zouave regiment during World War I. Following the cessation of hostilities Patou became a leading international couturier. He commissioned his fellow officer Bernard Boutet de Monvel, who was working for several fashion magazines, to illustrate many of his advertisements. Patou's salon was decorated by the leading art deco designers Louis Süe and André Mare, who painted the interior and upholstered the furniture in a color described as ash-beige, and installed huge mirrors to accentuate the building's elegant eighteenth-century proportions. At the same time that Patou was a shrewd businessman, however, he was also a playboy and a heavy gambler.

Patou did not regard himself as a skilled draftsman; he claimed that not only could he not draw, but also that a pair of scissors was a dangerous weapon in his hands. Each season he provided the designers in his "laboratory" with various antique textiles, fragments of embroidery, and documents annotated with special instructions for the styles and colors he wanted to develop. His staff would then develop these ideas and present him with *toiles* (sample garments made using inexpensive fabric to check cut and fit), which Patou modified until he was satisfied. At the height of Patou's career in the mid-1920s, he made around six hundred models each season, which he refined down to some three hundred. A collection of this size would be considered enormous by contemporary standards, as the Chambre Syndicale de la Couture Parisienne specifies that a couture collection must comprise a minimum of only fifty models.

The Early Twenties

Patou's early 1920s garments, like those of his archrival Chanel, were embellished with colorful folkloric Russian embroidery. His bell-skirted, high-waisted evening dresses, often made in georgette crêpe, were beaded—he particularly liked diamanté—delicately embroidered, or embellished with fine lace, which he felt was more youthful than heavy lace. Beige was Patou's primary color for spring–summer 1922, and his collection was received with acclaim. A gown of beige kasha cloth featured a deep V-neckline that was emphasized by a lingerie-style collar, while beige chiffon was combined with kasha to form pleated side panels and full undersleeves that were finished with a tight cuff. Patou was an exceptional colorist, and this season he offered a high-collared evening cape in an unusual shade of beige verging on green; its sole trimming was twisted silk openwork. A beige jersey costume was self-trimmed with bias-cut bands around the collar, cuffs, and hem of the hip-length coat.

Patou and Chanel were the leading exponents of the *garçonne* look that dominated the fashions of the 1920s. Patou was particularly well-known for his geometric designs. Most famous are the sweaters he designed from 1924 with cubist-style blocks of color inspired by the paintings of Braque and Picasso. This ultramodern motif was then applied to matching skirts, bags, and bathing costumes. Although Patou was influenced by the fine arts, he was emphatic that he himself was not an artist, and that a successful couturier did not have to be one. "What is needed is taste, a sense of harmony, and to avoid eccentricity" (Etherington-Smith, p. 38). His eminently wearable sweaters, with horizontal stripes in contrasting colors teamed with box-pleated skirts, were regularly featured in *Vogue* magazine.

Although Patou was renowned for his smart daywear, his *robes d'intérieur* (negligées) were unashamedly romantic. In 1923 he offered a design in rose-pink satin draped with silk lace dyed to match, and trimmed with clipped brown marabou. British *Vogue* described the gown as shown with "sabot" slippers with upturned toes in white glacé kid, decorated with red leather cutwork and red heels. Another robe was of crystal-embroidered satin worn with Turkish trousers, a "Capuchin hood" and fringed mules of orange and gold brocade. Patou's shoes were made by Greco (January 1923, p. 45).

Patou's sportswear. Patou's brother-in-law Raymond Barbas introduced the designer to the world of sport and many of its champions. On meeting the androgynous, smartly elegant tennis star Suzanne Lenglen, Patou recognized instantly that she personified the fashionable "new woman." In 1921 Lenglen appeared on court at Wimbledon wearing a white pleated silk skirt that skimmed her knees (and flew above them when she ran, revealing her knotted stockings), a sleeveless white sweater based on a man's cardigan, and a vivid orange headband—she was dressed head to toe by Patou. The audience gasped at Lenglen's audacity, but the women attending were soon to appropriate similar styles of dress for themselves. Lenglen may have been the first sports champion to endorse the look of a specific fashion designer.

By 1922 Patou had introduced sportswear styles for his fashionable clientele, who wanted to look sporty even if they did not undertake any form of exercise. The same year he introduced his "JP" monogram on his garments; he was the first fashion designer to exploit the cachet of a well-known name. He has also been credited as the originator of the triangular sports scarf worn knotted at one shoulder. In 1924 Patou opened additional branches of his house at the fashionable French seaside resorts of Deauville and Biarritz to sell his ready-made sportswear and accessories. The following year he opened a specialized sportswear boutique called "le coin des sports" within his couture house. This boutique consisted of a suite of rooms, each devoted to a different sport, including aviation, yachting, tennis, golf, riding, and fishing. Patou worked closely with the French textile manufacturers Bianchini-Ferrier and Rodier to develop functional sportswear fabrics.

Patou's fashions always appealed to the American market, and he brought himself plentiful publicity through his regular contributions to News Enterprise Association (N.E.A.), the nationwide syndication service. To highlight the fact that his designs were as well suited to the "American Diana" as the "Parisian Venus," the couturier brought six American models to Paris in 1924 (Chase, p. 163). Patou had placed an advertisement in which he advised aspiring applicants that they "must be smart, slender, with well-shaped feet and ankles and refined of manner" (Chase, p. 164). Five hundred women responded, of which six were chosen by a committee consisting of society interior decorator Elsie de Wolfe; fashion photographer Edward Steichen; Edna Woolman Chase, the editor of American *Vogue*; Condé Nast; and Patou himself. The successful applicants were Josephine Armstrong, Dorothy Raynor, Carolyn Putnam, Edwina Prue, Rosalind Stair, and Lillian Farley. The French couture industry was fiercely nationalist, however, and Patou's action caused a furor.

Patou's perfumes. Patou developed his first perfumes in collaboration with Raymond Barbas. In 1925 he introduced three fruit-floral fragrances—Amour Amour, Que sais-je?, and Adieu Sagesse—each designed for a different feminine profile. Downstairs in his couture house he installed a cubist-style cocktail bar complete with a "bartender" who mixed special perfumes for his clients. Other fragrances that Patou introduced include Moment Suprême (1929), Le Sien and Cocktail (both 1930), Invitation (1932), Divine Folie (1933), Normandie (1935), and Vacances (1936). The most famous of all, however, was Joy (1930), which required 10,600 jasmine flowers and 336 roses to make just one ounce of perfume, and which was promoted even during the Great Depression as the costliest fragrance in the world.

The Later Twenties

For spring–summer 1927 Patou presented knitted sweaters in bois-de-rose wool and jersey with wide and narrow horizontal stripes, and a two-piece costume in palest green whose matching kasha coat was lined in very faint mauve and collared with lynx. All-black and all-white evening dresses were in vogue this season—Patou's collection included a white gown fashioned from crêpe Roma, with a graceful fluid cut, an uneven hemline, and rhinestone trimming running in diagonal lines across the front. This was also the year he introduced the first suntan oil, called Huile de Chaldée (which was relaunched in 1993).

By winter 1928 Patou was anticipating the silhouettes of the 1930s: his skirts were slightly fuller, there was an impression of length, and his garments were generally more body-conscious. *Vogue* described as "ideal for days on the Riviera" a three-piece ensemble with a coat and skirt with godet of black asperic (a lightweight wool) and a sweater of gray jersey with tiny black diamonds. An evening gown made in a rich caramel-beige crêpe featured a draped bodice that created a higher waistline, while winglike draperies provided extra length.

Edna Woolman Chase recalls an evening in 1929, when after staring across a room at a group of women clad in short dresses and suits designed by Chanel, Patou rushed to his workroom and started feverishly making frocks that swept the ground with natural waistelines. Fashion usually evolved gradually in the 1920s, so when one designer with international influence suddenly presented a new silhouette, it caused a sensation. Patou's sports costumes were worn four inches below the knee; woolen day dresses worn a little longer, and afternoon dresses a little longer still. His evening gowns—there were several in red with gold lamé—touched the floor on three sides and just skimmed the top of the wearer's feet at the front. Many items had lingerie details, and Patou's new color, "dark dahlia" (a red so deep that it was almost black), often replaced black for evening dresses. Other designers immediately followed suit.

The Thirties

Although Patou was to remain a leading couturier during the 1930s, he was no longer an innovator. A long white evening dress with a print of huge pink and gray flowers for spring–summer 1932, featuring a striking diagonal cut and fabric that trailed over the shoulders and down across the bare back, was perfectly in tune with current fashion trends, but was not instantly identifiable as a Patou model. Where the designer continued to make his mark was in sportswear. He showed a day dress for the same season in thin white woolen crêpe, with a cardigan in navy-blue jersey and a scarf in red, white, and blue tussore. *Vogue* singled out the ensemble as perfect for summer life in the country, for tennis, boating, and spectator sports. Likewise a navy-blue flannel suit, consisting of a semi-fitted jacket with brass buttons, a straight-cut skirt, and a white crêpe blouse was considered correct for yachting, while looking equally proper on shore. In tune with the fashionable neoclassical styles of the mid-1930s, Patou presented asymmetric evening gowns in white romaine. For fall–winter 1935, dinner suits were important fashion news for semi-formal wear, and Patou offered them stylishly tailored, with one featuring a fantail.

Patou had been renowned for his dramatic openings and first-night parties, but his presentation of his spring–summer collection for 1936 was reported to be strictly businesslike. His new colors were tones situated between violet and pink as well as a clear lime green; several of his evening gowns featured fine shirring and tucking, and his stitched taffeta hoop hats with great bunches of flowers tumbling over one eye.

The 1936 presentation was Patou's final collection. Later the same year he died suddenly and unexpectedly. Various reasons were given for his death, including apoplexy, exhaustion from work and frenetic gambling, and the after-effects of a car wreck.

Recent History

Following Patou's death, Raymond Barbas became chairman of the House of Patou. Barbas had been particularly involved with the designer's perfumes since the mid-1920s, and the company went on to launch several new perfumes after 1936, including Colony (1938), L'Heure Attendue (1946), and Câline (1964). Designers for the House of Patou have included Marc Bohan and his assistant, Gérard Pipart (1953–1957); Karl Lagerfeld (1958–1963), Michel Goma and his assistant, Jean-Paul Gaultier (1963–1974); Angelo Tarlazzi (1973–1976); Gonzalés (1977–1981); and Christian Lacroix (1981–1987). The last fashion collection to be offered under the Patou label was shown for fall–winter 1987.

Since then the company has focused upon fragrances, continuing to produce new ones for both the American and European markets, and since 1984 on recreating a dozen of Patou's original fragrances under the direction of Jean Kerléo at the request of longstanding clients. As of 2004 Jean Patou was run by P&G Prestige Beauté, a division of Procter and Gamble.

See also Chanel, Gabrielle (Coco); Gaultier, Jean-Paul; Haute Couture; Lacroix, Christian; Lagerfeld, Karl; Paris Fashion; Perfume; Sportswear; Swimwear; Vogue.

Bibliography

Chase, Edna Woolman, and Ilka Chase. *Always in Vogue*. London: Gollancz, 1954. Fashion memoirs of the editor of American *Vogue*. Includes accounts of the competition for editorial space between Chanel and Patou, rival houses that copied Patou's clothes, and the designer's recruitment of American models.

Etherington-Smith, Meredith. *Patou*. London: Hutchinson, 1983. Includes biographical details and major design achievements. Illustrated in black and white. Line drawings from *Vogue* magazine and the Patou archive are not attributed or dated.

Amy de la Haye

PATTERNS AND PATTERN MAKING

Clothing production was originally the responsibility of women. After the advent of form-fitting clothing in the thirteenth century, the responsibility expanded to include professional tailors and dressmakers. From the mid-fourteenth century, tailors authored published works on methods for cutting and constructing clothing. "How-To" books for the home dressmaker were published by the late eighteenth century and by the 1830s, small diagrams of pattern shapes appeared in various professional journals and women's magazines. Full-size patterns as free supplements with fashion periodicals emerged in the 1840s in Germany and France. In the United States, fashion periodicals introduced full-size pattern supplements by 1854. Unlike their European contemporaries, American pattern manufacturers produced patterns for the retail and mail-order market, thereby establishing the commercial pattern industry.

The earliest surviving tailors' patterns appeared in Juan de Alcega's *Libro de Geometria pratica y trac a para* (1580). Garasault's *Descriptions des arts et mètiers* (1769), and Diderot's *L'Encyclopédie Diderot et D'Alembert: arts de l'habillement* (1776), played a crucial role during the Enlightenment to disseminate practical knowledge (Kidwell, p. 4). Intended for the professional tailor, the pattern drafts were the first that were generally available to the public. A number of publications, such as the American *The Tailors' Instructor* by Queen and Lapsley (1809), and other journals specifically for the professional tailor proliferated in the nineteenth century. These included tailored garments for both sexes.

For the home dressmaker, manuals with full-size patterns and pattern drafts written for charitable ladies sewing for the poor included *Instructions for Cutting out Apparel for the Poor* (1789) and *The Lady's Economical Assistant* (1808). These featured full-size patterns for caps, baby linen, and men's shirts. *The Workwoman's Guide* (1838) contains pattern drafts, drawings of the finished piece, and pattern drafting instructions.

Small pattern diagrams became a popular method of promoting the latest women's and children's fashions. Appearing in *Godey's Lady's Book* and *Peterson's Magazine* in the early 1850s, these were unsized with no scale given for enlarging the diagram. Full-scale, foldout patterns were issued as supplements in periodicals as early as 1841 in France and Germany, and in England in *The World of Fashions* (1850).

First Generation

In the United States, Godey's sold full-scale patterns by Mme Demorest through mail order in 1854. *Frank Leslie's Gazette of Fashions* included full-scale, foldout Demorest patterns in the monthly periodical as well as offering patterns by mail. The patterns were one size only. Because they were offered through retail or mail order, Demorest patterns were the first commercial patterns in the United States (Emery, p. 1999). They offered a wide range of ladies, children's, and men's tissue-paper patterns, either plain or trimmed.

Ebenezer Butterick began to make patterns for children's clothing and men's shirts in 1863. He expanded the line to include ladies' garments in 1866 and incorporated Butterick & Company in 1867. A former tailor, he was familiar with graded sizes and offered patterns in a range of sizes from the beginning. The competition expanded in 1873 when James McCall began to manufacture McCall's Patterns, offering a range of sizes for all patterns.

Even though varying sizes had a strong appeal, two imports—German and French—were competing for the market. *Harper's Bazaar*, an American version of *Der Bazar* of Berlin, introduced a weekly periodical with a pull-out pattern supplement sheet with 24 or more patterns printed on two sides. The one-size-only patterns are defined by different line codes for each piece super-imposed on each other. By 1871, *Harper's* was offering cut-paper patterns, although they continued the overlay pattern sheets until the early 1900s. From France, S. T. Taylor Company imported and marketed full-scale tissue patterns as supplements to each issue of *Le Bon Ton*, beginning in 1868. Taylor also offered made-to-measure patterns.

Two more companies joined the competition in 1873, Domestic and A. Burdette Smith. Domestic was a subsidiary of the Domestic Sewing Machine Company, and their patterns were available in a variety of sizes. Smith's patterns offered a cloth model to facilitate the fitting process.

Competition and Mergers

The success of the pattern industry encouraged new competitors. In 1887 Frank Keowing, a former Butterick employee, formed Standard Fashion Company and sold Standard Designer patterns through leading department stores. Between 1894 and 1900 several noteworthy pattern companies were formed: New Idea

(1894), Royal (1895), Elite (1897), Pictorial Review (1899), and Vogue (1899). Subsequently, these were joined by Ladies' Home Journal (1901), May Manton (1903), and Peerless (1904). Competition was keen, and each company touted the superiority of their patterns and the excellence of fit.

Demorest was the first to go out of business after Mme Demorest, née Ellen Curtis, retired in 1887. Domestic ceased pattern production in 1895; Smith in 1897, *Le Bon Ton* in 1907 and *Harper's* in 1913. Further realignment of the companies occurred through mergers. For example, Butterick acquired Standard Fashion in 1900 and New Idea in 1902, although each retained its identity until 1926. Royal merged with Vogue in 1924.

The New Generation

Joseph M. Shapiro formed the Simplicity Pattern Company in 1927. Depending on the pattern manufacturer, patterns in 1927 sold for 25¢ to $1.00. Shapiro's approach was to produce a less expensive pattern. Simplicity patterns sold for 15¢. In 1931 Simplicity formed a partnership with the F. W. Woolworth Company to produce DuBarry patterns, initially selling for 10¢. The company thrived and in 1936 acquired Pictorial Review and Excella, founded in 1922.

Condé Nast, publisher of Vogue patterns, introduced Hollywood patterns for 15¢ in 1932 to appeal to the mass market and the national fascination with the movies. Hollywood patterns ended production in 1947. Advance Pattern Company produced another 15¢ pattern. Established in 1932, evidence suggests Advance was affiliated with J.C. Penney Company (Emery 2001). Advance ceased production in 1964.

Syndicated pattern services such as Famous Features and Reader's Mail flourished in the 1920s. These companies produced inexpensive patterns for sale through newspapers. Mail-order patterns were a popular editorial feature, drawing the homemaker's attention to the paper's advertising pages. Patterns such as *Anne Adams*, *Sue Brunett*, and *Marion Martin* continued to be sold outright to the newspaper as a loss leader. Designs were targeted specifically for families in the middle-income and lower brackets.

Fashion Periodicals

Patterns were first advertised in existing periodicals such as *Godey's Lady's Book* and *Peterson's Magazine*. In 1860, Demorest introduced its own publication, *The Mirror of Fashion*. It was first offered as a quarterly and later was incorporated in *Demorest's Monthly Magazine*, which established publication practices for subsequent pattern manufactures. The history of U.S. fashion magazines is inextricably linked to the history of the U.S. pattern companies. The advantage of owning and publishing their own periodical was economically sound. Subscriptions were profitable. Extensive portions of the magazines offered ample coverage of the patterns available as well as articles extolling the virtues of the pattern styles. Further in-house production of give-away flyers and pattern catalogs were cost-efficient.

Such periodicals as Butterick's *Delineator*, McCall's *Queen of Fashion*, and Standard's *Designer* were house organs to promote the patterns with additional editorial features, short stories, and essays on various women's issues. Other established periodicals such as *Ladies' Home Journal* and *Vogue* incorporated sections on their patterns when these lines were established. Pattern companies produced fashion periodicals until the 1930s. These were gradually phased out or purchased by other publishers and the companies concentrated on catalogs to promote their fashions.

Technology and Pattern Production

Four key factors supported the development of the pattern industry: the inch tape measure, c. 1820; the availability of the sewing machine by the 1850s; the expansion of the U.S. Postal Service in 1845; and availability of

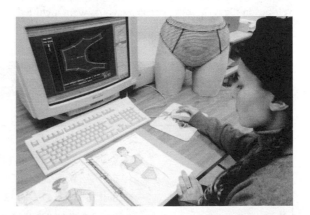

Computerized pattern-making. The use of computers in producing patterns has reduced the amount of time for a new pattern to be placed in stores. © Annebicque Bernard/Corbis Sygma. Reproduced by permission.

dress forms for the home sewer by the 1860s. These elements were essential components for the proliferation of pattern sales.

Making a Pattern

The pattern-making process is virtually unchanged from that developed by Demorest. Once approved, the designer's sketch is drafted to size by the pattern maker in muslin and fitted for an average size—usually size 36 for women. The line and fit of the mock-up is checked before being sent to the grading department for translation to various sizes and transferred to master pattern blocks. The blocks include darts, seams, notches, and other pertinent information. Until McCall introduced the printed pattern in 1921, tissue-paper patterns were made with a series of perforations cut into each piece. The perforation system was partially derived from tailor's markings. The process for making cut and punched patterns remained unchanged and was still practiced by Famous Features Pattern Company until 1996. When McCall's patent for all-printed patterns expired in 1938, other companies converted to printing, although Vogue retained perforated patterns until 1956. With the introduction of computerized-design systems, the time for a new pattern to reach the market has been reduced from 2.5 months to as little as four weeks (Chatzky, p. 154).

Early patterns had scant information on how to cut the garment and little instruction on how to make it.

Initially patterns were folded and pinned together with an attached label to identify the garment and the number of its pieces. Demorest introduced pattern envelopes in 1872. By 1906, pattern layouts were included on the envelopes by many pattern companies. Instructions for making up the garment were introduced by Butterick in 1916. The instruction sheet was called the Deltor, named for the first and last three letters from Butterick's magazine, *The Delineator*. Both the pattern layouts and instruction sheets, which are now standard practice, were done by hand for each pattern style. Today layouts and instruction sheets are done on computer. For the latter, templates such as how to insert a zipper or set in a sleeve, are plugged into the instructions. Most illustrations, which were originally done by hand, are now done on computer, as are the paste-ups for counter catalogs and other promotional materials.

Fitting Everyone

Proportional systems based on bust or chest measurements combined with height for adults or age (girls and boys) are the foundation for sizing patterns. Developed by tailors, the systems assume that all human bodies are shaped according to common geometric or proportional rules. Thus the patterns are made for an idealized figure. Early pattern diagrams and full-size patterns such as Mme Demorest and Harper's Bazar in the 1850s and 1860s, and Vogue as late as 1905, were not available in a range of sizes. Women's patterns were usually made for an idealized figure of 5' 5" with a 36" bust. Fitting was done by pinning the pattern on the body or form to adjust it to the individual's proportions. Alternatively, the customer could send in detailed measurements to special order a pattern made-to-measure from the pattern company. (Butterick still offers this service.)

Table 1 TYPICAL SIZING		
Years	**Size 14**	**Size 18**
1920s	Bust 32", Waist 27", Hip 35"	Bust 36", Waist 28", Hip 39"
1940s	Bust 32", Waist 26.5", Hip 35"	Bust 36", Waist 30", Hip 39"
Late 1950s	Bust 34", Waist 26", Hip 36"	Bust 38", Waist 30", Hip 40"
1967 (new sizing)	Bust 36", Waist 27", Hip 38"	Bust 38", Waist 31", Hip 42"
1970s	Bust 36", Waist 28", Hip 38"	Bust 38", Waist 32", Hip 42"
1980s-2000	Bust 36", Waist 28", Hip 38"	Bust 40", Waist 32", Hip 42"

Sizing Shift. Pattern companies use similar but not standard sizing systems, the proportions of which have shifted over time.

Current fashions and undergarments influence proportional systems. As explained in Butterick's *The Metropolitan* in 1871, a lady with a bust measure of 32" usually has a waist of 24", or 8" less than the bust; but a girl of 10 years usually has a bust measure of 27", with the waist usually 24". By 1905 when the flat-front corset was in vogue, the proportion for the 32" bust changed to a 22" waist.

Each company uses its own proportional system; they are similar but not standardized. By the 1920s, sizes for misses generally dropped the age reference and kept the sizes. Data compiled from the Commercial Pattern Archive digital database (CoPA) illustrate the shifts in typical sizing for size 14 and 18 from the 1920s through 2000 (see Table 1).

Each company continues to offer a wide range of sizes including misses, women's, half-size, petite, junior petite, maternity, toddler, girl/boy, child, men, and infant. Teenage fashions were introduced by Simplicity in the 1940s. In the 1980s Butterick instituted letter-coded sizes called *Today's Fit*, which are designed for the changing proportions of today's figure of about 5'5"with slightly larger waist and hips than misses' sizes. A full range of current size charts can be found in the catalogs and the Web sites of the pattern companies.

Realignment: 1960–2003

Four major companies currently produce patterns. Butterick acquired Vogue in 1961 producing patterns under both signatures. McCall acquired Butterick and Vogue in 2001 but is producing patterns under all three imprimaturs. Simplicity joined Conso Products Company in 1998.

Diversity is a major incentive. The companies have developed global markets, producing patterns in multiple languages. African American models were included in promotional materials in the 1960s. The style lines have been expanded to include more emphasis on crafts, patterns for period costumes, children's costumes, and vintage reproductions of previous eras.

Patterns are a valuable historical reference for everyday clothing, American ingenuity, entrepreneurship, and the democratization of fashion.

See also Godey's Lady's Book; Sewing Machine; Tailoring.

Bibliography

Alcega, Juan de. *Tailor's Pattern Book, 1589.* Translated by Jean Pain and Cecilia Bainton. Bedford, U.K.: Ruth Bean, 1979.

Arnold, Janet. *Patterns of Fashion: 1560–1620.* London: Macmillan Publishing Company, 1985. One of three in the *Patterns of Fashion* series. Introductions in each contains an excellent overview of clothing production.

Burman, Barbara, ed. *The Culture of Sewing: Gender, Consumption and Home Dressmaking.* Oxford: Berg, 1999. Excellent series of essays covering a breadth of topics related to clothing production.

Chatzky, Jean Sherman. "Reaping from Sewing," *Forbes* 25 (May 1992): 154–158. Informative article for the pattern business in the early 1990s.

Emery, Joy S. "Development of the American Commercial Pattern Industry, 1850–1880." *Costume* 31 (1997): 78–91.

——."Dress like a Star: Hollywood and the Pattern Industry." *Dress* 28 (2001): 92–99.

Kidwell, C. B. *Cutting a Fashionable Fit: Dressmakers Drafting Systems in the United States.* Washington D.C.: Smithsonian Institution Press, 1979. Concise introduction on the origins of clothing production.

Mott, Frank L. *A History of the American Magazines.* 5 vols. Cambridge: Harvard University Press, 1938–1968. Thorough coverage of fashion periodicals, especially volumes 3–5.

Ross, Ishbel. *Crusades and Crinolines: The Life and Times of Ellen Curtis Demorest and William Jennings Demorest.* New York: Harper and Row, 1963. The only full-length bibliography on Mme. Demorest.

Seligman, Kevin L. *Cutting for All!: The Sartorial Arts, Related Crafts and the Commercial Paper Pattern.* Carbondale, Ill.: Southern University Press, 1996. A comprehensive bibliographical reference related to clothing production.

Joy Spanabel Emery

PENIS SHEATH

A penis sheath is a supplement to the male body enclosing the glans and penis, leaving the scrotum uncovered. Sometimes the term "phallocrypt" is used as a synonym, but Peter Ucko observes that "phallocrypt" refers to dress supplements that cover both the penis and scrotum, whereas the penis sheath conforms and is attached to the penis only. Archeological evidence suggests the practice of applying a penis sheath dates to the prehistoric Near East, Minoan Crete, archaic Greece, and Roman Italy. In the early 2000s, people living in small-scale tribal societies all around the world, including Africa, the Pacific Islands, North and South

America, and the Himalayas, still used penis sheaths. Isolated examples have been documented in Japan and among the Inuit and Eskimo American Indians.

Penis sheaths are constructed of a wide variety of materials, including gourds, leaves, grass, raffia, bamboo, netting, basketry, shell, cocoons, ivory, horn, metal, leather, tapa cloth, and woven cotton trade cloth, depending on the culture. The sheath is attached to the body in a variety of ways depending on the style of sheath. The sheath can be shaped to cover and adhere to the penis; it can be attached directly to the glans; or it can be fastened to the end of the foreskin. Sometimes a cord or cloth wrap is used to hold the penis sheath on or at a particular angle. The sheath might be carved, painted, and/or tasseled. It can be as small as five or six centimeters or extend up to the ear of the wearer. The sheaths are not time consuming to make. Even a carved bamboo sheath will require only thirty to forty minutes to complete. The sheath is part of a whole ensemble of dress that can range from body painting and bead necklaces to shirt and trousers.

The function of the penis sheath in any society is the subject of some debate among scholars and requires more research. What tribal men report and what ethnographers interpret can differ. However, some anthropologically sound functions of the penis sheath can be identified, such as it acting as a carrying pouch, protection, display, or a marker of age, status, or tribal identity.

Informants report that the sheath protects their genitals from the natural environment, particularly bugs and insects when sitting on the ground. Since some sheaths are open at the end, do not cover the scrotum, and are not worn by all groups in the same geographic area, physical protection is not the only function. The penis sheath and its wrappings can serve as a place to store dry tinder and tobacco. Sheaths also act as spiritual protection from evil influences that can enter body orifices, particularly through the genitals. Some scholars suggest the penis sheath functioned as a threat or dominance display in battle. As threat displays became more symbolic than practical, some societies have developed penis sheaths for different occasions, from ceremonial use to everyday wear.

In the early days of anthropology, modesty was considered a function of the sheath. This idea has fallen to the wayside because human groups vary in their ideas of what is "naked" and "shameful." For many men, wearing the penis sheath is part of their definition of being dressed appropriately for interaction with others.

A comparable example is the codpiece, which was fashionable in the sixteenth century, and part of the well-dressed European man's ensemble. In any case, one can see by looking at various examples of the penis sheath that it both conceals the penis and draws attention to the genital region. The codpiece and the twenty-first century men's Speedo or thong swimming-suit function the same way. The act of revealing while concealing appears to be a panhuman use of dress in general.

The age when a boy begins wearing a penis sheath varies from society to society. In some cultures, when the boy has his first semen emission, there is a ritual donning of his first sheath. In other cultures, the first sheathing is part of the process of coming of age from youth to adult. Throughout life, a change in style of sheath may mark achieved status from child to warrior to husband to elder. For example, in A. F. Gell's study of penis sheathing in a West Sepik village spanning the border of New Guinea and West Irian, there were both secular and ritual penis sheaths called *pedas* used across the lifespan, and the pattern of their use is cyclic in opposition to each other. Peter J. Ucko points out that in some groups the youth wear penis sheaths at a time in their lives when virility is alluring and the elders are freed from the responsibility of this signal. By contrast, in other groups the older men wear penis sheaths and the young do not, denoting changing times. Often, the morphology of the penis sheath will differ from place to place, so the individual can be visually identified as a member of one group or another. In Gell's study, we can see that in one part of the valley, egg-shaped penis sheaths were used in the north and elongated sheaths in the south.

Even though different groups may have a general style of penis sheath unique to them, there may be little standardization within the group, allowing the individual the opportunity for aesthetic expression. Similarly, absence of a penis sheath communicates state of mind. For some groups, not wearing a penis sheath means the man is an adulterer (implying one function of the penis sheath as contraception by inconvenience), feeble minded, or in mourning and temporarily withdrawing from social life.

With a handful of exceptions, the penis sheath is exclusively a masculine symbol. It is more than a covering or a display. It is a unique form of material culture that draws one in to an understanding of the physical, social, and aesthetic life of people.

See also Cache-Sexe; Codpiece.

Bibliography

Gell, A. F. "Penis Sheathing and Ritual Status in a West Sepik Village." *Man* 6, no. 2 (June 1971): 165–181.

Heiser, Charles B., Jr. "The Penis Gourd of New Guinea." *Annals of the Association of American Geographers* 63, no. 3 (September 1973): 312–318.

Ucko, Peter J. "Penis Sheaths: A Comparative Study." *Proceedings of the Royal Anthropological Institute of Great Britain and Ireland* (1970): 24A–67.

Wickler, W. "Ursprung und biologische Deutung des Genitalpräsentierens männlicher Primaten." *Z Tierpsychol* 23: 422–437.

Sandra Lee Evenson

PENN, IRVING

Irving Penn, who was born in 1917 in Plainfield, New Jersey, is considered one of the great American photographers of the mid-twentieth century, not solely one of its masters of fashion photography, in which he initially made his name. His reputation might equally have been secured by a command of portraiture and austere still life. In a career spanning six decades, he has had success too with botanical studies, the beauty photograph (most markedly for advertising purposes), ethnographical documents of cultural types, studies of voluptuous nudes, and with his book *Dancer* (2001), meditations on movement and the body. He disallows any of these disciplines from taking precedence in his oeuvre, but his name is inescapably synonymous with fashion photography. Since 1943 Penn's photographs have appeared regularly in *Vogue*, where his career was nurtured by Alexander Liberman, the magazine's art director from 1943 to 1962.

Beginnings at *Vogue*

Penn studied at the Philadelphia Museum School of Industrial Art (1934–1938). Alexey Brodovitch, art director of *Harper's Bazaar*, whose design seminars Penn attended, introduced him to fashion magazines; moreover, he hired Penn to be his assistant during two summers. Brodovitch published some of Penn's illustrations in 1937. In the same year, Penn undertook a series of street photographs of the shop signs and facades of

New York, where he was laying the groundwork for a career in the fashion world by working as a freelance graphic designer and consultant art director for Saks Fifth Avenue.

By 1942, having spent a year painting in Mexico, Penn recognized that his future lay elsewhere. In 1943 Liberman hired him as a creative assistant in the art department of *Vogue*. Penn found *Vogue's* photographers mostly ambivalent about his ideas for the magazine's cover artwork and instead put them into practice himself. His first *Vogue* cover, a still life composition of accessories, was published in October 1943. Over the next sixty years he photographed nearly 170 more. Shortly after his 1943 debut, he embarked on the photography of clothes. He followed this with a short-lived but inventive series, *Portraits with Symbols*, a stylish fusion of still life and portraiture in which well-known figures posed with objects that evoked aspects of their personalities.

Portraits

Between 1944 and 1950 Penn completed more than three hundred portrait sittings for *Vogue*, the subjects for which ranged from the Spanish artist Salvador Dalí to Senator Hubert Humphrey. He rarely photographed outside the formal confines of the studio during this period and approached these sessions as he did his still life studies that punctuated *Vogue's* pages at this time: his models faced the lens in carefully arranged poses against the simplest of studio backdrops, where nothing was left to chance. His intention was to eschew artifice and flattery in favor of a timeless clarity. His celebrated "corner portraits" date from this period (1948–1949), too. Placing two studio flats at an acute angle to create a confining space for his sitters, Penn recalled that "the walls were a surface to lean on or push against. . . . [L]imiting the subjects' movement seemed to relieve me of part of the problem of holding on to them" (Penn, 1991, p. 50).

Apogee at *Vogue*

Penn's *Vogue* fashion photography reached its apogee with his coverage of the Paris collections of 1950. Stripped bare of props and artifice, the results appeared monumental in their simplicity, in the light of which the tableaux of Horst, Cecil Beaton, and Erwin Blumenfeld, his contemporaries in the pages of *Vogue*, suddenly seemed as overdressed as stage sets. Penn's uncluttered compositions against seamless gray paper, as taut and as concentrated as his portraits, remain unsurpassed as documents of haute couture at its zenith. For many of these fashion photographs he collaborated with the model Lisa Fonssagrives (1911–1992), whom he married shortly after their completion. His most famous cover for *Vogue*, a monochromatic study of the model Jean Patchett in fashion by Larry Aldrich, dates from 1950 and marks the first occasion *Vogue* ran a black-and-white photographic cover.

Ethnographic Photography

Besides his important work for *Vogue* at mid-twentieth-century, Penn began pointing his camera in new directions. In 1949, while on a fashion story for *Vogue* in Peru, he found a nineteenth-century daylight studio in the town of Cuzco. There, over three days, he photographed the town's residents (wearing their exotic clothing) and visitors against a painted cloth backdrop, thereby initiating a regular series of portraits documenting different cultures. This pursuit led him far afield in later years, to such locales as Dahomey, Nepal, Cameroon, New Guinea, and Morocco. He brought the same spirit of wonderment to chronicling these exotic dresses as he brought to his photographs of ethnic types and his celebrated series of tradespeople in Paris, London, and New York, which he also initiated in 1950.

New Directions

Penn embarked on his nude studies in 1949, continuing to work on them intermittently between *Vogue* fashion assignments, to which they stand in stark contrast. His subjects were in his own words "soft and fleshy, some very heavy." But he required the same of them as he did his fashion models: it was "more important [that] they were comfortable with their bodies" (Penn, 1991, p. 66). *Vogue* commissions and other commercial work, mostly advertising, occupied Penn for the remainder of the 1950s. In 1960 he published his first book, *Moments Preserved*, which contained the best of his fashion photography of the previous decade. The following year, in tandem with his *Vogue* duties, he began a series of annual photographic essays for *Look* magazine (1961–1967).

In 1964 Penn began to experiment with printing in precious metals, most notably platinum, palladium, and iridium. He continued refining these processes for exhibition pieces, which have included fashion masterworks such as *Lisa in Harlequin Dress by Jerry Parnis* (1950) and *Sunny Harnett in Ben Reig Silk-Chiffon Blouse* (1951). Penn became increasingly disenchanted with fashion photography in the 1960s and from then on his photographs in *Vogue*'s fashion pages became something of a rarity. "Nowadays," he told one commentator, "all that is required is a banal photograph of a girl in a dress." From the mid-1970s Penn regarded original work for exhibitions and books as more creatively fulfilling than editorial commissions. However, his beauty and still life compositions, and occasionally fashion pictures, continue to be published by *Vogue* almost on a monthly basis; thus, with more than sixty years contributing to the magazine, he is its longest-serving photographer. With an undeniable imprimatur on *Vogue*, he is one of the most influential fashion photographers of the twentieth century.

See also Beaton, Cecil; Fashion Photography; Horst, Horst P.; Vogue.

Bibliography

Fielden, Jay, ed. *Grace: Thirty Years of Fashion at Vogue*. Paris: Edition 7L, 2002.

Fraser, Kennedy. *On the Edge: Images from 100 Years of Vogue*. New York: Random House, 1992.

Hall-Duncan, Nancy. *The History of Fashion Photography*. New York: Alpine Books, 1979.

Hambourg, Maria Morris. *Earthly Bodies: Irving Penn's Nudes, 1949–1950*. Boston: Little, Brown, 2002.

Harrison, Martin. *Appearances: Fashion Photography since 1945*. New York: Rizzoli, 1991.

——. *Lisa Fonssagrives: Three Decades of Classic Fashion Photography*. New York: St. Martin's Press, 1996.

Howell, Georgina. *In Vogue: Six Decades of Fashion*. London: Allen Lane, 1975.

Kazanjian, Dodie, and Calvin Tomkins. *Alex: The Life of Alexander Liberman*. New York: Alfred A. Knopf, 1993.

Liberman, Alexander. *The Art and Technique of Color Photography*. New York: Simon and Schuster, 1951.

Penn, Irving. *Moments Preserved: Eight Essays in Photographs and Words*. New York: Simon and Schuster, 1960.

——. *Worlds in a Small Room*. New York: Grossman, 1974.

——. *Inventive Paris Clothes 1909–1939: A Photographic Essay*. New York: Viking, 1977.

——. *Irving Penn: Photographs in Platinum Metals: Images 1947–1975*. New York: Marlborough Gallery, 1977. An exhibition catalog.

——. *Flowers: Photographs.* New York: Harmony Books, 1980.

——. *Recent Still Life: Negatives 1979–1980, Prints in Platinum Metals 1980–1982.* New York: Marlborough Gallery, 1982. An exhibition catalog.

——. *Issei Miyake.* New York: New York Graphic Society, 1988.

——. *Passage: A Work Record,* New York: Alfred A. Knopf, 1991.

——. *Irving Penn Photographs: A Donation in Memory of Lisa Fonssagrives-Penn.* Stockholm: Moderna Museet, 1995.

——. *Irving Penn Regards the Work of Issey Miyake: Photographs 1975–1988.* London: Jonathan Cape, 1999.

——. *Irving Penn.* New York: Pace/MacGill Gallery, 1999.

——. *Drawings.* New York: Apparition, 1999.

——. *The Astronomers Plan a Voyage to Earth.* New York: Apparition, 1999.

——. *Irving Penn: Objects for the Printed Page.* Essen, Germany: Museum Folkwang, 2001.

——. *Dancer.* Tucson, Ariz.: Nazraeli Press, 2001.

——. *Still Life: Photographs 1938–2000.* New York: Bulfinch Press, 2001.

Szarkowski, John. *Irving Penn.* New York: The Museum of Modern Art, 1984.

Westerbeck, Colin, ed. *Irving Penn: A Career in Photography.* Boston: The Art Institute of Chicago in association with Bulfinch Press/Little, Brown, 1997.

Robert Muir

PERFUME

Perfume, from the Latin *per fumum*, meaning through smoke, has been a barometer of society and its mores throughout recorded history. Like fashion, it provides a road map to people's strivings for individuality, self-aggrandizement, social standing, and feelings of well-being.

Early Egyptians are credited as one of the first groups to improve their lives and deaths through the use of fragrance and fragrance ingredients, particularly blended for burning during religious services and burial. Historical references cite Ishmaelite traders who, in 2000 B.C.E., bore aromatic treasures to eager customers in Egypt via what was known as the Incense Road. Considered more precious than gold, flowers, herbs, and spices, perfumes were an expression of exaltation and admiration. The importance of perfumes gradually reached far beyond Egypt thanks to traders, crusaders, and shifting populations who took their precious fragrances with them. This was a fortuitous turn of events for the future of fragrance.

Perfume ingredients became indispensable in religious services, as medicants, to enhance personal environments, and to be applied to the skin for protection against the elements. Perfume was also used as an aphrodisiac. The famous and infamous embraced fragrance and made it their own. Cleopatra (60–30 B.C.E.) doused the sails of her ship to entice Mark Antony. The Queen of Sheba won the heart and devotion of King Solomon by bringing him gifts of rare spices all the way from Yemen. He particularly favored the fabled myrrh. It is said that each drop of Muhammad's sweat, as he ascended to heaven, morphed into the most precious of flowers—the rose.

It was the Egyptians who learned how to press the oils from flowers and leaves that they then smoothed on their sun-scorched skins. The Arabian doctor Avicenna is credited with developing the method of distillation, in the tenth century, which led to the creation of liquid perfume.

Little has changed in the gathering and processing of perfume ingredients. Flowers and plants are picked and gathered by hand, and distillation, in which steam separates the essential oils from the flowers and plants, remains one of the prime methods for extraction. (It is one of six methods: expression, maceration, enfluverage, extraction, and headspace technology.) In modern times, the greatest change has taken place in the fragrance laboratories where computer technology has become a basic tool, not only in establishing and maintaining quality standards, but also in allowing perfumers around the world to communicate with each other in developing unique new fragrance formulas.

Hand in Glove

Fragrance and fashion were linked for the first time in the thirteenth century. The setting was Grasse, France (located between Nice and Cannes) that at the time was the center of the glove-making industry. The problem these artisans faced, however, was the unbearable smell of the leather that was tanned with urine.

The fragrant flowers of Grasse, the province of the local perfumers, came to the rescue of the tanners and perfumed gloves became the rage throughout fashionable Europe. As a result, industrious glove-makers added the title of perfumer. They enjoyed great success until the early 1800s when they were taxed out of business and as a result moved away, leaving a talented coterie of flower growers and perfumers. Grasse flourished as the perfect source of flowers, especially lavender, jasmine, and tuberose that grew on the sun-drenched hills. In the twenty-first century, Grasse is a shadow of its former self, as real-estate developers usurped much of the land in the latter part of the twentieth century. It no longer is the prime source of flowers, roots, and herbs sought by the modern fragrance industry. The whole world serves the perfumers' fragrant needs.

Scents of Royalty

The desire to adorn the body with sweet smells and beautiful jewelry created a marriage of fashion and fragrance that reached its heights in the early 1700s, particularly during the reign of Louis XIV. It was then that European royalty decided to have their fragrances at hand night and day no matter where they might be. Aromatic jewelry designed by master craftsmen was in great demand. In fact, royalty had their own private jewelers and perfumers to cater to their every whim. Chatelaines, rings, earrings, belts, and bracelets were considered indispensable. Wealthy men, women, and children all wore decorative aromatic accessories.

Courting Perfume

In 1533, when Catherine de Medici left Italy to marry Henry II, she took all of her personal perfumes and perfumers with her. It was not uncommon for royalty and wealthy citizens to employ their own perfumers and jewelers who were responsible for creating exquisite one-of-a-kind containers for each perfume. The marriage of Marie Antoinette to the future king of France, Louis XVI, united two intense devotees of perfume. Both reveled in environments heavy with scent. But it was Louis XIV who became known as "The Perfumed King" in the seventeenth and early eighteenth centuries. His retinue of perfumers created different scents for him and his court to wear morning, noon, and night. In his court, the wings of doves were drenched with fragrance to be released after a great banquet to fill the air with refreshing scents. Extravagance was the coin of the realm. Vessels were designed to allow incense to be sprinkled on carpets and in dresser drawers. Incense was also burned to fumigate clothes, living quarters, and to induce sleep.

Street Scents and Scenes

The growth of the urban environment in the eighteenth century gave meaning to fragrance for the masses. Overcrowding, lack of sanitation, and pollution made life unbearable. Fears of unknown diseases lurking in the water kept people from bathing. Perfumes emerged as the panacea for the great-unwashed populace. Crudely made perfumes and colognes could be bought on the street by roving self-appointed perfumers who hawked their fragrant wares from garments which looked like cook's aprons. Scent bottles filled the many pockets. The French Revolution put a stop to royalty's fragrant revelries and perfume didn't regain its popularity until the early nineteenth century, when Napoleon became emperor. There was no limit to his fragrance indulgences. He virtually bathed in *eau de cologne*, and never went into battle without a full supply of his favorites. His wife, Josephine, loved roses and musk, and she surrounded herself with them night and day. But, when Napoleon left her for Marie Louise, Josephine filled the rooms of Malmaison with the overpowering scent of musk, which she knew Napoleon disliked intensely. Visitors to Versailles report they smell it still.

The twentieth century saw the birth of fashion designer fragrances (primarily of French origin). They were referred to as the invisible accessory by merchants and the media, to be worn on special occasions. Then, in 1921, the great couturier, Gabrielle Chanel, set the fashion world on fire when she launched her breakthrough creation, Chanel No. 5. It was the first aldehydic type that is characterized by its rich sparkling quality. It became an overnight sensation and established a new category for the perfume world.

Chanel was not the first designer to sniff the potential of scents, however. Credit must be given to Paul Poiret, whose exotic designs were inspired by the mysteries of the Far East and who achieved recognition and applause for his art deco costumes for theater and ballet. Fascinated by the imaginative and ephemeral, he adored fragrance and became a perfume entrepreneur in the early 1900s. He established his own laboratory and facilities for blowing glass and packaging his "small wonders." His company, Parfumes Rosine, was named for one of his daughters. Of the more than fifty perfumes (floral, spicy, and oriental types dominated) introduced between 1911 and 1924, several carried his daughter's name. La Rose de Rosine was presented to the public in the mid-twenties as was La Chemise de Rosine and Mon Choix de Rosine. In 1927, inspired by the flight of

Charles Lindbergh, Poiret launched Spirit of St. Louis, which was one of his last fragrance creations.

Poiret's couture clients, artists, actresses, and the wealthy, in the U.S. and abroad, quickly became his fragrance customers as he encouraged them to consider fragrance one of his most important fashion accessories. They responded enthusiastically. After World War I, however, his fashion house floundered. His fragrances continued to enjoy popularity in the United States where they were reintroduced. Poiret closed his business in 1930.

Designers and Grand Dames

The fascination with fragrance did not lose its momentum thanks to Chanel and an unending parade of designers who became arbiters of styles in scents with innovations of their own: Worth (Dans La Nuit, 1922), Jeanne Lanvin (My Sin, 1925). The legendary Arpege wasn't introduced until 1927. What was described as the most expensive perfume in the world, Joy, was launched by Jean Patou in 1930. Elsa Schiaparelli startled twentieth century women with a sexy scent which she appropriately called Shocking. Women flocked to her salon to add the scent in its unique "torso" bottle to their dressing tables. The bottle was said to have been inspired by the measurements of the voluptuous American actress Mae West. It is considered one of the great collectibles in the twenty-first century.

Peacetime Scent-Sations

A fashion/fragrance explosion following World War II was led by Christian Dior who not only dropped skirts to the floor in 1947 with his New Look, but also intrigued his customers with the legendary Miss Dior perfume. Nina Ricci introduced her romantic perfume, L'Air du Temps, in 1948 in its unforgettable "double doves" bottle. In 1951, the elegant Hubert Givenchy took his place in the perfume pantheon, with L'Interdit, inspired by his muse, Audrey Hepburn.

Hints of Globalization

In the second half of the twentieth century, the French couture world spawned a splendid group of designers including Yves Saint Laurent, Karl Lagerfeld, Guy Laroche, Pierre Cardin, and Paco Rabanne. Before long, all became perfume aficionados as fragrance and fashion became inextricably connected.

Fragrance in the United States, at the time was primarily French and considered a luxury to be worn only on special occasions. An interest in American fragrances began to accelerate when Estée Lauder introduced Youth Dew in 1953. The first perfume in an oil base (versus alcohol), it was particularly long lasting and became a nationwide success. The launch of Norell, however, catapulted America into the fashion/fragrance arena. Norell was the first American designer to lend his name to a perfume. Revlon introduced it in 1969. The sophisticated floral became the olfactory touchstone for executive women throughout the country. It suddenly became *de rigueur* for these career women to keep Norell perfume bottles in full view on their desks.

By the 1970s, American designer fragrances multiplied. Halston led the way with his first fragrance in 1975. Presented in the famed Elsa Peretti bean bottle, it was an immediate favorite. Ralph Lauren set new fragrance standards with Lauren and Polo in 1978. Calvin Klein rocked the fragrance world in 1985 with Obsession and its provocative, risqué advertising. He followed up in 1994 with the first important unisex fragrance, CK-1. It created a sensation. America's designers Oscar de la Renta, Liz Claiborne, Bill Blass, and Donna Karan moved quickly to join the fragrance explosion.

Designing a Fragrant Future

France's commitment to fragrance and its formidable fashion designers also continued unabated. In the 1980s, new cutting-edge designers made their mark: The 1990s witnessed fragrance launches from Jean-Paul Gaultier and Issey Miyake. By the time the century was over, fashion designers from Italy (Armani, Moschino, and Dolce & Gabbana), Spain (Carolina Herrera and Paco Rabanne), and Germany (Jil Sander and Hugo Boss) were international fragrance stars.

In the twenty-first century, competition heated up with fragrance blockbusters from the newest fashion leaders in the United States and abroad: the namesake fragrances of Marc Jacobs, Michael Kors, and Vera Wang have joined John Galiano's Kingdom. The everwidening development of odor identical molecules and computer-generated techniques that extract and reproduce scents previously undetected or available has dramatically expanded the perfumer's palette. Amongst the original olfactory experiences that emerged are food, oceanic, and ozone notes. Researchers have explored scents emitted by coral growing in the Caribbean.

Flowers have been sent into space to determine how the weightlessness impacts the flower's odor stability. Work has been undertaken to develop pleasing odor environments and delivery systems for future space stations. Research has revealed that humans are not comfortable living under odorless or negative odor conditions.

The key to the success of the designer scents has always depended on how well each designer interprets his or her fashion image in the packaging, name, advertising, and, of course, the fragrance. The appeal is especially powerful to the majority of consumers who could not afford the couture designs that appear alluringly in the pages of magazines, in store windows, and on popular TV shows. The perfumes have made it possible for almost everyone to experience the panache of the designers. As a result, designer fragrance successes have multiplied and captured the imagination and dedication of women everywhere.

There are eight basic fragrance categories: Green, single florals, floral bouquet, oriental blend, modern blend, fruity, spicy, and woodsy mossy. In recent years, fantasy formulations have grown increasingly popular. These are fragrances that defy description and are olfactory experiences based on the perfumers imagination.

In the twenty-first century, creating a fragrance demands scientific, technical, and artistic expertise. The time frame from start to finish can be as long as three years. Usually, a team of perfumers, assistants, and evaluators work against what the industry calls a "perfume profile." The profile identifies the type of fragrance (floral, spicy citrus, woodsy, green, or oriental), the characteristics of the type of woman who would wear the fragrance (sophisticated, conservative, sporty, adventurous), the pricing, the packaging, and among other factors, imagery. A number of perfumers from different supplier companies compete to win the assignment. Once the winning fragrance is selected, it is market-tested, which could take another six to eight months. During this period, the packaging, advertising, marketing, and sales promotion (including sampling) strategies are finalized.

There are only a handful of great perfumers and like all fine artists they are considered key to the success of creating a great luxury brand. They are in demand and remunerated accordingly. Because of the many elements involved in bringing a fragrance to market, there is no hard and fast rule for allocation of costs.

The future promises to expand the rarity and enjoyment of designer-inspired fragrances. New technologies and packaging concepts will make them available in a myriad of forms for personal wear and travel, as well as in the home and in public spaces. The olfactory adventure of the twenty-first century absolutely knows no bounds.

See also Cosmetics, Nonwestern; Cosmetics, Western.

Bibliography

Ackerman, Diane. *A Natural History of the Senses.* New York: Random House, 1990.

Classen, Constance, ed. *Aroma: The Cultural History of Smell.* London and New York: Routledge, 1994.

Corbin, Alain, ed. *The Foul and the Fragrant: Odor and the French Social Imagination.* Cambridge, Mass.: Harvard University Press, 1986

Cunningham, Donna. *Flower Remedies Handbook: Emotional Healing and Growth: With Bach and Other Flower Essences.* New York: Sterling Publishing Company, 1992.

Dyett, Linda, and Annette Green. *Secrets of Aromatic Jewelry.* New York: Flammarion, 1998.

Le Guerer, Annick. *Scent: The Mysterious and Essential Powers of Smell.* Translation by Richard Miller. New York: Turtle Bay Books/Random House, 1992.

Murris, Edwin T. *The Story of Perfume from Cleopatra to Chanel.* New York: Charles Scribner's Sons, 1984.

White, Palmer. *Elsa Schiaparelli: Empress of Fashion.* New York: Rizzoli, 1986.

Annette Green

PETTICOAT

The petticoat is derived from the *jupe* or underskirt of the eighteenth century. As the skirts of women's robes were open at the front, the *jupe* had to be as highly decorative as the robe, and was often constructed of the same rich material. Around 1715 the petticoat became an undergarment that gave structure to the outer skirt by means of a series of whalebone hoops.

The Nineteenth Century

By the nineteenth century, petticoats had several functions. They were used as underlinen to provide warmth and protect outer clothing from an unclean body, to give a structure to the skirt depending on the fashionable silhouette of the time, and to disguise the shape of the legs to give a modest appearance to a woman. It formed part of an extensive range of underwear as worn by the Victorian woman, which was comprised of a chemise, drawers, corset, and several petticoats. Petticoats were generally in two forms until the end of the nineteenth century: a petticoat with a bodice attached or a separate waisted garment which was corded, that is, it had tucks with cords threaded through and drawn in to the waist to provide initial support for the crinoline skirt.

Made out of cotton, linen, cambric, and flannel for winter, several petticoats would be worn at once in the 1840s to provide a bell-shaped structure for the skirt and were stiffened with horsehair at the hem. With the invention of the cage crinoline, petticoats became less structural, and usually only one was worn under the crinoline cage for warmth and modesty as the cage had a habit of flying up when a wearer sat down too rapidly. Another petticoat was customarily worn over the crinoline to soften the steel rings of its outline and tended to have an ornately decorative hem, usually of *broderie anglaise* or crochet as it was likely to be exposed when the wearer was walking. The shape of the petticoat was very much determined by the fashionable shape of outerwear and thus changed over the century from the narrower shapes of the 1860s to the gored cuts of the 1870s and the overly frilled and flounced *froufrou* of the Edwardian Era. The slimmer cut of 1920s fashions and bias cut of the 1930s necessitated a different kind of underwear—usually French knickers and bias-cut slips derived from the petticoat and attached bodice of the nineteenth century.

Post–World War II

In 1947 Christian Dior's *Corolle Line*, later dubbed the New Look, heralded the revival of the bouffant skirt, a round crinoline shape with an understructure comprised of several petticoats. The look was incorporated into teenage culture in the 1950s as young women adopted the petticoat and wore several at once—usually of sugar-starched net and paper nylon, or (for evening) taffeta, at least one of which was stiffened with plastic hoops. The look was particularly associated with rock 'n' roll and jiving as the petticoats preserved the dancer's modesty when exhibiting twirls with her male partner. In the 1960s the petticoat disappeared in daywear and, in much the same way as the corset, became the preserve of fetishism. The allure of the petticoat can be explained by the way it exaggerates certain characteristics

of the female body, by emphasizing the hips it highlights a fragile waist. It has thus earned a place in fetish culture as a signifier of femininity, and magazines such as *Petticoat Discipline* allude to the popular cross-dressing scenario of a little boy being forced to parade in front of his family and friends in petticoats as a punishment for some misdemeanor. The frisson of pleasure achieved through shame thus creates a fetishist.

British designer Vivienne Westwood revived the petticoat in the late 1970s and 1980s as a result of theatrical New Romantic dressing and the experiments with the mini-crini. The wedding of Lady Diana Spencer to Prince Charles in 1981 heralded a revival of the nineteenth-century silhouette in bridal design as a result of her crinoline-skirted wedding gown designed by David and Elizabeth Emmanuel. Thus, the contemporary petticoat is often used as an understructure in women's formal wear, in particular bridal gowns and in outfits worn by female country and western singers; Wynona Judd is associated with this look.

See also Crinoline; Corset; Petticoat; Underwear.

Bibliography

Carter, Alison. *Underwear: The Fashion History*. London: Batsford, 1992.

Cunnington, C. Willet and Phillis. *The History of Underclothes*. London: Dover Publications, 1992.

Saint-Laurent, Cecil. *History of Women's Underwear*. London: Academy Editions, 1986.

Caroline Cox

PLASTIC AND COSMETIC SURGERY

Cosmetic surgery began to be practiced in the last part of the nineteenth century as surgical intervention became increasingly possible because of the development of anesthesia and sterile techniques. One of the first cases to be reported in the last part of the nineteenth century had to do with correcting what was known as saddle nose, a deep depression in the middle of the nose. There are several causes of this condition, but one of them was syphilis. This association with syphilis made those with such noses particularly willing to try to get some surgical change. Large noses were also an issue and intranasal rhinoplasty (hiding the incisions inside the nose) was first done in the 1880s.

Public knowledge of the possibility of plastic surgery came during World War I (1914–1918) as surgeons treated patients in unprecedented number with bad facial and other visible scars. The "miracles" wrought by the surgeons brought plastic surgery out of the closet, and there were enough physicians engaged in it to found the American Association of Oral Surgeons in 1921, later called the American Association of Oral and Plastic Surgeons, and still later, the American Association of Plastic Surgeons.

These early-organized plastic surgeons were cautious about their reconstructive surgery, determined to use their skills to help the maimed but not to do frivolous surgery designed to make people more "beautiful." Not all would-be surgeons agreed with them, and a separate group popularly called "beauty surgeons" developed. These surgeons were looked down upon for their promises to improve the looks of their patients. They took shortcuts, avoiding some of the time-consuming operations involving bone and cartilage grafts. Instead, they relied upon the injection of paraffin, which for a time in the 1920s, was seen as a panacea for all soft-tissue defects. It was widely used to fill facial wrinkles. Unfortunately paraffin had a tendency to migrate to other areas, particularly if the patient spent time in the sun. That tended to disfigure the patient, who then had to go through the process again. One of the best known of these beauty surgeons was Charles C. Miller of Chicago, who wrote an early textbook entitled *Cosmetic Surgery: The Correction of Featural Imperfections.*

The attempt to distinguish between plastic surgery and beauty essentially failed. While surgery was still done for people whose bodily features had been altered by wounds or fires, increasingly it was used to meet personal beauty standards or to change identifiable ethnic features or to make someone appear younger by removing facial wrinkles or having eye tucks. Surgery was also done to change the contours of the body, particularly among women where breast augmentation or breast reduction became an important specialty. By 1988 breast enlargement surgery had become a $300 million business. Some urologists got into the business of penile augmentation, although this was far more controversial. One San Francisco urologist in the 1990s claimed to have done 3,500 such operations even though many urologists condemned the operations as unnecessary and potentially dangerous.

Silicone implants gave a big boost to the breast augmentation industry, and it became second only to lipo-suction (fat removal) as the most common cosmetic surgery. Some women complained that the silicone in their breast implants ruptured or leaked, causing them to have chronic fatigue, arthritis, and damage to the immune system. The result was a lawsuit that resulted in the largest fee ever negotiated in a class-action lawsuit. Dow Corning, Bristol-Myers Squibb Company, and others agreed to pay more $4 billion to 25,000 women. Breast-implant surgery grew even more prevalent, however, when the silicone was replaced by saline. Still the silicone worked better and research both before the lawsuit and after has tended to disprove the validity of the claims about the dangers of silicone. In 2003 there was an unsuccessful campaign to return to silicone as an option. The last word, however, has not been said on this issue. While many women want to increase the size of their breasts, others want to lessen theirs, and breast reduction remains an important part of cosmetic surgery. By 1992, 40,000 women a year were having reduction surgery.

Probably the most radical of plastic or cosmetic surgery is that involved in transsexual surgery. Surgery to change males to female has changed drastically in the last 40 years, and skilled surgeons can use the penis and testicles to make functional labia and vaginas. The surgery for changing females to males is less well-developed since it has proved difficult to make a penis that can be used for both urination and sexual intercourse, but research is still continuing in the field.

See also Body Building and Sculpting; Body Piercing; Branding; Implants; Scarification; Tattoos.

Bibliography

Haiken, Beth. "Plastic Surgery and American Beauty at 1921." *Bulletin of the History of Medicine* 68 (1994): 429–453.

Haiken, Elizabeth. *Venus Envy: A History of Cosmetic Surgery.* Baltimore, Md.: Johns Hopkins University Press, 1997.

Miller, Charles C. *Cosmetic Surgery: The Correction of Featural Imperfections.* Chicago: Oak Printing Company, 1907.

Yalom, Marilyn. *A History of the Breast.* New York: Alfred A. Knopf, 1998.

Vern L. Bullough

POIRET, PAUL

Before Paul Poiret (1879–1944), there was the couture: clothing whose raison d'être was beauty as well as the display of wealth and taste. Paul Poiret brought a new element of fashion to the couture; thanks to him fashion can be a mirror of the times, an art form, and a grand entertainment. Poiret, in the opinion of many, was fashion's first genius.

Born into a solidly bourgeois Parisian family (his father, Auguste Poiret, was a respectable cloth merchant), Poiret attended a Catholic *lycée*, finishing as was typical in his early teens. Following school came an apprenticeship to an umbrella maker, a *métier* that did not suit him. At the time, it was possible to begin a couture career by shopping around one's drawings of original fashion designs. Couture houses purchased these to use as inspiration. Poiret's first encouragement came when Mme. Chéruit, a good but minor couturière, bought a dozen of his designs. He was still a teenager when, in 1896, he began working for Jacques Doucet, one of Paris's most prominent couturiers.

Auspiciously, Doucet sold four hundred copies of one of Poiret's first designs, a simple red cape with gray lining and revers. And in four years there, the novice designer rose up in the ranks to become head of the tailoring department. His greatest coup was making an evening coat to be worn by the great actress Réjane in a play called *Zaza*. The biggest splash fashion could make in those days was on the stage, and Poiret made sure to design something attention-worthy: a mantle of black tulle over black taffeta painted with large-scale iris by a well-known fan painter. Next came the custom of more actresses, and then, while working on the play *L'Aiglon* starring Sarah Bernhardt, Poiret snuck into a dress rehearsal where his scathing critique of the sets and costumes were overheard by the playwright, costing him his job. (The remarks could not have alienated Madame Bernhardt, as he would dress her for several 1912 films.) He fulfilled his military service during the next year and then joined Worth, the top couture house as an assistant designer in 1901. There he was given a sous chef job of creating what Jean Worth (grandson of the founder) called the "fried potatoes," meaning the side dish to Worth's main course of lavish evening and reception gowns. Poiret was responsible for the kind of serviceable, simple clothes needed by women who took the bus as opposed to languishing in a carriage, and while he felt himself to be looked down on by his fellow workers, his designs were commercial successes.

In September 1903 he opened his own couture house on the avenue Auber (corner of the rue Scribe). There he quickly attracted the custom of such former clients as the actress Réjane. In 1905 he married Denise Boulet, the daughter of a textile manufacturer, whose waiflike figure and nonconventional looks would change the way he designed. In 1906 Poiret moved into 37, rue Pasquier, and by 1909 he was able to relocate to quite grand quarters: a large eighteenth-century *hôtel particulier* at 9 avenue d'Antin (perpendicular to the Faubourg Saint-Honoré and since World War II known as Avenue Franklin-Roosevelt). The architect Louis Süe oversaw the renovations; the spectacular open grounds included a parterre garden. Poiret also purchased two adjoining buildings on the Faubourg St. Honore, which he later established as Martine and Rosine.

Les Robes of Paul Poiret

Until the October 1908 publication of *Les Robes de Paul Poiret*, Poiret was merely an up-and-coming couturier, likely to assume a place in the hierarchy as secure as that of Doucet or Worth. However, the limited edition deluxe album of Poiret designs as envisioned and exquisitely rendered by new artist Paul Iribe would have far-reaching impact, placing Poiret in a new uncharted position, that of daringly inventive designer and arbiter of taste. Fashion presentation up to then had been quite straightforward: magazines showed clothes in a variety of media, based on what was possible technically: black-and-white sketches, hand-colored woodblock prints, or colored lithographs, and, in the case of the French magazine *Les Modes*, black- and-white photographs or pastel-tinted black-and-white photographs. The poses were typical photographer's studio ones, carefully posed models against a muted ground, vaguely landscape or interior in feeling.

Using the pochoir method of printing, resulting in brilliantly saturated areas of color, Paul Iribe juxtaposed Poiret's graphically striking clothes against stylishly arranged backgrounds including pieces of antique furniture, decorative works of art, and old master paintings. The dresses, depicted in color, popped out from the black-and-white backgrounds. This inventive approach was tremendously influential, not only affecting future fashion illustration and photography, but cementing the relationship between art and fashion and probably

THE POIRET ROSE

While there are some designers associated with specific flowers (Chanel and the camellia, Dior and the lily-of-the-valley) no one can claim the achievement of having reinvented a flower in such a way as to have it always identified with them. The Poiret rose (reduced to its simplest elements of overlapping curving lines) may have appeared for the first time in the form of a three-dimensional silk chiffon flower sewn to the empire bodice of Josephine, one of the 1907 dresses featured in the 1908 album Les Robes de Paul Poiret. Flat versions of the Poiret rose, embroidered in beads, appeared on the minaret tunic of the well-known dress Sorbet, 1913. Poiret's characteristically large and showy label also featured a rose.

inspiring the launch of such exquisitely conceived publications as the Gazette du Bon Ton.

The dresses were no less newsworthy and influential. When Poiret introduced his lean, high-waisted silhouette of 1908, it was the first time (but hardly the last) that a radically new fashion would be based fairly literally on the past. The dresses, primarily for evening, feature narrow lines, high waists, covered arms, low décolletés. Their inspiration is both Directoire and medieval. In abandoning the bifurcated figure of the turn of the twentieth century, Poiret looked back to a time when revolutionary dress itself was referencing ancient times. Suddenly the hourglass silhouette was passé.

Poiret, Bakst, and Orientalism

Poiret had an affinity with all things Eastern, claiming to have been a Persian prince in a previous life. Significantly, the first Asian-inspired piece he ever designed, while still at Worth, was controversial. A simple Chinese-style cloak called Confucius, it offended the occidental sensibilities of an important client, a Russian princess. To her grand eyes it seemed shockingly simple, the kind of thing a peasant might wear; when Poiret opened his own establishment such mandarin-robe-style cloaks would be best-sellers.

The year 1910 was a watershed for orientalism in fashion and the arts. In June, the Ballet Russe performed Scheherazade at the Paris Opera, with sets and costumes by Leon Bakst. Its effect on the world of design was immediate. Those who saw the production or

Bakst's watercolor sketches reproduced in such luxurious journals as Art et Decoration (in 1911) were dazzled by the daring color combinations and swirling profusion of patterns. Since the belle époque could be said to have been defined by the delicate, subtle tints of the impressionists, such a use of color would be seen as groundbreaking.

Although color and pattern were what people talked about, they serve to obscure the most daring aspect of the Ballet Russe costumes: the sheerness (not to mention scantiness) of the materials. Even in the drawings published in 1911, nipples can be seen through sheer silk bodices, and not just legs, but thighs in harem trousers. Midriffs, male and female, were bare altogether. Whether inspired or reinforced by Bakst, certain near-Eastern effects: the softly ballooning legs, turbans, and the surplice neckline and tunic effect became Poiret signatures.

The cover of Les Modes for April 1912 featured a Georges Barbier illustration of two Poiret enchantresses in a moonlit garden, one dressed in the sort of boldly patterned cocoon wraps for which Poiret would be known throughout his career, the other in a soft evening dress with high waist, below-the-knee-length overskirt, narrow trailing underskirt, the bodice sheer enough to reveal the nipples.

While Poiret's claim to have single-handedly banished the Edwardian palette of swooning mauves can be viewed as egotistical, given Bakst's tremendous influence, his assertions about doing away with the corset have more validity. In each of the numerous photographs of Denise Poiret she is dressed in a fluid slide of fabric; there is no evidence of the lumps ands bumps of corsets and other underpinnings. Corsetry and sheerness are hardly compatible and boning would interrupt Poiret's narrow lines.

The Jupe-Culotte

In the course of producing his (hugely successful) second album of designs Les Choses de Paul Poiret (1911), Poiret asked his latest discovery, the artist Georges Lepape, to come up with an idea for a new look. It was Mme. Lepape who sketched her idea of a modern costume and put it in her husband's pocket. When Poiret asked where the new idea was, Lepape had to be reminded to fish it out. The next time they met, Poiret surprised the couple with a mannequin wearing his version of their design: a long tunic with boat neck and high waist worn over dark pants gathered into cuffs at the ankle. And so, at the end of the album under the heading: Tomorrow's Fashions, there appeared several dress/trouser hybrids, which would become known as *jupe-culottes*.

The jupe-culotte caused an international sensation. The Victorian age had left the sexes cemented in rigid roles easily visible in their dress—men in the drab yet freeing uniform of business, and women in an almost literal gilded cage of whalebone and steel, brocade and lace. While Poiret's impulse seems to have been primarily aesthetic, the fact that it coincided with the crusade of suffragists taking up where Amelia Bloomer had left off, served to bring about a real change in how women dressed. For months anything relating to the jupe-culotte was major news. In its most common incarnation, a kind of high-waisted evening dress with tunic lines revealing soft chiffon harem pants, the jupe-culotte was wildly unmodern, requiring the help of a maid to get in and out of and utterly impractical for anything other than looking au courant. Poiret did design numerous more tailored versions, however, often featuring military details and his favorite checked or striped materials; these do look ahead (about fifty years) to the high-fashion trouser suit.

Martine

In the space of five years, Poiret had become a world-renown success. Now came another influential act. Martine, named after one of Poiret's daughters, opened 1 April 1911 as a school of decorative art. Poiret admitted to being inspired by his 1910 visit to the Wiener Werkstätte, but his idea for Martine entailed a place where imagination could flourish as opposed to being disciplined in a certain style. Young girls, who, in their early teens had finished their traditional schooling, became the pupils. Their assignment was to visit zoos, gardens, the aquarium, and markets and make rough sketches. Their sketches were then developed into decorative motifs. Once a wall full of studies had been completed, Poiret would invite artist colleagues and wallpaper, textile, or embroidery specialists for a kind of critique. The students were rewarded for selected designs, but also got to see their work turned into such Martine wares as rugs, china, pottery, wallpaper, textiles for interiors, and fashions. The Salon d'Automne of 1912 displayed many such items made after designs of the École Martine and Poiret opened a Martine store at 107, Faubourg Saint-Honoré.

Within a few years, a typical Martine style of interior had been developed, juxtaposing spare, simple shapes with large-scale native designs inspired in the main from nature. A 1914 bathroom featured micro-mosaic tiles turning the floor, sink case, and tub into a continuous smooth expanse punctuated by murals or tile panels patterned with stylized grapes on the vine. There were Martine departments in shops all over Europe; although more decorative than what would become known as art deco and art moderne, Martine deserves an early place in the chronology of modern furniture and interior design.

Also in 1911 Poiret inaugurated a perfume concern, naming it after another daughter, Rosine, and locating it at the same address as Martine. Poiret's visionary aesthetic was perfectly suited to the world of scents and he was involved in every aspect of the bottle design, packaging, and advertising, including the Rosine advertising fans. He was also interested in new developments of synthetic scents and in expanding the idea of what is a fragrance by adding lotions, cosmetics, and soaps. Fellow couturiers like Babani, the Callot Soeurs, Chanel, and Patou were among the first to follow suit; thanks to Poiret, perfumes continue to be an integral part of the image (and business) of a fashion house.

Poiret the Showman

At a time when the runway had yet to be invented and clothes were shown on models in intimate settings in couture houses, Poiret's 1911 and 1914 promotional tours of Europe with models wearing his latest designs made a tremendous splash.

On 24 June 1911 the renowned 1,002-night ball was held in the avenue d'Antin garden featuring Paul Poiret as sultan and Denise Poiret as the sultan's favorite in a combination of two of Poiret's greatest hits, a jupe-culotte with a minaret tunic. The invitations specified how the guests should dress: Dunoyer de Segonzac was told to come as Champagne, His Majesty's Valet and Raoul Dufy as The King's Fool. If one of the 300 guests showed up in Chinese (or, worse, conventional evening) dress, he or she was sent to a wardrobe room to be decked out in Persian taste. Although fancy dress balls had been all the rage for several decades, this one seems to have struck a chord; perhaps it was the first hugely luxurious (champagne, oysters, and other delicacies flowed freely) event staged by a creative person (in trade no less) rather than an aristocrat. Future fêtes, each with a carefully thought-out theme, failed to achieve the same level of excitement. After the war, Poiret's thoughts had turned toward increasingly zany moneymaking ventures. The nightclub was the latest diversion after World War I and Poiret turned his garden first into a nightspot, and then in 1921 it became an open-air theater, Oasis, with a retractable roof devised for him by the automobile manufacturer Voisin. This venture lasted six months.

His last truly notable bit of showmanship was his display at the 1925 Paris Exposition des Arts Décoratifs et Industriels. Rather than set up a display in an approved location in an official building, Poiret installed three barges on the Seine. Decorated in patriotic French colors, Delices was a restaurant decorated with red anemones; Amours was decorated with blue Martine carnations; and Orgues was white featuring fourteen canvases by Dufy depicting regattas at Le Havre, Ile de France, Deauville; and races at Longchamps, showing some of Poiret's last dress designs under his own label. It was clear that his zest for ideas was being directed elsewhere other than fashion. Typically over the top, he also commissioned a merry-go-round on which one could ride figures of Parisian life, including him and his *midinettes*, or shop-girls.

The Poiret Milieu

Poiret's interest in the fine, contemporary arts of the day began while he was still quite young. His artist friends included Francis Picabia and André Derain, who painted his portrait when they were both serving in the French army in 1914. His sisters were Nicole Groult, married to Andre Groult, the modern furniture designer; and Mme. Boivin, the jeweler; another was a poet. Besides discovering Paul Iribe and Georges Barbier, he reinvigorated the career of Raoul Dufy by commissioning woodcut-based fabric designs from him and starting him off on a long career in textile design and giving new life to his paintings as well. Bernard Boutet de Monvel worked on numerous early projects for Poiret, including, curiously, writing catalog copy for his perfume brochures. While quite young, Erté saw (and sketched) Poiret's mannequins in Russia in 1911; after emigrating to Paris he worked as an assistant designer to Poiret from the beginning of 1913 to the outbreak of war in 1914. His illustrations accompanied articles about Poiret fashion in *Harper's Bazaar* and reveal a signature Erté style that might not have developed without the inspiration of Poiret. He also launched the careers of Madeleine Panizon, a Martine student who became a milliner, and discovered shoemaker Andre Perugia, whom he helped establish in business after World War I.

Poiret's Clientele

Not surprisingly, Poiret's clients were more than professional beauties, clotheshorses, or socialites. Besides the very top actresses of his time, Réjane and Sarah Bernhardt, the entertainer Josephine Baker, and the celebrated Liane de Pougy, one of the last of the grandes horizontales, there were: the Countess Grefulhe, muse of Marcel Proust, and Margot Asquith, wife of the English prime minister, who invited him to show his styles in London, creating a political furor for her (and her husband's) disloyalty to British designers. Nancy Cunard, ivory bracelet–clad icon of early twentieth-century style, recalled that she had been wearing a gold-panniered Poiret dress in 1922 at a ball where she was bored dancing with the Prince of Wales but thrilled to meet and chat with T. S. Eliot.

The international cosmetics entrepreneur Helena Rubinstein met Poiret while he was a young design assistant at Worth and followed him as he struck out on his own. She was photographed in one of his daring jupeculottes in 1913 and wore a Poiret Egyptian style dress in her advertisements in 1924. The quintessentially French author Colette was a client. Boldini painted the Marchesa Casati in a chic swirl of Poiret and greyhounds. The American art patrons Peggy Guggenheim and Gertrude Whitney dressed in high bohemian Poiret and Natasha Hudnut Rambova, herself a designer and the exotic wife of the matinee idol Rudolf Valentino, went to Poiret for her trousseau.

Postwar Poiret

Poiret was involved for the duration of the war as a military tailor, and although he occasionally made news with a design or article, when he was demobilized in 1919 he had to relaunch his fashion, decorating, and perfume businesses. His first collection after the war, shown in the summer of 1919, was enthusiastically received and fashion magazines like *Harper's Bazaar* continued to regularly feature his luxurious creations, typically made in vivid colors, lush-patterned fabrics, and trimmed lavishly with fur. Poiret's work perfectly suited the first part of the 1920s. The dominant silhouette was tubular, and fairly long, and most coats were cut on the full side with kimono or dolman sleeves. Such silhouettes were perfect for displaying the marvelous Poiret decorations, either Martine-inspired or borrowed from native clothing around the world. He continued to occasionally show such previous greatest hits as jupe-culottes and dresses with minaret tunics. In 1924 he left his grand quarters in the avenue d'Antin, moving to the Rond Point in 1925. He would leave that business in 1929.

Obscurity

By 1925 Poiret had begun to sound like a curmudgeon, holding forth against chemise dresses, short skirts, flesh-colored hose, and thick ankles with the same kind of ranting tone once used by M. Worth to criticize Poiret's trouser skirt. Financially, he did poorly too, and he sold his business in 1929.

In 1931, *Women's Wear Daily* announced that Paul Poiret was reentering the couture, using as a business name his telephone number "Passy Ten Seventeen." Prevented from using his own name by a legal arrangement, he told the paper that he planned to print his photograph on his stationery, since presumably he still owned the rights to his face. This venture closed in 1932. After designing some for department stores such as Liberty in London in 1933, he turned his attention to an assortment of endeavors including writing (an autobiography called *King of Fashion*) and painting. He succumbed to Parkinson's disease on 28 April 1944.

While Gabrielle Chanel is credited with being the first woman to live the modern life of the twentieth century (designing accordingly), it is Poiret who created the contemporary idea of a couturier as wide-reaching arbiter. His specific fashion contributions aside, Poiret was the first to make fashion front-page news; to collaborate with fine artists; develop lines of fragrances; expand into interior decoration; and to be known for his lavish lifestyle. Poignantly he was also the first to lose the rights to his own name.

Poiret's earliest styles were radically simple; these would give way to increasingly lavish "artistic" designs and showman-like behavior. By 1913 *Harper's Bazaar* was already looking back at his notable achievements: originating the narrow silhouette, starting the fashion for the uncorseted figure, doing away with the petticoat, being the first to show the jupe-culotte and the minaret tunic. That the fashion world was already nostalgic about his achievements proved oddly prescient: his ability to transform how women dressed would pass with World War I.

See also Doucet, Jacques; Fashion Designer; Orientalism; Paris Fashion; Worth, Charles Frederick.

Bibliography

Deslandres, Yvonne, with Dorothée Lalanne. *Poiret Paul Poiret 1879–1944.* New York: Rizzoli International, 1987.
Poiret, Paul. *King of Fashion: The Autobiography of Paul Poiret.* Philadelphia and London: J. B. Lippincott, 1931.
Remaury, Bruno, ed. *Dictionnaire de la Mode Au XXe Siecle.* Paris: Editions du Regard, 1994.
Sweeney, James Johnson. "Poiret Inspiration for Artists, Designers, and Women." *Vogue,* 1 September 1971, 186–196.
White, Palmer. *Poiret.* New York: Clarkson N. Potter Inc., 1973.

Caroline Rennolds Milbank

POLITICS AND FASHION

Every large society and social group develops a system of social control or polity that is shared by the members of the group and relates in some way to their system of dress. The power to address diverse problems and needs of a society is invested in people who become specialists in delivery of the services of social control. Only those individuals so designated and recognized have the right to power and authority over group members. This system of control or government is reflected in the rules of the organization and evolves from the normative order and moral beliefs of the group. The moral ideas of a group both mold and reflect the group's beliefs concerning what is right or wrong behavior for members. Developing expectations for appearance, dress, and the extent to which one participates in fashion (defined here as the accepted way of behaving of the majority of individuals at a specific time and place) are social behaviors that are frequently subject to control by social organizations.

Control over dress and fashion participation is exercised both informally and formally through the political structure of an organization and its power. The governing body serves several functions, including: (a) developing, delineating, and assessing rules and regulations so that the beliefs of the organization are molded by and reflected in them; (b) establishing a framework regarding the rights and responsibilities of members of the group; and (c) developing a process for applying and enforcing the rules for all members. A process for adding new regulations and a method to dispute existing regulations can be developed along with penalties and sanctions for violations of these rules. The court system in Western societies is an example of a process used to manage power in interpreting and applying regulations, which may prohibit members from participation in some activities as well as prescribe participation in others. Government also has power over relations with other societies in matters that involve group interests including mobilizing legitimate use of force to defend the group against infringement of others. Government also involves relationships with other societies in the form of trade agreements and regulations. For example, when foreign manufacturers can produce apparel products at a lower cost than domestic manufacturers, the domestic industries are threatened. Governments may make regulations to control the flow of foreign-produced products into domestic markets to force consumers to purchase domestic products and maintain domestic industries.

Another area related to dress where the government uses power is in developing regulations for consumer protection. Laws can be developed to protect consumers from unsafe or unhealthy apparel products as well as protect the environment from human exploitation. An example of the former are the laws that prohibit the use of flammable fabrics in apparel. An example of the latter are endangered species laws that prohibit the use of skin and furs of specific animals in apparel.

Examples of power conveyed through dress are common in all societies. Topics frequently addressed through formal and informal regulations include body exposure and gender differences. Societies have regulations concerning under what circumstances, if any, different aspects of both male and female bodies can appear uncovered or covered. The amount or type of skin exposed tends to be interpreted as symbolic of certain sexual behaviors. General societal efforts to control sexual behavior may include regulations regarding appearing naked in public, exposure of genitals, appearing in clothing associated with the opposite sex (cross-dressing), or the separation of the sexes (such as governmentmandated separate swimming pools or even separate cash register lines for men and women). These regulations may be formal, as in the case of health laws concerning body exposure and food service (no shoes, no shirt, no service), or informal, as in the case of amount of body exposure on public beaches. Informal regulations often vary depending on the situation. For example, a brassiere and briefs worn by a female can offer as much if not more body coverage than a swimsuit. However, a garment defined as a swimsuit

is acceptable at locations like the beach or swimming pool, while a brassiere and briefs in the same place would be considered inappropriate.

Rules and regulations of social organizations vary in their degree of importance, in how they came into being, in the degree of emotional response that violating regulations might evoke, and the type of sanctions that might be applied to individuals who violate them. There are both positive and negative sanctions associated with engaging in or failing to participate in fashion. Positive sanctions such as praise or emulation reinforce behaviors perceived as correct. In contrast, a continuum in scope and intensity of negative sanctions can apply to individuals who fail to comply with the expectations of the group or group norms concerning dress and participation in fashion.

The type of negative sanction that results when individuals violate group norms for dress are tied to the degree of emotional response evoked. If the violation evoked a low degree of emotional response, concern is with violating a customary dress practice of the group. Violation of a customary practice generally does not create a great disturbance in the social organization of the group. If a sanction is applied by members of the group to influence the individual to change their behavior in keeping with the existing norm, the sanction may be in the form of gossip or teasing. In small organizations or societies where all members are known to each other, a negative sanction like gossip is probably all that is needed to force compliance with the expectations of group members. It is also possible that a mild sanction may result where a slight deviation from the group norm is tolerated if not accepted as only a minor deviation.

If the violation of the expectation for dress evokes a strong emotional response from group members, the violation is concerned with a moral standard of the group. Moral standards may be informally controlled, as is the case with customs concerning dress. Customs are associated with a history of practice, and violations may meet with negative sanctions from the group in the form of ridicule, avoidance, or ostracism. Moral standards concerning dress may also become codified into laws and formally controlled. Negative sanctions for violating laws concerning dress can include arrest, incarceration, or death.

Development of power through the rules of an organization or society do not guarantee that the rules equally reflect all members' interests. Whether the interests of men are favored over the interests of women was at issue in Terengganu, Malaysia, where the state government was said to have supported gender-based discrimination through dress codes as well as other practices. According to Endaya (2002), the government supported Islamic law as dress codes were developed that barred women from wearing bikinis and other clothing that exposed their bodies. Other dress codes that imposed restrictions based on gender included a requirement for young Muslim women to cover their heads. Laws of this kind have become commonplace in the contemporary Islamic world. Another dress code exemplifying promotion of the interests of one group over another was a decree in 2002 made by King Mswati III of Swaziland, in southern Africa, who banned women from wearing trousers in the capital of Mbabane because the practice "violated the country's traditions" (Familara 2002, p 4).

Few laws exist in the United States that regulate appearance, dress, or fashion in the workplace or in schools. However, dress codes are used to regulate appearances in the workplace as well as in schools, and judicial decisions (case laws) have developed concerning dress. In general, most courts uphold an employer's right to set appearance standards through dress codes as long as the codes are related to a legitimate business interest, government interest, or for health and sanitation reasons (Rothstein et al, 1994). As a result, few complaints brought forward by employees have been upheld in the courts unless the dress code differs between men and women, the code is demeaning, or is more costly to one sex versus the other (Lennon, Schultz, and Johnson 1999).

The courts have also held that students retain their constitutional rights when they enter the school building, although student conduct, including their appearance, can be regulated. Dress codes in schools are generally considered valid if they promote safety or if they prevent disruption or distraction of peers (Alexander and Alexander 1984). Since dress is a form of communication, students in the United States have voiced the complaint that some school dress codes violate their constitutional right to freedom of speech, which is guaranteed by the First Amendment (Lennon, Schultz, and Johnson 1999). Lewin (2003) reported on a student that was sent home from school for wearing a T-shirt with a picture of President Bush and the words "international terrorist." The high school junior wore the T-shirt to express his antiwar sentiment and believed his right to express his political beliefs were violated when he was sent home from school. In this case, the school would have to

---

FREEDOM OF EXPRESSION IN DRESS

While the right to express a political opinion through dress may be protected by the constitution, customs concerning appropriate dress based upon gender may not be protected. In the United States, a reported case where clothing was disruptive of the learning process occurred when a young man was suspended from school for wearing a long peasant dress with a plunging neckline (Rabinovotz 1998). The issue was not only that the young man appeared in clothing customarily associated with young women, but that he stuffed tissue paper down the front. School officials noted that they did not want to create "a carnival-like atmosphere in the school" (p. B5).

---

prove that the student's T-shirt was so different and disruptive that it detracted from the educational process.

The classic case concerning dress codes and students' freedom of speech in the United States is *Tinker* vs. *Des Moines Independent School District* (1969). The Tinker case involved a plan by students to wear black armbands to school to symbolize their opposition to the Vietnam War. Officials of the school learned of the students' decision two days before it happened and implemented a special dress code banning armbands in school. The U.S. Supreme Court held that wearing armbands constituted a form of speech protected by the constitution. The court held that for student activity to be prohibited, school officials must reasonably forecast disruption in the school and must have some evidence to support their forecast. The courts also ruled that the predicted disruption must be substantial, and judged to be physical and damaging to the learning environment at school (Alexander and Alexander 1984).

Regulations of an organization, such as dress codes, can shape the dress of its members. Dress can also serve as a platform for protest against such regulations. In 2001, King Mswati III of Swaziland also revived an old law requiring girls to wear chastity belts with tassels. The belts, according to the king, would not only preserve a young girl's virginity but also prevent HIV-AIDS. Subsequently, Swazi women protested and showed defiance against the law by dropping tassels in front of the royal palace (Familara 2002).

Interpersonal Social Power and Dress

While the government of a society is involved in regulations concerning dress, customs concerning dress often involve the use of dress as a symbol to communicate interpersonal social power. Interpersonal social power is defined as the potential to have social influence (French and Raven 1959). Social influence refers to a change in the behavior or belief of a person as a result of the action or presence of another person (Raven 1992). A typology originally developed by French and Raven and subsequently refined by Raven (1992; 1993) outlines six sources of social power that an influencing agent can draw upon to affect change in another person: legitimate power, reward power, coercion power, expert power, referent power, and the power of information. These sources of social power can be either formal or informal and can be communicated through dress.

Legitimate power is influence that is based on a social position or rank within the organization. This is power that is assigned to a position by the group to enforce the rules of the group (described previously as government). Symbolic of legitimate power is the uniform of an officer in the military or the robes of a judge. Reward power is influence derived from the ability to provide social approval or some form of compensation. Fashion editors and other arbiters of taste may exercise reward power as they name individuals to best-dressed lists or feature individuals repeatedly on the cover of magazines. A woman's beauty may also yield reward power as many men consider physical attractiveness in women to be highly desirable (Buss 1989). A woman's attractiveness may be rewarding to a man who is seen with her. Coercive power is reflective of influence that is achieved as a result of threats of punishment or rejection. Symbolic of coercive power is the uniform of a police officer because of their power to deter, detain, and arrest citizens. Expert power is influence stemming from knowledge or experience. Symbolic of this type of influence are the cap and gown of the academic or the lab coats of scientists and physicians. These individuals offer recommendations that are followed because individuals' believe in their expertise. Referent power is influence derived from the desire to identify with someone. Fashion models and movie stars wield referent power when individuals copy their dress. Information power is influence that is based on a logical presentation of information by the influencing agent, which persuades the individual to comply. Lennon (1999) noted that to Catholics the white clothing of the pope might represent informational power as a result of the belief that the pope has direct communication with God. Fashion is shaped by each of these types of social power.

As noted, legitimate power over fashion is in evidence when societies develop regulations concerning dress. Sumptuary laws have been used to maintain class and gender distinctions by disallowing certain individuals to wear certain styles or colors of clothing as well as requiring certain individuals to wear specific forms of dress. When the communist party came into power in China, coercive power became evident. According to Scott (1958), communists developed a standardization of dress that made no distinction between the sexes or on the basis of rank. The military uniform of the communists consisted of a high-collared tunic, trousers with puttees, and Chinese shoes or rubber boots. After troops occupied the cities, the industrial workers adopted dress styled more or less identical to the military uniform except the color differed. Soon afterward, students, clerical workers, and manual workers adopted the party uniform. According to Scott, no one issued directives but citizens tacitly understood that clothes other than the uniform seemed unpatriotic, and those not adopting the new style were publicly reprimanded or lectured.

The effect of reward power on fashion becomes evident through the practice of naming certain highly visible individuals to "best dressed" lists. Other individuals emulate the appearance of those named to the list and fuel fashion change in terms of speeding the diffusion of a style as well as providing an impetus for change. The impact of expert power and information power on the direction of fashion comes from numerous fashion magazines sharing perspectives on what styles comprise the fashion of a time or place. From all the styles made available by designers and manufacturers, fashion editors select and feature those styles they believe will appeal to the readers of their publications. In this way, they weld their knowledge and expertise and hence attempt to shape fashion. Newspapers feature advice columnists who answer questions about what is appropriate dress for specific social events, and subsequently impact their readers about what styles are acceptable for a given time and place (and what is the current fashion).

See also Dress Codes; Military Style; Religion and Dress.

Bibliography

Alexander, K., and M. D. Alexander. *The Law of School, Students, and Teachers in a Nutshell.* St. Paul, Minn.: West Publishing Co., 1984.

Buss, D. M. "Sex Differences in Human Mate Preferences: Evolutionary Hypotheses Tested in 37 Cultures." *Behavioral and Brain Sciences* 12 (1989): 1–49.

French, J. R. P., and B. Raven. "The Bases of Social Power." In *Studies in Social Power*. Edited by D. Cartwright. Ann Arbor, Mich.: University of Michigan, 1958, pp. 150–167.

Lennon, S. J. "Sex, Dress and Power in the Workplace: Star Trek, the Next Generation." In *Appearance and Power*, pp. 103–126. Edited by K. Johnson and S. Lennon. Oxford: Berg, 1999.

Lennon, S. J., T. L. Schultz, and K. K. P. Johnson. "Forging Linkages Between Dress and the Law in the U.S., Part II: Dress Codes." *Clothing and Textiles Research Journal* 17, no. 3 (1999): 157–167.

Lewin, T. "High School Tells Student to Remove Antiwar Shirt." *New York Times* (23 February 2003): A12.

Raven, B. "A Power Interaction Model of Interpersonal Influence: French and Raven Thirty Years Later." *Journal of Social Behavior and Personality* 7 (1992): 217–244.

——. "The Bases of Power: Origins and Recent Developments." *Journal of Social Issues* 49 (1993): 227–254.

Rothstein, M., C. B. Craver, E. P. Schroeder, E. W. Shoben, and L. S. Vandervelde. *Employment Law*. St. Paul, Minn.: West Publishing Company, 1994.

Scott, A. C. *Chinese Costume in Transition*. New York: Theatre Arts, 1958.

Tinker v. Des Moines Independence Community School District, 393 U.S. 503, 1969.

Internet Resources

Endaya, I. "Malaysian Government Reinforces Gender Segregation." *We* 19 (2002): 5. Available from <http://straits times.asia1.com.sg/women/0,3320,00.html>.

Familara, A. "Women Can't Wear Trousers, Orders Swazi King." *We* 20 (2002): 4. Available from <http://news.bbc.co.uk/hi/english/world/africa/newsid_206000/2062320.stm>.

Kim K. P. Johnson

PRADA*

Prada was founded in Milan in 1913 by Mario Prada as a luxury leather-goods firm, but it made little impact on the world of fashion until after Miuccia Prada took charge of her grandfather's company in 1978. Her first big success was a black nylon backpack with a triangular silver label. Soon her shoe and handbag designs became the focus of a veritable cult of fashionable consumers in Europe, America, and Japan. Miuccia Prada and her husband and business partner, Patrizio Bertelli, maintain close control over the company. They added a ready-to-wear line in 1989 and inaugurated the younger, slightly less expensive Miu Miu line in 1992, followed by Prada Sport, whose iconic red line is almost as recognized in certain circles as Nike's swoosh symbol. A string of shops and boutiques in Paris, New York, and San Francisco, designed in collaboration with the architect Rem Koolhaas, became instantly famous. Prada also engaged in a series of complex ownership maneuvers in the late 1990s, buying and selling stakes in Gucci, Fendi, and other companies and forming a partnership with Azzedine Alaïa in 2000.

Prada clothes and accessories have been described as both classic and eccentric, frumpy but hip, marked by an ambiguous techno-retro sensibility. On the one hand, Prada's style is modern, drawing on northern Italian traditions of discreet elegance and fine craftsmanship. On the other hand, as Miuccia Prada said in 1995, "I make ugly clothes from ugly material. Simply bad taste. But they end up looking good anyway." She may have been referring to that season's "bad taste" collection, featuring such styles as a Formica check design, which evoked the look of 1970s polyester. Several years later she said, "I have always thought that Prada clothes looked kind of normal, but not quite normal. Maybe they have little twists that are disturbing, or something about them that's not quite acceptable. . . . Prada is not clothing for the bourgeoisie."

The eccentricity and intellectual purity of Miuccia Prada's clothes appeal to intellectuals and artists, while fashion editors are drawn to her constant experimentalism. Prada produced very strong collections in 2003 and 2004 that reaffirm her own aesthetic sensibilities and the stature of her company. Prada has also become famous for its corporate patronage of avant-garde art.

Prada made a number of important acquisitions and other financial transactions in the first decade of the 21st century that have had a strong influence on the position and financial health of the company. For example, Prada's stake in Fendi was sold to LVMH in 2001 at a substantial loss, damaging Prada's financial position. Especially notorious was Prada's acquisition of rival companies Helmut Lang and Jil Sander. These were later sold off, and the founding designers left their respective companies.

See also Alaïa, Azzedine; Fendi; Gucci; Handbags and Purses; Retro Styles; Shoes.

Bibliography

Buxbaum, Gerda, ed. *Icons of Fashion: The Twentieth Century.* New York: Prestel, 1999.

Prada, Miuccia et al. *Prada.* New York: Abrahms, 2010.

John S. Major

PSYCHEDELIC FASHION

Psychedelia—the range of sensations, epiphanies, and hallucinations induced by chemical stimulants—was an epochal cultural phenomenal of the 1960s; in retrospect, it seems not only a key component of the decade's sensibility, but an apt symbol of the 1960s re-ordering of social, political, and artistic structures. It was inevitable that fashion and psychedelic experience would go hand-in-hand since one of the effects of an LSD [lysergic acid diethylamide) "trip" was a height-ened appreciation of color, texture, and line. Psyche-delic fashion did more than evoke or pay tribute to the mind-alerting experience; it became a way to enhance participation. Given that the LSD—popularly called acid—experience involved erasing discreet bound-aries, it was appropriate to dress in clothes that en-hanced the ability of the communicant to merge into an experience that for many became nearly sacerdotal rite.

The Big Bang

Partaking of LSD was central to the hippie credo, and the outlandish clothes of the hippies disseminated the psychedelic sensibility. Flowing shapes seemed to re-late to the unbinding of restrictions unloosed by the hallucinogenic experience. The prevalence of tactile fabrics in hippie fashions spoke to the sense-enhancing properties of the acid trip. Most visible were its in-novations in palette and imagery: equally provoca-tive vibrating patterns and colors. Certain traditional motifs—the amoebalike crawl of Indian paisley, for example—were appropriated as psychedelic imagery. The accoutrements included face painting in Day-

glo neon colors that recreated the incandescence of acid chimeras. But the principal topos of psychedelic fashion were portraits of light as it was fractured, made mobile by the lens of the acid trip. The awak-ened kineticism of light made flat surfaces seem to churn and roil. Colors bled, emulsified, and merged kaleidoscopically.

LSD existed for thirty years before reaching the widespread cultural acceptance and curiosity it aroused during the 1960s. Similarly, slightly before the apogee of psychedelic fashion in the mid to late 1960s, fashion in-spired by the oscillatory geometries of op art deployed a pleasurable hoodwinking of perceptual faculties. Psy-chedelic experience and psychedelic fashion's incongru-ous reshuffling of identifiable reference points recalled surrealistic art and Dada, which also were the progeni-tors to some extent of pop art. Pop art functioned in the 1960s as its own sometimes surreal rebuke to nonrepre-sentational abstract expressionism.

The Total Environment

Psychedelic fashion became a way for external reality to seemingly be transformed by the visions projected on the mind's internal screen. Psychedelic fashions existed within a cultural context that encompassed the radical lifestyles of the hippies, the transcendent "acid" experi-ence as well as constructed environments that sought to simulate the acid experience. These encompassed communal affirmations such as the "be-in," and perfor-mance art "happenings." Psychedelic fashion became an indispensable component of the total environment cre-ated in discotheques or rock palaces; it allowed an in-tegration of the reformed environment and the remade self. The *dereglement de tous les sens* that Artur Rimbaud had once propounded, was heightened orally by the fuzz box and "wah-wah" pedal distortions. Light shows at the rock concerts and at the discotheque hurled pul-sating apparitions at the spectator. The blinking strobe light atomized the continuity, the gestalt of visual per-ception. It might be said that under the strobe light, all fashion became psychedelic.

Psychedelic fashion was a quintessential 1960s movement. Although it was eventually, and to some degree opportunistically, embraced by virtually every mainstream design and sector of the fashion industry, it would be hard to isolated a single designer or even a cluster of designers who could be credited for its in-vention or promotion. Nevertheless, the psychedelic preoccupation with light and the total environment reached a paradigm at the Manhattan boutique Paraphernalia in 1966, when electrical engineer Diana Dew devised a vinyl dress that turned-on at the command of the wearer. A miniaturized potentiometer fit on the belt of the dress and regulated the frequency of the blinking hearts or stars, which could be coordinated to the throbbing beat of the disco soundtrack. That same year, Yves Saint Laurent brought psychedelic light and color to pop art's disembodied trademarks with a bridal gown that flashed an incandescent flower, which enlivened the runway show's traditional finale.

Psychedelic sensibility was essential to the second phase of 1960s' fashion vocabulary, the move away from some of the sleeker and brusquer characteristics of mod fashion. It was consanguineous with the second phase's absorption of folk and tribal lexicon, the experimentation in role playing and persona construction made possible by the improvised costumes adopted by youth cultures and spilling out into the Western world's clothes-wearing population at large. The unprecedented outfits certainly owed something to the phantasmagoria of acid visions. Tribal and psychedelic converged with mottled patterns of African and Indonesian fabrics, the phosphorescent splotches and showers of tie-dye.

Psychedelic fashion was a grass-roots groundswell, a radically demotic movement that eventually generated a ubiquitous acknowledgment. In New York, for example, one could buy made-to-order tie-dye ensembles at both The Fur Balloon on West 4th Street in Greenwich Village and at Halston's salon on East 68th Street on the Upper East Side.

Cycles of renewal

Ultimately, the lexicon and the fashion became degraded. New adjectives introduced into colloquial language and the language of fashion, "psychedelic" and "trippy" among them, no longer retained their original referents but became generic adjectives of approval. Psychedelia not only offered the keys to the cosmos but became the latest marketing ploy. "Call it psychedelic and it will sell fast, some merchants say," was a page-one headline on *The Wall Street Journal* in 1968. Psychedelic fashion petered out in the early 1970s, partly from overkill and over-exposure, and partly from the changing zeitgeist. Yet it remained popular with students until enjoying a full-scale revival in the mid-1980s, and has continued as a recurring motif.

See also Art and Fashion; Paisley; Saint Laurent, Yves; Subcultures.

Bibliography

Lobenthal, Joel. *Radical Rags: Fashions of the Sixties.* New York: Abbeville Press, 1990.

Masters, Robert E. L., and Jean Houston. *Psychedelic Art.* New York: Grove Press, 1968.

Joel Lobenthal

PUCCI, EMILIO*

Emilio Pucci, the *marchese di Barsento a Cavallo*, was born in Naples on 20 November 1914. The scion of an illustrious family tracing its heritage to the thirteenth century, Pucci grew up in the Palazzo Pucci on the *via dei Pucci* in Florence.

Education and Early Career

Reared within a strict aristocratic environment, Pucci turned out to be a rebel both personally and professionally. He graduated from the Università di Firenze in 1941 with a doctorate in political science, after having attended the University of Georgia in Athens, Georgia, and Reed College in Portland, Oregon. His decision to study in the United States, however, introduced him to the American way of life.

Proficiency in skiing started Pucci's fashion career. He had been a member of the Italian Olympic skiing team in 1934 and had gone to Reed College on a skiing scholarship in 1937. In 1947 the photographer Toni Frissell took photographs of Pucci and his female companions in Zermatt, Switzerland, wearing form-fitting, colorful, but practical ski clothes that Pucci had designed. These photographs were shown to the head buyer for Lord and Taylor, Marjorie Griswold, and the fashion editor of *Harper's Bazaar*, the legendary Diana Vreeland. The pictures were published in the December 1948 issue of *Bazaar*, while several Pucci models were ordered for Lord and Taylor's New York store. This order was Pucci's first retail success in the United States.

Pucci, however, needed additional financial security after World War II. In 1949 he opened a boutique in Capri, Italy, where he sold the tapered pants that became known as Capri pants, as well as sexy silk shirts fitted to show off the female figure. With the return of peace, people were again traveling for pleasure. Pucci astutely surmised that his boutique, which he named Emilio of Capri, and his casual, colorful resort fashions would be popular with the new visitors. International sophisticates like Consuelo Crespi, Mona Harrison von Bismarck, and Maxime de la Falaise were frequent customers at Emilio of Capri. Diana Vreeland praised Pucci as "divinely Italian" (Kennedy, p. 57). Although it was extremely unusual at that time for an aristocrat to be a shop owner and designer or dressmaker, Pucci enjoyed the creative process.

Post-World War II Innovations

The next phase of Pucci's career began at the first fashion show of Italian designers, which was organized by Giovanni Battista Giorgini in 1951 and held in the *Sala Bianca* at the Palazzo Pitti in Florence. Other designers who presented their work at the show included Simonetta, the Fontana sisters, Alberto Fabiani, and Emilio Schuberth. Major American stores like Neiman Marcus and Saks Fifth Avenue sent their buyers, who brought Italian, postwar, ready-to-wear fashion back across the Atlantic. Pucci's sleek, lightweight T-shirts, jersey dresses, silk shirts, and tapered pants made for an exciting new style.

Once the original and somewhat daring look of Pucci's designs appeared in the top U.S. stores, he was on the way to celebrity-designer status. Pucci won the coveted Neiman Marcus Award in 1954. He won the award a second time in 1967. Marcus, the head of the Dallas-based store, said, "Postwar fashion was hungry for a color explosion and [Pucci's] exotic, vivid color combinations were timed to perfection" (Kennedy, p. 67). Marjorie Griswold, Pucci's major retail supporter, had already suggested that he sign his name in script within the print design because the motifs themselves could be copied. Hence, the authenticity of a Pucci garment can be verified when the signature "Emilio" is visible throughout the print. Pucci used his first name rather than his family name because it was considered shocking for a member of the Italian nobility to work as a dressmaker or tradesman instead of a diplomat or politician. He said,

Italian designer Emilio Pucci at a Berlin fashion show, 1972. Pucci stands on the runway with the models that presented his exotic silk and chiffon gowns. Bold, wild patterns adorn the sleek sheath dresses, reflecting Pucci's rebellious spirit. CHARISSA CRAIG, MODEL. REPRODUCED BY PERMISSION.

"I am the first member of my family to work in a thousand years" (Kennedy, p. 42).

Pucci introduced a very lightweight, wrinkle-free, silk jersey that could be rolled up and packed easily—a feature appreciated by growing numbers of jet-set travelers. Technically advanced fabrics allowed him to fashion nonrestrictive clothes that were modern yet glamorous. Pucci also introduced an exciting array of colors, boldly mixing espresso and azure, tangerine and fuchsia, lime and turquoise, plum, and many other shades.

In addition to designing sleek silhouettes that allowed easy movement, using packable fabrics in an abundance of joyful colors, and insisting on top-quality workmanship, Pucci also designed his own prints. His prints included swirls, filigrees, arabesques, geometric figures, and kaleidoscopic or mosaic patterns. They were inspired by his far-flung travels to North and South America, Bali, Africa, the Middle East, Australia, and Asia. Pucci's finely-engineered prints also represented rich aspects of Italian history and cultural events as well as Mediterranean land- and seascapes. His prints from the 1950s, for example, featured motifs from Renaissance art, Florentine landmarks, the sunscapes and flowers of Capri, the mosaics of the Duomo di Monreale in Sicily, nightlife in Naples, and the flags from the famous annual Palio race in Siena. From the 1960s to the 1980s, his prints were inspired by his travels to Cuba, Bali, India, Hong Kong, and Tanzania. The American space program, underwater explorations, pop art, op art, rock music, and psychedelia also influenced his designs. One of Pucci's most famous prints, called Vivara, was inspired by the island Ischia; it became the name of his first fragrance in 1965. He even found time to sketch ideas for new print patterns during plane trips or sessions of the Italian Parliament, where he served from 1963 to 1972.

Designer Accessories

Emilio Pucci became one of the first designers with a recognizable high-status label and signature style. He was a leading pioneer of diversification and paved the way to widespread fashion licensing. He designed various products from perfumes to accessories, including handbags, scarves, sunglasses, tights, shoes, and lingerie—the last made by the American company Formfit Rogers. In 1977 Pucci even designed the interior of an automobile for a special edition of the Lincoln Continental Mark IV.

Pucci personally supervised the design of all his products. He designed colorful, sexy, and futuristic uniforms for the flight hostesses of Braniff Airways in 1965 and Quantas Airways in 1974. He also found time to design uniforms for the policewomen of Florence and clothes for Barbie dolls. Pucci took special pleasure in designing the mission patch for the Apollo 15 space mission in 1971.

Pucci married Christina Nannini and had two children, Laudomia and Alessandro. The family's elegant palazzo lifestyle was chronicled in fashion magazines. The "Prince of Prints" became as famous as the women who wore his designs—a list that included Marilyn Monroe (who was buried in a green Pucci dress), Elizabeth Taylor, Audrey Hepburn, Sophia Loren, Gina Lollobrigida, Lauren Bacall, Jacqueline Kennedy, Grace Kelly, Barbara ("Babe") Paley, Gloria Guinness, Barbara Walters, Gloria Steinem, and many others. Helen Gurley Brown, the author and former editor of *Cosmopolitan*, said, "The dresses were spare, sexy, and liberating!" (Kennedy, p. 8). Not to be outdone by fashionable women, men also wore wild and colorful Pucci ties, bowties, jackets, and beach attire.

The Pucci Revival

The wave of enthusiasm for Pucci's clothes known as "Puccimania" reached its height in 1967. Pucci's dresses became less popular in the 1970s as fashion trends changed, but the early 1990s saw a resurgence of interest in current Pucci styles and a blossoming market for vintage fashion—especially Puccis from the 1960s. Pucci collectors of the early 2000s included Madonna, Jennifer Lopez, Nicole Kidman, Julia Roberts, Paloma Picasso, and Ivana Trump. Vintage Puccis were sold in specialty shops and at auction for as much as $500 in 2002, whereas as a Pucci silk jersey dress from Saks Fifth Avenue in New York had been priced at $150 to $200 in the mid-1960s. When Pucci died on 29 November 1992, the fashion editor Carrie Donovan wrote in the *New York Times*, "He personified a moment, rather a long one in history" (1 December 1992).

After Pucci's death, his company continued under the guidance of his daughter, Laudomia, and wife, Cristina. The rich archive of fabrics maintained in the Palazzo Pucci provided an ongoing source of fashions for the Pucci boutiques. As creative director, Laudomia Pucci hired talented designers to continue her father's concepts. In February 2000 LVMH, the French luxury goods conglomerate headed by Bernard Arnault, purchased 67 percent of the Emilio Pucci SRL company, with the Pucci family retaining the rest of the business. More Pucci boutiques were opened around the world, from Bangkok to Palm Beach.

Christian Lacroix, the contemporary French designer known for his fantastical, exuberant, and exotically colorful fashions, became artistic director of the Emilio Pucci collection in April 2002. He said in the December 2002 issue of *Vogue*, "Emilio Pucci's vision is still very modern. . . . It's a way of life" (p. 76). Lacroix left the company in 2006 and was followed as head designer by Matthew Williamson. Peter Dundas then replaced Matthew Williamson in 2008.

See also Brands and Labels; Fontana Sisters; Italian Fashion; Lacroix, Christian; Perfume; Ski Clothing; Vintage Fashion.

Bibliography

Biennale di Firenze. *Looking at Fashion, Emilio Pucci.* Milan: Skira Editore, 1996.

Collins, Amy Fine. "Pucci's Jet-Set Revolution." *Vanity Fair* (October 2000): 380–393.

Kennedy, Shirley. *Pucci: A Renaissance in Fashion.* New York: Abbeville Press, 1991.

Tally, Andre Leon. "Style Fax." *Vogue* (December 2002): 76.

Vergani, Guido. *The Sala Bianca: The Birth of Italian Fashion.* Milan: Electa, 1992.

Shirley Kennedy

PUNK

Punk as dress cannot be discussed without at least some reference to its musical underpinnings. It has to be recognized that within the field of cultural studies, it both energized and produced a series of new responses to the theoretical construction of youth culture. Thus, it can be regarded as a formative movement in both its sartorial and visual presentation, and the consequent analysis of it as a subcultural style. It can be further argued that punk culture stands at a pivotal point in the relationship between youth cultural style and its commodification.

The United States

Punk had its roots in inner city America at the beginning of the 1970s. While its inspiration could be traced farther back, as a movement with a set of cohesive identities, New York appears to be its birthplace. But as befits its urban nature, punk cannot be said to have a singular geographic location. Detroit, Cleveland, and possibly Los Angeles are other sites that could also claim an emergent aesthetic and style identified as punk.

One of the many effects of the post–World War II consumer boom within the United States and Europe was an ever-expanding market for goods, particularly within a youth cultural market that led to an active struggle from young people to shape and realize their own identities through the consumption of music and fashion. This popularization of "youth" as "style" and "surface" was in part reflected in the breakdown of distinctions between high and low culture within the pop art movements—of Britain's Independent Group and its U.S. equivalent—of the 1950s and 1960s. In the latter grouping was Andy Warhol and the Factory. Symptomatic of pop, Warhol's work, its repetitive nature, and its insistence in articulating nothing more than the surface engaged with a youth cultural perspective of nihilism that revolved around the adage of "live fast, die young." As such, alongside Warhol's desire to surround himself with a coterie of the young, dangerous, and beautiful, the seeds of an avantgarde music scene began to be established.

Set around Warhol's Factory and the Lower East Side in a time of political and financial meltdown in New York, the music of these artists, in particular the

Punk fashion, 1983. Standing around in London's Brockwell Park, punks show off wild hairstyles and metal-studded black leather clothing, typical of the later punk fashion. While earlier years saw various other styles within the movement, it was this look that became the iconic punk image. © RICHARD OLIVIER/CORBIS. REPRODUCED BY PERMISSION.

Velvet Underground, reflected the repetivity and surface of the Factory's output. Playing at seedy venues such as Max's Kansas City, CBGBs, and Mother's, the music of the Stooges, New York Dolls, MC5's, Wayne County, and Patti Smith took their influences from a variety of sources all intent in demolishing what was seen as the pompous, sterile sound of contemporary music in the guise of "progressive" and "stadium" rock. So a disillusionment with all things commercial and the be-suited executives at the record companies led to a desire to perform music that would shock people to their senses, bringing music back to the poverty/richness of the everyday. While this was going on in the United States, Britain was in the grip of glam rock, a pub rock sound characterized in part by the clothing of its performers that looked to the transgressive in their stage presence. Of these perhaps the most original was David Bowie. Under a string of different pseudonyms and increasingly bizarre record personalities, David Bowie proved influential in his effect on both music and clothing in Britain and the United States.

By 1975 the American "punk scene" had evolved into a subculture characterized by the music of Television, and perhaps most famously The Ramones who wore clothes that reflected their rent boy street personas. Given that many of the musicians had gravitated from a bohemian inner-city scene detailed in the writings of William Burroughs and Alexander Trocchi, it seemed like a natural continuation of this aesthetic. The black leather jacket, T-shirt, straight jeans, and sneakers of the hustler proved the initial look of an American underground scene. While there were those such as the New York Dolls, who followed an English glam rock look of androgyny—made up with leather and knee-length boots, chest hair, and bleach—the majority pursued an understated street look. It was this musical explosion within the United States that brought a youngish Malcolm McLaren over to the United States to manage the New York Dolls where he fell into the punk scene and made clear his intentions to ship it back to the United Kingdom.

The United Kingdom

While it is obvious that Malcolm McLaren and his partner, Vivienne Westwood, are central to any definition of punk, especially in relation to its clothing, it is also clear that the self-aggrandizing machine which is Malcolm McClaren has skewed any historical understanding. In part this is justified, as McClaren and Westwood's string of shops on the Kings Road defined a particular look and McLaren's desire to exploit punk as a scene in the United Kingdom led directly to his management and dressing of the Sex Pistols, the most notorious of all punk bands.

Starting out on the Kings Road in 1972 as *Let It Rock* a shop that catered to a late working-class Teddy Boy revival, drape coats, and brothel creepers, Vivienne West-wood and Malcolm McLaren's shop then moved through a number of reincarnations, including *Too Fast to Live* and the fetish-orientated *Sex*, and later *Seditionaries*, and finally *World's End*. As in the United States, McLaren encouraged those who railed against society to hang around the shop. His and Westwood's antiestablishment aesthetic soon earned them a place in the London underground scene. However, we are not talking of the sophistication of New York, but a more rag-tag army of disillusioned teenagers. And it is from this group that the Sex Pistols were formed. Apart from the "rock" posturing of Glen Matlock, the rest of the band—Johnny Rotten, Sid Vicious, Steve Jones, and Paul Cook—were wholly working class and outside any artistic or intellectual clique. While many of the other emerging punk bands had members from an art school background, the *Sex Pistols* could claim to

be the genuine thing: an authentic working-class group of kids celebrating the boredom of their socially proscribed position.

Theoretical Angles

It is this notion of authenticity and working class that, in part, has always demarcated a British and U.S. understanding of punk as a philosophy or cultural experience. Whereas in the United Kingdom youth counter cultures had generally been a central experience of working-class youth—an expression of dissent and isolation from their parents and a reaction against a dominant ideology that on the surface worked to repress their ambition, in the United States the readings had not taken on such class-bound strictures.

The result in the United Kingdom was the publication in 1977, the peak of punk in Britain, of Dick Hebdige's *Subculture: The Meaning of Style*. Using punk as its central example, Hebdige employed a series of methodologies from Marxism to Structuralism and Semiotics to chart a view of post–World War II British youth cultures that were constructed through their working-class credentials and a desire to react against the dominant powers that appeared to shape their lives. In this analysis, Hebdige applied the notion of "bricolage" as the stylistic combination of disparate coded objects to juxtapose and create fresh meaning to punk dress and style. The safety pin's original meaning as something to hold together a diaper and to prevent injury to the child was pierced through a nose or stuck onto ripped jeans and jackets. Its once certain assigned meaning through was contextually redefined through its wearing as a stylistic device.

Clothing

In Britain the spectacular nature of punk as a style surpassed that of the United States. Westwood's designs—from "Destroy" T-shirts, bum bags, tartan bondage trousers, safety-pinned and ripped muslin shirts, and sloganed clothing—were a visible affront to a population who, for the most part, regarded long hair on a man as a concern. While youth cultures had previously been vilified within the national press for violence and drug taking, punk directly challenged the dress aesthetic and morals of a conservative nation. Beyond the Kings Road in 1976, 1977, and 1978, the influence of McLaren and Westwood diminished rapidly. Though they may have attracted a contingent of followers in London and their home counties, punk was a nationwide phenomenon and as such developed a style that was perhaps more coherent and less showy than Westwood's ready-to-wear clothing.

This do–it–yourself (D.I.Y.) aesthetic consisted of Hebdige's "bricolage" as the throwing together of a series of looks based around a few staple elements, such as mohair sweaters, tight jeans, and "jelly shoes." There was also the widespread use of secondhand clothing from charity shops and rummage sales—suits with T-shirts and basketball boots, collarless granddad shirts, and peroxided hair—with or without the ubiquitous stenciling and letter art of favorite bands, anarchist slogans, or the Situationist politicizing of groups such as The Clash.

This aesthetic was perhaps more subdued than the Kings Road look, but is more representative of punk as a dress code within the United Kingdom both for individuals and bands such as The Buzzcocks, The Damned, The Adverts, 999, and out on a style limb The Undertones. By 1977 punk's popularity as a musical form had seen by then the infamous Grundy television interviews; the Sex Pistols single "God Save the Queen" reaching number one in the week of the Queen's Golden Jubilee; and the interest of record companies in signing up groups who claimed in any manner, shape, or form to espouse a punk belief.

Commercialization

By 1979 the first stage of punk in the United Kingdom was coming to an end. Its commercial status became assured, from advertisements in music papers such as NME and Sounds advertising punk clothing, badges, and T-shirts to the record companies' desires to promote a gentler, more public-friendly "new wave" and to the release of various compilations that promised to tell the whole punk story. However, punk itself as both a music and a style attempted to change in order to avoid its co-option/commercialization by hardcore bands such as The Exploited and political bands such as Crass. In terms of dress, there was a reengagement with the motorcycle jacket, the use of Dr. Martin workwear boots, and the introduction of a wide variety of commercial rainbow hair colorants, along with the ubiquitous Mohawk haircut, which, along with a penchant for black, crossed over into both Goth and the New Romantic movements of the early 1980s. It is this

look that for many years characterized, and as such became the iconic image of, punk.

As a direct result of the energy of punk and the diffusion of a whole series of offshoots from punk with fanzines such as Punk in the United States and Sniffin' Glue in Britain, it became clear that there was a market for hard-edged youth journalism, which dealt specifically with an urban street scene. Punk fostered the emergence in 1980 of street-style magazines such as The Face, iD, and Blitz. Yet, as a consequence of these magazines trying to locate and expose scenes bubbling up from the streets, it became increasingly difficult for "subcultural" movements to resist commercialization through exposure. And it is this that is perhaps punk's greatest legacy to youth cultural style. While it would be inaccurate to suggest that youth cultures prior to punk were left to get on without the prying eyes of parents and large commercial operations intent on supplying, if not co-opting, youth culture toward their own ends, it is clear that punk stood at the crossroads of a contemporary "lifestyle" aesthetic. That youth culture in the early 2000s is so heavily mediated and prey to the intense gaze of commercial pressures is perhaps one of the less-appreciated consequences of punk as an historical event.

From the sounds of Seattle and grunge, through to a swathe of bands in 2004 that look more like The Ramones than The Ramones, punk has endured. For the fashion industry, its stylistic conceptualization as both "bricolage" and "rebellion" makes it the perfect vehicle to reappropriate the old in the spirit of the new, which gives rise to the interpretation of punk as a seasonal look on a cyclical basis. As such, its legacy is assured within both its musical and stylistic qualities. Yet whether its politics of change or its celebration of the bored and nihilistic attitude of teenagers can ever be faithfully played out again is another question.

See also Fashion and Identity; Subcultures; Teenage Fashions; T-Shirt.

Bibliography

Anscombe, Isabelle. *Not Another Punk Book*. London: Aurum Press, 1978.

Colegrave, Stephen, and Chris Sullivan. *Punk*. New York: Thunder's Mouth Press, 2001.

Coon, Caroline. *1988: The New Wave Punk Rock Explosion*. London: Orbach and Chambers Ltd, 1977.

Hebdige, Dick. *Subculture: The Meaning of Style*. London: Methuen, 1979.

Heylin, Clinton. *From the Velvets to the Voidoids: A Pre-Punk History for a Post-Punk World*. New York: Penguin USA, 1993.

Laing, David, and Milton Keynes. *One Chord Wonders: Power and Meaning in Punk Rock*. Philadelphia: Open University Press, 1985.

Makos, Christopher. *White Trash*. London: Stonehill Publishing, 1977.

McNeil, Legs and Gillian McCain. *Please Kill Me: The Uncensored Oral History of Punk*. New York: Penguin USA, 1996.

Perry, Mark. *Sniffin' Glue: The Essential Punk Accessory*. London: Sanctuary Publishing, 2000.

Sabin, Roger, ed. *Punk Rock: So What?* London and New York: Routledge, 1999.

Savage, Jon. *England's Dreaming: Sex Pistols and Punk Rock*. London: Faber, 1991.

Frank Cartledge

Q

QUANT, MARY

Mary Quant was born in London on 11 February 1934. A self-taught designer, she cut up bedspreads to make clothes when she was only six; as a teenager, she restyled and shortened her gingham school dresses. She recalled admiring the appearance of a child at a tap-dancing class who wore a black "skinny" sweater, pleated skirt, and pantyhose with white ankle socks and black patent shoes (Quant: 1966, p. 16). From the mid-1950s she transformed styles like these into amusing and sexy clothes for young women, and paved the way for London to become a center of irreverent youth-oriented fashion.

Quant's parents would not accept her attending a school of fashion design, but compromised by allowing her to go to art school. She met Alexander Plunkett Greene while she was studying illustration at Goldsmith's College of the University of London. Plunkett Greene later became her business partner and husband. After leaving art school, Quant was apprenticed to Erik of Brook Street, a Danish milliner working in London. In 1955 Quant's husband purchased Markham House in London's King's Road to start a shop named Bazaar, and open a restaurant called Alexander's in the basement. Mary was responsible for buying the stock for Bazaar, Alexander for sales and marketing, while Archie McNair, an exsolicitor who ran a photography business, handled the legal and commercial side of the business. Quant designed a black five-petaled daisy logo during this period; it eventually became her worldwide trademark.

Quant sourced innovative jewelry from art students and bought clothes from various wholesalers to stock the boutique. One of the items designed for Bazaar's opening was a pair of "mad" house-pajamas, which were featured in *Harper's Bazaar* and purchased by an American manufacturer to copy. Encouraged by her success as well as dissatisfied with the styles on the market, Quant decided to design her own stock. After attending a few evening classes on cutting, she adjusted some Butterick patterns to achieve the look she wanted. Quant was designing for Butterick by 1964; some of her pattern designs sold over 70,000 copies. Each day's sales at Bazaar paid for the cloth made up that evening into the next day's stock. As business took off, Quant employed a dressmaker to help her, and then another, and another, and so on.

Quant brought a groundbreaking approach to fashion retailing by providing an informal shopping experience. In contrast to traditional fashion retail outlets, which ranged from high-class couturiers through staid town-center department stores and chain stores such as C and A Modes to High Street dress shops, Bazaar set out to make shopping for clothes enjoyable: loud music played, wine flowed, and the boutique stayed open until late in the evening. Most importantly, the stock was constantly replenished with new and highly desirable designs. "The clothes were very simple. Basically tunic dresses, and very easy to wear, unlike the couturier clothes which were very structured. And put together with other things—tights and knickers in ginger and prune and a grapey colour, that people weren't used to" (Harris, 1994). Quant persuaded theatrical costume manufacturers to make the tights she sold, as there were no panty-hose in the color that Quant required on the market. While Quant's prices were reasonable in comparison to those of the traditional fashion houses, her clothes were made to a high standard—many were silk-lined—and were not cheap.

Quant was probably the first designer to acknowledge the influence of youth subcultures, and she credits the Mods as an important source of inspiration. Mods were a sub-cultural youth group characterized by their immaculate dress—their 'sharp' tailoring and love of Italian sportswear, and the parka coat that they wore to protect their clothes whilst traveling by scooter. One of her most successful early designs was a white plastic collar to be added to a sweater or dress. One of Quant's trademark innovations was the mini skirt: by 1960 her

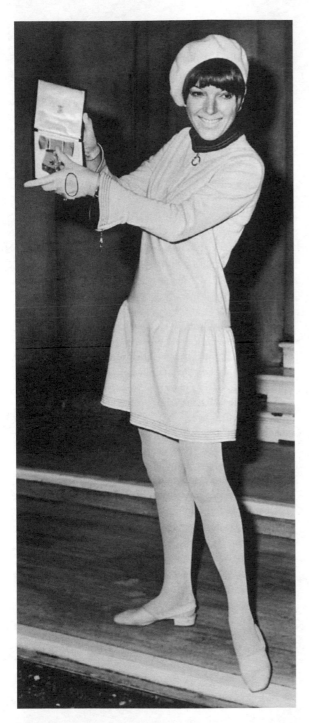

Mary Quant showing off her Order of the British Empire award. The self-taught Quant was the recipient of several awards for her innovative, progressive fashion designs. © BETTMAN/CORBIS. REPRODUCED BY PERMISSION.

hemlines were above the knee and crept up the leg to reach thigh level by the mid-1960s. She also derived inspiration from school uniforms and menswear, especially traditional country clothes—knickerbockers, Norfolk jackets, "granddaddy" tab-collared shirts, Liberty bodices or combinations (one-piece garments), and traditional children's underwear. Quant undertook much of her research at London's Victoria and Albert Museum. She bought her fabrics, notably Prince of Wales checks and herringbone weaves, from Harrod's, and persuaded knitwear manufacturers to make their men's cardigans 25 centimeters longer so that they could be worn as dresses. Whereas fashion designers had traditionally looked to Paris for stylistic guidance, Quant and her husband watched youth programs on television and attended fashionable London nightspots to identify new trends.

One example of Quant's work from 1956/57 was a dress in black-and-white checked wool cut in a sleeveless balloon style and teamed with a skinny-rib black sweater. For the winter of 1957/58 Quant designed an ensemble comprised of a rust-red Norfolk-style jacket, Harris tweed knickerbockers—she favored knickerbockers—, and a pinafore dress. Another pinafore of the same year, made of striped menswear suiting, featured two bold pockets at the bust. Her popular hipster pants were based on the styles that her husband had the fashionable tailor Dougie Hayward make for him. Quant was the first designer to use Polu-Vinyl-Chloride (PVC) in fashion; the first to introduce pantyhose in stunning colors to match her knitwear; and the first to introduce "fashion" lingerie—her seamless brassieres were called "booby traps," and her uplifting brassieres "bacon savers."

Quant also exerted a profound influence upon the representation of fashion by designing and commissioning young-looking animated mannequins and staging witty window displays. In her 1966 autobiography, she recalled one display in which "we had all the figures in bathing suits made of Banlon stretch fabric with madly wide coloured stripes like rugger sweat shirts. . . . The models were sprayed completely white with bald heads" (p. 8). In 1957 the trio (Mary, Alexander, and Archie) opened a second branch of Bazaar, designed by their friend Terence Conran, in London's Knightsbridge neighborhood. At the launch party, Quant's models danced to loud jazz music with glasses of champagne in their hands, "and floated around as if they had been to the wildest party or looking dreamily intellectual with a copy of Karl Marx or Engels in the other hand. . . . No one had ever used this style of showing. . . . At the end, the place just exploded!" (Quant, 1966, p. 95).

In 1962 Quant entered into a lucrative design contract with J. C. Penney, which had 1,700 retail outlets across the United States; and in 1963 she launched her own cheaper diffusion line, called the Ginger Group. Her talent was acknowledged that same year by the *Sunday Times*, which gave her its International Award for "jolting England out of its conventional attitude towards clothes" (Quant, 1966, p. 96). In 1966 she was awarded the Order of the British Empire and in 1967 she won the Annual Design Medal of the Royal Society of Arts. In the same year she opened her third shop, designed by Jon Bannenberg, in London's New Bond Street. Quant was awarded the Hall of Fame Award for Outstanding Contribution to British Fashion by the British Fashion Council in 1969.

Quant remained in fashion's vanguard throughout the first half of the 1970s. In 1971 she designed a spotted summer playsuit in cotton jersey called "Babygro," named after the ubiquitous babies' romper suits, and a long flared skirt printed with dots and daisies called "Sauce," which was teamed with a matching "Radish" bra-top. Summer evening dresses with plunging necklines, puffed sleeves, and ruffled skirts were made in pretty Liberty floral prints—once again borrowed from childrenswear—and glamorous striped Lurex. Quant's sporty styles for 1975 included brightly colored and striped jumpsuits, many with drawstring waists and ankle ties, and sailor-inspired slit-sided tunic dresses worn over pants. In 1978 she introduced her own range of childrenswear. She has also designed furnishings and bed linens since the 1980s, and won numerous awards for her carpet designs.

Mary Quant always wanted to create a total fashion look—her own geometric hairstyle, cut by Vidal Sassoon, was widely copied. As an art student she had used Caran d'Ache crayons and a box of watercolors for her own makeup. In 1966 she startled the cosmetics industry by offering makeup in a staggering choice of wild colors as well as a more natural palette. The range was advertised using top model Penelope Tree, and photographed by Richard Avedon. Her book *Colour by Quant* was published in 1984, followed by *Quant on Make-Up* in 1986, and the *Classic Make-Up and Beauty Book* in 1996.

In 1990 Quant was awarded the British Council's Award for Contribution to British Industry, and in 1993 she became a Fellow of the Society of Industrial Artists and Designers. Her cosmetics business is thriving as of the early 2000s; she has over 200 shops in Japan as well as outlets in London, Paris, and New York City.

See also Avedon, Richard; Children's Clothing; Cosmetics, Western; Fashion Marketing and Merchandising; London Fashion; Miniskirt; Retailing; Youthquake Fashions.

Bibliography

Harris, Martin, Interviewer. "Quantum Leap Back to the Street." *Daily Telegraph*, 22 June 1994.

Morris, Brian. *Mary Quant's London.* Museum of London, London, 1973. Extensively illustrated with an introduction by Ernestine Carter.

Quant, Mary. *Classic Make-Up and Beauty.* London: Dorling Kindersley, 1996.

——. *Quant by Quant.* London: Cassell and Company, Ltd., 1966. An entertaining and informative autobiographical insight into London's postwar youth scene and the rise of Quant's fashion empire.

——. *Make 'Up' by Mary Quant.* New York: Harper Collins, 1987.

Quant, Mary, and Felicity Green. *Colour by Quant.* London: Octopus Books, 1984.

Amy de la Haye

R

RABANNE, PACO

Paco Rabanne (1934–) was born Francisco Rabaneda y Cuervo in Pasagès de San Pedro in the Basque region of Spain. His family fled to France in 1939 after his father was captured and executed by Francisco Franco's troops. Rabanne studied architecture at the École nationale supérieure des Beaux-arts in Paris from 1951 to 1963. In 1963 he won an award at the Biennale de Paris for an inhabitable garden sculpture, which was exhibited at the Musée d'art moderne de la ville de Paris.

Early Career

Rabanne's drawing skills made it possible for him to enter the world of fashion as early as 1955; indeed, to finance his architecture studies, he regularly supplied drawings of handbags for Roger Model and shoes for Charles Jourdan until 1963. In 1959 *Women's Wear Daily* published seven sketches of dresses signed "Franck Rabanne." Though this was the first time the designer's name appeared in public, he chose "Franck" because the number of letters in the first and last names totaled a lucky thirteen. (He did not begin using the name Paco professionally until 1965.) These dresses bore the imprint of the style of Balenciaga, whose work was familiar to the young Rabanne through his mother, a former chief seamstress in the master's workshop in San Sebastián in Spain.

Rabanne put his artistic gifts and the skills of his family to good use between 1962 and 1966: together they hand-produced unusual buttons and embroideries for the houses of haute couture. His clients at the time included Nina Ricci, Cristóbal Balenciaga, Maggy Rouff, Philippe Venet, Pierre Cardin, and Hubert de Givenchy.

In 1965, Rabanne's creation of oversized *rhodoïd* jewelry in various geometric forms and bright colors brought him his first major commercial and media success. It also established one of the principles of his style:

the use of rigid divisible materials held together by metallic rings or rivets.

Paco Rabanne's first show took place on 1 February 1966 at the Hotel George V. This collection, which the designer called "Twelve Unwearable Dresses in Contemporary Materials," was worn by barefoot models parading to the sounds of Pierre Boulez's *Le marteau sans maître*, which Rabanne chose to reflect modernity and to shock the audience. It was a veritable fashion manifesto and helped to establish Rabanne's reputation as a revolutionary. On 21 April 1966, the dancers of the celebrated Parisian cabaret, the Crazy Horse Saloon, presented Rabanne's collection of beachwear made of rhodoïd disks or leather. The dancers modeled the unconventional clothes in the form of a strip tease, creating another scandal. Rabanne also set up his workshop in 1966 at 33, rue Bergère, with a black décor accented with industrial scaffolding and bicycle seats for chairs.

Experiments in Design

Following the example of contemporary artists who had given up the traditional media of paint and canvas, Paco Rabanne chose to base his fashion experiments on a systematic challenge to the art of cutting and sewing. His work was characterized from the beginning by a complete rejection of traditional couture techniques in favor of the exploration of unusual materials and methods of assemblage.

Rabanne followed up his experiments in rhodoïd with garments made of metal, making metal something of a distinctive signature. He used it from one collection to the next in all its forms: disks and rectangles normally used to make protective aprons for butchers, coats of mail, hammered plates, aluminum jerseys, or elements of jewelry or decoration used as modified ready-mades. This work led Coco Chanel to call him "the metal worker." Rabanne readily acknowledged that the recycling of ready-mades was very much in the tradition of the dadaists, such as his acknowledged master Marcel Duchamp.

He experimented with other materials, whether previously unknown to fashion or reimagined and redirected from their original purposes. Among Rabanne's most notable creations were: paper dresses, which were presented in his collections in 1967, 1988, and 1992; molded clothing known by the name of the patented Giffo process, in which all the individual parts, including the buttons and pockets, were molded in a single block (1968); designs made from knitted fur (1967); and several made entirely of buttons (1970), wood (1977), coconuts (1993), or laser discs (1988). Far from being incidental, these experiments were developed according to a rigorous artistic and ideological perspective. In the process, they helped to free the art of clothing design from its strictly utilitarian context, and they inspired many other designers to adopt their current positions.

The innovative and nonconformist character of Rabanne's work was recognized in avant-garde artistic circles. The gallery owner Iris Clert exhibited Paco Rabanne's creations in 1966 among those of other artists she supported, like Lucio Fontana. Salvador Dalí referred to his young compatriot as the second Spanish genius for his Unwearable Dresses collection. Rabanne's clothes also appealed to such 1960s icons as Brigitte Bardot and Françoise Hardy. It was also in this period that

Paco Rabanne with several of his designs, 1977.
Rabanne was famous for creating strikingly unusual clothing from unlikely materials such as plastic, paper, and various metals.
© James L. Amos/Corbis. Reproduced by permission.

the cinema made the most frequent use of his dresses, so singular in appearance and so photogenic.

Other Activities

In the 1960s and 1970s Rabanne was in great demand as a costume designer for theatrical productions and ballets as well as films. His many noteworthy contributions to the cinema include: *Two or Three Things I Know About Her*, directed by Jean-Luc Godard (1967); *The Adventurers (Les aventuriers)* also known as "The Last Adventure," directed by Robert Enrico (1967); *Two for the Road*, directed by Stanley Donen (1967); *Casino Royale*, directed by John Huston (1967); and *Barbarella*, directed by Roger Vadim (1968).

In addition to Rabanne's work in costume design, he produced a series of sophisticated perfumes. Calandre, launched in 1969 by the Spanish company Puig (which bought out Paco Rabanne in 1986), has proven to be one of the most successful contemporary fragrances. Subsequent fragrances have sold well also. Rabanne's perfumes, as well as his numerous licenses for other products around the world, have made it possible for the designer to continue his fashion experiments without suffering unduly from the low profit margins of haute couture.

In 1999, Rabanne decided to put an end to haute couture activity, while the ready-to-wear sector that he had developed since 1990 experienced new growth, particularly with the arrival in 2000 of Rosemary Rodriguez as the head of Rabanne's creative studio. Rodriguez has developed several collections in harmony with the very particular stylistic grammar of Paco Rabanne.

On the occasion of Rabanne's thirtieth anniversary as a designer, the first retrospective exhibition of his fashions was presented in 1995 at the Musée de la Mode in Marseille, followed in 1996 by the bilingual publication of the first monograph devoted to his work.

Paco Rabanne has been involved since the late 1980s in several artistic projects beyond the confines of fashion, including the production of Mira Nair's film *Salaam, Bombay!* The film was awarded the Caméra d'Or at the Festival de Cannes in 1988.

In 1991 Rabanne published his first book, *Trajectoire*. He has since written several other works of reflection on mystical subjects and practices.

See also Balenciaga, Cristóbal; Extreme Fashions; Givenchy, Hubert de; High-Tech Fashion; Paper Dresses; Paris Fashion; Perfume; Theatrical Costume.

Bibliography

Kamitsis, Lydia. *Paco Rabanne: les sens de la recherche*. Translated by Sylvia Carter. Paris: M. Lafon, 1996.

——. *Paco Rabanne*. Paris: Editions Assouline, 1997. Translated by Harriet Mason. London: Thames and Hudson, Inc., 1999.

Rabanne, Paco. *Trajectoire: d'une vie à l'autre*. Paris: M. Lafon, 1991.

Lydia Kamitsis

READY-TO-WEAR

The textile and apparel industry constitutes the largest global manufacturing employer with approximately 200 nations involved in production resulting in $313.5 billion in trade during 1996. Of this amount, $163.3 billion was derived from apparel, the tenth largest trade category in the world. The apparel industry comprises many small but interrelated firms. Making garments to sell as ready-to-wear is labor intensive but to initiate production requires less capital investment and less advanced technology than many other businesses. Women constitute the majority of the labor force worldwide and have found apparel a continuing source of employment throughout history. These factors have made the business of ready-to-wear clothing of particular importance to the economies of developing nations in the twentieth and early twenty-first centuries, and to entrepreneurs in many earlier eras.

The illustrated chart shows the relationships of the many associated firms involved in the production of all price levels of ready-to-wear. In the modern industry, these firms are located in many different parts of the world. Thus production emphasis is now placed on the coordination and logistics of each aspect of the process.

There are four aspects of ready-to-wear with historic antecedents that remain important businesses in the twenty-first century. The most common is the speculative production of fashionable garments to be sold at retail as described in the chart. Secondly, commissioned garment production, for example military uniforms, differs from speculative production in the nature of financial risk because there is no need to sell at retail. Thirdly, the used-clothing market has traditionally been a ready-made clothing source for the poor.

However, the enormous growth of used clothing as a viable and expanding business in the late twentieth and early twenty-first centuries is notable for the breadth of its market, which reaches almost all socioeconomic levels through resale and thrift shops as well as auctions. Due in part to the relaxation of standards of dress, in part to popular culture and in part to affluence in the last quarter of the twentieth century, used clothing is an important sector of the current ready-to-wear market. Firms that provide services for international trade via shipping and logistics constitute a fourth important and profitable aspect, especially because of the decentralization of the modern industry.

Pre-Industrial Ready-to-Wear: Speculative Production

Speculative production began in antiquity with garments and accessories traded internationally. For example, ready-to-wear was part of ancient Babylonian business life as recorded on clay tablets dating from 1400 to 1200 B.C.E. A merchant there wrote to his associates to instruct them to open his warehouse, take out garments from his sealed chests and from the chests of garments returned to him by another merchant. He instructed them to "Write your tablets as follows: they have taken so-and-so many garments from the chest, so-and-so many from the regular deliveries have not been received, so-and-so many are from the garments returned to me— and send all the tablets to me" (Oppenheim, p. 85). These instructions are not unlike inventories taken in modern industry.

Speculative production requires capital investment and the ability to assume the risks inherent in recouping investment through the sale of merchandise at a profit. In the pre-industrial era such production included useful but semi-fitted garments. After 1350, as clothing became more fitted, shirts and accessories such as collars, hair nets, hats, and gloves became the primary kinds of products traded. In Renaissance Florence, embroidered detachable sleeves could be purchased ready-made and were also exported. London customs records for the second half of the sixteenth century show gloves from Belgium, Spain, and Italy imported by the gross; hair nets, straw hats, and caps from France by the dozen; as well as knitted nightcaps, gloves, stockings, and petticoats. Sixteenth-century London silkwomen, who processed imported raw silk from Italy into thread, could weave ribbons and other trimmings to make silk accessories which they sold in their own shops along with imported silk items, such as hair nets, netted neckwear, and netted sleeves. Elsewhere, women did most of the work of making small accessories, and such products were ordered and sold through men's trade guilds.

Pre-Industrial Ready-to-Wear: Commissions and Donations

Commissions were given for the provisioning of armies, household retainers, or charitable donations. In ancient Rome records indicate that garments were produced in factory-like settings with perhaps 100 workers, and that some early form of mass production outfitted the Roman legions. Commissions also feature in later European religious rituals and charitable donations. For example, in the annual Maundy Thursday foot-washing ceremony, Elizabeth I of England (1533–1603) provided a woolen gown, a pair of shoes, and a smock—mass produced at her expense—to as many women as equaled the years of the queen's age. In another sixteenth-century example, a wealthy citizen of Nuremberg, Germany, provided in his will of 1577 that each year on 31 October, 100 poor men would be provided with a coat, waistcoat, and trousers of black wool, a black hat, a white linen shirt, and a pair of shoes. This particular donation continued until 1809 and required two master tailors and their journeymen to use specific patterns, standard measures, and materials purchased from specified vendors,

requirements similar to practices in twenty-first century ready-to-wear. Wealthy individuals might also provide in their wills for mourning clothes to be made and given to mourners at their funerals.

Pre-Industrial Ready-to-Wear: Used Clothing

By far the most widespread and common source of ready-to-wear clothing in the pre-industrial era was the used clothing market. Throughout Europe records beginning in the Middle Ages document dealers in used clothing, often women, who supplied many in the lower socioeconomic levels for whom new clothing was too expensive. Used clothing dealers sometimes rented stalls in market areas designated for their trade, or simply sold their wares on the streets. A retail guild including dealers in secondhand clothing was organized in Florence, Italy, in 1266. The necessity for having used clothing available is apparent in the following examples from Nuremberg, Germany, in 1509 where a new coat given to a servant girl by her employer was equal to 56 percent of her annual income, and the fabric provided for a servant's coat and trousers was 148 percent of his annual wage. Some members of the upper classes also purchased used clothing, most of which was acquired by dealers at estate sales. During plague years, when there was fear of infection, used clothing markets were closed.

Pre-Industrial Ready-to-Wear: International Trade

International trade in ready-to-wear garments and accessories increased as other regions of the world opened to European business in the sixteenth century. By the seventeenth century some larger ready-made garments, such as the *banyan* or *Indian gown* for men, and the *mantua* for women, were imported to Europe. Both were T-shaped garments similar to caftans, and were considered informal dress.

The first merchant ship to fly the flag of the United States, *The Empress of China*, sailed for the Orient in 1784. Its cargo of Virginia ginseng was traded at Canton, China, for porcelains and soft goods including ready-made umbrellas, 600 pairs of ladies' mitts; six pairs of ladies' satin shoes, more than 250 pairs of men's satin breeches, and a large number of textiles. On the second voyage in 1786, the ship returned with similar wares that included more than 600 pairs of satin

New York tailors, circa 1890. Around the turn of the century, many arriving immigrants with tailoring skills found work producing clothing in New York City, the center of the American ready-to-wear industry. © Hulton-Deutch Collection/Corbis. Reproduced by permission.

breeches. These cargos were consigned to merchants who advertised the contents up and down the east coast of the United States.

Bristol, England, had more than 200 merchant houses trading internationally by the late eighteenth century, exporting felt hats, worsted caps, stockings, hosiery, footwear, and wearing apparel such as canvas frocks, trousers, shirts, jackets, and drawers. As part of the slave trade, this kind of ready-made clothing was traded in Africa to buy slaves and sold in America and the West Indies to provide clothing for slaves. Similar ill-fitting loose clothing was provided for sailors and was known as slops.

Early Industrialization of Ready-to-Wear in the United States

Merchant tailors, long prevented from making clothing on speculation because of guild restrictions and lack of capital, began to work in mass production during the nineteenth century. Systems of standardized and proportional measurements enabled them to make better fitting ready-to-wear at more affordable prices. The introduction by 1820 of a tape measure marked in inches made more standardization possible. Statistics kept for soldiers in the American Civil War helped determine how men's measurements could be better adapted for mass production. Ebeneezer Butterick's 1863 patent for the sized paper pattern provided increased standardization for women's garments. During the first half of the nineteenth century, mass produced ready-to-wear clothing was almost exclusively for men. Only mantles and cloaks with little fit were produced for women.

In the early years of industrialization, labor costs remained cheaper than fabric, with women and boys doing much of the sewing by hand at home while the pattern making, cutting, and inspection of finished goods were under the supervision of the tailor in his shop. At the end of the nineteenth century, immigrants met the growing need for labor. Many arriving with tailoring and dressmaking skills found work producing ready-to-wear in New York City, the center of the American ready-to-wear industry.

Early Industrialization: The Sewing Machine

The first technological innovation impacting industrial garment making directly was the sewing machine.

Following developments by Elias Howe and Isaac Singer among others, Nathan Wheeler and Allen B. Wilson made and marketed a machine clothing manufacturers found efficient because it allowed fabric to feed evenly on curved seams. The sewing machine made possible the piecework concept of factory organization where each step was performed by a different person, eliminating the need for skilled workers.

Steam-powered sewing machines in factory workrooms were used from the early 1850s to produce men's shirts and collars, and were then adapted for the production of suits for men and boys. Overcoats of heavy cloth could be sewn by machine in three days instead of six by hand. The business of women's cloaks and mantles as well as crinolines and hooped petticoats was improved by the use of the sewing machine, and consequently these items became cheaper when ready-made. Women's fashions using braids and trimmings increased as machines made the application easier.

Improvements to the sewing machine continued, with 7,339 patents for sewing machines and accessories granted between 1842 and 1895. Technologies for cutting and pressing were the last fundamental industrial processes to be developed. The most successful mechanism for cutting multiple layers of cloth arrived in 1890, and the modern pressing machine was developed in the first years of the twentieth century.

Clothing Distribution after 1850

The nature of clothing distribution changed in the second half of the nineteenth century with the creation of department stores in large urban centers in Europe and North America. With these stores came greater variety for the consumer and the advent of advertising to influence choice. Department stores appeared in the early 1850s, and, by the end of the century had become enormous architectural wonders that encompassed many kinds of merchandise including ready-made garments for men, women, and children. Although these large stores offered products through illustrated catalogs, their focus was on the urban population.

In the United States, Aaron Montgomery Ward established a mail-order business in 1872 offering to furnish "Farmers and Mechanics throughout the Northwest with all kinds of Merchandise at Wholesale Prices." Sears, Roebuck and Company followed in 1893. By 1920, Ward's catalog had grown from a single sheet to 872 pages, and Sears' 1921 edition was 1,064 pages with the first 96 pages devoted to women's clothing, followed by

40 pages for men and boys. In addition to illustrated catalogs, women's magazines, first appearing in Europe at the end of the eighteenth century, proliferated throughout the nineteenth century. Initially limited fashion coverage focused on illustrations featuring the latest fashions, their materials and colors, and sometimes the providers. By the end of the nineteenth century, more pages were given over to product advertisements.

Speculative Production of Ready-to-Wear as a Mature Industry

By the 1920s mass production and mass merchandising were fully integrated into the ready-to-wear industry. The focus of advertising had shifted from declarations of quality to exhortations urging readers to keep up with fashion, and from an emphasis on men's wear to one on women's wear. This gave impetus to the modern industry's strategy of rapid fashion change. The women's ready-to-wear industry in the United States became concentrated in New York City between Sixth Avenue and Ninth Avenue from 35th Street to 41st Street, where 65 percent of the women's garment workers were employed by 1940. The proximity of manufacturers to labor and suppliers as well as associated businesses gave New York firms the flexibility to react quickly and efficiently to changing fashions. Employment in the domestic American apparel industry peaked in 1950 at 1.4 million.

Jerry Silverman, Inc., a manufacturer of women's better dresses, organized in 1959, provides an example of typical production processes. In 1970 Silverman sold dresses at wholesale from $39.75 to $89.75 to about 3,000 stores nationwide, where they cost the consumer from $70 to $175. Not including CMT (cut, make, trim) contractors, the firm employed about eighty people. Shannon Rodgers, the firm's designer, had his name on the label, an unusual acknowledgment when most designers working for manufacturers remain anonymous.

To develop a concept for his ready-to-wear line in a given season, Rodgers went to Europe to view collections. The industry in the United States usually depends on Parisian fashion ideas, especially for silhouette and color. However, the complex and detailed French haute couture (fine, luxurious made-to-order clothing) cannot be directly copied for ready-to-wear garments intended to fit thousands of consumers. Rodgers was skilled at taking single elements of a haute couture design, for example, a skirt detail, a neckline treatment, or a sleeve style, and incorporating them into various garments, getting perhaps six ready-to-wear ideas from

a single haute couture garment. These trips also gave Rodgers ideas for fabric choices that would give the finished garment the texture, volume, and movement he envisioned.

After sketches for the line were completed, fabrics and trimmings were purchased and a sample produced in company workrooms. Once the sample had been approved, it was sent to the pattern maker, graded into various sizes, and sent out to be duplicated for fashion show and showroom use. The Silverman fashion show for retail buyers and the fashion press usually featured about 100 different styles. Initial orders from buyers were confirmed after approval from the stores they represented. The success of the business depended on the quantity of confirmed orders and timely delivery—first of the fabrics and trimmings for production and then of the finished garments to the stores—as well as keeping production costs minimized.

Outside contractors cut the garments, bundled the pieces of each individual dress, and sent the bundles to machine operators for sewing. After sewing, the garments were finished, pressed, and returned to the Silverman Company for a final quality check and proper labeling. Labels included the firm's label, "Shannon Rodgers for Jerry Silverman," the union label, fiber content and cleaning instructions, style and size, and the store label and price tag.

Next came the firm's promotion and advertising to prepare customers for the new season. Once the finished garments had been shipped and received by the store, retail display, promotion, and advertising began. The salesperson and the customer at the point-of-sale completed the business process.

U.S. Ready-to-Wear Production in the Late Twentieth Century

By the early 1960s, manufacturers in the United States began to look for cheaper labor costs and production facilities off-shore. This resulted in a decrease in domestic apparel employment to 684,000 by 1999. It also resulted in a new focus on the logistics of coordinating off-shore production facilities where each part of an ensemble might be manufactured in a different country but is expected to reach the stores as a complete look. Modern communication and transportation make this kind of decentralized production process possible. Another significant change in late twentieth and early twenty-first century ready-to-wear is the importance of marketing strategies to product development.

Procedures associated with a retailer acting as manufacturer, or jobber, for merchandise bearing the store's private label, offer an instructive comparison with mid-twentieth century processes. In the 1990s, beginning at least 15 months in advance of the arrival of the garments in the store, the design director, color specialist, and product merchandisers would consult color and textile services and view collections in Europe and America. Fabric specialists and product merchandisers then shopped for yarns and textiles at major textile trade fairs. The initial line concept including color, mood, theme, silhouette, fabrics, and key components was presented to the product management team. The design team planned their internal strategy and refined the line concept before they joined the product merchandisers to make a final presentation to store committee members and management. Samples were reviewed and target prices agreed to before trips abroad to select contractors. Five months before the products were due to be shipped, the line was finalized and contracts signed. The products reached the stores six to eight weeks from the shipping date.

In order to track production at distant sites and cut costs even further, some mass-market firms use videoconferencing and other sophisticated technologies to send and receive information, thereby insuring product quality without the need to travel to the producer. As the time frame for fashion changes in ready-to-wear becomes more compressed, communication technology becomes more essential to success.

Conclusion

Innovations in transportation, communication, and technology have been major forces for change throughout the history of ready-to-wear clothing production. Additionally, rapid fashion changes have influenced the modern apparel industry by compressing the production timetable. However, the production of ready-to-wear apparel has been consistently labor intensive, leading modern manufacturers to seek lower labor costs by repeatedly moving production facilities. Challenges faced by the industry in the early twenty-first century remain similar to those faced in earlier eras, particularly in the area of speculative production where the customer must be inclined to purchase at a price that yields a profit to the manufacturer.

See also Fashion Industry; Seventh Avenue; Sewing Machine; Sweatshops.

Bibliography

Arnold, Janet. "Smocks, Shirts, Falling Bands and Mantuas: Evidence of Loosely-Fitting Garments and Neckwear Produced for the Ready-to-Wear Market, c. 1560–1700." In *Per una Storia della Moda Pronta, Problemi e Ricerche* (A History of Ready to Wear, Problems and Research). Proceedings of the Fifth International Conference of CISST (The Italian Center for the Study of the History of Textiles), Milan, 26–28 February, 1990. Firenze: EDI-FIR, 1991.

CISST. *Per una Storia della Moda Pronta, Problemi e Ricerche* (A History of Ready to Wear, Problems and Research). Proceedings of the Fifth International Conference of CISST (The Italian Center for the Study of the History of Textiles), Milan, 26–28 February, 1990. Firenze: EDI-FIR, 1991.

Dickerson, Kitty G. *Textiles and Apparel in the Global Economy.* 3rd ed. Upper Saddle River, N.J.: Prentice-Hall, Inc., 1999.

Druesedow, Jean L. "Designing for Off-shore Manufacture in the New York Ready-to-Wear Industry." In *Per una Storia della Moda Pronta, Problemi e Ricerche* (A History of Ready to Wear, Problems and Research). Proceedings of the Fifth International Conference of CISST (The Italian Center for the Study of the History of Textiles), Milan, 26–28 February 1990. Firenze: EDIFIR, 1991.

Frick, Carole Collier. *Dressing Renaissance Florence.* Baltimore: The Johns Hopkins University Press, 2002.

Kidwell, Claudia B., and Margaret C. Christman. *Suiting Everyone: The Democratization of Clothing in America.* Washington, D.C.: The Smithsonian Institution Press, 1974.

Levitt, Sarah. "Bristol Clothing Trades and Exports in the Georgian Period." In *Per una Storia della Moda Pronta, Problemi e Ricerche* (A History of Ready to Wear, Problems and Research). Proceedings of the Fifth International Conference of CISST (The Italian Center for the Study of the History of Textiles), Milan, 26–28 February, 1990. Firenze, EDIFIR, 1991.

Oppenheim, A. Leo. *Letters from Mesopotamia: Official Business and Private Letters on Clay Tablets from Two Millennia.* Translated and with an introduction by A. Leo Oppenheim. Chicago: University of Chicago Press, 1967.

Rath, Jan, ed. *Unravelling the Rag Trade: Immigrant Entrepreneurship in Seven World Cities.* Oxford and New York: Berg, 2002.

Seidel, Jutta Zander, "Ready-to-Wear Clothing in Germany in the Sixteenth and Seventeenth Centuries: New Ready-Made Garments and Second-Hand Clothes Trade." In

Per una Storia della Moda Pronta, Problemi e Ricerche (A History of Ready to Wear, Problems and Research). Proceedings of the Fifth International Conference of CISST (The Italian Center for the Study of the History of Textiles), Milan, 26–28 February, 1990. Firenze: EDI-FIR, 1991.

Smith, Philip Chadwick Foster. *The Empress of China*. Philadelphia: The Philadelphia Maritime Museum, 1984.

Tortora, Phyllis G., and Keith Eubank. *A Survey of Historic Costume: A History of Western Dress*. 3rd ed. New York: Fairchild Publications, 1996.

Zhou, Yu. "New York: Caught under the Fashion Runway." In *Unravelling the Rag Trade: Immigrant Entrepreneurship in Seven World Cities*. Edited by Jan Rath. Oxford and New York: Berg, 2002.

Jean L. Druesedow

RETAILING

Retailing consists of the set of business activities involved in selling products and services to consumers for their personal, family, or household use. Traditionally, a retailer serves as the last distribution channel that links manufacturers and consumers; however, in order to have control and exclusivity with their merchandise, most large retailers, such as Wal-Mart and the Gap, are vertically integrated and perform more than one set of activities in the distribution channel, such as both wholesaling and retailing activities or both manufacturing and retailing activities.

Retailing is a significant portion of world commerce. The world's 200 largest retailers generated $2.14 trillion in sales during 2002 and captured 30 percent of worldwide sales. These firms represent a variety of nations and such categories as department stores, specialty stores, category killers, discount stores, mail order, and so forth. However, the top nine largest retailers are discount stores or category killers, indicating a consumer trend to demand low prices. With increasing globalization, 56 percent of the top 200 retailers operated in more than one country. Geographically, U.S. companies, including Wal-Mart, Home Depot, Kroger, and Target, represented 53 percent of the total sales from the top 200 global retailers. Wal-Mart was the world's largest retailer in terms of sales and number of stores in the world. It was more

than three times the size of the second largest retailer, France's Carrefour.

Retailers are characterized by their retail mix, including the type of merchandise sold, the price of the merchandise, the variety and assortment of merchandise, and the level of customer service. Retailers are also categorized by a primary channel that they use to reach their customers such as store-based (specialty stores, department stores, discount stores) or non-store (catalog, TV home shopping, Internet) retailers. However, successful retailers in the early 2000s are multichannel retailers that sell products or services through more than one channel. For example, retailers such as Wal-Mart (discount store) and Macy's (department store) use Internet and catalog channels, and utilize the unique feature provided by each channel.

Store-Based Retail Channel

Store-based retailers use brick-and-mortar stores as primary modes of operation. Major types of store-based retailers include department stores, specialty stores, category killers, discount stores, off-price stores, outlet stores, and boutiques.

Department stores. A department store is a large-scale retail unit that carries a wide and in-depth assortment of merchandise that is classified into section divisions by product type and brand name. While department stores originated in downtown areas of major cities in the nineteenth century, with the advent of car travel and suburban flight, they came to be located in regional malls and have a typical size of between 100,000 and 200,000 square feet (930–1860 square meters). Merchandise quality, pricing, and customer service (sales help, credit card, and delivery) range from average to quite high. Accordingly, department stores target consumers with household incomes that are at least average. Two types of department store are commonly noted: the full-line department store and the specialized department store. Full-line department stores such as Macy's and Marshall Field's carry both hard goods (such as furniture, housewares, and home electronics) and soft goods (apparel, accessories, and bedding). Except for Sears, most full-line department stores no longer offer major appliances. Specialized department stores or limited-line department stores restrict their inventories rather than carry full lines. For example, Saks Fifth Avenue, Neiman Marcus, and Nordstrom focus on apparel and wearable accessories and may not carry lines such as furniture and home electronics. Other merchants emphasize jewelry and home furnishings, such as Fortunoff.

In the early twenty-first century, the largest department stores in the United States in terms of sales include Sears ($41.4 billion), JCPenny ($32.3 billion), Federated Department Stores, which owns Macy's and Bloomingdale's among others ($15.4 billion), and the May company, which owns such entities as Filene's, Lord & Taylor, and Famous-Barr ($13.5 billion). With the fierce competition that arises from specialty stores and discount stores, department stores' market shares have fallen since the mid-1990s. This decline has resulted in the reduced perceived-value for merchandise and services, unproductive selling space, low turnover merchandise, and fuzzy store images. A vast majority of department-store merchants in the early 2000s place great emphasis on soft goods and accessories, and less emphasis on hard goods.

Specialty stores. Specialty stores, also called limited-line stores, focus on selling one line of merchandise (such as jewelry) or serving one particular market (for example, maternity apparel). Specialty stores offer a narrow but deep assortment in the chosen category and tailor selection of products to a defined market segment. Specialty stores also feature a high level of customer service with knowledgeable sales personnel and customer service policies and intimate store size and atmosphere. A typical size of specialty stores is less than 8,000 square feet. Some specialty stores target affluent consumers with high price and upscale merchandise, whereas others target price-conscious consumers with discount merchandise. Popular product categories of specialty stores include apparel, personal care, home furnishings, jewelry, and sporting goods. The largest U.S. specialty stores in sales include GAP brands, which includes Gap, Baby Gap, Banana Republic, Gap Kids, and Old Navy ($14.4 billion), and Limited brands, which includes The Limited, Henri Bendel, Intimate Brands, Lane Bryant, Lerner New York, Limited Too, Structure, and Express ($8.4 billion).

Category killers. Also known as category specialist, category killers combine attributes of both specialty stores and discount stores because they feature a great breadth of assortment in one classification of merchandise (e.g., toys, electronics) and low prices. Because of the large volume of merchandise they require from suppliers, category killers can use their buying power to negotiate for low prices. Category killers provide consumers a warehouse environment with a typical store size of 50,000 to 120,000 square feet. Few sales people are available for assistance, but some category killers such as Office Depot (office supply) make knowledgeable salespeople available throughout the store to answer questions and make suggestions. The largest U.S. category killers in sales are Home Depot ($58.2 billion), Lowe's ($26.5 billion) and Best Buy ($20.9 billion). Home Depot and Lowe's offer equipment and material used to make home improvements while Best Buy carries consumer electronics.

Discount stores. Discount stores offer customers broad assortments of merchandise, limited services, and low prices. Discount stores are also referred to full-line discount stores or discount department stores. For their commonly recognizable huge retail format, discount stores are also referred to as big box retailers. The biggest U.S. discount stores in terms of sales include Wal-Mart ($246.5 billion), Target ($42.7 billion), and Kmart ($30.8 billion). In discount stores, customers can expect a similar range of product lines as those offered by full-line department stores, such as electronics, furniture, appliances, auto accessories, housewares, apparel, and wearable accessories, but these product lines in discount stores are less fashion-oriented than the product lines in department stores. Discount stores usually sell on only one floor rather than in a multi-floored building, as traditional department stores do. A typical size of a discount store is between 60,000 and 80,000 square feet, but a supercenter that combines a discount store with a supermarket ranges from 150,000 to 220,000 square feet. Wal-Mart, Kmart, and Target all operate supercenters.

The maintenance of low prices and lean gross margin contribute to the fast growing business of discount stores. Due to intense competition from category killers, the trends for discount stores are to create attractive shopping environments, to provide consumers branded merchandise (such as Levi Strauss in Wal-Mart) or to develop licensing agreements (for example, Isaac Mizrahi in Target).

Off-price stores. Off-price stores offer an inconsistent assortment of fashion-oriented and brand-name products at low prices and limited customer services. The leading U.S. off-price retailers are T.J. Maxx and Marshalls (both owned by TJX), Ross Stores, and Burlington Coat Factory. Most merchandise is purchased opportunistically from manufactures or from other retailers late in a selling season in exchange for low prices. This merchandise might be end-of-season excess inventory, unpopular styles and colors, returned merchandise, or irregulars. Due to this opportunistic buying practice, consumers cannot expect consistent offerings of merchandise. However, off-price stores appeal to budget and fashion-conscious consumers.

Outlet stores. Outlet stores are retailing units owned by manufacturers or by retailers that sell their leftover, low-quality, discontinued, irregular, out-of-season, or over-stock merchandise at prices less than full retail prices of their regular stores. Manufacturer-owned outlet stores are frequently referred to as factory outlets. Outlet stores were traditionally located at or near the manufacturing plant. Contemporary outlet stores are typically clustered in outlet centers or malls and located far enough from key department stores or specialty stores to avoid jeopardizing sales at full retail prices. There are 14,000 U.S. outlet stores and many are located in one of the 260 outlet centers nationwide. These stores generated total sales of $14.3 billion in 1999. Stores are characterized by few services, low rents, limited displays, and plain store fixtures, which reduce operating costs of the stores. Outlet retailing has been a popular way of disposing of unwanted merchandise by manufacturers and retailers. Even popular designers such as DKNY, Ralph Lauren, Calvin Klein, and Gucci use outlet stores to dispose of leftover items. However, most outlets also have product made especially for them—which is not just unwanted merchandise but low-quality product produced specially for that market.

Boutiques. A boutique is a small store that concentrates on a specific and narrow market niche and features topof-the-line merchandise. "Boutique" is a French term for little shop; the term was first used for small stores run by Paris couturiers. American boutique retailers include many top designers, such as Donna Karan, Calvin Klein, and Ralph Lauren. Boutiques offer high-priced, fashion-oriented merchandise and attract customers who want more sophisticated and individualized products than mass-produced goods. Boutiques cater to narrow, well-defined customer segments that usually consist of affluent men and women. Key to a boutique's attraction is its personal one-to-one service. Many designers are building flagship stores in their home country as well as in foreign markets.

Nonstore Retail Channels

Nonstore retailers utilize their retail mix in environments that are not store-based. U.S. nonstore retailers generated a total of $156 billion in 2001, accounting for roughly 5 percent of all U.S. retail sales. The major appeal of nonstore retailers is the convenience of shopping: shopping anytime and anywhere. Three major types of nonstore retailers include catalog retailers, electronic retailers (e-tailing), and television home-shopping retailers.

Catalog retailers. Catalog retailers promote products by mailing merchandise directly to a target market and process sales transactions using the mail, telephone, or fax, or Internet. Many catalog retailers embrace the Internet. When customers are mailed a catalog from the retailer, they either can order products by telephone or mail, or through the retailer's Web site. According to *Catalog Age* (2001), the most popular catalogers recognized by U.S consumers include J.C. Penny, Land's End, L.L. Bean, and Sears.

Television home-shopping retailers. Television home-shopping retailers use a program to promote and demonstrate their merchandise and process transaction over the telephone or Internet or through the mail. The two biggest home shopping retailers are QVC ("Quality, Value, Convenience") and HSN (Home Shopping Network). The best-selling merchandise of TV home shopping is inexpensive jewelry. Other categories include apparel, cosmetics, and exercise equipment.

E-tailers. The fastest-growing form of nonstore retailing is electronic retailing (e-tailing). Electronic retailers interact with customers and provide products or services for sale using the Internet. During the last five years of the 1990s, electronic retailing had a rapid growth with the creation of more than 10,000 entrepreneurial electronic retailing ventures. However, a large number of electronic retailers, especially electronic retailers that only used the Internet for selling products or services, have gone out of business since the Internet bubble burst in 2000. In 2001, U.S. electronic retailers generated about $50 billion in sales, accounting for 1.5 percent of total retail sales. The best-selling merchandise online includes computers and electronics, sporting goods, books and CDs, toys, and apparel. Due to continued consumer interest in shopping using the Internet, store-based and catalog retailers have also began to sell their merchandise using the Internet.

See also Department Store; Fashion Marketing and Merchandising; Shopping.

Bibliography

Berman, Barry, and Joel R. Evans. *Retail Management.* 9th ed. Upper Saddle River, N.J.: Prentice Hall, 2004.

Levy, Michael, and Barton A. Weitz. *Retailing Management.* 5th ed. New York: McGraw-Hill/Irwin, 2004.

Internet Resources

"Catalog Age Top Ten." Catalog Age June 2001. Available from <http://catalogagemag.com/ar/marketing_catalog_age_top_2>.

"Research Data: Outlet Industry Data." Value Retail News (2003). Available from <http://www.valueretailnews.com/research/research_index.htm>.

"Top 100 retailers." Stores July 2003. Available from <http://www.stores.org/archives/TopRetailers.asp?year=2003>.

"2003 Global Power of Retailing." Stores January 2003. Available from <http://www.stores.org>.

Seung-Eun Lee

RETRO STYLES

The fashion meaning of retro, first applied to clothes in the 1970s, refers to styles that are either copied or adapted from earlier periods. The retro reference was coined by London designers, and soon became a common coin throughout the fashion world. Thus the prefix for backward became a catchword for fashion in retrograde, fashion in retrogression—or retrospective fashion. While the word retro was "new" in the style context, the concept of bornagain fashion was not.

Fashion has often taken the past as inspiration. In the 1910s, Paul Poiret's fashions were inspired by the Directoire, the style of French design in the mid-1790s, which itself used Greco-Roman forms and Egyptian motifs.

The Neoclassicism of the 1790s alluded to the political heritage of Greek democracy and the Roman Republic, while later Egyptian motifs memorialized Napoleon's conquest of Egypt. Poiret's Neoclassicism, however, seems to have had no political significance, although it certainly emphasized physical freedom. In the 1930s, French fashion surrealists were influenced by the second empire of Louis Napoleon (1852–1870).

The mannish styles of World War II gave way in 1947 to Christian Dior's New Look. His wasp-waisted, hippadded, full-skirted silhouette represented a release from wartime austerity, and was in itself a homage to his mother and her *fin de siècle* finery. Dior's fitted jacked segued into the 1970s and 1980s, becoming a template for designers such as Claude Montana, Thierry Mugler, Azzedine Alaia, and Christian Lacroix, all of whom grew up in the Dior oeuvre. The full, petticoated skirts that marked the 1950s (which were in many respects a continuation of the New Look) reflected a societal return to pre–World War II gender stereotypes and Cold War social conservatism.

The 1960s relaunched aspects of the 1920s, the two decades sharing the same spirit of youth and anarchy—although sixties fashion originated on the streets of London (Mary Quant and the miniskirted Mods) instead of the salons of Paris. Perhaps because the 1960s symbolized the Youthquake and the mini, they have been resuscitated more than any other decade, most obviously every time designers show thigh-high miniskirts.

As the twenty-first century progresses, the 1970s, especially the mid-1970s, which were nostalgic for the 1930s, have been a favorite playback by designers in their forties. The shoulder-padded 1980s, which owe a big debt to the 1940s, were first returned to by designers in their thirties. And the minimalist, less-is-more 1990s are waiting to be rehashed when designers born in that decade reach their twenties. It seems that designers are inspired by the period when they first became interested in fashion—usually during their teens or twenties—or the period in which their design heroes lived. (One reason the 1960s have had so many sequels is that the designers of that decade were legends whose work was photographed, cataloged, and exhibited in museums as perhaps no other until that time.)

At the beginning of the twenty-first century, a new fashion amalgam appeared, one based on borrowing from other times, therefore retro, but one tweaked with "newness." This idea of taking bits of someone else's original work and either copying it or mixing it and then calling it one's own is also seen in other art forms. In the art world, it is called "appropriation." In music, it is "sampling." In the movies, it is sequels or "part twos." And in fashion, as in food, it is known as fusion. Another favorite expression for retro styles is called is referencing.

In fusion, the originality consisted in how the old was made "new." For example, the original space-age designs worn by Paris designer Andre Courrèges's moon maidens were worn with low-heeled, calf-high, white patent-leather boots. In the fused versions, Courrèges's A-line jumpers were subverted with high heels or combat boots, and some of the minis were layered over evening dresses or paired with leggings.

To this day, there are designers who plunder the past verbatim, seam-for-seam, stitch-for-stitch, line-for-line. Some credit the originals. To his credit, the late Bill Blass, in his book, *Bare Blass*, edited by the *New York Times*'s fashion critic Cathy Horyn, writes about First Lady Nancy Reagan wearing his gown to the Washington gala the night before Ronald Reagan's first inauguration: ". . .she wore a black velvet dress of mine. Which *Women's Wear* said was a knock-off of Saint Laurent's. Which indeed it was." Other designers cite no provenance. Those who do not are usually not called for copying for three reasons. First, few seem to care if a designer such as Nicolas Ghesquiere of Balenciaga calls a design by Kaisik Wong his own, even when confronted with visual proof. Appropriation is now considered not just acceptable, but expected. Second, few magazine editors can risk jeopardizing the loss of advertising pages if they offend the big-advertising designer by accusing him of stealing—whoops, appropriation. And third, there are not too many fashion journalists in the media mix of the early 2000s who would recognize a purloined design if they saw one.

One of the reasons retro styles became a fashion byword during the late twentieth and early twenty-first centuries can be attributed to the rage for vintage clothes. After almost a decade of simple, spare, less-is-more fashion, many women sought relief from the minimalist mode at swap meets, thrift shops, and vintage boutiques, where the old looked suddenly newer than the new.

It's the nature of the fashion beast to feed on the past. This apologia by TV host/designer Isaac Mizrahi hits the mark. He says that to complain about revivals of clothes from other decades is to complain about chicken. "A good classic recipe for *poulet* has existed for centuries, yet people still make chicken dishes. They may change some of the spices, but the basis is still chicken. In the same way, a classic dress from any period attained classic status because it is a good, time-tested design that is worthy of being modernized with new fabrics and new accessories. In other words, you just change the recipe to suit modern tastes."

See also Fashion, Historical Studies of.

Marylou Luther

ROMA AND GYPSY

Roma is the Romani word used to refer to Gypsies, a label that has pejorative connotations. Since many Roma use the term Gypsy with outsiders, and there are contexts in which Gypsy is the broader term, its use is still applicable in certain settings and certainly appears in literature as well as search engines. In Europe and the British Isles, terms such as Romanies, Travelers, or Tinkers are also used. Many different groups form the Roma population based on a common sense of belonging, although they may have very diverse characteristics and call themselves by different names.

Roma live in the United States, South America, Europe, Russia, Middle East, North Africa, and North and Central Asia. Some have migrated to Australia, Hawaii, and Alaska as well. The Roma migrated into Eastern and Western Europe in the fourteenth century through Persia en route from India, which they left approximately 1,000 years ago. Since leaving India, Roma have always lived within another culture or country as a minority and pariah group. They have been subjected to extreme discrimination and persecution throughout history, especially in Western and Central Europe where they were enslaved in the Middle Ages. Between 500,000 and 600,000 European Roma perished under the Nazis in World War II. In the nineteenth century they migrated to North and South America where they continue to be a nomadic or semi-nomadic group.

Roma in the United States are estimated to range between 100,000 and 300,000 members of various groups (such as Vlach Roma, Boyash, Irish Travelers, and Hungarian Roma) living in all parts of the country. Estimates of Roma in Europe are between 4 and 10 million, with the largest numbers concentrated in Central European and Balkan countries (as much as 5 percent of the population). Different groups have taken up various occupations, including music, metal work, buying and selling horses or cars, fortune-telling (primarily women), and selling craft items. Middle-class Roma have entered the professions, but in the early 2000s this was still a relatively small group.

Roma trace descent through both parents but take on patriline names and have a patrilocal marriage preference. Authority is based on age, with both older women and men enjoying a high status. Men are powerfully situated in the system of juridical authority, and women hold power through the complex system of religious, spiritual, and medical authority. Roma have no religious specialists other than older women, but they use clergy from local churches to conduct baptisms. In the United States their own religion is punctuated by certain rituals, including the baptism of a six-week-old child, marriage, the *pomana* (death ritual), *slava* (Saint's Day feast) and some American holidays, such as Easter and Thanksgiving.

In the United States, Roma generally live in urban areas, usually on main streets and in the poorer parts of towns. They are not as easily recognizable to the American population as they are in Europe, where they stand out more. They often prefer to represent themselves as a member of an ethnic group other than Roma since it abates the stereotyping and discrimination against them. One of their survival mechanisms is to keep to themselves and avoid contact with non-Roma except in work-related circumstances.

The Roma wear clothing that reflects their religion, customs, and ethics. Many Roma, both men and women (but not children), treat clothes worn on the upper body separately from clothes worn on the lower body. Upper and lower body clothes may be washed separately as the lower body is considered "impure," and it is desirable not to "pollute" the upper body. The head in particular is protected from impurity. Hats worn by men and scarves worn by married women are kept away from any surface (such as the seat of a chair) or other clothes that touch the lower body. In addition, men's clothes may be kept separate from women's clothes, and women's skirts are considered dangerously polluting to a man. Women must wear a skirt long enough to cover their legs at least to the mid-calf. Items (such as dish towels) that are used with food are also given particular attention to purity.

During ritual occasions, the Roma often purchase or make new clothes to wear. New clothes have never touched anyone's body and therefore are guaranteed to be pure. A Saint's Day feast, wedding, or pomana (death ritual) are occasions when special pure clothing is desirable. During the pomana, a living person representing

Roma men. A group of four young Roma men in Brasov, Romania. In Roma tradition, hats are kept away from any surface and must not touch any clothing on the lower body. © Wolfgang Kaehler/Corbis. Reproduced by permission.

the deceased is dressed in new clothes and is called "the wearer of the clothes." This person stands in for the spirit of the deceased who is thought to be watching the po-mana to make sure the relatives are displaying the proper respect for the dead.

The presentation of self through dress and fashion is very important to the Roma and part of their public performance as Roma. Roma fashions do change over time and place. Furthermore, fashions for men and women seem to be based on different criteria. Whereas men dress to present an image to the outside world that they associate with power and authority, women dress to present an image to the Roma that is associated with Roma ideas of the power of purity and pollution.

Men

In the United States Roma have adopted fashions that project a particular masculine stereotype, often gleaned from the movies. Their public and private appearance is a performance of a certain recognizable style that they associate with masculinity and authority. They are not concerned with being stylishly up-to-date, rather they are concerned with the images of power projected by the clothing. Examples of commonly seen styles include:

1. Urban cowboy—hat, cowboy shirt, bolo tie, jeans, and boots; sometimes a Western-style jacket.

2. 1930s Chicago gangster—loose pants, two toned shoes, wide splashy tie, and double breasted jacket.
3. Palm Springs golfer—white or loud color pants, red golf shirt, Irish hat.
4. Casual modern—polo shirts, white shirts, or Hawaiian shirts, long pants.

Young men who are not yet old enough to present an image of power may adopt a more youthful modern dress. For example: (1) Beatles attire—pencil thin tie, loud tight shirt, and stove pipe pants; (2) Spanish or Hungarian Gypsy musician—longish hair, red diklo at the neck, "Gypsy" shirt; or (3) Modern—shirt and baggy shorts.

Women

Women are interested in fashion that shows their sense of "shame" and their status as guardians of purity for the family. Because of this role, women are expected to cover their legs at least to the mid-calf. Married women traditionally cover their head with a scarf and tie their long hair up or braid it. There is no shame associated with showing a low-cut neckline; in fact, it is rare to see a woman who does not wear low-cut tops. Women may wear modern western clothing when they do not want to be recognized as Roma. Some, for example, wear "Hopi" Indian dress to "pass" as American Indians. Even within these limitations, women have a great deal of leeway to adopt different styles:

1. Traditional Serbian or Russian Roma—homemade, long, pleated, light chiffon, sari-like skirt; tight lowcut blouse with V-neck showing cleavage; bra that acts as a pocketbook and place for cigarettes; hair put up in a chignon or bun; pocket handkerchief or larger style scarf on the head; flat shoes.
2. 1970s fashion—store-bought suit with A-line maxi-skirt and fitted jacket; floppy straw Easter bonnet hat; high heels.
3. Eastern European Roma contemporary—flowered, bright calf-length skirt; short puffed-sleeved peasant blouse with gold coins around the neck; and scarf on head; barefoot or in flat shoes. (Located in Bulgaria, Romania, Hungary.)
4. Spanish Roma entertainment—flamenco dress that is calf-length; bright polka-dot material; sleeveless low-cut top.

Children

In general, children are considered pure until puberty and do not have to worry about being polluting or being polluted. Mostly they wear current store-bought American clothes. Very small children can wear shorts or tank tops. Boys wear jeans and a shirt, and on special occasions a suit. Girls wear dresses or pants, and on special occasions long dresses. They usually have long hair hanging down or a ponytail.

See also Ethnic Dress; Fashion and Identity; Religion and Dress.

Bibliography

Gay y Blasco, Paloma. *Gypsies in Madrid: Sex, Gender and the Performance of Identity*. Oxford: Berg, 1999.

Sutherland, Anne. *Gypsies: The Hidden Americans*. Prospect Heights, Ill.: Waveland Press, 1986.

——. "Pollution, Boundaries and Beliefs," In *Dress and Identity*, pp. 436–444. Edited by Roach-Higgens, Mary Ellen, Joanne Eicher and Kim Johnson. New York: Fairchild Publications, 1995.

Anne Hartley Sutherland

ROYAL AND ARISTOCRATIC DRESS

Rules governing ceremonial court and aristocratic dress not only reflected power ranking in the premodern world, but also were designed to reaffirm the legal status of royal and aristocratic privilege, and thus to secure the influence of the ruling class. Elisabeth Mikosch (1999, pp. 18–19) points out a dramatic example of how the wearing of royal clothes was taboo to others:

> After her flight from Lochleven to Carlisle, Mary [Stuart of Scotland] was in dire need of clothes and asked [Queen] Elizabeth to send her some dresses. Elizabeth harshly denied her request, because Mary had not asked Elizabeth for just any kind of clothes, but for used dresses from Elizabeth's own wardrobe. As a reply, Elizabeth sent some lengths of black velvet, black satin and black taffeta. With this gift Elizabeth not only

King Charles I and Queen Zita of Austria-Hungary. The elaborate ceremonial dress worn by royals prior to World War I was an indication of exclusive power and prestige. © Underwood & Underwood/Corbis. Reproduced by permission.

denied Mary royal dignity but also sent a sharp reprimand for Mary's personal behavior.

Ceremonial dress rules were also used by rulers to express their political opinions. In 1766 Emperor Joseph II decided to abolish the wearing of Spanish-style dress at the Viennese court, as the "Spanish cloak dress" was understood as a symbol for "an absolute ruler, who represented the entire state" (Mikosch 1999, pp. 49–50). Thus, it was inappropriate for the court of an Enlightenment monarch. The "Spanish cloak dress" was a fashionable predecessor of the uniform court dress or *justaucorps*. It was the obligatory court dress for gentlemen at the Vienna imperial court from the seventeenth century until 1766. Court ceremonial required that one had to wear it whenever the emperor was in residence. Mikosch traces its antiquated form back to the fashion of the second half of the sixteenth century and describes it as follows:

> The dress consisted of a tightly fitted short doublet with a collar and cuffed sleeves as well as breeches and a circular wide cloak or cape [Spanish *cappa*] reaching to the knees and displaying a flat collar. A rich lace collar or a falling band of lace or fine linen, called a *rabat*, and a large hat decorated with ostrich plumes, completed the ceremonial male dress.

Comparing the state portraits of the emperors Leopold I, Joseph I, Charles VI, and Joseph II, one finds that the main features remained unchanged throughout their reigns, but certain details were altered to conform to changing fashions. For special occasions the clothes were made of silk fabrics richly woven with gold threads (*drap d'or*), lined with silver fabric (*drap d'argent*), and abundantly trimmed with gold lace.

Lady Mary Wortley Montagu notes that in Vienna in 1716 "I saw t'other day the gala for Count Altheim, the emperor's favourite, and never in my life saw so many fine clothes illfancied. They embroider the richest gold stuffs; and provided they can make their clothes expensive enough, that is all the taste they shew in them" (*Letters of Lady Montagu*, vol. 1. p. 249).

Austrian books of emblems or *impresa* from the beginning of the eighteenth century show ladies' Spanish court dresses. The cut of these resembled the pattern of the *grand habit* or *robe manteau*, modeled after late seventeenth-century French court dress from Louix XIV's new palace at Versailles. The ensemble consisted of a skirt with a train and a matching stiff bodice that was drawn into a long point toward the waist; it had short sleeves and a very décolleté neckline that displayed the shoulders and bosom. Rows of lace ruffles and *engageantes* of fine lace decorated the short sleeves. The wide skirt had a long train and it was generally open in the front and turned back to reveal a petticoat. The skirt was supported by stays, and its shape, whether slender, round, or wide, depended on contemporary fashions. False or hanging sleeves were reminiscent to the original Spanish roots of the dress and called "*Adlerflügel*" (eagle's wings).

Lady Wortley Montagu observed of the Viennese court: "Their dress agrees with the French or English in no one article but wearing petticoats, and they have many fashions peculiar to themselves; as that it is indecent for a widow ever to wear green or rose colour, but all the other gayest colours at her own descretion" (*Letters of Lady Montagu*, 1866, vol. 1, p. 248; fine examples given by Bönsch 1990, 176/14 and 15). A letter from Johanna Theresia, countess of Harrach, to her husband, Ferdinand, on 9 December 1676, illustrates the importance of fashionable dress at court. The countess wrote that she had bought light-colored underwear for herself and their daughter from a merchant, "for when the Empress arrives, one has to have something to wear, for it is impossible to show up wearing nothing" (Bastl 2001, p. 365).

The impact of fashionable dress worn in elite circles, and the ability of rulers to make political statements through their dress can be seen in Charles Le Brun's tapestry series called *History of the King*. The scene illustrating the meeting between Louis XIV and Philip IV of Spain on 7 June 1660 shows that Le Brun gave precedence to the French king by placing him on the more distinguished left side of the tapestry and by making him larger than the Spanish king. The fashionable clothes of Louis draw the attention of the spectator, while Philip's clothing looks modest and old-fashioned.

The French court was seen as the new cultural leader of Europe in fashion and court ceremony, and Louis XIV used sartorial rules as a means of exercising power. For example, in 1665 the king awarded to a select group of cavaliers who enjoyed special favors personally granted by the king, the right to wear a blue *justaucorps à brevet* (warrant coat), lined in red and richly embroidered with gold and silver thread according to a prescribed pattern. (Mikosch 1999, 65/57). Paintings of King Louis XIV and his aristocracy provide vivid visual evidence of the importance of fashion at the royal court.

Roderick Random (1748), Tobias Smollett's (1721–1771) first novel, shows a boisterous and unprincipled hero who answers life's many misfortunes with a sledgehammer; but sometimes he does very well and then he acquires possessions like the following:

"My wardrobe consisted of five fashionable coats full mounted, two of which were plain, one of cut velvet (velvet having the pile cut so as to form patterns), one trimmed with gold, and another with silver-lace; two frocks, one of white drab (sort of woollen cloth) with large plate buttons, the other of blue, with gold binding; one waistcoat of gold brocade; one of blue satin, embroidered with silver; one of green silk, trimmed with broad figured gold lace; one of black silk, with figures; one of white satin; one of black cloth, and one of scarlet; six pair of cloth breeches; one pair of crimson, and another of black velvet; twelve pair of white silk stockings, as many of black silk, and the same number of fine cotton; one hat, laced with gold *point d'Espagne* [kind of lace], another with silver-lace scalloped, a third with gold binding, and a fourth plain; three dozen of fine ruffled shirts, as many neckcloths; one dozen of cambrick handkerchiefs, and the like number of silk" (Smollett, p. 256).

Conspicuous consumption, which expressed social distinction through a lavish lifestyle, was an instrument of royal and aristocratic self-esteem in the eternal contest over rank and prestige. In general, expenditures for clothing correlate less with a person's wealth than with his or her wish to achieve distinction through dress, but in the case of the European aristocracy there was also considerable pressure to dress appropriately to one's status. Maria Magdalena, countess of Hardegg (1595–1657) complained to her father, Georg Friedrich Prüschenk, count of Hardegg (1568–1628, in Vienna), that others made fun of her because of her attire:

> I cannot describe to your Lordship how they make fun of me because of my attire; they say it is a shame that I am dressed thus, that my attire ruins a person's looks, and I laugh with them when they criticize my dress, which I would not change for anyone if it were not on your will and order. (Bastl 2001, p. 362)

Aristocratic country life in premodern Europe was relatively simple, even boring; the pace of life was determined by the seasons and by ordinary everyday events, punctuated by celebrations and festive occasions. Festivals appealed to the eye and used a vocabulary of peculiar attributes that are difficult to decipher nowadays, but that constituted a wordless but well understood language at court in early modern times. There was an inevitable tendency for nonmembers of the elite to engage in what is called "power dressing" in the twenty-first century by appropriating elements of elite dress. One sees in this behavior that dress is both intimate and potent as a means of expressing power; much dressing is power dressing, and power dressing is by its very nature political, in that it is public.

In this context the "big event" of a wedding became a celebration that, like everything else, needed to be regulated within the order of a hierarchical society. When Anna of Starhemberg (1513–1551) had to wed her niece Elizabeth to Marquart of Kuenring in 1536, she was in charge of putting together the bride's wardrobe. In one of her letters (15 November 1536) she writes to her husband Erasmus about Elizabeth's wedding dress:

> Since you wrote to me that Els [Elizabeth] needed a white beret for her white damask dress, I want to let you know that she is not going to wear a beret but a wreath, which she has to wear at her betrothal. Also, when you said that she is going to need a red beret, I don't think it

is necessary because she has a pretty one with a pearl border although it is only black; give it to her, with the jewels on it. But if you want her to have a red one to go with her red velvet jacket, you can get one that has nothing on it so that we can sew the jewels on to it. (Bastl 2001, pp. 363–364)

This letter is revealing for various reasons: For one, it is an early documentation of a white wedding dress, which was already worn with a wreath at the engagement party, although the "beret" (Bönsch 1990, pp. 174–175) was also considered to be appropriate headwear at a wedding. Secondly, it is clear that the color red for garments also achieved similar, perhaps even greater, popularity with the nobility and was worn in matching shades for the dress and the hat. Apparently velvet was also considered to be a fabric similar in value to damask, since they seem to have been interchangeable for wedding attire. Most generally, it is understood that clothing itself is a matter of intense concern for the family of the bride at an elite wedding.

Clothing was precious and expensive and was worn throughout a lifetime. In 1595 Helena of Schallenberg was a lady-in-waiting at the court of the duke of Bavaria, and she wrote to her brother:

BLACK AND WHITE

The color or rather the non-color, black was associated with the grave impersonality of authority. In Europe its oldest association is with death, with grief, and with the fear of death. As the color worn by mourners, its use is very old. It is sometimes suggested that the use of black for mourning was a medieval development: but its use at that time was a revival, not an invention. Roman mourners wore black togas (though the deceased body itself was wrapped in a white toga). And funeral processions in ancient Greece wore black. We are dealing in death with a reversal of the dress code, which converts elegant court attire "a bright red-colored precious dress with trim of silver lace of Spain"—to a funeral dress, or as Anna Maria Countess of Trauttmansdorff writes in her last will of 1704, "the black court gown: the clothing of my corpse in a dark taffeta nightgown." This is an ambivalent procedure in more ways than one: on the one hand, the clothing of the live body in garments that are considered to be beautiful and that maintain or promote status; on the other, the clothing of the dead body with garments that are ugly, and hence diminish or reduce status (Bastl 2001, p. 371).

I am asking you with all my heart to ask our father for a martenskin—I cannot go without one. I have not had one made since I was a child. I have had a coat long enough—all my life—for which one cannot buy a lining at the market. I cannot wait any longer. We have to go to the Reichstag in appropriate dress and other necessary things; but I don't know how to go about it. (Bastl 2001, p. 365)

In the above-mentioned letters, Maria Magdalena of Hardegg wrote to her father in September 1616 that her late mother's lambskin has become too small for her and her little sister Sidonia might have her dressing gown, which she was not able to wear any more. The implication is that were she still able to fit into these clothes she would expect (and be expected) to continue wearing them, rather than replacing them with new clothing.

Aristocratic families must have had collections of clothes, for the tailor Hans Janoss found "an old tan-colored wool fabric dress, completely redone, sewn with fringes on it" in Regina Sybilla Countess Khevenhüller's trousseau in 1627. The same was true in sixteenth-century England, where Anne Basset had been criticized by Queen Jane Seymour and her ladies for her smocks and sleeves because they were "too coarse" and asked Lady Lisle to send finer material for new ones. Instead, "the Countess of Sussex had decided to have Anne's old gowns made into kirtles (skirts, or skirts and bodices) to save some expense" (Harris 2002, p. 229).

The discourse about court culture and aristocratic behavior and clothing in late nineteenth- and early twentieth-century Germany came to a curious conclusion. French *civilisation*, which implicated the art and artifice of fashion (expressed, for example, in the imperial court of Napoleon III), was dismissed as superficial, opposed philosophically in the emerging ideology of German nationalism by "deep" German *Kultur*, which was hostile to fashion (Duindam 2003, p. 295). At the same time, fashionable clothing was readily available to a much wider segment of the population than ever before; the court and its clothing no longer held a privileged position as the leader of fashion.

By the end of World War I, aristocratic titles survived in some European countries and were abolished in others, but royal and aristocratic dress lost its distinctiveness and exclusivity throughout European society. In the twentieth century, some royals were fashion leaders (Edward, Prince of Wales; Princess Grace of Monaco) and others were models of bourgeois respectability (Queen Beatrix of the Netherlands, Elizabeth II of England), but royals and aristocrats as a group no longer dressed in distinctive and regulated clothing, and were no longer society's principal leaders of fashion.

See also Court Dress; Uniforms, Diplomatic.

Bibliography

Arnold, Janet. *English Women's Dresses and Their Construction c. 1660–1860.* London: Macmillan, 1964.

——. *Patterns of Fashion: The Cut and Construction of Clothes for Men and Women c.1560–1620.* London: Drama Publishers, 1985.

Bastl, Beatrix. "Das Österreichische Frauenzimmer. Zur Rolle der Frau im höfischen Fest-und Hofleben 15.–17. Jahrhundert." In *Slavnost ia zábavy na dvorech a v residencních mestech raného novoveku.* Edited by Václav Buzek and Pavel Král, 79–105. České Budějovice, Czech Republic: 1996. Gives an overview about expenses for clothes for the lady-in-waiting Anna Josepha von Thürheim 1709–1711.

——. *Tugend, Liebe, Ehre. Die adelige Frau in der Frühen Neuzeit.* Wien, Köln, and Weimar, Germany: Böhlau, 2000.

——. "Das Österreichische Frauenzimmer. Zum Beruf der Hofdame in der Frühen Neuzeit." In *Residenzenforschung 11: Das Frauenzimmer.* Edited by Werner Paravicini, 355–375. Wiesbaden Germany: 2000. Edition of the *trousseau* for the court of Anna Maria Thurn 1559.

——. "Clothing the Living and the Dead: Memory, Social Identity and Aristocratic Habit in the Early Modern Habsburg Empire." *Fashion Theory* 5, no. 4 (2001): 1–32.

Bourdieu, Pierre. *Distinction. A Social Critique of the Judgement of Taste.* London: Routledge, 1999.

Duindam, Jeroen. *Vienna and Versailles. The Courts of Europe's Dynastic Rivals, 1550–1780.* Cambridge, U.K.: Cambridge University Press, 2003.

Elias, Norbert. *The Civilizing Process.* Oxford and Malden, U.K.: Blackwell, 2000.

Harris, Barbara J. *English Aristocratic Women 1450–1550: Marriage and Family, Property and Careers.* Oxford: Oxford University Press, 2002.

Hollander, Anne. *Seeing Through Clothes.* Berkeley, Los Angeles, and London: University of California Press, 1993.

The Letters and Works of Lady Mary Wortley Montagu, edited by her great grandson Lord Wharncliffe in two volumes. London, 1866.

Mikosch, Elisabeth. "Court Dress and Ceremony in the Age of the Baroque. The Royal/Imperial Wedding of 1719 in Dresden: A Case Study." Ph.D. diss., Institute of Fine Arts, New York University, 1999.

Pallmert, Sigrid. "Kleider machen Leute—Könige machen Mode. Ein Aspekt des sogenannten Allianzteppichs." *Zeitschrift für Schweizer Archäologie und Kunstgeschichte* 47 (1990): 49–54.

Roche, Daniel. *The Culture of Clothing. Dress and Fashion in the Ancient Regime.* Cambridge, U.K.: Cambridge University Press, 1994.

Smollett, Tobias. *The Adventures of Roderick Random.* Oxford: Oxford University Press, 1979.

Zander-Seidel, Jutta. *Textiler Hausrat. Kleidung und Hausextilien in Nürnberg von 1500–1650.* München: Deutscher Kunstverlag, 1990.

Beatrix Bastl

S

SAINT LAURENT, YVES*

A direct heir of the couture tradition of Gabrielle (Coco) Chanel, Cristóbal Balenciaga, and Christian Dior, Yves Saint Laurent explored, discovered, and polished, in the course of a career lasting more than forty years, the infinite resources of his vocabulary. Taming the signs and codes of his age, he created the grammar of the contemporary wardrobe and imposed his language, which became the inescapable reference of the twentieth century. In search of a uniform for elegance, Saint Laurent combined the greatest rigor of production with extreme sophistication of form to create clothing of impeccable cut with harmonious proportions, where the aesthetic of the detail was transformed into an absolute necessity. "Fashion is like a party. Getting dressed is preparing to play a role. I am not a couturier, I am a craftsman, a maker of happiness" (Teboul 2002).

Yves Mathieu Saint Laurent was born on 1 August 1936 in the Algerian city of Oran, the oldest of the three children of Lucienne-Andrée and Charles Mathieu Saint Laurent. He said later: "As long as I live I will remember my childhood and adolescence in the marvelous country that Algeria was then. I don't think of myself as a *pied noir*. I think of myself as a Frenchman born in Algeria" (Teboul 2002). He entered the Collège du Sacré-Cœur in September 1948. Strongly influenced by the play *L'École à deux têtes* of Jean Cocteau, he designed his first dresses: stage costumes for paper puppets with which he performed for his sisters. "I had a terrible time in class, and when I got home at night I was completely free. I thought only of my puppets, my marionettes, which I dressed up in imitation of the plays I had seen" (Benaïm, p. 451).

Saint Laurent designed a good deal, imitating Jean Gabriel-Domergue, Christian Bérard, René Gruau, Christian Dior, Cristóbal Balenciaga, and Hubert de Givenchy. In February 1949 he created his first dresses, made for his mother and his two sisters. At the age of sixteen he attended a performance of Molière's *L'École des femmes*, performed and directed by Louis Jouvet. Bérard had designed both sets and costumes. Seeing this play inspired in Saint Laurent a passion that he never surrendered for the theater. In December 1953 he went with his mother to Paris to receive the third prize in the competition of the Secrétariat de la Laine. There he was introduced to Michel de Brunhoff, who was then editor of the French edition of the essential fashion magazine *Vogue*.

Back in Oran, he began a correspondence with de Brunhoff, sending him fashion and theater sketches. The following year, armed with his baccalaureat (earning second prize for the philosophy essay and a score of 20 out of 20 in drawing), Saint Laurent settled in Paris and attended the École de la Chambre Syndicale de la Haute Couture for three months. He won first prize for dresses in the Secrétariat de la Laine competition. It was at about this time that, struck by the similarity of Saint Laurent's designs to those of the fall–winter collection of Christian Dior, de Brunhoff decided to introduce him to Dior, who promptly hired him as an assistant. During the next two years—years of apprenticeship and intense collaboration—a lasting complicity was established between the two men. "I remember him above all. . . . The elegance of his feelings matched the elegance of his style" (Yves Saint Laurent, p. 31).

On 24 October 1957 Christian Dior died from a heart attack at the age of fifty-two. On 15 November Saint Laurent was designated his successor. At age twenty-one he became the youngest couturier in the world. He presented his first collection in January 1958 and had his first triumph with the Trapeze line, which propelled him onto the international scene with its enormous success. He was given the Neiman Marcus Award. That same year he met Pierre Bergé, who soon became his companion and business partner.

While designing six collections a year for the house of Dior, Saint Laurent satisfied his passion for the theater, and he designed his first stage costumes (*Cyrano de Bergerac*, Ballets de Paris de Roland Petit,

1959). Influenced by Chanel, the spring–summer collection had solid success and provoked a craze, but the autumn–winter collection saw the appearance of a more controversial style: turtleneck knits and the first black leather jackets. Singularly prophetic, Saint Laurent had taken his inspiration directly from the street. Drafted into the Algerian armed forces in 1960, he was replaced at Dior by Marc Bohan.

Saint Laurent was soon declared unfit for service and hospitalized for nervous depression, and it was thanks to Bergé that he was able to leave the army. "Victoire" Doutrouleau, one of Dior's star models and a "marvelous muse" for Saint Laurent, recalls: "He left the hospital anxious, dazed, and alone. Yves a soldier? You might as well try changing a swan into a crocodile!" (Benaïm, p. 108). In open conflict with the Dior fashion house, which he sued for breach of contract, Saint Laurent decided to establish his own couture house in 1961, in association with Bergé. The financial support came from an American businessman, J. Mack Robinson: "I was impressed by such great talent in such a young man. I knew nothing about fashion, and I didn't want to get involved. This was the realm of Yves, the creator, and I immediately saw that he was a genius" (Yves Saint Laurent, p. 16).

The house opened officially on 4 December 1961. Former employees of Christian Dior left Dior to work for Saint Laurent, and more than half the seamstresses came from the Dior workshops. The graphic designer Cassandre created the YSL logo. Saint Laurent designed his first dress—labeled 00001—for Mrs. Arturo Lopez Willshaw, followed by the famous white feather costume for the dancer Zizi Jeanmaire. In 1962, on rue Spontini in Paris, the house presented its first show, described by Life as "the best suitmaker since Chanel" (p. 49). Dino Buzzati, special correspondent for the Corriere della sera, wrote: "Closing the show, a wedding dress in goffered white piqué brought an ovation from the public. The pale face of the young couturier then appeared for a moment from backstage; only for a moment, because a swarm of admirers surrounded him, embraced him, devoured him." This collection was memorable for the Norman jacket, the smock, and the pea jacket, which became "foundations" of the Saint Laurent style.

Saint Laurent designed the sets and costumes for Les chants de maldoror and Rapsodie espagnole, staged by Roland Petit, and the dresses for Claudia Cardinale in Blake Edwards's film The Pink Panther (1964). In April 1963, accompanied by Pierre Bergé, who had become his Pygmalion, he made his first trip to Japan, where he presented shows in Osaka and Tokyo.

The year 1964 saw the launch of a perfume for women, called "Y." But Saint Laurent's new collection was showered with negative criticism. The press spoke only of the André Courrèges' bombshell collection. Saint Laurent explained: "I have never been able to work on a wooden mannequin; I play by unrolling the fabric on the model, walking around her, making her move. . . . The only collection that I made a mess of, a complete fiasco, the very year when Courrèges's came on the scene and succeeded, I did not have good models, and I was not inspired" (Vacher, p. 68). Still drawn to the theater, he designed the costumes for Le mariage de Figaro and Il faut passer par les nuages for the Renaud-Barrault company.

In 1965 he triumphed with the Mondrian collection (named for the modern artist Piet Mondrian), which was surprising for its strict cut and the play of colors. Show-ered with praise by the American fashion press, he had become, according to Women's Wear Daily, "the Young King Yves of Paris." It was at this time that he made his first trip to New York, accompanied by Bergé. Richard Salomon (of Charles of the Ritz) acquired all the stock of the Yves Saint Laurent design company. At this time, too, Saint Laurent began a long friendship with the dancer Rudolph Nureyev, for whom he designed stage costumes and street clothes. He also created the wardrobe that Sophia Loren wore in Stanley Donen's film Arabesque (1966), as well as the costumes for Roland Petit's Notre-Dame de Paris.

For his summer 1966 haute couture show Saint Laurent presented the first see-through garments, the "nude look," and the first dinner jacket: "If I had to choose a design among all those that I have presented, it would unquestionably be the tuxedo jacket. . . . And since then, it has been in every one of my collections. It is in a sense the 'label' of Yves Saint Laurent" (Vacher, p. 64). For his haute couture collection of winter 1966–1967 he introduced the Pop Art collection. He met Andy Warhol and Loulou de la Falaise, his future muse. On 26 September 1966 Saint Laurent opened his first ready-to-wear shop, Saint Laurent Rive Gauche, at 21, rue de Tournon, with Catherine Deneuve, for whom he had designed the costumes in Luis Buñuel's film Belle de jour (1967), as godmother.

With the designs of Saint Laurent, ready-to-wear fashion established its pedigree, for he himself supervised the creation, manufacture, and distribution of the clothing: "The ready-to-wear is not a poor substitute for couture. It is the future. We know that we are dressing younger, more receptive women. With them it is easy to be bolder" (Benaïm, p. 153). That same year he won the *Harper's Bazaar* Oscar award; published an illustrated book, *La vilaine Lulu*; and launched his so-called African dresses. It was at that time that Saint Laurent and Bergé discovered Marrakesh, where they bought a house. For the spring–summer 1968 show, he presented the first jacket for the safari look, more see-through garments, and the jumpsuit, which would be successfully repeated in 1975. The style "Il" or "He" was born, comprising mini evening dresses and men's suits: "I was deeply struck by a photograph of Marlene Dietrich wearing men's clothes. A tuxedo, a blazer, or a navel officer's uniform—any of them. A woman dressed as a man must be at the height of femininity to fight against a costume that isn't hers" (Buck, p. 301). In September, the first Saint Laurent Rive Gauche shop was opened in New York. In a television interview, Chanel identified Saint Laurent as her spiritual heir, while galleries in London and New York exhibited his theater drawings.

The autumn–winter 1969 collection was dominated by the tapestry coat, patchwork furs, and jeweled dresses created by his sculptor friends the Lalannes. He continued to work in the cinema, designing costumes for Catherine Deneuve in François Truffaut's *La sirène du Mississippi* (1969); then, with Bergé, he opened the first Saint Laurent Rive Gauche shop for men at 17, rue de Tournon. In 1971, inspired by the designer Paloma Picasso, who bought her clothes at flea markets, he created the Libération collection, also known as Quarante, which provoked a scandal with its "retro" style. Saint Laurent later said that this collection—featuring puffed sleeves, square shoulders, platform shoes, and his famous green fox short jacket—was a humorous reaction to new fashion tendencies. In its wake, he posed nude for the photographer Jean-loup Sieff to advertise his first eau de toilette for men, YSL pour Homme, provoking another scandal.

Beginning in 1972 great changes took place. Pierre Bergé, whose ultimate aim was to recover all the stock of Yves Saint Laurent, repurchased from Charles of the Ritz (which had become a subsidiary of the American pharmaceutical giant Squibb) its shares in the couture house, thereby taking control of the couture and ready-to-wear businesses. Bergé and Saint Laurent then developed a licensing policy; although it had existed earlier, it was strengthened and enforced. The designs presented in the spring of 1972 (embroidered cardigans, padded jackets, "Proust" dresses with taffeta frills) were greeted triumphantly by a press once again overflowing with praise: "the man is pure and simple, the greatest fashion designer in the world today," said *Harper's Bazaar* (March 1972, p. 93). To close the season with a flourish, Andy Warhol did a series of portraits of Saint Laurent.

The following years found Saint Laurent ever more in demand in the world of film and theater. He designed costumes in succession for Anny Duperey in Alain Resnais's film *Stavisky . . .*, for Ellen Burstyn in the same director's *Providence*, and for Helmut Berger in Joseph Losey's *The Romantic Englishwoman*. He created the costumes for the ballets *La rose malade* (1973) and *Schéhérazade* (1974) for Roland Petit; for *Harold and Maude* (1973), a play by Colin Higgins; and for Jeanne Moreau and Gérard Depardieu in *The Ride across Lake Constance* (1974) by Peter Handke. In 1974 an exhibition of his costume and stage set sketches was staged in the Proscenium gallery in Paris. In July of the same year, the couture house moved from its cramped quarters to a Second Empire mansion at 5, avenue Marceau.

In 1976 the Opéra-Ballets Russes collection (homage to the Russian ballet producer Sergey Diaghilev) enjoyed international success and was featured on the front page of the *New York Times*. Saint Laurent, who was celebrating his fortieth birthday, said: "I don't know if this is my best collection, but it is my most beautiful collection" (August 16, 1976, p. 39). At about this time, Saint Laurent suffered a severe depression, and beginning in 1977 rumors circulated about his impending death. He replied with major colorful collections with exotic themes: the Espagnoles, with dresses straight out of a painting by Diego Velázquez, and the Chinoises, celebrating the annals of imperial China. He also launched a new perfume, Opium, the advertising for which, orchestrated by the Mafia agency, created a scandal with the slogan "For those who are addicted to Yves Saint Laurent."

In 1978, having just designed the sets and costumes for Cocteau's *L'Aigle à deux têtes* and for Ingrid Caven's cabaret show and written the preface for Nancy Hall-Duncan's book *The History of Fashion Photography* (1979), Saint Laurent demonstrated with his spring-summer collections, "Broadway suits" that he was still in touch with the current climate. He said, "This collection is very elegant, provocative, and at the same time wildly modern, which might appear contradictory. I have sought for purity, but I have interjected unexpected accessories: pointed collars, little hats, shoes with pompons. With these kinds of winks, I wanted to bring a little humor to haute couture, . . . give it the same sense of freedom one feels in the street, the same provocative and arrogant appearance as, for example, punk fashion. All of that, of course, with dignity, luxury, and style" (Yves Saint Laurent, p. 23).

During the ensuing decade Saint Laurent carried on with his favorite themes—the now classic blazer, dinner jacket, smock, pea jacket, raincoat, pants suit, and safari jacket—while presenting his collections in the form of the homage to various artists and writers. Pablo Picasso, the surrealist poet Aragon, the French poet Guillaume Apollinaire, Cocteau, the French artist Henri Matisse, Shakespeare, the American painter David Hockney, the French artist Georges Braque, the French painter Pierre Bonnard, and the Dutch painter Vincent van Gogh were invoked in turn, inspiring strongly colored garments in which were inscribed the emblematic forms of the painters and the verses of the poets. His creations were "setting static things in motion on the body of a woman," he said in *Paris-Match* (12 Février 1988, p. 69). The press around the world never stopped singing his praises.

The 1980s were full and rich for Saint Laurent. In 1981 he designed the uniform for the writer Marguerite Yourcenar, the first woman elected to the Académie Française, and launched a men's perfume, Kouros. The year 1982 was the twentieth anniversary of the founding of his couture house; the occasion was celebrated at the Lido, where he received the International Fashion Award of the Council of Fashion Designers of America.

In 1983 he showed the Noire et Rose collection, introduced the perfume Paris, designed costumes for the play *Savannah Bay* by Marguerite Duras, and enjoyed the opening of the exhibition "Yves Saint Laurent, 25 Years of Design" at the Metropolitan Museum of New York, the largest retrospective ever devoted to a living couturier. One million visitors attended the exhibition, organized by Diana Vreeland. As Vreeland put it, "Saint Laurent has been built into the history of fashion now for a long time. Twenty-six years is proof that he can please most of the people most of the time four times a year. That's quite a reputation" (*Time*, December 12, 1983, p. 56). That same year he made his appearance in the *Larousse* dictionary.

President François Mitterrand awarded Saint Laurent the medal of Chevalier de la Légion d'Honneur in 1985, the same year the African Look collection debuted. Accompanied by Pierre Bergé, he traveled to China for the exhibition devoted to his work at the Fine Arts Museum of Beijing (which recorded 600,000 visitors) and

received, at the Paris Opera, the award for Best Couturier for the body of his work. In 1986 he presented his fiftieth haute couture collection, and a retrospective of his work was given at the Musée des Arts de la Mode in Paris. Bergé and Saint Laurent, with the participation of Cerus, purchased Charles of the Ritz, owner of Yves Saint Laurent perfumes, for $630 million.

The next year retrospectives were mounted in the U.S.S.R. (Hermitage, Saint Petersburg) and in Australia (Art Gallery of New South Wales, Sydney). That season five hundred of his pieces sold, principally to a foreign clientele. In 1988, Saint Laurent became the first couturier to present a show for the French Communist Party, at the Fête de l'Humanité. Shares of the Saint Laurent group were introduced on the secondary market of the Paris Bourse in 1989, and the revenues of the house of Saint Laurent reached 3 million francs.

The decade of the 1990s began with an exhibition at the Sezon Museum of Art in Tokyo; the opening of the first shop for accessories, at 32, rue du Faubourg Saint-Honoré; and the presentation of the collection Hommages, considered a "farewell" by some of the press. Scandal arose, however, from an interview Saint Laurent gave to *Le figaro*, in which he spoke of detoxification, his homosexuality, his overuse of alcohol, and his fits of nervous depression. But in 1992, like the phoenix reborn from his ashes, he presented his 121st collection, Une Renaissance, and celebrated the thirtieth anniversary of the Saint Laurent fashion house by inviting 2,800 guests to the Opéra Bastille.

In May 1993 the Yves Saint Laurent group merged with the Elf-Sanofi company. With this acquisition, Elf-Sanofi became the third-largest international prestige perfume and cosmetic company, after L'Oréal and Estée Lauder. Saint Laurent then launched the perfume Champagne, "for happy, lighthearted women, who sparkle." On 21 July, he presented his 124th haute couture collection, with models parading to the melody of *The Merry Widow*. In a major spectacle at the Stade de France, for the opening of the 1998 World Cup of soccer Saint Laurent and Bergé paraded three hundred models before a packed stadium, while two billion spectators watched the event on television. In November of that year, in order to devote himself entirely to haute couture, Saint Laurent turned women's ready-to-wear over to Albert Elbaz and men's ready-to-wear to Hedi Slimane.

In 1999 François Pinault, owner of the department store Printemps, bought Saint Laurent from Elf for 1.12 billion euros and pumped in an additional 78 million euros to take control of all rights to the label, which he turned over to Tom Ford, the Texas-born designer for Gucci, a house also controlled by Pinault. In 2000, Bergé announced the opening of the Centre de Documentation Yves Saint Laurent, in Paris, which has since mounted a number of handsome exhibitions on aspects of Yves Saint Laurent's work, based on the Centre's outstanding collection.

After forty-four years of fashion designing, Saint Laurent announced the closing of his house at a press conference given on 7 January 2002. He took his leave of haute couture with these words: "I have always stood fast against the fantasies of some people who satisfy their egos through fashion. On the contrary, I wanted to put myself at the service of women. . . . I wanted to accompany them in the great movement of liberation that they went through in the last century. . . . I am naïve enough to believe that [my designs] can stand up to the attacks of time and hold their place in the world of today. They have already proved it."

Saint Laurent fixed the ephemeral and constantly sought beauty, shifting between classicism and provocation. Favoring methodical work, recurrent themes, and improvisations in the form of homages, he referred to other artists as catalysts. Shakespeare, Velázquez, Picasso, Proust, and Mondrian each, in turn, served as an inspiration to him. By pushing to extremes the exoticism of the street and delving into forgotten folk traditions, he brought forth a new spirit that illuminated his palette, for example, in the African, Ballets Russes, and Chinoises collections. In an even more radical shift, he took on the male wardrobe, diverting and transposing the dinner jacket, pants suit, safari jacket, and pea jacket to bring masculine and feminine together in a single design. But, it is Pierre Bergé who best describes Yves Saint Laurent's contribution for Yves—and herein lies his uniqueness—each collection is a means of bringing dreams to life, expressing fantasies, encountering myths, and creating out of them a contemporary fashion" (Saint Laurent, p. 27). Yves Saint Laurent died on June 1, 2008.

After Tom Ford left the company, Stefano Piloti became head designer of women's ready-to-wear at Saint Laurent, where his collections have been very well received.

See also Art and Fashion; Ballet Costume; Fashion Shows; Film and Fashion; Haute Couture; Paris Fashion; Perfume; Ready-to-Wear; Retro Styles; Theatrical Costume.

Bibliography

Benaïm, Laurence. *Yves Saint Laurent*. Paris: Grasset, 1993.

Bowles, Hamish and Müller, Florence. *Yves Saint Laurent: Style*. New York: Abrams, 2008.

Buck, Joan Juliet. "Yves Saint Laurent on Style, Passion, and Beauty." *Vogue* (December 1983): 301.

Saint Laurent, Yves, Diana Vreeland, et al. *Yves Saint Laurent*. New York: Clarkson N. Potter, Inc., 1983.

Teboul, David. *Yves Saint Laurent: 5, Avenue Marceau, 75116 Paris, France*. Paris: Martinière, 2002.

Vacher, Irène. "Lesgens." Paris Match, 4 décembre 1981, p. 68.

Yves Saint Laurent par Yves Saint Laurent, 28 ans de création. Paris: editions Herscher, 1986.

Pamela Golbin

SAPEURS

The words *sape* (*Société des Ambiançeurs et des Personnes Élégantes*) and *sapeurs* are neologisms that were coined by Congolese diasporic youth living in Western metropolises, especially Paris and Brussels, to authenticate and validate their quest for a new social identity through high fashion. The *sape*'s history, however, dates back to the first years of the colonial encounter in the Congolese capital cities of Kinshasa and Brazzaville.

As early as 1910, the *sape* was in full bloom in Brazzaville, as several observers complainingly noted. In 1913, French Baron Jehan De Witte demurred at what he thought was "overdressing" among the Brazzaville locals: "[. . .] on Sunday, those that have several pairs of pants, several cardigans, put these clothes on one layer over the other, to flaunt their wealth. Many pride themselves on following Parisian fashion . . ." (p. 164). In an article arguing that colonial subjects encountered European modernity first through fashion, Phyllis Martin notes that in 1920s Brazzaville "men wore suits and used accessories such as canes, monocles, gloves, and pocketwatches on chains. They formed clubs around their interest in fashion, gathering to drink aperitifs and dance to Cuban and European music played on the phonograph" (p. 407). Most of these young people who prided themselves on being unremitting consumers and fervent connoisseurs of Parisian fashion were domestic servants, civil servants, and musicians. They spent their meager wages to order, through catalogs, the latest fashions from France.

The 1950s witnessed the creation of several associations of urban youth, whose main interests seemed to have revolved around sartorial display. Bars had sprouted in every corner of the Congolese twin capitals, owing to the emergence in the 1940s of Congolese popular rumba. These venues provided a natural platform for the youth.

Sapeurs in the early 2000s represent at least the third generation of Congolese dandyism. But what sets them apart from their colonial counterparts is their migratory trajectory to European cities and their social dereliction in countries that adopt discriminatory policies toward Third World immigrants. For these young people, the *sape* therefore becomes a refuge and a vehicle through which to forge new identities away from their chaotic homeland. Before the 1990s, *sapeurs* living in Paris or elsewhere in Europe were conferred this status only by returning to Kinshasa or Brazzaville during their summer vacation to flaunt their wardrobe. With the two countries in the throes of civil war, and given that many of these youth live in Europe without proper and lawful immigrant documents, they are more reticent to go back home and thus are redefining their relationship to their homeland. The *sape* thus allows them to avoid the dreadful connivance of Scylla (sojourn) and Charibdis (return). Although confined to the bottom rung of society, these young people are loyal customers of the most prestigious fashion designers of Paris and sport Cerruti or Kenzo suits that can cost as much as $1,000 apiece. This said, it would be erroneous to define the *sape* solely as a paradoxical fashion statement. *Sapeurs* justify some of their deviant (such as loud talking in public places), sometimes delinquent (cheating public transportation) attitudes by arguing that they are making the French and the Belgians pay for colonization (the colonial debt). *Sapeurs* from Congo-Kinshasa could be said to have reacted against Mobutuese Seko's longtime ban on Western suits (and ties) by adopting a more exuberant form of *sape*. On the other hand, those from Congo-Brazzaville, predominantly southern Balaris, have used the *sape* to oppose the northerners (in power since 1969), whom they accuse of squandering the country's wealth by building lavish mansions and buying expensive cars. Indeed, these political attitudes remain inseparable from the hedonistic quest for perfection through fashion and speak to the ways African youth are attempting to negotiate and shape the marginal situation they have been confined to within the global village.

See also Africa, Sub-Saharan: History of Dress; Paris Fashion.

Bibliography

Bazenguissa, Rémy. "'Belles maisons' contre S.A.P.E.: Pratiques de valorisation symbolique au Congo." In *État et société dans le Tiers-Monde: de la modernisation à la démocratisation*. Edited by Maxime Haubert et al. Paris: Publications de la Sorbonne, 1992, pp. 247–255.

——, and Janet MacGaffey. "Vivre et briller à Paris. Des jeunes Congolais et Zaïrois en marge de la légalité économique," *Politique africaine* 57 (March 1995): 124–133.

——, and Janet MacGaffey. *Congo-Paris: Transnational Traders on the Margins of the Law*. Bloomington: Indiana University Press, 2000.

Friedman, Jonathan. "The Political Economy of Elegance: An African Cult of Beauty." *Culture and History* 7 (1990): 101–125.

Gandoulou, Justin-Daniel. *Entre Bacongo et Paris*. Paris: Centre Georges Pompidou, 1984.

——. *Dandies à Bacongo. Le culte de l'élégance dans la société congolaise contemporaine*. Paris: L'Harmattan, 1989.

Gondola, Ch. Didier. "Popular Music, Urban Society, and Changing Gender Relations in Kinshasa, Zaire." In *Gendered Encounters: Challenging Cultural Boundaries and Social Hierarchies in Africa*. Edited by Maria Grosz-Ngaté and Omari H. Kokole. London and New York: Routledge, 1996, pp. 65–84.

——. "La contestation politique des jeunes à Kinshasa à travers l'exemple du mouvement 'Kindoubill' (1950–1959)." *Brood und Rozen, Tijdschrift voor de Geschiedenis van Sociale Bewegingen* 2 (January 1999): 171–183.

——. "Dream and Drama: The Search for Elegance among Congolese Youth." *African Studies Review* 42 (April 1999): 23–48.

——. "La sape des *mikilistes*: théâtre de l'artifice et représentation onirique." *Cahiers d'études africaines* 153, no. 39-1 (1999): 13–47.

——. "La Sape: Migration, Fashion, and Resistance among Congolese Youth in Paris." *Elimu. Newsletter of the University of California, San Diego African and African-American Studies Research Project* 4 (Summer/Fall 2000): 4, 12.

Phyllis, Martin. "Contesting Clothes in Colonial Brazzaville." *Journal of African History* 35 (1994): 401–426.

——. *Leisure and Society in Colonial Brazzaville*. Cambridge, New York: Cambridge University Press, 1995.

Thomas, Dominic. "Fashion Matters: La Sape and Vestimentary Codes in Transnational Contexts and Urban Diasporas." *Francophone Studies: New Landscapes, Modern Language Notes* 118 (September 2003): 947–973.

Witte, Baron Jehan de. *Les deux Congo*. Paris: Plon, 1913.

Ch. Didier Gondola

SARI

The word "sari" has come into general use to cover a generic category, including any draped untailored textile of about five meters in length, worn by the women of South Asia. In common parlance outside the region, the term "sari" refers to an increasingly standardized form of drape. More urban and cosmopolitan women have adapted the Nivi style, but this drape is a relatively new phenomenon. In India alone, around a hundred other forms of drapes continue to be worn. These vary from the eight-yard Koli drape of fisherwomen in Maharashtra to the thrice-wrapped drape of Bengal.

There is a general belief that the sari as a draped and seamless garment is the contemporary representative of the traditional female attire of Hindu South Asia that became diluted by the introduction from the North of tailored and stitched garments under the influence of Islam. Historical and archaeological sources do not support this reading, however. Representations on statues, wall paintings, and other sources suggests that for as far back as there are records, women in the South Asia area wore a wide variety of regional styles that included both stitched and unstitched garments, tailored and untailored. Indeed in the twenty-first century, a sari is as likely to be associated with Muslim women in the Bengal region as Hindus in the South of India. Furthermore, the seamless piece of cloth of the sari is increasingly worn along with two stitched garments, a full-length underskirt tied at the waist with a drawstring, and a fitted waist-length blouse done up at the front. The sari itself covers little of the body that is not already hidden by these accompanying garments, although conceptually a woman would see herself as unclothed without the final addition. Most women also wear underwear to make a third layer of clothing.

In the latter half of the twentieth century, the emergence of the Nivi style of draping the sari may be attributed to middle-class women entering the public sphere during the struggle for independence. It was considered more suitable to public appearances and greater mobility. This style consists of the sari being wrapped around the lower body with about a meter of cloth pleated and tucked into the waist at the center and the remainder used to cover the bosom and then falls over the left shoulder. The loose end of the sari that hangs from the shoulder is known as the *pallu*. Younger and less confident women or those wearing the sari as a uniform (such as nurses, policewomen, or receptionists) usually pin the *pallu* to their shoulder in carefully arranged pleats. As a result of the development of this pan-Indian cosmopolitan drape of the sari, the influence of local regional traditions of draping has declined in urban spaces and has become either confined to being worn within the home or in rural areas. The Nivi style of wearing the sari was further popularized through its increased association with other pan-Indian phenomena, such as the film industry and national politicians. As a result this has become the style that is symbolic of India as a state and women's sense of themselves as Indian (although it may also be found more widely in South Asia, in Bangladesh and Nepal). As a result of this development, women in areas of India where the sari was not traditional garb adopted the sari for specific formal occasions such as weddings and important public events.

Saris can be made of natural or synthetic fibers, and can be woven on hand looms or power looms. Natural fibers such as silk and cotton, which are also more fragile, are worn mostly by middle-and upper-class women. They are named after the regions in which they are made such as Kanchipuram, Sambhalpur, or Kota. Each style is associated with particular weaves, motifs, and even colors. Some saris can be very ornate and may include real gold wash on silver thread (*zari*) in their embroidery (though most *zari* work in the early 2000s is nonmetal). Other varieties may include highly elaborate embroidery styles such as *chikan* work from Lucknow. These saris may cost hundreds of dollars and are often associated with the glamour attached to the Bollywood (the film industry based in India) and politicians such as Indira Gandhi who is famous for having chosen her wardrobe carefully to reflect aesthetic taste and populist appeal. Hand-loom saris are adopted by women not only for their traditional designs and beauty but also as a statement of support for the threatened cottage industry of weaving.

However, the vast majority of saris worn by working women in the early 2000s are made of synthetic materials. While the yarn is largely spun in major mills, the large mills make up only around 4 percent of sari production (hand-looms make up around 9 percent); the rest are the product of a vast, largely unregulated, power-loom sector, that varies from a couple of machines in someone's home to factory units consisting of two hundred looms, to whom the mill sector subcontracts the weaving process. By far the main fashion influence in

The Sari: a roadmap

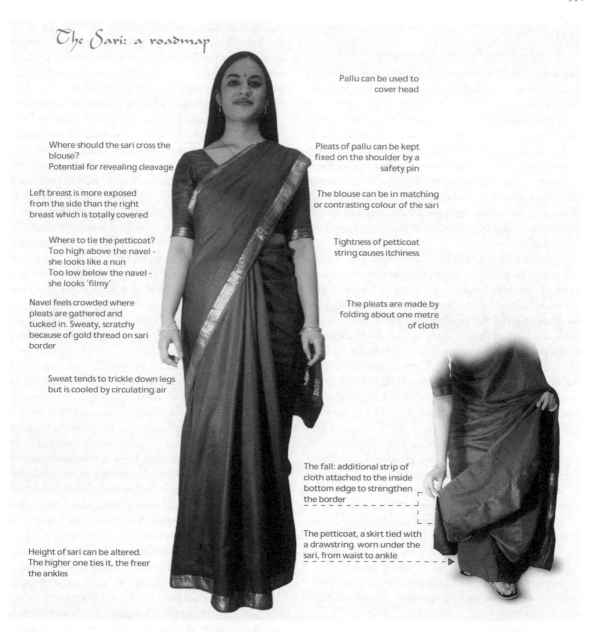

Pallu can be used to cover head

Where should the sari cross the blouse?
Potential for revealing cleavage

Pleats of pallu can be kept fixed on the shoulder by a safety pin

Left breast is more exposed from the side than the right breast which is totally covered

The blouse can be in matching or contrasting colour of the sari

Where to tie the petticoat?
Too high above the navel - she looks like a nun
Too low below the navel - she looks 'filmy'

Tightness of petticoat string causes itchiness

Navel feels crowded where pleats are gathered and tucked in. Sweaty, scratchy because of gold thread on sari border

The pleats are made by folding about one metre of cloth

Sweat tends to trickle down legs but is cooled by circulating air

The fall: additional strip of cloth attached to the inside bottom edge to strengthen the border

The petticoat, a skirt tied with a drawstring worn under the sari, from waist to ankle

Height of sari can be altered. The higher one ties it, the freer the ankles

The sari. The sari is a versatile garment worn by women throughout South Asia. The *Nivi* style shown here is the most familiar to the rest of the world, but many other styles are in use. Courtesy of Dixie. Reproduced by permission.

the early 2000s upon these synthetic saris is the rise of television soap operas and films. Typically a market or shop includes saris that have labels attached associating them with particular characters from popular culture.

The sari is not worn by young girls anywhere in India. Girls tend to wear what are locally called frocks.

Traditionally, wearing the sari was associated with puberty, but many regions have specific clothing associated with adolescence, such as the half-sari or *salwaar-kameez*, and these have grown in importance as fewer girls are married at puberty. Many mothers of girls start to collect saris from an early age, building up toward a wedding trousseau. The high point of sari wearing is commonly the wedding itself, which is (given sufficient resources) a series of events each demanding a particular sari. The color of the sari worn by the bride for the main ceremony is strictly prescribed and can vary from red in the north and east to white in Kerala. The wedding is also the occasion for much sari gifting among relatives of the bride and groom.

The period immediately after the wedding is usually the time when women are most likely to wear a sari in exclusion to all other types of clothing. As a new bride she is expected to sport the most expensive, dazzling, and bright saris. Through her years as a married woman and mother, the bright colors of her sari are expected to reflect the fecundity of her life. With age, however, the widow or elderly woman is expected to wear mainly simple and less elaborate saris. There is a cosmological significance to this shift in which the fading of the sari stands for the gradual detachment from an interest in and engagement with material things in general and with the specificity of a particular person and their occupation.

The sari as a possession is strongly correlated with wealth. Most village women keep their saris in a small trunk. They may have only one or two working saris that they wear on a daily basis, with another two or three better-quality saris kept for special occasions, such as weddings or visits to town. Some have even less than this number and most village women obtain the bulk of their saris as gifts associated with particular occasions, such as festivals. Poorer women may hardly buy any saris themselves during their lives. By contrast, middle-class salaried women in the towns may possess two or three hundred saris, often kept in steel cupboards, which reflect a wide spectrum of colors and styles. Many of these may also be gifts and are associated with particular relationships and events.

A more intimate examination of the consequences of wearing the sari demonstrates that there may be profound differences in the experience of wearing a sari as compared to wearing western dress. The existence of the *pallu* as a loose-end that comes over the shoulder and is then available to be manipulated in a wide variety of ways means that the relationship of women to their clothing can often take on a much more dynamic form. For example, most women are expected to appear in a particularly modest, if not veiled, manner in relation to various contexts, such as the presence of certain male relatives. Covering one's head with the *pallu* is a common response. Urban women, who are not subject to such restrictions, may be seen using the *pallu* to constantly change their appearance, for example, by tucking it into the waist to express anger or allowing it to reveal the bosom in order to flirt. The *pallu* is also very important in establishing key relationships, such as those between mother and child. The *pallu* may be used as a cradle, as a support to the child in learning to walk, and as a kind of "transitional object" that helps the child to separate from the mother into an independent person. This ability to manipulate one's clothing during the day and not be constrained by choices made when getting dressed in the morning makes the sari more of a companion in playing out a number of different social roles. This flexibility is what makes the sari a perfect garment to inhabit the multiplicity of roles which modernity brings to women's lives.

In areas of India where the sari was ubiquitous, women of the early 2000s are turning to alternative attire, especially the *salwar-kameez*, which is considered a more informal garment and thought better suited to commuting and work. In rural areas, the association of the *salwar-kameez* with the educated girl has given it more progressive connotations and has led to an increased availability and acceptance of this garment even in the heartlands of sari-wearing areas, such as Tamil Nadu and West Bengal.

In summary, the significance of sari wearing as opposed to other available options in South Asia lies in the dynamism and ambiguity that is the defining characteristic of the garment. While this has left open a niche which is being increasingly colonized by the *salwarkameez* as a "functional" garment associated with educational values and rationality, the combination of the two has in the early 2000s effectively prevented the adoption in South Asia of western dress, which is mainly worn by a small number of elite or by unmarried women.

See also India: Clothing and Adornment; Textiles, South Asian.

Bibliography

Banerjee, Mukulika, and Daniel Miller. *The Sari*. Oxford: Berg, 2003.

Boulanger, Chantal. *Saris: An Illustrated Guide to the Indian Art of Draping*. New York: Shakti Press International, 1997.

Chishti, Rta Kapur, and Amba Sanyal. *Saris of India: Madhya Pradesh*. New Delhi: Wiley Eastern, 1989.

Ghurye, Govind Sadashiv. *Indian Costume*. Bombay: Popular Book Depot, 1951.

Lynton, Linda, and Sanjay K. Singh. *The Sari: Styles, Patterns, History, Techniques.* New York: Harry N. Abrams, 1995.

Mukulika Banerjee and Daniel Miller

SARONG

The *sarong* is a wrapper sewn together into a tube. Both men and women in Indonesia and other parts of Southeast Asia wear it. In Indonesia the sarong is an item of everyday dress as well as an essential component of formalized ethnic dress. It is made in a variety of fabrics, including woven plaids, batik, warp ikats, songkets, or silk plaid and/or silk weft ikats. Hollywood's appropriation of the sarong has imbued it with exotic and erotic overtones and reinterpreted it as a wrapper rather than a tube. As a result, in the Western hemisphere the sarong has come to be defined in popular usage as a cloth wrap-per, not as a tube.

The Southeast Asian sarong is typically made of mill-woven cloth and is about 100 centimeters high and up to 220 centimeters in circumference. The wearer steps into a sarong, secures it at the hip (or under the arms, a variant for women) either by lapping both ends to meet in the center or by pulling the sarong taut at one side of the body and lapping the remaining fabric to the front, and then rolling the top down and tucking it in or tying the ends in a knot. In this way, hip to ankle are covered.

As a multipurpose garment, the sarong is worn in other ways as well. For women it might be secured under the arms to sleep in or to walk to the river for a bath. Male laborers in T-shirts and shorts hike it at their hips or wear it over their shoulder like a sash when working, only to wear it about their legs on the return home. Enveloped about a person, the sarong serves as a blanket against cool nights.

Origin of the Sarong

The sarong was the dress of the seafaring peoples of the Malay Peninsula near Sumatra and Java; according to Gittinger, it was subsequently introduced on the island of Madura and along the north coast of Java. In the late nineteenth century, an observer recorded its absence in the Java interior. Early sea traders in these waters were Moslems from India, and Islam spread from the coastal areas, so it is thought that these early sarongs may have been woven plaids, which were associated with Moslem men.

What makes the cloth produced for sarongs unique is the decorative panel (*kepala*, head) that contrasts with the rest of the fabric (*badan*, body), seen at the front when lapped over and secured. In a plaid, this panel may vary in color and/or weave.

One of the earliest panel configurations in batik sarongs of the north coast of Java and Madura is two rows of triangles (*tumpal*) whose points face each other. Traders brought chintzes from the Coromandel Coast of eastern India whose ends were rows of triangles. When sewn together, this created what is now the *kepala*, and eventually the two bands of triangles were positioned as a set at the end of the pre-sewn batik sarong. The *tumpal* motif is found on gold thread *songkets* of Sumatra and triangle end borders are seen in ikats, perhaps an influence from Indian chintzes.

In the clothing traditions of Java and adjacent western Indonesian islands, the sarong is an alternative to the *kain* (cloth wrapper). North coast batik sarongs are noted for their floral bouquet *kepala* and exuberant colors. At the turn of the twentieth century, Eurasian batik makers experimented with new chemical dyes and motifs, and the thigh-length jacket blouse (*kebaya*) worn with the sarong was shortened to hip length to better show off the *kepala* panel. The sarong is not as long as the *kain panjang* (long, cloth wrapper) batiks of court traditions of Yogyakarta and Surakarta in central Java. The *kain panjang* batiks are of an overall pattern, without a *kepala* panel; they are usually made with subdued colors such as browns, indigos, creams, and whites. When wrapped about the lower body, the end might be fan-folded in tight pleats, or with a loose drape.

The sarong varies in size and material. In all of Indonesia's twenty-six provinces, there are representative forms of ethnic dress in which sarongs, worn with a sleeved upper garment, figure prominently. In southern Sulawesi the Buginese silk sarong is extra wide. In Maluku sarongs are layered, the first one is long, and the second one is folded and worn at the hips, often revealing a *tumpal* motif. In Rote, the handwoven warp ikat sarong is narrow and tall; it is about twenty-five inches in circumference and would almost conceal the wearer's head. Here, the sarong is secured at the breasts and the excess folded over, and secured again at the waist with a belt. Another ikat (not a sarong) would be draped over the woman's shoulders. Generally speaking, the overall silhouette was tubular.

International Appropriation of Sarong

The sarong as appropriated by Hollywood bears little resemblance to the original. Hedy Lamarr in *White Cargo* (1942) and Dorothy Lamour in *Road to Bali* (1952) both wear wrappers (more like pareos), tied at the side in a way that emphasizes, rather than concealing, the curve of the hips. We know that what the actresses are wearing is a "sarong," because in *Road to Bali* Bob Hope specifically refers to Lamour's wrapper by that term. The draped, lapped frontal portion creates a diagonal line revealing the actress's entire leg. Both protagonists wear form-fitting tops baring midriff and shoulder, bangles, heavy necklaces and earrings. Lamarr and Lamour are seated in languorous poses to show off even more skin. The sarong here is a presentation of exotic femininity that is meant to titillate the western film audience. While *White Cargo* is set in Africa and *Road to Bali* is set in Indonesia on an unnamed island near Bali, the specifics of place and culture are immaterial. Tondelayo (Lamarr) and the Princess (Lamour) are not "natives," but rather a nebulous mixture of the Western and the "other." They conform to western ideals of beauty and allure, while the "ethnic" dress they wear is a fabrication of Hollywood costume designers, unrelated to anything attested in the anthropological record. What is depicted is the "East" as orientalized by the West.

According to Jones and Leshkowich, "Oriental" elements of clothing and decorative arts became part of the Western retail lifestyles markets in the 1990s at a time when Asian economic prowess was on the rise. The fashionable sarong as interpreted by Western fashion designers followed Hollywood's imagined version of the sarong as a knee-or thigh-length wrapper, tied at the side. Indonesian fashion designers, participating in self-orientalizing, also offered these Western-interpreted sarongs to cosmopolitan Indonesian women. Clearly, for these designers the sarong now referred to two kinds of dress, one local and one global, where the global one was an orientalizing of the local.

See also Asia, Southeastern Islands and the Pacific: History of Dress; Ikat; Kain-kebaya.

Bibliography

Achjadi, Judi. *Pakaian Daerah Wanita Indonesia [Indonesian Women's Costumes]*. Jakarta, Indonesia: Djambatan, 1976.

Djumena, Nian S. *Batik dan Mitra [Batik and its Kind]*. Jakarta, Indonesia: Djambatan, 1990.

Elliot, Inger McCabe. *Batik: Fabled Cloth of Java*. New York: Clarkson N. Potter, Inc., 1984.

Gittinger, Mattiebelle. *Splendid Symbols: Textiles and Tradition in Indonesia*. Washington, D.C.: The Textile Museum, 1979.

Jones, Carla, and Ann Marie Leshkowich. "Introduction: Globalization of Asian Dress." In *Re-Orienting Fashion: The Globalization of Asian Dress*. Edited by Sandra Niessen, Ann Marie Leshkowich, and Carla Jones. Oxford: Berg Press, 2003.

Taylor, Jean G. "Costume and Gender in Colonial Java." In *Outward Appearances: Dressing State and Society in Indonesia*, edited by Henk Schulte Nordholt. Leiden: KITLV Press, 1997.

Heidi Boehlke

SAVILE ROW

Savile Row is a typical central London street of fairly modest eighteenth-and nineteenth-century brick town houses mixed with late twentieth-century developments. It stretches from Vigo Street in the south to Conduit Street in the north, running parallel with Regent and New Bond Streets. Sitting at the heart of the city's West End luxury shopping district, the Row is particularly famous as the center of the British bespoke tailoring trade.

The Row traces its beginnings back to the late seventeenth century when Richard Boyle, the first Earl of Burlington, acquired a mansion on nearby Piccadilly (now Burlington House, home of the Royal Academy). Burlington protected the privacy of his estate by buying up the surrounding land, which was eventually developed by his descendant, the enlightened third Earl from the 1730s on. Savile Row was one of the resulting streets of genteel residences, which were generally rented by members of the nobility and affluent professionals who formed part of the new fashionable trend for living "in town" during the social season. The aristocratic atmosphere of the Row was an important component of its rise as a center of style. Its residents required expensive and well-made goods that befitted their rank, and thus attracted the attention of manufacturers and traders in luxury commodities. The high proportion of top-rank military and medical men living in the district also ensured that the provision of smart uniforms and civilian suits were prominent in this commercial expansion.

By the early nineteenth century, the Row had become synonymous with the London-based dandy craze, popularized by personalities such as Beau Brummel, and several ambitious tailors were establishing their reputations in nearby streets. Henry Creed and Meyer & Mortimer for example, were based in Conduit Street, with a rapidly expanding customer-base, thanks to the demand for uniforms initiated by the Napoleonic Wars. The first major incursion of tailoring into Savile Row itself was made by Henry Poole in the late 1840s. A few smaller tailors had opened workshops there in the 1820s, but Poole's were of a different order. They enjoyed the custom of high-profile clients, including royalty, statesmen, sporting stars, and literary and theatrical celebrities, and put unprecedented effort into the design of their showrooms and marketing ventures. Arguably it was Poole who established the international fame of the Row as a "Mecca" for men's fashion (though like most tailors he also fitted women with riding outfits and "tailor-mades").

Through the remainder of the Victorian age and into the twentieth-century, Savile Row shifted its character from that of a residential enclave to a thriving street of tailoring concerns. Distancing themselves from the sweated trades that were providing the mass-manufactured suits of the modern office worker, the tailors of the Row prided themselves on their mastery of traditional handcrafts, the quality of their textiles, and their attention to the individualized needs of their customers. Savile Row firms also came to be associated with a particularly English "look": restrained, narrow shouldered with a long waist; though each company pioneered a subtly differentiated version of the Savile Row staple. Huntsman, for example, was known for their heavy tweed sporting jackets while Gieves provided a sleek naval cut. By the mid-twentieth century, tailors such as Davies, Kilgour, and Anderson & Sheppard pioneered a more glamorous version of Savile Row style through their fitting-out of fashion leaders such as the Duke of Windsor and Hollywood stars including Cary Grant and Fred Astaire. This greater attention to "fashion" was also marked by the presence of couturier Hardy Amies in the street from 1945. The Row had adapted following the decline of the British Empire from its role as Imperial outfitter to a new incarnation as the epitome of urbane sophistication.

The final decades of the twentieth century saw further flowerings of talent on Savile Row. Echoing the explosion of boutique culture on Carnaby Street and the King's Road in the 1960s, Tommy Nutter and Rupert Lycett Green of Blades introduced the Row to styles that were well suited to the culture of Swinging London, a phenomenon brought to the heart of the Row by the arrival of the Beatles's management company, Apple, at number 3 in 1968. And in the 1990s and 2000s, the association of the Row with "cool" was reinforced once more by the innovations of a new generation of tailor/retailers, including Ozwald Boateng, Richard James, and Spencer Hart who attracted a younger, less hidebound clientele to their bright and airy emporia. Thus, it can be seen that Savile Row has been highly adaptable to the vagaries of styles in clothing and social trends, maintaining its reputation for traditional manufacturing methods while subtly embracing the challenges of novelty. It is still the premier street in the world for male fashion aficionados.

See also Boutique; Dandyism; London Fashion; Tailoring.

Bibliography

Breward, Christopher. *The Hidden Consumer: Masculinities, Fashion and City Life 1860–1914*. Manchester, U.K.: Manchester University Press, 1999.

——. *Fashioning London: Clothing and the Modern Metropolis*. New York: Berg Publishers, 2004.

Chenoune, Farid. *A History of Men's Fashion*. Paris: Flammarion, 1992.

Walker, Richard. *The Savile Row: An Illustrated History*. New York: Rizzoli, 1989.

Christopher Breward

SCHIAPARELLI, ELSA

The Italian-born Elsa Schiaparelli (1890–1973) was in many ways an outsider, yet one who successfully made her way to the heart of French haute couture in the interwar years, operating her business between 1927 and 1954. Born in Rome in 1890, the daughter of an orientalist scholar, she first left Italy in 1913. She traveled via Paris to London, where she married a theosophist named

Wilhelm Went de Kerlor in 1914. During World War I, she and her husband moved in artistic and cosmopolitan circles between Europe and the United States. When Schiaparelli separated from her husband in the early 1920s, she returned to Paris with her young daughter. There she came to know Paul Poiret, who often loaned the impoverished young woman dresses to wear.

Early Career

With Poiret's encouragement, Schiaparelli began to design clothes and sell her designs on a freelance basis to small fashion houses. She briefly became the designer of a small house, Maison Lambal, in 1925 before setting up an atelier in her own name in 1927. Schiaparelli's first collection featured hand-knitted trompe l'oeil sweaters, including an extremely successful black-and-white "bow-knot" sweater that was illustrated in *Vogue* and immediately sold in the United States. Her subsequent collections extended beyond sweaters to include dresses and suits, swimsuits and beach pyjamas, ski costumes and sports jackets. In the early 1930s her "Mad Cap," a simple knitted hat with distinctive pointed ends that could be pulled into any shape, was a runaway success in the United States, where, like the "bow-know" sweater, it was widely copied by mass-market manufacturers. In 1928 she launched her first perfume, S.

In the late 1920s and early 1930s Schiaparelli was primarily a designer of sportswear whose geometric patterns and sleek lines were in keeping with the mood of the moment. Yet these early collections contained many hallmarks of her styles of the later 1930s: the innovative use of fabrics, often synthetic; striking color contrasts; such unusual fastenings as zippers; and such eccentric or amusing costume jewelry as a white porcelain "Aspirin" necklace designed by the writer Elsa Triolet.

Schiaparelli's designs proved popular with Parisians and New Yorkers alike. Despite the 1929 economic crash, which significantly depleted the fortunes of French haute couture, Schiaparelli was still able to work successfully with American manufacturers in the early 1930s, and to sell her models to exclusive importers like William H. Davidow and such stores as Saks Fifth Avenue in New York. Later she was to remark that the more outrageous her designs became, the better they sold to a conservative clientele. Despite Schiaparelli's reputation as an artistic designer, she was always commercially successful.

Throughout the 1930s the fashionable silhouette changed; from the early 1930s Schiaparelli developed the boxy padded shoulders that were to characterize her mature style. Notable designs from 1934 included a "tree-bark" dress—actually crinkled rayon—and a "glass" evening cape made from a new synthetic material called Rhodophane. Schiaparelli benefited from significant developments in textiles in the 1930s, but she was never purely technologically driven. Rather, her work was galvanized by the themes of masquerade, artifice, and play—themes that related closely to the changing status of women in the interwar years, as well as to the avant-garde discourse of the surrealist artists and their circles, some of whom she worked with in the 1930s.

The Later 1930s

Schiaparelli moved her boutique to the Place Vendôme in 1935, commissioning Jean-Michel Franck to decorate her new premises. Their ever-changing décor incorporated, at various times, a stuffed bear that the artist Salvador Dalí had dyed shocking pink and fitted with drawers in its stomach, a life-size dummy of Mae West, and a gilded bamboo birdcage for the perfume boutique. In 1935 Schiaparelli inaugurated themed collections, starting with Stop, Look and Listen for summer 1935. "Schiaparelli collection enough to cause crisis in vocabulary," read a contemporary review of Stop, Look and Listen (Schiaparelli, p. 87). Following the Music Collection of 1937, Schiaparelli surpassed herself in 1938 and showed four collections in a single year: the Circus Collection for summer 1938, the Pagan Collection for autumn 1938, the Zodiac or Lucky Stars Collection for winter 1938–1939, and the Commedia dell'Arte Collection or A Modern Comedy for spring 1939. Her presentations were more like shows or plays than the conventional mannequin parade. Incorporating stunts, tricks, jokes, music, and light effects, they were dramatic and lively, and entry to them was as much sought after as tickets to a new play.

In 1937 Schiaparelli launched the color of vivid pink that she named "shocking," alongside her perfume Shocking!, packaged in a bottle designed by the artist Leonor Fini and based on the shape of Mae West's torso. The same year saw the designer's Shoe Hat ensemble, a black suit with pockets embroidered with lips and an inverted high-heeled shoe for a hat. The hat came in two versions, one that was all black, and the other, black with a shocking pink heel. The 1938 Circus collection featured a black evening dress with a padded skeleton stitched on it, boleros heavily embroidered with circus themes, and an inkwell-shaped hat whose feather resembled a quill pen. The 1938 Zodiac collection featured more highly encrusted embroidery such as the mirror suit, in which inverted baroque mirrors were embroidered on the front panels of the jacket and incorporated pieces of real mirrored glass. Schiaparelli encouraged the embroidery firm Maison Lesage to revive techniques from both medieval ecclesiastical vestments and eighteenth-century military uniforms. The result was a series of highly wrought evening jackets and accessories in which the decoration of the garment became a carapace or form of female armor.

While Schiaparelli was clearly established commercially as a fashion designer, she also retained many links, both personal and professional, with surrealist artists. In New York during World War I she knew Francis Picabia and his then wife Gabrielle, who introduced her to the artistic photographer Man Ray and the painter/sculptor Marcel Duchamp. Schiaparelli was photographed by Man Ray in the early 1920s and then again in 1930. Man Ray regularly took photographs for fashion magazines, including *Vogue* and *Harper's Bazaar*; some of these photographs also appeared in the surrealist magazine *Minotaure*, which was published between 1933 and 1939. An essay of 1933 by the surrealist writer Tristan Tzara was illustrated by Man Ray's photographs of Schiaparelli's hats. She in turn employed many surrealist artists to design accessories for her. The writer Elsa Triolet made jewelry for Schiapiarelli and other couturiers, with her husband Louis Aragon acting as the salesman. Alberto Giacometti made brooches for Schiaparelli, while Meret Oppenheim produced furlined metal bracelets. Christian Bérard illustrated Schiaparelli's designs and many of the program covers for her openings or fashion shows. In 1937 the designer used drawings done for her by the artist Jean Cocteau as trompe l'oeil embroidery on two evening garments, a blue silk coat and a grey linen jacket.

Schiaparelli's collaboration with Salvador Dalí, however, which began in 1936, produced a series of the most striking designs: chest of drawer suits (with horizontal pockets that looked like drawers and buttons that resembled drawer handles) from 1936, an evening dress with lobster print and a shoe hat and suit from 1937, and an evening dress with a tear design from 1938.

Apart from these accredited collaborations Schiaparelli produced many surrealist designs of her own from the start of her career, some clearly in homage to her contemporaries, others apparently her own inspiration: black suede gloves appliquéd with red snakeskin fingernails inspired by Man Ray; a telephone-shaped handbag inspired by Dalí and a brain-shaped hat made of corrugated pink velvet; buttons in the shape of peanuts, padlocks, and paper clips; multicolored wigs coordinated with gowns; and the first fabric designed to mimic newsprint, printed with Schiaparelli's own reviews in several languages. Meanwhile, Schiaparelli maintained her contacts with fashion-related industries in both the United States and Britain, collaborating with textile and accessory designers on specific ranges as well as selling model gowns through exclusive importers. She also worked in both theater and the cinema as a costume designer, most notably dressing Mae West for the film *Every Day's a Holiday* (1937).

Throughout the 1930s Schiaparelli continued to travel, many times to the United States, and once in 1935 to a trade fair in the Soviet Union. Although based in Paris, she had opened a branch of her salon in London in 1933. Schiaparelli's international clientele included Lady Mendl, Wallis Simpson, and various titled Englishwomen; she frequently designed costumes for such elaborate costume balls of the decade as the honorable Mrs. Reginald Fellowes's Oriental Ball in 1935 and Lady Mendl's Circus Ball of 1938. The chic and distinctive Daisy Fellowes was Schiaparelli's unofficial mannequin; the designer dressed her for free and she in turn attracted international publicity in newspapers and magazines as one of the few women who wore Schiaparelli's more outré designs. If Daisy Fellowes personified the Schiaparelli look, the American Bettina Bergery, née Jones, personified the designer's spirit. Equally elegant and rakish in her own person, Bergery was the editor of French *Vogue* between 1935 and 1940 as well as Schiaparelli's assistant, responsible in the late 1930s for the witty and iconoclastic window displays in Schiaparelli's salon on the Place Vendôme.

The 1940s and 1950s

Schiaparelli, who had taken French citizenship in 1931, set out on an American lecture tour after the Germans occupied Paris in 1940. She chose to return to the occupied city in January 1941, but within a short period was forced to leave again for New York, where she spent the remainder of the war. Schiaparelli's Paris house remained open throughout the war and produced collections, although they were not designed by Schiaparelli herself. Her early wartime designs, made before she departed for the United States, often used military themes but in a playful way, such as a one-piece "air-raid shelter" trouser suit. She also pioneered many innovative pocket designs in her Cash and Carry collection for spring 1940. She returned to Paris immediately after the end of the occupation in

1945 and resumed designing, picking up where she had left off in 1940, but focusing more on unusual cuttings and draping. Schiaparelli's designs from this period included a hat like a bird's nest with nesting birds; illusion bustle dresses; and inverted necklines that rose to cover the cleavage but dipped to reveal the breasts.

Throughout the late 1940s and early 1950s Schiaparelli continued to make merchandising and licensing deals with several American companies, but in terms of innovative design Cristóbal Balenciaga and Christian Dior took the lead in the 1950s. Dior's New Look of 1947 ushered in a new era in fashion. Schiaparelli's fortunes declined gradually after that; in 1954, the same year that Coco Chanel returned to Paris couture, Schiaparelli's Paris salon filed for bankruptcy. Thereafter the designer spent much of her time in Tunisia, where she had bought a house in 1950. Her autobiography, *Shocking Life*, was published in 1954. Schiaparelli died in Paris in 1973 at the age of 83, survived by her daughter Gogo and her granddaughters, the actresses Marisa Berenson and Berinthia ("Berry") Berenson Perkins.

Shiaparelli's fashion legacy was a vast body of endlessly inventive and original designs. She made elaborate visual jokes in garments that layered images deceptively on the body, to explore the themes of illusion, artifice, and masquerade. One of her couture clients, Nadia Georges Port, recalled: "For us 'Schiap' was much more than a natter of mere dresses: through clothes she expressed a defiance of aesthetic conventions in a period when couture was in danger of losing itself in anemic subtitles" (Musée de la mode, p. 125). Less well known, however, is the fact that, despite her apparently avante garde designs, she always maintained successful business relationships with American middle market manufacturers. In this respect she is a paradigm of the modern designer, marrying a fertile imagination and dramatic showman-ship to a pragmatic and commercial base.

See also Art and Fashion; Cardin, Pierre; Fashion Designer; Givenchy, Hubert de; Paris Fashion; Poiret, Paul; Vogue; Windsor, Duke and Duchess of.

Bibliography

Ballard, Bettina. *In My Fashion*. New York: David McKay and Co., Inc., 1960.

Blum, Dilys E. *Shocking! The Art and Fashion of Elsa Schiaparelli*. Philadelphia, New Haven, Conn., and London: Philadelphia Museum of Art in association with Yale University Press, 2003.

Evans, Caroline. "Masks, Mirrors and Mannequins: Elsa Schiaparelli and the Decentered Subject." *Fashion Theory* 3 (1999): 3–32.

Musée de la mode et du costume, Palais Galliera. *Hommage à Elsa Schiaparelli: exposition organisée au Pavillon des arts... Paris, 21 juin–30 août 1984*. Paris: Ville de Paris, Musée de la mode et du costume, 1984.

Schiaparelli, Elsa. *Shocking Life*. New York: E. P. Dutton and Co., 1954.

White, Palmer. *Elsa Schiaparelli: Empress of Paris Fashion*. London: Aurum Press, 1986.

——. *Haute Couture Embroidery: The Art of Lesage*. Paris: Vendôme Press, 1988; and Berkeley, Calif.: Lacis Publications, 1994.

Caroline Evans

SEAMSTRESSES

Seamstresses formed the main labor force, outside tailoring, which fueled the expansion of clothing production and related trades from the seventeenth century onward. This expansion was not dependent initially on technological developments or the introduction of a factory system, but on the pool of women workers. Their expendability and cheapness to their employers was effectively guaranteed by the sheer number of available women able and willing to use a needle, their general lack of alternative employment, and by the fact they then worked outside the control of guilds and latterly have been under-unionized. These seamstresses sewed goods for the increasing market for ready-made basic clothes such as shirts, breeches, waistcoats, shifts, and petticoats for working people, or slops as they were known (after the practice of sailors who stored their working clothes in slop chests). Their history is largely anonymous. However, social and economic historians with an interest in gender are now extending the knowledge of seamstresses' central role in the historical growth of clothing production and consumption.

At the cheaper end of the trade, the work of seamstresses did not involve complex cutting, fitting, or designing, though there were no hard and fast rules. "Seamstress" has always been a flexible term, with the work involved dependent on local conditions and the agency of individuals. Some elaboration and finishing was involved, such as tucking or buttonholes. While of sewing and mending tasks, in exchange for a day rate of pay and meals. This practice lingered until World War II in some areas of Britain.

The widespread use of the sewing machine from the 1860s increased the pace of production of clothing because it could stitch up to thirty times faster than a hand sewer, but it did not immediately result in centralized factories becoming the dominant means of production. Clothing production remained characterized by many small-scale businesses, often subcontracting work, and by the subdivision of the various tasks involved in the making of a garment, using many outworkers and home work-ers. This drove down prices and wages and produced the sweatshop system in which many seamstresses worked very long hours for low wages. Despite well-meant attempts to reform the trade, pay and conditions remained bad throughout the nineteenth century and well into the twentieth. It was said that a practiced observer could identify a seamstress in the street because of her stooped carriage. Seamstresses in outworking were vulnerable to employers who could withhold or delay payment if work was deemed substandard. It was common practice for seamstresses in this kind of work to have to pay for their own thread, needles, and candles, in addition to their heating and costs of collecting and returning the work. "My usual time of work is from five in the morning till nine at night—winter and summer. . . . But when there is a press of business, I work earlier and later. . . . I clears about 2s 6d a week. . . . I know it's so little I can't get a rag to my back" (London shirt maker talking to Henry Mayhew in 1849, cited in Yeo, p. 145). Despite enormous disadvantages, it was seamstresses who staged the first all-female strike in America, in New York in 1825. Apprenticeship provided one means, however, unreliable and open to abuse, for women to learn the better end of the trade. Some women found that the clothing trade presented opportunities for them to trade effectively as seamstresses on their own account or to work as middle women, putting out work. Health and safety legislation, greater unionization, and factory production have combined to improve the lot of women working in the late twentieth and early twenty-first centuries in the clothing trades; nevertheless, globally, it remains a fragmented industry with widespread homework and low wages.

work done in this style continued, seamstresses were generally distinguished from dressmakers, milliners, mantua-makers, stay-makers, embroiderers, and tailoresses by their lower levels of craft and skill, but at the top-end of the market fine sewing was valued. Their existence was precarious and exacerbated by layoffs due to seasonal demand and unpredictable changes of fashion. In the Victorian period, widespread demand for mourning clothes, short notice given for elaborate evening dresses, and fickle customers were commonly cited as causes of distress through overwork.

There were large numbers of seamstresses in a wide range of situations. They frequently worked as outworkers, on per-piece pay, in small workshops or in their homes. Having learned their trade in waged work, many seamstresses continued to use their skills after marriage by taking in work, often making simple garments or restyling old ones in their own poor communities where they played an important role in the provision of cheap clothing outside the regular retail trade. Some seamstresses were employed in a temporary but regular visiting capacity in wealthier households where they supplemented existing domestic staff and worked by arrangement through an accumulation

Popular Debates and Imagery

Prints and paintings, often sympathetic if moralistic, frequently showed individual women bent over their sewing, in shabby interiors, sewing either to support themselves or their families. Middle-class women, fallen on hard times, were also depicted eking out a living in this way, a particular anxiety in Victorian Britain. Allegations of immorality, including prostitution, were frequently made, based on perceptions of the effects of poverty or, in better-class workrooms, the supposed temptations caused by familiarity of young seamstresses with fashion and luxury beyond their means. In Britain in 1843, Thomas Hood's poem *The Song of the Shirt* dramatized their plight and helped focus attention on potential reforms to wages and conditions, mostly without long-term effect. In 1853 Elizabeth Gaskell's novel *Ruth* expanded on the theme of exploitation of seamstresses and the suffering caused by extravagant demands of selfish or ignorant customers; the subject was treated in the United States in Charles Burdett's 1850 *The Elliott Family or the Trial of New York Seamstresses.*

See also Sewing Machine; Sweatshops; Textile Workers.

Bibliography

Coffin, Judith. *The Politics of Women's Work: The Paris Garment Trades 1750–1915.* Princeton, N.J.: Princeton University Press, 1996.

Flint, Joy. *Thomas Hood: Selected Poems.* Manchester, U.K.: Carcanet, 1992.

Gamber, Wendy. *The Female Economy: The Millinery and Dressmaking Trades, 1860–1930.* Urbana: University of Illinois Press, 1997.

Green, Nancy. *Ready-to-Wear and Ready-to-Work: A Century of Industry and Immigrants in Paris and New York.* Durham, N.C.: Duke University Press, 1997.

Jenson, Joan M., and Davidson, Sue, eds. *A Needle, a Bobbin, a Strike: Women Needleworkers in America.* Philadelphia: Temple University Press, 1984.

Lemire, Beverly. *Dress, Culture and Commerce: The English Clothing Trade before the Factory, 1660–1800.* New York: St. Martin's Press, 1997.

Schmiechen, James A. *Sweated Industries and Sweated Labour: The London Clothing Trades 1860–1914.* Urbana: University of Illinois Press, 1984.

Stansell, Christine. *City of Women: Sex and Class in New York 1789–1860.* Urbana: University of Illinois Press, 1987.

Stewart, Margaret, and Hunter, Leslie. *The Needle Is Threaded: The History of an Industry.* London: Heinemann/Newman Neame, 1964.

Yeo, Eileen, and E. P. Thompson. *The Unknown Mayhew.* New York: Pantheon Books, 1971.

Walkley, Christina. *The Ghost in the Looking Glass: The Victorian Seamstress.* London: Peter Owen, 1981.

Barbara Burman

SEVENTH AVENUE

When a famed street is both conceptual and geographic, as Seventh Avenue in New York City is, commenting on it becomes many-pronged. To David Wolfe, the creative director of the Doneger Group, a major buying office, Seventh Avenue is a state of the mind, the creative epicenter of American fashion. He believes that where it once was a vital apparel and distribution center, it now functions as a showcase for designers and manufacturers. To Wolfe, "It is more than a street or a neighborhood, it is the geographic symbol of the power of American style."

In the 1930s, the Garment Center, as this area was called—between 6th and 9th Avenues from 30th to 42nd Streets—was the city's largest industry, and the fourth largest in the country. Three-quarters of ready-made coats and dresses, and four out of five fur coats worn by American women, were made here.

Surprisingly, over the years, not that many books have been written about Seventh Avenue, the reality, but one author (and manufacturer) who tackled it was Murray Sices, who in 1953, could still write in his tome, not surprisingly, called *Seventh Avenue*, "Seventh Avenue in the city of New York, between 35th and 40th Street, is not merely a geographic location. It's a legend. It's the birthplace of miracles. It's the fast-beating heart of an industry whose bloodstreams course through America.... Here with almost 4,000 firms crowded into a few square blocks, you have a concentration of apparel manufacturers such as the world has never seen elsewhere."

That was then, this is now, and there have been many changes, most of them disastrous for Seventh Avenue and its environs. In 2000 alone, citywide garment-making jobs fell to 60,700 down from 70,100 in 1998. There were 3,260 apparel-making shops in 2000 as opposed to 3,591 in 1999, according to *Crain's New York Business Magazine.* The publication reported in 2001, "Voluntarily or not, garment workers in New York are mobbing the exits." Industry watchers were shocked at what was happening, especially those who thought the employment drop had bottomed out in the late 1990s. Historically, however, there has been a loss of manufacturing jobs going back more than thirty years. Gone are many wholesalers and textile companies as well as companies that supplied everything. Garment manufacturing has dropped along with everything else, from buttons to zippers and other necessities for a complete garment; even jobbers have disappeared and positions in showrooms also have evaporated.

Also there is the major question of rents that have reportedly increased in double or triple digits. Cheap imports, too, have become major culprits in the changing face of Seventh Avenue.

On the slightly brighter side, even though manufacturing of apparel is down from the 300,000 workers at its peak in the 1950s, clothing accounts for about one-fourth of the manufacturing jobs in the city, and it's still a most important entry into the business world for immigrants from everywhere. Seventh Avenue and its surrounding businesses probably will endure, because designers, even in the age of the computer, will still need workers nearby to whip up small runs of high-end clothing.

However, that segment of the business is also no longer so significant. At a time when conglomerates have swallowed up many of the major department stores, and specialty stores and discounters swamp shopping malls, the ability to ship quickly is no longer so vital. Bud Konheim, the head of Nicole Miller Inc., one of Seventh Avenue's stalwarts, still refers to himself as a "quick turnaround guy," and retains his belief in "Made in the U.S.A." through thick and thin.

In the early 2000s, *Crain's* reported that the New York Industrial Retention Network would release a study showing 60 percent of apparel leases in the garment district will expire momentarily, putting the entire local industry in a negative position.

Even though everything is changing, there is still plenty of excitement just walking Seventh Avenue and the adjacent Broadway buildings like 1410 Broadway or 550 Seventh Avenue. Models still run to do a day's work at a manufacturer's showroom during New York Fashion Week. The Tower of Babel voices from different cultures still are part of street life and lore. There are still plenty of small cafés doing takeout, or one can sit and have bagels or more exotic fare served fast and furiously.

Plenty of New Yorkers, including the mayor and other politicians, want to keep Seventh Avenue and its environs as vital as they have ever been. In 1993 the Fashion Center Business Improvement Center was inaugurated, its mission to promote garment manufacturing, but ten years later BID's concept had changed. The idea is to perhaps create for the district (running

roughly from Fifth to Ninth Avenues and West 35th to 41st streets) a 24-hour seven-day-a-week place with diverse and residential units, including a fashion museum and more retail stores. BID's design center will add to the neighborhood's continuing unique personality, and allow it to remain, if not strictly a garment manufacturing area, a fashion district.

Gerald Scupp, the deputy director of the Fashion Center (which has its street of famous designers, called the Fashion Walk of Fame, similar to Grauman's Chinese Theatre in Hollywood which has its famous actors' hand-and footprints) notes many initiatives have failed, but he believes, and the report suggests, that abolishing special zoning that restricts non-manufacturing uses and keeps rents low for manufacturers could work. There will be those who will object, however.

Rent alone does not explain the declining job numbers, nor do cheap imports, for some manufacturers have defected to cheaper spaces in Brooklyn and Queens, but even this has not been entirely satisfactory. Another factor is the sub rosa conversion to office space with city officials looking the other way, rather than upholding the special district concept, according to Adam Friedman, the network's executive director. He notes the city stopped inspections in 1993.

Also taking a toll on legitimate design houses in New York City are manufacturers who violate the law by not paying overtime or taxes, so many of their workers do not show up on official job statistics. If all workers were truly accounted for, the number of city garment workers might double, according to Louis Vanegas, district director of the Wage and Hour Division of the U.S. Department of Labor. But even Vanegas agrees the uncounted jobs are declining and don't really account for the precipitous drop in manufacturing.

So, what will happen to Seventh Avenue and its environs if jobs decline at historic rates? According to the BID report in the early 2000s, only about 17,000 of the city's 50,000 apparel manufacturing positions will be around by 2010. However, as of early 2004, fashion-related businesses still make up the majority of the district—64 percent or 4,245—but more of these are showrooms or mixed uses. Other tenants range from printers, ad agencies, theaters, and an unknown number of illegal residential tenants who are tucked away in lofts and other spaces. Actually, the area is becoming more residential legally, and BID supports the idea. Many property owners would love to see zoning laws changed.

That the problems of Seventh Avenue remain is borne out by a *Woman's Wear Daily* article on June 10,

2003 headed "U.S. Makers Fading Away." The piece, by Scott Malone, notes, "The withering of the nation's production base has gotten to the point where even the makers of high-end apparel, who typically were able to digest the higher costs of domestic production because of their higher prices, have begun to break into camps on the question of whether making clothing in the U.S. will remain a viable strategy for the years to come."

The article maintains that the same economic pressures that pushed most mainstream apparel manufacturing out of the country are taking hold in the top-drawer designer market. "Eventually all that will be left in this country will be a small clique of sample makers."

But all is not lost for the Seventh Avenue of the early twenty-first century. The article makes clear there is still a shrinking group of high-end designers whose dresses carry three or even four-figure price tags who contend that domestic manufacturing in New York continues to make sense. These businessmen argue that being close to their factories allows a higher level of quality control and a faster rate of turnaround than is available overseas. Bud Konheim, "the quick turnaround guy" of Nicole Miller says, "The advantage of being domestic has nothing to do with cost." What keeps half of his company's manufacturing here are garment-district contractors. Konheim says, "You can get cheaper prices by going offshore, but then you've got a longer lead time; you have to make your decisions earlier, and you have to cut bigger quantities, so you have a lack of control. And, lack of control, in this marketplace, is very dangerous because some orders you take are not real orders. You have people canceling." He adds that domestic manufacturing is viable only if a brand's fashions are sufficiently distinctive so that retailers can't get a similar product elsewhere.

Another major manufacturer, who is also a highly prized designer, Oscar de la Renta, whose firm has long been on Seventh Avenue, still makes the majority of his line in the United States. For him also, quality concerns are a key reason for staying here. The firm's mixture of local and foreign sourcing has not changed since the early 1990s.

Famed handbag and accessories firm Judith Leiber continues to manufacture on West 33rd Street because so many of its workers have been with the company for a long time and their talents are specialized.

However, one of the problems of the apparel industry decline is that so many of the businesses that supported companies like trim suppliers or firms that stocked replacement parts died because of lack of customers. Konheim said his company has to contract many operations overseas including beading, embroidering, and hand knitting, because it no longer can find domestic companies doing that work. Ironically, at a time when going global has caused so many problems for unique Seventh Avenue and its environs, the cachet of a "Made in the U.S.A." label remains high in Asian markets as well as in the United States and throughout the world, so there is hope.

Nowhere where apparel and its appurtenances are created is there the excitement that was and is Seventh Avenue with its polyglot charisma, its smells and street noises, its buying and selling, its rushing and stopping, its garment racks flying down the street in competent hands. Clothing is manufactured around the world, but no one has a Seventh Avenue except New York, New York.

See also Fashion Designer; Garments, International Trade in; Leiber, Judith; Ready-to-Wear.

Bibliography

Curan, Catherine. "More Fashionable Garment Area Plan." *Crain's New York Business* (10 March 2003).

Fredrickson, Tom. "Garment Area Jobs Stripped." *Crain's New York Business* (26 March 2001).

Malone, Scott. "U.S. Makers Fading Away." *Women's Wear Daily* (10 June 2003): 10.

Sices, Murray. *Seventh Avenue.* New York: Fairchild Publications, 1953. Outdated, but provides interesting earlier background information on Seventh Avenue.

Margot Siegel

SHOEMAKING

Shoemaking continues to be the work of a family member in many cultures of the early 2000s. Inuit and other circumpolar peoples continue the tradition of footwear production by the mother of the family—the craft learned from her mother and passed on to her daughters, as it has always been.

The earliest professional shoemakers can only be supposed from Egyptian friezes where laborers are depicted making sandals, using tools not dissimilar to tools still used by hand shoemakers. However, leatherworkers also used the same tools as the shoemaker, and so it is impossible to define the period in which shoemaking as a singular profession developed.

During the Roman Empire shoemaking progressed from artisans working alone in small settlements to congregating in streets near the town's center or marketplace, where guilds became established. Guilds protected and regulated the shoemakers, their suppliers, and their clients from unfair business practices and pricing, and ensured quality products. Apollo was chosen patron deity of Roman shoemakers, with images and statues of him gracing the entrance to streets reserved for members of that profession.

Similarly, images of the Christian patron saints of shoemakers adorned the churches and guildhalls of medieval Europe. During the third century, noble Roman brothers Crispin and Crispinian were converted to Christianity and went to Gaul to preach the gospel, working as shoemakers at night. They were eventually tortured for their faith and put to death. Although the legend is unreliable and Saints Crispin and Crispinian have lost their status of sainthood, they have remained the patron saints of shoemakers since the fifteenth century, and their feast day, October 25, is still celebrated as a holiday for the shoe industry in France.

There is evidence that by the fourteenth century, shoemakers were already making footwear for speculative sale, essentially "ready to wear." This was aided by the adoption of standardized measurement. In England in 1324, measurements for distance were standardized under King Edward II. Consistent in size, three barleycorns laid end-to-end equaled one inch and the foot-long "ruler" became the foot measurement of King Edward,

the ruler of England. The other standard of measurement was the hand, used since biblical times, and used to this day for measuring the height of horses. A hand equals 4⅓ inches or 13 barleycorns. When a standardized measurement for shoe sizing began in the late seventeenth century, children's sizes were deemed to be less than the measurement of a hand and adult sizes were those over a hand. Adult sizes began with the deduction of 4⅓ inches, so an adult woman's size 4 shoe means it is made for a foot 8⅓ inches long. Under Louis XIV the Paris Point system was standardized as ⅔ centimeter, and became the standard for most of Europe, but Germany continued to follow the English measuring system.

By 1400 most large European cities had shoemakers' guilds. This did not include cobblers, who were shoe repairers and not part of the shoemakers' guild. Shoemakers are capable of doing repairs but this is considered inferior work. In England shoemakers were more prop-erly known as *cordwainers*, and in France as *cordonniers*, after the fine Cordwain leather tanned in Cordoba, Spain, and imported in great quantities. Their very name suggested the quality of their goods.

Shoemaking 1600 to 1850

In the late sixteenth century, welted shoe construction became standard whereby the upper was sewn to a welt with a second row of stitches made through the welt into the outer sole. From this development until the introduction of machinery in the mid-nineteenth century there is very little change in the tools or methods used for shoemaking. And for hand shoemakers, changes in this tradition have been minimal. The tools to achieve this construction consisted of a knife, last, dogs, hammer, awl, and shoulder stick.

The first and most important step in making a shoe is to measure the foot accurately, translating these measurements to a corresponding wooden last. The word *last* comes from the old English word for foot and is the wooden form used as a mold for making the shoe. The last is made to the same shape and size as the client's foot, or a standard last is adjusted adding built-up layers of leather to attain the same measurements. The last is frequently made up of at least two pieces, so that it can be more easily removed from the finished shoe.

After measuring the foot and translating those calculations onto a pattern, cutting out, or *clicking*, the leather is the first step in constructing a pair of shoes. The round, or moon knife is an early tool that can be seen as far back as ancient Egypt. Used by most workers

Jimmy Choo. Fashion clothing and footwear designer Jimmy Choo in his London workshop, 1997. © TIM GRAHAM/CORBIS. REPRODUCED BY PERMISSION.

in leather until the nineteenth century, the skill to use it to its full advantage was acquired during apprenticeship. Straight knives were also used but it was only with the mass entry of workers into the shoe factories of the nineteenth century that straight knives and scissors were preferred by the less-skilled labor force, resulting in the extinction of the moon knife.

Lasting pincers or *dogs* are used for pulling the top of the shoe, or upper, tight around the last so that it may be secured with tacks to the underside. Most dogs have serrated teeth that help to pull the upper taut and often have a hammer's peen on the other side to set the tacks so that the welted shoe can then be sewn. A hammer is rarely used to set the tacks into the last but rather is used for *peening* the leather. Once soaked, leather is hammered to flatten the fibrous tissues creating a surface that is more resilient to wear and dampness.

Shoes are traditionally not sewn with a needle, but rather holes are created using awls through which a waxed linen thread is inserted with a pig's bristle. The shapes of awl blades vary according to their intended use. A stitching awl has a straight blade and is used for making holes through multiple layers of leather. The closing awl has a curved blade and is used for joining the sole to the upper.

The shoulder stick, made of wood, burnished the welt and edge of the sole after the shoe was sewn, trimmed, and waxed. The shoulder stick was displaced in the nineteenth century with the use of heated irons, which did the same job but more quickly.

Heels began to be added to footwear beginning in the 1590s. Lasts are required to obtain the correct slope of the sole to accommodate the lift of the heel and as it is too expensive to have a huge inventory of lasts representing the various heel heights as well as for each foot, so most footwear would now be made without left or right definition. This practice of making shoes with straight soles would remain for the next two hundred years, gradually falling from favor throughout the nineteenth century and only finally disappearing in the 1880s. Many surviving examples of lightweight leather and textile footwear from this period show evidence of wear on the uppers where the widths of feet have splayed the upper onto the ground where the sole was insufficiently narrow. However, sturdy leather footwear, like riding boots, continued to be made to order with left and right foot definition for fit and comfort.

With standardized shoe measurements well established and the ease of production for shoemakers of straight soles, it became profitable for shoemakers to pre-make quantities of footwear. No doubt when the shoemaker was not employed by client's orders, he created shoes for speculative sale. Extant shoes dating as early as the 1740s and increasingly toward the end of the eighteenth century display sizes written on linings, suggesting pre-made footwear, as well as shoemaker's names printed on paper labels, usually with their address, suggesting an attempt by shoemakers to encourage repeat business. Footwear had become the first ready-to-wear clothing article sold through shoemaker shops, and also haberdashers and "cheap shoe" warehouses, another name for off-the-rack retailers. Standardized measurements ensured a good fit for length, but it would not be until the 1880s that American shoe manufacturers introduced width sizing.

Shortages of military footwear, and in fact all leather footwear, were a problem in the late eighteenth and early nineteenth centuries. According to period journals, boots and shoes from fallen soldiers were usually taken for reuse at the battle's end. All sides suffered from a lack of product, and methods to bypass the long years of apprenticeship to make a proficient shoemaker were sought. Improvements in the pantograph allowed for mirror images of lasts to be made proficiently, allowing for sturdy leather footwear to be made economically on speculation. The English developed a sole-riveting machine for military footwear in 1810 and also devised a press for cutting out leather around the same time. The French improved quotas by streamlining elements of construction, using a factory method for cottage production. Americans devised soles attached with wooden pegs rather than stitching, a process that had been used since the sixteenth century for attaching heels and repairing soles. And in 1823, the metal eyelet was introduced, eventually displacing the more time-consuming task of hand stitching lace holes.

Shoemaking 1850 to the Present

By 1830, exports of women's footwear from France and men's footwear from England dominated the fashionable marketplace. Shoemaking centers were now firmly established in Paris and Northampton, but the United States, whose shoe industry was centered in and around Lynn, Massachusetts, was about to change everything. Factory-style mass production using semi-skilled work-ers could undercut imported goods and with the American perfection of the lock-stitch sewing machine by 1860, shoes could be made as quickly as the machine-sewn uppers could be attached to the soles.

The invention of the sewing machine was primarily initiated by the need for sewing leather, not cloth, more proficiently. Chain-stitching machines were introduced in early French shoemaking factories in the 1830s, resulting in Luddite-like revolts by workers who smashed the machines in fear of losing their jobs to technology. However, chain stitching was found to be more suitable for decorative work than seam construction. It was the American Isaac Singer's patented lock-stitch sewing machine for leather in 1856 that was to begin a series of major changes to the shoemaking industry over the next thirty years.

In 1858 the McKay Closing Machine was perfected that sewed the sole to the upper efficiently without the need of a trained shoemaker. The Goodyear welting machine, developed in 1875 by Charles Goodyear Jr., the son of the man who invented the process of vulcanizing rubber, imitated the difficult stitching of a leather shoe through an upper, welt, and sole. Unlike the McKay closing machine, a Goodyear welting machine did not puncture the bottom of the sole, resulting in a suitable walking shoe for outdoor wear. The Lasting machine, invented in 1883 by Jan Matzelinger, copied the multiple motions of pulling leather around a last and tacking it into position—a time-consuming job.

These machines, all invented in the United States, secured the American ability to mass-produce footwear, as shoes could now be made at great speed and little cost. By the end of the nineteenth century, American shoes were flooding every market. Even the American idea of shoe boxes allowed for more efficient stock management and exporting of goods to Europe and the rest of the world. The European tradition of hand shoemaking was all but ruined.

Some European shoemakers survived the onslaught of cheaper American footwear by catering to the elite, creating footwear of exceptional quality and beauty. However, this worked for only a few small shoemakers. In order to survive, many European shoe companies modernized their factories, fitting them out with the latest machinery to compete with American goods, and many were successful, such as Clarks in England, Bally in Switzerland, Pelikan in Germany, and Bata in Czechoslovakia.

Through a changing workforce and insecure economy due to World War I, postwar recession, and the Great Depression, many shoe companies found it difficult to survive. However, a new process for cemented, or glued, soles in the mid-1930s brought production costs down and eliminated the need for many of the American machines. The 1930s put a focus on women's shoes in the wardrobe, now fully visible under shorter hemlines and thus a necessity for the fashion conscious. The importance of style, color, and decoration enabled European manufacturers the chance to regain supremacy. Companies such as I. Miller and Delman in the United States now saw competition from manufacturers such as Charles Jourdan in France, Rayne in England, and Ferragamo in Italy, who catered to a fashion-conscious clientele.

World War II changed the focus from style to durability. Shoe manufacturers did not suffer, because they were kept busy producing military footwear and other goods under military contract, but fashion footwear was limited by availability of materials.

As part of their postwar recovery, the Italian state aided indigenous shoe companies that were less wieldy than the huge American shoe manufacturers. Undercutting production costs, Italian shoe manufacturers quickly found a niche in the high-fashion footwear industry. By the 1960s French designers were going to Italy to have their shoes made, bypassing their own shoe-manufacturing nationals. Similar sized and modeled companies in Spain and South America with access to cheap and plentiful hides also found success in the 1970s and 1980s, at the cost of American, English, German, and French shoe manufacturers.

But the death knell for many American and European shoe manufacturers came in the development of Southeast Asian shoe industries in the late 1950s and 1960s. Cheaper labor costs for traditionally sewn footwear combined with the new slush molded plastic footwear, which could be produced by machine alone, resulted in the most profitable center in the world for the production of sports shoes—the most popular shoe style since the late 1960s.

While hand shoemakers still exist in London, Venice, and other locales, their numbers are limited and their clients few. High-fashion footwear is produced with a modicum of skilled labor in the finishing; workers whose greatest skill is computer programming make most of the shoes of the early 2000s. Cost, durability, and branding are what drive footwear production in the twenty-first century.

See also Inuit and Arctic Footwear; Ready-to-Wear; Sewing Machine; Shoes; Shoes, Children's Shoes, Men's; Shoes, Women's.

Bibliography

Bondi, Federico, and Giovanni Mariacher. *If the Shoe Fits.* Venice, Italy: Cavallino Venezia, 1983

Durian-Ress, Saskia. *Schuhe: vom späten Mittelalter bis zur Gegenwart Hirmer.* Munich: Verlag, 1991.

Ferragamo, Salvatore. *The Art of the Shoe, 1927–1960.* Florence, Italy: Centro Di, 1992,

Rexford, Nancy E. *Women's Shoes in America, 1795–1930.* Kent, Ohio: Kent State University Press, 2000.

Swann, June. *Shoes.* London: B.T. Batsford, Ltd., 1982.

——. *Shoemaking.* Shire Album 155. Jersey City, N.J.: Parkwest Publications, 1986.

Walford, Jonathan. *The Gentle Step.* Toronto: Bata Shoe Museum, 1994.

Jonathan Walford

SHOES

Neil Armstrong uttered, "One small step for man—one giant leap for mankind" upon his first step on the moon on 20 July 1969. In Teflon-coated nylon and rubber boots, Armstrong became the first man to come into contact with an unknown, hostile extraterrestrial environment. Ten thousand years earlier, dwellers of caves in the Pyrenees emerged from the Ice Age also wearing footwear, made from the hides of the animals they hunted, to protect them from the elements and environment.

Footwear's primary purpose is to protect, but in 10,000 years of history, footwear has taken nearly every form possible to service and compliment human bodies, influenced by environment, morality, practicality, economy, and beauty. Footwear is literally the foundation of fashion. It is the only article of clothing required to come into regular contact with the earth, taking the punishment of hundreds of pounds per square inch with every step. At the same time, it is usually expected to resist dampness, comfort the foot, last a long time, and also look attractive.

Footwear has been the subject of literature and folklore. From Cinderella and Dutch clogs laid out for Sinter Claus, to tying shoes to a newlywed's car bumper, and fetish boots—footwear is steeped in tradition and cultural meaning. From biblical times, the sandal or slipper has been used as a symbol. The Assyrians and Hebrews gave a sandal as a token of good faith and to signify the transfer of property. In Jewish ritual, the shoe represents wealth as when a loved one dies, the grieving family goes shoeless during the shivah as a sign of poverty, for without the deceased they are poor.

Five Basic Styles

Hot, dry climates generally saw the development of the sandal. Believed to be the world's first crafted foot covering, the sandal was a basic footwear style of the ancient Egyptians of the Nile valley and the Anasazi of the ancient American Southwest. Sandals have been the dominant footwear of Africa, Asia, and Central and South America. Their firm soles protect the feet from scorching surfaces, while the minimal uppers allow air to circulate. Sandals can be made of almost any material that is readily at hand, from woven grasses and leather to wood and even metal.

The moccasin, an Algonquian Native American word for footwear, is essentially a shoe made up of one piece of hide drawn up around the foot and sewn with no seams on the lower part. Moccasin-like foot coverings, gathered on top of the foot with a drawstring were the style of ancient northern Europeans. A descendant of this style survives in folk dress from the Balkans to the Baltic, most often referred to by its Croatian name—the *opanke.*

The shoe may have been the result of a union between the Roman *sandallium* and the *opanke* of northern Europe, essentially being a closed sandal. However, it is most aptly traced to the Christian Copts who developed the turnshoe in the first century. The turnshoe was made, as the names suggests, inside out and turned, with a seam along the edge of the hard sole attaching to the upper. Improvements to this style developed in Europe during the twelfth century when a welt was sewn in the seam to aid the shoe in keeping out water.

Similar in construction, boots provide protection to not only the foot, but also the lower leg. It is conjectured that boots originated in arctic Asia and over time spread across the circumpolar region. Certainly, boots are the dominant traditional footwear for natives of the coldest regions on earth, but ancient examples from Mesopotamia, among many hot climate cultures, prove that boots can also offer protection from desert heat and scrubby brush-lands, as well as insect and snakebites. Boots also developed in nomadic cultures where riders of horses or camels wore them to protect their legs from chafing.

Clogs most likely originated from the wooden-soled footwear discovered by the Romans to be worn in Gaul (ancient France). Their wooden-soled footwear was made for inclement weather, which is the origin of the modern word "galosh." Similar overshoes were made throughout the medieval period in Europe to protect good footwear from the filth of the streets. By the fourteenth century a shoe carved from one piece of wood became common for many northern European peasants who required waterproof, warm, inexpensive, and long-wearing footwear.

All footwear is based on these five historic styles. Created for different ranks, rituals, occupations, and uses, footwear can take on many looks when made of different materials and ornamentation. And the main cause for change in footwear is fashion.

From the tenth to twelfth centuries, Europe emerged from the dark ages by uniting itself into nations and developing a mercantile capitalist economy. Crusaders, sent to free the Holy land from Islamic occupation, brought back technical knowledge and fineries from the Arabs, which whetted the appetites of nobles who craved more novelty. By the fourteenth century, quality cloth and fine leathers were being fashioned into shoes that were conspicuous displays of style and elegance, worn with the purpose of expressing personal status.

During the fourteenth century, a fashion for pointed toes spread across Europe. The style originated in Poland, as it became known as the *poulaine* or *cracow*. Edicts were proclaimed limiting its use according to the wealth and social standing of its wearer. When the style fell from fashion at the end of the fifteenth century, it was replaced by wide-toe fashions, known variously as the *hornbill*, *cowmouth*, or *bearpaw*.

A curious woman's fashion, which was at its height of popularity during the 1590s, was the *chopine*—a platform-soled mule that raised the wearer sometimes as high as 39 inches (one meter) off the ground. By the time this fashion had subsided in the early seventeenth century, heels had emerged as a standard addition to both men's and women's footwear.

As Europe positioned itself into nations of power and wealth, the elite distinguished themselves from the masses through conspicuous refinement and extravagant ornamentation. Through the Rococo and Baroque arts, a noble's status was visible in everything he or she did and wore. High-heeled footwear made of expensive silks expressed the idle lifestyles and accumulated wealth of the well heeled. Buckles became a fashionable way of closing shoes during the 1660s, and a century later these large and showy objects had become the feature of the shoe.

By the late eighteenth century, the industrial revolution had brought wealth to the middle classes and the French Revolution ended the divine right of the ruling monarchy. These events empowered the middle classes who would now become the brokers of taste. As everyone was now born on the same level, heels disappeared, fancy buckles were elitist and were replaced by shoelaces, and expensive silk footwear was displaced by more affordable and better-wearing leather footwear. The industrial production of shoes, beginning in the nineteenth century, made attractive, good-quality footwear affordable to almost everyone.

Fashion footwear became a commodity available to all levels of society. Its style was now disseminated through the new communicator—the fashion magazine. Elitism still existed by the quality of the shoe's construction and decoration but what became the real elitist separator was the ability to remain "au courante." Styles, materials, colors, and ornaments changed noticeably enough each season to keep the unfashionable out of the game.

See also Boots; High Heels; Inuit and Arctic Footwear; Sandals; Shoes, Children's; Shoes, Men's; Shoes, Women's; Sneakers; Sport Shoes.

Bibliography

Bondi, Federico, and Giovanni Mariacher. *If the Shoe Fits.* Venice, Italy: Cavallino Venezia, 1983

Durian-Ress, Saskia. *Schuhe: vom späten Mittelalter bis zur Gegen-wart Hirmer.* Munich: Verlag, 1991.

Ferragamo, Salvatore. *The Art of the Shoe, 1927–1960.* Florence, Italy: Centro Di, 1992,

Rexford, Nancy E. *Women's Shoes in America, 1795–1930.* Kent, Ohio: Kent State University Press, 2000.

Swann, June. *Shoes.* London: B.T. Batsford, Ltd., 1982.

——. *Shoemaking.* Shire Album 155. Jersey City, N.J.: Parkwest Publications, 1986.

Walford, Jonathan. *The Gentle Step.* Toronto: Bata Shoe Museum, 1994.

Jonathan Walford

SHOES, MEN'S

In the medieval period new shoes were available only to a tiny elite of aristocrats and wealthy merchants.

However, it appears that in Britain almost all of the poor wore some kind of footwear, which was made possible through the widespread practice of remaking and repairing old shoes. Medieval shoes were made from leather, silk, and other cloths and up to the end of the sixteenth century, all men's footwear tended to be flat. The most extreme style of the fourteenth and fifteenth centuries was the "poulaine," or "pike," which featured extremely pointed toes, sometimes up to four inches (10 centimeters) in length.

Shoes with an arched sole and heel emerged at the end of the sixteenth century, a novelty that was to become a predominant feature of men's shoes in the seventeenth and eighteenth centuries. During the reign of James I (1603–1625), masculine court fashions became particularly flamboyant and stockings and shoes became a key focus of attention. The shoes of the wealthy began to be decorated with large bows, rosettes, or "roses." These styles were superseded in the reign of Charles I (1625–1649), when political instability and war in Britain and Europe encouraged the popularity of military-inspired, knee-high, leather boots. These were fashionable from the 1620s to the 1690s and despite their practical origins as riding wear, they were often elegant and decorative.

Early Modern Period

The rise of France as an international fashion center under Louis XIV (1643–1715) promoted the popularity of French court styles. Shoes were adorned with decorative buckles, a style that remained highly fashionable until the 1780s. Buckles were bought as separate items and by the late eighteenth century they were available for all tastes and pockets, from sparkling precious stones for the wealthy, to plain steel, brass, and pinchbeck for the lower orders.

New shoes became more accessible to the middle classes in the eighteenth century, owing to relative increases in incomes and new manufacturing methods. The development of large workshops, which produced ready-made shoes by hand helped to make shoes more affordable.

Modernity and Men's Footwear

The Enlightenment and the French Revolution (1789–1799) stimulated tastes for the plain, English, country mode of dress, which dominated international fashion from the 1780s. An important element of this style was the jockey or top boot, which featured a top of lighter colored leather. Popular men's wear styles of the early nineteenth century included laced-up walking shoes, flat leather evening pumps, and boots of various styles including top boots, Wellington, Hessian, and Blucher boots. The latter three illustrate the tendency for boot styles of the era to be named after significant military figures or developments.

By the mid-nineteenth century, ankle boots, such as the Balmoral, became the most common type of footwear for men and popular shoe styles included the Oxford and the Derby. These shoe types along with the brogue were widely worn in the twentieth century and are still common in the twenty-first century.

Shoe production was increasingly mechanized in the mid-nineteenth century and by 1900 most people wore shoes made in factories and sold by shoe retailers, rather than patronizing shoemakers. By the 1890s, relative increases in wealth, increased participation in sport and leisure activities such as tennis, golf, and cycling, and improvements in mass-manufacturing techniques led to middle-class consumption of an increasingly diverse range of styles, suitable for various contexts and activities. Despite these transformations in the production and consumption of shoes, leading bespoke shoemakers from this era such as John Lobb Ltd., London, and New & Lingwood, London, have survived into the twenty-first century.

Men's Shoes Post-1945

The predominant features of men's shoes in the post-1945 period have been an expanding diversity of styles and price levels and a more rapid turnover of fashionable designs. The manufacture of ready-made shoes became global after 1945, with low-cost production now concentrated in Asian countries and more exclusive shoes being made in Italy. From the 1950s the rise of youth fashion generated a greater degree of experimentation in men's footwear, with the emergence of designs such as brothel creepers, winklepickers, Chelsea boots, and Doctor Martens boots.

> "A sewing machine for leather was in use by the 1850s . . . and by the end of the century most shoes were made in large factories. The personal relationship between shoemaker and wearer disappeared except at the most expensive end of the market" (Mitchell, p. 34).

Since the mid-1970s, the trainer or sneaker has come to be ubiquitous footwear for men of all ages and tastes. This has partly been owing to a general move toward informality in male appearances, but is also linked to the influence of black street fashion and the aggressive marketing efforts of global sportswear companies like Nike, Puma, and Adidas.

The 1970s saw the appropriation of men's shoe styles such as Dr. Martens by women, a trend that was linked to the influence of feminist ideas and the punk subculture. Unisex or androgynous footwear has continued as a feature of mainstream dress in the early twenty-first century. However, despite these developments, there remain significant differences between men's and women's shoes. High heels are still seen as exclusively feminine and men's businesswear remains focused around variations on the Derby and Oxford styles.

See also Boots; Inuit and Arctic Footwear; Sandals; Shoemaking; Shoes; Shoes, Women's; Sneakers; Sport Shoes.

Bibliography

Baynes, Ken, and Kate Baynes. *The Shoe Show: British Shoes since 1790*. London: The Crafts Council, 1979.

Boydell, Christine. "The Training Shoe: 'Pump Up the Power.'" In *The Gendered Object*. Edited by Pat Kirham. Manchester, U.K.: Manchester University Press, 1996.

Cohn, Nik. *Today There Are No Gentlemen*. London: Weidenfeld and Nicolson, 1971.

de la Haye, Amy. *The Cutting Edge: 50 Years of British Fashion 1947–1997*. London: V & A Publications, 1996.

Mitchell, Louise. *Stepping Out: Three Centuries of Shoes*. Sydney: Powerhouse Publishing, 1997.

Woolley, Linda, and Lucy Pratt. *Shoes*. London: V & A Publications, 1999.

Fiona Anderson

SHOES, WOMEN'S

In cultures where bare feet are customary or only simple sandals are worn, little interest exists in the female foot as a sensual appendage. However, hidden away in tight, decorative shoes and boots, the female foot has been revered as a powerful sexual stimulus in many cultures. Smaller and narrower than a man's foot, the attributes of a woman's comparatively delicate foot has been appreciated and accentuated throughout much of history. This is most apparent in the extreme practice of Chinese foot binding.

For a thousand years in China it was considered refined and sexually attractive for a woman to have bound feet. Outside of weekly washing and perfuming, the feet were kept bound tightly at all times. Several attempts over the years to outlaw the practice by the ruling Manchurians failed and even the Republic made an attempt at stopping the tradition in 1912 when it came to power. The tradition slowly discontinued over time, being finally eliminated in 1949 under the communists. This is by far the most extreme example of sexual differentiation in footwear history. Most cultures cover the female foot differently than the male foot, but in a far less dramatic manner.

Amongst the traditional Inuit of central Northern Canada inlaid furred sealskin boots are designed with vertical patterns for men and horizontal patterns for women. In some cultures it is a matter of who wears the boots. Native Southwestern American Zuni women wear tall white skin boots, while the men wear shorter boots or shoes. Greenlander women's traditional costume includes thigh-high blood-red sealskin boots with decorative appliqués while men wear shorter, darker colored boots.

Fashion Footwear to 1600

In Western culture, it is women who generally wear more architecturally significant or decorous foot coverings. With few exceptions, until the Renaissance, women's footwear was generally less interesting for the simple reason that it was less visible under the longer garments worn, and it was men who were the peacocks in the footwear department.

In ancient Egypt, Greece, and Rome, women wore sandals consisting of fewer straps and less decoration than men's sandals, baring more toe cleavage. During the late Roman or Byzantine Empire, Christianity brought about radical change from the ancient classical ways. Christian morality considered it sinful to expose the body. St. Clement of Alexandria, in the third century, was already preaching humility for women, commanding them not to bare their toes. Byzantine footwear was designed to cover the feet, and shoes replaced sandals. Roman-style sandals remained the privilege of high-ranking church officials, and abundant decoration was seen as too worldly for the people to wear, appropriate only for the Pope and other prelates.

The largest threat to the Byzantine Empire came with the expansion of Islam that, by 750, had grown to include most of the old Roman territory including Egypt and its Christian Copt population. By the eighth century, Coptic steles (gravestones) depict the deceased wearing shoes and mules, sometimes decorated with gilded figures and etched linear designs, often in sacred imagery. The shoe had evolved to include a pointed toe and peaked throat and was often made of red kid. Called *mulleus* in Latin, referring to the red color, it is from this connection that the modern term "mule"—for a backless shoe—originates. This style can still be found in parts of the Middle and Far East.

Christianity reinforced the alliance of what was once Rome's domain. During the Carolingian age of Charlemagne (768–814) a close relationship between the various kings and the pope secured the Church in much of Europe unifying the European kingdoms.

Europe began to emerge from the Dark Ages in about 1000 C.E. Christian Europe was uniting into nations, headed by monarchies. These European states began crusades into the Holy Land, bringing themselves into contact with Islamic thought and products. The crusaders brought back silk, embroidery, and the button, whetting the appetites of nobles who craved finery and novelty. The textile arts flourished with the production of quality weavings, embroideries, leather goods, and felts. At the same time, merchants became wealthy importing and exporting these goods, making enough money to dress like nobles. Fashion was now a commodity that expressed the status of its wearer. Elitism could be expressed through a sumptuous display of fashion excess.

The first footwear fashion excess was the elongated pointed toe, said to have originated in the late 1100s. The style was popular in the late 1100s but subsided from fashion, and when reintroduced from Poland in the early 1300s it had become known as a *poulaine* or *crakow*, reflecting its supposed Polish origin.

Expensive materials and excessive styles were royalty's way of staying ahead of the moneyed bourgeoisie. If the sheer cost of dressing well did not create enough of a gap between the well-to-do and the have-nots, then edicts were placed upon materials, styles, and decorations restricting their use to persons of appropriate status. The church also set restrictions against obscene or excessive fashions. Together, these governing bodies attempted to keep the classes in their place, making each identifiable by their dress.

In England, in 1363, Edward III proclaimed a sumptuary law that limited the length of the toe to the wearer's income and social standing; commoners earning less than 40 *livres* per year were forbidden the use of long toes; those who made more than 40 *livres* annually could wear a toe no longer than six inches; a gentleman no more than twelve inches; a nobleman no more than 24 inches; and a prince was unlimited in the length he chose.

Northern Europe continued to don the style until the end of the fifteenth century, even though Italy, southern France, and Spain essentially stopped wearing the protrusive toe, choosing instead to have less pointed footwear made of the finest kid leather or silk.

When length finally became old fashioned, width became the next fashion excess. Popular in the English Tudor court and other northern European states of the sixteenth century, shoes with widths that extended well beyond the foot were known variously as the *hornbill*, *cow-mouth*, or *bearpaw*. This new dimension suffered the same excesses as the long toe. Under England's Queen Mary, another sumptuary law was passed, and although its wording is lost, it can be assumed that the width of the toe was similarly limited according to social status and wealth of its wearer.

The last dimension was now to be explored—height. The ancient Greeks first put platform sandals on the feet of their actors to give them distinction, suggesting the performer was playing an important person. Ancient Greek women adopted cork-soled versions, called *Cothurnus*. Fifteenth-century aristocratic Venetian women donned stilted mules or shoes, called *chopines*, to reflect their high social status. Fashioned in velvet with tack-work or white alum tanned kid with punch-work brogueing, *chopines* not only added height, but also décor to the silhouette. Although called "depraved" and "dis-solute" by the church, the style traveled across Europe where by 1600 even Shakespeare wrote in Hamlet "Your Ladyship is nearer to heaven than when I saw you last by the altitude of a *chopine*." Maidservants were required to steady the wearers of some of the tallest *chopines* that could reach a height of up to 39 inches (one meter). *Chopines* fell from fashion when prostitutes donned them, ruining their status for women of breeding. Heels, introduced in the 1590s, eventually displaced the platform mules, although some extant examples of *chopines* date as late as 1620.

Seventeenth and Eighteenth Centuries

When heels were first added to shoes in the 1590s they were only about an inch in height. Women's heels took on greater elevations during the reign of Louis XIV (1643–1715) in France. Heels towered two to three inches, although "well-heeled" women's skirts made their shoes virtually invisible. The heel expressed the status of the wearer as they were quite literally at a higher level than the hordes of common folk. Under Louis XIV, red heels were worn strictly at court. Although this law existed only in France, by restriction the color came to represent the power and status of the aristocratic elite across Europe.

Three different heel types developed in Europe during the eighteenth century. The Italian heel was tall and spiked, like a stiletto. The French heel was of mid-height and curvaceous and later became known as the Louis heel; and the English heel was thicker and generally low to mid-height. Fashionable continental European women were more inclined to be at court or at home in an urban setting, so their heels could generally be more delicate, while English women of breeding tended to live at their country estates for most of the year, so a thicker heel was necessary for the more natural terrain they traversed.

When the skirts of French gowns inched toward the ankles in the mid-eighteenth century, suddenly there seemed to be an erotic interest in the high-heeled shoe, as it made the foot appear smaller and narrower, and gave the ankle a delicate shape. In the meantime, due to practicality, men were now solidly planted on the ground with heels of less than an inch. It was appropriate for a gentleman to walk upon a muddy, cobbled street that required a low-heeled shoe or boot. A lady of quality, however, did not walk the streets and likely traveled by coach or other means, so a high heel was appropriate for most occasions she would encounter.

Throughout the seventeenth and eighteenth centuries an increasing fondness for luxurious fabrics and decorative trimmings ensued. European-made damask and brocaded silks had been produced in Italy and France until the emigration of Protestant French Huguenots in the last quarter of the seventeenth century. They brought with them the knowledge of silk production when they resettled throughout Protestant Europe, from Spitalfields, England, to Krefeld, Germany. The costly development of this new industry, however, kept domestically produced silks at a higher price than imported Chinese silks.

Chinese silks were usually brocaded patterns of abstract geometric designs, made specifically for the western market. To support the development of a domestic silk industry, England banned the wearing of Chinese silk in 1699; other countries proclaimed similar edicts. Silks produced in Europe followed the Oriental taste of abstract patterns and became known as "bizarres," remaining in fashion until the 1730s when tastes changed and grand floral designs came into vogue.

The decoration of shoes used many techniques: silk embroidery, applied cord *passementerie*, and silver and gold thread embroidery that was made by professional male embroiderers who belonged to embroidery guilds.

Originally, buckles came into fashion because of their utility. Samuel Pepys refers to putting on buckles for the first time in 1660. By the end of the seventeenth century, buckles overtook the standard of ribbon laces. Both men and women increasingly suffered from buckle mania throughout the eighteenth century. Buckles grew in size and became more elaborate, set with showy paste and semiprecious stones. Men's buckles were larger but both sexes displayed their shoe jewelry during a bow and curtsy with extended foot—the appropriate method of introduction of the day.

By the end of the eighteenth century mercantile and industrial wealth had created a strong, affluent, educated, yet politically under-represented middle class who were set between an ever-deepening rift of the noble elite and the working poor. The American and French revolutions exploded out of this imbalance, and, in the end, demo-graphics won. The middle classes rose to power and would become the brokers of taste.

Illustration of woman wearing chopines. In the fifteenth century, aristocratic Venetian women began wearing platform shoes as a symbol of status, and the style quickly spread across Europe. THE GRANGER COLLECTION LTD. REPRODUCED BY PERMISSION.

In the early months of the French Revolution, the French National Assembly demanded that all deputies give up their valuable shoe buckles for the benefit of the treasury. The legislative session of 22 November 1789 opened with le Marechal de Maille making the patriotic gift of his gold buckles.

The Nineteenth Century

Following the French Revolution, plain leather footwear became the mode. Durable and affordable, it was considered more democratic than the fussily embroidered and expensive silk shoes previously preferred by the elite. Heels also fell from use after the French Revolution, in keeping with the new democratic philosophy that all people are born equal. The new French and American republics looked to classical models of democracy for inspiration and excavations at Pompeii and from Napoleon's military campaigns in Egypt brought renewed interest in the ancient world and provided inspiration for neoclassical designs.

Women's fashion took on the silhouette of a Greek column. Neutrals of white and tan were complimented by dark tones of the classical world: Pompeiin red, crocodile green, and rich gold. The sandal was revived during the neoclassical period, although not with great success, especially in the colder northern European climates where instead, shoes were fashioned with cutouts lined with colored underlays or painted with stripes to emulate sandals. During the Napoleonic wars an inconsistent fashion image existed. In shoes, the use of heels and the shapes of toes varied, with no one style predominating. The square toe, introduced as early as the 1790s, did not become the main style until the late 1820s but would remain so for the next half century.

As factories disfigured the horizon, many longed for the picturesque qualities of an unspoiled landscape. A naturalism movement brought long country promenades into fashion; ladies began to wear "spatterdashes," leggings adapted from men's military dress that protected stockings from spatters and dashes of mud. Walking became a fad called "pedestrianism" and a prescribed activity for women. Boots were worn for this activity as a sensible alternative to fashion shoes. Ankle boots, referred to as demi-boots or half boots, found international appeal in this period.

By the time Queen Victoria ascended the throne in 1837 a sentimental, romanticized movement had swept popular thought. Women became expressions of virtue and femininity, their conservative costume and demure decorum reflected conscious gentility. Fine slippers of kid and silk were made in great quantities in Paris and exported around the world. Soles, which had been made without left or right definition for more than 200 years, were exceptionally narrow now and the delicate uppers tended not to last long as they were pulled under the sole at the ball of the foot, deteriorating with one wearing. Colored footwear found favor during the 1830s with ankle-length skirts, but fell from use for the next two decades. The long, full skirts of the mid-nineteenth century hid the feet from view, with perhaps the occasional peep at a vamp when the woman walked or waltzed across a floor. By the mid-1850s, black or white footwear was deemed by fashion delineators to be the most elegant and tasteful choice, a standard that would last for many years.

However, after the mid-1850s, with the introduction of wire frame "crinoline" skirt supports, skirts tended to tip and swing, exposing the foot and ankle. This brought about interest in the decoration of shoe vamps. Machine chain-stitched designs with colorful silk underlays, dubbed "chameleons," became fashionable for home and evening wear. For daytime, however, boots became modest essentials underneath the wire-frame supported skirts. Side-laced boots called "Adelaides" in England, after William IV's consort, were made for most outdoor occasions until improvements in the elasticity of rubber resulted in the development of elastic thread which, woven into webbing, was used for ankle-boot gussets. Elastic-sided boots were referred to as "Garibaldi" boots in Europe after the Italian statesman who united Italy during the 1860s, and as "Congress" boots in the United States after the American Congress. Front-laced boots came back into fashion by 1860. Called "Balmorals," after Queen Victoria's Scottish home, the style was deemed suitable for informal daywear and sporting occasions at first, but by the 1870s had become the more common closure of all boots. Button boots were introduced in the 1850s, but were generally not favored until the 1880s when their tight fit and elegant closure flattered the slim ankle and foot more than laced styles.

Heels were reintroduced on ladies' footwear during the late 1850s, but did not find universal appeal until the late 1870s. Historicism was an important movement of the mid-nineteenth century; Rococo and Baroque styling was evident on shoes in the 1860s with a return to buckles and bows. Large, multiple loop bows were called "Fenelon," after the seventeenth-century French writer. Mules, too, came back into fashion as part of the historical revival of the *ancien regime.*

Exoticism was another important movement of the nineteenth century. Via the Crimean war, Turkish embroideries were exported for the production of shoe uppers in the late 1850s and when Japan opened its doors to foreign trade in 1867, a taste for all-things Oriental made a strong comeback. Chinese embroidered silks or European embroidered silks in the taste of Chinese and Japanese textiles were in fashion and a Japanese-influenced palette of colors resulted in brown leather footwear coming into vogue, which would become a fashion staple.

By the late 1880s the square toe had finally fallen from fashion, replaced by rounded and even almondshaped toes and all shoes were now being made with right and left sole definitions. Business began to decline for hand shoemakers as mass manufacturers standardized sizes and provided widths for customer fit. Improvements in American manufacturing methods and machinery, as well as cheaper production costs positioned the Americans as the leading footwear manufacturers for the next fifty years.

The Twentieth Century

Black, brown, and white footwear predominated until the 1920s. Colored footwear was made almost entirely for evening dress, as it was seen as inappropriately gaudy for street or daywear. After the start of World War I in 1914, hemlines began a steady climb up the leg, so that by armistice the sensuous curves of the instep and ankle were exposed. The climbing hemline made the gap between the top of the boot and bottom of the hemline an unsightly distraction. The boot was generally abandoned from fashion, although a "Cossack" boot, or pull-on style was introduced and found some success in the late 1920s.

The impact of the shoe on the complete silhouette now had to be calculated to find a complimentary style. During the 1920s, short and curvy heels grew taller and straighter, which tightened the calf muscle, slimming the appearance of the ankle and foreshortening the foot making it appear smaller. Even the vamp was cut lower to expose more of the instep.

By the 1930s, shoemakers had become shoe designers. Color, shape, and decoration literally exploded at the feet of fashion. A wide variety of spectators, oxfords, pumps, sandals, brogues, and other styles filled the shoe stores. Salvatore Ferragamo revived the *chopine* in 1937, using cork to create platform soles. Internationally, the style found limited success, but with the beginning of World War II (1939–1945) the style grew in popularity. The war resulted in a shortage of leather for civilian footwear; thick wood or cork soles and substitute leather uppers made of raffia, hemp, or textile substituted. In the United States, where rationing was less severe than in Europe, platform shoes were more often made of leather, but women were rationed to two pairs of shoes per year.

The tall tapered heel remained in fashion from the late 1920s to the mid-1950s with only subtle changes in form until the Italian heel, renamed the "stiletto," became the fashion in the late 1950s. Tall and very slender with a metal core, the heel was named after the weapon for a reason. The narrow heel created pressure of hundreds of pounds per square inch with every step, pockmarking linoleum and wooden floors. Visitors to the Louvre were required to don plastic heel caps to protect the ancient floors. The stiletto heel, paired with a sharp pointed toe, was the most aesthetically complimentary shoe style ever designed. The pointed toe visually narrowed the foot and the high heel tightened the calf muscle, slimming the ankle. Medically, it was the worst combination ever created. Many women turned their ankles on the metal spikes, catching the tips in manholes, subway grates, or even cracks in the sidewalk; the high heel forced the foot forward into the pointed toe, which curtailed the toes, causing bunions and hammertoes.

In reaction, a low-heeled, square boot came back into fashion in the mid-1960s. Paired with miniskirts, the boot highlighted the leg and gave a youthful élan to the fashions of the day. Boots came on the fashion scene at the same time as the popular "go-go" dances of the day and quickly became known as go-go boots—usually white ankle boots.

The early 1970s saw the return of the platform that accomplished two feats at once. Women's liberation was reflected in the elevated soles that put women on an equal footing to men. At the same time, platforms were complimentary to the length of the leg, made apparent in hot pants, miniskirts, and long-legged pants.

Since the early 1970s fashion footwear has been eclipsed by the sports-shoe phenomenon. More runners, joggers, cross-trainers, and basketball shoes have been sold than high-fashion shoes on an annual basis. Scientific advances in fit and comfort has been paired with conscious design and celebrity marketing, creating a mad frenzy for every new design released. Fashion experts may scoff at sports shoes as fashion, but many designers have paid homage to the style in upscale versions over the past thirty years.

High-fashion footwear of the last quarter of the twentieth century consisted almost entirely of revivals. The stiletto-heeled, pointed-toe shoe of the late 1950s and early 1960s was the mainstream high-fashion style of the late 1980s and early 1990s. Every time the platform shoe has come back into fashion it has been heavily inspired by its previous incarnation. The platform shoes of the 1990s were many times perfect recreations of their 1970s predecessors, to the point where it was nearly impossible to tell the difference between the retro and the true vintage versions.

Subtle tweaking of heel shapes, toe shapes, decorations, colors, and materials, and the combinations in which they are used are the only elements that define the past thirty years of fashion footwear from previous styles. Multiplicity is key to the fashion footwear of the early 2000s: stilettos, platforms, chunky heels, low heels, pointed toes, square toes, boots, shoes, and ballerina flats. Virtually all styles are available at the same time, and all of them are at the height of fashion.

See also Boots; Footbinding; High Heels; Inuit and Arctic Dress; Sandals; Shoes; Shoes, Men's; Sneakers; Sports Shoes.

Bibliography

Bondi, Federico, and Giovanni Mariacher. *If the Shoe Fits.* Venice, Italy: Cavallino Venezia, 1983.

Durian-Ress, Saskia. *Schuhe: vom späten Mittelalter bis zur Gegenwart Hirmer.* Munich: Verlag, 1991.

Ferragamo, Salvatore. *The Art of the Shoe, 1927–1960.* Florence, Italy: Centro Di, 1992.

Rexford, Nancy E. *Women's Shoes in America, 1795–1930.* Kent, Ohio: Kent State University Press, 2000.

Swann, June. *Shoes.* London: B.T. Batsford, Ltd., 1982.

——. *Shoemaking.* Shire Album 155. Jersey City, N.J.: Parkwest Publications, 1986.

Walford, Jonathan. *The Gentle Step.* Toronto: Bata Shoe Museum, 1994.

Jonathan Walford

SIMMEL, GEORG

The German sociologist and philosopher Georg Simmel was born in Berlin on 1 March 1858 to assimilated Jewish parents. Between 1876 and 1881 Simmel studied history and philosophy in Berlin. His doctoral thesis (1881) and post-doctoral dissertation (1885) both dealt with Immanual Kant. His rhetorical gift proved to be successful with academic and nonacademic audiences alike, and his lectures became social events. In 1890 he married the writer Gertrud Kinel. A year later they had their only son, Hans. In 1894 he published the essay "The Problem of Sociology," which inaugurated a separate social science. Simmel and his wife were at the center of cultural circles in Berlin; their friends included the poets Rainer Maria Rilke and Stefan George as well as the sculptor Auguste Rodin. In 1903 his essay "The Metropolis and Mental Life" constituted an early study of urban modernity. Latent anti-Semitism, reservations about the academic validity of sociological studies, and envy of Simmel's social popularity hindered his professional progress in Berlin, and in 1914 he accepted a call to the university in Strasbourg, where he died on 26 September 1918.

Simmel's discussion of fashion, significant for its early date within academic discourse, its conceptual rigor, as well as its metaphysical breadth are defined by his simultaneous adherence to philosophical tradition and the formation of a sociological methodology. Accordingly, he viewed fashion both as an abstract concept that generates and influences cultural perception and as a defining factor in social and interpersonal relations. Simmel's beginnings as a neo-Kantian philosopher prepared his view of cognition as a biological process of adaptation by human beings to their environment, a view which is not only situated in a scientific (neo-Darwinian) discourse but also extended to culture—intellectual as well as sensory—within a contemporary (modern and urban) environment. Simmel defined the truth within expressions of reality pragmatically through its appropriateness for living practice. This led him to the emerging discipline of sociology, which developed the ground for direct application of such concepts to sociopolitical existence. His precursors herein were Auguste Comte, Herbert Spencer, and Gabriel Tarde, and among his contemporaries were Ferdinand Tönnies, Werner Sombart, Émile Durkheim, and Marcel Mauss.

Early Investigations

The methodological mix of metaphysics, economics, and social theory generated for Simmel an interest in fashion, which he viewed as a theoretical and material field of investigation that offered space for emphatic, almost literary, evocations of clothing but also for a formal description of (dress) codes as visual and structural primers for social groups and settings. He began to investigate the topic in an 1895 essay titled "Zur Psychologie der Mode" (On the psychology of fashion). In this essay, Kantian heritage accounts for a philosophical focus on the subject-object relation. Simmel asks where cognition is founded, in the objects of cognition or in the cognitive subject itself. He applies the question to fashion: Is cognition founded in the clothes we choose to wear, or is it the human mind that chooses the clothes? In this, his first essay about fashion, cognition and self-awareness are regarded as creative achievements of the subject, aided by guidelines extracted from the conglomerate of experience.

In his book *The Philosophy of Money*, Simmel returned to the progressive division of subject and object in modernity, this time applying socioeconomic criteria. In this work Simmel devotes a telling passage to fashion, describing how "the radical opposition between subject and object has been reconciled in theory by making the object part of the subject's perception," partly through a practice that produces the object by a single subject for a single subject. In modernity, mass production—with its division of labor—renders such reconciliation impossible. The analogy that Simmel draws here is "the difference . . . between the modern clothing store, geared towards utmost specialisation, and the work of the tailor whom one used to invite into one's home" (Simmel, p. 457). The example is indicative of Simmel's approach. Not only does the object of fashion—more than any other object of consumption that must remain at a distance from the body—allow for an introduction of sensuality and haptic experience within theory, but it also applies abstract concepts directly to corporeality. In discussing the production and consumption of fashion, Simmel leads the reader directly back to his or her own experience as a wearer of clothes and as a modern consumer, thus generating an important link to personal experience that coined contemporary philosophy (Simmel's subsequent term *Lebensphilosophie* [metaphysics of existence] would follow French philosopher Henri-Louis Bergson's *élan vital*, or nature's creative impulse).

In 1904–1905 two extended essays by Simmel were published—one in English under the simple heading "Fashion" and one in German titled "Philosophie der Mode" (Philosophy of fashion). They share a similar structure, but the former set an empiricist or rationalist tone that would determine Simmel's reception in Anglo-Saxon social sciences as a formal sociologist and precursor to the Chicago school of empiricist, urban sociology.

Akin to set theory, Simmel describes in his sociology the developmental process of social differentiation as a confluence of the homogeneous segments of heterogeneous circles. In modern (especially urban) culture both psychological and social differentiation are geared to minimizing physical friction and channeling the energy of personal collisions into dynamic movement as an economic principle (e.g., competition). Fashion exemplifies this process acutely. The complex mix within modern dressing between invention and imitation, between socially sanctioned conformity for societal survival and necessary independence for personal gratification and the formation of the self (even cognition), is found in all clothing rituals and codification. The abstract and generalized tone with which fashion is debated makes Simmel's analyses still pertinent in the twenty-first century, because he eschewed historicity, romanticism, or concreteness vis-à-vis sartorial styles.

Key Observations about Fashion

Two sets of his observations, in particular, render fashion a generic model both for the recognition of societal procedures and a phenomenology of modernity itself. The first is the import of fashion by strangers from out-side a given set or circle. Here the term "role-playing," which would become so significant for modern sociology, is prefigured. In his essays Simmel analyzes how a style or appearance of dress undergoes a developmental process of rejection to acceptance. "Because of their external origin," he wrote in 1904, "these imported fashions create a special and significant form of socialization, which arises through mutual relation to a point without the circle. It sometimes appears as though social elements, just like the axes of vision, converge best at a point that is not too near. . . . Paris modes are frequently created with the sole intention of setting a fashion elsewhere" (Simmel; 1904, p. 136). The methodological move from anthropology to economics here is characteristic for the formation of early social theory. Also, the strong interest in temporal structures (partly influenced through Bergson's *durée*, the natural milieu of a person's "deep self, or the true foundation of one's spiritual identity") and accelerated rhythm of modernity leads Simmel to a contemplation of sartorial transitoriness.

In the last of his four essays on fashion, "Die Mode" (Fashion, 1911), he explains how wider acceptance and distribution of a fashion herald its demise, since a widely accepted dress code no longer poses to the individual a challenge that is associated with the constitutive process of fractious assimilation. Accordingly, a novel form or style of clothing needs to be introduced to generate anew the dualities of innovation and imitation, social separation and inclusion. As soon as fashion manages to determine the totality of a group's appearance—which has to be its ultimate creative and economic aim—fashion will, owing to the logical contradiction inherent in its characteristics, die and become replaced. And the more subjective and individualized a style of clothing is, the quicker it perishes. For Simmel, this transitory character of fashion remains its essence and elevates its material objects to transhistorical significance. "The question of fashion is not 'to be or not to be,'" he concluded in 1911, ". . . but it always stands on the watershed between past and future" (Simmel: 1911, p. 41).

See also Benjamin, Walter; Fashion, Theories of.

Bibliography

Böhringer, Hannes, and Karlfried Gründer, eds. *Ästhetik und Soziologie um die Jahrhundertwende: Georg Simmel*. Frankfurt am Main, Germany: Vittorio Klostermann Verlag, 1976.

Dahme, Heinz-Jürgen, and Otthein Rammstedt, eds. *Georg Simmel und die Moderne*. Frankfurt am Main, Germany: Suhrkamp, 1984.

Frisby, David. *Fragments of Modernity: Theories of Modernity in the Work of Simmel, Kracauer, and Benjamin*. Cambridge, U.K.: Polity Press, 1985.

——. *Sociological Impressionism: A Reassessment of Georg Simmel's Social Theory*. 2nd ed. London: Routledge, 1992.

Kaern, Michael, Bernard S. Phillips, and Robert S. Cohen, eds. *Georg Simmel and Contemporary Sociology*. Dordrecht, Germany: Kluwer Academic Publishers, 1990.

Lehmann, Ulrich. *Tigersprung: Fashion in Modernity*. Cambridge, Mass.: MIT Press, 2000.

Lichtblau, Klaus. *Kulturkrise und Soziologie um die Jahrhundertwende*. Frankfurt am Main, Germany: Suhrkamp, 1996.

Rammstedt, Otthein, ed. *Simmel und die frühen Soziologen: Nähe und Distanz zu Durkheim, Tönnies, und Max Weber*. Frankfurt am Main, Germany: Suhrkamp, 1988.

Remy, Jean, ed. *Georg Simmel: Ville et modernité*. Paris: Éditions L'Harmattan, 1995.

Simmel, Georg. *On Individuality and Social Forms: Selected Writings*. Edited by Donald N. Levine. Chicago: University of Chicago Press, 1971.

——. *Georg Simmel on Women, Sexuality, and Love*. New Haven, Conn.: Yale University Press, 1984.

——. *Gesamtausgabe*. Edited by Ottheim Rammstedt. Frankfurt am Main, Germany: Suhrkamp, 1989–2002.

Wolff, Kurt H., ed. *The Sociology of Georg Simmel*. Glencoe, Ill.: Free Press, 1950.

Ulrich Lehmann

SMITH, PAUL

Paul Smith is renowned for classic garments that also demonstrate a discreet eccentricity that is essentially as British as his name. Committed to the idea of creative independence, he is Britain's most commercially successful designer, with a turnover of £230 million and retail outlets in forty-two countries.

Born in the city of Nottingham in 1946, he left school at age fifteen and began his career running errands in a fashion warehouse. When he was only seventeen, he was instrumental in the success of a local boutique, running the men's wear department and sourcing labels that were previously unavailable outside of London. In 1970 he opened his first shop, a three-meter-square room at the back of a tailor's space, together with a basement that he turned into a gallery, where he sold limited edition lithographs by Warhol and Hockney. He recalled,

> I had . . . [m]odern classics you couldn't get anywhere else. I knew that . . . if I started selling clothes that I didn't like, but that lots of people did want, then the job would have changed me. I called the boutique Paul Smith as a reaction to the silly names . . . [of] the time (Fogg, p. 130).

Smith began manufacturing and retailing shirts, trousers, and jackets under his own label, and in 1976 he showed for the first time in Paris. The opening of the first Paul Smith store in London's Covent Garden in 1979 coincided with a resurgence in the money markets of the city and subsequent changes in social attitudes. His suits for men became standard wear for the 1980s young urban professional, the "yuppie." "Young people were willing to wear suits and were not embarrassed about saying that they had money. That was what the 1980s were all about and my clothes reflected the times" (Smith p. 148). Smith's amalgamation of traditional tailoring skills with a witty and subversive eye for detail, together with his quirky use of color and texture, allowed his customers the reassurance that it was permissible to be fashion conscious without being outrageous. It was this particular brand of Britishness that appealed to the Japanese market, where Smith has a £212 million retail business of more than 240 shops. As the Paul Smith style infiltrated mainstream retail chains on the High Street, his company developed a stronger fashion emphasis, and in 1993 he introduced a women's wear collection.

An important element of Smith's shops has always been his ability to source quirky and idiosyncratic objects to sell alongside the clothes. With the opening of the Westbourne Grove shop in London's Notting Hill Gate in 1998, he introduced another retail concept, that of the shop as home, and he has diversified into home furnishings. Smith has always been concerned that each shop is individual and reflects the unique quality of the city in which it is placed, rather than presenting a homogeneous ideal that is brand-and-marketing-led. In the year 2000 Queen Elizabeth II knighted him for his services to the British fashion industry.

See also Suit, Business; Tailored Suit; Tailoring.

Bibliography

Fogg, Marnie. *Boutique: A '60s Cultural Phenomenon*. London: Mitchell Beazley, 2003.
Smith, Paul. *You Can Find Inspiration in Anything: (And If You Can't, Look Again!)*. London: Violette Editions, 2001.

Marnie Fogg

SNEAKERS

The first athletic shoes were created thousands of years ago to protect the foot from rough terrain when hunting and participating in combat games (Cheskin 1987, pp. 2–3). In Mesopotamia (c. 1600–1200 B.C.E.) soft shoes were worn by the mountain people who lived on the border of Iran. These shoes were constructed with crude tools such as bone needles and stone knives; and made of indigenous materials like leaves, bark, hide, and twine. With the available manufacturing processes and materials, primitive shoes were only constructed as sandals or wraparound moccasins. In a sandal construction the foot is attached to a platform with straps,

bands, or loops. A moccasin construction entails a piece of material wrapped under and over the top of the foot then anchored with a drawstring. As sports became more competitive throughout history, athletic shoes needed to perform better and be sport-specific. Functional attributes like weight, flexibility, cushioning, and traction became key features to making successful athletic shoes.

Folklore

According to some historians, King Henry VIII of England expressed ideas related to an athletic sneaker-type construction in the 1500s. According to folklore, the king was getting a bit overweight, and he decided playing tennis would be a good way to get in shape. But he was not happy with the shoes he had. He ordered his servant to get "syxe paire of shooys with feltys, to pleye in at tennis" (six pairs of shoes with felt bottoms to play tennis in), from the local cobbler (Paquin 1990). Although the king was not exactly ordering sneakers, as we technically know them, he had the right idea—to make lightweight shoes with a separate functional outsole to play tennis better.

What Is a Sneaker?

The word "sneaker" was a marketing term coined in the United States many years after the actual shoe construction was created. "Sneaker" is one of many names given to a shoe that consists of a canvas upper attached to a vulcanized rubber outsole. A shoe made any differently (e.g., a shoe with a foam midsole and a stability shank) is not technically a sneaker.

The first shoes constructed with canvas uppers and vulcanized rubber outsoles were called "Sand Shoes." These shoes were an evolution of a former sand shoe design that had a cotton canvas upper and outsole made from flat leather or jute rope. In the 1830s an English company called Liverpool Rubber evolved the original sand shoe, by bonding canvas to rubber, making the out-sole more durable. The name "sand shoe" came from the fact that they were worn on the beach, by the Victorian middle class (Kippen 2004). Sand shoes were revolutionary as they replaced heavy and more expensive leatherwork boots. Around the 1860s, a croquet shoe was created that had a rubber outsole with a canvas upper fastened with cotton laces. Sand shoes were different than the croquet shoe as they had a T-strap upper construction fastened with a metal buckle. Sand shoes were also the basis for traditional English school sandals, sometimes called "Sandies" (Wagner 1999).

In the 1870s, a more robust sand shoe was created; it was called a "Plimsoll" (also spelled Plimsol or Plimsole). The name came from Samuel Plimsoll (1824–1898), a British merchant and shipping reformer who designated the "Plimsoll Mark"—a mark on the hull of cargo ships that designated the waterline when it was at full capacity (*Britannica Student Encyclopedia* 2004). The term Plimsoll was adopted by the shoe industry because the point where the canvas upper and vulcanized rubber outsole bonded together looked similar to a ship's Plimsoll line. This line aesthetically made the shoe look more expensive than previous models and became adopted by all social classes for a variety of athletic activities.

Around the same time the Plimsoll was popular in England, the term "sneaker" was coined in the United States. There are several cited origins and dates of the term. Some say the word is merely an Americanism, made from the word "sneak" (1870), because the shoe was noiseless (Coye 1986, pp. 366–369). There is also a reference that the noise-less rubber shoes were preferred by "sneak thieves" (1891) hence the name sneakers (Vanderbuilt 1998, p. 9). There is even a source that mentions the shoe got its name from "sneaky" (1895) baseball players who liked stealing bases in them (Hendrickson 2000). Many sources reference Henry Nelson McKinney (1917), an advertising agent for N. W. Ayer & Son. He came up with the name "sneaker," because the rubber outsole allowed the shoe to be quiet or "sneaky" (Bellis 2004)

No matter how the name was born, shoes with a canvas upper and a vulcanized rubber outsole evolved into many forms. These evolutions allowed people to enhance their athletic skills and provided an aesthetic opportunity for casual shoe design. In the 1880s, vulcanized rubber was added to the toe box to stop the big toenail from breaking through the canvas. It also provided abrasion resistance in sports where the forefoot was dragged to provide balance (e.g., tennis). Functional outsole patterns (e.g., herringbone) were also created to add traction, facilitate player movements, and cushion the load when jumping. Similar types of shoes became useful for sailing and yachting, since they provided traction on the wet deck. The military also used them, and had them colored according to rank. Schools recommended them to students for gym class. Athletes wore them at the first modern Olympics in Paris (1900), and Robert Falcon Scott wore them on his Antarctic expedition (1901–1904) (Kippen 2004).

Names

Since the creation of the sand shoe, there have been numerous names used globally to describe a shoe with a canvas upper and vulcanized rubber outsole. In the beginning, plimsoll and sneaker were popular names. Over time, a variety of other names have been created. Some are based on function, while others are based on materials, people, and even street slang. A few of the names include: Bobos, Bumper Boots, Chuck's, Creepers, Daps, Felonies, Fish Heads, Go Fasters, Grips, Gym Shoes, Gymmers, Joggers, Jumps, Kicks, Outing Shoes, Pumps, Runners, Sabogs, Skiffs, Sneaks, Tackies, Tennies, Trainers, and Treads (Perrin 2004).

Materials and Construction

Although athletes have been wearing performance-related footwear for thousands of years, the "sneaker" is only a recent creation based upon serendipity and adaptations of several industrial revolution inventions.

The most recognized feature of a sneaker is its vulcanized rubber outsole. Natural or India rubber, a byproduct of trees, has been cultivated since 1600 B.C.E. (by the Mayans). However, natural rubber "as is," is not really appropriate for shoes. In hot and sticky weather it melts; in cold weather it becomes brittle and hard. In 1839, Charles Goodyear from the United States serendipitously created the modern form of rubber used for sneakers when he was trying to come up with a waterproof mailbag material for the U.S. government. Goodyear's recipe, later named "vulcanization" was discovered when he accidentally dropped a mixture of rubber, lead, and sulfur onto a hot stove. His accident resulted in a substance that was not affected by the weather, and would snap back to its original shape when stretched (Goodyear 2003). The same type of rubber was reinvented and patented in England (1843), by a rubber pioneer named Thomas Hancock, who analyzed and copied samples from Goodyear. A friend of Hancock's coined the term "vulcanization" after Vulcan, the Roman god of fire (Goodyear 2003).

Sewing Machine

Cotton canvas was around for a long time before the creation of the first sneaker-type construction; however, sewing small pieces of canvas into a three-dimensional shape that conforms to the foot is quite tedious by hand. The lockstitch sewing machine was invented and patented in 1845 by Elias Howe, which allowed fabrics of all weights and constructions to be quickly and neatly stitched together. In 1851, Isaac Merrit Singer improved upon Howe's invention (and also infringed on Howe's patent), and started his own sewing machine business that still prospers among home sewers and clothing factories (Bellis 2004). Singer's sewing machine was further evolved for the shoe industry by one of his own employees: Lyman Reed Blake. In 1856, Blake became a partner in a shoemaking company and was dedicated to inventing machines that helped automate the shoe-manufacturing process. In 1858, he received a patent for a machine that could stitch shoe uppers to outsoles. He sold his patent to Gordon McKay in 1859, and worked for McKay from 1861 until his retirement in 1874. The shoes made on this machine were known as "McKays" (United Shoe Machinery Corporation 2004).

Lasting Machine

The sewing machine was helpful in automating the shoemaking process, but it was not the ultimate solution of joining an upper to an outsole. A typical sewing machine cannot manipulate around small, curvy parts that exist in a shoe design, and it takes great skill to bend, shape, and hold the upper while it is stitched to the outsole. American immigrant Jan Matzeliger (from Dutch Guiana) helped revolutionize the shoe industry by developing a shoe lasting machine that could attach an outsole to an upper in one minute. His shoe lasting machine was able to adjust an upper snugly over a last (a foot form used for shoemaking), arrange the upper under the outsole and pin it in place with nails while the outsole is stitched to the upper. On March 20, 1883, the United States Patent Office awarded Matzeliger patent number 274,207 for his do-it-all shoe lasting machine (Tenner 2000, p. 37). The lasting machine revolutionized the shoe-making process as it could make hundreds of pairs of shoes a day and enabled the mass production of affordable shoes.

Early Sneaker Marketing

There are hundreds of companies that produce sneakers for the global marketplace. The first sneakers were manufactured and marketed by rubber companies, as they were the major producers of vulcanized rubber.

Dunlop Green Flash. The Dunlop rubber company in England can trace their first marketed sneaker (plimsoll) back to the 1870s. In 1933, their Green Flash collection was launched and proved to be very popular. It had a higher quality canvas upper and a better outsole (with a herringbone pattern) to provide good traction on grass tennis courts. Dunlop's Green Flash was worn by Fred Perry to win three Wimbledon titles (Heard 2003, pp. 290–291).

U.S. Rubber Keds. Keds was the first mass-marketed sneaker brand in the United States (1917), by U.S. Rubber. Much debate took place around naming U.S. Rubber's sneaker, as the initial favorite was Peds meaning, "foot" in Latin. Unfortunately another company trademarked the name, so U.S. Rubber narrowed the name down to two other possibilities—"Veds or Keds." Keds was chosen because the company felt that "K" was the strongest letter in the alphabet (Paquin). Another story says that the letter "K" represents the word "Kids," and that Keds is rhyming slang for Peds—the name that U.S. Rubber originally wanted to use for their sneaker (Vanderbuilt 1998, p. 22).

Converse Chuck Taylor. In 1908, Marquis M. Converse from Massachusetts was producing rubber galoshes and decided that he would like a more exciting career. In 1917, he introduced the Converse All-Star, a high-top sneaker designed especially for basketball. At the same time, Charles H. Taylor, a basketball player for the Akron Firestones, believed so much in Converse's shoe that he joined the sales force in 1921 and traveled across the United States promoting the All-Star Sneaker. He was so successful in promoting, selling, and making important changes to the original design that in 1923 his signature "Chuck Taylor" appeared on the ankle patch and the shoes were known as "Chucks" (Heard 2003, pp. 278–279). Converse's Chuck Taylor design is still popular around the world.

SHOELACES

Before shoelaces, shoes were typically fastened with metal buckles. The shoelace (lace and shoe holes) was invented in England (1790). An aglet is the small plastic or metal tube that binds the end of a shoelace to prevent it from fraying. It also allows the lace to pass easily through the shoe's eyelets or other openings (e.g., webbing/leather loops). The term "aglet" comes from the Latin word for "needle" (Bellis).

Modern Sneaker Marketing

Once the basic processes were established to make and market sneakers, companies other than rubber manufacturers were founded. These companies evolved technologies and created competition in the marketplace. Some of the most influential companies are reviewed chronologically.

Reebok. In the 1890s, Joseph William Foster from Bolton, England made some of the world's first known track spikes. Although track spikes are technically different than sneakers, Foster was interested in making athletes run faster by evolving shoe technologies. By 1895, he was in business making spikes for an international circle of distinguished runners. In 1924, J. W. Foster and Sons made the spikes worn in Summer Olympic Games by the athletes celebrated in the film *Chariots of Fire* (Vanderbuilt 1998, p. 11). In 1958, two of Fosters' grandsons started a companion company named Reebok (which went on to make sneakers), after the African gazelle. Reebok has grown to be one of the world's largest athletic shoe manufacturers, producing products for many sports like tennis, basketball, and cross-training.

New Balance. Location was another commonality between the first sneaker manufacturers, as talent and machinery were important in keeping manufacturers in business. Most came from England or the New England region of the United States, particularly Massachusetts. New Balance was one of those companies, and was established in 1906, by William J. Riley from Watertown, Massachusetts. Riley was a 33-year-old English immigrant who committed to help people with troubled feet by making personal arch supports and prescription footwear to improve shoe fit. Arch supports and prescription footwear remained the core of New Balance's business until 1961, when they manufactured the "Trackster," a performance running shoe (weighing 96 grams) that was made with a rippled rubber outsole and came in multiple widths (Heard 2003, pp. 48–49). The Trackster was the preferred shoe of college running coaches and YMCA fitness directors. Since the 1960s, New Balance's reputation for manufacturing performance footwear in multiple widths has grown through word of mouth and "grassroots" marketing programs for which they are still known.

Adidas. The first major non-English or American sneaker manufacturers were the Dassler brothers,

Adolf (nicknamed Adi) and Rudolf (nicknamed Rudi) who setup business in Herzogenaurach, Germany (1926). Their first sneakers cost two German Reich marks, and followed three guiding principles: to be the best shoes for the requirements of the sport, to protect athletes from injury, and to be durable. The Dasslers developed many firsts in the athletic shoe industry. Some of them included shoes with spikes and studs for soccer, track, and field. They also looked at constructing shoes with materials other than leather and canvas to reduce weight. By 1936, the Dasslers' shoes were internationally known, and were worn by many great athletes like Jesse Owens. In the Berlin 1936 Olympics, Owens won in almost every track and field event he competed in, earning four gold medals while wearing the Dasslers' shoes (Cheskin 1987, p. 11). Due to irreconcilable differences, Adi Dassler parted from his brother Rudi (1948), and they formed two separate shoe companies (Vanderbuilt 1998, p. 29). Rudi's company was called Puma, named after the powerful wild cat. Adi's company was called Adidas, where he took the first two syllables of his first and last name to create the famous name for his product line. To give support to the runner's midfoot, Adi created the three side stripes trademark in 1949 which is still used in almost every Adidas athletic shoe design (Heard 2003, pp. 90–93).

Onitsuka Tiger (ASICS). Although most sneakers in the early 2000s are manufactured in Asia, Onitsuka Tiger (later named ASICS) was the first Asian brand to make a statement in the sneaker market. Established in Kobe, Japan (1949), by Kihachiro Onitsuka, the company's philosophy was based on "bringing-up sound youth through sports." Onitsuka believed that playing sports was a solution to keeping kids out of prison, especially after World War II. The company's first shoes were made in Onitsuka's living room and resembled the Converse All-Star. Another philosophy of Onitsuka's was "harmony between human and science." In an interview with Onitsuka, he said: "We try to analyze all phenomena which affect a human body during sports and to make shoes which will meet the needs of the users is our principle toward the shoe making" (ASICS 2004). The company's name evolved to ASICS in 1977 based on the Latin phrase "Anima Sana In Corpore Sano," which translates to "A Sound Mind in a Sound Body." Although ASICS is a smaller company compared to the others mentioned, it is important to note, as it inspired the creation of Nike. Nike's founders,

Bill Bowerman and Phil Knight, started their careers in the sneaker business working for ASICS, where they designed, developed, and sold their products.

Nike. Of all the major sneaker companies, Nike is the youngest, yet the largest globally. Nike was a business venture between the track coach Bill Bowerman from the University of Oregon and Phil Knight (who ran for Bowerman). Bowerman always had a desire for better quality running shoes and was always tinkering with new ideas. He even made customized shoes for his own athletes. Bowerman was very inspirational to Knight, and while studying for his MBA at Stanford University in the early 1960s, he devised a small business plan for making quality running shoes, producing them in Japan, and shipping to the United States for distribution. After graduation, Knight traveled in 1963 to Japan to seek a way to live his dream. Representing Blue Ribbon Sports (BRS), he met with the president of Tiger ASICS (Onitsuka Company) and they agreed to go into business. Knight traveled throughout the West Coast of the United States and sold ASICS out of his car. Even Bowerman got involved and evolved some of the designs. Eventually the partners decided to split from the Onitsuka Company and create their own company. In 1971, Jeff Johnson (the first Nike employee) coined the name "Nike," and the Swoosh was created. The name originates from the Greek goddess of victory, and the famous Swoosh design was the creation of student Caroline Davidson, who was paid only $35 (Nike 2004). The first Nike shoe to feature the Swoosh was the Cortez in 1972. Product innovation and marketing has been key to Nike's success. By the end of the twentieth century, technologies like the waffle outsole, AIR, SHOX and legacies like Michael Jordan and Tiger Woods were just a few things that contributed to making Nike the largest sneaker company in the world.

Trainers. Technically, a sneaker is a shoe made of a canvas upper and a soft rubber outsole. What some refer to as a sneaker is much different and a more correct term to use is "trainer or "athletic shoe." Since the creation of the first sneaker-type construction, technology, fashion, and the desire for athletes to perform more efficiently and accurately have led to design evolution. The most typical types of sneakers are: running, cross-training, walking, basketball, and tennis. Technologies in materials have allowed sneakers to be made of synthetic leathers and 3D knits that are lightweight, breathable, and waterproof. A modern-day trainer could be as complicated as a shoe with an upper, midsole, insole, outsole, and shank. Within those parts, there are often subparts that better define each particular technology and give it its own specific performance advantage to others in the marketplace.

See also Shoemaking; Shoes.

Bibliography

Cheskin, Melvyn P. *The Complete Handbook of Athletic Footwear.* New York: Fairchild Publications, 1987.

Coye, Dale. "The Sneakers/Tennis Shoes Boundary." *American Speech* 61 (1986): 366–369.

Heard, Neal. *Sneakers: Over 300 Classics from Rare Vintage to the Latest Designs.* London: Carlton Books, 2003.

Hendrickson, Robert. *Facts on File Encyclopedia of Word and Phrase Origins.* New York: Facts on File Inc., 2000.

Tenner, Edward. "Lasting Impressions: An Ancient Craft's Surprising Legacy in Harvard's Museums and Laboratories." *Harvard Magazine* 103, no. 1 (September–October 2000): 37.

Vanderbuilt, Tom. *The Sneaker Book: Anatomy of an Industry and an Icon.* New York: The New Press, 1998.

Internet Resources

ASICS. "Special Interview: The Reasons Why I Keep Making Sports Shoes." ASICS Shoe History: Epochs of 1949–2000. Available from <http://asics.cyplus.com/index_e.html>.

Bellis, Mary. "Footware and Shoes: What You Need to Know About." Available from <http://inventors.about.com/library/inventors/blshoe.htm>.

Goodyear. "Charles Goodyear and the Strange Story of Rubber." Goodyear. Available from <http://www.goodyear.com/corporate/strange.html>.

"The History of Your Shoes." Shoe Info Net. Available from <http://www.shoeinfonet.com>.

Kippen, Cameron. "History of Sport Shoes." Curtin University of Technology: Department of Podiatry. Available from <http://podiatry.curtin.edu.au/sport.html#science>.

Nike Inc. "Niketimeline: From Humbling Beginnings to a Promising Future." Nikebiz.com, The Inside Story. Available from <http://www.nike.com/nikebiz>.

Paquin, Ethel. "From Creepers to High-tops: A Brief History of the Sneaker." Lands' End Catalog. Available from <http://www.landsend.com>.

Perrin, Charles L. "Athletic Shoes: Many Types, Many Nicknames." Charlie's Sneaker Pages. Available from <http://sneakers.pair.com>.

"Plimsoll Line." *Britannica Student Encyclopedia*. Encyclopedia Britannica Premium Service. Available from <http://www.britannica.com>.

Wagner, Christopher. "School Sandals." Historical Boys Clothing (HBC). Available from <http://histclo.hispeed.com/index3.html>.

Susan L. Sokolowski

SOCIAL CLASS AND CLOTHING

Display of wealth through dress became customary in Europe in the late thirteenth century. Therefore, a person's class affiliation could be assessed with relative ease. Because dress was recognized as an expressive and a potent means of social distinction, it was often exploited in class warfare to gain leverage. Dress was capable of signifying one's culture, propriety, moral standards, economic status, and social power, and so it became a powerful tool to negotiate and structure social relations as well as to enforce class differences.

For example, the sumptuary laws in Europe in the Middle Ages emerged as a way to monitor and maintain social hierarchy and order through clothes. People's visual representation was prescriptive, standardized, and regulated to the minutest detail. The types of dress, the length and width of the garment, the use of particular materials, the colors and decorative elements, and the number of layers in the garment, for instance, were confined to specific class categories. However, after society's lower-class groups relentlessly challenged the class structure and evaded the sumptuary laws' strictures, the laws were finally removed from statute books in the second half of the eighteenth century.

The sartorial expression of difference in social rank is also historically cross-cultural. For example, in China, a robe in yellow, which stood for the center and the earth, was to be used only by the emperor. In Africa among the Hausa community, members of the ruling aristocracy wore large turbans and layers of several gowns made of expensive imported cloth to increase their body size and thus set them apart from the rest of the society. In Japan, the colors of the kimono, its weave, the way it was worn, the size and stiffness of the obi (sash), and accoutrements gave away the wearer's social rank and gentility.

The History and Substance of Social Class System

Social class is a system of multilayered hierarchy among people. Historically, social stratification emerged as the consequence of surplus production. This surplus created the basis for economic inequality, and in turn prompted a ceaseless striving for upward mobility among people in the lower strata of society.

Those who possess or have access to scarce resources tend to form the higher social class. In every society this elite has more power, authority, prestige, and privileges than those in the lower echelons. Therefore, society's values and rules are usually dictated by the upper classes.

Social Class Theories

Philosopher and economist Karl Marx argued that class membership is defined by one's relationship to the means of production. According to Marx, society can be divided into two main groups: people who own the means of production and those who do not. These groups are in a perpetual, antagonistic relationship with one another, attempting either to keep up or reverse the status quo. Sociologist Max Weber extended Marx's ideas by contending that social class refers to a group of people who occupy similar positions of power, prestige, and privileges and share a life style that is a result of their economic rank in society.

Social class theories are problematic for a number of reasons. They often conceptualize all classes as homogenous entities and do not adequately account for the disparities among different strata within a particular social class. These theories also tend to gloss over geographic variants of class manifestations, such as urban and rural areas. A host of other factors, such as gender, race, ethnicity, religion, nationality, and even age or sexuality, further complicate the theories.

Social Class in the Twenty-First Century

In the twenty-first century, assessing one's social class is no longer a straightforward task because categories have become blurred and the boundaries are no longer well defined or fixed. Now one's social class would be decided by one's life-style choices, consumption practices, time spent on leisure, patterns of social interaction, occupation, political leanings, personal values, educational level, and/or health and nutritional standards.

Since, in global capitalism, inter-and intra-class mobility is not only socially acceptable but encouraged, people do not develop a singular class-consciousness or distinct class culture. Instead, they make an effort to achieve self-representation and vie for the acceptance of their chosen peer group. The progress of technology has also helped provide access to comparable and often identical status symbols to people of different class backgrounds across the globe. At the same time, however, as sociologist Pierre Bourdieu argues in his treatise *Distinction* (1984), the dominant social classes tend to possess not only wealth but "cultural capital" as well. In matters of dress, this capital manifests itself in the possession of refined taste and sensibilities that are passed down from generation to generation or are acquired in educational establishments.

Conspicuous Leisure, Consumption, and Waste

According to economist and social commentator Thorstein Veblen, the drive for social mobility moves fashion. In his seminal work, *The Theory of the Leisure Class* (1899), Veblen claims that the wealthy class exercised fashion leadership through sartorial display of conspicuous leisure, consumption, and waste. The dress of people in this group indicated that they did not carry out strenuous manual work, that they had enough disposable income to spend on an extensive wardrobe, and that they were able to wear a garment only a few times before deeming it obsolete.

Imitation and differentiation: Trickle-down, bubble-up, and trickle-across theories. Although sociologist Georg Simmel is not the sole author of the "trickle-down" theory, the general public still attributes it to him. In his article, *Fashion* (1904), Simmel argued that upper-class members of society introduce fashion changes. The middle and lower classes express their changing relationship to the upper classes and their social claims by imitating the styles set by the upper classes. However, as soon as they complete this emulation, the elite changes its style to reinforce social hierarchy. But as Michael Carter's research in *Fashion Classics* (2003) demonstrates, imitation and differentiation does not occur necessarily one after the other in a neat fashion.

Instead, there is an ongoing, dynamic interaction between the two. Besides, within each class as well as among the different classes, there is an internal drive to express and assert one's unique individuality.

By the 1960s, the fashion industry had begun to produce and distribute more than enough products for everyone to be able to dress fashionably. This democratization of fashion means that by the twenty-first century anyone across the world could imitate a new style instantaneously. The direction of fashion change is no longer unilinear—it traverses geographical places, and flows from both the traditional centers of style as well as "the periphery." Through global media and popular culture, members of the lower classes, and subcultural and marginal groups, have been able to influence fashion as much as those in the upper classes. Therefore, it has become more appropriate to talk about a "bubbleup" or "trickle-across" theory.

Although social class is no longer a significant category of social analysis, one remains cognizant of it. The display of one's social standing through dress has become more subtle, eclectic, and nonprescriptive. The key to assessment in the early 2000s is often in the details. Higher status is indicated by a perfectly cut and fitted garment, the use of natural and expensive fabrics, and brand-name wear. One's class affiliation is often given away only by the choice of accessories, such as eyeglasses, watches, or shoes. A stylish haircut, perfect and even teeth, and especially a slender body often have become more of a class signifier than dress itself.

See also Gender, Dress, and Fashion.

Bibliography

Bourdieu, Pierre. *Distinction*. Cambridge, Mass.: Harvard University Press, 1984.

Carter, Michael. *Fashion Classics from Carlyle to Barthes*. New York: Berg, 2003.

Crane Diana. *Fashion and Its Social Agendas*. Chicago: University of Chicago Press, 2000.

Damhorst, Mary Lynn, Kimberley A. Miller, and Susan O. Michelman, eds. *The Meanings of Dress*. New York: Fairchild Publications, 1999.

Davis, Fred. *Fashion, Culture, and Identity*. Chicago: University of Chicago Press, 1992.

Kaiser, Susan. *The Social Psychology of Clothing*. New York: Macmillan Publishing Company, 1990.

Simmel, Georg. "Fashion." *International Quarterly* 10: 130–155.

Veblen, Thorstein. *The Theory of the Leisure Class.* New York: Macmillan, 1899.

Katalin Medvedev

SPACE AGE STYLES

Humans did not walk on the moon until 1969, but their imminent arrival was slotted on the world's calendar from the very beginning of the decade. Space exploration's grip on the popular consciousness during the 1960s contributed to a new fashion philosophy, becoming a pool of design inspiration; an analog to speculation about a radically transformed future that preoccupied the sensibilities of the decade. In the April 1965 issue of *Harper's Bazaar*, Richard Avedon photographed British fashion model Jean Shrimpton wearing an astronaut's helmet and flight uniform. But it was hardly necessary to don an actual flight suit to be part of the styles that came to be known as "space age." Sleek as a fuselage, space age fashion emulated the aerodynamic simplicity and severity of a space capsule. Frills and flounces were eschewed in favor of a new, hard-edged and streamlined silhouette that also incorporated industrial materials. Space age fashion created a brusque and frequently shocking brave new universe within the 1960s fashion cosmos.

Blast off. As a design movement, space age fashion was above all a French phenomenon, promulgated mostly by men in their thirties who had been trained in the old-guard Paris couture, but saw the need to refute some of their pedigree. André Courrèges was perhaps the most creative. Courrèges was a member of Balenciaga's couture house for ten years before beginning his own business in 1961 in partnership with his wife Coqueline, who had also worked for Balenciaga. It took him but a couple of years to find his own feet, and when he did he kicked out the props from under establishment couture. "Things have never been the same since Courrèges had his explosion," Yves Saint Laurent said in a 1966 *Women's Wear Daily* (9 December, p. 1).

Before turning to fashion, Courrèges had dallied in both architecture and engineering, and this was reflected in his clothes. His dresses, suits, and trouser suits might be fitted, semi-fitted, or tubular, but they presented a bold and graphic silhouette, delineated as interlocking geometries by welt seaming and strategic piping. He preferred a restricted palette of monochromes and pastels, and was partial to aggressive checks and stripes. Courrèges used white a great deal, exploiting its myriad and contradictory connotations of sterility and/or purity as well as all-inclusive spectrum-spanning synergy.

Courrèges's work surely owed a debt to London ready-to-wear, but ever present in his work was the active, constructing hand of the couturier. His fabrics were flat, tailored wools, more intractable than what ready-to-wear was espousing. In a Courrèges suit a woman herself became a Brancusi-like distillation, an avatar of streamlined strength. Courrèges inveighed against the traditional appurtenances of femininity and foreswore the curvilinear. Reaching his meridian in 1964 and 1965, he advocated very short skirts as well as pants for all occasions, at the time a highly controversial proposition.

Women of the future. "Working women have always interested me the most," Courrèges said in *Life Magazine* in 1965. "They belong to the present, the future" (21 May, p. 57). Yet what he produced could not be easily transferred to the workplace, although his clothes and mass-manufactured imitations were seen on streets around the world. He offered what might be considered fashion manifestos. For him, high heels were as absurd as the bound feet of Asian women. He outfitted his models, instead, in flat Mary Jane slippers, or white boots that enhanced the graphic rectangularity of his silhouette.

After six years working for Balenciaga, Emanuel Ungaro assisted Courrèges for one year before opening his own doors in 1965. He also promised a radical departure from couture business-as-usual, pledging that there would be no evening clothes in this first collection, since he did not believe in them. He was certainly Courrèges's disciple during these years but his suits and dresses in childlike flaring shapes were gentle and more ingratiating. Essential to the success of the young house as unique fabrics designed exclusively for him by his partner Sonia Knapp. Knapp worked as closely with Ungaro as Coqueline Courrèges did with her husband.

A decade older than Courrèges or Ungaro, Pierre Cardin began his own business in 1957 after apprenticeships at several couture houses. During the epoch of space age, Cardin offered some of the couture's most outré designs, offered like so much during the 1960s as provocative hypothesis rather than empirical prototype. His shapes might resemble floral abstractions that devoured conventional clothing dimensions. His enormous collars and frequent use of vinyl evoked outerspace gear. Cardin was a Renaissance man whose many endeavors included his own theater. Both Courrèges and Ungaro established ready-to-wear and licensing franchises, but Cardin's endeavors were waged on an exponential scale. His empire included a highly successful men's wear line—"Cardin's cosmonauts" presented a complementary vision of men's apparel.

Like much of Cardin's ideas, Paco Rabanne pushed space age fashion toward wearable art. He too trained as an architect, then designed accessories, before the young designer created a sensation in 1966 with ready-to-wear sheaths of plastic squares and discs attached to fabric backing. They were *le dernier cri* of Paris fashion, memorably commemorated in William Klein's film of the same year, *Qui Etes Vous Polly McGoo*. For him the new and ultimate frontier of fashion had become "the finding of new materials." His investigation of plastics and other hardware as possible human carapaces proclaimed a new epoch in Paris's wonted tradition of clothes so intricately constructed that they could stand on their own.

Space age fashion was gestated in a salon environment that was just as stark and unadorned as the clothes. New-style fashion shows went hand in hand with the fashion experiments they showcased. They were hectic rather than stately, built around mysterious theatrical effects rather than the old-style hauteur.

Splashdown. In the early 2000s, space age styles seem a paradigm of the teleological mentality of the 1960s, a last glorification of industrialization before the realization of its downside. Hard-edged fashion stayed influential all through the 1960s, eventually being vanquished by the unconstructed fashion that prevailed during the first half of the 1970s. The leaders of space age fashion have all remained in vogue, and from time to time pay homage to their bellwether work of the 1960s.

See also Extreme Fashions; Futurist Fashion, Italian.

Bibliography

Lobenthal, Joel. *Radical Rags: Fashions of the Sixties*. New York: Abbeville Press, 1990.

Ryan, Ann, and Serena Sinclair. "Space Age Fashion." In *Couture*. Garden City, N.Y.: Doubleday, 1972.

Joel Lobenthal

SPORTSWEAR

At the beginning of the twenty-first century, "sportswear" describes a broad category of fashion-oriented comfortable attire based loosely on clothing developed for participation in sports. "Active sportswear" is the term used to cover the clothing worn specifically for sport and exercise activities. Now generally accepted as the most American of all categories of dress, sportswear has become, from the second half of the twentieth century, the clothing of the world. It consists of separate pieces that may be "mixed and matched," a merchandising term meaning that articles of clothing are designed to be coordinated in different combinations: trousers or shorts or skirts with shirts (either woven or knit, with or without collars, long-sleeved or short) and sweaters (either pullovers or cardigans) or jackets of a variety of sorts.

Pre-Twentieth Century

The origins of sportswear, so intimately tied to the rise of sports, are complex, arising from pervasive social change and cultural developments in the mid-nineteenth century. Previously, sport had been the domain of the landed well-to-do, revolving mostly around horses, shooting, and the hunt. Clothing generally was modified fashion wear, but distinctions between the clothing of the country and of town had appeared as early as the eighteenth century. Men, especially young men, wore the new collared, sometimes double-breasted, skirtless but tailed frock for shooting or country wear, itself probably adapted from the military uniform of the early eighteenth century. This coat was quickly adopted into fashionable dress for young gentlemen. Fox or stag hunting called for skirted coats and high boots to protect the legs, and for trim tailoring that would not hamper the rider maneuvering rough terrain and the new fences that were an outcome of the British Enclosure Acts (1760–1840). These acts, by transferring common grazing lands to private holdings, resulted in fences never needed before, thereby adding new challenges to cross-country riding and revolutionizing the sport of hunting.

The long, straight, narrow, severely tailored riding coats that emerged toward the end of eighteenth-century England traveled to France as the *redingote*, to become a high-fashion garment for both men and women for the next several decades, through the 1820s. Eventually, red coats became the acceptable color for the hunt, possibly for the obvious reason of making the riders more easily visible. As early as the eighteenth-century, women also adopted severely tailored riding coats based directly on men's styles, creating a standard that still characterizes women's sportswear in the early twenty-first century. Americans, both men and women, followed the English lead in sporting activity. These upper-class choices set the tone and provided the models for the future, but it took democratization to effect change overall. That came with the industrial revolution and the rise of leisure activity among even the poorer classes.

With the movement of the population away from its agrarian past into the cities, reformers realized that the working classes had no real outlets other than drinking for what little leisure time they had. In an era of revivalist fervor that preached temperance, the concerned middle classes sought other, safer avenues of activity for the poorer classes. Both active and spectator sport and games helped fill that gap. European immigrants to the United States, particularly those from Germany and the Scandinavian countries, brought a variety of outdoor sports and games for men with them, and an accompanying culture of health and exercise that they nurtured in their private clubs. Clothing for these activities was more relaxed than the street clothes of the time, and consisted often of a shirt and trouser combination. Native-born Americans also had had a long history of team games, early versions of various ball games that continued to be played once the population moved to the cities. However, it was baseball, with its singular attire, that most influenced men's clothing for sport. Baseball had emerged as a popular team game with new rules after the first meeting of the elite New York Knickerbocker Base Ball Club with the New York Nines at Elysian Fields in Hoboken, New Jersey, on 19 June 1846. By the 1850s, many other more democratic clubs of workers played the game as well, quickly turning it into America's favorite sport. In 1868, the Cincinnati Redstockings were the first major team to adopt a uniform of bloused shirt, baggy knee breeches, and sturdy knee socks. The unusual pants, so different from the long stove-pipe trousers of the time, were named after Washington Irving's seventeenth-century character, Dietrich Knickerbocker—not coincidentally the same surname the first baseball team in America had adopted as its own. These became the accepted trouser for active sports in general, and were dubbed "knickerbockers" after the original team. Knickerbockers's success may be seen in their appearance for the next

century for shooting, bicycling, hiking, and golf. By the 1920s, they were even worn by women.

Active sports uniforms and clothing grew out of necessity. Players needed protection from bodily harm in contact sports like football and hockey; they also needed to let the body breathe and enable it to move as easily and freely as possible while performing the sport. The entire history of active sports clothing is tied to higher education, the increasingly rapid developments in textile technology, and the Olympics. For example, football, a new and favorite game in men's colleges in the late nineteenth century, adopted a padded leather knickerbocker, pairing it with another innovation, the knitted wool jersey pullover. Lightweight wool jersey, an English invention of the 1880s, was perfect for men's sporting pullovers (which soon were referred to as "jerseys"). Perhaps the most enduring of these has been the rugby shirt—striped, collared, and ubiquitous. It had its beginnings as the uniform for the "new" nineteenth-century game begun at the venerable British school, Rugby, but proved so enduring that it is still worn in the early 2000s, by men, women and children who never thought of playing the game. Jersey was equally adopted into women's dress for sport as well. The new lawn tennis of the 1870s was ripe for a flexible fabric that allowed greater movement, and jersey filled that need by the 1880s. In that same decade, students in the new women's colleges left behind their corsets, petticoats, and bustles for simpler gathered dirndl-style skirts and jersey tops taken directly from men's styles in order to participate in sports like crew and baseball. At the same time, men's schools added a heavier outer layer of wool knit to keep the body warm, and since athletic activity brought on healthy sweating, "sweater" clearly described its role. When a high roll collar was added, the "turtleneck," still a staple of sportswear, was born. The college environment was important because it allowed a looser, less rigid, more casual kind of clothing on campuses frequently isolated from the formality of fashionable urban attire. Soon after the introduction of these pieces of specific clothing for sports in collegiate settings, women borrowed them, wearing them for their own sports and leisurewear from the end of the nineteenth century and on.

The modern Olympic Games introduced new generations of active sportswear. From the first meet in 1896, men appeared in very brief clothing to compete in track and field and swimming events: singlets, or tank tops, with above-the-knee shorts, and knit—sometimes fine wool and sometimes silk—skin-baring one-piece suits for swim competition. More surprising than these were the bikini-like liners that men wore under the sheer silk suits, without the tops, as typical practice garb. These items became the clothing for sport for men as the century progressed; even the briefs under the suits found their way into swimwear for men and women some half-century or so after their introduction.

Twentieth Century

Fabrics have played an important role in the development of active sportswear. As with sheer knits at the turn of the twentieth century, so too did stretch fabrics form a second skin shaving seconds off time in competition. From the introduction of Lastex in the 1930s to the spandex of the twenty-first century, clothing for active sports has reflected the attention to sleek bodies, to speed. Speedo, the Australian swimwear company, first introduced its one-piece stretchy suit in the 1950s. From that time on, swimwear became sleeker, tighter but more comfortable because of the manufactured stretch fibers. The concept proved irresistible for men and women in all active sports: new stretch textiles produced ski pants in the 1930s fashioned with stirrups to anchor the sleek lines, bicycle shorts in the 1970s, all-in-one cat suits for skiing, sledding, sailing, speed skating, even running in the 1980s and 1990s. With the biannual Olympic publicity, the new active suits, shorts, and tops found their way into active sportswear and onto athletic bodies everywhere. Even the nonathlete wanted the look, pressing fashion-wear manufacturers to adopt the tight-fitting yet comfortable clothing that technology had made possible.

Sportswear, as opposed to active sportswear, fulfills an entirely different role. Though their roots are the same, sportwear concerns the fashionable aspect of clothing for sport rather than the athletic. Individual items such as jerseys, sweaters, and turtlenecks came directly out of active sports. Certain jackets also became linked with sports and therefore sportswear. The most notable of these, still a staple of modern dress, is the blazer. This standard straight-cut lounge jacket of the late nineteenth century was adapted both by colleges and early sports clubs, the new tennis, golf, or country clubs that emerged in the 1870s and 1880s, who used their own club colors for these jackets, often fashioning them in stripes called "blazes." Hence, blazers. Striped blazers, popular through the 1920s, have had revivals since, most notably in the late 1950s and 1960s. Generally, however, they gave way to single-colored blazers

in the 1930s. The best recognized of these is the bright green Masters jacket of golf.

For women's leisure wear (and it must be noted that women never wore this casual, "new" clothing in any other setting), women adopted men's clothing, as they had earlier. This had been noticeable in the 1890s with the clothes of the New Woman, with her blazer, shirtwaist, and easy skirt, or even, on occasion (though not as routinely as is now believed) with divided skirts for such activities as bicycling. By the turn of the twentieth century, young women wore jerseys, turtleneck sweaters, and cardigans, borrowed directly from their brothers. In addition, many chose to leave off their corsets when participating in active activities, opting instead for lighter, unboned "sporting waists." This last move was perhaps the most forward-thinking of all in affecting change in women's dress. Magazines of the day picked up the new "daring" fashions, with illustrations, to spread them across the country. Early movies, even those prior to the 1920s, also helped distribute and popularize the new styles, showing beautiful young women dressed for all sorts of activities: swimming, golf, tennis and, as time went on, simply for leisure. So the foundations had been laid in the nineteenth century, but the phenomenon of sportswear for women really began in the 1920s with the post–World War I emergence of mass production in women's wear.

The new loose, unfitted styles of the 1920s allowed a much freer approach to women's dress for play and leisure. Although women still clung to skirts, the dresses for such sports as golf and tennis were so admired

Rugby players. A group of rugby players, wearing the striped shirts after which their sport is named. © Duomo/Corbis. Reproduced by permission.

(to say nothing of the sports figures who wore them, like Suzanne Lenglen, a French tennis champion, and later, Babe Didrickson) that they became day dresses for women whose lifestyles and pocketbooks allowed variety in their clothing. These golf and tennis dresses, with their pleated skirts and tailored tops, sometimes two-piece and sometimes one, comfortable and washable, became the prototypes for the most American of all clothing, the shirtwaist dress. So welcome were tennis dresses that in the 2000s they still prevail over shorts for competition tennis and, as early as the 1940s, offered a new, short skirt length that eventually became accepted into fashion wear.

Trousers for women were another matter. The struggle for their acceptance was a long one, dating from the early nineteenth century when, as baggy "Turkish trowsers," they were introduced for water cures and exercise, then later adopted as dress reform. It was sport, however, that provided the reason for their acceptance, as long as they were kept within strictly sex-segregated environments like the emerging women's colleges or all-women gyms. The heavy serge bifurcated bloomers worn for the new game of basketball were the first acceptable pants for women, and worn with turtlenecked sweaters in the early part of the twentieth century, became an outfit for magazine pinups. The bloomers slimmed down by the 1920s, becoming the popular knickers of that decade, and the introduction of beach pajamas for leisurewear at the same time led to further acceptance, even if not worn in town settings.

The movies helped to sell the image of women in trousers, especially in the 1930s with actresses like Katharine Hepburn and Marlene Dietrich. Even then, women did not wear pants for fashion wear. World War II changed their image, when trousers became the norm for factory workers, but still, pants were not acceptable for the average woman except when she was on vacation or in the country. Indeed, trousers were not accepted for professional working women until the end of the 1970s or early 1980s. But since that time, trousers have become the norm for women everywhere, professionals and vacationers alike, proving once again that women borrow their most comfortable clothing from men's wear.

Mass manufacturing made the simple items of ready-to-wear sportswear inexpensive and practical for everyone. The notion of designing separates to go together in coordinated fashion, a key concept of sportswear, began in New York in the mid-1920s

when Berthe Holley introduced a line of separates that could be interchanged to suggest a larger wardrobe. The concept of easy separates for leisurewear in resort or casual surroundings, if not for more formal wear, grew in the 1930s and finally took hold for more general wear in the 1940s, during World War II. American designers such as Claire McCardell, Clare Potter, and Bonnie Cashin turned to designing ready-made American sportswear, using inexpensive fabrics and following the easy, comfortable styles that made it so popular in the United States. Companies such as B. H. Wragge in the 1940s marketed well-designed separates, particularly to the college-aged crowd, at inexpensive prices that they could afford. After the war, with manufacturing back to prewar norms and the introduction of the more formal New Look from France, the distinction between American and Parisian clothing became even more evident. American designers more and more turned to the casual expressions in fashion that American women loved. By midcentury, the great designers who captured the essence of American style, Bill Blass and Geoffrey Beene, had begun to be recognized, and were turning their attention to ready-to-wear sportswear. Eventually they even brought sportswear ideas into eveningwear, directly translating the shirts, sweaters, and skirts women were so attached to into elegance for evening. Finally, toward the later twentieth century, Ralph Lauren took what had become the staples of sportswear—jackets, sweaters, shirts, pants, and skirts—and gave them a distinctly upper-class edge by reviving the elegance of the club-based sports clothing of the 1930s and 1940s. These later twentieth-century designers captured the American Look and made it their own, turning the higher end of sportswear back to its origins by appealing to the upper classes. But by then, the style of dress known as sportswear was open to all, in all classes and levels of society, through mass manufacturing and mass marketing. A truly American style, sportwear has spread throughout the world, representing a first in clothing history.

See also Activewear; Blazer; Lauren, Ralph; Sport Shirt; Sweater; Swimwear.

Bibliography

Armitage, John. *Man at Play: Nine Centuries of Pleasure Making.* London and New York: Frederick Warne and Co., 1977.

Mackay-Smith, Alexander, et al. *Man and the Horse*. New York: The Metropolitan Museum of Art and Simon and Schuster, 1984.

Milbank, Caroline Rennolds. *New York Fashion: The Evolution of American Style*. New York: Harry N. Abrams, 1996.

Schreier, Barbara A. "Sporting Wear." In *Men and Women: Dressing the Part*. Edited by Claudia Brush Kidwell and Valerie Steele. Washington, D.C.: Smithsonian Institution, 1989, pp. 102–103.

Warner, Patricia Campbell. "The Gym Suit: Freedom at Last." In *Dress in American Culture*. Edited by Patricia A. Cunningham and Susan Voso Lab. Bowling Green, Ohio: Popular Press, Bowling Green State University, 1992, pp. 140–179.

Patricia Campbell Warner

STREET STYLE

Street style has always existed. It is, however, only since the mid-1950s that its significance has been recognized, valued, and emulated.

Why this change? Arguably the most profound and distinctive development of the twentieth century was this era's shift from high culture to popular culture—the slow but steady recognition that innovation in matters of art, music, and dress can derive from all social strata rather than, as previously, only from the upper classes. As much as, for example, the twentieth century's accreditation of jazz, blues, folk, and tango as respected musical forms, the reevaluation of street style as a key source of innovation in dress and appearance—in the early 2000s, a principle engine of the clothing industry—demonstrates this democratization of aesthetics and culture.

With the development of that system of perpetual style change that is called "fashion" (in the Renaissance), most new designs "trickled down" the socioeconomic ladder to be copied by anyone who could afford to do so. This system was still the order of the day in 1947 when Christian Dior launched his "New Look": first available only to a tiny, wealthy elite, the tight-waisted and full, voluminous hem of this design rapidly became available in department stores (and via patterns for home sewing) throughout the West. (Interestingly, one of the first prominent British street style "tribes," the Teddy Boys, might be seen as another example of the "trickle down" principle in that the distinctive styling of their extra-long jackets—and even their name—was copied from the "edwardian" style fashionable amongst some upper-class British men.)

Yet even as the "New Look" demonstrates the extent to which—in the middle of the twentieth century—the high-fashion world remained largely impervious to influences from outside the tight sphere of elite designers and their wealthy customers, a broader perspective on dress reveals a growing appreciation of styles and fabrics with distinct, explicit working or lower-class roots and connotations. Denim is a good example of this: originally worn only by male manual workers, the 1947 and 1948 Sears & Roebuck catalogs both feature casual wear for women and children made from this material. While the designs and catalog presentation of these garments promotes the symbolic context of cowboys and the "Wild West" rather than urban manual labor, it could be argued that the cowboy was the first "working-class hero." At around the same time, the flamboyant, extrovert, and extravagant zoot-suited "hipster" styles of black jazz musicians and (at the other extreme stylistically) the rough and ready look of the Bikers (models for Brando in *The Wild One*) were increasingly influencing the dress style of the sort of middle-class male who previously had looked only to upper-class style (and upper-class sports) for sartorial inspiration. Thus, even before the end of the first half of the twentieth century, one finds significant examples of "bubble up" replacing the previously all-pervasive "trickle down" process; of the upper class loosening its stranglehold on "good taste" in matters of dress and, therefore, the emergence of street style as a potent and energizing force.

A Positive View of Street Style

The dramatic increase in the standardization of life after World War II (suburbanization, mass marketing, the franchising of restaurant and retail chains, the spread of television, and so on) may have increased the appeal of "alternative" lifestyles for individuals in search of "authenticity." The clothing styles of both the "outlaw" and those "from the wrong side of the tracks" became attractive as symbolic totems of escape from the bland (un)reality of what many cultural theorists have termed "late capitalism."

Important also was the astounding demographic blip of the "baby boomers" born just after World War II. As this generation grew up in the late 1950s and early

1960s, they came to represent a new sociocultural category—the "teenager"—who, by sheer dint of numbers and the fact that, by and large, they had money to spend, became a significant focus of the economic and cultural worlds. Slow off the mark in its embrace of "youth culture" (and still determinedly upper class and elitist), high fashion had little to offer the average baby-boom teenager who saw street style as a hipper, more authentic, and relevant source of stylistic inspiration. Every street "look" (beat, mod, rockabilly, biker, etc.) brought with it an entire lifestyle package of values and beliefs, a philosophy and, it was often hoped, a new, alternative, community.

This admiration of street style was especially true of young males. Fashionable male dress reached a crescendo of blandness in the 1950s with the typical, middle-class Western male reduced to near sartorial invisibility. It comes as no surprise, therefore, that street style in the twentieth century was as biased toward men (hipsters, beats, teddy boys, bikers, mods, hippies, psychedelics, skinheads, glam rockers, punks, new romantics, goths, casuals, b-boys, etc.) as fashion has been biased toward women. The rise of street style represents the return of the peacock male from near extinction and this undoubtedly plays a key part in its rising popularity and importance.

Finally, mention should be made of the importance of street style as a facilitator of group identity and subcultural cohesion. Since the close of World War II, Western culture has seen a dramatic decline in the significance of the traditional sociocultural divisions such as class, race, religion, ethnicity, regionalism, nationalism, and so on in defining and limiting personal identity. While liberating and egalitarian, this diminishing of the importance of such traditional sociocultural groupings created a huge amorphous, undifferentiated, homogenous mass within which a sense of community— "People Like Us"—became more problematic. The "tribelike" groupings of, for example, bikers, beats, and teddy boys in the 1950s; mods, hippies, and skinheads in the 1960s; headbangers, punks, and b-boys in the 1970s; and goths, new age travelers and ravers in the 1980s, offered a much needed sense of community—especially for teenagers who, beginning to separate from the parental family but not yet having created their own family unit, feel this need most acutely. Significantly, while throughout human history sociocultural groups have always used dress and body decoration styles to signal and reinforce their group identities and their shared culture, now, for the first time, one's appearance and

style became a sociocultural glue which, it was hoped, would bind together disparate strangers—most of whom would never meet but all of whom shared a culture encrypted in a particular style of dress and music.

From the 1940s through the 1980s street style coalesced into dozens if not hundreds of alternative "tribes"—each with its own complex, integrated subcultural system of style, values, and beliefs. Many of these evolved, distinguishing one from the other (hipsters to beats to hippies) while others developed in an antagonistic process energized by opposition (mods/rockers, hippies/punks). In the process, a complex family tree of "styletribes" has spanned (and in many ways defined) several generations.

An Advertisement of Self

Street style "tribes" offered (and, for many, seem to have provided) that sense of community and shared identity that is so difficult to find in contemporary society. But while significant remnants of many of these subcultures remain scattered around the globe, such commitment and group identity have become less typical of the twenty-first century. Such looks are now, typically, plucked off the shelf of the post-modern "supermarket of style," tried out, promiscuously mixed with other looks, and then discarded.

However, while street style may now have entered a post-tribal phase, this is not to suggest that its

Skateboarders. A group of teenage skateboarders pose for a picture in Manhattan. Many teenagers reject conventional fashions, instead developing their own street styles to better reflect their identities. © Rose Hartman/Corbis. Reproduced by permission.

importance has diminished, since fashion, in its strict, traditional sense, no longer structures and empowers most of the clothing industry. As the supreme expression of modernism, fashion's orderly, lineal production of new, "New Looks" and the consensus in the form of a singular, progressive "direction" that it demanded, is ill-suited to the complexity and pluralism of the postmodern age within which the possibility of progress, the value of uniformity, and the desirability of transience are increasingly questioned.

Originally attractive because of its perceived "authenticity," its offer of "alternative" choice and its capacity to "say" something significant about those who wear it, street style has moved into a key position within the clothing industry in a postmodern age characterized by a crises of identity, truth, and meaning. This is to say, not only has the "fashion industry" come to increasingly and persistently look to "the street" for design inspiration, but, more significantly, that how clothing functions in the early 2000s from the perspective of the consumer—how it is purchased, worn, and valued—is more rooted in the history of street style than in the history of high fashion. Consumers have, in other words, moved a very long way indeed from the world of Dior's "New Look" in 1947 and the direction of this movement is commensurate with that approach to dress and appearance that has come to be known as "street style."

The "bubbling up" of stylistic inspiration (often, modeled by up-and-coming pop musicians) has become widespread within every segment of the clothing industry including "High Fashion." Moreover, street style's delight in "timeless classics" and its disdain for the ephemeral (Hell's Angels never coveted "This Season's New Biker Look") is seen in a widespread resistance to throwing out everything in one's wardrobe just because some fashion journalist might claim that "brown is the new black." While once the consumer sought out a "total look" from a particular designer, it is increasingly thought that only a pathetic "fashion victim" takes such a passive approach. Thus, the construction of a presentation of self is increasingly seen as the work of the creative individual.

To this end, in a process that can be traced directly back to the Punks, the twenty-first century consumer—using garments and accessories from different designers, brands, or charity shops as "adjectives"—samples and mixes an eclectic (often even contradictory) range of looks into a personal style statement. This emphasis on what a look has to "say" also largely derives from street style. While pure fashion articulated only "This

Motorcycle gang from *The Wild One*. Johnny Strabler (Marlon Brando, center) and his motorcycle gang from the 1953 film *The Wild One*, which helped to popularize the tough, leather-clad look of bikers, is an early example of a street style influencing fashion. © John Springer Collection/Corbis. Reproduced by permission.

is new and I am therefore fashionable," street style was always deeply resonate with more complex personal (even philosophical and political) meanings—a choice of cut or color or fabric calculated to convey a precise summary of attitude and lifestyle. Street style obliged the individual to wear his or her values and beliefs on the sleeve—in a way that more often than not required commitment and courage. Arguably, it is this capacity to give visual expression to where one is "at"—to articulate personal differences and, therefore, to create the possibility of interpersonal connection between like-minded individuals—which, in an age of too much communication and too little meaning, is street style's most valuable legacy.

See also Hippie Style; Punk; Subcultures; Teenage Fashions; Zoot Suit.

Bibliography

Chenoune, Farid. *A History of Men's Fashion*. Paris: Flammarion, 1993.

Hebdige, Dick. *Subculture: The Meaning of Style*. London: Methuen and Co., 1979. A key text in the development of subcultural theory.

MacInnes, Colin. *Absolute Beginners*. London: Allison and Busby, 1992. A novel that was originally published in 1959.

McRobbie, Angela, ed. *Zoot Suits and Second-hand Dresses: An Anthology of Fashion and Music*. London: Macmillan, 1989.

Melly, George. *Revolt into Style: The Pop Arts in the 50s and 60s*. Oxford: Oxford University Press, 1989. A classic text; originally published in 1970.

Muggleton, David. *Inside Subculture: The Post-Modern Meaning of Style*. Oxford: Berg, 2000.

Muggleton, David, and Rupert Weinzierl, eds. *The Post-Subcultures Reader*. New York: New York University Press, 2003.

Olian, JoAnne. *Everyday Fashions of the Forties: As Pictured in Sears Catalogs*. New York: Dover Publications, Inc., 1992.

Polhemus, Ted. *Streetstyle: From Sidewalk to Catwalk*. London: Thames and Hudson, Inc., 1994. A summary of all significant "styletribes" from 1940s to 1990s; includes book, music, and film references for all groups in "Further Information."

———. *Style Surfing: What to Wear in the 3rd Millennium*. London: Thames and Hudson, Inc., 1996.

Redhead, Steve. *Subculture to Clubcultures: An Introduction to Popular Cultural Studies*. Oxford: Blackwell Publishers, 1997.

———, ed. *The Clubcultures Reader: Readings in Popular Cultural Studies*. Oxford: Blackwell Publishers, 1998.

Ted Polhemus

STRIPTEASE

Publicists coined the word striptease in the late 1920s. It is still an evocative word, bringing to mind the lurid image of a busty, 1950s performer bumping and grinding in tasseled pasties and a sequined g-string. This icon of overtly commercial sexuality had its heyday in the 1950s, but the history of the striptease reaches as far back as the nineteenth century.

Starting in the 1850s, what is often referred to as the "scandal of tights" swept through America. Flesh-colored stockings were worn on the stage by comediennes, chorines, and cancan dancers revealing limbs that had been all but eliminated from the fashionable silhouette. The costume shocked audiences, but was allowed by censors since it had originated on ostensibly respectable stages in Europe, such as the Gaiety in London and the Folies Bergère in Paris. These nineteenth-century performers never actually disrobed, but they

were harassed, fined, and occasionally jailed for pulling up their skirts, flashing their underwear, and swiveling their hips in a way that evoked the throes of passion. In 1893, the American purveyors of the tights-clad leg show, found mainly in burlesque and vaudeville theaters, shed even more clothes in order to adapt the "exotic" dance of the Chicago World's Fair's Little Egypt (whose performance launched the first and longest-lived euphemism for the stripteaser: exotic dancer).

The element of bare flesh was introduced around the turn of the century at the tea parties of socialite ladies. Early modern dancers like Isadora Duncan, Ruth St. Denis, and Maud Allan scandalized moralists with the degree of physical exposure in the costumes for their dances that were launched through the patronage of wealthy women interested in Orientalist art and culture. Duncan performed at ladies' matinees in bare feet and without tights, dressed only in a classical gown (made at first of her mother's muslin curtains). St. Denis adopted the exotic dance of the World's Fairs and dressed in ultra-sheer and bejeweled net garments. Allan developed a Dance of the Seven Veils based on the biblical story of Salome that was so popular that prominent women were inspired to hold a costume party of Salome-style dress. Through the popularity of modern dancers, a formula was filtered into American popular theater where numerous young women reduced their stage costumes to gauzy skirts, beaded bras, and bared midriffs in an effort to interpret foreign cultures, real and imagined, through the art of dance.

By the 1910s, the first accounts of striptease appeared on the heels of the advent of modern dance. Vaudeville historian Joe Laurie, Jr. claimed that vaudeville headliner Eva Tanguay let the veils drop in her version of the Salome dance in 1912. Morton Minsky claimed that burlesque performer Mae Dix invented it when she removed the detachable collar and cuffs of her costume in full view of the audience in order to save on her cleaning bill. Former stripteaser Ann Corio credited Hinda Wassau with inventing the act when forced to shimmy out of a chorus costume that had caught on the beads of the ensemble worn beneath for purposes of a quick change. The "Glorified Girls" featured in the mainstream Broadway revue of Florenz Ziegfeld, Jr. also made nudity more and more acceptable on the stage with opulent *tableaux* such as "Lady Godiva's Ride" in the *Follies of 1919*.

The acceptance of nudity necessitated bawdy entertainment to up the ante further in order to secure their lucratively raunchy reputations. The result was striptease. The precedent of nudity established by modern dancers implied artistic motives. The striptease represented a return to the flash-and-tickle approach of populist vaudeville dancers. That was infinitely more appealing to male audiences and it was achieved not through nudity, but through an undressing that mimicked the disrobing which preceded a sexual encounter. The formula was simple: the slow parade of a beautiful girl in a beautiful gown; the removal of stockings, gloves, hairpins; the slow shimmy out of the clinging, formal dress; and the briefest wriggle in only a g-string. Nudity made artistic became artistry made erotic.

Four burlesque producer brothers named Minsky became inextricably connected with striptease in the 1920s. Their publicists, George Alabama Florida and Mike Goldreyer, came up with the name for it and promoted its finest practitioners. These included Margie Hart, Georgia Southern, Ann Corio, and the incomparable Gypsy Rose Lee. When the Great Depression came, the Minskys were able to lease a theater on Broadway. Gypsy Rose Lee thrived in Minsky shows during this era and set the tone for high-style striptease as an extremely beautiful woman who was also an engaging comedienne and natural-born celebrity. The Minskys were so successful that theater producers and real-estate interests (along with some conservative religious organizations) banded together to get the act of striptease itself banned in New York City. They succeeded in 1937 when the word burlesque and the name Minsky were banned in New York City, and all the theaters that featured striptease were shut down. Similar bans followed in other cities across the nation.

Throughout the 1940s, a few burlesque houses survived and Minsky strippers used their fame to headline shows on carnival midways. In the years following the crackdown on striptease, some concessions were made to avoid trouble with the law. The use of pasties to cover the aureolas was the most noticeable change, but the addition of sequins, rhinestones, and tassels changed pasties from a handicap to an innovation. As nightclubs entered a boom following World War II, striptease came back in style again. A 1954 Newsweek article reported that the number of stripteasers had quadrupled since the 1930s and that 50 nightclubs in New York City featured striptease. The article gleefully recounts the props in the shows (snakes, monkeys, macaws, doves, parakeets, stuffed horses, swimming tanks, and bubble baths); the cost of the costumes ($850 to $1,000 for Lili St. Cyr's Vegas act); and the stage names in use (Carita La Dove—the Cuban Bombshell, Evelyn West—the

$50,000 Treasure Chest Girl). The star performers of this era employed all the over-the-top shtick of 50 years of vaudeville in their acts. Blaze Starr had a red settee, which she had tricked out with a fan, canned smoke, and a piece of bright silk that would appear to go up in flames. Lili St. Cyr did interpretive striptease based on *Salome, Carmen, The Picture of Dorian Gray*, and *Sadie Thompson*. Tempest Storm promoted herself relentlessly, dating celebrities and accepting a mock award from Dean Martin and Jerry Lewis for having the two biggest props in Hollywood. These acts were so popular that in 1951 Frenchman Alain Bernadin opened the Crazy Horse Saloon in Paris to bring American-style striptease to European cabaret audiences. Another garish heyday for striptease had arrived. But by the 1960s, that heyday had come and gone.

In the decades that followed, striptease was rejected in favor of the direct appeal of already bare flesh. The topless trend kicked off in the mid-1960s when a go-go dancer at a San Francisco strip club performed in Rudi Gernreich's topless bathing suit without getting arrested. Topless lunches, topless shoeshines, and other mundane acts improved by toplessness were featured in the clubs that had showcased striptease. Bottomlessness logically followed. By the 1970s, the hugely profitable pornography industry almost eclipsed live nude girls altogether. Crackdowns on the pornography industry in the 1980s encouraged a resurgence of striptease, but much of the glamour and humorous shtick of 1950s striptease was excised in favor of the intimacy of the lap dance for an audience of one and as a result, the theatrically-inclined tassel-twirling stripteaser was replaced by the more readily accessible silicone-enhanced bottle blond with one leg wrapped around a metal pole.

Bibliography

Alexander, H. M. *Strip Tease: The Vanished Art of Burlesque.* New York: Knight Publishers, 1938.

Allen, Robert C. *Horrible Prettiness: Burlesque and American Culture.* Chapel Hill: University of North Carolina Press, 1991.

Cherniasky, Felix. *The Salome Dancer: The Life and Times of Maud Allan.* Toronto, Ontario: McClelland and Stewart, Inc., 1991.

Corio, Ann with Joseph DiMona. *This Was Burlesque.* New York: Madison Square Press/Grosset and Dunlap, 1968.

Derval, Paul. *Folies-Bergere.* New York: E. P. Dutton and Co., Inc., 1955.

Fields, Armond, and L. Marc Fields. *From the Bowery to Broadway: Lew Fields and the Roots of American Popular Theater.* New York and Oxford, U.K.: Oxford University Press, 1993.

Jarret, Lucinda. *Stripping in Time: A History of Erotic Dancing.* London: Pandora-Harper, 1977.

Laurie, Joe, Jr. *Vaudeville: From the Honky-Tonks to the Palace.* New York: Henry Holt and Company, 1953.

Lee, Gypsy Rose. *Gypsy.* Berkeley, Calif: Frog, Ltd., 1957.

Macdougall, Allan Ross. *Isadora: A Revolutionary in Art and Love.* New York: Thomas Nelson and Sons, 1960.

Mariel, Pierre and Jean Trocher. *Paris Cancan.* Translated by Stephanie and Richard Sutton. London: Charles Skilton Ltd., 1961.

Minsky, Morton. *Minsky's Burlesque.* New York: Arbor, 1986.

Parker, Derek and Julia Parker. *The Natural History of the Chorus Girl.* Indianapolis, Ind., and New York: Bobbs-Merrill, 1975.

Shelton, Suzanne. *Divine Dancer: A Biography of Ruth St. Denis.* New York: Doubleday, 1981.

Sobel, Bernard. *Burleycue: An Underground History of Burlesque Days.* New York: Farrar and Rinehart, Inc., 1931.

——. *A Pictorial History of Burlesque.* New York: Bonanza Books, 1956.

Starr, Blaze and Huey Perry. *Blaze Starr: My Life as Told to Huey Perry.* Warner Paperback Library Edition. New York: Praeger Publishers, Inc., 1975.

Stencell, A. W. *Girl Show: Into the Canvas World of Bump and Grind.* Toronto, Ontario, Canada: ECW Press, 1999.

Storm, Tempest. *The Lady Is a Vamp.* Atlanta, Ga.: Peachtree Publishers, Ltd., 1987.

Zeidman, Irving. *The American Burlesque Show.* New York: Hawthorn Books, Inc., 1967.

Ziegfeld, Richard and Paulette. *The Ziegfeld Touch: The Life and Times of Florenz Ziegfeld, Jr.* New York: Harry N. Abrams, 1993.

Jessica Glasscock

SUBCULTURES

A point on which many costume historians have concurred is that fashion, as it is currently understood—the propensity for continual change in clothing designs, colors, and tastes—is a relatively recent phenomenon in the history of humankind, virtually unknown before the fourteenth century and occurring only with the emergence of mercantile capitalism, the concomitant growth in global trade, and the rise of the medieval city. (Among the few exceptions are Tang Dynasty China and Heian Period Japan.) Other scholars have analyzed fashion as an aspect of a distinctively modern and Western consumer culture that first gained impetus in the eighteenth century, concurrent with the onset of the industrial revolution. Either way, to be "fashionable" in this sense of the term must not be understood as a natural, universal, or biologically given aspect of human behavior, but as a socially and historically specific condition. Fashion is, in other words, a cultural construction. Its very existence, form, and direction are dependent on the complex interplay of quite specific economic, political, and ideological forces.

If fashion is cultural then fashion subcultures are groups organized around or based upon certain features of costume, appearance, and adornment that render them distinctive enough to be recognized or defined as a subset of the wider culture. Depending on the group in question, subcultures may be loosely or tightly bounded; their collective identification may be self-attributed or imputed to them by outsiders. A particular gender, age span, social class, or ethnic identity may dominate membership. Subcultures often create their own distinctiveness by defining themselves in opposition to the "mainstream"—the accepted, prescribed, or prevailing fashion of the period. They may be either radical and forward-looking or reactionary and conservative in relation to the dominant mode of dressing: in either case, they aim toward exclusivity. Thus, while these subcultures may depend upon fashion for their very existence, their members may dispute the relevance of fashion (as both phenomenon and terminology) to their own identity, perhaps preferring to orient themselves around the idea of "style" or "anti-fashion." "Anti-fashion is that 'true chic' which used to be defined as the elegance that never draws attention to itself, the simplicity that is 'understated' . . . Anti-fashion attempts a timeless style, tries to get the essential element of change out of fashion altogether" (Wilson, pp. 183–184).

Early Examples

Elizabeth Wilson's *Adorned in Dreams* includes a useful introductory discussion of certain forms of early, European fashion subcultures that favored rebellious, or oppositional, dress. Along with the "great masculine renunciation" of the early nineteenth century, in which men forsook foppish perfumed effeminacy for classic understated sobriety, came the figure of the Regency dandy. Although English in origin, dandyism soon found a resonance in post-revolutionary France, where it was adopted by the avant-garde youth subculture, the Incroyables. The typical dandy was undoubtedly motivated by a narcissistic obsession with image, display, and the presentation of the self through dress; yet his overriding concern was with sheer quality of fabric, fit, and form, not overbearing or ostentatious ornamentation. This coterie of young gentlemen was thus characterized by an ethos of stoical heroism, a disciplined quest for refinement, elegance, and excellence, the diverse historical legacy of which can be seen in male Edwardian dress, the 1960s mod subculture, and the character of John Steed in the cult TV show, *The Avengers*.

The fastidiousness of the dandy can be contrasted with the flamboyance of the bohemian, who also emerged in the early nineteenth century, but as a romantic reaction against the perceived de-humanizing utilitarianism and rationalism of the industrial revolution. Although often solidly upper-middle class in origin, the romantic rebel—as artist, visionary, or intellectual—was fundamentally anti-bourgeois in tastes and outlook, their moral quest for self-renewal through art synonymous with a desire to escape the inhibitions of conventional lifestyles and appearances. Bohemian countercultures have been a feature of many major Western urban centers of creativity—Paris, London, New York, Berlin, San Francisco—at regular intervals over the past two hundred years. From the casual neckties, romantic robes, and ethnic exoticism of the early French bohemians, via the existentiallyinspired black uniform and pale complexions of the 1950s beatniks, to the natural fibers, Eastern-influenced designs, and psychedelic aesthetic of the 1960s hippies, Wilson's book provides descriptions of their many and varied forms of sartorial dissent.

Because calls to free the physical self from the strictures imposed by social conventions of dress can imply a need for either increased functionality of design or a relaxation of hitherto too rigid forms, oppositional fashions and attempts at reformist dress can display both puritan rational and aesthetic romantic elements. Artistic or aesthetic dress of the nineteenth century called for the natural and free-flowing draping of the female body at a time when the tightly corseted, narrow-waisted, and heavily bustled female was the height of popular fashion; yet it is interesting that a movement founded in 1881 to free women from precisely these restrictions and impediments of conventional Victorian dress should be called "The Rational Dress Society." In the Soviet Union of the 1920s, the rational aspects of dress design were underpinned by the scientific tenets of Marxist-Leninism. Constructivist artists such as Vladimir Tatlin, Liubov' Popova, and Varvara Stepanova combined geometric Modernist motifs with the principle that form follows function to address the utilitarian clothing needs of urban industrial workers. The resulting revolutionary garments, intended for mass production, were destined, however, to remain—like aesthetic dress—a minority taste—the artistic expression of an avant-garde subculture.

Youth Subcultural Styles

The British context. Despite assumptions to the contrary, working-class youth subcultures, based around distinctive, dissenting styles, were not confined to the period after World War II. Geoffrey Pearson, for example, in a study of the "history of respectable fears," notes the presence in late-nineteenth-century Britain of the troublesome teenage "hooligan" (an Australian equivalent of the same period was known as the "larrikin"). Notwithstanding some regional variations in style between the different hooligan groups—the Manchester "Scuttlers" and the Birmingham "Peaky Blinders," for example—there was adopted a quite distinct uniform of large boots, bell-bottomed trousers, a loosely worn muffler or scarf, and a peaked cap worn over a donkey-fringe haircut. The whole peculiar ensemble was set off with a broad, buckled, leather belt.

There were six or more intervening decades between the demise of the original "hooligans" and the emergence of the more familiar and clearly documented British youth subcultures of the post-1945 era—the teddy boys, mods, rockers, hippies, skinheads, and punks. Yet Pearson sees no fundamental difference between the way the Victorian gangs constructed clearly recognizable styles by appropriating elements from the range of fashionable sources available to them and the attempts by the more recent "spectacular" youth subcultures to create new, oppositional meanings through the recontextualization of raw commodities from the market—a process that the Centre for Contemporary Cultural Studies (CCCS) at the University of Birmingham, England, termed "bricolage." Hence, the working-class teddy boys of the early 1950s appropriated the long lapeled neo-Edwardian drape suit from exclusive London tailors who aimed to bring back the pre-1914 look for upper-class young men. But the teds combined this item with bootlace ties (from Western movies), greased-back haircuts, drainpipe trousers, and thick creped-soled shoes.

CCCS writers such as John Clarke and Dick Hebdige had adopted an analysis whereby subcultural styles were "decoded" or read as a text for their hidden meanings. Hence, the fastidious and narcissistic neatness of the mods, with their two-tone mohair suits, button-down collared shirts, and short, lacquered hair, could be interpreted as an attempt by young working-class people in menial and routine employment to live out on a symbolic level the affluent, consumerist, and classless aspirations of the early 1960s. By contrast, the skinheads who emerged later in the same decade typically sported very close-cropped hair or shaven heads, Ben Sherman shirts and suspenders, and short, tight jeans or sta-press trousers with Dr. Martens boots—a combination of elements that signified a "magical" desire to return to the puritan masculinity of a rapidly disappearing traditional proletarian lifestyle. By the end of the 1970s subcultural fashions had become less easy to decipher in this way. Hebdige, analyzing punk style in his classic text *Subculture*, was driven to assert that the punks' "cut-up" wardrobe of bondage trousers, school ties, safety pins, bin liners, and spiky hair signified meaningfully only in terms of its very meaninglessness, as a visual illustration of chaos.

American and Australian examples. In Britain during the early 1960s, the natural enemy of the cool, clean-looking, scooter-riding mods were the leather and denim-clad, insignia-decorated, greasy-haired rockers, or motorbike boys as Paul Willis called them, renowned for their macho, rock 'n' roll image and "ton-up" speeding runs on heavy-duty Triumph Bonnevilles. Yet the reputation of the British rockers was tame by comparison with the notoriety of the American "outlaw" biker gangs of the postwar era, the most famous of which were—and still are—the Hell's Angels. Organized territorially in "chapters," and espousing an ideology of personal freedom and conservative patriotism, the "Angels" rode their collective "runs" on "chopped hogs"—customized Harley-Davidson bikes. Their famous Death-Head emblem or logo, as described by Hunter Thompson, is a cloth patch embroidered with a biker helmet atop a winged skull, and a band inscribed with the words Hell's Angels and the local chapter name. These "colors," as they are known, are typically sewn to the back of a sleeveless denim shirt.

Heavy Metal is a rock music genre that has given rise to a virtually global fashion, arguably derived from a crossover of elements from biker, glam, and hippie culture. Headbangers or metalers, as they are known, are characterized by their typical dress of black T-shirt, often bearing a heavy metal band name, faded denim jeans, and a leather or denim jacket, perhaps decorated with various badges, patches, and band insignia. For both men and women, hair is usually long, the body or arms are often tattooed, and jewelry may be worn. The music itself has fragmented into various subgenres such as thrash-, death-and sleaze-metal, each with its own variant on the general metaler look. Jeffrey Arnett views young American metalheads (as they are named in the title of his book) as particularly prone to the alienation, anomie, and hyper-individualism that, from his point of view, characterize contemporary American youth more generally.

Because of the immense power of its market, and the dependence of subcultural fashions upon commodity production and consumption, styles originally developed or popularized in America have rapidly spread to other cultural contexts. In a chapter in Rob White's edited book on the Australian experience of youth subcultures, Stratton discusses the case of the 1950s bodgies and widgies—terms used to denote male and female members respectively. The style of the bodgie and widgies was originally jazz-and jive-oriented and loosely derived from the zoot suit (discussed below)

The New Avengers. The stars of the 1970s British television series *The New Avengers*, (from left to right) Gareth Hunt, Joanna Lumley, and Patrick McNee. McNee's character, John Steed, epitomized the style of the later-day Edwardian dandy. © HULTON-DEUTSH COLLECTION/CORBIS. REPRODUCED BY PERMISSION.

worn by young black and Hispanic Americans in the 1940s. Later, however, this Australian subculture became influenced by American biker culture and also began to incorporate elements from rock 'n' roll. Boys wore leather jackets or drapes with thin ties, drainpipe trousers, and winkle-picker shoes; girls had pencil skirts, stilettos or pedal-pusher shoes, and beehive or ponytail hairstyles.

Neglected Dimensions and New Developments

Gender and ethnicity. In a chapter in *Resistance through Rituals*, Angela McRobbie and Jenny Garber noted that most of the subcultures and styles examined by the CCCS appeared overwhelmingly male in both composition and orientation. They concluded that girls *had* actually been present in such subcultures, but were rendered marginalized and invisible by the masculinist bias of the writers. It was only with the publication nearly a quarter of a century later of *Pretty in Punk*, Lauren Leblanc's noteworthy text on Canadian female punk rockers, that females in a male-dominated style subculture were studied comprehensively, in their own right and on their own terms. Leblanc's sample displayed a range of punk signifiers, including hair brightly dyed and worn in a Mohawk style, facial piercings, tattoos, and the "street-" or gutter-punk look—dark, baggy T-shirts and trousers with black boots. Leblanc concludes that women's presence in a largely male punk subculture can be explained by the way their membership enables them to resist certain normative and stylistic aspects of fashionable (i.e. mainstream) femininity.

Although ethnicity, like gender, has been a relatively neglected dimension in the writings of subcultural style, the American "zooties" of the 1940s are one of the better-documented examples of black and Hispanic rebellious fashion. Derived from black, hipster jazz culture, the zoot suit comprised an oversized, draped and pleated jacket with hugely padded shoulders, worn with high-waisted, baggy-kneed and ankle-taped pants, often set off with a wide-brimmed hat worn over a ducktail hairstyle. During a period of wartime rationing of material, the wearing of such an extravagant, luxurious, and ostentatious style led to rising tensions between the young black and Hispanic male zooties and white U.S. servicemen, sparking off full-scale riots in a number of U.S. cities.

Within the British literature on subcultures, the ethnic dimension has been more typically viewed in terms of the effects of postwar British "race relations" and black style on the formation of indigenous rebellious youth fashions. A noted example of such an approach is Dick Hebdige's discussion of the Jamaican rude boy and Rastafarian subcultures. Elements from the first of these styles—the cool look, shades, porkpie hat, and slim trousers with cropped legs—fed first into 1960s mod and then the Two-Tone movement of the late 1970s. Rastafarians, to symbolize their oppression by white society (Babylon) and their prophesied return to Zion (Africa), have adopted knitted caps (called "tams"), scarves, and jerseys in red, gold, and green, the colors of the Ethiopian flag. It is, though, the Rasta's dreadlock hairstyle that has most significantly been taken up by certain groups of white youth, particularly new-age hippies and anarchopunks, to show subcultural disaffection toward the dominant social order.

Post-Modernism and Post-Subculture

The practice of borrowing ethnic signifiers has reached extreme proportions in the contemporary, transatlantic example of the Modern Primitive subculture. The chapter by Winge, in David Muggleton and Rupert Weinzierl's *The Post-Subcultures Reader*, details how this subculture with its largely white membership adopts aspects of so-called "primitive" tribal cultures, such as black-work tattoos, brandings, keloids, and septum piercings. While subcultural styles have typically been constructed by a borrowing of elements from other sources, this relocation of traditional elements in a modern, urban setting could be seen as a prime example of a tendency toward a more complex cross-fertilization of time-compressed stylistic symbols in an increasingly global context. It is further argued that the identities fashioned from these diverse sources are themselves ever more eclectic, hybrid, and fragmented. Such a position has led some writers to proclaim that subculture—traditionally used to denote a coherent, stable, and specific group identification—is no longer a useful concept by which to comprehend these so-called "post-modern" or "post-subcultural" characteristics of contemporary styles.

That attempts at reconceptualizing the term subculture, such as "neo-tribe," or "post-subculture," have proceeded on the terrain of post-modernism owes much to the American anthropologist Ted Polhemus. His *Streetstyle* is particularly worth singling out here, most obviously for its vividly illustrated genealogy of late-twentieth-century subcultures, from the 1940s zootsuiters to the 1990s new-age travelers, but also for its attempt in the final chapters to conceptualize a new stage of development in the history of popular street fashion—"the supermarket of style." "Those who frequent the Supermarket of Style display . . . a stylistic promiscuity which is breathtaking in its casualness. 'Punks' one day, 'Hippies' the next, they fleeting leap across ideological divides—converting the history of street style into a vast theme park. All of which fits very neatly within postmodern theory" (Polhemus, p. 131).

Muggleton's *Inside Subculture* represents the first attempt to test such theoretical propositions about post-modern fashions. Using data from interviews with members from a range of subcultures, Muggleton generally agrees with post-modern claims concerning the fluidity, fragmentation, and radical individuality of dissident youth styles. He describes, for example, those such as the respondent with a Chinese hairstyle, baggy skateboarder shorts, leather biker jacket, and boots, whose eclecticism arguably leads them to disavow any affiliation to a group identity. Paul Hodkinson's *Goth* is a qualitative study of self-identifying members of the gothic subculture. Both male and female goths are noted for their dark and macabre appearance, typical features being black clothes, whitened faces, long, dyed black hair, plus dark eyeliner and lipstick. *Goth* differs somewhat from *Inside Subculture* in its stress on the continuing cultural coherence and stylistic substance of the British subcultural scene. Yet the potential reader is advised to seek out these two texts for their complimentary rather than conflicting assessments of the contemporary fashion subculture situation.

See also Extreme Fashions; Punk; Retro Styles; Zoot Suit.

Bibliography

Arnett, Jeffrey. *Metalheads: Heavy Metal Music and Adolescent Alienation.* Boulder, Colo.: Westview, 1996.

Hall, Stuart, and Tony Jefferson, eds. *Resistance Through Rituals: Youth Subcultures in Post-War Britain.* London: Hutchinson, 1976.

Hebdige, Dick. *Subculture: The Meaning of Style.* London: Methuen, 1979.

Hodkinson, Paul. *Goth: Identity, Style and Subculture.* Oxford: Berg, 2002.

Leblanc, Lauren. *Pretty in Punk: Girls' Gender Resistance in a Boys' Subculture.* New Brunswick, N.J., and London: Rutgers University Press, 2002.

Muggleton, David. *Inside Subculture: The Postmodern Meaning of Style.* Oxford: Berg, 2000.

——, and Rupert Weinzierl, eds. *The Post-Subcultures Reader.* Oxford: Berg, 2003.

Pearson, Geoffrey. *Hooligan: A History of Respectable Fears.* London: Macmillan, 1983.

Polhemus, Ted. *Streetstyle: From Sidewalk to Catwalk.* London: Thames and Hudson, Inc., 1994.

Thompson, Hunter. *Hell's Angels.* New York: Random House, 1966.

White, Rob, ed. *Youth Subcultures: Theory, History and the Australian Experience.* Hobart: National Clearinghouse for Youth Studies, 1993.

Willis, Paul. *Profane Culture.* London: Routledge and Kegan Paul, 1978.

Wilson, Elizabeth. *Adorned in Dreams: Fashion and Modernity.* London: Virago, 1985.

David Muggleton

SUMPTUARY LAWS

Sumptuary laws can be dated to at least the fourth century B.C.E., and while they have largely disappeared in name, they have by no means disappeared in fact. By definition, they are intended to control behavior, specifically the excessive consumption of anything from foodstuffs to household goods. By convention, they have come to be largely associated with the regulation of apparel, their most frequent target. Typically, those issued by executive or legislative entities—and that are thus laws in the legal sense—have lasted no more than a few decades before being repealed or annulled. Infinitely more enduring have been extra-legal pronouncements that codify social or religious precepts, such as the injunction against garments woven of wool and linen proclaimed in Leviticus 19:19 and still obeyed by Orthodox Jews. (The longevity of restrictions on women's dress issued by modern theocracies remains to be seen, now that these have passed from custom into law.)

Types

Sumptuary regulation is of two general types: prescriptive and proscriptive. The first defines what people must purchase, wear, or use, the second what they may not. Although both approaches limit choice, proscriptive laws can be seen as less onerous in so far as individual freedom is concerned since they imply acceptance of anything not expressly forbidden.

Goals and Outcomes

Personal liberty is never a factor in such legislation; however, actual statutes are written to address any of a number of sociocultural objectives deemed important by the issuing authority. Rulings in effect between 1337 and 1604 in medieval and renaissance England, for example, reflect multiple (and by no means mutually exclusive) goals: resisting new fashions, protecting public morals, preserving the public peace, maintaining social distinctions, and—extremely important to this commercial nation—defending the domestic economy and promoting home industries. Across the Channel, particularly in Protestant countries, sumptuary laws were more likely to assume the deity to be as offended by sartorial choices as was the government. Here, one might compare an English statute of 1483, which banned without explanation the stylishly short gowns that failed to mask "privy Members and Buttocks" (*Statues of the Realm*, p. 22) with a Bavarian injunction that prohibited uncovered codpieces because these were offensive to God. After the conclusion of the Thirty Years War in 1648, however, the sumptuary laws of the German states began to resemble those of England in their emphasis on economic issues.

One of the intended outcomes of much sumptuary law is that of separation, the division of people into explicit categories. Modern examples tend to differentiate by religion, whether by choice (the Amish cap) or by coercion (the yellow star). In earlier times, a populace was more likely to be divided by class than by creed; and in hierarchical societies in which ritualized honors were due those of superior rank, status had to be readily recognizable if people were neither to insult their betters (by failing to offer the proper marks of respect) nor embarrass themselves (by extending undeserved courtesies to those beneath them).

Parameters

The desire for upward mobility may be both innate and unquenchable; however, much of sumptuary legislation is concerned with defining the degrees of rank and wealth that govern the wearing of metals, textiles, colors, decorative techniques, furs, and jewels.

Limitations on gold, silks, purples, lace, embroidery, sable, and precious stones are, thus, recurring elements, as are injunctions against certain fashions (including short robes, long-toed shoes or *poulaines*, and great hose) considered unacceptable for moral, patriotic, or economic reasons. Improving economies raised not only the earnings but also the aspirations of, especially, the merchant classes, however, and England was not unusual in its continuing reformulation of vestimentary prohibitions relative to disposable income. While the threshold most commonly cited in English law is £40, in 1337 Edward III limited the wearing of furs to those with a disposable income of at least £100, and in 1554 Queen Mary lowered the minimum for silk to £20 (although she also insisted on a net worth of £200, an amount reiterated in a Massachusetts law of 1651).

Penalties

Most sumptuary legislation provides penalties for lawbreakers that could include confiscation of the offending garment, fines (up to £200 in England), tax auditing, the pillory, or even jail. That legislators were themselves subject to (and breakers of) these statutes may help to explain both their lax enforcement and their frequent repeal. In England, at least, lack of compliance was so general that in 1406 Henry IV vainly requested that violators be excommunicated. In 1670, women who used dress and cosmetics to "betray into matrimony any of his majesty's subjects" (Geocities.com Web site) were to be punished as witches.

Women

As might be expected, the attention paid to women in sumptuary law varies with time and country, and does so in ways that reflect their place in society. Generally speaking, early modern sumptuary legislation treats women in one of four ways: it exempts them specifically or ignores them completely (implying that women were of no consequence); or, conversely, it subjects them either to the same requirements as men or to parallel requirements (implying that women were not to be disregarded). There are of course exceptions. A few statutes imply fear of gender confusion. In the third century C.E., for example, the emperor Aurelian barred men from wearing shoes of yellow, green, white, or red since these colors were reserved for women. Others were aimed at keeping women in the home, as did an edict enacted in Rome in the second century B.C.E., that forbade their riding in a carriage in or near populated areas. More (both written and unwritten) were intended to keep them modest—Hebrews, Romans, early Christians, and early Americans alike mandated simplicity in feminine hairstyles, clothing, and accessories. Perhaps not surprisingly, prostitutes received special attention, as did courtesans, who, finding their consorts among the nobility, rather naturally rivaled well-born women in their dress. From at least the thirteenth century onward, European prostitutes were commonly enjoined to wear some form of distinctive clothing, whether striped hoods, striped stockings, colored patches, or bells (interestingly, such markers were prescribed for other social outcasts, among them lepers and Jews).

Summary

Collectively, sumptuary laws reflect a need for permanence that is shared by governments, religions, and smaller societal groups alike. That so many have been written and so few endure speaks to the fundamental dissonance between the institutional need for stability and the personal desire for independence.

See also Colonialism and Imperialism; Europe and America: History of Dress (400–1900 C.E.).

Bibliography

Baldwin, Frances Elizabeth. *Sumptuary Legislation and Personal Regulation in England.* Vol. 44: *Johns Hopkins University Studies in Historical and Political Science.* Baltimore: The Johns Hopkins Press, 1926.

Benhamou, Reed. "The Restraint of Excessive Apparel: England 1337–1604." *Dress* 15 (1989), 27–37.

Great Britain. *Statutes of the Realm.* London: 1890. Reprint, London: Dawson, 1963.

Vincent, John Martin. *Costume and Conduct in the Laws of Basel, Bern, and Zurich 1370–1800.* New York: Greenwood, 1969. Original edition published in 1935.

Internet Resource

Geocities.com. "Platform Shoes of the 1600s." Available from <http://www.geocities.com/FashionAvenue/1495/1600.html>.

Reed Benhamou

SUPERMODELS

"Supermodel" ranks with "genius" and "original" as one of the most-abused terms in the fashion lexicon. Indeed, it has been so overused that by the late 1990s, when the Supermodel phenomenon (personified by larger-than-life mannequins such as Cindy Crawford, Claudia Schiffer, Naomi Campbell, and Christy Turlington) had long-since peaked and passed, the word had lost almost all meaning, becoming a generic gossip-column descriptive promiscuously pinned on almost any fashion model with, or in some cases, merely wanting, a public profile.

Though many claimed to have coined the term, notably the 1970s model Janice Dickinson, the first recorded use of the word was in a 1948 book, *So You Want to Be a Model!* by a small-time model agent named Clyde Matthew Dessner. It came into more general usage in 1981, when *New York* magazine published "The Spoiled Supermodels," in which Anthony Haden-Guest, the incisive British journalist, chronicled the myriad misbehaviors of highly paid models and photographers in the cocaine-clouded world of post-Studio-54 New York City.

In pure terms, there had been supermodels long before that—at least, if supermodels are defined, as they

Designer Gianni Versace and supermodels. Fashion designer Gianni Versace stands amidst models (*From left*: Unknown, Unknown, Shalom Harlow, Linda Evangelista, Kate Moss, Naomi Campbell, Amber Valletta) for his autumn-winter 1996–1997 hautecouture collection. © PHOTO B.D.V./CORBIS. REPRODUCED BY PERMISSION.

properly should be, as mannequins whose renown and activities stretch beyond the bubble-world of fashion.

Supermodels don't just look the part—they have to live it. The earliest one was probably Anita Colby, who began her career in the 1930s as a model with the Conover Agency in New York, but was soon lured to Hollywood where, in 1944, she served as ringleader of a gang of models who co-starred with Rita Hayworth in the big-budget film, *Cover Girl*. Colby's success in publicizing the film—she arranged an average three magazine cover stories per cover girl—won her a job as image consultant for the great producer, David O. Selznick, an appearance on the cover of *Time* magazine, a recurring spot on the *Today Show* (where a young Barbara Walters wrote her scripts), and marriage proposals from Clark Gable and James Stewart.

The 1940s and 1950s were dominated by the supermodel sisters Dorian Leigh and Suzy Parker. Leigh, the older sister, lived large; she had affairs with Harry Bela-fonte, Irving Penn, and the Marquis de Portago, and a two-day marriage to drummer Buddy Rich; she founded two modeling agencies, and gave Martha Stewart her first job when she owned a catering business. Sister Suzy Parker, best known as photographer Richard Avedon's muse, was also a gossip column staple and a Hollywood star before she settled into domesticity as the wife of actor Bradford Dillman.

The next generation of supermodels was led by Britons Jean Shrimpton and Twiggy. Shrimpton had the good fortune to hook up with David Bailey, the best of a batch of trendsetting British photographers known as the Terrible Trio, just as the 1960s were getting started. She was a pouty-lipped, saucer-eyed, eighteen-year-old modeling school graduate; he was a twenty-three-yearold East End rake-in-the-making. Together, they kicked off the Youthquake before he went on to marry actress Catherine Deneuve, and she to an affair with actor Terence Stamp and an appearance on the cover of *Newsweek*.

A year later, The Shrimp was replaced by a Twig, or rather Leslie Hornby, a.k.a Twiggy, who catapulted to worldwide fame (and another *Newsweek* cover) with the help of a hairdresser at Vidal Sassoon who called himself Justin de Villeneuve. Twiggy was the first model to gain a profile outside fashion before making the jump into film. But she was also a comet—by 1968, she'd burned out. In 1971, she made a comeback as an actress, but despite some success, never again saw super-stardom. "I used to be a thing," she said in 1993. "I am a person now" (Gross, p. 183).

By then, of course, many other women had donned the rainments of the supermodel, only to be disrobed by a public eager for the next new . . . thing. Thanks to a lift from *Sports Illustrated*'s swimsuit issue, Cheryl Tiegs revived the poster girl, and the supermodel phenomenon, when she crossed over from fashion into the worlds of the pinup and then the eponymous product marketer—a trajectory many wanna-be "supes" would follow thereafter. Hers wasn't the only path to stardom. Janice Dickinson made it by doffing her clothes at every opportunity, Iman by hooking up with the socialite photographer Peter Beard, who billed her as fresh out of the African bush, even though she was the educated daughter of a diplomat. Christie Brinkley parlayed her moment into several decades, and in the early 2000s is a star-billed political activist. Patti Hansen and Jerry Hall married Rolling Stones and became celebrities through sexual association. But that path to staying power didn't always lead to the same destination. After Elaine Irwin married rocker John Mellen-camp, she fell from view, apparently content to be a wife and mother.

Irwin was one of ten supermodels photographed for *Harper's Bazaar* by Patrick Demarchelier in 1992, the peak of Supermodeldom. With her in the picture were Christy Turlington, Cindy Crawford, Naomi Campbell, Linda Evangelista, Yasmeen Ghauri, Karen Mulder, Claudia Schiffer, Niki Taylor, and Tatjana Patitz. Along with Helena Christensen, Stephanie Seymour, and later, Kate Moss, this baker's dozen formed the core of the real Supermodel Corps, aided and abetted by image-conscious designers such as Karl Lagerfeld, Calvin Klein, and Gianni Versace, photographers such as Patrick Demarchelier, Peter Lindberg, and Steven Meisel, and the Parisian model agent Gerald Marie. All of their behind-the-scenes machinations helped create the supermodel moment.

Each, in his own way, had seen a window of opportunity open in 1987, when fashion's excesses of the preceding ten years, followed hard by a stock-market crash on Wall Street, and a worldwide recession, put an end to the designer decade that had been launched along with Calvin Klein jeans back in the pre-super 1970s. When the pouf dress—symbol of those heady days—went pop, the air went out of fashion and designers lost their way, just at the moment when the mass market seemed to have discovered them. The supermodels were used as a placeholder, a distraction, a way to keep the attention of the audience focused on fashion, while behind the scenes, the designers scurried around looking for a new message better suited to their times and their greatly expanded audience. Only problem was the supes soon became the tail that wagged the dog of fashion.

But truth be told, they couldn't sustain their "suzerainity." By 1995, the public had tired of the supes and were ready for something, anything, else. The fashion business was tired of them, too. They were too demanding, too expensive (Evangelista had famously remarked that she wouldn't get out of bed for less than $10,000; by 1995, that price had risen to $25,000), too overexposed. The shelf life of models is generally seven years. The supermodels were pert nose up against their use-by date. "I won't use her," as designer Todd Oldham said of Campbell, then the worst behaved of the lot (Gross, p. 438).

In 1996, just in time, a new model movement came along. The small, unassuming girls who were newly in favor were called waifs, and they dressed in a style with the unappealing name, grunge. Unfortunately, although it did take to Kate Moss, the last of the era's supermodels, the public didn't go along with the rest of the trend, and soon enough a new crop of larger-than-life models appeared. But fashion had been downsized—and they were too. Amber Valletta and Shalom Harlow made a run for the top but fell short. In their wake came other girls (for that's what the business calls them, even though they are its representation of womanhood), but few supes. Had you asked a boy tossing a football in Indiana to name the supermodels of 2003, he would probably say Gisele Bundchen and Heidi Klum (both stars of the ad campaigns run by Victoria's Secret, which replaced *Sports Illustrated*'s bathing suit issue as the source of all fashion knowledge for American men) . . . and then he would pause, searching for more names but not finding them.

Which means that as surely as long hems follow short ones, the time is probably nigh for the return of the supermodel.

See also Fashion Models; Grunge; Twiggy.

Bibliography

Conover, Carole. *Cover Girls: The Story of Harry Conover.* Englewood Cliffs, N.J.: Prentice-Hall, 1978.

Gross, Michael. *Model: The Ugly Business of Beautiful Women.* New York: William Morrow, 1995.

Leigh, Dorian, with Laura Hobe. *The Girl Who Had Everything: The Story of "The Fire and Ice Girl."* Garden City, N.Y.: Doubleday, 1980.

Moncur, Susan. *They Still Shoot Models My Age.* London: Serpent's Tail, 1991.

Sims, Naomi. *How To Be A Top Model.* New York: Doubleday, 1989.

Michael Gross

SWEATSHOPS

Sweatshops are workplaces run by unscrupulous employers who pay low wages to workers for long hours under unsafe and unhealthy conditions. For example, in a clothing sweatshop in California in the early 2000s, Asian women sewed for ten to twelve hours per day, six or seven days per week, in a dim and unventilated factory loft where the windows were sealed and the emergency doors locked. The workers had no pension or health-care benefits and were paid at a piece rate that fell far below the legal minimum wage. When the company went bankrupt, the owner sold off the inventory, locked out the workers without paying them, moved his machines in the middle of the night to another factory, and reopened under a different name.

The term "sweatshop" is derived from the "sweating system" of production and its use of "sweated labor." At the heart of the sweating system are the contractors. A large company distributes its production to small contractors who profit from the difference between what they charge the company and what they spend on production. The work is low skilled and labor intensive, so the contractors do best when their workers are paid the least. Workers employed under these conditions are said to be doing sweated labor.

Sweatshops are often used in the clothing industry because it is easy to separate higher and lower skilled jobs and contract out the lower skilled ones. Clothing companies can do their own designing, marketing, and cutting, and contract out sewing and finishing work. New contractors can start up easily; all they need is a few sewing machines in a rented apartment or factory loft located in a neighborhood where workers can be recruited.

Sweatshops make the most fashion-oriented clothing—women's and girls'—because production has to be flexible, change quickly, and done in small batches. In less style-sensitive sectors—men's and boys' wear, hosiery, and knit products—there is less change and longer production runs, and clothing can be made competitively in large factories using advanced technology.

Since their earliest days, sweatshops have relied on immigrant labor, usually women, who were desperate for work under any pay and conditions. Sweatshops in New York City, for example, opened in Chinatown, the mostly Jewish Lower East Side, and Hispanic neighborhoods in the boroughs. Sweatshops in Seattle are near neighborhoods of Asian immigrants.

The evolution of sweatshops in London and Paris—two early and major centers of the garment industry—followed the pattern in New York City. First, garment manufacturing was localized in a few districts: the *Sentier* of Paris and the Hackney, Haringey, Islington, the Tower Hamlets, and Westminster boroughs of London. Second, the sweatshops employed mostly immigrants, at first men but then primarily women, who had few job alternatives. The source of immigrant workers changed over time. During the late nineteenth and twentieth century, most workers in the garment sweatshops of Paris were Germans and Belgians, then Polish and Russian Jews and, into the 2000s, Yugoslavs, Turks, Southeast Asians, Chinese and North African Jews. Eastern European Jews initially worked in London sweatshops, but most of these workers were replaced by Cypriots and Bengali immigrants. Also, sweatshop conditions in the two cities were the result of roughly similar forces;

New York City sweatshop. A scene from a sweatshop on New York City's Lower East Side, 1908, as photographed by Lewis Hines. The workers here are probably recent Jewish immigrants. Modern-day American sweatshops continue to exist and continue to rely on recent immigrants willing to work long hours for very low pay. © CORBIS. REPRODUCED BY PERMISSION.

in the nineteenth century, production shifted to lower-grade, ready-made clothing that could be made by less skilled workers; skill requirements further declined with the introduction of the sewing machine and the separation of cutting and less skilled sewing work; frequent style changes, particularly in ready-made women's wear, led to production in small lots and lower entry barriers to new entrepreneurs who sought contracts for sewing; and, as contractors competed among themselves, they tried to lower labor costs by reducing workers' pay, increasing hours, and allowing working conditions to deteriorate.

In developing countries, clothing sweatshops tend to be widely dispersed geographically rather than concentrated in a few districts of major cities, and they often operate alongside sweatshops, some of which are very large, that produce toys, shoes (primarily athletic shoes), carpets, and athletic equipment (particularly baseballs and soccer balls), among other goods. Sweatshops of all types tend to have child labor, forced unpaid overtime, and widespread violations of workers' freedom of association (i.e., the right to unionize). The underlying cause of sweat-shops in developing nations—whether in China, Southeast Asia, the Caribbean or India and Bangladesh—is the intense cost-cutting done by contractors who compete among themselves for orders from larger contractors, major manufacturers, and retailers.

Clothing was not always produced with the sweating system. Throughout much of the nineteenth century, seamstresses made clothing by working long hours at home for low pay. They sewed precut fabric to make inexpensive clothes. Around the 1880s, clothing work shifted to contract shops that opened in the apartments of the recently arrived immigrants or in small, unsafe factories.

The spread of sweatshops was reversed in the United States in the years following a horrific fire in 1911 that destroyed the Triangle Shirtwaist Company, a women's blouse manufacturer near Washington Square in New York City. The company employed five hundred workers in notoriously poor conditions. One hundred and forty-six workers, mostly young Jewish and Italian women, perished in the fire; many jumped out windows to their deaths because the building's emergency exits were locked. The Triangle fire made the public acutely aware of conditions in the clothing industry and led to pressure for closer regulation. The number of sweatshops gradually declined as unions organized and negotiated improved wages and conditions and as government regulations were stiffened (particularly under the 1938 Fair Labor Standards Act, which imposed a minimum wage and required overtime pay for work of more than forty hours per week).

Unionization and government regulation never completely eliminated clothing sweatshops, and many continued on the edges of the industry; small sweatshops were difficult to locate and could easily close and move to avoid union organizers and government inspectors. In the 1960s, sweatshops began to reappear in large numbers among the growing labor force of immigrants, and by the 1980s sweatshops were again "business as usual." In the 1990s, atrocious conditions at a sweatshop once again shocked the public.

In 1995, police raided a clandestine sweatshop in El Monte, California (outside Los Angeles), where seventy-two illegal Thai immigrants were sewing clothing in near slavery in a locked and gated apartment complex. They sewed for up to seventeen hours per day and earned about sixty cents per hour. When they were not working, they slept ten to a room. The El Monte raid showed an unsuspecting public that sweatshop owners continued to prey on vulnerable immigrants and were ignoring the toughened workplace regulations. Under intense public pressure, the federal government worked with unions, industry representatives, and human rights organizations to attack the sweatshop problem. Large companies pledged to learn more about their contractors and avoid sweat-shops. Congress proposed legislation that would make clothing manufacturers responsible for the conditions at their contractors. College students formed coalitions with labor unions and human rights organizations to organize consumer boycotts against clothing made in sweatshops. Despite these efforts, the old sweatshops continued and many new ones were opened.

In the early twenty-first century, about a third of garment manufacturers in the United States operate without licenses, keep no records, pay in cash, and pay no overtime. In New York City, about half of the garment manufacturers could be considered sweatshops because they repeatedly violate pay and workplace regulations. In Los Angeles, the nation's new sweatshop center, around three-quarters of the clothing contractors pay less than the minimum wage and regularly violate health regulations.

The resurgence of sweatshops in the United States is a byproduct of globalization—the lowering of trade barriers throughout the world—and the widespread use of sweatshops to make garments in developing countries. American clothing companies must compete against producers elsewhere that can hire from a nearly endless supply of cheap labor.

In the clothing industry, one sees a classic case of the "race to the bottom" that can come with unrestrained globalization. As trade barriers are reduced, clothing retailers face intensive competitive pressure and, squeezed for profits, they demand cheaper goods from manufacturers. The manufacturers respond by paying less to contractors, and the contractors lower their piece rates and spend less money maintaining working conditions. Quite often, the contractors move abroad because the "race to the bottom" also happens worldwide. Developing countries outbid each other with concessions (for example, wages are set below the legal minimum, child labor and unhealthy work conditions are overlooked) to attract foreign investors.

The fight against sweatshops is never a simple matter; there are mixed motives and unexpected outcomes. For example, unions object to sweatshops because they are genuinely concerned about the welfare of sweated labor, but they also want to protect their own members' jobs from low-wage competition even if this means ending the jobs of the working poor in other countries.

Also, sweatshops can be evaluated from moral and economic perspectives. Morally, it is easy to declare sweatshops unacceptable because they exploit and endanger workers. But from an economic perspective, many now argue that without sweatshops developing countries might not be able to compete with industrialized countries and achieve export growth. Working in a sweatshop may be the only alternative to subsistence farming, casual labor, prostitution, and unemployment. At least most sweatshops in other countries, it is argued, pay their workers above the poverty level and provide jobs for women who are otherwise shut out of manufacturing. And American consumers have greater purchasing power and a higher standard of living because of the availability of inexpensive imports.

The intense low-cost competition spurred by the opening of world markets is creating a resurgence of sweatshops in the United States. The response has been a large and energetic anti-sweatshop movement aimed at greater unionization, better government regulation, and consumer boycotts against goods produced by sweated labor. But despite the historical rise and fall and rise again of sweatshops in the clothing industry, their fundamental cause remains the same. The sweating system continues because contractors can profit by offering low wages and harsh conditions to workers in the United States and abroad who have no alternatives.

See also Globalization.

Bibliography

Piore, Michael. "The Economics of the Sweatshop." In *No Sweat: Fashion, Free Trade, and the Rights of Garment Workers.* Edited by Andrew Ross. New York: Verso, 1997, pp. 135–142. A brief, well-written review of the economic factors behind the operation of sweatshops in the garment industry.

Rath, Jan, ed. *Unraveling the Rag Trade: Immigrant Entrepreneurship in Seven World Cities.* New York: Berg, 2002. A collection of articles about immigrant workers and entrepreneurs in the emerging garment industries of seven major production centers including New York, Paris, and London.

Rosen, Ellen Israel. *Making Sweatshops: The Globalization of the U.S. Apparel Industry.* Berkeley: University of California Press, 2002. A comprehensive study of the impact of globalization on sweatshops in the American garment industry, with detailed analyses of their historical development and present condition.

Stein, Leon, ed. *Out of the Sweatshop: The Struggle for Industrial Democracy.* New York: Quadrangle, 1977. A collection of classic essays, news stories, and workers' firsthand accounts of sweatshops with particularly strong sections on immigrants, early sweatshops, and union organizing and strikes.

Von Drehle, David. *Triangle: The Fire that Changed America.* New York: Atlantic Monthly Press, 2003. A vivid and informative account of the 1911 Triangle fire—the deadliest workplace fire in American history and an early turning point in the evolution of sweatshops and the government regulation of work.

Gary Chaison

SWIMWEAR

Clothing for swimming, bathing, and seaside wear has been an important and influential area of fashionable dress since the late nineteenth century. The evolution of swimming and bathing costumes has been closely associated with trends in mainstream fashion and advancements in textile technology, but has also reflected broader societal attitudes about personal hygiene, body exposure, and modesty, and whether or not it was appropriate for women to participate in active sports.

Bathing Costumes

Swimming and bathing were common activities in the ancient world, and the Romans built public baths in even the most remote parts of their empire. After declining during the Middle Ages, bathing was revived in the seventeenth century, when it became popular as a medicinal treatment. At spas such as Bath and Baden, where bathers sought out the warm mineral waters for their therapeutic effects, linen bathing garments—knee-length drawers and waistcoats for men, and long-sleeved linen smocks or chemises for women—were in use by the late seventeenth century. These garments were worn for modesty rather than appearance, and could be hired from the baths by those who did not wish to purchase their own.

In the eighteenth century, medical authorities began to prescribe salt-water bathing, and seaside towns, along with large floating baths in most major cities, began to cater to large numbers of health-conscious visitors. Bathing usually consisted of a quick dip, often in the early morning, and was considered more a duty than a pleasure. Until the mid-nineteenth century, male and female bathers were almost always segregated from each other, either through the provision of separate bathhouses or stretches of beach, or by using the same area at different assigned times. Modesty was also preserved by the use of "bathing machines"—small buildings mounted on wheels, in which the bather would change from street clothes into a bathing costume while a horse and driver pulled the machine into the sea. The steps by which the bather would descend into the water were often covered with an awning to ensure that he or she would not be seen until mostly underwater. Thus protected from the eyes of the opposite sex, men generally bathed nude, or in simple trunks with a drawstring waist; women's bathing gowns were cut much like the chemise (undergarment) of the period, but were often made of stiffer material so as not to cling to the figure, and sometimes incorporated weights in the hem to keep the gown from floating. The only purpose of bathing garments at this time was to keep the bather warm and sufficiently covered up, and little thought was given to their appearance.

In the early nineteenth century, bathing began to be considered a recreational as well as beneficial activity, and seaside holidays grew in popularity. Each locality had its own standards for appropriate attire, and the costumes worn varied widely from place to place. In general, however, as women began to be more active in the water, rather than simply immersing themselves, their bathing dresses became slightly shorter, and were gathered or fitted around the waist. At the same time, ankle-length drawers or pantaloons, similar to the drawers worn as underwear by ladies in the 1840s, began to be worn underneath.

From the mid-century on, mixed bathing became more acceptable, and as stationary beach huts began to replace bathing machines, bathing costumes were more visible, and attention began to be paid to making them more attractive. Bathing styles began to be covered by popular magazines, which both standardized bathing costumes and brought them into the realm of fashion, with new styles introduced each season. Women's costumes began to follow the silhouette of street fashions more closely in this period, but also developed their own fashion vocabulary; they were usually made of wool flannel or serge, in dark colors (which were less revealing of the figure when wet), and enlivened by jaunty details such as sailor collars and braid trim in contrasting colors. Bathing costumes also now required many fashionable accessories. Hats, rubberized and oilcloth caps, and a variety of turban-like head-wraps kept hair neat and protected from salt water. Full-length dark stockings kept the legs modestly covered, and flat-soled bathing shoes, often with ribbon ties crossing up the leg, protected the feet and set off the ankles. As wool bathing dresses became quite heavy when wet, and clung to the figure in a way that was considered unattractive and immodest, bathing capes and mantles were

BATHING BEAUTIES

Beautiful aquatic women have been important fantasy figures since ancient times, when sirens, mermaids, and water nymphs led heroes of mythology astray. The modern-day bathing beauty, however, did not appear until the late nineteenth century, when bathing dresses were first seen in public. As these were the most revealing costumes allowed for women at the time, images of pretty bathing girls, both in wholesome advertisements and on naughty postcards, soon proliferated. Around 1914, the comedies of silent film producer Mack Sennett began to feature a bevy of young women in exaggerated and revealing bathing dress, whom he called his Bathing Beauties. Their popularity inspired beach resorts such as Venice Beach, California, and Galveston, Texas, to stage annual bathing girl parades and beauty contests; the Miss America pageant started as one such bathing girl contest, held in Atlantic City, New Jersey in 1920 to encourage late-season tourism. Over the years this and other beauty pageants, with their parades of women in bathing suits and high heels featured in newsreels and television broadcasts, have been instrumental in associating swimwear with feminine beauty in the popular imagination. (This connection was not lost on Catalina Swimwear, a major pageant sponsor, which started the Miss USA and Miss Universe pageants after the 1951 Miss America refused to pose in a swimsuit during her reign.)

The Hollywood bathing beauty came of age in the 1930s, when photographs of stars and starlets posing in fashionable swimwear began appearing in large numbers. These images had an impact on fashions, as women sought to emulate the look of their favorite stars, and achieved iconic status during World War II, when pinups of Betty Grable and Rita Hayworth came to symbolize "what we're fighting for" to many American servicemen. Another, more active kind of bathing beauty was showcased in the aquatic ballets of Billy Rose's Aquacades at the 1939–1940 World's Fair, in the water-skiing spectaculars at Cypress Gardens in Florida, and, most memorably, in the lavish MGM films featuring Esther Williams, the first of which was the 1944 Bathing Beauty. Miss Williams, a 1939 national swimming champion, was a top box-office draw through the mid-1950s, and her film costumes, together with her ability to look glamorous before, during, and after swimming, did much to inspire the desired poolside look of the era.

Since its debut in 1964, *Sports Illustrated*'s annual swimsuit issue has probably been the most relevant modern incarnation of the bathing beauty tradition, and has come to symbolize its contradictions. Widely credited with popularizing the active, healthy California look in the 1960s, and thus encouraging women to be more athletic, the swimsuit issue has also been criticized for displaying women as sex objects for the enjoyment of a predominantly male audience. Seen as empowering, exploitative, or both, the bathing beauties seen in Sports Illustrated continue to influence swimwear fashion, and to act as a kind of barometer for changing cultural attitudes and standards of beauty.

also considered necessary for the walk from the water to the changing room.

Later in the century, bathing dresses (the term "bathing suit" also came into use at this time) became more practical, with both skirt and pantaloons gradually shortened, necklines lowered, and sleeves shortened or even eliminated. In the United States, where it took longer for these styles to catch on, the one-piece (or "princess-style") costume became a popular alternative in the 1890s; this consisted of an attached blouse and knee-length drawers, with a separate knee-length or shorter skirt that could be removed for swimming. Even so, most bathing costumes were essentially variations of street fashions, intended largely for promenading by the sea and wading or frolicking in the surf; many required the wearing of a corset underneath, and were made of materials that would be ruined if they ever got wet. In the early twentieth century, the term "bathing dress" came to mean this kind of fashionable, skirted costume, as opposed to the utilitarian "swimming suit." Chemise-style silk bathing dresses with bloomers or tights continued to be worn by some women into the 1920s, but by the 1930s they were obsolete, and the terms "bathing suit" and "swimsuit" had become interchangeable.

Swimming Suits

Until the mid-nineteenth century, swimming was an activity almost entirely limited to men. While men and women were segregated at baths and beaches, men were free to practice swimming unencumbered by clothes. As mixed bathing became more popular, however, they were forced to find a suitable costume, and by the 1850s men generally wore one-piece knit suits very similar to contemporary one-piece underwear (called union suits), but usually with short sleeves and legs cut off at the knees. Later in the century, there was also a two-piece version available, consisting of a short-sleeved or sleeveless tunic over knee-length drawers. To avoid any hint of impropriety caused by appearing in garments so similar to underwear, men's bathing suits were usually dark in color, sometimes with contrasting bands at the edges; striped suits were also popular, especially in France. This practical knit costume remained basically unchanged until the 1930s.

Women who wished to swim, however, found it much more difficult to find a suitable costume. Beginning in the 1860s, women were encouraged to take up swimming for exercise, and by the 1870s many women were learning to swim at pools and bathhouses, which had separate times designated for male and female bathers. In these sex-segregated situations, and for swimming competitions and demonstrations, female swimmers adopted simple "princess-style" one-piece suits, knitted garments similar to men's suits, or suits with long tights similar to those worn by circus performers. However, these garments were still not acceptable in mixed company, or for public wear out of the water, until the early twentieth century. The Australian swimmer Annette Kellerman became famous early in the century for her long-distance swimming feats and exhibitions of fancy diving, for which she wore sleeveless, form-fitting one-piece suits of black wool knit, sometimes with full-length stockings attached. She was an outspoken advocate for practical swimwear for women, and when she was arrested for indecent exposure for wearing a one-piece suit to a public beach in Boston in 1907, the resulting trial and publicity helped to change public attitudes on the subject. In 1912, the Olympic Games in Stockholm were the first to include women's swimming events, and by the beginning of World War I, one-piece knit suits had gained wide acceptance. In many places, however, local authorities passed strict bathing suit regulations, and the battle over the alleged indecency of abbreviated suits, particularly when worn without stockings, continued in many places into the 1920s.

The Modern Swimsuit

After World War I, several factors combined to produce a radical change in swimwear. Women had achieved new levels of independence during the war, and fashions began to allow them more freedom of movement. Interest in active sports of all kinds increased during the 1920s, and sportswear achieved new importance in fashion. Swimming also gained in popularity due to an increase in the number of municipal swimming pools, and the publicity given to such celebrities as Gertrude Ederle, who in 1926 became the first woman to swim the English Channel. Form-fitting knitted wool tank suits, almost identical to those worn by men, were promoted as active swimwear for the modern woman, and soon became the dominant style. At the same time, beach resorts on the Riviera or at Palm Beach became an important part of the fashionable calendar, and beach fashions assumed new significance in society wardrobes. Paris couturiers such as Jean Patou, Jeanne Lanvin, and Elsa Schiaparelli used crisply detailed knit suits—both two-piece suits of tunic and trunks and one-piece suits (known as maillots)—as a canvas for geometric designs in bold, contrasting colors. Spending long leisurely days at the beach also required an extensive on-shore wardrobe, including sunsuits and sunbathing dresses, beach coats and capes, bathing shoes and sandals, close-fitting hats for swimming and wide-brimmed hats for shade, colorful beach umbrellas, beach pajamas (very popular in the late 1920s) and, to hold it all, large canvas beach bags.

By the early 1930s, the growing popularity of sunbathing inspired suits with very low-cut "evening-gown" backs, suits with removable straps for sunning, and suits with large cutouts at the sides and back. The one-piece maillot, with or without a vestigial skirt or skirt front (called a "modesty panel"), was still the most common style, but two-piece suits, consisting of a high-waisted skirt or trunks and a brassiere or halter top, were introduced early in the decade. These sometimes coordinated with matching separates to convert into sundresses or playsuits, which succeeded beach pajamas as the most fashionable form of on-shore beachwear. So-called dressmaker suits were another popular style; these were skirted suits with attached trunks, cut like dresses and usually made of printed or textured woven fabrics (sometimes with an elastic liner).

The Swimwear Industry

In the years following World War I, American manufacturers of ready-made swimwear, most of them based on the West Coast, played a major role in setting fashion trends, and in creating a mass market for fashionable swimwear. The first Jantzen swimming suits, introduced in the late 1910s, were knit in a double-sided rib stitch, which added elasticity and made knitted suits much more practical. The company's innovative advertising campaigns in the 1920s, often featuring Olympic champion swimmers such as Johnny Weissmuller, helped to popularize swimming as well as Jantzen bathing suits, and by 1930 Jantzen was the largest swimwear manufacturer in the world. Catalina and Cole of California, which became major competitors to Jantzen in the late 1920s, emphasized appearance and styling in their suits and advertisements; Catalina became associated with the Miss America pageant, and Cole with Hollywood glamour. Competition between these manufacturers, joined by B.V.D. in 1929, drove changes in swimwear styles and technology through much of the twentieth century.

When feminine curves returned to fashion around 1930, manufacturers began to find ways of shaping the body within the suit, using darts, seaming, and strategically placed elastic to uplift and emphasize the bust. The most important innovation, however, was Lastex, an elastic yarn consisting of an extruded rubber core covered in cotton, rayon, silk, acetate, or wool, which was introduced in 1931 and soon revolutionized the industry. It could be used in both knitted and woven fabrics, gave improved fit and figure control, and allowed designers to add supporting layers, such as brassieres and tummy-control panels, without adding bulk to the silhouette. Lastex-based fabrics, some also incorporating new synthetic yarns, were soon available in a variety of textures and surface treatments, including stretch satins, velvets, shirred cottons, and novelty knits. All-rubber suits, made of embossed rubber sheeting, were introduced in 1932, and were an inexpensive option throughout the decade, though they were easily torn, and sometimes peeled away from the body in pounding surf. Rubber found more practical application in bathing caps, which now fit close to the head to keep the hair dry, and in bathing shoes, many of which were molded rubber facsimiles of street footwear.

The 1930s were also when swimwear manufacturers first turned to Hollywood for style ideas and promotional tie-ins. Jantzen, Catalina, and B.V.D. began to use Hollywood stars in their advertising campaigns, and formed alliances with movie studios and studio designers, lending mass-produced suits an air of Hollywood glamour. Bathing suits worn by stars in films and publicity photos became a major source of swimwear fashion. For example, the strapless sarong-like costumes worn by Dorothy Lamour, first seen in the 1936 film *Jungle Princess*, immediately inspired manufacturers to include sarong suits in their lines, and helped set a fashion for tropical prints in swimwear.

New Styles for Men

While the detailing of men's suits had been somewhat updated by the late 1920s, and their construction and performance had been improved, decency regulations in many places still required men to wear suits thst covered the chest up to the level of the armpits. As sunbathing became more popular, manufacturers tried to work around these regulations, producing suits with side and back cutouts to permit more sun exposure. Pressure to reduce the amount of fabric in suits also came from competitive swimmers, who quickly adopted the silk knit racer-back suits (with low-cut sides and a single back strap to reduce drag) introduced by the Australian company Speedo in 1928. By the early 1930s, public opinion on the decency of the male chest had begun to shift, and American manufacturers developed convertible suits, with tops that could be zipped off where shirtless bathing was allowed. Swimming trunks, although sold with matching shirts in more conservative markets, began selling well in 1934, and by 1937 had almost completely supplanted the one-piece tank suit. The more abbreviated and close-fitting styles of Lastex with built-in athletic supporters were given outerwear details, such as belts, pockets, and fly fronts, to distinguish them from underwear. Around 1940, the looser boxer-short style, usually boldly patterned, became another popular alternative, with matching short-sleeved sports shirts worn as cover-ups.

Postwar Styles

By the early 1940s, women could choose from a wide variety of styles and fabrics, and were encouraged to have a wardrobe of suits appropriate for different activities and occasions. The bust was increasingly emphasized in both one- and two-piece suits, through strategically placed cutouts, ruffles, and bra sections ruched or tied at the center to form a sweetheart neckline. Dressmaker suits made of woven fabrics were popular, in part because Lastex was in short supply during World War II; these included a new category of dressier suits, meant largely for lounging by the pool, with details borrowed from evening wear and an emphasis on firm figure control. Figure control became even more important after the war, as swimwear adopted the dramatic corseted silhouette made fashionable by Christian Dior's 1947 "New Look" collection. Lastex was once more available, and new synthetic fibers such as nylon were quickly adopted for use in swimwear. Suits began to be constructed like foundation garments, with boning, under-wires, interfacing, and padding producing the desired high, pointed breasts, tiny waist, and jiggle-free figure.

Though the first bikini was introduced in 1946, the reaction in America was to move toward more covered up suits, exemplified by the ladylike designs of Rose Marie Reid. In the 1950s, amid growing prosperity and increasing amounts of leisure time, and as more Americans had access to resort vacations and backyard pools, swimwear became more than ever a vehicle for display and fantasy. Swimwear manufacturers found design inspiration in exotic locales such as Mexico and Polynesia, and tropical print and batik ensembles, worn with printed cotton cover-ups and rustic accessories of straw, wood, and raffia, were popular throughout the decade. Exotic animals, especially felines, were another popular theme, as exemplified by the seductive leopard-spotted suits of Cole of California's "Female Animal" collection. Some glamorous poolside ensembles were made of waterproof taffeta and lamé, cut like strapless evening gowns, and decorated with beading and sequins to evoke ancient Egypt or the Arabian Nights. A wide variety of sunsuits, terry-cloth robes, footwear, bathing caps, and sunglasses, along with waterproof makeup, allowed women to maintain a polished appearance, both in and out of the water.

While most 1950s suits were designed to mold the figure to an artificial ideal, a few American designers, including Claire McCardell, Carolyn Schnurer, and Tina Leser, took a different approach. Beginning in the 1940s, they designed unpretentious swimwear and playsuits, usually of wool jersey or printed cotton, which emphasized practicality and freedom of movement over static display. McCardell's ingeniously draped and wrapped jersey suits were praised by the fashion media, but her body-conscious approach had little impact on mainstream styles until the mid-1950s, when swimwear in a similar spirit by designer Rudi Gernreich began to receive attention. Gernreich's sleek wool knit suits, inspired by dancewear, offered a stylish alternative to structured suits, and embodied the casual spirit of California, the source of many lifestyle trends in the late 1950s.

The 1960s to the Present

By the early 1960s, changing attitudes toward body exposure, together with the growing influence of the youth market, brought a new mood to swimwear. The new ideal of a youthful, tanned, and healthy look, with girls in bikinis and boys in cut-off blue jeans or baggy trunks (known as "jams"), was disseminated by beach party movies and the surf music craze. As the decade progressed, swimwear became briefer and more daring, with tiny bikinis, cutouts, mesh and transparent panels, and Rudi Gernreich's famous topless suit. Designs were drawn from an eclectic variety of sources, including pop art, scuba-diving gear, science fiction, and tribal costumes from around the world. The most important swimwear development, however, was the availability of spandex, a lightweight synthetic polyurethane fiber much stronger and more elastic than rubber, which was introduced for use in foundation garments in 1958. Spandex expanded the range of novelty fabrics available to designers, and that meant suits could now be made to fit like a second skin without heavy linings and supporting layers.

In the 1970s and 1980s, a fit, sculpted, and toned body became the new ideal. Rather than shaping the body, fashionable swimwear and beachwear was now designed to frame and reveal it, and difficult-to-tone areas such as the buttocks and upper thighs became the new erogenous zones. Athletic styles, such as racerback tank suits and the Speedo briefs worn by Mark Spitz at the 1972 Olympics, were a major influence. One-piece suits returned to fashion, though many of them were essentially complex networks of crossed and wrapped straps joining small areas of fabric, and offered little more coverage than contemporary thongs and string bikinis. Stretch fabrics could be made lighter than ever, and bright, solid colors and metallic finishes were used for sleek maillots with thin spaghetti straps, which with the addition of a wrap skirt could double as disco wear.

Since the 1980s, despite warnings about the dangers of ultraviolet radiation, swimwear and beachwear have remained an important part of most wardrobes. Swimwear has been in what might be called its postmodern phase, with a wide variety of styles and influences operating simultaneously. Retro styles first appeared in the early 1980s, when designers such as Norma Kamali revived the glamorous shirred and skirted styles of the 1940s, and designs recalling every decade of the twentieth century have since appeared. Other recurring themes have been underwear-as-outerwear styles, with visible boning and underwires; minimalism; and streamlined athletic styles, emphasizing high-tech fabrics and finishes. Men have also been able to choose from a range of retro looks and amounts of coverage, from skimpy bikini briefs to baggy knee-length surfer styles; extremely baggy shorts with low-rise waists are a popular look in the early 2000s. Two late-1990s innovations were the tankini, a two-piece suit with the coverage and figure control of a one-piece, and the concept of mix-and-match swim separates, with a variety of bra styles, trunks, and skirted bottoms recalling the versatile playsuits of the 1930s and 1940s, and offering consumers unprecedented freedom of choice.

See also Bikini; Gernreich, Rudi; Kamali, Norma; McCardell, Claire; Patou, Jean.

Bibliography

Cunningham, Patricia. "Swimwear in the Thirties: The B.V.D. Company in a Decade of Innovation." *Dress* 12 (1986): 11–27.

Johns, Maxine James, and Jane Farrell-Beck. "Cut Out the Sleeves: Nineteenth-Century U.S. Women Swimmers and Their Attire." *Dress* 28 (2001): 53–63.

Kidwell, Claudia. *Women's Bathing and Swimming Costume in the United States*. Washington, D.C.: Smithsonian Institution Press, 1968.

Lansdell, Avril. *Seaside Fashions 1860–1939*. Princes Risborough, U.K.: Shire Publications, 1990.

Lenček, Lena, and Gideon Bosker. *Making Waves: Swimsuits and the Undressing of America*. San Francisco: Chronicle Books, 1989.

Martin, Richard, and Harold Koda. *Splash!: A History of Swimwear*. New York: Rizzoli International, 1990.

Probert, Christina. *Swimwear in Vogue*. New York: Abbeville Press, 1981.

Internet Resource

Miss America Organization. "Miss America History." Available from <http://www.missamerica.org/meet/history/default.asp>.

Susan Ward

T

TAILORING

Tailoring is the art of designing, cutting, fitting, and finishing clothes. The word tailor comes from the French *tailler*, to cut, and appears in the English language during the fourteenth century. In Latin, the word for tailor was *sartor*, meaning patcher or mender, hence the English "sartorial," or relating to the tailor, tailoring, or tailored clothing. The term bespoke, or custom, tailoring describes garments made to measure for a specific client. Bespoke tailoring signals that these items are already "spoken for" rather than made on speculation.

As a craft, tailoring dates back to the early Middle Ages, when tailors' guilds were established in major European towns. Tailoring had its beginnings in the trade of linen armorers, who skillfully fitted men with padded linen undergarments to protect their bodies against the chafing of chain mail and later plate armor. Men's clothing at the time consisted of a loosely fitted tunic and hose. In 1100 Henry I confirmed the royal rights and privileges to the Taylors of Oxford. In London, the Guild of Taylors and Linen Armorers were granted arms in 1299. They became a Company in 1466 and were incorporated into the company of Merchant Taylors in 1503. In France, the tailors of Paris (*Tailleurs de Robes*) received a charter in 1293, but there were separate guilds for Linen Armorers and Hose-Makers. In 1588, various guilds for French tailors were united as the powerful *Maitres Tailleurs d'Habits*. Tailoring has traditionally been and remains a hierarchical and male-dominated trade, though some women tailoresses have learned the trade.

Products

In the sixteenth and seventeenth centuries, tailors were responsible for making a variety of outer garments including capes, cloaks, coats, doublets, and breeches. They gave shape to them by using coarse, stiff linen and canvas for interlining, horsehair cloth and even cardboard stiffened with whalebone for structural elements. Imperfect or asymmetrical body shapes could be evened out with wool or cotton padding. Luxury garments were often lined with satins or furs to keep their wearers warm. Tailors were the structural engineers for women's fashions and made whalebone stays or corsets until the nineteenth century. Women largely made relatively unshaped undergarments and shirts for men, women, and children. The nineteenth-century tailor added trousers, fancy waistcoats, and sporting clothing of all sorts to his repertoire. The tailor was particularly adept at working woolen fabrics, which he shaped and sculpted using steam and heavy irons. Menswear had long used wool as a staple fabric. In Britain wool connoted masculinity, sobriety, and patriotism but in the early nineteenth century, it became extremely fashionable, almost completely replacing the silks and velvets used in the previous century. At the same time, men began to wear trousers rather than breeches and by the 1820s, tightly cut trousers or pantaloons could be worn as evening wear. Though they no longer made corsets, women's sidesaddle riding habits and walking suits remained the province of the tailor and were cut and fashioned from the same fabrics as male garments.

Early Tailoring Manuals

Because tailoring was taught by traditional apprenticeships, skills were passed on from master to apprentice without the need for written manuals. The most skilled aspect of the trade was cutting out garments from the bolt of cloth. In G. B. Moroni's painting *The Tailor* (c. 1570), the fashionably dressed artisan prepares to use his shears on a length of cloth marked with tailor's chalk. These markings would probably have been based on a master pattern. The earliest tailors used cloth patterns because paper and parchment were too expensive at this period. Paper patterns became widespread and commercially available in the nineteenth century.

The earliest known tailoring manuals are Spanish. These are Juaan de Alcega's *Libro de Geometric Practica y Traca* of 1589 and La Rocha Burguen's *Geometrica y Traca* of 1618. These books illustrate ways of drawing patterns to use fabric in the most economical manner, but have no information on technique. Later manuals, such as the important *L'Art du Tailleur* by de Garsault (1769) have more detailed instructions as to measurement, cutting, fit, and construction. The typical workshop had a master tailor, who dealt directly with the client and cut out garments. There might be several cutters in a large establishment and they were at the top of the tailoring hierarchy, for cutting out was the most skilled part of the trade. Under them other journeymen tailors were responsible for a variety of activities, including padding and sewing in interlinings, pockets, and the difficult task of assembling the sleeve and turning the collar, as well as manipulating the heavy shaping iron called a goose. Apprentices were usually responsible for running errands and sweeping up scraps of fabric before being taught basic sewing skills. When sewing machines were introduced, machinists, who might be women, were also added to the workshop floor. The tailors who sewed the garment together sat on a workbench near natural light with legs crossed, hunched over their work. To sit cross-legged in French is still to be *assis en tailleur*, or sitting in the tailor's pose.

The first manual in the English language is the anonymous *The Taylor's Complete Guide*, published in 1796. After this publication, there were many important manuals produced during the nineteenth century, including Compaing and Devere's *Tailor's Guide* (1855) and most importantly, E. B. Giles's *History of the Art of Cutting* (1889) which has been reprinted and provides great insight into the nineteenth-century techniques from a master tailor who knew many of its practitioners personally.

A spirit of competition and enterprise marked the first half of the nineteenth century, when tailors patented a multitude of inventions, manuals, systems of measurement, and fashion journals aimed at the man-about-town and his tailor. Some of the most important of these were the *Tailor and Cutter* and *West-End Gazette*. The endless cycles and revivals of women's fashions seemed illogical and capricious compared to the more rational, linear, and technologically innovative development of men's dress. The finest tailoring combined the principles of science and art to produce clothing that was both engineered and sculptural.

Measurement

Systems of measurement changed radically during the history of tailoring. Tailors have always had the difficult task of creating three-dimensional garments for asymmetrical and highly varied body shapes. Unlike static sculpture, garments also had to allow the wearer to move freely and gracefully during their daily pursuits. Early tailors developed complex systems for measuring the bodies of their clients. However, as most manuals observe, no system could replace the observant eye and hand of the tailor, who noted the more subtle nuances of his client's posture and anatomy and could make allowances for a slight hunch, uneven shoulders, or a protruding stomach. In his tailoring manual of 1769, de Garsault illustrated the strip of paper he used for taking measure. His system involved cutting notches in the strip to measure the breadth of the back and the length of the arm to the elbow. Each client was measured against shifts in his own body's size and shape.

The modern tape measure was introduced in about 1800. In Britain, cloth had been accurately measured in ells (short for elbows), but the body was not quantified in units. In post-revolutionary France the metric system was used to measure the body, whereas British tailors favored inches. The tape measure was soon joined by a compass, ruler, and tracing paper to produce elaborate geometric systems used throughout the nineteenth century. These mathematical patterns could be produced in scaled sizes and were designed around the more abstract idea of a bodily norm or average. In their most elaborate forms these systems used machines like Delas's somatometer or body meter of 1839, which was an adjustable metal cage for measuring the bodies of clients. Entrepreneurs who used them to produce ready-made clothing in standardized sizes gratefully appropriated systems designed to ensure a more accurate fit. Reporting on the inroads made by ready-made tailoring exhibited at the 1867 World's Fair in Paris, Auguste Luchet wrote that the age of the sculptural tailors was over: "There are no more measurements, there are sizes . . . Meters and centimeters. One is no longer a *client*, one is a *size eighty*! A hundred vestimentary factories are leading us toward the absolute and indifferent uniform." Though loosely fitting, ready-made clothing for the lower classes had existed since the seventeenth century, the nineteenth century saw the introduction of high-quality, fitted tailored garments sold off the rack.

Shop Displays

The fully equipped tailor's establishment of the nineteenth and twentieth centuries could be sparsely or luxuriously fitted. The basic requirements of the trade included shelving for the display of cloth bales, a counter where swatches could be consulted, a space where the client could be measured, a fitting room with mirrors, a sturdy table for cutting out, and possibly blocks for saddles to fit riding clothes properly. Fashion prints were also hung as decoration or shown to clients as models. The shop might or might not include a space for workshops. More prestigious firms made garments on the premises while "jobbing" tailors sent bundles of pieces to outworkers, often women, who would assemble the garments at home or in sweatshops. At the top end of the scale, establishments like Henry Poole on Savile Row at the turn of the twentieth century combined more functional elements with the thick carpets, mahogany fittings, satin upholstery and gilded mirrors of the palace or exclusive gentlemen's club. In the twentieth century many tailors kept traditional interiors, though some, like Simpsons of Piccadilly and Austin Reed innovated with modern, Art Deco, or Bauhaus styles and included amenities such as barbershops. In the middle of the nineteenth century, the tailor was joined by hosiers, who specialized in high-end accessories and outfitters, whose trade was based on made-to-measure shirts, but who also sold suits, coats, hats, boots, and all manner of accessories. Their shop window displays tended to emphasize orderliness and neatness to appeal to the male customer.

Tailoring in the Twentieth Century

Bond Street, Savile Row, and St James's Street in the fashionable West End of London have been the center for elite, traditional tailoring since the turn of the eighteenth century. However, tailoring spanned the whole class spectrum, from tailors with royal warrants to immigrants working in the warehouses of the East End. One of the most important shifts in Savile Row tailoring was the transition from a more traditional client base of British gentry and aristocracy to a more international, clientele including American financiers and eventually Hollywood celebrities. Though Savile Row rose to prominence in the late eighteenth century, dressing such figures as the Prince Regent and dandy Beau Brummel, in the twentieth it created the movie wardrobes of Fred Astaire, Cary Grant, and Roger Moore. Though many American stars sought the cachet of Savile Row, there were very talented tailors in the United States. In Harlem, the exaggerated shapes and bright colors of the zoot suit were launched by stylish young black men in the mid-1930s. When the War Production Board tried to curtail this "antipatriotic" tailoring because of wool rationing in 1942, race riots ensued. In Britain, there was a brief revival in elegant Edwardian tailoring after World War II, when so-called Teddy Boys—working-class men who spent large sums on their wardrobes—adopted it. In 1960s London, fashionable men's goods were democratized in the "Peacock Revolution," which saw the center of fashion gravitate toward Carnaby Street and the King's Road—along with Cecil Gee, John Stephen, John Michael, John Pears, Michael Rainey, and Rupert Lycett Green. One of the most important figures in the rejuvenation of menswear was the celebrity tailor Tommy Nutter. He created unique suits for both men and women, including suits for the Beatles, Mick and Bianca Jagger, and Twiggy.

In the 1980s, Italian tailoring began to receive more attention on the international fashion scene. With their "unstructured" suits, designers such as Giorgio Armani catered to a desire for more informal, lighter weight garments for both men and women. At the turn of the millennium, the Italian tailoring firm Brioni dressed the British movie icon James Bond, played by the actor Pierce Brosnan. In Britain, a new generation of designers combine the flawless cut and construction of traditional tailoring with the flair of haute couture. Ozwald Boateng is an Anglo-Ghanian whose work displays a dazzling sense of color and who prefers to describe his work as "bespoke couture." Alexander McQueen, who trained for a short two years on Savile Row, also incorporates tailoring's emphasis on structure and materials into his couture womenswear.

Though it represents a very small part of the contemporary menswear market, custom tailoring still has pride of place in the wardrobe of the sharply dressed man. Whether it applies to computer software or kitchens, the expression "tailor-made" still carries positive connotations of individualized, customized service. In the clothing trade, as long as the suit remains the classic form of formal attire, tailors will elegantly dress their clients. These may include men whose bodies may not fit the norms of the ready-made clothing industry, as well as royalty, businesspeople, or celebrities who turn to the tailor for a classic or innovative suit of clothing made to their precise measure.

See also Armani, Giorgio; Cutting; Savile Row; Sewing Machine; Suit, Business.

Bibliography

Breward, Chris. *The Hidden Consumer: Masculinities, Fashion and City Life 1860–1914*. New York and Manchester, U.K.: Manchester University Press, 1999.

——, ed. *Fashion Theory* 4, no. 4 (December 2000). Special issue focusing on "masculinities."

Chenoune, Farid. *A History of Men's Fashion*. Paris: Flammarion, 1993.

Garsault, M. de. *L'Art du Tailleur* [The art of the tailor]. Paris: Académie Royale des Sciences, 1769.

Giles, E. B. *The History of the Art of Cutting in England*. London: F. T. Prewett, 1887.

Luchet, Auguste. *L'Art Industriel à l'exposition universelle de 1867* [Industrial art at the 1867 World's Fair]. Paris: Librairie Internationale, 1868.

Walker, Richard. *The Savile Row Story*. London: Prion, 1988.

Waugh, Norah. *The Cut of Men's Clothes, 1600–1900*. London: Faber and Faber, 1964.

Alison Matthews David

TATTOOS

Tattooing is a process of creating a permanent or semipermanent body modification that transforms the skin. The word tattoo comes from the Tahitian *tatau*, which means "to mark something"; it is also hypothesized that the term comes from the sound the tatau sticks make when clicking together to mark the skin with ink. Tattooing is a process of puncturing the skin and depositing pigments, usually indelible ink, by a variety of methods beneath the skin to create a desired design or pattern. Tattoos range from "blackwork," large areas of heavy black ink in designs, to fine details and elaborate color schemes including fluorescent inks.

Historic Tattoos

The earliest evidence of tattooing includes tattooing tools and tattooed mummies. At 10,000-year-old sites in Tanzoumaitak, Algeria, tattooing instruments used for puncturing the skin were found with the female tattooed mummy of Tassili N'Ajje. In 1991, Ötzi, a Stone Age male mummy, was found in the Ötztal Alps, bordering Austria and Italy. This mummy had numerous tattoos, which were hypothesized as being used for medicinal cures, spiritual ceremonies, or indicating social status. Two well-preserved Egyptian mummies from 4160 B.C.E., a priestess and a temple dancer for the fertility goddess Hathor, bear random dot and dash tattoo patterns on the lower abdomen, thighs, arms, and chest. In 1993, a fifth-century B.C.E. Ukok priestess mummy, nicknamed the Siberian Ice Maiden, was found on the steppes of eastern Russia. She had several tattoos believed to have had medicinal, spiritual, and social significance. Most of the 4,000-year-old adult mummies from Xinjiang, China, had tattoos that related to their gender or social position.

Classical authors have written about tattoos used by the Thracians, Greeks, Romans, ancient Germans, ancient Celts, and ancient Britons. Tattooing has been practiced in most parts of the world, although it is rare among people with darker skins, such as those of Africa, who more often practice scarification and cicatrisation. Scholars hypothesize that tattooing was a permanent version of the desired aesthetic of body painting. Motivations, meanings, and exact techniques relating to tattoos vary from culture to culture. Tattoos have emphasized social and political roles; indicated cultural values and

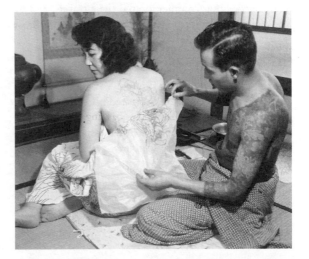

A Japanese artist tattoos a pattern to a customer's back, 1955. These elaborate and symbolic Japanese tattoos became a popular fashion during the late eighteenth to nineteenth century. © BETTMANN/CORBIS. REPRODUCED BY PERMISSION.

created an identity for the individual; reinforced aesthetic ideals; encouraged sexual attraction; eroticized the body; served medicinal and healing roles; communicated group affiliation or membership, and emphasized ritual and spiritual roles and customs of a culture.

Polynesia. In 1787, a French expedition led by Jan Francoise de la Perouse landed on Samoa and reported the men's thighs were heavily painted or tattooed, which gave the appearance of wearing pants. Samoan tattoos were applied with ink, tattoo combs, and hammer. Male tattoos had larger black areas than females, who had lighter, more filigreed lines.

Borneo. In the nineteenth century, Americans with tattoos were sailors and naval personnel, who wrote about their tattoo experiences in ships' logs, letters, and journals. During World Wars I and II, some U.S. soldiers and sailors decorated their bodies with tattoos. Usually these tattoos were from a set of stereotypical symbols—courage, patriotism, and defiance of death—later referred to as "flash." In the early 2000s, flash includes a wide variety of stock art used for tattoos.

Central America. In the nineteenth century most of Europe did not allow tattooing because the Catholic Church admonished it. However, tattooing flourished in England, due primarily to the tradition of tattooing in the British Navy. Many British sailors returned home with tattoos that commemorated their travels, and by the eighteenth century most British ports had at least one tattoo practitioner in residence.

In 1862, Prince Edward of Wales had a Jerusalem cross tattooed on his arm to commemorate his visit to the Holy Land. Later, as King Edward VII, he acquired additional tattoos, and even instructed his sons, the Duke of Clarence and the Duke of York (King George V), to obtain tattoos to commemorate their visit to Japan.

In 1941, the Nazis registered all prisoners entering the Auschwitz concentration camp who were not ethnic Germans with a tattooed serial number. This tattoo was first placed on the left side of the chest; later, the location was moved to the inner forearm.

Contemporary Tattoos

During the latter part of the twentieth century, tattoos were primarily utilized by microcultures, such as motorcycle gangs, street gangs, and punks. In the twenty-first century, tattoos have gained popularity in Western culture and become commonplace and even fashion statements.

At the same time, some microcultures, such as the Modern Primitives, have sought alternative and perhaps more extreme tattooing methods and designs. Often these methods and designs have been borrowed from anthropological texts about ancient cultures and related tattooing practices. There are tattoo practitioners who specialize in "tribal tattoos" and "primitive technologies." "Tribal tattoos" are typically heavy black ink and focus on designs that resemble Polynesian designs, ancient Celtic knotwork, or archaic languages. "Primitive technologies" include a wide variety of manual tattoo application methods, such as sharpened bones and ink; bone combs, hammer and ink; and tatau sticks and soot-based ink. These methods require lengthy tattooing sessions even for the smallest tattoos.

Electric Tattooing Practices

In 1891, the first electric tattooing implement was patented in the United States. In the early twenty-first century, many tattoos are applied in tattoo parlors using hand-held electric tattooing machines controlled by a foot pedal. These machines have a needle bar that holds from one to fourteen needles. The type or specific area of the tattoo design being worked on determines the number of needles. A single needle is used to make fine, delicate lines and shading. Additional needles are used for dense lines and filling with color. Even with the use of all fourteen needles, large or heavily detailed tattoos could take several months to complete.

Each needle extends a couple of millimeters beyond its own ink reservoir, which is loaded with a small amount of ink. Only one color is applied at a time. The tattoo practitioner holds the machine steady and guides the dyeloaded needles across the skin to create the desired pattern or design. A small motor moves the needles up and down to penetrate and deposit ink in the superficial (epidermis) and middle (dermis) layers of the skin.

Tattoo Health-Related Risks

Licensed tattoo establishments are required by law to take measures to ensure the health and safety of their clients. Since puncturing the skin and inserting the inks cause inflammation and bleeding, precautions are taken to prevent the possible spread of blood-borne infections, such as hepatitis B and C. Rooms used in the tattooing process are disinfected before and after each client. An autoclave, a regulated high-temperature steamer that kills blood-borne pathogens and bacterial agents, is used to sterilize the needle bar and reservoirs before each tattoo session. Sterile needles are removed from individual packaging in front of the client. The area of skin to be tattooed is shaved and disinfected by the tattoo practitioner. During the tattooing process, the skin is continually cleaned of excess ink and blood that seep from punctures with absorbent sanitary tissues.

Tattoo Removal

Tattoos have become part of fashion trends, resulting in the need for effective tattoo removal. Past methods of removing tattoos have often left scars. Tattoo removal with laser technology has become the most effective method used and has a minimal risk of scarring. Despite advances in laser technology, many tattoos cannot be completely removed, due to the unique nature of each tattoo. Successful tattoo removal depends on the tattoo's age, size, color, and type, as well as the patient's skin color and the depth of the pigment.

Semipermanent and Temporary Tattoos

Cosmetic tattoos are semipermanent makeup, such as eyeliner and lip color, tattooed on the face. These tattoos use plant-derived inks that are deposited in the superficial skin layer, resulting in a tattoo that lasts up to five years. Temporary tattoos come in a wide variety of designs and patterns. Unlike permanent and semipermanent tattoos, most temporary tattoos can be applied and removed by the wearer. These tattoos are burnished onto the skin and secured with an adhesive. Most temporary tattoos can be removed with soap and water or acetone, depending on the adhesive. Another type of temporary tattoo is henna or *mehndi*, which is a shrublike plant that grows in hot, dry climates, mostly in India, North African countries, and Middle Eastern countries. The leaves are dried, ground into a powder, and made into a paste, which is applied in desired designs to the skin. After several hours of drying, a reddish-brown stain temporarily tattoos the skin. This tattoo begins to fade as the skin exfoliates and renews itself.

See also Body Piercing; Scarification.

Bibliography

Beck, Peggy, Nia Francisco, and Anna Lee Walters, eds. *The Sacred: Ways of Knowledge, Sources of Life.* Tsaile, Ariz.: Navajo Community College Press, 1995.

Camphausen, Rufus C. *Return to the Tribal: A Celebration of Body Adornment.* Rochester, Vt.: Park Street Press, 1997.

Demello, Margo. *Bodies of Inscription: A Cultural History of the Modern Tattoo Community.* Durham, N.C.: Duke University Press, 2000.

Gilbert, Steve. *Tattoo History: A Source Book.* New York: Juno Books, 2001.

Hadingham, Evan. "The Mummies of Xinjiang." *Discover* 15, no. 4 (April 1994): 68–77.

Polosmak, Natalya. "A Mummy Unearthed from the Pastures of Heaven." *National Geographic* 186, no. 4 (October 1994): 80–103.

Simmons, David R. *Ta Moko: The Art of Maori Tattoo.* Auckland: Reed Methuen Publishers, Ltd., 1986.

Tanaka, Shelley. *Discovering the Iceman: What Was It Like to Find a 5,300-Year-Old Mummy?* Toronto: The Madison Press, Ltd., 1996.

Theresa M. Winge

TEA GOWN

The tea gown is an interior gown that emerged in England and France in the 1870s at a time when increased urbanization affected social behavior. The growing number of etiquette manuals and lady's periodicals produced at this time contributed to the revival of teatime by the middle classes and to the adoption of a whimsical type of gown worn by hostesses in their homes at five o'clock tea. Marked by Victorian eclecticism, this unique gown often incorporated elements of fashionable European dress from previous centuries, with exotic fabrics and stylistic components of foreign dress. The tea gown provided respectable women with an outlet for fantasy and innovation within the codified system of nineteenth-century dress and behavioral codes.

The nature and origin of teatime had considerable impact on the development of tea gowns. As tea was worth its weight in gold at the time of its introduction in Europe in the early seventeenth century, its consumption was reserved for the elite. Although this exotic beverage had become widely accessible in Europe and America by the mid-eighteenth century, tea drinking had been established as a class-conscious social event through which a network of selected individuals attained group membership. A sign of hospitality and politeness, serving tea to one's friends and relations retained an air of gentility and exclusivity that appealed to the rising middle classes. This mode of refined social entertainment entailed distinct refreshments, equipment, and rituals and would foster the emergence of a distinctive form of dress.

Specialization was also perceptible in interior spaces and manners, and gave rise to the development of the dining room and parlor. Both have significance in the tea gown's rise in popularity. The emergence of the dining room and the refinement of table etiquette in the mid-nineteenth century led to increased cost and formality when hosting dinners to repay social obligations and entertain friends. In comparison, teatime was far less costly and formal and could host a greater number of individuals, as custom required that guests stay between fifteen minutes and half an hour. With increased urbanization, social circles expanded rapidly and teatime became a more accommodating and feasible event in a system of reciprocity that was often daunting, and where hosting anxieties were on the rise. The parlor was in nature more flexible and became a stage for public display where teatime was held. As socializing was frequently conducted in private residences, home was also a public stage, and many late nineteenth-century parlors aimed to convey to visitors the owners' artistic sensibilities. This contributed to the popularity of the tea gown, which was considered to be the appropriate form of dress for artistic and exotic features. Many such gowns were aesthetically coordinated with their surroundings. This also influenced artist James Abbott McNeil Whistler and architect Henry van de Velde to design tea gowns for sitters or clients.

As teatime had long been conducted in private residences, the type of gown worn for the occasion was derived from interior gowns, which fit into the category of "undress." Nineteenth-century dress code was mainly divided in three categories: "undress," "half dress," and "full dress." Although this classification suggests a crescendo from least to most formal, elevated levels of formality existed within each category. As both men and women participated in social tea-drinking, and because teatime could be attended by distant acquaintances, tea gowns worn by hostesses did not stray far from Victorian propriety and became very formal interior gowns that were

fit for public exposure. The state of "undress" could thus include gowns that were loose or semi-fitted to those, like the tea gown, that could be as fitted as other day and evening dresses. However, artistic elements such as Watteau pleats (wide pleats emerging from the center back neckline borrowed from eighteenth-century gowns) and draped front panels were among the features often added to a fitted understructure that gave the impression of looseness. These elements gave way to very elaborate interior gowns that were not labeled as "tea gowns" until the late 1870s.

The earliest labeled tea gowns discovered to date appeared in the 1878 British periodical, *The Queen, The Lady's Newspaper*. These one-piece gowns with long sleeves, high necklines, and back trains were made to give the impression of being closely fitted open robes with under dresses. One had the Watteau pleats and was named "The Louis XV Tea Gown." This is of interest as it names its source of inspiration and reinforces the eighteenth-century salon connection that was mentioned by writers of the period, and helped to intellectualize and elevate the status of teatime. Such tea gowns co-exist with numerous other elaborate interior gowns of the same style, which, until the turn of the century, were as likely to be named with the new term "tea gown" as they were to be labeled by the variant French term, *robe de chambre*. The words *robe* and *toilette* were also used interchangeably, as were *chambre* and *intérieur*. Terminology is thus a problem because tea gowns were derived from interior gowns, but not all interior gowns were fit to be worn in mixed company at teatime.

Nineteenth-century tea gowns seen in fashion plates followed the bustled styles of their times, and descriptions mentioned elaborate fashion fabrics and trims. This serves to differentiate these gowns further from other interior gowns. Although loose and artistic features were acceptable in tea gowns, their public use mandated the adoption of the fashionable and highly-fitted silhouette.

As wearing underpinnings such as bustles without a corset was not a Victorian practice, the contrived fashionable silhouette present in tea gowns observed in fashion plates and in surviving specimens in museum collections suggests that corsets were worn under some of theses gowns.

From the late 1870s to the mid-1910s, tea gowns were immensely popular. Their magnificence was on the rise and leading designers joined in with fanciful creations that could easily have been mistaken for fancy dresses.

As Edwardian dress gave rise to a love of different colors and fabrics and introduced Empire revival features in high fashion, a progressive blurring occurred. The appropriateness of historically inspired gowns with looser and exotic elements was no longer confined to teatime. This also expanded the tea gown's use to other day and evening events. As the revivalist Empire silhouette gained ground and exoticism became the rage, it became hard to differentiate tea gowns from other types of gowns. Changes also occurred in the physical settings of teatime, which migrated to newly-popular tea pavilions and helped the *thés dansants* of the 1910s supersede teatime in the home as the fashionable thing to do.

See also Empire Style; Europe and America: History of Dress (400–1900 C.E.); Robe.

Bibliography

Kasson, John F. *Rudeness and Civility: Manners in Nineteenth-Century Urban America.* New York: Hill and Wang, 1990.

Roth, Rodris. "Tea-Drinking in Eighteenth-Century America: Its Etiquette and Equipage." In *Material Life in America, 1600–1860.* Edited by Robert Blair St. George. Boston: Northeastern University Press, 1988, pp. 439–462.

Montgomery, Maureen E. *Displaying Women: Spectacles of Leisure in Edith Wharton's New York.* New York: Routledge, 1998.

Anne Bissonnette

THEATRICAL COSTUME

Western theater tradition has its foundations in the Greek celebrations performed in the sixth century B.C.E., honoring Dionysus, the god of wine and revelry. The revels (dances, songs, and choral responses) evolved into spoken drama in 535 B.C.E., when the playwright Thespis introduced an actor to respond to the chorus leader. The result was dialogue.

Another playwright, Aeschylus (525–456 B.C.E.), is credited with establishing what became the traditional costume for Greek tragedy. It consisted of a long, sleeved, patterned tunic, a stylized mask for instant character recognition, and a pair of high-soled shoes called corthunae. All of these garments were exclusively for theatrical use. One cannot act the hero in everyday wear.

Actors in Greek comedies also wore masks to indicate which characters they portrayed. Additionally, they would often add exaggerated body parts, padded bottoms or stomachs, and oversize phalluses to heighten the comic effect. Short tunics, much like those worn by ordinary citizens, were thought appropriate to comedy.

Although the Romans added their own twists, the costume conventions established by the Greeks essentially remained the same until the fall of the Roman Empire, when Western theater virtually disappeared for eight hundred years.

The Middle Ages and the Renaissance

When theater reemerged, it did so, ironically, in the context of the church. The Christian church was the sworn enemy of the drama (perceiving it to be both immodest and akin to devil-worshiping). But, since services were performed in Latin, which fewer and fewer parishioners could understand, priests had to devise a way to dramatize the liturgy.

From the fifth century C.E. forward, mystery plays, dramatizing events in the scriptures, and miracle plays, which depicted the lives of the saints, were increasingly performed both inside the church and on church grounds. As they became more elaborate, they moved into the market square.

Costumes worn in the early religious dramas were ecclesiastical garments. As the scripts became more secular, often involving townspeople in addition to the clergy, lay performers assumed responsibility for any costume pieces not owned by the church. Contemporary religious art provided inspiration for such characters as Daniel, Herod, the Virgin Mary, and assorted devils.

It was during the Renaissance that production elements, both scenery and costume, came to be even more important than the text. Throughout Europe, the nobility staged lavish court masques and pageants to entertain their guests. Costumes depicted gods, animals, and mythological creatures, as well as such emotions as hope and joy. Designers for these festivities included Leonardo da Vinci and Inigo Jones.

The Commedia Dell'arte

Commedia dell'arte, a form of popular street comedy, emerged in Italy during the sixteenth century. Groups of itinerant actors presented largely improvised plays throughout Italy and Europe.

Like the Greek comedies (to which commedia is thought to be linked), commedia actors portrayed stock characters identifiable by their masks and by their traditional costumes. Pantaloon, the archetypal doddering old man, was often dressed in the wide trousers that now bear his name. The wily servant Brighella had a coat of horizontal green stripes, the forerunner of nineteenth-century British livery. Other comic characters include Arlecchino, or Harlequin, Il Dottore, a pedantic academic always dressed in black, and Il Capitano, a cowardly Spaniard. The serious characters in commedia, two pair of lovers and a servant girl, wore contemporary clothing.

The works of William Shakespeare, Jean-Baptiste Moliere, and Jean-Antoine Watteau all show evidence of the influence of this important popular art form.

The Sixteenth through the Eighteenth Century

Costumes for Shakespeare's plays were a mixture of various periods that audiences accepted as the standard convention. Most parts were performed in contemporary dress either owned by the actor (all were men) or provided by the theater's patron. On occasion, a helmet or breastplate might indicate a soldier. Fairies and nymphs might wear classical draperies.

The same principle applies to costume in the seventeenth and eighteen centuries. Most actors and especially actresses dressed as fashionably as possible. A turban indicated an Eastern character. A plumed helmet signified a soldier. Performers provided their own wardrobe with the exception of specialty items provided by the theater.

The Nineteenth and Early Twentieth Centuries

The period between the 1770s and the 1870s saw a drive toward historical accuracy in costume design. As travel became relatively easier, reports, both written and visual, increased people's knowledge of other cultures. International exhibitions such as the Crystal Palace Exhibition in London in 1851 brought the material culture of exotic places to the public. They wanted what they saw and read about to be reflected on the stage.

In the German principality of Saxe-Meiningen, Duke George II established his own theatrical troupe called the Meiningers. The Duke used every available resource to create authentic costumes for his actors.

The Meiningers toured the continent widely, and the style of their productions greatly influenced such bastions of nineteenth century realism as the Théâtre Libre in Paris, and the Moscow Art Theater in Russia. In the United States, the productions of impresario David Belasco reflected his admiration for this new, realistic style.

An inevitable backlash followed. In Russia, to cite just one example, constructivist artists designed highly conceptual costumes whose only relationship to clothing was that they were worn by human beings.

Eventually both styles were recognized as valid, leading to the mixture of historically accurate or concept driven productions that continues in the twenty-first century.

Current Practice

Theatrical costumes are designed to support the script. If realism or historicism is central to the text, the costumes will accurately reflect the clothing appropriate to the period or to the environment. Examples include Henrik Ibsen's *The Master Builder*, which requires clothing of the early 1890s, or David Storey's *The Changing Room*, which calls for uniforms and street wear appropriate for a group of rugby players in the North of England.

Other scripts require a more fanciful approach. Shakespeare's *The Tempest* must be set on an island, but that island can be anywhere in the world. Prospero and Miranda can inhabit any time period agreed upon by the director and the design team.

Costume's Influence on Fashionable Dress

While film costume often influences fashionable clothing, theatrical costume almost never does. A film is seen by millions of people across the country in the first week of its release. By contrast, the average Broadway theater can accommodate only eight thousand people in the same one-week period.

Moreover, there is typically an interval of a year or more between the end of shooting and the film's release. In this interval fashion magazines and other periodicals can run spreads showcasing the costumes, creating customer demand. Historically, film studios, manufacturers, department stores, and dressmaker pattern companies entered into partnerships to promote both the film and the ready-to-wear (or ready-to-sew) garments which the film inspired.

A classic example is the "Letty Lynton" dress worn by Joan Crawford in the 1932 film of the same name. More than 500,000 copies of Adrian's design were reputedly sold at every price point as soon as the film opened. In 1967, Theodora von Runkle's costumes for *Bonnie and Clyde* sparked the trend for 1930s revival styles that were so popular in the late 1960s. Ruth Morley's costumes for Diane Keaton produced *Annie Hall* look-alikes throughout the United States and Europe in the late 1970s.

Another reason why there can be little relationship between theatrical clothing and street wear is scale. A costume is designed to be seen from a distance of thirty or forty feet. Details are exaggerated to make them visible. Film, in contrast, is largely about close-ups. Movie costumes have to be "real" in a way that successful theatrical costumes cannot be.

A few exceptions exist, but they are rare. A red suit designed by Patricia Zipprodt for the 1969 Broadway production of Neil Simon's *Plaza Suite* was subsequently manufactured for Bergdorf Goodman. In 2002, Bloom-ingdale's introduced a collection of plus-size garments based on William Ivey Long's designs for the musical *Hairspray*.

The audience for a theatrical event is so small relative to the number of people who attend films that it makes little economic sense to use the theater as a design source. Contemporary clothing for the stage may reflect fashionable dress, but it does not influence it.

Special Requirements

Above everything, a theatrical costume is designed for movement. Armholes are cut higher than they are in mass-produced clothing to permit the actor to raise his arms without the whole garment following. Crotches are cut higher to allow for kicks without splitting a seam.

Costumes must be constructed to be strong enough to withstand eight wearings a week for months or even years, with infrequent cleaning or laundering. If the script calls for a "quick change," meaning that the performer makes a complete change of clothing in under a minute, the costume will be constructed to facilitate the change. To change a shirt quickly, for example, the buttons are sewn on top of the buttonholes. The shirt is held closed by snaps or hook and loop tape so that it can literally be ripped off the performer.

Dancers shoes must have soles thin enough to allow the dancer to flex and point her foot. When custom-made, elk skin is the material of choice.

Trends and Developments

Theatrical costumes rely heavily on natural fibers (cotton, linen, silk, and wool). Synthetics do not handle or drape like natural fibers. That said, however, the development of new materials has had a tremendous effect on the industry.

Before the late 1950s, for example, dancer's tights were made from elasticized cotton, given to sags and bags, or they were knitted and prone to runs. The invention of Lycra, spandex, and other two-way stretch fabrics eliminated such problems. Braided nylon horsehair can be used to make ruffs that simulate the starched linen originals but which hold their shape when laundered.

No firm manufactures textiles exclusively for use in costumes. The market is far too small. Costumers, however, are extremely creative in discovering theatrical uses for products designed for other purposes. Veri-form, a brand name for a type of thermoplastic sheeting, for example, is an open weave, plastic mesh fabric used by orthopedic surgeons for lightweight casts. It makes excellent armor and masks, is nontoxic and easy to work with.

The plastic netting used to ventilate baseball caps makes indestructible and inexpensive crinolines. Air conditioning and other types of foam can be cut and sculpted to form the understructure of lightweight mascot or other costumes that are taller and broader than the actor inside them. Birdseed, encased in a body suit, is excellent to simulate the movement of sagging breasts.

The most significant development in the field in the last twenty years has undoubtedly been a heightened awareness of health and safety issues. As late as the 1970s both designers and costume makers routinely treated fabrics with highly toxic paints, solvents, and glues with no understanding of the risks involved. In the twenty-first century, not only are less toxic products available, but material safety data sheets, respirators, spray booths, and other protective devices are the norm.

While materials continue to evolve, and styles of costume design go in and out of fashion, the principle remains constant. As Robert Edmond Jones wrote in 1941, "A stage costume is a creation of the theater. Its quality is purely theatrical and taken outside the theater it loses its magic at once. It dies as a plant dies when uprooted" (p. 91).

See also Actors and Actresses, Impact on Fashion; Art and Fashion; Ballet Costume; Theatrical Makeup.

Bibliography

Bieber, Margaret. *The History of the Greek and Roman Theater.* Princeton, N.J.: Princeton University Press, 1961.

Cheney, Sheldon. *The Theatre: Three Thousand Years of Drama, Acting and Stagecraft.* New York, London, and Toronto: Longmans, Green and Co., 1952.

Gascoine, Bamber. *World Theater: An Illustrated History.* Boston and Toronto: Little, Brown and Co., 1968.

Jones, Robert Edmond. *The Dramatic Imagination.* New York: Theatre Arts, 1941.

Laver, James. *Costume in the Theatre.* New York: Hill and Wang, 1965.

Molinari, Cesare. *Theater through the Ages.* New York: McGraw Hill Book Company, 1975.

Whitney Blausen

THEATRICAL MAKEUP

Thousands of years ago, people in many parts of the world discovered that powdered pigments mixed into a base of wax or grease could be used to create striking effects of personal adornment and transformation. The survival of that practice is reflected in a common term for theatrical makeup, "grease-paint." Select types or styles of makeup were often used for special occasions, which could include going to war, celebrating stages of life, and religious festivals. The latter often included performative aspects, such as dance and reenactments of mythical events. Modern theatrical makeup therefore is heir to a very ancient performance tradition.

Some ancient theatrical traditions have relied on masks for the creation of visual characters; others have relied on makeup for the same purpose. In Asia, for example, one can point to the masked theater of Java and the elaborately made-up Kathakali dance theater of southwestern India, or the masked religious dances of Tibet and the strikingly masklike makeup of the Peking Opera and related theatrical forms in China. In Japan, the Noh drama is masked, while Kabuki drama employs extravagant makeup.

Ancient Greek theater was masked, but later European theater usually used stage makeup to create characters, heighten facial features, and compensate for the effects of stage lighting. (The Italian Commedia del'Arte, which continued to employ masks, was an important exception.) Until well into the twentieth century, performers were expected to do their own makeup, as they were expected to supply their own stage costumes. The professional theatrical makeup artist is a modern phenomenon, as is the theatrical costume designer.

Theatrical makeup is inseparable from the act of performance itself. The aim of theatrical makeup is to delineate and enhance the role of a character and to give performers an additional tool for conveying the characters being performed. Stage makeup is often used to create visual stereotypes or clichés that will be readily understood by the audience. Stage makeup is usually much more colorful and graphic than ordinary cosmetic makeup. When viewed closely, it can seem excessive and exaggerated, but it works when the performer is on stage being seen at a distance by the audience. Theatrical makeup itself is also heavier, more dense, and more strongly colored than ordinary cosmetics, and it is often produced in the form of lipstick-like waxy crayons or pencils. For many performers, the act of putting on makeup is an important part of the ritual of preparing for a performance; it allows the performer to move psychologically into the role of the character as the makeup is being applied.

Makeup artists are employed today in a variety of roles, and they often specialize in, for example, theatrical makeup, cinema makeup, fashion photography and runway makeup, or special effects. Regardless of specialty, they typically require years of training and practice to perfect their skills. Special effects makeup is particularly prominent in the world of film, but has also played an important role in the success of many popular Broadway productions, such as *Jekyll and Hyde* and *Beauty and the Beast.* In the film trilogy *The Lord of the Rings*, the prosthetic feet worn by the hobbits were made by a team of special effects makeup artists. Hundreds of pairs were made, as a new pair had to be worn daily by each actor in a hobbit role. In executing such assignments, makeup artists have to draw on skills in sculpture and other plastic arts as well as in the use of cosmetics.

Whether in the dramatic makeup of a horror film or the powerful aesthetic appeal of the unique makeup employed by the Cirque du Soleil, makeup plays an important part in establishing the characterization and impact of a performed role. Baz Luhrmann's successful films of *Romeo and Juliet* and *Moulin Rouge*, and his stage production of *La Bohême*, owed a significant part of their theatricality and audience appeal to his production team's careful use of makeup techniques that evoked a period style. As these examples indicate, by the early twenty-first century makeup in different theatrical and fashion genres began to cross previously rigid barriers. The world of film, especially in special effects, has had a profound impact on the development of new techniques of stage makeup, and today theatrical makeup shows up regularly on fashion catwalks as well. Recent fashion shows by Dior and Givenchy, for example, have been notable for their strong sense of theater. Fashion makeup artists have begun to borrow liberally from traditional stage makeup techniques to create striking new designs that help to showcase the fashions on display. Meanwhile, theatrical makeup is enriched by new developments in film, fashion photography, and other media.

See also Makeup Artists.

Bibliography

Corson, Richard. *Fashions in Makeup: From Ancient to Modern Times.* London: Peter Owen Ltd., 1972.

Delamar, Penny. *The Complete Make-up Artist: Working in Film, Television, and Theater.* 2nd edition. Evanston, Ill.: Northwestern University Press, 2002.

Kehoe, Vincent. *The Technique of the Professional Make-up Artist.* New York: Focal Press, 1995.

Elizabeth McLafferty

TIGHT-LACING

The term "tight-lacing" refers to the laces that tighten a corset. There is no generally accepted definition of what constitutes tight-lacing since it could be argued that any corset that is not loose is tight. Furthermore, there is no agreement as to how tightly corsets were usually laced. Some nineteenth-century writers argued that any use

of the corset was dangerously unhealthy, whereas others tolerated or praised "moderate" corsetry, reserving their criticism for tight-lacing, however this might be defined. When they mentioned measurements at all, they variously defined tight-lacing as a reduction of the waist by anywhere from three to ten inches. That is, depending on the definition, a natural waist of, say, 27 inches might be reduced to a circumference of anywhere between 24 inches and 17 inches.

John Collet's caricature *Tight Lacing, or Fashion Before Ease* (1770–1775) depicts a fashionable woman clutching a bedpost, while several people tug strenuously at her stay laces. Anyone who has seen the movie *Gone with the Wind* (1939) can picture Scarlett O'Hara in a similar situation, exclaiming that if she cannot be laced down to 18 inches, she will not be able to fit into any of her dresses.

Published accounts of extreme tight-lacing in Victorian periodicals, such as *The Englishwoman's Domestic Magazine* (EDM), describe young women reducing their waists to sixteen inches or less. For example, a letter signed Nora was published in the *EDM* in May 1867, claiming to have attended "a fashionable school in London" where "it was the custom for the waists of the pupils to be reduced one inch per month. When I left school ... my waist measured only thirteen inches." Another letter signed Walter appeared in November 1867: "I was early sent to school in Austria, where lacing is not considered ridiculous in a gentleman ... and I objected in a thoroughly English way when the doctor's wife required me to be laced. A sturdy *mädchen* was stoically deaf to my remonstrances, and speedily laced me up tightly ... The daily lacing tighter and tighter produced inconvenience and absolute pain. In a few months, however, I was ... anxious ... to have my corsets laced as tightly as a pair of strong arms could draw them."

Between 1867 and 1874 *EDM* printed dozens of letters on tight-lacing, as well as on topics such as flagellation, high heels, and spurs for lady riders. Later in the century, other periodicals, such as *The Family Doctor*, published letters and articles on tight-lacing. The notorious "corset correspondence" has been cited by some writers, such as David Kunzle, as evidence of extreme tight-lacing during the Victorian era.

However, most scholars in the early 2000s believe that these accounts represent fantasies. Indeed, by the end of the century, the tight-lacing literature becomes increasingly pornographic, as fetishist themes overlap with sadomasochistic and transvestite scenarios. Such accounts may well indicate the existence in the later nineteenth century of sexual subcultures where corset fetishists (most of whom were probably men) enacted their fantasies in settings such as specialized brothels, where they paid prostitutes to role-play as sadistic governesses. Yet this is a far cry from the use of corsets in ordinary women's lives.

The popular belief that many Victorian women had 16-inch waists is almost certainly false. Corset advertisements in the second half of the nineteenth century usually give waist measurements of 18 to 30 inches, and larger sizes were also available. Within museum costume collections, it is rare to find a corset measuring less than 20 inches around the waist. Moreover, as the author of *The Dress Reform Problem* (1886) noted, "A distinction should be made between actual and corset measurements, because stays as ordinarily worn, do not meet at the back. Young girls, especially, derive intense satisfaction from proclaiming the diminutive size of their corset. Many purchase 18- and 19-inch stays, who must leave them open two, three, and four inches. 15, 16, and 17 inch waists are glibly chattered about . . . [yet] we question whether it is a physical possibility for women to reduce their natural waist measure below 17 or 18 inches."

This is not to say that women did not use corsets to reduce their waists. Writing in 1866, the English author Arnold Cooley claimed that, "The waist of healthy women . . . is found to measure 28 to 29 inches in circumference. Yet most women do not permit themselves to exceed 24 inches round the waist, whilst tens of thousands lace themselves down to 22 inches, and many deluded victims of fashion and vanity to 21 and even to 20 inches."

The discourse on tight-lacing needs to be analyzed in ways that move beyond simple measurements. Because the practice of tight-lacing was so ill-defined and yet was perceived as being so ubiquitous in the nineteenth century, it became the focus of widespread social anxieties about women.

Tight-lacing disappeared as a social issue with the decline of the corset as a fashionable garment in the early twentieth century. However, there still existed individuals who wore tightly laced corsets. In the mid-twentieth century, Ethel Granger was listed in the *Guinness Book of World Records* for having "the world's smallest waist," which measured 13 inches. In the early twenty-first century, the most famous tight-lacer is probably the corsetier Mr. Pearl, who claims to have a 19-inch waist. His friend Cathie J. boasts of having reduced her waist to 15 inches.

See also Corset; Fetish Fashion.

Bibliography

Kunzle, David. *Fashion and Fetishism*. Totowa, N.J.: Rowman and Littlefield, 1982.

Steele, Valerie. *Fetish: Fashion, Sex and Power*. New York: Oxford University Press, 1996.

——. *The Corset: A Cultural History*. New Haven and London: Yale University Press, 2001.

Summers, Leigh. *Bound to Please*. Oxford: Berg, 2001.

Ward, E. *The Dress Reform Problem: A Chapter for Women*. London: Hamilton, Adams, 1886.

Valerie Steele

TOGA

The toga was a wrapped outer garment worn in ancient Rome. Its origin is probably to be found in the *tebenna*, a semicircular mantle worn by the Etruscans, a people who lived on the Italian peninsula in an area close to that occupied by the Romans. Several Roman kings were Etruscan and many elements of Etruscan culture were taken over by the Romans. The toga may have been one of these elements.

The toga was a highly symbolic garment for the Romans. It had numerous forms, but the *toga pura* or *toga virilis* was the most significant. In its earliest form the toga pura was a semicircle of white wool.

At the time of the Roman Republic (509 B.C.E. to 27 B.C.E.) and after, only free male citizens of Rome who were at least sixteen years of age could wear this toga. It was the symbol of Roman citizenship and was required dress for official activities. Men wore togas to audiences with the Emperor and to the games played in the Roman arena.

The toga was worn outermost, over a tunic. (A tunic was a T-shaped woven garment, similar in form to a long, modern T-shirt.) The toga wrapped around the body. The straight edge was placed at the center of the body, perpendicular to the floor. The bulk of the fabric was carried over the left shoulder, across the back and under the right arm, after which it was draped across the chest and over the left shoulder.

By the time of the Roman Empire, the earlier half-circle toga had changed its form and had an extended section added to the semicircle at the straight edge. The system of draping remained the same, however the extended section was first folded down. The overfold section fell at the front of the body and formed a pocketlike pouch, called the *sinus*, into which the wearer could place objects such as a scroll of paper. As the toga became still more elaborate and larger, the sinus eventually was too open and loose for holding things, so a knot of fabric was pulled up from underneath to form an area called the *umbo*, and this being smaller and more compact became the "pocket" area. The umbo may also have helped to hold the toga in place.

Individuals of some significant status wore special togas. Although both men and women had worn togas in early Roman times, by the time of the Republic only men wore togas. However, a vestige of the earlier practice remained. Sons and daughters of Roman citizens wore the *toga praetexta*, a toga with a purple border about two or three inches wide. Boys wore this toga until age fourteen to sixteen when they assumed the *toga pura*, while girls gave up the garment around the age of puberty. Certain priests and magistrates also wore the *toga praetexta*.

Political candidates wore a *toga candida* that was bleached very white. The English word "candidate" derives from the name of this garment.

A *toga picta* was purple with gold embroidery. Victorious generals and others who had been singled out for special honors were awarded the opportunity to wear this toga. A *toga pulla* appears to have been worn for mourning, and was dark or black in color. The *toga trabea* seems to have been worn by religious augurs or important officials.

The toga was an awkward garment. Roman writers speak of the difficulties in keeping the toga properly arranged. Apparently it was acceptable for men to wear longer or shorter togas. A poor man might wear a shorter toga in order to save money, while one seeking to impress others might wear an especially large and long toga. In order to keep this garment clean, it had to be washed often, which caused it to wear out frequently. Replacing a worn toga was an expense that is commented on by some Roman satirists.

By the time of the Roman Republic and after, respectable adult women did not wear togas. Prostitutes were said to wear togas, as were women who had been divorced for adultery. The connotation of a woman wearing a toga implied disapproval.

The form of the toga continued to change. It seems as if men were constantly searaching for variations that made the toga easier to keep in place. In one version dating from circa 118–119 C.E. and after, the umbo was eliminated by wrapping the section under the right arm at a higher point and twisting that upper section to form a sort of band. This band was called a *balteus*. In the third century it was an easy step from this to "the toga with the folded bands."

In the toga with the folded bands, the twisted balteus became an overfold that was folded and refolded over itself in order to form a flat, layered band of fabric that may have been fastened in place by either pinning or sewing. As the toga wrapped around the body, the bands lay flat, fitting smoothly in a diagonal band across the front of the body.

In the latter years of the Roman Empire, discipline in following prescribed forms of dress grew somewhat lax, and men preferred to wear the *pallium* instead of the toga. The pallium itself was an evolved form of a Greek wrapped garment, the himation, which draped much the same way as the toga. The pallium was a rectangular panel of fabric that, like the toga, ran perpendicular to the floor, around the left shoulder, under the right arm, and across the body, draping over the arm. It was a sort of skeletal form of the toga, retaining its draping but losing its semi-circular form and most of its bulk.

Although the toga in its exact Roman form has not been revived in contemporary fashion, the name "toga" is often loosely applied to fashions that feature one covered and one uncovered shoulder. Examples include the "toga dress" defined by Calasibetta (2003) as an "Asymmetric dress or at-home robe styled with one shoulder bare, the other covered" or the "toga nightgown," which could be "styled with one shoulder." Both were styles introduced in the 1960s (Calasibetta 2003).

See also Ancient World: History of Dress.

Bibliography

Calasibetta, C. M., and P. Tortora. *The Fairchild Dictionary of Fashion.* New York: Fairchild Publications, 2003.

Croom, A. T. *Roman Clothing and Fashion.* Charleston, S.C.: Tempus Publishing Inc., 2000.

Goldman, N. "Reconstructing Roman Clothing." In *The World of Roman Costume*. Edited by J. L. Sebesta and L. Bonfante, pp. 213–237. Madison: University of Wisconsin Press, 1994.

Houston, M. G. *Ancient Greek, Roman, and Byzantine Costume*. London: Adam and Charles Black, l966.

Rudd, N., trans. *The Satires of Horace and Persius*. Baltimore, Md.: Penguin Books, 1973.

Stone, S. "The Toga: From National to Ceremonial Costume." In *The World of Roman Costume*. Edited by J. L. Sebesta, and L. Bonfante, pp. 13–45. Madison: University of Wisconsin Press, 1994.

Tortora, P., and K. Eubank. *Survey of Historic Costume*. New York: Fairchild Publications, 1998.

Wilson, L. M. *The Roman Toga*. Baltimore, Md.: Johns Hopkins Press, 1924.

Phyllis Tortora

TOLEDO, ISABEL AND RUBEN*

Ruben and Isabel Toledo are a husband-and-wife team who work closely together in several fields of fashion. She is a fashion designer known for producing clothing that combines sophisticated simplicity and meticulous craftsmanship. He is a fashion artist whose distinctive drawings have appeared in many fashion publications and whose work extends to designing mannequins and painting murals for fashionable restaurants; Isabel is his muse and almost invariably his model. He also is responsible for managing the business side of her clothing business. Theirs is a true creative partnership; it is impossible to delineate the boundaries of the contribution of each to the work of the other.

Born in Cuba in 1961, Isabel learned to sew as a child, when she was fascinated by her grandmother's sewing machine. She describes Cuban culture as one in which mastering the techniques of fine sewing was an admired accomplishment for women. When she first began designing clothes, she adopted the technique, associated with such great couturieres as Mmes. Grès and Madeleine Vionnet, of working directly with fabric by draping and cutting, designing in three dimensions. Like Claire McCardell, she works in simple materials such as denim, cotton jersey, and cotton flannel. She describes her garments as forward-looking and optimistic.

Ruben Toledo was born in Cuba in 1960; he and Isabel met in school as members of the large Cuban expatriate community of northern New Jersey. They quickly recognized one another as kindred spirits and began collaborating in art and design. They were married in 1984.

Isabel showed her first collection in 1985 and was immediately acclaimed as an important new talent on the New York fashion scene. Her clothes—architectural, slightly severe, with black or shades of gray dominating her palette—became highly prized by wearers of fashion-forward, "downtown" styles and were praised in such publications as the *Village Voice*, *Paper*, and *Visionaire*. Acquiring a cult following in New York, Paris, and Tokyo, Isabel nevertheless has had difficulties finding sufficient long-term financial backing to break out of niche markets to reach more widespread recognition.

The Toledos had a major exhibition, *Toledo/Toledo: A Marriage of Art and Fashion*, at the museum at the Fashion Institute of Technology (FIT) in 1999. Ruben's illustrations reached a wide audience in his witty book, *Style Dictionary* (1997). In one of his iconoclastic fashion illustrations, entitled "Fashion history goes on strike," Ruben portrayed dresses from the past, from New Look to Mod, parading across the page in a militant demonstration, carrying placards reading, "Let us rest in peace! No more retro! Look forward, not backward!" Both of the Toledos remain on the cutting edge of style, moving fashion forward.

First Lady Michelle Obama wore a lemongrass-yellow Isabel Toledo dress and coat ensemble for her husband's inauguration as president in January 2009. This world-famous ensemble was later featured in a major exhibition, "Isabel Toledo: Fashion from the Inside Out," at the Museum at FIT in New York in the summer of 2009. It was subsequently acquired by the Smithsonian Institute in Washington, D.C., for its popular display of First Ladies' Dresses.

See also Art and Fashion.

Bibliography

Hastreiter, Kim. "Isabel Toledo." *Paper* (Fall 1998).

Mason, Christopher. "A Pair of Muses, above It All." *New York Times* (27 February 1997).

Steele, Valerie and Mears, Patricia. *Isabel Toledo: Fashion from the Inside Out*. New Haven, Conn., and London: Yale University Press, 2009.

Toledo, Isabel and Toledo. *Toledo/Toledo: A Marriage of Art and Fashion*. Kyoto: Korinsha Press, 1998. An exhibition catalog.

Toledo, Ruben. *Style Dictionary: A Visualization, Exploration, Transformation, Mutation, Documentation, Investigation, Classification, Free-association, Interpretation and Exact Quotations of Fashion Terms and a Collection of Past Works.* New York: Abbeville, 1997.

Valerie Steele

TRENDSETTERS

Functionally, clothes provide warmth and protection. Socially, clothes express status and identity. The first trendsetters were members of the ruling class, particularly monarchs and aristocrats. Queen Elizabeth I, for example, adorned herself as if her person were the state, creating an unassailable image for herself as Britain's monarch. Similarly, Louis XIV of France dressed to impress, and also set rules regulating what members of the court aristocracy were to wear. By the eighteenth century, however, trends were increasingly set by individuals in urban centers, such as Paris and London, rather than at court.

In the mid-nineteenth century, the wife of Napoleon III, working with the couturier Charles Frederick Worth, set fashions for an eclectic array of nouveaux riches, social climbers, old aristocrats, and members of the demimonde. Women of the demimonde were often entertainers, actresses, and dancers, as well as courtesans. In some ways, they were precursors of modern stars.

By the beginning of the twentieth century, theatrical stars such as Sarah Bernhardt were joined by film stars such as Clara Bow, Marlene Dietrich, and Greta Garbo in setting sartorial trends. For example, the ballroom dancer Irene Castle helped to popularize the post–World War I trend for short hair when she cut her own hair in a "Castle bob." By the early 2000s, actresses remained among the most important trendsetters, joined by pop singers such as Madonna, arguably the most trendsetting woman of the twentieth century.

Fashion magazines—notably *Vogue*—have also played an important part in launching "the Beautiful People" as celebrity trendsetters. Among them were girls of good family, dressed and posed and photographed by fashion editors and photographers. The 1957 film *Funny Face* starred the gamine Audrey Hepburn, whose character lived out the transformation from duckling to swan.

What is a trendsetter? A woman put on a pedestal, an icon that others want to follow. In magazines, they fall into a few categories: the society girl (Gloria Guinness, sometimes known as "the swan," and Babe Paley); the model girl (Jean Shrimpton, Veruschka, Kate Moss); the entertainer (Katharine Hepburn, Sarah Jessica Parker). Gabrielle (Coco) Chanel is a rare case of the designer as trendsetter, since she was the best model of her own clothes.

The qualities these women possess include beauty, status, and larger-than-life personas. In the late twentieth century, models gave way to the phenomenon of super-models, who commodified trendiness through brand association. Actresses also became associated with particular styles and designers. Trendsetters have become figures thrown into the light by the flare of the paparazzo's flash. Whereas yesterday's social elite had money and status, and actresses and models had beauty, contemporary trendsetters possess a lifestyle (encompassing fashion) that whets the appetite of a global public.

See also Actors and Actresses, Impact on Fashion; Celebrities; Supermodels.

Bibliography

Howell, Georgina. *Vogue Women*. New York and London: Pavilion Books Ltd., 2000.
Keenan, Brigid. *The Women We Wanted to Look Like*. New York: St. Martin's Press, 1978.
Shakar, Alex. *The Savage Girl*. New York: Harper Collins, 2001.

Laird Borrelli

TRICKLE-DOWN

The "trickle-down" theory offers a straightforward way of predicting fashion diffusion: a hierarchical process whereby individuals with high status establish fashion trends, only to be imitated by lower-status individuals wearing cheaper versions of the styles. Subsequently, high-status individuals become motivated to differentiate themselves by moving on to a new trend. Initially based upon an explanation of social-class dynamics within western modernity, the theory has since been applied to gender and age relations.

The origin of the theory is generally attributed to sociologist Georg Simmel, although he was actually only one of several writers (e.g., Spencer, Grosse, Veblen) who sought to explain fashion through class structure and social mobility in the late nineteenth century. Through a contemporary lens, Simmel (like others of his day) placed an inordinate emphasis on social class in his explanation of fashion (see Blumer; Davis; Crane). However, in many ways Simmel's analysis was especially nuanced in its blend of psychology and philosophy; it can be read as elaborating a fundamental blend of imitation and differentiation that surpasses social class alone (Lehmann; Carter).

Carter (2003) suggests that a modern scientific goal of assigning order to a seemingly disorderly phenomenon (fashion) led to the restricted (economic-based) naming and life of the trickle-down theory. The historical evidence of such an orderly trickling-down fashion is not very convincing (see Breward; Crane). By the late 1960s, the theory had come under attack, as class-based explanations could not explain the number of styles that bubbled or percolated up from working-class youth or diverse ethnicities (Blumer; King). Furthermore, the speed with which fashion could be "knocked off" in cheaper versions had accelerated to the point that any trickling that occurred was blurry. Indeed, in the twenty-first century's global economy, counterfeit versions of high-fashion handbags appear almost simultaneously with "original" handbags, on the sidewalks outside designer stores in major cities around the world.

McCracken (1985) attempted to rehabilitate the trickle-down theory by relating it to gender. He noted a process whereby women imitate men's fashions in order to obtain more status, only to be usurped by further changes in men's attire. Although McCracken has been critiqued for not demonstrating the differentiation function (on the part of men) adequately, if one goes back to Simmel's analysis, it is possible to establish how the dialectical process of fashion simultaneously articulates twin opposites in a single "masculine" or "feminine" look.

More recently, Huun and Kaiser (2000) demonstrated how the basic elements of imitation and differentiation can explain changing infants' and young children's fashions—in terms of age, as well as gender. And, Cook and Kaiser (2004) reinterpreted the trickle-down theory to explain the recent "downsizing" of teen and adult fashion into children's and "tweens'" styles. Although the hierarchical (class-based) flow of the trickle-down theory may be challenged in many ways, the basic dynamic underlying Simmel's analysis

of imitation and differentiation remains a critical part of fashion theory.

See also Veblen, Thorstein.

Bibliography

Blumer, Herbert. "Fashion: From Class Differentiation to Collective Selection. "*Sociological Quarterly* 10 (Summer 1969): 275–291.

Breward, Christopher. *The Culture of Fashion*. Manchester, U.K.: Manchester University Press, 1995.

Carter, Michael. *Fashion Classics: From Carlyle to Barthes*. Oxford, U.K., and New York: Berg Press, 2003.

Cook, Daniel, and Susan B. Kaiser. "Be Twixt and Be Tween: Age Ambiguity and the Sexualization of the Female Consuming Subject." *Journal of Consumer Culture* 4, no. 2 (2004): 203–227.

Crane, Diana. *Fashion and Its Social Agendas: Class Gender, and Identity in Clothing*. Chicago: University of Chicago Press, 2000.

Davis, Fred. *Fashion, Culture, and Identity*. Chicago: University of Chicago Press, 2002.

Huun, Kathleen, and Susan B. Kaiser. "The Emergence of Modern Infantwear, 1896–1962: Traditional White Dresses Succumb to Fashion's Gender Obsession." *Clothing and Textiles Research Journal* 19, no. 3 (2001): 103–119.

King, Charles W. "Fashion Adoption: A Rebuttal to the 'Trickle-Down' Theory." In *Toward Scientific Marketing*. Edited by S. A. Greyser. Chicago: American Marketing Association, 1963, pp. 108–125.

Lehmann, Ulrich. *Tigersprung: Fashion in Modernity*. Cambridge, Mass.: MIT Press, 2000.

McCracken, Grant. "The Trickle-Down Theory Rehabilitated." In *The Psychology of Fashion*. Edited by Michael R. Solomon. Lexington, Mass.: Heath, 1985.

Simmel, Georg. "Fashion." *American Journal of Sociology* 62 (May 1957): 541–558.

Susan B. Kaiser

T-SHIRT

From its origins as men's underwear to its complex role in modern fashion, the T-shirt is today one of the most universally worn items of clothing. Cheap, hygienic, and comfortable, the T-shirt has become an essential basic wardrobe item worn by people of all social classes and ages. Technically, the T-shirt evolved and proliferated at an astonishing rate, aided by the increased availability of American cotton and the invention of the circular knitting machine in the mid-nineteenth century. Its current shape and style developed during the 1930s and it became universally worn as an outer-garment after World War II. In 2004 over two billion were sold worldwide. Contemporary versions range from inexpensive multi-packaged units to haute couture editions to high-tech fiber versions used in sports and health industries.

Shirts of T-shaped construction were worn as early as the medieval times to protect the body from chafing by heavy, metal armor. Civilians adopted the shirt as a protective and hygienic barrier between the body and costly garments. Made of cotton or linen, the shirt was more easily washable than silk or woolen outer garments with complex ornamentation. These shirts were made with long tails that wrapped around the body serving as underpants. The shirt was still always worn with a waistcoat or vest and jacket over the shirt. Wearing a clean, laundered shirt showed off a gentleman's wealth and gentility. Shirts changed very little in shape from their introduction in medieval times through the mid-nineteenth century. They were loose fitting, made of a woven fabric, and constructed with rectangular pieces that formed a T shape.

In the late nineteenth century when health-oriented concerns became prevalent, doctors and physicians advised wearing warm undershirts to protect from colds and rheumatism. Dr. Jaeger lauded the healthful benefits of wearing knitted underwear made of wool and manufactured his own line of knit undershirts. The circular knitting machine patented in 1863 made it possible to mass-produce knit jersey undershirts and hosiery for wide distribution. This technology created a greater range of types and refinement in undergarments. Its closer fit looked more like the modern T-shirt than earlier loose-fitting, woven shirts.

Sailors in the nineteenth century wore white flannel undershirts under their woolen pullovers. These shirts were worn alone on deck for work that required freedom of movement. The white cotton knit T-shirt was adopted as official underwear for the U.S. Navy in 1913. Fast drying, quick, and easy to put on, sailors responded positively to the new garment. The U.S. Army adopted it in 1942, in its classic form. Nicknamed skivvies, each soldier's name was stenciled on. In 1944 the army colored the shirt khaki to camouflage with the

extreme tropical environment of the South Pacific. The vast media coverage of World War II popularized the T-shirt as a symbol of victorious, modern America and glorified it as a masculine, military icon. Returning soldiers retained the style after the war because of its comfort, practicality, and image. A Sears, Roebuck and Co. catalog slogan in the 1940s took advantage of the heroic image that had developed during the war, "You needn't be a soldier to have your own personal T-shirt." Since that time it has been used in every war and has been appropriated by paramilitary factions. Like the trench coat it has also become an integral part of civilian dress from street fashion to haute couture.

Fruit of the Loom was the manufacturer who began marketing T-shirts on a large scale in the 1910s, first supplying the U.S. Navy and then universities with white T-shirts. The company manages its own cotton fields and yarn production. Each shirt undergoes 60 inspections before it is packaged. From the rebels of the 1950s to preppies who paired them with pearl necklaces in the 1980s, the company remained a number one producer of T-shirts through the 1990s and is still a competitive brand. The P. H. Hanes Knitting Company, founded in 1901, introduced a new style of men's two-piece underwear. They have been a major supplier of T-shirts to the military and to the Olympics in addition to vast civilian distribution.

An increase in sports and leisure activities gave rise to new forms of clothing in the latter part of the nineteenth century. Close-fitting knitted woolen swimsuits made in the tank-shaped style of undershirts accustomed the eye to seeing more skin and one's body shape in a public place. By the 1930s T-shirts were standard sporting wear at colleges and universities. The earliest shirts printed with school logos served as uniforms for school sport teams. These sport uniforms encouraged a new casualness in dress among the middle classes that was important to the T-shirt's general acceptance. The cotton T-shirt has remained a mainstay of sports activities because it is absorbent, quick-drying, and allows free range of movement. The T-shirts' role in sports has moved beyond team identification and practical function; it is crucial to the marketing, promotion, and profitability of the sports industry.

In post–World War II years, the T-shirt was primarily worn for athletics, informally at home, or by blue-collar workers for physical labor. Marlon Brando's portrayal of Stanley Kowalski in *A Streetcar Named Desire* (1951), wearing a visibly sweaty T-shirt clinging to his musculature, captured an erotic power of the shirt. The strong associations of masculinity developed earlier in patriotic form in military images, now had an amplified sexual expression. The silver-screen images of Marlon Brando in *The Wild Ones* (1953) and James Dean in *Rebel Without a Cause* (1955) embodied the spirit of American youth in the 1950s. The impact of these movies was profoundly influential on society in solidifying a language and image of rebellion. Through these movies the white T-shirt, blue jeans, and black leather motorcycle jacket became the uniform of nonconformists searching for meaning in conservative postwar consumerist society. Other important musicals, films, and television programs from *West Side Story* (1961) to *Happy Days* (1974) to *American Graffiti* (1973) repeated and confirmed the rebellious meanings. Young people recognized this style as a new American fashion. Administrators prohibited wearing the T-shirt to school in an era when most people still wore shirts with collars. Not only was it rejected because of its informality, but the knit quality of the T-shirt is more clinging than a shirt or blouse. The Underwear Institute declared in 1961 that the T-shirt had become a dual-purpose garment that was acceptable as both outer-wear and underwear. In the early 1960s, a female image was promoted in the pivotal French film, *Breathless* (1960). Jean Seberg was featured as a young American selling the *Herald Tribune*, wearing a white T-shirt silk-screened with the newspaper logo that showed off her curvaceous figure and at the same time embodied a new, youthful androgynous style of seduction and feminine power. This film did much to introduce the style into female fashion. The erotic aspect of the T-shirt has been exploited in wet T-shirt contests that not only make use of the clinging quality of the fabric, but also its semi-transparency when wet.

Since the late 1960s and 1970s, the T-shirt has evolved and proliferated at a rapid rate. Decorative techniques used to create expressive statements on T-shirts became popular from the 1960s onward. Graphic designs, novelty patterns, and written words lionize rock 'n' roll bands, promote products and places, and express political and community-minded causes. Rapidly made and inexpensive, imprinted T-shirts can respond quickly to popular and political events. The first political use was in 1948 when the Republican candidate Thomas Dewey distributed T-shirts that read "Dew it with Dewey." The graphics for one of the most printed and widely copied designs, "I Love New York," was created in 1976 by graphic artist Milton Glaser.

Technological advancements in inks used for silk-screen printing in the early 1960s made this ancient technique easy, inexpensive, and fast. Underground artists who were decorating surfboards and skateboards on a cottage-industry level were some of the first to put designs on T-shirts. The shirts were an inexpensive canvas for expression. The hot iron transfer technique introduced in 1963 was even easier and faster to use. The fast-heat pressure-press widely available in the 1970s gave consumers the ability to choose the color of the shirt and its image or wording, and have it custom prepared in the store within minutes. In a 1976 *Time* magazine article, a Gimbels department store executive claimed that the Manhattan store sold over 1,000 imprinted shirts a week. Current digital processes allow for the printing of complex images with a professional appearance. Flocking, bubble coating, and embroidery are all used to create textured designs. With these two techniques the design area is coated with glue and then dusted with fibers that are attracted by electro-static means that affix them perpendicularly to the surface of the fabric leaving a velvety surface. Embroidered designs, whether done mechanically or manually, can be enhanced with beads, sequins, feathers, and other materials.

Community-minded causes were print designs that were most popular in the 1960s and 1970s. Images and messages about the Vietnam War, Civil Rights, peace and love, and feminist movements were prevalent. "Make Love Not War" and "Save the Whales" were two of the most popular messages. British designer Katherine Hamnett created a revival in T-shirts bearing political written messages in 1984 when she wore an oversized T-shirt bearing the message "98% of people don't want Pershings" in a public meeting with British Prime Minister Margaret Thatcher at the height of the Falklands War.

More than a passing fad, imprinted T-shirts have become an integral part of brand marketing, whether distributed as promotional gifts or to generate revenue. In 1939, Metro-Goldwyn-Mayer used the T-shirt to promote one of the first color movies made in Hollywood, *The Wizard of Oz*. Budweiser started stamping its logo on shirts in 1965 but it was the following decade that the idea was spread to all types of brands, from Bic to Xerox. In the case of the Hard Rock Café, collecting logoed T-shirts from its locations around the world has become a significant portion of the draw to the restaurant.

In 1983 the *New Yorker* reported that the industry sold 32 million dozen items in 1982. Although there are fads for different styles and colors, the imprinted T-shirt is unique in that men, women, and children of all ages, shapes, and social standings universally wear it.

Pop artists Andy Warhol, Keith Haring, and Jenny Holzer pioneered the use of the T-shirt as a work of art. In the 1980s contemporary fashion's inclusion in museum exhibitions considered the many designer versions. Also in the 1980s, with the explosion of marketing of museums, masterworks of art were reproduced on T-shirts and sold in their gift stores.

High fashion adopted the T-shirt as early as 1948. A model appeared on the cover of *Life* magazine and ran a story that featured T-shirts by American designers Claire McCardell, Ceil Chapman, and Valentina. The article demonstrated how the sports shirt was now a street and evening style. The 1960s saw it go from street fashion to silk haute couture versions in the collections of such designers as Pierre Balmain and Christian Dior. From Woodstock to Yves Saint Laurent Rive Gauche to Vivienne Westwood, by the 1970s the T-shirt was part of all sectors of dress. Logoed shirts by Lacoste and Polo Ralph Lauren of the 1980s and 1990s were popular indicators of status. The black T-shirt became the uniform of the trendy and hip in the 1980s. Bruce Weber's photos of models wearing Calvin Klein's T-shirts became an icon of 1990s sexuality and minimalism. Designers such as Donna Karan, Giorgio Armani, Tom Ford, Jean Paul Gaultier, and Helmet Lang have worn the T-shirt as their own identifying uniform. Designer shirts are usually made from a high-quality cotton, have an elegant neckline, and well-cut and sewn sleeves. Japanese designers Issey Miyake and Yohji Yammamoto have led new ways of thinking about the T-shirt in their deconstructionist work through cutting, slashing, and knotting. Miyake's vision has ranged from his Janice Joplin and Jimi Hendrix T-shirt of the 1970s to his piece of cloth shirts by the yard of 1999. The T-shirt has been pivotal to the revolution in lifestyles and attitudes that formed the second half of the twentieth century and its impact on fashion continues.

See also Politics and Fashion; Sportswear; Underwear.

Bibliography

Bayer, Ann. "What's the Message on Your T-Shirt?" *Seventeen* (April 1981): 186–187.

——. "1951 T-Shirt." *Life* (16 July 1951): 73–76.

——. "T-Shirts: Sports Standby is Now a Street and Evening Style." *Life* (7 June 1948): 103–106.

——. "Imprinted Sportswear." *New Yorker* (11 April 1983): 33.

Brunel, Charlotte. *The T-Shirt Book*. New York: Assouline, 2002.

Harris, Alice. *The White T*. New York: Harper Collins, 1996.

——. "The T-Shirt: A Startling Evolution." *Time* (1 March 1976): 48–50.

Russell, Mary. "The Top on Top." *Vogue* (March 1983): 316–317.

Dennita Sewell

TURBAN

The turban is essentially a headgear that uses fabric of varying width and length, which is twisted and turned around the head. The wrapped folds derived produce a "fitted effect" akin to a stitched or an engineered head covering. Though length, style, color, and fabric may vary as geographical locations change, the basic concept and construction of the turban remains unaltered. This is probably the widest and most flexible definition of this garment considering the many forms in which it exists.

Little is conclusively known of the origins of the turban. The earliest evidence of a turban-like garment is from Mesopotamia in a royal sculpture dating from 2350 B.C.E. Thus, it is known that the turban was in use before the advent of Islam and Christianity, therefore the origin of the turban cannot be ascribed to religious reasons alone. It is also mentioned in the Old Testament and Vedic literature from India. Sculpture from Central India (100 B.C.E.) provides detailed visual evidence of the use of turbans. These headdresses were originally worn by royalty and spiritual leaders and used to commute power, often being adorned with jewels and accessories to display wealth and grandeur.

In some form or another, the turban has been important in many cultures and religions. It is still in use in rural areas in Persia, the Middle East, Turkey, parts of Africa, and the Indian subcontinent where wrapped, as opposed to stitched headgear, continues to be preferred. Historically, draped clothing has always had a special significance in eastern culture. Watson notes that "certain strict Hindus still do not wear cut or stitched cloth as for them a garment composed of several pieces sewn together is an abomination and defilement" (p.11). Though turbans are worn primarily by men, literary evidence reveals that they were used by women on rare occasions in the past. "In Vedic literature Indrani, wife of Indra, wears a headdress known as usnisa" (Ghuyre, p. 68). Some of the earliest terms for the turban in English are *turbant*, *tolibanl*, and *turband*. These represent the French adaptation of the Turkish *tulbend*, a vulgarism for the term *dulbend* from Persia, *didband*, a scarf or sash wound around the neck.

In India this headdress is known by many different names locally. *Potia*, *usnisa*, *pag*, *pagri*, *safa*, and *veshtani* are some of the names used for the turban. The Sikhs, a community that dictates its followers to wear the turban, call it *dastaar*, while the Muslim religious leaders refer to it as the *kalansuwa*. In the earliest times, cotton was the fabric most commonly used as turban material. This is because it was affordable and abundant, apart from being the most comfortable fabric to use in tropical or temperate climates where it was most worn. Fabrics such as silk and satin saw limited usage among the more affluent and powerful class. Though there are innumerable variations in the turban, they can easily be divided into two broad types—long turbans and square turban pieces. The long piece is seven to ten meters long with the width varying from twenty-five to one hundred centimeters. The square pieces could vary in size between one to three meters per side, with one to one-and-a-half meters constituting the most useful size. There are an amazingly wide variety of turbans across different cultures and religions. Distinctions are made on the basis of size, shape, material, color, ornamentation, and method of wrapping. In the Muslim world, religious elders often wear a turban wrapped around a cap known in Arabic as a *kalansuwa*. The shape of these caps can be spherical or conical and this produces variations in the turban shape. In Iran, leaders wear black or white turbans wrapped in the flat, circular style. In the Indian state of Rajasthan the style of turban may vary even within the distance of a few miles. The Rajput turbans are remarkably different from the kind worn in any other region in India. There are specialists called *pagribands* whose skill is in the art of tying the turban and were employed by the erstwhile royalty for their services. Some famous styles from Rajasthan are the *Jaipur pagri* and the *Gaj Shahi* turban, the fabric of which is dyed in five distinctive colors and was

developed by Maharaja Gaj Singh II from the Jodhpur royal family.

The turban as a headdress is not merely a fashion statement or cultural paraphernalia; it has symbolic meaning beyond the obvious. It serves to identify the wearer as a member of a particular group, tribe, or community, and serves as an introduction to their cultural, religious, political, and social orientations. Sikh men commonly wear a peaked turban, that serves partly as a covering for their hair, which is never cut out of respect for God's creation. The turban has significant associations with the concepts of respect and honor. A man's turban is supposed to signify his honor and the honor of his people. The exchange of turbans is considered a sign of everlasting friendship, while presenting someone with a turban is considered a great token of esteem. An exchange of turbans also signifies a long relationship and forges relationships between families. Thus, the turban is an intrinsic part of all ceremonies from birth until death.

Conversely, it is considered a grave insult to step over or pick up another man's turban. It is linked intrinsically to the "ego" of a person. To remove a turban and lay it at another's feet symbolizes submission and an expression of humbleness. The turban at a glance conveys the social and economic status of the wearer, the season, festival, community, and the region. It is also distinctive by the style of wrapping—each fold telling its own story. The tightness of the drape of the headgear, the lengths of the hanging end, the types of bands which are created on the surface, all say something about its wearer.

The colors of turbans vary in different cultures and are imbued with complex connotations, emotional context, and rich association. They are used to convey mood, religious values, customs, and ceremonial occasions. In India, ocher is the color of the saint, saffron denotes chivalry, and prosperity. White turbans, considered by some Muslims to be the holiest color, are used for mourning and by older men, whereas dark blue is reserved for a condolence visit. Among Sikhs of north India, blue and white cotton turbans are essentially religious in nature. In the Middle East, green turbans, thought to be the color of paradise, are worn by men who claim descent from the prophet Muhammad. Shape and size of the turban are determined by many conditions. Chief among these are the climate, status, and occupation of a person. Turbans are big and loose without hanging tails in the hot desert and thus serve a protective function. Merchants involved in more sedentary activities would wear ornamental turbans with long hanging tails.

The turban was introduced into fashionable European dress in the early fifteenth century and its usage continued until the sixteenth century. It has been revived many times in women's fashion at intervals since the sixteenth century. The turban has acquired a more contemporary form in the twenty-first century. Though it continues to exist in various parts of the world in its more traditional form, of late various fashion designers and couturiers have adapted the turban to give it a more fashionable and chic look, making it a popular fashion accessory. Even though in its more contemporary form the turban may not retain the same symbolism that is attached to its more traditional form, it nevertheless reinforces the importance of this garment.

See also Headdress.

Bibliography

Bhandari, Vandana. *Women's Costume in Rajasthan.* Ph.D. diss., Delhi University, 1995.

——. "Mystical folds: The Turban in India." *Fashion and Beyond* (October 2001): 22–25.

Boucher, Francois. *A History of Costume in the West.* London: Thames and Hudson, Inc., 1987.

Ghurye, Govind Sadashiv. *Indian Costumes.* Bombay: Popular Book Depot, 1951.

Mathur, U. B. *Folkways in Rajasthan.* Jaipur: The Folklorists, 1986.

Nagar, Mahender Singh. *Rajasthan ki pag pagriyan.* Jodhpur: Mehranarh Museum Trust, 1994.

Singh, C. et al. *The Costumes of Royal India.* New Delhi: Festival of India in Japan, 1988.

Watson, John Forbes. *The Textile Manufacturers and the Costumes of the People of India.* Varanasi, India: Indological Book House, 1982. Originally published in London in 1866.

Yarwood, Doreen. *The Encyclopaedia of World Costume.* London: B. T. Batsford, Ltd., 1988.

Vandana Bhandari

TUXEDO

Throughout the twentieth century, the tuxedo was emblematic of occasions when men were requested to dress formally after dark, whether for drinks, dinner, or some other gathering. The garment developed at a time in the late nineteenth century when men in the upper levels of society began to demand that their clothes be cut to accommodate the increasingly casual nature of leisure time. As with many fashion innovations, credit for the new style of jacket intended to be worn by men in the evening was claimed by many individuals. In fact the tuxedo jacket arose from sartorial innovations in both America and England. It succeeded in ushering in a new level of formality, intermediate between full white-tie formal wear and the lounge suit, that is only now showing signs of fading from usage.

The term tuxedo derives from Tuxedo Park, a residential club colony of rustic mansions in the outer suburbs of New York, founded in 1886 by the wealthy Lorillard family and some of their friends. The Tuxedo Club's annual Autumn Ball was an important event in the New York social calendar; the dress code for the ball would normally have been white-tie and tails. However, in 1885 James Brown Potter, a charter member of the Tuxedo Club and friend of the Lorillard family, had been introduced to the idea of the dinner jacket by the Prince of Wales, who was later to become Edward VII. The Prince had recently created a new evening jacket to be worn at his country estate at Sandringham; it was a black jacket without tails, inspired by the smoking jackets that men would wear when retiring to the smoking room after a meal. A year later, Pierre Lorillard and his son Griswold had their tailor design similar dinner jackets with satin lapels, with a cut similar to the equestrian jackets worn for fox hunting. These "Tuxedo jackets" soon caught on as the customary attire for semiformal evening events in New York society.

In a separate development, the French responded to the need for a lighter semiformal jacket for warm Mediterranean evenings by creating the Monte Carlo. Although all of these developments show the influence of sporting, hunting, and leisure dress as a means of modernizing a garment by the simplification of its attributes and by the easing of bodily restriction in its cut and construction, it is from the American sense of casualness in formality that the tuxedo derives most of its meaning.

As an alternative to the black tailcoat, the tuxedo was differentiated from the lounge jacket through a fairly strict definition of what constituted it and what it could be worn with. Principally in black, the jacket could bear peak lapels or a shawl collar faced in either silk or gros-grain, and was matched to a pair of trousers with a plain silk stripe running down the side of each leg, without turned-up cuffs. The obligatory furnishings of a black bow tie and cummerbund (when worn without a waistcoat) did not become fully established until the 1920s. At that time, too, the Duke of Windsor refined the narcissistic possibility of the tuxedo by having a dinner jacket made in midnight blue. Ever conscious of his own appearance, the Duke had noted that under artificial light, midnight blue seemed blacker than black. Better still, it also registered darker in photographic terms on newsprint giving the garment the weight of royal authority executed as a self-conscious exercise in style.

The co-option of the tuxedo by women from the late 1960s on indicates a performative sense of playfulness, transgressing the costume's once rigid gender implications. Yves Saint Laurent's *le smoking* (named after the French term for the tuxedo) was launched in spring 1967 as the singular concept for his entire couture collection. Saint Laurent's technique was to soften the tailoring while retaining the angularity of the cut which, when accessorized with stiletto heels and dramatic makeup, formed a contradictory image of femininity without compromise. This proposition is most clearly articulated in a photograph by Helmut Newton where a woman, unaccompanied in a street at night, pauses to light a cigarette. As a statement of style it is unsurpassed. All designers who have followed on from this deviation, including Ralph Lauren's form-following tuxedo suits, Giorgio Armani's textured interpretations, and Viktor and Rolf's historical pastiches, underline the singular importance of this sartorial appropriation in women's dress as expressive of modernity.

The modulations in the details of the tuxedo across the postwar period are reflected in the sartorial taste of the literary and filmic figure James Bond. More than any other figurehead, Bond has been the model that most men have looked to when considering a style of tuxedo when occasion demands. Sean Connery's depiction of Bond in early films such as *Dr. No* (1962) and *Diamonds Are Forever* (1971) crystallized an early 1960s sensibility of a black "tux" with lean lapels, satin cuffbacks, covered buttons, and a folded white handkerchief in the top pocket. The clipped and minimal detailing was suggestive of both acumen and agility in a louche world to which many men aspired. The contradiction is that Bond is better known in the public imagination for the white rather than the black tuxedo jacket, necessitated by the range of tropical settings and number of casinos that the character frequented.

The other institution that upholds the suitability of the tuxedo for special-occasion dress is the Oscar ceremony. As a necessary foil to the elaborate costumes worn by the invited actresses, the tuxedo lends a certain formal gravity to support the very unstable nature of dress designs that appear on the red carpet on a yearly basis. In the vogue for women to reveal the actuality of their bodies in the dresses they wear, the tuxedo becomes the monochromatic means for men to encase the actuality of their own bodies in a formal armor that reveals very little of the true self.

Originating as a relaxed alternative to formal wear, the tuxedo has become emblematic of celebration and special occasions and a potent sartorial symbol of ceremony. When worn well, it conjures up a ritualistic sense of propriety and the debonair expression of a lost era.

See also Formal Wear, Men's.

Bibliography

Curtis, Bryan, and John Bridges. *A Gentleman Gets Dressed Up: Knowing What to Wear, How to Wear It, and When to Wear It.* New York: Rutledge Hill Press, 2003.
Flusser, Alan. *Dressing the Man: Mastering the Art of Permanent Fashion.* New York: Harper Collins, 2002.
Hollander, Anne. *Sex and Suits: The Evolution of Modern Dress.* Tokyo and New York: Kodansha International, 1995.

Internet Resource

"The History of the Tuxedo." Village of Tuxedo Park official website. Available from <http://www.votuxpk.com>.

Alistair O'Neill

TWIGGY

In 1949 Lesley Hornby, later rechristened "Twiggy," was born in Neasden, an unfashionable suburb in North London, where she grew up. Only sixteen when she began modeling in 1966, she introduced the cult of the "celebrity model" and left an indelible legacy in other, more significant ways. Models in the 1950s, in both America and Britain, were styled and made up to look mature, sophisticated, and "ladylike," to complement

Twiggy. Unlike the feminine and sophisticated looks of models in the 1950s, Twiggy became the celebrity model who typified the new, young, and boyish style of the 1960s. © HULTON-DEUTSCH COLLECTION/CORBIS. REPRODUCED BY PERMISSION.

the fashionable clothes of the time. In England many were young women from respectable families who had followed a modeling course at Lucie Clayton's Modeling and Grooming School in Mayfair. In America, such top models as Suzy Parker were also well-groomed girls from middle-class backgrounds. New photographic techniques allowed mass-circulation newspapers and magazines to print high-fashion images, and the models' names soon became familiar to the public.

The social and demographic changes that followed created need for new designs and new models. Mary Quant's clothes for *Bazaar* were aimed at a young clientele, while the early 1960s saw the opening of innumerable boutiques in London, which, unlike Quant's shop, were intended for girls of far more limited means. The first model whose image reflected this climate was Jean Shrimpton. Although she had attended Miss Clayton's school, her success was a result of the partnership she had formed with the working-class photographer David Bailey. The early pictures, which made them both famous, showed off her youth and her tomboy persona.

Lesley Hornby was working as a hairdresser in a salon near her home when an older man recognized the way in which she might personify the new London.

Nigel Davies, a former boxer and stallholder, who called himself "Justin de Villeneuve," changed her name and transformed her appearance; it was at his suggestion that she painted on eyelashes under her eyes so as to resemble a porcelain doll and had her hair cut short. The photographer Barry Lategan took a picture for the salon, and, by chance, the fashion editor Deirdre McSharry saw it. In the February 1966 issue of the *Daily Express*, she used a center spread to portray this "Cockney Kid" as "the Face of '66." One of the shots showed Twiggy wearing homemade trousers and sweater, which accentuated both her androgynous appearance and her democratic appeal.

She was smaller than most models and invariably posed so as to emphasize her childlike qualities. In 1967 she was photographed for British *Vogue* by Ronald Traeger, who portrayed her riding a miniature bike in knee-high socks. Cecil Beaton sat her on a high shelf, and Helmut Newton asked her to jump toward the camera with arms outstretched. There followed a shoot with Richard Avedon and a cover for American *Vogue* in August of that year. At one point she was on twelve covers simultaneously; as a model, she was used by both traditional "glossies" and new, youth-oriented publications.

Although the syndication of her name to dresses, dolls, and other merchandise meant that she could retire from modeling by 1969 to pursue a career as actress and singer, she had permanently changed magazine culture. Now, to the deification of youth was added the idea of instant fame, the notion that class barriers that could be painlessly transcended, and the problematic pursuit of a pre-pubescent ideal of beauty.

See also Fashion Photography; Fashion Magazines; London Fashion; Quant, Mary.

Bibliography

Aitken, Jonathan. *The Young Meteors*. New York: Atheneum, 1967.
Green, Jonathon. *All Dressed Up: The Sixties and the Counterculture*. London: Jonathan Cape, 1998.
Levy, Shawn. *Ready, Steady, Go! The Smashing Rise and Giddy Fall of Swinging London*. New York: Doubleday, 2002.
Melly, George. *Revolt into Style: The Pop Arts in Britain*. London: Allen Lane, 1970.
Twiggy. *Twiggy: An Autobiography*. London: Hart-Davis, MacGibbon, 1975.

Pamela Church Gibson

U

UMBRELLAS AND PARASOLS

The origins of the word "umbrella" lie in the Latin *umbra*, meaning shade, while "parasol" comes from the Latin *sol*, meaning sun, and the two words were used interchangeably up until the middle of the eighteenth century (Farrell 1985). Since then, "parasol" has come to denote specifically a shade that protects against the sun, while "umbrella" indicates an item that provides protection from the rain.

Most umbrellas and parasols consist of a central stick to which a number of ribs are attached. The ribs support the cover or canopy and, in turn, they are supported by stretchers from the center of their length to the tubular runner that slides up and down the stick (Farrell 1985). Historians indicate that while umbrellas were always designed to fold, some parasols were made rigid, with the cover consisting of a single circular piece of waxed cloth or taffeta supported on cane ribs.

Umbrellas date from over 3,000 years ago, and according to Crawford (1970), from early times they had religious and mythological symbolism. Most histories of the umbrella and parasol cite Egypt, China, and India as being important geographical locations in the pre-European history of the umbrellas.

In all such cultures where it has had a presence, the umbrella appears to have been associated with high status. Moreover, Stacey notes that: "The Oxford English Dictionary does in fact date the use of the word umbrella from 1653 as 'an Oriental or African symbol of dignity'" (1991, p. 114).

Many Asian countries have used the parasol in symbolic relation to their dignitaries, and Sangster notes: "In all eastern countries, with the exception of China and Turkey, the Parasol was reserved exclusively for the great men of the land." (1855, p. 18). According to Crawford (1970), Burma and Siam are two Asian countries that have the most regard for the umbrella as a symbol of sovereignty, and subsequently reports that the ruler of the ancient capital of the Burmese empire

had the title of "King of the White Elephants and Lord of the Twenty-Four Umbrellas." The use of the umbrella as a symbol of respect appears to have continued into the twentieth century as Jacqueline Kennedy, widow of the American President John Kennedy, was accorded the privilege of the ceremonial umbrella when she visited Burma in 1967 (Crawford 1970).

In China, too, umbrellas have been used to denote status from as early as the eleventh century B.C.E. Frames at that time were made of cane or sandalwood and the covers of leather or feathers, for wet and dry days (Stacey 1991). During the period of the Ming dynasty (1368–1644), Crawford (1970) notes that ordinary people were not allowed to use umbrellas covered with cloth or silk: they had to use less prestigious items constructed from stout paper. Cheaper East Asian umbrellas are still made of paper manufactured from cotton rags, although better models use paper made from the bark bast of mulberry, which is much stronger. Covers are painted or lacquered and may be decorated with pictorial motifs or auspicious phrases (Crawford 1970).

Evidence of early European use of umbrellas is mentioned by Sangster: "We find frequent reference to the Umbrella in the Roman Classics, and it appears that it was, probably, a post of honour among maid-servants to bear it over their mistresses" (1855, p. 15). However, most historians indicate that the first European umbrellas were probably ceremonial items associated with the pope. There are extant depictions of the Emperor Constantine presenting Pope Sylvester I—who was in office from C.E. 314 to 335—with a brown and white striped umbrella (Crawford 1970) and Pope Eugenius IV (1431–1447) incorporated an *ombrellino* into his coat of arms. Although the emblem is no longer used by the pope himself, it still appears on certain institutions and seminaries (Stacey 1991).

It is likely that trading activity in Asian colonies from the sixteenth century onward ultimately brought the umbrella to wider European attention. Portuguese women in India in the sixteenth century, for instance, would not venture out without an escort of slaves, one of whom bore a shade over his mistress to protect her from the sun and to emphasize her prestige, Crawford (1970) writes. The umbrella subsequently became a custom that returned with the Portuguese to Europe.

The umbrella or parasol started to appear elsewhere in Europe around this time and the French king, Louis XIII, is reported to have owned a good number of umbrellas. Between 1619 and 1637 he enlarged his collection to include eleven sunshades made of taffeta and three umbrellas made of oiled cloth trimmed with gold and silver lace (Crawford 1970).

However, the umbrella had no significant presence in Britain until the eighteenth century. Although there are records of some eighteenth century "church umbrellas" designed specifically for use by members of the clergy, the traveler and philanthropist Jonas Hanway is generally credited with introducing the umbrella to London (Stacey 1991). Born in 1712, he traveled extensively to the British colonies and to Europe. On returning to London to carry out his philanthropic work, he was reportedly ridiculed by sedan chair carriers for his use of the umbrella, possibly because they perceived it as a threat to their business (Stacey 1991). Hanway's now infamous umbrella is most likely to have been French in origin (Farrell 1985).

But it took time for the waterproof umbrella to attain popularity in Britain, perhaps because to be seen with one was regarded as indicative of insufficient funds

Asian woman decorating an umbrella. In many Asian cultures, umbrellas, often painted with decorations, are associated with status and dignity. © Bohemian Nomad Picturemakers/Corbis. Reproduced by permission.

for a carriage (Farrell 1985). Moreover, Sangster writes that: "The earliest English Umbrellas . . . were made of oiled silk, very clumsy and difficult to open when wet; the stick and furniture were heavy and inconvenient, and the article very expensive" (1855, p. 31). The ribs of umbrellas at this time were made of whalebone—which lost its elasticity when wet—and the oiled silk or cotton cover would quickly become saturated and leaky. Furthermore, walking-stick umbrellas were uncommon in England in the eighteenth century (although they were being marketed in France), so they generally had to be carried under the arm or slung across the back (Crawford 1970).

In terms of production, Stacey (1991) notes that the first patent was taken out on an umbrella in 1786, and there was subsequently a proliferation of developments with over 121 patents filed in the 1850s alone. But as Sangster points out, "The most important improvement dates from the introduction of steel instead of whalebone." (Sangster 1855, p. 58). The most successful umbrella designs involving metal ribs were those patented by Henry Holland of Birmingham in 1840, and later by Samuel Fox in 1852 (Farrell 1985).

By the middle of the nineteenth century, there was a thriving umbrella and parasol industry in Britain, and Sangster notes that these items were well represented in the great exhibition of 1851. In particular, the elaborate umbrella belonging to the Maharajah of Najpoor captured the imagination of visitors and drew attention from visitors: "The ribs and stretchers, sixteen in number, divided the Umbrella into as many segments, covered with silk, exquisitely embroidered with gold and silver ornaments" (1855, p. 63). There is, perhaps, just a hint of umbrella envy in his subsequent statement that "we were glad to find that the visitors turned away from this display of barbaric pomp to the plainer, but more valuable productions of our own land" (1855, p. 63). It was at this exhibition that two of the Sangster brothers, who were themselves umbrella manufacturers, won a prize medal for their alpaca-covered umbrellas. Inferior to silk, but far cheaper and sturdier, alpaca became a highly popular textile for umbrellas in Britain in the 1850s (Crawford 1970).

By the end of the nineteenth century, umbrellas had become less of a novelty and more of an item of convenience. Best quality umbrellas had covers made of silk, cheaper ones of cotton, and green was the most popular color although blue, red, and brown umbrellas were also available. Handles were made of horn, ivory, antler, or wood, and were often decorated with bands of gold or silver (Farrell 1985). By the close of the nineteenth century, *The Tailor and Cutter* reported that "fashionable men are wedded to them" (Stacey 1991, p. 27).

Throughout the eighteenth and nineteenth centuries, manufacturers of quality umbrellas and parasols had their own outlets, while cheaper products were sold in the streets by itinerant vendors (Crawford 1970). Many retailers would offer a repair service as well as new products, and by the nineteenth century there was a healthy trade in refurbished umbrellas (Farrell 1985).

Compared to umbrellas, parasols were light and elegant, and throughout the early nineteenth century a wide range of styles and color were available. They were frequently referred to in magazines and newspapers of the time (Crawford 1970), although parasols were not generally carried by men (Farrell 1985).

Covers were made of chiffon, silk, taffeta, or satin and were often decorated with fringes, lace details, and embroidery. Long wooden bone or ivory handles were elaborately carved to feature animals and insects, porcelain handles were painted with delicate floral designs and some parasol handles even featured gimmicks such as inlaid watches (Bordignon Elestici 1990). Around the mid-1800s, the *en-tout-cas* became popular, as it fulfilled the function of protecting against both the sun and the rain (Farrell 1985), but one of the most remarkable parasols documented belonged to Queen Victoria, which she had lined with chain mail following an attempt to assassinate her (Stacey 1991).

The introduction of the automobile in the early years of the twentieth century initially encouraged the development of driving-specific parasols and umbrellas (Farrell 1985), but the new vehicles probably precipitated the decline of umbrella use, as people were less often on foot when out of doors (Crawford 1970). However, even during the interwar years (1918–1939), an umbrella was still regarded as "part of the unofficial uniform of a gentleman in London" (Farrell 1985, p. 79).

Although parasols, particularly those that emulated the style of flat, oriental sunshades, were popular up until the 1920s, the growing fashion for tanned skin effectively put an end to widespread use of the parasol by the 1930s. Looking to North America, Stacey notes that "neither the umbrella nor the parasol gained quick acceptance in America (1991, p. 59) and although Sidney Fisher's *Men, Woman and Manners of Colonial Days*, published in 1898, recorded sightings of umbrellas and parasols in Philadelphia in 1771, as a means of keeping off the sun they were reportedly regarded as a "ridiculous effeminacy" (Stacey 1991, p. 59). By the 1950s, however, Americans had championed the "unisex" umbrella, a distinct shift away from the gender-specific umbrella styles of Europeans (Stacey 1991).

The British umbrella trade had flourished in the last quarter of the eighteenth century, as the colonies could be relied on to supply raw materials including canes, whalebone, horn, and ivory, and a thriving textile industry provided fabrics such as silk and cotton gingham for making covers. As a result, by 1851 London had about 1,330 workers in the trade, a third of whom were in the Stepney area of East London. But following the collapse of the parasol market in the 1930s and the domination of the umbrella market by cheap imports from the 1940s onward, the British umbrella industry effectively disappeared (Crawford 1970).

Farrell (1985) indicates that over time, each part of the umbrella and parasol has been the object of improvement, including the innovation of the cranked stick, which allowed the open umbrellas to be centered over the head rather than to one side, and the cycloidal umbrella, which had the stick placed off-center. Since the nineteenth century, however, the only significant structural development has been Hans Haupt's telescopic umbrella in 1930, and improvements to allow automatic opening, but patents continue to be filed at the rate of about twenty a year (Stacey 1991). Use of nylon covers since the 1950s was the only other notable development in umbrella design in the twentieth century (Farrell 1985).

Europe's oldest and biggest umbrella shop continues, in the early 2000s, to trade under the name of James Smith & Sons (Umbrellas) Ltd., which was established in 1830. According to the London and Home Counties Survey (1957), "at one period umbrellas were actually manufactured inside the shop in a space four feet wide, and stock had to be stored in the window," and the company was one of the first to use "Fox Frames" in their umbrellas. In addition to conventional umbrellas, the firm has also specialized in the production of ceremonial umbrellas for traditional rulers in Africa.

Despite its pan-global origins, the umbrella has come to be regarded, in literature at least, as a quintessentially English item, perhaps due to the inclement weather for which Britain is famous. Stacey notes that Max Beerbohm said: "What is an Englishman without his umbrella? . . . It is the umbrella which has made Englishmen what they are, and its material is the stuff of which Englishmen are made" (cited in Stacey 1991, p. 7). In the twenty-first century, however, cheap and poorly made folding umbrellas have become disposable items, displacing durable, high-quality umbrellas in most parts of the world.

See also Protective Clothing; Raincoat; Rainwear.

Bibliography

Bordignon Elestici, Letizia. *Gli Ombrelli* [Umbrellas]. Milan: BE-MA Editrice, 1990.

Crawford, T. S. *A History of the Umbrella*. New York: Taplinger Publishing Company, 1970.

Farrell, Jeremy. *Umbrellas and Parasols*. London: B. T. Batsford, Ltd., 1985.

"Histories of Famous Firms." London and Home Counties Survey (part 4), 1957.

Sangster, William. *Umbrellas and Their History*. London: Effingham Wilson, Royal Exchange, 1855.

Stacey, Brenda. *The Ups and Downs of Umbrellas*. Stroud, U.K.: Alan Sutton Publishing, 1991.

Anna König

V

VALENTINA*

Working in New York City from the mid-1920s until 1957, Valentina Sanina Nicholaevna Schlée (known professionally as Valentina) was one of a very small, select coterie of mid-century female designers who achieved commercial success and maintained influential careers during the formative years of American fashion.

Working for a carefully chosen, exclusive clientele, Valentina turned out exquisitely cut and constructed evening, cocktail, and day ensembles that were commissioned and crafted in the manner of the French haute couture; every Valentina creation was made to order and was subject to multiple meticulous fittings and hand-finishing until the designer deemed the resulting garment worthy of her label. Known for her floor-gracing, draped, silk jersey gowns; body-skimming evening dresses with lowcut backs; deep décolleté; and bolero evening ensembles, Valentina also designed pared-down day dresses, linens, and undecorated cocktail dresses—all of which exuded a frank, forward-looking minimalist aesthetic.

Early Life and Marriage

Born in 1904 in the Kiev region of Russia, Valentina escaped the revolution in the late teens with her new husband and soon-to-be business manager, George Schlée, arriving in America in 1923 after several years spent in Paris, Athens, and various other European cities. Much like the French designer Coco Chanel, who offered as many versions of her colorful past as her admirers cared to indulge, Valentina was prone to invent and embroider her early life as it suited her. As a result, Valentina's origins are shrouded in mystery. But as one delves further, it becomes increasingly clear that this mystery is largely of her own making.

While U.S. immigration records indicate that she and her husband were affiliated with a traveling dance troupe known as the Revue Russe, Valentina was not above stretching that period to "her time in Paris with [dance impresario] Diaghilev." One account of her life after escaping Russia finds her dancing as part of a cabaret act with the Chauve Souris theater group in Paris. And while the Chauve Souris and the Revue Russe were hardly Diaghilev, one thing is certain: Valentina's early training as a performing artist played a critical role in the formation of her talent for costuming actors as well as her uniquely dramatic personal style. Graced with an undeniably compelling natural beauty, and enhanced by a theatrical presence, Valentina became as famous for the disciplined elegance and reductive simplicity of her clothing as she was for her meticulously crafted public persona. Self-created in virtually every aspect of her existence, Valentina offered an exotic beauty and charmingly mangled English that played to her favor in America, adding a veil of dazzlingly misleading allure to an already intriguing personality.

Formation of Valentina Gowns

In operation from 1928 to 1956, Valentina Gowns, Inc., was preceded by two early businesses, one the mid-1920s operating under the spelling "Valentena," and another venture called "Valentina & Sonia." Both of these concerns had folded by 1928 when Valentina Gowns was formed on more solid ground—this time backed by the Wall Street lawyer and financier Eustace Seligman. With George Schlée as business manager and Schlée's extended family employed in the workrooms, what became the most exclusive and most expensive American house of couture actually began as a rather simple, family-run business under the shrewd and watchful eye of the firm's only designer, Valentina.

Providing a formidable livelihood for the entire Schlée family, Valentina and George lived with great flair and panache on the swelling coffers of an almost immediate success. Within the first decade of business, Valentina's client list read like a who's who of blue-book society. With customers ranging from Park Avenue matrons to stars of the stage and silver screen, Valentina soon claimed Millicent Rogers, Lillian Gish, Gloria Swanson, Katharine Hepburn, Jennifer Jones, and even White House wives among her loyal following. Eleanor Lambert, the pioneer fashion publicist who represented Valentina for more than twenty-two years, claimed that Valentina was the dominant fashion designer of the 1930s and 1940s.

Designs for Stage and Screen

From the early 1930s on, Valentina designed costumes for Broadway productions, operas, and (by the early 1940s) Hollywood films. Drawing on her experience in theater, she was keenly aware of the character-specific, problem-solving needs of performers. Not surprisingly, Valentina's costume design quickly gained renown for helping to define a character's role without challenging an actor's stage presence. Aptly summing up Valentina's contribution to theater design, the drama critic Brooks Atkinson noted that "Valentina has designed clothes that act before ever a line is spoken." From Lily Pons to Rosa Ponselle to Gladys Swarthout, Valentina dressed and accessorized the world's most sought-after opera divas of the mid-twentieth century. Her stage and screen credits include longstanding working relations with Alfred Lunt and Lynn Fontanne, Norma Shearer, Paulette Goddard, Ginger Rogers, and Jennifer Jones, to name but a few. Her designs for and association with the reclusive film star Greta Garbo (who lived in the same Upper East Side apartment house as the Schlées) inspired endless sensationalistic journalism, but perhaps Valentina's most influential and highly publicized work was for Katharine Hepburn, whom she dressed in 1939 for Hepburn's starring role in the stage version of *The Philadelphia Story*. The white crepe, corselet-tied gown Hepburn wore was widely copied by designers at every price point across the nation for years.

In many ways, Valentina's work influenced fashion well beyond the scope of her limited elite clientele. In the 1940s, fashion editors coined the phrase "a poor-man's Valentina" to describe an affordable, simple, well-cut black dress devoid of any decoration. One of the first designers to promote monochromatic dressing, opaque and black stockings, and simple, short dresses for formal eveningwear, Valentina launched fashion trends that immediately trickled down to the masses. If Valentina's most recognizable calling card was simplicity, it should be remembered that hers was a carefully studied, highly disciplined simplicity. Her signature

fragrance, "My Own," which was in production by the 1950s, was remembered by one ardent admirer as "Just like Valentina. Deceptively simple. But wildly complex." This carefully measured restraint during a time when floral appliqué, sequins, and pussycat bows were the ubiquitous choice of American dressmakers lent Valentina's designs a cool, modernist edge and earned her the respect and patronage of many of the most celebrated names in art, theater, and society. Wary of obvious fads and proudly declaring herself an American designer, Valentina insisted that true style and well-designed clothing were, in their ideal form, timeless, and she duly advised women to "Fit the century. Forget the year!"

In 1957, Valentina Gowns closed its doors—an event that coincided with the end of Valentina's marriage to George Schlée. The business was jointly owned and run, and it was George's role to manage the business while Valentina created—a two-person performance that simply could not be accomplished by Valentina on her own. In retrospect, however, it appears that Valentina's career might have run its course. By the late 1950s, both in the press and on the streets, the sophisticated ladies of café society were reluctantly giving way to the youth-driven and fast-approaching 1960s, which would witness the imperious and haughty glamour of the preceding era slowly fading away like the lingering scent of a once ravishing perfume. From the very beginning of her career, up until her very last days, Valentina had remained at the very top of the most competitive, most exclusive, and perhaps least understood area of twentieth-century fashion history—American couture. She died in New York City in 1989 at the age of ninety. There was a major display of Valentina's work in 2009 at the Museum of the City of New York, accompanied by a book by Kohle Yohannan.

See also Film and Fashion; Hollywood Style; Theatrical Costume.

Bibliography

Milbank, Caroline Rennolds. *New York Fashion: The Evolution of American Style*. New York: Harry N. Abrams, 1989.
Steele, Valerie. *Women of Fashion: Twentieth-Century Designers*. New York: Rizzoli International, 1991.
Watt, Melinda. *Valentina: American Coutouriere*. Thesis New York University catalog holdings, n.d.
Yohannan, Kohle. *Valentina: American Couture and the Cult of Celebrity*. New York: Rizzoli, 2009.

Kohle Yohannan

VALENTINO*

Valentino Garavani (1932–) was born in Voghera, a city in Lombardy, on 11 May. Even as a young man he was fascinated by fashion and decided to study design in Milan. When he was seventeen he discovered the extraordinary shade of red that would remain a design element throughout his career at a premiere of the Barcelona Opera.

Early Career

In 1950 Valentino went to Paris, where he studied design at the schools of the Chambre Syndicale de la Couture Parisienne. He obtained his first position as a designer with Jean Dessès. In 1957 Valentino went to work in Guy Laroche's new atelier, where he remained for two years. His training in France provided him with both technical skill and a sense of taste. In 1959 he decided to return to Italy and opened his own fashion house on the via Condotti in Rome with financial assistance from his family. In November he made his debut with his first couture collection, displaying 120 luxurious outfits notable for their stoles and draped panels that emphasized the shoulders. The *Sunday Times* of London was quick to take note of the new designer, singling him out for the refined lines of his tailoring and the sophistication of his garments.

In 1960 Valentino met Giancarlo Giammetti, who became his business administrator. At this time he moved his fashion house to via Gregoriana, 54. Valentino quickly became the favorite designer of the movie stars who were often found at Cinecittà, known as the new Hollywood during the years of Italy's economic boom. One of the first stars who wore Valentino's clothes was Elizabeth Taylor, who was in Rome for the filming of *Cleopatra*. In 1960 Valentino signed an agreement with a British firm, Debenham and Freebody, to reproduce some of his couture designs. That same year he designed costumes for Monica Vitti in Michelangelo Antonioni's film *La Notte*. In 1963 Valentino's summer line was photographed on the set of Federico Fellini's film *8 1/2*.

Valentino's collection for fall–winter 1961–1962 featured twelve white outfits inspired by Jacqueline Kennedy. But what secured Valentino's fame was the success of his first fashion show on the runway of the Sala Bianca in the Palazzo Pitti in Florence in July 1962. For the first time French *Vogue* dedicated its cover to an Italian designer.

International Success

Valentino's fall–winter collection for 1963–1964 was inspired by wild animals. American *Vogue* published a photograph of the contessa Consuelo Crespi wearing one of his zebra-patterned models, which anticipated his op art and pop art-inspired collection of spring–summer 1966. The 1966 collection has become famous for its prints and geometric designs, its stylized animals, and its large dots. That same year Valentino started a lingerie line and stunned his audience with a winter show that included pink and violet furs. Ethel Kennedy chose a Valentino dress for her meeting with Pope Paul VI in June 1966.

In 1967 Valentino received the Neiman Marcus Award in Dallas, which spurred him to further develop his creative ideas. The award was the direct impetus for his first men's collection, Valentino Uomo. The designer's accessories, especially his handbags with a gold "V," became essential items for the elegant women of the jet set. In 1968 Valentino introduced his famous Collezione Bianca, a spring–summer line of white and off-white garments that included suits, wraps, coats, and legwear in white lace. The show took place at a critical moment in international fashion and helped alleviate the crisis in haute couture—a crises due to changes in international society in 1968 when people started looking at less exclusive models. In March of that year Valentino opened a store in Paris, followed by one in Milan in 1969. In October 1968 he designed Jacqueline Kennedy's dress for her wedding to Aristotle Onassis. He was the most acclaimed designer of the moment and expanded his circle of clients to include Paola di Liegi, Princess Margaret of England, Farah Diba, the Begum Aga Khan, Marella Agnelli, Princess Grace of Monaco, Sophia Loren, and many other well-known women.

Valentino lengthened hemlines and introduced folk and gypsy motifs in the early 1970s. He started his first boutique line in 1969. It was originally produced by Mendes, although ready-to-wear production was turned over to Gruppo Finanziario Tessile (GFT) in 1979. Valentino also opened a prêt-à-porter shop in the center of Rome in 1972. Throughout the 1970s his designs alternated between slender suits and harem pants coupled with maxi coats. These designs often evoked a Liberty and art deco atmosphere, as in his 1973 collection inspired by the art of Gustav Klimt and the Ballets Russes. In 1974 he opened new stores in London, Paris, New York, and Tokyo (in the early 2000s there are twenty-five stores throughout the world). In 1976 he decided to show his boutique line in Paris, while keeping his couture line in Rome. Valentino launched his first perfume, named Valentino, in 1978. The following year he introduced a line of blue jeans at a famous discothèque, Studio 54 in New York City, which was publicized through an advertising campaign photographed by Bruce Weber.

The collections of the 1980s were characterized by sarong skirts gathered on the hip, draped garments, ruched fabrics, breathtaking necklines, and dramatic slits in a range of colors that emphasized the famous Valentino red, together with black and white. In 1982 the designer presented his fall–winter collection at the Metropolitan Museum of Art. In 1986 he introduced Oliver, a more youthful line named after his faithful dog, which he used as a logo. Three years later, Valentino decided to show his couture line in Paris, a series of garments inspired by ancient and modern art.

Valentino's collections of the 1990s integrated the themes of revival and self-reference—flounces, embroidery, and dots—partly as a way of emphasizing his thirty years in fashion, which were celebrated in several short films, exhibitions, and books. In January 1998, after a difficult period, Valentino sold his brand to the Holding di Partecipazioni Industriali SpA (HdP) group run by Maurizio Romiti, although Valentino remained the creative director. In 2002 HdP sold the fashion house to Gruppo Marzotto.

Elements of Style

Valentino has paid his own personal tribute to contemporary fashion, inventing a recognizable look, modern yet sophisticated, which balances tradition and innovation through the image of an iconic femininity that is both classic and chic. Valentino's designs have as a common denominator the technical precision of fine tailoring, which he applies not so much for the sake of innovation but rather to provide a sense of stylistic continuity. Bows, ruching, and draping are distinctive features of many of his designs, together with the famous Valentino red. All these features are used strategically, serving to give the brand its mythic quality. Valentino's fabrics are printed with flowers, dots, and his own initial, which has doubled as a logo since the 1960s, highlighting the interplay between ornamental texture and effective communication.

A forceful interpreter of the lines and ambiance of the nineteenth century, with references ranging from the neoclassical with its fine drapery through the Second

Empire with its crinolines, Valentino plays with the idea that his garments serve as a kind of aesthetic memory, a modern reference to a different time. Because of the designer's ability to work with tradition, he has found a unique, although elitist, stylistic solution that has satisfied sophisticated women throughout the world.

See also **Celebrities; Italian Fashion; Vogue.**

Bibliography

Bianchino, Gloria, and Arturo Carlo Quintavalle. *Moda: Dalla fiaba al design.* Novara, Italy: De Agostini, 1989.
Cosi, Marina. *Valentino che veste di nuovo.* Milan: Camunia Editrice, 1984.
Golbin, Pamela. *Valentino: Themes and Variations.* New York: Rizzoli, 2008.
Menkes, Suzy. *Valentino.* New York: Taschen America, 2009.
Morris, Bernadine. *Valentino.* Florence: Octavo, 1997.
Pellé, Marie-Paule. *Valentino's Magic.* Milan: Leonardo Arte Editore, 1998.
Sozzani, Franca. *Valentino's Red Book.* Milan: Rizzoli International, 2000.
Valentino. *Trent'anni di magia. Le opere. Le immagini.* Milan: Bompiani Editore, 1991.

Aurora Fiorentini

VEBLEN, THORSTEIN

A North American economist and sociologist, Thorstein Veblen (1857–1929) was an unrelenting critic of late nineteenth-century industrial society and in particular of the hierarchy of values associated with its dominant group, which Veblen named the *leisure class.* Clothing and fashion, he argued, were important as a way in which this group competed among themselves for prestige and social status.

Veblen sought to understand the aims and ambitions of the leisure class by uncovering the economic motives that were at the center of their actions and values. In his classic text, *The Theory of the Leisure Class: An Economic Study in the Evolution of Institutions* (1899), he concluded that the economic activity of the leisure class is driven by a way of life given over to either the maintenance or the acquisition of "honorable repute." The key to gaining status, argued Veblen, is for the households within the leisure class to dispose publicly of their wealth according to the principles of conspicuous consumption and conspicuous leisure. Adherence to these principles shows that a household and its members are able to consume without participating in the "demeaning and unworthy" activities attached to the "the industrial process."

Although Veblen scrutinized a wide range of expenditures—including houses, food, gardens, and household pets—he singled out clothing for special consideration. As he observed, "no line of consumption affords a more apt illustration than expenditure on dress" (p. 123). This is because clothing is a social necessity and to be in public is, by necessity, to be clothed. By being on show, clothing becomes a prime indicator of its wearer's "pecuniary repute" (p. 123), and since, in modern industrial society, clothing is a universal item of consumption, it is difficult for anyone to ignore the pressures of competitive emulation. Dress, therefore, is ideally placed as a vehicle with which to assert superior status in relation to one's peers within the leisure class, as well as collectively displaying the superiority of this class over all others. Veblen concluded that dress has only a tentative connection to protection and bodily comfort, observing that "it is by no means an uncommon occurrence, in an inclement climate, for people to go ill clad in order to appear well dressed" (p. 124).

Dress and Conspicuous Consumption

Veblen argued that a prime function of dress within the leisure class is to display the wearer's wealth by their consumption "of valuable goods in excess of what is required for physical comfort" (p. 125). According to Veblen the most immediate form of conspicuous consumption is *quantity*, or the possession of items of clothing (for instance shoes or suits) far beyond the requirements of reasonable daily wear. However, dress in the leisure class is also subject to considerations of *quality*. Ability to pay can also be demonstrated by the ownership of garments distinguished by the expensiveness of their materials, such as the goat hair used to weave pashmina shawls. Time-consuming methods of garment construction, and therefore expense, can, Veblen argued, insinuate itself into the esteem in which its wearer will be held. The comparison between a handmade garment and a machine-made one is almost always in favor of the former. Finally, the *scarcity* of a garment can also be a factor in adding to the repute of its wearer. An original item from the studio of a famous designer, or a garment bearing the label of a chic fashion house, carries more prestige than an undistinguished item of clothing.

One final way that members of the leisure class exhibit pecuniary strength is always to appear in fashionable, up-to-date clothing. Veblen observed that "if each garment is permitted to serve for but a brief term, and if none of last season's apparel is carried over and made further use of during the present season, the wasteful expenditure on dress is greatly increased" (p. 127).

Conspicuous Leisure

Veblen's exploration of the dress of the leisure class extends beyond the ways in which individuals consume items of clothing and engages with the very forms and styles assumed by these garments. As he wrote, "Dress must not only be conspicuously expensive; it must also be 'inconvenient'" (p. 127). This is because, within the competitive logic of the leisure class, overt displays of wealth can be supplemented by wearing clothes that show the person in question "is not engaged in any kind of productive labour" (p. 125). Veblen uses this idea of conspicuous leisure to great effect in explaining the enormous differences in the form taken by men's and women's clothing at the end of the nineteenth century.

In scrutinizing contemporary men's clothing for evidence of the principle of conspicuous leisure, Veblen argued that there should be an absence on the male garments of any evidence of manual labor such as stains, shiny elbows, or creasing. Rather, elegant men's dress must exhibit signs that the wearer is a man of leisure. As he states, "Much of the charm that invests the patent-leather shoe, the stainless linen, the lustrous cylindrical hat, and the walking stick . . . comes of their pointedly suggesting that the wearer cannot when so attired bear a hand in any employment that is directly and immediately of any human use" (p. 126).

The dress of the women of the leisure class, while embodying the salient principles of conspicuous consumption and conspicuous leisure, is also influenced by the inferior social position they occupy within the leisure-class household. It is the job of the woman, argued Veblen, "to consume for the [male] head of the household; and her apparel is contrived with this object in view" (p. 132). By wearing garments that are both expensive and inconvenient, such as ornate dresses, corsets, and complicated hats, women show that they do not need to work and so increase the "pecuniary repute" in which the head of the family is held. Veblen was one of the first modern thinkers to relate the appearance of women to their weak social and economic position.

Although Veblen's analysis of dress and fashion has proved fruitful in social and historical contexts beyond what he originally envisaged, he always considered his study to be an explanation applicable primarily to what took place within the leisure class, not as a universal theory of dress. Strongly influenced by Charles Darwin's theory of evolution, Veblen believed that in the future men and women would progress beyond the restless changes of dress styles encouraged by "pecuniary culture." In their place would emerge a set of relatively stable costumes similar to those Veblen imagined had existed in ancient Greece and Rome, China, and Japan.

See also Fashion, Theories of; Fashion and Identity.

Bibliography

Bell, Quentin. *On Human Finery*. London: Hogarth Press, 1976. An extended interpretation of Veblen's ideas on dress and fashion.

Carter, Michael. *Fashion Classics from Carlyle to Barthes*. Oxford and New York: Berg, 2003. See chapter 3, "Thorstein Veblen's Leisure Class."

Dorfman, Joseph. *Thorstein Veblen and His America*. New York: Viking Press, 1934. The standard biography of Veblen. Contains fascinating details of his personal taste in clothing.

Riesman, David. *Thorstein Veblen: A Critical Interpretation*. New York and London: Charles Scribner's Sons, 1953. See chapter 8 for a discussion of Veblen's analysis of the corset.

Veblen, Thorstein. "The Economic Theory of Women's Dress." In *Essays in Our Changing Order*. Edited by Leon Ardzrooni. New York: Viking Press, 1964. This is Veblen's account of the historical and economic origins of women's dress.

———. *The Theory of the Leisure Class*. New York: The Modern Library, Random House, 2001.

Michael Carter

VERSACE, GIANNI AND DONATELLA*

Gianni Versace (1946–1997) was a defining figure in the world of design in the 1980s and 1990s. He dressed the independent spirits, celebrities, and the rich, young, and fearless. His exclusive clique personified his ideals of men's and women's ready-to-wear and couture clothing. He also created accessories, linens, and a collection for the home inspired by his preference for the baroque style. Versace's knowledge was encyclopedic and his sense of history prophetic; his genius was the successful linkage of fashion and culture.

Following Versace's tragic death in July 1997, his sister Donatella was catapulted into the international limelight. Only three months later, no longer her brother's muse and collaborator, she assumed creative direction over the development of a dozen highly demanding collections. An earlier agreement between brother and sister had established that she would be the one to carry on his work if it were ever necessary. As a result the signature Versace Atelier collection was presented as usual in Paris in 1998.

Donatella Versace was born in Reggio Calabria, in southern Italy in 1955. She was one of four children born to a businessman and an accomplished seamstress. During Donatella's childhood, Gianni designed clothing for his younger sister, who became the embodiment of his standards. After she completed her studies in Italian literature at the Università di Firenze to supplement her sense of culture, she followed Gianni to Milan, where he had established his career. Initially he sketched his first ready-to-wear collections for the manufacturing firms of Genny, Complice, and Callaghan.

Donatella arrived with the intention of shaping her brother's public image through deft management of his public relations. When he established his signature company in 1978, she became his spirited muse-in-residence. Santo Versace, an older sibling, assisted in the organization of the business, which he continues to direct.

As the house's driving creative force since 1997, Donatella has forged on to energize her international team of fashion designers. Her entrance-making gowns, as well as practical, elegant ready-to-wear clothes and men's wear maintained a high profile in her design studios and corporate offices in the center of Milan. The Versace family estates are located in nearby Como, within an hour's drive from the Milan corporate headquarters.

Business Innovations

Donatella's larger-than-life approach to creating fashion mirrored her brother's maxim that fashion must fuse with the media, the performing arts, celebrity, vitality, and sexuality. Donatella staged the audacious, high-powered Versace runway shows after Gianni's death, enlisting the friendship and devotion of many of the supermodels. Her brother had initiated successful advertising campaigns with photographers and artists beginning in the late 1970s: Richard Avedon and Andy Warhol, among others, shared his flamboyant taste for self-promotion. Donatella continued in this vein, preferring to work with such photographers as Steven Meisel and Bruce Weber. The company continued to unleash dynamic, sexually charged media campaigns in the early 2000s as it expanded its share of the luxury trades.

Gianni Versace's penchant for extreme styling and unconventional choices of sumptuous and radiant fabrics combined themes from his studies in art history with new technology. The Versace label was more focused on the modern career woman in the early twenty-first century, a change reflected in the variety of garments it produced. Donatella's hallmarks included flashy materials fluidly draped. She presented herself on the international stage as the model of an invincible woman. Donatella also launched the fragrance Versace Woman in 2001.

Personal Image

During their adolescence and early adult years, brother and sister remained loyal to each other. Gianni created vibrant garments for Donatella that embodied his personal rationale of expression. The freedom to dare, to make personal choices, was one of the Versace duo's resonant manifestos. During their nineteen years of collaboration, Versace consulted his younger sibling in all important decisions. Her bravura and dedication made her an integral part of the company as it developed. In early 2000 she epitomized the liberation he sought as a designer. Gianni paid tribute to Donatella when he named his 1995 perfume Blonde to honor her trademark long, platinum locks. Surrounded by revelers, her frequent tours of nightspots provided her with access to the younger generation. In due course, Donatella became chief designer for Versace's Versus collection, where she further empowered her success with their dual vision of bold patterns and high glamour infused with sex appeal, designed for a younger clientele. While Donatella was independent in her thinking, she was also committed to her brother's enduring legacy. She continued to style flashy and extreme ready-to-wear clothing as well as a couture line, as she did during her apprenticeship with Gianni and in her position as an accessory designer and creator of a line of children's clothing in 1993.

Donatella's camaraderie with celebrities, including Elton John, Elizabeth Hurley, and Courtney Love, reflected her belief in the significance of uncompromising friendships. Madonna, Jon Bon Jovi, Sting, and Trudy Skyler were among her closest confidantes. Like her older brother, she combined music with the media and the spectacle of contemporary urban life. Donatella's designs affirmed sensuality, employing short skirts and plunging necklines as devices of freedom. "Fashion can be freedom or it can be a way to live with no freedom," she avowed in *Interview*.

Donatella married the former model Paul Beck, with whom she had two children—Allegra, her uncle's beneficiary, born in 1986, and Daniel, born in 1991.

Donatella Versace reveled in the attention she received in fashion and popular lifestyle magazines. She pursued visibility at all levels of society and was always ready to convey the glamorous extravagance that identified her company. Her fashion edicts remained consistent: "If I want to be blonde, I am not going to be a medium blonde. I am going to be totally blonde. If I am going to wear heels, they are not going to be two inches high. They are going to be much higher than that. It's the freedom of extremes that I love" (*Interview*). Her confident design ethic mirrored that of her late brother, who became a creative genius in high-end apparel and of bold gestures in the media.

There have been several important museum exhibitions devoted to Versace—at the Museum at FIT, at the Costume Institute of the Metropolitan Museum of Art, and most recently in 2002–3 at the Victoria and Albert Museum in London, the last of which also included Donatella's work.

See also Avedon, Richard; Celebrities; Fashion Photography; Italian Fashion; Madonna; Meisel, Steven; Supermodels.

Bibliography

"Friendship is Freedom." *Interview* 30, no. 3 (March 2000): 212.
Martin, Richard. *Versace*. New York: Universe/Vendome, 1997.
——. *Gianni Versace*. New York: The Metropolitan Museum of Art and Harry N. Abrams, Inc., 1998.
Spindler, Amy M. "Style: The Great Gianni." *New York Times* (18 February 2001).

Wilcox, Claire. *The Art and Craft of Gianni Versace*. London: Victoria and Albert Museum, 2002.

Gillion Carrara

VIKTOR & ROLF*

The Dutch saying, *Doe normaal, dan ben je al gek genoeg* (literally, Just be normal, then you are crazy enough) sheds light on the work of design team Viktor & Rolf. Viktor Horsting (b. 1969) and Rolf Snoeren (b. 1969) met while they were students at the Arnhem Academy of Art, the Netherlands, in 1988. They both sought to escape the boredom they experienced while growing up in small, quiet, suburban towns in southern Holland. "We had nothing to relate to, never saw glamour except for fashion magazines, and longed to escape to those dream worlds," Horsting once said to an interviewer. By pushing the boundaries of what defines fashion, Viktor & Rolf inspired a new generation of Dutch fashion designers and helped to expose the international fashion media to a country known more for wooden clogs than high fashion.

Viktor & Rolf are characterized in Stephen Gan's *Visionaire 2000* (1997) as "fashion's biggest fans and its toughest critics." While their works celebrate the detailed craftsmanship of tailoring and consistently reference classic silhouettes from the legendary couturiers Cristóbal Balenciaga, Coco Chanel, Christian Dior, and Yves Saint Laurent, they also critique the twentieth- and twenty-first century's fashion industry, tackle the stereotypes of fashion, and expose its vulnerabilities to a runway audience.

The Early Experiments

Viktor & Rolf's first collection won the grand prize at the *Salon européen des jeunes stylists* (1993), a fashion festival in the southern French city of Hyères. When deconstruction was the trend, Viktor & Rolf reconstructed by piling layers of men's button-down shirts to form ball gowns. The following year they suspended flashy gold garments adorned with oversized ribbons and excessive decorations from the ceiling in their installation *L'Apparence du vide* (1994) at the Galerie Patricia Dorfman, Paris, which sought to critique the aura and hype surrounding fashion. In another experiment,

sleek marketing for *Viktor & Rolf, le parfum* (1996) served to critique the superficial, banal beauty of fragrance advertising. The neatly packaged, limited-edition (2,500) perfume bottles were deliberately designed so that they could not be opened. The bottles sold out at the Parisian boutique Colette. In *Launch* (1996), presented at the Torch Gallery in Amsterdam, Viktor & Rolf's dream world of the fashion process was realized on a small scale. They explained that, with a doll-sized runway, sketch and draping session, and photo shoot setup, "we created the ultimate goals we wanted to achieve in fashion (but felt unable to). These miniatures represented some of the most emblematic situations in fashion we wanted to become reality" (Personal interview, 23 December 1999). Their dream was realized soon thereafter in the form of an haute couture collection.

The Haute Couture Collections

Viktor & Rolf brought an intellectual approach to the fashion process via art. They pursued haute couture because they found it to be "the most sublime" aspect of fashion. With Dutch government support and the Groninger Museum, the Netherlands, as their sole client, Viktor & Rolf were able to develop creatively without the pressure of maintaining profitability that most young designers experience. In their second spring/summer 1998 collection at the Thaddeus Ropac Gallery in Paris, Viktor & Rolf created their signature "atomic bomb silhouette"—exaggerated on top and pencil-skinny on the bottom. The clothes were dedicated to the millennium (fit either for the biggest celebration ever or apocalyptic destruction) and were deformed with silk balloons, streamers, and other brightly colored party elements. The Viktor & Rolf label was recognized by the Federation de la couture, the umbrella organization that over-sees the Parisian haute couture houses and their events. This prestigious invitation for inclusion occurred even though Viktor & Rolf did not conform to the organization's rules and guidelines. Viktor & Rolf presented their entire fall/winter 1999–2000 collection on the shoulders of one model, Maggie Rizer. As she stood on a revolving platform, Viktor & Rolf layered, in nine successive stages à la Russian-doll style, precisely-engineered jute dresses decorated with Swarovski crystals. Through this mechanism they attempted to showcase their feelings about haute couture as a precious and unattainable jewel.

Viktor & Rolf in the Twenty-first Century

The fashion media's attraction to their exaggerated silhouettes and noteworthy runway performances has always played an integral role in the shaping of the Viktor & Rolf brand identity. With no advertising campaigns, no self-standing boutiques, and no mass-produced clothes to sell, their early relationship with the public depended heavily on the generous amounts of press coverage they received each season. (Close collaborations with photography teams Inez van Lamsweerde and Vinoodh Matadin, as well as Anouschka Blommers and Niels Schumm, also helped further their vision.) The media's acknowledgment of Viktor & Rolf as a leading avantgarde haute couture label was instrumental to the commercial success of their ready-to-wear line. Their first collection sold immediately to sixty stores worldwide during its launch in February 2000.

Viktor Horsting and Rolf Snoeren understand that a fashion designer's public image is nearly as important as the clothes that are created. Oftentimes referred to as "the Gilbert & George of fashion," the two present themselves as mirror images of each other: matching dark-rimmed glasses, closely trimmed dark hair, and a serious demeanor despite the humor in their shows. They performed a tap-dance finale with tuxedos, top hats, and canes to "Putting on the Ritz" and "Singin' in the Rain" for their spring/summer 2001 collection. Additionally, they used themselves as models for the launch of their fall/winter 2003–2004 men's wear collection, Monsieur, as they synchronized changes into looks depicting clichés of traditional men's wear.

Viktor & Rolf continue to push the boundaries of fashion in ready-to-wear by using the catwalk as a stage for performance art. Models were cast as walking shadows, for example, in their "Black Hole" collection (fall/winter 2001–2002) when they were covered head-totoe in black silhouettes and black makeup. Two years later (fall/winter 2003–2004) their models appeared as fair-skinned, red-haired clones of the actress Tilda Swinton. In 2006, Viktor and Rolf designed a line for H&M, greatly expanding their public recognition. Renzo Rossi, the owner of Diesel, took a controlling stake in the company in 2008. There have been several museum exhibitions of their work, of which the most striking was the one at the Barbican Gallery, London, in 2008.

Through their shows Viktor & Rolf try to bring fantasy, beauty, and magic back to fashion as they forge a path for the viewer to enter their dream. "For us," explains Rolf Snoeren, "it's always about escaping reality, so in that sense the clothes are meant to show beauty first. Beauty and hope. Because cynicism, you know, kills everything."

See also Fashion Designer; Fashion Shows.

Bibliography

Alonso, Roman, and Lisa Eisner. "Double Dutch." *New York Times* (8 December 2002): 109. This in-depth interview reveals the personalities and fantasy worlds of Horsting and Snoeren.

Evans, Caroline. *The House of Viktor & Rolf.* London: Merrell Publishers, 2008.

Horsting, Viktor, and Artimo. *Viktor & Rolf.* Breda, Netherlands: Artimo Foundation, 1999. This artist's book covers Viktor & Rolf's early work, 1993–1999.

Lowthorpe, Rebecca. "The Gilbert & George of Fashion." *The Independent on Sunday* (30 September 2001): 35–38.

Martin, Richard. "A Note: Art & Fashion, Viktor & Rolf." *Fashion Theory: The Journal of Dress, Body & Culture* 3 (1999). Martin analyzes Viktor & Rolf's early works and emphasizes their importance in crossing the boundaries of fashion with art.

Spindler, Amy. *Viktor & Rolf Haute Couture Book.* Groningen, Netherlands: Groninger Museum, 2001. A retrospective exhibition catalog featuring the haute couture collections at the Groninger Museum.

Angel Chang

VIONNET, MADELEINE*

Born in Chilleurs-aux-Bois in 1876, Madeleine Vionnet was apprenticed to a dressmaker while still a child. She began her career in fashion working for makers of lingerie, as well as dress-makers and couturiers in London and Paris. These early experiences of craft skills and, in particular, the relationship between body and fabric involved in making under-garments, influenced the future direction of her own designs. She learned to respect the intricate skills of craftspeople, who were able to produce delicate effects through, for example, drawn threadwork and fagoting, which created spatial patterns by moving and regrouping the fabric's threads. This fascination with minute detail and the possibilities of fabric manipulation formed the foundation of her approach. Her background in the couture trade was fundamental to her later status, since it distinguished her as a craftsperson who was knowledgeable about the various dressmaking skills and decorative trades that supported designers. She was therefore not only tutored in practical skills but was also aware of the status and treatment of young women who worked in the ateliers.

Birth of Vionnet's Design Philosophy

Around 1900 Vionnet moved to Callot Soeurs's celebrated couture house in Paris. There she began to understand the significance of garment design that sprang from draping fabric directly onto a live model, rather than sketching a design on paper and then translating it into fabric. This approach necessarily focused attention on the body and its relationship to the way fabric was draped and sculpted around its contours. Vionnet exploited this technique to the full. For Vionnet, draping—in her case on a miniature, eighty-centimeter mannequin—became crucial to her design philosophy. It enabled her to think of the body as a whole and to mobilize the full potential of the springy, malleable, silk crêpes she came to favor.

At Callot Soeurs these methods were combined with an acute awareness of fashion and style, as skillful designers and saleswomen sought to mold couture's elite tastes to each client's particular figure and requirements. Vionnet encountered high fashion and learned its seasonal rhythms, while she experimented with the dressmaking skills she had acquired over the years. An example of this was her adaptation of Japanese kimono sleeves to Western dress, which produced deeper armholes that made the silhouette less restrictive and enabled the fabric to flow and drape around the upper body. This early innovation incorporated several of what were to become Vionnet's trademarks. For example, her use of Asian and classical techniques freed fabric from established Western dressmaking methods that tended to fix the cloth, and therefore the body, into position. Her focus upon draping and wrapping rather than cutting and tailoring to the figure enabled her to achieve maximum fluidity, enhancing movement and flexibility. Her concentration on experimental construction techniques tested the boundaries

of design and dressmaking and allowed her to create clothing that derived its significance from subtle reconfigurations of cloth, rather than from dramatic surface decoration. For Vionnet minute attention to detail was paramount.

Vionnet's career may have started during the late nineteenth century when fashion was predicated upon exaggeration, novelty, and decoration, but there were already intimations of new types of femininity and clothing that would enable greater physical freedom. These came partly from utopian dress reform movements, but also from other designers, such as Fortuny, who used historical dress as a source for comfortable yet luxurious dress.

Daring Designs

When Vionnet moved to the house of Doucet in 1907, she became more daring in her display of the female figure, inspired by avant-garde dancer Isadora Duncan's barefoot movements and by her own desire to strip fashion to its essential elements: fabric and body. She insisted that Doucet's models walk barefoot and corsetless into the couturier's salon for his seasonal fashion show. Her dramatic exposure of the models' skin enhanced the fall of the fabric as they moved and brought sudden focus onto the natural figure.

Vionnet helped to instigate modern fashion's exploration of private and public, with her designs' reliance upon a sophisticated interplay between sheer and opaque fabrics draped to swirl about the skin. Many found her work too controversial, and her main clients were stage performers, used to their public roles and more ready to experiment with avant-garde fashions. The *déshabillé*, a fashionable and fluid garment previously worn in private, became acceptable, if still daring, for entertaining at home. In Vionnet's hands its light drapes created a shimmering cocoon reminiscent of lingerie. For example, the French actress Lantelme was photographed in 1907 in a loose tea gown, the pastel tones and matte glow of its layered chiffon illuminated by beading and sequins.

Classical Influences and Cutting on the Bias

In 1912 Vionnet opened her own house in the rue de Rivoli. It was closed, however, at the outbreak of war in

1914, and Vionnet moved to Rome for the duration. Her experience there, as well as her studies of ancient Greek art in museum collections, became another crucial aspect of her work. Classicism, both as an aesthetic and design philosophy, provided Vionnet with a language to articulate her belief in geometrical form, mathematical rhythm, and the strength of proportion and balance as a basis for the garments she created.

During the late teens Vionnet focused on the process of wrapping lengths of fabric onto the body in the style of the Greek chiton. Through these experiments she exploited the advances made in fabric technology during World War I that had produced yarns that could be made into more supple fabrics, and she had extra wide lengths of material created for her to allow even greater drape. Vionnet was thus able to push her examination of construction methods that not only draped but twisted fabric still further than before; moreover, she formulated the potential of the bias cut for which she is so often remembered. To do this she cut the fabric diagonally, across the grain, to produce a springy, elastic drape. Although cutting on the bias had been used for accessories and had been applied to fixed, molded dress forms, it had not been used this extensively for the body of a garment. Vionnet took an experimental leap forward in her desire to release both fabric and figure from the tight-fitting ethos of traditional Western dressmaking.

Vionnet reduced the use of darts, often eliminating them completely and therefore allowing bias-cut fabric to hover freely around the body. She also introduced lingerie techniques—such as roll-tucked hems or fagoting to disguise the line of a seam—to both day and evening wear. Her designs aimed for simplicity of overall form and impact, while they frequently employed complex construction techniques.

One of the most dramatically minimal of her designs was a dress from 1919–1920, now in the collection of the Costume Institute at the Metropolitan Museum in New York. It demonstrates Vionnet's search during this period of her career for new ways to push the boundaries of the fabric while maintaining tight control over the ultimate hang of the garment. In this example she used four rectangles of ivory silk crêpe, two at the back and two at the front, held together at one point to form the shoulders of the dress. The rectangles hang down the body from these two points, to form two diamond forms of mobile fabric at front and back. Vionnet, in the act of turning the geometric shapes onto the diagonal for the final dress, swung

the weave onto the bias. Thus the dress is stripped of dressmaking's usual devices to nip and sew the material for a "fit" with the body beneath; Vionnet instead used the movement released in the fabric to flow and drape around the wearer as she walked and danced. The deep drape of the fabric created vertical bands of light flowing down the figure. These elongated the silhouette, which was first blurred and then brought into relief as the wearer's movements caused the swathes of fabric to shift and form anew.

In Vionnet's hands the bias cut was a means to rethink the relationship between fabric and flesh. She constantly tested the methods she had learned during her early career, and her attention to anatomy led to her use of bias cutting not just to allow material to cocoon the figure, but to produce sophisticated forms of decoration. She varied the direction of the material's grain to encourage light to bounce off contrasting matte and shiny pattern pieces. The complexity of her construction techniques meant that her designs came alive only when worn or draped on the stand. They were conceived for the three dimensions of the body and cut to smooth over the figure: evening dresses dipped into the small of the back; day dresses slid under the clavicle to form a soft cowl neckline; and bias-cut fabric draped artfully to allow for the curve of the stomach or the arch of hip bones.

Futurist Influences

Such effects were only enhanced as the wearer moved, and Vionnet's interest in contemporary art, and in particular futurism, served to develop this exploration of movement as a further expression of modernism. The illustrations that artist Thayaht produced for the *Gazette du bon ton* in the 1920s expound futurism's view that art should represent the dynamics of the body in movement. His drawings show women in Vionnet outfits, with lines tracing the curves of the dress into the surrounding environment to suggest the flow of the body, and the fabric, as they walked. He wanted to express the sensation of the space between body and material, and between the material and the space the wearer inhabits, as alive with friction and loaded with the potential to blur air and matter.

Vionnet's approach explored women's modern lives and sought to express an adult, liberated femininity. Like modern artists she was interested in the integrity of the materials she used. She also exploited technology by experimenting with new ways to dye fabric, and

"My efforts have been directed towards freeing material from the restrictions imposed on it, in just the same way that I have sought to liberate the female form. I see both as injured victims . . . and I've proved that there is nothing more graceful than the sight of material hanging freely from the body."

Madeleine Vionnet, quoted in Milbank 1985.

she was driven to create clothes that broke away from highly decorative, constraining forms of fashion that relied upon historical notions of femininity. However, while she described her clothing as appropriate for any body size or shape, its revelatory exposure of the natural form, and the prevailing ideal of youth and athleticism, meant her designs can be seen as part of the twentieth century's shift toward bodies controlled from within, through diet and exercise, rather than through restrictive undergarments.

Classicism and Ornamentation

In 1923 Vionnet moved her couture house to 50 avenue Montaigne, where its salons were decorated in a classically inspired, modernist manner that formed a suitable backdrop to her work. The salon used for her seasonal shows contained frescoes that showed contemporary women clad in some of her most popular designs, intermingled with images of ancient Greek goddesses. Thus clients could measure themselves against classical ideals and see Vionnet's designs through the prism of a revered, idealized past. This placed her designs, which could seem so daring in their simplicity, within the context of classical antiquity's noble precedent and articulated the link between her own focus upon mathematical harmony and that of the past.

The various ateliers that produced her collections showed the diversity of her output and her ability to imbue a whole range of different types of clothing, from sportswear to furs, lingerie, and tailored clothes, with her ethos of creative pattern-cutting and subtle, supple silhouettes. Her daywear also relied upon the material's inherent properties and the possibilities to be explored in her integration of construction techniques and decoration. Discreet day dresses were pintucked in neat rows, whose spacing gently pulled fabric in toward the figure at the waist and curved diagonally across the body from shoulders, across the bust, around the hips, and round

toward the small of the back to shape the dress. Thus Vionnet's garments were given shape while maintaining smooth, uncluttered silhouettes, and the tucks of materials created a pattern on the fabric's surface.

During the 1920s, when heavy beadwork and embroidery proliferated, Vionnet was committed to search for methods of ornamentation that took part in shaping the whole garment. Narrow pintucks were used to form her signature rose motif, its size subtly graduated to pull dresses toward the wearer's figure. For Vionnet such exact craftsmanship enabled her to challenge traditional methods continually. Even when she used beadwork, most famously on the 1924 Little Horses dress, she demanded an innovative approach. She commissioned couture embroiderer Albert Lesage to explore new ways to apply bugle beads to bias-cut silk, so that the flow of the fabric would not be interrupted and the images of glittering horses inspired by the stylized, representational forms on Grecian red figure vases would not be distorted by the beads' weight. Even thick furs and tweeds could be given greater fluidity and form through her manipulation of their drape and use of pattern pieces cut to sculpt and form around the figure.

Business Growth

Vionnet's couture house grew during the 1920s, and she opened a branch in Biarritz to provide everything from spectator sportswear and travel garments—a growing market as women led increasingly active lives—to her supple evening wear for dinners and dances. By 1932 her Paris establishment had grown, despite the impact of the Great Depression, to twenty-one ateliers. Her attitude toward her employees was as enlightened as her design approach. She remembered her own path through the studios' hierarchy and ensured that workers, while paid the same as in other couture houses, were provided with dental and medical care, had paid breaks and holidays, and were given help with maternity leave and proper teaching in her favored design techniques, such as bias cutting.

Vionnet set up her company, Vionnet et cie, in 1922, and with the support of her backers, she pursued a series of business schemes. These included several attempts during the mid-twenties to capitalize on America's reliance upon Parisian fashion for new trends and Vionnet's popularity there, through a number of deals with companies to produce ready-to-wear. Although innovative, these ventures were brief and did nothing to stem the tide of copyists, both in the United States and in France, who cost the couture industry large sums of money each season by plagiarizing original models and mass producing them at lower prices. This practice damaged Vionnet's profits and also reduced the cachet of particular outfits, since couture clients were paying, at least in part, for exclusivity. Despite Vionnet's involvement with a series of couture organizations pledged to track down copyists, and a landmark case in 1930, when Vionnet and Chanel successfully sued a French copyist, this plagiarism was a recurrent problem that haunted the couture industry.

Legacy and Influence on Fashion Design

The last collection Vionnet produced was shown in August 1939 and acknowledged the current vogue for romantic, figure-enhancing styles. Fragile-looking black laces were traced over palest silver lamé, with appliquéd velvet bows to pull out and shape the lighter weight lace overdress and add fashionable fullness to skirts. Vionnet closed her house on the outbreak of World War II. Her work had been hugely influential in both Europe and the Americas during the period between the wars. While she sought to stand outside fashion and create timeless clothing, her liquid bias cut became a defining emblem of 1930s sophistication and style and inspired Hollywood designers to use bias-cut gowns to create iconic images of actresses such as Jean Harlow. Her experiments with fabric control and manipulation and the advances she made in testing the boundaries of fabric construction left a complex legacy which has inspired designers as diverse as Claire McCardell, Ossie Clark, Azzedine Alaïa, Issey Miyake, Yohji Yamamoto, and John Galliano.

When Vionnet died in 1975, her place within the history of fashion in the early twentieth century was assured. Perhaps because of the lack of drama in her private life and her unwillingness to give many interviews, she was less well known than some of her contemporaries. However, Vionnet's focus on experimentation and her desire continually to redefine the relationship between body and fabric provided women with clothing that expressed the period's dynamic modernity.

Vionnet embraced the dressmaking skills she had learned as a child apprentice and elevated them to new levels of complexity, yet she always strove to produce finished garments that preserved, and indeed celebrated, the integrity of the materials she used and the natural shape of the wearer's body. She viewed couture as a testing ground for the new identities that the twentieth century created. Her clients became living embodiments of modern femininity, clad in garments inspired by contemporary art, Asian wrapping techniques, and classical antiquity. In Vionnet's hands these elements were united into dramatically simple silhouettes. Vionnet's intimate knowledge of cutting and draping enabled her to create clothing that expressed the dynamism and potential of women's increasingly liberated lives.

The House of Vionnet was acquired in 1996 by the Lummen family. Their initial focus was on perfume and accessories; after many delays, the first collection of the revived house was presented in 2006. Marc Audibet became the house's artistic director in 2007 but resigned that same year. The House of Vionnet was acquired from the Lummen family by Matteo Marzotto in 2009 and all of its operations were moved to Milan.

See also Cutting; Embroidery; Film and Fashion; Lingerie; Tea Gown.

Bibliography

Chatwin, Bruce. *What Am I Doing Here.* London: Picador, 1990.

Demornex, Jacqueline. *Vionnet.* London: Thames and Hudson, Inc., 1991.

Evans, Caroline, and Minna Thornton. *Women and Fashion: A New Look.* London: Quartet, 1989.

Golbin, Pamela. *Madeline Vionnet.* New York: Rizzoli, 2009.

Kirke, Betty. *Madeleine Vionnet.* San Francisco: Chronicle Books, 1998.

Koda, Harold, Richard Martin, and Laura Sinderbrand. *Three Women: Madeleine Vionnet, Claire McCardell, and Rei Kawakubo.* New York: Fashion Institute of Technology, 1987. Exhibition catalog.

Milbank Rennolds, Caroline. *Couture: The Great Designers.* New York: Stewart, Tabori, and Chang, Inc., 1985.

Rebecca Arnold

VOGUE

Vogue is fashion's bible, the world's leading fashion publication. It was founded in 1892 as a weekly periodical focused on society and fashion, and was subscribed to by New York's elite. Condé Nast (1873–1942) bought the magazine in 1909 and began to transform it into a powerhouse.

Vogue delivered beautifully presented, authoritative content under the leadership and watchful eyes of a few talented editors-in-chief. One of the most notable, Edna Woolman Chase, became editor in 1914 and remained at its helm for thirty-eight years, until 1952. Caroline Seebohm, Nast's biographer, credits Chase with introducing new American talents to the fashion audience. Chase gave full coverage to European, and especially Parisian, fashions, but her approach also suggested that American women might exercise a certain independence of taste.

Chase's successor, Jessica Daves, served as editor in chief from 1952 to 1963 and is remembered primarily for her business acumen. She was followed by the flamboyant Diana Vreeland, whose eight-year tenure (1963–1971) documented "Youthquake," street-influenced youth fashions, and space age and psychedelic fashions. Vreeland's successor was her colleague Grace Mirabella, who served as editor-in-chief from 1971 to 1988. Mirabella was the antithesis of Vreeland; her watchwords for fashion were functionality and affordability. Whereas Vreeland wrote in 1970, "In the evening we go east of the sun and west of the moon—we enter the world of fantasy," Mirabella countered, in 1971, "When you come to evening this year, you do not come to another planet." Mirabella approached the "antifashion" 1970s with a levelheaded stance that addressed a growing constituency of the magazine: the working woman.

Anna Wintour became editor-in-chief of the magazine in 1988 and combined a shrewd and appealing mix of high and low. Her first cover for the magazine, in November 1988, featured model Michaela in a jeweled Lacroix jacket—worn with blue jeans.

A controlling interest in Condé Nast Publications was acquired in 1959 by S. I. Newhouse, who subsequently became the sole owner of the corporation. There are now more than twelve editions of *Vogue*: American, Australian, Brazilian, British, French, German, Greek, Italian, Japanese, Spanish, Taiwanese, Chinese, and Korean. *Teen Vogue* was launched in 2003. (Nast inaugurated the international editions with British *Vogue* in 1916 and French *Vogue* in 1920.)

Nast's original "formula" for *Vogue* was based on service, which Seebohm translates as disseminating fashion information to his readers as efficiently and clearly as possible. Clarity did not exclude creativity, and the magazine became well known for its own stylish look. *Vogue's* most famous art and creative directors were M. F. (Mehmed Fehney) Agha, who started at *Vogue* in 1929, and Alexander Liberman, who joined the staff in 1941. The magazine has employed the foremost illustrators and photographers of its times. (The first photographic cover appeared in 1932; color printing was introduced in the following year.) Its glossy pages maintain the highest standards for the visual presentation of fashion. *Vogue* is still the stuff that many dreams are made of.

See also Fashion Editors; Vreeland, Diana.

Bibliography

Chase, Edna Woolman, and Ilka Chase. *Always in Vogue.* New York: Doubleday and Company, 1954.

Daves, Jessica. *Ready-Made Miracle.* New York: G. P. Putnam's Sons, 1967.

Dwight, Eleanor. *Diana Vreeland.* New York: William Morrow and Company, 2002.

Mirabella, Grace. *In and Out of Vogue: A Memoir.* New York: Doubleday and Company, 1995.

Seebohm, Caroline. *The Man Who Was Vogue: The Life and Times of Condé Nast.* New York: Viking Penguin, 1962.

Laird Borrelli

VREELAND, DIANA

Diana Vreeland (1903–1989) was, and continues to be, an iconic figure in fashion history, whose distinctive personal style and penchant for fantasy influenced her work at *Vogue* and the exhibitions she organized at the Costume Institute of the Metropolitan Museum of Art. Diana Vreeland was born in Paris in 1903 to Emily Key Hoffman and Frederick Young Dalziel. The Dalziels moved to New York in 1904, where the socially eminent family enjoyed a prosperous lifestyle. According to Vreeland's biographer, she was a vivacious child who was interested in fantasy and the transforming powers of artifice from a very young age. In 1924, Diana married Thomas Reed Vreeland, a socially prominent banker. The couple moved to London in 1929, where they remained until 1933. In London Vreeland started her career in fashion by opening a lingerie shop in the city, and her frequent visits to Paris familiarized her with haute couture. As a patron of designers such as Jean Patou, Elsa Schiaparelli, Madeleine Vionnet, and Main-bocher,

Vreeland's flair for dressing, combined with her social standing, made her the subject of commentary in the social pages and in magazines such as American *Vogue*, *Harper's Bazaar* and *Town and Country*.

Harper's Bazaar and *Vogue*

The Vreelands moved back to New York in 1935. Diana began her first job in fashion editorial work at *Harper's Bazaar* in 1937. She was promoted to the position of fashion editor in 1939, working under editor-in-chief Carmel Snow, and remained at the magazine until 1962. Vreeland first came to the readership's attention with her 1936 column entitled "Why Don't You?" The feature encapsulated her personal belief in the ability of fashion to transform women by offering such extravagant and fantastic suggestions to her readers as "Why don't you . . . Turn your child into an Infanta for a fancy dress party?" (August 1936) and "Why don't you own, as does one extremely smart woman, twelve diamond roses of all sizes?" (January 1937) Vreeland honed her editorial skills at *Harper's Bazaar* by working closely with such photographers as Richard Avedon and Louise Dahl-Wolfe to implement her ideas and transfer her imaginative vision to the fashion pages.

Vreeland became publicly known as the archetypal fashion editor, famous for such proclamations as "Pink is the navy blue of India" (Donovan). Her inimitable persona was further popularized when she was parodied in the 1957 film *Funny Face*.

In 1962, Vreeland moved to American *Vogue* as associate editor. In 1963, Sam Newhouse, the owner of Condé Nast, promoted her to editor-in-chief in an effort to reinvigorate the magazine. Having complete control over the look of the magazine, she imbued its pages with her distinctive style and flair for the fantastic. During Vreeland's tenure, the magazine's editorial spreads presented a popular audience with exoticism, aristocratic glamour, and such atypical models (atypical because of their youth, multicultural appearance, and unisex body types) as Veruschka, Penelope Tree, Twiggy, and Lauren Hutton. Vreeland firmly believed that the magazine had the ability to transport the reader, just as clothing had the ability to transform the wearer. The mundane realities of life did not interest her.

The Costume Institute

By the late 1960s, Vreeland's extravagant fashion editorials were deemed out of touch with the times and

> "Mrs. Vreeland is unquestionably the Madame de Sévigné of fashion's court: witty, brilliant, intensely human, gifted like Madame de Sévigné with a superb flair for anecdotes that she communicates verbally rather than in epistles, Mrs. Vreeland is more of a connoisseur of fashion than anyone I know."
> (Beaton, p. 359)

her position at *Vogue* was terminated in 1971; she was replaced by Grace Mirabella. In 1972, Vreeland became involved with the Costume Institute at the Metropolitan Museum of Art, the museum's acclaimed collection of historic costumes. Vreeland's fashionable and colorful personality was perceived as an opportunity to revitalize the costume exhibitions. Vreeland was brought in with the title of special consultant and acted as a creative director for twelve exhibitions from 1972 through 1985. Through these highly popular exhibitions, which included "Balenciaga," "The Eighteenth-Century Woman," "Romantic and Glamorous Hollywood Design," "The Glory of Russian Costume," "La Belle Époque," and "Yves Saint Laurent," Vreeland succeeded in placing her distinctive stamp upon the museum world. She transferred her unique style of fashion marketing to the museum gallery, taking inspiration from the runway, retail trends, fashion editorials, and her own fertile imagination. Her costume exhibitions were spectacular sensory experiences; as she herself admitted in her autobiography, she was interested more in effect than historical accuracy.

In 1976, she received the medal of the Legion d'Honneur from France for her contributions to the fashion industry. In 1984, she published her memoirs, entitled *D.V.* Vreeland died in New York City in 1989, but her status as an icon has had a lasting influence on the world of fashion. In 1993, the Costume Institute celebrated her memory with an exhibition entitled "Diana Vreeland, Immoderate Style." She was the subject of a one-person off-Broadway play entitled *Full Gallop* in 1995. The repeated reexamination of Vreeland's impact on fashion attests to her impact as an arbiter of style who fostered the visibility of fashion on a popular level.

See also Avedon, Richard; Dahl-Wolfe, Louise; Fashion Editors; Fashion Icons; Fashion Magazines; Fashion Models; Fashion Museums and Collections; Vogue.

Bibliography

Beaton, Cecil. *The Glass of Fashion*. Garden City, N.Y.: Doubleday, 1954.

Donovan, Carrie. "Diana Vreeland, Dynamic Fashion Figure, Joins *Vogue.*" *New York Times* (28 March 1952).

Dwight, Eleanor. *Diana Vreeland.* New York: HarperCollins Publishers, Inc., 2002.

Martin, Richard, and Harold Koda. *Diana Vreeland: Immoderate Style.* New York: Metropolitan Museum of Art, 1993.

Silverman, Debora. *Selling Culture: Bloomingdale's, Diana Vreeland, and the New Aristocracy of Taste in Reagan's America.* New York: Pantheon Books, 1986.

Vreeland, Diana. *D.V.* Edited by George Plimpton and Christopher Hemphill. New York: Alfred A. Knopf, 1984.

Michelle Tolini Finamore

VUITTON, LOUIS*

Born in 1821 in Anchay, France, Louis Vuitton worked as an apprentice for the packing-case maker M. Maréchal, where he created personal luggage for Empress Eugénie before setting up his own business in 1854. Vuitton's career as a craftsman trunk maker quickly brought him an ever-expanding roster of clients, requiring him to move to workshops at Asnières, on the outskirts of Paris, in 1859. The workshops remain at the original site, and this is where all the luggage and accessories are still made. Annexed to the workshops is the family home, which is now a museum.

Vuitton's first innovation was to pioneer a gray, waterproof canvas (Trianon), which was stretched across the poplar wood structure of the trunk, eliminating the need for a dome-shaped lid, which had been essential for repelling rain from the trunk during transit atop a horse-drawn carriage. This innovation enabled porters to stack trunks one on top of the other, allowing travelers to take more luggage with them on trips.

Vuitton's success in the luxury luggage market was due to his willingness to modify and custom-build luggage that was adaptable to new forms of transportation. For example, cabin trunks for ocean liners were designed to fit under daybeds so as to maximize use of space. Yet what the luggage contained was never a secondary concern, but of equal value in the definition of first-class travel. To meet the needs of these elite travelers, Vuitton devised the wardrobe trunk with interior drawers and hanging space with the advice of the couturier Charles Frederick Worth.

As the company prospered, its products were widely imitated, forcing Vuitton to change the canvas design from a striped to a checkerboard (or Daumier) design. His son Georges created the famous monogram canvas in 1896. The design was intended primarily to combat commercial piracy, although its orientalist, decorative design also reflected the fashion for all things Japanese at the end of the nineteenth century. Beyond the initials that feature as a tribute to his father, Georges's design bears three abstracted flowers, based upon a Japanese *mon* or family crest that, not unlike a coat of arms, was traditionally used to identify items made for and owned by a particular family.

International stature was assured for the company by the opening of a London store in 1885, a French store opposite the Grand Hotel in 1871, and distribution in America through Wanamaker's department store in 1898. Design awards at the Exposition International d'Industrie et des Arts Decoratives of 1925 secured the company's reputation for grand luxe in the art deco style.

Later in the twentieth century, handbags, wallets, and other small leather goods became increasingly important parts of the company's product line, as luxe travel with numerous trunks and suitcases became largely a thing of the past. In 1997, the company hired the American fashion designer Marc Jacobs to design accessories and clothing. A commercial and critical success, the ready-to-wear collections have been central to the continued success of Louis Vuitton. Limited edition pieces produced in collaboration with other creative artists have resulted in some of the wittiest and shrewdest reworkings of brand identity. Fashion designer Stephen Sprouse (2001), British fashion illustrator Julie Verhoeven (2002), and Japanese artist Takashi Murakami (2003) have created some of the most popular designs.

The Stephen Sprouse collaboration was inspired by a visit Marc Jacobs made to Charlotte Gainsbourg's apartment, where he noticed a Louis Vuitton trunk that had once belonged to her father, the French singer Serge Gainsbourg. Gainsbourg had so disliked the status implied by the canvas design that he had tried to erase the symbols with black paint. Yet as the design is produced as a woven jacquard, he only made the design appear subtler, and in turn, more sophisticated. Sprouse was inspired to add graffiti over the monogram canvas in fluorescent colors as an ironic act of defilement. Yet the graffiti design only served to reinforce the status of the brand and its association with street credibility. Even more successful was Murakami's 2003 re-design of the famous Louis Vuitton monogram logo, using a radiant palette of colors. This was followed by two additional collections, featuring cherries and *animé*-like symbols that brought J-Pop into high fashion.

The consumption of luxury brands by American hiphop performers, termed *bling-bling*, created a new and younger market for Louis Vuitton. This new market was memorably represented by the performing artist Lil' Kim, who posed on the cover of the November 1999 issue of *Interview* magazine naked, her body painted with the Louis Vuitton monogram. In recent years head designer Marc Jacobs has also transformed himself into a hard-bodied sex symbol, given to posing semi-naked, adorned with tattoos.

Because they are such desirable status symbols, Louis Vuitton products are subject to intense counterfeiting, which the company vigorously combats. Vuitton remains the most prestigious and easily recognized brand of luggage.

See also Leather and Suede; Logos.

Bibliography

Foley, Bridget. *Marc Jacobs*. New York: Assouline, 2004.

Forestier, Nadege, and Nazanine Ravai. *The Taste of Luxury: Bernard Arnault and the Moët-Hennessy Louis Vuitton Story*. London: Bloomsbury Publishing, 1993.

Gasparina, Jill *et al. Louis Vuitton: Art, Fashion, and Architecture*. New York: Rizzoli, 2009.

Gerschel, Stephane. Louis *Vuitton: Icons*. Paris: Assouline, 2007.

Pasols, Paul-Gerard. *Louis Vuitton: The Birth of Modern Luxury*. New York: Abrahms, 2005.

Alistair O'Neill

W

WAISTCOAT

The waistcoat, or vest (as it is known in the United States), is a close-fitting sleeveless garment originally designed for men that buttons (or occasionally zips) down the front to the waist. Produced in either single or double-breasted styles, the waistcoat is designed to be worn underneath a suit or jacket, although it does not necessarily have to match. Similar garments are worn by women.

History

Originating in Persia, waistcoats first became fashionable in the middle of the seventeenth century. The new style was noticed by Samuel Pepys in 1666: "The King hath . . . declared his resolution of setting a fashion for clothes which he will never alter," he wrote in his diary. "It will be a vest."

King Charles II was persuaded that, after the Great Plague and the Great Fire of London, a much more sober form of attire should be worn by gentlemen, particularly in view of the gross extravagance displayed in the French court at the time. The vest was a knee-length garment that would follow the cut of the coat but would be much tighter in fit. It was designed to discourage the use of lavish materials (such as lace) by covering much of the body in plainer and cheaper material. By 1670, vests had become one of the most important European fashion trends of the time, particularly among nobility who would soon forget the notion of sobriety in favor of opulence and excessive decoration.

1700 to 1900

By 1700, many waistcoats became much shorter, with skirts reaching above the knee, and few had collars or sleeves. Waistcoat styles designed for sporting purposes did away with any skirt almost completely. As the waistcoat became short it also became more and more

cut away in a curve at the front to reveal the wearer's breeches. Whereas elaborately embroidered waistcoats were fastened with hooks and eyes, the majority were fastened with buttons that would match those of the coat being worn.

Double-breasted waistcoats were the most popular style during the first few decades of the eighteenth century and featured small pockets with flaps. By the middle of the century, rather than following the older style of having cuff-length sleeves, the majority of waistcoats were sleeveless; skirts were much shorter and by 1790 were cut square to the waist. Toward 1800, decorated single-breasted waistcoats with small lapels became fashionable; fabrics with horizontal or vertical stripes were particularly favored, especially if the waistcoat was finished with a silk trim.

By 1800, the waistcoat had become an increasingly decorative and flamboyant addition to the male wardrobe. Through various style trends at the time, the overriding principle was that as long as a waistcoat was highly conspicuous, ostentatious, and embroidered, it was deemed fashionable. Single-breasted, double-breasted, waist-length, square-cut, roll-collared, low stand-collared and flap-pocketed styles all were worn. Dandies at the time even took to wearing two waistcoats at once. One would be as elaborate as the other, with the upper unbuttoned to show the one underneath.

Generally speaking, after the mid-nineteenth century, waistcoats became much more sober. The majority were produced to match the jackets or suits they would be worn with, rather than being outward expressions of originality and wealth.

The 1900s and Onward

Although the waistcoat was still deemed fashionable at the beginning of the twentieth century, its popularity soon began to wane. Rather than being worn as a show of wealth or decadence, the waistcoat was considered little more than a functional item to house a pocket watch or to finish off a formal evening wear outfit. With suits becoming softer and men opting for the growing trend of the wristwatch, the waistcoat was deemed less than essential for the male wardrobe.

That is not to say that the waistcoat simply died. Many men continued to wear a knitted waistcoat in the winter and a lighter version in the summer; however, it was now seen as an item simply to accompany and harmonize the rest of the outfit.

After World War II, few businessmen were wearing waistcoats to work, and right up to the Peacock Revolution in the 1960s, they had become all but extinct except with the more conservative dressers and those of an older generation. The waistcoat began to revive among fashionable young men, however, who associated themselves with style tribes such as Neo-Edwardians and Teddy boys.

The 1960s also saw the waistcoat move away from being a formal item when it was adopted by the hippies and incorporated as part of their ethnic-inspired or countrified look. The hippy version of the waistcoat still followed the contours of the body, but it tended to be longer than the waistcoat of a business suit; some were knee-length and featured heavy floral embroidery, fringing, and patchwork; some were tie-dyed (a look that would be recreated for the spring/summer 1993 collection by Dolce & Gabbana).

In the early twenty-first century, the waistcoat is seldom worn, except by businessmen trying to show some form of individuality or personality with a suit. Among conservative members of some professions, such as corporate law and banking, a three-piece suit (i.e., trousers, jacket, and matching waistcoat) is still regarded as the most appropriate business attire. But aside from designers such as Jean Paul Gaultier and Dolce & Gabbana reviving waistcoats for men during the 1980s and early 1990s, they are now more likely to be worn as novelty items than to be part of a classic tailored look.

See also Dandyism; Jacket; Trousers; Uniforms, Occupational.

Bibliography

Amies, Hardy. *A, B, C's of Men's Fashion*. London: Cahill & Company Ltd., 1964.

Byrde, Penelope. *The Male Image: Men's Fashion in England 1300–1970*. London: B. T. Batsford, Ltd., 1979.

Chenoune, Farid. *A History of Men's Fashion*. Paris: Flammarion, 1993.

De Marley, Diana. *Fashion For Men: An Illustrated History*. London: B. T. Batsford, Ltd., 1985.

Keers, Paul. *A Gentleman's Wardrobe*. London: Weidenfield and Nicolson, 1987.

Roetzel, Bernhard. *Gentleman: A Timeless Fashion*. Cologne, Germany: Konemann, 1999.

Schoeffler, O. E., and William Gale. *Esquire's Encyclopedia of 20th Century Men's Fashions*. New York: McGraw-Hill, 1973.

Tom Greatrex

WEDDING COSTUME

A wedding dress is apparel used in conjunction with wedding ceremonies, including accessories that may differentiate nonmatrimonial dress from that worn specifically for weddings.

Contemporary Overview

As of the late twentieth and early twenty-first centuries, the global, urbanized standard of wedding apparel has followed the Western tradition of a bride dressed in white or off-white, with a head-covering, whether a veil or head-piece, and carrying flowers, a book, or some other object. The groom is attired in keeping with the degree of formality of the bride. Attendants are generally present, the number, gender, age, and dress of whom being peculiar to each culture. Family members usually attend, playing a prominent role, and are dressed in equally formal, but generally more subdued styles of clothing than the bridal party. Other accessories have become standard, some of which are mandated by religion or culture, and others of which are remnants of folk practice. The former may include specific types of headgear, for both bride and groom, and possibly all attendees. These range from yarmulkes at Jewish weddings, to crowns held over the heads of the bridal couple in Orthodox Christian ceremonies. Anglo-phone folkloric touches suggest the inclusion of "some-thing old, something new, something borrowed, and something blue," as well as a single garter, a remnant of the days when the public removal of one's garters was a significant symbolic gesture. The throwing of the garter to the male attendants serves more or less the same function as the tossing of the bridal bouquet to the females: that of determining the next to wed, although the previous stipulation that all attendants be unmarried having disappeared, this old "good luck" charm is vitiated.

In contemporary non-western industrial societies, the situation is complex. There are generally local or national traditions, based on religious and/or societal norms that have developed over time to provide identifiable wedding apparel. This can range from Japanese kimonos to long body-and face-concealing robes in Islamic cultures, to elaborate saris in India, to hand-embroidered and metal-encrusted Hmong dress. However, the primacy of the "western wedding style"— that of a bride dressed in a white gown and a groom in typical western formal attire, has supplanted many local traditions, at least for the middle and upper classes. Even in countries with strong local traditions, if there are no specific religious strictures that would prohibit them and the economic resources are available, couples may opt to hold two ceremonies, one in the tradition of their own country and one of the western variety. This has been particularly popular in Japan and Korea, where the couple dresses according to the religion and architecture of the wedding chapel, or holds two separate ceremonies, and might change ensembles five to seven times during the course of the celebrations. Even in Islamic societies such as Saudi Arabia, this doubling up of wedding attire has proven popular among the upper classes.

History

It is not possible to determine from archaeological evidence whether or not prehistoric societies celebrated marital unions in a specific manner or marked those celebrations through the use of special garb. Information is nearly as scarce for the first great urban societies, where nothing is known of the wedding dress or practices of the bulk of the population and only dynastic marriages survive in the written record. However, it appears that even at the dynastic level, dress for weddings was less occasion-specific than a matter of showing off one's best garments and accessories.

The first clear references to specific wedding apparel, in the form of bridal crowns and veils, come from the Hellenistic period of Greece. These too, while spec-ified for use in weddings, and ranging from simple flow-ers to elaborate metal tiaras, were accessories. It is not until many centuries later that most cultures adopted recognizable ensembles to mark the occasion. This stems, in part, from simple economics. In pre-industrial times,

the idea of ceremony-specific clothing, particularly for a one-time event, was beyond the means of the vast majority of the population. Even at the court level, wardrobe inventories discuss the fact that royalty and courtiers alike tended to wear their most fashionable garments, with no real consideration of one-time use or symbolism of color or style. Again, it is the use of accessories that gives the garments their meaning.

It was during the long rule of Queen Victoria (1837–1901) that the Western notion of what the bride and her party should look like solidified, first in Britain, and subsequently the rest of the industrialized world. However, certain aspects, such as identically dressed attendants, appeared in many other cultures for more symbolic reasons than simply to honor, support, and, perhaps impress. The generation previous to Queen Victoria's introduced the white wedding gown, when Victoria's cousin, Crown Princess Charlotte, was married in 1816. According to reports, and a controversial garment in the collection of the Museum of London, her bridal gown consisted of a silver tissue and lace overgown worn over a white underdress. That this probably had more to do with the Regency fashion of white dresses than any symbolic intent did not stop it from exerting the same fashion influence of twentieth-century "royalty" such as Princess Grace of Monaco; Diana, Princess of Wales; or Carolyn Bessette Kennedy. The ideal of a white wedding dress was codified in 1840, when Queen Victoria wore a creamy white Spitalfields silk satin and lace gown. It was endlessly reproduced in fashion journals, setting a fashion standard for some appreciable time.

With the advent of industrialization in the West, the combination of readily available and comparatively cheap fabric meshed with the aspirations and needs of a nolonger self-sustaining population to acquire more garments, particularly those for festive occasions. Improved communication, in the form of newspapers, magazines, and their delivery methods of roads, railroads, and improved shipping speeds, as well as the establishment of dependable rural postal delivery at the turn of the twentieth century, allowed even isolated or working-class women to aspire to new fashion trends. However, economics and practicality continued to play a significant role, particularly among these populations. Societal norms decreed that appropriately formal dress be worn for significant occasions, from confirmation, to weddings, to church attendance, to funerals. Frequently, such a dress was presented to a young woman at her coming of age; if funding permitted, another was obtained for her wedding. However, this dress would be expected to serve, not only for the festive occasion for which it was purchased, but also for all others in the foreseeable future, including funerals. It tended toward a conservative cut for this reason, and often had large seam allowances that could accommodate pregnancy and possible weight gain. With the long-standing tradition of black for funerals and mourning, most of these "good" dresses were black, and often worn for the first time at the woman's wedding. This tendency continued into the late nineteenth and even early twentieth century among rural women. Women of the higher classes wore colors; frequently, but not invariably, white. After a death in the family, when the period of strict mourning was over, marriage could take place, but the bride would wear either gray or lavender. Among the working classes, as soon as it was economically feasible, colors were adopted, although the white, one-time only dress was still a rarity. Even the more affluent often assumed their gowns would see use more than once, and colored wedding dresses were still common into the first decade of the twentieth century, after which the ideal of a white, often anachronistic gown, meant to be worn only once, was only supplanted by extraordinary conditions, such as war.

With nods to changes in silhouette and length, the now-immutable tradition of the bride in white, surrounded by equally formally dressed family and attendants, became the norm, not only in Western culture, but wherever Western fashion was emulated, and frequently in the face of centuries-old local tradition. Occasional vagaries of lifestyle, including nude hippie weddings and thematic concoctions ranging from period or folk evocations to camouflage in honor of a deploying soldier, did not dislodge the basic formal make-up of the wedding party, or its concentration on white or off-white and a fairly conservative cut. However, in the 1980s, this began to change, first among the attendants and guests, who began to wear colors such as black, previously considered taboo for twentieth-century weddings. New materials began to appear, including leather, sequins, and even tattoos, as part of the wedding ensemble which itself frequently displayed significantly more flesh than had previously been considered appropriate. Now even brides were sporting colors such as red and black, and indeed, even getting tattoos for the occasion.

The symbolism of both color and cut for the wedding party, solidified over the nineteenth century and even earlier in the case of many of the accessories, is

accepted in the early 2000s with no understanding of origin or is ignored by many modern brides. The idea of wearing a one-time only dress is more prevalent, as most medium-priced gowns have their beaded or pearl decoration glued on rather than sewn. Alternatively the bride simply rents her gown, a tendency common in Japan, but that is making inroads in Europe and the United States.

Accessories and Their Symbolism

It is often the accessories that historically have provided clothing with bridal significance. Some can be traced to specific time periods while others appear to predate written records. One example of this is the headpiece. Depending on the culture, both men and women may have a specific type of head covering, but it is most unusual for the bride to be bareheaded. The earliest were undoubtedly simple wreaths of plant material: flowers, grain, or leaves, most of which appear to have had fertility symbolism, and possibly served to identify the wedding party. Later, head ornaments of cloth, metal, gems, and even wood began to be used. These were often accompanied by an additional piece of cloth, which might simply cover the hair or be draped over the entire head of the bride, obscuring her features. Certain religions dictate this kind of modesty, historically as well as in the early twenty-first century. However, in European culture, the veil also served as a disguise, a pre-Christian remnant of hiding the bride lest she be attacked by the forces of evil. Identically dressed attendants served not only to assist her, but to also confuse demonic presence.

Bouquets or other objects, such as fans or books, are also important accessories and are symbolic on several different levels. The carrying of flowers or other plants, such as wheat, is not only decorative, but refers to the fertility of the union. Flowers have been accorded symbolism in nearly every culture, but they also express wealth and taste in their choice and cost. In the early 2000s it is most common for Western brides to carry expensive flowers, with only very religious or economically prudent women opting for a prayer book. However, in earlier times, the owning and display of such a luxury item as a book would have lent the bride additional status, and frequently formed one of her betrothal gifts. The wedding ring, a token of affection, an exchange of property in the form of precious metal, and a none-too-subtle warning of future unavailability, is not a universal accessory. This is even more true of the engagement ring, a staple in North America, but not as common in other cultures, even in the West. Additionally, the finger or hand on which the rings are worn vary from culture to culture, as well as historically. Sixteenth-century examples of wedding portraits show the bride wearing a ring on her thumb.

Color symbolism did not play a role in weddings until relatively recently in the West, although now it signifies virginity, and, as mentioned above, the primacy of the white wedding dress flies directly in the face of many other cultures' norms. White is the color of mourning in most Asian cultures. Red, the one color still forbidden to most mainstream Western brides, due to its connotations of immorality ("scarlet woman," "red-light district"), is completely appropriate in other cultural settings. In India, it is the color of purity, and is often worn by brides. In much of East Asia, it is the color of celebration and luck, and therefore appropriate for bridal attire. However, the tendency toward adopting the Western white wedding, established only in the mid-nineteenth century, seems to be continuing throughout the world, sometimes alone, and sometimes in conjunction with local traditions. At the same time, the white wedding in the West is proving to be far less static than previously thought, evolving as fashions and societal norms do.

See also Ceremonial and Festival Costumes; Religion and Dress.

Bibliography

Baker, Margaret. *Wedding Customs and Folklore*. Devon, U.K.: David and Charles, 1977. An early work exploring the symbolism of marriage and its dress.

Baldizzone, Tiziana, and Gianni Baldzonne. *Wedding Ceremonies: Ethnic Symbols, Costume, and Ritual*. Paris: Flam-marian, 2002. One of many new studies that look at modern global practice.

Cunnington, Phillis, and Catherine Lucas. *Costume for Births, Marriages, and Deaths*. New York: A & C Black, 1972. One of the first, and still important studies of Western ceremonial clothing.

Foster, Helen Bradley, and Donald Clay Johnson. *Wedding Dress: Across Cultures*. Oxford: Berg, 2003. A rather good exploration of modern global wedding practices.

Kaivola-Bregenhøj, Annikki. *Bondebryllup*. Copenhagen, 1983. Excellent discussion of European peasant weddings.

Mordecai, Carolyn. *Weddings, Dating and Love: Customs and Cultures Worldwide, including Royalty*. Phoenix, Ariz.:

Nittany, 1998. An imperfect but broad compendium of modern practices.

Newton, Stella Mary. *Fashion in the Age of the Black Prince: A Study of the Years 1340–1365*. Woodbridge, Suffolk: Boydell, 1980. Reprint, Totowa, N.J.: Rowman and Littlefield, 1999. One of the best studies of fourteenth-century dress, including weddings, using difficult to find primary sources.

Noss, Aagot. *Lad og Krone: frå jente til brur*. Oslo: Universitetsforlaget, 1991. The most careful case study to date of ethnic wedding traditions, focusing on those of Norway, by one of the pioneers of costume history fieldwork.

Piponnier, Françoise, and Perrine Mane. *Dress in the Middle Ages*. New Haven, Conn., and London: Yale University, 1997. A book that is significant because it presents much compressed information, and its discussion of garments signifying rites of passage is important.

Tobin, Shelley, Sarah Pepper, and Margaret Willes. *Marriage à la Mode: Three Centuries of Wedding Dress*. London: The National Trust, 2003.

Michelle Nordtorp-Madson

WESTWOOD, VIVIENNE*

Born Vivienne Swire in Glossop in Derbyshire in 1941, Vivienne Westwood originally set out to become a teacher. She married Derek Westwood in 1962; her first child was born a year later and she seemed destined to lead a quiet, suburban life. However, in 1965 she met Malcolm McLaren, a publicist and impresario, whose subversive ideas and alternative lifestyle gave Westwood the opportunity and momentum to break free from her former life and embark on a highly successful career of fashion.

Vivienne Westwood's designs are a reaction against traditional British standards of morality—against petty bourgeois notions of etiquette and propriety. Since her early street style-based collaborations with McLaren, Westwood has defied the ideal of polite, anonymous clothes that express the wearer's ascribed social status. She seeks to transcend definitions of class, gender, ethnicity, and sexual orientation and create outfits that are dramatic—that encourage wearers to carry themselves confidently as they masquerade in theatrical assimilations of eighteenth-century aristocratic dress or traditionally tailored suits adorned with fetish bondage

Vivienne Westwood. Two models flank designer Vivenne West-wood, displaying her designs for the 1996 spring-summer pret-aporter collection. Westwood's unconventional fashions often reference historical and traditional dress. © B.D.V./CORBIS. REPRODUCED BY PERMISSION.

buckles. West-wood is a utopian. Through her work and the ideas she expresses in interviews, she strives to construct new personae for future cultures that draw upon idealized visions of the past inspired by portraiture and film.

During the early to mid-1970s, she and McLaren merged tough biker leather jackets with pornographic imagery and traditional tartans to produce the DIY (doit-yourself) aesthetic that expressed the antiestablishment spirit of punk. Based in London's King's Road, they changed the name of their shop from time to time to enhance the current collection's ideals, from Let It Rock (1971) to Too Fast to Live, Too Young to Die (1973) to Sex (1974) and finally to Seditionaries (1976)—a name and anarchic style that coincided with the increased notoriety of the Sex Pistols, a punk rock band that McLaren managed. Punk enabled Westwood to break free from the suburbs she had felt trapped in and experiment with fashion's power to shock and challenge. Her sex shop-style plastic miniskirts worn with ripped fishnet stockings, buckles, and chains, fractured traditional notions of femininity and beauty. Along with her straggly-knit sweaters, Karl Marx portrait print shirts, and bondage trousers, they became emblems of pop cultural revolt.

Westwood's subsequent work with McLaren was just as closely linked to youth culture, music, and clubs. As her King's Road shop settled into its final

incarnation as World's End in 1980, she embarked on a series of collections that explored historical construction techniques. One example was Pirates, presented at her first catwalk show in 1981. She continued to play with the relation-ship between body and fabric in the multilayered bulk of the Buffalo collection of 1982–1983 and the Witches collection of 1983–1984, which used sweatshirt fabric cut to pull away from the figure. These collections have inspired other designers; for example, punk was revisited in the early 1990s by Jean-Paul Gaultier and Karl Lagerfeld. Westwood's asymmetrical sportswear-based designs, highlighted with the neon colors that she used in her last collections with McLaren between 1983 and 1984, were seen on catwalks and in such High Street stores as Topshop and H & M in 2002–2003.

Westwood's split from McLaren prompted her shift away from pop culture and street style toward a more thorough exploration of history and tradition. She no longer wanted to be seen as a creator of subcultural dress, but rather as a designer of high fashion posing serious questions about culture, art, and identity. While her standing as one of the most significant British designers of the period was already established in mainland Europe, America, and Japan, she remained an outsider in Britain itself. It was not until the late 1980s that such high fashion magazines as *Vogue* began to feature her work on a regular basis. Before that time, her clothes were seen mainly in style magazines like *The Face* and *i-D*.

Westwood's first post-McLaren collection, Mini Crini (1986), indicated the direction she was to take, with its juxtaposition of eighteenth-century corsets, the "crini" (abbreviated 1860s-style crinolines), and huge curved wooden platform shoes that laced up the leg and rocked forward as the wearer walked in them. This collection was fashion created to make an impact; Westwood wanted to distinguish her wearers through references to grandeur, royalty, and the Establishment. In 1987 this dramatic aura was tempered by Westwood's ironic wit and her expertise with rich traditional fabrics: Harris tweed, John Smedley fine knits, and wool barathea were enlivened with such flourishes as a tweed crown worn with a tiny cape and crini. "You have a much better life if you wear impressive clothes," she remarked at the time (Jones, p. 57).

Westwood's philosophy, a mixture of contempt for late twentieth-century casual dress and reverence for the eighteenth-century Enlightenment's use of classical references, was encapsulated in her collections from

1988 through 1991 under the broad title Britain Must Go Pagan. These collections, like the punk fashions before them, sought to challenge existing ideas of status, gender, and display. In this case, however, Westwood strove for refinement and education rather than youthful rebellion. She used togas to add grandeur to traditional suiting, and contrasted light, floating chiffons that evoked both ancient Greece and prerevolutionary France with thick Scottish tweeds and corsets photoprinted with Boucher paintings of rural idylls. The clothing that resulted from these combinations relied heavily upon an idealized vision of the past and required its wearers to take on new personae that suggested their awareness of the fine arts.

Westwood appropriated emblems of aristocratic status and elitism for their power and theatricality. She encouraged people to dress up in princess-style coats like those the Queen wore as a child, or in delicate silk coats with rose-strewn edges like an eighteenth-century gentleman's garment. She has continued to draw on these themes of heritage and culture in her subsequent work. While Westwood is always considered inherently British, and has undoubtedly drawn upon her own country's past, she has been equally transfixed by French art and style. This attraction was summarized in her autumn–winter 1993–1994 collection, Anglomania, which harked back to Parisians' fascination with Englishness in the 1780s.

Westwood has consolidated her label since the late 1990s. In 1993 she diversified her collections to appeal to different audiences: the Red Label for ready-to-wear styles, the Gold Label for made-to-measure garments, and in 1998, and the diffusion line Anglomania (a less expensive collection aimed at a younger market), which reinterprets such staples as the pirate shirts from her earlier collections. Along with her perfumes, Boudoir, launched in 1998, and Libertine, launched in 2000, this diversification has enabled her to widen her market and build upon her previous successes. A major exhibition of Westwood's fashions was held at the Victoria and Albert Museum, London, in 2004.

See also Extreme Fashions; Gaultier, Jean-Paul; Lagerfeld, Karl; London Fashion; Perfume; Punk; Vogue.

Bibliography

Arnold, Rebecca. "Vivienne Westwood's Anglomania." In *The Englishness of English Dress*. Edited by Christopher Breward, Becky Conekin, and Caroline Cox. Oxford: Berg, 2002.

Evans, Caroline, and Minna Thornton. *Women and Fashion: A New Look*. London: Quartet, 1989.

Jones, Dylan. "Royal Flush: Vivienne Westwood." *i-D* (August 1987): 57.

Mulvagh, Jane. *Vivienne Westwood: An Unfashionable Life*. London: HarperCollins, 1998.

Wilcox, Claire. *Vivienne Westwood*. London: Victoria and Albert Museum, 2004.

Rebecca Arnold

WIGS

Wigs are artificial heads of hair, either cunningly concealing baldness or glaringly obvious fashion items in their own right. The Jewish *sheitel*, for instance, is worn for religious reasons where a woman's natural hair is shielded from the gaze of all men who are not her husband. The Talmud teaches that the sight of a woman's hair constitutes an arousal or sexual lure; thus a woman hiding her hair helps protect the fabric of Jewish society. The entertainer Elton John's obvious ginger weave is, of course, completely different, worn to retain an air of youth and as a disguise for baldness.

Early Wigs

The earliest Egyptian wigs (c. 2700 B.C.E.) were constructed of human hair, but cheaper substitutes such as palm leaf fibers and wool were more widely used. They denoted rank, social status, and religious piety and were used as protection against the sun while keeping the head free from vermin. Up until the 1500s, hair tended to be dressed as a foundation for headdresses, but by the end of the century hairstyles became higher and more elaborate constructions in which quantities of false hair were used to supplement the wearer's own. Hair was gummed and powdered, false curls and ringlets were in fashion, and, in some cases, a complete head of false hair called a *perruque*, was worn. The French perruque was colloquially known as a peruke, periwyk, periwig, and eventually the diminutive *wig* by 1675.

Seventeenth and Eighteenth Centuries

The seventeenth century saw the complete resurgence of the wig and it became the height of fashion for both men and women, with many shaving their heads beneath for both comfort and fit. Hair historian Richard

Corson sees the ascendance of Louis XIV to the French throne as pivotal. The king supplemented his thinning hair with false pieces until "eventually he agreed to have his head shaved, which was done daily thereafter, and to wear a wig." (Corson, p. 215) By the eighteenth century, those who had the finances had a large wig for formal occasions and a smaller one for use in the home. The larger or more "full bottomed" the wig, the more expensive, thus they were also a mark of class and income and the target of wig snatch-ers. If one was unable to afford a wig, one made one's natural hair look as wiglike as possible. By the mid-eighteenth century, white was the favored color for wigs, and they were first greased then powdered with flour or a mixture of starch and plaster of paris in the house's wig closet using special bellows. Lucrative trades were constructed around their care and maintenance, such as hairdressing, so-called because hair was dressed rather than cut. Women's wigs were particularly high, powdered, and bejeweled, and the subject of much caricature. To achieve the look, hair was harvested from the heads of the rural working classes. Richard Corson noted that the full wig was disappearing by about 1790, however, "when there was a good deal of natural hair in evidence" (Corson, p. 298).

Nineteenth and Early Twentieth Centuries

After this brief period of respite during the French Revolution, when a natural look and thus natural hair was fashionable, the elaborately dressed hairstyles of the Victorian and Edwardian era demanded a myriad of false pieces or fronts and transformations. As the feminine ideal in the Edwardian era required enormous hairstyles, the natural bulk of the hair was padded out. Lady Violet Harvey recalled,

> Enormous hats often poised on a pyramid of hair, which if not possessed, was supplied, pads under the hair to puff it out were universal and made heads unnaturally big. This entailed innumerable hairpins. My sister and I were amazed to see how much false hair and pads were shed at 'brushing time.' (Hardy, p. 79)

The building of massive hairstyles was dependent on the use of *postiche*, the French word for "added hair" and styles included fringes, fronts, switches, pompadour rolls, and frizettes. All hairdressers had a workroom in which postiches were made for sale wherein the posticheur prepared hair. Hair combings were saved and then drawn through a hackle (a flat board with metal teeth sticking upward) to straighten them. Hair was sorted into bundles ready to be curled into false pieces or curled by a device called a *bigoudis* made of wood or hardened clay. Sections of hair were rolled up on the bigoudis and then dropped into water mixed with soda. After being boiled for several hours the dry hair was then unwound and stored—a method that dates back to the Egyptians. If too little hair was obtained from combings it came from other women. It was a commodity to be exploited and one famous source was the Hair Market at Morlans in the Pyrenees, one of a number of hiring fairs where dealers literally bought the hair from women's heads. Much hair was also imported from Asia Minor, India, China, and Japan and boiled in nitric acid to remove the color and vermin. Men wore wigs, too, but this was to hide baldness.

1920s to Present

With the introduction of the new bobbed hairstyle in the 1920s, wigs fell out of favor and were worn by older women who were not interested in the newly shorn look. Their use returned in the 1950s, but only as a way of having temporary fantasy hairstyles. The most renowned wigmakers and hairdressers in Europe were Maria and Rosy Carita. In black hairdressing, though, the wig was of supreme importance allowing for fashionable styles without undergoing the time-consuming, and in some instances painful, process of straightening. Black stars such as Diana Ross were known for their stylish wig collections in the mid-1960s. It was not really until the late 1960s that wigs underwent a massive renaissance in white hairdressing practices. Rapidly changing fashion, a space-age chic and the vogue for drip-dry clothes in new man-made fabrics led to a vogue for the artificial over the natural. By 1968 there was a wig boom and it is estimated that one-third of all European women wore what hair-dressers called a "wig of convenience." Men still tended to wear wigs differently moving further toward the naturalism that many women were rejecting. Until the early 1950s, all wigs were made by hand. However, the invention of the machine-made, washable, nylon and acrylic wig in Hong Kong led to cheap, mass-produced wigs flooding the market. The novelty fashion wig or hair-piece became one of Hong Kong's fastest growing exports and by 1970 the industry employed 24,000 workers. In 1963 British imports of wigs and hairpieces from Hong Kong was worth £200,000 ($350,000); by 1968 it was almost £5 million ($8.78 million). By 1969 around forty percent of wigs were synthetic and the leading companies in wig development were the American firm Dynel and the Japanese Kanekalon, who both used modacrylics to create wigs that were easy to care for and held curl well. In the late twentieth century, many false forms of hair are used and the change from a long to a short hair-style can be completed at a whim with extensions that have moved from black hairdressing to white hairdressing. Singers such as Beyoncé and Britney Spears use weaves of all styles and colors openly.

See also Acrylic and Modacrylic Fibers; Caricature and Fashion; Hair Accessories; Hairdressers; Hairstyles; Headdress.

Bibliography

Corson, Richard. *Fashions in Hair: The First Five Thousand Years.* London: Peter Owen, 1965.

Cox, Caroline. *Good Hair Days: A History of British Hairstyling.* London: Quartet, 1999.

Hardy, Lady Violet. *As It Was.* London: Christopher Johnson, 1958.

Caroline Cox

WILDE, OSCAR

Oscar Wilde (1854–1900) was one of the most prominent and influential figures of the fin de siècle. Playwright, author, journalist, dandy-aesthete, wit, and homosexual social critic, his life and work fore-shadowed many of the features of twentieth-century popular and creative subcultures, not least their obsession with the cult of celebrity and the act of self-fashioning. Wilde's constant concern with surface appearance and its power also ensured that his distinctive and constantly changing personal image became a style-template for those who wish to dress in extravagant and innovative ways, from actors and artists to pop stars and clubbers.

Born in Dublin in 1854, Wilde was the second son of a leading surgeon, Dr. William Wilde, and Jane Francesca Speranza Elgee, an Irish nationalist poet and translator. Following the traditional route for a boy of his social background and aptitude, Wilde studied classics at Trinity College, Dublin before winning a scholarship to Magdalen College, Oxford in 1874. In photographs of this period Wilde appeared quite the student "masher" in loudly checked suits and bowler hats. There was little to indicate his later espousal of artistic fashions, though his hair was a little longer than the norm for the 1870s. During his time at Oxford Wilde immersed himself in the ideas of Walter Pater and John Ruskin, honing an acute appreciation of ancient and renaissance art on study visits to Greece and Italy. He graduated with a first class degree in 1878. Having established a reputation as a promising poet with the award of the Newdigate Prize for his poem "Ravenna" in the same year, Wilde launched himself on the London social and literary circuit, where he skillfully adapted the learned theories of Ruskin and Pater for a less erudite audience. His talent for self-publicizing soon earned him notoriety as the "Professor of Aesthetics" in such satirical publications as *Punch*, where his flowing hair, loosely tied collars, floral accessories, and velvet suits formed an obvious target for the caricaturists.

By 1881, Wilde's reputation was such that he found his opinions and appearance lampooned in the Gilbert and Sullivan operetta *Patience*, whose libretto ridiculed the current metropolitan taste for "aesthetic" clothing, interior design, and amateur philosophizing. Wilde turned this critique to his advantage by spearheading a promotional lecture tour for the operetta in the United States and Canada during the following year. Dressed in extreme aesthetic garb—which now included breeches, stockings and pumps, fur-trimmed overcoats, cloaks, and wide-brimmed hats—he delivered talks to American audiences on such subjects as "The House Beautiful." Wilde had his image from this period immortalized in a series of striking portraits by the society photographer Napoleon Sarony that idealized him as a romantic bohemian.

Back in London, Wilde married Constance Lloyd in 1884, setting up an elegant home with her in Chelsea where they raised two sons, Cyril (born 1885) and Vyvyan (born 1886). For the remainder of the 1880s, Wilde had a successful career as a reviewer and editor of the progressive magazine *Woman's World*, while honing his talents as an essayist and writer of exquisite short stories. During this time, he exchanged the long locks and soft velvets of the *Patience* era for dramatic "Neronian" curls—a subversive reference to the pagan moral code of imperial Rome—and urbane Savile Row tailoring, the better to represent himself as the epitome of cosmopolitan stylishness.

By the late 1880s Wilde was beginning to explore the then dangerous territory of male to male desire, both in his personal life and as a subject for artistic expression. He experienced his first homosexual relationship with a Cambridge undergraduate named Robert Ross in 1886, which partly inspired him to write an essay on Shake-speare's sonnets, "The Portrait of Mr. W. H.," exploring the thesis that Shakespeare's creativity was derived from his love for a boy actor. Wilde published the first version of his most explicit investigation of the demimonde in which he was now operating in 1890. *The Picture of Dorian Gray* was not only heavily informed by French decadent literature in terms of style and subject matter, but also contained expressions of the amoral out-look that would bring Wilde into contact in 1891 with his most infamous lover, Lord Alfred Douglas. In tandem with this search for hedonistic sensation, which was the ultimate outcome of the "art for art's sake" philosophy of aestheticism, Wilde was also a supporter of the socialism espoused by William Morris. He wrote his influential essay "The Soul of Man under Socialism" during the same period. In fashion terms, the ideals of socialism found a corollary in the rational Liberty style of "anti-fashion" dressing adopted by Constance Wilde and promoted by Oscar in his journalistic output.

Wilde's popularity as an author of astringent drawing-room comedies for the London stage peaked during the first half of the 1890s. Following the success of *Lady Windermere's Fan* in 1892, he went on to produce *A Woman of No Importance*, *An Ideal Husband*, and *The Importance of Being Earnest*. Besides opening the mores and hypocrisies of contemporary fashionable life to devastating scrutiny, these plays also afforded an opportunity for sophisticated costume designs that influenced the modes of the day. While the drawing-room plays enjoyed the critical acclaim of polite society, Wilde was also developing further his interest in decadent and erotic themes. These were represented most forcefully in Wilde's association with the avant-garde journal *The Yellow Book* and in his play *Salome*, which was refused a license for production in London on the grounds of obscenity.

The tension between Wilde's public and private interests snapped in 1895, when he rashly brought charges of criminal libel against the Marquess of Queensbury, who was enraged by Wilde's liaison with his son, Lord Alfred Douglas. The marquess had been accusing Wilde of "unnatural acts" to all who would listen. On the collapse of the libel trial Wilde was himself arrested for "acts of gross indecency with other male persons," for which he was eventually found guilty and sentenced to two years' imprisonment with hard labor. In 1897, during his incarceration, Wilde authored *De Profundis*, a confessional account of his fall. He published "The Ballad of Reading Gaol," a poem that captured the suffering of prison life, after his release and exile to Paris in 1898. Though the image of Wilde in convict's clothing provided a fitting costume for the final act of a drama that he himself might have written, he never fully recovered from the shame and physical discomfort caused by his punishment, and died a broken man in Paris in 1900. His remains were transferred to the Cimetière du Père-Lachaise in 1909, where they were marked by Jacob Epstein's powerful sculptured angel.

Following decades when his name, works and image were associated in the puritanical Anglo-Saxon world with "unmentionable vices," Wilde's reputation as a gifted writer was gradually restored from the 1950s onwards. Sympathetic film treatments of his life and plays helped bring his sparkling legacy to a new generation, and the counterculture of the 1960s interpreted Wilde as a sexual and aesthetic revolutionary. By the 1980s and 1990s Wilde's complex personality and self-contradictory proclamations made him once again the focus of intense study and speculation. For the fashion theorist and historian, Wilde's life and work undoubtedly offer a rich seam of material for further research.

See also Aesthetic Dress; Dandyism; Fashion and Homosexuality; Fashion and Identity; Gender, Dress, and Fashion; Savile Row; Theatrical Costume.

Bibliography

Cohen, Ed. *Talk on the Wilde Side: Toward A Genealogy of a Dis-course on Male Sexualities*. London: Routledge, 1993. An examination of the relevance of Wilde's trial to modern understandings of homosexual identities.

Ellmann, Richard. *Oscar Wilde*. London: Hamish Hamilton, 1987. The most authoritative and comprehensive biography of Wilde published to date.

Holland, Merlin. *The Wilde Album*. London: Fourth Estate Limited, 1997. An excellent visual resource for images of Wilde and his milieu.

Kaplan, Joel, and Sheila Stowell. *Theatre and Fashion: Oscar Wilde to the Suffragettes*. Cambridge, U.K.: Cambridge University Press, 1994. An innovative study of the relationship between the theater and sartorial culture in the 1890s.

Sinfield, Alan. *The Wilde Century: Effeminacy, Oscar Wilde and the Queer Movement.* London: Cassell, 1994. A sophisticated account of the political and theoretical afterlife of Wilde in the twentieth century.

Sloan, John. *Oscar Wilde.* Oxford, U.K.: Oxford University Press, 2003. A useful summary of the social and literary contexts of Wilde's life and work.

Christopher Breward

WINDSOR, DUKE AND DUCHESS OF

If Bet-tina Zilkha's International Best Dressed List extended to couples, the Duke and Duchess of Windsor would be its king and queen. As individuals, their influence on twentieth century fashion was considerable, but combined it was unassailable. From the 1930s to the 1960s, the influence they exercised was all the more apparent for the media attention that magnified their sway on the public's imagination.

Biography

The Duke of Windsor was born Prince Edward of York on 23 June 1894. With the death of his grandfather, King Edward VII in 1910, his father was crowned King George V. Upon his father's accession, Prince Edward of York became Duke Edward of Cornwall, and on his sixteenth birthday, Prince Edward of Wales.

Bessie Wallis Warfield, who was to become the Duchess of Windsor, was born in Pennsylvania on 19 June 1896. Her upbringing, by her own admission, was modest and unexceptional. When she met Prince Edward of Wales for the first time around 1930, she had been married twice. Her first husband was Earl Winfield Spencer Jr., and her second was Ernest Aldrich Simpson, an American living in London.

It is generally accepted that the Prince of Wales and Mrs. Simpson began their affair in 1934. Following the death of King George V, the prince was crowned King Edward VIII on 20 January 1936. That summer, he took Mrs. Simpson on a yachting holiday in the Eastern Mediterranean. Press coverage of the trip created a scandal, complicating the king's decision to marry Mrs. Simpson. Parliament refused the king's marriage request on the grounds of Mrs. Simpson's status as a twice-divorced foreign commoner. A "Constitutional Crisis" ensued, which resulted in the king's abdication on 11 December 1936. In his abdication speech he explained, "You must believe me when I tell you that I have found it impossible to carry out the heavy burden of responsibility and discharge my duty as King as I would wish to do, without the support of the woman I love" (Ziegler, p. 331).

Upon his abdication, he became His Royal Highness the Duke of Windsor, and with his marriage to Mrs. Simpson on 3 June 1937, she became the Duchess of Windsor. The title Her Royal Highness, however, was never conferred upon her. Apart from spending time in the Bahamas during World War II, the Duke and Duchess of Windsor remained in exile in France for the rest of their lives. The duke died on 18 May 1972, while the duchess, who was last seen in public in 1975, died on 24 April 1986.

The Duke: Trend Setter

More than any other individual, the Duke of Windsor was responsible for a transformation of men's dress in the twentieth century. His personal preference for rejecting the received notions of Victorian and Edwardian "proprieties" not only influenced the men of his generation, but also—as Chanel is credited for having done with women—created a modern paradigm that persists to this day. What Nicholas Lawford said of him in the 1930s remained true of the Duke all his life, "In a world where men tend to look more and more alike, he seems more than ever endowed with the capacity to look like no one else" (Menkes, p. 95).

The Duke of Windsor preferred comfortable clothes that allowed freedom of movement, a style that he described as "dress soft" (The Duke of Windsor, 1960, p. 110). In the 1930s, he was one of the first men to wear unlined, unstructured jackets. From 1919–1959, these were made for him by Frederick Scholte, a Dutch-born, London-based tailor who disapproved of any form of exaggeration in the style of a jacket. As the duke commented in *A Family Album*, his treatise on style written in 1960, "Scholte had rigid standards concerning the perfect balance of proportions between shoulders and waist in the cut of a coat to clothe the masculine torso" (The Duke of Windsor, 1960, p. 99). The sleeves of the duke's jackets were usually adorned with four buttons, and he preferred welted pockets rather than pocket flaps.

Before World War II, Forster and Son in London tailored the duke's trousers. "I never had a pair of trousers made by Scholte," the duke explained. "I disliked the cut of them; they were made, as English trousers usually are, to be worn with braces high above the waist. So preferring as I did to wear a belt rather than braces with trousers, in the American style, I invariably had them made by another tailor" (The Duke of Windsor, 1960, p. 103). For every jacket the duke had made, two pairs of trousers were produced. These he wore in strict rotation. In 1934, along with his brother, the Duke of York, and his cousin, Lord Louis Mountbatten, he replaced the conventional button flies with zip flies. A heavy smoker all his life, the duke instructed Forster and Son to make his trousers with a slightly wider left pocket with no fastening, allowing him easy access to his cigarette case, which he always carried in his left pocket. The duke preferred trousers with cuffs or turn-ups. With the adoption of rationing restrictions in Britain during World War II, which banned turn-ups, he placed all subsequent orders with H. Harris, a tailor based in New York.

The London firm of Peal and Co. made the duke's shoes, Lock and Co. his hats, and Hawes and Curtis his shirts and ties. He favored shirts with soft, unstarched cuffs and collars and wore his ties, which he ordered with thick inner linings, with a wide "four-in-hand" knot. Despite popular opinion, the Duke of Windsor did not, in fact, wear a style known as the "Windsor knot." As he explains, "The so-called 'Windsor knot,' was I believe regulation wear for G.I.s during the war, when American college boys adopted it too. But in fact I was in no way responsible for this. The knot to which the Americans gave my name was a double knot in a narrow tie—a "Slim Jim" as it is sometimes called" (The Duke of Windsor, 1960, p. 116).

As a keen sportsman, the Duke of Windsor paid particular attention to his sporting attire. In the 1920s, he popularized the wearing of plus fours, which became his standard dress for hunting and sporting pursuits. Disliking the traditional style with fastenings below the knees, he developed a loose-fitting version with a soft cotton lining, which he wore slightly lower than the traditional four inches below the knee. When playing golf, he would wear them with brightly colored Argyle socks and Fair Isle sweaters. Commenting on the Prince at play, Law-ford noted, "He was quite loud in the way he mixed his checks, but he represented style to his generation" (Menkes, p. 102).

Like his sportswear, the duke's highland dress expressed his theatrical and audacious use of color, pattern and texture. He wore kilts, often made by

Chalmers of Oban or William Anderson and Sons in Scotland, in casual settings, usually at "The Mill," the Windsor's weekend retreat just outside Paris. These he would wear with a leather sporran, in which he would store his cigarettes. The duke preferred "tartans which I have the right to wear—Royal Stuart, Hunting Stuart, Rothesay, Lord of the Isles, Balmoral" (The Duke of Windsor, 1960, p. 128). In A Family Album, the duke describes wearing a suit of Rothesay hunting tartan, originally belonging to his father, that triggered a vogue for tartan in the 1950s,

> I happened to wear it one evening for dinner at La Croe near Antibes, where the Duchess and I lived for a while after the last war. One of our guests mentioned the fact to a friend in the men's fashion trade, who immediately cabled the news to America. Within a few months tartan had become a popular material for every sort of masculine garment, from dinner jackets and cummerbunds to swimming-trunks and beach shorts. Later the craze even extended to luggage (The Duke of Windsor, p. 129).

One of the Duke of Windsor's most notable sartorial innovations was the introduction, in the 1920s, of the midnight blue evening suit, an alternative to the traditional black evening suit. Wanting to enhance his well-dressed standing in the popular press as well as soften men's formal wear, he explained,

> I was in fact 'produced' as a leader of fashion, with the clothiers as my showmen and the world as my audience. The middle-man in this process was the photographer, employed not only by the Press but by the trade, whose task it was to photograph me on every possible occasion, public or private, with an especial eye for what I happened to be wearing (The Duke of Windsor, 1960, p. 114).

The Prince of Wales understood that in black and white photography, unlike black, midnight blue allowed the subtle details of tailoring, such as lapels, buttons, and pockets, to become more apparent.

It is through these photographs that the Duke of Windsor influenced fashionable men of his generation, and, indeed, continues to influence fashionable men today. Through their designs, Ralph Lauren, Paul Smith, Sean John Combes, and a host of other men's wear designers pay homage to the Duke of Windsor's witty and idiosyncratic approach to self-presentation.

As Diana Vreeland (1906–1989), editor of *Harper's Bazaar* and *Vogue*, said of him, "Did he have style? The Duke of Windsor had style in every buckle of his kilt, every check of his country suits" (Menkes, p. 126).

The Duchess: Trend Follower

Unlike the Duke of Windsor's innate sense of style, the Duchess of Windsor's self-presentation, as Suzy Menkes, fashion editor for the International Herald Tribune, has observed, was "a product of rigorous effort rather than inherited or natural taste" (p. 95). She was a picture of elegance, preferring simple, tailored clothes with no superfluous details or decoration. She remained on the International Best Dressed List for more than forty years, and upon her death in 1986, Elle commented, "She elevated sobriety to an art form" (Menkes, p. 95).

Being immaculate was the hallmark of the Duchess of Windsor's personal style. As Cecil Beaton (1904–1980), a British portrait photographer, commented, "She reminds one of the neatest, newest luggage, and is as compact as a Vuitton travelling-case" (Beaton, p. 27). Beaton's first impression of the Duchess, formed in 1930 before she had acquired her title, was less than favorable. He recalled her as "brawny and raw-boned in her sapphire blue velvet" (Tapert and Edkins, p. 92). Four years later, however, when they met again, the Duchess had changed. Beaton commented, "I liked her immensely. I found her bright and witty, improved in looks and chic" (Tapert and Edkins, p. 92). Lady Mendl (Elsie de Wolfe), who remained the Duchess of Windsor's friend and mentor throughout her life, was largely responsible for Mrs. Simpson's transformation. It was Lady Mendl who introduced her to Mainbocher, who was to dress her until he retired in 1971. As Vreeland commented, "Mainbocher was responsible for the Duchess's wonderful simplicity and dash" (Menkes, p. 98).

Mainbocher was to make the Duchess of Windsor's wedding ensemble and trousseau. The wedding ensemble included a simple, floor-length dress and matching long-sleeved jacket in "Wallis Blue" silk crepe. The color was specially developed by Mainbocher to equal that of the Duchess of Windsor's eyes. The dress complemented the duchess's style of fashion austerity, being modest but not prudish. Shortly after her marriage, copies of the dress were sold at retailers for a small fraction of the original's cost, from $25 at Benwit Teller to a mere $8.90 at Klein's cash-and-carry. Within a few months, the "Wally" dress made its way to the United

States, where it was available from department stores in a variety of styles, colors, and materials.

Cecil Beaton became the Duchess of Windsor's unofficial photographer. In this position, he was able to play an important role in the construction and depiction of her public image. Beaton, in fact, took photographs of the royal wedding the day before the actual ceremony. Several weeks before the marriage, he also took a series of famous photographs of the Duchess of Windsor wearing models from Elsa Schiaparelli's Spring/Summer 1937 collection, including the legendary "Lobster Dress" with a print designed by Salvador Dalí. Like Mainbocher's designs, Schiaparelli's clothes appealed to the Duchess of Windsor's rigorous, restrained aesthetic. She liked Schiaparelli's evening suits, in particular, and made them her trademark. Indeed, the duchess was at her most elegant in smart, impeccably tailored suits, a look that Cecil Beaton referred to as her "trim messenger-boy's suits" (Menkes, p. 102).

While the Duchess of Windsor's daywear tended to be plain and simple, her evening wear revealed a more feminine, romantic sensibility. As Danielle Porthault of Yves Saint Laurent commented, "Her Royal Highness's style was sobriety by day and fantasy and originality at night" (Menkes, p. 116). During the 1930s, the Duchess of Windsor favored Mainbocher, Schiaparelli, and Vionnet, while after World War II she preferred Dior, Givenchy, and Yves Saint Laurent. These she would wear with shoes by Roger Vivier, who began working for the House of Dior in 1953. According to Vreeland, one of the Duchess of Windsor's many sartorial innovations was the short evening dress.

The Duchess of Windsor's recipe of "sobriety by day and fantasy at night" included ingredients of wit and irony, often expressed in her exuberant use of jewelry. Her two favorite jewelers, Cartier and Van Cleef and Arpels, competed with each other to provide the Duchess with ever more lavish and innovative creations. The Duchess of Windsor's simple day suits proved the perfect backdrop for her flamboyant broaches, bracelets, earrings and necklaces, as did her more romantic confections worn at night. One of her more memorable pieces of jewelry was a bracelet made from jeweled crosses, which she wore at her wedding. Each cross represented "a stepping stone in their love story, and a cross they had to bear" (Menkes, p. 151).

The Duchess of Windsor once told her friend and confidante Elsa Maxwell, "My husband gave up everything for me . . . I'm not a beautiful woman. I'm nothing to look at, so the only thing I can do is dress better than anyone else" (Tapert and Edkins, p. 97). But she did much more than this. Not only did she dress to enhance the idiosyncrasies of her physicality, enhanced by her coiffure by Alexandre, but she dressed with a consciousness of how her image would be received by both the press and public. As Vreeland observed, "She had a position and dressed to it" (Menkes, p. 138). In this respect, she had a lasting influence on royal women and stateswomen alike, perhaps most notably Jacqueline Kennedy and Diana, Princess of Wales.

See also Diana, Princess of Wales; Fashion Icons; Fashion Magazines; Formal Wear, Men's; Mainbocher; Neckties and Neckwear; Royal and Aristocratic Dress; Schiaparelli, Elsa; Tartan.

Bibliography

Beaton, Cecil. *Cecil Beaton's Scrapbook.* New York: Charles Scribner's Sons, 1937.

Duchess of Windsor. *The Heart Has Its Reasons.* New York: D. McKay Company, 1956.

Duke of Windsor. *A King's Story.* New York: Putnam, 1951.

——. *A Family Album.* London: Cassell, 1960.

Menkes, Suzy. 1988. *The Windsor Style.* Topsfield, Mass.: Salem House Publishers, 1988.

Sothebys. *The Duke and Duchess of Windsor.* New York: Sothebys, 1997.

Tapert, Annette, and Diana Edkins. *The Power of Style: The Women Who Defined the Art of Living Well.* New York: Crown, 1994.

Ziegler, Philip. *King Edward VIII.* London: Collins, 1990.

Andrew Bolton

WOMEN'S WEAR DAILY

Its own motto is "the retailer's daily newspaper," but within the fashion industry, *Women's Wear Daily* is widely referred to as "the bible of the business." It is far more than just a trade publication serving an industry. With its unique mix of hard business, financial stories, society gossip, and biting fashion reviews, *WWD* (as it is commonly known) is a high-impact cultural voice.

Women's Wear first appeared as a supplement to the 21 May 1910 edition of the *Daily Trade Record*, a broad-sheet that tracked the burgeoning, if rather dry,

textiles imports and apparel manufacturing businesses. Both were products of Fairchild Publications, started by Edmund Wade (E.W.) Fairchild and his brother Louis E. Fairchild But with department stores booming and women's fashion becoming a business unto itself, it seemed obvious to the Fairchilds that the *Women's Wear* supplement could succeed as a stand-alone publication. "There is probably no other line of human endeavor in which there is so much change as in the product that womankind wears," opined an editorial in one of the first editions. *Women's Wear* became a daily on 15 July 1910, publishing every day but Sunday and selling for 15 cents.

The next year, E. W. Fairchild opened a Paris bureau, since that city's houses basically dictated the course of fashion; correspondents would wire stories about the trends in French fashion, such as the "universally repudiated hobble skirt," or Paul Poiret's scandalous Turkish trousers of 1913. In 1912, one of the paper's Paris correspondents, Edith L. Rosenbaum, happened to be on the maiden voyage of the Titanic; she survived and gave *Women's Wear* a version of the tragedy that noted which prominent retailers were on the ship (Isidore Straus, a founder of Abraham & Straus, perished with his wife) and what some of the survivors wore in the lifeboats ("Lady Duff-Gordon made her escape in a very charming lavender bathrobe").

The paper by then was based at 822 Broadway and had three Linotype machines dedicated to rolling out its copies. In 1927, Fairchild added the "Daily" to its name. Although the paper acknowledged world events, high society, Hollywood movies, and the like, its content was always within the context of the fashion industry. Coverage was always focused on business, not personalities. *WWD* adopted the mind-set of its readers slavishly following Paris designers like Christian Dior, Cristóbal Balenciaga, and Coco Chanel while essentially ignoring homegrown talents. It was first and foremost a trade paper, with a fairly narrow, albeit loyal and influential readership.

The second generation took over in 1948 when Louis E. Fairchild passed the president's title to his nephew, Louis W. But it wasn't until the charismatic, confident, worldly Princeton-educated John B. Fairchild (son of Louis W.) arrived in 1960, after a stint in the Paris office, that *WWD* shook off its old identity as a niche-market trade paper and became a cultural chronicler crackling with opinion. "It was as if a tornado hit 7 East 12th Street," recalled fashion journalist Etta Froio, then just starting her *WWD* career as a market editor. "In just a few weeks, he swept away every trace of the musty, stodgy newspaper we had known and set out to create a new era of style and status."

During his time in Paris, Fairchild had decided that the most interesting thing about fashion wasn't the clothes as much as the people who made and wore them. He began establishing the new tone of *WWD* there, as he befriended Coco Chanel, Christian Dior, Yves Saint Laurent, Pierre Bergé, and Pierre Cardin, among others. Once back in New York, he expanded that vision to include the entire industry. Before John B., *WWD* had more or less ignored society, except as it pertained to the fashion business. Now, the paper began running on-the-street pictures of chic socialites and interviews with sexy young starlets like Julie Christie, Brigitte Bardot, Vanessa Redgrave, Jane Fonda, and Faye Dunaway. Even counterculture artists, rock stars, and scandalous trends (Andy Warhol, Patti Smith, braless women, the invasion of blue jeans), barely acknowledged in the mainstream press, were investigated and reported on.

Fairchild and *WWD* were instrumental in shifting the world's attention to the merits of American designers, giving their clothes and their personal style more attention than either had ever received. He covered designers such as Halston, Perry Ellis, Oscar de la Renta, and Calvin Klein as much for their social lives as for their collections. "We became fascinated with the personalities of the business executives and the social world," said John B. Fairchild in an interview he gave for *WWD*'s 90th Anniversary edition in 2001. "We were looking for people who made the world tick. That's what it has to be about. All the other coverage then was just endless descriptions of clothes. Nothing to me is more boring than that!" This new approach to fashion was seen in the paper's spin-off magazine *W*, founded in 1972, which combines edgy coverage of fashion with features such as celebrity interviews and news of society events.

When it came to modern women, Fairchild was particularly obsessed with Jacqueline Kennedy Onassis, sending photographers to wait outside restaurants like La Grenouille and Le Cote Basque where she regularly lunched. He also tracked chic young socialites like Babe Paley, Slim Keith, and CZ Guest. He had his editors write stinging reviews of collections that sometimes infuriated the designers (and occasionally resulted in banishment, which never lasted more than a season) but always delighted the readers. The phrases *WWD* invented to describe this gilded group have entered the common lexicon: the BPs (beautiful people), Nouvelle Society, Social Cyclones, Walkers (the men who escort Social Cyclones to events), and HotPants, coined in 1970 to describe indecently short shorts. The paper's power grew to the point that its decrees could make a trend or a designer; *Time* magazine put Fairchild on the cover of its 14 September 1970 issue, labeling him "The Man Behind Midi Mania."

WWD courted controversy, frequently needling designers—its review of Saint Laurent's first collection for Dior said the dresses looked like toothpaste tubes on top of a brioche—and occasionally banishing them from the pages. The most famous example was an estrangement lasting for several years between the paper and Geoffrey Beene. Under John B. Fairchild's editorship, *WWD* added theater, restaurant and movie reviews, lengthy interviews with celebrities such as Truman Capote, Barbra Streisand, Alfred Hitchcock, and Cassius Clay (pre-Muhammad Ali), and even coverage of the social doings of the White House. The paper's Washington coverage prompted Henry Kissinger to complain that it was giving his active social life too much attention. *WWD* became a must-read not just for retail and business executives, but also for socialites, public-relations people, talent agents, and even politicians.

A new round of conspicuous consumption in the 1980s fit perfectly with the paper's exuberant coverage of the worlds of fashion and society. *WWD* gave the Reagan White House ample play. Couture came back, exemplified by Christian Lacroix's bubble dress and the swept-up hairdo, and a new generation of celebrities designed and wore the high-end fashions of the decade. Designer Carolyne Roehm, for example, was married to the wealthy Henry Kravitz, and appeared in the pages of *WWD* both as a designer and a socialite. The recession of the late 1990s that accompanied the bursting of the dot-com bubble was like a morning-after hangover after the long party of the 1980s and early 1990s. The pages of *WWD* began to fill with news of liquidations and reorganizations in the fashion industry, and the flight of manufacturing to Asia and the developing world. But the paper remained the must-read publication for everyone connected with the world of fashion.

In 1968, the family decided to sell Fairchild Publications (which had grown to include trade papers dedicated to footwear, home furnishings, even electronics) to Capital Cities Broadcasting, thus becoming part of a publicly owned media empire. In 1986 *WWD* editors retired their typewriters and moved into the computer age. In 1991, Fairchild Publications moved from its woefully outdated Greenwich Village headquarters to modern offices in a more convenient, if less attractive, neighbor-hood across the street from the Empire State Building. John B. Fairchild retired in 1997 at age 70, naming Patrick McCarthy to be his successor as chairman and editorial director of Fairchild Publications. After a series of media mergers and acquisitions that gave Fairchild Publications various corporate parents in the 1980s and 1990s, the company was acquired in 1999 by Advance Publications Inc., the publishing empire (and publishers of *Vogue*), owned by the Newhouse family.

WWD remains one of the most influential voices in the world of fashion. It is famous as a sort of prep school for fashion journalists. Its alumni are on the masthead of almost every American consumer magazine, from *Condé Nast Traveller* to *Time*, although the concentration is heaviest, naturally, at fashion magazines. *New York Times* theater critic Ben Brantley and Bernadine Morris worked at *WWD*, as did former CNN correspondent Elsa Klensch, *Vogue* editor-at-large André Leon Talley, photographer Bill Cunningham, former French *Vogue* editor Joan Juliet Buck, and even Calvin Klein, who had a brief, unsuccessful stint as a copy boy in 1961.

See also Fashion Advertising; Fashion Editors; Fashion Icons; Fashion Industry; Fashion Journalism; Fashion Magazines; Fashion Photography.

Bibliography

Agins, Teri. *The End of Fashion: How Marketing Changed the Clothing Business Forever.* New York: Quill, 2000.

Kelly, Katie. *The Wonderful World of Women's Wear Daily.* New York: Saturday Review Press, 1972.

Janet Ozzard

WORKING-CLASS DRESS

For much of the period between the eighteenth century and the present, most people in western countries could be characterized as working class. Many occupations and styles of living are encompassed, ranging from independent skilled artisans in regular work to unskilled laborers or the unemployed. Despite a numerical majority and their central place in social, cultural, and economic history, working-class people, like women as a group, until recently have been hidden from written history and their clothing has been overlooked or subject to only generalized or romanticized interest. What they wore also remained under-represented in museums, due to a low survival rate caused by the thrifty reuse of clothing or its worn-out condition, and the tendency of museums to collect and preserve elite fashions rather than utilitarian clothing. In the early 2000s there is widespread interest in occupational dress, the clothing of the poor, and the role of working-class clothing consumption in the development of a consumer society during this period. Academic studies in this field make use of an array of sources including inventories, court records, and household accounts to pursue this interest in the earlier part of the period and the use of oral history, film, and photography helps ensure the more recent past is better documented.

Occupation, Social Position, and Clothing

One of the most marked gulfs between the appearance of working people and their employers was the use of livery for retainers and household servants. This practice of providing uniform clothing in the colors and style of a particular household was used to augment wages, and it served to embody hierarchy by distinguishing between employees and employer and between ranks of employees themselves. Livery was in widespread use during the period, as it had been since medieval times. It was far from universally popular with its recipients. By the nineteenth century it had become archaic in appearance, such as breeches and wigs for footmen, and had become very limited in use. It has been superseded to some extent by corporate uniforms. Domestic service was a major employer of women until World War I and generated styles of clothing representative of moral and practical notions of order and cleanliness.

Working people in the eighteenth and nineteenth centuries who did not get livery or other clothing as part

> "Everybody knows that good clothes, boots or furniture are really the cheapest in the end, although they cost more money at first; but the working classes can seldom or never afford to buy good things; they have to buy cheap rubbish which is dear at any price." (Tressell, p. 296)

> "To imagine New York City in 1789 is to conjure up . . . tattered beggars, silk-stockinged rich men, pomadoured ladies and their liveried footmen, leather-aproned mechanics and shabby apprentice boys, sleek coach horses, pigs . . . where the riotous world of the labouring poor surrounded a small, self-enclosed enclave of the wealthy and urbane." (Stansell, p. 3)

of their employment often struggled not only to clothe themselves and their families at a basic level, but also to keep up certain levels of cleanliness and respectable appearances on which their continuing employment or their participation in local and church life depended. However, throughout these centuries, employers and the elite, in general, expressed anxiety about the consumption of clothing by working people. Increasing use, more styles, and a variety of available textiles, and the so-called democratization of fashion were judged to weaken conventional distinctions between social classes. Expenditure on clothing by working people was thought to indicate potential extravagance, vanity, and improvidence. There were numerous Victorian cartoons mocking both the domestic servant and her employer as the servant appeared in stylish crinolines or other finery. This was frequently observed in Britain, where social distinctions in dress are thought to have prevailed for longer than in the United States. In the twentieth century, new synthetic materials, simpler styles, affordable fashion magazines, dance halls, and the cinema especially, spurred greater access to fashionable clothing for working women. More recent adoption of homogeneous leisure wear means that social distinctions may be less visible than ever before outside work.

Working Clothes and Fashion

Modish and symbolic use of working-class dress entered general consumption in various ways and in general over the last three centuries; there has been a significant flow of garment types and textiles from utilitarian and occupational clothing into fashion. Examples include appropriation of military combat styles into everyday wear and the rough and thorn-proof warmth of local Scottish and Irish tweeds that were adopted for fashionable urban use in Victoria's reign. Sailors wore "trowsers" long before they entered fashionable male wardrobes. What was produced in nineteenth-century

America as denim work wear for men is, in the early 2000s, universally available as fashionable leisure wear for men, women, and children alike and authentic antique jeans command high prices among collectors.

Doc Marten boots had a similar pattern of appropriation and cult status. English agricultural smocks of the nineteenth century were adopted and revived as artistic dress, popularized by Liberty's for well-off urban women and children at the end of the century, echoing nostalgia for a largely imagined idyll of rural England.

Politicians have made use of the symbolic value of materials or garments associated with working-class life, such as when Keir Hardy, elected as one of Britain's first working-class members of parliament, insisted on wearing a rough-spun tweed suit and a flat wool cap instead of the more formal garb usually seen in parliament. President Lyndon Johnson famously wore a cowboy hat to signify his allegiance, and President Jimmy Carter often wore a sweater rather than more formal attire.

In the arts, performers and actors such as Dolly Parton, James Dean, Marlon Brando, and Charlie Chaplin have used working and utilitarian dress to powerful effect. Subcultures, as disparate as Hell's Angels, hippies, punks, and New Agers, have often demonstrated their nonconformism by blending garments from a variety of sources, including working clothes. In the 1970s many pioneer feminists adopted dungarees as a sartorial rejection of fashion and conventional gender roles.

The making and wearing of replica working clothing from the past has become widespread through the popularity of historical reenactment and the use of living history to interpret historic sites. The shift such clothing makes in its esteem and value may have no single explanation; rather, it may embody a complex range of social, cultural, and economic factors over time. Mass production of clothing, urbanization, and more recently, new attitudes to work and leisure, money, and credit, may change not only our clothing but the identities they represent.

Provision

Before the advent of systematic state support in the twentieth century, various local or parish bodies and charitable organizations took responsibility for those unable to help themselves, and clothing for such men, women, and children was often part of the provision. Outside this framework, provision was uncertain because it was dependent on income, locality, and luck.

Secondhand clothes were an important element in the clothing strategies of working people. These could be obtained as cast-offs from employers, or from markets and specialist shops in urban areas. There were large warehouses buying and selling secondhand clothing in bigger cities by the eighteenth century, and Henry Mayhew describes a vibrant trade in the wholesale and export of old clothes in 1850s London.

Where women possessed adequate sewing skills, much clothing was made over or recycled: For example, children's clothes were made from cut-down adult garments. The pawning of best clothes played a central part in many household economies. This provided regular cash, and often clothes left all week in the pawnshop were stored in better conditions than was possible in damp or overcrowded homes. In many working households, mothers were traditionally in charge of the budget, and there is evidence that they often clothed and shod working husbands, sons, and school-age children before meeting their own needs.

Sewing clothes at home was assisted by the advent of the sewing machine and effective paper patterns from the 1860s onward, but these were unaffordable for many women. Others sewed at home to earn cash by making or renovating garments for local customers.

Theft played its part in the provision of clothes for use or resale, and in the eighteenth century there are numerous records of vanished household servants who took quantities of clothing with them to pawn or sell. Peddlers traveled around selling clothing, accessories, and cloth to individual households in the eighteenth century before communications and transport improved.

Many working people continued to clothe themselves and their families in ways more suited to their circumstances than traveling to expensive shops. Local or workplace clothing clubs and, by the mid-nineteenth century, mail order with payment by installments played an important part in enabling them to be adequately and fashionably clothed.

Huge markets for slops and utilitarian clothing, including uniforms for the military, led to the development of the mass manufacture of ready-mades from the eighteenth century onward. In America the manufacture of jeans for men demonstrates the growth of factory-based specialist clothing companies. As urbanization coupled with expanding markets during the nineteenth century, new jobs grew up in service industries such as banking and insurance, which resulted in large numbers of low-paid white collar jobs for men and women. A big manufacturing sector developed for affordable clothes for this work, such as suits, blouses, collars, and shoes, which could be widely distributed through growth in urban retailing.

Specific Modes and Items

The common utilitarian dress for laboring men before the twentieth century was made up of breeches or trousers, jackets, and waistcoats of hard-wearing materials such as moleskin, fustian, or corduroy. In some situations, working women were the first women to don breeches or trousers. This occurred in the second half of the nineteenth century in Britain (in pits and mines, in work associated with fishing, and in brickworks), and in the United States (where women did agricultural work), and in some utopian communities.

In many manual occupations, until shorter skirts were widely accepted, women simply hitched up long skirts in various ways. Commonly, in many countries, they wore aprons and woolen shawls. In eighteen-and early nineteenth-century Britain, the red woolen, hooded cloak was commonly worn by rural women. Women used boots instead of shoes; pattens and then clogs were valuable assets for workingmen and -women on dirt roads and later in factories and mills. Stout and durable footwear has always been a major investment for those undertaking physical labor. Similarly in the United States, denim became widely used by the second half of the nineteenth century for tough work by cattlemen, on the railways and in the mines. Roomy and rugged work shirts accompanied these. Leather and suede have been used in working garments for centuries and persists to the present day, providing hard-wearing and durable covering in the form of aprons for blacksmiths and chaps, gaiters, gloves, and various specialist items and outerwear for other occupations.

Although Britain differed from continental Europe in having no recognizable regional folk dress, two agricultural garments stand out as characteristic of rural workers, and these were worn either at work or as Sunday best. These were smocks for men, from the eighteenth century onwards, which provided a measure of protection and warmth; and the cotton sunbonnet for women, which was decorated with tucks and piping and had strikingly long panels to protect the neck. Fishermen have always had special clothing needs to protect them against the elements. In this context, oilskin was developed in the nineteenth century, and the woolen hand-knitted, close-fitting and ornamented upper garment for fishermen known variously as a gansy, jersey, Guernsey, knitfrock, and later sweater or jumper, became associated with the island fishing communities of Britain. Versions of it were later widely adopted as warm, informal attire for both sexes.

Occupational dress evolves as new occupations emerge, and innovative protective elements are introduced as new risks appear. In the industrializing period, boiler suits accompanied the use of steam power, and since the advent of forms of power that propel us into alien environments, special forms of clothing have been developed for, among others, pilots, divers, and astronauts. To an extent, occupational dress has often represented social and local or regional identities. In this sense, it has shown more style and commanded more loyalty than is strictly utilitarian. In 2002 in northern England a local bus driver was fired for refusing to exchange his habitual cloth cap for a baseball-style company cap. The dramatic fantail hats of the garbage collectors of early nineteenth century England or the intricate patterning on fishermen's knitwear have all testified to expressive and creative elements in occupational dress.

See also Secondhand Clothes, History of; Uniforms, Occupational.

Bibliography

Crane, Diana. *Fashion and its Social Agendas: Class, Gender and Identity in Clothing*. Chicago: University of Chicago Press, 2000.

De Marly, Diana. *Working Dress: A History of Occupational Clothing*. London: B. T. Batsford, Ltd., 1986.

Hall, Lee. *Common Threads: A Parade of American Clothing*. London: Little, Brown and Company, 1992.

Kidwell, Claudia, and Margaret Christman. *Suiting Everyone: The Democratisation of Clothing in America*. Washington, D.C.: Smithsonian Institution Press, 1974.

Partington, Angela. "Popular Fashion and Working-Class Affluence." In *Chic Thrills: A Fashion Reader*. Edited by Juliet Ash and Elizabeth Wilson. London: Pandora, 1992.

Quennell, Peter, ed. *Mayhew's London: Henry Mayhew*. London: Bracken Books, 1984.

Severa, Joan. *Dressed for the Photographer: Ordinary Americans and Fashion, 1840–1900*. Kent, Ohio, and London: Kent State University Press, 1995.

Stansell, Christine. *City of Women: Sex and Class in New York 1789–1860*. Urbana: University of Illinois Press, 1987.

Textile History. Special Issue on the Dress of the Poor. Vol. 33, no. 1 (May 2002).

Tressell, Robert. *The Ragged Trousered Philanthropists*. London: Flamingo, 1993. The original edition was published in 1914.

Barbara Burman

WORTH, CHARLES FREDERICK

Four generations of Worths are associated with perhaps the most enduring name in fashion history. Indeed, without the house's contributions to fashion, the French Second Empire would not be remembered as an unending parade of luxurious confections in women's dress, and the Gilded Age would not seem so golden.

Charles Frederick Worth (1825–1895) was the founder of a fashion house usually credited with establishing the highest level of fashion creativity: haute couture. Originally the French phrase meant the highest level of sewing. Later it was employed to identify that portion of fashion—particularly French fashion—that both exemplified the pinnacle of dressmaking techniques and produced new styles. Unfortunately, the phrase *haute couture* has lost its original meaning through overuse.

Early Career

Charles Frederick Worth was uncommonly astute in recognizing that his talents were better directed toward artistic creativity rather than managing a business. Following a period of working in London dry-goods shops, Worth set out for Paris. In 1846 he found a position at the prominent dry-goods and dressmaking firm of Gagelin et Opigez. This position gave Worth the experience that later enabled him to build his own business. At Gagelin he was exposed to the best resources for fabrics and trims, and allowed to develop his design skills. He also learned the value of live models and met his future business partner, a Swede named Otto Bobergh (1821–1881). What eventually became the House of Worth was established in late 1856 or early 1857 as Worth and Bobergh at 7, rue de la Paix, with Worth as the artistic head and Bobergh as the financial director. The partnership dissolved in 1870–1871, when Bobergh decided to retire due to major political unrest in France.

Worth's wife, née Marie Vernet (1825–1898), was a former Gagelin model. Mme. Worth easily attracted the attention of the ladies of the French court and then the Empress Eugénie herself, by wearing Worth's creations. Taken with promoting French industries, including the once-dying silk industry of Lyon, the empress thrived on lavish gatherings and equally lavish dress at these events. The empress appointed Worth the court couturier in 1860. To make sure his house could keep up with the growing demand for his dresses, Worth introduced a new way of creating an outfit. Instead of designing a complete dress, he pioneered the concept of mixing and matching skirts and bodices, which insured that ladies did not appear at a function in look-alike attire. Worth also developed inter-changeable pattern pieces in constructing these garments, further insuring the uniqueness of a completed ensemble.

At the House, clients could preview evening attire in rooms illuminated by various forms of light—natural light, candlelight, gas lamps, and later, electric bulbs. While the House maintained the usual fitting and modeling rooms, it also offered rooms for fabric selection that were distinguished by color. An understanding of the play of colors and textures was one of the enduring achievements of the House, and was successfully passed from generation to generation. Charles Worth's sense of color was particularly noteworthy—he preferred nuanced hues to bold primary colors.

Merchandising Innovations

Throughout the House of Worth's existence, it catered to the rich and titled, although it also served those of more limited means. Garments could be ordered from afar with no personal fittings required. The client supplied a comfortably fitted garment from which appropriate measurements were taken. Worth's models also could be made from commercial paper patterns. The House initially advertised its creations in obscure but aesthetically interesting nineteenth-century publications before entering the mainstream at the end of the century with full-page images in *Harper's Bazaar* and *The Queen* as well as their French counterpart *La mode illustrée*. In the twentieth century, the House's models were advertised in such selective fashion publications as the *Gazette du bon ton*, and such newer entries as *Vogue*. The former type of publication carried on the centuries-old tradition of hand-drawn and hand-colored illustrations, while the latter featured modern photographs.

Late-nineteenth-century publicity images of Charles Frederick Worth depict a man who saw himself as an artist, wearing a bow at the neck or a beret. Many of the images of his son Jean-Philippe also show someone intent on conveying an impression of creativity. Like many classically trained painters and sculptors of their day, the Worths drew on historical prototypes. The House's designs included references to garments in historical paintings gleaned from museum visits, published descriptions of works of art, and personal familiarity with historic costume. Large numbers of Worth garments from the period of Charles and Jean-Philippe referenced seventeenth-and eighteenth-century styles, but none of them will ever be confused with their prototypes, thanks to construction detail and fabric choice. The Worths employed several distinguishing features in their garments beyond the waistband label that they first introduced in the mid-1860s. Although often credited with the innovation, Worth was not the first dressmaker to use a label. The earliest Worth examples were stamped in gold, but they became a woven signature in the late 1870s. This signature label would last the duration of the House. Attempts to defraud the public with spurious labels were made, especially in the United States in the early twentieth century.

Dress Construction and Materials

Contrary to Worth family mythology, the vast majority of the House's garments were trimmed with machine-made rather than handmade lace. Many Worth clients had collections of lace that had been acquired as investments. Sometimes such lace was used on a garment but almost always removed later and returned to the client. The same procedure was followed if gemstones were incorporated into a garment's design. An additional feature employed by the House was the use of selvage as a decorative touch as well as functional finishing.

Perhaps the House's most important contribution was the type of fabrics that it employed. Following the collapse of the Second Empire in 1870, Worth became an even more important client for the textile and trim producers of Lyon and its environs. There is evidence that Worth both used preexisting yard goods and worked with manufacturers to come up with patterns for new materials.

Charles Worth had begun his designing career by following the expansion of women's skirts in the 1850s, when they were supported by layer upon layer of petticoats. In the later 1850s Worth draped yards of fabric over the skirts' increasing width, as the newly devised crinoline cage, or hoop, permitted expansion without increased bulk. Many Worth dresses from this period, sadly, were frothy, cloudlike confections in silk tulle that have now melted into oblivion. An impression of their impact, however, can be seen in portraits by such artists as Franz Xaver Winterhalter.

Worth introduced hooped dresses with flatter fronts in the early 1860s. It is evident, however, that he was careful not to diminish the amount of material needed; he merely pushed the fabric to the back of the dress. During this decade Worth is also credited with developing the princess-cut dress. These less expansive styles posed an economic challenge. Having been trained in dry-goods shops, Worth recognized the danger of weakening trades that contributed to the success of his own business. Therefore he had to either incorporate large quantities of material into his garments or support the production of costlier luxury goods. In order to maintain a high level of consumption, the House moved material throughout much of the 1870s and 1880s from draped overskirts to trains, bustled backs, and a variety of combinations of these styles. Just as the Empress Eugénie's patronage of the French textile industries had been crucial before 1870, so also was Worth's business vital for the looms of Lyon and Paris that created spectacular luxury materials afterward.

Many of the House's early garments had been constructed of unpatterned silks—tulles, taffetas, reps, and satins—or nominally patterned fabrics featuring stripes and small floral sprays—in other words, typical dress goods. Beginning in the 1870s, almost as a move to fill the void left by the departed French court, the house increasingly employed more expensive textiles usually associated with household furnishing in its garments. Worth boldly utilized grand-scale floral motifs designed for wall coverings in garments whose skirts were often not long enough to include a full repeat of the pattern. Such luxury fabrics, exhibiting astonishing richness of material and the highest level of technical skill, were a feature of the House's models into the first years of the twentieth century. With the exception of machine-made laces, Worth's trims and embroideries matched the ground fabric to which they were applied. The consensus among Worth's clients was that these costly toilettes were worth the price.

Charles Worth and his house did not merely purchase materials; they are also known to have worked closely with textile manufacturers. From such concerns as A. Gourd et Cie, J. Bachelard et Cie, and Tassinari et Chatel, the Worths either commissioned specific designs or ordered preexisting patterns. Often the fabrics they chose had been displayed at important international exhibitions. Many of the fabrics found in late-nineteenth-or early-twentieth-century Worth garments feature subjects that were especially popular with the House: feathers, stalks of grain, stars, butterflies, carnations, iris, tulips, chestnut and oak leaves, scallops and scales, and bowers of roses.

The First Couturier

Worth was not the first man to be an acclaimed creator of fashion. LeRoy had been held in similar esteem as a milliner and dressmaker to the Empress Josephine. Worth was, however, the first clothing designer to be called a couturier. Nevertheless, Worth had the good fortune to be a man entering a field that had become dominated by women, a position that automatically made him a curiosity in the 1850s. During the heady days of the Second Empire, the magic of the "man milliner" called Worth drew the fashion-conscious to the rue de la Paix. Worth's clients were decried as slaves to this dictatorial monarch. Nor was it lost on the House that the theater was an active agent for the propagation of fashion. Even when dressing actresses of the stature of Sarah Bernhardt, however, Worth would insist on full payment for garments. British actress Lillie Langtry was a faithful client, as were such other *grandes horizontales* (courtesans), actresses, and opera stars as Cora Pearl, Eleanora Duse, and Nellie Melba. Such Bostonians as Lillie Moulton, Isabella Stewart Gardner, and Mrs. J. P. Morgan were dressed by the House, as were their counterparts of the Vanderbilt, Astor, Hewitt, Palmer, McCormick, and Stanford families in New York, Chicago, and San Francisco. The House dressed members of the royal families of Russia, Italy, Spain, and Portugal as well as the noblewomen of numerous German principalities.

The first challenge to the house's primacy came with the founding of the House of Paquin in 1891. During the 1890s Worth began to lose clients to this concern. An analysis of the order numbers found in late nineteenth-and early twentieth-century garments reveals not only the year of manufacture but also the fact that orders were declining during this period. But for nearly fifty years, however, a Worth garment had been the most coveted of all apparel, particularly among American women. Perhaps this popularity developed because women from the United States felt at ease discussing their dressmaking needs with a man who could speak English. In return, Charles Worth appreciated his American clients because they had faith in him, figures that displayed his creations to advantage, and perhaps most importantly—francs to pay his bills.

Worth's Successors

Charles Frederick Worth was officially succeeded on his death by his sons Jean-Philippe and Gaston, who had established important roles within the House in the 1870s. Jean-Philippe (1856–1926) worked as a designer alongside his father, and Gaston (1853–1924) functioned as business manager. Throughout the years and over the span of four generations, the Worths never lost sight of the need for astute financial as well as artistic direction.

During the period when Charles and Jean-Philippe worked together as designers within the House it is impossible to separate their designs. Even though later house labels carry the signature of the elder Worth, others may have been responsible for the garment's inspiration.

World War I and the subsequent devaluations of European currencies were particularly devastating to the Worths, because the house had dressed so many female members of the royal families of Europe. In addition, many of the House's older clients died during this period, while fashions were making the transition from Edwardian modes to jazz age styles. When Jean-Philippe and Gaston retired in the early 1920s, they were succeeded by Gaston's sons; Jean-Charles Worth became the new designer, and his brother Jacques the financial director. Jean-Charles easily moved the House's designs from the more staid yet elaborate models of the prewar period into the simpler and more practical styles of the 1920s. In the process, however, fewer and fewer of the characteristics that had been exclusively associated with the House's production can be discerned in the garments that survive from this period.

Worth's grandsons were followed in the 1930s by his great-grandsons Maurice and Roger, the latter assuming the couturier role. They attempted to breathe new life into the House; in 1936 they moved the Paris store to 120, rue du Faubourg St.-Honoré. At the end of World War II, however, both the London and Paris branches of the house merged with Worth's old rival Paquin. The London branches, the first established in 1911, survived the Paris branch by eight years. Worth's heirs also shut-tered the branches of the House that had been established in Cannes and Biarritz.

As of the early 2000s, the Worth name survived in perfume, although the company has long been out of direct family control.

See also Crinoline; Fancy Dress; Fashion Marketing and Merchandising; Haute Couture; Paquin, Jeanne; Paris Fashion; Perfume; Royal and Aristocratic Dress.

Bibliography

Coleman, Elizabeth A. *The Opulent Era: Fashions of Worth, Doucet and Pingat.* New York: The Brooklyn Museum in association with Thames and Hudson, 1989.

De Marly, Diana. *Worth: Father of Haute Couture.* 2nd ed. New York: Holms and Meier, 1990.

Saunders, Edith. *The Age of Worth.* London and New York: Longmans, Green, 1954.

Internet Resources

Charles Frederick Worth Organization. Available from <http://www.charlesfrederickworth.org>.

House of Worth. Available from <http://www.houseofworth.co.uk>.

Elizabeth Ann Coleman

X

XULY BËT

The Paris-based African fashion designer Lamine Kouyaté is the creator of the XULY.Bët brand. The company is best known for its use of recycled clothing to create high fashion, reshaping found garments by cutting, stitching, and silk-screening, or making modifications that range from the subtle shaping of a seam to the complete transformation of a garment's function. XULY.Bët's recycled clothing embodies several seemingly contradictory attributes: simultaneously mass-produced and unique, new and old, African and European, exclusive and accessible, emerging out of the rarified fantasy of fashion runways and the gritty practicality of the streets. This work turns the notion of haute couture inside out, since it relies on the creation of garments that are one of a kind because they are made of used clothing that has been discarded.

Personal Background

Lamine Badian Kouyaté is the product of the cosmopolitan African culture of both urban Africa and the African diaspora. He was born in Bamako, the capital of the West African country Mali, in 1962. His father was a government minister in the first postcolonial administration, and his mother was a doctor from Senegal. Kouyaté's father was imprisoned during the 1968 coup d'état, when President Modibo Keita was overthrown by Moussa Traoré, who led a repressive, dictatorial government until 1992. The family left the country, moving to Paris when Kouyaté was fourteen, then to Dakar when he was sixteen, where his father worked for the United Nations. Dakar and Bamako are cosmopolitan centers whose cultural influences draw upon African, European, American, and myriad other sources. Kouyaté described the global perspective of youth culture in the African cities: "I knew more about rock and funk in the 70's than any of the kids in Paris when I got here" (Spindler, p. 1). At age twenty-four,

he left Dakar to study architecture at the University of Strasbourg in France.

Before completing his architecture degree, Kouyaté moved to Paris and began working as a clothing designer. He founded his XULY.Bët label in 1989. Kouyaté's background in architecture may in part explain his tendency to reveal and rework the structure of garments, often by disassembling them at the seams. Kouyaté's fashion sensibilities were also shaped by his interests in music and performance. He participated in the underground Parisian music and nightclub scene of the early 1980s and, as part of that environment, began designing clothes for performances and for his friends in the clubs. He continues to perform as a musician with his band, "This Is Not A Machine Gun." His attention to the expressive potential of music and performance continues to be manifested in his work, including most notably his presentation of designs at fashion shows.

Recycled Clothing

Kouyaté's line of recycled garments debuted in 1992 as part of the first major collection of the XULY.Bët brand. The garments were made of previously owned shirts, sweaters, dresses, pants, hosiery, and other clothing purchased in flea markets, charity shops, and lowend department stores. Kouyaté altered each garment, responding to the fabrics and the shape of the piece, cutting, removing, and restitching seams using bright red thread. His energetic technique is preserved in the threads left hanging at the end of seams, their red hue emphasizing the process of transformation from discarded garment to designer statement. Kouyaté's reshaping of garments includes the transformation of dresses into skirts, skirts into bags, stockings into halter tops, and sweaters stitched together to create dresses.

The previous lives of XULY.Bët recycled garments are deliberately preserved; Kouyaté leaves the original labels in the collars of used shirts and the waistbands of pants purchased at flea markets. These labels provide vivid evidence of the histories of clothing that has been used, discarded, and later returned to the fashion market by the designer. The original label alludes to the garment's first life; the bright red XULY.Bët label, usually placed on the outside of the garment, declares its current identity. The used garments Kouyaté works with provide an endless source of constantly changing raw material, like an archaeological record of past styles that are rein-troduced into the fashion market.

Rethinking the Fashion Show

XULY.Bët's first major fashion show, held during the spring 1992 season in Paris, illustrates Kouyaté's interest in the tension between the theatrical and the mundane. His debut fashion show's innovative staging emphasized the brand's raw, edgy aesthetic. Kouyaté presented the show outside the conventional precincts of the fashion industry, at a public park. He did not use a runway or a sound system. Instead, models emerged from a bus that pulled up at the site, each carrying a boombox that provided her own soundtrack to the event. No stage, no lights, no delineation of theatrical space separated the audience from the performers, just as the garments themselves were but subtly separated from their previous, mundane lives.

African Elements

Kouyaté's work incorporates aspects of his own biography, which encompasses contemporary, urban Africa as well as the fashion worlds of Paris and New York. His company's name draws immediate attention to his African origins. In Oulouf (or Wolof), the predominant language of Senegal, *xuly bët* is a colloquial term that can be roughly translated as "voyeur," or, in a more nuanced definition, as someone who breaks through appearances to see the reality beneath the surface. This notion, peeling back the exterior to reveal the often uneven surfaces layered beneath, is embodied by Kouyaté's exposed seams and loose threads. He has cited his roots in Africa as an important source of inspiration for his recycled fashion, reflecting a widespread African ethic of reusing resources that is born out of necessity. Kouyaté draws on Africa in a more literal sense, using African fabrics in several of his designs and, in the early twenty-first century, working with dyers in Mali to create fabrics that he uses in his other clothing lines.

International Presence

Kouyaté is among the few African designers to have achieved an international profile; XULY.Bët clothing and the designer himself have been featured in prominent publications, including French *Glamour*, the *New York Times*, *Le Figaro*, and *Essence*. His clothing played a prominent role in Robert Altman's film *Ready To Wear* (1994), in which a fashion show in an underground subway station presents XULY.Bët clothing as the work of one of the film's main characters. The designer's personal background as well as his work drew substantial attention from both the fashion and the popular press, particularly in the early 1990s. In the early 2000s Kouyaté continued to design actively, marketing his clothing through several shops in Paris and for international clients.

See also Fashion Designer; Fashion Shows; Recycled Textiles; Textiles, African.

Bibliography

Jacobs, P. "XULY Bet: A Brother from the 'Mother' Turns Fashion Inside Out." *Essence* 15 (May 1994): 26–27, 144. Introduction to Kouyaté's background and his work, with several illustrations.

Renaux, P. "Pari Dakar de Xuly Bët." *Glamour* (April 1994). Focuses on the designer's African background, documenting a trip home to Dakar to visit his family.

Revue Noire 27 (March 1998). Special issue on African fashion includes a large spread devoted to XULY. Bët, with generous illustrations of his recycled line of clothing. An important publication for readers seeking insight into African fashion design as an international phenomenon.

Spindler, A. M. "Prince of Pieces." *New York Times* (2 May 1993): section 9, pp. 1, 13. Most substantive coverage of the designer available, including an overview of his career and extensive quotations from interview with Kouyaté.

Van der Plas, E., and M. Willemsen, eds. *The Art of African Fashion*. Lawrenceville, N.J.: Africa World Press, 1998. Kouyaté is one of a handful of African designers featured in this important publication. Several essays by academics and fashion practitioners situate African fashion design within global markets.

Victoria L. Rovine

Y

YAMAMOTO, YOHJI*

Yohji Yamamoto is widely regarded as ranking among the greatest fashion designers of the late twentieth and early twenty-first centuries. He is one of the few in his profession who have successfully broken the boundaries between commodity and art, by creating clothing that ranges from basics like athletic shoes and denim jeans to couture-inspired gowns that are nothing short of malleable mobile sculptures. Lauded as a blend of master craftsman and philosophical dreamer, Yamamoto has balanced the seemingly incompatible extremes of fashion's competing scales.

Despite the magnitude of his talent and the importance of his work, however, Yamamoto has yet to be the subject of serious critical discourse among fashion journalists and historians. It is perhaps ironic that the only probing analysis of Yamamoto—both the man and the designer—came from someone who possessed little knowledge of or interest in fashion. Wim Wenders, the renowned German filmmaker, produced a documentary in 1989 entitled *Notebook on Cities and Clothes*. Throughout the film, Wenders dramatized Yamamoto's creative genius by setting the words of the late German philosopher Walter Benjamin against the urban backdrops of both Tokyo and Paris. Yet the director's probing failed to illuminate the crucial elements that constituted Yamamoto's fashions. Neither the elements particular to the art of dressmaking nor Yamamoto's particular aesthetic contributions were discussed.

Inspiration from the intangible, mainly images of historical dress from sources such as photographs, has been a mainstay in Yamamoto's work. The crumpled collar in a August Sander portrait, the gauzy dresses captured by Jacques-Henri Lartigue while vacationing on the Riviera, and the gritty realism of Françoise Huguier's travels among the Inuit of the Arctic Circle are but a few examples. It is not surprising that the riveting catalogs created for each of Yamamoto's high-end ready-to-wear women's collections have included the work of such notable photographers as Nick Knight, Paolo Roversi, Inez van Lamsweerde, and Vinoodh Matadin. Whether Yamamoto is evoking historicism via the ancien régime or the belle epoque, or ethnic garments made of richly woven silks and woolens, he has come to epitomize the vast range of creative possibilities in the art of dress.

Early Career

Yamamoto was born in Tokyo on 3 October 1943. He never knew his father, who died in Manchuria during World War II; he was reared by his widowed mother Yumi. A dressmaker by trade, Yumi suffered what Yamamoto recalls as the indignities of a highly skilled worker whose gender and station in life afforded her little opportunity to make a rewarding living or to obtain recognition for her talents. Yumi encouraged her son to become an attorney—he graduated with a law degree from Keio University but never practiced. The lure of becoming a designer, however, pulled Yamamoto into fashion.

After completing his university studies in 1966, Yamamoto studied fashion design at the famous Bunka-fukuso Gakuin, a fashion institute in Tokyo. Despite his skills as a master craftsman, he started his career as an anonymous creator around 1970. Two years later he marketed his own designs under the label Y's. Clothing under this label is now considered to be Yamamoto's lower-priced, or "bridge," line. In 1977 he presented his Y's collection for the first time in Tokyo. Along with his compatriot Rei Kawakubo, he designed his first high-end women's ready-to-wear collection in 1981 and presented it in Paris. Over the next two years, Kawakubo and Yamamoto pioneered the idea of deconstructed fashions. Their revolutionary aesthetic shocked the world with clothing that appeared to be unfinished, tattered, and haphazardly put together. Yamamoto's loose, flowing silhouettes and ubiquitous use of black further enhanced his groundbreaking work, which became the favored look of the 1980s urban aesthetic. In 1984 Yamamoto presented a deluxe menswear line that incorporated many of these same elements.

Yamamoto's Aesthetic

From the moment Kawakubo and Yamamoto presented their first fashion collections to an international audience in the 1980s, they were defined as Japanese designers. Virtually every article about them as well as the critical reviews of their collections began by describing them as inseparable from and encapsulated in their Asian heritage. Many journalists inaccurately assumed that they produced clothing worn by all Japanese people. The reality was that the loose, dark-colored, and seemingly tattered garments were as startling to the average Japanese as they were to the Western audiences that first viewed them. Although Yamamoto's work changed and evolved over the next two decades, it retained several key elements—the ambiguities of gender, the importance of black, and the aesthetics of deconstruction.

Gender ambiguity. Yamamoto's professed love of and respect for women has not been evident to many because his clothes were often devoid of Western-style gender markers. He expressed an aversion to overtly sexualized females, and often dressed women in designs inspired by men's wear. Such cross-gender role-playing has long been a part of Japanese culture, and a persistent theme among performers and artists for centuries. The fact that Yamamoto on more than one occasion chose women as models for his menswear fashion shows was another small piece of his sexual identity puzzle.

Even when his later work embraced the sweeping romanticism of postwar Parisian haute couture, Yamamoto's historical recontextualizations contrasted sharply with the work of other marquee designers. Deliberately absent from his runway presentations were the requisites of the contemporary high-fashion wardrobe for women: high heels, rising hemlines, plunging necklines, and sheer fabrics. These characteristics might be the reason that Yamamoto's dark tailored suits and white shirts for both men and women have been some of his most enduring and compelling products. Worn by Western men of all classes for two centuries, the dark-colored suit and the white shirt have a combined ability to convey both sexuality and power through conformity. This blend of erotic appeal and strength was a perfect template for Yamamoto to express his postwar version of male and female sexuality.

Basic black. No color in the fashion palette has been as important in the work of Yohji Yamamoto as black. This early unrelenting black-on-black aesthetic earned his devotees the nickname *karasuzoku*, or members of the crow tribe. Black has certain associations in the history of the West that have been processed through a kaleidoscope of self-conscious modernist or postmodernist theories and assumptions. As a result of historical recontextualization, black had by the last quarter of the twentieth century acquired a range of meanings, such as poverty and devastation for some fashion critics, and sobriety, intellectualism, chic, self-restraint, and nobility in dress for others.

The aesthetic attributes of traditional Japan and contemporary culture, as well as the role black plays in fashion, can be seen in the color's association with poverty. For some observers, black is an illusion of—or perhaps an allusion to—rusticity, simplicity, and self-restraint. In Japan, black dyes may connote rural origin as well as noble warrior status. An important connection between black and the symbolic associations of old Europe, traditional Japan, and the modern urban landscape may also be derived from the couture atelier. Yamamoto, like Cristóbal Balenciaga, often created day suits, dresses, ball gowns, and coats devoid of any ornament. Charcoal gray, navy blue, and of course black woolens were often molded and manipulated into pure sculptural forms that displayed both marvelous engineering and tailoring techniques as well as a love of dramatic form.

Deconstructed styles. The connection between deconstruction, originally a French philosophical movement, and contemporary fashion design has yet to be fully explored by fashion historians. There is no direct evidence that such ideas were the motivating force in the early designs of Yohji Yamamoto. It is more likely that he combined a mélange of influences: the devastation and rapid rebuilding of Japan in the postwar era; the revolt against bourgeois tastes; an affiliation with European street styles; and a desire, like that of the early proponents of abstraction in fine art, to find a universal expression of design by erasing elements that assign people to specific socioeconomic and gender roles.

Aesthetically, the dressmaking techniques that gave Yamamoto's work its deconstructed look were also related to traditional non-Western methods of clothing construction as well as to the concept that natural, organic, and imperfect objects can also be beautiful. Yamamoto's clothes masked the body with voluminous folds and layers of dark fabric; in addition, they diminished such evident elements of clothing as frontality and clear demarcations between the inside and outside of a garment.

Yamamoto's version of deconstruction fashion more likely began by questioning the very essence of his postwar existence. Japan's initial efforts to rebuild its physical and political infrastructure, and its later economic ascendancy, did provide the right environment to foster the talents of an amazingly creative generation that included the architects Tadao Ando, Arata Isozaki, and Kenzo Tange as well as the furniture designer Shiro Kuramata and the fashion designers Yamamoto and Kawakubo.

It seems more plausible that Yamamoto was fueled by the anger typical of the generation that spearheaded the social changes of the 1960s. Thus he arrived at a new vision for fashion that railed against the bourgeois conformity that resulted from what Yamamoto obliquely referred to as American colonialism. Though the exact elements that led him to the creation of his particular style may not be known, more than one journalist concluded that Yamamoto's clothing reflected a kind of anger that evoked images of nuclear holocaust survivors and were labeled the "Hiroshima bag lady" look by some. A few critics even made an alliance between his fashions and a coven of witches.

Despite such misunderstandings, the designs of Yamamoto paralleled the rise of punk fashions and street style, and their connection with mid-twentieth-century urban degradation. In fact, more than one writer noted that the look established by Yamamoto was neither a pure invention on his part nor a derivative of Asian culture. Such London-based designers as Malcolm McLaren and Vivienne Westwood, like other disenfranchised English youth, turned clothing into a medium for political expression and were at the forefront of the punk movement.

Yamamoto's ability to see beauty in degradation, however, and to strip things to their foundation in a search for the inherent integrity of each object is profoundly Japanese. This aesthetic of imperfection, incompleteness, or poverty, is a hallmark of *wabi-sabi*. A worldview that originated in Zen Buddhism, *wabi-sabi* was later applied to the creation of objects characterized by external lack of ornamentation and internal refinement (*wabi*) and an emphasis on the ephemeral nature of all things that eventually leads to decay (*sabi*). While Yamamoto did not formally study *wabi-sabi*, he is the product of his culture, one that is arguably the most aesthetically refined in the world.

Mature Work

The initial impact of Yamamoto's designs began to diminish as the 1980s came to a close; the designer fell into a self-professed decline for the next few years. By the mid-1990s, however, Yamamoto experienced a resurgence of creativity rare in contemporary fashion. His output was vastly different from his work of a decade earlier, in that it fully embraced the most lyrical and fleeting elements of historical modes. His designs became a blend of street-style realism and Victorian romanticism, reshaped and reconfigured for a contemporary audience. At both extremes, Yamamoto retained his very personal vision—creating clothes for an ideal woman who, according to the couturier, does not exist.

Perhaps the most potent quality that Yamamoto displayed was his brilliant ability to recontextualize the familiar into wearable creations that came as close to works of art as any clothing designed in the early 2000s. Although he created several lines of clothing for both men and women, it was his couture-inspired creations for women that manifested this concept most completely. One of the best fashion presentations in recent memory was the spring 1999 collection that Yamamoto created around the theme of a wedding. All the Yamamoto hallmarks were evident: the play on androgyny as seen through an array of masculine-tailored suits; the reliance on a neutral color scheme of black, white and khaki; and magnificent three-dimensional gowns that evoked both the Victorian era and the golden age of twentieth-century Parisian haute couture. The glory of the garments was further enhanced by the lyrical presentation itself, with the highlight being a young bride who performed a reverse striptease. Rather than disrobing, as is usually the case in fashion shows, the mannequin, dressed in an unadorned hoop-skirted wedding gown, pulled her mantle, a pair of sandals, a hat, gloves, and finally, a bouquet of flowers from pockets hidden in the gown. Fittingly, the usually jaded fashion journalists found themselves shedding tears before giving Yamamoto a standing ovation. After the success of this collection, he was honored as international designer of the year by the Council of Fashion Designers of America in New York City in June 2000.

Yamamoto continued to evolve in the early 2000s. His spring 2003 collection was not shown during the Paris ready-to-wear fashion week in October of 2002, but instead during the haute couture presentations earlier that year. Simultaneously, he became the designer for a new line of clothing produced in conjunction with the Adidas sportswear company called Y's 3. This agreement came about after Yamamoto first designed an astoundingly successful set of trainers, athletic shoes, and sports shoes for Adidas in 2001. Deeply in debt, Yohji Yamamoto filed for bankruptcy in October 2009. Soon afterwards the Integral Corporation announced that it had acquired the company and that it would remain in business with Yohji Yamamoto as its chief designer.

See also Benjamin, Walter; Fashion, Theories of; Film and Fashion; Japanese Fashion; Punk; Street Style; West-wood, Vivienne.

Bibliography

Armstrong, Lisa. "Deconstructing Yohji." British *Vogue* (August 1998): 134–137.

Chua, Lawrence. "Exploring the Yamamoto Cult." *Women's Wear Daily* (April 1988).

Hildreth, Jean C. *A New Wave in Fashion: Three Japanese Designers, March 1–April 24, 1983.* Phoenix, Ariz.: The Arizona Costume Institute of the Phoenix Art Museum, 1983.

Hirokawa, Taishi. *Sonomama Sonomama: High Fashion in the Japanese Countryside.* San Francisco: Chronicle Books, 1988.

Kondo, Dorinne. *About Face: Performing Race in Fashion and Theater.* New York: Routledge, 1997.

Koren, Leonard. *New Fashion Japan.* Tokyo: Kodansha International, 1984.

Martin, Richard. "Destitution and Deconstruction: The Riches of Poverty in the Fashions of the 1990s." *Textile and Text* 15 (1992): 3–12.

Takashina, Shuji. "Japonism: An Aesthetic of Shadow and Fragment." In *Japonism in Fashion.* Edited by A. Fukai. Tokyo: Kyoto Costume Research Foundation, 1996.

Wenders, Wim. *Aufzeichnungen zu Kleidern und Städten* (*Notebook on Cities and Clothes.*) Berlin: Road Movies Filmproduktion in cooperation with Centre National d'Art et du Culture Georges Pompidou, 1989.

Patricia Mears

YOUTHQUAKE FASHIONS

A tag, a slogan, and a rallying cry, "Youthquake" exemplifies the slickness as well as the conviction, the spontaneous ebullience as well as the commercial aggression that during the 1960s marked the triumph of London ready-to-wear. Powered by the momentum of a cresting youth culture, a cadre of British designers, mostly women, wrenched dominance away from the Paris couture houses and profoundly altered global fashion.

Youthquake fashion cannot be explored or understood without acknowledging its social and political context. In *Fifty Years of Fashion*, Valerie Steele notes that the "narrow, apolitical approach," preferred by many fashion journalists "becomes insupportable when dealing with the 1960s" (p. 49). These clothes garbed armies of protagonists in the ongoing narrative of women's economic, sexual, and social independence, and the consequent and reciprocal expansion of men's personas. In 1988, Mary Quant recalled: "Women had been building to this for a long time, but before the pill there couldn't be a true emancipation. It's very clear in the look, in the exuberance of the time—a rather childlike exuberance. "Wow—look at me!—isn't it lovely? At last, at last!'" (Conversation with author, December, 1988).

Youthquake fashion was also a lever as well as a product of the increased social mobility engendered by the postwar Labor governments of Britain. Due to governmentsubsidized tuition, an unprecedented number of students of humble origin were now able to pursue careers in the fine and commercial arts. At the Royal College of Art, Madge Garland, formerly editor in chief of British *Vogue*, had developed a graduate program in fashion design. Professor Janey Ironside became the program's principal in 1956. "We were trained to see, to explore, to enjoy ourselves," recalled RCA alumna Sally Tuffin, one half of celebrated Youthquake design team (Marion) Foale and Tuffin. "We felt as though we could go off and do anything, without restriction." (Conversation with author, November, 1988).

Boutiques

Throughout the 1950s, British fashion was dominated by the Paris couture, and the long shadow it cast over London couturiers such as Norman Hartnell and Hardy Amies. British manufacturers followed the parameters laid out by the high end of fashion. But the emerging generation wanted something entirely different and entirely their own. They were out of sympathy with the mores of expensive made-to-order clothing. "The couture was for kept women," said Barbara Hulanicki, who opened the London boutique Biba after working as a fashion illustrator in the late 1950s and early '60s. As she sketched the couture for London newspapers, Hulanicki objected as well to "the snobbery that was designed to make everyone feel inferior." (Conversation with author, November, 1988)

Youthquake fashion found its own staging ground as the boutique replaced the couture salon as fashion incubator. The Youthquake boutique was somewhere between a neighborhood dressmaker's atelier and the auxiliary shops maintained within some Paris couture strongholds, in which accessories and related bagatelles might be sold. Youthquake fashion could be said to have begun in November 1955, when Quant, recently graduated from art college, opened her boutique "Bazaar" in the London district of Chelsea. A year later she started designing because she couldn't find the type of clothes she wanted to stock her store.

"What was wrong at that stage was that fashion only came through one route," Quant recalled, "which designed for a way of life which was very much that of a minority."....She instead would design for "women who had a job and a fantasy life that took that job into account" (conversation with author, December 1988). The daughter of schoolteachers, Quant was married to Alexander Plunkett Greene, scion of an aristocratic lineage. Their marriage became emblematic of falling class barriers.

The Miniskirt Emerges

Chelsea had long been a magnet for London artists and bohemians, and during the 1950s it was a haunt for the city's Beatnik culture. Quant paid tribute to their minimal and monochromatic uniforms. As the couture never could, Quant and her brethren acknowledged, even asserted defiantly, that a primary design inspiration was the clothes of the young wandering the streets outside their workrooms. Quant was enamored, too, of the look of tap dancing students she'd watched as a child, as they practiced wearing short skirts, black tights, and patent-leather shoes. She kept on raising hemlines, and eventually Quant became known as "Mother of the Miniskirt." Some accounts have her showing skirts above the knee by 1958, although Quant's claims to precedence were challenged by Paris couturier André Courrèges. But who was first, or if there indeed was a first, is of peripheral importance. As far back as the late 1920s, hemlines were almost above the knee, and it was inevitable that after the long skirts of the late 1940s, they would rise again. As well, the inexorable shifts in society provided an historical imperative. In 1968, British fashion historian James Laver described the miniskirt as "the final word in

the emancipation of women—in proving her economic independence. . .Long, hampering skirts were fetters to keep a woman at home. The very short ones scream: 'I am stepping out'" (*WWD* March 22, 1968, p.8).

King's Road

Eventually, there were three Bazaars in London. They survived until 1968, by which time Quant was presiding over a vast wholesale and licensing empire. Bazaar was a catalyst in King's Road's transformation into a streaming, coursing artery of fashion and display. Kiki Byrne, who had worked as Quant's assistant, also opened a celebrated boutique there, where Hulanicki was enthralled by Byrne's "wonderful black dresses . . . shifts that weren't over-designed" (conversation with author, November 1988). Her generation wanted something much looser both philosophically and structurally even than the unfitted shape that was being shown in the Paris couture as the 1950s progressed. The Youthquake silhouette was less determined, less sculptural, less constructed, and usually less decorated. "Our clothes *had* to be comfortable," Tuffin recalled. "That was the main requirement" (conversation with author, November 1988).

While the Paris couture continued to take itself very seriously, the kingdom of Youthquake teemed with humor and irreverence. Quant gave droll names to her clothes and arranged gag tableau in her store windows. Foale and Tuffin put Y's across the front of shift dresses—"Y-fronts" were men's underwear briefs.

Where pants for women were concerned, London was more adventurous than the Paris couture or even the "ye-yes," the young ready to wear designers of Paris. The Foale and Tuffin trouser suit became a global prototype—"The cut was incredible," Betsey Johnson recalled, "the best I've ever seen" (conversation with author, August, 1987). They were strongly advocating trousers well before Courrèges's pants-dominated couture collections of the mid-1960s. Yet in 1961, when they first began teaming pants instead of skirts with jackets, the combination seemed so incongruous that "we actually fell about laughing," Tuffin recalled. Lines were straight, shoulders natural, the jacket semi-fitted like riding attire, but devoid of constructed reinforcement. The trouser suit was one of Youthquake fashion's most controversial provocations, but also one of its most enduring legacies.

Youthquake fashion at its most egalitarian and inclusive was represented by London's Biba boutique, which Hulanicki opened with her husband Stephen Fitz-Simon in 1964. "We practically gave our things away to the public," Hulanicki claimed. Biba practiced a rapid response to the trends of the street, alternately spurring and parrying the restless experimentation of the young. "I couldn't stand wholesale," Hulanicki said, "because it's just between you and the buyer, and the buyers are always wrong, anyway. They want what sold last year, but we were working right on the moment, all the time" (conversation with author, November 1988). Biba kept moving to larger and large quarters, its decor an iconoclastic mise-en-scène of oddments and antiques. With Biba, the Youthquake boutique reached its apogee as destination, event, parade ground, and crossroads.

Although at Biba the use of inexpensive synthetics was dictated by the need to keep prices down, synthetics were also championed by Youthquake fashion for reasons other than necessity. Rather then simply a pallid imitation of natural fibers, they could manifest novel textures and appearances. Machine-tooled fabrics were celebrated as a threshold to a utopia of increased leisure and lessened drudgery. Quant extolled their ability to look "like a delicious soufflé that happened with a pure kind of joy—without anybody's tears on them" (conversation with author, December 1988).

Youthquake designers were certainly gratified by the boggled attention their work received by mainstream manufacturers, journalists, and even the couture itself. But they were primarily concerned with designing for themselves and their contemporaries, and because of the exploding youth market, were able to do so without compromise. Certainly mature women could legitimately complain that the ubiquitous narrow armholes of the Youthquake silhouette were not easy to fit into. Women who'd been brought up on the postwar British rations were not robust. Hulanicki noted that the average women's shoe size during the 1960s was 3 1/2 or 4, while twenty years later it had jumped two sizes. The somewhat androgynous silhouette privileged by Youthquake fashion was also an aesthetic and sexual statement, however, a rejection of the overblown ideal of hourglass femininity that been promulgated during the 1950s by the couture and, perhaps more oppressively, by the imagery of popular culture.

Men's New Look

Women's reassessment of gender-specific clothes and behavior, unleashed from men a rejection of the dour clothes that had been obligatory since the Regency epoch of the nineteenth century. Young working-class men of the late 1950s organized themselves into coteries—The Teddy Boys, The Mods, the Rockers—each with its own odd and distinctive uniform. Around this time, Scottish-born retailer John Stephens began to transform London's Carnaby Street into a chockablock concentration of stores inviting men to cast off the fetters of old. Once all but completely polarized, men's and women's clothes could now converge into unisex outfits designed to be worn by either sex. A colony of men's and unisex boutiques sprung up around London, allowing men a selection unlike anything previously imaginable.

Clothing Anarchy

Biba's enveloping of new world fashions in the warm patina of vintage furnishings could be seen to anticipate the historical bent of late '60s London fashion. The city's archival closets were turned inside out and its streets became a fantastic masquerade. The rage for antique clothing, as well as the folklore and psychedelic panoply of the hippies dominated this second phase of Youthquake. The hippies' sartorial revolution evolved from the fashions of the Beats and the British ready-to-wear sisterhood; its founding mothers smoothly negotiated this second phase of Youthquake. The late '60s also saw the rise of designers like Ossie Clark and Zandra Rhodes, whose gossamer and fanciful creations recalled the romanticism of Arts and Crafts dress of the previous century. Vanguard London fashion of the late '60s was more anarchic than earlier in the decade. The laissez-faire of the hippies necessitated less homogeneous internal consistency to broadcast its sartorial and cultural message.

The End of an Era

By the mid-1970s, however, the very moniker Youthquake was superannuated. Many of the movers and shakers were in states of decompression or stately retreat. Quant was by now concentrating entirely on licensing. Foale and Tuffin disbanded. After Hulanicki and Fitz-Simon's alliance with outside capital, Biba suffered a bitter demise not long after reaching its apotheosis taking over a huge Art Deco department store. On the other hand, designers like Rhodes thrived amid a London fashion environment that continued to appreciate the eccentric. Conversely, the more muted and classic designs of Youthquake's Jean Muir became more popular than ever.

The plucky young firebrands of Youthquake had succeeded in radically upending global fashion markets. London itself has never returned to the fashion backwaters it was in the 1950s. The social and economic leveling proclaimed by Youthquake's habits and habiliments were not defeated by reactionary political developments during Britain in the 1980s. The Youthquake movement will always be an inspiration to those who seek to democratize fashion and tap the creative vitality of youth.

See also Biba; Miniskirt; Quant, Mary.

Bibliography

Lobenthal, Joel. *Radical Rags: Fashions of the Sixties.* New York: Abbeville Press, 1990.

Mulvagh, Jane. *Vogue History of 20th Century Fashion.* London: Viking, 1988.

Quant, Mary. *Quant by Quant.* London: Cassell, 1966.

Steele, Valerie. *Fifty Years of Fashion: New Look to Now.* New Haven, Conn.: Yale University Press, 1997.

Joel Lobenthal

Z

ZIPPER

More generically called a "slide fastener," the zipper is used as a closure in garments and a variety of other articles. Zippers were first introduced in a primitive form in the 1890s, but were not widely accepted in clothing until the 1930s.

The fastener that Americans most commonly call "zippers" can be traced to the invention of a Midwestern traveling salesman, Whitcomb Judson, in the early 1890s. Judson patented his device as a "clasp locker or unlocker" for shoes; this invention resembled the later zipper only superficially. It consisted of a series of hooks and eyes, each pair of which was engaged by the action of a key or slider. Over the next few years, Judson designed modifications of this device, none of which worked very effectively. The idea of an "automatic hook-and-eye," however, caught the attention of entrepreneurs, so Judson was given money and encouragement to continue engineering his invention, and in the first years after 1900, the first devices came to market under the aegis of the Universal Fastener Company of Hoboken, New Jersey.

After several years of futile design and sales efforts, the Hoboken company gained the services of a Swedish immigrant, Gideon Sundback. Trained as an electrical engineer, Sundback was a remarkably clever and astute mechanic. He analyzed with care the key elements of the automatic hook-and-eye, and concluded that the hook-and-eye model was not a suitable one for any kind of automatic fastener. Late in 1913, Sundback introduced his "Hookless Fastener," based on novel principles and resembling in all important respects the modern metal zipper.

Sundback's hookless fastener depended on the action of a series of closely spaced elements, technically called "scoops," whose precise spacing and ingenious shape are key to the fastener's success. Each scoop has a dimple on one side and a protruding nib on the other. The fastener consists of two opposing rows of scoops,

spaced so that the scoops from one side engage in the spaces between the scoops on the other side. The nib from one scoop fits into the dimple in the facing scoop, whose nib in turn fits into the next dimple down the row. Sundback likened the action to a series of spoons in which the bowls of alternating spoons fitted into one another. If the spoons at each end of the rows are held in place, the intermediate spoons cannot disengage one another. The slider's function is simply to bring the two rows of scoops together (or to separate them) in a continuous, serial action.

The entrepreneurs who had backed Judson and then Sundback readily saw the efficacy of the hookless fastener design. Sundback's contributions went further to include the construction of machinery that made fastener manufacture rapid and economical. The Hookless Fastener Company was organized in Meadville, Pennsylvania, and efforts to market the novel device began in 1914. The fastener makers encountered challenges every bit as formidable as the technical ones they had overcome after such effort. The early hookless fastener was an unquestionably clever device, and it worked reasonably reliably and consistently. It was, however, expensive compared to the buttons or hooks and eyes that it was designed to replace, and it posed a host of difficulties for the designers and makers of most garments.

The clothing industry initially rejected the new fastener. It might, in fact, have died an ignominious early death if its salesmen had not cultivated small niche markets that sustained it for several years. Money belts for World War I sailors were followed by tobacco pouches, which in turn were followed, in the early 1920s, by rubber overshoes. The manufacturers of this last, the B. F. Goodrich Rubber Company, came up with a moniker for their new product, "Zippers," that became even more popular than the overshoes themselves, and the term "zipper" came to be the common American term for the fastener (despite Goodrich's trademark claims). Through most of the 1920s, expanding niche markets brought the fastener to a wider public, although garment makers still resisted wider adoption. Hookless Fastener adopted the trademark "Talon" in 1928 (and changed the corporate name to Talon, Inc., a decade later).

Only in the 1930s did zippers come to be accepted elements of men's and women's clothing, and even then only by steps. The famous haute couture designer, Elsa Schiaparelli, chose to set her designs of 1935 off by liberal use of zippers—even in places where no fastener was needed or expected. A couple of years later, in 1937, zippers began to appear widely in high fashion lines—Edward Molyneux's pencil-slim coats, for example, used zippers to emphasize the sleek silhouette. At about the same time, the designers of the best tailored men's clothing let it be known that zippered flies were acceptable, and by the end of the decade, zippers were common in the better men's trousers and were making their way into the ready-to-wear market. The combination of a reduction in prices (due to higher volume production) and the growing association of the zipper with modernity and fashion overcame the long-standing resistance of the garment makers and buyers. The widespread use of zippers in military uniforms during World War II was associated by many with the final popularization of the fastener, but its usage was already well on its way to becoming common before the war. By the 1950s, the zipper was the default fastener for everything from skirt plackets and trouser flies to leather motorcycle jackets and backpacks.

Even before the war, some manufacturers experimented with replacing the copper-nickel alloy standard in zippers with plastic, but this substitution was not very successful until Talon and the DuPont Company collaborated on a very new zipper design, in which the metal scoops were replaced by nylon spirals. The nylon zipper, after a few difficult years, became the standard appliance for lightweight applications, as garment makers were particularly attracted to the ease with which the nylon could be colored to match fabric dyes. Other materials were used for more specialized purposes: surgeons even adopted inert Teflon zippers for postoperative applications.

The zipper was by no means a strictly American phenomenon. Within only a few years of its introduction, British manufacturers sought to establish manufacture, and by the mid-1920s, French, German, and other suppliers followed. The chief British manufacturer, the Lightning Fastener Company of Birmingham, gave its name to the fastener itself in a wide range of languages; in France it became known as a "fermature éclair," and in Germany as a "Blitzverschluss" (*Reissverschluss* became the more common German word later).

As the zipper became increasingly common in the twentieth century, it acquired an unusual cultural status. It became a widely recognized and used symbol with a host of associations. Aldous Huxley used zippers throughout his 1932 novel, *Brave New World*, to allude to the impersonal and mechanical nature of sex in his nightmarish world of the future. Broadway and Hollywood began in the same decade to use the zipper to convey images of promiscuity: Rodgers and Hart's 1940 musical *Pal Joey* included a famous pantomime striptease with the refrain of "zip" throughout. Rita Hayworth, in her 1946 movie *Gilda*, used the zipper more than once as an instrument of sexual provocation. Even in the realm of urban legend, the zipper quickly became a common trope, conveying the awkwardness of relying on the mechanical in the intimate realms of daily life.

In the course of the twentieth century, the zipper became so ubiquitous as to become almost invisible. It has multiplied in form, size, style, and function; ranging from the simple plastic of the Ziploc bag to the zippers used in surgery and spacesuits. Arguably the most characteristic fastener of the twentieth century, the zipper has still not, even in the twenty-first century, lost its symbolic power to convey sexuality, opening and closing, separating and joining. And, despite the apparent allure of alternatives from old-fashioned buttons to modern Velcro, zippers appear in no danger of being displaced as the leading fastener.

See also Fasteners; Uniforms, Military.

Bibliography

Friedel, Robert. *Zipper: An Exploration in Novelty.* New York: W. W. Norton, 1994.

Gray, James. *Talon, Inc.: A Romance of Achievement.* Meadville, Pa.: Talon Inc., 1963.

Robert Friedel

ZOOT SUIT

The zoot suit cut a suave silhouette. Initially popularized by black "hipsters" in the mid-to late-1930s, but embraced more generally by swing jazz enthusiasts of all colors, the zoot suit jacket exaggerated the upper male body with wide padded shoulders and broad lapels, tapering dramatically down to the waist and flaring out to the knees. The pants were flowing, high waisted, and pleated, flaring at the knees and angling radically down to a tight fit around the ankles. The look was usually completed with a porkpie hat, long watch chain, thin belt, and matching shoes. It was a style androgynous enough to be worn by either men or women, but the fashion was most popular among men.

Eastern zooters favored eye-catching colors and patterns, but youth on the West coast preferred a more discreet appearance, possibly prompted by the March 1942 ruling of the War Production Board restricting the measurements for men's suits and rationing the availability of material for civilian use. Men's fashion in general became more moderate, and "the drape" was the more conservative version of the zoot suit. The length of the drape jacket was considerably shorter than the zoot jacket, falling at mid-thigh, and otherwise looked little different from a man's oversized business suit. Some women in Los Angeles took to wearing pleated skirts underneath the drape jacket with hosiery and huarache sandals.

Contemporary accounts placed the origins of the zoot suit in the African American communities of Gainesville, Georgia; Chicago; and Harlem, but the stylistic foundations of the zoot suit trace back to Edwardian fashion at the turn of the century. In the Northeast, the style was known as the "root suit," "suit suit," and "zoot suit"; in the South as "killer diller"; and in the West as "drape shape" or in Spanish as "el tacuche" (the wardrobe).

Jobs in war production allowed young people to experiment with consumption and a popular culture largely inspired by the African American jazz artists they admired. Jazz music, dance, clothing, and language that youth across the color line shared allowed for recreations of social identities. For some, jazz music and the hipster style were audacious celebrations of life in spite of the difficulties blacks faced during the 1930s. For others, wearing the fashion was a show of newfound but modest wealth from wartime employment that signaled their move from square to cool or from "country" to urbane. At the same time, the zoot suit was a dashing if not scandalous image because of its association with hipsters, drugs, and sex. Such layered meanings promised rich possibilities for transforming cultural expression into a form of resistance to the social conventions of segregation.

Although a few saw the popularity of the zoot suit as a harmless development, many more had visceral reactions to it as a symbol of the breakdown of social convention. Critics of jazz fashion seemed unable to accept that working-class youth of color could afford such an expensive suit through honest means. Some saw the suit as a waste of rationed material and an unabashed disregard for community values of thrift and sacrifice. Others projected the antiwar sympathies that some black hipsters expressed to all jazz enthusiasts who wore the zoot suit.

In many communities, the zoot suit grew into a powerful symbol of subversion by the mid-1940s, transformed by different sources of tension over changing social boundaries. As people of color challenged racial barriers across the nation, many whites violently resisted integration. To them, the popularity of the zoot suit seemed to epitomize growing concerns over juvenile delinquency as young people of color increasingly refused to defer to white privilege.

In early June 1943, sailors, soldiers, and some civilians in Los Angeles rioted for a week, setting off a wave of race riots in cities large and small across the nation. The Zoot Suit Riot in Los Angeles was the longest, but the Detroit Race Riot in mid-June was the deadliest. Growing tensions over integration led to a day and a half of rioting, leaving twenty-five blacks and nine whites dead and more than 1,800 arrested. Conversely, in Los Angeles, no murders, rapes, deaths, or serious damage to property were reported in connection with the riot, and only a few cases of serious injury. The mob of mostly white military men seemed focused on reasserting segregation, breached by "uppity" young men of color, by destroying their public displays of wealth and beating those who refused to yield their drapes.

Jazz followed wherever American troops were stationed abroad, and for a moment zoot suits were fashionable among jazz enthusiasts in France, England, and as far away as South Africa. The zoot suit fell out of fashion in the postwar years as the jazz world moved from swing to be-bop, but it served as the inspiration for the Teddy Boys' distinctive look in postwar London.

Decades later the zoot suiter arose immortalized in the dramatic and scholarly works of Chicano artists and intellectuals who saw the wartime generation as cultural nationalists. A zoot suit revival inspired by Luis Valdez's stage and screen musical continues in popular venues, and productions of Zoot Suit continue to draw large audiences in the Southwest. Some businesses and Internet sites cater to customers interested in zoot suits, and zoot-suited youth are a staple at some low rider car shows. For many Mexican American youth, putting on the zoot suit serves as a way to connect with a past that was self-assertive and stylish, pay homage to community elders, and assume a place in the continuum of cultural resistance and affirmation.

High-end designers such as Stacey Adams, Vittorio St. Angelo, and Gianni Vironi produce suits that could well be considered next-generation zoot suits. Updated zoot suits no longer elicit the public censure received in the 1940s, because the social context in which the fashion was first received has changed so dramatically.

See also African American Dress; Latin American Fashion.

Bibliography

Capeci, Dominic J., and Martha Wilkerson. *Layered Violence: The Detroit Rioters of 1943.* Jackson: University of Mississippi, 1991.

Mazón, Mauricio. *The Zoot Suit Riots: The Psychology of Symbolic Annihilation.* Austin: University of Texas, 1984.

Pagán, Eduardo Obregón. *Murder at the Sleepy Lagoon: Zoot Suits, Race, and Riot in Wartime L.A.* Chapel Hill: University of North Carolina Press, 2003.

White, Shane, and Graham White. *Stylin': African American Expressive Culture From Its Beginnings to the Zoot Suit.* Ithaca, New York: Cornell University Press, 1998.

Eduardo Pagán

Index

afrocentric fashion, 14–17
adoption of, 17
assimilation within, 15–16
bubas, 16
in Dancehall culture, 16
dashiki, 16
foundations of, 14–15
negritude and, 14–15
as self-expression, 15–16
in US, 16–17
artistic influences on, 16
for Rastafarians, 16
Western dress v., 15
Afrocentrism, 14–15
Afro hairstyles, 11–14
among artists, 12
civil rights movement and, 11–13
cultural significance of, 14
curly, 14
declining popularity of, 14
early reactions to, 13
origins of, 11–12
popularization of, 13–14
through commercialization, 13
in fashion industry, 13
straightened hair and, 11–12
for women, 12–13
Alaïa, Azzedine (Tunisia), 17–18
collections of, 17–18
early career, 17
as fashion influence, 18
ready-to-wear of, 17–18
style technique for, 18
with Lycra, 18
Albini, Walter (Italy), 19–20
Chanel as influence on, 19
design collections of, 19
"total look" in, 20
fashion design study for, 19
fashion reforms by, 19
fashion shows for, 20
fashion specialization under, 19
FTM and, 19–20
A-line dress, 20–1
contemporary design for, 21
definition of, 20
design style for, 21
development of, 21
Dior and, 21
"Trapeze Line" and, 21
see also chemise dress
American Gigolo, 26

"American Look," 504–3
Amies, Hardy (England), 21–3
design awards for, 23
as designer for royalty, 21
early life of, 22
at Lachasse firm, 22
men's wear designs of, 23
during World War II, 22
Androver, Miguel (US), 106
anti-Semitism, Nazi dress and, 272–3
Antoinette, Marie, 72–3
chemise dress and, 144
Antonio, Juan Carlos see Galliano, John
Antwerp, Belgium, as fashion city, 67–8
"Antwerp Six," 67
A Piece of Cloth (APOC) concept, 515
APOC concept see A Piece of Cloth
"apron men," 23
aprons, 23–5
"apron men," 23
decorative, 24
definition of, 23
early history of, 23–4
as instant uniforms, 24
in US, 24
see also protective clothing
The Arcades Project (Benjamin), 70
Arickx, Filip (Belgium), 67
aristocratic dress see royal dress
Arlen, Michael, 52
Armani, Giorgio (Italy), 25–7, 431
collections, 26
commercial expansion for, 26
costume design by, 26, 335
design philosophy for, 25–7
contemporary influences on, 26
for female dress, 27
early career, 25
Emporio Armani, 26
GFT and, 26
international recognition for, 25–6
as social influence, 26–7
subsidiary lines for, 26
textile choice for, 27
armor, 27–30
in ceremonial costumes, 133–4
contemporary, 29–30
decline in use of, 28–9
design development of, 28

earliest versions of, 27
chain mail, 27–8
lamellar, 27
Roman style, 28–9
in terra cotta army, 27
during Enlightenment, 29
flak jackets as, 29–30
manufacture of, 28
during middle ages, 27–8
symbolism in, 28
during Renaissance, 28–9
for equestrian events, 29
garniture and, 29
Maximilian style of, 28–9
Armstrong, James, 2
Art Deco movement, fashion influenced, 36–7
for Barbier, 52
in contemporary fashion, 37
development of, 36
fashion illustration and, 37
in films, 37
in haute couture, 37
for Poiret, 36
retro versions of, 37
see also Orientalism
art, fashion and, 30–5
for avant-gardes, 32–3
body consciousness and, 32–3
consumption of, 33–5
through media, 34–5
contemporary, 33
cultural hierarchy for, 33
evolution of, 30
haute couture and, 33
history and, 31
inspiration for, 31–2
à la mode, 31
modern, 35
modernism and, 34
politics as influence on, 33
production similarities for, 32–4
ready-to-wear as influence, 33
role of artists, 32
St. Laurent and, 32
Art nouveau movement, fashion influenced, 36–7
designers influenced by, 36
as high art, 36
historical content of, 36
popular versions of, 36
retro versions of, 37